CROSS-TALK IN COMP THEORY

CROSS-TALK IN COMP THEORY

A Reader

Third Edition

Edited by

Victor Villanueva
Washington State University

Kristin L. Arola
Washington State University

National Council of Teachers of English
1111 W. Kenyon Road, Urbana, Illinois 61801-1096

Staff Editor: Bonny Graham
Interior and Cover Design: Precision Graphics

NCTE Stock Number: 09779

It is the policy of NCTE in its journals and other publications to provide a forum for the open discussion of ideas concerning the content and the teaching of English and the language arts. Publicity accorded to any particular point of view does not imply endorsement by the Executive Committee, the Board of Directors, or the membership at large, except in announcements of policy, where such endorsement is clearly specified.

Every effort has been made to provide current URLs and email addresses, but because of the rapidly changing nature of the Web, some sites and addresses may no longer be accessible.

Library of Congress Cataloging-in-Publication Data

Cross-talk in comp theory : a reader / edited by Victor Villanueva, Kristin L. Arola.–3rd ed.
    p. cm.
  Includes bibliographical references and index.
  ISBN 978-0-8141-0977-9 ((pbk))
  1. English language–Composition and exercises–Study and teaching.
2. English language–Rhetoric–Study and teaching. I. Villanueva, Victor, 1948-
II. Arola, Kristin L.
  PE1404.C755 2011
  808'.042071–dc22

                                     2011002598

To my Carol
        my children
                their children
        my students
                their teachers
                        —Victor Villanueva

To the teachers who've inspired me,
The students who keep me on my toes,
The friends and family who keep me honest,
And to Jeff, for everything.
                        —Kristin Arola

Contents

SECTION SIX

Virtual Talk: Composing Beyond the Word   697

Contents

Preface to the Third Edition

FROM VICTOR

My father was a mechanic for the army during World War II. And he used to state proudly that he had attended a school for auto mechanics under the GI Bill (essentially, his ninth-grade education). So he would tell me about cars, and as a good son, I would listen. I got the basics of the internal combustion engine. So I know that that squeaky sound under the hood means a belt needs tightening and that the jerkiness of the chassis means time for new plugs or distributor (and usually both). I listen to Click and Clack on NPR on Sundays and usually guess right before Tom and Ray finish chortling. But for all of that, I can't say that I know anything really about cars, apart from being glad to own one (fossil fuel issues notwithstanding).

My relation with cars is somewhat analogous to my relation with computers. I worked as a computer operator when I was eighteen years old, the Honeywell H200, one of the seven competitors to IBM. And even as I worked for an IBM competitor, I started to learn FORTRAN (but dropped out) and began to learn (well, for a few weeks) what would become Pascal, even took a night course on programming (which I never finished). I wrote my dissertation on the first Apple model. Did DOS a few years later, and friends across the nation and I tried to figure out how to make email work in 1992. Returned to Apple in 1995, even as a friend who worked for Microsoft told me that there would be no Apple in a couple of years. And now when things explode (remember the little Mac bomb?), I tend to figure my way around. I don't shout obscenities at the machine; I go "hmm." Yet my interest in computers, apart from my "driving" them, was never piqued. So while there has been a conversation going on in composition studies for as long as I've been in this profession, I have been willfully deaf.

But I have students who force me to think about computer gaming or the new ways ideologies are represented in digital media, hypertextually. Just two examples: Chris Ritter had me consider how racial stereotypes are morphed into racialized stereotypes in the avatars of *World of Warcraft*, and Paul Muhlhauser looked to all kinds of representations in the human gamete industry. Patty Ericsson makes my head spin as she tells of discussions she assumes I know about—but don't. And through her students I learn of the rhetorics of bureaucracy in a digitized world. Jason Farman had me look at "mobile interface theory." Kristin Arola makes me think of Web design and identity. I read, discuss, and learn.

The discussions concerning computers and composition studies are rich, and have been for some time. So we offer one more edition of *Cross-Talk*, to include a glimpse at the conversation concerning the digital paradigm. But since I can't really compensate for a quarter-century of ignorance, I have asked a colleague, Kristin Arola, to help me out. She did more than help, however. She constructed the new Section Six of the collection—"Virtual Talk." In keeping with the basic premise of this book, this section is not comprehensive, but is, rather, fuel with which to prime the pump: some talk and some cross-talk, the utopic and the dystopic, maybe.

Otherwise, the collection remains pretty much the same, some additions and some deletions to reflect current conversations (and to satisfy publisher-imposed page limits). My hope—our hope, Kristin's and mine—is that this collection will continue to serve the needs of those coming into the conversations in our community of theorists of the teaching of writing.

FROM KRISTIN

Cross-Talk has always been with me: in the hallways of Northern Arizona University as a wide-eyed first-year master's student; at my family holiday dinners when I tried to explain what it was that I was actually *doing* in graduate school; and as I wrote my dissertation at Michigan Tech, when I tried to place my work within a larger narrative of composition studies. Yet I often found myself holding the history of composition in one hand and the history of computers and writing in the other. We all come from similar training, and we all are concerned with how to best teach first-year composition, but at times I found it difficult to pull these two strands together.

Truthfully, for me, coming of age in the digital era and going to graduate school when you couldn't swing a dead cat without hitting a PhD student whose research focused on digital-or-visual-something-or-other, I found it easy to stick with the computers and writing canon. I knew that Composition (capital C) and Computers and Writing (capital CW) were

xiv

inextricable, yet the latter felt like the sexy choice. Even today, I feel this pull when I choose one conference over another, or read one journal over the other. Yet I think there's a lot to be learned when we place folks like Donald Murray alongside Cindy Selfe, or James Berlin alongside Richard Ohmann. They might not be talking directly to each other, but if we listen closely enough we'll hear the resonances and the dissonances, and perhaps be able to see how the digital is not, and should not be, relegated to its own corner of the field.

As Victor has (repeatedly) reminded me, it is nearly impossible to encapsulate thirty years of conversation in six essays. Yet I hope the essays that constitute Section Six create a cross-talk not only with one another, but also with the other pieces in the collection. We need to be talking with one another and finding connections, because even if we don't research the digital, it informs, and is, the stuff with which we work every day.

Preface to the Second Edition

Second editions are like movie sequels. And I don't figure I've got a Part II to *The Godfather* or *Aliens*. But the profession has continued to move ahead, so the sequel to *Cross-Talk* seems like a good idea. One of the editors kept referring to it as "Son of Cross-Talk."

The acorn hasn't landed far from the tree, though. The book isn't all that different from the first edition. It's still divided into the same categories. My biases remain my biases, though as in the first edition, I try to remain true to the profession by giving preference to essays that are most frequently cited. And as in the first edition, there are a lot of interesting things going on in composition studies that don't get addressed, things like empirical research, assessment, or linguistics.

But some things have happened since I conducted the research for the first edition in 1992 to 1994. The most remarkable has been the technological explosion, with new software packages that affect our work coming out weekly, or so it seems, and with the pervasiveness of the Internet and its World Wide Web. The Net changed the way I conducted the research for this volume, a two-year process reduced to a few weeks on computerized databases and journal archives on the Web—often with whole texts available at the stroke of a few keys. Yet for all that, it doesn't appear as if technology has made its way into our theoretical discussions. Despite the great work of Cynthia Selfe and Gail Hawisher, not much has emerged in our journals that can stand the test of time—not because of any shortcoming in our scholars but because of the speed with which the things written about become archaic, this morning's innovation becoming this evening's anachronism. Technology has been included in this version, but not significantly, surely not as significantly as its presence in our lives would suggest.

In a very real sense, *Cross-Talk* is intended as a historical artifact, a way of tracking theoretical discussions in a field that continues to find itself forming its theoretical foundations. Even the givens of comp—writing as process—are contending with cross-talk, like post-process theory. It's hard to track the history we're in.

The other big change in composition studies—at least in our journals—has been the increased presence of writers of color and the greater acceptance of critical pedagogy. As I point out in the final essay to this volume, writers of color are still not present in this profession in the kinds of numbers that would affect our discussions on racism in truly meaningful ways, but something did happen in the second half of the 1990s: the beginnings of rich discussion on racism clearly centered on the concerns of this profession (a somewhat different set of discussions on racism from those which took place in journals like *College English* at the beginning of the second half of the twentieth century).

Readers of the first edition will likely miss the discussion between Peter Elbow and David Bartholomae. It was, I recognize, an interesting discussion centering on academic discourse versus other kinds of writing. It's gone because the discussion has taken a different turn—the personal versus the academic. That discussion has its representatives here, through Gesa Kirsch and Joy Ritchie, through Jacqueline Jones Royster, and in some sense through Richard Miller. Joy Ritchie and Kathleen Boardman broaden the discussion on feminism. And service learning is introduced, a relatively new entry into the conversation on composition.

Composition studies has moved on. New students are learning of our field, a field still in flux, still growing. It was time to account for the 1990s in the conversation, in the talk and cross-talk. Something gets lost with a sequel, I know, even a good sequel. Robert De Niro might have been great, but I missed Brando. Some of the Brandos will be missed in Son of Cross-Talk, but I trust this sequel will continue to serve, to initiate graduate students and more experienced teachers into the theories that inform composition studies.

Preface to the First Edition

I wanted to prepare a healthier pancake for the children. The whole-wheat recipe in the healthier cookbook hadn't quite gone over. But my adjustments made for pretty pancakes that came out, time and again, uncooked at the center. I figured I'd better add another egg to the batter next time around. And that worked. That egg added just the touch more leavening the batter needed, the touch more air to cook the batter through. If I had wanted to go just a bit healthier, I could have substituted that egg with two egg whites, beaten to a froth, since the fat of the yolk wouldn't have been necessary to the batter, as it would have been for, say, a custard. I made healthy pancakes that the kids would (and did and do) eat.

The point is this: I could adjust, take control of the process, because I had an understanding of how eggs work in cooking. I understood the theory.

But then, theories of leavening have been pretty well worked out. Theories of written composition have not. And operating from the gut, what feels right, what sounds right, what might be fun for the students, can too easily lead to theoretical contradictions. And students know. I don't know how they know, but they seem to sense or maybe outwardly recognize theoretical inconsistencies, reacting too often with passive compliance, never arriving at the full benefits possible in engaging—really engaging—in written discourse.

What those benefits of literacy might be aren't exactly clear, though. Plato tells of the god Thoth claiming that writing would be the key to remembrance. And writing was, we are told, used as a memory aid, a mnemonic device. In recent times, as we will find in the articles to follow, writing has been credited with learning, cognitive development, social cohesion, political power. What writing can provide has never been altogether clear.

So composition studies has divided itself, either to find out what writing is, or how to teach it better, or to discern the degree to which it either removes or bestows power. Composition studies finds its historicists (with some compositionists as revisionist historicists), current-traditionalists, cognitivists, expressionists, social-constructionists (who tend also to be epistemicists), empiricists, anti-foundationalists, and leftists, among others. Academic books

on composition studies tend to historicize, theorize, polemicize, or synthesize, as well as proselytize. Composition is complex and diverse.

But with the greater diversity and sophistication has come greater confusion. I have seen teachers come to accept writing as a process, a common-
enough notion nowadays, without recognizing the theoretical bases to
different approaches to process. I have heard a new compositionist on the
job market betray his confusion, claiming a Marxist bent, yet aligning himself with Kenneth Bruffee and Peter Elbow—highly respected compositionists, but hardly representatives of the political left. Another candidate clearly
knew research on composition (for which there are several good collections)
but seemed not to know of the philosophical objections to classical-
empirical research. The overwhelming majority of candidates—even those
fortunate enough to study with prestigious compositionists—seem unable to
navigate their ways through composition's currents.

What follows, then, is an aid for you—the teacher of graduate composition theory, the graduate student of composition, the veteran teacher of
composition back in the graduate comp course. What follows is a book of
readings whose objective is to introduce you to some of the concepts and
methods available to writing teachers today and to have you regard some of
the controversy. This is a reader of previously published works, mainly by
those who tend to be mentioned in the works of others. The book's further
objective is to have you begin to consider your own predispositions toward
language, discourse, writing, and writing instruction, predispositions which
can then be considered critically and discussed knowledgeably. The list of
suggested readings adds book-length considerations. With the books I have
suggested, the books and articles cited in the essays that pique your interest,
and the essays themselves, you should be able to come up with quite the
pancake recipe, something you can swallow.

I mention the readings and the works the essays themselves cite
because, though this book is comprehensive, it is not complete. It is not
intended to establish a canon of comp. It's an overview, manageable within
an academic quarter or semester. So the readings contained herein do not
encompass all there is to composition studies. There are gaps. Writing
across the curriculum is absent. Linguistics is minimally represented,
which means there is little here on research on those who come into the
classroom speaking a nonstandard dialect or those whose primary language
is other than English (which includes sociolinguistic and applied linguistic
studies of the hundreds of American Indian languages still spoken in the
United States today). There is little on grammar, and the current discussions on multiculturalism and the comp classroom aren't explicitly represented. But all of these concerns really are here, in large terms, in the

theoretical discussions concerning those who have been traditionally excluded or underrepresented in the academy.

Nor is evaluation explicitly represented. I know that the teacher is always concerned with evaluation and assessment. And how a teacher decides to respond, evaluate, and grade essays should be a reflection of the philosophy or theory of writing that the classroom curriculum embodies. But the subject of evaluation is large, almost another theoretical sphere, more concerned with what you do with writing in the classroom than with what writing is or even what writing instruction might be. I've relegated evaluation to the list of suggested readings. In other words, to learn more you'll still have to read those more complete academic books on composition contained in the list of readings or mentioned in the collection. But after going through this book, you will have a sense of who you might want to read. This book is intended as a primer, drops to activate the pump.

Selection suggests a selector, one with particular biases. But though my own biases in selecting the readings will no doubt come through, no single viewpoint is presented. The readings are presented in such a way as to establish a dialectic—a way for you to come to your own conclusions by considering opposing viewpoints. The process approach espoused in the first section receives a critical assessment in the "Mulligan Stew" article. Walter Ong provides a necessary reconsideration of product. The cognitive explanations of basic writers' problems advanced by Andrea Lunsford and by Frank D'Angelo are countered by Mike Rose's article on cognitive development. Cognitive explanations generally are countered by social-construction's explanations, with Patricia Bizzell explicitly drawing the comparison, offering the critique; both the cognitivist and the social-constructionist become subject to ideological critiques. Points find counterpoints throughout the book—talk and cross-talk.

Some articles will address matters of race or ethnicity, gender, the poor or working class. Considerations of race and the like have had a great deal to do with establishing the theoretical controversies. One compositionist of note, at least, Maxine Hairston, has argued that our changing theories of composition are in part the result of the introduction into our college classrooms of those we have come to call basic writers, those who come to college not quite prepared to undertake college writing, most often people of color and the poor. There are always a few in every composition classroom, at every level, from first-year college students to seniors. To ponder how composition might affect the more troublesome, those basic writers, would inform our approach to the less troublesome.

Although the book's layout is principally concerned with establishing a dialectic, presenting varying views, there is something of a chronology to the ordering, a near chronology of the profession's changes—process to cohesion to cognition to social construction to ideology. The first two sections present the views that seem to have lasted: writing-as-process, writing as a means of learning, James Kinneavy's aims of discourse, some basic research. Yet even these sections contain some controversial matters: the generalizability of case studies, Frank D'Angelo's ontogeny recapitulating phylogeny (terms you'll come to understand through the reading). The third section looks to the cognitive sciences and developmental psychology, pretty popular till recently. The fourth section addresses that which has compromised cognition's popularity: social construction. It introduces Kenneth Bruffee and something of a counter in John Trimbur; there is also Charles Schuster's reading of Mikhail Bakhtin as informing social construction. Section five looks to the debate over whether freshman composition courses should concern themselves with narration or with academic discourse, with the discourses about and by those traditionally excluded from the academy—women, people of color. Then an important set of postscripts. And so the profession stands, kind of, for the moment.

The Givens in Our Conversations
The Writing Process

That writing is a process sounds pretty obvious. We know that texts don't appear magically on pages as whole products. There is a process in getting from mind to page. As obvious as that might be, however, teachers of writing have until relatively recently been trained to behave as literary critics—looking at texts so as to analyze what happens within those texts. Students in composition classes were enjoined to look at texts, analyze and discuss what happens in those texts, and then produce something of their own that followed the patterns they found in those texts. Ideas were to be provided by the text, the form provided by the text, with evaluation based on how well the student paper emulated the ideal text. The process was rather like having students watch and discuss a videotape of a prima ballerina and having the students attempt the same dance, with the students then being evaluated based on how well they approximated the ballerina's performance—without knowing how the ballerina came to master those steps. No attention was given to the process of arriving at the product.

In 1959 the National Academy of Sciences sponsored the Woods Hole Conference. Its director was a cognitive psychologist with a keen interest in education and language—Jerome Bruner. The result of the conference was a shift in emphasis for all schooling to the process of cognitive development. *Process* became the new catchword. In 1966, about fifty teachers of English from England and from the United States met to discuss common problems. What the Americans discovered was that the British did not teach writing as discipline specific. The British, rather than teach writing to serve some external purpose or genre, taught writing as a process of individual development, a matter of self-discovery. This was the Dartmouth Conference. Its discoveries fit well with the Woods Hole discoveries.

1

Woods Hole and Dartmouth made for a new attention to the whole concept of process. Writers and teachers like Donald Murray, Ken Macrorie, and Peter Elbow turned to what they knew as writers and as teachers to shed light on what writers do when they write. At about the same time, researchers in composition were heeding the call provided by Richard Braddock, Richard Lloyd-Jones, and Lowell Schoer's *Research in Written Composition,* a collection of research on composing to 1963. Their call? More research on writing itself (as opposed to products or pedagogy). Janet Emig's *The Composing Processes of Twelfth Graders* was the first significant answer to the call. Others presented here looked to what professional writers do when they revise that students in writing classes don't do, and what Basic Writers—students not quite ready for the tasks of college literacy—do when they write.

So writing is a process. But that doesn't mean that at the end of the process there won't be a product. The idea is to place greater emphasis on the process than on the product. Rhetorician Walter Ong reminds us in a classic article that combines matters of literary criticism with rhetoric and the teaching of writing, that there are consequences to the writing produced, that what is written affects and is affected by audiences, by readers. Lisa Ede and Andrea Lunsford broaden the picture on audience. Then comes the question as to whether "process" has overshadowed other concerns with writing. This comes to be called "post-process theory," a reconsideration of the givens of our conversation. Lee-Ann M. Kastman Breuch tells us about post-process.

Teach Writing as a Process Not Product

Donald M. Murray

Most of us are trained as English teachers by studying a product: writing. Our critical skills are honed by examining literature, which is finished writing; language as it has been used by authors. And then, fully trained in the autopsy, we go out and are assigned to teach our students to write, to make language live.

Naturally we try to use our training. It's an investment and so we teach writing as a product, focusing our critical attentions on what our students have done, as if they had passed literature in to us. It isn't literature, of course, and we use our skills, with which we can dissect and sometimes almost destroy Shakespeare or Robert Lowell to prove it.

Our students knew it wasn't literature when they passed it in, and our attack usually does little more than confirm their lack of self-respect for their work and for themselves; we are as frustrated as our students, for conscientious, doggedly responsible, repetitive autopsying doesn't give birth to live writing. The product doesn't improve, and so, blaming the student—who else?—we pass him along to the next teacher, who is trained, too often, the same way we were. Year after year the student shudders under a barrage of criticism, much of it brilliant, some of it stupid, and all of it irrelevant. No matter how careful our criticisms, they do not help the student since when we teach composition we are not teaching a product, we are teaching a process.

And once you can look at your composition program with the realization you are teaching a process, you may be able to design a curriculum which works. Not overnight, for writing is a demanding, intellectual process;

Pulitzer Prize–winning journalist Donald M. Murray presented this paper at the 1972 convention of the New England Association of Teachers of English; it appeared in their journal, *The Leaflet*, in November 1972. Reprinted with permission.

3

but sooner than you think, for the process can be put to work to produce a product which may be worth your reading.

What is the process we should teach? It is the process of discovery through language. It is the process of exploration of what we know and what we feel about what we know through language. It is the process of using language to learn about our world, to evaluate what we learn about our world, to communicate what we learn about our world.

Instead of teaching finished writing, we should teach unfinished writing, and glory in its unfinishedness. We work with language in action. We share with our students the continual excitement of choosing one word instead of another, of searching for the one true word.

This is not a question of correct or incorrect, of etiquette or custom. This is a matter of far higher importance. The writer, as he writes, is making ethical decisions. He doesn't test his words by a rule book, but by life. He uses language to reveal the truth to himself so that he can tell it to others. It is an exciting, eventful, evolving process.

This process of discovery through language we call writing can be introduced to your classroom as soon as you have a very simple understanding of that process, and as soon as you accept the full implications of teaching process, not product.

The writing process itself can be divided into three stages: *prewriting, writing,* and *rewriting*. The amount of time a writer spends in each stage depends on his personality, his work habits, his maturity as a craftsman, and the challenge of what he is trying to say. It is not a rigid lock-step process, but most writers most of the time pass through these three stages.

Prewriting is everything that takes place before the first draft. Prewriting usually takes about 85% of the writer's time. It includes the awareness of his world from which his subject is born. In prewriting, the writer focuses on that subject, spots an audience, chooses a form which may carry his subject to his audience. Prewriting may include research and daydreaming, note-making and outlining, title-writing and lead-writing.

Writing is the act of producing a first draft. It is the fastest part of the process, and the most frightening, for it is a commitment. When you complete a draft you know how much, and how little, you know. And the writing of this first draft—rough, searching, unfinished—may take as little as one percent of the writer's time.

Rewriting is reconsideration of subject, form, and audience. It is researching, rethinking, redesigning, rewriting—and finally, line-by-line editing, the demanding, satisfying process of making each word right. It may take many times the hours required for a first draft, perhaps the remaining fourteen percent of the time the writer spends on the project.

4

How do you motivate your student to pass through this process, perhaps even pass through it again and again on the same piece of writing?

First by shutting up. When you are talking he isn't writing. And you don't learn a process by talking about it, but by doing it. Next by placing the opportunity for discovery in your student's hands. When you give him an assignment you tell him what to say and how to say it, and thereby cheat your student of the opportunity to learn the process of discovery we call writing.

To be a teacher of a process such as this takes qualities too few of us have, but which most of us can develop. We have to be quiet, to listen, to respond. We are not the initiator or the motivator; we are the reader, the recipient.

We have to be patient and wait, and wait, and wait. The suspense in the beginning of a writing course is agonizing for the teacher, but if we break first, if we do the prewriting for our students they will not learn the largest part of the writing process.

We have to respect the student, not for his product, not for the paper we call literature by giving it a grade, but for the search for truth in which he is engaged. We must listen carefully for those words that may reveal a truth, that may reveal a voice. We must respect our student for his potential truth and for his potential voice. We are coaches, encouragers, developers, creators of environments in which our students can experience the writing process for themselves.

Let us see what some of the implications of teaching process, not product, are for the composition curriculum.

Implication No. 1. The text of the writing course is the student's own writing. Students examine their own evolving writing and that of their classmates, so that they study writing while it is still a matter of choice, word by word.

Implication No. 2. The student finds his own subject. It is not the job of the teacher to legislate the student's truth. It is the responsibility of the student to explore his own world with his own language, to discover his own meaning. The teacher supports but does not direct this expedition to the student's own truth.

Implication No. 3. The student uses his own language. Too often, as writer and teacher Thomas Williams points out, we teach English to our students as if it were a foreign language. Actually, most of our students have learned a great deal of language before they come to us, and they are quite willing to exploit that language if they are allowed to embark on a serious search for their own truth.

Implication No. 4. The student should have the opportunity to write all the drafts necessary for him to discover what he has to say on this particular subject. Each new draft, of course, is counted as equal to a new paper. You are not teaching a product, you are teaching a process.

Implication No. 5. The student is encouraged to attempt any form of writing which may help him discover and communicate what he has to say. The process which produces "creative" and "functional" writing is the same. You are not teaching products such as business letters and poetry, narrative and exposition. You are teaching a product your students can use—now and in the future—to produce whatever product his subject and his audience demand.

Implication No. 6. Mechanics come last. It is important to the writer, once he has discovered what he has to say, that nothing get between him and his reader. He must break only those traditions of written communication which would obscure his meaning.

Implication No. 7. There must be time for the writing process to take place and time for it to end. The writer must work within the stimulating tension of unpressured time to think and dream and stare out windows, and pressured time—the deadline—to which the writer must deliver.

Implication No. 8. Papers are examined to see what other choices the writer might make. The primary responsibility for seeing the choices is the student. He is learning a process. His papers are always unfinished, evolving, until the end of the marking period. A grade finishes a paper, the way publication usually does. The student writer is not graded on drafts any more than a concert pianist is judged on his practice sessions rather than on his performance. The student writer is graded on what he has produced at the end of the writing process.

Implication No. 9. The students are individuals who must explore the writing process in their own way, some fast, some slow, whatever it takes for them, within the limits of the course deadlines, to find their own way to their own truth.

Implication No. 10. There are no rules, no absolutes, just alternatives. What works one time may not another. All writing is experimental.

None of these implications require a special schedule, exotic training, extensive new materials or gadgetry, new classrooms, or an increase in federal, state, or local funds. They do not even require a reduced teaching load. What they do require is a teacher who will respect and respond to his students, not for what they have done, but for what they may do; not for what they have produced, but for what they may produce, if they are given an opportunity to see writing as a process, not a product.

Writing as a Mode of Learning

JANET EMIG

Writing represents a unique mode of learning—not merely valuable, not merely special, but unique. That will be my contention in this paper. The thesis is straightforward. Writing serves learning uniquely because writing as process-and-product possesses a cluster of attributes that correspond uniquely to certain powerful learning strategies.

Although the notion is clearly debatable, it is scarcely a private belief. Some of the most distinguished contemporary psychologists have at least implied such a role for writing as heuristic. Lev Vygotsky, A. R. Luria, and Jerome Bruner, for example, have all pointed out that higher cognitive functions, such as analysis and synthesis, seem to develop most fully only with the support system of verbal language—particularly, it seems, of written language.[1] Some of their arguments and evidence will be incorporated here.

Here I have a prior purpose: to describe as tellingly as possible *how* writing uniquely corresponds to certain powerful learning strategies. Making such a case for the uniqueness of writing should logically and theoretically involve establishing many contrasts, distinctions between (1) writing and all other verbal languaging processes—listening, reading, and especially talking; (2) writing and all other forms of composing, such as composing a painting, a symphony, a dance, a film, a building; and (3) composing in words and composing in the two other major graphic symbol systems of mathematical equations and scientific formulae. For the purposes of this paper, the task is simpler, since most students are not permitted by most curricula to discover the values of composing, say, in dance, or even in film; and most students are not sophisticated enough to create, to originate formulations, using the highly abstruse symbol system of equations and formulae. Verbal language

Reprinted from *College Composition and Communication* 28.2 (May 1977): 122–28. Copyright © 1977 by Janet Emig. Used with permission.

represents the most *available* medium for composing; in fact, the significance of sheer availability in its selection as a mode for learning can probably not be overstressed. But the uniqueness of writing among the verbal languaging processes does need to be established and supported if only because so many curricula and courses in English still consist almost exclusively of reading and listening.

WRITING AS A UNIQUE LANGUAGING PROCESS

Traditionally, the four languaging processes of listening, talking, reading, and writing are paired in either of two ways. The more informative seems to be the division many linguists make between first-order and second-order processes, with talking and listening characterized as first-order processes; reading and writing, as second-order. First-order processes are acquired without formal or systematic instruction; the second-order processes of reading and writing tend to be learned initially only with the aid of formal and systematic instruction.

The less useful distinction is that between listening and reading as receptive functions and talking and writing as productive functions. Critics of these terms like Louise Rosenblatt rightfully point out that the connotation of passivity too often accompanies the notion of receptivity when reading, like listening, is a vital, construing act.

An additional distinction, so simple it may have been previously overlooked, resides in two criteria: the matters of origination and of graphic recording. Writing is originating and creating a unique verbal construct that is graphically recorded. Reading is creating or re-creating *but not* originating a verbal construct that is graphically recorded. Listening is creating or re-creating but not originating a verbal construct that is *not* graphically recorded. Talking is creating *and* originating a verbal construct that is *not* graphically recorded (except for the circuitous routing of a transcribed tape). Note that a distinction is being made between creating and originating, separable processes.

For talking, the nearest languaging process, additional distinctions should probably be made. (What follows is not a denigration of talk as a valuable mode of learning.) A silent classroom or one filled only with the teacher's voice is anathema to learning. For evidence of the cognitive value of talk, one can look to some of the persuasive monographs coming from the London Schools Council project on writing: *From Information to Understanding* by Nancy Martin or *From Talking to Writing* by Peter Medway.[2] We also know that for some of us, talking is a valuable, even necessary, form of pre-writing. In his curriculum, James Moffett makes the value of such talk quite explicit.

8

But to say that talking is a valuable form of pre-writing is not to say that writing is talk recorded, an inaccuracy appearing in far too many composition texts. Rather, a number of contemporary trans-disciplinary sources suggest that talking and writing may emanate from different organic sources and represent quite different, possibly distinct, language functions. In *Thought and Language*, Vygotsky notes that "written speech is a separate linguistic function, differing from oral speech in both structure and mode of functioning."[3] The sociolinguist Dell Hymes, in a valuable issue of *Daedalus*, "Language as a Human Problem," makes a comparable point: "That speech and writing are not simply interchangeable, and have developed historically in ways at least partly autonomous, is obvious."[4] At the first session of the Buffalo Conference on Researching Composition (4–5 October 1975), the first point of unanimity among the participant-speakers with interests in developmental psychology, media, dreams and aphasia was that talking and writing were markedly different functions.[5] Some of us who work rather steadily with writing research agree. We also believe that there are hazards, conceptually and pedagogically, in creating too complete an analogy between talking and writing, in blurring the very real differences between the two.

What Are These Differences?

1. Writing is learned behavior; talking is natural, even irrepressible, behavior.

2. Writing then is an artificial process; talking is not.

3. Writing is a technological device—not the wheel, but early enough to qualify as primary technology; talking is organic, natural, earlier.

4. Most writing is slower than most talking.

5. Writing is stark, barren, even naked as a medium; talking is rich, luxuriant, inherently redundant.

6. Talk leans on the environment; writing must provide its own context.

7. With writing, the audience is usually absent; with talking, the listener is usually present.

8. Writing usually results in a visible graphic product; talking usually does not.

9. Perhaps because there is a product involved, writing tends to be a more responsible and committed act than talking.

10. It can even be said that throughout history, an aura, an ambience, a mystique has usually encircled the written word; the spoken word

has for the most part proved ephemeral and treated mundanely (ignore, please, our recent national history).

11. Because writing is often our representation of the world made visible, embodying both process and product, writing is more readily a form and source of learning than talking.

UNIQUE CORRESPONDENCES BETWEEN LEARNING AND WRITING

What then are some *unique* correspondences between learning and writing? To begin with some definitions: Learning can be defined in many ways, according to one's predilections and training, with all statements about learning of course hypothetical. Definitions range from the chemo-physiological ("Learning is changed patterns of protein synthesis in relevant portions of the cortex")[6] to transactive views drawn from both philosophy and psychology (John Dewey, Jean Piaget) that learning is the re-organization or confirmation of a cognitive scheme in light of an experience.[7] What the speculations seem to share is consensus about certain features and strategies that characterize successful learning. These include the importance of the classic attributes of re-inforcement and feedback. In most hypotheses, successful learning is also connective and selective. Additionally, it makes use of propositions, hypotheses, and other elegant summarizers. Finally, it is active, engaged, personal—more specifically, self-rhythmed—in nature.

Jerome Bruner, like Jean Piaget, through a comparable set of categories, posits three major ways in which we represent and deal with actuality: (1) enactive—we learn "by doing"; (2) iconic—we learn "by depiction in an image"; and (3) representational or symbolic—we learn "by restatement in words."[8] To overstate the matter, in enactive learning, the hand predominates; in iconic, the eye; and in symbolic, the brain.

What is striking about writing as a process is that, by its very nature, all three ways of dealing with actuality are simultaneously or almost simultaneously deployed. That is, the symbolic transformation of experience through the specific symbol system of verbal language is shaped into an icon (the graphic product) by the enactive hand. If the most efficacious learning occurs when learning is re-inforced, then writing through its inherent re-inforcing cycle involving hand, eye, and brain marks a uniquely powerful multi-representational mode for learning.

Writing is also integrative in perhaps the most basic possible sense: the organic, the functional. Writing involves the fullest possible functioning of the brain, which entails the active participation in the process of both the left and the right hemispheres. Writing is markedly bispheral, although in some popular accounts, writing is inaccurately presented as a chiefly left-hemisphere activity, perhaps because the linear written product is somehow regarded as analogue for the process that created it; and the left hemisphere seems to process material linearly.

The right hemisphere, however, seems to make at least three, perhaps four, major contributions to the writing process—probably, to the creative process generically. First, several researchers, such as Geschwind and Snyder of Harvard and Zaidal of Cal Tech, through markedly different experiments, have very tentatively suggested that the right hemisphere is the sphere, even the *seat*, of emotions.[9] Second—or perhaps as an illustration of the first—Howard Gardner, in his important study of the brain-damaged, notes that our sense of emotional appropriateness in discourse may reside in the right sphere:

> Emotional appropriateness, in sum—being related not only to *what* is said, but to how it is said and to what is *not* said, as well—is crucially dependent on right hemisphere intactness.[10]

Third, the right hemisphere seems to be the source of intuition, of sudden gestalts, of flashes of images, of abstractions occurring as visual or spatial wholes, as the initiating metaphors in the creative process. A familiar example: William Faulkner noted in his *Paris Review* interview that *The Sound and the Fury* began as the image of a little girl's muddy drawers as she sat in a tree watching her grandmother's funeral.[11]

Also, a unique form of feedback, as well as reinforcement, exists with writing, because information from the *process* is immediately and visibly available as that portion of the *product* already written. The importance for learning of a product in a familiar and available medium for immediate, literal (that is, visual) re-scanning and review cannot perhaps be overstated. In his remarkable study of purportedly blind sculptors, Géza Révész found that without sight, persons cannot move beyond a literal transcription of elements into any manner of symbolic transformation—by definition, the central requirement for reformulation and re-interpretation, i.e., revision, that most aptly named process.[12]

As noted in the second paragraph, Vygotsky and Luria, like Bruner, have written importantly about the connections between learning and writing. In his essay "The Psychobiology of Psychology," Bruner lists as one of six axioms regarding learning: "We are connective."[13] Another correspondence then between learning and writing: in *Thought and Language*, Vygotsky notes that writing makes a unique demand in that the writer must engage in "deliberate semantics"—in Vygotsky's elegant phrase, "deliberate structuring of the web of meaning."[14] Such structuring is required because, for Vygotsky, writing centrally represents an expansion of inner speech, that mode whereby we talk to ourselves, which is "maximally compact" and "almost entirely predicative"; written speech is a mode which is "maximally detailed" and which requires explicitly supplied subjects and topics. The medium then of written verbal language requires the establishment of systematic connections and relationships. Clear writing by definition is that writing which signals without ambiguity the nature of conceptual relationships, whether they be coordinate, subordinate, superordinate, causal, or something other.

Successful learning is also engaged, committed, personal learning. Indeed, impersonal learning may be an anomalous concept, like the very notion of objectivism itself. As Michael Polanyi states simply at the beginning of *Personal Knowledge*: "the ideal of strict objectivism is absurd." (How many courses and curricula in English, science, and all else does that one sentence reduce to rubble?) Indeed, the theme of *Personal Knowledge* is that

> into every act of knowing there enters a passionate contribution of the person knowing what is being known, . . . this coefficient is no mere imperfection but a vital component of his knowledge.[15]

In *Zen and the Art of Motorcycle Maintenance*, Robert Pirsig states a comparable theme:

> The Quality which creates the world emerges as *a relationship* between man and his experience. He is a *participant* in the creation of all things.[16]

Finally, the psychologist George Kelly has as the central notion in his subtle and compelling theory of personal constructs man as a scientist steadily and actively engaged in making and re-making his hypotheses about the nature of the universe.[17]

We are acquiring as well some empirical confirmation about the importance of engagement in, as well as self-selection of, a subject for the student learning to write and writing to learn. The recent Sanders and Littlefield study, reported in *Research in the Teaching of English*, is persuasive evidence on this point, as well as being a model for a certain type of research.[18]

As Luria implies in the quotation above, writing is self-rhythmed. One writes best as one learns best, at one's own pace. Or to connect the two processes, writing can sponsor learning because it can match its pace. Support for the importance of self-pacing to learning can be found in Benjamin Bloom's important study "Time and Learning."[19] Evidence for the significance of self-pacing to writing can be found in the reason Jean-Paul Sartre gave last summer for not using the tape-recorder when he announced that blindness in his second eye had forced him to give up writing:

> I think there is an enormous difference between speaking and writing. One rereads what one rewrites. But one can read slowly or quickly: in other words, you do not know how long you will have to take deliberating over a sentence. . . . If I listen to a tape recorder, the listening speed is determined by the speed at which the tape turns and not by my own needs. Therefore I will always be either lagging behind or running ahead of the machine.[20]

Writing is connective as a process in a more subtle and perhaps more significant way, as Luria points out in what may be the most powerful paragraph of rationale ever supplied for writing as heuristic:

> Written speech is bound up with the inhibition of immediate synpractical connections. It assumes a much slower, repeated mediating process of analysis and synthesis, which makes it possible not only to develop the required thought, but even to revert to its earlier stages, thus transforming the sequential chain of connections in a simultaneous, self-reviewing structure. Written speech thus represents a new and powerful instrument of thought.[21]

But first to explicate: writing inhibits "immediate synpractical connections." Luria defines *synpraxis* as "concrete-active" situations in which language does not exist independently but as a "fragment" of an ongoing action "outside of which it is incomprehensible."[22] In *Language and Learning,* James Britton defines it succinctly as "speech-cum-action."[23] Writing, unlike talking, restrains dependence upon the actual situation. Writing as a mode is inherently more self-reliant than speaking. Moreover, as Bruner states in explicating Vygotsky, "Writing virtually forces a remoteness of reference on the language user."[24]

Luria notes what has already been noted above: that writing, typically, is a "much slower" process than talking. But then he points out the relation of this slower pace to learning: this slower pace allows for—indeed, encourages—the shuttling among past, present, and future. Writing, in other words, connects the three major tenses of our experience to make meaning. And the two major modes by which these three aspects are united are the processes of analysis and synthesis: analysis, the breaking of entities into their constituent parts; and synthesis, combining or fusing these, often into fresh arrangements or amalgams.

13

Finally, writing is epigenetic, with the complex evolutionary development of thought steadily and graphically visible and available throughout as a record of the journey, from jottings and notes to full discursive formulations.

For a summary of the correspondences stressed here between certain learning strategies and certain attributes of writing see Figure 1.

This essay represents a first effort to make a certain kind of case for writing—specifically, to show its unique value for learning. It is at once over-elaborate and under specific. Too much of the formulation is in the off-putting jargon of the learning theorist, when my own predilection would have been to emulate George Kelly and to avoid terms like *reinforcement* and *feedback* since their use implies that I live inside a certain paradigm about learning I don't truly inhabit. Yet I hope that the essay will start a crucial line of inquiry; for unless the losses to learners of not writing are compellingly described and substantiated by experimental and speculative research, writing itself as a central academic process may not long endure.

Figure 1 Unique cluster of correspondences between certain learning strategies and certain attributes of writing.

Selected Characteristics of Successful Learning Strategies	Selected Attributes of Writing Process and Product
1. Profits from multi-representational and integrative re-inforcement	1. Represents process uniquely multi-representational and integrative
2. Seeks self-provided feedback:	2. Represents powerful instance of self-provided feedback:
a. immediate	a. provides product uniquely available for *immediate* feedback (review and re-evaluation)
b. long-term	b. provides record of evolution of thought since writing is epigenetic as process-and-product
3. Is connective:	3. Provides connections:
a. makes generative conceptual groupings, synthetic and analytic	a. establishes explicit and systematic conceptual groupings through lexical, syntactic, and rhetorical devices
b. proceeds from propositions, hypotheses, and other elegant summarizers	b. represents most available means (verbal language) for economic recording of abstract formulations
4. Is active, engaged, personal— notably, self-rhythmed	4. Is active, engaged, personal— notably, self-rhythmed

NOTES

1. Lev S. Vygotsky, *Thought and Language*, trans. Eugenia Hanfmann and Gertrude Vakar (Cambridge: The M.I.T. Press, 1962); A. R. Luria and F. Ia. Yudovich, *Speech and the Development of Mental Processes in the Child*, ed. Joan Simon (Baltimore: Penguin, 1971); Jerome S. Bruner, *The Relevance of Education* (New York: W. W. Norton and Co., 1971).

2. Nancy Martin, *From Information to Understanding* (London: Schools Council Project Writing Across the Curriculum, 11–13, 1973); Peter Medway, *From Talking to Writing* (London: Schools Council Project Writing Across the Curriculum, 11–13, 1973).

3. Vygotsky, p. 98.

4. Dell Hymes, "On the Origins and Foundations of Inequality Among Speakers," *Daedalus*, 102 (Summer, 1973), 69.

5. Participant-speakers were Loren Barrett, University of Michigan; Gerald O'Grady, SUNY/Buffalo; Hollis Frampton, SUNY/Buffalo; and Janet Emig, Rutgers.

6. George Steiner, *After Babel: Aspects of Language and Translation* (New York: Oxford University Press, 1975), p. 287.

7. John Dewey, *Experience and Education* (New York: Macmillan, 1938); Jean Piaget, *Biology and Knowledge: An Essay on the Relations between Organic Regulations and Cognitive Processes* (Chicago: University of Chicago Press, 1971).

8. Bruner, pp. 7–8.

9. Boyce Rensberger, "Language Ability Found in Right Side of Brain," *New York Times*, 1 August 1975, p. 14.

10. Howard Gardner, *The Shattered Mind: The Person After Brain Damage* (New York: Alfred A. Knopf, 1975), p. 372.

11. William Faulkner, *Writers at Work: The Paris Review Interviews*, ed. Malcolm Cowley (New York: The Viking Press, 1959), p. 130.

12. Géza Révész, *Psychology and Art of the Blind*, trans. H. A. Wolff (London: Longmans-Green, 1950).

13. Bruner, p. 126.

14. Vygotsky, p. 100.

15. Michael Polanyi, *Personal Knowledge: Toward a Post-Critical Philosophy* (Chicago: University of Chicago Press, 1958), p. viii.

16. Robert Pirsig, *Zen and the Art of Motorcycle Maintenance* (New York: William Morrow and Co., Inc., 1974), p. 212.

17. George Kelly, *A Theory of Personality: The Psychology of Personal Constructs* (New York: W. W. Norton and Co., 1963).

18. Sara E. Sanders and John H. Littlefield, "Perhaps Test Essays Can Reflect Significant Improvement in Freshman Composition: Report on a Successful Attempt," *RTE*, 9 (Fall, 1975), 145–153.

19. Benjamin Bloom, "Time and Learning," *American Psychologist*, 29 (September 1974), 682–688.

20. Jean-Paul Sartre, "Sartre at Seventy: An Interview," with Michel Contat, *New York Review of Books*, 7 August 1975.

21. Luria, p. 118.

22. Luria, p. 50.

23. James Britton, *Language and Learning* (Baltimore: Penguin, 1971), pp. 10–11.

24. Bruner, p. 47.

The Composing Processes
of Unskilled College Writers

SONDRA PERL

This paper presents the pertinent findings from a study of the composing processes of five unskilled college writers (Perl, 1978). The first part summarizes the goals of the original study, the kinds of data collected, and the research methods employed. The second part is a synopsis of the study of Tony, one of the original five case studies. The third part presents a condensed version of the findings on the composing process and discusses these findings in light of current pedagogical practice and research design.

GOALS OF THE STUDY

This research addressed three major questions: (1) How do unskilled writers write? (2) Can their writing processes be analyzed in a systematic, replicable manner? and (3) What does an increased understanding of their processes suggest about the nature of composing in general and the manner in which writing is taught in the schools?

In recent years, interest in the composing process has grown (Britton, 1975; Burton, 1973; Cooper, 1974; Emig, 1967, 1971). In 1963, Braddock, Lloyd-Jones, and Schoer, writing on the state of research in written composition, included the need for "direct observation" and case study procedures in their suggestions for future research (pp. 24, 31–32). In a section entitled "Unexplored Territory," they listed basic unanswered questions such as, "What is involved in the act of writing?" and "Of what does skill in writing actually consist?" (p. 51). Fifteen years later, Cooper and Odell (1978)

Reprinted from *Research in the Teaching of English* 13.4 (December 1979): 317–36. Used with permission.

edited a volume similar in scope, only this one was devoted entirely to issues and questions related to research on composing. This volume in particular signals a shift in emphasis in writing research. Alongside the traditional, large scale experimental studies, there is now widespread recognition of the need for works of a more modest, probing nature, works that attempt to elucidate basic processes. The studies on composing that have been completed to date are precisely of this kind; they are small-scale studies, based on the systematic observation of writers engaged in the process of writing (Emig, 1971; Graves, 1973; Mischel, 1974; Pianko, 1977; Stallard, 1974).

For all of its promise, this body of research has yet to produce work that would insure wide recognition for the value of process studies of composing. One limitation of work done to date is methodological. Narrative descriptions of composing processes do not provide sufficiently graphic evidence for the perception of underlying regularities and patterns. Without such evidence, it is difficult to generate well-defined hypotheses and to move from exploratory research to more controlled experimental studies. A second limitation pertains to the subjects studied. To date no examination of composing processes has dealt primarily with unskilled writers. As long as "average" or skilled writers are the focus, it remains unclear as to how process research will provide teachers with a firmer understanding of the needs of students with serious writing problems.

The present study is intended to carry process research forward by addressing both of these limitations. One prominent feature of the research design involves the development and use of a meaningful and replicable method for rendering the composing process as a sequence of observable and scorable behaviors. A second aspect of the design is the focus on students whose writing problems baffle the teachers charged with their education.

DESIGN OF THE STUDY

This study took place during the 1975–76 fall semester at Eugenio Maria de Hostos Community College of the City University of New York. Students were selected for the study on the basis of two criteria: writing samples that qualified them as unskilled writers and willingness to participate. Each student met with the researcher for five 90-minute sessions (see Table 1). Four sessions were devoted to writing with the students directed to compose aloud, to externalize their thinking processes as much as possible, during each session. In one additional session, a writing profile on the students' perceptions and memories of writing was developed through the use of an open-ended interview. All of the sessions took place in a soundproof room in the

Table 1   Design of the study.

	Session 1 (S1)	Session 2 (S2)	Session 3 (S3)	Session 4 (S4)	Session 5 (S5)
Mode	Extensive	Reflexive		Extensive	Reflexive
Topic	Society & Culture	Society & Culture	Interview: Writing Profile	Capitalism	Capitalism
Directions	Students told to compose aloud; no other directions given	Students told to compose aloud; no other directions given		Students told to compose aloud; also directed to talk out ideas before writing	Students told to compose aloud; also directed to talk out ideas before writing

college library. Throughout each session, the researcher assumed a noninterfering role.

The topics for writing were developed in an introductory social science course in which the five students were enrolled. The "content" material they were studying was divided into two modes: extensive, in which the writer was directed to approach the material in an objective, impersonal fashion, and reflexive, in which the writer was directed to approach similar material in an affective, personalized fashion. Contrary to Emig's (1971) definitions, in this study it was assumed that the teacher was always the audience.

DATA ANALYSIS

Three kinds of data were collected in this study: the students' written products, their composing tapes, and their responses to the interview. Each of these was studied carefully and then discussed in detail in each of the five case study presentations. Due to limitations of space, this paper will review only two of the data sets generated in the study.

Coding the Composing Process

One of the goals of this research was to devise a tool for describing the movements that occur during composing. In the past such descriptions have taken the form of narratives which detail, with relative precision and insight, observable composing behaviors; however, these narratives provide no way of ascertaining the frequency, relative importance, and place of each behavior within an individual's composing process. As such, they are cumbersome and difficult to replicate. Furthermore, lengthy, idiosyncratic narratives run the risk of leaving underlying patterns and regularities obscure. In contrast, the method created in this research provides a means of viewing the composing process that is:

1. Standardized—it introduces a coding system for observing the composing process that can be replicated;

2. Categorical—it labels specific, observable behaviors so that types of composing movements are revealed;

3. Concise—it presents the entire sequence of composing movements on one or two pages;

4. Structural—it provides a way of determining how parts of the process relate to the whole; and

5. Diachronic—it presents the sequences of movements that occur during composing as they unfold in time.

In total, the method allows the researcher to apprehend a process as it unfolds. It lays out the movements or behavior sequences in such a way that if patterns within a student's process or among a group of students exist, they become apparent.

The Code

The method consists of coding each composing behavior exhibited by the student and charting each behavior on a continuum. During this study, the coding occurred after the student had finished composing and was done by working from the student's written product and the audiotape of the session. It was possible to do this since the tape captured both what the student was saying and the literal sound of the pen moving across the page. As a result, it was possible to determine when students were talking, when they were writing, when both occurred simultaneously, and when neither occurred.

The major categorical divisions in this coding system are talking, writing, and reading; however, it was clear that there are various kinds of talk and various kinds of writing and reading operations, and that a coding system would need to distinguish among these various types. In this study the following operations were distinguished:

1. General planning [PL]—organizing one's thoughts for writing, discussing how one will proceed.
2. Local planning [PLL]—talking out what idea will come next.
3. Global planning [PLG]—discussing changes in drafts.
4. Commenting [C]—sighing, making a comment or judgment about the topic.
5. Interpreting [I]—rephrasing the topic to get a "handle" on it.
6. Assessing [A(+); A(−)]—making a judgment about one's writing; may be positive or negative.
7. Questioning [Q]—asking a question.
8. Talking leading to writing [T→W]—voicing ideas on the topic, tentatively finding one's way, but not necessarily being committed to or using all one is saying.
9. Talking and writing at the same time [TW]—composing aloud in such a way that what one is saying is actually being written at the same time.
10. Repeating [re]—repeating written or unwritten phrases a number of times.
11. Reading related to the topic:
    a. Reading the directions [R_D]
    b. Reading the question [R_Q]
    c. Reading the statement [R_S]
12. Reading related to one's own written product:
    a. Reading one sentence or a few words [R^a]
    b. Reading a number of sentences together [R^{a-b}]
    c. Reading the entire draft through [R^{W1}]
13. Writing silently [W].
14. Writing aloud [TW].
15. Editing [E]:
    a. Adding syntactic markers, words, phrases, or clauses [Eadd]
    b. Deleting syntactic markers, words, phrases, or clauses [Edel]
    c. Indicating concern for a grammatical rule [Egr]
    d. Adding, deleting, or considering the use of punctuation [Epunc]

    e. Considering or changing spelling [Esp]

    f. Changing the sentence structure through embedding, coordination or subordination [Ess]

    g. Indicating concern for appropriate vocabulary (word choice) [Ewc]

    h. Considering or changing verb form [Evc]

16. Periods of silence [s].

By taking specific observable behaviors that occur during composing and supplying labels for them, this system thus far provides a way of analyzing the process that is categorical and capable of replication. In order to view the frequency and the duration of composing behaviors and the relation between one particular behavior and the whole process, these behaviors need to be depicted graphically to show their duration and sequence.

The Continuum

The second component of this system is the construction of a time line and a numbering system. In this study, blank charts with lines like the following were designed:

10	20	30	40	50	60	70

A ten-digit interval corresponds to one minute and is keyed to a counter on a tape recorder. By listening to the tape and watching the counter, it is possible to determine the nature and duration of each operation. As each behavior is heard on the tape, it is coded and then noted on the chart with the counter used as a time marker. For example, if a student during prewriting reads the directions and the question twice and then begins to plan exactly what she is going to say, all within the first minute, it would be coded like this:

Prewriting

RdRoRdRoPLL

10

If at this point the student spends two minutes writing the first sentence, during which time she pauses, rereads the question, continues writing, and then edits for spelling before continuing on, it would be coded like this:

At this point two types of brackets and numbering systems have appeared. The initial sublevel number linked with the TW code indicates which draft the student is working on. TW_1 indicates the writing of the first draft; TW_2 and TW_3 indicate the writing of the second and third drafts. Brackets such as [Esp] separate these operations from writing and indicate the amount of time the operation takes. The upper-level number above the horizontal bracket indicates which sentence in the written product is being written and the length of the bracket indicates the amount of time spent on the writing of each sentence. All horizontal brackets refer to sentences, and from the charts it is possible to see when sentences are grouped together and written in a chunk (adjacent brackets) or when each sentence is produced in isolation (gaps between brackets). (See Appendix for sample chart.)

The charts can be read by moving along the time line, noting which behaviors occur and in what sequence. Three types of comments are also included in the charts. In bold-face type, the beginning and end of each draft are indicated; in lighter type-face, comments on the actual composing movements are provided; and in the lightest type-face, specific statements made by students or specific words they found particularly troublesome are noted.

From the charts, the following information can be determined:

1. the amount of time spent during prewriting;
2. the strategies used during prewriting;
3. the amount of time spent writing each sentence;
4. the behaviors that occur while each sentence is being written;
5. when sentences are written in groups or "chunks" (fluent writing);
6. when sentences are written in isolation (choppy or sporadic writing);
7. the amount of time spent between sentences;
8. the behaviors that occur between sentences;
9. when editing occurs (during the writing of sentences, between sentences, in the time between drafts);
10. the frequency of editing behavior;

11. the nature of the editing operations; and

12. where and in what frequency pauses or periods of silence occur in the process.

The charts, or *composing style sheets* as they are called, do not explain what students wrote but rather *how* they wrote. They indicate, on one page, the sequences of behavior that occur from the beginning of the process to the end. From them it is possible to determine where and how these behaviors fall into patterns and whether these patterns vary according to the mode of discourse.

It should be noted that although the coding system is presented before the analysis of the data, it was derived from the data and then used as the basis for generalizing about the patterns and behavioral sequences found within each student's process. These individual patterns were reported in each of the five case studies. Thus, initially, a style sheet was constructed for each writing session on each student. When there were four style sheets for each student, it was possible to determine if composing patterns existed among the group. The summary of results reported here is based on the patterns revealed by these charts.

Analyzing Miscues in the Writing Process

Miscue analysis is based on Goodman's model of the reading process. Created in 1962, it has become a widespread tool for studying what students do when they read and is based on the premise that reading is a psycholinguistic process which "uses language, in written form, to get to the meaning" (Goodman, 1973, p. 4). Miscue analysis "involves its user in examining the observed behavior of oral readers as an interaction between language and thought, as a process of constructing meaning from a graphic display" (Goodman, 1973, p. 4). Methodologically, the observer analyzes the mismatch that occurs when readers make responses during oral reading that differ from the text. This mismatch or miscueing is then analyzed from Goodman's "meaning-getting" model, based on the assumption that "the reader's preoccupation with meaning will show in his miscues, because they will tend to result in language that still makes sense" (Goodman, 1973, p. 9).

In the present study, miscue analysis was adapted from Goodman's model in order to provide insight into the writing process. Since students composed aloud, two types of oral behaviors were available for study: encoding processes or what students spoke while they were writing and decoding processes or what students "read"[1] after they had finished writing. When a discrepancy existed between encoding or decoding and what was on the paper, it was referred to as miscue.

24

For encoding, the miscue analysis was carried out in the following manner:

1. The students' written products were typed, preserving the original style and spelling.
2. What students said while composing aloud was checked against the written products; discrepancies were noted on the paper wherever they occurred.
3. The discrepancies were categorized and counted.

Three miscue categories were derived for encoding:

1. Speaking complete ideas but omitting certain words during writing.
2. Pronouncing words with plural markers or other suffixes completely but omitting these endings during writing.
3. Pronouncing the desired word but writing a homonym, an approximation of the word or a personal abbreviation of the word on paper.

For decoding, similar procedures were used, this time comparing the words of the written product with what the student "read" orally. When a discrepancy occurred, it was noted. The discrepancies were then categorized and counted.

Four miscue categories were derived for decoding:

1. "Reading in" missing words or word endings;
2. Deleting words or word endings;
3. "Reading" the desired word rather than the word on the page;
4. "Reading" abbreviations and misspellings as though they were written correctly.

A brief summary of the results of this analysis appears in the findings.

SYNOPSIS OF A CASE STUDY

Tony was a 20-year-old ex-Marine born and raised in the Bronx, New York. Like many Puerto Ricans born in the United States, he was able to speak Spanish, but he considered English his native tongue. In the eleventh grade, Tony left high school, returning three years later to take the New York State high school equivalency exam. As a freshman in college, he was also working part-time to support a child and a wife from whom he was separated.

Behaviors

The composing style sheets provide an overview of the observable behaviors exhibited by Tony during the composing process. (See Appendix for samples of Tony's writing and the accompanying composing style sheet.) The most salient feature of Tony's composing process was its recursiveness. Tony rarely produced a sentence without stopping to reread either a part or the whole. This repetition set up a particular kind of composing rhythm, one that was cumulative in nature and that set ideas in motion by its very repetitiveness. Thus, as can be seen from any of the style sheets, talking led to writing which led to reading which led to planning which again led to writing.

The style sheets indicated a difference in the composing rhythms exhibited in the extensive and reflexive modes. On the extensive topics there was not only more repetition within each sentence but also many more pauses and repetitions between sentences, with intervals often lasting as long as two minutes. On the reflexive topics, sentences were often written in groups, with fewer rereadings and only minimal time intervals separating the creation of one sentence from another.

Editing occurred consistently in all sessions. From the moment Tony began writing, he indicated a concern for correct form that actually inhibited the development of ideas. In none of the writing sessions did he ever write more than two sentences before he began to edit. While editing fit into his overall recursive pattern, it simultaneously interrupted the composing rhythm he had just initiated.

During the intervals between drafts, Tony read his written work, assessed his writing, planned new phrasings, transitions or endings, read the directions and the question over, and edited once again.

Tony performed these operations in both the extensive and reflexive modes and was remarkably consistent in all of his composing operations. The style sheets attest both to this consistency and to the densely packed, tight quality of Tony's composing process—indeed, if the notations on these sheets were any indication at all, it was clear that Tony's composing process was so full that there was little room left for invention or change.

Fluency

Table 2 provides a numerical analysis of Tony's writing performance. Here it is possible to compare not only the amount of time spent on the various

Table 2 Tony: Summary of four writing sessions (time in minutes).

	Drafts	Words	Time	Drafts	Words	Time
			S1 TW$_1$			**S4 T→W**
Extensive Mode			Prewriting: 7.8			Prewriting: 8.0
	W1	132	18.8	W1	182	29.0
	W2	170	51.0	W2	174	33.9
	Total	302	Total composing: 91.2*	Total	356	Total composing: 82.0*
			S2 TW$_1$			**S5 T→W**
Reflexive Mode			Prewriting: 3.5			Prewriting: 5.7
	W1	165	14.5	W1	208	24.0
	W2	169	25.0	W2	190	38.3
	W3	178	24.2	W3	152	20.8
	Total	512	Total composing: 76.0*	Total	550	Total composing: 96.0*

* Total composing includes time spent on editing and rereading, as well as actual writing.

composing operations but also the relative fluency. For Sessions 1 and 2 the data indicate that while Tony spent more time prewriting and writing in the extensive mode, he actually produced fewer words. For Sessions 4 and 5, a similar pattern can be detected. In the extensive mode, Tony again spent more time prewriting and produced fewer words. Although writing time was increased in the reflexive mode, the additional 20 minutes spent writing did not sufficiently account for an increase of 194 words. Rather, the data indicate that Tony produced more words with less planning and generally in less time in the reflexive mode, suggesting that his greater fluency lay in this mode.

Strategies

Tony exhibited a number of strategies that served him as a writer whether the mode was extensive or reflexive. Given my topic, the first operation he performed was to focus in and narrow down the topic. He did this by rephrasing the topic until either a word or an idea in the topic linked up with something in his own experience (an attitude, an opinion, an event). In this way he established a connection between the field of discourse and himself and at this point he felt ready to write.

Level of Language Use

Once writing, Tony employed a pattern of classifying or dividing the topic into manageable pieces and then using one or both of the divisions as the basis for narration. In the four writing sessions, his classifications were made on the basis of economic, racial, and political differences. However, all of his writing reflected a low level of generality. No formal principles were used to organize the narratives nor were the implications of ideas present in the essay developed.

In his writing, Tony was able to maintain the extensive/reflexive distinction. He recognized when he was being asked directly for an opinion and when he was being asked to discuss concepts or ideas that were not directly linked to his experience. However, the more distance between the topic and himself, the more difficulty he experienced, and the more repetitive his process became. Conversely, when the topic was close to his own experience, the smoother and more fluent the process became. More writing was produced, pauses were fewer, and positive assessment occurred more often. However, Tony made more assumptions on the part of the audience in the reflexive mode. When writing about himself, Tony often did not stop to explain the context from which he was writing; rather, the reader's understanding of the context was taken for granted.

Editing

Tony spent a great deal of his composing time editing. However, most of this time was spent proofreading rather than changing, rephrasing, adding, or evaluating the substantive parts of the discourse. Of a total of 234 changes made in all of the sessions, only 24 were related to changes of content and included the following categories:

1. Elaborations of ideas through the use of specification and detail;
2. Additions of modals that shift the mood of a sentence;
3. Deletions that narrow the focus of a paper;
4. Clause reductions or embeddings that tighten the structure of a paper;
5. Vocabulary choices that reflect a sensitivity to language;

6. Reordering of elements in a narrative;

7. Strengthening transitions between paragraphs;

8. Pronoun changes that signal an increased sensitivity to audience.

The 210 changes in form included the following:

Additions	19	Verb changes	4
Deletions	44	Spelling	95
Word choice	13	Punctuation	35
Unresolved problems	89		

The area that Tony changed most often was spelling, although, even after completing three drafts of a paper, Tony still had many words misspelled.

Miscue Analysis

Despite continual proofreading, Tony's completed drafts often retained a look of incompleteness. Words remained misspelled, syntax was uncorrected or overcorrected, suffixes, plural markers, and verb endings were missing, and often words or complete phrases were omitted.

The composing aloud behavior and the miscue analysis derived from it provide one of the first demonstrable ways of understanding how such seemingly incomplete texts can be considered "finished" by the student. (See Table 3 for a summary of Tony's miscues.) Tony consistently voiced complete sentences when composing aloud but only transcribed partial sentences. The same behavior occurred in relation to words with plural or marked endings. However, during rereading and even during editing, Tony supplied the missing endings, words, or phrases and did not seem to "see" what was missing from the text. Thus, when reading his paper, Tony "read in" the meaning he expected to be there which turned him into a reader of content rather than form. However, a difference can be observed between the extensive and reflexive modes, and in the area of correctness Tony's greater strength lay in the reflexive mode. In this mode, not only were more words produced in less time (1,062 vs. 658), but fewer decoding miscues occurred (38 vs. 46), and fewer unresolved problems remained in the text (34 vs. 55).

When Tony did choose to read for form, he was handicapped in another way. Through his years of schooling, Tony learned that there were sets of rules to be applied to one's writing, and he attempted to apply these rules of form to his prose. Often, though, the structures he produced were far more

Table 3 Tony—Miscue analysis.

	ENCODING			
	Speaking complete ideas but omitting certain words during writing	Pronouncing words with plural markers or other suffixes completely but omitting these endings during writing	Pronouncing the desired word but writing a homonym, an approximation of the word or a personal abbreviation of the word on paper	Total
S1	1	4	11	16
S2	8	0	14	22
S4	4	0	16	20
S5	3	1	15	19
	16	5	56	77

	DECODING			
	Reading in missing words or word endings	Deleting words or word endings	Reading the desired word rather than the word on the page	Reading abbreviations and misspellings as though they were written correctly	Total
S1	10	1	1	15	27
S2	5	1	2	10	18
S4	3	3	0	13	19
S5	7	1	2	10	20
	25	6	5	48	84

complicated than the simple set of proofreading rules he had at his disposal. He was therefore faced with applying the rule partially, discarding it, or attempting corrections through sound. None of these systems was completely helpful to Tony, and as often as a correction was made that improved the discourse, another was made that obscured it.

Summary

Finally, when Tony completed the writing process, he refrained from commenting on or contemplating his total written product. When he initiated writing, he immediately established distance between himself as writer and his discourse. He knew his preliminary draft might have errors and might need revision. At the end of each session, the distance had decreased if not entirely disappeared. Tony "read in" missing or omitted features, rarely perceived syntactic errors, and did not untangle overly embedded sentences. It was as if the semantic model in his head predominated, and the distance with which he entered the writing process had dissolved. Thus, even with his concern for revision and for correctness, even with the enormous amount of time he invested in rereading and repetition, Tony concluded the composing process with unresolved stylistic and syntactic problems. The conclusion here is not that Tony can't write, or that Tony doesn't know how to write, or that Tony needs to learn more rules: Tony is a writer with a highly consistent and deeply embedded recursive process. What he needs are teachers who can interpret that process for him, who can see through the tangles in the process just as he sees meaning beneath the tangles in his prose, and who can intervene in such a way that untangling his composing process leads him to create better prose.

SUMMARY OF THE FINDINGS

A major finding of this study is that, like Tony, all of the students studied displayed consistent composing processes; that is, the behavioral subsequences prewriting, writing, and editing appeared in sequential patterns that were recognizable across writing sessions and across students.

This consistency suggests a much greater internalization of process than has ever before been suspected. Since the written products of basic writers often look arbitrary, observers commonly assume that the students' approach is also arbitrary. However, just as Shaughnessy (1977) points out that there is "very little that is random . . . in what they have written" (p. 5), so, on close observation, very little appears random in *how* they write. The students observed had stable composing processes which they used whenever they were presented with a writing task. While this consistency argues against seeing these students as beginning writers, it ought not necessarily imply that they are proficient writers. Indeed, their lack of proficiency may be attributable to the way in which premature and rigid attempts to correct and edit their work truncate the flow of composing without substantially improving the form of what they have written. More detailed findings will be reviewed in the following subsections which treat the three major aspects of composing: prewriting, writing, and editing.

Prewriting

When not given specific prewriting instructions, the students in this study began writing within the first few minutes. The average time they spent on prewriting in sessions 1 and 2 was four minutes (see Table 4), and the planning strategies they used fell into three principal types:

1. Rephrasing the topic until a particular word or idea connected with the student's experience. The student then had "an event" in mind before writing began.

2. Turning the large conceptual issue in the topic (e.g., equality) into two manageable pieces for writing (e.g., rich vs. poor; black vs. white).

3. Initiating a string of associations to a word in the topic and then developing one or more of the associations during writing.

When students planned in any of these ways, they began to write with an articulated sense of where they wanted their discourse to go. However, frequently students read the topic and directions a few times and indicated that they had "no idea" what to write. On these occasions, they began writing without any secure sense of where they were heading, acknowledging only that they would "figure it out" as they went along. Often their first sentence was a rephrasing of the question in the topic which, now that it was in their own handwriting and down on paper in front of them, seemed to enable them to plan what ought to come next. In these instances, writing led to planning which led to clarifying which led to more writing. This sequence of planning and writing, clarifying and discarding, was repeated frequently in all of the sessions, even when students began writing with a secure sense of direction.

Although one might be tempted to conclude that these students began writing prematurely and that planning precisely what they were going to write ought to have occurred before they put pen to paper, the data here suggest:

1. that certain strategies, such as creating an association to a key word, focusing in and narrowing down the topic, dichotomizing and classifying, can and do take place in a relatively brief span of time; and

2. that the developing and clarifying of ideas is facilitated once students translate some of those ideas into written form. In other words, seeing ideas on paper enables students to reflect upon, change and develop those ideas further.

Table 4 Overview of all writing sessions.

	Prewriting time*				Total words / Total composing time				Editing changes		Unresolved problems	Miscues during reading
	S1	S2	S4	S5	S1	S2	S4	S5	Content	Form		
Tony	7.8	3.5	8.0	5.7	302 / 91.2	512 / 76.0	356 / 82.0	550 / 96.0	24	210	89	84
Dee	2.5	2.9	5.0	5.0	409 / 55.5	559 / 65.0	91 / 24.5	212 / 29.0	7	24	40	32
Stan	3.5	4.3	14.8	14.7	419 / 62.0	553 / 73.1	365 / 73.0	303 / 68.0	13	49	45	55
Lueller	2.0	1.5	4.0	13.0	518 / 90.8	588 / 96.8	315 / 93.0	363 / 77.8	2	167	143	147
Beverly	5.5	7.0	32.0	20.0	519 / 79.0	536 / 80.3	348 / 97.4	776 / 120.0	21	100	55	30

* Due to a change in the prewriting directions, only Sessions 1 and 2 are used to calculate the average time spent in prewriting.

33

Writing

Careful study revealed that students wrote by shuttling from the sense of what they wanted to say forward to the words on the page and back from the words on the page to their intended meaning. This "back and forth" movement appeared to be a recursive feature: at one moment students were writing, moving their ideas and their discourse forward; at the next they were backtracking, rereading, and digesting what had been written.

Recursive movements appeared at many points during the writing process. Occasionally sentences were written in groups and then reread as a "piece" of discourse; at other times sentences and phrases were written alone, repeated until the writer was satisfied or worn down, or rehearsed until the act of rehearsal led to the creation of a new sentence. In the midst of writing, editing occurred as students considered the surface features of language. Often planning of a global nature took place: in the midst of producing a first draft, students stopped and began planning how the second draft would differ from the first. Often in the midst of writing, students stopped and referred to the topic in order to check if they had remained faithful to the original intent, and occasionally, though infrequently, they identified a sentence or a phrase that seemed, to them, to produce a satisfactory ending. In all these behaviors, they were shuttling back and forth, projecting what would come next and doubling back to be sure of the ground they had covered.

A number of conclusions can be drawn from the observations of these students composing and from the comments they made: although they produced inadequate or flawed products, they nevertheless seemed to understand and perform some of the crucial operations involved in composing with skill. While it cannot be stated with certainty that the patterns they displayed are shared by other writers, some of the operations they performed appear sufficiently sound to serve as prototypes for constructing two major hypotheses on the nature of their composing processes. Whether the following hypotheses are borne out in studies of different types of writers remains an open question:

1. Composing does not occur in a straightforward, linear fashion. The process is one of accumulating discrete bits down on the paper and then working from those bits to reflect upon, structure, and then further develop what one means to say. It can be thought of as a kind of "retrospective structuring"; movement forward occurs only after one has reached back, which in turn occurs only after one has some sense of where one wants to go. Both aspects, the reaching back and the sensing forward, have a clarifying effect.

2. Composing always involves some measure of both construction and discovery. Writers construct their discourse inasmuch as they begin with a sense of what they want to write. This sense, as long as it remains implicit, is not equivalent to the explicit form it gives rise to. Thus, a process of constructing meaning is required. Rereading or backward movements become a way of assessing whether or not the words on the page adequately capture the original sense intended. Constructing simultaneously affords discovery. Writers know more fully what they mean only after having written it. In this way the explicit written form serves as a window on the implicit sense with which one began.

Editing

Editing played a major role in the composing processes of the students in this study (see Table 5). Soon after students began writing their first drafts, they began to edit, and they continued to do so during the intervals between drafts, during the writing of their second drafts and during the final reading of papers.

While editing, the students were concerned with a variety of items: the lexicon (i.e., spelling, word choice, and the context of words); the syntax (i.e., grammar, punctuation, and sentence structure); and the discourse as a whole (i.e., organization, coherence, and audience). However, despite the students' considered attempts to proofread their work, serious syntactic and stylistic problems remained in their finished drafts. The persistence of these

Table 5 Editing changes.

	Tony	Dee	Stan	Lueller	Beverly	Totals
Total number of words produced	1720	1271	1640	1754	2179	8564
Total form	210	24	49	167	100	550
Additions	19	2	10	21	11	63
Deletions	44	9	18	41	38	150
Word choice	13	4	1	27	6	51
Verb changes	4	1	2	7	12	26
Spelling	95	4	13	60	19	191
Punctuation	35	4	5	11	14	69
Total content	24	7	13	2	21	67

errors may, in part, be understood by looking briefly at some of the problems that arose for these students during editing.

Rule Confusion

(1) All of the students observed asked themselves, "Is this sentence [or feature] correct?" but the simple set of editing rules at their disposal was often inappropriate for the types of complicated structures they produced. As a result, they misapplied what they knew and either created a hypercorrection or impaired the meaning they had originally intended to clarify; (2) The students observed attempted to write with terms they heard in lectures or class discussions, but since they were not yet familiar with the syntactic or semantic constraints one word placed upon another, their experiments with academic language resulted in what Shaughnessy (1977, p. 49) calls, "lexical transplants" or "syntactic dissonances"; (3) The students tried to rely on their intuitions about language, in particular the sound of words. Often, however, they had been taught to mistrust what "sounded" right to them, and they were unaware of the particular feature in their speech codes that might need to be changed in writing to match the standard code. As a result, when they attempted corrections by sound, they became confused, and they began to have difficulty differentiating between what sounded right in speech and what needed to be marked on the paper.

Selective Perception

These students habitually reread their papers from internal semantic or meaning models. They extracted the meaning they wanted from the minimal cues on the page, and they did not recognize that outside readers would find those cues insufficient for meaning.

A study of Table 6 indicates that the number of problems remaining in the students' written products approximates the number of miscues produced during reading. This proximity, itself, suggests that many of these errors persisted because the students were so certain of the words they wanted to have on the page that they "read in" these words even when they were absent; in other words, they reduced uncertainty by operating as though what was in their heads was already on the page. The problem of selective perception, then, cannot be reduced solely to mechanical decoding; the semantic model from which students read needs to be acknowledged and taken into account in any study that attempts to explain how students write and why their completed written products end up looking so incomplete.

Table 6   The talk-write paradigm.
         Miscues—Decoding behaviors

	Tony	Dee	Stan	Lueller	Beverly	Totals
Unresolved problems	89	40	45	143	55	372
"Reading in" missing words or word endings	25	13	11	44	11	104
Deleting words or word endings	6	2	4	14	9	35
"Reading" the desired word rather than the word on the page	5	6	18	15	8	52
"Reading" abbreviations and misspellings as though they were written correctly	48	11	22	74	2	157
	84	32	55	147	30	348

Egocentricity

The students in this study wrote from an egocentric point of view. While they occasionally indicated a concern for their readers, they more often took the reader's understanding for granted. They did not see the necessity of making their referents explicit, of making the connections among their ideas apparent, of carefully and explicitly relating one phenomenon to another, or of placing narratives or generalizations within an orienting, conceptual framework.

On the basis of these observations one may be led to conclude that these writers did not know how to edit their work. Such a conclusion must, however, be drawn with care. Efforts to improve their editing need to be based on an informed view of the role that editing already plays in their composing processes. Two conclusions in this regard are appropriate here:

1. Editing intrudes so often and to such a degree that it breaks down the rhythms generated by thinking and writing. When this happens the students are forced to go back and recapture the strands of their thinking once the editing operation has been completed. Thus, editing occurs prematurely, before students have generated enough discourse to approximate the ideas they have, and it often results in their losing track of their ideas.

2. Editing is primarily an exercise in error-hunting. The students are prematurely concerned with the "look" of their writing; thus, as soon as a few words are written on the paper, detection and correction of errors replaces writing and revising. Even when they begin writing with a tentative, flexible frame of mind, they soon become locked into whatever is on the page. What they seem to lack as much as any rule is a conception of editing that includes flexibility, suspended judgment, the weighing of possibilities, and the reworking of ideas.

IMPLICATIONS FOR TEACHING AND RESEARCH

One major implication of this study pertains to teachers' conceptions of unskilled writers. Traditionally, these students have been labeled "remedial," which usually implies that teaching ought to remedy what is "wrong" in their written products. Since the surface features in the writing of unskilled writers seriously interfere with the extraction of meaning from the page, much class time is devoted to examining the rules of the standard code. The pedagogical soundness of this procedure has been questioned frequently,[2] but in spite of the debate, the practice continues, and it results in a further complication, namely that students begin to conceive of writing as a "cosmetic" process where concern for correct form supersedes development of ideas. As a result, the excitement of composing, of constructing and discovering meaning, is cut off almost before it has begun.

More recently, unskilled writers have been referred to as "beginners," implying that teachers can start anew. They need not "punish" students for making mistakes, and they need not assume that their students have already been taught how to write. Yet this view ignores the highly elaborated, deeply embedded processes the students bring with them. These unskilled college writers are not beginners in a *tabula rasa* sense, and teachers err in assuming they are. The results of this study suggest that teachers may first need to identify which characteristic components of each student's process facilitate writing and which inhibit it before further teaching takes place. If they do not, teachers of unskilled writers may continue to place themselves in a defeating position: imposing another method of writing instruction upon the students' already internalized processes without first helping students to extricate themselves from the knots and tangles in those processes.

A second implication of this study is that the composing process is now amenable to a replicable and graphic mode of representation as a sequence of codable behaviors. The composing style sheets provide researchers and teachers with the first demonstrable way of documenting how individual students write. Such a tool may have diagnostic as well as research benefits. It may be used to record writing behaviors in large groups, prior to and after instruction, as well as in individuals. Certainly it lends itself to the longitudinal study of the writing process and may help to elucidate what it is that changes in the process as writers become more skilled.

A third implication relates to case studies and to the theories derived from them. This study is an illustration of the way in which a theoretical model of the composing process can be grounded in observations of the individual's experience of composing. It is precisely the complexity of this experience that the case study brings to light. However, by viewing a series of cases, the researcher can discern patterns and themes that suggest regularities in composing behavior across individuals. These common features lead to hypotheses and theoretical formulations which have some basis in shared experience. How far this shared experience extends is, of course, a question that can only be answered through further research.

A final implication derives from the preponderance of recursive behaviors in the composing processes studied here, and from the theoretical notion derived from these observations: retrospective structuring, or the going back to the sense of one's meaning in order to go forward and discover more of what one has to say. Seen in this light, composing becomes the carrying forward of an implicit sense into explicit form. Teaching composing, then, means paying attention not only to the forms or products but also to the explicative process through which they arise.

APPENDIX

Composing Style Sheet

Name: __Tony__   Mode: __Extensive TW1__   Date: __October 31, 1975__

Session: __1__   Topic: __Society & Culture__   Time: __11:00 AM – 12:30 PM__

Prewriting   1

RDRQAPL   QWCRIQPLRQ   PLRQPLRQRI   PLRQPLRQPLRQ   TA(-)QRIP L   RIRI RQ T   QDQTPLRQPLG   RQ   TW1   AR^1[E$_{sp}$] R^1 PL RQPLG T

10   20 rephrasing   30   40   50   60   70   80   90   100
question

     2   3

RW1RQTQRW1 TO   PL   RW1RW1RQRQ   RQ TPL   TW1[E(-)]   RW1→TW1   R^{2}T   RW1 RW1 E RW1   TW1   PLL R1-3   TW1 PLL TW1

10 developing 20   30   40   50 developing 60   70   80   90   200
ideas   not a good way to   narrative
start a sentence

4   5   6   7   8+9

R3T→TW1 TW1 TW1T→TW1   PLT TW1[re]   TW1 T RQ   PL   R^2 TW1   [re]   TW1   PLG RQ RW1   [PL→E]   RW1   TE   RW1 [Eadd] PL

10   20 ending   30   effects 40   ending 50   60 End of W1 70   80   read for 90   300
                 of crisis   content first

                                                 1

RW1   A(-)   TPL   RW1   A(+)   RW1   [E$_{os}$] T   RW1   PLW2   TW2   [E$_{gr}$]   TW2 [E$_{gr}$] TW2 PL

go into 10   20   30   40   50   60   70 Begin W2 80   90   400
more depth   elaborating
                 lay-offs – jobs

    2   3

R2A(+) TW2   [R2]A(+) TW2   [E$_{sp}$]   R^2 R^3 PL   T[E$_{os}^{gr}$]PL   A(+)TW2 [PL→ E] TW2 [E$_{del}^{add}$] TW2[E$_{gr}$] TW2 PLR^3 PL-R^3 Tadd

10   20   30   40   50   60   70   80   90   500
                       there is
                       there are

    4   5

TW2—[EPL   ]TW2   PL RW2 [E PL]RW2[EWC]RIQ   RW1 [EWC^{add}]   A(+) TW2   [re] TW2   T   TW2[re]RW1 T   PL   RW1 T   [re]   TW2 [re]

10   20   30   40   50   60   70 elaborating 80   90   600

            6

[re][re]TW2 [re]   TW2   [re]   TW2   PLRW1   RW2 [re] RW2   A(+) RW2 TE   PL   RW1   RW2   PL

10   20   30   40   50   60   70   80   90   700
                               explaining
                               changes

                                 7

RW1 T PI   RW2 T R^4 T   R$^+$TW2   [re]   TW2   [re] TW2   R$^{6-7}$ [Eadd] R$^{6-7}$ [re]   PL R$^{5-7}$ A(+)PIRW1

10   20   30   40   50   60   70   80   90   800
      elaborating new sentence

                     8   9   10

TS→PL   RQ   PL   T RW1→TW2[re]   R^8 TW2   Tadd   RQ   A(-)   RW1 A(+) R^9 TW2   PL   RQ   RW2

should 10   20   30   40   50 changes 60   70   80   90   900
I add more?   elaborating   mind   ending   End of W2

RW2   WS to 960

10   Total   20   30   40   50   60   70   80   90   1000
     composing
     finished

Writing Sample
TONY
Session 1
W1

All men can't be consider equal in a America base on financial situation.[1] Because their are men born in rich families that will never have to worry about any financial difficulties.[2]

         are
And then theyre / ~~the~~ another type of Americans that is born to a poor family and al-
     may
way / have some kind of fina—difficulty.[3] Espeicaly nowadays in New York city With
            and all   If he is able
the budgit Crisis /   .[4] ~~He may~~ be able To get a job.[5] But are now he lose the job just as easy as he got it.[6] So when he loses his job he'll have to try to get some fina—assistance.[7]

                        here
A Then he'll probley have even more fin—diffuicuty.[8] So right / you can't see that In Amerian, all men are not create equal in the fin—sense.[9]

Writing Sample
TONY
Session 1
W2

All men can not be consider equal in America base on financial situation.[1] Because their are men born in rich families that will never have to worry about any financial ~~diffuel~~
         ~~the~~
diffuliculties.[2] And then they're are / another type of ameraicans that are born to a poor
                   may
famitly.[3] And This is the type of Americans that ~~will~~ / alway have some kind of fininacal diffuliculty.[4] Espeical today ~~today~~ ~~the~~in new york The way the city has fallen ~~has fallen~~
                         working
into fin—debt.[5] It has become such a big crisis for the ~~people~~ people, in the [6] If the
                with the   the   ~~is~~
working man is able to find a job, espeicaly ~~for~~ / ~~city~~ a city The way ~~the way~~ city / fin— sitionu is set up now, ~~h~~He'll probley lose the job a whole lot faster than what he got it.[7] When he loses his job he'll ~~p~~ have even more fin—difficulty.[8] And then he'll be force to got to the city for some fini—assi—.[9] So right here you can see that all men in America are not create equal in the fin—sense.[10]

NOTES

1. The word "read" is used in a particular manner here. In the traditional sense, reading refers to accurate decoding of written symbols. Here it refers to students' verbalizing words or endings even when the symbols for those words are missing or only minimally present. Whenever the term "reading" is used in this way, it will be in quotation marks.

41

2. For discussions on the controversy over the effects of grammar instruction on writing ability, see the following: Richard Braddock, Richard Lloyd-Jones, and Lowell Schoer, *Research in Written Composition* (Urbana, Ill.: National Council of Teachers of English, 1963); Frank O'Hare, *Sentence Combining* (NCTE Research Report No. 15, Urbana, Ill.: National Council of Teachers of English, 1973); Elizabeth F. Haynes, "Using Research in Preparing to Teach Writing," *English Journal*, 1978, 67, 82–89.

REFERENCES

Braddock, R., Lloyd-Jones, R., & Schoer, L. *Research in written composition*. Urbana, Ill.: National Council of Teachers of English, 1963.

Britton, J., Burgess, T., Martin, N., McLeod, A., & Rosen, H. *The development of writing abilities (11–18)*. London: Macmillan Education Ltd., 1975.

Burton, D. L. Research in the teaching of English: The troubled dream. *Research in the Teaching of English*, 1973, 1, 160–187.

Cooper, C. R. Doing research/reading research. *English Journal*, 1974, 63, 94–99.

Cooper, C. R., & Odell, L. (Eds.) *Research on composing: Points of departure*. Urbana, Ill.: National Council of Teachers of English, 1978.

Emig, J. A. *The composing processes of twelfth graders*. Urbana, Ill.: National Council of Teachers of English, 1971. (Research Report No. 13) (Ed. D. Dissertation, Harvard University, 1969).

Emig, J. A. On teaching composition: Some hypotheses as definitions. *Research in the Teaching of English*, 1967, 1, 127–135.

Goodman, K. S. (Ed.) *Miscue analysis: Applications to reading instruction*. Urbana, Ill.: NCTE and ERIC, 1973.

Graves, D. H. Children's writing: Research directions and hypotheses based upon an examination of the writing process of seven year old children (Doctoral dissertation, State University of New York at Buffalo, 1973). *Dissertation Abstracts International*, 1974, 34, 6255A.

Haynes, E. F. Using research in preparing to teach writing. *English Journal*, 1978, 67, 82–89.

Mischel, T. A case study of a twelfth-grade writer. *Research in the Teaching of English*, 1974, 8, 303–314.

O'Hare, F. *Sentence-combining: Improving student writing without formal grammar instruction*. Urbana, Ill.: National Council of Teachers of English, 1973. (Research Report No. 15)

Perl, S. *Five writers writing: Case studies of the composing processes of unskilled college writers*. Unpublished doctoral dissertation, New York University, 1978.

Pianko, S. *The composing acts of college freshmen writers*. Unpublished Ed.D. dissertation, Rutgers University, 1977.

Shaughnessy, M. P. *Errors and expectations: A guide for the teacher of basic writing*. New York: Oxford University Press, 1977.

Stallard, C. K. An analysis of the writing behavior of good student writers. *Research in the Teaching of English*, 1974, 8, 206–218.

Revision Strategies of Student Writers and Experienced Adult Writers

Nancy Sommers

Although various aspects of the writing process have been studied extensively of late, research on revision has been notably absent. The reason for this, I suspect, is that current models of the writing process have directed attention away from revision. With few exceptions, these models are linear; they separate the writing process into discrete stages. Two representative models are Gordon Rohman's suggestion that the composing process moves from prewriting to writing to rewriting and James Britton's model of the writing process as a series of stages described in metaphors of linear growth, conception — incubation — production.[1] What is striking about these theories of writing is that they model themselves on speech: Rohman defines the writer in a way that cannot distinguish him from a speaker ("A writer is a man who . . . puts [his] experience into words in his own mind" — p. 15); and Britton bases his theory of writing on what he calls (following Jakobson) the "expressiveness" of speech.[2] Moreover, Britton's study itself follows the "linear model" of the relation of thought and language in speech proposed by Vygotsky, a relationship embodied in the linear movement "from the motive which engenders a thought to the shaping of the thought, *first* in inner speech, *then* in meanings of words, and *finally* in words" (quoted in Britton, p. 40). What this movement fails to take into account in its linear structure — "first . . . then . . . finally" — is the recursive shaping of thought by language; what it fails to take into account is *revision*. In these linear

Reprinted from *College Composition and Communication* 31.4 (December 1980): 378–88. Used with permission.

conceptions of the writing process revision is understood as a separate stage at the end of the process—a stage that comes after the completion of a first or second draft and one that is temporally distinct from the prewriting and writing stages of the process.[3]

The linear model bases itself on speech in two specific ways. First of all, it is based on traditional rhetorical models, models that were created to serve the spoken art of oratory. In whatever ways the parts of classical rhetoric are described, they offer "stages" of composition that are repeated in contemporary models of the writing process. Edward Corbett, for instance, describes the "five parts of a discourse"—*inventio, dispositio, elocutio, memoria, pronuntiatio*—and, disregarding the last two parts since "after rhetoric came to be concerned mainly with written discourse, there was no further need to deal with them,"[4] he produces a model very close to Britton's conception [*inventio*], incubation [*dispositio*], production [*elocutio*]. Other rhetorics also follow this procedure, and they do so not simply because of historical accident. Rather, the process represented in the linear model is based on the irreversibility of speech. Speech, Roland Barthes says, "is irreversible":

> "A word cannot be retracted, except precisely by saying that one retracts it. To cross out here is to add: if I want to erase what I have just said, I cannot do it without showing the eraser itself (I must say: 'or rather. . . ' 'I expressed myself badly. . . '); paradoxically, it is ephemeral speech which is indelible, not monumental writing. All that one can do in the case of a spoken utterance is to tack on another utterance."[5]

What is impossible in speech is *revision*: like the example Barthes gives, revision in speech is an afterthought. In the same way, each stage of the linear model must be exclusive (distinct from the other stages) or else it becomes trivial and counterproductive to refer to these junctures as "stages."

By staging revision after enunciation, the linear models reduce revision in writing, as in speech, to no more than an afterthought. In this way such models make the study of revision impossible. Revision, in Rohman's model, is simply the repetition of writing; or to pursue Britton's organic metaphor, revision is simply the further growth of what is already there, the "preconceived" product. The absence of research on revision, then, is a function of a theory of writing which makes revision both superfluous and redundant, a theory which does not distinguish between writing and speech.

What the linear models do produce is a parody of writing. Isolating revision and then disregarding it plays havoc with the experiences composition teachers have of the actual writing and rewriting of experienced writers. Why should the linear model be preferred? Why should revision be forgotten, superfluous? Why do teachers offer the linear model and students accept it? One reason, Barthes suggests, is that "there is a fundamental tie between teaching and speech," while "writing begins at the point where speech becomes *impossible*."[6] The spoken word cannot be revised. The possibility of revision distinguishes the written text from speech. In fact, according to Barthes, this is the essential difference between writing and speaking. When we must revise, when the very idea is subject to recursive shaping by language, then speech becomes inadequate. This is a matter to which I will return, but first we should examine, theoretically, a detailed exploration of what student writers as distinguished from experienced adult writers *do* when they write and rewrite their work. Dissatisfied with both the linear model of writing and the lack of attention to the process of revision, I conducted a series of studies over the past three years which examined the revision processes of student writers and experienced writers to see what role revision played in their writing processes. In the course of my work the revision process was redefined as *a sequence of changes in a composition—changes which are initiated by cues and occur continually throughout the writing of a work.*

METHODOLOGY

I used a case study approach. The student writers were twenty freshmen at Boston University and the University of Oklahoma with SAT verbal scores ranging from 450–600 in their first semester of composition. The twenty experienced adult writers from Boston and Oklahoma City included journalists, editors, and academics. To refer to the two groups, I use the terms *student writers* and *experienced writers* because the principal difference between these two groups is the amount of experience they have had in writing.

Each writer wrote three essays, expressive, explanatory, and persuasive, and rewrote each essay twice, producing nine written products in draft and final form. Each writer was interviewed three times after the final revision of each essay. And each writer suggested revisions for a composition written by an anonymous author. Thus extensive written and spoken documents were obtained from each writer.

The essays were analyzed by counting and categorizing the changes made. Four revision operations were identified: deletion, substitution, addition, and reordering. And four levels of changes were identified: word, phrase, sentence, theme (the extended statement of one idea). A coding system was developed for identifying the frequency of revision by level and operation. In addition, transcripts of the interviews in which the writers interpreted their revisions were used to develop what was called a *scale of concerns* for each writer. This scale enabled me to codify what were the writer's primary concerns, secondary concerns, tertiary concerns, and whether the writers used the same scale of concerns when revising the second or third drafts as they used in revising the first draft.

REVISION STRATEGIES OF STUDENT WRITERS

Most of the students I studied did not use the terms *revision* or *rewriting*. In fact, they did not seem comfortable using the word *revision* and explained that revision was not a word they used, but the word their teachers used. Instead, most of the students had developed various functional terms to describe the type of changes they made. The following are samples of these definitions:

> *Scratch Out and Do Over Again:* "I say scratch out and do over, and that means what it says. Scratching out and cutting out. I read what I have written and I cross out a word and put another word in; a more decent word or a better word. Then if there is somewhere to use a sentence that I have crossed out, I will put it there."
>
> *Reviewing:* "Reviewing means just using better words and eliminating words that are not needed. I go over and change words around."
>
> *Reviewing:* "I just review every word and make sure that everything is worded right. I see if I am rambling; I see if I can put a better word in or leave one out. Usually when I read what I have written, I say to myself, 'that word is so bland or so trite,' and then I go and get my thesaurus."
>
> *Redoing:* "Redoing means cleaning up the paper and crossing out. It is looking at something and saying, no that has to go, or no, that is not right."
>
> *Marking Out:* "I don't use the word rewriting because I only write one draft and the changes that I make are made on top of the draft. The changes that I make are usually just marking out words and putting different ones in."
>
> *Slashing and Throwing Out:* "I throw things out and say they are not good. I like to write like Fitzgerald did by inspiration, and if I feel inspired then I don't need to slash and throw much out."

The predominant concern in these definitions is vocabulary. The students understand the revision process as a rewording activity. They do so because they perceive words as the unit of written discourse. That is, they concentrate on particular words apart from their role in the text. Thus one student quoted above thinks in terms of dictionaries, and, following the eighteenth century theory of words parodied in *Gulliver's Travels*, he imagines a load of things carried about to be exchanged. Lexical changes are the major revision activities of the students because economy is their goal. They are governed, like the linear model itself, by the Law of Occam's Razor that prohibits logically needless repetition: redundancy and superfluity. Nothing governs speech more than such superfluities; speech constantly repeats itself precisely because spoken words, as Barthes writes, are expendable in the cause of communication. The aim of revision according to the students' own description is therefore to clean up speech; the redundancy of speech is unnecessary in writing, their logic suggests, because writing, unlike speech, can be reread. Thus one student said, "Redoing means cleaning up the paper and crossing out." The remarkable contradiction of cleaning by marking might, indeed, stand for student revision as I have encountered it.

The students place a symbolic importance on their selection and rejection of words as the determiners of success or failure for their compositions. When revising, they primarily ask themselves: can I find a better word or phrase? A more impressive, not so cliched, or less hum-drum word? Am I repeating the same word or phrase too often? They approach the revision process with what could be labeled as a "thesaurus philosophy of writing"; the students consider the thesaurus a harvest of lexical substitutions and believe that most problems in their essays can be solved by rewording. What is revealed in the students' use of the thesaurus is a governing attitude toward their writing: that the meaning to be communicated is already there, already finished, already produced, ready to be communicated, and all that is necessary is a better word "rightly worded." One student defined revision as "redoing"; "redoing" meant "just using better words and eliminating words that are not needed." For the students, writing is translating: the thought to the page, the language of speech to the more formal language of prose, the word to its synonym. Whatever is translated, an original text already exists for students, one which need not be discovered or acted upon, but simply communicated.[7]

The students list repetition as one of the elements they most worry about. This cue signals to them that they need to eliminate the repetition either by substituting or deleting words or phrases. Repetition occurs, in large part, because student writing imitates—transcribes—speech: attention to repetitious words is a manner of cleaning speech. Without a sense of the developmental possibilities of revision (and writing in general) students seek, on the authority of many textbooks, simply to clean up their language and prepare to type. What is curious, however, is that students are aware of lexical repetition, but not conceptual repetition. They only notice the repetition if they can "hear" it; they do not diagnose lexical repetition as

47

symptomatic of problems on a deeper level. By rewording their sentences to avoid the lexical repetition, the students solve the immediate problem, but blind themselves to problems on a textual level; although they are using different words, they are sometimes merely restating the same idea with different words. Such blindness, as I discovered with student writers, is the inability to "see" revision as a process: the inability to "re-view" their work again, as it were, with different eyes, and to start over.

The revision strategies described above are consistent with the students' understanding of the revision process as requiring lexical changes but not semantic changes. For the students, the extent to which they revise is a function of their level of inspiration. In fact, they use the word *inspiration* to describe the ease or difficulty with which their essay is written, and the extent to which the essay needs to be revised. If students feel inspired, if the writing comes easily, and if they don't get stuck on individual words or phrases, then they say that they cannot see any reason to revise. Because students do not see revision as an activity in which they modify and develop perspectives and ideas, they feel that if they know what they want to say, then there is little reason for making revisions.

The only modification of ideas in the students' essays occurred when they tried out two or three introductory paragraphs. This results, in part, because the students have been taught in another version of the linear model of composing to use a thesis statement as a controlling device in their introductory paragraphs. Since they write their introductions and their thesis statements even before they have really discovered what they want to say, their early close attention to the thesis statement, and more generally the linear model, function to restrict and circumscribe not only the development of their ideas, but also their ability to change the direction of these ideas.

Too often as composition teachers we conclude that students do not willingly revise. The evidence from my research suggests that it is not that students are unwilling to revise, but rather that they do what they have been taught to do in a consistently narrow and predictable way. On every occasion when I asked students why they hadn't made any more changes, they essentially replied, "I knew something larger was wrong, but I didn't think it would help to move words around." The students have strategies for handling words and phrases and their strategies helped them on a word or sentence level. What they lack, however, is a set of strategies to help them identify the "something larger" that they sensed was wrong and work from there. The students do not have strategies for handling the whole essay. They lack procedures or heuristics to help them reorder lines of reasoning or ask questions about their purposes and readers. The students view their compositions in a linear way as a series of parts. Even such potentially useful concepts as "unity" or "form" are reduced to the rule that a composition, if it is to have form, must have an introduction, a body, and a conclusion, or the sum total of the necessary parts.

The students decide to stop revising when they decide that they have not violated any of the rules for revising. These rules, such as "Never begin a sentence with a conjunction" or "Never end a sentence with a preposition," are lexically cued and rigidly applied. In general, students will subordinate the demands of the specific problems of their text to the demands of the rules. Changes are made in compliance with abstract rules about the product, rules that quite often do not apply to the specific problems in the text. These revision strategies are teacher-based, directed towards a teacher-reader who expects compliance with rules—with pre-existing "conceptions"—and who will only examine parts of the composition (writing comments about those parts in the margins of their essays) and will cite any violations of rules in those parts. At best the students see their writing altogether passively through the eyes of former teachers or their surrogates, the textbooks, and are bound to the rules which they have been taught.

REVISION STRATEGIES OF EXPERIENCED WRITERS

One aim of my research has been to contrast how student writers define revision with how a group of experienced writers define their revision processes. Here is a sampling of the definitions from the experienced writers:

> *Rewriting:* "It is a matter of looking at the kernel of what I have written, the content, and then thinking about it, responding to it, making decisions, and actually restructuring it."

> *Rewriting:* "I rewrite as I write. It is hard to tell what is a first draft because it is not determined by time. In one draft, I might cross out three pages, write two, cross out a fourth, rewrite it, and call it a draft. I am constantly writing and rewriting. I can only conceptualize so much in my first draft—only so much information can be held in my head at one time; my rewriting efforts are a reflection of how much information I can encompass at one time. There are levels and agenda which I have to attend to in each draft."

> *Rewriting:* "Rewriting means on one level, finding the argument, and on another level, language changes to make the argument more effective. Most of the time I feel as if I can go on rewriting forever. There is always one part of a piece that I could keep working on. It is always difficult to know at what point to abandon a piece of writing. I like this idea that a piece of writing is never finished, just abandoned."

Rewriting: "My first draft is usually very scattered. In rewriting, I find the line of argument. After the argument is resolved, I am much more interested in word choice and phrasing."

Revising: "My cardinal rule in revising is never to fall in love with what I have written in a first or second draft. An idea, sentence, or even a phrase that looks catchy, I don't trust. Part of this idea is to wait a while. I am much more in love with something after I have written it than I am a day or two later. It is much easier to change anything with time."

Revising: "It means taking apart what I have written and putting it back together again. I ask major theoretical questions of my ideas, respond to those questions, and think of proportion and structure, and try to find a controlling metaphor. I find out which ideas can be developed and which should be dropped. I am constantly chiseling and changing as I revise."

The experienced writers describe their primary objective when revising as finding the form or shape of their argument. Although the metaphors vary, the experienced writers often use structural expressions such as "finding a framework," "a pattern," or "a design" for their argument. When questioned about this emphasis, the experienced writers responded that since their first drafts are usually scattered attempts to define their territory, their objective in the second draft is to begin observing general patterns of development and deciding what should be included and what excluded. One writer explained, "I have learned from experience that I need to keep writing a first draft until I figure out what I want to say. Then in a second draft, I begin to see the structure of an argument and how all the various sub-arguments which are buried beneath the surface of all those sentences are related." What is described here is a process in which the writer is both agent and vehicle. "Writing," says Barthes, unlike speech, "develops like a seed, not a line,"[8] and like a seed it confuses beginning and end, conception and production. Thus, the experienced writers say their drafts are "not determined by time," that rewriting is a "constant process," that they feel as if (they) "can go on forever." Revising confuses the beginning and end, the agent and vehicle; it confuses, *in order to find*, the line of argument.

After a concern for form, the experienced writers have a second objective: a concern for their readership. In this way, "production" precedes "conception." The experienced writers imagine a reader (reading their product) whose existence and whose expectations influence their revision process. They have abstracted the standards of a reader and this reader seems to be partially a reflection of themselves and functions as a critical and productive collaborator—a collaborator who has yet to love their work. The anticipation of a reader's judgment causes a feeling of dissonance when the writer

50

recognizes incongruities between intention and execution, and requires these writers to make revisions on all levels. Such a reader gives them just what the students lacked: new eyes to "re-view" their work. The experienced writers believe that they have learned the causes and conditions, the product, which will influence their reader, and their revision strategies are geared towards creating these causes and conditions. They demonstrate a complex understanding of which examples, sentences, or phrases should be included or excluded. For example, one experienced writer decided to delete public examples and add private examples when writing about the energy crisis because "private examples would be less controversial and thus more persuasive." Another writer revised his transitional sentences because "some kinds of transitions are more easily recognized as transitions than others." These examples represent the type of strategic attempts these experienced writers use to manipulate the conventions of discourse in order to communicate to their reader.

But these revision strategies are a process of more than communication; they are part of the process of *discovering meaning* altogether. Here we can see the importance of dissonance; at the heart of revision is the process by which writers recognize and resolve the dissonance they sense in their writing. Ferdinand de Saussure has argued that meaning is differential or "diacritical," based on differences between terms rather than "essential" or inherent qualities of terms. "Phonemes," he said, "are characterized not, as one might think, by their own positive quality but simply by the fact that they are distinct."[9] In fact, Saussure bases his entire *Course in General Linguistics* on these differences, and such differences are dissonant; like musical dissonances which gain their significance from their relationship to the "key" of the composition which itself is determined by the whole language, specific language (parole) gains its meaning from the system of language (langue) of which it is a manifestation and part. The musical composition — a "composition" of parts — creates its "key" as in an over-all structure which determines the value (meaning) of its parts. The analogy with music is readily seen in the compositions of experienced writers: both sorts of composition are based precisely on those structures experienced writers seek in their writing. It is this complicated relationship between the parts and the whole in the work of experienced writers which destroys the linear model; writing cannot develop "like a line" because each addition or deletion is a reordering of the whole. Explicating Saussure, Jonathan Culler asserts that "meaning depends on difference of meaning."[10] But student writers constantly struggle to bring their essays into congruence with a predefined meaning. The experienced writers do the opposite: they seek to discover (to create) meaning in the engagement with their writing, in revision. They seek to emphasize and exploit the lack of clarity, the differences of meaning, the dissonance, that writing as opposed to speech allows in the possibility of revision. Writing has spatial and temporal features not apparent in speech—words are recorded in space and fixed in time—which is why writing is susceptible to reordering and later addition. Such features make possible the dissonance that both provokes revision and promises, from itself, new meaning.

For the experienced writers the heaviest concentration of changes is on the sentence level, and the changes are predominantly by addition and deletion. But, unlike the students, experienced writers make changes on all levels and use all revision operations. Moreover, the operations the students fail to use—reordering and addition—seem to require a theory of the revision process as a totality—a theory which, in fact, encompasses the *whole* of the composition. Unlike the students, the experienced writers possess a nonlinear theory in which a sense of the whole writing both precedes and grows out of an examination of the parts. As we saw, one writer said he needed "a first draft to figure out what to say," and "a second draft to see the structure of an argument buried beneath the surface." Such a "theory" is both theoretical and strategical; once again, strategy and theory are conflated in ways that are literally impossible for the linear model. Writing appears to be more like a seed than a line.

Two elements of the experienced writers' theory of the revision process are the adoption of a holistic perspective and the perception that revision is a recursive process. The writers ask: what does my essay as a *whole* need for form, balance, rhythm, or communication. Details are added, dropped, substituted, or reordered according to their sense of what the essay needs for emphasis and proportion. This sense, however, is constantly in flux as ideas are developed and modified; it is constantly "re-viewed" in relation to the parts. As their ideas change, revision becomes an attempt to make their writing consonant with that changing vision.

The experienced writers see their revision process as a recursive process—a process with significant recurring activities—with different levels of attention and different agenda for each cycle. During the first revision cycle their attention is primarily directed towards narrowing the topic and delimiting their ideas. At this point, they are not as concerned as they are later about vocabulary and style. The experienced writers explained that they get closer to their meaning by not limiting themselves too early to lexical concerns. As one writer commented to explain her revision process, a comment inspired by the summer 1977 New York power failure: "I feel like Con Edison cutting off certain states to keep the generators going. In first and second drafts, I try to cut off as much as I can of my editing generator, and in a third draft, I try to cut off some of my idea generators, so I can make sure that I will actually finish the essay." Although the experienced writers describe their revision process as a series of different levels or cycles, it is inaccurate to assume that they have only one objective for each cycle and that each cycle can be defined by a different objective. The same objectives and sub-processes are present in each cycle, but in different proportions. Even though these experienced writers place the predominant weight upon finding the form of their argument during the first cycle, other concerns exist as well. Conversely, during the later cycles, when the experienced writers' primary attention is focused upon stylistic concerns, they are still attuned, although in a reduced way, to the form of the argument. Since writers are limited in what they can attend to during each cycle (understandings are temporal), revision strategies help balance competing demands on attention. Thus, writers can concentrate on more than one objective at a time by developing strategies to sort out and organize their different concerns in successive cycles of revision.

It is a sense of writing as discovery—a repeated process of beginning over again, starting out new—that the students failed to have. I have used the notion of dissonance because such dissonance, the incongruities between intention and execution, governs both writing and meaning. Students do not see the incongruities. They need to rely on their own internalized sense of good writing and to see their writing with their "own" eyes. Seeing in revision—seeing beyond hearing—is at the root of the word *revision* and the process itself; current dicta on revising blind our students to what is actually involved in revision. In fact, they blind them to what constitutes good writing altogether. Good writing disturbs: it creates dissonance. Students need to seek the dissonance of discovery, utilizing in their writing, as the experienced writers do, the very difference between writing and speech—the possibility of revision.

NOTES

1. D. Gordon Rohman and Albert O. Wlecke, "Pre-writing: The Construction and Application of Models for Concept Formation in Writing," Cooperative Research Project No. 2174, U.S. Office of Education, Department of Health, Education, and Welfare; James Britton, Anthony Burgess, Nancy Martin, Alex McLeod, Harold Rosen, *The Development of Writing Abilities (11–18)* (London: Macmillan Education, 1975).

2. Britton is following Roman Jakobson, "Linguistics and Poetics," in T. A. Sebeok, *Style in Language* (Cambridge, Mass: MIT Press, 1960).

3. For an extended discussion of this issue see Nancy Sommers, "The Need for Theory in Composition Research," *College Composition and Communication*, 30 (February, 1979), 46–49.

4. *Classical Rhetoric for the Modern Student* (New York: Oxford University Press, 1965), p. 27.

5. Roland Barthes, "Writers, Intellectuals, Teachers," in *Image-Music-Text*, trans. Stephen Heath (New York: Hill and Wang, 1977), pp. 190–191.

6. "Writers, Intellectuals, Teachers," p. 190.

7. Nancy Sommers and Ronald Schleifer, "Means and Ends: Some Assumptions of Student Writers," *Composition and Teaching*, II (in press).

8. *Writing Degree Zero* in *Writing Degree Zero and Elements of Semiology*, trans. Annette Lavers and Colin Smith (New York: Hill and Wang, 1968), p. 20.

9. *Course in General Linguistics*, trans. Wade Baskin (New York, 1966), p. 119.

10. Jonathan Culler, *Saussure* (Penguin Modern Masters Series; London: Penguin Books, 1976), p. 70.

Acknowledgment: The author wishes to express her gratitude to Professor William Smith, University of Pittsburgh, for his vital assistance with the research reported in this article and to Patrick Hays, her husband, for extensive discussions and critical editorial help.

The Writer's Audience
Is Always a Fiction

WALTER J. ONG, S.J.

Epistola . . . non erubescit.
  —*Cicero,* Epistolae ad familiares *v. 12.1.*

Ubi nihil erit quae scribas, id ipsum scribes.
  —*Cicero,* Epistolae ad Atticum *iv.8.4.*

I

Although there is a large and growing literature on the differences between oral and written verbalization, many aspects of the differences have not been looked into at all, and many others, although well known, have not been examined in their full implications. Among these latter is the relationship, of the so-called "audience" to writing as such, to the situation that inscribed communication establishes and to the roles that readers as readers are consequently called on to play. Some studies in literary history and criticism at times touch near this subject, but none, it appears, take it up in any detail.

The standard locus in Western intellectual tradition for study of audience responses has been rhetoric. But rhetoric originally concerned oral communication, as is indicated by its name, which comes from the Greek word for public speaking. Over two millennia, rhetoric has been gradually extended to include writing more and more, until today, in highly technological cultures, this is its principal concern. But the extension has come

Reprinted by permission of the Modern Language Association of America from *PMLA* 90.1 (January 1975): 9–21. Copyright © 1975 by the Modern Language Association of America.

gradually and has advanced pari passu with the slow and largely unnoticed emergence of markedly chirographic and typographic styles out of those originating in oral performance, with the result that the differentiation between speech and writing has never become a matter of urgent concern for the rhetoric of any given age: when orality was in the ascendancy, rhetoric was oral-focused; as orality yielded to writing, the focus of rhetoric was slowly shifted, unreflectively for the most part, and without notice.

Histories of the relationship between literature and culture have something to say about the status and behavior of readers, before and after reading given materials, as do mass media studies, readership surveys, liberation programs for minorities or various other classes of persons, books on reading skills, works of literary criticism, and works on linguistics, especially those addressing differences between hearing and reading. But most of these studies, except perhaps literary criticism and linguistic studies, treat only perfunctorily, if at all, the roles imposed on the reader by a written or printed text not imposed by spoken utterance. Formalist or structuralist critics, including French theorists such as Paul Ricoeur as well as Roland Barthes, Jacques Derrida, Michel Foucault, Philippe Sollers, and Tzvetan Todorov, variously advert to the immediacy of the oral as against writing and print and occasionally study differences between speech and writing, as Louis Lavelle did much earlier in *La Parole et l'écriture* (1942). In treating of masks and "shadows" in his *Sociologie du théâtre* (1965), Jean Duvignaud brilliantly discusses the projections of a kind of collective consciousness on the part of theater audiences. But none of these appear to broach directly the question of readers' roles called for by a written text, either synchronically as such roles stand at present or diachronically as they have developed through history. Linguistic theorists such as John R. Searle and John L. Austin treat "illocutionary acts" (denoted by "warn," "command," "state," etc.), but these regard the speaker's or writer's need in certain instances to secure a special hold on those he addresses,[1] not any special role imposed by writing.

Wayne Booth in *The Rhetoric of Fiction* and Walker Gibson, whom Booth quotes, come quite close to the concerns of the present study in their treatment of the "mock reader," as does Henry James, whom Booth also cites, in his discussion of the way an author makes "his reader very much as he makes his character."[2] But this hint of James is not developed—there is no reason why it should be—and neither Booth nor Gibson discusses in any detail the history of the ways in which readers have been called on to relate to texts before them. Neither do Robert Scholes and Robert Kellogg in their invaluable work, *The Nature of Narrative*: they skirt the subject in their chapter on "The Oral Heritage of Written Narrative,"[3] but remain chiefly concerned with the oral performer, the writer, and techniques, rather than with the recipient of the message. Yet a great many of the studies noted here as well as many others, among which might be mentioned Norman N. Holland's *The Dynamics of Literary Response* (1968), suggest the time is ripe for a study of the history of readers and their enforced roles, for they show that we have ample phenomenological and literary sophistication to manage many of the complications involved.

So long as verbal communication is reduced to a simplistic mechanistic model which supposedly moves corpuscular units of something labeled "information" back and forth along tracks between two termini, there is of course no special problem with those who assimilate the written or printed word. For the speaker, the audience is in front of him. For the writer, the audience is simply further away, in time or space or both. A surface inscribed with information can neutralize time by preserving the information and conquer space by moving the information to its recipient over distances that sound cannot traverse. If, however, we put aside this alluring but deceptively neat and mechanistic mock-up and look at verbal communication in its human actuality, noting that words consist not of corpuscular units but of evanescent sound and that, as Maurice Merleau-Ponty has pointed out,[4] words are never fully determined in their abstract signification but have meaning only with relation to man's body and to its interaction with its surroundings, problems with the writer's audience begin to show themselves. Writing calls for difficult, and often quite mysterious, skills. Except for a small corps of highly trained writers, most persons could get into written form few if any of the complicated and nuanced meanings they regularly convey orally. One reason is evident: the spoken word is part of present actuality and has its meaning established by the total situation in which it comes into being. Context for the spoken word is simply present, centered in the person speaking and the one or ones to whom he addresses himself and to whom he is related existentially in terms of the circumambient actuality.[5] But the meaning caught in writing comes provided with no such present circumambient actuality, at least normally. (One might except special cases of written exchanges between persons present to one another physically but with oral channels blocked: two deaf persons, for example, or two persons who use different variants of Chinese and are orally incomprehensible to one another but can communicate through the same written characters, which carry virtually the same meanings though they are sounded differently in the different varieties of Chinese.)

Such special cases apart, the person to whom the writer addresses himself normally is not present at all. Moreover, with certain special exceptions such as those just suggested, he must not be present. I am writing a book which will be read by thousands, or, I modestly hope, by tens of thousands. So, please, get out of the room. I want to be alone. Writing normally calls for some kind of withdrawal.

How does the writer give body to the audience for whom he writes? It would be fatuous to think that the writer addressing a so-called general audience tries to imagine his readers individually. A well-known novelist friend of mine only laughed when I asked him if, as he was writing a novel, he imagined his real readers—the woman on the subway deep in his book, the student in his room, the businessman on a vacation, the scholar in his study. There is no need for a novelist to feel his "audience" this way at all. It may be, of course, that at one time or another he imagines himself addressing one or another real person. But not all his readers in their particularities. Practically speaking, of course, and under the insistent urging of editors and publishers, he does have to take into consideration the real social, economic, and psychological state of possible readers. He has to write a book that real persons will buy and read. But I am speaking—or writing—here of the "audience" that fires the writer's imagination. If it consists of the real persons who he hopes will buy his book, they are not these persons in an untransmuted state.[6]

Although I have thus far followed the common practice in using the term "audience," it is really quite misleading to think of a writer as dealing with an "audience," even though certain considerations may at times oblige us to think this way. More properly, a writer addresses readers—only, he does not quite "address" them either: he writes to or for them. The orator has before him an audience which is a true audience, a collectivity. "Audience" is a collective noun. There is no such collective noun for readers, nor, so far as I am able to puzzle out, can there be. "Readers" is a plural. Readers do not form a collectivity, acting here and now on one another and on the speaker as members of an audience do. We can devise a singularized concept for them, it is true, such as "readership." We can say that the *Reader's Digest* has a readership of I don't know how many millions—more than it is comfortable to think about, at any rate. But "readership" is not a collective noun. It is an abstraction in a way that "audience" is not.

The contrast between hearing and reading (running the eye over signals that encode sound) can be caught if we imagine a speaker addressing an audience equipped with texts. At one point, the speaker asks the members of the audience all to read silently a paragraph out of the text. The audience immediately fragments. It is no longer a unit. Each individual retires into his own microcosm. When the readers look up again, the speaker has to gather them into a collectivity once more. This is true even if he is the author of the text they are reading.

To sense more fully the writer's problem with his so-called audience let us envision a class of students asked to write on the subject to which school-teachers, jaded by summer, return compulsively every autumn: "How I Spent My Summer Vacation." The teacher makes the easy assumption, inviting and plausible but false, that the chief problem of a boy and a girl in writing is finding a subject actually part of his or her real life. In-close subject matter is supposed to solve the problem of invention. Of course it does not. The problem is not simply what to say but also whom to say it to. Say? The student is not talking. He is writing. No one is listening. There is no feedback. Where does he find his "audience"? He has to make his readers up, fictionalize them.

If the student knew what he was up against better than the teacher giving the assignment seemingly does, he might ask, "Who wants to know?" The answer is not easy. Grandmother? He never tells grandmother. His father or mother? There's a lot he would not want to tell them, that's sure. His class-mates? Imagine the reception if he suggested they sit down and listen quietly while he told them how he spent his summer vacation. The teacher? There is no conceivable setting in which he could imagine telling his teacher how he spent his summer vacation other than in writing this paper, so that writing for the teacher does not solve his problems but only restates them. In fact, most young people do not tell anybody how they spent their summer vacation, much less write down how they spent it. The subject may be in-close; the use it is to be put to remains unfamiliar, strained, bizarre.

How does the student solve the problem? In many cases, in a way somewhat like the following. He has read, let us say, *The Adventures of Tom Sawyer*. He knows what this book felt like, how the voice in it addressed its readers, how the narrator hinted to his readers that they were related to him and he to them, whoever they may actually have been or may be. Why not pick up that voice and, with it, its audience? Why not make like Samuel Clemens and write for whomever Samuel Clemens was writing for? This even makes it possible to write for his teacher—itself likely to be a productive ploy—whom he certainly has never been quite able to figure out. But he knows his teacher has read *Tom Sawyer*, has heard the voice in the book, and could therefore obviously make like a *Tom Sawyer* reader. His problem is solved, and he goes ahead. The subject matter now makes little difference, provided that it is something like Mark Twain's and that it interests him on some grounds or other. Material in-close to his real life is not essential, though, of course, it might be welcome now that he has a way to process it.

If the writer succeeds in writing, it is generally because he can fictionalize in his imagination an audience he has learned to know not from daily life but from earlier writers who were fictionalizing in their imagination audiences they had learned to know in still earlier writers, and so on back to the dawn of written narrative. If and when he becomes truly adept, an "original writer," he can do more than project the earlier audience, he can alter it. Thus it was that Samuel Clemens in *Life on the Mississippi* could not merely project the audience that the many journalistic writers about the Midwestern rivers had brought into being, but could also shape it to his own demands. If you had read Isaiah Sellers, you could read Mark Twain, but with a difference. You had to assume a part in a less owlish, more boisterous setting, in which Clemens' caustic humor masks the uncertainty of his seriousness. Mark Twain's reader is asked to take a special kind of hold on himself and on life.

II

These reflections suggest, or are meant to suggest, that there exists a tradition in fictionalizing audiences that is a component part of literary tradition in the sense in which literary tradition is discussed in T. S. Eliot's "Tradition and the Individual Talent." A history of the ways audiences have been called on to fictionalize themselves would be a correlative of the history of literary genres and literary works, and indeed of culture itself.

What do we mean by saying the audience is a fiction? Two things at least. First, that the writer must construct in his imagination, clearly or vaguely, an audience cast in some sort of role—entertainment seekers, reflective sharers of experience (as those who listen to Conrad's Marlow), inhabitants of a lost and remembered world of prepubertal latency (readers of Tolkien's hobbit stories), and so on. Second, we mean that the audience must correspondingly fictionalize itself. A reader has to play the role in which the author has cast him, which seldom coincides with his role in the rest of actual life. An office worker on a bus reading a novel of Thomas Hardy is listening to a voice which is not that of any real person in the real setting around him. He is playing the role demanded of him by this person speaking in a quite special way from the book, which is not the subway and is not quite "Wessex" either, though it speaks of Wessex. Readers over the ages have had to learn this game of literacy, how to conform themselves to the projections of the writers they read, or at least how to operate in terms of these projections. They have to know how to play the game of being a member of an audience that "really" does not exist. And they have to adjust when the rules change, even though no rules thus far have ever been published and even though the changes in the unpublished rules are themselves for the most part only implied.

A history of literature could be written in terms of the ways in which audiences have successively been fictionalized from the time when writing broke away from oral performance, for, just as each genre grows out of what went before it, so each new role that readers are made to assume is related to previous roles. Putting aside for the moment the question of what fictionalizing may be called for in the case of the audience for oral performance, we can note that when script first came on the scene, the fictionalizing of readers was relatively simple. Written narrative at first was merely a transcription of oral narrative, or what was imagined as oral narrative, and it assumed some kind of oral singer's audience, even when being read. The transcribers of the *Iliad* and the *Odyssey* presumably imagined an audience of real listeners in attendance on an oral singer, and readers of those works to this day do well if they can imagine themselves hearing a singer of tales.[7] How these texts and other oral performances were in fact originally set down in writing remains puzzling, but the transcribers certainly were not composing in writing, but rather recording with minimal alteration what a singer was singing or was imagined to be singing.

Even so, a scribe had to fictionalize in a way a singer did not, for a real audience was not really present before the scribe, so it would seem, although it is just possible that at times one may have been (Lord, pp. 125–28). But, as transcription of oral performance or imagined oral performance gave way gradually to composition in writing, the situation changed. No reader today imagines *Second Skin* as a work that John Hawkes is reciting extempore to a group of auditors, even though passages from it may be impressive when read aloud.

III

We have noted that the roles readers are called on to play evolve without any explicit rules or directives. How readers pick up the implicit signals and how writers change the rules can be illustrated by examining a passage from a specialist in unpublished directives for readers, Ernest Hemingway. The passage is the opening of *A Farewell to Arms*. At the start of my comment on the passage, it will be clear that I am borrowing a good deal from Walker Gibson's highly discerning book on modern American prose styles, *Tough, Sweet, and Stuffy*.[8] The Hemingway passage follows:

> In the late summer of that year we lived in a house in a village that looked across the river and the plain to the mountains. In the bed of the river there were pebbles and boulders, dry and white in the sun, and the water was clear and swiftly moving and blue in the channels.

Hemingway's style is often characterized as straightforward, unadorned, terse, lacking in qualifiers, close-lipped; and it is all these things. But none of them were peculiar to Hemingway when his writing began to command attention. A feature more distinctive of Hemingway here and elsewhere is the way he fictionalizes the reader, and this fictionalizing is often signaled largely by his use of the definite article as a special kind of qualifier or of the demonstrative pronoun "that," of which the definite article is simply an attenuation.

"The late summer of that year," the reader begins. What year? The reader gathers that there is no need to say. "Across the river." What river? The reader apparently is supposed to know. "And the plain." What plain? *"The* plain"— remember? "To the mountains." What mountains? Do I have to tell you? Of course not. *The* mountains—*those* mountains we know. We have somehow been there together. Who? You, my reader, and I. The reader—every reader—is being cast in the role of a close companion of the writer. This is the game he must play here with Hemingway, not always exclusively or totally, but generally, to a greater or lesser extent. It is one reason why the writer is tight-lipped. Description as such would bore a boon companion. What description there is comes in the guise of pointing, in verbal gestures, recalling humdrum, familiar details. "In the bed of the river there were pebbles and boulders, dry and white in the sun." The known world, accepted and accepting. Not presentation, but recall. The writer needs only to point, for what he wants to tell you about is not the scene at all but his feelings. These, too, he treats as something you really had somehow shared, though you might not have been quite aware of it at the time. He can tell you what was going on inside him and count on sympathy, for you were there. You *know.* The reader here has a well-marked role assigned him. He is a companion-in-arms, somewhat later become a confidant. It is a flattering role. Hemingway readers are encouraged to cultivate high self-esteem.

The effect of the definite article in Hemingway here is quite standard and readily explicable. Normally, in English, we are likely to make an initial reference to an individual object by means of the indefinite article and to bring in the definite only subsequently. "Yesterday on the street *a* man came up to me, and when I stopped in my stride *the* man said. . . ." "A" is a modified form of the term "one," a kind of singular of "some." "A man" means "one man" (of many real or possible men). The indefinite article tacitly acknowledges the existence or possibility of a number of individuals beyond the immediate range of reference and indicates that from among them one is selected. Once we have indicated that we are concerned not with all but with one-out-of-many, we train the definite article or pointer article on the object of our attention.[9] The definite article thus commonly signals some previous, less definite acquaintanceship. Hemingway's exclusion of indefinite in favor of definite articles signals the reader that he is from the first on familiar ground. He shares the author's familiarity with the subject matter. The reader must pretend he has known much of it before.

Hemingway's concomitant use of the demonstrative distancing pronoun "that" parallels his use of "the." For "the" is only an attenuated "that." It is a modified form of the demonstrative pronoun that replaced the original Old English definite article "seo." Both hold their referents at a distance, "that" typically at a somewhat greater distance than "the." *That* mountain you see ten miles away is indicated there on *the* map on *the* wall. If we wish to think of the map as close, we would say, *"This* map on this wall." In distancing their objects, both "that" and "the" can tend to bring together the speaker and the one spoken to. "That" commonly means that-over-there at a distance from you-and-me here, and "the" commonly means much the same. These terms thus can easily implement the Hemingway relationship: you-and-me.

This you-and-me effect of the distancing demonstrative pronoun and the definite article can be seen perhaps more spectacularly in romance etymology. The words for "the" in the romance languages come from the Latin word *ille, illa, illud,* which yields in various romance tongues *il, le, la, el, lo,* and their cognates. *Ille* is a distancing demonstrative in Latin: it means "that-over-there-away-from-you-and-me" and stands in contrastive opposition to another Latin demonstrative which has no counterpart in English, *iste, ista, istud,* which means "that-over-there-by-you" (and thus can readily become pejorative — "that-little-no-account-thing-of-yours"). *Ille* brings together the speaker and the one spoken to by contrast with the distanced object; *iste* distances from the speaker the one spoken to as well as the object. *Ille* yields the romance definite articles, which correspond quite closely in function to the English "the," and thus advertises the close tie between "the" and "that."

Could readers of an earlier age have managed the Hemingway relationship, the you-and-me relationship, marked by tight-lipped empathy based on shared experience? Certainly from antiquity the reader or hearer of an epic was plunged in medias res. But this does not mean he was cast as the author's boon companion. It means rather that he was plunged into the middle of a narrative sequence and told about antecedent events only later. A feeling of camaraderie between companions-in-arms is conveyed in epics, but the companions-in-arms are fictional characters; they are not the reader or hearer and the narrator. *"Forsan et haec olim meminisse iuvabit"* — these words in the *Aeneid,* "perhaps some day it will help to recall these very things," are spoken by Aeneas to his companions when they are undergoing a period of hardships. They are one character's words to other characters, not Virgil's words to his hearer or reader. One might urge further that, like Hemingway's reader, the reader or hearer of an epic—most typically, of an oral folk epic—was hearing stories with which he was already acquainted, that he was thus on familiar ground. He was, but not in the sense that he was forced to pretend he had somehow lived as an alter ego of the narrator. His familiarity with the material was not a pretense at all, not a role, but a simple fact. Typically, the epic audience had heard the story, or something very much like it, before.

The role in which Hemingway casts the reader is somewhat different not only from anything these situations in early literature demand but also from anything in the time immediately before Hemingway. This is what makes Hemingway's writing interesting to literary historians. But Hemingway's demands on the reader are by no means entirely without antecedents. The existence of antecedents is indicated by the fact that Hemingway was assimilated by relatively unskilled readers with very little fuss. He does not recast the reader in a disturbingly novel role. By contrast, the role in which Faulkner casts the reader is a far greater departure from preceding roles than is Hemingway's. Faulkner demands more skilled and daring readers, and consequently had far fewer at first, and has relatively fewer even today when the Faulkner role for readers is actually taught in school. (Perhaps we should say the Faulkner roles.)

No one, so far as I know, has worked up a history of the readers' roles that prepared for that prescribed by Hemingway. But one can discern significantly similar demands on readers beginning as early as Addison and Steele, who assume a new fashionable intimacy among readers themselves and between all readers and the writer, achieved largely by casting readers as well as writer in the role of coffeehouse habitués. Defoe develops in his own way comparable author-reader intimacy. The roots of these eighteenth-century intimacies are journalistic, and from earlier journalism they push out later in Hemingway's own day into the world of sportswriters and war correspondents, of whom Hemingway himself was one. With the help of print and the near instantaneousness implemented by electronic media (the telegraph first, later radio teletype and electronic transmission of photography), the newspaper writer could bring his reader into his own on-the-spot experience, availing himself in both sports and war of the male's strong sense of camaraderie based on shared hardships. Virgil's *forsan et haec olim meminisse iuvabit* once more. But Virgil was telling a story of the days of old and, as has been seen, the camaraderie was among characters in the story, Aeneas and his men. Sports and war journalism are about the here and now, and, if the story can be got to the

reader quickly, the camaraderie can be easily projected between the narrator and the reader. The reader is close enough temporally and photograph-
ically to the event for him to feel like a vicarious participant. In journalism
Hemingway had an established foundation on which to build, if not one
highly esteemed in snobbish literary circles. And he in turn has been built
upon by those who have come later. Gibson has shown how much the
style of *Time* magazine is an adaptation of Hemingway (pp. 48–54). To
Hemingway's writer-reader camaraderie *Time* adds omniscience, solemnly
"reporting," for example, in eyewitness style, the behavior and feelings of a
chief of state in his own bedroom as he answers an emergency night telephone call and afterward returns to sleep. Hemingway encouraged his
readers in high self-esteem. *Time* provides its readers, on a regular weekly
basis, companionship with the all-knowing gods.

When we look the other way down the corridors of time to the period
before the coffeehouses and the beginnings of intimate journalism, we find
that readers have had to be trained gradually to play the game Hemingway
engages them in. What if, *per impossibile,* a Hemingway story projecting the
reader's role we have attended to here had turned up in Elizabethan
England? It would probably have been laughed out of court by readers
totally unable to adapt to its demands upon them. It would certainly have
collided with representative literary theory, as propounded for example by
Sir Philip Sidney in *The Defense of Poesie.* For Sidney and most of his age,
poetry—that is to say, literature generally—had as its aim to please, but even
more basically to teach, at least in the sense that it gave the reader to know
what he did not know before. The Hemingway convention that the reader
had somehow been through it all before with the writer would have been to
Sidney's age at best confusing and at worst wrongheaded. One could argue
that the Hemingway narrator would be telling the reader at least something
he did not know before—that is, largely, the feelings of the narrator. But
even this revelation, as we have seen, implies in Hemingway a covert awareness on the part of the reader, a deep sympathy or empathy of a basically
romantic, nonpublic sort, grounded in intimacy. Sidney would have sent
Hemingway back to his writing table to find something newer to write
about, or to find a way of casting his material in a fresher-sounding form.

Another, and related, feature of the Hemingway style would have
repelled sixteenth-century readers: the addiction to the "the" and "that" to
the calculated exclusion of most descriptive qualifiers. There is a deep irony
here. For in the rhetorical world that persisted from prehistoric times to the
age of romanticism, descriptive qualifiers were commonly epithetic,
expected qualifiers. The first chapter of Sidney's *Arcadia* (1590) presents the
reader with "the hopeless shepheard," the "friendly rival," "the necessary

65

food," "natural rest," "flowery fields," "the extreme heat of summer," and countless other souvenirs of a country every rhetorician had trod many times before. Is this not making the reader a recaller of shared experience much as Hemingway's use of "the" and "that" does? Not at all in the same way. The sixteenth-century reader recalls the familiar accouterments of literature, which are the familiar accouterments or commonplaces also of sculpture, painting, and all art. These are matters of shared public acquaintanceship, not of private experience. The sixteenth-century reader is walking through land all educated men know. He is not made to pretend he knows these familiar objects because he once shared their presence with this particular author, as a Hemingway reader is made to pretend. In Sidney, there is none of the you-and-I-know-even-if-others-don't ploy.

IV

To say that earlier readers would have been nonplussed at Hemingway's demands on them is not to say that earlier readers did not have special roles to play or that authors did not have their own problems in devising and signaling what the roles were. A few cases might be instanced here.

First of all, it is only honest to admit that even an oral narrator calls on his audience to fictionalize itself to some extent. The invocation to the Muse is a signal to the audience to put on the epic-listener's cap. No Greek, after all, ever talked the kind of language that Homer sang, although Homer's contemporaries could understand it well enough. Even today we do not talk in other contexts quite the kind of language in which we tell fairy stories to children. "Once upon a time," we begin. The phrase lifts you out of the real world. Homer's language is "once upon a time" language. It establishes a fictional world. But the fictionalizing in oral epic is directly limited by live interaction, as real conversation is. A real audience controls the narrator's behavior immediately. Students of mine from Ghana and from western Ireland have reported to me what I have read and heard from many other sources: a given story may take a skilled or "professional" storyteller anywhere from ten minutes to an hour and a half, depending on how he finds the audience relates to him on a given occasion. "You always knew ahead of time what he was going to say, but you never knew how long it would take him to say it," my Irish informant reported. The teller reacts directly to audience response. Oral storytelling is a two-way street.

Written or printed narrative is not two-way, at least in the short run. Readers' reactions are remote and initially conjectural, however great their ultimate effects on sales. We should think more about the problems that the need to fictionalize audiences creates for writers. Chaucer, for example, had a problem with the conjectural readers of the *Canterbury Tales*. There was no established tradition in English for many of the stories, and certainly none at all for a collection of such stories. What does Chaucer do? He sets the stories in what, from a literary-structural point of view, is styled a frame. A group of pilgrims going to Canterbury tell stories to one another: the pilgrimage frames the individual narratives. In terms of signals to his readers, we could put it another way: Chaucer simply tells his readers how they are to fictionalize themselves. He starts by telling them that there is a group of pilgrims doing what real people do, going to a real place, Canterbury. The reader is to imagine himself in their company and join the fun. Of course this means fictionalizing himself as a member of a nonexistent group. But the fictionalizing is facilitated by Chaucer's clear frame-story directives. And to minimize the fiction by maximizing real life, Chaucer installs himself, the narrator, as one of the pilgrims. His reader-role problem is effectively solved. Of course, he got the idea pretty much from antecedent writers faced with similar problems, notably Boccaccio. But he naturalizes the frame in the geography of southeast England.

The frame story was in fact quite common around Europe at this period. Audience readjustment was a major feature of mature medieval culture, a culture more focused on reading than any earlier culture had been. Would it not be helpful to discuss the frame device as a contrivance all but demanded by the literary economy of the time rather than to expatiate on it as a singular stroke of genius? For this it certainly was not, unless we define genius as the ability to make the most of an awkward situation. The frame is really a rather clumsy gambit, although a good narrator can bring it off pretty well when he has to. It hardly has widespread immediate appeal for ordinary readers today.

In the next period of major audience readjustment, John Lyly's *Euphues* and even more Thomas Nashe's *The Unfortunate Traveler* can be viewed as attempts to work out a credible role in which Elizabethan readers could cast themselves for the new medium of print. Script culture had preserved a heavy oral residue signaled by its continued fascination with rhetoric, which had always been orally grounded, a fascination that script culture passed on to early print culture. But the new medium was changing the noetic economy, and, while rhetoric remained strong in the curriculum, strain was developing. Lyly reacts by hyperrhetoricizing his text, tongue-in-cheek, drowning the audience and himself in the highly controlled gush being purveyed by the schools. The signals to the reader are unmistakable, if unconsciously conveyed: play the role of the rhetorician's listener for all you are worth (*Euphues* is mostly speeches), remembering that the response the rhetorician commands is a serious and difficult one—it takes hard work to assimilate the baroque complexity of Lyly's text—but also that there is something awry in all the isocola, apophonemata, and antisagogai, now that the reader is so very much more a reader than a listener. Such aural iconographic equipment had been functional in oral management of knowledge, implementing storage and recall, but with print it was becoming incidental—which is, paradoxically, why it could be so fantastically elaborated.

Nashe shows the same uneasiness, and more, regarding the reader's role. For in the phantasmagoria of styles in *The Unfortunate Traveler* he tries out his reader in every role he can think of: whoever takes on Nashe's story must become a listener bending his ear to political orations, a participant in scholastic disputations, a hanger-on at goliardic Woodstocks, a camp follower fascinated by merry tales, a simpering reader of Italian revenge stories and sixteenth-century true confessions, a fellow conspirator in a world of picaresque cheats, and much more.

Nashe gives a foretaste of other trial-and-error procedures by which recipes were to be developed for the reader of the narrative prose works we now call novels. Such recipes were being worked out in other languages, too: in French notably by Rabelais, whose calls for strenuous shifts in the reader's stance Nashe emulated, and in Spanish by Cervantes, who explores all sorts of ironic possibilities in the reader's relationship to the text, incorporating into the second part of *Don Quixote* the purported reactions of readers and of the tale's characters to the first part of the work. Picaresque travels, well known at least since Apuleius' *Golden Ass*, multiplied, with major audience adjustments, in English down through *Tom Jones*: the unsettled role of the reader was mirrored and made acceptable by keeping the hero himself on the move. Samuel Richardson has his readers pretend they have access to other persons' letters, out of which a story emerges. Journals and diaries also multiplied as narrative devices: the reader becoming a snooper or a collector of seeming trivia that turn out not to be trivia at all. Ultimately, Laurence Sterne is able to involve his reader not only in the procreation of his hero Tristram Shandy but also in the hero's writing of his autobiography, in which pages are left blank for the reader to put his "own fancy in." The audience-speaker interaction of oral narrative here shows the reader in a new ironic guise—somewhat destructive of the printed book, toward which, as an object obtruding in the person-to-person world of human communication, the eighteenth century was feeling some ambiguous hostilities, as Swift's work also shows.

The problem of reader adjustment in prose narrative was in great part due to the difficulty that narrators long had in feeling themselves as other than oral performers. It is significant that, although the drama had been tightly plotted from classical antiquity (the drama is the first genre controlled by writing, and by the same token, paradoxically, the first to make deliberate use of colloquial speech), until the late eighteenth century there is in the whole Western world (and I suspect in the East as well) no sizable prose narrative, so far as I know, with a tidy structure comparable to that known for two millennia in the drama, moving through closely controlled tensions to a climax, with reversal and denouement. This is not to say that until the modern novel emerged narrative was not organized, or that earlier narrators were trying to write modern novels but regularly fell short of their aims. (Scholes and Kellogg have warned in *The Nature of Narrative* against this retroactive analysis of literary history.) But it is to say that narrative had not fully accommodated itself to print or, for that matter, to writing, which drama had long before learned to exploit. *Tom Jones* is highly programed, but in plot it is still episodic, as all prose narrative had been all the way back through the Hellenic romances. With Jane Austen we are over the hurdle: but Jane Austen was a woman, and women were not normally trained in the Latin-based academic, rhetorical, oral tradition. They were not trained speechmakers who had turned belatedly to chirography and print.

Even by Jane Austen's time, however, the problem of the reader's role in prose narrative was by no means entirely solved. Nervousness regarding the role of the reader registers everywhere in the "dear reader" regularly invoked in fiction well through the nineteenth century. The reader had to be reminded (and the narrator, too) that the recipient of the story was indeed a reader—not a listener, not one of the crowd, but an individual isolated with a text. The relationship of audience-fictionalizing to modern narrative prose is very mysterious, and I do not pretend to explain it all here, but only to point to some of the strange problems often so largely overlooked in the relationship. Tightly plotted prose narrative is the correlative of the audiences fictionalized for the first time with the aid of print, and the demands of such narrative on readers were new.

V

The present reflections have focused on written fictional narrative as a kind of paradigm for the fictionalizing of writers' "audiences" or readers. But what has been said about fictional narrative applies ceteris paribus to all writing. With the possible[10] exception noted above of persons in the presence of one another communicating by writing because of inability to communicate orally, the writer's audience is always a fiction. The historian, the scholar or scientist, and the simple letter writer all fictionalize their audiences, casting them in a made-up role and calling on them to play the role assigned.

Because history is always a selection and interpretation of those incidents the individual historian believes will account better than other incidents for some explanation of a totality, history partakes quite evidently of the nature of poetry. It is a making. The historian does not make the elements out of which he constructs history, in the sense that he must build with events that have come about independently of him, but his selection of events and his way of verbalizing them so that they can be dealt with as "facts," and consequently the overall pattern he reports, are all his own creation, a making. No two historians say exactly the same thing about the same given events, even though they are both telling the truth. There is no *one* thing to say about anything; there are many things that can be said.

The oral "historian" captures events in terms of themes (the challenge, the duel, the arming of the hero, the battle, and so on), and formulas (the brave soldier, the faithful wife, the courageous people, the suffering people), which are provided to him by tradition and are the only ways he knows to talk about what is going on among men. Processed through these conventions, events become assimilable by his auditors and "interesting" to them. The writer of history is less reliant on formulas (or it may be he has such a variety of them that it is hard to tell that is what they are). But he comes to his material laden with themes in much vaster quantity than can be available to any oral culture. Without themes, there would be no way to deal with events. It is impossible to tell everything that went on in the Pentagon even in one day: how many stenographers dropped how many sheets of paper into how many wastebaskets when and where, what they all said to each other, and so on ad infinitum. These are not the themes historians normally use to write what really "happened." They write about material by exploiting it in terms of themes that are "significant" or "interesting." But what is "significant" depends on what kind of history you are writing— national political history, military history, social history, economic history, personal biography, global history. What is significant and, perhaps even more, what is "interesting" also depends on the readers and their interaction with the historian. This interaction in turn depends on the role in which the historian casts his readers. Although so far as I know we have no history of readers of history, we do know enough about historiography to be aware that one could well be worked out. The open-faced way the reader figures in Samuel Eliot Morison's writings is different from the more conspiratorial way he figures in Perry Miller's and both are quite different from the way the reader figures in Herodotus.

Scholarly works show comparable evolution in the roles they enforce on their readers. Aristotle's works, as has often been pointed out, are an agglomerate of texts whose relationship to his own holographs, to his students' notes, and to the work of later editors will remain always more or less a puzzle. Much of Aristotle consists of school logia or sayings, comparable to the logia or sayings of Jesus to his followers of which the Gospels chiefly consist. Aristotle's logia were addressed to specific individuals whom he knew, rather than simply to the wide world. Even his more patently written compositions retain a personal orientation: his work on ethics is the *Nicomachean Ethics*, named for his son. This means that the reader of Aristotle, if he wants to understand his text, will do well to cast himself in the role of one of Aristotle's actual listeners.

The practice of orienting a work, and thereby its readers, by writing it at least purportedly for a specific person or persons continues well through the Renaissance. The first edition of Peter Ramus' *Dialectic* was the French *Dialectique de Pierre de la Ramée à Charles de Lorraine Cardinal, son Mécène* (Paris, 1555), and the first edition of the far more widely used Latin version preserved the same personal address: *Dialectici Libri Duo . . . ad Carolum Lotharingum Cardinalem* (Paris, 1556). Sidney's famous romance or epic is *The Countess of Pembroke's Arcadia.* Often in Renaissance printed editions a galaxy of prefaces and dedicatory epistles and poems establishes a whole cosmos of discourse which, among other things, signals the reader what roles he is to assume. Sidney's, Spenser's, and Milton's works, for example, are heavily laden with introductory material—whole books have been devoted to the study of Sidney's introductory matter alone.

Until recent times the rhetorical tradition, which, with the allied dialectical or logical tradition, dominated most written as well as oral expression, helped in the fictionalizing of the audience of learned works in a generic but quite real way. Rhetoric fixed knowledge in agonistic structures.

For this reason, the roles of the reader of learned works until fairly recent times were regularly more polemic than those demanded of the reader today. Until the age of romanticism reconstituted psychological structures, academic teaching of all subjects had been more or less polemic, dominated by the ubiquitous rhetorical culture, and proceeding typically by proposing and attacking theses in highly partisan fashion. (The academic world today preserves much of the nomenclature, such as "thesis" and "defense" of theses, but less of the programed fighting spirit, which its members let loose on the social order more than on their subject matter or colleagues.) From Augustine through St. Thomas Aquinas and Christian Wolff, writers of treatises generally proceeded in adversary fashion, their readers being cast as participants in rhetorical contests or in dialectical scholastic disputations.

Today the academic reader's role is harder to describe. Some of its complexities can be hinted at by attending to certain fictions which writers of learned articles and books generally observe and which have to do with reader status. There are some things the writer must assume that every reader knows because virtually every reader does. It would be intolerable to write, "Shakespeare, a well-known Elizabethan playwright," not only in a study on Renaissance drama but even in one on marine ecology. Otherwise the reader's role would be confused. There are other things that established fiction holds all readers must know, even though everyone is sure all readers do not know them: these are handled by writing, "as everyone knows," and then inserting what it is that not quite everyone really does know. Other things the reader can safely be assumed not to know without threatening the role he is playing. These gradations of admissible ignorance vary from one level of scholarly writing to another, and since individual readers vary in knowledge and competence, the degree to which they must fictionalize themselves to match the level of this or that reading will vary. Knowledge of the degrees of admissible ignorance for readers is absolutely essential if one is to publish successfully. This knowledge is one of the things that separates the beginning graduate student or even the brilliant undergraduate from the mature scholar. It takes time to get a feel for the roles that readers can be expected comfortably to play in the modern academic world.

Other kinds of writing without end could be examined in our reflections here on the fictionalizing of readers' roles. For want of time and, frankly, for want of wider reflection, I shall mention only two others. These are genres that do not seem to fall under the rule that the writer's audience is always a fiction since the "audience" appears to be simply one clearly determined person, who hardly need fictionalize himself. The first of the genres is the familiar letter and the second the diary.

The case of the letter reader is really simple enough. Although by writing a letter you are somehow pretending the reader is present while you are writing, you cannot address him as you do in oral speech. You must fictionalize him, make him into a special construct. Whoever saluted a friend on the street with "Dear John"? And if you try the informal horrors, "Hi!" or "Greetings!" or whatever else, the effect is not less but more artificial. You are reminding him that you wish you were not writing him a letter, but, then, why are you? There is no way out. The writer has to set up another relationship to the reader and has to set the reader in a relationship to the writer different from that of nonchirographical personal contact.

The dimensions of fiction in a letter are many. First, you have no way of adjusting to the friend's real mood as you would be able to adjust in oral conversation. You have to conjecture or confect a mood that he is likely to be in or can assume when the letter comes. And, when it does come, he has to put on the mood that you have fictionalized for him. Some of this sort of adjustment goes on in oral communication, too, but it develops in a series of exchanges: a tentative guess at another's mood, a reaction from him, another from yourself, another from him, and you know about where you are. Letters do not have this normal give-and-take: they are one-way movements. Moreover, the precise relationships of writer to reader in letters vary tremendously from age to age even in intensively role-playing correspondence. No one today can capture exactly the fiction in Swift's *Journal to Stella*, though it is informative to try to reconstruct it as fully as possible, for the relationships of children to oldsters and even of man to woman have subtly altered, as have also a vast mesh of other social relationships which the *Journal to Stella* involves.

The epistolary situation is made tolerable by conventions, and learning to write letters is largely a matter of learning what the writer-reader conventions are. The paradoxes they involve were well caught some years ago in a Marx Brothers movie—if I recall correctly where the incident occurred. Letters start with "Dear Sir." An owlish, bemused businessman calls his secretary in. "Take this letter to Joseph Smithers," he directs. "You know his address. 'Dear Sir: You dirty rat. . . .'" The fiction of the exordium designed to create the *lector benevolens* is first honored and then immediately wiped out.

The audience of the diarist is even more encased in fictions. What is easier, one might argue, than addressing oneself? As those who first begin a diary often find out, a great many things are easier. The reasons why are not hard to unearth. First of all, we do not normally talk to ourselves—certainly not in long, involved sentences and paragraphs. Second, the diarist pretending to be talking to himself has also, since he is writing, to pretend he is somehow not there. And to what self is he talking? To the self he imagines he is? Or would like to be? Or really thinks he is? Or thinks other people think he is? To himself as he is now? Or as he will probably or ideally be twenty years hence? If he addresses not himself but "Dear Diary," who in the world is "Dear Diary"? What role does this imply? And why do more women than men keep diaries? Or if they don't (they really do—or did), why do people think they do? When did the diary start? The history of diaries, I believe, has yet to be written. Possibly more than the history of any other genre, it will have to be a history of the fictionalizing of readers.

The case of the diary, which at first blush would seem to fictionalize the reader least but in many ways probably fictionalizes him or her most, brings into full view the fundamental deep paradox of the activity we call writing, at least when writing moves from its initial account-keeping purposes to other more elaborate concerns more directly and complexly involving human persons in their manifold dealings with one another. We are familiar enough today with talk about masks—in literary criticism, psychology, phenomenology, and elsewhere. Personae, earlier generally thought of as applying to characters in a play or other fiction (dramatis personae), are imputed with full justification to narrators and, since all discourse has roots in narrative, to everyone who uses language. Often in the complexities of present-day fiction, with its "unreliable narrator" encased in layer after layer of persiflage and irony, the masks within masks defy complete identification. This is a game fiction writers play, harder now than ever.

But the masks of the narrator are matched, if not one-for-one, in equally complex fashion by the masks that readers must learn to wear. To whom is *Finnegans Wake* addressed? Who is the reader supposed to be? We hesitate to say—certainly I hesitate to say—because we have thought so little about the reader's role as such, about his masks, which are as manifold in their own way as those of the writer.

Masks are inevitable in all human communication, even oral. Role playing is both different from actuality and an entry into actuality: play and actuality (the world of "work") are dialectically related to one another. From the very beginning, an infant becomes an actual speaker by playing at being a speaker, much as a person who cannot swim, after developing some ancillary skills, one day plays at swimming and finds that he is swimming in truth. But oral communication, which is built into existential actuality more directly than written, has within it a momentum that works for the removal of masks. Lovers try to strip off all masks. And in all communication, insofar as it is related to actual experience, there must be a movement of love. Those who have loved over many years may reach a point where almost all masks are gone. But never all. The lover's plight is tied to the fact that every one of us puts on a mask to address himself, too. Such masks to relate ourselves to ourselves we also try to put aside, and with wisdom and grace we to some extent succeed in casting them off. When the last mask comes off, sainthood is achieved, and the vision of God. But this can only be with death.

No matter what pitch of frankness, directness, or authenticity he may strive for, the writer's mask and the reader's are less removable than those of the oral communicator and his hearer. For writing is itself an indirection. Direct communication by script is impossible. This makes writing not less but more interesting, although perhaps less noble than speech. For man lives largely by indirection, and only beneath the indirections that sustain him is his true nature to be found. Writing, alone, however, will never bring us truly beneath to the actuality. Present-day confessional writing—and it is characteristic of our present age that virtually all serious writing tends to the confessional, even drama—likes to make an issue of stripping off all masks. Observant literary critics and psychiatrists, however, do not need to be told that confessional literature is likely to wear the most masks of all. It is hard to bare your soul in any literary genre. And it is hard to write outside a genre. T. S. Eliot has made the point that so far as he knows, great love poetry is never written solely for the ear of the beloved (p. 97), although what a lover speaks with his lips is often indeed for the ear of the beloved and of no other. The point is well made, even though it was made in writing.

NOTES

1. See, e.g., J. R. Searle, *The Philosophy of Language* (London: Oxford Univ. Press, 1971), pp. 24–28, where Austin is cited, and Searle's bibliography, pp. 146–48.

2. *The Rhetoric of Fiction* (Chicago: Univ. of Chicago Press, 1961), pp. 49–52, 138, 363–64.

3. *The Nature of Narrative* (New York: Oxford Univ. Press, 1966), pp. 17–56. Among recent short studies exhibiting concerns tangent to but not the same as those of the present article might be mentioned three from *New Literary History*: Georges Poulet, "Phenomenology of Reading," 1 (1969–70), 53–68; Geoffrey H. Hartman, "History-Writing as Answerable Style," 2 (1970–71), 73–84; and J. Hillis Miller, "The Still Heart: Poetic Form in Wordsworth," 2 (1970–71), 297–310, esp. p. 310; as well as Gerald Prince, "Introduction à l'étude du narrataire," *Poétique*, No. 14 (1973), pp. 178–96, which is concerned with the "narrataire" only in novels ("narratee" in a related English-language study by the same author as noted by him here) and with literary taxonomy more than history. See also Paul Ricoeur, "What Is a Text? Explanation and Interpretation," Appendix, pp. 135–50, in David Rasmussen, *Mythic-Symbolic Language and Philosophical Anthropology: A Constructive Interpretation of the Thought of Paul Ricoeur* (The Hague: Martinus Nijhoff, 1971).

4. *Phenomenology of Perception*, trans. Colin Smith (London: Routledge, 1962), pp. 181–84.

5. See my *The Presence of the Word* (New Haven and London: Yale Univ. Press, 1967), pp. 116–17.

6. T. S. Eliot suggests some of the complexities of the writer-and-audience problem in his essay on "The Three Voices of Poetry," by which he means (1) "the voice of the poet talking to himself—or to nobody," (2) "the voice of the poet addressing an audience," and (3) "the voice of the poet when he attempts to create a dramatic character speaking" (*On Poetry and Poets*, New York: Noonday Press, 1961, p. 96). Eliot, in the same work, states that these voices often mingle and indeed, for him, "are most often found together" (p. 108). The approach I am here taking cuts across Eliot's way of enunciating the problem and, I believe, brings out some of the built-in relationships among the three voices which help account for their intermingling. The "audience" addressed by Eliot's second voice not only is elusively constituted but also, even in its elusiveness, can determine the voice of the poet talking to himself or to nobody (Eliot's first sense of "voice"), because in talking to oneself one has to objectify oneself, and one does so in ways learned from addressing others. A practiced writer talking "to himself" in a poem has a quite different feeling for "himself" than does a complete illiterate.

7. See Albert B. Lord, *The Singer of Tales*, Harvard Studies in Comparative Literature, No. 24 (Cambridge, Mass.: Harvard Univ. Press, 1964), pp. 124–38.

8. *Tough, Sweet, and Stuffy* (Bloomington and London: Indiana Univ. Press, 1966), pp. 28–54. In these pages, Gibson gets very close to the concern of the present article with readers' roles.

9. The present inclination to begin a story without the initial indefinite article, which tacitly acknowledges a range of existence beyond that of the immediate reference, and to substitute for the indefinite article a demonstrative pronoun of proximity, "this," is one of many indications of the tendency of present-day man to feel his lifeworld—which is now more than ever the whole world—as in-close to him, and to mute any references to distance. It is not uncommon to hear a conversation begin, "Yesterday on the street this man came up to me, and. . . ." A few decades ago, the equivalent would very likely have been, "Yesterday on the street a man came up to me, and. . . ." This widespread preference, which Hemingway probably influenced little if at all, does show that Hemingway's imposition of fellowship on the reader was an indication, perhaps moderately precocious, of a sweeping trend.

10. "Possible," because there is probably a trace of fictionalizing even when notes are being exchanged by persons in one another's presence. It appears unlikely that what is written in such script "conversations" is exactly the same as what it would be were voices used. The interlocutors are, after all, to some extent pretending to be talking, when in fact they are not talking but writing.

Audience Addressed/ Audience Invoked

The Role of Audience in Composition Theory and Pedagogy

LISA EDE AND ANDREA LUNSFORD

One important controversy currently engaging scholars and teachers of writing involves the role of audience in composition theory and pedagogy. How can we best define the audience of a written discourse? What does it mean to address an audience? To what degree should teachers stress audience in their assignments and discussions? What *is* the best way to help students recognize the significance of this critical element in any rhetorical situation?

Teachers of writing may find recent efforts to answer these questions more confusing than illuminating. Should they agree with Ruth Mitchell and Mary Taylor, who so emphasize the significance of the audience that they argue for abandoning conventional composition courses and instituting a "cooperative effort by writing and subject instructors in adjunct courses. The cooperation and courses take two main forms. Either writing instructors can be attached to subject courses where writing is required, an organization which disperses the instructors throughout the departments participating; or the composition courses can teach students how to write the papers assigned in other concurrent courses, thus centralizing instruction but diversifying topics."[1] Or should teachers side with Russell Long, who asserts that those advocating greater attention to audience overemphasize the role of "observable physical or occupational characteristics" while

Reprinted from *College Composition and Communication* 35.2 (May 1984): 155–71. Used with permission.

ignoring the fact that most writers actually create their audiences. Long argues against the usefulness of such methods as developing hypothetical rhetorical situations as writing assignments, urging instead a more traditional emphasis on "the analysis of texts in the classroom with a very detailed examination given to the signals provided by the writer for his audience."[2]

To many teachers, the choice seems limited to a single option—to be for or against an emphasis on audience in composition courses. In the following essay, we wish to expand our understanding of the role audience plays in composition theory and pedagogy by demonstrating that the arguments advocated by each side of the current debate oversimplify the act of making meaning through written discourse. Each side, we will argue, has failed adequately to recognize (1) the fluid, dynamic character of rhetorical situations; and (2) the integrated, interdependent nature of reading and writing. After discussing the strengths and weaknesses of the two central perspectives on audience in composition—which we group under the rubrics of *audience addressed* and *audience invoked*[3]—we will propose an alternative formulation, one which we believe more accurately reflects the richness of "audience" as a concept.[*]

AUDIENCE ADDRESSED

Those who envision audience as addressed emphasize the concrete reality of the writer's audience; they also share the assumption that knowledge of this audience's attitudes, beliefs, and expectations is not only possible (via observation and analysis) but essential. Questions concerning the degree to which this audience is "real" or imagined, and the ways it differs from the speaker's audience, are generally either ignored or subordinated to a sense of the audience's powerfulness. In their discussion of "A Heuristic Model for Creating a Writer's Audience," for example, Fred Pfister and Joanne Petrik attempt to recognize the ontological complexity of the writer-audience relationship by noting that "students, like all writers, must fictionalize their audience."[4] Even so, by encouraging students to "construct in their

---

[*]A number of terms might be used to characterize the two approaches to audience which dominate current theory and practice. Such pairs as identified/envisaged, "real"/fictional, or analyzed/created all point to the same general distinction as do our terms. We chose "addressed/invoked" because these terms most precisely represent our intended meaning. Our discussion will, we hope, clarify their significance; for the present, the following definitions must serve. The "addressed" audience refers to those actual or real-life people who read a discourse, while the "invoked" audience refers to the audience called up or imagined by the writer.

78

imagination an audience that is as nearly a replica as is possible of *those many readers who actually exist in the world of reality,*" Pfister and Petrik implicitly privilege the concept of audience as addressed.[5]

Many of those who envision audience as addressed have been influenced by the strong tradition of audience analysis in speech communication and by current research in cognitive psychology on the composing process.[6] They often see themselves as reacting against the current-traditional paradigm of composition, with its a-rhetorical, product-oriented emphasis.[7] And they also frequently encourage what is called "real-world" writing.[8]

Our purpose here is not to draw up a list of those who share this view of audience but to suggest the general outline of what most readers will recognize as a central tendency in the teaching of writing today. We would, however, like to focus on one particularly ambitious attempt to formulate a theory and pedagogy for composition based on the concept of audience as addressed: Ruth Mitchell and Mary Taylor's "The Integrating Perspective: An Audience-Response Model for Writing." We choose Mitchell and Taylor's work because of its theoretical richness and practical specificity. Despite these strengths, we wish to note several potentially significant limitations in their approach, limitations which obtain to varying degrees in much of the current work of those who envision audience as addressed.

In their article, Mitchell and Taylor analyze what they consider to be the two major existing composition models: one focusing on the writer and the other on the written product. Their evaluation of these two models seems essentially accurate. The "writer" model is limited because it defines writing as either self-expression or "fidelity to fact" (p. 255) — epistemologically naive assumptions which result in troubling pedagogical inconsistencies. And the "written product" model, which is characterized by an emphasis on "certain intrinsic features [such as a] lack of comma splices and fragments" (p. 258), is challenged by the continued inability of teachers of writing (not to mention those in other professions) to agree upon the precise intrinsic features which characterize "good" writing.

Most interesting, however, is what Mitchell and Taylor *omit* in their criticism of these models. Neither the writer model nor the written product model pays serious attention to invention, the term used to describe those methods designed to aid in retrieving information, forming concepts, analyzing complex events, and solving certain kinds of problems."[9] Mitchell and Taylor's lapse in not noting this omission is understandable, however, for the same can be said of their own model. When these authors discuss the writing process, they stress that "our first priority for writing instruction at every level ought to be certain major tactics for structuring material because these structures are the most important in guiding the reader's comprehension and memory" (p. 271). They do not concern themselves with where "the material" comes from—its sophistication, complexity, accuracy, or rigor.

Mitchell and Taylor also fail to note another omission, one which might be best described in reference to their own model (Figure 1). This model has four components. Mitchell and Taylor use two of these, "writer" and "written product," as labels for the models they condemn. The third and fourth components, "audience" and "response," provide the title for their own "audience-response model for writing" (p. 249).

Mitchell and Taylor stress that the components in their model interact. Yet, despite their emphasis on interaction, it never seems to occur to them to note that the two other models may fail in large part because they overemphasize and isolate one of the four elements—wrenching it too greatly from its context and thus inevitably distorting the composing process. Mitchell and Taylor do not consider this possibility, we suggest, because their own model has the same weakness.

Mitchell and Taylor argue that a major limitation of the "writer" model is its emphasis on the self, the person writing, as the only potential judge of effective discourse. Ironically, however, their own emphasis on audience leads to a similar distortion. In their model, the audience has the sole power of evaluating writing, the success of which "will be judged by the audience's reaction: 'good' translates into 'effective,' 'bad' into 'ineffective.'" Mitchell and Taylor go on to note that "the audience not only judges writing; it also motivates it" (p. 250),[10] thus suggesting that the writer has less control than the audience over both evaluation and motivation.

Despite the fact that Mitchell and Taylor describe writing as "an interaction, a dynamic relationship" (p. 250), their model puts far more emphasis on the role of the audience than on that of the writer. One way to pinpoint

Figure 1   Mitchell and Taylor's "general model of writing" (p. 250).

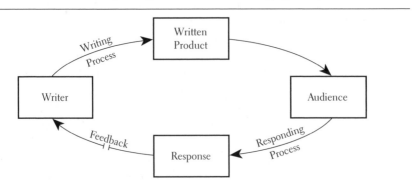

the source of imbalance in Mitchell and Taylor's formulation is to note that they are right in emphasizing the creative role of readers who, they observe, "actively contribute to the meaning of what they read and will respond according to a complex set of expectations, preconceptions, and provocations" (p. 251), but wrong in failing to recognize the equally essential role writers play throughout the composing process not only as creators but also as *readers* of their own writing.

As Susan Wall observes in "In the Writer's Eye: Learning to Teach the Rereading/Revising Process," when writers read their own writing, as they do continuously while they compose, "there are really not one but two contexts for rereading: there is the writer-as-reader's sense of what the established text is actually saying, as of this reading; and there is the reader-as-writer's judgment of what the text might say or should say. . . ."[11] What is missing from Mitchell and Taylor's model, and from much work done from the perspective of audience as addressed, is a recognition of the crucial importance of this internal dialogue, through which writers analyze inventional problems and conceptualize patterns of discourse. Also missing is an adequate awareness that, no matter how much feedback writers may receive after they have written something (or in breaks while they write), as they compose writers must rely in large part upon their own vision of the reader, which they create, as readers do their vision of writers, according to their own experiences and expectations.

Another major problem with Mitchell and Taylor's analysis is their apparent lack of concern for the ethics of language use. At one point, the authors ask the following important question: "Have we painted ourselves into a corner, so that the audience-response model must defend sociologese and its related styles?" (p. 265). Note first the ambiguity of their answer, which seems to us to say no and yes at the same time, and the way they try to deflect its impact:

> No. We defend only the right of audiences to set their own standards and we repudiate the ambitions of English departments to monopolize that standard-setting. If bureaucrats and scientists are happy with the way they write, then no one should interfere.
>
>   But evidence is accumulating that they are not happy. (p. 265)

Here Mitchell and Taylor surely underestimate the relationship between style and substance. As those concerned with Doublespeak can attest, for example, the problem with sociologese is not simply its (to our ears) awkward, convoluted, highly nominalized style, but the way writers have in certain instances used this style to make statements otherwise unacceptable to lay persons, to "gloss over" potentially controversial facts about programs and their consequences, and thus violate the ethics of language use. Hence, although we support Mitchell and Taylor when they insist that we must better understand and respect the linguistic traditions of other disciplines and professions, we object to their assumption that style is somehow value free.

As we noted earlier, an analysis of Mitchell and Taylor's discussion clarifies weaknesses inherent in much of the theoretical and pedagogical research based on the concept of audience as addressed. One major weakness of this research lies in its narrow focus on helping students learn how to "continually modify their work with reference to their audience" (p. 251). Such a focus, which in its extreme form becomes pandering to the crowd, tends to undervalue the responsibility a writer has to a subject and to what Wayne Booth in *Modern Dogma and the Rhetoric of Assent* calls "the art of discovering good reasons."[12] The resulting imbalance has clear ethical consequences, for rhetoric has traditionally been concerned not only with the effectiveness of a discourse, but with truthfulness as well. Much of our difficulty with the language of advertising, for example, arises out of the ad writer's powerful concept of audience as addressed divorced from a corollary ethical concept. The toothpaste ad that promises improved personality, for instance, knows too well how to address the audience. But such ads ignore ethical questions completely.

Another weakness in research done by those who envision audience as addressed suggests an oversimplified view of language. As Paul Kameen observes in "Rewording the Rhetoric of Composition," "discourse is not grounded in forms or experience or audience; it engages all of these elements simultaneously."[13] Ann Berthoff has persistently criticized our obsession with one or another of the elements of discourse, insisting that meaning arises out of their synthesis. Writing is more, then, than "a means of acting upon a receiver" (Mitchell and Taylor, p. 250); it is a means of making meaning for writer *and* reader.[14] Without such a unifying, balanced understanding of language use, it is easy to overemphasize one aspect of discourse, such as audience. It is also easy to forget, as Anthony Petrosky cautions us, that "reading, responding, and composing are aspects of understanding, and theories that attempt to account for them outside of their interaction with each other run the serious risk of building reductive models of human understanding."[15]

AUDIENCE INVOKED

Those who envision audience as invoked stress that the audience of a written discourse is a construction of the writer, a "created fiction" (Long,

p. 225). They do not, of course, deny the physical reality of readers, but they argue that writers simply cannot know this reality in the way that speakers can. The central task of the writer, then, is not to analyze an audience and adapt discourse to meet its needs. Rather, the writer uses the semantic and syntactic resources of language to provide cues for the reader—cues which help to define the role or roles the writer wishes the reader to adopt in responding to the text. Little scholarship in composition takes this perspective; only Russell Long's article and Walter Ong's "The Writer's Audience Is Always a Fiction" focus centrally on this issue.[16] If recent conferences are any indication, however, a growing number of teachers and scholars are becoming concerned with what they see as the possible distortions and over-simplifications of the approach typified by Mitchell and Taylor's model.[17]

Russell Long's response to current efforts to teach students analysis of audience and adaptation of text to audience is typical: "I have become increasingly disturbed not only about the superficiality of the advice itself, but about the philosophy which seems to lie beneath it" (p. 221). Rather than detailing Long's argument, we wish to turn to Walter Ong's well-known study. Published in *PMLA* in 1975, "The Writer's Audience Is Always a Fiction" has had a significant impact on composition studies, despite the fact that its major emphasis is on fictional narrative rather than expository writing. An analysis of Ong's argument suggests that teachers of writing may err if they uncritically accept Ong's statement that "what has been said about fictional narrative applies ceteris paribus to all writing" (p. 17).

Ong's thesis includes two central assertions: "What do we mean by saying the audience is a fiction? Two things at least. First, that the writer must construct in his imagination, clearly or vaguely, an audience cast in some sort of role. . . . Second, we mean that the audience must correspondingly fictionalize itself" (p. 12). Ong emphasizes the creative power of the adept writer, who can both project and alter audiences, as well as the complexity of the reader's role. Readers, Ong observes, must learn or "know how to play the game of being a member of an audience that 'really' does not exist" (p. 12).

On the most abstract and general level, Ong is accurate. For a writer, the audience is not *there* in the sense that the speaker's audience, whether a single person or a large group, is present. But Ong's representative situations—the orator addressing a mass audience versus a writer alone in a room—oversimplify the potential range and diversity of both oral and written communication situations.

Ong's model of the paradigmatic act of speech communication derives from traditional rhetoric. In distinguishing the terms audience and reader, he notes that "the orator has before him an audience which is a true audience, a collectivity. . . . Readers do not form a collectivity, acting here and now on one another and on the speaker as members of an audience do" (p. 11). As this quotation indicates, Ong also stresses the potential for interaction among members of an audience, and between an audience and a speaker.

But how many audiences are actually collectives, with ample opportunity for interaction? In *Persuasion: Understanding, Practice, and Analysis,* Herbert Simons establishes a continuum of audiences based on opportunities for interaction.[18] Simons contrasts commercial mass media publics, which "have little or no contact with each other and certainly have no reciprocal awareness of each other as members of the same audience" with "face-to-face work groups that meet and interact continuously over an extended period of time." He goes on to note that: "Between these two extremes are such groups as the following: (1) the *pedestrian audience,* persons who happen to pass a soap box orator . . . ; (2) the *passive, occasional audience,* persons who come to hear a noted lecturer in a large auditorium . . . ; (3) the *active, occasional audience,* persons who meet only on specific occasions but actively interact when they do meet" (pp. 97–98).

Simons' discussion, in effect, questions the rigidity of Ong's distinctions between a speaker's and a writer's audience. Indeed, when one surveys a broad range of situations inviting oral communication, Ong's paradigmatic situation, in which the speaker's audience constitutes a "collectivity, acting here and now on one another and on the speaker" (p. 11), seems somewhat atypical. It is certainly possible, at any rate, to think of a number of instances where speakers confront a problem very similar to that of writers: lacking intimate knowledge of their audience, which comprises not a collectivity but a disparate, and possibly even divided, group of individuals, speakers, like writers, must construct in their imaginations "an audience cast in some sort of role."[19] When President Carter announced to Americans during a speech broadcast on television, for instance, that his program against inflation was "the moral equivalent of warfare," he was doing more than merely characterizing his economic policies. He was providing an important cue to his audience concerning the role he wished them to adopt as listeners—that of a people braced for a painful but necessary and justifiable battle. Were we to examine his speech in detail, we would find other more subtle, but equally important, semantic and syntactic signals to the audience.

We do not wish here to collapse all distinctions between oral and written communication, but rather to emphasize that speaking and writing are, after all, both rhetorical acts. There are important differences between speech and writing. And the broad distinction between speech and writing that Ong makes is both commonsensical and particularly relevant to his subject, fictional narrative. As our illustration demonstrates, however, when one turns to precise, concrete situations, the relationship between speech and writing can become far more complex than even Ong represents.

Just as Ong's distinction between speech and writing is accurate on a highly general level but breaks down (or at least becomes less clear-cut) when examined closely, so too does his dictum about writers and their audiences. Every writer must indeed create a role for the reader, but the constraints on the writer and the potential sources of and possibilities for the reader's role are both more complex and diverse than Ong suggests. Ong stresses the importance of literary tradition in the creation of audience: "If the writer succeeds in writing, it is generally because he can fictionalize in his imagination an audience he has learned to know not from daily life but from earlier writers who were fictionalizing in their imagination audiences they had learned to know in still earlier writers, and so on back to the dawn of written narrative" (p. 11). And he cites a particularly (for us) germane example, a student "asked to write on the subject to which schoolteachers, jaded by summer, return compulsively every autumn: 'How I Spent My Summer Vacation'" (p. 11). In order to negotiate such an assignment successfully, the student must turn his real audience, the teacher, into someone else. He or she must, for instance, "make like Samuel Clemens and write for whomever Samuel Clemens was writing for" (p. 11).

Ong's example is, for his purposes, well-chosen. For such an assignment does indeed require the successful student to "fictionalize" his or her audience. But why is the student's decision to turn to a literary model in this instance particularly appropriate? Could one reason be that the student knows (consciously or unconsciously) that his English teacher, who is still the literal audience of his essay, appreciates literature and hence would be entertained (and here the student may intuit the assignment's actual aim as well) by such a strategy? In Ong's example the audience—the "jaded" schoolteacher—is not only willing to accept another role but, perhaps, actually yearns for it. How else to escape the tedium of reading 25, 50, 75 student papers on the same topic? As Walter Minot notes, however, not all readers are so malleable:

> In reading a work of fiction or poetry, a reader is far more willing to suspend his beliefs and values than in a rhetorical work dealing with some current social, moral, or economic issue. The effectiveness of the created audience in a rhetorical situation is likely to depend on such constraints as the actual identity of the reader, the subject of the discourse, the identity and purpose of the writer, and many other factors in the real world.[20]

An example might help make Minot's point concrete.

Imagine another composition student faced, like Ong's, with an assignment. This student, who has been given considerably more latitude in her choice of a topic, has decided to write on an issue of concern to her at the moment, the possibility that a home for mentally-retarded adults will be built in her neighborhood. She is alarmed by the strongly negative, highly emotional reaction of most of her neighbors and wishes in her essay to persuade them that such a residence might not be the disaster they anticipate.

This student faces a different task from that described by Ong. If she is to succeed, she must think seriously about her actual readers, the neighbors to whom she wishes to send her letter. She knows the obvious demographic factors—age, race, class—so well that she probably hardly needs to consider them consciously. But other issues are more complex. How much do her neighbors know about mental retardation, intellectually or experientially? What is their image of a retarded adult? What fears does this project raise in them? What civic and religious values do they most respect? Based on this analysis—and the process may be much less sequential than we describe here—she must, of course, define a role for her audience, one congruent with her persona, arguments, the facts as she knows them, etc. She must, as Minot argues, *both* analyze and invent an audience.[21] In this instance, after detailed analysis of her audience and her arguments, the student decided to begin her essay by emphasizing what she felt to be the genuinely admirable qualities of her neighbors, particularly their kindness, understanding, and concern for others. In so doing, she invited her audience to see themselves as *she* saw them: as thoughtful, intelligent people who, if they were adequately informed, would certainly not act in a harsh manner to those less fortunate than they. In accepting this role, her readers did not have to "play the game of being a member of an audience that 'really' does not exist" (Ong, "The Writer's Audience," p. 12). But they did have to recognize in themselves the strengths the student described and to accept her implicit linking of these strengths to what she hoped would be their response to the proposed "home."

When this student enters her history class to write an examination she faces a different set of constraints. Unlike the historian who does indeed have a broad range of options in establishing the reader's role, our student has much less freedom. This is because her reader's role has already been established and formalized in a series of related academic conventions. If she is a successful student, she has so effectively internalized these conventions that she can subordinate a concern for her complex and multiple audiences to focus on the material on which she is being tested and on the single audience, the teacher, who will respond to her performance on the test.[22]

We could multiply examples. In each instance the student writing—to friend, employer, neighbor, teacher, fellow readers of her daily newspaper—would need, as one of the many conscious and unconscious decisions required in composing, to envision and define a role for the reader. But *how* she defines that role—whether she relies mainly upon academic or technical writing conventions, literary models, intimate knowledge of friends or neighbors, analysis of a particular group, or some combination thereof—will vary tremendously. At times the reader may establish a role for the reader which indeed does not "coincide[s] with his role in the rest of actual life" (Ong, p. 12). At other times, however, one of the writer's primary tasks may be that of analyzing the "real life" audience and adapting the discourse to it. One of the factors that makes writing so difficult, as we know, is that we have no recipes: each rhetorical situation is unique and thus requires the writer, catalyzed and guided by a strong sense of purpose, to reanalyze and reinvent solutions.

Despite their helpful corrective approach, then, theories which assert that the audience of a written discourse is a construction of the writer present their own dangers.[23] One of these is the tendency to overemphasize the distinction between speech and writing while undervaluing the insights of discourse theorists, such as James Moffett and James Britton, who remind us of the importance of such additional factors as distance between speaker or writer and audience and levels of abstraction in the subject. In *Teaching the Universe of Discourse*, Moffett establishes the following spectrum of discourse: recording ("the drama of what is happening"), reporting ("the narrative of what happened"), generalizing ("the exposition of what happens"), and theorizing ("the argumentation of what will, may happen").[24] In an extended example, Moffett demonstrates the important points of connection between communication acts at any one level of the spectrum, whether oral or written:

> Suppose next that I tell the cafeteria experience to a friend some time later in conversation. . . . Of course, instead of recounting the cafeteria scene to my friend in person I could write it in a letter to an audience more removed in time and space. Informal writing is usually still rather spontaneous, directed at an audience known to the writer, and reflects the transient mood and circumstances in which the writing occurs. Feedback and audience influence, however, are delayed and weakened. . . . *Compare in turn now the changes that must occur all down the line when I write about this cafeteria experience in a discourse destined for publication and distribution to a mass, anonymous audience of present and perhaps unborn people.* I cannot allude to things and ideas that only my friends know about. I must use a vocabulary, style, logic, and rhetoric that anybody in that mass audience can understand and respond to. I must name and organize what happened during those moments in the cafeteria that day in such a way that

this mythical average reader can relate what I say to some primary moments of experience of his own. (pp. 37–38; our emphasis)

Though Moffett does not say so, many of these same constraints would obtain if he decided to describe his experience in a speech to a mass audience—the viewers of a television show, for example, or the members of a graduating class. As Moffett's example illustrates, the distinction between speech and writing is important; it is, however, only one of several constraints influencing any particular discourse.

Another weakness of research based on the concept of audience as invoked is that it distorts the processes of writing and reading by overemphasizing the power of the writer and undervaluing that of the reader. Unlike Mitchell and Taylor, Ong recognizes the creative role the writer plays as reader of his or her own writing, the way the writer uses language to provide cues for the reader and tests the effectiveness of these cues during his or her own rereading of the text. But Ong fails adequately to recognize the constraints placed on the writer, in certain situations, by the audience. He fails, in other words, to acknowledge that readers' own experiences, expectations, and beliefs do play a central role in their reading of a text, and that the writer who does not consider the needs and interests of his audience risks losing that audience. To argue that the audience is a "created fiction" (Long, p. 225), to stress that the reader's role "seldom coincides with his role in the rest of actual life" (Ong, p. 12), is just as much an oversimplification, then, as to insist, as Mitchell and Taylor do, that "the audience not only judges writing, it also motivates it" (p. 250). The former view overemphasizes the writer's independence and power; the latter, that of the reader.

RHETORIC AND ITS SITUATIONS[25]

If the perspectives we have described as audience addressed and audience invoked represent incomplete conceptions of the role of audience in written discourse, do we have an alternative? How can we most accurately conceive of this essential rhetorical element? In what follows we will sketch a tentative model and present several defining or constraining statements about this apparently slippery concept, "audience." The result will, we hope, move us closer to a full understanding of the role audience plays in written discourse.

Figure 2 represents our attempt to indicate the complex series of obligations, resources, needs, and constraints embodied in the writer's concept of audience. (We emphasize that our goal here is *not* to depict the writing process as a whole—a much more complex task—but to focus on the writer's

Figure 2   The concept of audience.

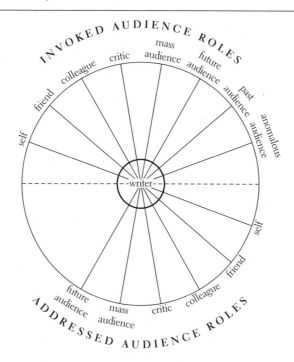

relation to audience.) As our model indicates, we do not see the two perspectives on audience described earlier as necessarily dichotomous or contradictory. Except for past and anomalous audiences, special cases which we describe paragraphs hence, all of the audience roles we specify—self, friend, colleague, critic, mass audience, and future audience—may be invoked or addressed.[26] It is the writer who, as writer and reader of his or her own text, one guided by a sense of purpose and by the particularities of a specific rhetorical situation, establishes the range of potential roles an audience may play. (Readers may, of course, accept or reject the role or roles the writer wishes them to adopt in responding to a text.)

Writers who wish to be read must often adapt their discourse to meet the needs and expectations of an addressed audience. They may rely on past experience in addressing audiences to guide their writing, or they may engage a representative of that audience in the writing process. The latter occurs, for instance, when we ask a colleague to read an article intended for scholarly publication. Writers may also be required to respond to the intervention of others—a teacher's comments on an essay, a supervisor's suggestions for improving a report, or the insistent, catalyzing questions of an editor. Such intervention may in certain cases represent a powerful stimulus to the writer, but it is the writer who interprets the suggestions—or even commands—of others, choosing what to accept or reject. Even the conscious decision to accede to the expectations of a particular addressed audience may not always be carried out; unconscious psychological resistance, incomplete understanding, or inadequately developed ability may prevent the writer from following through with the decision—a reality confirmed by composition teachers with each new set of essays.

The addressed audience, the actual or intended readers of a discourse, exists outside of the text. Writers may analyze these readers' needs, anticipate their biases, even defer to their wishes. But it is only through the text, through language, that writers embody or give life to their conception of the reader. In so doing, they do not so much create a role for the reader—a phrase which implies that the writer somehow creates a mold to which the reader adapts—as invoke it. Rather than relying on incantations, however, writers conjure their vision—a vision which they hope readers will actively come to share as they read the text—by using all the resources of language available to them to establish a broad, and ideally coherent, range of cues for the reader. Technical writing conventions, for instance, quickly formalize any of several writer-reader relationships, such as colleague to colleague or expert to lay reader. But even comparatively local semantic decisions may play an equally essential role. In "The Writer's Audience Is Always a Fiction," Ong demonstrates how Hemingway's use of definite articles in A Farewell to Arms subtly cues readers that their role is to be that of a "companion in arms . . . a confidant" (p. 13).

Any of the roles of the addressed audience cited in our model may be invoked via the text. Writers may also invoke a past audience, as did, for instance, Ong's student writing to those Mark Twain would have been writing for. And writers can also invoke anomalous audiences, such as a fictional character—Hercule Poirot perhaps. Our model, then, confirms Douglas Park's observation that the meanings of audience, though multiple and complex, "tend to diverge in two general directions: one toward actual people external to a text, the audience whom the writer must accommodate; the other toward the text itself and the audience implied there: a set of suggested or evoked attitudes, interests, reactions, conditions of knowledge which may or may not fit with the qualities of actual readers or listeners."[27] The most complete understanding of audience thus involves a synthesis of the perspectives we have termed audience addressed, with its focus on the reader, and audience invoked, with its focus on the writer.

One illustration of this constantly shifting complex of meanings for "audience" lies in our own experiences writing this essay. One of us became interested in the concept of audience during an NEH Seminar, and her first audience was a small, close-knit seminar group to whom she addressed her work. The other came to contemplate a multiplicity of audiences while working on a textbook; the first audience in this case was herself, as she debated the ideas she was struggling to present to a group of invoked students. Following a lengthy series of conversations, our interests began to merge: we shared notes and discussed articles written by others on audience, and eventually one of us began a draft. Our long distance telephone bills and the miles we travelled up and down I-5 from Oregon to British Columbia attest most concretely to the power of a co-author's expectations and criticisms and also illustrate that one person can take on the role of several different audiences: friend, colleague, and critic.

As we began to write and re-write the essay, now for a particular scholarly journal, the change in purpose and medium (no longer a seminar paper or a textbook) led us to new audiences. For us, the major "invoked audience" during this period was Richard Larson, editor of this journal, whose questions and criticisms we imagined and tried to anticipate. (Once this essay was accepted by *CCC*, Richard Larson became for us an addressed audience: he responded in writing with questions, criticisms, and suggestions, some of which we had, of course, failed to anticipate.) We also thought of the readers of *CCC* and those who attend the annual CCCC, most often picturing you as members of our own departments, a diverse group of individuals with widely varying degrees of interest in and knowledge of composition. Because of the generic constraints of academic writing, which limit the range of roles we may define for our readers, the audience represented by the readers of *CCC* seemed most vivid to us in two situations: (1) when we were concerned about the degree to which we needed to explain concepts or terms; and (2) when we considered central organizational decisions, such as the most effective way to introduce a discussion. Another, and for us extremely potent, audience was the authors—Mitchell and Taylor, Long, Ong, Park, and others—with whom we have seen ourselves in silent dialogue. As we read and reread their analyses and developed our responses to them, we felt a responsibility to try to understand their formulations as fully as possible, to play fair with their ideas, to make our own efforts continue to meet their high standards.

Our experience provides just one example, and even it is far from complete. (Once we finished a rough draft, one particular colleague became a potent but demanding addressed audience, listening to revision upon revision and challenging us with harder and harder questions. And after this essay is published, we may revise our understanding of audiences we thought we knew or recognize the existence of an entirely new audience.

The latter would happen, for instance, if teachers of speech communication for some reason found our discussion useful.) But even this single case demonstrates that the term *audience* refers not just to the intended, actual, or eventual readers of a discourse, but to *all* those whose image, ideas, or actions influence a writer during the process of composition. One way to conceive of "audience," then, is as an overdetermined or unusually rich concept, one which may perhaps be best specified through the analysis of precise, concrete situations.

We hope that this partial example of our own experience will illustrate how the elements represented in Figure 2 will shift and merge, depending on the particular rhetorical situation, the writer's aim, and the genre chosen. Such an understanding is critical: because of the complex reality to which the term audience refers and because of its fluid, shifting role in the composing process, any discussion of audience which isolates it from the rest of the rhetorical situation or which radically overemphasizes or underemphasizes its function in relation to other rhetorical constraints is likely to oversimplify. Note the unilateral direction of Mitchell and Taylor's model (p. 5 [p. 80]), which is unable to represent the diverse and complex role(s) audience(s) can play in the actual writing process—in the creation of meaning. In contrast, consider the model used by Edward P. J. Corbett in his *Little Rhetoric and Handbook*[28] (see Figure 3). This representation, which allows for interaction among all the elements of rhetoric, may at first appear less elegant and predictive than Mitchell and Taylor's. But it is finally more useful since it accurately represents the diverse range of potential interrelationships in any written discourse.

We hope that our model also suggests the integrated, interdependent nature of reading and writing. Two assertions emerge from this relationship. One involves the writer as reader of his or her own work. As Donald Murray notes in "Teaching the Other Self: The Writer's First Reader," this role is

Figure 3   Corbett's model of "The Rhetorical Interrelationships" (p. 5).

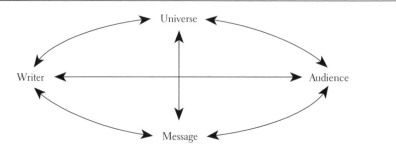

critical, for "the reading writer—the map-maker and map-reader—reads the word, the line, the sentence, the paragraph, the page, the entire text. This constant back-and-forth reading monitors the multiple complex relationships between all the elements in writing."[29] To ignore or devalue such a central function is to risk distorting the writing process as a whole. But unless the writer is composing a diary or journal entry, intended only for the writer's own eyes, the writing process is not complete unless another person, someone other than the writer, reads the text also. The second assertion thus emphasizes the creative, dynamic duality of the process of reading and writing, whereby writers create readers and readers create writers. In the meeting of these two lies meaning, lies communication.

A fully elaborated view of audience, then, must balance the creativity of the writer with the different, but equally important, creativity of the reader. It must account for a wide and shifting range of roles for both addressed and invoked audiences. And, finally, it must relate the matrix created by the intricate relationship of writer and audience to all elements in the rhetorical situation. Such an enriched conception of audience can help us better understand the complex act we call composing.

NOTES

1. Ruth Mitchell and Mary Taylor, "The Integrating Perspective: An Audience-Response Model for Writing," *CE*, 41 (November, 1979), 267. Subsequent references to this article will be cited in the text.

2. Russell C. Long, "Writer-Audience Relationships: Analysis or Invention," *CCC*, 31 (May, 1980), 223 and 225. Subsequent references to this article will be cited in the text.

3. For these terms we are indebted to Henry W. Johnstone, Jr., who refers to them in his analysis of Chaim Perelman's universal audience in *Validity and Rhetoric in Philosophical Argument: An Outlook in Transition* (University Park, PA: The Dialogue Press of Man & World, 1978), p. 105.

4. Fred R. Pfister and Joanne F. Petrik, "A Heuristic Model for Creating a Writer's Audience," *CCC*, 31 (May, 1980), 213.

5. Pfister and Petrik, 214; our emphasis.

6. See, for example, Lisa S. Ede, "On Audience and Composition," *CCC*, 30 (October, 1979), 291–295.

7. See, for example, David Tedlock, "The Case Approach to Composition," *CCC*, 32 (October, 1981), 253–261.

8. See, for example, Linda Flower's *Problem-Solving Strategies for Writers* (New York: Harcourt Brace Jovanovich, 1981) and John P. Field and Robert H. Weiss' *Cases for Composition* (Boston: Little Brown, 1979).

9. Richard E. Young, "Paradigms and Problems: Needed Research in Rhetorical Invention," in *Research on Composing: Points of Departure*, ed. Charles R. Cooper and Lee Odell (Urbana, IL: National Council of Teachers of English, 1978), p. 32 (footnote #3).

10. Mitchell and Taylor do recognize that internal psychological needs ("unconscious challenges") may play a role in the writing process, but they cite such instances as an "extreme

case (often that of the creative writer)" (p. 251). For a discussion of the importance of self-evaluation in the composing process see Susan Miller, "How Writers Evaluate Their Own Writing," *CCC*, 33 (May, 1982), 176–183.

11. Susan Wall, "In the Writer's Eye: Learning to Teach the Rereading/Revising Process," *English Education*, 14 (February, 1982), 12.

12. Wayne Booth, *Modern Dogma and the Rhetoric of Assent* (Chicago: The University of Chicago Press, 1974), p. xiv.

13. Paul Kameen, "Rewording the Rhetoric of Composition," *Pre/Text*, 1 (Spring-Fall, 1980), 82.

14. Mitchell and Taylor's arguments in favor of adjunct classes seem to indicate that they see writing instruction, wherever it occurs, as a skills course, one instructing students in the proper use of a tool.

15. Anthony R. Petrosky, "From Story to Essay: Reading and Writing," *CCC*, 33 (February, 1982), 20.

16. Walter J. Ong, S. J., "The Writer's Audience Is Always a Fiction," *PMLA*, 90 (January, 1975), 9–21. Subsequent references to this article will be cited in the text.

17. See, for example, William Irmscher, "Sense of Audience: An Intuitive Concept," unpublished paper delivered at the CCCC in 1981; Douglas B. Park, "The Meanings of Audience: Pedagogical Implications," unpublished paper delivered at the CCCC in 1981; and Luke M. Reinsma, "Writing to an Audience: Scheme or Strategy?" unpublished paper delivered at the CCCC in 1982.

18. Herbert W. Simons, *Persuasion: Understanding, Practice, and Analysis* (Reading, MA: Addison-Wesley, 1976).

19. Ong, p. 12. Ong recognizes that oral communication also involves role-playing, but he stresses that it "has within it a momentum that works for the removal of masks" (p. 20). This may be true in certain instances, such as dialogue, but does not, we believe, obtain broadly.

20. Walter S. Minot, "Response to Russell C. Long," *CCC*, 32 (October, 1981), 337.

21. We are aware that the student actually has two audiences, her neighbors and her teacher, and that this situation poses an extra constraint for the writer. Not all students can manage such a complex series of audience constraints, but it is important to note that writers in a variety of situations often write for more than a single audience.

22. In their paper on "Student and Professional Syntax in Four Disciplines" (unpublished paper delivered at the CCCC in 1981), Ian Pringle and Aviva Freedman provide a good example of what can happen when a student creates an aberrant role for an academic reader. They cite an excerpt from a third year history assignment, the tone of which "is essentially the tone of the opening of a television travelogue commentary" and which thus asks the reader, a history professor, to assume the role of the viewer of such a show. The result is as might be expected: "Although the content of the paper does not seem significantly more abysmal than other papers in the same set, this one was awarded a disproportionately low grade" (p. 2).

23. One danger which should be noted is a tendency to foster a questionable image of classical rhetoric. The agonistic speaker-audience relationship which Long cites as an essential characteristic of classical rhetoric is actually a central point of debate among those involved in historical and theoretical research in rhetoric. For further discussion, see: Lisa Ede and Andrea Lunsford, "On Distinctions Between Classical and Modern Rhetoric," in *Classical Rhetoric and Modern Discourse: Essays in Honor of Edward P. J. Corbett*, ed. Robert Connors, Lisa Ede, and Andrea Lunsford (Carbondale, IL: Southern Illinois University Press, 1984).

24. James Moffett, *Teaching the Universe of Discourse* (Boston: Houghton Mifflin, 1968), p. 47. Subsequent references will be mentioned in the text.

25. We have taken the title of this section from Scott Consigny's article of the same title, *Philosophy and Rhetoric*, 7 (Summer, 1974), 175–186. Consigny's effort to mediate between two opposing views of rhetoric provided a stimulating model for our own efforts.

26. Although we believe that the range of audience roles cited in our model covers the general spectrum of options, we do not claim to have specified all possibilities. This is particularly the case since, in certain instances, these roles may merge and blend—shifting subtly in character. We might also note that other terms for the same roles might be used. In a business setting, for instance, colleague might be better termed co-worker; critic, supervisor.

27. Douglas B. Park, "The Meanings of 'Audience,'" *CE*, 44 (March, 1982), 249.

28. Edward P. J. Corbett, *The Little Rhetoric & Handbook*, 2nd edition (Glenview, IL: Scott, Foresman, 1982), p. 5.

29. Donald M. Murray, "Teaching the Other Self: The Writer's First Reader," *CCC*, 33 (May, 1982), 142.

Post-Process "Pedagogy"

A Philosophical Exercise

Lee-Ann M. Kastman Breuch

Recently, "post-process" theories of composition instruction have suggested that process (prewriting, writing, rewriting) is no longer an adequate explanation of the writing act. Many post-process scholars, largely influenced by postmodernist and anti-foundationalist perspectives, suggest that the process paradigm has reduced the writing act to a series of codified phases that can be taught. These critics suggest that process pedagogy simply offers us another foundational explanation of writing.[1] Indeed, the dominant contention of post-process scholars is that process has come to represent Theory with a capital "T."[2] Gary Olson explains, for example, that the process approach is problematic because it attempts to generalize the writing act:

> The problem with process theory, then, is not so much that scholars are attempting to theorize various aspects of composing as it is that they are endeavoring (consciously or not) to construct a model of the composing process, thereby constructing a Theory of Writing, a series of generalizations about writing that supposedly hold true all or most of the time. (8)

This generalization can be especially problematic if teachers of writing present the writing process as one universal process rather than as plural processes (see Russell 80).

The suggestion that process is no longer a viable explanation for the writing act has spurred further discussion about the nature of the writing

First published in JAC 22.1 (Winter 2002): 119–50. Reprinted with permission.

process. For example, while some scholars suggest that the process approach may attempt to represent the act of writing universally, others find this characterization of process inaccurate. Bruce McComiskey notes his disagreement with this characterization: "Invention and revision strategies, as I understand and teach them, do not assume a stable and predictable linguistic system for generating universal meaning; their function is, instead, to harness the polyphonic character of language in communities, to develop rather than constrict a writer's sense of purpose" (39–40). David Russell also argues that the idea of a universal process—"*the* process," as he puts it—is less accurate than the idea of plural processes. He argues for a "progressively wider understanding of writing processes as they are played out in a range of activity systems in our culture(s)" (88). Joseph Petraglia suggests that we should not abandon or reject process, but simply move past it:

> Of course, the fundamental observation that an individual produces text by means of a writing process has not been discarded. Instead, it has dissolved and shifted from figure to ground. . . . We now have the theoretical and empirical sophistication to consider the mantra "writing is a process" as the right answer to a really boring question. We have better questions now, and the notion of process no longer counts as much of an insight. (53)

Because process is so often the topic of discussion in post-process scholarship, post-process has come to mean a critique of the process movement in composition studies. In response, I argue that post-process scholarship is shortchanged by the continued emphasis on process in that the broader implications of post-process theory have very little to do with process. Furthermore, I suggest that the only importance process has to post-process theory is in the form of an illustration—and a poor one at that. That is, "process" as it is cast by post-process scholarship is the scapegoat in an argument to forward postmodern and anti-foundationalist perspectives that are critical to post-process theory.

In this article, I attempt to clarify what I believe post-process theory can contribute to composition pedagogy. In accordance with Sidney Dobrin, who suggests that post-process theory should not fall into the "pedagogical imperative," I suggest that there is no identifiable post-process pedagogy that we can concretely apply to writing classrooms; however, I believe post-process theory offers many insights for the profession of teaching that we all should consider (*Constructing* 63). Specifically, I argue that post-process theory encourages us to reexamine our definition of writing as an activity rather than a body of knowledge, our methods of teaching as indeterminate activities rather than exercises of mastery, and our communicative interactions with students as dialogic rather than monologic. My mission to highlight these insights is driven by what I perceive to be a lack of clarity in post-process theory, fueled by a diversion into discussions of process and by arguments that seemingly resist pedagogical application. When we look past arguments that dominate current scholarship in post-process theory and instead uncover the assumptions that guide post-process theory, we may find helpful and even profound contributions that inform our pedagogical practice—if not in specific pedagogical agendas, then in philosophical principles that guide our practice.

In the next section, I explain how post-process theory may seemingly defy pedagogical application. I specifically review central arguments made by Thomas Kent, a prominent post-process scholar, and I offer a critique of current scholarship on post-process theory.

POST-PROCESS RESISTANCE

On the surface, post-process theory seems to resist pedagogical application because of post-process claims that writing cannot be taught, vague pedagogical agendas, and divergent depictions of post-process pedagogy. If one were to casually explore post-process theory, these three characterizations might leave the impression that teaching writing is a hopeless endeavor. I argue that the wrong arguments are highlighted in this scholarship—arguments that focus on the negatives of process pedagogy rather than on the possibilities of post-process theory. In this section, I explore these arguments further to uncover central assumptions that inform the post-process perspective.

Pedagogical resistance is perhaps most apparent in the claim that writing cannot be taught, which stems from the argument forwarded by Kent that writing is a situated, interpretive, and indeterminate act. In *Paralogic Rhetoric*, Kent suggests that accepting a post-process perspective (at least in a paralogic sense) means rejecting process as the ultimate explanation for the writing act and instead recognizing the role of interpretation and indeterminacy in the writing act. Consequently, if we consider writing as an indeterminate and interpretive activity, he asserts, then "writing and reading—conceived broadly as processes or bodies of knowledge—cannot be taught, for nothing exists to teach" (161). This statement is critical to the post-process perspective for its rejection of process as both an explanation of the writing act and a method of teaching writing. Indeed, this claim seems to have spurred discussions about what Petraglia has called "life after process," so it is necessary to examine it more closely.

Certainly, the claim that writing cannot be taught—and that writing process is inadequate to explain the writing act—on the surface indicates resistance to pedagogical application. However, when investigating more closely, we see that Kent does not completely abandon writing pedagogy, as the following passage from *Paralogic Rhetoric* about his "externalist pedagogy" reveals:

> Stated baldly, an externalist pedagogy endorses the following claims: (1) writing and reading are kinds of communicative interaction; (2) communicative interaction requires triangulation; (3) triangulation requires us to make hermeneutic guesses about how others will interpret our utterances; (4) the process we employ to make our hermeneutic guesses cannot be codified; (5) consequently, no system or framework theory can predict in advance how our utterances will be interpreted; (6) therefore, neither writing nor reading can be reduced to a systemic process or to a codifiable set of conventions, although clearly some of the background knowledge useful for writing—like grammar, sentence structure, paragraph cohesion, and so forth—can be codified and reduced to a system. However, we should remember that knowing a framework or process is necessary but not sufficient for communicative interaction; knowing a grammar, for example, only prepares us to write or to read. (161)

I argue that this passage demonstrates not a total resistance to pedagogy, but rather a careful pedagogical position, for Kent's stance on teaching writing depends on the definition of *writing* that he has outlined in this passage. Kent distinguishes background knowledge—grammar systems and so forth—from the writing act, which he says is indeterminate and dynamic and defies systems. That is, while grammar and rules about cohesion or sentence structure can be easily codified and transmitted to students, these systems should not be confused with the writing act—an act that he describes as uncertain and indeterminate: "Certain background skills, such as an understanding of grammar, can be taught, but the acquisition of these skills never guarantees that a student will be able to communicate effectively; no framework theory of any kind can help a student predict in advance the interpretation that someone else may give to an utterance" (161).

It is important to note that Kent does not reject the instruction of system-based content such as grammar; rather, he suggests that these skills do not in themselves comprise the writing act and that we cannot reduce the writing act to a system that can then be taught. These statements help us to understand that in saying "nothing exists to teach," Kent is not rejecting pedagogical application altogether, but rather the specific pedagogical application of process pedagogy, which he claims attempts to reduce the writing act (not background knowledge) into content that can be taught to students:

> So, any composition or literature pedagogy that presupposes such a frame-work assumes that writing and reading consists of a well-defined process that, once mastered, allows us to engage unproblematically in communicative interaction. These process-oriented pedagogies generally assume that discourse production and reception are cognitive activities that may be reduced either to frameworks that describe the mental processes writers and readers employ or to social activities that describe the conventions or conceptual schemes that hold together a discourse community. (161–62)

Let's take this claim for what it's worth. Kent suggests that writing is not a system or process and therefore cannot be taught as such. Consequently, he does not suggest that teaching writing is impossible; he suggests that teaching writing *as a system* is impossible. Thus, while some may take the claim that "nothing exists to teach" to mean that writing pedagogy is an impossible project, I argue that the claim exists to attack process pedagogy specifically.

While Kent's project here seems to be to dismantle process pedagogy, he does provide suggestions for reconceptualizing pedagogy based on the theoretical framework he has outlined. Yet these, too, demonstrate resistance to pedagogical application. As some scholars have pointed out, Kent's discussions of pedagogy are "vague," "cautious," and "less developed" than his theoretical framework (Dobrin, *Constructing* 89; Ward 158). Nonetheless, in order to illustrate the ways in which Kent moves away from process pedagogy, it is important to review the pedagogical insights he does offer. Kent's reconceptualization of pedagogy begins with the suggestion that we use a new vocabulary to discuss writing in relation to communicative interaction:

> As strong externalists, we would stop talking about writing and reading as processes and start talking about these activities as determinate social acts. This shift from an internalist conception of communicative interaction—the notion that communication is a product of the internal workings of the mind or the workings of the discourse communities in which we live—to an externalist conception that I have outlined here would challenge us to drop our current process-oriented vocabulary and to begin talking about our social and public uses of language. (169)

What results from this proposal is an increased emphasis on communicative interaction between teachers and students. Kent discusses at length how this emphasis would affect teacher-student roles in writing classrooms:

> Instead of dialecticians who initiate students into new knowledge, mentors who endorse a paralogic rhetoric become co-workers who actively collaborate with their students to help them through different communicative

situations both within and outside the university. As co-workers, these mentors—by relinquishing their roles as high priests—engender a new relationship with their students in that they actively collaborate with their students and become, in a sense, students themselves. (166)

Kent's (re)vision of writing pedagogy, then, pushes past process and toward a dialogic understanding of meaning-making. This dialogic pedagogy requires two-way rather than one-way communication, suggesting that teachers move away from a transmission model of education and toward a transformative model that includes active participation from both teachers and students as collaborators.

While Kent's comments about pedagogy do provide direction beyond process, some scholars have been quick to point out that his comments are not specific enough to outline any pedagogy that could be labeled "post-process," thus increasing the resistance to applying post-process theory to pedagogy. Indeed, the vagueness of Kent's proposed pedagogy has indicated to some that post-process theory should remain a theoretical enterprise. Dobrin in particular supports this viewpoint: "Perhaps Kent's own glossing of classroom application should serve as an indication that these theories, while informative about the nature of discourse, are not necessarily practice-oriented theories, a recognition which, of course, puts us at an awkward crossroads" (*Constructing* 86). Dobrin argues that post-process theory is not yet developed enough for pedagogical application: "Even those who see the classroom potential of post-process theory have too hastily fallen into the pedagogical imperative and seek to create pedagogies from theories we are just beginning to discuss" (64). Warning of the "pedagogical imperative," or the idea that a theory must have direct classroom application, Dobrin says that rushing to outline pedagogical application is "frivolous" (86).

Further resistance to pedagogical application of post-process theory exists in the inevitable trap of trying to specify a pedagogy that upholds anti-foundationalist and postmodern beliefs. That is, post-process theory as outlined by Kent upholds the anti-foundationalist view that knowledge is situated, indeterminate, and thoroughly hermeneutic. Thus, in advocating a pedagogy based on anti-foundationalism, one must wrestle with the paradox of any pedagogical agenda it forwards. David Wallace explains:

If we recognize that structural understandings of language and rhetoric are not *objective* and have no intrinsic basis in *reality*, then we must also recognize that any act of pedagogy that requires (or encourages) conformity to convention is ultimately a power move. . . . Thus *any* pedagogical act must be seen as socially and culturally implicated because asking students to move in any direction—whether that be toward mastery of the conventions of standard written English or toward a critical awareness of the social and political consequences of acts of literacy—is to ask them to change not just what they know but who they are. (110–11)

Wallace claims that any pedagogy—postmodern or anti-foundationalist—adopts a stance and therefore cannot be considered indeterminate or ambiguous. Note that Wallace suggests that *any* pedagogical act is an act of power, thus reinforcing the paradox of any anti-foundationalist pedagogy.

What results from this inherent paradox of pedagogical application is confusion about any pedagogical insights post-process theory might offer; in addition, the resistance to a single pedagogical agenda encourages pluralism. For example, in recent years, various "post-process pedagogies" have emerged that bear no resemblance to one another. One example of post-process pedagogy is offered by McComiskey, who openly rejects what he calls Kent's "anti-process" and builds a post-process pedagogy on the idea of "social-process rhetorical inquiry," which he defines as "a method of invention that usually manifests itself in composition classes as a set of heuristic questions based on the cycle of cultural production, contextual distribution, and critical consumption" (40, 42). Raúl Sánchez, who stays closer to Kent's arguments and advocates pedagogy as a one-to-one mentored relationship between teacher and student, articulates another pedagogy that claims to be post-process. In this proposed pedagogy, Sánchez suggests that writing courses no longer focus on process as content, but rather use class time to engage in discourse about writing (see Dobrin, *Constructing* 84). Irene Ward also builds on Kent's ideas to articulate a "functional dialogism" for writing pedagogy, which includes the following forms of dialogue in the writing classroom:

♦ internal dialogues between a self and an internalized audience

♦ dialogue between teacher and student

♦ dialogue between students and other larger social institutions, including but not limited to the educational institution or some other social institution within any one or more of the student's immediate communities

♦ dialogues among students about the formal matters of the composition or the ideas or subject of the discourse

♦ composing using dialogic forms in order to understand an issue or group of issues from various points of view and gain insight into one's relationship to those ideas and into multiple perspectives represented by many voices that have already entered into public dialogue. (171)

Still others articulate different visions for how post-process theory might apply to pedagogy. For example, Barbara Couture suggests that pedagogy must move beyond modeling a process and toward the development of agency in students:

> Our current scholarship on diverse ways of knowing, meaning, and communicating strongly suggests that modeling specific conventions and procedures will not ensure that writers learn all they need to know in order to communicate effectively to others. . . . Writers need to become subjective agents, making willful judgments effected in concrete actions that convey them successfully to others. (42)

Russell takes a different approach and does not advocate rejecting process outright but, rather, extending the notion of process—or, as he puts it, "to extend the activity system of the discipline of composition studies, to offer to teachers and students more and more refined tools for helping people in and entering various activity systems to write and learn to write and transform their activity through writing" (91).

Lest we become confused by these divergent attempts to apply post-process theory to pedagogy, Petraglia reminds us that given the increase in scholarship about writing in the past two decades, both qualitative and quantitative, it is "natural" for post-process theory to exhibit such complexity (53). Yet, this does not help us understand with any clarity just what post-process theory can offer. Kent admits to the hybrid nature of scholarship about post-process theory in the introduction to his edited collection about post-process theory: "Although the authors appearing in these pages may disagree about the nature of the 'post' in 'post-process' theory, all of them agree that change is in the air" (5). Further, he describes three assumptions that he claims most post-process scholars share: writing is public; writing is interpretive; and writing is situated (1). Perhaps these assumptions clarify to some degree how we might understand post-process theory, and I return to them later in this essay.

In sum, there are good reasons to believe that post-process theory resists pedagogical application: the declaration that writing cannot be taught, the lack of a clear pedagogical agenda, and the divergent applications thus far of post-process theory. With respect to Dobrin's insistence that we too easily fall into the "pedagogical imperative," I suggest that there are implications for pedagogy but that they are not highlighted in a productive way. The first implication is the recognition that writing is more than a body of knowledge to be mastered, which I address in the next section.

POST-PROCESS REJECTION OF MASTERY

While it is unclear what post-process theory offers in the way of concrete assignments or classroom environment, post-process theory does make an important pedagogical contribution through its rejection of mastery. Not coincidentally, many post-process scholars associate the process movement with mastery, suggesting (as Kent does) that process represents a system of writing that can be learned and perfected.[3] Couture explains: "We pay a price . . . by reducing those acts that make us uniquely human—speaking and writing—to a device or technology to be mastered, ignoring their more central role in shaping the way we are and live" (39). In this section, I explain in further detail the assumptions of mastery that post-process scholars have articulated (and rejected) about process pedagogy. I argue that whether or not we agree with the depiction of process as mastery, the post-process rejection of mastery is an important recognition for writing scholars and teachers.

One way post-process theorists depict process as mastery is by suggesting that writing process is a "thing"—a system, body of knowledge, or model—that can be skillfully practiced and conquered. When we reexamine Kent's claim about writing pedagogy, this language becomes apparent: "Writing and reading—conceived broadly as processes or bodies of knowledge—cannot be taught, for nothing exists to teach" (161). Helen Ewald observes that Kent's claim "seems based on the assumption that the ability to teach a subject rests on its having a codified body of knowledge that can be transmitted" (122). Of course, Kent ultimately rejects the idea that writing can be described as a body of knowledge, but in doing so process becomes the scapegoat, representing little more than a body of knowledge. Dobrin, also speaking from a post-process perspective, makes this point clear: "Certainly, process pedagogy is convenient; process pedagogy makes it easy to define texts and to write texts. We can unproblematically, clearly present a body of knowledge and evaluate students' abilities to absorb and rehash that body of knowledge, that process" ("Paralogic" 139). According to these and other post-process scholars, process means little more than content—a body of knowledge.

This depiction of process as a body of knowledge often leads to what Erika Lindemann calls "what-centered" teaching approaches, in which teachers emphasize subject matter above all else. It is helpful to examine process pedagogy in this light to better understand the post-process critique that process leads to mastery. According to Lindemann, a what-centered writing course might emphasize subject matter such as literature, films, linguistic systems (grammar and sentence structure), or even modes of writing. In contrast, "how-centered" approaches emphasize activities that occur in a writing class (Lindemann includes process pedagogy here) such as prewriting, writing, and rewriting, in addition to activities such as listening to and discussing the writing of students in class (251, 252). She suggests that "what-centered" courses emphasize nouns (content), while "how-centered" courses emphasize verbs (activities).

The distinction between what-centered and how-centered approaches is particularly important where process pedagogy is concerned. If process pedagogy is considered an approach that reduces writing to a thing—a body of knowledge that can be transmitted to students—then process pedagogy would certainly be considered a what-centered approach to teaching writing. However, Lindemann notes (and I agree) that process pedagogy as it was originally introduced in composition represents a *how-centered* approach because of its emphasis on the activities involved in process approaches to writing (prewriting, writing, rewriting). Indeed, process pedagogy and the research of Janet Emig, Ken Macrorie, and Peter Elbow in many ways encouraged a shift away from content-based approaches, such as current-traditional pedagogy, which emphasized grammatical structures. But viewed through post-process lenses, process seems to have lost its luster. Indeed, post-process scholarship has ignored process as how-centered and has curiously assumed that process is content-based.

Thinking about process or writing as "what-centered" facilitates mastery, as Lindemann explains: "We turn process-centered courses into what-centered courses every time we're tempted to interrupt students engaged in writing with an explanation of some subject matter. Or, if we 'explain' prewriting strategies during the first few weeks and never refer to them again, we've made prewriting a subject matter, a body of information to learn about rather than an activity to practice" (252). Lindemann argues that this turn is not productive and that teachers should be conscious of their efforts to uphold process as how-centered. However, post-process theory seems to be certain that this turn toward content has in fact occurred. Couture explains that instructors have emphasized process as content as a result of a historical habit of modeling writing in the classroom: "How did the emphasis upon process, like so many ideas about writing that are derived from scholarship and research, lose so much when applied en masse in our classrooms? At least one reason can be traced back to how we traditionally have approached composition instruction, teaching students to model technique rather than to emulate expression" (30). As Couture explains, our tendency to perceive process as mastery is historically consistent with past pedagogy, such as current-traditional approaches:

Teaching the writing process as the modeling of technique certainly is consistent with a tradition of composition pedagogy extending from the practice of imitating good writing by good writers; through the practice of perfecting the argumentative strategies of deduction, induction, comparing, contrasting, and defining; to following the basic pattern of the five-paragraph theme, mastered by most of us in high school English and freshman composition classes. And, too, emphasis on process as model has reflected an overt desire of many composition instructors to identify methods for improving writing instruction so as to "right" their students' writing. . . . (33)

Couture explains well how we—both students and teachers—might interpret process as mastery of writing techniques. From a student's perspective, process could be presented as a technique that could be mastered to improve student writing. From a teacher's perspective, process could be viewed as a pedagogical method that could be mastered in the classroom. Either way, the argument presented here suggests that process has been treated as a thing to master in writing pedagogy. Yet, this characterization of process as mastery seems too simple. Lisa Ede reminds us, for example, that research on writing process has displayed enormous complexity. To illustrate this complexity, she reviews the work of several process scholars such as Emig, Elbow, Donald Murray, Linda Flower, and John Hayes, and she reminds us of their divergent approaches to process. But, as Ede articulates, process became "co-opted and commodified—by textbooks that oversimplified and rigidified a complex phenomenon, by overzealous language arts coordinators and writing program administrators who assumed that the process approach to teaching could be 'taught' in one or two in-service sessions" (35–36; see also Russell 84).

I review these arguments to problematize the assumption that process is "what-centered," based solely on content or a body of knowledge. While it may be true that process has been "co-opted," as Ede suggests, I argue that this commodification of process should be considered as a slip and not as a fact. As Lindemann reminds us, the characterization of process as how-centered is more true to the origins of the process movement. Simply stated, before accepting post-process arguments about the failure of process, we need to examine the assumptions informing them. When we do, we can find value in the post-process insistence that we reexamine the way we think of process in the writing classroom, as well as our approaches to mastery. That is, post-process scholars seem most concerned about writing being characterized as a thing, whether that thing is process, grammatical systems, discourse conventions, and so on. When considering these arguments, the value in post-process scholarship appears not to be the rejection of process, but the rejection of mastery—the rejection of the belief that writing can be categorized as a thing to be mastered.

Post-process opposition to mastery is also apparent in arguments that characterize process as Theory—or process as having universal explanatory power. And, as in the "what-centered" characterization of process, process as a Theory is rejected by post-process scholars, as Olson reminds us:

> The problem with process theory, then, is not so much that scholars are attempting to theorize various aspects of composing as it is that they are endeavoring (consciously or not) to construct a model of the composing process, thereby constructing a Theory of Writing, a series of generalizations about writing that supposedly hold true all or most of the time. (8)

Couture's observation that process is a way to teach writing the "right" way also supports the argument that process presents a Theory. Like the rejection of mastery, these arguments illustrate the postmodern and anti-foundationalist influences on post-process theory. As Olson explains, "The postmodern critique of theory serves as a useful corrective in that it alerts us to the dangers of creating master narratives and then adhering to these explanations as if we have obtained truth" (8). Postmodern critique is especially helpful in deconstructing what Pullman describes as the "rhetorical narrative" of process pedagogy, a "motivated selection and sequencing of events that sacrifices one truth in order to more clearly represent another" (16; see also Foster 149). Indeed, the postmodern influences on post-process theory denounce the search for universal truth. Kent reminds us of the "master narrative of objectivity," the idea that truth resides outside of language and that knowledge is systematic rather than interpretive (*Paralogic* 63). At the root of the post-process critique of process pedagogy is the idea that process is a systematic method for learning writing—one that is objective rather than subjective.

Again, considering the post-process opposition to mastery, we must reexamine the claim that process represents a Theory or a grand narrative. I suggest that given the postmodern and anti-foundationalist influences on post-process theory, post-process scholars are more concerned with the rejection of universal theories in general than the rejection of process pedagogy in particular. Process appears to be merely a convenient illustration of the post-process perspective. For example, because process scholarship has been the dominant perspective in writing pedagogy, it is easy to paint it as an illustration of a master narrative, a Theory, or a model to be imitated. It is tempting to wonder if the purpose of post-process scholarship is to simply knock process off of its pedestal. Similar moves have been made in the past regarding the current-traditional movement in composition studies. Pullman describes the rush to associate the term *current-traditional* with a movement, theory, or label about teaching writing effectively:

> We forget that [this] expression did not refer to a theory but was instead a shorthand and off-the-cuff way of alluding to the way the tradition of rhetoric was currently being purveyed in the Freshman Composition textbooks of [the] day. Because we forget this, we tend to think that current-traditional rhetoric was a bogus theory based on prejudice and misunderstanding, a kind of mindless application of traditional folklore or naive interpretations of Aristotle's *Rhetoric* when in fact it did not exist as a theory except to the extent one could extrapolate a theory from the textbooks current at the time. (22)

Pullman asserts that the rush to define current-traditional rhetoric forwarded the process movement: "The writing process was not, in other words, so much discovered as created . . ." (23). Further, he suggests that this "creation" of process gave scholars reason to reject current-traditional rhetoric: "In a sense, the reified expression *current-traditional rhetoric* does little more than create a daemon for the sake of expelling it" (23).

In describing the building and rejecting of current-traditional rhetoric, Pullman illustrates his perception of the rhetorical narrative of process. Ede makes a similar observation of this rhetorical move, suggesting that advocates of the process movement depicted current-traditional rhetoric negatively. She claims that the process movement "in effect constituted itself through a denial of origins that involves creating that which it wishes to oppose and then erasing the shared ground that made the original construction of the other possible. In an important sense current-traditional rhetoric did not exist until advocates of writing as a process created it" (37). Ede calls this strategy "a characteristic move of the western intellectual project," and the point I wish to make is that this same move may be apparent in post-process scholarship (37). Here, process is described as a master narrative, a Theory, a content- and what-centered approach. Process is first described as a thing and is then promptly rejected. Petraglia articulates this move: "As I understand it, 'post-process' signifies a rejection of the generally formulaic framework for understanding writing that process suggested" (53). It could easily be argued that post-process scholars have created their own rhetorical narrative of process as content-based, thus casting process as the scapegoat.

As I suggested previously, I disagree with the depiction of process as a formula, model, or "thing," but I do agree with Petraglia's assertion that post-process scholarship signifies a rejection of generally formulaic frameworks for explaining writing. This broader understanding of post-process scholarship—focused not on process, but on the rejection of formulaic explanations of writing—is a key contribution to the reconceptualization of writing. Petraglia explains this well: "This reconceptualization requires that the discipline let go of its current pedagogical shape (i.e., its focus on supplying students with productive rhetorical skills that can be exercised through writing) and instead deploy its efforts to inculcate *receptive* skills" (61–62). Thus, I argue that rather than the rejection of process, the post-process critique contributes to our discipline through the rejection of mastery—the description of writing as a "thing," and the description of a master narrative or theory of writing. In giving up the search for a way to teach writing, post-process theory advocates, in the words of Petraglia, the "letting go" of the discipline. As I explain in the next section, post-process theory can be more fully explained by reviewing key assumptions critical to the theory, assumptions that are informed by postmodern and anti-foundationalist perspectives.

POST-PROCESS ASSUMPTIONS ABOUT WRITING

In moving away from writing as a "thing," post-process theory encourages us to examine writing again as an activity—an indeterminate activity. By "indeterminate" I mean that the writing act cannot be predicted in terms of how students will write (through certain formulas or content) or how students will learn (through certain approaches). The shift from writing as content to writing as activity can be more fully explained by assumptions that are central to the post-process perspective. These are, according to Kent, the following: "(1) writing is public; (2) writing is interpretive; and (3) writing is situated" (Introduction 1). As I suggest in this section, because so much post-process scholarship has focused on the rejection of process, we need further explanation about assumptions that support a post-process view of writing. In my attempt to provide more background and explanation of these assumptions, I refer to the work of Donald Davidson, Richard Rorty, Thomas Kuhn, Stanley Fish, and scholars in composition who have discussed these assumptions.

Writing Is Public

The assumption that writing is public grows out of the post-process perspective that meaning making is a product of our communicative interaction with others rather than a product of an individual.[4] Acknowledging the public nature of writing means acknowledging a reading audience—people to whom the writing matters—whether that audience is oneself, another person, a group of people, or any other reader. Emphasizing the public nature of writing reminds us that beyond writing correctly, writers must work toward communicating their message to an audience. It is this goal—being understood—that Kent suggests cannot be "guaranteed"; therefore, we cannot know with certainty if students are successful, nor can we know how to teach students to be successful in communicative interaction. However, we *can* encourage students to become more aware of their interactions with others.

We can further understand the assumption that writing is public by examining the Davidsonian perspective of "language-in-use," a concept that has influenced some post-process scholars, particularly Kent. Davidson explains in "A Nice Derangement of Epitaphs" that language-in-use does not rely on some sort of foundational structure (like Noam Chomsky's deep structure) or even conventions of language. His description of language-in-use has radical implications for the idea that language is contextually or "convention" bound:

> There is no such thing as a language, not if a language is anything like what many philosophers and linguists have supposed. There is therefore no such thing to be learned, mastered, or born with. We must give up the idea of a clearly defined shared structure which language-users acquire and then apply to cases. And we should try again to say how convention in any important sense is involved in language; or, as I think, we should give up the attempt to illuminate how we communicate by appeal to conventions. (446)[5]

Davidson's version of communicative interaction suggests that meaning is not relative to a community or to discourse conventions but is a product of language-in-use, and language-in-use, as Reed Way Dasenbrock explains, is always public and accessible to other language users:

> Networks of meaning, thus, are both inner and outer, including ourselves and others in a web. It is not that we have something unique to say stemming from our personal experience before we negotiate the public structures of meaning, but what we have to say forms as a response to that public structure, to what has come before us and what is being said and done around us. (29)

Davidson terms this public interaction "triangulation," which he understands as the connection between language users and the world.[6] In explaining triangulation, Davidson writes that the "basic idea is that our concept of objectivity—our idea that our thoughts may or may not correspond to the truth—is an idea that we would not have if it weren't for interpersonal relations. In other words, the source of objectivity is intersubjectivity: the triangle consists of two people and the world" (Kent, "Language" 7–8). Triangulation is a key concept for explaining how meanings are located within our communicative interactions with others, and it suggests that we can't know things without knowing others.

The public aspect of writing, which incorporates Davidson's depiction of language-in-use, is already apparent in some writing pedagogies; however, these pedagogies are often described as "dialogic" instead of "post-process" because they emphasize communicative interaction in the teaching of writing. Sánchez outlines a writing pedagogy, for example, as a one-to-one mentored relationship between teacher and student that emphasizes communicative interaction. In this proposed pedagogy, writing instruction is no longer focused on process as content, but rather on class time used to engage students in discourse about writing (see Dobrin, *Constructing* 83–85). Similarly, Ewald suggests that a pedagogy emphasizing communicative interaction would "enjoy an intimate connection between instructional subjects and methods. Writing instruction could be organized around discourse moves" (128).

Other pedagogies that emphasize dialogue employ concepts from Bakhtin—particularly the concepts of heteroglossia and addressivity. Ward explains how these concepts relate to writing pedagogy: "The self in a dialogic pedagogy is not autonomous and solitary but multiple, composed of all the voices or texts one has ever heard or read and therefore capable of playing an infinite number of roles in service of the internal dialogic interaction" (172–73). Using Bakhtinian concepts of dialogue, Ward describes a "functional dialogism," a pedagogy that encourages students to interact with others, thus reinforcing the public aspect of writing:

> Because learning takes place best in communicative interaction, a functional dialogic pedagogy will have to employ a great deal of public writing—that is, writing directed to others capable of and interested in responding—if we are to produce students who are able to generate not only correct, readable prose, but also prose that can elicit a response from others, thereby enabling students to become active participants in communities beyond the classroom. (170)

Dialogue is even more prominent in Kay Halasek's *A Pedagogy of Possibility*, in which she argues that "dialogue has replaced writing as a process as a defining metaphor for the discipline" (3–4). Halasek's decidedly post-process pedagogy emphasizes Bakhtinian scholarship, which she conceptualizes as "a world that recognizes the viability and necessity of existing social, economic, and national languages. Through the concept of dialogism, Bakhtin establishes the critical need to sustain dialogue in the unending quest to maintain difference and diversity, hallmarks of intellectual growth and health . . ." (8). Emphasizing the importance of communicative interaction, Halasek suggests that heteroglossia—reflexivity and response— ought to characterize writing pedagogy.

The assumption that writing is public, therefore, incorporates the idea that meaning is made through our interactions. Terms used to describe this emphasis include language-in-use, communicative interaction, and dialogue, but they all point to the idea that writing is an activity—an interaction with others—rather than content to be mastered.

Writing Is Interpretive

A second assumption of the post-process perspective is that writing is interpretive. That is, the production—not just the reception—of discourse is thoroughly interpretive (or what Rorty calls "interpretation all the way down").[7] This assumption supports the belief that writing is indeterminate, for saying writing is interpretive suggests that meaning is not stable. We can better understand this assumption by reviewing what has been called the "interpretive turn" in philosophy, the claim that what we know is shaped by our interpretations. The interpretive turn, as described by James Bohman, David Hiley, and Richard Shusterman, follows previous philosophical movements such as the "epistemological turn" of the eighteenth century (where knowledge was equated with rational thought, especially the kind of rational thought exemplified by the scientific method) and the "linguistic turn" early in this century, where emphasis was placed on the structure of language and the meanings generated through language systems. According to Bohman, Hiley, and Shusterman, the interpretive turn breaks with these previous traditions by giving up the notion that the essence or the foundations of knowledge and meaning can be discovered: "The views about the foundations of knowledge and the knowing subject that were the basis for the epistemological turn have been called into question, and it has seemed to many philosophers that language and meaning cannot bear the kind of weight the linguistic turn required" (1). When we give up our search for the foundations of knowledge, and when we relinquish our attempts to reduce knowledge and meaning to foundational categories of linguistic or mental states, we encounter the interpretive turn—the acknowledgment that meaning is shaped by our interpretive acts.

Critical to the assumption that writing is interpretive is the degree to which interpretation penetrates. That is, are there some things, ideas, concepts, that are not subject to interpretation? The post-process assumption is that writing is thoroughly interpretive, or what Rorty calls "interpretation all the way down." Bohman, Hiley, and Shusterman explain that the move toward interpretation can take one of two forms: either "hermeneutic universalism" or "hermeneutic contextualism" (7). Hermeneutic universalism holds that interpretation never stops—that communication itself constitutes an interpretive act. Hermeneutic contextualism holds that interpretation takes place within some context, community, or background (7). In short, contextualism suggests that there are limits to interpretation, while universalism does not.

These competing conceptions of interpretation characterize a recurring debate within current hermeneutic theory, and clear examples of this debate are found in the writings of Kuhn and Rorty. For example, in "The Natural and the Human Sciences," Kuhn, a hermeneutic contextualist, notes that both the natural and the human sciences rely on interpretation, but the human sciences rely on interpretation more completely: "The natural sciences, therefore, though they may require what I have called a hermeneutic base, are not themselves hermeneutic enterprises. The human sciences, on the other hand, often are, and they may have no alternative." Kuhn endorses the idea that the natural sciences are more objective, and, finally, more "truthful" than the human sciences because the natural sciences "are not themselves hermeneutic enterprises" (23).

In contrast, Rorty, a hermeneutic universalist, argues that interpretation goes "all the way down": "My fantasy is of a culture so deeply anti-essentialist that it makes only a sociological distinction between sociologists and physicists, not a methodological or philosophical one" (71). In "Inquiry as Recontextualization," Rorty asserts that our minds are "webs of beliefs and desires, of sentential attitudes—webs that continually reweave themselves so as to accommodate new sentential attitudes" (59). For Rorty, both the human sciences and the natural sciences are thoroughly hermeneutic enterprises, and he argues that what we know or could ever know about the world derives from the webs of beliefs and desires that we continually reweave or "recontextualize":

> As one moves along the spectrum from habit to inquiry—from instinctive revision of intentions through routine calculation toward revolutionary science or politics—the number of beliefs added to or subtracted from the web increases. At a certain point in this process it becomes useful to speak of "recontextualization." The more widespread the changes, the more use

> we have for the notion of "a new context." This new context can be a new explanatory theory, a new comparison class, a new descriptive vocabulary, a new private or political purpose, the latest book one has read, the last person one talked to; the possibilities are endless. (60–61)

According to Rorty, interpretation—what he calls "reinterpretation" and "recontextualization"—never ceases, for every interpretation is based on a previous interpretation. The different views about the power of interpretation held by Rorty and Kuhn exemplify the current debate concerning hermeneutic universalism and hermeneutic contextualization that we encounter in studies of both the reception and the production of discourse.

To understand writing as a thoroughly interpretive activity (in the spirit of hermeneutic universalism) means accepting that no foundational knowledge is the basis for writing as a discipline. Given this assumption, we can better understand the post-process rejection of mastery and its depiction and consequent rejection of process as a foundational body of knowledge. In addition, when we understand writing as thoroughly interpretive, we must also accept the indeterminate nature of the writing activity. Writing becomes an activity that requires an understanding of context, interaction with others, and our attempts to communicate a message. Understanding interpretation as universal helps illuminate the third post-process assumption: that writing is situated.

Writing Is Situated

The assumption that writing is situated also illustrates the indeterminacy of the writing act, as writing must correspond to specific contexts that naturally vary. Of all three post-process assumptions, the assumption that writing is situated has been discussed most frequently by scholars interested in postmodern or anti-foundationalist perspectives. For example, James Sosnoski asserts that postmodern classrooms "do not have to follow a single blueprint and should change according to the situation" (210). Also endorsing situatedness, Thomas Barker and Fred Kemp explain that postmodernism is "a self-conscious acknowledgment of the immediate present and an attempt to respond to it in new ways" (1). James Berlin draws on postmodern thought and social-epistemic rhetoric to suggest that pedagogy becomes enforced through "dialectical interaction, working out a rhetoric more adequate to the historical moment and the actual conditions of teacher and students" (25). Situatedness, for these postmodern scholars, refers to the ability to respond to specific situations rather than rely on foundational principles or rules.

Situatedness has been discussed similarly in the anti-foundationalist perspective. For example, Patricia Bizzell asserts that "an anti-foundationalist understanding of discourse would see the student's way of thinking and interacting with the world, the student's very self, as fundamentally altered by participation in any new discourse" (43). She includes situatedness in her definition of rhetoric: "Rhetoric is the study of the personal, social and historical elements in human discourse—how to recognize them, interpret them, and act on them, in terms both of situational context and of verbal style" (52). Likewise, Susan Wells suggests that technical writing pedagogy should help students enter into communicative action and to help them understand their situatedness (264). Further, in "Teaching Professional Writing as Social Praxis," Thomas Miller suggests that we need to teach technical writing not as *techné* (or cognitive skills) but as *praxis*, which means that writers must understand the situations and contexts that surround them: "We can foster such 'practical wisdom' by developing a pedagogy that contributes to our students' ability to locate themselves and their professional communities in the larger public context" (68).

While situatedness has been addressed more explicitly in these passages, we can see traces of all three post-process assumptions in this scholarship. They are evident in assertions that writing should *change with the situation*, that students *interact with the world* through *dialectical interaction*, and that rhetoric involves *interpretation of social and historical elements of human discourse*. Given these similarities, we see that post-process scholarship is not advocating new directions, but rather endorsing anti-foundationalist and postmodern approaches that have already been articulated. To see writing in terms of post-process assumptions—as public, interpretive, and situated— encourages us to think of writing as an indeterminate activity rather than a body of knowledge to be mastered. These post-process assumptions (strongly influenced by postmodern and anti-foundationalist perspectives) finally shed light on how post-process theory might inform teaching.

POST-PROCESS PEDAGOGY?

My purpose thus far has been to reveal the post-process rejection of mastery and to outline the anti-foundationalist assumptions informing post-process theory. In doing so, I have suggested that post-process theory rejects system-based explanations of writing and embraces indeterminacy in the writing act. Given this understanding of post-process theory, in this final section I assert that post-process theory resists pedagogical agendas that are comprised of content, but that it offers valuable pedagogical principles about the activity of teaching. I discuss implications of these principles, which include mentoring and tutorial approaches to writing instruction.

Understanding the anti-foundationalist nature of post-process theory places us, as Dobrin suggests, "at an awkward crossroads" *(Constructing* 86). To articulate any kind of pedagogy based on anti-foundationalism would be to support the claim that knowledge can be rooted in a particular approach or system and, therefore, would no longer be anti-foundational. It is for this reason that I do not advocate a specific pedagogical agenda that espouses post-process theory, for I believe doing so presents an inherent paradox. Fish more clearly explains that we ought not to place too much pedagogical stock in anti-foundationalist assumptions such as situatedness:

> To put the matter in a nutshell, the knowledge that one is in a situation has no particular payoff for any situation you happen to be in, because the constraints of that situation will not be relaxed by that knowledge. It follows, then, that teaching our students the lesson of anti-foundationalism, while it will put them in possession of a new philosophical perspective, will not give them a tool for operating in the world they already inhabit. Being told that you are in a situation will help you neither to dwell in it more perfectly nor to *write* within it more successfully. (351)

Similarly, if we accept the post-process perspective that writing is indeterminate, public, interpretive, and situated, there is little we can do with this knowledge.

When it comes to pedagogy, however, the temptation is to turn our revelations into content to be delivered in the classroom, thereby falling prey to what Dobrin calls the "pedagogical imperative." While we may want to translate the post-process assumptions (writing is public, interpretive, and situated) into content to have our students learn, what good does this do? I completely agree with Dobrin that the force of the "pedagogical imperative" is alive and well and also that it is premature in relation to post-process theory. Dobrin suggests that post-process theory is too new to generate pedagogical insights — that its discussions should be theoretical at this point *(Constructing* 64). While I agree with Dobrin, I suggest that because of the anti-foundationalist influence on post-process theory, it is unlikely that we will *ever* see a "post-process pedagogy," complete with neat, bulleted points about applying a specific approach to the writing classroom. Fish is again insightful here, for he argues a similar point in declaring that the project to develop a postmodern or anti-foundationalist pedagogy should be abandoned — not simply because the project would be difficult, but because it is impossible. According to Fish, anti-foundationalism only helps us understand *that* we are situated. He argues that we can do nothing with this knowledge, and we certainly can't put it to use. In the conclusion of "Anti-Foundationalism, Theory Hope, and the Teaching of Composition," Fish offers a kind of apology for this view: "Perhaps I should apologize for taking up so much of your time in return for so small a yield; but the smallness of the yield has been my point. It is also the point of anti-foundationalism, which offers you nothing but the assurance that what it is unable to give you—knowledge, goals, purposes, strategies—is what you already have" (355). Similarly, I offer a kind of apology that I have no specific pedagogical agenda to offer that I could claim would be "post-process pedagogy," for I don't believe such an agenda is compatible with the theory.

More to the point, Fish's viewpoint actualizes, in my opinion, the "letting go" of the discipline that Petraglia spoke of in terms of post-process theory. Petraglia suggests that instructors of writing need to let go of the idea that writing is built on a foundational body of knowledge and accept the idea that we need to focus on situational response. Likewise, we must resist the temptation to turn our understanding of post-process assumptions into content to be delivered and mastered by students. Accepting post-process assumptions truly implies a "letting go" of the desire to find a right way to learn and teach writing.

While post-process theory does not offer concrete pedagogical agendas based on content, I believe that it offers valuable pedagogical principles that guide our practice as teachers. I see two main principles that post-process theory can offer pedagogy: the rejection of mastery and the engagement in dialogue rather than monologue with students. I have already illustrated these principles in my explanation of post-process assumptions (writing is public, interpretive, and situated), so I won't explain them again here. It is worth noting, however, that these principles have been present in previous scholarship about composition pedagogy, alternative pedagogies, and pragmatic theories dating back to John Dewey. We need to recognize that these post-process principles are not out in left field but, rather, that they support excellent scholarship in education. It is worth briefly reviewing these principles, most notably in the scholarship of Dewey and Paulo Freire.

We find traces of the rejection of mastery and engagement in dialogue in Dewey's declaration that education is a social process instead of subject matter (230). In "My Pedagogic Creed," Dewey suggests that "the only true education comes through the stimulation of the child's powers by the demands of the social situations in which he finds himself," that education is a lifelong process, and that school "must represent present life—life as real and vital to the child as that which he carries on in the home, in the neighborhood, or on the playground" (229, 230–31). In declaring these beliefs, he rejects the idea that education is a fixed body of knowledge to be transmitted passively to the student: "I believe, therefore, that the true centre of correlation of the school subjects is not science, nor literature, nor history, nor geography, but the child's own social activities" (232). The idea is that the rote learning of subject matter, without understanding its relevance to one's situation and the world, does not improve one's education. Dewey's ideas resonate with the post-process rejection of system-based writing approaches and its emphasis on language-in-use.

In some regards, an even more striking resemblance exists between post-process principles and the work of Freire, particularly his notion of the "banking concept." In *Pedagogy of the Oppressed*, Freire describes the banking concept as "an act of depositing, in which the students are the depositories and the teacher is the depositor. Instead of communicating, the teacher issues communiques and makes deposits which the students patiently receive, memorize, and repeat" (67). Freire considers the banking method of teaching to be a dehumanizing practice that ultimately reinforces teachers as oppressors, controlling knowledge, and students as the oppressed, incapable of response (68). In place of the banking concept of education, Freire advocates a "problem-posing" concept of education, which would require students to play active rather than passive roles:

> Those truly committed to liberation must reject the banking concept in its entirety, adopting instead a concept of women and men as conscious beings and consciousness intent upon the world. They must abandon the educational goal of deposit-making and replace it with the posing of the problems of human beings in their relationship with the world. (74)

By suggesting that critical consciousness requires that students must communicate with the world, not just be in the world, Freire illustrates the post-process emphasis on writing as public interaction with others and the world. And he emphasizes the social aspect of education when he asserts that human life can only have meaning through communication (72). He encourages the teacher-student relationship to be a "partnership" in which teacher and student engage in two-way dialogue. To do so requires a dialogic relationship between students and teacher in which roles of the traditional banking concept of education no longer exist and in which "the students—no longer docile listeners—are now critical co-investigators in dialogue with the teacher" (70, 75). Although Freire's pedagogy is thoroughly ideological—a premise Dewey's pedagogy does not share to the same degree—both principles of rejection of mastery and engagement of dialogue can be seen in this scholarship.

In composition studies, we have also heard these principles before. As I outlined earlier in this essay, postmodern and anti-foundationalist "pedagogies" have advocated writing as situated, interpretive, and public rather than based on foundational knowledge, and several "dialogic" pedagogies have also been discussed in composition scholarship. Although the principles of rejection of mastery and engagement in dialogue have been discussed in previous scholarship, what is different about post-process theory is the combination of these principles in one theoretical perspective, as well as its sharp criticism of the dominant paradigm in composition studies. These features of post-process theory push the discipline forward in a most pronounced way, as its very name suggests.

Although I am unable to produce specific content-based pedagogical agendas that can be immediately transferred to the classroom, I do suggest that the rejection of mastery and engagement in dialogue lead to an important implication for how we teach writing: such a stance helps us reconsider teaching as an act of mentoring rather than a job in which we deliver content. To think of teaching as mentoring means spending time and energy on our interactions with students—listening to them, discussing ideas with them, letting them make mistakes, and pointing them in the right direction. This type of teacher-student relationship demonstrates instruction that is collaborative and dialogic, and it in fact reflects Kent's suggestions for pedagogy in *Paralogic Rhetoric:* "By working in partnership with their students, mentors would no longer stand outside their students' writing and reading experiences. Instead, they would become an integral part of their students' learning experiences . . ." (166). This type of mentoring suggests a release of the idea of mastery and the embrace of indeterminacy in teaching situations. Indeed, the connection could be made that like the post-process description of writing, the act of *teaching* is also public, interpretive, and situated—another type of indeterminate activity.

Given this emphasis on mentoring, I believe the strongest application of post-process theory is in the practice of one-to-one instruction that manifests itself in teacher-student interactions. Kent, Sánchez, Ward, and Halasek have come to similar conclusions, drawing attention to dialogue between teacher-student and to student-student interactions in the classroom. I support the kind of one-to-one, dialogic instruction these scholars have advocated; however, their descriptions of one-to-one interactions tend to be broad and abstract, leaving readers with little concrete sense of how post-process theory might apply to one-to-one instruction. For purposes of illustration, a more immediate and tangible application of post-process theory might exist in tutorial interactions between tutors and students in writing centers. Writing centers provide a concrete context for post-process theory because one-to-one interactions are the primary practice of writing center tutors, as well as the subject of writing center research. For example,

Christina Murphy and Steve Sherwood suggest that the essence of tutoring is *conversation*, or language-in-use (2). Similarly, Eric Hobson suggests that writing center scholarship often derives its credibility from practice, or "lore." In addition, illustrations of one-to-one teaching interactions abound in writing center literature; many scholars have addressed the dynamics of teaching interactions, teacher-student roles, and methods involved in one-to-one writing instruction.[8] Given that post-process theory emphasizes dialogue in writing instruction, as well as the importance of mentoring, and given that such dialogue in writing instruction is the core of writing center work, the connection between post-process theory and writing center pedagogy is easy to support.

Post-process theory, then, could find immediate application in writing center work and could benefit from writing center scholarship about one-to-one teaching. Alternatively, writing centers could benefit from post-process theory in exploring theoretical avenues to support writing center practice. There exists a wonderful irony in this connection because of the sometimes perceived gap in prestige between post-process theory and writing center practice. That is, post-process theory, at least in the terms Dobrin describes, appears on the surface to be an ivory-tower endeavor. Writing centers, on the other hand, because of their focus on practice, have historically been marginalized and have consequently struggled to legitimize scholarship based on tutorial practice. The connection between the two might result in a happy marriage. For instance, anti-foundationalist and postmodernist perspectives are appearing more frequently in writing center scholarship.[9] Traces of the public, situated, and interpretive aspects of post-process theory in writing centers exist in Joan Mullin's suggestion that writing centers "provide spaces where the personal and public, the individual and other, struggle to honor the singular voice, to recognize different language communities" (xiii). In addition, claims such as that expressed by Hobson ("no single theory can dictate writing center instruction") are reminiscent of the post-process rejection of a grand theory or narrative to describe communicative practice (8). The union of post-process theory and writing center practice could potentially demonstrate how theory and practice could live in harmony, providing both illustration and explanation of one-to-one writing instruction. Of course, while there are some interesting overlaps between post-process theory and writing center work, asserting a strong connection would require another lengthy and careful discussion, which I do not have time to develop here. But I do see this connection as a fruitful area for future research, and I see writing centers as an immediate illustration of the kind of instructional dialogue post-process theory endorses.

For the purposes of my discussion here, however, I wish to suggest that post-process theory is, at its very core, concerned with pedagogical practice.

In asserting this claim, I disagree with those scholars who suggest post-process theory should remain a theoretical enterprise, and I suggest that post-process theory is most decidedly connected to a *how-centered* approach to teaching. Critiques that deny any pedagogical relevance of post-process theory are, I believe, based on the expectation that pedagogy is what-centered and needs to produce a concrete pedagogical agenda based on content. The real pedagogical thrust of post-process theory has to do not with content or subject matter, but rather with *what we do with content*. As such, post-process theory has much to offer teachers in any discipline, whether they teach writing, math, physics, women's studies, history, or occupational therapy, for the pedagogical thrust of post-process theory is in its reminder that teaching does not equal mastery of content but rather how teachers and students can interact with one another *about* content. Thus, in addition to posing the question "what does it mean to write?" post-process theory also poses the question "what does it mean to teach?"

LETTING GO

As discerning scholars, we must not take post-process theory at face value, associating it only with a critique of process. If, as many post-process scholars articulate, post-process theory means accepting an anti-foundationalist perspective and adopting language-in-use, then its relevance to pedagogy is to encourage us to reexamine the "foundations" from which we may have been operating, as well as our communicative practices with students. Even if this examination does not make anti-foundationalists out of us, it reminds us to think carefully about our teaching practices, to avoid co-opting or reducing complex research in composition studies, and to become more aware of our interactions with students in the classroom.

"Letting go" in the case of post-process theory does not mean an avoidance of the teaching of writing; it does not mean becoming irresponsible teachers. It means, quite frankly, the opposite. It means becoming teachers who are more in tune to the pedagogical needs of students, more willing to discuss ideas, more willing to listen, more willing to be moved by moments of mutual understanding. It means, in sum, to be more conscientious in our attempts to meet the needs of students in their educational journeys. Post-process theory does not prescribe a pedagogy and ask us to adopt it blindly. Rather, it enhances our sensitivity as teachers, our knowledge and expertise, and the way we communicate with students to help them learn. In short, post-process theory asks us to take a close look at ourselves as teachers. Thinking through the principles of rejection of mastery and engagement in dialogue provides all teachers with a valuable philosophical exercise.[10]

NOTES

1. See, for example, Olson; Pullman; Kent, "Introduction."
2. See Petraglia; Dobrin, "Constructing"; Kent, "Introduction"; Pullman.
3. See, for example, Pullman, Olson, Couture.
4. In his *Paralogic Rhetoric*, Kent identifies this assumption with "externalism."
5. We can note similarities between Davidson's argument that "there is no such thing as language" and Kent's argument that "we cannot teach writing . . . for nothing exists to teach." Both arguments reject the idea that language and writing are comprised of foundational systems.
6. The term "triangulation" that Davidson uses is not to be confused with the term "triangulation" that denotes qualitative research methodology in which data are compiled from three or more perspectives to establish a more verifiable analysis.
7. While much has been discussed about interpretation in the reception of discourse—for example, Stanley Fish's concept of interpretive communities and how meaning is received—little has been discussed about the interpretive nature of writing or speaking.
8. See, for example, Murphy and Sherwood; Hobson; Harris; Black; Clark; Mullin and Wallace.
9. See Nancy Grimm's fine book, *Good Intentions: Writing Center Work for Postmodern Times*, as well as scholarship by Hobson and Abascal-Hildebrand.
10. I wish to thank colleagues who reviewed this article and provided comments that contributed to substantive improvements: Peter T. Breuch, Thomas Kent, Mary Lay, John Logie, David Beard, and James Thomas Zebroski.

WORKS CITED

Abascal-Hildebrand, Mary. "Tutor and Student Relations: Applying Gadamer's Notions of Translation." Mullin and Wallace 172–83.
Barker, Thomas T., and Fred O. Kemp. "Network Theory: A Postmodern Pedagogy for the Writing Classroom." *Computers and Community: Teaching Composition in the Twenty-First Century.* Ed. Carolyn Handa. Portsmouth: Boynton, 1990. 1–27.
Berlin, James A. "Poststructuralism, Cultural Studies, and the Composition Classroom: Postmodern Theory in Practice." *Rhetoric Review* 11 (1992): 16–33.
Bizzell, Patricia A. "Foundationalism and Anti-Foundationalism in Composition Studies." *Pre/Text* 7.1–2 (1986): 37–56.
Black, Laurel Johnson. *Between Talk and Teaching: Reconsidering the Writing Conference.* Logan: Utah State UP, 1998.
Bohman, James F., David R. Hiley, and Richard Shusterman. "Introduction: The Interpretive Turn." Hiley, Bohman, and Shusterman 1–14.
Clark, Gregory. *Dialogue, Dialectic, and Conversation: A Social Perspective on the Function of Writing.* Carbondale: Southern Illinois UP, 1990.
Couture, Barbara. "Modeling and Emulating: Rethinking Agency in the Writing Process." Kent, *Post-Process* 30–48.
Dasenbrock, Reed Way. "Do We Write the Text We Read?" *Literary Theory After Davidson.* Ed. Reed Way Dasenbrock. University Press: Pennsylvania State UP, 1993. 18–36.

———. "The Myths of the Subjective and of the Subject in Composition Studies." *Journal of Advanced Composition* 13 (1993): 21–32.

Davidson, Donald. "A Nice Derangement of Epitaphs." *Inquiries into Truth and Interpretation: Perspectives on the Philosophy of Donald Davidson.* Ed. Ernst LePore. New York: Oxford UP, 1984. 433–46.

Dewey, John. "My Pedagogic Creed." 1897. *The Essential Dewey: Pragmatism, Education, Democracy.* Ed. Larry A. Hickman and Thomas M. Alexander. Vol. 1. Bloomington: Indiana UP, 1998. 229–35.

Dobrin, Sidney I. *Constructing Knowledges: The Politics of Theory-Building and Pedagogy in Composition.* Albany: State U of New York P, 1997.

———. "Paralogic Hermeneutic Theories, Power, and the Possibility for Liberating Pedagogies." Kent, *Post-Process* 132–48.

Ede, Lisa. "Reading the Writing Process." *Taking Stock: The Writing Process Movement in the '90s.* Ed. Lad Tobin and Thomas Newkirk. Portsmouth: Boynton, 1994. 31–43.

Elbow, Peter. *Writing without Teachers.* New York: Oxford UP, 1973.

Emig, Janet. *The Composing Processes of Twelfth Graders.* Urbana, IL: NCTE, 1971.

Ewald, Helen Rothschild. "A Tangled Web of Discourses: On Post-Process Pedagogy and Communicative Interaction." Kent, *Post-Process* 116–31.

Fish, Stanley. "Anti-Foundationalism, Theory Hope, and the Teaching of Composition." *Doing What Comes Naturally: Change, Rhetoric, and the Practice of Theory in Literary and Legal Studies.* Durham: Duke UP, 1989. 315–41.

———. "Consequences." *Doing What Comes Naturally: Change, Rhetoric, and the Practice of Theory in Literary and Legal Studies.* Durham: Duke UP, 1989. 342–55.

Flower, Linda, and John Hayes. "Identifying the Organization of the Writing Processes." *Cognitive Processes in Writing.* Ed. Lee W. Gregg and Erwin R. Steinberg. Hillsdale: Erlbaum, 1980. 3–30.

Foster, David. "The Challenge of Contingency: Process and the Turn to the Social in Composition." Kent, *Post-Process* 149–62.

Freire, Paulo. *Pedagogy of the Oppressed.* Rpt. in *The Paulo Freire Reader.* Ed. Ana Maria Araujo Freire and Donaldo Macedo. New York: Continuum, 1998.

Grimm, Nancy Maloney. *Good Intentions: Writing Center Work for Postmodern Times.* Portsmouth: Boynton, 1999.

Halasek, Kay. *A Pedagogy of Possibility: Bakhtinian Perspectives on Composition Studies.* Carbondale: Southern Illinois UP, 1999.

Harris, Muriel. *Teaching One to One: The Writing Conference.* Urbana, IL: NCTE: 55–75, 1986.

Hiley, David R., James F. Bohman, and Richard Shusterman, eds. *The Interpretive Turn: Philosophy, Science, Culture.* Ithaca: Cornell UP, 1991.

Hobson, Eric H. "Writing Center Practice Often Counters Its Theory. So What?" Mullin and Wallace 1–10.

Kent, Thomas. Introduction. Kent, *Post-Process* 1–6.

———. "Language Philosophy, Writing, and Reading: A Conversation with Donald Davidson." *Journal of Advanced Composition* 13 (1993): 1–20.

———. *Paralogic Rhetoric: A Theory of Communicative Interaction.* Lewisburg: Bucknell UP, 1993.

———, ed. *Post-Process Theory: Beyond the Writing-Process Paradigm.* Carbondale: Southern Illinois UP, 1999.

Kuhn, Thomas S. "The Natural and the Human Sciences." Hiley, Bohman, and Shusterman 17–24.

Lindemann, Erika. *A Rhetoric for Writing Teachers.* 3rd ed. New York: Oxford UP, 1995.

Macrorie, Ken. *Writing to Be Read.* Rochelle Park, NJ: Hayden, 1976.

McComiskey, Bruce. "The Post-Process Movement in Composition Studies." *Reforming College Composition: Writing the Wrongs.* Ed. Ray Wallace, Alan Jackson, and Susan Lewis Wallace. London: Greenwood, 2000. 37–53.

Miller, Thomas P. "Treating Professional Writing as Social *Praxis.*" *Journal of Advanced Composition* 11 (1991): 57–72.

Mullin, Joan A. "Introduction: The Theory Behind the Centers." Mullin and Wallace vii–xiii.

Mullin, Joan A., and Ray Wallace, eds. *Intersections: Theory-Practice in the Writing Center.* Urbana, IL: NCTE, 1994.

Murphy, Christina, and Steve Sherwood. "The Tutoring Process: Exploring Paradigms and Practices." *The St. Martin's Sourcebook for Writing Tutors.* New York: St. Martin's, 1995. 1–18.

Murray, Donald M. *A Writer Teaches Writing.* Boston: Houghton, 1968.

Olson, Gary A. "Toward a Post-Process Composition: Abandoning the Rhetoric of Assertion." Kent, *Post-Process* 7–15.

Petraglia, Joseph. "Is There Life after Process? The Role of Social Scientism in a Changing Discipline." Kent, *Post-Process* 49–64.

Pullman, George. "Stepping Yet Again into the Same Current." Kent, *Post-Process* 16–29.

Rorty, Richard. "Inquiry as Recontextualization: An Anti-Dualist Account of Interpretation." Hiley, Bohman, and Shusterman 59–80.

Russell, David. "Activity Theory and Process Approaches: Writing in School and Society." Kent, *Post-Process* 80–95.

Sosnoski, James J. "Postmodern Teachers in Their Postmodern Classrooms: Socrates Begone!" *Contending with Words: Composition and Rhetoric in a Postmodern Age.* Ed. Patricia Harkin and John Schilb. New York: MLA, 1991. 198–219.

Wallace, David. "Reconsidering Behaviorist Composition Pedagogies: Positivism, Empiricism, and the Paradox of Postmodernism." *Journal of Advanced Composition* 6 (1996): 103–17.

Ward, Irene. *Literacy, Ideology, and Dialogue: Towards a Dialogic Pedagogy.* Albany: State U of New York P, 1994.

Wells, Susan. "Jürgen Habermas, Communicative Competence, and the Teaching of Technical Discourse." *Theory in the Classroom.* Ed. Cary Nelson. Urbana: U of Illinois P, 1986. 245–69.

Young, Richard E. "Paradigms and Problems: Needed Research in Rhetorical Invention." *Research on Composing: Points of Departure.* Ed. Charles R. Cooper and Lee Odell. Urbana: NCTE, 1978. 29–47.

Talking in Terms of Discourse

What It Is; How It's Taught

Research and introspection became the ways of discovering something about how one goes about writing. And part of that writing involves the writer's intentions in directing what is written to an audience: readers located in particular social contexts. In effect, then, the givens of our conversations include how our acts are rhetorical acts. That is, writing is a matter of someone saying something to someone within a given context using the tools of writing. The writer, the reader, and the text constitute the essential elements of the rhetorical triangle contained in classical rhetoric's *ethos*, *pathos*, and *logos*. James Kinneavy makes explicit the implicit fourth element in that triangle — the context. It is in this tradition of ancient rhetoric that James Kinneavy and Frank D'Angelo classify the various elements of written discourse, D'Angelo explicitly creating an ontology of discourse.

To some extent, each essay in this section is concerned with matters of mind: ontology, epistemology, psychology. The precedent is old. The second book to Aristotle's rhetoric, in many ways still the basis of academic rules of written discourse, provides a psychology of audiences. Eighteenth-century rhetorician George Campbell, and the nineteenth century's Alexander Bain, each turns to psychology to explain the processes involved in rhetorical acts. Kenneth Burke, perhaps the most noted rhetorician of the twentieth century, writes of a newly invigorated rhetoric that would turn to the insights of the "new sciences," including psychology. As we have seen, psychological matters influence the research that emerges as writing-as-process. Psychology also influences James Britton's looks to how early-childhood fluency in writing is accomplished.

James Berlin outlines the different epistemological assumptions that arise within the history of western rhetoric and their implications for composition theory by looking to the dynamic interplay among the various elements of the epistemological field. In other words, Berlin outlines what he sees as the underlying assumptions about the relations among words, thoughts, and the things represented in those words and thoughts that are implicit in various approaches to teaching composition. His categories (as presented both in his essay in this section and in another included later in this collection) become the terms with which we discuss ideological and epistemological assumptions about discourse and writing instruction. The other essays in this section look to the parts of a discourse in order to understand the whole more readily, asking how rigidly writers construct paragraphs or thesis sentences within paragraphs, and what it is that constitutes grammar and grammar instruction as part of teaching writing. All try to define what we're talking about when we talk about written discourse.

The Basic Aims of Discourse

James L. Kinneavy

INTRODUCTION

Most of us make implicit assumptions about the aims of discourse when we loosely distinguish expository writing from literature or creative writing, and, no doubt, there is some validity to the distinction. Many college composition textbooks often assume a similar distinction and address themselves to the province of expository writing. But it may be that this simple distinction is too simple and that other aims of discourse ought to be given some consideration. It is this question which I would like to investigate in this paper.

First, at least one working definition. I am concerned with complete discourse, not individual sentences or even paragraphs. It is often impossible to determine the aim of an individual sentence or paragraph without its full context. The same sentence or even paragraph in another context may have a very different aim. "Discourse" here means the full text, oral or written, delivered at a specific time and place or delivered at several instances. A discourse may be a single sentence, "Fire," screamed from a hotel window, or a joke, or a sonnet, or a three-hour talk, or a tragedy, or Toynbee's twelve volumes of *A Study of History*. Sometimes the determination of text is difficult: a conversation may trail off into another one; a novel like *Sanctuary* may pick up years later in *Requiem for a Nun*; there are trilogies in drama and novel, etc.; but usually the determination of text is a fairly simple matter.

By aim of discourse is meant the effect that the discourse is oriented to achieve in the average listener or reader for whom it is intended. It is the intent as embodied in the discourse, the intent of the work, as traditional

Reprinted from *College Composition and Communication* 20.4 (December 1969): 297–304. Used with permission.

philosophy called it. Is the work intended to delight or to persuade or to inform or to demonstrate the logical proof of a position? These would be typical aims.

The determination of the basic aims of discourse and some working agreement in this area among rhetoricians would be a landmark in the field of composition. For it is to the achievement of these aims that all our efforts as teachers of composition are directed.

Yet a classification of diverse aims of discourse must not be interpreted as the establishing of a set of iron-clad categories which do not overlap. Such an exercise must be looked upon as any scientific exercise—an abstraction from certain aspects of reality in order to focus attention on and carefully analyze the characteristics of some feature of reality in a scientific vacuum, as it were. The scientist who is attempting to formulate the law of gravity isolates the gravitational forces from air resistance, from surface variations, from electric attraction, etc., and hopefully postulates a principle of gravity. The re-insertion into real situations wherein wind, surface variations, electricity and other forces intervene comes later. Similarly, an attempt to formulate the nature of information, as such, must operate in a discourse vacuum which momentarily abstracts from the fact that information can be used in propaganda or be a component of a literary discourse. In actual practice such pure discourses as information devoid of persuasion, or persuasion devoid of information, or literature without some personal expression, and so forth, are almost non-existent or as rare as the laboratory concept of gravitation. But that does not destroy the validity of the classifications.

THE DETERMINATION OF THE AIMS OF DISCOURSE

Some Negative and Some External Norms

There are some useful cautions about determination of aims made in literary theory by W. K. Wimsatt and Monroe Beardsley which can be extended to discourse theory. It is dangerous in literature (and even more in persuasion) to assume that what the author says he is trying to do is actually what the work really accomplishes. To determine the aim by author intent is to run the risk of the "intentional fallacy." A parallel danger is to assume that the reaction of a given reader is an accurate indication of purpose. This fallacy has been termed the "affective fallacy" by Wimsatt and Beardsley.[1] The stated intentions of the author and the reactions of a given reader are useful markers that can point to significant evidence in the discourse itself, as the linguist Michael Riffaterre points out;[2] for this reason they should not be disregarded. Similarly, many authors advise us to take into account the cultural conventions of the genre employed; anthropologists like Malinowski warn of the importance of the immediate historical context; McLuhan emphasizes the significance of the medium used; Kenneth Burke writes a whole book on the influence of the semantic range, the grammar he calls it, of the motivational field; and even the grammatical choices offered by the language can restrict and modify the aim, as Sapir and Whorf caution us. All of these, external to the discourse, are nonetheless weighty determinants of aim and are so many arguments against the mythical autonomy of the text.

Internal Norms of Aim

Among the writers who have sought to establish the aims of discourse by norms internal to the discourse there is considerable variation in the kind of norm singled out. Yet there is a surprising measure of agreement among the analysts on so fundamental an issue. In Figure 1, I have attempted to show some of these various approaches, together with the principle of division and the resulting classifications of aims of discourse. The parallel classifications of the various systems are indicated in the horizontal rows. All of the authorities whom I have analyzed could not be presented on a single page, so I have only indicated typical representatives of various approaches.

The eldest and most persistent approach in western civilization is that beginning in Plato, codified by Aristotle, continued by the medieval Arab philosophers Averröes and Avicenna, Aquinas and Albertus Magnus, and passed on to modern times by the classical tradition and some comparative philologists, like Joshua Whatmough. Aristotle and Aquinas distinguish a *scientific* use of language achieving certainty, a *dialectical* use of language operating in the area of probability, a *rhetorical* or persuasive use of language based on seeming probability, and a *poetic* use of language incorporating a rigid but internal probability. The principle of division is obviously a scale of diminishing probability.[3]

Ernst Cassirer, examining the historical sequence of Greek views on the functions of language, sees first a *mythological* view of language as a medium for expressing the aspirations of early Greek society. This partially (though not at all totally) corresponds to Aristotle's poetic function. This was followed by a period in which it was felt by the philosophers that language was admirably suited to mirror or represent the universe. This *metaphysical* period, as he calls it, corresponds to Aristotle's scientific use of language. The practical or *pragmatic* use of language by the sophists and rhetoricians

Figure 1 A comparison of some systems of aims of discourse.

SCHOOL	Aristotle and Aquinas	Cassirer	Morris	Miller	Russell	Reichenbach	Richards	Bühler, Jakobson, Kinneavy
PRINCIPLE OF DIVISION	Level of Probability	Historical Sequence in Greece	Behavioral Reactions of Animals to Stimuli	Socio-Psych. Motives for Communications	Grammar (Kinds of Sentences)	Faculty Addresses to	Proportions of Reference and Emotion	Component of Communication Process Stressed
	Scientific —certain	Metaphysical —representative of the world	Informative	Informative —to increase uniformity of information	Informative —declarative	Communicative (thoughts to be believed)	Scientific (pure reference)	Reference / Informative / Scientific
	Dialectical —probable		Valuative	Opinion —to increase uniformity of opinions	Questioning —interrogative			Exploratory
	Rhetorical —seemingly probable	Pragmatic —practical use by Sophists	Incitive	Status change	Imperative —imperative	Promotive (actions to be accomplished)	Rhetorical (mixed reference and emotion)	Persuasive
	Poetic —internally probable						Poetic (pure emotion)	Literary
		Mythological —expressive of aspirations / Interjectional	Systemic	Emotive	Expressive (of emotion) —exclamatory	Suggestive (emotions to be aroused)		Expressive

132

came next. Finally, Democritus pointed to a basic and initial *interjectional* or emotive use of language — to which Aristotle has no direct parallel.[4]

In the next column of Figure 1, C. W. Morris, the semiotician, bases his aims of discourse on a behavioral analysis of how animals react to stimuli. The animal first *informs* itself of the features of its environment, then *evaluates* the seemingly useful features, then responds to these as *incitive* "stimuli," and finally *systematizes* his signs in order to achieve the purpose for which he engaged in this expressive activity. There is a rough approximation here to Aristotle's scientific, dialectic, and rhetorical functions. Morris' systemic has some affinity with the expressive function of the others on the chart.[5]

George Miller, a communication theorist, establishes his distinctions on the socio-psychological motives for the communications which are revealed in the discourse. The *informative* use of language attempts to increase uniformity of fact and information in the community; the *opinion* use of language attempts to increase uniformity of the probable in the society; the *status change* use of language is oriented to improve one's societal position; and the *emotive* use is oriented to individual satisfaction in an expressive use of language. The similarities to the preceding systems are fairly obvious.[6]

In an interesting chapter on "The Uses of Language" in *Human Knowledge, Its Scope and Limits*, Bertrand Russell takes issue with the dominant logical positivist view of a simple dichotomy of referential and emotive uses of language and distinguishes the informative, the questioning, the promotive, and the emotional uses of language. These correspond quite naturally to the kinds of rhetorical sentences in the language: declarative, interrogative, imperative, and exclamatory. These *image* quite closely Miller's, Morris' and Aristotle's categories, though the principle of division is different in each.[7]

Hans Reichenbach, a logical positivist, in a brief introduction to his book on symbolic logic, differentiates functions of language by the faculty appealed to in the discourse. He therefore distinguishes a communicative use emphasizing thoughts to be believed by the intellect, from a promotive use directed to actions to be accomplished, from a suggestive use oriented to emotions to be aroused.[8]

Both Reichenbach and Richards take the logical positivist position as their springboard. Richards emphasizes the kind of reference found in the discourse. In his various books, Richards suggests various categories of discourse. I have followed here the distinctions to be found in *How to Read a Page* and *Principles of Literary Criticism* rather than some of his other works. Discourses exist in a continuum with decreasing referential and increasing emotive affirmations. Pure reference discourse is scientific, pure emotive discourse is poetic. Any appreciable mixture of the two is rhetoric. Further subdivisions of the mixed area (rhetoric) are generally useless.[9]

The equating of poetry with emotive discourse in Richards is a common phenomenon among these classificatory systems—a fact the figure illustrates. Sometimes poetry is subsumed under emotive, sometimes poetry is equated to the emotive (as in Richards). Sometimes there is no provision for one or the other—thus Aristotle makes no room for expressive discourse as such, though emotion is important for his concept of catharsis in poetry and in the whole second book of his *Rhetoric*.

The last column of the figure distinguishes aims by the focus on the component of the communication process which is stressed in a given discourse. At one time I thought that this principle of classification was original with me, but I later found that Karl Bühler, a German psychologist, had used it in depth in the 1930's and that Roman Jakobson, acknowledging Bühler as his source, had also used it to classify aims of discourse in the early 1960's. The beginnings of this norm can be found in Aristotle who calls science language directed to things and rhetoric language directed to persons. Alan Gardiner, the linguist, had also suggested this principle of classification in the 1950's.[10]

This principle can be seen illustrated in Figure 2. If one represents the components of the communication process as a triangle composed of an encoder (writer or speaker), a decoder (reader or listener), a signal (the linguistic product), and a reality (that part of the universe to which the linguistic product refers), then a focus on one of these tends to produce a specific kind of discourse. Discourse dominated by subject matter (reality talked about) is called referential discourse. There are three kinds of referential discourse: exploratory, informative, and scientific. These correspond to elements in the first and second rows across Figure 1. Here, however, it seems important to distinguish the merely informative kind of writing (such as news stories in journalism, simple encyclopedia or textbook presentations) from the strictly scientific, though few authorities make the distinction. Aristotle, for example, has no theory of information, though he has one of science. And Miller has provision for informative, though he has no specific provision for the scientific. And it is equally important to distinguish a kind of discourse which asks a question (exploratory, dialectical, interrogative in some formulations) from discourse which answers it (informative) and proves the answer (scientific). Yet all three of these kinds of discourse are subject-matter or reference dominated. Examples of all three are given in Figure 2. These subdistinctions of reference discourse are my own and differ somewhat from Jakobson's.

Figure 2 The basic purposes of composition.

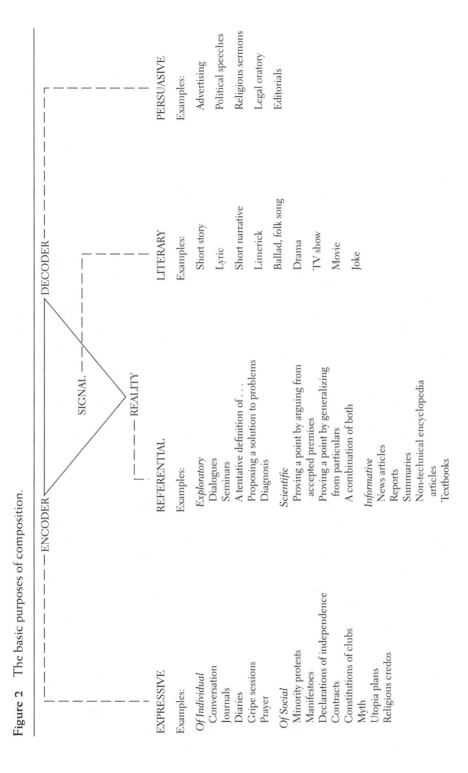

Secondly, as Bühler, Jakobson, and Aristotle point out, discourse which focuses on eliciting a specific reaction from the decoder and is dominated by this request for reaction emerges as persuasion or rhetoric. In this use, the encoder may purposely disguise his own personality and purposely distort the picture of reality which language can paint in order to get the decoder to do something or believe something (as in dishonest advertising or some political propaganda). These distortions are not essential to persuasion, however. What is essential is that encoder, reality, and language itself all become instrumental to the achievement of some practical effect in the decoder. Obvious examples of such aims of discourse are given in the last column of Figure 2.

Thirdly, when the language product is dominated by the clear design of the writer or speaker to discharge his emotions or achieve his own individuality or embody his personal or group aspirations in a discourse, then the discourse tends to be expressive. The expressor or encoder here dominates the communication process. Sometimes in such uses the decoder and the referential components even become negligible—as with curse words uttered in private. But often such uses carry strong sub-components of information and persuasion, as in the *Declaration of Independence*. Some examples of such uses are given in the first column of the figure we have been analyzing.

Finally, the product or text or work itself may be the focus of the process as an object worthy of being appreciated in its own right. Such appreciation gives pleasure to the beholder. In this use of language, language calls attention to itself, to its own structures, not as references to reality or as expressions of personal aspirations or as instruments of persuasion, but as structures worthy of contemplation in their own right. Of course, reference, author personality, and persuasion may and usually are involved. But they are not rigidly relevant as primary foci. Indeed the reality may be fictional or very distorted; the author may be hidden under dramatic projections; and the persuasions involved may be quite trivial on occasion. This last use of language is called literature. It appears in such varied forms as the pun, the salacious joke, the sonnet, the novel, the TV drama, the epic, etc.

If a comparison may be drawn, it could be said that language is like a windowpane. I may throw bricks at it to vent my feelings about something; I may use a chunk of it to chase away an intruder; I may use it to mirror or explore reality; and I may use a stained-glass window to call attention to itself as an object of beauty. Windows, like language, can be used expressively, persuasively, referentially, and esthetically.

SOME CONCLUSIONS ABOUT
AIMS OF DISCOURSE

I have not included in Figure 1 many of the other approaches to aims of discourse, most of which are fairly symmetrical to those given here. These would include the several groups interested in the functions of language at its origin (was it imitative of reality, the bow-wow theory, was it a utilitarian rhetorical tool, the yo-he-ho theory, was it an expressive emotional theory, the ah-ah, pooh-pooh theory, or did language begin in play and poetry, the ding-dong theory). These theories, like the child function theories, do parallel the four functions arrived at. Some anthropologists, like Malinowski and Doob, have examined primitive societies and isolated the functions of language found there (they do not find a literary or play use, I might add, though Lévi-Strauss did). Nor have I mentioned the semanticists; Hayakawa's four uses of language also parallel the model sketched here. The uses of language, established by the Nebraska high school composition program and drawn heavily from the ordinary language philosophers, also closely parallel these distinctions.

The important lesson to be drawn from this almost fearful symmetry is that no composition program can afford to neglect any of these basic aims of discourse. There have been periods in the history of the teaching of composition, whether in the elementary or secondary or college level, when one or the other has been unduly prominent and others slighted or entirely neglected. The results have usually been educationally disastrous. In speech departments where persuasion was, for too long a time, too prominent, two cancerous effects have often followed: first, expository or reference discourse is assimilated into and made equivalent to persuasion and Aristotelian rhetorical proofs are extended to all discourse; secondly, even literature is reduced to persuasion, and some modern theories of oral interpretation now speak of the oral interpreter's function as one of coercing the audience into a desired emotional attitude. At the elementary and secondary school during the Deweyite progressive period, the reduction of all language to self-expression destroyed alike any objective scientific or literary norms. At the college level, in English departments during the period immediately preceding the present, the restriction of composition to expository writing and the reading of literary texts has had two equally dangerous consequences. First, the neglect of expressionism, as a reaction to progressive education, has stifled self-expression in the student and partially, at least, is a cause of the unorthodox and extreme forms of deviant self-expression now indulged in by college students on many campuses today.

Secondly, the neglect of persuasion has often caused persuasion to be assimilated and absorbed into literature in many cases. Expressionism has often been similarly absorbed so that literature has become prostituted to propaganda or the most weird forms of formless self-expression. In philosophy, with the logical positivists, interested solely in scientific statements, the ignoring of other uses of discourse has caused all of them to be lumped into the general category of nonsensical or meaningless. None of these situations is healthy. It is to the good of each of the aims of discourse to be studied in conjunction with the others.

The reason for this is to be seen in the various principles of classification used in the establishing of the aims by various writers. Scientific discourse is generally different in its logic, its level of probability, from the other aims of discourse. In fact, each aim of discourse has its own logic, its own kind of references, its own communication framework, its own patterns of organization, and its own stylistic norms. Sometimes these logics and stylistic principles even contradict each other. Overlaps certainly occur but the ultimate conflation and confusion of any of the aims of discourse with any other is pedagogically disastrous.

The study of these distinct aims of discourses is only a continuation of the basic liberal arts tradition. That tradition, coalesced into the trivium of grammar, rhetoric, and logic or dialectic, simply meant the study of literature, the study of persuasion, and the study of scientific and exploratory discourse. When the English departments presided over the dissolution of the liberal arts tradition in the early 1900's by exiling persuasion to speech departments and by exiling logic to philosophy departments, only literature (grammar) remained and literature, as such, had never been the only basis of the liberal arts. My plea is simply for a preservation of the liberal arts tradition with composition as the foundation stone.

NOTES

1. For the treatment of both fallacies, see W. K. Wimsatt and Monroe Beardsley, *The Verbal Icon* (Lexington, Kentucky, 1965), pp. 3–18, 21–39.

2. "Criteria for Style Analysis," in *Essays on the Language of Literature*, eds. Seymour Chatman and Samuel R. Levin (Boston, Massachusetts, 1967), pp. 419 ff.

3. For a historical survey of this school, see J. Craig LaDrière, "Rhetoric and 'Merely Verbal' Art," in *English Institute Essays, 1948*, ed. D. A. Robertson (New York, 1949), pp. 123–153.

4. See Ernst Cassirer, *An Essay on Man* (New Haven, 1944), pp. 109 ff.

5. See C. W. Morris, *Signs, Language and Behavior* (Englewood Cliffs, New Jersey, 1946), pp. 95 ff.

6. See George A. Miller, *Language and Communications* (New York, 1951), p. 253.

7. See Bertrand Russell, *Human Knowledge, Its Scope and Limits* (New York, 1948), pp. 58 ff.

8. See Hans Reichenbach, *Introduction to Symbolic Logic* (New York, 1947), pp. 17 ff.

9. See I. A. Richards, *How to Read a Page* (London, 1943), p. 100; and *Principles of Literary Criticism* (London, 1925), p. 261.

10. See Roman Jakobson, "Linguistics and Poetics," in *Essays on the Language of Literature*, eds. Seymour Chatman and Samuel R. Levin (Boston, 1967), pp. 299 ff.

An Ontological Basis
for a Modern Theory
of the Composing Process

FRANK J. D'ANGELO

In a recent article entitled "Tradition and Theory in Rhetoric," S. M. Halloran comments that, in the past, the rhetorical tradition was built on the cultural ideal of the orator, the good man skilled in speaking who embodied the wisdom and knowledge of the culture. Because modern values are unstable and fragmented, Halloran continues, the orator no longer embodies the communal wisdom. Therefore, to base modern rhetorical theories on the cultural ideal of the orator would be difficult, if not impossible. Halloran concludes that "one cannot simply graft modern rhetorical or communication theory onto classical rhetoric."[1] Modern theorists, therefore, must base their rhetorical theories on different ontological assumptions.

I believe that a modern theory of the composing process can be based directly on evolutionary theory as it relates to the origins and history of consciousness. The composing process, being an aspect of consciousness, must necessarily develop along the same general lines as consciousness itself. What I have in mind, however, is not evolution conceived of in mechanistic terms, but evolution understood in teleological terms. In this view, the composing process is analogous to universal evolutionary processes, in which an original, amorphous, undifferentiated whole gradually evolves into a more complex, differentiated one. Like the processes of teleological evolution, the composing process is progress toward a goal that is directed by a conscious or

Reprinted from *Quarterly Journal of Speech* 64.1 (February 1978): 79–85. Used by permission of the National Communication Association (www.natcom.org).

unconscious intention or intelligence. My thesis is that *the process of composing is a movement from an undifferentiated to a differentiated whole.* It repeats in microcosm the history of the evolution of consciousness.[2]

THE COMPOSING PROCESS AND THE EVOLUTION OF CONSCIOUSNESS

The rhetorical topics themselves can be viewed as differentiations of basic mental processes that have evolved over thousands of years. So, also, can the figures of speech in Greek rhetoric. Paragraphing is the process of differentiating the parts from the whole. Invention, arrangement, and style are differentiations of a single, ongoing mental process.[3]

From the evolutionary point of view, composition is an organic development that begins with a kind of intuitive grasp of the end to be achieved and that concludes when that end is brought to fruition. The problem of composing is the problem of how an intention or purpose that is already partially realized in the mind gets what it needs to complete itself.[4]

It is not enough that in the process of composing the writer see the subject whole. One may know in general the end one wants to achieve without knowing all the details. The gestalt has to be brought to fulfillment, slowly, bit by bit, by linear methods. Thus the process of composing begins with a general idea, but the main process consists in filling in the details. Once the mind intuitively grasps the initial gestalt, then the rational mental processes can take over and the process of composition can be brought to completion in a logical, analytical manner.

Invention always seems to take place within a system. Some kind of structure always underlies the process. To invent is to extend a system which is already present in the mind.

There is purpose in the mind itself. The mind takes an active part in the composing process, supplying at one and the same time the ends and the means. Thus, a kind of necessity inheres in the process of invention. The mind, when faced with a problem, attempts to incorporate this problem within an existing structure. The mind of necessity must then invent because it is constantly active, always in process; it seeks to understand and to incorporate into its knowledge structure whatever is placed before it.

In the composing process, it seems that both conscious and subconscious processes take part. The subconscious mind provides the design, and the conscious mind provides its development. (A reverse process is also possible.) Actually, this is probably a simplification since there is a constant

142

interplay between these two modes of consciousness. Since the subconscious part of the mind is not always accessible for invention, the writer must aid the subconscious as much as possible by a deliberate and conscious effort, by defining the problem, by filling in the details, by carefully working out the design—in brief, by preparing the mind so that the subconscious can take over.

STAGES OF EVOLUTION AND THE DEVELOPMENT OF CONSCIOUSNESS

I have said that the composing process is analogous to universal evolutionary processes, in which an original, amorphous, undifferentiated whole gradually evolves into a more complex, differentiated whole. The idea that evolution is taking us toward increasing complexity, differentiation, and unity has been admirably set forth by Pierre Teilhard de Chardin, who notes that historically the universe is becoming more and more concentrated into organized forms. In the beginning, the stuff of the universe was "virtually homogeneous," but with the passage of time, it segments, complicates, and differentiates itself into hierarchical units:

> . . . the ramifications of evolution reappear and go on close to us in a thousand social phenomena which we should never have imagined to be so closely linked with biology; in the formation and dissemination of languages, in the development and specialisation of new industries, in the formulation and propagation of philosophic and religious doctrines. In each of these groups of human activity a superficial glance would only detect a weak and haphazard answer to the procedure of life. It would accept without questioning the strange fact of parallelism—or it would account for it in terms of some abstract necessity.[5]

This differentiation is not merely fragmentation, though fragmentation there is, for the results of this differentiation are eventually being incorporated into a highly unified and organized pattern.

Differentiation manifests itself everywhere—on an inorganic level, on a biological level, and on a cultural level. Differentiation, together with its resulting and increasing complexity, is leading "to the evolution of progressively more conscious mind." As life advances, it transforms itself in depth, moving toward higher and higher levels of consciousness. It is gaining the "psychic zones of the world." As a result, humanity is achieving a more

143

complex mental activity to guide it along "the path of progress" to higher levels of consciousness.[6]

Teilhard believes that humanity is approaching a critical level of social organization. Evolution has reached a point where it is becoming conscious of itself, and in order to see where evolution is taking us, we must envision humankind as a single organism, growing, changing, and developing in a single direction. As a result of education, research, and the mass media, the human race has developed a collective memory and a generalized nervous system which is resulting in the super-organization of matter. Not only the individual, but the race as a whole is becoming *totally reflexive upon itself.* Consequently, not only are we seeing a general heightening of consciousness in the individual, but also in the world:[7]

> What we see taking place in the world today is not merely the multiplication of *men* but the continued shaping of *Man. Man* . . . is not yet zoologically mature. Psychologically he has not spoken his last word. In one form or another something ultrahuman is being born which, through the direct or indirect effect of socialisation, cannot fail to make its appearance in the near future: a future that is not simply the unfolding of Time, but which is being constructed in advance of us.[8]

In his study of the origins and history of consciousness, Erich Neumann contends that the development of consciousness in the individual can be regarded as a repetition of the racial history of consciousness, that is, ontogeny repeats phylogeny. According to Neumann, "The individualized conscious man of our era is a late man, whose structure is built on early, pre-individual human stages from which individual consciousness has only detached itself step by step."[9] We can trace the stages in the evolution of consciousness, states Neumann, in mythological types, for ego consciousness in its evolution passes through a series of images or archetypes which are projections of the psyche and therefore must necessarily reveal themselves in dreams, fantasies, and myths. These images or archetypes are structural elements of the mind. To trace the stadial progression of archetypes in myths, therefore, is to trace the psychological stages in the development of the individual consciousness and the history of consciousness.[10]

To trace the mythological stages in the evolution of consciousness is not my main purpose, except insofar as it illuminates the study of the psychological stages in the development of consciousness. The three main stages of archetypal development are the creation myth, the hero myth, and the transformation myth. The creation myth symbolizes original unity, that stage of consciousness in which the ego is still submerged in the unconscious. The hero myth symbolizes separation from this original unity (the birth of the hero) and the growth of consciousness. The transformation myth symbolizes increasing differentiation of consciousness; it is the stage of the reflecting, self-conscious ego, the return to original unity in which the whole and its parts are synthesized into a unified system.[11]

What do these myths signify in terms of the ontogenetic and phylogenetic development of consciousness? We can imagine a time in prehistory when the person was not yet separated from nature, when the individual was a part of the group, the ego a part of the unconscious. All were parts of an undifferentiated whole. Just as the individual had, gradually, to escape the domination of the group, so also the ego had to emerge slowly from the sway of the unconscious. At this stage, states Neumann, consciousness was "still in abeyance, being not yet developed or only partially developed." This early stage in the development of consciousness corresponds to the dream state in which the individual consciousness breaks down easily and dissolves itself into images and symbols. This stage also corresponds to the state of consciousness of primitives, who are easily tired by any kind of self-conscious activity. Even in the modern individual the margin of conscious awareness is somewhat limited. Consciousness in prehistory, then, is characterized by non-differentiation and indeterminateness.[12] But slowly, over the course of thousands and thousands of years, the human mind becomes increasingly more complex and differentiated, and this differentiation is built into the structure of the brain. As the ego begins to gain its independence from the unconscious, it separates from it, yet still remains partially dependent on it. This splitting off of the ego from its origins in the unconscious leads to a kind of fragmentation in which the ego tries to become autonomous. As long as the ego attempts to cut off all of its ties with the unconscious, it is in danger of becoming sterile, emptied of all content. Like the hero in mythology, it must occasionally make a "descent" into the depths of the unconscious to recover its emotional components and images if it is to remain emotionally stable and creative.[13]

Neumann believes that Western civilization is in danger of upsetting the compensating balance of the unconscious forces of the psyche with the conscious forces. He claims that the human race is becoming increasingly more egocentric and that this egocentricity is responsible for the restlessness and meaninglessness of modern life. Not only are our traditional systems of values disintegrating, but also the very meaning of existence is being questioned.[14]

This increasing complexity and differentiation of consciousness is not necessarily bad in itself, argues Neumann. In fact, it is a necessary result of the process of evolution: "The development that has brought about the division of the two systems is in accord with a necessary process of psychic differentiation, but, like all differentiation, it runs the risk of becoming over-differentiated and perverse."[15] Creative processes, then, must not exclude the unconscious. Although the ego is the directive force in the creative process, it must somehow assimilate aspects of the unconscious if it is to function properly. In so doing, it will be able to synthesize the differentiated parts previously broken down by the analytical mind into a new whole, into a new unity of the conscious and unconscious elements.

STAGES OF EVOLUTION AND THE ORGANIZATION OF KNOWLEDGE

In almost every field, the idea that evolution is moving from an undifferentiated to a differentiated whole manifests itself. For example, according to the Russian psychologist L. S. Vygotsky, in the acquisition of language the child begins with an undifferentiated whole. Vygotsky asserts that in terms of meaning, "the first word of the child is a whole sentence. Semantically, the child starts from the whole, from a meaningful complex, and only later begins to master the separate semantic units, the meanings of words, and to divide his formerly undifferentiated thought into those units."[16] Vygotsky continues: "A child's thought, precisely because it is born as a dim amorphous whole, must find expression in a single word. As his thought becomes more differentiated, the child is less apt to express it in single words but constructs a composite whole."[17]

The development of concept formation in the child seems to follow the same evolutionary stages as those enumerated by Neumann and Teilhard. In his study of *Thought and Language*, Vygotsky enumerates three basic stages of concept formation. The first stage is the placing of objects into unorganized heaps or congeries (that is, into undifferentiated wholes). In the first stage, in trying to solve a problem, the child brings together the most diffuse, seemingly unrelated objects into a highly unstable mental image. The concept, or rather perception, is vague and indefinite. The second stage consists of thinking in complexes. In this stage, the child no longer groups things together on the basis of subjective impressions alone, but brings them together by noting connections that actually exist between and among them. The final stage is that of abstracting, the process of isolating elements from a concrete experience and viewing them apart. At this time, the child is not only able to abstract and to analyze, but also to synthesize these abstracted elements into a coherent whole.[18]

A study of the history of the paragraph reveals that the paragraph as a differentiated unit is a relatively recent development. Edwin Lewis states that there has long been a unit of discourse in English prose larger than the sentence, but this unit was not really differentiated as our modern paragraph is: "In other words English writers have thought roughly in long stages before they have analyzed such stages into smaller steps."[19] Lewis then discusses the chief influences leading to the development of the modern paragraph: the scribal tradition which considers the paragraph as a unit of thought, the Latin tradition which regards the paragraph as a unit of emphasis, and the oral tradition which breaks up long stretches of discourse into easily understood smaller units for an uncultivated audience. In the eighteenth and nineteenth centuries, the tendency of writers was to reduce the length of the paragraph to a succession of smaller units of a more or less constant length.[20]

Supporting Lewis' point of view, Virginia Burke observes that "the paragraph was not sharply defined in the minds of many English prosaists, for it was often not distinguished from larger units (chapter and section) or from smaller units (sentences). Some writers frequently produced short paragraphs of fewer than three sentences. . . . Some writers. . . produced a high number of single sentence paragraphs, in which the single sentences were usually inordinately long. This practice seems to indicate that these writers frequently regarded sentences and paragraphs as identical or, more precisely, equivalent."[21] Burke concludes that "if the paragraph, as we know it, is possible only when internal arrangement is possible, and if internal arrangement is possible only when there are several sentences to organize, then the paragraph is a recent phenomenon."[22]

The foregoing examples suffice to demonstrate the extent to which scholars working in isolation in completely different fields have come to the realization of the importance of the stages of evolutionary development as a way of understanding and organizing knowledge. Yet, despite the significance of these ideas in other fields, little attempt has been made to apply them to the study of rhetoric.[23] I have already suggested that the composing process repeats in microcosm the history of the evolution of consciousness, in the mind's movement from an undifferentiated whole to a differentiated whole. Once the underlying pattern is grasped, almost anything can be assimilated to the overall design. Thus Alfred North Whitehead's three stages of education—the stage of romance, the stage of precision, and the stage of generalization—fit the pattern. So also do Piaget's psychological stages in the mental development of the child. For example, the first stage, the stage of egocentricity, is characterized by a high degree of subjectivity and little self-consciousness on the part of the child, who is hardly able to distinguish between the subjective and objective aspects of the world. The second stage is characterized by increasing differentiation of the subjective and objective. The third stage, the stage of abstract formal operations, is characterized by the child's ability to discern causal connections and general principles, and to relate the differentiated parts to the whole.

CONSIDERATION OF POSSIBLE OBJECTIONS

Let me at this point take up one or two possible objections. The first is that a part of my evidence seems to rest on outworn psychological knowledge. *Because our knowledge of the structure and functions of the human brain has increased, have not the ideas of psychoanalysts such as Jung or Freud grown increasingly irrelevant?* On the contrary, studies in psychoneurology suggest increasing specialization and differentiation in the two hemispheres of the cerebral cortex of the brain and that the psychoanalytical concepts of the ego and the id, the conscious and the subconscious, the rational and the intuitive, and the masculine and the feminine can easily be accommodated to the functions of the two hemispheres.[24]

A much more important objection, however, may be: *But doesn't the idea that the composing process must necessarily follow certain lines of development smack of a kind of evolutionary determinism? After all, rhetoric has traditionally been concerned with free choice.* The answer to this objection is that, as both Neumann and Teilhard point out, the evolutionary process that leads to greater complexity and differentiation can take a negative path. It can lead to egocentricity, fragmentation, and alienation. So free choice is still possible. That is why the task of rhetoric in the coming years is so important. Evolution has reached a point where it is partially self-controlled. According to Teilhard, it is up to us to further the progress of what he calls *hominisation*, that is, human beings rising from their animal natures toward higher things. This progress will take a very long time and will undoubtedly suffer setbacks along the way. Nevertheless, the ultimate goal is nothing less than universal convergence.

The function of rhetoric, therefore, is to guide individuals who are distinct and separate toward greater unity and identification of purpose and action. Of all the arts and sciences, rhetoric seems to be the discipline best able to induce cooperation among humankind. As Teilhard puts it: "Forced against one another by the increase in their numbers and the multiplication of their interrelations—compressed together by the activation of a common force and the awareness of a common distress—the men of the future will form, in some way, but one single consciousness."[25]

I realize, of course, that I have not necessarily shown a precise analogous relationship between the composing process and the evolution of consciousness. Yet the similarities between the two processes are so striking that we must either "accept without questioning the strange fact of parallelism" or "account verbally for it in terms of some abstract necessity."[26]

NOTES

1. S. M. Halloran, "Tradition and Theory in Rhetoric," *Quarterly Journal of Speech*, 62 (1976), 235–38, 241.

2. Dorothy C. Higginbotham, in some correspondence to me, has commented that what I "have defined as the composing process has relevance for the ontogeny of language in terms of spoken discourse long before the individual is capable of anything like written composition." This suggests that the composing process is "an example of the larger language organizing behavior that has evolved in man."

3. For one attempt at a theoretical application of these ideas to rhetoric, see Frank J. D'Angelo, *A Conceptual Theory of Rhetoric* (Cambridge, Ma.: Winthrop, 1975); for a pedagogical application, see Frank J. D'Angelo, *Process and Thought in Composition* (Cambridge, Ma.: Winthrop, 1977), especially Chapters 2, 3, and 8.

4. The generalized discussion of the composing process which follows is taken from D'Angelo, *A Conceptual Theory*, pp. 52–54.

5. Pierre Teilhard de Chardin, *The Phenomenon of Man*, intro. Sir Julian Huxley (New York: Harper Torchbooks, 1961), pp. 221–22.

6. Ibid., pp. 16, 17, 219.

7. Pierre Teilhard de Chardin, *The Future of Man*, trans. Norman Denny (New York: Harper Torchbooks, 1964), pp. 137–39.

8. Ibid., p. 275.

9. Erich Neumann, *The Origins and History of Consciousness*, foreword C. G. Jung, trans. R. F. C. Hull (Princeton: Princeton Univ. Press, 1954), p. xx.

10. Ibid., p. xvi.

11. Ibid., pp. 261–418, passim.

12. Ibid., pp. 266–70, 280–81, passim.

13. Ibid., p. 343.

14. Ibid., pp. 389–91.

15. Ibid., p. 383.

16. L. S. Vygotsky, *Thought and Language*, ed. and trans. Eugenia Hanfmann and Gertrude Vakar (Cambridge: The M.I.T. Press, 1962), p. 126.

17. Ibid.

18. Ibid., pp. 51, 60–61, 76.

19. Edwin H. Lewis, "The History of the Paragraph," in *Prose Style: A Historical Approach Through Studies*, ed. James R. Bennett (San Francisco: Chandler, 1971), p. 14.

20. Ibid., p. 14.

21. Virginia M. Burke, "The Continuity of the Paragraph," in *Prose Style: A Historical Approach Through Studies*, ed. James R. Bennett (San Francisco: Chandler, 1971), p. 19.

22. Ibid., p. 20.

23. Walter J. Ong's work, of course, is the most important attempt to study rhetoric in terms of evolving consciousness. See, especially, his *The Presence of the Word* (New Haven:

Yale Univ. Press, 1967) and *Rhetoric, Romance, and Technology* (Ithaca: Cornell Univ. Press, 1971).

24. See, for example, Stuart Dimond, *The Double Brain* (Edinburgh: Churchill Livingstone, 1972); Stuart J. Dimond and J. Graham Beaumont, eds., *Hemispheric Function in the Human Brain* (New York: Wiley, 1974); Michael S. Gazzaniga, *The Bisected Brain* (New York: Appleton-Century-Crofts, 1970); Julian Jaynes, *The Origin of Consciousness in the Breakdown of the Bicameral Mind* (Boston: Houghton Mifflin, 1977); Robert E. Ornstein, *The Psychology of Consciousness* (New York: Viking, 1972).

25. Teilhard, *Future of Man*, p. 321.

26. Teilhard, *Phenomenon of Man*, pp. 221–22.

Spectator Role
and the Beginnings of Writing

JAMES BRITTON

*Only by understanding the entire history of sign development in the child
and the place of writing in it can we approach a correct solution of the psychology of writing.*
—L. S. Vygotsky, Mind in Society, p. 106

IN SEARCH OF A THEORY

Literary and Nonliterary Discourse

Works of literature constitute a form of discourse: We have theories of
GENRE to distinguish among works of literature, but no satisfactory theory to
account for what is common to all such works and in what general ways
they differ from nonliterary discourse. The 1958 interdisciplinary symposium on "Style in Language" at Indiana University attempted to make
such a distinction, but the only consensus that seemed to emerge was the
low-level generalization that literary discourse is "noncasual discourse."
Moreover, in summing up that symposium, George Miller remarked, "I
gradually learned to understand a little of what the linguist has on his mind
when he begins to talk; his verbal behavior during these past days has not
puzzled me quite the way it once would have. But the critics have some
mystic entity called a 'poem' or 'literature,' whose existence I must take on
faith and whose defining properties still confuse me. (The fact that they

Reprinted from *What Writers Know: The Language, Process, and Structure of Written Discourse.* Ed. Martin Nystrand. New York: Academic, 1982. 149–69. Used by permission of
Emerald Group Publishing Limited.

cannot agree amongst themselves on what a poem is adds to the mystery.) [Sebeok, 1960, p. 387]."

Since a great deal of (mostly unpublished) writing by nonprofessionals, by children in school and students in college, takes on forms that are clearly related to literary forms, it seems appropriate that any study of the psychology of writing should attempt to deal with this problem; and that the theory adumbrated should seek both to relate the artlike writings to literary works of art, and to distinguish between them.

One of the most important contributors to the Indiana symposium was Roman Jakobson who put forward his model of the 'constitutive factors' in a speech situation:

$$
\begin{array}{ccc}
 & \text{Context} & \\
 & \text{Message} & \\
\text{Addressor} & \text{Contact} & \text{Addressee} \\
 & \text{Code} &
\end{array}
$$

and the functions assignable to an utterance or part utterance in accordance with the factor on which it focuses:

$$
\begin{array}{ccc}
 & \text{Referential} & \\
\text{Emotive (or} & \text{Poetic} & \text{Conative} \\
\text{Expressive)} & \text{Phatic} & \\
 & \text{Metalingual} &
\end{array}
$$

He made it clear that a verbal message was very unlikely to be fulfilling one function only, but that in taking account of the various functions liable to be copresent we might expect to find them hierarchically ordered, one function being **dominant.** "The verbal structure," he added, "depends primarily on the dominant function [Sebeok, 1960, p. 353]."

I want to accept as starting point his view that the poetic function (in the broad sense of 'poetic,' equivalent to the verbal arts) may be defined as a "focus on the message for its own sake," and to agree in principle that the poetic function may be either dominant or merely accessory. But Jakobson goes on to say:

> Any attempt to reduce the sphere of poetic function to poetry or to confine poetry to poetic function would be a delusive oversimplification. Poetic function is not the sole function of verbal art but only its dominant, determining function, whereas in all other verbal activities it acts as a subsidiary, accessory constituent [Sebeok, 1960, p. 356].

Any linguistic choice made on the sole grounds that "it sounds better that way" would seem to exemplify Jakobson's conception of the poetic function in an accessory role. Yet it seems to me that the urgent necessity is to characterize the structure and status of verbal messages in which the poetic function is dominant, that is, to find ways of distinguishing poetic from nonpoetic discourse. Jakobson's model itself might even suggest a dichotomy of this kind, a dominant focus on the message itself for its own sake being in contrast with a message dominantly focused on something beyond or outside itself.

Susanne Langer (1953) recognizes such a dichotomy when she comments on the switch required when readers or listeners turn their attention from nonliterary to literary discourse. An "illusion of life," she says,

> is the primary illusion of all poetic art. It is at least tentatively established by the very first sentence, which has to switch the reader's or hearer's attitude from conversational interest to literary interest, i.e., from actuality to fiction. We make this shift with great ease, and much more often than we realize, even in the midst of conversation; one has only to say "You know about the two Scotchmen, who . . ." to make everybody in earshot suspend the actual conversation and attend to "the" two Scots and "their" absurdities. Jokes are a special literary form to which people will attend on the spur of the moment [1953, p. 213].

And, speaking of Blake's poem *Tyger*, she comments, "The vision of such a tiger is a virtual experience, built up from the first line of the poem to the last. But nothing can be built up unless the very first words of the poem EFFECT THE BREAK WITH THE READER'S ACTUAL ENVIRONMENT [p. 214, emphasis added]."

In *The Reader, the Text, the Poem*, Louise Rosenblatt (1978) makes a broad distinction between two types of reading process, **efferent** and **aesthetic**. In efferent reading the reader's concern is with what he takes away from the reading (hence "efferent" from *effero* [I carry away]). In aesthetic reading, in contrast, "the reader's primary concern is with what happens during the actual reading event. . . . The reader's attention is centered directly on what he is living through during his relationship with that particular text [1978, pp. 24–25]." She is careful to point out that this is no hard and fast division but rather a continuum between two poles. Thus, "given the assumption that the text offers a potentially meaningful set of linguistic symbols, the reader is faced with the adoption of either a predominantly efferent or a predominantly aesthetic stance [1978, p. 78]." We shall return to this matter of the relation between a reader's and a writer's options.

Support for a general distinction between literary and nonliterary discourse comes also from a linguist's work in stylistics. Widdowson (1975) claims that what is crucial to the character of literature is that "the language of a literary work should be fashioned into patterns over and above those required by the actual language system [1975, p. 47]." I shall return to consider this claim in a later section.

Spectator and Participant Roles

As we have noted, many of the features we find in poetic discourse (the language of literature) we find also widely distributed in many other forms of discourse. A mere study of the distribution of such features will not, I believe, add up to an adequate description of the verbal structure of a message in which the poetic function is dominant. We have no difficulty in practice in recognizing the difference between a novel with a political purpose and a piece of political rhetoric or persuasive discourse. What are the factors that shape the literary work as a whole?

The theory I want to pursue is one that I first put forward many years ago (Britton, 1963), in what seems to me now a crude form. My purpose then was to find common ground between much of the writing children do in school and the literature they read. I was concerned that, unlike the arts of painting and music, literature, as far as schools and universities were concerned, was not something that students do, but always something that other people HAVE DONE. To bridge this gap, I looked for what seemed to be the informal spoken counterparts of written literature—not the anecdote as such, I decided (Langer's tale of the two Scotsmen)—but the kind of gossip about events that most of us take part in daily. To quote from that account, "The distinction that matters . . . is not whether the events recounted are true or fictional, but whether we recount them (or listen to them) as spectators or participants: and whenever we play the role of spectator of human affairs I suggest we are in the position of literature [Britton, 1963, p. 37]." The roles of spectator and participant were differentiated in this way:

> When we talk about our own affairs, clearly we can do so either as participant or as spectator. If I describe what has happened to me in order to get my hearer to do something for me, or even to change his opinion about me, then I remain a participant in my own affairs and invite him to become one. If, on the other hand, I merely want to interest him, so that he savours with me the joys and sorrows and surprises of my past experiences and appreciates with me the intricate patterns of events, then not only do I invite him to be a spectator, but I am myself a spectator of my own experience. . . . I don't think it is far-fetched to think of myself talking not about

my own past, but about my future, and, again, doing so in either of the two roles. As participant I should be planning, and asking my listener to partici- pate by helping or advising or just 'giving me the necessary permission'. As spectator I should be day-dreaming, and inviting my listener to share in that kind of pleasure [Britton, 1963, p. 39].

To complete the account, I then made reference to taking up the role of spectator of imagined experiences in fantasy or fiction.

Three years later I prepared an advance paper for discussion at the Anglo-American Seminar at Dartmouth, a paper on "Response to Litera- ture" (Britton, 1968), and as a brief postscript to that document, I referred to the "unorthodox view of literature" that characterized it as a written form of language in the role of spectator and so related it to the spoken form, gossip about events. The paper was discussed by a study group under the chair- manship of the British psychologist, D. W. Harding. It was not until the first meeting of the study group was over that he asked me whether I knew his own papers putting forward a similar view; and that evening, in Dartmouth College Library, I read for the first time "The Role of the Onlooker" (Hard- ing, 1937) and "Psychological Processes in the Reading of Fiction" (Hard- ing, 1962). There I found a fully and carefully argued case for distinguishing the role of an onlooker from that of a participant in events and for relating gossip to literature as activities in the former role.

The final report of that study group was prepared by Harding and included this comment:

> Though central attention should be given to literature in the ordinary sense, it is impossible to separate response to literature sharply from response to other stories, films, or television plays, or from children's own personal writing or spoken narrative. In all of these the student contem- plates represented events in the role of a spectator, not for the sake of active intervention. But since his response includes in some degree accepting or rejecting the values and emotional attitudes which the narration implicitly offers, it will influence, perhaps greatly influence, his future appraisals of behavior and feeling [Harding, 1968, p. 11].

D. W. Harding

In the two articles I have referred to, Harding explored the relationship between three processes that seemed to him to have much in common: (*a*) watching events without taking part in them; (*b*) exchanging gossip—infor- mal recounting or description of events; and (*c*) reading (or writing) fiction. An understanding of the first of these, that of being literally in the role of spectator, is essential to an understanding of his view of the other two. An onlooker, he says, (*a*) ATTENDS (and this will range from "a passing glance" to a "fascinated absorption") and (*b*) EVALUATES (within a range from "an attitude of faint liking or disliking, hardly above indifference" to one of "strong, perhaps intensely emotional" response). What we attend to, he suggests, reflects our interests (if we take interest to mean "an enduring disposition to respond, in whatever way, to some class of objects or events"); how we evaluate reflects our sentiments, if we take a sentiment to be "an enduring disposition to evaluate some object or class of objects in a particular way [Harding, 1972, p. 134]."

A major aspect of a spectator's response to the events he witnesses will be a concern for the people involved and an interest in the way they react, but there is likely to be present also an interest in and evaluation of the pattern events take, with a sense that what is happening here might one day happen to him. Both aspects are, in a broad sense, learning experiences: As spectators we not only reflect our interests and sentiments but also modify and extend them. "In ways of this kind," Harding writes,

> the events at which we are "mere onlookers" come to have, cumulatively, a deep and extensive influence on our systems of value. They may in certain ways be even more formative than events in which we take part. Detached and distanced evaluation is sometimes sharper for avoiding the blurrings and bufferings that participant action brings, and the spectator often sees the event in a broader context than the participant can tolerate. To obliterate the effects on a man of the occasions on which he was only an onlooker would be profoundly to change his outlook and values [1962, p. 136].

To be one of a number of spectators is to take part in a mutual challenging and sanctioning of each other's evaluations. "Everything we look on at is tacitly and unintentionally treated as an object lesson by our fellow spectators; speech and gesture, smiles, nudges, clicks, tuts and glances are constantly at work to sanction or correct the feelings we have as spectators [Harding, 1937, p. 253]."

This aspect of a spectator's experience is sharply emphasized when we turn to the second of the three processes I have listed, that of deliberately taking up the role of spectator of represented or recounted experiences, as for example when we go home in the evening and chat about the day's events. We HAVE BEEN participants but are so no longer; taking up the role of spectator, we invite our listener to do the same. Harding goes so far as to imply that this familiar habit is something we indulge in for the purpose of testing out our modes of evaluating; having, in fact, our value systems sanctioned or modified by others whose values, in general, we reckon to share. We do not recount everything that happens to us: What we select constitutes a first level of evaluation. But it is as we recount the events in a manner designed to arouse in our listeners attitudes towards them that chime with our own that we more specifically invite corroboration of our ways of evaluating. On this basis, I think it is no distortion of Harding's account to suggest that as participants we APPLY our value systems, but as spectators we GENERATE AND REFINE the system itself. In applying our value systems we shall inevitably be constrained by self-interest, by concern for the outcome of the event we are participating in; as spectators we are freed of that constraint.

Harding goes on to suggest that what takes place informally in chat about events is in essence similar to what is achieved by a work of fiction or drama. "True or fictional, all these forms of narrative invite us to be onlookers joining in the evaluation of some possibility of experience [1962, p. 138]."

The London Writing Research Project

At the time of the Dartmouth Seminar my colleagues and I at the University of London Institute of Education were beginning to plan the Schools Council Project on the written language of 11- to 18-year-olds. Our first and major task was to devise modes of analysis of children's writings by means of which the development of writing abilities might be documented. We envisaged a multidimensional analysis and worked on what seemed to us two of the essential dimensions. The first resulted in a set of categories we called "sense of audience" (Who is the writing for?) and the second in a set of function categories (What is the writing for?). These are fully described in *The Development of Writing Abilities, 11–18* (Britton, Burgess, Martin, McLeod, & Rosen, 1975) and for my present purpose I need only indicate how the spectator-participant distinction was taken up and developed as the basis of the function category set.

To relate gossip to literature is not only to show a similarity in that they are both utterances in the spectator role, but also to indicate a difference. The formal and informal ends of the spectrum have very different potentials. One of the important ways in which we frame an evaluation and communicate it is by giving a particular shape to the events in narrating them; at the formal end of the scale all the resources of literary art, all the linguistic and conceptual forms that a literary artist molds into a unity, are at the service of that shaping and sharing.

Clearly, an account given of an experience in a letter to an intimate friend might also be placed at the informal end of the scale, in contrast perhaps to the same event narrated by the same writer as part of a short story or a published autobiography. (Dr. Johnson wrote a letter from the Hebrides to a friend in which he said, "When we were taken upstairs, a dirty fellow bounced out of the bed on which one of us was to lie"; this appears in his *Journal* as "Out of one of the couches on which we were to repose there started up at our entrance a man black as a Cyclops from the forge"—more of a parody of the point I am making than an illustration, I think!)

The informality of a chat or a personal letter is certainly in part a reflection of a relaxed relationship between the communicating parties—closeness rather than distance, warmth rather than coldness. Perhaps influenced also by Moffett's model of kinds of discourse in which he sees the **I–you** rhetorical relationship and the **I–it** referential relationship as intimately connected (Moffett, 1968, p. 33), we came to identify the informal end of this continuum with expressive language as Sapir (1961, p. 10) has defined it; further, to see that the "unshaped," loosely structured end of the spectator role continuum merged into the informal pole of language in the role of participant. This gave us three major categories of function: transactional, expressive, and poetic. **Transactional** is the form of discourse that most fully meets the demands of a participant in events (using language to get things done, to carry out a verbal transaction). **Expressive** is the form of discourse in which the distinction between participant and spectator is a shadowy one. And **poetic** discourse is the form that most fully meets the demands associated with the role of spectator—demands that are met, we suggested, by MAKING something with language rather than doing something with it.

Though our principal source for the term "expressive" was Edward Sapir, we found it was one widely used by other linguists. Jakobson labeled the function arising from a focus on the addressor either "emotive" or "expressive" and saw it as offering "a direct expression of the speakers attitude towards what he is speaking about [Sebeok, 1960, p. 354]"; a point that Dell Hymes later glossed: "A sender cannot help but express attitudes towards each of the other factors in a speech event, his audience, the style of the message, the code he is using, the channel he is using, his topic, the scene of the communication [1908, p. 106]." Labov (1966, p. 13) characterizes the expressive function as "the role of language as self-identification," and it is this aspect that Gusdorf elaborates: "The relation to others is only meaningful insofar as it reveals that personal identity within the person who is himself speaking. To communicate, man *expresses* himself, i.e. he actualizes himself, he creates from his own substance [1965, p. 69]." Thus the expressive function in our model is not simply the informal end of two scales, the neutral point between participant and spectator role language, but has its own positive function to perform—a function that profits from the indeterminacy between carrying out a verbal transaction and constructing a verbal object to be shared. The positive function of expressive speech is, in simple terms, to make the most of being with somebody, that is, to enjoy their company, to make their presence fruitful—a process that can profit from exploring with them both the inner and outer aspects of experience.

But in expressive writing the presence, the "togetherness" is simulated: The writer invokes the presence of the reader as he writes; the reader invokes the presence of the writer as he reads. Thus a working definition of expressive writing would be "writing that assumes an interest in the writer as well as in what he has to say about the world." We might add that it would be foolish to underestimate the importance of expressive speech or writing as means of influencing people and events. Advertisers and propagandists are only too ready to exploit its effectiveness.

Our description of expressive writing thus distinguished it from a verbal transaction on the one hand and a verbal object on the other. The verbal transaction and the verbal object are communicative rather than expressive, being in both cases language in the public domain; yet they communicate in very different ways. Expressive and referential strands, as Sapir explains, intermingle in all discourse, but the degree to which the former predominates is criterial in distinguishing expressive from transactional discourse. The change from expression to communication on the poetic side is brought about by an increasing degree of organization—organization into a single complex verbal symbol.

H. G. Widdowson

It is this last distinction that is illuminated by the work in stylistics of Widdowson (1975). He cites from literature examples of nongrammatical expressions that are nevertheless interpretable, finds such expressions in nonliterary texts, but concludes that they occur randomly in nonliterary writing, "whereas in literature they figure as part of a pattern which characterizes the literary work as a separate and self-contained whole [p. 36]." Interpretation of these expressions that violate the grammatical code relies on viewing them in the light of the context; and he goes on to show that this is also true of most metaphorical expressions (which again occur randomly in ordinary discourse but as part of a total pattern in a work of literature). Context, however, in ordinary language will include aspects of the social situation in which the utterance takes place and remarks that have gone before; whereas in literature context consists of the verbal fabric alone. Widdowson identifies patterns of three kinds to be found in literary works: phonological (metre and verse form are obvious examples), syntactical (parallel structures, for example, can invest an item with meaning which is, so to speak, by halo effect from other items in the series), and patterns formed by semantic links between individual lexical items. "At the heart of literary discourse," he concludes, "is the struggle to devise patterns of language which will bestow upon the linguistic items concerned just those values which convey the individual writer's personal vision [1975, p. 42]."

He goes on to suggest that the effect of the patterning over and above the patterns of the language code is "to create acts of communication which are self-contained units, independent of a social context and expressive of a reality other than that which is sanctioned by convention. In other words, I want to suggest that although literature need not be deviant as text it must of its nature be deviant as discourse [1975, p. 47]." This he achieves principally by pointing out that normal discourse features a sender of a message who is at the same time the addressor, and a receiver of a message who is also the addressee, whereas in literary discourse the author, as sender, is distinguished from the addressor, and the reader, as receiver, from the addressee. Striking examples of this disjunction illustrate his point ("I am the enemy you killed, my friend" from Owen; "With how sad steps, O moon" from Sidney), but he goes on to indicate that this modified relationship holds in general for works of literature. An addressor thus fuses meanings associated with a grammatical first person with those associated with a third, an addressee those of the second and third persons. This account of a systematic modification of the grammatical code he completes by showing how third person and first person are fused when in fiction a narrator describes the experiences of a third person sometimes in terms of what might have been observed, sometimes in terms of inner events that only the experiencer could know. On these grounds he concludes: "It would appear then that in literary discourse we do not have a sender addressing a message directly to a receiver, as is normally the case. Instead we have a communication situation within a communication situation and a message whose meaning is self-contained and not dependent on who sends it and who receives it [p. 50]."

In defending this view against likely objections, he makes two interesting points that are relevant to my theme. In many literary works, particularly perhaps in lyric poems, it is evident that the "I" of the work is the writer himself. In arguing that "it is not the writer as message sender, the craftsman, the 'maker' that the 'I' refers to but to the inner self that the writer is objectifying, and the very act of objectifying involves detaching this self and observing it as if it were a third person entity [1975, p. 53]," Widdowson sketches out, somewhat loosely, three forms of discourse in terms of the role of the "I": (a) In diaries and personal letters there is no distinction between sender and addressor: The writer may reveal his inner thoughts and feelings, and in doing so he takes responsibility—his readers may assume that he is "telling the truth." (*b*) In all other forms of nonliterary language, the writer, as sender and addressor, adopts a recognized social role and what he says and how he says it are determined by that role: "he is not at liberty to express his own individual sentiments at will. . . . [H]is addressee will be concerned with what he has to say in his role and not with his private and individual thoughts [p. 52].'"; (*c*) literary discourse, where the sender and addressor are disjoined, is concerned with the private thoughts and feelings of the writer, but in "bringing them out of hiding" he objectifies them and may explore them through the creation of personae, so that "we cannot assume that when a literary writer uses the first person he is describing his own experiences or making a confession." The literary writer, in fact, aware of the convention that distinguishes sender from addressor, is "relieved from any social responsibility for what he says in the first person [p. 53]." (Love letters, he notes, count as evidence in a court of law, love poems don't!)

This analysis provides an interesting gloss on the three major function categories in our model: expressive, transactional, and poetic.

The second objection Widdowson anticipates relates to the familiar problem of "the novel with a message." Our claim that a literary work was a verbal object and not a verbal transaction was objected to on just these grounds, and we argued in reply that a poetic work achieved its effect indirectly, via the poetic construct taken as a whole. Widdowson's claim that a literary work is a self-contained unit independent of a social context risks the same kind of objection: His answer is

> that it may indeed be the purpose of a writer to stir the social conscience but he does not do so by addressing himself directly to those whose consciences he wishes to stir. He expresses a certain reality, a personal vision, and the reader, as an *observer* of this reality, might then feel constrained to act in a certain way. But he is not directed to act by the writer (1975, p. 53).

Widdowson then develops a point that will be familiar to readers of Jakobson (1971, e.g., p. 704); he explores the way paradigmatic relationships invade the area of syntagmatic relationships in poetic discourse, and illustrates this at the level of phonemes and the grammatical level of words and phrases. Phonological distinctions that by the normal language code exist as a range from which **selection** is made (the story for example is about a cat and not about a hat, a bat, or a mat) invade the syntagmatic relationship, the process of **combination** in a literary work, as for example when a poet chooses "bright" in preference to "shining" because that word fits into the sound pattern, including perhaps both rhythm and rhyme, of his poem.

More germane to his principal argument is Widdowson's example of a series of verbal groups any one of which might have served to complete a sentence in a T. S. Eliot poem. Widdowson then shows how Eliot in fact does not SELECT, but COMBINES: "Words strain, Crack and sometimes break . . ." etc. This strategy, Widdowson notes, reflects the writer's struggle to resolve ambiguities and allows him to invite the reader to take part in that process. By such means works of literature communicate "an individual awareness of a reality other than that which is given general social sanction but nevertheless related to it [1971, p. 70]."

Contextualization

One of the important ways in which we may characterize the difference between transactional and poetic discourse is by reference to the way a reader grasps the message. If what a writer does when he draws from all he knows and selectively sets down what he wants to communicate is described as 'decontextualization', then the complementary process on the part of a reader is to 'contextualize', interpreting the writer's meaning by building it into his existing knowledge and experience. We have suggested (Britton et al., 1975, pp. 85–86) that in reading a piece of transactional discourse we contextualize the material in piecemeal fashion; passing over what is familiar, rejecting what is incomprehensible to us or perceived as inconsistent with our own thinking, accepting in piecemeal fashion what seems to us interesting, building our own connections between these fragments and our existing knowledge (which is open to modification, of course, in the process). With poetic discourse, on the other hand (and much of what Widdowson has said will support this difference), we apply our own knowledge and experience to the reconstruction of the writer's verbal object, and until we have done this, until we have the sense of a completed whole, a single unique symbol, we are in no position to reexamine our own thoughts and feelings in the light of the author's work. This we have called **global contextualization.** I think our response to a novel with a message may sometimes be a deliberate reexamination of the kind this suggests, but I have come to believe that in most cases global contextualization is a process that goes on over time and one we may not even be conscious of. We are constantly learning from our own first-hand experiences and mostly, because of the wide-ranging and diffuse nature of the process, without being aware that we are doing so. I am inclined to think that our response to a work of literature is like that.

We do of course contextualize in piecemeal fashion while reading works of literature: We pick up clues as to what life is like in places we have never visited, what it was like at times before we were born. But this is quite subsidiary, for most of us, to the main effects of literature; and it has its risks, since the verbal object, as Widdowson shows, deals with a reality "other than that which is given social sanction." There may be pygmies in the Australian rain forests the novelist describes, but that is no guarantee that they exist in fact. Nevertheless, for historians or sociologists, say, to study literature for the information they can glean is of course a legitimate option; they will be employing a process of piecemeal contextualization where what the author offered was a work to be contextualized globally. Louise Rosenblatt (1978), as we have mentioned, has paid close attention to this matter of the reader's options and raised some important issues. In defining a literary work of art as "what happens when a reader and a text come together [p. 12]," she is I think loading the dice in the reader's favor, but the weight has for so long been on the author's side that this is understandable. There are of course anomalies, as when a text produced by an author as propaganda survives when its injunctions are no longer appropriate, and survives as a piece of literature; or when an informative text (Gibbon's *Decline and Fall* is the stock example) survives when much of its information has been superseded and even discredited, to be read now not as information but for the unique and individual qualities typical of a work of literature.

There are anomalies, but without wishing in any way to infringe on the reader's freedom to choose, I do suggest that in the vast majority of cases the general conventions chosen by the writer—whether to produce expressive, transactional, or poetic discourse—are in fact the conventions by which the reader chooses to interpret.

YOUNG FLUENT WRITERS

L. S. Vygotsky

I have known a number of children who by the age of 5 or 6 had taught themselves to write. In each case it was stories that they wrote, and usually the stories were made up into little books, with pictures as well as writing. I take it as some evidence of the extraordinary ability human beings have of succeeding in doing what they want to do. One of these young children, under the age of 4, began by producing a little book with "pretend writing" in it—and surely, just as we pretend to be someone we want to be, so we pretend to do something we want to do. Some 20 months later the scribbled lines had given place to a decipherable story. Evidence of this kind is too often ignored, and it takes a Vygotsky, speaking across the decades since his death, to observe that the attempt to teach writing as a motor skill is mistaken (Vygotsky, 1978, p. 117); that psychology has conceived of it as a motor skill and "paid remarkably little attention to the question of written language as such, that is, a particular system of symbols and signs whose mastery heralds a critical turning-point in the entire cultural development of the child [p. 106]." It was his view that make-believe play, drawing and writing should be seen as "different moments in an essentially unified process of development of written language [p. 116]." And this he contrasted with what he found in schools: "Instead of being founded on the needs of children as they naturally develop and on their own activity, writing is given to them from without, from the teacher's hands [p. 105]."

I suggest that the 4-year-old I have referred to made what Vygotsky calls "a basic discovery—namely that one can draw not only things but also speech [1978, p. 115]." Since pictorial representation is first-order symbolism and writing is second-order symbolism (designating words that are in turn signs for things and relationships), Vygotsky saw this discovery as a key point in the development of writing in a child; yet he recognized there was little understanding of how the shift takes place, since the necessary research had not been done (p. 115). We are not much wiser today, though the labors of Donald Graves and others give us good reason to hope.

Outline for a Case Study

My records of the development of Clare, the 4-year-old whose pretend writing I have referred to, may illustrate some of the points Vygotsky has made in his account of "the developmental history of written language."

(1) Her conversational speech was quite well developed by the time she was 2 years old. Much of her talk was playful (seeing me at the washbasin, *What have you got off, Daddy?*—at 2:3) and she used made-up forms freely (*I'm spoonfuling it in, I'm see-if-ing it will go through, smuttered in your eyes*—for uncombed hair—all at 2:7). Her curiosity about language was in evidence early (*When it's one girl you say "girl" and when it's two three four girls you say "girl s." Why when it's two three four childs you say "child ren?"*—at 2:10; *"Fairy girl with curly hair," that makes a rhyme, doesn't it?*—at 2:11; on hearing something described as 'delicious,' *Is delicious nicer than lovely?*—at 3:1).

(2) Extended make-believe play, involving her toy animals in family roles, was established by the time she was 3. Storytelling developed from it, the animals becoming the audience. The toy animals (she was given dolls from time to time but they were never adopted into the family) seem to have

sustained a key role. They were the *dramatis personae* of her make-believe play, the subject of the stories she told, of her drawings, and later of the stories she wrote. Vygotsky's point that in make-believe play the plaything is free to take on a meaning that does not rely on perceptual resemblance is amusingly illustrated by the fact that when Clare enacted a queen's wedding, the least suitable of the animals—a scraggy, loose-knit dog—was chosen for the role of queen!

(3) Her earliest recognizable drawings came just before she was 2 and though they are clearly attempts at human figures, the talk that always accompanied the drawing was often in anthropomorphic terms (*the mummy bird, the daddy bird*). A picture drawn in colored chalks at 3:5 shows a large figure of a girl on the left-hand side and a house on the right. Her commentary as she drew explained: *The girl is carrying a yellow handbag and she has a brown furry dog on a lead. Her feet are walking along. . . . I have put a car outside the house. I am putting blue sky, now I am putting in the sunshine.* (Here the diagonal blue strokes that had indicated the sky were interspersed with yellow ones.) *She's got a tricycle with blue wheels and a chain. Mrs. Jones across the road has yellow and brown on her windows. I shall put yellow and red on mine.*

It is an important part of Vygotsky's thesis that a young child's drawing is "graphic speech," dependent on verbal speech: The child draws, that is to say, from the memory of what he knows rather than from what he presently observes; and that what he knows has been processed in speech and is further processed in the speech that accompanies the drawing. The space in Clare's picture is well filled, but not in terms of topographical representation: The girl and the house are upright; the car is drawn vertically standing on its head; the dog vertically sitting on its tail; and the tricycle has its frame, wheels and chain spread out, looking more like an assembly kit.

(4) What circumstances could be supposed to facilitate the process that Vygotsky calls the move from drawing objects to drawing speech? Imitating the general pattern of writing behavior, Clare at the age of 3:6 produced parallel horizontal lines of cursive scribble, saying that she was *doing grown-up's kind of writing.* At 3:11 she produced the little story book I have described with similar lines of scribble but interspersed with words she could actually write (*mummy, and, the*) and with a drawing on the cover. The stories she wrote from 5:6 onward were in cursive script with headings in capitals. She was by this time reading a good deal, mainly the little animal stories by Beatrix Potter and Alison Uttley.

Turning from the general pattern to the detail, Clare at the age of 3 played very often with a set of inch-high letters made of plastic in various colors. Among more random, playful uses, she learned to make her name in these letters and she was interested in what each letter was called. (One effect of this play was evident: When first she attempted to write words, an "E," for example, was an "E" for her whether it faced right or left or up or down.) One of her activities represented a link between letter recognition and writing behavior in general: At 3:5, in imitation of picture alphabets she knew, she was drawing a series of objects and writing the initial letter of each beside the drawing. Most of them she knew, but she came to one she did not: "rhubarb." When I told her, she said, *R—that's easy—just a girl's head and two up-and-downs!*

(5) The final stage in Vygotsky's "developmental history" is that by which the written language ceases to be second-order symbolism, mediated by speech, and becomes first-order symbolism. I can offer no evidence of this from the records of Clare, and indeed I seriously doubt whether that transition is ever entirely appropriate to the written language we have been concerned with, that of stories.

(6) I think the most important conclusion to be drawn from the case of Clare and other children who have taught themselves to write by writing stories is a point that is central to Vygotsky's argument, that of the effect of INTENTION on a child's performance. It would appear that the spoken language effectively meets young children's needs in general, and we must surmise that it is only as they come to value the written language as a vehicle for stories that they are likely to form an intention to write. Much of Clare's behavior indicated that she had done so. Slobin and Welsh (1973) have effectively demonstrated that mastery of the spoken language cannot be adequately assessed without account of "the intention to say so-and-so"—a lesson that as teachers or researchers we have been slow to learn.

Writing and Reading

Clare continued to read and write stories for many years. Animal fantasies predominated until the age of 7, pony stories and adventure stories (often featuring an animal) followed until, from the ages of 12 to 14 she gave herself up almost entirely to reading women's magazine stories and writing herself at great length in that vein. Here, to represent successive stages, are some opening lines:

At 6: *I am a little Teddy Bear. I've got a pony called Snow and I live in a little house with a thatched roof.*

At 8½: *Mrs. Hedgehog had just had three babies. Two of them were like ordinary hedgehog babies, covered with soft prickles. But the third had none. It was a dead calm as the Sand Martin and crew glided out of the small harbour at Plymouth. Phillip and Jean were the eldest. They were twins of fourteen.*

At 11: *Fiona Mackenzie lay in bed in her small attic bedroom. She turned sleepily over, but the morning sun streaming in at her small window dazzled her, and she turned back.* (A story about horses in the Highlands.)

At 12: *Derek looked into her face, and his green eyes burning fiercely with the white hot light of intense love gazed into the liquid depth of her melting, dark brown ones.*

At 14: *The dance was in full swing, and Giselle was the acknowledged belle of it. More radiant, more sparkling than ever before, she floated blissfully in the arms of James Wainforth.*

Her comments on her reading and writing were sometimes illuminating. At 3:8 she described the Cinderella story as *A bit sad book about two ugly sisters and a girl they were ugly to.* At 8:7 she was asked what sort of things she liked reading. *Well,* she said, *there's* Treasure Island—*that's a bloody one for when I'm feeling boyish. And* Little Men, *that's a sort of half-way one.* "And don't you ever feel girlish?" she was asked. *Yes. When I'm tired and then I read* The Smallest Dormouse. At 10:2 she wrote a story about children finding a treasure: *It's like Enid Blyton's story mostly,* she said, *except longer words.* A few months later she was struggling to get through Mrs. Craik's *John Halifax, Gentleman,* but gave up with the comment, *It's a bit Lorna Doonish, a lot of cissy boys in it. It's so sort of **genteel**—I can't stand it!*

That her writing was influenced by her reading shows up dramatically (though from a limited aspect) in the following figures relating to mean T-unit length and subordination at four age-points. The figures for a passage from a women's magazine story she had read are shown in parentheses.

Age:	6	9	13	(Magazine)	17
Number of words taken:	331	332	340	(330)	322
Mean T-Unit length:	4.1	8.0	6.9	(6.7)	11.5
Number of subordinate clauses:	7	17	6	(9)	19

Spectator Role and the Beginnings of Writing

In the light of current school practices, it is as important as ever today to stress Vygotsky's view that learning to read and learning to write must be seen as inseparable aspects of one process, that of mastering written language. We have come to recognize the way this process is grounded in speech but have not yet acknowledged the essential contribution of other forms of symbolic behavior, gesture, make-believe play, pictorial representation. In my account of Clare's development, I have added one other activity, that of manipulative play with the substance of written language. Bruner (1975) has pointed out that such play contributes to learning because it is a 'meta-process,' one that focuses on the nature itself of the activity. (Children learn to walk for the purpose of getting where they want to be; PLAY with walking—early forms of dancing—involves a concern with the nature of the walking process, an exploration of its manifold possibilities.)

It remains for me to point out that make-believe play (embracing the social environment children construct with their playthings), storytelling, listening to stories, pictorial representation and the talk that complements it, story reading and story writing—these are all activities in the role of spectator. As I have suggested, I believe it is this characteristic that develops a need for the written language in young children and the intention to master it. In such activities children are sorting themselves out, progressively distinguishing what is from what seems, strengthening their hold on reality by a consideration of alternatives. Clare, for example, at the age of 8:6, writes what at first sight appears to be a variant of the kind of animal fable she was familiar with from earlier reading of Beatrix Potter:

HEDGEHOG
Mrs. Hedgehog had just had three babies. Two of them were like ordinary hedgehog babies, covered with soft prickles.

But the third had none. He was like a hedgehog in any other way. He ate like a hedgehog and he lived like a hedgehog and he rolled up in a ball like a hedgehog, and he went to sleep in the winter like a hedgehog. But he had no prickles like a hedgehog.

When he was a year old a fairy came to him and said, "Go to China and get three hairs from the Emperor Ching Chang's seventh guinea-pig. Throw the hairs in the fire, and then put it out with six bucketfuls of water. Put some of the ash on your head, and leave it for the night. In the morning you will be covered with prickles." Then she faded away.

[The story tells how he carried out these instructions, and concludes:]

He went to sleep beside the stream. In the morning he woke up feeling rather strange. He looked at his back. It was covered in prickles. He spent four days in China, then he went home in the boat. His family were very surprised to see him!

For those who knew Clare, it was not difficult to recognize here an account of her own struggle to establish herself in the family in competition with a more confident and more relaxed younger sister. *His family were very surprised to see him!* Without knowing the writer, one might guess that a similar self-exploration was taking place, unconsciously, in the 6-year-old girl who wrote:

> *There was a child of a witch who was ugly. He had pointed ears thin legs and was born in a cave. he flew in the air holding on nothing just playing games.*
> *When he saw ordinary girls and boys he hit them with his broomstick. A cat came along. he arched his back at the girls and boys and made them run away. When they had gone far away the cat meeowed softly at the witch child. the cat loved the child. the child loved the cat the cat was the onlee thing the child loved in the world.*

It has often been pointed out that in one sense a tiny infant is lord of his universe, and that growing from infancy into childhood involves discovering one's own unimportance. But the world created in the stories children write is a world they control and this may be a source of deep satisfaction. As one of the children recorded by Donald Graves remarked, she liked writing stories because "you are the mother of the story."

Whether to read or to write, a story makes fewer demands than a piece of transactional writing since one essential element of the latter process is missing in the former. The reader of an informative or persuasive piece must construct himself the writer's meaning and inwardly debate it (an essential part of the piecemeal contextualization process); the reader of a story accepts, so to speak, an invitation to enter a world and see what happens to him there. The writer of a transactional piece must attempt to anticipate and make provision for the reader's inner debate; the writer of a story constructs a situation to his own satisfaction, though thereafter he may be willing, even eager, to share it.

Expressive Writing

Edward Sapir observed that "ordinary speech is directly expressive [1961, p. 10]." Because expressive writing, though it differs in substantial ways from speech, is the form of written discourse closest to speech, the London Writing Research team suggested that it provided a "natural" starting point for beginning writers, assisting them at a time when they have rich language resources recruited through speech, but few if any internalized forms of the written language. Progress from this point consists, we believe, in shuttling between those spoken resources and an increasing store of forms internalized from reading and being read to. (It may prove that vocal reading, whether their own or somebody else's, is in the early stages a more effective route to that internalization.)

We might describe this early form as an all-purpose expressive. As the writer employs it to perform different tasks, fulfill different purposes, and increasingly succeeds in meeting the different demands, his all-purpose expressive will evolve: He will acquire by dissociation a variety of modes. Expressive writing is thus a matrix from which will develop transactional and poetic writing, as well as the more mature forms of the expressive.

What the Young Writer Needs to Know

My argument has been that Vygotsky's account offers an explanation of the phenomenon I have noted, that of Clare and the other children who mastered written language by producing storybooks at an early age. Let me now go on to ask, "What does a writer acquiring mastery in this way need to know?"

First and foremost he must know from experience the SATISFACTION that can come from a story—perhaps first a story told to him, but then certainly a story read to him. Sartre (1967, p. 31) has commented on the difference: Accustomed to having his mother tell him stories, he describes his experience when first she reads to him: *The tale itself was in its Sunday best: the woodcutter, the woodcutter's wife and their daughter, the fairy, all those little people, our fellow-creatures, had acquired majesty; their rags were magnificently described, words left their mark on objects, transforming actions into rituals and events into ceremonies.*

Then he must know something of the structure of a story, a learning process that Applebee (1978) has very helpfully described in developmental terms for stories told by children between the ages of 2 and 5 (but with implications for later stages). He sees two principles at work, one of **centering,** a concern for the unity of a story, and one of **chaining,** a concern for sequence; and in terms of these two principles he outlines a series of plot structures that parallel the stages of concept development described by Vygotsky (1962). It should be noted, at the same time, that recall of events in narrative form is something that all children achieve a year or more before they are ready to tackle the written language.

Some forms of story writing will only be possible if the writer is familiar with the conventional associations that govern our expectations in listening to stories—the role expected of a wolf, a lion, a fox, a witch, a prince, and so on (Applebee, 1978, chap. 3). Such built-in associations are, of course, a resource that a young writer may in his own stories exploit, improvise on, invert, or ignore.

Knowledge of the linguistic conventions of stories—the *Once upon a time* and *happily ever after* conventions—are often familiar to children before they can read or write, as are more general features of the language of written stories. (I saw a story dictated by a 3-year-old which contained the sentence, *The king went sadly home for he had nowhere else to go*—a use of *for* which is certainly not a spoken form.)

But production of these and all other written forms relies, of course, on a knowledge of the written code itself, the formation of letters, words, sentences. How this is picked up from alphabet books and cornflake packets, picture books, TV advertisements, and street signs remains something of a mystery, though two governing conditions seem likely: a context of manipulative play and picture-making, and the association of this learning with the purpose of producing written stories. I am sure we underestimate the extent of such learning when a powerful interest is in focus. In my recent experience of reading stories to a 3-year-old, I have been amazed at her ability to fill the words into gaps I leave when the story I am reading is one she cannot have heard very often. Michael Polanyi's account of the relation of subsidiary to focal awareness certainly helps us to see this learning process as feasible (Polanyi, 1958, chap. 4).

Finally, the writer must know from experience the sound of a written text read aloud. How else can he come to hear an inner voice dictating to him the story he wants to produce? An apprenticeship of listening to others will enable him later to be aware of the rhythms of the written language in the course of his own silent reading.

A Final Speculation

I believe the successful writer learns all these things implicitly; that is to say, in Polanyi's terms, by maintaining a focal awareness of the desired performance that acts as a determining tendency guiding and controlling his subsidiary awareness of the means he employs. I believe, further, that any attempt to introduce explicit learning would be likely to hinder rather than help at this early stage. When we are dealing with poetic writing, there is much that could not in any case be made explicit: We simply do not know by what organizing principles experience is projected into a work of art.

It is this problem that Susanne Langer has been investigating over many years. Her distinction between discursive and presentational symbolism—between a message encoded in a symbol system and a message embodied in a single unique complex symbol; her recognition of the key role of the arts as offering an ordering of experience alternative to the cognitive, logical ordering achieved by discursive symbolism—these are foundation stones in our theory of language functions.

From her exploration of the laws governing a work of art she makes one very interesting suggestion: that in all works of art there is a building-up and resolution of tensions and that the intricate pattern of these movements, this rhythm, somehow reflects the "shape of every living act [Langer, 1967, chap. 7]."

To speculate on her speculations: We give and find shape in the very act of perception, we give and find further shape as we talk, write or otherwise represent our experiences. I say "give and find" because clearly there is order and pattern in the natural world irrespective of our perceiving and representing. At the biological level man shares that order, but at the level of behavior he appears to lose it: The pattern of his actions is more random than that of the instinctual behavior of animals. In learning to control his environment he has gained a freedom of choice in action that he may use constructively and harmoniously or to produce disharmony, shapelessness, chaos. When, however, he shapes his experience into a verbal object, an art form, in order to communicate it and to realize it more fully himself, he is seeking to recapture a natural order that his daily actions have forfeited. Understanding so little of the complexities of these processes, we can do no more than entertain that idea as a fascinating speculation.

REFERENCES

Applebee, A. N. *The child's concept of story.* Chicago: University of Chicago Press, 1978.

Britton, J. N. Literature. In J. N. Britton (Ed.), *The arts and current tendencies in education.* London: Evans, 1963. Pp. 34–61.

Britton, J. N. Response to literature. In J. R. Squire (Ed.), *Response to literature.* Champaign, Ill.: National Council of Teachers of English, 1968. Pp. 3–10.

Britton, J. N., Burgess, T., Martin, M., McLeod, A., and Rosen, H. *The development of writing abilities, 11–18.* London: Macmillan, 1975.

Bruner, J. S. The ontogenesis of speech acts. *Journal of Child Language,* 1975, 2, 1–19.

Gusdorf, G. *Speaking.* Evanston: Northwestern University Press, 1965.

Harding, D. W. The role of the onlooker. *Scrutiny,* 1937, 6, 247–258.

Harding, D. W. Psychological processes in the reading of fiction. *British Journal of Aesthetics,* 1962, 2, 133–147.

Harding, D. W. Response to literature: The report of the study group. In J. R. Squire (Ed.), *Response to literature.* Champaign, Ill.: National Council of Teachers of English, 1968. Pp. 11–27.

Hymes, D. The ethnography of speaking. In J. A. Fishman (Ed.), *Readings in the sociology of language.* The Hague: Mouton, 1968.

Jakobson, R. *Selected writings* (Vol. 2). *Word and language.* The Hague: Mouton, 1971.

Labov, W. *The social stratification of English in New York City.* Washington, D.C.: Center for Applied Linguistics, 1966.

Langer, S. K. *Feeling and form.* London: Routledge and Kegan Paul, 1953.

Langer, S. K. *Mind: An essay on human feeling.* Baltimore: Johns Hopkins Press, 1967.

Moffett, J. *Teaching the universe of discourse.* Boston: Houghton Mifflin, 1968.

Polanyi, M. *Personal knowledge.* London: Routledge and Kegan Paul, 1958.

Rosenblatt, L. *The reader, the text, the poem.* Carbondale, Ill.: Southern Illinois University Press, 1978.

Sapir, E. *Culture, language and personality.* Berkeley: University of California Press, 1961.

Sartre, J. P. *Words.* Harmondsworth: Penguin Books, 1967.

Sebeok, T. *Style in language.* Cambridge: M.I.T. Press, 1960.

Slobin, D. I., & Welsh, C. A. Elicited imitation as a research tool in developmental psycholinguistics. In C. A. Ferguson & D. I. Slobin (Eds.), *Studies of child language development.* New York: Holt, Rinehart and Winston, 1973.

Vygotsky, L. S. *Mind in society.* Cambridge: Harvard University Press, 1978.

Widdowson, H. G. *Stylistics and the teaching of literature.* London: Longman, 1975.

A Discourse-Centered Rhetoric of the Paragraph

PAUL C. RODGERS, JR.

Today's textbook paragraph, the paragraph taught by so many to so few—with its vision of triune organic integrity and its philosophy of mechanism—was unveiled almost precisely a century ago, in March 1866, by an unprepossessing Scottish logician and composition teacher named Alexander Bain. Bain laid no claim to infallibility as a rhetorician, and was more or less ignored in his own day, but the late nineteenth century chose to magnify his authority in retrospect: long after the man was forgotten, his dicta assumed something of the aura of revealed truth. In all the intervening years since 1866, though Bain's six "rules" have undergone considerable refinement and elaboration, virtually no one has ever challenged his basic concept of the paragraph or its underlying suppositions. In essence the paragraph today is just what it has been since the beginning, an "expanded sentence"—logically, structurally, semantically.[1]

Yet it has been obvious all along that Bain's analysis simply does not comprehend what goes on in many sound and effective paragraphs, and the language of its successive formulations never has given the student writer adequate guidance. As commonly defined (à la Bain), the paragraph is a group of sentences which develops the single idea conveyed in its topic sentence. Each of the key words in this definition offers pitfalls. What, for instance, is an "idea"? Does a noun or noun phrase express an idea, or must every idea be a proposition? Must the topic idea be carried as the major predication of the topic sentence? If not, then how does one distinguish

Reprinted from *College Composition and Communication* 17.1 (February 1966): 2–11. Used with permission.

topic material from its context? Can the topic be merely suggested, as by a question or exclamation or negative declaration or figure of speech, or must it be spelled out? If the paragraph is a group of sentences, how small can the group be? Do two sentences constitute a group? Does one? That is, can a paragraph properly be conterminous with its own topic sentence?

Bain and his immediate successors worked by deduction, first assuming a close organic parallel between sentence and paragraph and then applying traditional sentence-law to the paragraph. But questions like the ones suggested above provoked inductive study of actual paragraphs and eventually produced a mass of inductive qualifications grafted upon the original deductive formula:

♦ A proper paragraph always has a single central topic idea, except when it has two, three, or more.

♦ Development of the topic is always limited to the paragraph in which the topic is broached, except when the topic requires that exposition continue in the next.

♦ The topic sentence always expresses the topic idea, but the work of expression may be disposed of in a minor segment of the sentence; or, on the other hand, a complicated topic may take several sentences, and these sentences may be widely separated in the paragraph.

♦ There is always a topic sentence, yet it may not actually be stated. In this case, it is "implied," and serves as a sort of offstage influence directing the action in the paragraph.

♦ A paragraph by definition is a series of sentences, but now and then it turns out to be one sentence only. If the sentence-series seems too long for presentation as a unit, it can be subdivided into several paragraphs without loss of unity. Conversely, a series of short paragraphs can be combined into a single unit, sometimes with the original components identified by number or letter.

♦ Moreover there are certain very useful and common paragraph types that show little interest in amplifying topics: transitional, introductory, directive, summary, and concluding paragraphs.

In short, the paragraph is what the textbook says it is, except . . . it isn't. At least, not always; and if one happens to be working with the wrong handbook or the wrong anthology of prose models, it often isn't.

Faced with this congeries of paradoxes, recent commentators have tended to reject or simply ignore traditional theory:

> Since every paragraph of the essay is part of the general flow, it is difficult to find in many paragraphs anything so static that it can be isolated as the single idea, or topic, of that paragraph. The notion that every paragraph must have a topic sentence is hence a misleading one.[2]
>
> Obviously any piece of composition possessing even a minimum of unity may be summed up in some kind of sentence. The "implied" topic sentence, therefore, is an abstraction—a not very useful kind of ghost sentence.[3]
>
> [The paragraph] is simply a convenient grouping of sentences. In a progression of sentences a few places will be more suited to indentations than others, but you can justify an indentation before almost any sentence of sophisticated prose.[4]

However well grounded such pronouncements may be, they contribute little to prose criticism. If ideas flow, how shall we measure and define the current? If a sequence of ideas can be introduced without interpretive comment, how does the sequence relate to its context, the discourse? If indentations can occur almost anywhere, upon what basis shall we justify or challenge a given decision to indent?

The current situation may be summed up as follows: Deduction has failed to yield a fully satisfactory model of the paragraph, and interest in the putative organic parallel between paragraph and sentence has declined sharply. Reviewing Barrett Wendell's epochal commentary of 1890 in its reincarnation of 1963, one marvels at the man's poise and aplomb; and inevitably, and perhaps a bit sadly, one also notes the anachronism:

> A paragraph is to a sentence what a sentence is to a word. The principles which govern the arrangement of sentences in paragraphs, then, are identical with those that govern the arrangement of words in sentences.[5]

Piecemeal inductive observations over the years have so far undermined this notion of the paragraph that it scarcely seems worthwhile to state it. Yet we have not broken cleanly with the past: to the contrary, many teachers and textbook writers, possibly a majority, finding some value still in sentence-based tradition, seem to be fearful of pitching the baby out with the bath. As recently as October 1965, Francis Christensen prefaced his trail-breaking "Generative Rhetoric of the Paragraph" with these words:

> My purpose here is. . . to show that the paragraph has, or may have, a struc-
> ture as definable and traceable as that of the sentence and that it can be
> analyzed in the same way. In fact . . . I have come to see that the parallel
> between sentence and paragraph is much closer than I suspected, so close,
> indeed, that as Josephine Miles put it (in a letter) the paragraph seems to
> be only a macro-sentence or meta-sentence.[6]

Christensen later went on to qualify his commentary with several of the
usual exceptions.

My intention here is not to criticize Professor Christensen's approach,
which strikes me as having great promise, but rather to argue for a concept
of the paragraph that will comprehend *all* paragraphs.

Let me begin by pointing out again that the sentence-based notion of
the paragraph was first introduced in words written, not in the skies, but at
the University of Aberdeen, and by a man of strong logical predisposition.
Secondly, when one explores its historical origin, one finds that the paragraph (from Gr. *para*, beside, + *graphos*, mark) began as a punctuation
device, a symbol placed in the margin to indicate a noteworthy break in the
flow of discourse; only later did the word come to signify the stretch of language between breaks. The original notion persists in our transitive verb *to
paragraph*.

Thus paragraph structure precedes, in a certain very vital sense, the
indentation that marks its physical limit; and rhetoric's proper task is to
understand why indentations occur when they do, rather than to devise
some Procrustean formula for governing the behavior of sentences between
breaks, and to insist upon applying it over and over again throughout all
written discourse. What we need is a philosophy of paragraph punctuation,
a flexible, open-ended *discourse-centered* rhetoric of the paragraph.

What, then, may be the aspects or qualities of discourse that writers recognize when they indent? The late nineteenth century visualized discourse
as a series of horizontal "leaps and pauses," a stream that "shoots toward
some point of interest, eddies about it for a moment, then hurries on to
another," with the paragraph indentations indicating successive conceptual
leaps and lingerings.[7] As Edwin Lewis observed in 1894, the writer

> conceives his paragraph topic before he develops it, though of course in
> the process of development the associations of the symbols used may lead
> him afield. He thinks, so to speak, in successive nebulous masses, perceiv-
> ing in each a luminous centre before he analyses the whole.[8]

This horizontal image still appears regularly in textbooks, but a second
image now has been added. In 1946 the late Wendell Johnson pointed out

that when the mind is "interested," attention fluctuates vertically, up and down the abstraction ladder:

> If you will observe carefully the speakers you find to be interesting, you are very likely to find that they play, as it were, up and down the levels of abstraction quite as a harpist plays up and down the strings of her harp.. . . . the speaker who remains too long on the same general level of abstraction offends our evaluative processes — no matter what his subject may be.[9]

In 1964, John Lord applied Johnson's insight to prose analysis, visualizing good writing as "a constant weaving up and down between the concrete and the abstract, as well as a constant forward movement from a beginning through a middle to an end."[10]

The vertical image ties in nicely with traditional ideas of paragraph structure. Topic sentences coincide with certain emphasized peaks of abstraction. The most common methods of "amplification" — clarification of the topic by use of definition, analogy, comparison, or contrast; presentation of causes or logical proof; citation of examples, instances, and illustrations; accumulation of supporting details — all these methods tend strongly toward lower-level statement. The two main types of "movement" — variously spoken of as loose and periodic, deductive and inductive, regressive and progressive, and (perhaps most satisfactorily) as analytic and synthetic — refer simply to the upward or downward thrust of attention, toward or away from the abstract topic. Our thought-movement normally is synthetic, and moves upward from the particulars of experience to the high-level generalities of conceptual thought. The particulars "generate" the abstraction. When we write, however, we usually proceed by analysis, first stating the available generality, which stands first in consciousness, and then recovering or discovering ("generating") a sufficient bulk of particulars to support it. Extended synthetic movement accordingly is fairly uncommon in written discourse.

But neither horizontal leaps nor the vertical seesaw obligates a writer to indent. Both types of movement exist at all levels of discourse, in units smaller than the sentence and larger than the paragraph. Indentation frequently does mark major horizontal and vertical phases (which tend to coincide), but sometimes other considerations take precedence.

Like music, writing is a complex sequence of events in time. Subordinate patterns occur within the sequence, many of them interpenetrating and partly coinciding with others. The writer has at his disposal various punctuation devices with which he can tag and call attention to some of them. The paragraph break is only one such device, the most emphatic.

About all we can usefully say of *all* paragraphs at present is that their authors have marked them off for special consideration as *stadia of discourse*, in preference to other stadia, other patterns, in the same material. "At this point," the writer tells us with his indentation, "a major stadium of discourse has just been completed. Rest for a moment, recollect and consider, before the next begins." But his decision to indent may be taken for any one (or more) of at least half a dozen different reasons.

The great majority of stadia of course are logical, whatever else they may be, but thought-movement submits to very flexible partitioning; hence the size of a given logical paragraph frequently reflects secondary influences. Often the physical aspect of the paragraph must be controlled, especially in publications using narrow-column format. The reader must not be put off unnecessarily by paragraphs that seem overly bulky, and therefore indigestible, or by a long succession of thin, apparently anemic units. On the other hand, the need for rhetorical emphasis may dictate either bulk treatment or isolation of a short stadium in a paragraph of its own, and an impulse to vary paragraph length purely for variety's sake may have the same effect. To a lesser degree, patterns of prose rhythm may call for indentation;[11] so, too, may abrupt shifts in tone or strictly formal considerations, as when paragraphs are paired off for contrast or comparison or knit into some larger pattern involving paragraphs as units.

Thus the paragraph can be described very roughly as an autochthonous pattern in prose discourse, identified originally by application of logical, physical, rhythmical, tonal, formal, and other rhetorical criteria, set off from adjacent patterns by indentations, and commended thereby to the reader as a noteworthy stadium of discourse. Though all good paragraphs are distinct stadia, not all stadia are paragraphs. Many must always exist merely as emergent possibilities, potential paragraphs (as well as smaller units) dissolved in the flow of discourse. Paragraph structure is part and parcel of the structure of the discourse as a whole; a given stadium becomes a paragraph not by virtue of its structure but because the writer elects to indent, his indentation functioning, as does all punctuation, as a gloss upon the overall literary process under way at that point. Paragraphs are not composed; they are discovered. To compose is to create; to indent is to interpret. Accordingly, the qualities of the paragraph can no more be grasped through normative statement than can the qualities of discourse.

This conclusion is not wholly negative, of course. It denies only that the paragraph can be wrapped up conclusively in a tight deductive formula, and implies, positively, that inductive study of the art of paragraphing has an immense neglected potential. While intent upon determining what The Paragraph is, we have very largely failed to appreciate what real paragraphs are.

To test this contention, let us contrast the traditional and discourse-centered views of a familiar paragraph sequence, Walter Pater's descant on "Style" (1888), an essay that recommends itself to our purpose for several special reasons. In it, Pater stresses what he calls "the necessity of *mind* in style," "that architectural conception of work, which foresees the end in the beginning and never loses sight of it," the underlying structural framework, which is "all-important, felt, or painfully missed, everywhere" (14.3).[12] One of the greatest pleasures in reading good prose, he tells us, lies in "the critical tracing out of that conscious artistic structure, and the pervading sense of it as we read" (15.16). Surely he must have foreseen that readers would judge his essay by its own forceful pronouncements; and he must therefore have paragraphed with unusual care.

But Pater always composed laboriously and deliberately. For thirty-five years, George Saintsbury admired his "wonderful perfection of craftsmanship,"[13] noting especially his sensitive control of prose rhythm and adroit management of the paragraph:

> Above all, no one, it must be repeated, has ever surpassed, and scarcely any one has ever equalled Mr. Pater in deliberate and successful architecture of the prose-paragraph—in what may, for the sake of a necessary difference, be called the scriptorial in opposition to the oratorical manner.[14]
>
> . . . it must always be remembered that the care of the paragraph was one of Mr. Pater's first and greatest anxieties; when I remarked on it [in 1876, apropos of Pater's *Renaissance*], . . . he wrote to me expressing special gratification, and acknowledging that it had been one of his principal objects.[15]

Such a conscious, calculated devotion to paragraph technique warrants close inspection.

But "Style" holds particular interest for us because of its structural subtlety and flexibility. As A. C. Benson observed, "the bones do not show; not only does the rounded flesh conceal them, but they are still further disguised into a species of pontifical splendour by a rich and stiff embroidered robe of language."[16] The great variety in paragraph "shape" can be inferred from the following statistics. Though Pater's average paragraph in this essay is quite long (271 words), individual paragraphs range from 24 to 793 words, and the totals of sentences per paragraph range from one to 18. Two paragraphs have fewer than 100 words; 11 contain between 100 and 200 words; 9 contain between 200 and 300; and 9 run to more than 300. This breakdown corresponds almost exactly to Edwin Lewis's conclusions regarding English prose in general.[17]

The traditional analysis of the first three paragraphs would view each block of writing individually, describing P1 and P2 as introductory paragraphs, informally assembled, lacking clear-cut central ideas and topic sentences, serving mainly to carry the reader in to P3, a single directive statement which lays out the ground to be covered in the sequel and initiates the essay proper. P3 reads as follows:

> Dismissing then, under sanction of Wordsworth, that harsher opposition of poetry to prose, as savouring in fact of the arbitrary psychology of the last century, and with it the prejudice that there can be but one only beauty of prose style, I propose here to point out certain qualities of all literature as a fine art, which, if they apply to the literature of fact, apply still more to the literature of the imaginative sense of fact, while they apply indifferently to verse and prose, so far as either is really imaginative—certain conditions of true art in both alike, which conditions may also contain in them the secret of the proper discrimination and guardianship of the peculiar excellences of either.

Despite its complexity, this paragraph plainly leans upon the previous discussion for its full implication. Wordsworth's "sanction" has just been examined at the close of P2; the prejudiced claim that there can be but "one only beauty" of prose style refers to earlier comments about Dryden's notions of prose (2.3) and overly narrow conceptions of literature in general (P1 *passim*, esp. 1.4); the distinction between verse and prose recalls a major motif recurring throughout both preceding paragraphs; the opposition of "fact" and "imaginative sense of fact" draws upon the climactic concluding clause of 2.5; and the unobtrusive reference to "discrimination and guardianship" reaches all the way back to 1.1, where Pater relates "the sense of achieved distinctions" to "progress of mind." Each of these references imparts vital meaning to the language of P3. In short, although P3 does direct the reader's attention forward, it simultaneously reminds him of ground already covered. Its gaze is at least as much retrospective as prospective. And it has to be, in view of the complexity of the idea it conveys.

Yet P3 does more than summarize: it selects, relates, disposes, and assigns varying degrees of emphasis to previously discrete ideas. Thus the task of P1-2 is not merely to introduce but to lay a necessary basis for P3; and the thought-movement throughout the sequence, despite occasional analytic eddies, can readily be identified as synthetic. Indeed, with only minor revisions, P1-3 could be combined into one huge synthetic paragraph, with the present P3 serving as its topic sentence.

Since an opening paragraph as bulky as this would obviously repel the reader, Pater divides his exposition into three manageable portions, arranging them in descending order of size as he moves toward his climax in P3. (The word count is 418-251-121; each succeeding unit contains roughly half as many words as its predecessor.) The pace is slow and even, transitions smooth. Although he regularly provides topic statements elsewhere, he omits them in P1 and P2—a further indication that he thinks of P1-3 as a single logical stadium. In a synthetic passage, the progression of ideas should unfold without interruption; otherwise it may not always be clear whether the writer is still approaching his as yet unstated conclusion, or making a new "leap." A topic sentence in either P1 or P2 would introduce just such an element of risk. Also, a terminal topic signals the close of a period of mental concentration. At this point, having surveyed the argument as a whole, and having judged it, the reader no longer feels obliged to bear in mind all the particulars from which the conclusion was drawn. He tends to relax his grip upon lesser elements as he pushes on toward the next major proposition. This is precisely what Pater has to prevent from happening: his reader must retain all the material of P1 and P2 till he arrives at P3.

To summarize, when we examine P1-3 closely, we discover a single synthetic logical stadium broken into three paragraphs, no doubt for physical or editorial reasons. Topic sentences are omitted, quite possibly deliberately, with the result that the thought-movement proceeds without that particular threat to continuity. Formal criteria may account for the length of the separate paragraphs, which descend in size to the relatively short and emphatic P3.

None of these observations could be made by a strict traditional paragraph analysis.

The next passage of interest is P4-6. Pater opens P4 by commenting on the difficulty of discriminating "fact" from "sense of fact" in prose, and then develops this topic at length with illustrations, remarking at the close of 4.8 that historical writing enters the domain of "art proper" when it reflects the historian's sensibility and bias. Then (4.9) he digresses sharply, explaining that prose becomes "fine" art when it transcribes the writer's sense of fact and (second clause) "good" art when it renders the inner vision "truthfully." In 4.10 he drifts further from his topic, praising truth as a fundamental requirement of all good writing; and in 4.11 drifts yet again, defining beauty as a by-product of goodness (i.e., truthfulness), "the finer accommodation of speech to that vision within."

Here the paragraph ends, but the line of thought pushes on into P5 without interruption, and Pater seals the transition, oddly, by opening the new paragraph with a dash followed by what amounts to an appositive depending from the predicate of 4.11:

> —The transcript of his sense of fact rather than the fact, as being prefera-
> ble, pleasanter, more beautiful to the writer himself.

Pater often opens a new phase of argument in a grammatically subordinate element emphasized by placement in terminal position; the present usage is unusual only because the appositive has been detached from the base construction and moved to the head of a new paragraph.

Logically complete and satisfying in itself, P5 nevertheless participates in the long disquisition upon fidelity-to-inner vision beginning at 4.9. And P6 extends the commentary even further. Not till the final phrase of 6.2 does Pater relinquish the theme he first introduced ostensibly to clarify the short prepositional phrase at the end of 4.8.

How shall we describe what happens in 4.9-6.2? The digression at the end of P4 is too long to be taken as a mildly irrelevant conclusion. Does it not then constitute a serious break in paragraph unity? Traditionalist critics doubtless would say it did. They might further object, on the same ground, to the weight of introductory material concentrated in 6.1-2, and probably would view the sequence 4.9-6.2 as a single unified paragraph which Pater has sadly misconceived.

Can Pater be defended? He can, I think, if we set aside our preconceptions and observe the general flow of discourse. A single logical stadium does of course exist, beginning at 4.9. It could easily be presented as a single analytic paragraph based on 4.9, conveying material which now requires 325 words. This would make a very substantial block of writing, but Pater's paragraphs frequently run to more than 300 words; so mere physical length cannot account for his decision to indent the way he has.

We can appreciate his strategy, once we note how deficient the whole passage is in "vertical" movement. His sole concern here is to clarify his notion of art, and this involves statement of four ideas: fact vs. sense of fact as the criterion for separating "fine" from "merely serviceable" art; adherence to inward truth as the criterion for recognizing "good" art; goodness in art as the foundation of beauty; and the inevitability of pleasure to be found in artistic self-expression. All these ideas are highly general and abstract, and he develops them mainly by repetition, a method which tends to maintain the same abstraction level as the topic. The passage consequently proceeds on a high abstraction plateau, and would surely risk boring the reader if it continued to its end without interruption.

Pater greatly reduces this hazard by dividing his material. Also, having worked out his four-point commentary in 4.9-5.1, he manages to repeat it in three separated contexts between 5.2 and 6.2, hammering his theses home not only by iteration but also by placement in terminal position, by isolation in a short paragraph, and by placement in initial position. He displays his argument much more forcefully in this way than he could have in a standard analytic paragraph. Further, if he had written such a paragraph, he probably would have felt obliged either to reduce the abstract exposition, thereby weakening its impact, or to introduce lower-level material—illustrations, causal statements, and the like—in order to generate interest.

Pater obviously found neither option appealing: to curtail treatment would have been to rob crucial ideas of emphasis they deserved—notably his doctrine of truth; to amplify them further, as by definition or illustration, would have been to raise problems he did not wish to handle, perhaps because of lack of space, perhaps because he sensed he could not handle them.[18]

Accordingly, rhetorical criteria in P4-6 take precedence over logical, the risk of dead-level dullness is reduced by partitioning, and a stadium of thought is allowed to straddle two paragraph breaks, exercising squatter's rights in paragraphs centered on other topics—to the dismay of traditionalist critics who perceive the massive breach of unity in P4, yet cannot honestly (I submit) find fault with it as they read.

Plainly, a stadium can be recognized as such without being punctuated as a paragraph. We have seen how Pater divides a stadium into separate paragraphs, and distributes portions of a divided stadium across paragraph breaks. He also does just the opposite, combines smaller stadia into a single paragraph. After a long series of routine analytic paragraphs dealing with diction and "contingent ornamentation" (P7-13), he broaches the general idea of structure in a synthetic transitional paragraph (P14), and then elaborates at great length in P15. The sequence 15.3-6 develops the topic by iteration; 15.7-8 concentrates on the structure of sentences; 15.9-10 deals with spontaneous structural elaborations, good and bad; 15.11-13 handles elaborations occurring after the main structure of a unit is complete; and 15.14-17 comments on the reader's pleasure in appreciating structure. Here, as elsewhere, Pater frequently advances in short, almost imperceptible steps taken in contexts otherwise devoted to illustration and repetition of previous points. His horizontal leaps, such as they are, often occur in minor subordinate structures within sentences, rather than across hiatuses between sentences, so that when a topic finally is granted full predication, it seems but an amplified echo. Heaping one "long-contending, victoriously intricate" sentence upon another, he pushes P15 to a length of 793 words and ends with the substance of a small essay, punctuated as a single paragraph.

Coherence, this passage undeniably possesses, but is it unified? Does it focus on one topic? Retracing the flow of ideas, we can argue with some difficulty that all this material is generated by 15.1-2. Or can we? Traditional criticism would point out that the paragraph moves in phases and could easily be broken at 15.7, 15.9, 15.10, 15.11, and 15.15, each resulting unit having its own topic sentence. As it is, we find several sub-topics, or possibly one "divided" topic, six identifiable stadia, all drawn into one union. The integrity of this union, assessed by the usual logical standards, is certainly open to question; to defend it on traditional grounds, we probably would have to abandon 15.1-2 as topic and invoke a ridiculously broad "implied" topic.

All the same, the paragraph reads well enough. And to mount a theoretical defense, we need only recognize that other legitimate criteria here have overridden the tug of logic. Obviously Pater wants to present his notion of structure as a single idea, regardless of its ramifications. Division of components would involve extensive expansion of this phase of the essay (cf. P4-6). By combining components, he avoids having to elaborate and at the same time stresses the whole by bulk treatment. However, I suspect that formal reasons also figured in the decision: P15 (793 words) and P16 (583 words) are by far the heaviest paragraphs in the essay,[19] and they deal with paired concepts, "mind" and "soul" in style. By cumulating the substance of P15 into one impressive mass, and juxtaposing it to the massive P16, he interprets the two concepts visually as a pair.

By contrast, the long stadium that follows, on Flaubert and the doctrine of the perfect word (P17-29), is far too heavy for block presentation. So he breaks it down into smaller stadia paragraphed in routine analytic fashion.

For the most part, of course, Pater's stadia follow the normal analytic pattern, whether or not they are set off as paragraphs. Synthesis is reserved for special situations. In P1-3 synthesis not only offers the advantages mentioned above but provides a gentle, gradual introit that accords well with his quiet tone and generally relaxed manner. In P14, where the movement sets up a definite contrast with the foregoing analytic sequence, it heralds an important phase of argument. At the conclusion of the essay (in P31), it allows him to end on a heavy note of emphasis.[20]

But the penultimate P30 is synthetic, too—the only synthetic paragraph in the essay that is not clearly an introduction or a conclusion. One wonders why, inevitably, for Pater rarely does anything without reason, yet the reason here is hard to find. I can offer only this suggestion: that P30 really is the conclusion of the essay, and was conceived and written as such originally. It rounds out the argument beautifully, summing up the essay's central thesis in its final sentence, and has the characteristic force and rhythmic impact of a conclusion. Upon reviewing what he had written, however, if not before, Pater saw that his literary theory lay wide open to the same moralistic objections that had led him to withdraw the famous "Conclusion" to the *Renaissance* (1873) in its second edition (1877). Admittedly, he had recently restored a slightly modified version of the "Conclusion" in the third edition (1888), but he may very well have felt the present essay would revive old criticisms.

So in P31, having brought his commentary to a very satisfying close, he resumes exposition. He has shown how good art is achieved, he now informs us, but "great" art is something else. Here the criterion is matter, substance, not truth or form. To be great, a work of art must be more than good; it must also have "something of the soul of humanity in it," must increase the sum of human happiness, enlarge the sympathies, ennoble, fortify, redeem . . . and find "its logical architectural place in the great structure of human life" (31.4).

With these words, having barely introduced a major new idea which places the whole foregoing discussion in a new perspective, Pater abruptly ends. Even so sympathetic a reader as Saintsbury objects to the "appearance of 'hedging'" in P31, the sudden return to subject matter, which "as easily rememberable and with a virtuous high sound in it, appears to have greatly comforted some good but not great souls."[21] Pater's own judgment upon his paragraph perhaps can be inferred from his willingness to let its synthetic predecessor stand unrevised: P31 is distinct and supernumerary, both logically and structurally.

The foregoing observations in no way exhaust the possibilities of discourse-centered paragraph analysis. I have said nothing of tonal fluctuation, which does not strike me as being particularly significant in this essay, nor of rhythm, which is definitely significant but very hard to describe. Nor have I noted adequately the methods used to launch topic ideas, or the rise and fall of the abstraction level, or the use of ellipsis and the dash to tighten transitions between stadia, or Pater's unusual penchant for underplaying important ideas grammatically while stressing them rhetorically.

Inductive analysis of Pater's "Style" shows us something of what a paragraph *can* be, not what it must be; another writer, or another essay by the same writer, would reveal different possibilities, further precedents. I have been concerned mainly to demonstrate that the paragraph is just one of several kinds of stadia, and that the logical partitioning of complex discourse into paragraphs can occur at so many junctures that additional non-logical criteria often have to be invoked to account for a given decision to indent.

To insist that logic establish every indentation is to ignore several of the prime resources of good prose—which elevate and help transmute it from a merely serviceable "good round-hand" (1.3) into fine art.

NOTES

1. See my "Alexander Bain and the Rise of the Organic Paragraph," *Quarterly Journal of Speech*, LI (December 1965), 399–408.

2. James McConkey, *The Structure of Prose* (New York, 1963), p. 4.

3. Cleanth Brooks and Robert Penn Warren, *Modern Rhetoric* (2nd ed; New York, 1958), pp. 269–270.

4. Leo Rockas, *Modes of Rhetoric* (New York, 1964), p. 6.

5. Barrett Wendell, *English Composition* (New York, 1963), p. viii.

6. Francis Christensen, "A Generative Rhetoric of the Paragraph," *College Composition and Communication*, XVI (October 1965), 144.

7. Fred N. Scott and Joseph V. Denney, *Paragraph-Writing* (Ann Arbor, 1891), p. 71.

8. Edwin Herbert Lewis, *The History of the English Paragraph* (Chicago, 1894), p. 43.

9. Wendell Johnson, *People in Quandaries: The Semantics of Personal Adjustment* (New York, 1946), pp. 277–278. For a partial adumbration of this idea, see the "Introduction" to Lane Cooper's translation of *The Rhetoric of Aristotle* (New York, 1932), pp. xxxiv–xxxv.

10. John B. Lord, *The Paragraph: Structure and Style* (New York, 1964), p. 73.

11. Herbert Read, *English Prose Style* (Rev. ed; New York, 1952), pp. 58–65.

12. To facilitate reference to Pater, I shall use numbers to specify a given sentence (14.3 = fourteenth paragraph, third sentence) and a capital P to indicate "paragraph" (P4-6 = paragraphs four through six, inclusive).

13. George Saintsbury, *A History of Nineteenth Century Literature* (New York, 1896), p. 401.

14. *Ibid.*, p. 400.

15. George Saintsbury, *A History of English Prose Rhythm* (London, 1912), p. 421.

16. A. C. Benson, *Walter Pater* (New York, 1911), pp. 147–148.

17. Of 73 representative English prose writers studied by Lewis (p. 171), 27 average between 100 and 200 words per paragraph, 25 average between 200 and 300, and 21 average either below 100 or above 300, presumably the latter. In establishing the Pater word-counts, I have included quoted material.

18. See Edmund Chandler, "Pater on Style: An Examination of the Essay on 'Style' and the Textual History of 'Marius the Epicurean,'" *Anglistica*, XI (Copenhagen, 1958), pp. 95–99.

19. With the exception of P17 (573 words). P17 appears to be much lighter, however, since more than half of it consists of an inset block quotation.

20. It can easily be argued that P31 is analytic, comprising a definition (31.1) followed by illustrations and expanded repetitions of the same idea (31.2-4). I classify the paragraph as synthetic because 31.1-3 seems to me to build toward and to reach a climax in 31.4, which is by far the fullest and most emphatic of the four statements.

21. George Saintsbury, *A History of English Criticism* (New York, 1911), p. 501.

The Frequency and Placement of Topic Sentences in Expository Prose

RICHARD BRADDOCK

Most textbooks on English composition have presented some concerted treatment of topic sentences, long hailed as means of organizing a writer's ideas and clarifying them for the reader. In the most popular composition textbook of the nineteenth century, for example, Alexander Bain recognized that topic sentences may come at the end of a descriptive or introductory paragraph, but he emphasized that expository paragraphs have topic sentences and that they usually come at the beginnings of paragraphs:

> 19. The opening sentence, unless obviously preparatory, is expected to indicate the scope of the paragraph. . . . This rule is most directly applicable to expository style, where, indeed, it is almost essential. (Bain, 1890, p. 108)

In one of the more popular composition textbooks of the present, Gorrell and Laird present a similar statement about topic sentences—a statement which is paralleled in many other textbooks these days:

> Topic sentences may appear anywhere, or even be omitted. . . . but most modern, carefully constructed prose rests on standard paragraphs, most of which have topic sentences to open them.

And of 15 items on "Paragraph Patterns" in a commercial test of "writing," three involve the identification of topic sentences in brief paragraphs. In

Reprinted from *Research in the Teaching of English* 8.3 (Winter 1974): 287–302. Used with permission.

each of the three, the correct answer is the first sentence in the paragraph (*Basic Skills,* 1970).

How much basis is there for us to make such statements to students or to base testing on the truth of them? To clarify the matter, I studied the paragraphs in representative contemporary professional writing, seeking the answers to these two questions:

1. What proportion of the paragraphs contain topic sentences?
2. Where in the paragraphs do the topic sentences occur?

PROCEDURE

As a body of expository material representing contemporary professional writing, I used the corpus of 25 complete essays in American English selected by Margaret Ashida, using random procedures, from 420 articles published from January, 1964, through March, 1965, in *The Atlantic, Harper's, The New Yorker, The Reporter,* and *The Saturday Review.* Ashida indicated possible uses of the corpus:

> . . . this corpus could be used for a wealth of investigations by students, teachers, and research scholars—for anything from a relatively superficial examination of controversial matters of usage, to the exploration of the deep (and equally controversial) questions being raised by theoreticians of the new rhetorics. Because the sample has its own built-in validity, it represents a *common* corpus for use by many different scholars—something we desperately need in rhetorical research. . . . (Ashida, 1968, pp. 14–23)

Paragraphs

Working one-by-one with zerographic copies of the 25 articles,[1] I numbered each paragraph from the first paragraph of the essay to the last. For this study, a paragraph was what we normally take to be one in printed material—a portion of discourse consisting of one or more sentences, the first line of type of which is preceded by more interlinear space than is otherwise found between lines in the text and the first sentence of which begins either with an indentation or with an unindented large initial capital.

Headnotes and footnotes were not counted as parts of the text for this study and hence were not numbered and analyzed. A problem appeared when one article included an insert, consisting of a diagram and some ten sentences of explanation, which was crucial to an understanding of the text proper.[2] This insert arbitrarily was not counted as a paragraph in the article. In those few essays in which dialog was quoted, each separately indented paragraph was counted as a paragraph, even though it consisted in one case merely of one four-word sentence (Taper, p. 138).

T-units

After numbering the paragraphs in an essay, I proceeded to insert a pen-cilled slash mark after each T-unit in each paragraph and to write the total number of T-units at the end of each paragraph.

The T-unit, or "minimal terminable unit," is a term devised by Kellogg Hunt to describe the "shortest grammatically allowable sentences into which . . . [writing can] be segmented" (Hunt, 1965, pp. 20–21). In other words, consideration of the T-units of writing permits the researcher to use a rather standard conception of a sentence, setting aside the differences occurring between writers when they use different styles of punctuation. A T-unit, then, "includes one main clause plus all the subordinate clauses attached to or embedded within it. . . ." (Hunt, p. 141). Hunt wrote that an independent clause beginning with "and" or "but" is a T-unit, but I also included "or," "for," and "so" to complete what I take to be the coordinat-ing conjunctions in modern usage.

Although in the vast majority of cases there was no difficulty knowing where to indicate the end of a T-unit, several problems did arise. Take, for instance, the following sentence:

> The Depression destroyed the coalfield's prosperity, but the Second World War revived it, and for a few years the boom returned and the miner was again a useful and honored citizen. (Caudill, p. 49)

Obviously, one T-unit ends with "prosperity" and another with "revived it," but is what follows "revived it" one T-unit or two? I made the judgment that "for a few years" was an integral part of both clauses following it and that "and for a few years the boom returned and the miner was again a useful and honored citizen" was one T-unit. Similarly, I counted the following sen-tence as one T-unit, not two, judging the intent of the first clause in the speech of the Protocol man to be subordinate, as if he had said "If you put an ambassador in prison":

> For another, as a Protocol man said recently, "You put an ambassador in prison and you can't negotiate with him, which is what he's supposed to be here for." (Kahn, p. 75)

In marking off T-units, a person must be prepared for occasional embedding. Sometimes a writer uses parentheses to help accomplish the embedding:

> Gibbs & Cox (Daniel H. Cox was a famous yacht designer who joined the firm in 1929, retired in 1943, and subsequently died) is the largest private ship-designing firm in the world. (Sargeant, p. 49)

That sentence, of course, has one T-unit embedded within one other. In the following example, dashes enclose two T-units embedded within another, and the entire sentence consists of four T-units:

> "They're condescending, supercilious bastards, but when the 'United States' broke all the transatlantic records—it still holds them, and it went into service in 1952—they had to come down a peg." (Sargeant, p. 50)

But embedding does not prove to be a problem in determining what is and what is not a T-unit. With the exception of perhaps a dozen other problems in the thousands of sentences considered in the 25 essays, marking off and counting the T-units was a fairly mechanical operation.

Topic Sentences

The next problem was to decide which T-unit, if any, constituted a topic sentence in each paragraph. After several frustrating attempts merely to underline the appropriate T-unit where it occurred, I realized that the notion of what a topic sentence is, is not at all clear.

Consultation of composition textbooks provided no simple solution of the problem. Gorrell and Laird, for example, offered this definition of a topic sentence:

> Most paragraphs focus on a central idea or unifying device expressed in topical material. Occasionally this topical material is complex, involving more than one sentence and some subtopics; sometimes it carries over from a previous paragraph and is assumed to be understood or is referred to briefly; but usually it simply takes the form of a sentence, sometimes amplified or made more specific in a sentence or two following it. This topic sentence may appear at the end of the paragraph as a kind of summary or somewhere within the paragraph, but most frequently it opens the paragraph or follows an opening introduction or transition. (Gorrell and Laird, p. 25)

The authors further clarify their definition (pp. 25–26) by stating that a topic sentence has three main functions: (1) to provide transition, (2) to suggest the organization of the paragraph, (3) to present a topic, either by naming or introducing a subject or by presenting a proposition or thesis for discussion. In the next several pages, the authors consider various types of "topic sentences as propositions" (or theses) and the problems in writing them with precision.

From my preliminary attempts to identify topic sentences in paragraphs, I could see the truth of a complex definition like Gorrell and Laird's. But such a comprehensive definition presents problems. Sometimes a paragraph opens with a sentence which we could all agree is transitional but which does not reveal much about the content of the paragraph. The second sentence may name the topic of the paragraph but not make a statement about it. The actual thesis of the paragraph may be stated explicitly in a succeeding sentence or in several sentences, or it may merely be inferred from what follows, even though it is never stated explicitly. In such a paragraph, which is the topic sentence—the first, second, a succeeding sentence, perhaps even all of them? Many of the sentences seem to fit the definition. An all-embracing definition does not seem helpful to me in deciding which sentence can be named the topic sentence.

Furthermore, as Paul Rodgers demonstrated (1966), paragraphing does not always correspond to a reader's perceived organization of ideas. Sometimes a paragraph presents an illustration of the thesis of the preceding paragraph. The second paragraph thus extends the previous paragraph, and the paragraph indentation seems quite arbitrary. Or sometimes a thesis is stated in a one-sentence paragraph and the following paragraph explains that thesis without restating it. In such situations, one cannot simply identify a topic sentence in each paragraph.

It seemed to me that the best test of topic sentences is the test a careful reader might make—the test offered when one constructs a sentence outline of the major points of an essay, drawing the sentences insofar as possible from the sentences the author has written. In constructing a sentence outline, one usually omits transitional and illustrative statements and concentrates on the theses themselves. Consequently, I decided to prepare a sentence outline of each of the 25 essays and *then* determine which paragraphs had topic sentences and where in the paragraphs they occurred.

Outlines

From the beginning of the first one, I was aware of the serious problems in constructing a sentence outline to study the organization of another person's writing. To what degree would I tend to impose on an essay my own inter-pretation of what was written? Does it do violence to discursive writing to cast it into the form of a sentence outline, trying to make the outline under-standable by itself when the essay includes details of thought and qualities of style omitted in the process? Would the paragraphing and other typographi-cal features of the edited essay distract me from the ideas and structure of the written essay? Of course I would try to preserve the author's intent in all of these matters, but what I actually did would be so much a matter of judg-ment that I should expose my outlines for the criticism of others, permitting comparison to the original articles. Moreover, the outlines might be helpful to other investigators who would like to use them without going to the exten-sive effort of preparing their own. Although it is impractical to include the outlines here, I will make them available to others for the cost of the copying.

In outlining an article, I read it through in sections of a number of para-graphs which seemed to be related, underlining topic sentences where I could find them and constructing topic sentences where they were not explicit in the article. In constructing a topic sentence, I tried to include phrases from the original text as much as possible. Whatever sentences, phrases, or key words I did use from the original I was careful to enclose in quotation marks, indicating by ellipsis marks all omissions and by brackets all of my own insertions. Opposite each entry in the outline I indicated the number of the paragraph and T-unit of each quotation used. Thus the nota-tion 20:2,3, and 4 indicates that quoted portions of the outline entry were taken from the second, third, and fourth T-units of the twentieth paragraph in the essay. On a few occasions where I took an idea from a paragraph but it did not seem possible to cast it in the author's original words at all, I put the paragraph number in parentheses to indicate that. But I tried to use the author's words as much as I could, even, in some cases, where it yielded a somewhat unwieldy entry in the outline.

To illustrate the approach, let me offer in Figure 1 the opening para-graphs from the first article in the corpus, indicating the corresponding entries in the outline.

Notice the different types of outline entries necessitated by the various kinds of paragraphs the author writes. Topic Sentence B is an example of what I would call a *simple topic sentence*, one which is quoted entirely or almost entirely from one T-unit in the passage, wherever that T-unit occurs. (Incidentally, the last sentence in Paragraph 2 is not reflected in Topic Sen-tence B because that last sentence is an early foreshadowing of the main idea of the entire article.)

Figure 1 Sample paragraphs and outline entries.

Opening Paragraphs from Drew, p. 33	Excerpt from Outline	
1. Among the news items given out to a shocked nation following the assassination of President Kennedy was the fact that Lee Harvey Oswald had purchased his weapon, a 6.5-mm Italian carbine, from a Chicago mail-order house under an assumed name. The rifle was sent, no questions asked, to one "A. Hidell," in care of a post-office box in Dallas. The transaction was routine in the mail-order trade; about one million guns are sold the same way each year.	I. "By the ordinary rules of the game, the events in Dallas should have ensured prompt enactment. . . ." of gun control legislation by Congress.	2:2
	A. "President Kennedy" had recently been shot with one of the "one million guns . . . sold . . . each year" through "the mail-order business in guns."	1:1,3,4
2. At the same time, a bill was pending in Congress to tighten regulation of the rapidly expanding mail-order business in guns. By the ordinary rules of the game, the events in Dallas should have ensured prompt enactment, just as the news of Thalidomide-deformed babies had provided the long-needed impetus for passage of stricter drug regulations in 1962. But Congress did not act—a testimonial to the deadly aim of the shotting lobby.	B. "At the same time, a bill was pending in Congress to tighten regulation of the rapidly expanding mail-order business in guns."	2:1
3. Two existing statutes presumably deal with the gun traffic. Both were passed in reaction to the gangsterism of the prohibition era. But, because of limited coverage, problems of proof, and various other quirks, they have had a negligible impact on the increasing gun traffic.	C. "Two existing statutes. . . . [had] a negligible impact on the increasing gun traffic."	3:1,3
4. The investigation of the mail-order traffic in guns began in 1961 under the auspices of the Juvenile Delinquency subcommittee. . . .		

Topic Sentence C is a fairly common type, one in which the topic sentence seems to begin in one T-unit but is completed in a later T-unit. In Paragraph 3, the first sentence does not make a specific enough statement about the two existing statutes to serve as a complete topic sentence, even though it reveals the subject of the paragraph. One must go to the third sentence to find the predicate for the topic sentence. Let us term this type a *delayed-completion topic sentence*. Not all delayed-completion topic sentences stem from separated subjects and predicates, though. Sometimes the two sentences present a question and then an answer (Fischer, 18: 1,2), a negative followed by a positive (Fischer, 38: 1,2), or metaphoric language subsequently explained by straight language (Drucker, 8: 1,2). The T-units from which a delayed-completion topic sentence is drawn are not always adjoining. In one instance, I discovered them separated by three T-units (Collado, 29: 1,2,6); in another, in adjoining paragraphs (Caudill, 17: 2 and 18: 1); in still another, nine paragraphs apart (Lear, 1: 1,2 and 10: 1).

Notice that Topic Sentence A is an example of a statement assembled by quotations from throughout the paragraph. The first sentence in Paragraph 1 cannot properly be considered the topic sentence: it includes such phrases as "the news item" and "a shocked nation" and such details as the name of the assassin, the size and make of the carbine, and the location of the mail order house—such matters as are not essential to the topic sentence; and it omits such a detail as the scope of the problem—"one million guns . . . sold . . . each year"—which helps convey the idea in Statement I. To ease later reference to this type of topic sentence, let us call it an *assembled topic sentence*.

Finally, there is what we might call an *inferred topic sentence*, one which the reader thinks the writer has implied even though the reader cannot construct it by quoting phrases from the original passage. Though the paragraph in Figure 2 comes out of context—from an article on cutting the costs of medical care—it may still be clear why the corresponding topic sentence had to be inferred.

As I was determining what were the topic sentences of an article, I was also keeping an eye out for what we might call the *major topic sentences* of the larger stadia of discourses. That is, a series of topic sentences all added up to a major topic sentence; a group of paragraphs all added up to what William Irmscher (1972) calls a "paragraph bloc" within the entire article. A major topic sentence (designated with a Roman numeral) might head as few as two topic sentences (designated with capital letters) in the outline or as many as 12 topic sentences (in the Kahn outline) or 15 (the most, in the Mumford outline). On the other hand, it was frequently apparent that the main idea of a paragraph was really a subpoint of the main idea of another

Figure 2 Sample of paragraph yielding inferred topic sentence.

Paragraph from Saunders, p. 24	Excerpt from Outline
Fortunately most ailments do not require such elaborate treatment. Pills cost a good deal less but even they are no small item in the medical bill. From 1929 to 1956 prescription sales climbed from $140 million to $1,466 million a year, and the average price per prescription rose from 85 cents to $2.62. Citing the findings of the Kefauver Committee, Professor Harris makes a strong case for more—and more stringent—regulation of the pharmaceutical industry by the government.	Prescription drug costs have risen.

paragraph. Let us call these *subtopic sentences*. As few as two and as many as seven subtopic sentences (in the Taper outline) were headed by a topic sentence. Sometimes a major topic sentence or a subtopic sentence was simply stated in a single T-unit, but sometimes it had to be assembled, sometimes inferred. Some occurred as delayed-completion topic sentences.

After completing the rest of the outline, I arrived at the main idea (the thesis) or, in the case of the Kahn and Sargeant articles (both *New Yorker* "Profiles"), the purpose. And as with the various types of topic sentences, I drew quoted phrases from the article to construct the statement of the main idea whenever possible, but with one exception—if a term or phrase occurred frequently in the article, I would not enclose it in quotations and note its location unless it seemed to me to have been put by the author in a particular place or signalled in a particular way to suggest that he was at that time intentionally indicating to readers the nature of his main idea.

After all of the outlines were completed, I went back through each one, classifying each topic sentence as one of the four types and checking the outline against the text of the original essay.

FINDINGS

A tabulation of the frequency of each type of topic sentence for each of the 25 essays is presented in Table 1. It should not escape the reader that the number of topic sentences in an outline does not correspond directly to the number of paragraphs in its essay. Sometimes a major topic sentence and a topic sentence occurred in the same paragraph, and sometimes several

Table 1 Frequency of types of topic sentences in each of the 25 essays.

Essay No.	Author	Magazine	Main Idea	Simple			Del-comp.			Assembled			Inferred			Total TS's	Total Pars.
				MTS	TS	STS	MTS	TS	STS	MTS	TS	STS	MTS	TS	STS		
1	Drew	*Reporter*	Inf.	3	8	2	0	2	0	2	2	2	0	0	0	22	20
2	Tebbel	*Sat. Rev.*	D-C	1	5	2	1	2	0	0	5	2	1	2	1	23	25
3	Collado	*Sat. Rev.*	Sim.	3	8	3	1	1	2	0	4	9	0	1	0	33	50
4	Sargeant	*New York.*	Inf.	1	3	0	0	0	0	1	13	6	3	3	1	32	26
5	Chamberlain	*Atlantic*	Inf.	3	5	2	0	2	0	1	7	3	0	0	0	24	24
6	Daniels	*Sat. Rev.*	Sim.	3	8	0	0	0	0	0	6	0	0	0	0	18	27
7	E. Taylor	*Reporter*	Ass.	3	8	0	0	2	0	1	2	0	1	0	0	17	19
8	Kaufman	*Atlantic*	Ass.	2	13	5	1	2	7	1	0	2	0	1	0	35	41
9	Kahn	*New York.*	Inf.	0	7	0	0	7	0	1	25	0	4	5	0	44	45
10	Handlin	*Atlantic*	Sim.	4	11	0	0	1	0	1	4	0	0	0	0	28	35
11	Francois	*Reporter*	Ass.	2	5	0	0	0	0	0	3	0	0	1	0	13	13
12	Sanders	*Harper's*	Sim.	3	12	0	0	4	0	1	6	0	2	3	0	32	35
13	Lear	*Sat. Rev.*	Sim.	0	7	0	2	2	0	2	15	0	2	1	0	32	67
14	Lyons	*Atlantic*	Sim.	4	8	0	1	1	0	1	13	0	0	2	0	31	53
15	Ribman	*Harper's*	Inf.	5	20	0	0	4	0	1	12	0	1	0	0	44	56
16	Taper	*New York.*	Inf.	4	14	1	0	3	0	3	16	11	0	0	0	53	53
17	Fischer	*Harper's*	Inf.	4	11	9	0	3	1	1	9	3	1	1	0	41	42
18	Mumford	*New York.*	Inf.	2	17	0	0	2	0	3	27	0	2	0	0	54	49
19	Drucker	*Harper's*	Sim.	5	15	1	0	5	1	0	16	1	0	0	0	45	53
20	Caudill	*Atlantic*	Sim.	2	10	3	0	7	0	2	6	0	0	0	0	31	39
21	C. Taylor	*Atlantic*	Sim.	1	11	0	0	1	1	2	7	3	1	1	0	29	29
22	Cousins	*Sat. Rev.*	Sim.	1	2	0	1	2	1	1	3	0	0	0	0	11	13
23	Clark	*Harper's*	Sim.	4	8	0	1	0	0	0	4	1	0	0	0	21	26
24	Durrell	*Atlantic*	Sim.	1	5	0	1	0	0	1	6	0	0	0	0	15	13
25	Rule	*Atlantic*	Ass.	3	15	0	1	3	0	1	9	0	0	0	0	33	36
Totals			25	64	236	28	10	56	13	27	220	43	16	21	2	761	889

MTS = major topic sentence   TS = topic sentence   STS = subtopic sentence paragraphs seemed devoted to the presentation of one topic sentence. (The total number of topic sentences—including the main idea or purpose, major topic sentences, topic sentences, and subtopic sentences, if any—and the total number of paragraphs are given in the two columns at the right of the table.)

One conclusion from Table 1 is that the use made of the different types of topic sentences varies greatly from one writer to the next. Another is that the four articles taken from the *New Yorker* (each one a "Profile") tend to have yielded a higher proportion of assembled topic sentences than most of the other essays.

Frequency of Types of Topic Sentences

Table 2 combines the data for the 25 essays, indicating the distribution of topic sentences of each type. It is clear that less than half of all the topic sentences (45%) are simple topic sentences and almost as many (39%) are assembled. It is also apparent that—except for the statements of the main idea or purpose—the more of the text that the topic sentence covers, the more likely it is to be a simple topic sentence. That is, of the 117 major topic sentences, 55% were simple; of the 533 topic sentences, 44% were simple; of the 80 subtopic sentences, 33% were simple.

One might well maintain that simple and delayed-completion topic sentences are relatively explicit, that assembled and inferred topic sentences are relatively implicit. Pairing the types of topic sentences in that fashion, Table 2 reveals no great changes in the tendencies of the percentages. Slightly more than half of all the topic sentences (55%) are explicit, slightly less than half (45%) implicit. Again, with the exception of statements of

Table 2 Percentages of topic sentences of various types.

Types of Topic Sentences	No.	Sim.	D-C	Explicit	Ass.	Inf.	Implicit
				Percentages			
Main idea or purpose	25	48	4	52	16	32	48
Major topic sentences	117	55	9	63	23	14	37
Topic sentences	533	44	11	55	41	4	45
Subtopic sentences	86	33	15	48	50	2	52
All types together	761	45	11	55	39	6	45

main idea and purpose, the more of the text which the topic sentence covers, the more likely it is to be explicit.

If what the composition textbooks refer to as "the topic sentence" is the same thing as this study terms the simple topic sentence, it is apparent that claims about its frequency should be more cautious. It just is not true that most expository paragraphs have topic sentences in that sense. Even when simple and delayed-completion topic sentences are combined into the category "explicit topic sentences"—a broader conception than many textbook writers seem to have in mind—the frequency reaches only 55% of all the entries in a sentence outline. And when one remembers that only 761 outline topic sentences represent the 889 paragraphs in all 25 essays, he realizes that considerably fewer than half of all the paragraphs in the essays have even explicit topic sentences, to say nothing of simple topic sentences.

Placement of Simple Topic Sentences

How true is the claim that most expository paragraphs open with topic sentences? To find out, I studied the paragraph location of the 264 topic sentences and subtopic sentences in the outline. Gorrell and Laird, like others, had written that the "topic sentence may appear at the end of the paragraph as a kind of summary or somewhere within the paragraph, but most frequently it opens the paragraph or follows an opening introduction or transition (p. 25). Thus I decided to tabulate the occurrence of each simple topic sentence as it appeared in each of four positions: the first T-unit in the paragraph, the second T-unit, the last, or a T-unit between the second and last. To do that, of course, I could consider only paragraphs of four or more T-units. Consequently, I excluded from consideration paragraphs with three or fewer T-units. The results are presented in Table 3.

More than a fourth (28%) of all those paragraphs presenting simple topic sentences or simple subtopic sentences contained fewer than four T-units. Of the rest, 47% presented a simple topic sentence or simple subtopic sentence in the first T-unit, 15% in the second T-unit, 12% in the last T-unit, and 26% elsewhere. But these figures are based on the 190 paragraphs of four or more T-units which contain simple topic sentences or simple subtopic sentences. There were 355 paragraphs from which other topic sentences or subtopic sentences were drawn—delayed-completion, assembled, and inferred. One cannot say that they "have topic sentences to open them." Consequently, it is obvious that much smaller percentages than the above pertain to expository paragraphs in general. Furthermore, there were at least 128 paragraphs from which no topic sentences at all

Table 3 Location of simple topic sentences and simple subtopic sentences.

Location	Essay Number																									Tot.	%
	1	2	3	4	5	6	7	8	9	10	11	12	13	14	15	16	17	18	19	20	21	22	23	24	25		
(Paragraph shorter than 4 T-units)	1	1	4	0	3	2	6	5	0	4	1	7	4	0	9	0	6	1	4	2	0	1	6	1	6	74	(28)
First T-unit	6	2	2	3	3	2	0	2	6	4	2	2	1	2	7	5	7	3	6	5	1	0	0	3	7	89	47
Second T-unit	1	4	2	0	0	1	1	2	0	1	0	1	0	1	1	0	4	5	0	2	2	1	1	0	0	29	15
Last T-unit	0	0	1	0	0	1	0	4	0	0	0	0	2	0	0	1	1	4	3	2	0	1	0	0	1	22	12
Elsewhere	2	2	0	1	2	2	1	5	1	2	2	0	0	5	3	9	2	4	3	2	0	0	1	1	1	50	26
Total no. of TS's and STS's in essay	10	7	11	3	7	8	8	18	7	11	5	12	7	8	20	15	20	17	16	13	11	2	8	5	15	264	
Total no. of paragraphs in essay	20	25	50	26	24	27	19	41	45	35	13	35	67	53	56	53	42	49	53	39	29	13	26	13	36	889	

were drawn. If one adds the 190, 355, and 128, he has a total of 673 from which percentages may be computed, if he wishes to estimate what percentage of *all* of the paragraphs in the 25 essays open with a topic sentence. Using those figures, I estimate that only 13% of the expository paragraphs of contemporary professional writers begin with a topic sentence, that only 3% end with a topic sentence.

IMPLICATIONS FOR TEACHING

Teachers and textbook writers should exercise caution in making statements about the frequency with which contemporary professional writers use simple or even explicit topic sentences in expository paragraphs. It is abundantly clear that students should not be told that professional writers usually begin their paragraphs with topic sentences. Certainly teachers of reading, devisers of reading tests, and authors of reading textbooks should assist students in identifying the kinds of delayed-completion and implicit topic statements which outnumber simple topic sentences in expository paragraphs.

This sample of contemporary professional writing did not support the claims of textbook writers about the frequency and location of topic sentences in professional writing. That does not, of course, necessarily mean the same findings would hold for scientific and technical writing or other types of exposition. Moreover, it does not all mean that composition teachers should stop showing their students how to develop paragraphs from clear topic sentences. Far from it. In my opinion, often the writing in the 25 essays would have been clearer and more comfortable to read if the paragraphs had presented more explicit topic sentences. But what this study does suggest is this: While helping students use clear topic sentences in their writing and identify variously presented topical ideas in their reading, the teacher should not pretend that professional writers largely follow the practices he is advocating.

NOTES

1. The copies were supplied through the generosity of the Department of English, University of Iowa.

2. Here and hereafter, reference to specific articles in the corpus will be made simply by using the author's last name—or, in the cases of the two articles by individuals of the same last name, by using the first initial and last name (see Table 1)—The paragraph referred to here is in Lear, p. 89.

REFERENCES

Ashida, M. E. Something for everyone: a standard corpus of contemporary American expository essays. *Research in the Teaching of English*, 1968, 2, 14–23.

Bain, A. *English Composition and Rhetoric*, enl. ed. London: Longmans, Green, 1890.

Basic skills system: writing test, Form A. New York: McGraw Hill, 1970.

Gorrell, R. M. and Laird, C. *Modern English handbook*, 4th ed. Englewood Cliffs, New Jersey: Prentice Hall, 1967.

Hunt, K. W. *Grammatical structures written at three grade levels.* Research Report No. 3. Urbana, Illinois: NCTE, 1965.

Irmscher, W. F. *The Holt guide to English.* New York: Holt, Rinehart and Winston, 1972.

Rodgers, P. Jr. A discourse-centered rhetoric of the paragraph. *College Composition and Communication*, 1966, 17, 2–11.

Grammar, Grammars, and the Teaching of Grammar

Patrick Hartwell

For me the grammar issue was settled at least twenty years ago with the conclusion offered by Richard Braddock, Richard Lloyd-Jones, and Lowell Schoer in 1963.

> In view of the widespread agreement of research studies based upon many types of students and teachers, the conclusion can be stated in strong and unqualified terms: the teaching of formal grammar has a negligible or, because it usually displaces some instruction and practice in composition, even a harmful effect on improvement in writing.[1]

Indeed, I would agree with Janet Emig that the grammar issue is a prime example of "magical thinking": the assumption that students will learn only what we teach and only because we teach.[2]

But the grammar issue, as we will see, is a complicated one. And, perhaps surprisingly, it remains controversial, with the regular appearance of papers defending the teaching of formal grammar or attacking it.[3] Thus Janice Neuleib, writing on "The Relation of Formal Grammar to Composition" in *College Composition and Communication* (23 [1977], 247–250), is tempted "to sputter on paper" at reading the quotation above (p. 248), and Martha Kolln, writing in the same journal three years later ("Closing the Books on Alchemy," *CCC*, 32 [1981], 139–151), labels people like me "alchemists" for our perverse beliefs. Neuleib reviews five experimental studies, most of them concluding that formal grammar instruction has no

---

Reprinted from *College English* 47.2 (February 1985): 105–127. Used with permission.

effect on the quality of students' writing nor on their ability to avoid error. Yet she renders in effect a Scots verdict of "Not proven" and calls for more research on the issue. Similarly, Kolln reviews six experimental studies that arrive at similar conclusions, only one of them overlapping with the studies cited by Neuleib. She calls for more careful definition of the word *grammar*—her definition being "the internalized system that native speakers of a language share" (p. 140)—and she concludes with a stirring call to place grammar instruction at the center of the composition curriculum: "our goal should be to help students understand the system they know unconsciously as native speakers, to teach them the necessary categories and labels that will enable them to think about and talk about their language" (p. 150). Certainly our textbooks and our pedagogies—though they vary widely in what they see as "necessary categories and labels"—continue to emphasize mastery of formal grammar, and popular discussions of a presumed literacy crisis are almost unanimous in their call for a renewed emphasis on the teaching of formal grammar, seen as basic for success in writing.[4]

AN INSTRUCTIVE EXAMPLE

It is worth noting at the outset that both sides in this dispute—the grammarians and the anti-grammarians—articulate the issue in the same positivistic terms: what does experimental research tell us about the value of teaching formal grammar? But seventy-five years of experimental research has for all practical purposes told us nothing. The two sides are unable to agree on how to interpret such research. Studies are interpreted in terms of one's prior assumptions about the value of teaching grammar: their results seem not to change those assumptions. Thus the basis of the discussion, a basis shared by Kolln and Neuleib and by Braddock and his colleagues—"what does educational research tell us?"—seems designed to perpetuate, not to resolve, the issue. A single example will be instructive. In 1976 and then at greater length in 1979, W. B. Elley, I. H. Barham, H. Lamb, and M. Wyllie reported on a three-year experiment in New Zealand, comparing the relative effectiveness at the high school level of instruction in transformational grammar, instruction in traditional grammar, and no grammar instruction.[5] They concluded that the formal study of grammar, whether transformational or traditional, improved neither writing quality nor control over surface correctness.

> After two years, no differences were detected in writing performance or language competence; after three years small differences appeared in some

206

minor conventions favoring the TG [transformational grammar] group, but these were more than offset by the less positive attitudes they showed towards their English studies. (p. 18)

Anthony Petrosky, in a review of research ("Grammar Instruction: What We Know," *English Journal*, 66, No. 9 [1977], 86–88), agreed with this conclusion, finding the study to be carefully designed, "representative of the best kind of educational research" (p. 86), its validity "unquestionable" (p. 88). Yet Janice Neuleib in her essay found the same conclusions to be "startling" and questioned whether the findings could be generalized beyond the target population, New Zealand high school students. Martha Kolln, when her attention is drawn to the study ("Reply to Ron Shook," *CCC*, 32 [1981], 139–151), thinks the whole experiment "suspicious." And John Mellon has been willing to use the study to defend the teaching of grammar; the study of Elley and his colleagues, he has argued, shows that teaching grammar does no harm.[6]

It would seem unlikely, therefore, that further experimental research, in and of itself, will resolve the grammar issue. Any experimental design can be nitpicked, any experimental population can be criticized, and any experimental conclusion can be questioned or, more often, ignored. In fact, it may well be that the grammar question is not open to resolution by experimental research, that, as Noam Chomsky has argued in *Reflections on Language* (New York: Pantheon, 1975), criticizing the trivialization of human learning by behavioral psychologists, the issue is simply misdefined.

> There will be "good experiments" only in domains that lie outside the organism's cognitive capacity. For example, there will be no "good experiments" in the study of human learning.
>
> This discipline . . . will, of necessity, avoid those domains in which an organism is specially designed to acquire rich cognitive structures that enter into its life in an intimate fashion. The discipline will be of virtually no intellectual interest, it seems to me, since it is restricting itself in principle to those questions that are guaranteed to tell us little about the nature of organisms. (p. 36)

ASKING THE RIGHT QUESTIONS

As a result, though I will look briefly at the tradition of experimental research, my primary goal in this essay is to articulate the grammar issue in different and, I would hope, more productive terms. Specifically, I want to ask four questions:

1. Why is the grammar issue so important? Why has it been the dominant focus of composition research for the last seventy-five years?
2. What definitions of the word *grammar* are needed to articulate the grammar issue intelligibly?
3. What do findings in cognate disciplines suggest about the value of formal grammar instruction?
4. What is our theory of language, and what does it predict about the value of formal grammar instruction? (This question—"what does our theory of language predict?"—seems a much more powerful question than "what does educational research tell us?")

In exploring these questions I will attempt to be fully explicit about issues, terms, and assumptions. I hope that both proponents and opponents of formal grammar instruction would agree that these are useful as shared points of reference: care in definition, full examination of the evidence, reference to relevant work in cognate disciplines, and explicit analysis of the theoretical bases of the issue.

But even with that gesture of harmony it will be difficult to articulate the issue in a balanced way, one that will be acceptable to both sides. After all, we are dealing with a professional dispute in which one side accuses the other of "magical thinking," and in turn that side responds by charging the other as "alchemists." Thus we might suspect that the grammar issue is itself embedded in larger models of the transmission of literacy, part of quite different assumptions about the teaching of composition.

Those of us who dismiss the teaching of formal grammar have a model of composition instruction that makes the grammar issue "uninteresting" in a scientific sense. Our model predicts a rich and complex interaction of learner and environment in mastering literacy, an interaction that has little to do with sequences of skills instruction as such. Those who defend the teaching of grammar tend to have a model of composition instruction that is rigidly skills-centered and rigidly sequential: the formal teaching of grammar, as the first step in that sequence, is the cornerstone or linchpin. Grammar teaching is thus supremely interesting, naturally a dominant focus for educational research. The controversy over the value of grammar instruction, then, is inseparable from two other issues: the issues of sequence in the teaching of composition and of the role of the composition teacher. Consider, for example, the force of these two issues in Janice Neuleib's conclusion: after calling for yet more experimental research on the value of teaching grammar, she ends with an absolute (and unsupported) claim about sequences and teacher roles in composition.

> We do know, however, that some things must be taught at different levels. Insistence on adherence to usage norms by composition teachers does improve usage. Students can learn to organize their papers if teachers do not accept papers that are disorganized. Perhaps composition teachers can teach those two abilities before they begin the more difficult tasks of developing syntactic sophistication and a winning style. ("The Relation of Formal Grammar to Composition," p. 250)

(One might want to ask, in passing, whether "usage norms" exist in the monolithic fashion the phrase suggests and whether refusing to accept disorganized papers is our best available pedagogy for teaching arrangement.)[7]

But I want to focus on the notion of sequence that makes the grammar issue so important: first grammar, then usage, then some absolute model of organization, all controlled by the teacher at the center of the learning process, with other matters, those of rhetorical weight—"syntactic sophistication and a winning style"—pushed off to the future. It is not surprising that we call each other names: those of us who question the value of teaching grammar are in fact shaking the whole elaborate edifice of traditional composition instruction.

THE FIVE MEANINGS OF "GRAMMAR"

Given its centrality to a well-established way of teaching composition, I need to go about the business of defining grammar rather carefully, particularly in view of Kolln's criticism of the lack of care in earlier discussions. Therefore I will build upon a seminal discussion of the word *grammar* offered a generation ago, in 1954, by W. Nelson Francis, often excerpted as "The Three Meanings of Grammar."[8] It is worth reprinting at length, if only to re-establish it as a reference point for future discussions.

> The first thing we mean by "grammar" is "the set of formal patterns in which the words of a language are arranged in order to convey larger meanings." It is not necessary that we be able to discuss these patterns self-consciously in order to be able to use them. In fact, all speakers of a language above the age of five or six know how to use its complex forms of organization with considerable skill; in this sense of the word—call it "Grammar 1"—they are thoroughly familiar with its grammar.

The second meaning of "grammar"—call it "Grammar 2"—is "the branch of linguistic science which is concerned with the description, analysis, and formulization of formal language patterns." Just as gravity was in full operation before Newton's apple fell, so grammar in the first sense was in full operation before anyone formulated the first rule that began the history of grammar as a study.

The third sense in which people use the word "grammar" is "linguistic etiquette." This we may call "Grammar 3." The word in this sense is often coupled with a derogatory adjective: we say that the expression "he ain't here" is "bad grammar." . . .

As has already been suggested, much confusion arises from mixing these meanings. One hears a good deal of criticism of teachers of English couched in such terms as "they don't teach grammar any more." Criticism of this sort is based on the wholly unproven assumption that teaching Grammar 2 will improve the student's proficiency in Grammar 1 or improve his manners in Grammar 3. Actually, the form of Grammar 2 which is usually taught is a very inaccurate and misleading analysis of the facts of Grammar 1; and it therefore is of highly questionable value in improving a person's ability to handle the structural patterns of his language. (pp. 300–301)

Francis' Grammar 3 is, of course, not grammar at all, but usage. One would like to assume that Joseph Williams' recent discussion of usage ("The Phenomenology of Error," *CCC*, 32 [1981], 152–168), along with his references, has placed those shibboleths in a proper perspective. But I doubt it, and I suspect that popular discussions of the grammar issue will be as flawed by the intrusion of usage issues as past discussions have been. At any rate I will make only passing reference to Grammar 3—usage—naively assuming that this issue has been discussed elsewhere and that my readers are familiar with those discussions.

We need also to make further discriminations about Francis' Grammar 2, given that the purpose of his 1954 article was to substitute for one form of Grammar 2, that "inaccurate and misleading" form "which is usually taught," another form, that of American structuralist grammar. Here we can make use of a still earlier discussion, one going back to the days when *PMLA* was willing to publish articles on rhetoric and linguistics, to a 1927 article by Charles Carpenter Fries, "The Rules of the Common School Grammars" (42 [1927], 221–237). Fries there distinguished between the scientific tradition of language study (to which we will now delimit Francis' Grammar 2, scientific grammar) and the separate tradition of "the common school grammars," developed unscientifically, largely based on two inadequate principles—appeals to "logical principles," like "two negatives make a positive," and analogy to Latin grammar; thus, Charlton Laird's characterization, "the grammar of Latin, ingeniously warped to suggest English" (*Language in America* [New York: World, 1970], p. 294). There is, of course, a direct link between the "common school grammars" that Fries criticized in 1927 and the grammar-based texts of today, and thus it seems wise, as Karl W. Dykema suggests ("Where Our Grammar Came From," *CE*, 22 (1961), 455–465), to separate Grammar 2, "scientific grammar," from Grammar 4, "school grammar," the latter meaning, quite literally, "the grammars used in the schools."

Further, since Martha Kolln points to the adaptation of Christensen's sentence rhetoric in a recent sentence-combining text as an example of the proper emphasis on "grammar" ("Closing the Books on Alchemy," p. 140), it is worth separating out, as still another meaning of *grammar*, Grammar 5, "stylistic grammar," defined as "grammatical terms used in the interest of teaching prose style." And, since stylistic grammars abound, with widely variant terms and emphases, we might appropriately speak parenthetically of specific forms of Grammar 5 — Grammar 5 (Lanham); Grammar 5 (Strunk and White); Grammar 5 (Williams, *Style*); even Grammar 5 (Christensen, as adapted by Daiker, Kerek, and Morenberg).[9]

THE GRAMMAR IN OUR HEADS

With these definitions in mind, let us return to Francis' Grammar 1, admirably defined by Kolln as "the internalized system of rules that speakers of a language share" ("Closing the Books on Alchemy," p. 140), or, to put it more simply, the grammar in our heads. Three features of Grammar 1 need to be stressed: first, its special status as an "internalized system of rules," as tacit and unconscious knowledge; second, the abstract, even counterintuitive, nature of these rules, insofar as we are able to approximate them indirectly as Grammar 2 statements; and third, the way in which the form of one's Grammar 1 seems profoundly affected by the acquisition of literacy. This sort of review is designed to firm up our theory of language, so that we can ask what it predicts about the value of teaching formal grammar.

A simple thought experiment will isolate the special status of Grammar 1 knowledge. I have asked members of a number of different groups — from sixth graders to college freshmen to high-school teachers — to give me the rule for ordering adjectives of nationality, age, and number in English. The response is always the same: "We don't know the rule." Yet when I ask these groups to perform an active language task, they show productive control over the rule they have denied knowing. I ask them to arrange the following words in a natural order:

French   the   young   girls   four

I have never seen a native speaker of English who did not immediately produce the natural order, "the four young French girls." The rule is that in English the order of adjectives is first, number, second, age, and third, nationality. Native speakers can create analogous phrases using the rule— "the seventy-three aged Scandinavian lechers"; and the drive for meaning is so great that they will create contexts to make sense out of violations of the rule, as in foregrounding for emphasis: "I want to talk to the French four young girls." (I immediately envision a large room, perhaps a banquet hall, filled with tables at which are seated groups of four young girls, each group of a different nationality.) So Grammar 1 is eminently usable knowledge— the way we make our life through language—but it is not accessible knowledge; in a profound sense, we do not know that we have it. Thus neurolinguist Z. N. Pylyshyn speaks of Grammar 1 as "autonomous," separate from common-sense reasoning, and as "cognitively impenetrable," not available for direct examination.[10] In philosophy and linguistics, the distinction is made between formal, conscious, "knowing about" knowledge (like Grammar 2 knowledge) and tacit, unconscious, "knowing how" knowledge (like Grammar 1 knowledge). The importance of this distinction for the teaching of composition—it provides a powerful theoretical justification for mistrusting the ability of Grammar 2 (or Grammar 4) knowledge to affect Grammar 1 performance—was pointed out in this journal by Martin Steinmann, Jr., in 1966 ("Rhetorical Research," CE, 27 [1966], 278–285).

Further, the more we learn about Grammar 1—and most linguists would agree that we know surprisingly little about it—the more abstract and implicit it seems. This abstractness can be illustrated with an experiment, devised by Lise Menn and reported by Morris Halle,[11] about our rule for forming plurals in speech. It is obvious that we do indeed have a "rule" for forming plurals, for we do not memorize the plural of each noun separately. You will demonstrate productive control over that rule by forming the spoken plurals of the nonsense words below:

thole   flitch   plast

Halle offers two ways of formalizing a Grammar 2 equivalent of this Grammar 1 ability. One form of the rule is the following, stated in terms of speech sounds:

a. If the noun ends in /s z š ž č ǰ/, add /ɨz/;

b. otherwise, if the noun ends in /p t k f Ø/, add /s/;

c. otherwise, add /z/.[11]

This rule comes close to what we literate adults consider to be an adequate rule for plurals in writing, like the rules, for example, taken from a recent "common school grammar," Eric Gould's *Reading into Writing: A Rhetoric, Reader, and Handbook* (Boston: Houghton Mifflin, 1983):

> *Plurals* can be tricky. If you are unsure of a plural, then check it in the dictionary. The general rules are
>   Add *s* to the singular: *girls, tables*
>   Add *es* to nouns ending in *ch, sh, x* or *s: churches, boxes, wishes*
>   Add *es* to nouns ending in *y* and preceded by a vowel once you have changed *y* to *i: monies, companies*. (p. 666)

(But note the persistent inadequacy of such Grammar 4 rules: here, as I read it, the rule is inadequate to explain the plurals of *ray* and *tray*, even to explain the collective noun *monies*, not a plural at all, formed from the mass noun *money* and offered as an example.) A second form of the rule would make use of much more abstract entities, sound features:

a. If the noun ends with a sound that is [coronal, strident], add /ɨz/;

b. otherwise, if the noun ends with a sound that is [non-voiced], add /s/;

c. otherwise, add /z/.

(The notion of "sound features" is itself rather abstract, perhaps new to readers not trained in linguistics. But such readers should be able to recognize that the spoken plurals of *lip* and *duck,* the sound [s], differ from the spoken plurals of *sea* and *gnu,* the sound [z], only in that the sounds of the latter are "voiced"—one's vocal cords vibrate—while the sounds of the former are "non-voiced.")

To test the psychologically operative rule, the Grammar 1 rule, native speakers of English were asked to form the plural of the last name of the composer Johann Sebastian *Bach,* a sound [x], unique in American (though not in Scottish) English. If speakers follow the first rule above, using word endings, they would reject a) and b), then apply c), producing the plural as /baxz/, with word-final /z/. (If writers were to follow the rule of the common school grammar, they would produce the written plural *Baches,* apparently, given the form of the rule, on analogy with *churches.*) If speakers follow the second rule, they would have to analyze the sound [x] as [non-labial, non-coronal, dorsal, non-voiced, and non-strident], producing the plural as /baxs/, with word-final /s/. Native speakers of American English overwhelmingly produce the plural as /baxs/. They use knowledge that Halle characterizes as "unlearned and untaught" (p. 140).

Now such a conclusion is counterintuitive—certainly it departs maximally from Grammar 4 rules for forming plurals. It seems that native speakers of English behave as if they have productive control, as Grammar 1 knowledge, of abstract sound features (± coronal, ± strident, and so on) which are available as conscious, Grammar 2 knowledge only to trained linguists—and, indeed, formally available only within the last hundred years or so. ("Behave as if," in that last sentence, is a necessary hedge, to underscore the difficulty of "knowing about" Grammar 1.)

Moreover, as the example of plural rules suggests, the form of the Grammar 1 in the heads of literate adults seems profoundly affected by the acquisition of literacy. Obviously, literate adults have access to different morphological codes: the abstract print -s underlying the predictable /s/ and /z/ plurals, the abstract print -ed underlying the spoken past tense markers /t/, as in "walked," /əd/, as in "surrounded," /d/, as in "scored," and the symbol /Ø/ for no surface realization, as in the relaxed standard pronunciation of "I walked to the store." Literate adults also have access to distinctions preserved only in the code of print (for example, the distinction between "a good sailer" and "a good sailor" that Mark Aranoff points out in "An English Spelling Convention," *Linguistic Inquiry*, 9 [1978], 299–303). More significantly, Irene Moscowitz speculates that the ability of third graders to form abstract nouns on analogy with pairs like *divine::divinity* and *serene::serenity*, where the spoken vowel changes but the spelling preserves meaning, is a factor of knowing how to read. Carol Chomsky finds a three-stage developmental sequence in the grammatical performance of seven-year-olds, related to measures of kind and variety of reading; and Rita S. Brause finds a nine-stage developmental sequence in the ability to understand semantic ambiguity, extending from fourth graders to graduate students.[12] John Mills and Gordon Hemsley find that level of education, and presumably level of literacy, influence judgments of grammaticality, concluding that literacy changes the deep structure of one's internal grammar; Jean Whyte finds that oral language functions develop differently in readers and non-readers; José Morais, Jésus Alegria, and Paul Bertelson find that illiterate adults are unable to add or delete sounds at the beginning of nonsense words, suggesting that awareness of speech as a series of phones is provided by learning to read an alphabetic code. Two experiments—one conducted by Charles A. Ferguson, the other by Mary E. Hamilton and David Barton—find that adults' ability to recognize segmentation in speech is related to degree of literacy, not to amount of schooling or general ability.[13]

It is worth noting that none of these investigators would suggest that the developmental sequences they have uncovered be isolated and taught as discrete skills. They are natural concomitants of literacy, and they seem best characterized not as isolated rules but as developing schemata, broad strategies for approaching written language.

GRAMMAR 2

We can, of course, attempt to approximate the rules or schemata of Grammar 1 by writing fully explicit descriptions that model the competence of a native speaker. Such rules, like the rules for pluralizing nouns or ordering adjectives discussed above, are the goal of the science of linguistics, that is, Grammar 2. There are a number of scientific grammars—an older structuralist model and several versions within a generative-transformational paradigm, not to mention isolated schools like tagmemic grammar, Montague grammar, and the like. In fact, we cannot think of Grammar 2 as a stable entity, for its form changes with each new issue of each linguistics journal, as new "rules of grammar" are proposed and debated. Thus Grammar 2, though of great theoretical interest to the composition teacher, is of little practical use in the classroom, as Constance Weaver has pointed out (*Grammar for Teachers* [Urbana, Ill.: NCTE, 1979], pp. 3–6). Indeed Grammar 2 is a scientific model of Grammar 1, not a description of it, so that questions of psychological reality, while important, are less important than other, more theoretical factors, such as the elegance of formulation or the global power of rules. We might, for example, wish to replace the rule for ordering adjectives of age, number, and nationality cited above with a more general rule—what linguists call a "fuzzy" rule—that adjectives in English are ordered by their abstract quality of "nouniness": adjectives that are very much like nouns, like *French* or *Scandinavian*, come physically closer to nouns than do adjectives that are less "nouny," like *four* or *aged*. But our motivation for accepting the broader rule would be its global power, not its psychological reality.[14]

I try to consider a hostile reader, one committed to the teaching of grammar, and I try to think of ways to hammer in the central point of this distinction, that the rules of Grammar 2 are simply unconnected to productive control over Grammar 1. I can argue from authority: Noam Chomsky has touched on this point whenever he has concerned himself with the implications of linguistics for language teaching, and years ago transformationalist Mark Lester stated unequivocally, "there simply appears to be no correlation between a writer's study of language and his ability to write."[15] I can cite analogies offered by others: Francis Christensen's analogy in an essay originally published in 1962 that formal grammar study would be "to invite a centipede to attend to the sequence of his legs in motion,"[16] or James Britton's analogy, offered informally after a conference presentation, that grammar study would be like forcing starving people to master the use of a knife and fork before allowing them to eat. I can offer analogies of my own, contemplating the wisdom of asking a pool player to master the physics of momentum before taking up a cue or of making a prospective driver get a degree in automotive engineering before engaging the clutch. I consider a hypothetical argument, that if Grammar 2 knowledge affected Grammar 1 performance, then linguists would be our best writers. (I can certify that they are, on the whole, not.) Such a position, after all, is only in accord with other domains of science: the formula for catching a fly ball in baseball ("Playing It by Ear," *Scientific American*, 248, No. 4 [1983], 76) is of such complexity that it is beyond my understanding—and, I would suspect, that of many workaday centerfielders. But perhaps I can best hammer in this claim—that Grammar 2 knowledge has no effect on Grammar 1 performance—by offering a demonstration.

The diagram below is an attempt by Thomas N. Huckin and Leslie A. Olsen (*English for Science and Technology* [New York: McGraw-Hill, 1983]) to offer, for students of English as a second language, a fully explicit

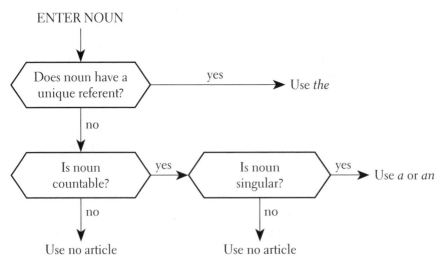

formulation of what is, for native speakers, a trivial rule of the language—the choice of definite article, indefinite article, or no definite article. There are obvious limits to such a formulation, for article choice in English is less a matter of rule than of idiom ("I went to college" versus "I went to a university" versus British "I went to university"), real-world knowledge (using indefinite "I went into a house" instantiates definite "I looked at the ceiling," and indefinite "I visited a university" instantiates definite "I talked with the professors"), and stylistic choice (the last sentence above might alternatively end with "the choice of the definite article, the indefinite article, or no article"). Huckin and Olsen invite non-native speakers to use the rule consciously to justify article choice in technical prose, such as the passage below from P. F. Brandwein (*Matter: An Earth Science* [New York: Harcourt Brace Jovanovich, 1975]). I invite you to spend a couple of minutes doing the same thing, with the understanding that this exercise is a test case: you are using a very explicit rule to justify a fairly straightforward issue of grammatical choice.

> Imagine a cannon on top of ___the___ highest mountain on earth. It is firing _____ cannonballs horizontally. _____ first cannonball fired follows its path. As _____ cannonball moves, _____ gravity pulls it down, and it soon hits _____ ground. Now _____ velocity with which each succeeding cannonball is fired is increased. Thus, _____ cannonball goes farther each time. Cannonball 2 goes farther than _____ cannonball 1 although each is being pulled by _____ gravity toward the earth all _____ time. _____ last cannonball is fired with such tremendous velocity that it goes completely around _____ earth. It returns to _____ mountaintop and continues around the earth again and again. _____ cannonball's inertia causes it to continue in motion indefinitely in _____ orbit around earth. In such a situation, we could consider _____ cannonball to be _____ artificial satellite, just like _____ weather satellites launched by _____ U.S. Weather Service. (p. 209)

Most native speakers of English who have attempted this exercise report a great deal of frustration, a curious sense of working against, rather than with, the rule. The rule, however valuable it may be for non-native speakers, is, for the most part, simply unusable for native speakers of the language.

COGNATE AREAS OF RESEARCH

We can corroborate this demonstration by turning to research in two cognate areas, studies of the induction of rules of artificial languages and studies of the role of formal rules in second language acquisition. Psychologists have studied the ability of subjects to learn artificial languages, usually constructed of nonsense syllables or letter strings. Such languages can be described by phrase structure rules:

$$S \Rightarrow VX$$
$$X \Rightarrow MX$$

More clearly, they can be presented as flow diagrams, as below:

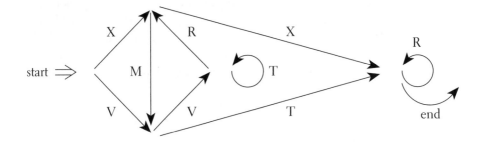

This diagram produces "sentences" like the following:

VVTRXRR.	XMVTTRX.	XXRR.
XMVRMT.	VVTTRMT.	XMTRRR.

The following "sentences" would be "ungrammatical" in this language:

*VMXTT.	*RTXVVT.	*TRVXXVVM.

Arthur S. Reber, in a classic 1967 experiment, demonstrated that mere exposure to grammatical sentences produced tacit learning: subjects who copied several grammatical sentences performed far above chance in judging the grammaticality of other letter strings. Further experiments have shown that providing subjects with formal rules—giving them the flow diagram above, for example—remarkably degrades performance: subjects given the "rules of the language" do much less well in acquiring the rules than do subjects not given the rules. Indeed, even telling subjects that they are to induce the rules of an artificial language degrades performance. Such laboratory experiments are admittedly contrived, but they confirm predictions that our theory of language would make about the value of formal rules in language learning.[17]

The thrust of recent research in second language learning similarly works to constrain the value of formal grammar rules. The most explicit statement of the value of formal rules is that of Stephen D. Krashen's monitor model.[18] Krashen divides second language mastery into *acquisition*— tacit, informal mastery, akin to first language acquisition—and formal learning—conscious application of Grammar 2 rules, which he calls "monitoring" output. In another essay Krashen uses his model to predict a highly individual use of the monitor and a highly constrained role for formal rules:

> Some adults (and very few children) are able to use conscious rules to increase the grammatical accuracy of their output, and even for these people, very strict conditions need to be met before the conscious grammar can be applied.[19]

In *Principles and Practice in Second Language Acquisition* (New York: Pergamon, 1982) Krashen outlines these conditions by means of a series of concentric circles, beginning with a large circle denoting the rules of English and a smaller circle denoting the subset of those rules described by formal linguists (adding that most linguists would protest that the size of this circle is much too large):

rules of English

rules described by formal linguists

(p. 92)

Krashen then adds smaller circles, as shown below—a subset of the rules described by formal linguists that would be known to applied linguists, a subset of those rules that would be available to the best teachers, and then a subset of those rules that teachers might choose to present to second language learners:

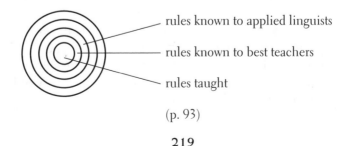

rules known to applied linguists

rules known to best teachers

rules taught

(p. 93)

219

Of course, as Krashen notes, not all the rules taught will be learned, and not all those learned will be available, as what he calls "mental baggage" (p. 94), for conscious use.

An experiment by Ellen Bialystock, asking English speakers learning French to judge the grammaticality of taped sentences, complicates this issue, for reaction time data suggest that learners first make an intuitive judgment of grammaticality, using implicit or Grammar 1 knowledge, and only then search for formal explanations, using explicit or Grammar 2 knowledge.[20] This distinction would suggest that Grammar 2 knowledge is of use to second language learners only after the principle has already been mastered as tacit Grammar 1 knowledge. In the terms of Krashen's model, learning never becomes acquisition (*Principles*, p. 86).

An ingenious experiment by Herbert W. Seliger complicates the issue yet further ("On the Nature and Function of Language Rules in Language Learning," *TESOL Quarterly*, 13 [1979], 359–369). Seliger asked native and non-native speakers of English to orally identify pictures of objects (e.g., "an apple," "a pear," "a book," "an umbrella"), noting whether they used the correct form of the indefinite articles *a* and *an*. He then asked each speaker to state the rule for choosing between *a* and *an*. He found no correlation between the ability to state the rule and the ability to apply it correctly, either with native or non-native speakers. Indeed, three of four adult non-native speakers in his sample produced a correct form of the rule, but they did not apply it in speaking. A strong conclusion from this experiment would be that formal rules of grammar seem to have no value whatsoever. Seliger, however, suggests a more paradoxical interpretation. Rules are of no use, he agrees, but some people think they are, and for these people, assuming that they have internalized the rules, even inadequate rules are of heuristic value, for they allow them to access the internal rules they actually use.

THE INCANTATIONS OF THE "COMMON SCHOOL GRAMMARS"

Such a paradox may explain the fascination we have as teachers with "rules of grammar" of the Grammar 4 variety, the "rules" of the "common school grammars." Again and again such rules are inadequate to the facts of written language; you will recall that we have known this since Francis' 1927 study. R. Scott Baldwin and James M. Coady, studying how readers respond to punctuation signals ("Psycholinguistic Approaches to a Theory of Punctuation," *Journal of Reading Behavior*, 10 [1978], 363–383), conclude that conventional rules of punctuation are "a complete sham" (p. 375). My own favorite is the Grammar 4 rule for showing possession, always expressed in terms of adding -'s or -s' to nouns, while our internal grammar, if you think about it, adds possession to noun phrases, albeit under severe stylistic constraints: "the horses of the Queen of England" are "the Queen of England's horses" and "the feathers of the duck over there" are "the duck over there's feathers." Suzette Haden Elgin refers to the "rules" of Grammar 4 as "incantations" (*Never Mind the Trees*, p. 9: see footnote 3).

It may simply be that as hyperliterate adults we are conscious of "using rules" when we are in fact doing something else, something far more complex, accessing tacit heuristics honed by print literacy itself. We can clarify this notion by reaching for an acronym coined by technical writers to explain the readability of complex prose—COIK: "clear only if known." The rules of Grammar 4—no, we can at this point be more honest—the incantations of Grammar 4 are COIK. If you know how to signal possession in the code of print, then the advice to add -'s to nouns makes perfect sense, just as the collective noun *monies* is a fine example of changing -*y* to -*i* and adding -*es* to form the plural. But if you have not grasped, tacitly, the abstract representation of possession in print, such incantations can only be opaque.

Worse yet, the advice given in "the common school grammars" is unconnected with anything remotely resembling literate adult behavior. Consider, as an example, the rule for not writing a sentence fragment as the rule is described in the best-selling college grammar text, John C. Hodges and Mary S. Whitten's *Harbrace College Handbook*, 9th ed. (New York: Harcourt Brace Jovanovich, 1982). In order to get to the advice, "as a rule, do not write a sentence fragment" (p. 25), the student must master the following learning tasks:

Recognizing verbs.

Recognizing subjects and verbs.

Recognizing all parts of speech. (*Harbrace* lists eight.)

Recognizing phrases and subordinate clauses. (*Harbrace* lists six types of phrases, and it offers incomplete lists of eight relative pronouns and eighteen subordinating conjunctions.)

Recognizing main clauses and types of sentences.

These learning tasks completed, the student is given the rule above, offered a page of exceptions, and then given the following advice (or is it an incantation?):

> Before handing in a composition, . . . proofread each word group written as
> a sentence. Test each one for completeness. First, be sure that it has at least
> one subject and one predicate. Next, be sure that the word group is not a
> dependent clause beginning with a subordinating conjunction or a relative
> clause. (p. 27)

The school grammar approach defines a sentence fragment as a conceptual error—as not having conscious knowledge of the school grammar definition of *sentence*. It demands heavy emphasis on rote memory, and it asks students to behave in ways patently removed from the behaviors of mature writers. (I have never in my life tested a sentence for completeness, and I am a better writer—and probably a better person—as a consequence.) It may be, of course, that some developing writers, at some points in their development, may benefit from such advice—or, more to the point, may think that they benefit—but, as Thomas Friedman points out in "Teaching Error, Nurturing Confusion" (*CE*, 45 [1983], 390–399), our theory of language tells us that such advice is, at the best, COIK. As the Maine joke has it, about a tourist asking directions from a farmer, "you can't get there from here."

REDEFINING ERROR

In the specific case of sentence fragments, Mina P. Shaughnessy (*Errors and Expectations* [New York: Oxford University Press, 1977]) argues that such errors are not conceptual failures at all, but performance errors—mistakes in punctuation. Muriel Harris' error counts support this view ("Mending the Fragmented Free Modifier," *CCC*, 32 [1981], 175–182). Case studies show example after example of errors that occur *because of* instruction—one thinks, for example, of David Bartholmae's student explaining that he added an *-s* to *children* "because it's a plural" ("The Study of Error," *CCC*, 31 [1980], 262). Surveys, such as that by Muriel Harris ("Contradictory Perceptions of the Rules of Writing," *CCC*, 30 [1979], 218–220), and our own observations suggest that students consistently misunderstand such Grammar 4 explanations (COIK, you will recall). For example, from Patrick Hartwell and Robert H. Bentley and from Mike Rose, we have two separate anecdotal accounts of students, cited for punctuating a *because*-clause as a sentence, who have decided to avoid using *because*. More generally, Collette A. Daiute's analysis of errors made by college students shows that errors tend to appear at clause boundaries, suggesting short-term memory load and not conceptual deficiency as a cause of error.[21]

Thus, if we think seriously about error and its relationship to the worship of formal grammar study, we need to attempt some massive dislocation of our traditional thinking, to shuck off our hyperliterate perception of the value of formal rules, and to regain the confidence in the tacit power of unconscious knowledge that our theory of language gives us. Most students, reading their writing aloud, will correct in essence all errors of spelling, grammar, and, by intonation, punctuation, but usually without noticing that what they read departs from what they wrote.[22] And Richard H. Haswell ("Minimal Marking," *CE*, 45 [1983], 600–604) notes that his students correct 61.1% of their errors when they are identified with a simple mark in the margin rather than by error type. Such findings suggest that we need to redefine error, to see it not as a cognitive or linguistic problem, a problem of not knowing a "rule of grammar" (whatever that may mean), but rather, following the insight of Robert J. Bracewell ("Writing as a Cognitive Activity," *Visible Language*, 14 [1980], 400–422), as a problem of metacognition and metalinguistic awareness, a matter of accessing knowledges that, to be of any use, learners must have already internalized by means of exposure to the code. (Usage issues—Grammar 3—probably represent a different order of problem. Both Joseph Emonds and Jeffrey Jochnowitz establish that the usage issues we worry most about are linguistically unnatural, departures from the grammar in our heads.)[23]

The notion of metalinguistic awareness seems crucial. The sentence below, created by Douglas R. Hofstadter ("Metamagical Themas," *Scientific American*, 235, No. 1 [1981], 22–32), is offered to clarify that notion; you are invited to examine it for a moment or two before continuing.

Their is four errors in this sentance. Can you find them?

Three errors announce themselves plainly enough, the misspellings of *there* and *sentence* and the use of *is* instead of *are*. (And, just to illustrate the perils of hyperliteracy, let it be noted that, through three years of drafts, I referred to the choice of *is* and *are* as a matter of "subject-verb agreement.") The fourth error resists detection, until one assesses the truth value of the sentence itself—the fourth error is that there are not four errors, only three. Such a sentence (Hofstadter calls it a "self-referencing sentence") asks you to look at it in two ways, simultaneously as statement and as linguistic artifact—in other words, to exercise metalinguistic awareness.

A broad range of cross-cultural studies suggest that metalinguistic awareness is a defining feature of print literacy. Thus Sylvia Scribner and Michael Cole, working with the triliterate Vai of Liberia (variously literate in English, through schooling; in Arabic, for religious purposes; and in an indigenous Vai script, used for personal affairs), find that metalinguistic awareness, broadly conceived, is the only cognitive skill underlying each of the three literacies. The one statistically significant skill shared by literate Vai was the recognition of word boundaries. Moreover, literate Vai tended to answer "yes" when asked (in Vai), "Can you call the sun the moon and the moon the sun?" while illiterate Vai tended to have grave doubts about such metalinguistic play. And in the United States Henry and Lila R. Gleitman report quite different responses by clerical workers and PhD candidates asked to interpret nonsense compounds like "house-bird glass": clerical workers focused on meaning and plausibility (for example, "a house-bird made of glass"), while PhD candidates focused on syntax (for example, "a very small drinking cup for canaries" or "a glass that protects house-birds").[24] More general research findings suggest a clear relationship between measures of metalinguistic awareness and measures of literacy level.[25] William Labov, speculating on literacy acquisition in inner-city ghettoes, contrasts "stimulus-bound" and "language-bound" individuals, suggesting that the latter seem to master literacy more easily.[26] The analysis here suggests that the causal relationship works the other way, that it is the mastery of written language that increases one's awareness of language as language.

This analysis has two implications. First, it makes the question of socially nonstandard dialects, always implicit in discussions of teaching formal grammar, into a non-issue.[27] Native speakers of English, regardless of dialect, show tacit mastery of the conventions of Standard English, and that mastery seems to transfer into abstract orthographic knowledge through interaction with print.[28] Developing writers show the same patterning of errors, regardless of dialect.[29] Studies of reading and of writing suggest that surface features of spoken dialect are simply irrelevant to mastering print literacy.[30] Print is a complex cultural code—or better yet, a system of codes—and my bet is that, regardless of instruction, one masters those codes from the top down, from pragmatic questions of voice, tone, audience, register, and rhetorical strategy, not from the bottom up, from grammar to usage to fixed forms of organization.

Second, this analysis forces us to posit multiple literacies, used for multiple purposes, rather than a single static literacy, engraved in "rules of grammar." These multiple literacies are evident in cross-cultural studies.[31] They are equally evident when we inquire into the uses of literacy in American communities.[32] Further, given that students, at all levels, show widely variant interactions with print literacy, there would seem to be little to do with grammar—with Grammar 2 or with Grammar 4—that we could isolate as a basis for formal instruction.[33]

224

GRAMMAR 5: STYLISTIC GRAMMAR

Similarly, when we turn to Grammar 5, "grammatical terms used in the interest of teaching prose style," so central to Martha Kolln's argument for teaching formal grammar, we find that the grammar issue is simply beside the point. There are two fully-articulated positions about "stylistic grammar," which I will label "romantic" and "classic," following Richard Lloyd-Jones and Richard E. Young.[34] The romantic position is that stylistic grammars, though perhaps useful for teachers, have little place in the teaching of composition, for students must struggle with and through language toward meaning. This position rests on a theory of language ultimately philosophical rather than linguistic (witness, for example, the contempt for linguists in Ann Berthoff's *The Making of Meaning: Metaphors, Models, and Maxims for Writing Teachers* [Montclair, N.J.: Boynton/Cook, 1981]); it is articulated as a theory of style by Donald A. Murray and, on somewhat different grounds (that stylistic grammars encourage overuse of the monitor), by Ian Pringle. The classic position, on the other hand, is that we can find ways to offer developing writers helpful suggestions about prose style, suggestions such as Francis Christensen's emphasis on the cumulative sentence, developed by observing the practice of skilled writers, and Joseph Williams' advice about predication, developed by psycholinguistic studies of comprehension.[35] James A. Berlin's recent survey of composition theory (*CE*, 45 [1982], 765–777) probably understates the gulf between these two positions and the radically different conceptions of language that underlie them, but it does establish that they share an overriding assumption in common: that one learns to control the language of print by manipulating language in meaningful contexts, not by learning about language in isolation, as by the study of formal grammar. Thus even classic theorists, who choose to present a vocabulary of style to students, do so only as a vehicle for encouraging productive control of communicative structures.

We might put the matter in the following terms. Writers need to develop skills at two levels. One, broadly rhetorical, involves communication in meaningful contexts (the strategies, registers, and procedures of discourse across a range of modes, audiences, contexts, and purposes). The other, broadly metalinguistic rather than linguistic, involves active manipulation of language with conscious attention to surface form. This second level may be developed tacitly, as a natural adjunct to developing rhetorical competencies—I take this to be the position of romantic theorists. It may be developed formally, by manipulating language for stylistic effect, and such manipulation may involve, for pedagogical continuity, a vocabulary of style. But it is primarily developed by any kind of language activity that enhances the awareness of language as language.[36] David T. Hakes, summarizing the research on metalinguistic awareness, notes how far we are from understanding this process:

> the optimal conditions for becoming metalinguistically competent involve growing up in a literate environment with adult models who are themselves metalinguistically competent and who foster the growth of that competence in a variety of ways as yet little understood. ("The Development of Metalinguistic Abilities," p. 205: see footnote 25)

Such a model places language, at all levels, at the center of the curriculum, but not as "necessary categories and labels" (Kolln, "Closing the Books on Alchemy," p. 150), but as literal stuff, verbal clay, to be molded and probed, shaped and reshaped, and, above all, enjoyed.

THE TRADITION OF EXPERIMENTAL RESEARCH

Thus, when we turn back to experimental research on the value of formal grammar instruction, we do so with firm predictions given us by our theory of language. Our theory would predict that formal grammar instruction, whether instruction in scientific grammar or instruction in "the common school grammar," would have little to do with control over surface correctness nor with quality of writing. It would predict that any form of active involvement with language would be preferable to instruction in rules or definitions (or incantations). In essence, this is what the research tells us. In 1893, the Committee of Ten (*Report of the Committee of Ten on Secondary School Studies* [Washington, D.C.: U.S. Government Printing Office, 1893]) put grammar at the center of the English curriculum, and its report established the rigidly sequential mode of instruction common for the last century. But the committee explicitly noted that grammar instruction did not aid correctness, arguing instead that it improved the ability to think logically (an argument developed from the role of the "grammarian" in the classical rhetorical tradition, essentially a teacher of literature—see, for example, the etymology of *grammar* in the *Oxford English Dictionary*).

But Franklin S. Hoyt, in a 1906 experiment, found no relationship between the study of grammar and the ability to think logically; his research led him to conclude what I am constrained to argue more than seventy-five years later, that there is no "relationship between a knowledge of technical grammar and the ability to use English and to interpret language" ("The Place of Grammar in the Elementary Curriculum,"

Teachers College Record, 7 [1906], 483–484). Later studies, through the 1920s, focused on the relationship of knowledge of grammar and ability to recognize error; experiments reported by James Boraas in 1917 and by William Asker in 1923 are typical of those that reported no correlation. In the 1930s, with the development of the functional grammar movement, it was common to compare the study of formal grammar with one form or another of active manipulation of language; experiments by I. O. Ash in 1935 and Ellen Frogner in 1939 are typical of studies showing the superiority of active involvement with language.[37] In a 1959 article, "Grammar in Language Teaching" (*Elementary English,* 36 [1959], 412–421), John J. DeBoer noted the consistency of these findings.

> The impressive fact is . . . that in all these studies, carried out in places and at times far removed from each other, often by highly experienced and disinterested investigators, the results have been consistently negative so far as the value of grammar in the improvement of language expression is concerned. (p. 417)

In 1960 Ingrid M. Strom, reviewing more than fifty experimental studies, came to a similarly strong and unqualified conclusion:

> direct methods of instruction, focusing on writing activities and the structuring of ideas, are more efficient in teaching sentence structure, usage, punctuation, and other related factors than are such methods as nomenclature drill, diagramming, and rote memorization of grammatical rules.[38]

In 1963 two research reviews appeared, one by Braddock, Lloyd-Jones, and Schorer, cited at the beginning of this paper, and one by Henry C. Meckel, whose conclusions, though more guarded, are in essential agreement.[39] In 1969 J. Stephen Sherwin devoted one-fourth of his *Four Problems in Teaching English: A Critique of Research* (Scranton, Penn.: International Textbook, 1969) to the grammar issue, concluding that "instruction in formal grammar is an ineffective way to help students achieve proficiency in writing" (p. 135). Some early experiments in sentence combining, such as those by Donald R. Bateman and Frank J. Zidonnis and by John C. Mellon, showed improvement in measures of syntactic complexity with instruction in transformational grammar keyed to sentence combining practice. But a later study by Frank O'Hare achieved the same gains with no grammar instruction, suggesting to Sandra L. Stotsky and to Richard Van de Veghe that active manipulation of language, not the grammar unit, explained the earlier results.[40] More recent summaries of research—by Elizabeth I. Haynes, Hillary Taylor

Holbrook, and Marcia Farr Whiteman—support similar conclusions. Indirect evidence for this position is provided by surveys reported by Betty Bamberg in 1978 and 1981, showing that time spent in grammar instruction in high school is the least important factor, of eight factors examined, in separating regular from remedial writers at the college level.[41]

More generally, Patrick Scott and Bruce Castner, in "Reference Sources for Composition Research: A Practical Survey" (*CE*, 45 [1983], 756–768), note that much current research is not informed by an awareness of the past. Put simply, we are constrained to reinvent the wheel. My concern here has been with a far more serious problem: that too often the wheel we reinvent is square.

It is, after all, a question of power. Janet Emig, developing a consensus from composition research, and Aaron S. Carton and Lawrence V. Castiglione, developing the implications of language theory for education, come to the same conclusion: that the thrust of current research and theory is to take power from the teacher and to give that power to the learner.[42] At no point in the English curriculum is the question of power more blatantly posed than in the issue of formal grammar instruction. It is time that we, as teachers, formulate theories of language and literacy and let those theories guide our teaching, and it is time that we, as researchers, move on to more interesting areas of inquiry.

NOTES

1. *Research in Written Composition* (Urbana, Ill.: National Council of Teachers of English, 1963), pp. 37–38.

2. "Non-magical Thinking: Presenting Writing Developmentally in Schools," in *Writing Process, Development and Communication*, Vol. II of *Writing: The Nature, Development and Teaching of Written Communication*, ed. Charles H. Frederiksen and Joseph F. Dominic (Hillsdale, N.J.: Lawrence Erlbaum, 1980), pp. 21–30.

3. For arguments in favor of formal grammar teaching, see Patrick F. Basset, "Grammar—Can We Afford Not to Teach It?" *NASSP Bulletin*, 64, No. 10 (1980), 55–63; Mary Epes, et al., "The COMP-LAB Project: Assessing the Effectiveness of a Laboratory-Centered Basic Writing Course on the College Level" (Jamaica, N.Y.: York College, CUNY, 1979) ERIC 194 908; June B. Evans, "The Analogous Ounce: The Analgesic for Relief," *English Journal*, 70, No. 2 (1981), 38–39; Sydney Greenbaum, "What Is Grammar and Why Teach It?" (a paper presented at the meeting of the National Council of Teachers of English, Boston, Nov. 1982) ERIC 222 917; Marjorie Smelstor, *A Guide to the Role of Grammar in Teaching Writing* (Madison: University of Wisconsin School of Education, 1978) ERIC 176 323; and A. M. Tibbetts, *Working Papers: A Teacher's Observations on Composition* (Glenview, Ill.: Scott, Foresman, 1982).

For attacks on formal grammar teaching, see Harvey A. Daniels, *Famous Last Words: The American Language Crisis Reconsidered* (Carbondale: Southern Illinois University Press, 1983); Suzette Haden Elgin, *Never Mind the Trees: What the English Teacher Really Needs to*

Know about Linguistics (Berkeley: University of California College of Education, Bay Area Writing Project Occasional Paper No. 2, 1980) ERIC 198 536; Mike Rose, "Remedial Writing Courses: A Critique and a Proposal." *College English*, 45 (1983), 109–128; and Ron Shook, "Response to Martha Kolln," *College Composition and Communication*, 34 (1983), 491–495.

4. See, for example, Clifton Fadiman and James Howard, *Empty Pages: A Search for Writing Competence in School and Society* (Belmont, Cal.: Fearon Pitman, 1979); Edwin Newman, *A Civil Tongue* (Indianapolis, Ind.: Bobbs-Merrill, 1976); and *Strictly Speaking* (New York: Warner Books, 1974); John Simons, *Paradigms Lost* (New York: Clarkson N. Potter, 1980); A. M. Tibbetts and Charlene Tibbetts, *What's Happening to American English?* (New York: Scribner's, 1978); and "Why Johnny Can't Write," *Newsweek*, 8 Dec. 1975, pp. 58–63.

5. "The Role of Grammar in a Secondary School English Curriculum." *Research in the Teaching of English*, 10 (1976), 5–21; *The Role of Grammar in a Secondary School Curriculum* (Wellington: New Zealand Council of Teachers of English, 1979).

6. "A Taxonomy of Compositional Competencies," in *Perspectives on Literacy*, ed. Richard Beach and P. David Pearson (Minneapolis: University of Minnesota College of Education, 1979), pp. 247–272.

7. On usage norms, see Edward Finegan, *Attitudes toward English Usage: The History of a War of Words* (New York: Teachers College Press, 1980), and Jim Quinn, *American Tongue in Cheek: A Populist Guide to Language* (New York: Pantheon, 1980); on arrangement, see Patrick Hartwell, "Teaching Arrangement: A Pedagogy," *CE*, 40 (1979), 548–554.

8. "Revolution in Grammar," *Quarterly Journal of Speech*, 40 (1954), 299–312.

9. Richard A. Lanham, *Revising Prose* (New York: Scribner's, 1979); William Strunk and E. B. White, *The Elements of Style*, 3rd ed. (New York: Macmillan, 1979); Joseph Williams, *Style: Ten Lessons in Clarity and Grace* (Glenview, Ill.: Scott, Foresman, 1981); Christensen, "A Generative Rhetoric of the Sentence," *CCC*, 14 (1963), 155–161; Donald A. Daiker, Andrew Kerek, and Max Morenberg, *The Writer's Options: Combining to Composing*, 2nd ed. (New York: Harper & Row, 1982).

10. "A Psychological Approach," in *Psychobiology of Language*, ed. M. Studdert-Kennedy (Cambridge, Mass.: MIT Press, 1983), pp. 16–19. See also Noam Chomsky, "Language and Unconscious Knowledge," in *Psychoanalysis and Language: Psychiatry and the Humanities*, Vol. III, ed. Joseph H. Smith (New Haven, Conn.: Yale University Press, 1978), pp. 3–44.

11. Morris Halle, "Knowledge Unlearned and Untaught: What Speakers Know about the Sounds of Their Language," in *Linguistic Theory and Psychological Reality*, ed. Halle, Joan Bresnan, and George A. Miller (Cambridge, Mass.: MIT Press, 1978), pp. 135–140.

12. Moscowitz, "On the Status of Vowel Shift in English," in *Cognitive Development and the Acquisition of Language*, ed. T. E. Moore (New York: Academic Press, 1973), pp. 223–260; Chomsky, "Stages in Language Development and Reading Exposure," *Harvard Educational Review*, 42 (1972), 1–33; and Brause, "Developmental Aspects of the Ability to Understand Semantic Ambiguity, with Implications for Teachers," *RTE*, 11 (1977), 39–48.

13. Mills and Hemsley, "The Effect of Levels of Education on Judgments of Grammatical Acceptability," *Language and Speech*, 19 (1976), 324–342; Whyte, "Levels of Language Competence and Reading Ability: An Exploratory Investigation," *Journal of Research in Reading*, 5 (1982, 123–132; Morais, et al., "Does Awareness of Speech as a Series of Phones Arise Spontaneously," *Cognition*, 7 (1979), 323–331; Ferguson, *Cognitive Effects of Literacy: Linguistic Awareness in Adult Non-readers* (Washington, D.C.: National Institute of

Education Final Report, 1981) ERIC 222 85; Hamilton and Barton, "A Word Is a Word: Metalinguistic Skills in Adults of Varying Literacy Levels" (Stanford, Cal.: Stanford University Department of Linguistics, 1980) ERIC 222 859.

14. On the question of the psychological reality of Grammar 2 descriptions, see Maria Black and Shulamith Chiat, "Psycholinguistics without 'Psychological Reality'," *Linguistics*, 19 (1981), 37–61; Joan Bresnan, ed., *The Mental Representation of Grammatical Relations* (Cambridge, Mass.: MIT Press, 1982); and Michael H. Long, "Inside the 'Black Box': Methodological Issues in Classroom Research on Language Learning," *Language Learning*, 30 (1980), 1–42.

15. Chomsky, "The Current Scene in Linguistics," *College English*, 27 (1966), 587–595; and "Linguistic Theory," in *Language Teaching: Broader Contexts*, ed. Robert C. Meade, Jr. (New York: Modern Language Association, 1966), pp. 43–49; Mark Lester, "The Value of Transformational Grammar in Teaching Composition," CCC, 16 (1967), 228.

16. Christensen, "Between Two Worlds," in *Notes toward a New Rhetoric: Nine Essays for Teachers*, rev. ed., ed. Bonniejean Christensen (New York: Harper & Row, 1978), pp. 1–22.

17. Reber, "Implicit Learning of Artificial Grammars," *Journal of Verbal Learning and Verbal Behavior*, 6 (1967), 855–863; "Implicit Learning of Synthetic Languages: The Role of Instructional Set," *Journal of Experimental Psychology: Human Learning and Memory*, 2 (1976), 889–894; and Reber, Saul M. Kassin, Selma Lewis, and Gary Cantor, "On the Relationship between Implicit and Explicit Modes in the Learning of a Complex Rule Structure," *Journal of Experimental Psychology: Human Learning and Memory*, 6 (1980), 492–502.

18. "Individual Variation in the Use of the Monitor," in *Principles of Second Language Learning*, ed. W. Richie (New York: Academic Press, 1978), pp. 175–185.

19. "Applications of Psycholinguistic Research to the Classroom," in *Practical Applications of Research in Foreign Language Teaching*, ed. D. J. James (Lincolnwood, Ill.: National Textbook, 1983), p. 61.

20. "Some Evidence for the Integrity and Interaction of Two Knowledge Sources," in *New Dimensions in Second Language Acquisition Research*, ed. Roger W. Anderson (Rowley, Mass.: Newbury House, 1981), pp. 62–74.

21. Hartwell and Bentley, *Some Suggestions for Using Open to Language* (New York: Oxford University Press, 1982), p. 73; Rose, *Writer's Block: The Cognitive Dimension* (Carbondale: Southern Illinois University Press, 1983), p. 99; Daiute, "Psycholinguistic Foundations of the Writing Process," *RTE*, 15 (1981), 5–22.

22. See Bartholomae, "The Study of Error"; Patrick Hartwell, "The Writing Center and the Paradoxes of Written-Down Speech," in *Writing Centers: Theory and Administration*, ed. Gary Olson (Urbana, Ill.: NCTE, 1984), pp. 48–61; and Sondra Perl, "A Look at Basic Writers in the Process of Composing," in *Basic Writing: A Collection of Essays for Teachers, Researchers, and Administrators* (Urbana, Ill.: NCTE, 1980), pp. 13–32.

23. Emonds, *Adjacency in Grammar: The Theory of Language-Particular Rules* (New York: Academic, 1983); and Jochnowitz, "Everybody Likes Pizza, Doesn't He or She?" *American Speech*, 57 (1982), 198–203.

24. Scribner and Cole, *Psychology of Literacy* (Cambridge, Mass.: Harvard University Press, 1981); Gleitman and Gleitman, "Language Use and Language Judgment," in *Individual Differences in Language Ability and Language Behavior*, ed. Charles J. Fillmore, Daniel Kempler, and William S.-Y. Wang (New York: Academic Press, 1979), pp. 103–126.

25. There are several recent reviews of this developing body of research in psychology and child development: Irene Athey, "Language Development Factors Related to Reading

Development," *Journal of Educational Research,* 76 (1983), 197–203; James Flood and Paula Menyuk, "Metalinguistic Development and Reading/Writing Achievement," *Claremont Reading Conference Yearbook,* 46 (1982), 122–132; and the following four essays: David T. Hakes, "The Development of Metalinguistic Abilities: What Develops?," pp. 162–210; Stan A. Kuczaj, II, and Brooke Harbaugh, "What Children Think about the Speaking Capabilities of Other Persons and Things," pp. 211–227; Karen Saywitz and Louise Cherry Wilkinson, "Age-Related Differences in Metalinguistic Awareness," pp. 229–250; and Harriet Salatas Waters and Virginia S. Tinsley, "The Development of Verbal Self-Regulation: Relationships between Language, Cognition, and Behavior," pp. 251–277; all in *Language, Thought, and Culture,* Vol. II of *Language Development,* ed. Stan Kuczaj, Jr. (Hillsdale, N.J.: Lawrence Erlbaum, 1982). See also Joanne R. Nurss, "Research in Review: Linguistic Awareness and Learning to Read," *Young Children,* 35, No. 3 [1980], 57–66.

26. "Competing Value Systems in Inner City Schools," in *Children In and Out of School: Ethnography and Education,* ed. Perry Gilmore and Allan A. Glatthorn (Washington, D.C.: Center for Applied Linguistics, 1982), pp. 148–171; and "Locating the Frontier between Social and Psychological Factors in Linguistic Structure," in *Individual Differences in Language Ability and Language Behavior,* ed. Fillmore, Kempler, and Wang, pp. 327–340.

27. See, for example, Thomas Farrell, "IQ and Standard English," *CCC,* 34 (1983), 470–484; and the responses by Karen L. Greenberg and Patrick Hartwell, *CCC,* in press.

28. Jane W. Torrey, "Teaching Standard English to Speakers of Other Dialects," in *Applications of Linguistics: Selected Papers of the Second International Conference of Applied Linguistics,* ed. G. E. Perren and J. L. M. Trim (Cambridge, Mass.: Cambridge University Press, 1971), pp. 423–428; James W. Beers and Edmund H. Henderson, "A Study of the Developing Orthographic Concepts among First Graders," *RTE,* 11 (1977), 133–148.

29. See the error counts of Samuel A. Kirschner and G. Howard Poteet, "Non-Standard English Usage in the Writing of Black, White, and Hispanic Remedial English Students in an Urban Community College," *RTE,* 7 (1973), 351–355; and Marilyn Sternglass, "Close Similarities in Dialect Features of Black and White College Students in Remedial Composition Classes," *TESOL Quarterly,* 8 (1974), 271–283.

30. For reading, see the massive study by Kenneth S. Goodman and Yetta M. Goodman, *Reading of American Children whose Language Is a Stable Rural Dialect of English or a Language other than English* (Washington, D.C.: National Institute of Education Final Report, 1978) ERIC 175 754; and the overview by Rudine Sims, "Dialect and Reading: Toward Redefining the Issues," in *Reader Meets Author/Bridging the Gap: A Psycholinguistic and Sociolinguistic Approach,* ed. Judith A. Langer and M. Tricia Smith-Burke (Newark, Del.: International Reading Association, 1982), pp. 222–232. For writing, see Patrick Hartwell, "Dialect Interference in Writing: A Critical View," *RTE,* 14 (1980), 101–118; and the anthology edited by Barry M. Kroll and Roberta J. Vann, *Exploring Speaking-Writing Relationships: Connections and Contrasts* (Urbana, Ill.: NCTE, 1981).

31. See, for example, Eric A. Havelock, *The Literary Revolution in Greece and its Cultural Consequences* (Princeton, N.J.: Princeton University Press, 1982); Lesley Milroy on literacy in Dublin, *Language and Social Networks* (Oxford: Basil Blackwell, 1980); Ron Scollon and Suzanne B. K. Scollon on literacy in central Alaska, *Interethnic Communication: An Athabascan Case* (Austin, Tex.: Southwest Educational Development Laboratory Working Papers in Sociolinguistics, No. 59, 1979) ERIC 175 276; and Scribner and Cole on literacy in Liberia, *Psychology of Literacy* (see footnote 24).

32. See, for example, the anthology edited by Deborah Tannen, *Spoken and Written Language: Exploring Orality and Literacy* (Norwood, N.J.: Ablex, 1982); and Shirley Brice Heath's continuing work: "Protean Shapes in Literacy Events: Ever-Shifting Oral and Literate Traditions," in *Spoken and Written Language*, pp. 91–117; *Ways with Words: Language, Life and Work in Communities and Classrooms* (New York: Cambridge University Press, 1983); and "What No Bedtime Story Means," *Language in Society*, 11 (1982), 49–76.

33. For studies at the elementary level, see Dell H. Hymes, et al., eds., *Ethnographic Monitoring of Children's Acquisition of Reading/Language Arts Skills In and Out of the Classroom* (Washington, D.C.: National Institute of Education Final Report, 1981) ERIC 208 096. For studies at the secondary level, see James L. Collins and Michael M. Williamson, "Spoken Language and Semantic Abbreviation in Writing," *RTE*, 15 (1981), 23–36. And for studies at the college level, see Patrick Hartwell and Gene LoPresti, "Sentence Combining as Kid-Watching," in *Sentence Combining: Toward a Rhetorical Perspective*, ed. Donald A. Daiker, Andrew Kerek, and Max Morenberg (Carbondale: Southern Illinois University Press, in press).

34. Lloyd-Jones, "Romantic Revels—I Am Not You," *CCC*, 23 (1972), 251–271; and Young, "Concepts of Art and the Teaching of Writing," in *The Rhetorical Tradition and Modern Writing*, ed. James J. Murphy (New York: Modern Language Association, 1982), pp. 130–141.

35. For the romantic position, see Ann E. Berthoff, "Tolstoy, Vygotsky, and the Making of Meaning," *CCC*, 29 (1978), 249–255; Kenneth Dowst, "The Epistemic Approach," in *Eight Approaches to Teaching Composition*, ed. Timothy Donovan and Ben G. McClellan (Urbana, Ill.: NCTE, 1980), pp. 65–85; Peter Elbow, "The Challenge for Sentence Combining"; and Donald Murray, "Following Language toward Meaning," both in *Sentence Combining: Toward a Rhetorical Perspective* (in press; see footnote 33); and Ian Pringle, "Why Teach Style? A Review-Essay," *CCC*, 34 (1983), 91–98.

For the classic position, see Christensen's "A Generative Rhetoric of the Sentence"; and Joseph Williams' "Defining Complexity," *CE*, 41 (1979), 595–609; and his *Style: Ten Lessons in Clarity and Grace* (see footnote 9).

36. Courtney B. Cazden and David K. Dickinson, "Language and Education: Standardization versus Cultural Pluralism," in *Language in the USA*, ed. Charles A. Ferguson and Shirley Brice Heath (New York: Cambridge University Press, 1981), pp. 446–468; and Carol Chomsky, "Developing Facility with Language Structure," in *Discovering Language with Children*, ed. Gay Su Pinnell (Urbana, Ill.: NCTE, 1980), pp. 56–59.

37. Boraas, "Formal English Grammar and the Practical Mastery of English." Diss. University of Illinois, 1917; Asker, "Does Knowledge of Grammar Function?" *School and Society*, 17 (27 January 1923), 109–111; Ash, "An Experimental Evaluation of the Stylistic Approach in Teaching Composition in the Junior High School," *Journal of Experimental Education*, 4 (1935), 54–62; and Frogner, "A Study of the Relative Efficacy of a Grammatical and a Thought Approach to the Improvement of Sentence Structure in Grades Nine and Eleven," *School Review*, 47 (1939), 663–675.

38. "Research on Grammar and Usage and Its Implications for Teaching Writing," *Bulletin of the School of Education*, Indiana University, 36 (1960), pp. 13–14.

39. Meckel, "Research on Teaching Composition and Literature," in *Handbook of Research on Teaching*, ed. N. L. Gage (Chicago: Rand McNally, 1963), pp. 966–1006.

40. Bateman and Zidonis, *The Effect of a Study of Transformational Grammar on the Writing of Ninth and Tenth Graders* (Urbana, Ill.: NCTE, 1966); Mellon, *Transformational Sentence Combining: A Method for Enhancing the Development of Fluency in English*

Composition (Urbana, Ill.: NCTE, 1969); O'Hare, *Sentence-Combining: Improving Student Writing without Formal Grammar Instruction* (Urbana, Ill.: NCTE, 1971); Stotsky, "Sentence-Combining as a Curricular Activity: Its Effect on Written Language Development," *RTE*, 9 (1975), 30–72; and Van de Veghe, "Research in Written Composition: Fifteen Years of Investigation," ERIC 157 095.

41. Haynes, "Using Research in Preparing to Teach Writing," *English Journal*, 69, No. 1 (1978), 82–88; Holbrook, "ERIC/RCS Report: Whither (Wither) Grammar," *Language Arts*, 60 (1983), 259–263; Whiteman, "What We Can Learn from Writing Research," *Theory into Practice*, 19 (1980), 150–156; Bamberg, "Composition in the Secondary English Curriculum: Some Current Trends and Directions for the Eighties," *RTE*, 15 (1981), 257–266; and "Composition Instruction Does Make a Difference: A Comparison of the High School Preparation of College Freshmen in Regular and Remedial English Classes," *RTE*, 12 (1978), 47–59.

42. Emig, "Inquiry Paradigms and Writing," *CCC*, 33 (1982), 64–75; Carton and Castiglione, "Educational Linguistics: Defining the Domain," in *Psycholinguistic Research: Implications and Applications,* ed. Doris Aaronson and Robert W. Rieber (Hillsdale, N.J.: Lawrence Erlbaum, 1979), pp. 497–520.

Contemporary Composition
The Major Pedagogical Theories

JAMES A. BERLIN

A number of articles attempting to make sense of the various approaches to teaching composition have recently appeared. While all are worth considering, some promote a common assumption that I am convinced is erroneous.[1] Since all pedagogical approaches, it is argued, share a concern for the elements of the composing process—that is, for writer, reality, reader, and language—their only area of disagreement must involve the element or elements that ought to be given the most attention. From this point of view, the composing process is always and everywhere the same because writer, reality, reader, and language are always and everywhere the same. Differences in teaching theories, then, are mere cavils about which of these features to emphasize in the classroom.

I would like to say at the start that I have no quarrel with the elements that these investigators isolate as forming the composing process, and I plan to use them myself. While it is established practice today to speak of the composing process as a recursive activity involving prewriting, writing, and rewriting, it is not difficult to see the writer-reality-audience-language relationship as underlying, at a deeper structural level, each of these three stages. In fact, as I will later show, this deeper structure determines the shape that instruction in prewriting, writing, and rewriting assumes—or does not assume, as is sometimes the case.

I do, however, strongly disagree with the contention that the differences in approaches to teaching writing can be explained by attending to the degree of emphasis given to universally defined elements of a universally defined

Reprinted from *College English* 44.8 (December 1982): 765–77. Used with permission.

composing process. The differences in these teaching approaches should instead be located in diverging definitions of the composing process itself—that is, in the way the elements that make up the process—writer, reality, audience, and language—are envisioned. Pedagogical theories in writing courses are grounded in rhetorical theories, and rhetorical theories do not differ in the simple undue emphasis of writer or audience or reality or language or some combination of these. Rhetorical theories differ from each other in the way writer, reality, audience, and language are conceived—both as separate units and in the way the units relate to each other. In the case of distinct pedagogical approaches, these four elements are likewise defined and related so as to describe a different composing process, which is to say a different world with different rules about what can be known, how it can be known, and how it can be communicated. To teach writing is to argue for a version of reality, and the best way of knowing and communicating it—to deal, as Paul Kameen has pointed out, in the metarhetorical realm of epistemology and linguistics.[2] And all composition teachers are ineluctably operating in this realm, whether or not they consciously choose to do so.

Considering pedagogical theories along these lines has led me to see groupings sometimes similar, sometimes at variance, with the schemes of others. The terms chosen for these categories are intended to prevent confusion and to be self-explanatory. The four dominant groups I will discuss are the Neo-Aristotelians or Classicists, the Positivists or Current-Traditionalists, the Neo-Platonists or Expressionists, and the New Rhetoricians. As I have said, I will be concerned in each case with the way that writer, reality, audience, and language have been defined and related so as to form a distinct world construct with distinct rules for discovering and communicating knowledge. I will then show how this epistemic complex makes for specific directives about invention, arrangement, and style (or prewriting, writing, and rewriting). Finally, as the names for the groups suggest, I will briefly trace the historical precedents of each, pointing to their roots in order to better understand their modern manifestations.

My reasons for presenting this analysis are not altogether disinterested. I am convinced that the pedagogical approach of the New Rhetoricians is the most intelligent and most practical alternative available, serving in every way the best interests of our students. I am also concerned, however, that writing teachers become more aware of the full significance of their pedagogical strategies. Not doing so can have disastrous consequences, ranging from momentarily confusing students to sending them away with faulty and even harmful information. The dismay students display about writing is, I am convinced, at least occasionally the result of teachers unconsciously offering contradictory advice about composing—guidance grounded in assumptions that simply do not square with each other. More important, as I have already indicated and as I plan to explain in detail later on, in teaching writing we are tacitly teaching a version of reality and the student's place and mode of operation in it. Yet many teachers (and I suspect most) look upon their vocations as the imparting of a largely mechanical skill, important only because it serves students in getting them through school and in advancing them in their professions. This essay will argue that writing teachers are perforce given a responsibility that far exceeds this merely instrumental task.[3]

I begin with revivals of Aristotelian rhetoric not because they are a dominant force today—far from it. My main purpose in starting with them is to show that many who say that they are followers of Aristotle are in truth opposed to his system in every sense. There is also the consideration that Aristotle has provided the technical language most often used in discussing rhetoric—so much so that it is all but impossible to talk intelligently about the subject without knowing him.

In the Aristotelian scheme of things, the material world exists independently of the observer and is knowable through sense impressions. Since sense impressions in themselves reveal nothing, however, to arrive at true knowledge it is necessary for the mind to perform an operation upon sense data. This operation is a function of reason and amounts to the appropriate use of syllogistic reasoning, the system of logic that Aristotle himself developed and refined. Providing the method for analyzing the material of any discipline, this logic offers, as Marjorie Grene explains, "a set of general rules for scientists (as Aristotle understood science) working each in his appropriate material. The rules are rules of validity, not psychological rules" (*A Portrait of Aristotle* [London: Faber and Faber, 1963], p. 69). Truth exists in conformance with the rules of logic, and logic is so thoroughly deductive that even induction is regarded as an imperfect form of the syllogism. The strictures imposed by logic, moreover, naturally arise out of the very structure of the mind and of the universe. In other words, there is a happy correspondence between the mind and the universe, so that, to cite Grene once again, "As the world is, finally, so is the mind that knows it" (p. 234).

Reality for Aristotle can thus be known and communicated, with language serving as the unproblematic medium of discourse. There is an uncomplicated correspondence between the sign and the thing, and—once again emphasizing the rational—the process whereby sign and thing are united is considered a mental act: words are not a part of the external world, but both word and thing are a part of thought.[4]

Rhetoric is of course central to Aristotle's system. Like dialectic—the method of discovering and communicating truth in learned discourse—rhetoric deals with the realm of the probable, with truth as discovered in the areas of law, politics, and what might be called public virtue. Unlike scientific discoveries, truth in these realms can never be stated with absolute certainty. Still, approximations to truth are possible. The business of rhetoric then is to enable the speaker—Aristotle's rhetoric is preeminently oral—to find the means necessary to persuade the audience of the truth. Thus rhetoric is primarily concerned with the provision of inventional devices whereby the speaker may discover his or her argument, with these devices naturally falling into three categories: the rational, the emotional, and the ethical. Since truth is rational, the first is paramount and is derived from the rules of logic, albeit applied in the relaxed form of the enthymeme and example. Realizing that individuals are not always ruled by reason, however, Aristotle provides advice on appealing to the emotions of the audience and on presenting one's own character in the most favorable light, each considered with special regard for the audience and the occasion of the speech.

Aristotle's emphasis on invention leads to the neglect of commentary on arrangement and style. The treatment of arrangement is at best sketchy, but it does display Aristotle's reliance on the logical in its commitment to rational development. The section on style is more extensive and deserves special mention because it highlights Aristotle's rationalistic view of language, a view no longer considered defensible. As R. H. Robins explains:

> The word for Aristotle is thus the minimal meaningful unit. He further distinguishes the meaning of a word as an isolate from the meaning of a sentence; a word by itself "stands for" or "indicates" . . . something, but a sentence affirms or denies a predicate of its subject, or says that its subject exists or does not exist. One cannot now defend this doctrine of meaning. It is based on the formal logic that Aristotle codified and, we might say, sterilized for generations. The notion that words have meaning just by standing for or indicating something, whether in the world at large or in the human mind (both views are stated or suggested by Aristotle), leads to difficulties that have worried philosophers in many ages, and seriously distorts linguistic and grammatical studies.[5]

It should be noted, however, that despite this unfavorable estimate, Robins goes on to praise Aristotle as in some ways anticipating later developments in linguistics.

Examples of Aristotelian rhetoric in the textbooks of today are few indeed. Edward P. J. Corbett's *Classical Rhetoric for the Modern Student* (1971) and Richard Hughes and Albert Duhamel's *Principles of Rhetoric* (1967) revive the tradition. Most textbooks that claim to be Aristotelian are operating within the paradigm of what has come to be known as Current-Traditional Rhetoric, a category that might also be called the Positivist.

The Positivist or Current-Traditional group clearly dominates thinking about writing instruction today. The evidence is the staggering number of textbooks that yearly espouse its principles. The origins of Current-Traditional Rhetoric, as Albert Kitzhaber showed in his dissertation (University of Washington, 1953) on "Rhetoric in American Colleges," can be found in the late nineteenth-century rhetoric texts of A. S. Hill, Barett Wendell, and John F. Genung. But its epistemological stance can be found in eighteenth-century Scottish Common Sense Realism as expressed in the philosophy of Thomas Reid and James Beattie, and in the rhetorical treatises of George Campbell, Hugh Blair, and to a lesser extent, Richard Whately.

For Common Sense Realism, the certain existence of the material world is indisputable. All knowledge is founded on the simple correspondence between sense impressions and the faculties of the mind. This so far sounds like the Aristotelian world view, but is in fact a conscious departure from it. Common Sense Realism denies the value of the deductive method—syllogistic reasoning—in arriving at knowledge. Truth is instead discovered through induction alone. It is the individual sense impression that provides the basis on which all knowledge can be built. Thus the new scientific logic of Locke replaces the old deductive logic of Aristotle as the method for understanding experience. The world is still rational, but its system is to be discovered through the experimental method, not through logical categories grounded in a mental faculty. The state of affairs characterizing the emergence of the new epistemology is succinctly summarized by Wilbur Samuel Howell:

> The old science, as the disciples of Aristotle conceived of it at the end of the seventeenth century, had considered its function to be that of subjecting traditional truths to syllogistic examination, and of accepting as new truth only what could be proved to be consistent with the old. Under that kind of arrangement, traditional logic had taught the methods of deductive analysis, had perfected itself in the machinery of testing propositions for consistency, and had served at the same time as the instrument by which truths could be arranged so as to become intelligible and convincing to other learned men. . . . The new science, as envisioned by its founder, Francis Bacon, considered its function to be that of subjecting physical and human facts to observation and experiment, and of accepting as new truth only what could be shown to conform to the realities behind it.[6]

The rhetoric based on the new logic can be seen most clearly in George Campbell's *Philosophy of Rhetoric* (1776) and Hugh Blair's *Lectures on*

Rhetoric and Belles Lettres (1783). The old distinction between dialectic as the discipline of learned discourse and rhetoric as the discipline of popular discourse is destroyed. Rhetoric becomes the study of all forms of communication: scientific, philosophical, historical, political, legal, and even poetic. An equally significant departure in this new rhetoric is that it contains no inventional system. Truth is to be discovered outside the rhetorical enterprise—through the method, usually the scientific method, of the appropriate discipline, or, as in poetry and oratory, through genius.

The aim of rhetoric is to teach how to adapt the discourse to its hearers—and here the uncomplicated correspondence of the faculties and the world is emphasized. When the individual is freed from the biases of language, society, or history, the senses provide the mental faculties with a clear and distinct image of the world. The world readily surrenders its meaning to anyone who observes it properly, and no operation of the mind—logical or otherwise—is needed to arrive at truth. To communicate, the speaker or writer—both now included—need only provide the language which corresponds either to the objects in the external world or to the ideas in his or her own mind—both are essentially the same—in such a way that it reproduces the objects and the experience of them in the minds of the hearers (Cohen, pp. 38–42). As Campbell explains, "Thus language and thought, like body and soul, are made to correspond, and the qualities of the one exactly to co-operate with those of the other."[7] The emphasis in this rhetoric is on adapting what has been discovered outside the rhetorical enterprise to the minds of the hearers. The study of rhetoric thus focuses on developing skill in arrangement and style.

Given this epistemological field in a rhetoric that takes all communication as its province, discourse tends to be organized according to the faculties to which it appeals. A scheme that is at once relevant to current composition theory and typical in its emulation of Campbell, Blair, and Whately can be found in John Francis Genung's *The Practical Elements of Rhetoric* (1886).[8] For Genung the branches of discourse fall into four categories. The most "fundamental" mode appeals to understanding and is concerned with transmitting truth, examples of which are "history, biography, fiction, essays, treatises, criticism." The second and third groups are description and narration, appealing again to the understanding, but leading the reader to "feel the thought as well as think it." For Genung "the purest outcome" of this kind of writing is poetry. The fourth kind of discourse, "the most complex literary type," is oratory. This kind is concerned with persuasion and makes its special appeal to the will, but in so doing involves all the faculties. Genung goes on to create a further distinction that contributed to the departmentalization of English and Speech and the division of English into literature and composition. Persuasion is restricted to considerations of experts in the spoken language and poetry to discussions of literature teachers, now first appearing. College writing courses, on the other hand, are to focus on discourse that appeals to the understanding—exposition, narration, description, and argumentation (distinct now from persuasion). It is significant, moreover, that college rhetoric is to be concerned solely with the communication of truth that is certain and empirically verifiable—in other words, not probabilistic.

Genung, along with his contemporaries A. S. Hill and Barrett Wendell, sets the pattern for most modern composition textbooks, and their works show striking similarities to the vast majority of texts published today.[9] It is discouraging that generations after Freud and Einstein, college students are encouraged to embrace a view of reality based on a mechanistic physics and a naive faculty psychology—and all in the name of a convenient pedagogy.

The next theory of composition instruction to be considered arose as a reaction to current-traditional rhetoric. Its clearest statements are located in the work of Ken Macrorie, William Coles, Jr., James E. Miller and Stephen Judy, and the so-called "Pre-Writing School" of D. Gordon Rohman, Albert O. Wlecke, Clinton S. Burhans, and Donald Stewart (see Harrington, et al., pp. 645–647). Frequent assertions of this view, however, have appeared in American public schools in the twentieth century under the veil of including "creative expression" in the English curriculum.[10] The roots of this view of rhetoric in America can be traced to Emerson and the Transcendentalists, and its ultimate source is to be found in Plato.

In the Platonic scheme, truth is not based on sensory experience since the material world is always in flux and thus unreliable. Truth is instead discovered through an internal apprehension, a private vision of a world that transcends the physical. As Robert Cushman explains in *Therepeia* (Chapel Hill: University of North Carolina Press, 1958), "The central theme of Platonism regarding knowledge is that truth is not brought to man, but man to the truth" (p. 213). A striking corollary of this view is that ultimate truth can be discovered by the individual, but cannot be communicated. Truth can be learned but not taught. The purpose of rhetoric then becomes not the transmission of truth, but the correction of error, the removal of that which obstructs the personal apprehension of the truth. And the method is dialectic, the interaction of two interlocutors of good will intent on arriving at knowledge. Because the respondents are encouraged to break out of their ordinary perceptual set, to become free of the material world and of past error, the dialectic is often disruptive, requiring the abandonment of long held conventions and opinions. Preparing the soul to discover truth is often painful.

Plato's epistemology leads to a unique view of language. Because ultimate truths cannot be communicated, language can only deal with the realm of error, the world of flux, and act, as Gerald L. Bruns explains, as "a preliminary exercise which must engage the soul before the encounter with 'the knowable and truly real being' is possible" (p. 16). Truth is finally inexpressible, is beyond the resources of language. Yet Plato allows for the possibility that language may be used to communicate essential realities. In the *Republic* he speaks of using analogy to express ultimate truth, and in the *Phaedrus*, even as rhetoric is called into question, he employs an analogical method in his discussion of the soul and love. Language, it would appear, can be of some use in trying to communicate the absolute, or at least to approximate the experience of it.

The major tenets of this Platonic rhetoric form the center of what are commonly called "Expressionist" textbooks. Truth is conceived as the result of a private vision that must be constantly consulted in writing. These textbooks thus emphasize writing as a "personal" activity, as an expression of one's unique voice. In *Writing and Reality* (New York: Harper and Row, 1978), James Miller and Stephen Judy argue that "all good writing is *personal*, whether it be an abstract essay or a private letter," and that an important justification for writing is "to sound the depths, to explore, and to discover." The reason is simple: "Form in language grows from content—something the writer has to say—and that something, in turn, comes directly from the self" (pp. 12, 15). Ken Macrorie constantly emphasizes "Telling Truths," by which he means a writer must be "true to the feeling of his experience." His thrust throughout is on speaking in "an authentic voice" (also in Donald Stewart's *The Authentic Voice: A Pre-Writing Approach to Student Writing*, based on the work of Rohman and Wlecke), indicating by this the writer's private sense of things.[11] This placement of the self at the center of communication is also, of course, everywhere present in Coles' *The Plural I* (New York: Holt, Rinehart, and Winston, 1978).

One obvious objection to my reading of these expressionist theories is that their conception of truth can in no way be seen as comparable to Plato's transcendent world of ideas. While this cannot be questioned, it should also be noted that no member of this school is a relativist intent on denying the possibility of any certain truth whatever. All believe in the existence of verifiable truths and find them, as does Plato, in private experience, divorced from the impersonal data of sense experience. All also urge the interaction between writer and reader, a feature that leads to another point of similarity with Platonic rhetoric—the dialectic.

Most expressionist theories rely on classroom procedures that encourage the writer to interact in dialogue with the members of the class. The purpose is to get rid of what is untrue to the private vision of the writer, what is, in a word, inauthentic. Coles, for example, conceives of writing as an unteachable act, a kind of behavior that can be learned but not taught. (See especially the preface to *The Plural I.*) His response to this denial of his pedagogical role is to provide a classroom environment in which the student learns to write—although he or she is not taught to write—through dialectic. *The Plural I*, in fact, reveals Coles and his students engaging in a dialogue designed to lead both teacher and class—Coles admits that he always learns in his courses—to the discovery of what can be known but not communicated. This view of truth as it applies to writing is the basis of Coles' classroom activity. Dialogue can remove error, but it is up to the individual to discover ultimate knowledge. The same emphasis on dialectic can also be found in the texts of Macrorie and of Miller and Judy. Despite their insistence on the self as the source of all content, for example, Miller and Judy include "making connections with others in dialogue and discussion" (p. 5), and Macrorie makes the discussion of student papers the central activity of his classroom.

This emphasis on dialectic, it should be noted, is not an attempt to adjust the message to the audience, since doing so would clearly constitute a violation of the self. Instead the writer is trying to use others to get rid of what is false to the self, what is insincere and untrue to the individual's own sense of things, as evidenced by the use of language—the theory of which constitutes the final point of concurrence between modern Expressionist and Platonic rhetorics.

Most Expressionist textbooks emphasize the use of metaphor either directly or by implication. Coles, for example, sees the major task of the writer to be avoiding the imitation of conventional expressions because they limit what the writer can say. The fresh, personal vision demands an original use of language. Rohman and Wlecke, as well as the textbook by Donald Stewart based on their research, are more explicit. They specifically recommend the cultivation of the ability to make analogies (along with meditation and journal writing) as an inventional device. Macrorie makes metaphor one of the prime features of "good writing" (p. 21) and in one form or another takes it up again and again in *Telling Writing*. The reason for this emphasis is not hard to discover. In communicating, language does not have as its referent the object in the external world or an idea of this object in the mind. Instead, to present truth language must rely on original metaphors in order to capture what is unique in each personal vision. The private apprehension of the real relies on the metaphoric appeal from the known to the unknown, from the public and accessible world of the senses to the inner and privileged immaterial realm, in order to be made available to others. As in Plato, the analogical method offers the only avenue to expressing the true.

The clearest pedagogical expression of the New Rhetoric—or what might be called Epistemic Rhetoric—is found in Ann E. Berthoff's *Forming/Thinking/Writing: The Composing Imagination* (Rochelle Park, N.J.: Hayden, 1978) and Richard E. Young, Alton L. Becker, and Kenneth L. Pike's *Rhetoric: Discovery and Change* (New York: Harcourt Brace Jovanovich, 1970). These books have behind them the rhetorics of such figures as I. A. Richards and Kenneth Burke and the philosophical statements of Susan Langer, Ernst Cassirer, and John Dewey. Closely related to the work of Berthoff and Young, Becker, and Pike are the cognitive-developmental approaches of such figures as James Moffett, Linda Flower, Andrea Lunsford, and Barry Kroll. While their roots are different—located in the realm of cognitive psychology and empirical linguistics—their methods are strikingly similar. In this discussion, however, I intend to call exclusively upon the textbooks of Berthoff and of Young, Becker, and Pike to make my case, acknowledging at the start that there are others that could serve as well. Despite differences, their approaches most comprehensively display a view of rhetoric as epistemic, as a means of arriving at truth.

Classical Rhetoric considers truth to be located in the rational operation of the mind, Positivist Rhetoric in the correct perception of sense impressions, and Neo-Platonic Rhetoric within the individual, attainable only through an internal apprehension. In each case knowledge is a commodity situated in a permanent location, a repository to which the individual goes to be enlightened.

For the New Rhetoric, knowledge is not simply a static entity available for retrieval. Truth is dynamic and dialectical, the result of a process involving the interaction of opposing elements. It is a relation that is created, not pre-existent and waiting to be discovered. The basic elements of the dialectic are the elements that make up the communication process—writer (speaker), audience, reality, language. Communication is always basic to the epistemology underlying the New Rhetoric because truth is always truth for someone standing in relation to others in a linguistically circumscribed situation. The elements of the communication process thus do not simply provide a convenient way of talking about rhetoric. They form the elements that go into the very shaping of knowledge.

It is this dialectical notion of rhetoric—and of rhetoric as the determiner of reality—that underlies the textbooks of Berthoff and of Young, Becker, and Pike. In demonstrating this thesis I will consider the elements of the dialectic alone or in pairs, simply because they are more easily handled this way in discussion. It should not be forgotten, however, that in operation they are always simultaneously in a relationship of one to all, constantly modifying their values in response to each other.

The New Rhetoric denies that truth is discoverable in sense impression since this data must always be interpreted—structured and organized—in order to have meaning. The perceiver is of course the interpreter, but she is likewise unable by herself to provide truth since meaning cannot be made apart from the data of experience. Thus Berthoff cites Kant's "Percepts without concepts are empty; concepts without percepts are blind" (p. 13). Later she explains: "The brain puts things together, composing the percepts by which we can make sense of the world. We don't just 'have' a visual experience and then by thinking 'have' a mental experience; the mutual dependence of seeing and knowing is what a modern psychologist has in mind when he speaks of 'the intelligent eye'" (p. 44). Young, Becker, and Pike state the same notion:

> Constantly changing, bafflingly complex, the external world is not a neat, well-ordered place replete with meaning, but an enigma requiring interpretation. This interpretation is the result of a transaction between events in the external world and the mind of the individual—between the world "out there" and the individual's previous experience, knowledge, values, attitudes, and desires. Thus the mirrored world is not just the sum total of eardrum rattles, retinal excitations, and so on; it is a creation that reflects the peculiarities of the perceiver as well as the peculiarities of what is perceived. (p. 25)

Language is at the center of this dialectical interplay between the individual and the world. For Neo-Aristotelians, Positivists, and Neo-Platonists, truth exists prior to language so that the difficulty of the writer or speaker is to find the appropriate words to communicate knowledge. For the New Rhetoric truth is impossible without language since it is language that embodies and generates truth. Young, Becker, and Pike explain:

> Language provides a way of unitizing experience: a set of symbols that label recurring chunks of experience. . . . Language depends on our seeing certain experiences as constant or repeatable. And seeing the world as repeatable depends, in part at least, on language. A language is, in a sense, a theory of the universe, a way of selecting and grouping experience in a fairly consistent and predictable way. (p. 27)

Berthoff agrees: "The relationship between thought and language is dialectical: ideas are conceived by language; language is generated by thought" (p. 47). Rather than truth being prior to language, language is prior to truth and determines what shapes truth can take. Language does not correspond to the "real world." It creates the "real world" by organizing it, by determining what will be perceived and not perceived, by indicating what has meaning and what is meaningless.

The audience of course enters into this play of language. Current-Traditional Rhetoric demands that the audience be as "objective" as the writer; both shed personal and social concerns in the interests of the unobstructed perception of empirical reality. For Neo-Platonic Rhetoric the audience is a check to the false note of the inauthentic and helps to detect error, but it is not involved in the actual discovery of truth—a purely personal matter. Neo-Aristotelians take the audience seriously as a force to be considered in shaping the message. Still, for all its discussion of the emotional and ethical appeals, Classical Rhetoric emphasizes rational structures, and the concern for the audience is only a concession to the imperfection of human nature. In the New Rhetoric the message arises out of the interaction of the writer, language, reality, and the audience. Truths are operative only within a given universe of discourse, and this universe is shaped by all of these elements, including the audience. As Young, Becker, and Pike explain:

> The writer must first understand the nature of his own interpretation and how it differs from the interpretations of others. Since each man segments experience into discrete, repeatable units, the writer can begin by asking how his way of segmenting and ordering experience differs from his reader's. How do units of time, space, the visible world, social organization, and so on differ? . . .
>
> Human differences are the raw material of writing—differences in experiences and ways of segmenting them, differences in values, purposes, and goals. They are our reason for wishing to communicate. Through communication we create community, the basic value underlying rhetoric. To do so, we must overcome the barriers to communication that are, paradoxically, the motive for communication. (p. 30)

Ann E. Berthoff also includes this idea in her emphasis on meaning as a function of relationship.

> *Meanings are relationships.* Seeing means "seeing relationships," whether we're talking about seeing as *perception* or seeing as *understanding*. "I see what you mean" means "I understand how you put that together so that it makes sense." The way we make sense of the world is to see something *with respect to, in terms of, in relation to* something else. We can't make sense of one thing by itself; it must be seen as being *like* another thing; or *next to, across from, coming after* another thing; or as a repetition of another thing. *Something* makes sense—is meaningful—only if it is taken with *something else*. (p. 44)

The dialectical view of reality, language, and the audience redefines the writer. In Current-Traditional Rhetoric the writer must efface himself; stated differently, the writer must focus on experience in a way that makes possible the discovery of certain kinds of information—the empirical and rational—and the neglect of others—psychological and social concerns. In Neo-Platonic Rhetoric the writer is at the center of the rhetorical act, but is finally isolated, cut off from community, and left to the lonely business of discovering truth alone. Neo-Aristotelian Rhetoric exalts the writer, but circumscribes her effort by its emphasis on the rational—the enthymeme and example. The New Rhetoric sees the writer as a creator of meaning, a shaper of reality, rather than a passive receptor of the immutably given. "When you write," explains Berthoff, "you don't follow somebody else's scheme; you design your own. As a writer, you learn to make words behave the way you want them to. . . . Learning to write is not a matter of learning the rules that govern the use of the semicolon or the names of sentence structures, nor is it a matter of manipulating words; it is a matter of making meanings, and that is the work of the active mind" (p. 11). Young, Becker, and Pike concur: "We have sought to develop a rhetoric that implies that we are all citizens of an extraordinarily diverse and disturbed world, that the 'truths' we live by are tentative and subject to change, that we must be discoverers of new truths as well as preservers and transmitter of old, and that enlightened cooperation is the preeminent ethical goal of communication" (p. 9).

This version of the composing process leads to a view of what can be taught in the writing class that rivals Aristotelian rhetoric in its comprehensiveness. Current-Traditional and Neo-Platonic Rhetoric deny the place of invention in rhetoric because for both truth is considered external and self-evident, accessible to anyone who seeks it in the proper spirit. Like Neo-Aristotelian Rhetoric, the New Rhetoric sees truth as probabilistic, and it provides students with techniques—heuristics—for discovering it, or what might more accurately be called creating it. This does not mean, however, that arrangement and style are regarded as unimportant, as in Neo-Platonic Rhetoric. In fact, the attention paid to these matters in the New Rhetoric rivals that paid in Current-Traditional Rhetoric, but not because they are the only teachable part of the process. Structure and language are a part of the formation of meaning, are at the center of the discovery of truth, not simply the dress of thought. From the point of view of pedagogy, New Rhetoric thus treats in depth all the offices of classical rhetoric that apply to written language—invention, arrangement, and style—and does so by calling upon the best that has been thought and said about them by contemporary observers.

In talking and writing about the matters that form the substance of this essay, at my back I always hear the nagging (albeit legitimate) query of the overworked writing teacher: But what does all this have to do with the teaching of freshman composition? My answer is that it is more relevant than most of us are prepared to admit. In teaching writing, we are not simply offering training in a useful technical skill that is meant as a simple complement to the more important studies of other areas. We are teaching a way of experiencing the world, a way of ordering and making sense of it. As I have shown, subtly informing our statements about invention, arrangement, and even style are assumptions about the nature of reality. If the textbooks that sell the most copies tell us anything, they make abundantly clear that most writing teachers accept the assumptions of Current-Traditional Rhetoric, the view that arose contemporaneously with the positivistic position of modern science. Yet most of those who use these texts would readily admit that the scientific world view has demonstrated its inability to solve the problems that most concern us, problems that are often themselves the result of scientific "breakthroughs." And even many scientists concur with them in this view—Oppenheimer and Einstein, for example. In our writing classrooms, however, we continue to offer a view of composing that insists on a version of reality that is sure to place students at a disadvantage in addressing the problems that will confront them in both their professional and private experience.

Neo-Platonic, Neo-Aristotelian, and what I have called New Rhetoric are reactions to the inadequacy of Current-Traditional Rhetoric to teach students a notion of the composing process that will enable them to become effective persons as they become effective writers. While my sympathies are obviously with the last of these reactions, the three can be considered as one in their efforts to establish new directions for a modern rhetoric. Viewed in this way, the difference between them and Current-Traditional Rhetoric is analogous to the difference Richard Rorty has found in what he calls, in *Philosophy and the Mirror of Nature* (Princeton, N.J.: Princeton University Press, 1979), hermeneutic and epistemological philosophy. The hermeneutic approach to rhetoric bases the discipline on establishing an open dialogue in the hopes of reaching agreement about the truth of the matter at hand. Current-Traditional Rhetoric views the rhetorical situation as an arena where the truth is incontrovertibly established by a speaker or writer more enlightened than her audience. For the hermeneuticist truth is never fixed finally on unshakable grounds. Instead it emerges only after false starts and failures, and it can only represent a tentative point of rest in a continuing conversation. Whatever truth is arrived at, moreover, is always the product of individuals calling on the full range of their humanity, with esthetic and moral considerations given at least as much importance as any others. For Current-Traditional Rhetoric truth is empirically based and can only be achieved through subverting a part of the human response to experience. Truth then stands forever, a tribute to its method, triumphant over what most of us consider important in life, successful through subserving writer, audience, and language to the myth of an objective reality.

One conclusion should now be incontestable. The numerous recommendations of the "process"-centered approaches to writing instruction as superior to the "product"-centered approaches are not very useful. Everyone teaches the process of writing, but everyone does not teach the *same* process. The test of one's competence as a composition instructor, it seems to me, resides in being able to recognize and justify the version of the process being taught, complete with all of its significance for the student.

NOTES

1. I have in mind Richard Fulkerson, "Four Philosophies of Composition," *College Composition and Communication*, 30 (1979), 343–348; David V. Harrington, et al., "A Critical Survey of Resources for Teaching Rhetorical Invention," *College English*, 40 (1979), 641–661; William F. Woods, "Composition Textbooks and Pedagogical Theory 1960–80," *CE*, 43 (1981), 393–409.

2. "Rewording the Rhetoric of Composition," *PRE/TEXT*, 1 (1980), 39. I am indebted to Professor Kameen's classification of pedagogical theories for the suggestiveness of his method; my conclusions, however, are substantially different.

3. There is still another reason for pursuing the method I recommend, one that explains why rhetorical principles are now at the center of discussions in so many different disciplines. When taken together, writer, reality, audience, and language identify an epistemic field—the basic conditions that determine what knowledge will be knowable, what not knowable, and how the knowable will be communicated. This epistemic field is the point of departure for numerous studies, although the language used to describe it varies from thinker to thinker. Examples are readily available. In *Science and the Modern World* (New York: Macmillan, 1926), A. N. Whitehead sees this field as a product of the "fundamental assumptions which adherents of all variant systems within the epoch unconsciously presuppose" (p. 71). Susanne Langer, in *Philosophy in a New Key* (Cambridge, Mass.: Harvard University Press, 1979), calls it the "tacit, fundamental way of seeing things" (p. 6). Michael Polanyi uses the terms "tacit knowledge" in *Personal Knowledge* (Chicago: University of Chicago Press, 1962). Michel Foucault, in *The Order of Things* (1971; rpt. New York: Vintage Books, 1973), speaks of the "episteme," and Thomas Kuhn, in *Structure of Scientific Revolutions* (Chicago: University of Chicago Press, 1970), discusses at length the "paradigm" that underlies a scientific discipline. The historian Hayden White, in *Metahistory: The Historical Imagination in Nineteenth-Century Europe* (Baltimore: Johns Hopkins University Press, 1973), has translated the elements of the composing process into terms appropriate to the writing of history, seeing the historical field as being made up of the historian, the historical record, the historical accounts, and an audience. One compelling reason for studying composition theory is that it so readily reveals its epistemic field, thus indicating, for example, a great deal about the way a particular historical period defines itself—a fact convincingly demonstrated in Murray Cohen's *Sensible Words: Linguistic Practice in England 1640–1785* (Baltimore: Johns Hopkins University Press, 1977), a detailed study of English grammars.

4. See Gerald L. Bruns, *Modern Poetry and the Idea of Language* (New Haven, Ct.: Yale University Press, 1974), p. 34.

5. *Ancient and Mediaeval Grammatical Theory in Europe* (London: G. Bell and Sons, 1951), pp. 20–21.

6. *Eighteenth-Century British Logic and Rhetoric* (Princeton, N.J.: Princeton University Press, 1971), pp. 5–6.

7. *The Philosophy of Rhetoric*, ed. Lloyd F. Bitzer (Carbondale: Southern Illinois University Press, 1963), p. 215.

8. For a more detailed discussion of Genung see my "John Genung and Contemporary Composition Theory: The Triumph of the Eighteenth Century," *Rhetoric Society Quarterly*, 11 (1981), 74–84.

9. For an analysis of modern composition textbooks, see James A. Berlin and Robert P. Inkster, "Current-Traditional Rhetoric: Paradigm and Practice," *Freshman English News*, 8 (1980), 1–4, 13–14.

10. Kenneth J. Kantor, "Creative Expression in the English Curriculum: A Historical Perspective," *Research in the Teaching of English*, 9 (1975), 5–29.

11. *Telling Writing* (Rochelle Park, N.J.: Hayden Book Company, 1978), p. 13.

SECTION THREE

Scientific Talk

Developmental Schemes

Among James Berlin's epistemological categories in "Contemporary Composition" there is positivism. The assumptions that are carried by positivism remain the most pervasive for our society and for composition studies (though not without some sharp criticism). Implicit in the term (and the concept) is that knowledge is scaffolded, building upon itself, always ascending. So given rhetoric's and thereby composition's concern with mind, and given the cognitive emphasis of Woods Hole, the positivistic schemes that composition found most attractive were those concerning cognitive development.

The stages of development were determined by Jean Piaget's developmental scheme, and the approach to tapping into the "natural" process of cognitive development was inductive reasoning, a process of discovery. In 1968, James Moffett published *Teaching the Universe of Discourse*, a developmental scheme for teaching discourse that spanned from the elementary grades to the secondary. The curricular stages he developed—from the egocentric to the public: interior dialogue to conversation to correspondence to public narrative—follow the cognitive stages of development offered by Piaget. Piaget's interpretation of the mind as structuring knowledge systematically, his genetic epistemology, continues to hold sway with the education community. And since language plays a crucial role in his developmental scheme, it holds a particular attraction for compositionists. This attraction becomes magnified in the work of Lev Vygotsky, a contemporary of Piaget's. For Vygotsky, language doesn't just play a role; language is central, that which provides for our conceptions of reality. Vygotsky's concept of "inner speech," in which Piaget's egocentric speech doesn't disappear but becomes internalized and removed from the sounds of discourse, causes Piaget to revise his theories.

251

So intriguing and suggestive are the language and thought connections provided by Piaget and Vygotsky that composition becomes obsessed with recognizing those stages, fostering their development, believing in their lack when expectations for student writing are not met. Other developmental schemes, like William Perry's scheme of ethical and intellectual development in college, gain new attention. Mina Shaughnessy—who first coins the term *basic writer* to describe college writers otherwise termed *developmental* or *remedial*—creates a parody of developmental schemes to discuss how teachers come to consider basic writers when first confronted with them. And although not developmental, Linda Flower and John R. Hayes turn to the cognitive sciences, the research method of protocol analysis developed by Carl Jung, to build a model of the composing process. Mike Rose, Ann Berthoff, and Patricia Bizzell provide the cross-talk: Rose using his own understanding of cognitive psychology to question some of the assertions arising within composition studies' cognitivists, Berthoff looking to other schemes, and Bizzell calling the whole turn to cognition into question.

A Cognitive Process Theory of Writing

LINDA FLOWER AND JOHN R. HAYES

There is a venerable tradition in rhetoric and composition which sees the composing process as a series of decisions and choices.[1] However, it is no longer easy simply to assert this position, unless you are prepared to answer a number of questions, the most pressing of which probably is: "What then are the criteria which govern that choice?" Or we could put it another way: "What guides the decisions writers make as they write?" In a recent survey of composition research, Odell, Cooper, and Courts noticed that some of the most thoughtful people in the field are giving us two reasonable but somewhat different answers:

> How do writers actually go about choosing diction, syntactic and organizational patterns, and context? Kinneavy claims that one's purpose — informing, persuading, expressing, or manipulating language for its own sake — guides these choices. Moffett and Gibson contend that these choices are determined by one's sense of the relation of speaker, subject, and audience. Is either of these two claims borne out by the actual practice of writers engaged in drafting or revising? Does either premise account adequately for the choices writers make?[2]

Rhetoricians such as Lloyd Bitzer and Richard Vatz have energetically debated this question in still other terms. Lloyd Bitzer argues that speech always occurs as a response to a rhetorical situation, which he succinctly defines as containing an exigency (which demands a response), an audience,

Reprinted from *College Composition and Communication* 32.4 (December 1981): 365–87. Used with permission.

and a set of constraints.[3] In response to this "situation-driven" view, Vatz claims that the speaker's response, and even the rhetorical situation itself, are determined by the imagination and art of the speaker.[4]

Finally, James Britton has asked the same question and offered a linguist's answer, namely, that syntactic and lexical choices guide the process.

> It is tempting to think of writing as a process of making linguistic choices from one's repertoire of syntactic structures and lexical items. This would suggest that there is a meaning, or something to be expressed, in the writer's mind, and that he proceeds to choose, from the words and structures he has at his disposal, the ones that best match his meaning. But is that really how it happens?[5]

To most of us it may seem reasonable to suppose that all of these forces — "purposes," "relationships," "exigencies," "language" — have a hand in guiding the writer's process, but it is not at all clear how they do so or how they interact. Do they, for example, work in elegant and graceful coordination, or as competitive forces constantly vying for control? We think that the best way to answer these questions — to really understand the nature of rhetorical choices in good and poor writers — is to follow James Britton's lead and turn our attention to the writing process itself: to ask, "but is that really how it happens?"

This paper will introduce a theory of the cognitive processes involved in composing in an effort to lay groundwork for more detailed study of thinking processes in writing. This theory is based on our work with protocol analysis over the past five years and has, we feel, a good deal of evidence to support it. Nevertheless, it is for us a working hypothesis and springboard for further research, and we hope that insofar as it suggests testable hypotheses it will be the same for others. Our cognitive process theory rests on four key points, which this paper will develop:

1. The process of writing is best understood as a set of distinctive thinking processes which writers orchestrate or organize during the act of composing.

2. These processes have a hierarchical, highly embedded organization in which any given process can be embedded within any other.

3. The act of composing itself is a goal-directed thinking process, guided by the writer's own growing network of goals.

4. Writers create their own goals in two key ways: by generating both high-level goals and supporting sub-goals which embody the writer's developing sense of purpose, and then, at times, by changing major

goals or even establishing entirely new ones based on what has been learned in the act of writing.

1. Writing is best understood as a set of distinctive thinking processes which writers orchestrate or organize during the act of composing.

To many this point may seem self-evident, and yet it is in marked contrast to our current paradigm for composing—the stage process model. This familiar metaphor or model describes the composing process as a linear series of stages, separated in time, and characterized by the gradual development of the written product. The best examples of stage models are the Pre-Write/Write/Re-Write model of Gordon Rohman[6] and The Conception/Incubation/Production model of Britton et al.[7]

STAGE MODELS OF WRITING

Without doubt, the wide acceptance of Pre-Writing has helped improve the teaching of composition by calling attention to planning and discovery as legitimate parts of the writing process. Yet many question whether this linear stage model is really an accurate or useful description of the composing process itself. The problem with stage descriptions of writing is that they model the growth of the written product, not the inner process of the person producing it. "Pre-Writing" is the stage before words emerge on paper; "Writing" is the stage in which a product is being produced; and "Re-Writing" is a final reworking of that product. Yet both common sense and research tell us that writers are constantly planning (pre-writing) and revising (re-writing) as they compose (write), not in clean-cut stages.[8] Furthermore, the sharp distinctions stage models make between the operations of planning, writing, and revising may seriously distort how these activities work. For example, Nancy Sommers has shown that revision, as it is carried out by skilled writers, is not an end-of-the-line repair process, but is a constant process of "re-vision" or re-seeing that goes on while they are composing.[9] A more accurate model of the composing process would need to recognize those basic thinking processes which unite planning and revision. Because stage models take the final product as their reference point, they offer an inadequate account of the more intimate, moment-by-moment intellectual process of composing. How, for example, is the output of one stage, such as pre-writing or incubation, transferred to the next? As every writer knows, having good ideas doesn't automatically produce good prose. Such models are typically silent on the inner processes of decision and choice.

A COGNITIVE PROCESS MODEL

A cognitive process theory of writing, such as the one presented here, represents a major departure from the traditional paradigm of stages in this way: in a stage model the major units of analysis are *stages* of completion which reflect the growth of a written product, and these stages are organized in a *linear* sequence or structure. In a process model, the major units of analysis are elementary mental *processes*, such as the process of generating ideas. And these processes have a *hierarchical* structure (see p. 288, below) such that idea generation, for example, is a sub-process of Planning. Furthermore, each of these mental acts may occur at any time in the composing process. One major advantage of identifying these basic cognitive processes or thinking skills writers use is that we can then compare the composing strategies of good and poor writers. And we can look at writing in a much more detailed way.

In psychology and linguistics, one traditional way of looking carefully at a process is to build a model of what you see. A model is a metaphor for a process: a way to describe something, such as the composing process, which refuses to sit still for a portrait. As a hypothesis about a dynamic system, it attempts to describe the parts of the system and how they work together. Modeling a process starts as a problem in design. For example, imagine that you have been asked to start from scratch and design an imaginary, working "Writer." In order to build a "Writer" or a theoretical system that would reflect the process of a real writer, you would want to do at least three things:

1. First, you would need to define the major elements or sub-processes that make up the larger process of writing. Such sub-processes would include planning, retrieving information from long-term memory, reviewing, and so on.

2. Second, you would want to show how these various elements of the process interact in the total process of writing. For example, how is "knowledge" about the audience actually integrated into the moment-to-moment act of composing?

3. And finally, since a model is primarily a tool for thinking with, you would want your model to speak to critical questions in the discipline. It should help you see things you didn't see before.

Obviously, the best way to model the writing process is to study a writer in action, and there are many ways to do this. However, people's after-the-fact, *introspective analysis* of what they did while writing is notoriously inaccurate and likely to be influenced by their notions of what they should have done. Therefore we turned to *protocol analysis*, which has been successfully used to study other cognitive processes.[10] Unlike introspective reports, thinking aloud protocols capture a detailed record of what is going on in the writer's mind during the act of composing itself. To collect a protocol, we give writers a problem, such as "Write an article on your job for the readers of *Seventeen* magazine," and then ask them to compose out loud near an unobtrusive tape recorder. We ask them to work on the task as they normally would—thinking, jotting notes, and writing—except that they must think out loud. They are asked to verbalize everything that goes through their minds as they write, including stray notions, false starts, and incomplete or fragmentary thought. The writers are *not* asked to engage in any kind of introspection or self-analysis while writing, but simply to think out loud while working like a person talking to herself.

The transcript of this session, which may amount to 20 pages for an hour session, is called a protocol. As a research tool, a protocol is extraordinarily rich in data and, together with the writer's notes and manuscript, it gives us a very detailed picture of the writer's composing process. It lets us see not only the development of the written product but many of the intellectual processes which produced it. The model of the writing process presented in Figure 1 attempts to account for the major thinking processes and constraints we saw at work in these protocols. But note that it does *not* specify the order in which they are invoked.

The act of writing involves three major elements which are reflected in the three units of the model: **the task environment, the writer's long-term memory, and the writing processes.** The task environment includes all of those things outside the writer's skin, starting with the rhetorical problem or assignment and eventually including the growing text itself. The second element is the writer's long-term memory in which the writer has stored knowledge, not only of the topic, but of the audience and of various writing plans. The third element in our model contains writing processes themselves, specifically the basic processes of **Planning, Translating, and Reviewing,** which are under the control of a Monitor.

This model attempts to account for the processes we saw in the composing protocols. It is also a guide to research, which asks us to explore each of these elements and their interaction more fully. Since this model is described in detail elsewhere,[11] let us focus here on some ways each element contributes to the overall process.

257

Figure 1 Structure of the writing model. (For an explanation of how to read a process model, please see endnote 11.)

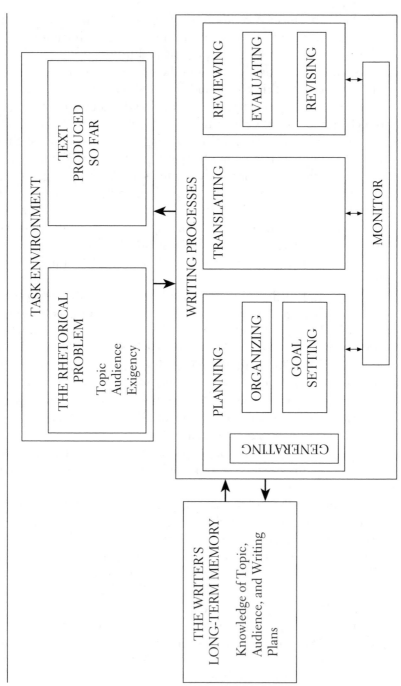

258

OVERVIEW OF THE MODEL

The Rhetorical Problem

At the beginning of composing, the most important element is obviously the **rhetorical problem** itself. A school assignment is a simplified version of such a problem, describing the writer's topic, audience, and (implicitly) her role as student to teacher. Insofar as writing is a rhetorical act, not a mere artifact, writers attempt to "solve" or respond to this rhetorical problem by writing something.

In theory this problem is a very complex thing: it includes not only the rhetorical situation and audience which prompts one to write, it also includes the writer's own goals in writing.[12] A good writer is a person who can juggle all of these demands. But in practice we have observed, as did Britton,[13] that writers frequently reduce this large set of constraints to a radically simplified problem, such as "write another theme for English class." Redefining the problem in this way is obviously an economical strategy as long as the new representation fits reality. But when it doesn't, there is a catch: people only solve the problems they define for themselves. If a writer's representation of her rhetorical problem is inaccurate or simply underdeveloped, then she is unlikely to "solve" or attend to the missing aspects of the problem. To sum up, defining the rhetorical problem is a major, immutable part of the writing process. But the way in which people choose to define a rhetorical problem to themselves can vary greatly from writer to writer. An important goal for research then will be to discover how this process of representing the problem works and how it affects the writer's performance.

The Written Text

As composing proceeds, a new element enters the task environment which places even more constraints upon what the writer can say. Just as a title constrains the content of a paper and a topic sentence shapes the options of a paragraph, each word in the growing text determines and limits the choices of what can come next. However, the influence that the growing text exerts on the composing process can vary greatly. When writing is incoherent, the text may have exerted too little influence; the writer may have failed to consolidate new ideas with earlier statements. On the other hand, one of the earmarks of a basic writer is a dogged concern with extending the previous sentence[14] and a reluctance to jump from local, text-bound planning to more global decisions, such as "what do I want to cover here?"

As we will see, the growing text makes large demands on the writer's time and attention during composing. But in doing so, it is competing with two other forces which could and also should direct the composing process; namely, the writer's knowledge stored in long-term memory and the writer's plans for dealing with the rhetorical problem. It is easy, for example, to imagine a conflict between what you know about a topic and what you might actually want to say to a given reader, or between a graceful phrase that completes a sentence and the more awkward point you actually wanted to make. Part of the drama of writing is seeing how writers juggle and integrate the multiple constraints of their knowledge, their plans, and their text into the production of each new sentence.[15]

The Long-Term Memory

The writer's long-term memory, which can exist in the mind as well as in outside resources such as books, is a storehouse of knowledge about the topic and audience, as well as knowledge of writing plans and problem representations. Sometimes a single cue in an assignment, such as "write a persuasive . . . ," can let a writer tap a stored representation of a problem and bring a whole raft of writing plans into play.

Unlike short-term memory, which is our active processing capacity or conscious attention, long-term memory is a relatively stable entity and has its own internal organization of information. The problem with long-term memory is, first of all, getting things out of it—that is, finding the cue that will let you retrieve a network of useful knowledge. The second problem for a writer is usually reorganizing or adapting that information to fit the demands of the rhetorical problem. The phenomena of "writer-based" prose nicely demonstrates the results of writing strategy based solely on retrieval. The organization of a piece of writer-based prose faithfully reflects the writer's own discovery process and the structure of the remembered information itself, but it often fails to transform or reorganize the knowledge to meet the different needs of a reader.[16]

Planning

People often think of planning as the act of figuring out how to get from here to there, i.e., making a detailed plan. But our model uses the term in its much broader sense. In the **planning** process writers form an internal *representation* of the knowledge that will be used in writing. This internal representation is likely to be more abstract than the writer's prose representation will eventually be. For example, a whole network of ideas might be represented by a single key word. Furthermore, this representation of one's knowledge will not necessarily be made in language, but could be held as a visual or perceptual code, e.g., as a fleeting image the writer must then capture in words.

Planning, or the act of building this internal representation, involves a number of sub-processes. The most obvious is the act of **generating ideas**, which includes retrieving relevant information from long-term memory. Sometimes this information is so well developed and organized *in memory* that the writer is essentially generating standard written English. At other times one may generate only fragmentary, unconnected, even contradictory thoughts, like the pieces of a poem that hasn't yet taken shape.

When the structure of ideas already in the writer's memory is not adequately adapted to the current rhetorical task, the sub-process of **organizing** takes on the job of helping the writer make meaning, that is, give a meaningful structure to his or her ideas. The process of **organizing** appears to play an important part in creative thinking and discovery since it is capable of grouping ideas and forming new concepts. More specifically, the organizing process allows the writer to identify categories, to search for subordinate ideas which develop a current topic, and to search for superordinate ideas which include or subsume the current topic. At another level the process of organizing also attends to more strictly textual decisions about the presentation and ordering of the text. That is, writers identify first or last topics, important ideas, and presentation patterns. However, organizing is much more than merely ordering points. And it seems clear that all rhetorical decisions and plans for reaching the audience affect the process of organizing ideas at all levels, because it is often guided by major goals established during the powerful process of **goal-setting**.

Goal-setting is indeed a third, little-studied but major, aspect of the **planning** process. The goals writers give themselves are both procedural (e.g., "Now let's see—a—I want to start out with 'energy'") and substantive, often both at the same time (e.g., "I have to relate this [engineering project] to the economics [of energy] to show why I'm improving it and why the steam turbine needs to be more efficient" or "I want to suggest that—that—um—the reader should sort of—what—what should one say—the reader should look at what she is interested in and look at the things that give her pleasure . . . ").

The most important thing about writing goals is the fact that they are *created* by the writer. Although some well-learned plans and goals may be drawn intact from long-term memory, most of the writer's goals are generated, developed, and revised by the same processes that generate and organize new ideas. And this process goes on throughout composing. Just as goals lead a writer to generate ideas, those ideas lead to new, more complex goals which can then integrate content and purpose.

Our own studies on goal setting to date suggest that the act of defining one's own rhetorical problem and setting goals is an important part of "being creative" and can account for some important differences between good and poor writers.[17] As we will argue in the final section of this paper, the act of developing and refining one's own goals is not limited to a "pre-writing stage" in the composing process, but is intimately bound up with the ongoing, moment-to-moment process of composing.

Translating

This is essentially the process of putting ideas into visible language. We have chosen the term **translate** for this process over other terms such as "transcribe" or "write" in order to emphasize the peculiar qualities of the task. The information generated in **planning** may be represented in a variety of symbol systems other than language, such as imagery or kinetic sensations. Trying to capture the movement of a deer on ice in language is clearly a kind of translation. Even when the **planning** process represents one's thought in words, that representation is unlikely to be in the elaborate syntax of written English. So the writer's task is to translate a meaning, which may be embodied in key words (what Vygotsky calls words "saturated with sense") and organized in a complex network of relationships, into a linear piece of written English.

The process of **translating** requires the writer to juggle all the special demands of written English, which Ellen Nold has described as lying on a spectrum from generic and formal demands through syntactic and lexical ones down to the motor tasks of forming letters. For children and inexperienced writers, this extra burden may overwhelm the limited capacity of short-term memory.[18] If the writer must devote conscious attention to demands such as spelling and grammar, the task of translating can interfere with the more global process of planning what one wants to say. Or one can simply ignore some of the constraints of written English. One path produces poor or local planning, the other produces errors, and both, as Mina Shaughnessy showed, lead to frustration for the writer.[19]

In some of the most exciting and extensive research in this area, Marlene Scardamalia and Carl Bereiter have looked at the ways children cope with the cognitive demands of writing. Well-learned skills, such as sentence construction, tend to become automatic and lost to consciousness. Because so little of the writing process is automatic for children, they must devote conscious attention to a variety of individual thinking tasks which adults perform quickly and automatically. Such studies, which trace the development of a given skill over several age groups, can show us the hidden components of an adult process as well as show us how children learn. For example, these studies have been able to distinguish children's ability to handle idea complexity from their ability to handle syntactic complexity; that is, they demonstrate the difference between seeing complex relationships and translating them into appropriate language. In another series of studies Bereiter and Scardamalia showed how children learn to handle the translation process by adapting, then eventually abandoning, the discourse conventions of conversation.[20]

Reviewing

As you can see in Figure 1, **reviewing** depends on two sub-processes: **evaluating** and **revising**. Reviewing, itself, may be a conscious process in which writers choose to read what they have written either as a springboard to further translating or with an eye to systematically evaluating and/or revising the text. These periods of planned reviewing frequently lead to new cycles of planning and translating. However, the reviewing process can also occur as an unplanned action triggered by an evaluation of either the text or one's own planning (that is, people revise written as well as unwritten thoughts or statements). The sub-processes of revising and evaluating, along with generating, share the special distinction of being able to interrupt any other process and occur at any time in the act of writing.

The Monitor

As writers compose, they also monitor their current process and progress. The **monitor** functions as a writing strategist which determines when the writer moves from one process to the next. For example, it determines how long a writer will continue generating ideas before attempting to write prose. Our observations suggest that this choice is determined both by the writer's goals and by individual writing habits or styles. As an example of varied composing styles, writers appear to range from people who try to move to polished prose as quickly as possible to people who choose to plan the entire discourse in detail before writing a word. Bereiter and Scardamalia have shown that much of a child's difficulty and lack of fluency lies in their lack of an "executive routine" which would promote switching between processes or encourage the sustained generation of ideas.[21] Children for example, possess the skills necessary to generate ideas, but lack the kind of monitor which tells them to "keep using" that skill and generate a little more.

IMPLICATIONS OF A COGNITIVE PROCESS MODEL

A model such as the one presented here is first and foremost a tool for researchers to think with. By giving a testable shape and definition to our observations, we have tried to pose new questions to be answered. For example, the model identifies three major processes (**plan, translate, and review**) and a number of sub-processes available to the writer. And yet the first assertion of this cognitive process theory is that people do not march through these processes in a simple 1, 2, 3 order. Although writers may spend more time in planning at the beginning of a composing session, planning is not a unitary stage, but a distinctive thinking process which writers use over and over during composing. Furthermore, it is used at all levels, whether the writer is making a global plan for the whole text or a local representation of the meaning of the next sentence. This then raises a question: if the process of writing is not a sequence of stages but a set of optional actions, how are these thinking processes in our repertory actually orchestrated or organized as we write? The second point of our cognitive process theory offers one answer to this question.

2. The processes of writing are hierarchically organized, with component processes embedded within other components.

A hierarchical system is one in which a large working system such as composing can subsume other less inclusive systems, such as generating ideas, which in turn contain still other systems, and so on. Unlike those in a linear organization, the events in a hierarchical process are not fixed in a rigid order. A given process may be called upon at any time and embedded within another process or even within another instance of itself, in much the same way we embed a subject clause within a larger clause or a picture within a picture.

For instance, a writer trying to construct a sentence (that is, a writer in the act of **translating**) may run into a problem and call in a condensed version of the entire writing process to help her out (e.g., she might generate and organize a new set of ideas, express them in standard written English, and review this new alternative, all in order to further her current goal of translating). This particular kind of embedding, in which an entire process is embedded within a larger instance of itself, is known technically in linguistics as recursion. However, it is much more common for writers to simply embed individual processes as needed—to call upon them as sub-routines to help carry out the task at hand.

Writing processes may be viewed as the writer's tool kit. In using the tools, the writer is not constrained to use them in a fixed order or in stages. And using any tool may create the need to use another. Generating ideas may require evaluation, as may writing sentences. And evaluation may force the writer to think up new ideas.

Figure 2 demonstrates the embedded processes of a writer trying to compose (translate) the first sentence of a paper. After producing and reviewing two trial versions of the sentence, he invokes a brief sequence of planning, translating, and reviewing—all in the service of that vexing sentence. In our example the writer is trying to translate some sketchily represented meaning about "the first day of class" into prose, and a hierarchical process allows him to embed a variety of processes as sub-routines within his overall attempt to translate.

A process that is hierarchical and admits many embedded sub-processes is powerful because it is flexible: it lets a writer do a great deal with only a few relatively simple processes—the basic ones being **plan**, **translate**, and **review**. This means, for instance, that we do not need to define "revision" as a unique stage in composing, but as a thinking process that can occur at any time a writer chooses to evaluate or revise his text or his plans. As an important part of writing, it constantly leads to new planning or a "re-vision" of what one wanted to say.

Embedding is a basic, omni-present feature of the writing process even though we may not be fully conscious of doing it. However, a theory of composing that only recognized embedding wouldn't describe the real complexity of writing. It wouldn't explain *why* writers choose to invoke the processes

Figure 2   An example of embedding.

(**Plan**)   Ok, first day of class. . . . . just jot down a possibility.

(**Translate**)   *Can you imagine what your first day of a college English class will be like?*

(**Review**)   I don't like that sentence, it's lousy—sounds like theme talk.

(**Review**)   Oh Lord—I get closer to it and I get closer—

(**Plan**)   Could play up the sex thing a little bit

(**Translate**)   *When you walk into an English class the first day you'll be interested, you'll be thinking about boys, tasks, and professor—*

(**Review**)   That's banal—that's awful.

---

they do or how they know when they've done enough. To return to Lee Odell's question, what guides the writers' decisions and choices and gives an overall purposeful structure to composing? The third point of the theory is an attempt to answer this question.

3. Writing is a goal-directed process. In the act of composing, writers create a hierarchical network of goals and these in turn guide the writing process.

This proposition is the keystone of the cognitive process theory we are proposing—and yet it may also seem somewhat counter-intuitive. According to many writers, including our subjects, writing often seems a serendipitous experience, as act of discovery. People start out writing without knowing exactly where they will end up; yet they agree that writing is a purposeful act. For example, our subjects often report that their writing process seemed quite disorganized, even chaotic, as they worked, and yet their protocols reveal a coherent underlying structure. How, then, does the writing process manage to seem so unstructured, open-minded, and exploratory ("I don't know what I mean until I see what I say") and at the same time possess its own underlying coherence, direction, or purpose?

One answer to this question lies in the fact that people rapidly forget many of their own local working goals once those goals have been satisfied. This is why thinking aloud protocols tell us things retrospection doesn't.[22] A second answer lies in the nature of the goals themselves, which fall into two distinctive categories: process goals and content goals. Process goals are essentially the instructions people give themselves about how to carry out the process of writing (e.g., "Let's doodle a little bit." "So . . . , write an introduction." "I'll go back to that later."). Good writers often give themselves many such instructions and seem to have greater conscious control over their own process than the poorer writers we have studied. Content goals and plans, on the other hand, specify all things the writer wants to say or to do to an audience. Some goals, usually ones having to do with organization, can specify both content and process, as in, "I want to open with a statement about political views." In this discussion we will focus primarily on the writer's content goals.

The most striking thing about a writer's content goals is that they grow into an increasingly elaborate network of goals and sub-goals as the writer composes. Figure 3 shows the network one writer had created during four minutes of composing. Notice how the writer moves from a very abstract goal of "appealing to a broad range in intellect" to a more operational definition of that goal, i.e., "explain things simply." The eventual plan to "write an

Figure 3   Beginning of a network of goals.

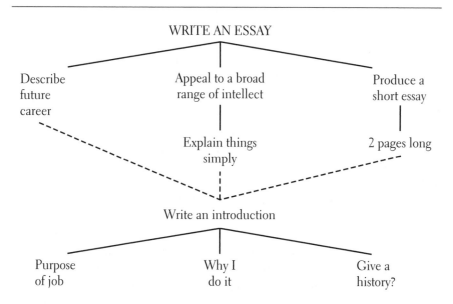

WRITE AN ESSAY

Describe future career

Appeal to a broad range of intellect

Produce a short essay

Explain things simply

2 pages long

Write an introduction

Purpose of job

Why I do it

Give a history?

introduction" is a reasonable, if conventional, response to all three top-level goals. And it too is developed with a set of alternative sub-goals. Notice also how this network is hierarchical in the sense that new goals operate as a functional part of the more inclusive goals above them.

These networks have three important features:

1. They are created as people compose, throughout the entire process. This means that they do not emerge full-blown as the result of "pre-writing." Rather, as we will show, they are created in close interaction with ongoing exploration and the growing text.

2. The goal-directed thinking that produces these networks takes many forms. That is, goal-setting is not simply the act of stating a well-defined end point such as "I want to write a two-page essay." Goal-directed thinking often involves describing one's starting point ("They're not going to be disposed to hear what I'm saying"), or laying out a plan for reaching a goal ("I'd better explain things simply"), or evaluating one's success ("That's banal—that's awful"). Such statements are often setting implicit goals, e.g., "Don't be banal." In order to understand a writer's goals, then, we must be sensitive to the broad range of plans, goals, and criteria that grow out of goal-directed thinking.

Goal-directed thinking is intimately connected with discovery. Consider for example, the discovery process of two famous explorers—Cortez, silent on his peak in Darien, and that bear who went over the mountain. Both, indeed, discovered the unexpected. However, we should note that both chose to climb a long hill to do so. And it is this sort of goal-directed search for the unexpected that we often see in writers as they attempt to explore and consolidate their knowledge. Furthermore, this search for insight leads to new, more adequate goals, which in turn guide further writing.

The beginning of an answer to Odell's question, "What guides composing?" lies here. The writer's own set of self-made goals guide composing, but these goals can be inclusive and exploratory or narrow, sensitive to the audience or chained to the topic, based on rhetorical savvy or focused on producing correct prose. All those forces which might "guide" composing, such as the rhetorical situation, one's knowledge, the genre, etc., are mediated through the goals, plans, and criteria for evaluation of discourse actually set up by the writer.

This does not mean that a writer's goals are necessarily elaborate, logical, or conscious. For example, a simple-minded goal such as "Write down what I can remember" may be perfectly adequate for writing a list. And experienced writers, such as journalists, can often draw on elaborate networks of goals which are so well learned as to be automatic. Or the rules of a genre, such as those of the limerick, may be so specific as to leave little room or necessity for elaborate rhetorical planning. Nevertheless, whether one's goals are abstract or detailed, simple or sophisticated, they provide the "logic" that moves the composing process forward.

3. Finally writers not only create a hierarchical network of guiding goals, but, as they compose, they continually return or "pop" back up to their higher-level goals. And these higher-level goals give direction and coherence to their next move. Our understanding of this network and how writers use it is still quite limited, but we can make a prediction about an important difference one might find between good and poor writers. Poor writers will frequently depend on very abstract, undeveloped top-level goals, such as "appeal to a broad range of intellect," even though such goals are much harder to work with than a more operational goal such as "give a brief history of my job." Sondra Perl has seen this phenomenon in the basic writers who kept returning to reread the assignment, searching, it would seem, for ready-made goals, instead of forming their own. Alternatively, poor writers will depend on only very low-level goals, such as finishing a sentence or correctly spelling a word. They will be, as Nancy Sommers' student revisers were, locked in by the myopia in their own goals and criteria.

Therefore, one might predict that an important difference between good and poor writers will be in both the quantity and quality of the middle range of goals they create. These middle-range goals, which lie between intention and actual prose (cf., "give a brief history" in Figure 3), give substance and direction to more abstract goals (such as "appealing to the audience") and they give breadth and coherence to local decisions about what to say next.

GOALS, TOPIC, AND TEXT

We have been suggesting that the logic which moves composing forward grows out of the goals which writers create as they compose. However, common sense and the folklore of writing offer an alternative explanation which we should consider, namely, that one's own knowledge of the topic (memories, associations, etc.) or the text itself can take control of this process as frequently as one's goals do. One could easily imagine these three forces constituting a sort of eternal triangle in which the writer's goals, knowledge, and current text struggle for influence. For example, the writer's initial planning for a given paragraph might have set up a goal or abstract representation of a paragraph that would discuss three equally important, parallel points on the topic of climate. However, in trying to write, the writer finds that some of his knowledge about climate is really organized around a strong cause-and-effect relationship between points 1 and 2, while he has almost nothing to say about point 3. Or perhaps the text itself attempts to take control, e.g., for the sake of a dramatic opening, the writer's first sentence sets up a vivid example of an effect produced by climate. The syntactic and semantic structure of that sentence now demand that a cause be stated in the next, although this would violate the writer's initial (and still appropriate) plan for a three-point paragraph.

Viewed this way, the writer's abstract plan (representation) of his goals, his knowledge of the topic, and his current text are all actively competing for the writer's attention. Each wants to govern the choices and decisions made next. This competitive model certainly captures that experience of seeing the text run away with you, or the feeling of being led by the nose by an idea. How then do these experiences occur within a "goal-driven process"? First, as our model of the writing process describes, the processes of **generate** and **evaluate** appear to have the power to interrupt the writer's process at any point—and they frequently do. This means that new knowledge and/or some feature of the current text can interrupt the process at any time through the processes of **generate** and **evaluate**. This allows a flexible collaboration among goals, knowledge, and text. Yet this collaboration often culminates in a revision of previous goals. The persistence and functional importance of initially established goals is reflected by a number of signs:

the frequency with which writers refer back to their goals; the fact that writers behave consistently with goals they have already stated; and the fact that they evaluate text in response to the criteria specified in their goals.

Second, some kinds of goals steer the writing process in yet another basic way. In the writers we have studied, the overall composing process is clearly under the direction of global and local *process* goals. Behind the most free-wheeling act of "discovery" is a writer who has recognized the heuristic value of free exploration or "just writing it out" and has chosen to do so. Process goals such as these, or "I'll edit it later," are the earmarks of sophisticated writers with a repertory of flexible process goals which let them use writing for discovery. But what about poorer writers who seem simply to free associate on paper or to be obsessed with perfecting the current text? We would argue that often they too are working under a set of implicit process goals which say "write it as it comes," or "make everything perfect and correct as you go." The problem then is not that knowledge or the text have taken over, so much as that the writer's own goals and/or images of the composing process put these strategies in control.[23]

To sum up, the third point of our theory—focused on the role of the writer's own goals—helps us account for purposefulness in writing. But can we account for the dynamics of discovery? Richard Young, Janet Emig, and others argue that writing is uniquely adapted to the task of fostering insight and developing new knowledge.[24] But how does this happen in a goal-directed process?

We think that the remarkable combination of purposefulness and openness which writing offers is based in part on a beautifully simple, but extremely powerful principle, which is this: *In the act of writing, people regenerate or recreate their own goals in the light of what they learn.* This principle then creates the fourth point of our cognitive process theory.

4. Writers create their own goals in two key ways: by generating goals and supporting sub-goals which embody a purpose; and, at times, by changing or regenerating their own top-level goals in light of what they have learned by writing.

We are used, of course, to thinking of writing as a process in which our *knowledge* develops as we write. The structure of knowledge for some topic becomes more conscious and assertive as we keep tapping memory for related ideas. That structure, or "schema," may even grow and change as a result of library research or the addition of our own fresh inferences. However, writers must also generate (i.e., create or retrieve) the unique goals which guide their process.

In this paper we focus on the goals writers create for a particular paper, but we should not forget that many writing goals are well-learned, standard ones stored in memory. For example, we would expect many writers to draw automatically on those goals associated with writing in general, such as, "interest the reader," or "start with an introduction," or on goals associated with a given genre, such as making a jingle rhyme. These goals will often be so basic that they won't even be consciously considered or expressed. And the more experienced the writer the greater this repertory of semi-automatic plans and goals will be.

Writers also develop an elaborate network of working "sub-goals" as they compose. As we have seen, these sub-goals give concrete meaning and direction to their more abstract top-level goals, such as "interest the reader," or "describe my job." And then on occasion writers show a remarkable ability to regenerate or change the very goals which had been directing their writing and planning: that is, they replace or revise major goals in light of what they learned through writing. It is these two creative processes we wish to consider now.

We can see these two basic processes—creating sub-goals and regenerating goals—at work in the following protocol, which has been broken down into episodes. As you will see, writers organize these two basic processes in different ways. We will look here at three typical patterns of goals which we have labeled **"Explore and Consolidate," "State and Develop," "Write and Regenerate."**

EXPLORE AND CONSOLIDATE

This pattern often occurs at the beginning of a composing session, but it could appear anywhere. The writers frequently appear to be working under a high-level goal or plan to explore: that is, to think the topic over, to jot ideas down, or just start writing to see what they have to say. At other times the plan to explore is subordinate to a very specific goal, such as to find out "what on earth can I say that would make a 15-year-old girl interested in my job?" Under such a plan, the writer might explore her own knowledge, following out associations or using more structured discovery procedures such as tagmemics or the classical topics. But however the writer chooses to explore, the next step is the critical one. The writer pops back up to her top-level goal and from that vantage point reviews the information she has generated. She then consolidates it, producing a more complex idea than she began with by drawing inferences and creating new concepts.

Even the poor writers we have studied often seem adept at the exploration part of this process, even to the point of generating long narrative trains of association—sometimes on paper as a final draft. The distinctive thing about good writers is their tendency to return to that higher-level goal and to review and consolidate what has just been learned through exploring. In the act of consolidating, the writer sets up a *new goal* which replaces the goal of explore and directs the subsequent episode in composing. If the writer's topic is unfamiliar or the task demands creative thinking, the writer's ability to explore, to consolidate the results, and to regenerate his or her goals will be a critical skill.

The following protocol excerpt, which is divided into episodes and sub-episodes, illustrates this pattern of **explore and consolidate**.

Episode 1 a, b

In the first episode, the writer merely reviews the assignment and plays with some associations as he attempts to define his rhetorical situation. It ends with a simple process goal—"On to the task at hand"—and a reiteration of the assignment.

> (la) Okay - Um . . . Open the envelope - just like a quiz show on TV - My job for a young thirteen to fourteen teenage female audience - Magazine - *Seventeen*. My job for a young teenage female audience - Magazine - *Seventeen*. I never have read *Seventeen*, but I've referred to it in class and other students have. (1b) This is like being thrown the topic in a situation - you know - in an expository writing class and asked to write on it on the board and I've done that and had a lot of fun with it - so on to the task at hand. My job for a young teenage female audience - Magazine - *Seventeen*.

Episode 2 a, b, c, d

The writer starts with a plan to explore his own "job," which he initially defines as being a teacher and not a professor. In the process of exploring he develops a variety of sub-goals which include plans to: make new meaning by exploring a contrast; present himself or his persona as a teacher; and affect his audience by making them reconsider one of their previous notions. The extended audience analysis of teen-age girls (sub-episode 2c) is in response to his goal of affecting them.

At the end of episode 2c, the writer reaches tentative closure with the statement, "By God, I can change that notion for them." There are significantly long pauses on both sides of this statement, which appears to consolidate much of the writer's previous exploration. In doing this, he dramatically extends his earlier, rather vague plan to merely "compare teachers and professors"—he has regenerated and elaborated his top-level goals. This consolidation leaves the writer with a new, relatively complex, rhetorically sophisticated working goal, one which encompasses plans for a topic, a persona, and the audience. In essence the writer is learning through planning and his goals are the creative bridge between his exploration and the prose he will write.

Perhaps the writer thought his early closure at this point was too good to be true, so he returns at 2d to his initial top-level or most inclusive goal (write about my job) and explores alternative definitions of his job. The episode ends with the reaffirmation of his topic, his persona, and, by implication, the consolidated goal established in Episode 2c.

(2a) Okay lets see - lets doodle a little bit - Job - English teacher rather than professor - I'm doodling this on a scratch sheet as I say it. -ah- (2b) In fact that might be a useful thing to focus on - how a professor differs from - how a teacher differs from a professor and I see myself as a teacher - that might help them - my audience to reconsider their notion of what an English teacher does. (2c) -ah- English teacher - young teen-age female audience - they will all have had English - audience - they're in school - they're taking English - for many of them English may be a favorite subject - doodling still - under audience, but for the wrong reasons - some of them will have wrong reasons in that English is good because its tidy - can be a neat tidy little girl - others turned off of it because it seems too prim. By God I can change that notion for them. (2d) My job for a young teenage female audience - Magazine - *Seventeen.* -ah- Job - English teacher - guess that's what I'll have to go - yeah - hell - go with that - that's a challenge - rather than - riding a bicycle across England that's too easy and not on the topic - right, or would work in a garden or something like that - none of those are really my jobs - as a profession - My job for a young teenage female audience - Magazine - *Seventeen.* All right - I'm an English teacher.

STATE AND DEVELOP

This second pattern accounts for much of the straightforward work of composing, and is well illustrated in our protocol. In it the writer begins with a relatively general high-level goal which he then proceeds to develop or flesh out with sub-goals. As his goals become more fully specified, they form a bridge from his initial rather fuzzy intentions to actual text. Figure 4 is a

Figure 4   Writer developing a set of sub-goals.

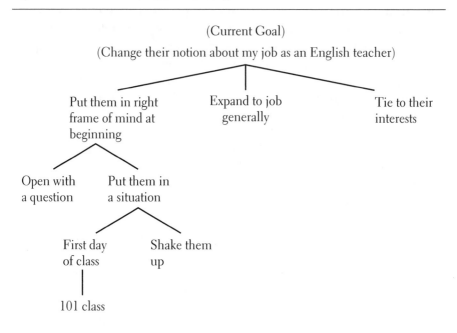

schematic representation of the goals and sub-goals which the writer eventually creates.

Episode 3 a, b, c

The episode starts with a sub-goal directly subordinate to the goal established in Episode 2 (change their notion of English teachers). It takes the pattern of a search in which the writer tries to find ways to carry out his current goal of "get [the audience?] at the beginning." In the process he generates yet another level of sub-goals (i.e., open with a question and draw them into a familiar situation). (A note on our terminology: in order to focus on the overall structure of goals and sub-goals in a writer's thinking, we have treated the writer's plans and strategies all as sub-goals or operational definitions of the larger goal.)

Notice how the content or ideas of the essay are still relatively unspecified. The relationship between creating goals and finding ideas is clearly reciprocal: it was an initial exploration of the writer's ideas which produced these goals. But the writing process was then moved forward by his attempt to flesh out a network of goals and sub-goals, not just by a mere "pre-writing" survey of what he knew about the topic. Episode 3c ends in an effort to test one of his new goals against his own experience with students.

(3a) All right - I'm an English teacher. I want to get at the beginning - I know that they're not going to be disposed - to hear what I'm saying - partly for that reason and partly to put them in the right, the kind of frame of mind I want - I want to open with an implied question or a direct one and put them in the middle of some situation - then expand from there to talk about my job more generally . . . and try to tie it in with their interest. (3b) So one question is where to begin - what kind of situation to start in the middle of - probably the first day of class. . . . They'd be interested - they'd probably clue into that easily because they would identify with first days of school and my first days are raucous affairs - it would immediately shake-em up and get them to thinking a different context. (3c) Okay - so - First day of class - lets see. - Maybe the first 101 class with that crazy skit I put on - that's probably better than 305 because 101 is freshmen and that's nearer their level and that skit really was crazy and it worked beautifully.

WRITE AND REGENERATE

This pattern is clearly analogous to the explore and consolidate pattern, except that instead of planning, the writer is producing prose. A miniature example of it can be seen in Figure 2, in which the writer, whose planning we have just seen, attempts to compose the first sentence of his article for *Seventeen.* Although he had done a good deal of explicit planning before this point, the prose itself worked as another, more detailed representation of what he wanted to say. In writing the sentence, he not only saw that it was inadequate, but that his goals themselves could be expanded. The reciprocity between writing and planning enabled him to learn even from a failure and to produce a new goal, "play up sex." Yet it is instructive to note that once this new plan was represented in language—subjected to the acid test of prose—it too failed to pass, because it violated some of his tacit goals or criteria for an acceptable prose style.

The examples we cite here are, for the purposes of illustration, small and rather local ones. Yet this process of setting and developing sub-goals, and—at times—regenerating those goals is a powerful creative process. Writers and teachers of writing have long argued that one learns through the act of writing itself, but it has been difficult to support the claim in other ways. However, if one studies the process by which a writer uses a goal to generate ideas, then consolidates those ideas and uses them to revise or regenerate new, more complex goals, one can see this learning process in action. Furthermore, one sees why the process of revising and clarifying goals has such a broad effect, since it is through setting these new goals that the fruits of discovery come back to inform the continuing process of writing. In this instance, some of our most complex and imaginative acts can depend on the elegant simplicity of a few powerful thinking processes. We feel that a cognitive process explanation of discovery, toward which this theory is only a start, will have another special strength. By placing emphasis on the inventive power of the writer, who is able to explore ideas, to develop, act on, test, and regenerate his or her own goals, we are putting an important part of creativity where it belongs—in the hands of the working, thinking writer.

NOTES

1. Aristotle, *The Rhetoric*, trans. Lane Cooper (New York: Appleton-Century-Crofts, 1932); Richard Lloyd-Jones, "A Perspective on Rhetoric," in *Writing: The Nature, Development and Teaching of Written Communication*, ed. C. Frederiksen, M. Whiteman, and J. Dominic (Hillsdale, NJ: Lawrence Erlbaum Associates, in press.)

2. Lee Odell, Charles R. Cooper, and Cynthia Courts, "Discourse Theory: Implications for Research in Composing," in *Research on Composing: Points of Departure*, ed. Charles Cooper and Lee Odell (Urbana, IL: National Council of Teachers of English, 1978), p. 6.

3. Lloyd Bitzer, "The Rhetorical Situation," *Philosophy and Rhetoric*, 1 (January, 1968), 1–14.

4. Richard E. Vatz, "The Myth of the Rhetorical Situation," in *Philosophy and Rhetoric*, 6 (Summer, 1973), 154–161.

5. James Britton et al., *The Development of Writing Abilities, 11–18* (London: Macmillan, 1975), p. 39.

6. Gordon Rohman, "Pre-Writing: The Stage of Discovery in the Writing Process," *CCC*, 16 (May, 1965), 106–112.

7. See Britton et al., *The Development of Writing Abilities*, pp. 19–49.

8. Nancy Sommers, "Response to Sharon Crowley, 'Components of the Process,'" *CCC*, 29 (May, 1978), 209–211.

9. Nancy Sommers, "Revision Strategies of Student Writers and Experienced Writers," *CCC*, 31 (December, 1980), 378–388.

10. John R. Hayes, *Cognitive Psychology: Thinking and Creating* (Homewood, IL: Dorsey Press, 1978); Herbert A. Simon and John R. Hayes, "Understanding Complex Task Instruction," in *Cognition and Instruction*, ed. D. Klahr (Hillsdale, NJ: Lawrence Erlbaum Associates, 1976), pp. 269–285.

11. John R. Hayes and Linda S. Flower, "Identifying the Organization of Writing Processes," in *Cognitive Processes in Writing: An Interdisciplinary Approach*, ed. Lee Gregg and Erwin Steinberg (Hillsdale, NJ: Lawrence Erlbaum Associates, 1980), pp. 3–30. Although diagrams of the sort in Figure 1 help distinguish the various processes we wish our model to describe, these schematic representations of processes and elements are often misleading. The arrows indicate that *information* flows from one box or process to another; that is, knowledge about the writing assignment or knowledge from memory can be transferred or used in

the **planning** process, and information from **planning** can flow back the other way. What the arrows *do not mean* is that such information flows in a predictable left to right circuit, from one box to another as if the diagram were a one-way flow chart. This distinction is crucial because such a flow chart implies the very kind of stage model against which we wish to argue. One of the central premises of the cognitive process theory presented here is that writers are constantly, instant by instant, orchestrating a battery of cognitive processes as they integrate planning, remembering, writing, and rereading. The multiple arrows, which are conventions in diagramming this sort of model, are unfortunately only weak indications of the complex and active organization of thinking processes which our work attempts to model.

12. Linda S. Flower and John R. Hayes, "The Cognition of Discovery: Defining a Rhetorical Problem," CCC, 31 (February, 1980), 21–32.

13. Britton et al., *The Development of Writing Abilities*, pp. 61–65.

14. Sondra Perl, "Five Writers Writing: Case Studies of the Composing Process of Unskilled College Writers," Diss. New York University, 1978.

15. Linda S. Flower and John R. Hayes, "The Dynamics of Composing: Making Plans and Juggling Constraints," in *Cognitive Processes in Writing: An Interdisciplinary Approach*, ed. Lee Gregg and Erwin Steinberg (Hillsdale, NJ: Lawrence Erlbaum Associates, 1980), pp. 31–50.

16. Linda S. Flower, "Writer-Based Prose: A Cognitive Basis for Problems in Writing," *College English*, 41 (September, 1979), 19–37.

17. Flower, "The Cognition of Discovery," pp. 21–32.

18. Ellen Nold, "Revising," in *Writing: The Nature, Development, and Teaching of Written Communication*, ed. C. Frederiksen et al. (Hillsdale, NJ: Lawrence Erlbaum Associates, in press).

19. Mina Shaughnessy, *Errors and Expectations* (New York: Oxford University Press, 1977).

20. Marlene Scardamalia, "How Children Cope with the Cognitive Demands of Writing," in *Writing: The Nature, Development and Teaching of Written Communication*, ed. C. Frederiksen et al. (Hillsdale, NJ: Lawrence Erlbaum Associates, in press). Carl Bereiter and Marlene Scardamalia, "From Conversation to Composition: The Role of Instruction in a Developmental Process," in *Advances in Instructional Psychology*, Volume 2, ed. R. Glaser (Hillsdale, NJ: Lawrence Erlbaum Associates, in press).

21. Bereiter and Scardamalia, "From Conversation to Composition."

22. John R. Hayes and Linda Flower, "Uncovering Cognitive Processes in Writing: An Introduction to Protocol Analysis," in *Methodological Approaches to Writing Research*, ed. P. Mosenthal, L. Tamor, and S. Walmsley (in press).

23. Cf. a recent study by Mike Rose on the power of ineffective process plans, "Rigid Rules, Inflexible Plans, and the Stifling of Language: A Cognitivist's Analysis of Writer's Block," CCC, 31 (December, 1980), 389–400.

24. Janet Emig, "Writing as a Mode of Learning," CCC, 28 (May, 1977), 122–128; Richard E. Young, "Why Write? A Reconsideration," unpublished paper delivered at the convention of the Modern Language Association, San Francisco, California, 28 December 1979.

Cognitive Development
and the Basic Writer

Andrea A. Lunsford

In her article, "Writing as a Mode of Learning," Janet Emig argues that

> Writing . . . connects the three major tenses of our experience to make
> meaning. And the two major modes by which these three aspects are
> united are the processes of analysis and synthesis: analysis, the breaking of
> entities into their constituent parts; and synthesis, combining or fusing
> these, often into fresh arrangements or amalgams.[1]

I agree with Professor Emig, and her work as well as that of Mina Shaughnessy has led me to ponder the relationship of writing and the processes of
analysis and synthesis to the teaching of basic writers. In general, my study of
basic writers—their strategies, processes, and products[2]—leads me to believe
that they have not attained that level of cognitive development which would
allow them to form abstractions or conceptions. That is, they are most often
unable to practice analysis and synthesis and to apply successfully the principles thus derived to college tasks. In short, our students might well perform a given task in a specific situation, but they have great difficulty
abstracting from it or replicating it in another context.

Let me offer one concrete example to illustrate this point. Asked to read
ten consecutive issues of a comic strip, choose one of the major characters,
and infer the basic values of that character from the information provided in
the ten issues, typical basic writing students find it almost impossible to
articulate anything about the values of characters unlike themselves. In
short, they have problems drawing inferences or forming concepts based on
what they have read. Instead, they tend either to describe the characters, or,

Reprinted from *College English* 41.1 (September 1979): 449–59. Used with permission.

more typically, to drop the comic strip character after a few sentences and shift to what they see as their own values. When I first began teaching basic writers, their response to this type of assignment gave me the first hint of how their difficulties were related to cognitive development.

In *Thought and Language*, the Russian psychologist Lev Vygotsky identifies three basic phases in the ascent to concept formation: the initial syncretic stage, in which "word meaning denotes nothing more to the child than a vague syncretic conglomeration of individual objects that have . . . coalesced into an image"; the "thinking in complexes" stage during which "thought . . . is already coherent and objective . . . , although it does not reflect objective relationships in the same way as conceptual thinking"; and, finally, the true-concept formation stage.[3] Vygotsky cautions, however, that

> even after the adolescent has learned to produce concepts, . . . he does not
> abandon elementary forms; they continue for a long time to operate, indeed
> to predominate, in many areas of his thinking. . . . The transitional character
> of adolescent thinking becomes especially evident when we observe the
> actual functioning of the newly acquired concepts. Experiments specially
> devised to study the adolescent's operations bring out. . . a striking discrepancy
> between his ability to form concepts and his ability to define them. (p. 79)

Vygotsky goes on to distinguish between "spontaneous" concepts, those which are formed as a result of ordinary, day-to-day experiences, and "scientific" concepts, which are formed largely in conjunction with instruction. The student described above by Vygotsky is like my basic writing students confronted with the comic strips in that they all are able to formulate spontaneous concepts, but not able to remove themselves from such concepts, to abstract from them, or to define them into the scientific concepts necessary for successful college work. In my experience, basic writing students most often work at what Vygotsky calls the "thinking in complexes" stage and the spontaneous-concept stage rather than at the true-concept formation stage. While these writers may have little difficulty in dealing with familiar every-day problems requiring abstract thought based on concepts, they are *not aware of the processes they are using.* Thus they often lack the ability to infer principles from their own experience. They are not forming the "scientific concepts" which are basic to mastery of almost all college material.

Jean Piaget categorizes mental development basically into four stages: the sensori-motor stage; the pre-operational stage; the concrete-operations stage; and the formal-operations stage characterized by the ability to abstract, synthesize, and form coherent logical relationships.[4] At the stage of concrete operations, the child's thought is still closely linked to concrete

280

[handwritten marginalia: Is there an implication of Lacanian Psychology here?]

data; completely representational, hypothetical, or verbal thought still eludes him. As the child moves through the stages of cognitive development, he goes through what Piaget calls the process of "de-centering," a process further defined by Lee Odell as "getting outside one's own frame of reference, understanding the thoughts, values, feelings of another person; . . . projecting oneself into unfamiliar circumstances, whether factual or hypothetical; . . . learning to understand why one reacts as he does to experience."[5] Although children first begin to "de-center" as early as the pre-operational stage, egocentricity is still strong in the concrete stage, and, indeed, we apparently continue the process of "de-centering" throughout our lives.

The relationship of Piaget's concrete stage to Vygotsky's "thinking in complexes" stage and "spontaneous-concept formation" stage is, I believe, clear. Furthermore, the work of both Piaget and Vygotsky strongly indicates that cognitive development moves first from doing, to doing consciously, and only then to formal conceptualization. As Eleanor Duckworth says in an essay in *Piaget in the Classroom*, "thoughts are our way of connecting things up for ourselves. If somebody else tells us about the connections he has made, we can only understand him to the extent that we do the work of making those connections ourselves."[6] This notion is directly related to the highly influential work of Gilbert Ryle. In *The Concept of Mind* (New York: Barnes and Noble, 1949), Ryle makes his crucial distinction between knowing *how* and knowing *that*.

> Learning *how* or improving in ability is not like learning *that* or acquiring information. Truths can be imparted, procedures can only be inculcated, and while inculcation is a gradual process, imparting is relatively sudden. It makes sense to ask at what moment someone became apprised of a truth, but not to ask at what moment someone acquired a skill. "Part-trained" is a significant phrase, "part-informed" is not. Training is the art of setting tasks which the pupils have not yet accomplished but are not any longer quite incapable of accomplishing. . . . Misunderstanding is a by-product of knowing how. Only a person who is at least a partial master of the Russian tongue can make the wrong sense of a Russian expression. Mistakes are exercises of competences. (pp. 59–60)

Chomsky's distinction between "competence" and "performance" has similar implications. Chomsky's views as expressed in *Aspects of the Theory of Syntax* (Cambridge, Mass.: MIT Press, 1965) can be used to argue against the notion that "language is essentially an adventitious construct, taught by 'conditioning' . . . or by a drill and explicit explanation" (p. 51). In other words, students learn by doing and *then* by extrapolating principles from their activities. This theory informs an educational model proposed by James Britton in a recent lecture at Ohio State University (and based on his 1970 *Language and Learning*). Essentially, this paradigm incorporates learning by doing as opposed to learning solely by the study of abstract principles or precepts.

Britton's model is closely related to that articulated in Michael Polanyi's discussion of skills in *Personal Knowledge* (New York: Harper and Row, 1964). Polanyi begins his discussion by citing "the well-known fact that the *aim of a skillful performance is achieved by the observance of a set of rules which are not known as such to the person following them*" (p. 49). Polanyi uses examples of the person who rides a bicycle, keeps afloat in the water, or plays a musical instrument without at all comprehending the underlying rules. "Rules of art can be useful," Polanyi says, "but they do not determine the practice of an art; they are maxims, which can serve as a guide to an art only if they can be integrated into the practical knowledge" (p. 50). Polanyi goes on to discuss the importance of apprenticeship in acquiring a skill or an art, by which he means that we learn by doing *with* a recognized "master" or "connoisseur" better than by studying or reading about abstract principles. Vygotsky puts it quite succinctly: "What a child can do in cooperation today he can do alone tomorrow. Therefore the only good kind of instruction is that which marches ahead of development and leads it; it must be aimed not so much at the ripe as at the ripening functions" (*Thought and Language*, p. 104).

I have attempted this very cursory theoretical review partially in support of the premise asserted at the beginning of my essay: that most of our basic writing students are operating well below the formal-operations or true-concept formation stage of cognitive development, and hence they have great difficulty in "de-centering" and performing tasks which require analysis and synthesis. But once we are convinced that our basic writing students are most often characterized by the inability to analyze and synthesize, what then? How can we, as classroom teachers, use what we know about theory and about our students' levels of cognitive development to guide the ways in which we organize our basic writing classes and create effective assignments?

The theory reviewed above offers, I believe, a number of implications which will help us answer these questions. First, basic writing classes should never be teacher-centered; set lectures should always be avoided. Instead, the classes should comprise small workshop groups in which all members are active participants, apprentice-writers who are "exercising their competence" as they learn *how* to write well. Class time should be spent writing, reading what has been written aloud to the group/audience, and talking about that writing. Such sessions require an atmosphere of trust, and they demand careful diagnosis and preparation by the teacher. But these suggestions offer only a very general guide. Exactly *what* preparation should the basic writing teacher do?

The best way to move students into conceptualization and analytic and synthetic modes of thought is to create assignments and activities which allow students to practice or exercise themselves in these modes continuously. While an entire course plan would take more space than is available here, I can offer a series of examples, from activities focusing on grammatical categories and sentence-building to essay assignments, each of which is designed to foster conceptualization and analytic thinking.

One reason drill exercises have so often failed to transfer a skill into a student's own writing is that the student is operating below the cognitive level at which he or she could abstract and generalize a principle from the drill and then apply that principle to enormously varied writing situations. Memorizing precepts has been equally ineffective. Instead of either one, why not present students with a set of data, from their own writing or from that of someone else, and help them approach it inductively? Following is an exercise on verb recognition which attempts to engage students in inferential reasoning.

RECOGNIZING VERBS

Read the following sentences, filling in the missing word(s) in each one:

a. The cow _____ over the moon.

b. The farmer _____ a wife.

c. Jack Sprat _____ _____ no fat; his wife _____ _____ no lean.

d. Jack Horner _____ in a corner.

e. Jack _____ over the candlestick.

f. Don't _____ on my blue suede shoes.

g. The cat _____ away with the spoon.

h. Sunshine on my shoulder _____ me happy.

i. Little Miss Muffett _____ on a tuffet.

j. He _____ for his pipe, and he _____ for his fiddlers three.

k. The three little kittens _____ their mittens.

l. Little Boy Blue, come _____ your horn.

m. They all _____ in a yellow submarine.

n. The three little pigs _____ to market.

o. Jack and Jill _____ up the hill.

p. One _____ over the cuckoo's nest.

q. Everywhere that Mary _____ the lamb was sure to _____

Whether or not you recognize the songs and rhymes these sentences come from, you will have filled in the blanks with VERBS. Look back over the verbs you have used, and then list five other lines from songs or rhymes and underline the verbs in them.

1.
2.
3.
4.
5.

Now try your hand at formulating the rest of the following definition: Verbs are words which _____

_____

You may have noted in your definition that verbs *do something;* or you may have remembered learning a traditional definition of verbs. No matter what definition we come up with, though, verbs are essential to our communication: they complete or comment on the subjects of our sentences. Now revise your definition so that it includes the major *function* which verbs have in sentences:

_____

_____

CHARACTERISTICS OF VERBS

In this assignment, your job is to discover some major characteristics of verbs. To find the first one, begin studying the following lists of verbs. Then try to determine what characterizes each group. How do the groups differ?

Group One	Group Two	Group Three
break	prayed	will go
sweep	climbed	will run
strikes	altered	will fall
say	passed	will listen
heeds	dug	will look
catch	failed	will move
engages	wrote	will organize
operates	chose	will win
arrests	swore	will answer
play	questioned	will ride
reads	promised	will act
study	gave	will sing

Can you state what characterizes each group? _____

_____

_____

If you are having difficulty answering this question, try answering the next three questions first.

The action named by the verbs in Group One takes place at what time?

_____

The action named by the verbs in Group Two takes place at what time?

_____

The action named by the verbs in Group Three takes place at what time?

_____

Now go back and fill in an answer to the first question about what characterizes each group.

By now, you will have been able to identify the TENSE of the verbs in the three groups. Tense, or relation to time, is one of the major characteristics of verbs; it distinguishes them from other kinds of words such as nouns. Do you know the names of the three tenses represented in Group One, Group Two, and Group Three?

This same inductive or analytic approach can be applied to any grammatical concept or convention we wish our students to become familiar with. Rather than asking students to memorize the functions of the semi-colon, for instance, workshop groups can be presented with a passage or short essay which uses semi-colons frequently. The students' task is to isolate those sentences which use semi-colons and then draw some conclusions based on their data: they might be asked to group sentences which use semi-colons in the same way, to define the semi-colon, etc. Whatever the task, the group will be engaged in inferential problem-solving rather than in isolated drill or memorization. In Vygotsky's terms, analytic thinking is the "ripening function" we are attempting to foster.

In spite of their general effectiveness, sentence-combining drills will often fail to transfer new patterns into the basic writer's own writing—unless the sentence-combining work helps build inferential bridges. The sequential sentence-combining exercise below is designed to give students practice in inferring and analyzing. It is based primarily on the ancient practice of *imitatio*, which we would do well to introduce in all of our basic writing classes. Rhetoric

285

Pattern Sentence: The General Motors assembly line grinds out cars swiftly, smoothly, and almost effortlessly.

A. After studying the sentence pattern, combine each of the following sets of sentences into a sentence which imitates the pattern.

1. The cat eyed its prey.
2. The cat was scruffy.
3. The cat was yellow.
4. The prey was imaginary.
5. The cat eyed it craftily.
6. It eyed it tauntingly.
7. It even eyed it murderously.

---

1. Oil massages you.
2. The oil is bath oil.
3. It is Beauty's oil.
4. The massaging is gentle.
5. The massaging is soothing.
6. The massaging is almost loving.

---

1. We tend to use technologies.
2. The technologies are new.
3. Our use of them is profuse.
4. Our use is unwise.
5. Our use is even harmful.

---

1. H. L. Mencken criticized foibles.
2. The foibles belonged to society.
3. The society was American.
4. The criticism was witty.
5. It was sarcastic.
6. It was often unmerciful.

---

1. The lecturer droned.
2. The lecturer was nondescript.
3. The lecturer was balding.
4. The droning went on and on.
5. The droning was mechanical.
6. It was monotonous.
7. It was interminable.

B. Now fill in appropriate words to complete the following sentence, again being careful to imitate the pattern sentence.

The _____ _____ wins _____ _____ly, _____ly, and almost _____ly.

C. Now write a series of seven sentences and then combine them into one sentence which imitates the pattern sentence. Then write at least one more sentence which imitates the pattern.

Such exercises are not difficult to create; they can easily be adapted to specialized interests of any particular group or class. And they can lead to the kind of paragraph- and theme-length sentence-combining exercises recommended recently by Donald Daiker, Andrew Kerek, and Max Morenberg of Miami of Ohio.[7] Furthermore, such exercises can be supplemented by visual stimuli, pictures or video tapes, which can be used as raw material from which to generate new sentences in imitation of the pattern. But to be maximally effective, sentence-combining exercises must be designed to lead basic writing students to bridge the cognitive gap between imitating and generating.

I have yet to offer any sample essay assignments, but I do not thereby mean to imply that writing whole essays should only occur at or toward the end of a basic writing course. On the contrary, basic writers should begin composing whole paragraphs and essays, practicing the entire process of writing, from the very onset of the course. A pitcher does not practice by articulating one mini-movement at a time but by engaging in an entire, continuous process, from warm-up and mental preparation, to the wind-up, the release, and the follow-through: an analogy, to be sure, but one which I hope is not overly-strained. In addition to having students write paragraphs and essays early in the course, I would like especially to emphasize the importance of working with analytic modes in basic writing classes. Basic writers often fall back on narrative and descriptive modes because these modes are more adaptable to their own experience, or to what Linda Flower has described as "writer-based prose."[8] Yet the work of Ed White in California and of James Britton and his colleagues in England has shown us that little correlation exists in student performance between the spatial and temporal modes of narration and description and the logical and analytic modes of exposition and argumentation. Therefore, the basic writing course that works exclusively on narration and description will probably fail to build the cognitive skills its students will need to perform well in other college courses.

The comic-strip assignment I described earlier in this essay helped me learn that my students needed practice in using and assimilating analytic modes; it also helped me see that I had made several crucial mistakes in giving that assignment. First, I assigned it when the students had had little or no formal practice in inferential reasoning; second, I asked students to do the assignment at home rather than in workshop groups. In short, I ignored one of the lessons both Polanyi and Vygotsky have taught us: that often we learn best by working at a task in cooperation with a "master" or "connoisseur." I have since profited from these mistakes, and that same assignment, properly prepared for by workshop discussion and practice, has proven considerably more effective. Following are two other assignments, one calling for a brief response, the other for a longer essay, which are designed to help students gain control of analytic modes.

WRITING ASSIGNMENT A

Study the following set of data:

1. New York City lost 600,000 jobs between 1969–76.
2. In 1975, twenty buildings in prime Manhattan areas were empty.
3. Between 1970–75, ten major corporations moved their headquarters from New York City to the Sunbelt.
4. In 1976, New York City was on the brink of bankruptcy.
5. Between February, 1977, and February, 1978, New York City gained 9,000 jobs.
6. Since January, 1978, one million square feet of Manhattan floor space has been newly rented.
7. AT&T has just built a $110 million headquarters in New York.
8. IBM has just built an $80 million building at 55th and Madison in New York.
9. Co-op prices and rents have increased since 1977.
10. Even $1 million luxury penthouses are sold out.
11. There is currently an apartment shortage in Manhattan.
12. The President recently signed a bill authorizing $1.65 billion in federal loan guarantees for New York City.

After reading and thinking about the information listed above, how would you describe the current economic trend in New York City? Using your answer to that question as an opening sentence, write a paragraph in which you explain and offer support for your conclusion by using the information provided in the original set of data.

An assignment like the one above, which gives students practice in analyzing, generalizing, and abstracting, can be readily adapted to workshop groups in which discussion, criticism, and revision can take place.

WRITING ASSIGNMENT B

Preparing: Choose a person (but NOT someone you know well) whom you can observe on at least 5–7 occasions. You might choose someone who rides the same bus as you do, or one of your instructors, or someone who is in one of your classes. Be sure that you are on no closer than "how are you today?" terms with the person you choose.

Gathering Data: Arrange the times you can observe your person so that you can make notes during or immediately after the observation. Note down anything that seems important to you. For a start, answer these questions after each observation.

1. What is X wearing? (Be detailed; include colors, types of fabric, etc.)
2. How is X's hair fixed? (What kind of hair-cut, length of hair, style, etc.)
3. What, if anything, does X have with him or her? (Bag, knapsack, purse, books, etc.)
4. What is X doing? (Be as detailed as possible.)
5. What does X say? (Get exact wording whenever you can.)
6. Who does X associate with?
7. What seems to be X's mood?

Grouping Data: Study all your notes. Then group them under the following headings: APPEARANCE, ACTIONS, WORDS. *[handwritten: cultural inference]*

Analyzing Data: Now study all the information you have categorized. Based on that information, what would you say is X's lifestyle? What does your observation suggest about X's top priorities? What is most important to X?

Writing About your Data: Write a short essay which begins by answering the questions asked under "Analyzing Data." Use the data you have grouped in your notes to explain and support your analysis of the lifestyle and priorities of X.

This assignment begins with workshop discussion; the results of each stage are discussed by the group. Revision, sorting, and excluding are thus continuous, with the teacher helping students move more and more surely from *describing* their subjects to *analyzing* them. To save space, I have omitted the revising stages, which involve group response to and criticism of the essays and which vary, of course, with the particular difficulties encountered by each group.

Writing projects based on inference-drawing and conceptualization are easily adapted to almost any topic. I have used excerpts from the *Foxfire* books as the basis for essays in which students draw conclusions and generalize about the people interviewed. David Bartholomae, of the University of Pittsburgh, recommends Studs Terkel's *Working* as the basis for similar assignments building conceptual skills. Role-playing exercises and persona paraphrases offer other effective means of helping students "de-center" and hence gain the distance necessary to effective analysis and synthesis. In fact, it is possible and, I would urge, highly profitable, to build an entire basic writing course on exercises like the ones described above, assignments which "march ahead of development and lead it." If we can do so successfully, and if we can find valid ways to substantiate our success, certainly we will have put all our theory to the best practical use. And as a bonus, we will help to establish what Janet Emig argues is the unique value of writing to the entire learning process.

NOTES

1. "Writing as a Mode of Learning," *CCC*, 28 (1977), 127.

2. "The Ohio State University Remedial English Pilot Project: Final Report and Follow-Up Study," Ohio State University, 1977, and "An Historical, Descriptive, and Evaluative Study of Remedial English in American Colleges and Universities," Diss. Ohio State University, 1977.

3. Lev Semenovich Vygotsky, *Thought and Language*, trans. Eugenia Hanfmann and Gertrude Vakar (Cambridge, Mass.: MIT Press, 1962), pp. 59–61.

4. *Six Psychological Studies* (New York: Random House, 1967).

5. "Teaching Reading: An Alternative Approach," *English Journal*, 22 (1973), 455.

6. "Language and Thought," in *Piaget in the Classroom*, ed. Milton Schwebel and Jane Raph (New York: Basic Books, 1973), p. 148.

7. *The Writer's Options: College Sentence Combining* (New York: Harper and Row, 1979).

8. Linda Flower and John R. Hayes, "Problem Solving Strategies and the Writing Process," *College English*, 39 (1977), 449–461.

Diving In

An Introduction to Basic Writing

MINA P. SHAUGHNESSY

Basic writing, alias remedial, developmental, pre-baccalaureate, or even handicapped English, is commonly thought of as a writing course for young men and women who have many things wrong with them. Not only do medical metaphors dominate the pedagogy (*remedial, clinic, lab, diagnosis,* and so on), but teachers and administrators tend to discuss basic-writing students much as doctors tend to discuss their patients, without being tinged by mortality themselves and with certainly no expectations that questions will be raised about the state of *their* health.

Yet such is the nature of instruction in writing that teachers and students cannot easily escape one another's maladies. Unlike other courses, where exchanges between teacher and student can be reduced to as little as one or two objective tests a semester, the writing course requires students to write things down regularly, usually once a week, and requires teachers to read what is written and then write things back and every so often even talk directly with individual students about the way they write.

This system of exchange between teacher and student has so far yielded much more information about what is wrong with students than about what is wrong with teachers, reinforcing the notion that students, not teachers, are the people in education who must do the changing. The phrase "catching up," so often used to describe the progress of BW students, is illuminating here, suggesting as it does that the only person who must move in the teaching situation is the student. As a result of this view, we are much more likely

Reprinted from *College Composition and Communication* 27.3 (October 1976): 234–39. Used with permission.

in talking about teaching to talk about students, to theorize about *their* needs and attitudes or to chart *their* development and ignore the possibility that teachers also change in response to students, that there may in fact be important connections between the changes teachers undergo and the progress of their students.

I would like, at any rate, to suggest that this is so, and since it is common these days to "place" students on developmental scales, saying they are eighth-graders or fifth-graders when they read and even younger when they write or that they are stalled some place on Piaget's scale without formal propositions, I would further like to propose a developmental scale for teachers, admittedly an impressionistic one, but one that fits the observations I have made over the years as I have watched traditionally prepared English teachers, including myself, learning to teach in the open-admissions classroom.

My scale has four stages, each of which I will name with a familiar metaphor intended to suggest what lies at the center of the teacher's emotional energy during that stage. Thus I have chosen to name the first stage of my developmental scale GUARDING THE TOWER, because during this stage the teacher is in one way or another concentrating on protecting the academy (including himself) from the outsiders, those who do not seem to belong in the community of learners. The grounds for exclusion are various. The mores of the times inhibit anyone's openly ascribing the exclusion to genetic inferiority, but a few teachers doubtless still hold to this view.

More often, however, the teacher comes to the basic-writing class with every intention of preparing his students to write for college courses, only to discover, with the first batch of essays, that the students are so alarmingly and incredibly behind any students he has taught before that the idea of their ever learning to write acceptably for college, let alone learning to do so in one or two semesters, seems utterly pretentious. Whatever the sources of their incompetence—whether rooted in the limits they were born with or those that were imposed upon them by the world they grew up in—the fact seems stunningly, depressingly obvious: they will never "make it" in college unless someone radically lowers the standards.

The first pedagogical question the teacher asks at this stage is therefore not "How do I teach these students?" but "What are the consequences of flunking an entire class?" It is a question that threatens to turn the class into a contest, a peculiar and demoralizing contest for both student and teacher, since neither expects to win. The student, already conditioned to the idea that there is something wrong with his English and that writing is a device for magnifying and exposing this deficiency, risks as little as possible on the page, often straining with what he does write to approximate the academic style and producing in the process what might better be called "written Anguish" rather than English—sentences whose subjects are crowded out by such phrases as "it is my conviction that" or "on the contrary to my opinion," inflections that belong to no variety of English, standard or non-standard, but grow out of the writer's attempt to be correct, or words whose idiosyncratic spellings reveal not simply an increase in the number of conventional misspellings but new orders of difficulty with the correspondences between spoken and written English. Meanwhile, the teacher assumes that he must not only hold out for the same product he held out for in the past but teach unflinchingly in the same way as before, as if any pedagogical adjustment to the needs of students were a kind of cheating. Obliged because of the exigencies brought on by open admissions to serve his time in the defense of the academy, he does if not his best, at least his duty, setting forth the material to be mastered, as if he expected students to learn it, but feeling grateful when a national holiday happens to fall on a basic-writing day and looking always for ways of evading conscription next semester.

But gradually, student and teacher are drawn into closer range. They are obliged, like emissaries from opposing camps, to send messages back and forth. They meet to consider each other's words and separate to study them in private. Slowly, the teacher's preconceptions of his students begin to give way here and there. It now appears that, in some instances at least, their writing, with its rudimentary errors and labored style has belied their intelligence and individuality. Examined at a closer range, the class now appears to have at least some members in it who might, with hard work, eventually "catch up." And it is the intent of reaching these students that moves the teacher into the second stage of development—which I will name CONVERTING THE NATIVES.

As the image suggests, the teacher has now admitted at least some to the community of the educable. These learners are perceived, however, as empty vessels, ready to be filled with new knowledge. Learning is thought of not so much as a constant and often troubling reformulation of the world so as to encompass new knowledge but as a steady flow of truth into a void. Whether the truth is delivered in lectures or modules, cassettes or computers, circles or squares, the teacher's purpose is the same: to carry the technology of advanced literacy to the inhabitants of an underdeveloped country. And so confident is he of the reasonableness and allure of what he is presenting, it does not occur to him to consider the competing logics and values and habits that may be influencing his students, often in ways that they themselves are unaware of.

Sensing no need to relate what he is teaching to what his students know, to stop to explore the contexts within which the conventions of academic discourse have developed, and to view these conventions in patterns large enough to encompass what students do know about language already, the teacher becomes a mechanic of the sentence, the paragraph, and the essay. Drawing usually upon the rules and formulas that were part of his training in composition, he conscientiously presents to his students flawless schemes for achieving order and grammaticality and anatomizes model passages of English prose to uncover, beneath brilliant, unique surfaces, the skeletons of ordinary paragraphs.

Yet too often the schemes, however well meant, do not seem to work. Like other simplistic prescriptions, they illuminate for the moment and then disappear in the melee of real situations, where paradigms frequently break down and thoughts will not be regimented. S's keep reappearing or disappearing in the wrong places; regular verbs shed their inflections and irregular verbs acquire them; tenses collide; sentences derail; and whole essays idle at one level of generalization.

Baffled, the teacher asks, "How is it that these young men and women whom I have personally admitted to the community of learners cannot learn these simple things?" Until one day, it occurs to him that perhaps these simple things—so transparent and compelling to him—are not in fact simple at all, that they only appear simple to those who already know them, that the grammar and rhetoric of formal written English have been shaped by the irrationalities of history and habit and by the peculiar restrictions and rituals that come from putting words on paper instead of into the air, that the sense and nonsense of written English must often collide with the spoken English that has been serving students in their negotiations with the world for many years. The insight leads our teacher to the third stage of his development, which I will name SOUNDING THE DEPTHS, for he turns now to the careful observation not only of his students and their writing but of himself as writer and teacher, seeking a deeper understanding of the behavior called writing and of the special difficulties his students have in mastering the skill. Let us imagine, for the sake of illustration, that the teacher now begins to look more carefully at two common problems among basic writers—the problem of grammatical errors and the problem of undeveloped paragraphs.

Should he begin in his exploration of error not only to count and name errors but to search for patterns and pose hypotheses that might explain them, he will begin to see that while his lessons in the past may have been "simple," the sources of the error he was trying to correct were often complex. The insight leads not inevitably or finally to a rejection of all rules and standards, but to a more careful look at error, to the formulation of what might be called a "logic" of errors that serves to mark a pedagogical path for teacher and student to follow.

Let us consider in this connection the "simple" *s* inflection on the verb, the source of a variety of grammatical errors in BW papers. It is, first, an alien form to many students whose mother tongues inflect the verb differently or not at all. Uniformly called for, however, in all verbs in the third person singular present indicative of standard English, it would seem to be a highly predictable or stable form and therefore one easily remembered. But note the grammatical concepts the student must grasp before he can apply the rule: the concepts of person, tense, number, and mood. Note that the *s* inflection is an atypical inflection within the modern English verb system. Note too how often it must seem to the student that he hears the stem form of the verb after third person singular subjects in what sounds like the present, as he does for example whenever he hears questions like "Does *she want* to go?" or "Can the *subway stop?*" In such sentences, the standard language itself reinforces the student's own resistance to the inflection.

And then, beyond these apparent unpredictabilities within the standard system, there is the influence of the student's own language or dialect, which urges him to ignore a troublesome form that brings no commensurate increase in meaning. Indeed, the very *s* he struggles with here may shift in a moment to signify plurality simply by being attached to a noun instead of a verb. No wonder then that students of formal English throughout the world find this inflection difficult, not because they lack intelligence or care but because they think analogically and are linguistically efficient. The issue is not the capacity of students finally to master this and the many other forms of written English that go against the grain of their instincts and experience but the priority this kind of problem ought to have in the larger scheme of learning to write and the willingness of students to mobilize themselves to master such forms at the initial stages of instruction.

Somewhere between the folly of pretending that errors don't matter and the rigidity of insisting that they matter more than anything, the teacher must find his answer, searching always under pressure for short cuts that will not ultimately restrict the intellectual power of his students. But as yet, we lack models for the maturation of the writing skill among young, native-born adults and can only theorize about the adaptability of other models for these students. We cannot say with certainty just what progress in writing ought to look like for basic-writing students, and more particularly how the elimination of error is related to their over-all improvement.

Should the teacher then turn from problems of error to his students' difficulties with the paragraphs of academic essays, new complexities emerge. Why, he wonders, do they reach such instant closure on their ideas, seldom moving into even one subordinate level of qualification but either moving on to a new topic sentence or drifting off into reverie and anecdote until the point of the essay has been dissolved? Where is that attitude of "suspended conclusion" that Dewey called thinking, and what can one infer about their intellectual competence from such behavior?

Before consigning his students to some earlier stage of mental development, the teacher at this stage begins to look more closely at the task he is asking students to perform. Are they aware, for example, after years of right/wrong testing, after the ACT's and the GED's and the OAT's, after straining to memorize what they read but never learning to doubt it, after "psyching out" answers rather than discovering them, are they aware that the rules have changed and that the rewards now go to those who can sustain a play of mind upon ideas—teasing out the contradictions and ambiguities and frailties of statements?

Or again, are the students sensitive to the ways in which the conventions of talk differ from those of academic discourse? Committed to extending the boundaries of what is known, the scholar proposes generalizations that cover the greatest possible number of instances and then sets about supporting his case according to the rules of evidence and sound reasoning that govern his subject. The spoken language, looping back and forth between speakers, offering chances for groping and backing up and even hiding, leaving room for the language of hands and faces, of pitch and pauses, is by comparison generous and inviting. The speaker is not responsible for the advancement of formal learning. He is free to assert opinions without a display of evidence or recount experiences without explaining what they "mean." His movements from one level of generality to another are more often brought on by shifts in the winds of conversation rather than by some decision of his to be more specific or to sum things up. For him the injunction to "be more specific" is difficult to carry out because the conditions that lead to specificity are usually missing. He may not have acquired the habit of questioning his propositions, as a listener might, in order to locate the points that require amplification or evidence. Or he may be marooned with a proposition he cannot defend for lack of information or for want of practice in retrieving the history of an idea as it developed in his own mind.

Similarly, the query "What is your point?" may be difficult to answer because the conditions under which the student is writing have not allowed for the slow generation of an orienting conviction, that underlying sense of the direction he wants his thinking to take. Yet without this conviction, he cannot judge the relevance of what comes to his mind, as one sentence branches out into another or one idea engenders another, gradually crowding from his memory the direction he initially set for himself.

Or finally, the writer may lack the vocabulary that would enable him to move more easily up the ladder of abstraction and must instead forge out of a nonanalytical vocabulary a way of discussing thoughts about thoughts, a task so formidable as to discourage him, as travelers in a foreign land are discouraged, from venturing far beyond bread-and-butter matters.

From such soundings, our teacher begins to see that teaching at the remedial level is not a matter of being simpler but of being more profound, of not only starting from "scratch" but also determining where "scratch" is. The experience of studenthood is the experience of being just so far over one's head that it is both realistic and essential to work at surviving. But by underestimating the sophistication of our students and by ignoring the complexity of the tasks we set before them, we have failed to locate in precise ways where to begin and what follows what.

But I have created a fourth stage in my developmental scheme, which I am calling DIVING IN in order to suggest that the teacher who has come this far must now make a decision that demands professional courage—the decision to remediate himself, to become a student of new disciplines and of his students themselves in order to perceive both their difficulties and their incipient excellence. "Always assume," wrote Leo Strauss, to the teacher, "that there is one silent student in your class who is by far superior to you in head and in heart." This assumption, as I have been trying to suggest, does not come easily or naturally when the teacher is a college teacher and the young men and women in his class are labeled remedial. But as we come to know these students better, we begin to see that the greatest barrier to our work with them is our ignorance of them and of the very subject we have contracted to teach. We see that we must grope our ways into the turbulent disciplines of semantics and linguistics for fuller, more accurate data about words and sentences; we must pursue more rigorously the design of developmental models, basing our schemes less upon loose comparisons with children and more upon case studies and developmental research of the sort that produced William Perry's impressive study of the intellectual development of Harvard students; we need finally to examine more closely the nature of speaking and writing and divine the subtle ways in which these forms of language both support and undo each other.

The work is waiting for us. And so irrevocable now is the tide that brings the new students into the nation's college classrooms that it is no longer within our power, as perhaps it once was, to refuse to accept them into the community of the educable. They are here. DIVING IN is simply deciding that teaching them to write well is not only suitable but challenging work for those who would be teachers and scholars in a democracy.

William Perry
and Liberal Education

PATRICIA BIZZELL

The work of psychologist William G. Perry, Jr. has attracted much attention recently from college writing teachers who seek a developmental model to inform composition courses and writing-across-the-curriculum programs. To assess Perry's usefulness to writing instruction, I would like first to summarize his work, giving his own interpretation of its significance, and then to say how I think we should, and should not, use it.

After taking a BA in psychology at Harvard College, Perry began his academic career teaching English literature at Williams College. In 1947 he returned to Harvard to head the Bureau of Study Counsel, and there he performed the research that led to the publication of his influential book, *Forms of Intellectual and Ethical Development in the College Years: A Scheme* (New York: Holt, Rinehart, and Winston, 1968). Perry describes how college students pass from childhood to adulthood by moving through nine developmental positions. The shape of this process and the nature of the positions were defined through a series of interviews with Harvard undergraduate men in each of their four years in college.

Perry's nine-position scheme chronicles movement through three world views, "Dualism," "Relativism," and "Commitment in Relativism." The young person typically passes through them in this order, sometimes pausing or backtracking. Each world view shapes value judgments on religion, politics, family relations, and so on. Drawing on the student interviews, Perry depicts each world view primarily in terms of the young person's attitude toward schoolwork.

Reprinted from *College English* 46.5 (September 1984): 447–54. Used with permission.

The first world view, "Dualism," is characterized by the belief that everything in the world can be ordered in one of two categories—right or wrong. These categories are defined by axiomatic statements or "Absolutes," which are possessed by "Authority," adults who have perfect knowledge of the Absolutes. The proper task of Authority is to convey the Absolutes to the ignorant. For the dualist, knowing the world means memorizing the Absolutes and applying them to individual instances. For the student Dualist, education is a process of finding right answers (correct applications of Absolutes), with the help of the teacher (Authority). The student Dualist resists exploring academic problems that have no one right solution, and prefers teachers who supply answers and disciplines in which answers can be securely quantified.

In the second world view, "Relativism," Absolutes either are unknowable or no longer exist. Without them Authority can no longer empower one to categorize the world as right or wrong. In place of these generally applicable standards, selfish interest becomes the basis for each individual's decisions. For the Relativist, knowing the world means devising an individual strategy for survival. For the student Relativist, education is a process of devising persuasive answers, since right answers no longer exist. The teacher judges persuasiveness according to idiosyncratic criteria, not Absolute standards. As the student Relativist learns how to satisfy teachers' demands, he or she enjoys exploring problematic questions and prefers disciplines in which they abound. This student also prefers teachers who do not stand on the (now unfounded) authority of their office but relate personally to the student.

In the third world view, "Commitment in Relativism," the world is still without Absolutes and Authority. Nevertheless, it is not without order, and decisions need not be based on solitary self-interest. For the Committed Relativist, knowing the world means understanding what has been rendered important by one's family, friends, religious and ethnic traditions, and intellectual interests. These priorities derived from social surroundings guide choices about the values that will order one's life, choices that Perry calls "Commitments." As one's Commitments develop, one can make confident judgments of what is better or worse relative to them, while still realizing that other people who have sufficiently examined their values may employ different but valid standards of judgment. For the student Committed Relativist, education is a process of achieving the knowledge necessary for making Commitments. Once Committed to a field of study, this student does not seek right or glib answers; rather he or she tries to start working productively in the chosen field. The teacher is neither Authority nor personal friend during this process, but rather a more experienced fellow worker, or mentor.

Perry does not clearly explain what his developmental scheme describes. Is it a process through which all normal 18- to 21-year-olds can be expected to pass, a process that is automatic, genetically determined? If so, Perry's scheme would extend the developmental scheme put forward for younger children by Jean Piaget. Piaget sees children moving through a series of stages of cognitive activity, from sensori-motor on to formal-operational; this process unfolds independent of a child's particular cultural context. Most researchers in the development of adolescents seek to complete Piaget's scheme, that is, to describe the stages children pass through after puberty; and Perry, too, nods in the direction of Piaget. He suggests that he follows Piaget in the notion that developmental processes repeat themselves on different levels—in other words, that we can expect to find some process in the adolescent analogous to the movement through cognitive stages in the young child.

Perry differentiates his study from Piaget's, however, when he says that *Forms of Intellectual and Ethical Development* focuses on "the level at which a person undertakes the development of his 'philosophical assumptions' about his world" (p. 29). I see two distinctions from Piaget here. First, Perry describes this development as something a person "undertakes"; in other words, it is a process of which the person is conscious and which he or she can guide to some extent. In contrast, Piaget describes cognitive development as unfolding naturally, with only occasional awareness on the child's part that changes are occurring, and without much possibility of anyone, child or observing adult, altering the course of the development. The second distinction follows from this self-conscious aspect of the development Perry describes: what are developed are "philosophical assumptions," not cognitive stages. Philosophical assumptions, I take it, can be examined, revised, and consciously affirmed by their possessor, unlike cognitive stages. Perry puts the phrase in quotation marks to indicate that he does not see the typical undergraduate as a systematic thinker; nevertheless, he wants to use such language because it suggests that the scheme focuses on beliefs consciously held in the mind. The process of developing philosophical assumptions may be analogous to that of developing mature cognitive abilities, but it is not the same kind of process.

But if Perry derives from Piaget only the concept of a developmental process, then what kind of process does Perry's scheme describe? Perry's answer to this question is not clear. I think, however, that in spite of Perry's nod to Piaget, his developmental scheme describes something that does not necessarily happen to all cognitively normal 18- to 21-year-olds. Perry drops many hints that what he is describing is what happens to young people when they receive an education. Furthermore, he suggests that an education-induced developmental process should not be regarded as value-neutral, as we would presumably have to regard a process that unfolded according to some genetic necessity, such as that described by Piaget. Education initiates one into the traditions, habits, and values of a community. Perry's scheme focuses particularly on liberal arts education and the world view it inculcates. Obviously, then, it is possible to pass through the ages of 18 to 21 quite "normally" from the psychological point of view without undergoing this kind of development.

Perry aims in his book to convince us that undergraduates in a liberal arts college do pass through the developmental process he describes, but he also does something more. He tries, I think, to persuade us that this development, although not necessary for normal cognition, is desirable. There is, of course, an implicit argument for the desirability of a developmental process in any work that claims simply to describe such a process. If the process is developmental, then by definition, movement through it must be good and arrest at an early stage bad. The researcher is not supposed to assign such values to the stages being described and therefore is not expected to defend the implicit values. Perry, however, has openly assigned values to his developmental stages: successful completion of a liberal arts education requires moving eventually into the world view of Committed Relativism. Perry must either defend the values or be charged with bias in his research.

Consequently Perry openly states: "The values built into our scheme are those we assume to be commonly held in significant areas of our culture, finding their most concentrated expression in such institutions as colleges of liberal arts, mental health movements, and the like" (p. 45). He understands that these values are "statements of opinion," with which others may differ (p. 45), and that framing these values in a developmental scheme implicitly argues for them by implying that the closer one adheres to them, the more one "grows" (p. 44). But he is unembarrassed at arguing for these values because he believes that they lead ultimately to the truest world view, or as he puts it, "an optimally congruent and responsible address to the present state of man's predicament" (p. 45). Ultimately Perry sees the achievement of this world view as having spiritual significance; he refers several times to his scheme's being a sort of modern-day *Pilgrim's Progress*, and he stresses the courage it takes for young people to win through to the end (see pp. 37, 44).

Perry's scheme, then, charts the creation of, not just any intellectually and ethically mature adult, but precisely "the liberally educated man," a man (or woman) "who has learned to think about even his own thoughts, to examine the way he orders his data and the assumptions he is making, and to compare these with other thoughts that other men might have" (p. 39). Perry characterizes the adult who cannot be self-reflective in this way as "anti-intellectual," even if he or she is otherwise intelligent (p. 39). To develop this kind of self-reflective intellectual maturity, Perry explicitly recommends a pedagogy of pluralism, which forces students to confront opposing views on an issue, forcing them out of the Dualist world view on into Relativism and beyond. Persuasively arguing for this pedagogy, Perry cites Socrates as its first practitioner and finds an American supporter for it in Henry Adams (p. 35). Pluralism is also the pedagogy of Harvard College. Perry recognizes that its pervasiveness at Harvard has conditioned his research results, but he does not seek to claim universality for his results. Rather, he argues for this particular education-induced development. Let other colleges, Perry implies, follow Harvard, as they have done in the past, in defining "the very heart of liberal education" (pp. 35–36).

Perry does not discuss the place of writing in the development for which he argues. He does not say, for example, that a Dualist student will write a particular kind of essay. Indeed, to determine a student's position in the scheme, Perry looks at nothing other than what the student tells the interviewer about his experiences. From the transcript of the interview Perry derives the student's attitudes toward schoolwork, which serve to characterize the positions in the scheme, as I explain above.

These general attitudes toward schoolwork presumably do inform particular kinds of academic performance, however. In a much anthologized essay Perry has distinguished between the attitudes that produce "cow" writing, or data unorganized by theory, and "bull" writing, or theory unsupported by data.[1] He does not use the descriptive terms from his scheme to characterize "cow" and "bull" writers, but he does connect students' papers with their understanding of academic ways of thinking.

With this indirect encouragement from Perry, many writing teachers have found it easy to match typical kinds of student essays with positions in the scheme. For example, a familiar sort of undergraduate essay is the one without an organizing thesis, the essay that is simply a collocation of facts strung together like beads with connectives such as "another" or "next." Typically, too, this kind of essay is either hypercorrect or fraught with errors that seem to have kept the student's attention fixed on the sentence level, so underdeveloped are the ideas in the whole paper. In place of generalizations from data this paper relies on maxims used so uncritically as to strike us as dreadful clichés. Mina Shaughnessy has found these characteristics in the writing of students at the most "basic" level of approximation to academic discourse (*Errors and Expectations* [New York: Oxford University Press, 1977], pp. 198–202). Building on Shaughnessy's work, Andrea Lunsford finds similar characteristics in the essays of some of her Basic Writers.[2] It seems easy to identify such writing as the work of what Perry calls Dualist students, with their belief in unquestionable Absolutes and their view of education as the collecting of right answers.

Much more research is needed, however, before we can use Perry's scheme to classify kinds of student writing. No doubt there are common kinds of undergraduate essays other than that described above, which seems to fit the scheme so neatly; we do not know whether Perry's scheme can provide an exhaustive explanation of variation in student writing. We should remember that Perry's scheme was based on the experiences of students who were highly successful academically and who were attending one of the most selective liberal arts colleges in the country. Although Shaughnessy and Lunsford, working with students somewhat different from Perry's, found signs in student writing of a development similar to the one he describes (neither of them refers to Perry), we do not know to what extent Perry's scheme can extend its explanatory power across a variety of student abilities, academic preparation, and college experiences. We should also note that Perry provides no timetable for progress through his scheme; nowhere does he suggest that all freshmen can be expected to be Dualists, who then as sophomores and juniors traverse Relativism and achieve Committed Relativism as seniors. The existence of these gaps in our knowledge of the scheme's application to student writing argues against using the scheme to classify student writing in any detailed way.

Furthermore, I would argue that we should not use Perry's scheme as a blueprint for writing curricula. Mechanical applications of Perry's scheme will tend to trivialize it while producing curricula that really tell us nothing new. For example, one freshman composition curriculum based on Perry uses his analysis of Relativism to justify the already familiar recommendation to ask students to read several essays that take opposing views on a controversial issue and then to develop their own argumentative positions.[3] The method is so familiar as already to have been embodied in numberless freshman composition anthologies. Furthermore, because students require prolonged exposure to pluralistic methods in many disciplines, and time to reduce the domain of Dualism, this curriculum does not do justice to the rather elaborate process whereby a student achieves the Relativist world view, according to Perry. Some research has suggested that Dualists make more progress if teachers initially take a nurturing, rather than a challenging, stance with them.[4] Moreover, students who have already achieved Relativism may not be greatly benefited by lessons in recognizing and arguing from opposing views on a controversial issue. Such practice may only entrench them in intransigently held personal views, a mind-set which, according to Perry, often retards students' progress through Relativism to Commitment.

If we agree with Perry that students pass through certain positions on their way to the kind of intellectual maturity valued in liberal arts colleges, it does not necessarily follow that we can get them to progress faster by forcing them to imitate more advanced positions until their brains kick on and hold these positions on their own. We should not, in other words, commit a version of what has come to be known as the "American heresy" with respect to the work of Piaget, that is, the attempt to find ways of moving children faster through the Piagetian levels. Perry's scheme describes the effects of a certain liberal arts curriculum, to be sure — Harvard's — but this does not mean that we can turn the effects into a model of causes for a new curriculum that will perform the same changes more efficiently. To try would be to neglect the emphasis Perry himself places on the function of education as acculturation, not training; inculcation of values, not practice in techniques.

Of what use, then, is Perry's work to college writing teachers? I think his scheme can help us to understand why the differences occur in student writing, even if we cannot apply his classification scheme rigidly. Shaughnessy and Lunsford do not agree on why such differences occur. Shaughnessy suggests that they arise from students' unequal ability to meet the expectations of the academic discourse community. Lunsford argues that the students are at different levels of cognitive development in the Piagetian sense — Basic Writers are "egocentric" (p. 284). Perry's scheme forges a link between these social and cognitive explanations because, as I argued above, he is describing a developmental process that is only analogous to but not identical with Piaget's. Perry's analysis describes the changes in student thinking that result from their socialization into the academic community. The great strength of his scheme is its focus on one important constant in the struggles of all college writers: the intellectual demands of liberal education.

Perry's work should make us realize that as we bring our students through the process of liberal education, we are not simply teaching them to think or to grow up, as we sometimes like to say that we are. Rather, we are teaching them to think in a certain way, to become adults with a certain set of intellectual habits and ethical predilections. We are asking them to accept a certain kind of relation to their culture, from among the range of relations that are possible.

Thus Perry's greatest use to writing teachers is to provide us with a sort of philosophical map of the changes liberal education seeks to induce in our students. Such a map can help us understand that certain typical problems students have with writing in college should be regarded as problems with accepting the academic community's preferred world view, and not necessarily as problems with achieving "normal" cognition. This is supported by the rough match between Perry's scheme and the characteristics Shaughnessy and Lunsford note in the writing of students who are different from those in Perry's research sample.

In short, Perry provides us with a useful picture of the kind of "cultural literacy" required in a liberal arts college. The term "cultural literacy" refers to the objects of knowledge and the ways of thinking that one must master in order to participate in a particular community.[5] Following Perry we come to realize that the academic community requires students to know, for example, not only what Genesis says about the creation of the earth but also what geologists, biologists, and other scientists say about it. A community of religious fundamentalists might require only knowledge of Genesis. Furthermore, the academic community requires students to know how to evaluate competing ideas according to criteria of logical structure, adequate evidence, and so on; this academic way of thinking might not be valued, for instance, in a fundamentalist community in which tradition or the judgment of a revered authority is sufficient to validate arguments.

Literacy in the more usual sense of the ability to read and write is also highly valued in the academic community. Clearly, literacy is not required for participation in every sort of community. Some communities, too, value reading over writing—when there is a sacred text to be chanted, for example. But the academic community places a high value on writing, and Perry can help us see why. The whole thrust of his developmental scheme is toward an increasing distance on the beliefs of one's childhood. These beliefs can no longer be accepted uncritically as Absolutes, once we realize that well-intentioned people may hold beliefs different from our own. As the pedagogical pluralism which Perry recommends widens the students' perspectives, it also fosters relativism by casting their beliefs into comparative relations with those of others.

Many theorists in composition studies have argued that writing is a unique mode of learning precisely because it fosters this kind of distancing.[6] One's ideas can be more easily examined, critiqued in comparison with other views, and reformulated as they are worked out in written form. Learning to write, then, can be seen as a process of learning to think about one's own thinking, a process which may well be unfamiliar to students in their home communities.

306

Furthermore, Perry's quasi-spiritual tone should remind us that we tend to invest teaching with moral fervor. I submit that most teachers will recognize in themselves a sort of moral repugnance about bad writing, a feeling that students "ought" to be able to organize and develop their ideas better, even while recognizing that this feeling partakes of the irrational blaming of the victim. Given that we do have this moral investment in the objects of knowledge and the ways of thinking that we teach, it seems hypocritical to pretend that academic activity is value-neutral, that we are merely teaching "thinking," not thinking in a certain way. And it seems more respectful to our students to see what we are doing when we teach as attempting to persuade them to accept our values, not simply inculcating our values.

Is this development desirable? The nature of Perry's scheme makes this question inevitable, fortunately. As in all discussions of cultural literacy the issue is, whose culture will be empowered to set the terms of literacy? Writing teachers are already acquainted with one such discussion in the debate over students' right to their own language. Personally, I believe that the kind of cultural literacy whose development is both chronicled and advocated in Perry's scheme is desirable for all students. But I do not want to begin here the lengthy argument that would be needed to defend that view.

Here I would simply like to make the point that our assumptions about the ends of education are strongly culture-bound, as Perry helps us see. Furthermore, Perry gives us a perspective on all college teachers as, in effect, rhetors. To a high degree we persuade students to our values through our use of language, in lectures, textbooks, informal discussions, and writing assignments. Writing-across-the-curriculum programs do not so much create important roles for writing in all disciplines as they render us self-conscious about the role writing already plays. Some college teachers may not be comfortable with the view of themselves as rhetors, preferring to see themselves as investigators, reporters, value-neutral conveyors of truth. Perry's most important contribution to writing instruction may well be the critique he implies of this positivistic view of the teacher's role.

NOTES

1. "Examsmanship and the Liberal Arts," in *Examining at Harvard College*, ed. L. Bramson (Cambridge, Mass.: Faculty of the Arts and Sciences, Harvard University, 1963).

2. "The Content of Basic Writers' Essays," *College Composition and Communication*, 31 (1980), 279–283, 285.

3. This new, experimental composition program was described in a paper presented by Professor Gene Krupa of the University of Iowa at the 1983 Conference on College Composition and Communication. Professor Krupa did not want to draw any conclusions yet about its worth.

4. See, for example, Kiyo Morimoto, "Notes on the Context for Learning," *Harvard Educational Review*, 43 (1973), 245–257.

5. For a definition of the term, and an argument in favor of a cultural literacy similar to that in Perry's scheme, see Richard Hoggart, "The Importance of Literacy," *Journal of Basic Writing*, 3 (1980), 74–87.

6. See, for example, Janet Emig, "Writing as a Mode of Learning," *College Composition and Communication*, 28 (1977), 122–128; and Linda Flower, "Writer-Based Prose: A Cognitive Basis for Problems in Writing," *College English*, 41 (1979), 19–37.

Is Teaching Still Possible?
Writing, Meaning, and Higher Order Reasoning

ANN E. BERTHOFF

In the memorable disquisition with which he begins *Permanence and Change* (Indianapolis, Ind.: Bobbs Merrill, 1954), Kenneth Burke explains how thinking which does not include thinking about thinking is merely problem-solving, an activity carried out very well by trouts.

> Though all organisms are critics in the sense that they interpret the signs about them, the experimental speculative technique made available by speech would seem to single out the human species as the only one possessing an equipment for going beyond the criticism of experience to a criticism of criticism. We not only interpret the characters of events. . . . We may also interpret our interpretations. (pp. 5–6)

That species-specific capacity for thinking about thinking, for interpreting interpretations, for knowing our knowledge, is, I think, the chief resource for any teacher and the ground of hope in the enterprise of teaching reading and writing.

I plan to be cheerful but there is a certain amount of setting aside which needs to be done before I can confidently claim that teaching is still possible. About half my time will go to nay-saying: I want first to assess the hazards of developmental models and the positivist views of language which underwrite them. I will turn then to a consideration of how alternative views of language and learning can help us invent a pedagogy that views reading and writing as interpretation and the making of meaning.

Reprinted from *College English* 46.8 (December 1984): 743–55. Used with permission.

What we have these days is properly described, I think, as a pedagogy of exhortation: "Feel comfortable. . . . Wake up! . . . Find something you're interested in. . . . Get your thesis statement. . . . Say what you really think. . . . Go over your paper and take out all unnecessary words." But exhortation, whether left-wing or right-wing, is not instructive. (No writer ever puts in words which he or she thinks are unnecessary; learning to discover that some *are* is one of the chief challenges in learning to write.) What must supplant the pedagogy of exhortation is a "pedagogy of knowing." The phrase is Paulo Freire's, and he means by it what Socrates, Montessori, Jane Addams, I. A. Richards, Roger Ascham, or other great teachers would have meant, namely, that unless and until the mind of the learner is engaged, no meaning will be made, no knowledge can be won.

What chiefly forestalls our moving from a pedagogy of exhortation to a pedagogy of knowing is a dependence on a view of language which cannot account *for* meaning nor give an account *of* meanings. A positivist conception of language as a "communication medium," as a set of muffin tins into which the batter of thought is poured, leads to question-begging representations and models of the composing process. Understanding what a pedagogy of knowing would involve is prevented by an unhealthy confusion about what development means and a damaging dependence on the stage models which cognitive psychologists have elaborated, supposedly for the benefit of rhetoricians as well as for guidance counsellors, therapists, curriculum designers, and the publishers of values clarification kits.

Let me begin with a passage from an article by a rhetorician who is discussing cross-disciplinary programs.

> Since the early 1970s evidence has been accumulating which suggests that up to fifty percent of the adolescent population in this country fail to make the transition from the concrete operational stage to formal operations by the time they have reached late high school or college age. Judging from this empirical research, it would appear that as many as half of our students from junior high on into adulthood are unable to think abstractly, to process and produce logical propositions.[1]

Three points are notable: First, the Piagetian model, which is of course intended to represent the stages of development of the language and thought of the child, is here applied to the reasoning of young adults; second, "empirical research" is taken as providing evidence in support of certain claims about learning; third, the failure to reach the stage of formal operations is made equivalent to an inability to "think abstractly," which, in turn, is identified as processing and producing logical propositions. These are all misconceptions. The attempt to apply the Piagetian stage model to non-children is futile; the claim that empirical research supports the efficacy of doing so is false; the identification of abstract thought with processing propositions begs the question of what constitutes that process.

What the child does or does not do may look like what the incompetent or deficient or uneducated adult does or does not do, but it does not follow that the two instances are alike so far as motivation or function are concerned. Just so, the savage is not a child; the lunatic is not a poet; the chimp who has been taught sign language cannot be said to be using it as either the hearing or deaf human being does. To see the similarities without noting the differences is to settle for pseudo-concepts, in Vygotsky's phrase.

If we do form a concept of language as not just a medium of communication but a means of making meaning, we preclude a dependence on empirical research to find out what is happening in our classrooms, to see what writers do when they compose. If you start with a working concept of language as a means of making meaning, you are recognizing that language can only be studied by means of language. Understood in such terms as *context, purpose, intention, import, reference, significance, ambiguity, representation*, and so on, linguistic structures or texts or speech acts can only be studied by interpreting the interdependencies of meanings—and by interpreting our interpretations. But if these conceptions are central, what is there for empirical researchers to investigate? Empiricists do not generally recognize that all method, including scientific method, entails interpretation; they do not generally recognize that there are no raw data; there are no self-sufficient facts; there is no context-free evaluation. Their method is not to recognize the fact that all knowledge is mediated and that facts must be formulated, but to proceed as if interpretation were supererogatory. Empirical researchers leave out of account meaning because they have no means of accounting for it. I. A. Richards observed of this kind of investigator that he "does not know how to respect the language."

> He does not yet have a conception of the language which would make it respectable. He thinks of it as a code and has not yet learned that it is an organ—the supreme organ of the mind's self-ordering growth. Despite all his claims to be expert in collecting, reporting, comparing, and systematizing linguistic facts, he has not yet apprehended the greatest of them all: that language is an instrument for controlling our becoming.[2]

Some of the human sciences have seen the folly of denying the very subject which should be at the heart of the study of the language animal, the *animal symbolicum*. The anthropologist Clifford Geertz, in a wonderful essay called "Thick Description," shows just what it means to ask questions about what human beings are doing.[3] He undertakes to explain how context and perspective function in interpretation by subjecting an example of Gilbert Ryle's to analysis: A boy is seen to wink; another boy has a tic which involves his eyelid; a third boy is seen practicing an imitation of the boy with the tic. Try describing these "behaviors," as the empirical researcher would call them, and watch two of them become human acts, motivated and meaningful—and subject to interpretation.

If meaning is set aside in the search for "data," the findings will not then be applicable to the making of meaning. But composition specialists who follow psycholinguistic principles of analysis want to have it both ways: their empirical research requires that meaning be left out of account, but they also want to claim that their findings are relevant to pedagogy. What writers do is thus confused with what psycholinguists want to study. This methodological pitfall is impossible to avoid when the investigator is guided by a conception of language as a code.[4]

The empiricist needs something to measure, and cohesive devices can be counted, once there is a taxonomy. They are a feature of discourse analysis, which is not, as one might have thought, a matter of studying the dialectic of what-is-said and what-is-meant; it is not the analysis of intention and recalcitrant linguistic structures in dialectic, the relationship that makes the representation of meaning possible; it is by no means simply a fancy name for "critical reading": discourse analysis is the study of "information management," "thematic structure," "sentence rules," and, preeminently, of "cohesion." Now the "cohesiveness" of a text is not the same thing as "coherence." Coherence is mentalistic; it isn't there on the page; it cannot be measured and graphed; it can only be interpreted in terms of the emergent meanings of the writer. But for the psycholinguistic investigator, it is not writers who produce texts; texts are created by cohesive devices.

At a recent conference I heard a psycholinguist explain how, in order to foreground the cohesive devices, he had to reduce the role of meaning. The first problem in the design of his experiment was to find a passage or a stretch of discourse in which meaning was not important so that it would be easier to measure the responsiveness of college students to cohesive devices. He spent some time in preparing the text, but I wondered why he didn't simply excise something from any textbook in any discipline published in any year, since they are generally written so that readers will not be irritated or distracted by the need to interpret what is being said in an attempt to understand what was intended.

This kind of empirical research institutionalizes the pedagogy of exhortation: "Does your paper flow? If not, check your transitions. Can your reader follow you? Be sure to give him clues." Thus we get papers full of roadsigns pointing in the wrong direction—*however,* when there is no *however* relationship; *on the other hand,* introducing a faulty parallel; redundancy (the uninstructed writer's only means of emphasis); end linkages—which I call Nixonian Syntactic Ligature—with the beginning of each sentence picking up the exact wording of the end of the preceding sentence. Research on cohesive devices easily seeps into composition theory because it sounds scientific and because anything that lets us count will seem helpful in evaluating what we think we are teaching. But the fact that cohesive ties may be identified and classified can easily distract us from the problem of learning how to help writers discover, in the very act of realizing their intentions, the discursive power of language itself, what Edward Sapir meant by calling language heuristic. Empirical research into "discourse acquisition" is likely, I think, to mislead us—to lead us away from thinking about thinking, to keep us from studying the process whereby writers discover the resources of language and learn to control them in the making of meaning.[5]

The challenge to experimental design should be not to reduce meaning or to try to eliminate it; this is a primitive conception of what disembedding involves. The challenge to experimental design is not to dispense with meaning but to control language so that there are not too many meanings at a time; so that the learners can discern, in I. A. Richards' words, "the partially parallel task" (*Speculative Instruments,* p. 96) when they confront it; so that the teacher, by means of a careful sequence of lessons or assignments, can assure that the students are conscious of their minds in action, can develop their language by means of exercising deliberate choice. Positivists see no virtue whatsoever in consciousness of consciousness since they model conceptualization on motor skills—and everybody knows that there consciousness becomes self-consciousness: you'll fall off the bicycle if you think hard about what you're doing. What is forgotten is that wherever language is concerned we are dealing with symbolic acts. Consciousness there is not that "self" consciousness which is so destructive but Freire's "conscientization" or Burke's "interpretation of our interpretations" or Richards' "comprehending our comprehensions more comprehensively" or Coleridge's "knowing our knowledge" or Cassirer's "confrontation of an act of awareness" and so on. Consciousness of consciousness is entailed in our activity as language animals.

If psychologists would read Susanne K. Langer's *Mind: An Essay on Human Feeling,* they would have a clearer idea of what they are about. Or they could read a little phenomenology, but psychology is usually about a generation behind. Thus psychologists have recently taken up structuralism, just as it's being laid to rest elsewhere. And before that it was operationalism, which fed itself on hard data. Robert Oppenheimer, in a brilliant talk to the American Psychological Association in 1955, urged the members not to mimic a determinist physics "which is not there any more" ("Analogy in Science," reprinted in *Reclaiming the Imagination*, pp. 189–202). He suggested, rather, that they listen to a man named Jean Piaget. Nowadays, when psychology is awash in Piagetian concepts, it is hard to imagine that this warning was necessary, but Oppenheimer realized that those in charge were the successors to those whom William James had called "brass instrument psychologists." Oppenheimer said: "I make this plea not to treat too harshly those who tell you a story, having observed carefully without having established that they are sure that the story is the whole story and the general story" (p. 201).

The story Piaget had to tell was certainly interesting, but it isn't the whole story or the general story, and some psychologists, by examining Piaget's experimental designs very carefully, have shown how and where he went wrong. I call your attention to an excellent little book, *Children's Minds*, by Margaret Donaldson (New York: Norton, 1979). (She is neither polemical about Piaget nor worshipful of some anti-Piaget.) Dozens of experiments are described which offer alternative explanations of children's responses to certain questions and situations designed to test their cognitive skills. They clearly establish that Piaget's findings, in instance after instance, are the artifacts of his procedures. The alleged incapacity to "decenter" is seen to be a matter of difficulty in locomotion and movement and not in a lack of "object concept" or an incapacity to entertain other points of view. It seems clear that children who made "egocentric" responses in various experiments of Piaget did not fully understand what they were supposed to do.

Margaret Donaldson writes in one of the summaries:

> Children are not at any stage as egocentric as Piaget has claimed . . . [they] are not so limited in ability to reason deductively as Piaget—and others—have claimed. . . . There is no reason to suppose that [the child] is born with an 'acquisitive device' which enables him to structure and make sense of the language he hears while failing to structure and make sense of the other features of his environment. (pp. 55–56)

The recent corrective experiments she discusses are fascinating, but there are precedents. What Margaret Donaldson's psychologists have done for the semantics and syntax of Piagetian questions, Rudolf Arnheim did for visual representation in Piagetian problems. Ever alert to the powers of visual thinking, Arnheim illustrates what he calls "visual illiteracy" with a pair of drawings in cross section of a water tap in open and closed position, schematic representations used in one of Piaget's perceptual problems. In a series of devastating questions in *Visual Thinking* (Berkeley: University of California Press, 1969) he points out the ambiguities and concludes as follows:

> I am not denying that a person, immunized and warned by years of expo-sure to mediocre textbook illustrations, mail order catalogues, and similar products of visual ineptness, can figure out the meaning of these drawings, especially if helped by verbal explanation. But surely, if a child passes the test he does so in spite of the drawing, not with the help of it; and if he fails, he has not shown that he does not understand the working of a tap. He may simply be unable to extricate himself from a visual pitfall. (p. 312)

But of course the centrally important critique of Piaget's work came from Lev Vygotsky as early as 1932. Vygotsky's strictures concern not only the rela-tionship of language and thought but also that of learning and instruction.[6] All study of language and thought, Vygotsky argued, must begin with the "unit of meaning," since neither language as element nor thought as element can be apprehended in its real character without the context provided by the other. Speech is not articulated sound plus intention; it is not speech until and unless it is meaningful. Neither language nor thought is meaningful out-side a social context—which is to say that purpose and intention are from the first constrained not by a need for "communication" but by a need for repre-sentation, which of course invites and demands interpretation. Language is symbolic activity and from the first establishes itself in a social setting. The crucial difference between Vygotsky's procedures and Piaget's is that lan-guage is built into Vygotsky's test design and the tester is actively involved in exchanges with the subject. Piaget, Vygotsky thought, did not appreciate the complex dialectic of the learning curve and the role of instruction. The explanation for the misleading questions and the ambiguous directions is to be sought in the fact that Piaget thought that the only way to test cognitive skills was to isolate them as far as possible from language-dependent settings. The failure to understand the interdependence of language and thought is consonant with the misconception of the role of instruction which, like test design, is considered by Piaget in mechanistic terms.

Why should we care about Piaget and his critics? Don't we have enough to do, taking care of course design and teacher training and writing across the curriculum and trying to assure the survival of departments of English and to assuage deans who are counting FTE's—don't we have enough to do without worrying over arguments which may or may not be intelligible or important? The answer is that if we don't understand the grounds for a critical appraisal of theories of cognitive development, if we let our practice be guided by whatever we are told has been validated by empirical research, we will get what we have got: a conception of learning as contingent on development in a straightforward, linear fashion; of development as a pre-set program which is autonomous and does not require instruction; of language as words used as labels; of meaning as a one-directional, one-dimensional attribute; of the human mind as an adaptive mechanism. Thus are we wrecked on the rocks of teaching seen as intervention; of the so-called student-centered classroom; of single-skill correction; of discourse analysis, in which the chief function of discourse is disregarded; of reading instruction in which language is considered solely as a graphic code; of writing seen as the assignment of topics sequenced according to the commonplaces of classical rhetoric, as interpreted by associationist psychology: narrative before description, compare-contrast separate from definition, expression way before exposition; an affective English 101 (Turn off your mind and float downstream) and a cognitive English 102 (Get your thesis statement! Generalize! Be brief! Don't generalize!).

Developmental models uncritically deployed lead to the kind of judgment exemplified in the final sentence of the text I took as my point of departure, the one stating that students can't think abstractly, that they can't "produce or process logical propositions." We should not be surprised that this writer goes on to say that "It is fairly obvious from work done in psychology that we cannot accelerate the transition from concrete to formal operations." What is surprising is the rest of the sentence: "but we may be able to promote its natural development by creating a more natural classroom environment" (Freisinger, p. 163). Why would we aim to promote its "natural development" if we don't think we can "accelerate the transition" to a stage now long overdue? Yet I am cheered by this absurd contradiction, cheered according to the same logic by which Gide was led to praise hypocrisy as a step in the right direction. I think the writer is a better teacher than the theory he explicitly depends on lets him be; so he discards it! He finds another which allows him to speak of promoting natural development in a natural environment. That sounds like somebody who believes that teaching is still possible!

I am now ready to be cheerful. The first piece of good news is that what college students find difficult—what everybody finds difficult, what diplomats and doctors, of medicine and of philosophy, find difficult, is not *abstraction* but *generalization*. These acts of mind are conflated by positivists, but they are not the same. Abstraction is not generalization. This is not a quibble; if it were, our enterprise would be futile and the very idea of education fatuous.

Abstraction is natural, normal: it is the way we make sense of the world in perception, in dreaming, in all expressive acts, in works of art, in all imagining. Abstraction is the work of the active mind; it is what the mind does as it forms. The name for this power of mind used to be imagination. We do not have to teach it: it is the work of our Creator. It is a God-given power or, if you prefer, it is a specific power the *animal symbolicum* has in lieu of a repertory of instincts which obviate the necessity of interpreting interpretations. We do not have to teach abstraction. What we do have to do is to show students how to reclaim their imaginations so that "the prime agent of all human perception" can be for them a living model of what they do when they write. What we must learn to do, if we are to move from the pedagogy of exhortation to a pedagogy of knowing, is to show our students how to use what they already do so cleverly in order to learn how to generalize—how to move from abstraction in the non-discursive mode to discursive abstraction, to generalization. We must strive to "raise implicit recognitions to explicit differentiations": that phrase comes from a book called *The Philosophy of Rhetoric*, published nearly fifty years ago by I. A. Richards. We do not yet have a philosophy of rhetoric, for the very good reason that we, teachers of reading and writing and those responsible for literacy at all levels, have not "taken charge of the criticism of our own assumptions," as Richards urged. The second piece of good news is that there is a semiotics which can guide that enterprise.

It starts from a triadic rather than a dyadic conception of the sign and you can represent it rather easily by drawing two triangles. Draw first an equilateral triangle, pointing upward. At the southwest corner write "Writer or encoder"; at the southeast, write "Audience or decoder" and at the top, write "Message." This constitutes what positivist rhetoricians call the triangle of discourse: It is worthless. As you can easily see, it leaves out purpose, meaning, and intention; it confuses message with signal. Now draw another equilateral triangle and make the base a dotted line. Label the southwest angle "representamen or symbol"; the southeast angle, "object or referent"; at the apex, write "interpretant or reference." You can get from the symbol to what it represents only by means of a meaning, a mediating idea. This curious triangle represents the triadicity central to C. S. Peirce's *semeiotics* and it appears in *The Meaning of Meaning* (New York: Harcourt, Brace, 1944) by Ogden and Richards, a work first published in 1922. I know of no evidence that Vygotsky had read either Peirce or Ogden and Richards, but the triangle with the dotted line appears in an excellent paper of his on symbolization as mediated activity, first published in 1930 ("Mind in Society," reprinted in *Reclaiming the Imagination*, pp. 61–72).

Triadicity is an idea whose time has surely come. It can help us take charge of the criticism of our assumptions about teaching because in the triadic conception of the sign, the symbol-user, the knower, the learner is integral to the process of making meaning. The curious triangle, by thus representing the mediating function of interpretation, can serve as an emblem for a pedagogy of knowing. Indeed, my third piece of good news is that triadicity can help us reclaim imagination and the idea of language as "the supreme organ of the mind's self-ordering growth." I will conclude now with a sketch of this view of language and how it can lead us towards an authentic pedagogy of knowing.

Language seen as a means of making meaning has two aspects, the hypostatic and the discursive. By naming the world, we hold images in mind; we remember; we can return to our experience and reflect on it. In reflecting, we can change, we can transform, we can envisage. Language thus becomes the very type of social activity by which we might move towards changing our lives. The hypostatic power of language to fix and stabilize frees us from the prison of the moment. Language recreates us as historical beings. In its discursive aspect language runs along and brings thought with it, as Cassirer puts it. Discourse grows from inner dialogue (and the differing accounts by Piaget and Vygotsky of that development make a fascinating study). From this earliest activity of the mind, language gradually takes on the discursive forms which serve the communicative function. Because of this tendency to syntax, we can articulate our thoughts; we can think about thinking and thus interpret our interpretations.

Seeing language in this perspective encourages the recognition that meaning comes first; that it is complex from the start; that its articulation is contingent on the mind's activity in a human world. The chief hazard of the developmental model is that it sanctions the genetic fallacy—that what comes first is simple, not complex, and that what comes after is a bigger version of a little beginning. Thus we have the idea that there is first one word and then another, another, another, until there is enough to fill out the awaiting syntactic structures. But this isn't the way it happens. The hypostatic word, the single uttered syllable, is a protosentence; syntax is deeply implicated, we might say, in every human cry. Children let a single word do the work of the sentence until the discursive power of language can draw out and articulate the meaning. The conception of a semantic component added to a syntactic structure is a mechanistic conception which must be supplanted. I suggest as an image of the growth and development of language one of those little wooden flowers which the Japanese used to make— before they turned to silicon chips—a tiny compacted form which, placed in a dish of water, opens and expands, blossoming in the shape of a fully articulated flower. Please note the dialectic: it is the water which acts to release the form. In my extended metaphor, the water is our social life, the essential context for the making of meaning. Cognitive psychologists who deliberately ignore it have not advanced over those early kings whose hobby it was to try to discover which language is oldest. They sequestered newborn twins in castle keep or cottage, in the care of a mute nurse, and breathlessly awaited news of what language it would be, when the babies came to speak. And you can safely bet that the court astrologer—that proto-psycholinguist—saw to it that the first reported syllables were construed as Swedish or Hebrew or whatever language it was that the monarch—that proto-funding agency—expected.

In my opinion the ambiguities of the determinism suggested by any account of natural, normal development can serve as the hinges of our thinking about thinking in the interest of discovering the laws of growth, the interdependency of nature and nurture, seed and soil. Language and learning, like syntax and semantics, are in a dialectical relationship which we must learn to construe and represent so that it is accessible to our students. Just so, we must guide their consciousness of consciousness so that it can become the means of freeing the self from itself: as a pleasant way of resolving that paradox, I recommend Walker Percy's new book, *Lost in the Cosmos: The Last Self-Help Book.* After a startling and instructive analysis of twenty versions of the lost self, we have a chapter on triadicity, the means of reclaiming the self. Dr. Percy is an artist, a scientist, and a philosopher for whom triadicity provides the means of conceiving that symbolic activity which defines the mind.

Because they make interpretation central, triadic models of the composing process are the trustworthy ones we need in developing a pedagogy of knowing. The two I consider most useful are perception and dialogue. Every course I teach begins with observation—with looking and looking again. It is my strong conviction that what is looked at should include organic objects, themselves compositions. But of course we must also "problematize the existential situation," as Freire rather infelicitously puts it. I bring seaweed and crab legs to class, the seed pods of sedges and five kinds of pine cones, but I also ask students to problematize the soda cans and milk cartons left from the last class.[7] (I haven't dared to undertake the archeology of the waste basket: God knows what we might find!) We use my version of the journalist's heuristic, *HDWDWW?*—deliberately constructed to resist becoming an acronym: *How does who do what and why?* How does that come to be on your desk? Who left it there? Why do you leave this junk around? What are these things in evidence of? What is the meaning of this litter? Looking and looking again helps students learn to transform things into questions; they learn to see names as "titles for situations," as Kenneth Burke puts it. In looking and naming, looking again and re-naming, they develop perspectives and contexts, discovering how each controls the other. They are composing; they are forming; they are abstracting.

Perception is non-discursive abstraction; the questioning of perceptions is the beginning of generalization, of discursive abstraction. Perception as a model of the composing process lets us capitalize on the hypostatic function of language. Students can discover that they are already thinking; by raising implicit recognitions to explicit differentiations, they can, as it were, *feel* the activity of their minds. By beginning with meaning, with complexity, we assure that minds will, indeed, be active. As I've been arguing, that complexity must be controlled by the way we use language or it will overwhelm, but the complexity entailed in making meaning should never be put off: *elements of what we want to end with must be present in some form from the first or we will never get to them.* That, I take it, is the chief law of growth.

Dialogue is the other triadic model. The "natural environment" necessary to the growth and development of the discursive power of language requires dialogue. Looking again starts that questioning which is the beginning of dialectic and it should be practiced in dialogue in class, of course, but also in what I call a "dialectical notebook," the facing pages offering a structure which enables the student to talk to herself. Dialogue is essential not only because it provides practice in those other uses of language—speaking and listening—but because it can model that constant movement from the particular to the general and back again which for Vygotsky is the defining characteristic of concept formation. But let me be explicit about this natural environment: it is a *prepared* environment, in the sense in which Montessori spoke of her classroom as a prepared environment. This dialectic of particularizing and generalizing, this conceptualizing, this thinking, though it is a power natural by reason of language itself, though it is natural to the human mind, must be put into practice. Like speech itself, it requires a social context in which purposes can be arrived at, intentions discovered and formulated and represented in different modes of discourse.

If college students find generalizing difficult, it's because nobody has ever taught them how to go about it, and abstraction which proceeds by means of generalizing—*concept formation*, as it is often called—must be deliberately learned and should therefore be deliberately taught. But few methods for doing so have been developed and those which have are, generally speaking, of the type Freire calls the banking model: the teacher deposits valuable information. Developmental models are most dangerous when they distract teachers from recognizing the deficiencies of their pedagogy. When we are told, as we are by almost everybody reporting research, that students are good at narrative but fall apart when faced with exposition, it is not necessary to hypothesize that students have come bang up against a developmental fence. The first step of the analysis should be to look at the character of the assignments, at the sequence of "tasks." In an interesting variation on this theme of "narrative good, exposition terrible," one researcher contrasts how well students do with persuasion and how poorly they do with argument.[8] She reports how intelligently students have jumped through the hoops of compare-contrast, "explain a process," "describe an incident," etc., etc.—all in the interest of composing in the persuasive mode—only to fall flat on their faces with the argumentation paper. And guess where it came from? Not from exploration or dialogue or observation or a close reading of texts. No: it came from an assigned topic on euthanasia. Why is anybody surprised when they get terrible writing from a terrible assignment? "Who is to get the kidney machine?" is no advance at all over "Which is greater, fire or water?" "Provocative" topics stimulate cant and cliché; they breed Engfish; they lead to debate, which is by no means dialectic. Nobody learns from debate because, as Richards often observed, the disputant is commonly too busy making a point to trouble to see what it is.

Assigning topics—the essential strategy of the pedagogy of exhortation—is no substitute for instruction. But the deeper reason for the failure in the argumentation paper is the same as for the proclaimed success in the persuasion paper. Persuasion is the air we breathe; it is the mode of advertisement. But where do our students hear argument? Mine do not have the faintest idea of the conventions of an editorial—and when have they ever heard an authentic, dialectical exchange on television information shows? The discourse we find familiar to the point of being able to reproduce it has nothing to do with developmental stages, once childhood is passed—or maybe even before. You may be sure that prepubescent Presbyterians in the eighteenth century were capable of composing arguments on natural depravity, while pre-pubescent Baptists were writing on grace abounding unto the chief of sinners, and little Methodists were writing on topics like "Must the drunkard be an unhappy man?" My advanced composition students find almost intolerably difficult Huxley's "On a Piece of Chalk," a public lecture which a century ago famously enthralled workers with no secondary education—but Huxley's audience had heard two or three sermons every week of their lives! Argument was the air you breathed, a hundred years ago. I am not, of course, claiming authenticity or moral superiority for those who can argue. I mean only that the capacity to manage disputation is a culture-bound skill and that its dependence on neurobiological development is a necessary but not a sufficient condition.

Ironically, it is sometimes students themselves who misconceive the developmental model. Especially older students fear that they must return to Square One. They have to make it all up, they think. When we ask them, like everybody else, to look and look again, we must, by a careful choice of reading—on the model of malt whiskey, not diet soda—lead them to discover that scientists and lawyers and poets look and look again. Of course we must begin with where they are—as meaning makers. We must, in I. A. Richards' phrase, offer them "assisted invitations" to look carefully at what they are doing—observing a weed or drawing up a shopping list—in order to discover *how* to do it.[9] Our job is to devise sequences of assignments which encourage conscientization, the discovery of the mind in action. That will not be accomplished by setting topics, no matter how nicely matched to the "appropriate" developmental stage they might be.

Rather, in our pedagogy of knowing, we will encourage the discovery of mind by assuring that language is seen not as a set of slots, not as an inert code to be mastered by drill, but as a means of *naming* the world; of holding the images by whose means we human beings recognize the forms of our experience; of reflecting on those images, as we do on other words. We teachers will assure that language is continually exercised to name and establish likes and differents so that by sorting and gathering, students will learn to define: they will learn to abstract in the discursive mode; they will learn to generalize. They will thus be able to "think abstractly" because they will be learning how meanings make further meanings possible, how form finds further form. And we will, in our pedagogy of knowing, be giving our students back their language so that they can reclaim it as an instrument for controlling their becoming.

NOTES

1. Randall Freisinger, "Cross-Disciplinary Writing Workshops: Theory and Practice," *College English*, 42 (1980), 163.

2. *Speculative Instruments* (New York: Harcourt Brace, 1955), p. 9. It is the lack of a philosophy of language that could properly account for meaning which invalidates the procedures so frequently recommended for students of the composing process. George Hillocks, for instance, suggests that inquiry procedures are well-modelled by ethology. (See his article "Inquiry and the Composing Process: Theory and Research," *College English*, 44 [1982], 659–673.) But as Susanne K. Langer has shown in the second volume of *Mind: An Essay on Human Feeling* (Baltimore, Md.: Johns Hopkins University Press, 1972), Frisch, Tinbergen, et al. are unaware of the role metaphor plays in their descriptions; of presuppositions which remain entirely unexamined; of distortions resulting from a failure to differentiate animal and human acts. Ethological interpretations are shown to be pseudoconcepts, generalizations about particular cases, not authentic concepts.

3. *The Interpretation of Cultures* (New York: Basic Books, 1973), pp. 3–30. Reprinted in my *Reclaiming the Imagination*, (Upper Montclair, N.J.: Boynton/Cook, 1984), pp. 226–248.

4. Max Black in an essay on Whorf entitled "Linguistic Relativity" notes "the linguist's fallacy of imputing his own sophisticated attitudes to the speakers he is studying" (*Models and Metaphors* [Ithaca, N.Y.: Cornell University Press, 1962], p. 247).

5. I do not deny the value of analyzing cohesive devices in the context of discourse; this, I take it, is precisely what Richards had in mind when he called rhetoric "the study of how words work." But "discourse analysis," as presently practiced, does not always take into account the interdependence of linguistic and rhetorical functions. It begs the question of the relationship of language and thought, because the positivist conception of language by which it is guided does not provide the means for accounting for meaning. Discourse analysts separate thinking from writing, which they conceive of as the manipulation of *devices*. When Charles R. Cooper tells us in "Procedures for Describing Written Texts" (in *Research on Writing*, ed. Peter Mosenthal and Shaun Walmsley [New York: Longman, 1983]) that the "thinking process leads the writer to choose appropriate strategies and forms for presenting the outcomes of thought *as written text*" (p. 291), he has not been alert to those hazards Vygotsky urges us to avoid by beginning with the unit of meaning. For Professor Cooper it is clearly not part of the procedure for describing, much less for producing, "texts" to take into account the heuristic powers of language or the interplay of feedback and what Richards calls "feedforward." Yet "shaping at the point of utterance" is not exclusively an oral phenomenon.

It should be noted that for Halliday and Hasan, whose taxonomy is widely used, the working concept of a text is as a semantic unit. For an excellent discussion of the interdependence of meaning and grammatical, logical, and rhetorical forms, see Jeanne Fahnestock, "Semantic and Lexical Coherence," *College Composition and Communication*, 34 (1983), 400–416. And see anything Josephine Miles has ever written.

6. See especially "Development of Scientifc Concepts in Childhood" in *Thought and Language*, trans. and ed. Eugenia Hanfman and Gertrude Vakar (Cambridge, Mass.: MIT Press, 1962). Vygotsky analyzes the theories of the relationship of learning and development held by Piaget, William James, and the Gestaltists and then goes on to outline his own theory, the central feature of which is "the zone of proximal development." The interdependence of "scientific" and "spontaneous" concepts is exactly analogous to that of discursive and mythic forms of thought in Cassirer's philosophy of symbolic forms and Susanne K. Langer's philosophy of mind. The idea of development "upward" in spontaneous conceptualization and "downward" in the formation of scientific concepts is fundamental to Vygotsky's dialectical conception of learning and development as set forth in *Mind in Society: The Development of Higher Psychological Processes*, ed. Michael Cole, Vera John-Steiner, Sylvia Scribner, and Ellen Souberman (Cambridge, Mass.: Harvard University Press, 1978). See especially pp. 78–91.

7. For excellent examples and interesting procedures, see Ira Shor, *Critical Teaching and Everyday Life* (Boston: South End Press, 1980), pp. 155–194.

8. Susan Miller, "Rhetorical Maturity: Definition and Development," in *Reinventing the Rhetorical Tradition*, ed. Aviva Freedman and Ian Pringle (Conway, Ark.: L & S Books, 1980), pp. 119–127.

9. I have borrowed the phrase "assisted invitations" for the exercises in *Forming/Thinking/Writing: The Composing Imagination* (Upper Montclair, N.J.: Boynton/Cook, 1982). Richards returns continually to the importance of the conscious and deliberate auditing of meaning as a means of making further meaning. See Ann E. Berthoff, "I. A. Richards and the Audit of Meaning," *New Literary History*, 14 (1982), 64–79.

Narrowing the Mind and Page
Remedial Writers and Cognitive Reductionism

MIKE ROSE

There has been a strong tendency in American education—one that took modern shape with the I.Q. movement—to seek singular, unitary cognitive explanations for broad ranges of poor school performance. And though this trend—I'll call it cognitive reductionism—has been challenged on many fronts (social and political as well as psychological and psychometric), it is surprisingly resilient. It re-emerges. We see it in our field in those discussions of basic and remedial writers that suggest that unsuccessful writers think in fundamentally different ways from successful writers. Writing that is limited to the concrete, that doesn't evidence abstraction or analysis, that seems illogical is seen, in this framework, as revealing basic differences in perception, reasoning, or language.[1] This speculation has been generated, shaped, and supported by one or more theories from psychology, neurology, and literary studies.

Studies of cognitive style suggest that people who can be characterized as "field-dependent" (vs. those who are "field-independent") might have trouble with analytical tasks. *Popular articles on brain research* claim a neurophysiological base for some humans to be verbal, logical, analytical thinkers and for others to be spatial, holistic, non-verbal thinkers. *Jean Piaget's work on the development of logical thought* seems pertinent as well: some students might not have completed their developmental ascent from concrete to abstract reasoning. And *orality-literacy theorists* make connections between literacy and logic and suggest that the thinking of some minority groups

Reprinted from *College Composition and Communication* 39.3 (October 1988): 267–98. Used with permission.

might be affected by the degree to which their culture has moved from oral to literate modes of behavior.

The applications of these theories to poor writers appear in composition journals and papers at English, composition, and remedial education conferences. This is by no means the only way people interested in college-age remedial writers talk about thinking-writing connections, but the posing of generalized differences in cognition and the invoking of Piaget, field dependence and the rest has developed into a way of talking about remediation. And though this approach has occasionally been challenged in journals, it maintains a popular currency and encourages a series of bold assertions: poor writers can't form abstractions; they are incapable of analysis; they perceive the world as an undifferentiated whole; the speech patterns they've acquired in their communities seriously limit their critical capacity.

I think we need to look closely at these claims and at the theories used to support them, for both the theories and the claims lead to social distinctions that have important consequences, political as well as educational. This is not to deny that the theories themselves have contributed in significant ways to our understanding of mental processes (and Piaget, of course, shaped an entire field of research), but their richness should not keep us from careful consideration of their limits, internal contradictions, and attendant critical discussions and counterstatements. Consideration of the theories leads us naturally to consideration of their applicability to areas beyond their original domain. Such application often overgeneralizes the theory: Ong's brilliant work on orality and literacy, for example, moves beyond its history-of-consciousness domain and becomes a diagnostic framework. A further problem—sometimes inherent in the theories themselves, sometimes a result of reductive application—is the tendency to diminish cognitive complexity and rely on simplified cognitive oppositions: independent vs. dependent, literate vs. oral, verbal vs. spatial, concrete vs. logical. These oppositions are textbook-neat, but, as much recent cognitive research demonstrates, they are narrow and misleading. Yet another problem is this: these distinctions are usually used in a way meant to be value-free (that is, they highlight differences rather than deficits in thinking), but, given our culture, they are anything but neutral. Social and political hierarchies end up encoded in sweeping cognitive dichotomies.

In this article I would like to reflect on the problems with and limitations of this particular discourse about remediation. To do this, I'll need to provide a summary of the critical discussion surrounding each of the theories in its own field, for that complexity is too often lost in discussions of thought and writing. As we move through the essay, I'll point out the problems in applying these theories to the thought processes of poor writers. And, finally, I'll conclude with some thoughts on studying cognition and writing in less reductive ways.

COGNITIVE STYLE:
FIELD DEPENDENCE-INDEPENDENCE

Cognitive style, broadly defined, is an "individual's characteristic and consistent manner of processing and organizing what he [or she] sees and thinks about" (Harré and Lamb 98). In theory, cognitive style is separate from verbal, quantitative, or visual intelligence; it is not a measure of how much people know or how well they mentally perform a task, but the manner in which they perform, their way of going about solving a problem, their style. Cognitive style research emerges out of the study of individual differences, and there have been a number of theories of cognitive style proposed in American and British psychology since the late 40's. Varied though they are, all the theories discuss style in terms of a continuum existing between two polar opposites: for example, reflectivity vs. impulsivity, analytic vs. global, complexity vs. simplicity, levelling vs. sharpening, risk-taking vs. cautiousness, field-dependence vs. field-independence. Field dependence-independence, first described by Herman A. Witkin in 1949, is, by far, the most researched of the cognitive styles, and it is the style that seems to be most discussed in composition circles.

The origins of the construct are, as Witkin, Moore, Goodenough, and Cox note, central to its understanding. Witkin's first curiosity concerned the degree to which people use their surrounding visual environment to make judgments about the vertical position of objects in a field. Witkin devised several devices to study this issue, the best known being the Rod and Frame Test. A square frame on a dark background provides the surrounding visual field, and a rod that rotates within it is the (potentially) vertical object. Both the frame and the rod can separately be rotated clockwise or counterclockwise, and "[t]he subject's task is to adjust the rod to a position where he perceives it as upright, while the frame around it remains in its initial position of tilt" ("Field-Dependent" 3). Witkin, et al.'s early findings revealed some interesting individual differences:

> For some, in order for the rod to be apprehended as properly upright, it must be fully aligned with the surrounding frame, whatever the position of the frame. If the frame is tilted 30 [degrees] to the right, for example, they will tilt the rod 30 [degrees] to the right, and say the rod is perfectly straight in that position. At the opposite extreme of the continuous performance

range are people who adjust the rod more or less close to the upright in making it straight, regardless of the position of the surrounding frame. They evidently apprehend the rod as an entity discrete from the prevailing visual frame of reference and determine the uprightness of the rod according to the felt position of the body rather than according to the visual frame immediately surrounding it. ("Field-Dependent" 3–4)

A subject's score is simply the number of degrees of actual tilt of the rod when the subject claims it is straight.

Witkin and his associates later developed another measure—one that was much less cumbersome and could be given to many people at once—The Embedded Figures Test.[2] Witkin, et al. considered the Embedded Figures Test to be similar to the Rod and Frame Test in its "essential perceptual structure." The subject must locate a simple geometric design in a complex figure, and "once more what is at issue is the extent to which the surrounding visual framework dominates perception of the item within it" (6). A subject's score on the test is the number of such items he or she can disembed in a set time.

The "common denominator" between the two tests is "the extent to which the person perceives part of the field as discrete from the surrounding field as a whole, rather than embedded in the field; or the extent to which the organization of the prevailing field determines perception of its components" (7). Put simply, how strong is our cognitive predisposition to let surrounding context influence what we see? Witkin soon began to talk of the differences between field dependence vs. independence as differences between articulated (or analytic) vs. global perception:

At one extreme there is a consistent tendency for experience to be global and diffuse; the organization of the field as a whole dictates the manner in which its parts are experienced. At the other extreme there is a tendency for experience to be delineated and structured; parts of a field are experienced as discrete and the field as a whole organized. To these opposite poles of the cognitive styles we may apply the labels "global and articulated." ("Psychological Differentiation" 319)

Witkin's tests were tapping interesting individual differences in perception and cognition, but the really tantalizing findings emerged as Witkin and his colleagues began pursuing a wide-ranging research agenda that, essentially, sought correlations between performance on field dependence-independence tests and performance on a variety of other cognitive, behavioral, and personality tests, measures, and activities. Hundreds of these studies followed, ranging from the insightful (correlating cognitive style with the way teachers structure social science concepts) to the curious (correlating cognitive style with the shortness of women's skirts). Some of the studies yielded low correlations, and some were inconclusive or were contradictory—but, in general, the results, as summarized by educational psychologist Merlin Wittrock, resulted in the following two profiles:

- ◆ To the degree that people score high on field independence they tend to be: "relatively impersonal, individualistic, insensitive to others and their reinforcements, interested in abstract subject matter, and intrinsically motivated. They have internalized frames of reference, and experience themselves as separate or differentiated from others and the environment. They tend to use previously learned principles and rules to guide their behavior" (93).

- ◆ To the degree that people score low on field independence they are, by default, field-dependent, and they tend to be: "more socially oriented, more aware of social cues, better able to discern feelings of others from their facial expressions, more responsive to a myriad of information, more dependent on others for reinforcement and for defining their own beliefs and sentiments, and more in need of extrinsic motivation and externally defined objectives" (93).

The tendency of the field-independent person to perceive particular shapes and orientations despite context, and the tendency of the field-dependent person to let "the organization of the field as a whole dictate the manner in which its parts are experienced" seemed to be manifesting themselves in motivation, cognition, and personality. A few relatively simple tests were revealing wide-ranging differences in the way people think and interact.

The psychometric neatness of this work seems a little too good to be true, and, in fact, problems have been emerging for some time. My discussion of them will be oriented toward writing.

You'll recall that it is central to the theory that cognitive style is not a measure of ability, of how well people perform a task, but a measure of their manner of performance, their style. If we applied this notion to writing, then, we would theoretically expect to find interesting differences in the way discourse is produced, in the way a rhetorical act is conceived and executed: maybe the discourse of field independents would be more analytical and impersonal while field-dependent discourse would be richer in social detail. But these differences should not, theoretically, lead to gross differences in quality. By some general measure, papers written by field-dependent and field-independent students should have equal possibility of being acceptable discourse. They would just be different. However, the most detailed and comprehensive cognitive style study of college-level writers I've yet seen yields this: papers written by field-dependent students are simply poor papers, and along most dimensions—spelling, grammar, development (Williams). This doesn't fit. Conclusions emerge, but they don't jibe with what the theory predicts.

Such conceptual and testing perplexities are rooted, I believe, in the field dependence-independence work itself. My review of the psychological literature revealed seven problems with the construct, and they range from the technical to the conceptual level.

For cognitive style to be a legitimate construct, it has to be distinct from general intelligence or verbal ability or visual acuity, because cognitive style is not intended to be a measure of how "smart" someone is, but of the manner in which she or he engages in an intellectual task. Unfortunately, there are a number of studies which suggest that field dependence-independence significantly overlaps with measures of intelligence, which are, themselves, complex and controversial. As early as 1960, Lee J. Cronbach wrote in his authoritative *Essentials of Psychological Testing:* "General reasoning or spatial ability accounts for much of Embedded Figures performance as does difficulty in handling perceptual interference" (549). In 1972, Philip Vernon, also a prominent researcher of individual differences, reviewed studies that investigated relations between scores on field dependence-independence and various measures of "visual intelligence." He concluded that "the strong positive correlation with such a wide range of spatial tests is almost embarrassing" (368). And after conducting his own study, Vernon declaimed that Embedded Figures Tests "do not define a factor distinct from general intelligence . . . and spatial ability or visualization" (386). Things become more complicated. Vernon, and other researchers (see, for example, Linn and Kyllonen), present factor-analytic data that suggest that determining the position of the rod within the frame and disembedding the hidden figures tap *different* mental constructs, not the unitary construct Witkin had initially postulated.[3] It is possible, of course, that different aspects of field dependence-independence are being tapped by the different tests and that two of them should be administered together—as Witkin, in fact, recommended. But even if researchers used multiple measures (as few have—most use only the Embedded Figures Test because of its utility), the problem of overlap with measures of intelligence would remain. In short, it's not certain just what the field dependence-independence tests are measuring, and it's very possible that they are primarily tapping general or spatial intelligence.

There is a further testing problem. In theory, each pole of a cognitive style continuum "has adaptive value in certain circumstances . . . neither end of [a] cognitive style dimension is uniformly more adaptive . . . adaptiveness depends upon the nature of the situation and upon the cognitive requirements of the task at hand" (Messick 9). Now, there have been studies which show that field-dependent people seem to attend more readily than field-independent people to social cues (though the effects of these studies tend to be small or inconsistent—see McKenna), but it is important to note that Witkin and his colleagues have never been able to develop a test that *positively* demonstrates field dependence. The Rod and Frame Test, the Embedded Figures Test—and all the other tests of field dependence-independence—assess how well a person displays field *in*dependence. Field dependence is essentially determined by default—the more a person fails at determining the true position of the rod or the slower he is at disembedding the figure, the more field dependent he is. This assessment-by-default would not be a problem if one were testing some level of skill or intellectual ability, say, mechanical aptitude. But where a bipolar and "value-free" continuum is being assessed—where one is not "deficient" or "maladaptive" regardless of score, but only different, where both field-independent and field-dependent people allegedly manifest cognitive strengths as well as limitations—then it becomes a problem if you can't devise a test on which field-dependent subjects would score well. Witkin, et al. admit that the development of such a test is "an urgent task" (16). It has not yet been developed.

But even if a successful test of field dependence could be created, problems with assessment would not be over. All existing tests of field dependence-independence are, as Paul L. Wachtel points out:

> in certain respects poorly suited for exploration of the very problem [they were] designed to deal with—that of style. It is difficult to organize ideas about different directions of development upon a framework which includes only one dimension, and only the possibility of "more" or "less." (186)

Consider the notion of style. It would seem that style is best assessed by the observation and recording of a range of behaviors over time. Yet the Rod and Frame and Embedded Figures Tests don't allow for the revelation of the cognitive processes in play as the person tries to figure them out. That is, there is no provision made for the subject to speak aloud her mental processes or offer a retrospective account of them or explain—as in Piagetian method—why she's doing what she's doing. We have here what Michael Cole and Barbara Means refer to as the problem of drawing process inferences from differences in task performance (65). It would be unfair to lay this criticism on Witkin's doorstep alone, for it is a general limitation with psychometric approaches to cognition. (See, for example, Hunt.) But Witkin's work, since it purports to measure style, is especially vulnerable to it.

Let us now rethink those composite profiles of field-independent vs. field-dependent people. You'll recall that the correlations of all sorts of measures suggest that field-dependent people are more socially oriented, more responsive to a myriad of information, etc., while field-independent people tend to be individualistic, interested in abstract subject matter, and so on. These profiles can be pretty daunting; they're built on hundreds of studies, and they complement our folk wisdom about certain kinds of personalities. But we must keep in mind that the correlations between tests of field independence and personality or cognitive measures are commonly .25 to .3 or .4; occasionally, correlations as high as .5 or .6 are recorded, but they are unusual. That means that, typically, 84% to 94% of the variance between one measure and the other remains to be accounted for by factors other than those posited by the cognitive style theorist. Such studies accrue, and eventually the theorist lays them all side by side, notes the seeming commonalities, and profiles emerge. You could consider these profiles telling and veridical, but you could also consider them webs of thin connection.

We in the West are drawn to the idea of consistency in personality (from Renaissance humors to Jungian types), and that attraction, I think, compels us to seek out similar, interrelated consistencies in cognition. Certainly there are regularities in the way human beings approach problems; we don't go at our cognitive tasks willy-nilly. But when cognitive researchers try to chart those consistencies by studying individual people solving multiple problems they uncover a good deal of variation, variation that is potentially efficient and adaptive. William F. Battig, for example, found in his studies of adult verbal learning that most subjects employed different strategies at different times, even when working on a single problem. At least in the cognitive dimension, then, it has proven difficult to demonstrate that people approach different problems, in different settings, over time in consistent ways. This difficulty, it seems to me, presents a challenge to the profiles provided by cognitive style theorists.

There are, finally, troubling conceptual-linguistic problems with field dependence-independence theory, and they emerge most dramatically for me when I try to rephrase some of Witkin's discussions of the two styles. Here is one example:

> Persons with a global style are more likely to go along with the field "as is," without using such mediational processes as analyzing and structuring. In many situations field-independent people tend to behave as if governed by general principles which they have actively abstracted from their experiences. . . . In contrast, for field-dependent people information processing systems seem to make less use of such mediators. (Witkin, et al. 21)

Statements like this are common in Witkin, and they flow along and make sense in the discussion he offers us—but you stop cold if you consider for a minute what it might mean for people to have a tendency to operate in the world "without using such mediational processes as analyzing and structuring" or, by implication, to not "behave as if governed by general principles which they have actively abstracted from their experiences." These seem like pretty extreme claims, given the nature and limitations of tests of cognitive style. All current theories of cognition that I'm familiar with posit that human beings bring coherence to behavior by abstracting general principles from experiences, by interpreting and structuring what they see and do. When people can't do this sort of thing, or can only do it minimally, we assume that something is seriously wrong with them.

Witkin and his colleagues faced the dilemma that all theory builders face: how to find a language with which to express complex, abstract ideas. (For a Wittgensteinian analysis of Witkin's language, see Kurtz.) And given the nature of language, such expression is always slippery. I think, though, that Witkin and company get themselves into more than their fair share of trouble. The language they finally choose is often broad and general: it is hard to operationalize, and, at times, it seems applicable post hoc to explain almost any result (see Wachtel 184–85). It is metaphoric in troubling ways. And it implies things about cognition that, upon scrutiny, seem problematic. I would suggest that if we're going to apply Witkin's notions to the assessment of writing and cognition we'll need more focussed, less problematic definitions. Now, Witkin does, in fact, occasionally provide such definitions, but they raise problems of a different order. And here again we see the complications involved in connecting Witkin's theory to composing.

In an admirably precise statement, Witkin, et al. note:

> The individual who, in perception, cannot keep an item separate from the surrounding field—in other words, who is relatively field-dependent—is likely to have difficulty with that class of problems, and, we must emphasize, *only* with that class of problems, where the solution depends

on taking some critical element out of the context in which it is presented and restructuring the problem material so that the item is now used in a different context. (9)

Consider rhetoric and the production of written language. For Witkin's formulation to apply, we would have to define rhetorical activity and written language production as *essentially* involving the disembedding of elements from contexts and concomitant restructuring of those contexts. It seems to me that such application doesn't hold. Even if there were a rhetorical-linguistic test of cognitive style—and there isn't; the tests are visual, perceptual-orientational—I think most of us would say that while we could think of linguistic-rhetorical problems that might fit Witkin's description, it would be hard to claim that it characterizes rhetorical activity and linguistic production in any broad and inclusive way.

Second of all, it's important to remember that Witkin is talking about a *general* disembedding skill, a skill that would be effective in a wide range of contexts: engineering, literature, social relations. A number of contemporary students of cognition, however, question the existence of such general cognitive skills and argue for more domain-specific strategies, skills, and abilities (see, for example, Carey; Fodor; Gardner, *Frames*; Glaser; Perkins). Given our experience in particular domains, we may be more or less proficient at disembedding and restructuring problem areas in literature but not in engineering. Our ability to disembed the hidden geometric figures in Witkin's test may be more related to our experience with such visual puzzles than to some broad cognitive skill at disembedding. If a student can't structure an essay or take a story apart in the way we've been trained to do, current trends in cognitive research would suggest that her difficulties have more to do with limited opportunity to build up a rich network of discourse knowledge and strategy than with some general difference or deficit in her ability to structure or analyze experience.

HEMISPHERICITY

The French physician Paul Broca announced in 1865 that "we speak with the left hemisphere"; neurologists have had clinical evidence for some time that damage to certain areas of the left side of the brain could result in disruptions in production or comprehension of speech-aphasia—and that damage to certain areas of the right could result in space and body orientation problems; laboratory experiments with healthy people over the last 25 or so years have demonstrated that particular linguistic or spatial capacities seem to require the function of regions in the left or right brain respectively (though it is also becoming clear that there is some degree of right hemisphere involvement in language production and comprehension and left hemispheric involvement in spatial tasks); and radical neurosurgery on a dozen or so patients with intractable epilepsy—a severing of the complex band of neural fibers (the commissures) that connect the left and right cerebral hemispheres—has provided dramatic, if highly unusual, illustration of the anatomical specialization of the hemispheres. It is pretty much beyond question, then, that different areas of the brain contribute to different aspects of human cognition. As with any biological structure there is variation, but in 98% of right handers and 70% of "non-right" handers, certain areas of the left hemisphere are critical for the processing of phonology and syntax and for the execution of fine motor control, and certain areas of the right hemisphere are involved in various kinds of visual and spatial cognition.

These conclusions evolve from either clinical observation or experimental studies. Most studies fit the following paradigm: a set of tasks is presented to a subject, and the tasks are either isomorphic with the process under investigation (e.g., distinguishing nonsense syllables like "pa," "ta," "ka," "ba" as a test of phonetic discrimination) or can be assumed, in a common sense way, to tap the activity under investigation (e.g., mentally adding a list of numbers as a test of serial processing). The subject's speed or accuracy is recorded and, in some studies, other measures are taken that are hypothesized to be related to the mental processes being studied (e.g., recording the brain wave patterns or blood flow or glucose metabolism of the cerebral hemispheres while the subject performs the experimental task).

Studies of this type have enabled researchers to gain some remarkable insight into the fine neuropsychological processes involved in understanding language and, to a lesser degree, in making spatial-orientational discriminations. But it is also true that, ingenious as the work has been, the field is still at a relatively primitive state: many studies are difficult to duplicate (a disturbing number of them yield conflicting results), and the literature is filled with methodological quarrels, competing theories, and conceptual tangles. (For a recent, and very sympathetic, overview see Benson and Zaidel.)

In spite of the conflicts, there are various points of convergence in the data, and, in the yearning for parsimony that characterizes science, the areas of agreement have led some neuroscientists to seek simple and wide-ranging characterizations of brain function. They suggest that beneath all the particular findings about syntax and phonetics and spatial discrimination lie *fundamental* functional differences in the left and right cerebral hemispheres: each is best suited to process certain kinds of stimuli and/or each processes

335

stimuli in distinct ways. A smaller number of neuroscientists—and many popularizers—go a step further and suggest that people tend toward reliance on one hemisphere or the other when they process information. This theory is commonly referred to as "hemisphericity" (Bogen, DeZure, TenHouton, and Marsh). And a few sociologically oriented theorists take another, truly giant, step and suggest that entire dominant and subdominant groups of people can be characterized by a reliance on left or right hemispheric processing (TenHouten). We have, then, the emergence of a number of cognitive dichotomies: the left hemisphere is characterized as being analytic while the right is holistic (or global or synthetic); the left is verbal, the right non-verbal (or spatial); the left a serial processor, the right a parallel processor—and the list continues: focal vs. diffuse, logical vs. intuitive, propositional vs. appositional, and so on.

The positing of hemispheric dichotomies is understandable. Human beings are theory-makers, and parsimony is a fundamental criterion by which we judge the value of a theory: can it account for diverse data with a simple explanation? But, given the current state of brain research, such generalizations, to borrow Howard Gardner's phrase, leapfrog from the facts ("What We Know" 114). Gardner is by no means alone in his criticism. My reading of the neuroscientific literature reveals that the notion of dichotomous hemispheric function is very controversial, and the further notion of hemisphericity is downright dismissed by a broad range of neuroscientists, psychologists, psycholinguists, and research psychiatrists:

> [T]he concepts [analytic/synthetic, temporal/spatial, etc.] are currently so slippery that it sometimes proves impossible to maintain consistency throughout one paper. (John C. Marshall in Bradshaw and Nettleton 72)

> [M]uch of perception (certainly of visual perception) is very difficult to split up this way. The alleged dichotomy [between temporal-analytic and spatial-holistic] is, if it exists at all, more a feature of laboratory experiments than of the real world. (M.J. Morgan in Bradshaw and Nettleton 74)

> [T]he idea of hemisphericity lacks adequate foundation and. . . because of the assumptions implicit in the idea of hemisphericity, it will never be possible to provide such a foundation. The idea is a misleading one which should be abandoned. (Beaumont, Young, and McManus 191)

The above objections rise from concerns about method, subjects, and conceptualization. Let me survey each of these concerns.

A significant amount of the data used to support hemisphericity—and certainly the most dramatic—is obtained from people in whom accident or pathology has highlighted what particular sections of the brain can or can't do. The most unusual group among these (and they are much-studied) is the handful of people who have had severe and life-threatening epilepsy alleviated through a radical severing of the neural fibers that connect the right and left hemispheres. Such populations, however, present a range of problems: tumors and wounds can cause disruptions in other areas of the brain; stroke victims could have had previous "silent strokes" and could, as well, be arteriosclerotic; long disease histories (certainly a characteristic of the severe epileptics who underwent split-brain surgery) can lead to compensatory change in brain function (Bogen, "The Dual Brain"; Whitaker and Ojemann). Furthermore, extrapathological factors, such as education and motivation, can, as Bradshaw and Nettleton put it, also "mask or accentuate the apparent consequences of brain injury" (51). And, as a final caution, there is this: the whole enterprise of localizing linguistic function through pathological performance is not without its critics (see Caplan).

Studies with healthy subjects—and there are increasing numbers of these—remove one major difficulty with hemisphericity research, though here methodological problems of a different sort arise. Concern not with subjects but with instruments and measures now comes into focus. Space as well as my own technological shortcomings prohibit a full review of tools and methods, but it might prove valuable to briefly survey the problems with a representative research approach: electroencephalographic methods. (Readers interested in critical reviews of procedures other than the one I cover can consult the following: Regional Cerebral Blood Flow: Beaumont; Lateral Eye Movements: Ehrlichman and Weinberger; Tachistoscopic Methods: Young; Dichotic-Listening Tests: Efron.)

If you hypothesize that certain kinds of tasks (like discriminating between syllables or adding a list of numbers) are primarily left-brain tasks and that others (like mentally rotating blocks or recognizing faces) are primarily right-brain tasks, then neuroelectric activity in the target hemisphere should vary in predictable ways when the subject performs the respective tasks. And, in fact, such variation in brain wave activity has been empirically demonstrated for some time. Originally, such studies relied on the electroencephalogram (EEG)—the ongoing record of brain wave activity—but now it is possible to gain a more sophisticated record of what are called event-related potentials (ERP). ERP methods use the electroencephalographic machinery, but rely on computer averaging and formalization to more precisely relate brain wave activity to repeated presentations of specific stimuli (thus the waves are "event-related"). The advantage of EEG and ERP methods is that they offer a direct electrophysiological measurement of brain activity and, especially in the case of ERP, "can track rapid fluctuation in brain electrical fields related to cognitive processing . . ." (Brown, Marsh, and Ponsford 166). Such tracking is important to hemisphericity theorists, for it can lend precision to their claims.

There are problems, however. EEG/ERP methods are among the most technically demanding procedures in psychology, and that technical complexity gives rise to a number of difficulties involving variation in cortical anatomy, electrode placement, and data analysis (Beaumont; Gevins, Zeitlin, Doyle, Schaffer, and Callaway). And, when it comes to the study of language processing—certainly an area of concern to writing researchers—ERP procedures give rise to problems other than the technical. Most ERP studies must, for purposes of computer averaging, present each stimulus as many as 50 times, and such repetition creates highly artificial linguistic processing conditions. Even relatively natural language processing studies have trouble determining which perceptual, linguistic, or cognitive factors are responsible for results (see, e.g., Hillyard and Woods). So, though hemispheric differences in brain wave patterns can be demonstrated, the exceptional technical and procedural difficulties inherent in the EEG/ERP studies of language processing make it hard to interpret data with much precision. Cognitive psychophysiologists Emanuel Donchin, Gregory McCarthy and Marta Kutas summarize this state of affairs:

> [A]lthough a substantial amount of clinical data support the theory of left hemisphere superiority in language reception and production, the ERP data regarding this functional asymmetry are far from consistent. The methodological and statistical shortcomings which exist in some of the studies cited [in their review article] along with inconsistencies in the others render any decision about the efficacy of ERP's as indices of linguistic processing inconclusive. (239. For similar, more recent, assessments, see Rugg; Beaumont, Young, and McManus.)

In considering the claims of the hemisphericity theorists, we have reviewed problems with subjects, techniques, and procedures. There is yet a further challenge to the notion of hemisphericity. Some hemisphericity theorists believe that since people can be characterized by a tendency to rely on one hemisphere or the other, then such reliance should manifest itself in the way people lead their lives: in the way they solve problems, in the jobs they choose, and so on. Yet the few studies that have investigated this dimension of the theory yielded negative results. Hemisphericity advocates Robert Ornstein and David Galin failed to find overall systematic EEG differences between lawyers (assumed to be left hemispheric) and sculptors and ceramicists (assumed to be right hemispheric). In a similar study, Dumas and Morgan failed to find EEG differences between engineers and artists, leading the researchers to conclude that "the conjecture that there are 'left hemispheric' people and 'right hemispheric' people seems to be an oversimplification" (227). In a more ambitious study, Arndt and Berger gave graduate students in law, psychology, and sculpture batteries of tests to assess verbal analytic ability (for example, a vocabulary test) and spatial ability (for example, a figure recognition test), and, as well, tests to assess hemisphericity (letter and facial recognition tachistoscopic tasks). While they found—as one would expect—a significant correlation between verbal or spatial ability and occupation (e.g., sculptors scored better than lawyers on the spatial tests), they *did not* find significant correlations between the verbal or spatial tests and the hemisphericity task; nor did they find significant correlation between the hemisphericity task and occupation.

A postscript on the above. Failures to find hemispheric differences between individuals of various occupational groups—along with the methodological difficulties mentioned earlier—throw into serious doubt the neurosociological claim that entire *groups* of people can be characterized as being left or right hemispheric. The neurosociological literature makes some remarkable speculative leaps from the existence of left-right dualities in cultural myth and symbol to asymmetries in left-right brain function, and relies, for empirical support, on the results of individual verbal and spatial tests (like the sub-tests in I.Q. assessments)—precisely the kinds of tests that a number of psychologists and neurologists have shown to be limited in assessing left or right hemispheric performance (see, e.g., DeRenzi).

Let me try to draw a few conclusions for rhetoric and composition studies.

It is important to keep in mind that the experimental studies that do support hemispheric specialization suggest small differences in performance capacities, and the differences tend to be of degree more than kind: in the range of 6–12%. Researchers have to expose subjects to many trials to achieve these differences. (One hundred and fifty to two hundred is common; one facial recognition study ran subjects through 700 trials.) And the experiments deal with extremely specific—even atomistic—functions. (Researchers consider the distinguishing of homonyms in a sentence— "bear" vs. "bare"—to be a "complex verbal task.") It is difficult to generalize from results of this type and magnitude to broad statements about one hemisphere being the seat of logic and the other of metaphor. What happens, it seems, is that theorists bring to very particular (though, admittedly, very important) findings about phonology or syntax or pattern recognition a whole array of cultural beliefs about analytic vs. synthetic thinking and logic vs. creativity and apply them in blanket fashion. There is a related problem here, and it concerns the hemisphericity theorists' assumption that, say, distinguishing phonemes is an analytical or serial or propositional task while, say, facial recognition is synthetic or holistic or appositional. These assumptions are sensible, but they are not proven. In fact, *one could argue the other way around*: e.g., that recognizing faces, for example, is not a holistic but a features analysis task. Unfortunately, neuroscientists don't know enough to resolve this very important issue. They work with indirect measures of information processing: differences in reaction time or variations in electrophysiological measures. They would need more direct access than they now have to the way information is being represented and problems are being solved.

Because the accounts of cerebral asymmetry can be so dramatic—particularly those from split-brain studies—it is easy to dwell on differences. But, in fact, there is wide-ranging similarity, overlap, and cooperation in the function of the right and left hemispheres:

> Complex psychological processes are not 'localized' in any one hemisphere but are the result of integration between hemispheres. (Alexander Luria cited in LeDoux 210)

If Luria's dictum applied anywhere, it would certainly be to the "complex psychological processes" involved in reading and writing. Under highly controlled laboratory conditions researchers can show that phoneme discrimination or word recognition can be relatively localizable to one hemisphere or the other. But attempts to comprehend or generate writing—what is perceived or produced as logical or metaphoric or coherent or textured—involve a stunning range of competencies: from letter recognition to syntactic fluency to an understanding of discourse structure and genre (see, e.g., Gardner and Winner 376–80). And such a range, according to everything we know, involves the whole brain in ways that defy the broad claims of the hemisphericity theorists. When students have trouble structuring an argument or providing imagistic detail, there is little neurophysiological evidence to support contentions that their difficulties originate in organic predisposition or social conditioning to rely on one hemisphere or the other.

JEAN PIAGET AND STAGES OF COGNITIVE DEVELOPMENT

Piaget's theory of cognitive development is generally held to be, even by its revisors and detractors, the modern West's most wide-ranging and significant account of the way children think. The theory, which Piaget began to articulate over 50 years ago, covers infancy to adolescence and addresses the development of scientific and mathematical reasoning, language, drawing, morality, and social perception; it has shaped the direction of inquiry into childhood cognition; and it has led to an incredible number of studies, a good many of which have been cross-cultural. In holding to the focus of this article, then, there's a lot I'll have to ignore—I'll be limiting myself to those aspects of Piaget's theory that have been most widely discussed in reference to college-age writers.

Though Piaget and his colleagues adjusted their theory to account for the wealth of data being generated by researchers around the world, there are several critical features that remain central to the theory. Piaget's theory is a stage theory. He posits four general stages (some with substages), and all children pass through them in the same order. A child's reasoning at each stage is *qualitatively* different from that at earlier or later stages, though the knowledge and strategies of earlier stages are incorporated into later ones. During any given stage, the child reasons in *similar* ways regardless of the kinds of problems she or he faces, and Piaget tended to rule out the possibility that, during a given stage, a child could be trained to reason in much more sophisticated ways. Passage, evolution really, from one stage to the next occurs over time, an interaction of genetic processes and engagement with the world. The child continually assimilates new information which both reshapes and is reshaped by the knowledge structures the child currently has—and, as the child continues to interact with the world, she or he experiences discontinuities between the known and the new, and these discontinuities lead to further development of knowledge of how things work. Thinking, then, gradually evolves to ever more complex levels, represented by each of the stages.

It is important to keep in mind that Piaget's perspective on cognition is fundamentally logical and mathematical. Late in his life he observed that he did not wish "to appear only as a child psychologist":

> My efforts, directed toward the psychogenesis of thought, were for me only a link between two dominant preoccupations: the search for the mechanisms of biological adaptation and the analysis of that higher form of adaptation which is scientific thought, the epistemological interpretation of which has always been my central aim. (in Gruber and Vonèche xi)

With this perspective in mind, let us very briefly consider the stages of Piaget's theory that are appropriated to discussions of college-age remedial writers.

♦ *Concrete Operational* (6–7 to 11–12 years). The cognitive milestone here is that children are freed from immediate perception and enter the realm of logical—if concrete—operations. They can use logic to solve everyday problems, can take other points of view, can simultaneously take into account more than one perspective. In many ways, though, the child's reasoning is still linked to the environment, to tasks that are concrete and well-specified: "Tasks that demand very abstract reasoning, long chains of deduction, or the recognition that the available evidence is insufficient to reach any conclusion are thought to be beyond the reach" of children at the concrete operational stage (Siegler 89). Children have trouble separating out and recombining variables, performing sophisticated conservation tasks, and solving proportionality problems. They also have trouble planning systematic experiments and understanding "purely hypothetical questions that are completely divorced from anything in their experience" (Siegler 90).

♦ *Formal Operational* (11–15 years). During this stage, children develop into sophisticated logical thinkers—Piaget compared them to scientists—and can solve problems that throw concrete-operational children: like the pendulum task described below. Flavell summarizes the ability of the formal-operational child this way: "His thinking is *hypothetico-deductive* rather than *empirico-inductive,* because he creates hypotheses and then deduces the empirical states of affairs that should occur if his hypotheses are correct . . . The older individual's thinking can . . . be totally abstract, totally formal-logical in nature." (145. For a critical discussion of the notion of stages, see Brainerd.)

Piaget and his colleagues developed a number of tasks to distinguish concrete from formal operational thinking. The pendulum task is representative:

Children observed strings with metal balls at their ends swinging from a metal frame. The strings varied in length and the metal balls varied in how much they weighed; the task was to identify the factor or combination of factors that determined the pendulum's period. Plausible hypotheses included the weight of the metal balls, the length of the strings, the height from which the strings were dropped, and the force with which they were pushed. Although the length of the string is in fact the only relevant factor . . . 10- and 11-year olds almost always concluded that the metal ball's weight played a key role, either as the sole determining factor or in combination with the string's length. Thus the children failed to disentangle the influence of the different variables to determine which one caused the effect. (Siegler 89–90)

In the 1970's a number of studies appeared reporting that up to 50% of American college freshmen could not solve formal-operational problems like the pendulum task. The conclusion was that an alarming number of our 18-year-olds were locked at the level of concrete operations, a stage Piaget contends they should have begun evolving beyond by early and certainly by mid-adolescence. These data quickly found their way to a more general readership, and some people in composition understandably saw relevance in them and began to use them to explain the problems with the writing of remedial students. With support of the data, they wrote that up to 50% of college freshmen were locked into the level of the concrete, couldn't think abstractly, couldn't produce logical propositions, couldn't conceptualize—and, borrowing further from Piagetian terminology, they speculated that these students couldn't decenter, couldn't take another's point of view, were cognitively egocentric. The last two stages of the Piagetian framework became in application a kind of cognitive dichotomy unto themselves. If students couldn't produce coherent abstractions in writing, if they wrote about what was in front of them and couldn't express themselves on the conceptual level, if they described something in writing as though their reader shared their knowledge of it—then those limits in written expression suggested something broad and general about the state of their thinking: they might be unable to form abstractions . . . any abstractions; they couldn't decenter . . . at all. There are problems with this line of reasoning, however, and they have to do with the application of the framework as well as with the framework itself.

As any developmental psychologist will point out, there are major conceptual problems involved in applying a *developmental* model to adults. Piaget's theory was derived from the close observation of infants, children, and early- to mid-adolescents; it was intended as a description of the way thinking evolves in the growing human being. Applying it to college-age students and, particularly, to adult learners is to generalize it to a population other than the one that yielded it. There are more specific problems to consider as well, and they have to do with testing.

It is important to underscore the fact that Piaget implies broad limitations in cognition from specific inadequacies on a circumscribed set of tasks. This is not an unreasonable induction—all sorts of general theories are built on the performance of specific tasks—but it must be pointed out that we are dealing with an inference of major consequence. As developmental psychologist Rochelle Gelman put it: "The child is said to lack cognitive principles of broad significance simply because he fails a particular task involving those principles" (326). It is, then, an inferential leap of some magnitude to say that because college students fail to separate out variables and formally test hypotheses in a few tasks typical of the physics lab, they cannot conceptualize or abstract or tease out variables in any other sphere of their lives. Piaget himself said as much in one of his late articles:

> In our investigation of formal structures we used rather specific types of experimental situations which were of a physical and logical-mathematical nature because these seemed to be understood by the school children we sampled. However, it is possible to question whether these situations are, fundamentally, very general and therefore applicable to any school or professional environment. . . . It is highly likely that [people like apprentice carpenters, locksmiths, or mechanics] will know how to reason in a hypothetical manner in their speciality, that is to say, dissociating the variables involved, relating terms in a combinatorial manner and reasoning with propositions involving negations and reciprocities. (10)

Piaget's tests are clever and complex. To assist in replication, Piaget and his colleagues provided explicit instructions on how to set up the tests, what to say, and how to assess performance. This clarity contributed to the welter of Piagetian studies conducted over the years, many of which supported the theory. A significant body of recent research, however, has raised serious questions about the social conditions created when these tests are given. Most of this research has been done with younger children, and probably the best summary of it is Donaldson's. The thrust of this work is contained in one of Donaldson's chapter titles; when a child performs poorly on a Piagetian task, is it because of a "failure to reason or a failure to understand"? The tasks might be unfamiliar; the child might misunderstand the instructions; because psychological experiments are new to her, she might confuse the experimenter's intentions and "not see the experiment as the experimenter hopes [she] will" (Gelman 324). (See also philosopher Jonathan Adler's Grician critique of Piagetian testing.) What psychologists like Donaldson have done is keep the formal requirements of Piagetian tasks but change the particular elements to make them more familiar (e.g., substituting a toy policeman and a wall for a doll and a mountain), provide a chance for children to get familiar with the tasks, and rephrase instructions to make sure children understand what is being asked. Children in these conditions end up performing remarkably better on the tasks; significantly higher percentages of them can, for example, adopt other points of view, conserve quantity and number, and so on. What limited some children on Piaget's tasks, then, seems to be more related to experimental conditions rather than some absolute restriction in their ability to reason.

A somewhat related set of findings has do with training—one of the more controversial issues in Piagetian theory. This is not the place to recap the controversy; suffice it to say that a large number of studies has demonstrated that brief training sessions can have dramatic results on performance. One such study has direct bearing on our discussion. Kuhn, Ho, and Adams provided training to college freshman who failed at formal-operational tasks. After training, the students were once again presented with the tests, and "most of the college subjects showed immediate and substantial formal reasoning." The authors go on to speculate that the absence of formal-operational performance "may to a large extent reflect cognitive processing difficulties in dealing with the problem formats, rather than absence of underlying reasoning competencies" (1128).

I will conclude this brief critique by considering, once again, the mathematico-logical base of Piaget's theory. There is a tradition in the 20th century West—shaped by Russell, Whitehead, Carnap, and others—to study human reasoning within the framework of formal, mathematical logic, to see logic not only as a powerful tool, but as a representation of how people actually reason—at least when they're reasoning effectively. This tradition had a strong influence on Piaget's theory. In Toulmin's words, Piaget's "overall intellectual goal" was to:

> discover how growing children "come to *recognize the necessity* of" conforming to the intellectual structures of logic, Euclidean geometry, and the other basic Kantian forms. (256)

And as Inhelder and Piaget themselves said: "[R]easoning is nothing more than the propositional calculus itself" (305).

Mathematical logic is so privileged that we tend to forget that this assumption about logic being isomorphic with reasoning is highly controversial; it lies at the center of a number of current debates in cognitive psychology, artificial intelligence, and philosophy. Here is one of many counterstatements:

> Considerations of pure logic . . . may be useful for certain kinds of information under certain circumstances by certain individuals. But logic cannot serve as a valid model of how most individuals solve most problems most of the time. (Gardner, *Mind's New Science* 370)

Formal logic essentially strips away all specific connections to human affairs and things of the world; it allows us to represent relations and interactions within a wholly abstract system. Our elevation of this procedure blinds us to the overwhelming degree to which powerful and effective reasoning can be practical, non-formal, and concrete. As psychologist Barbara Rogoff puts it, "thinking is intricately interwoven with the context of the problem to be solved" (2). She continues:

> Evidence suggests that our ability to control and orchestrate cognitive skills is not an abstract context-free competence which may be easily transferred across widely diverse problem domains but consists rather of cognitive activity tied specifically to context. (3)

Much problem-solving and, I suspect, the reasoning involved in the production of most kinds of writing rely not only on abstract logical operations, but, as well, on the rich interplay of visual, auditory, and kinesthetic associations, feeling, metaphor, social perception, the matching of mental representations of past experience with new experience, and so on. And writing, as the whole span of rhetorical theory makes clear, is deeply embedded in the particulars of the human situation. It is a context-dependent activity that calls on many abilities. We may well need to engage in formal-logical reasoning when writing certain kinds of scientific or philosophical papers or when analyzing certain kinds of hypotheses and arguments, but we cannot assume that the ability or inability to demonstrate formal-operational thought on one or two Piagetian tasks has a necessary connection to our students' ability or inability to produce coherent, effective discourse.

ORALITY-LITERACY

Orality-literacy theory draws on the studies of epic poetry by Milman Parry and Albert Lord, the classical-philological investigations of Eric Havelock, the wide-ranging theoretical work of Walter Ong, and, to a lesser degree, on the compelling, though dated, cross-cultural investigations of thought in primitive, non-literate cultures. The work is broad, rich, and diverse—ranging from studies of the structure of the epic line to the classification schemes of unlettered rural farmers—but as it comes to those of us in composition, its focus is on the interrelation of language and cognition. Various scholars say it in various ways, but the essential notion is that the introduction of literacy into a society affects the way the members of the society think. There seem to be strong and weak versions of this theory.

The strong version states that the acquisition of literacy brings with it not only changes in linguistic possibilities—e.g., subordinative and discursive rather than additive and repetitive styles, less reliance on epithets and maxims and other easily remembered expressions—but *necessarily* results in a wide variety of changes in thinking: only after the advent of literacy do humans possess the ability to engage in abstraction, generalization, systematic thinking, defining, logos rather than mythos, puzzlement over words as words, speculation on the features of language. And these abilities, depending on who you read, lead to even wider changes in culture, summarized, not without exasperation, by social historian Harvey Graff:

> These characteristics include, in typical formulations or listings, attitudes ranging *from* empathy, innovativeness, achievement orientation, "cosmopoliteness," information and media awareness, national identification, technological acceptance, rationality, and commitment to democracy, *to* opportunism, linearity of thought and behavior, or urban residence. ("Reflections" 307)

The operative verb here is "transformed." Writing *transforms* human cognition.

The weak version of the oral-literate construct acknowledges the role literacy plays in developing modes of inquiry, building knowledge, etc., but tends to rely on verbs like "facilitate," "favor," "enable," "extend"—the potential of human cognition is extended more than transformed. Here's Jack Goody, an anthropologist who is often lumped in with those holding to the "strong version," but who, at least in his late work, takes issue with the oral-literate dichotomy. In discussing various differences between literate and oral expression, for example, he warns that such differences "do not relate primarily to differences of 'thought' or 'mind' (though there are consequences for these) but to differences in the nature of communicative acts" (26). So though Goody grants that writing "made it possible to scrutinize discourse in a different kind of way" and "increased the potentiality for cumulative knowledge" and freed participants from "the problem of memory storage" dominating "intellectual life," (37), he also insists that:

> Even in non-literate societies there is no evidence that individuals were prisoners of pre-ordained schemes, of primitive classifications, of the structures of myth. Constrained, yes; imprisoned, no. Certain, at least, among them could and did use language in a generative way, elaborating metaphor, inventing songs and "myths", creating gods, looking for new solutions to recurring puzzles and problems, changing the conceptual universe. (33)

The theory is a sensible one: literacy must bring with it tremendous repercussions for the intellect. The problem is that when the theory, particularly the strong version, is applied to composition studies, it yields some troubling consequences. Late twentieth-century American inner-city adolescents and adults are thought to bear cognitive resemblance to (ethnocentric notions of) primitive tribesmen in remote third-world cultures (or these adolescents and adults think like children, and children think like primitives): they don't practice analytic thinking; they are embedded in the context of their lives and cannot analyze it; they see things only as wholes; they think that printed words are concrete things; they cannot think abstractly.

A little reflection on this application of orality-literacy theory—given its origins—reveals a serious problem of method. The theory emerges from anthropological work with primitive populations, from historical-philological study of Homeric texts, from folkloric investigations of non-literate taletellers, and from brilliant, though speculative, literary-theoretical reflection on what might have happened to the human mind as it appropriated the alphabet. It is, then, a tremendous conceptual leap to apply this theory to urban-industrial Americans entering school in the penultimate decade of the twentieth century. We have here a problem of generalizability.

Now one could admit these problems yet still see some analogic value in applying the oral-literate construct with a hedge—for it at least, as opposed to the other theories we've been exploring, is directly concerned with written language. Fair enough. Yet my reading has led me to doubt the strength and utility of the theory on its own terms. (My concern rests primarily with the strong version. The weak version makes less dramatic claims about cognition, though some of what I found would qualify weak versions as well.) There are problems with what the theory implies about the way written language emerges in society and the role it plays in determining how people lead their linguistic lives and conduct their cognitive affairs. This is not to deny the profound effects literacy can have on society; it is to question the strength of the orality-literacy construct in characterizing those effects. Let me briefly survey some of the difficulties.

Literacy and Society

The historical record suggests that the technology and conventions of literacy work their way slowly through a society and have gradual—and not necessarily linearly progressive—influence on commerce, politics, bureaucracy, law, religion, education, the arts. (See, e.g., Marrou; Clanchy; Cressy.) Furthermore, it is hard to maintain, as the strong version does, that literacy is the primum mobile in social-cultural change. What emerges, instead, is a complex interaction of economic, political, and religious forces of which literacy is a part—and not necessarily the strongest element. Though there is no doubt that literacy shapes the way commerce, government, and religion are conducted, it, as John Oxenham puts it: "would have followed, not preceded, the formation of certain kinds of society" (59). And Harvey Graff, pointing out all the "discontinuities" and "contradictions" in linear, evolutionary assumptions about the spread of literacy, emphasizes that "[n]either writing [n]or printing alone is an 'agent of change'; their impacts are determined by the manner in which human agency exploits them in a specific setting" ("Reflections" 307).[4]

Another way to view the problems with the transformational claims about literacy is to consider the fact that a number of societies have appropriated literacy to traditional, conservative purposes. In such societies literacy did not trigger various cultural-cognitive changes—changes in mores, attitudes, etc.—but reinforced patterns already in place. Again, John Oxenham:

> We have always to bear in mind that there have been literate social groups, who so far from being inventive and trusting, have been content merely to copy their ancient scriptures and pass them on virtually unaltered. It may be, then, that literate people can respond more readily to leadership for change in culture, technology, social mores, but that literacy by itself does not induce appetites for change, improvement or exploration. (52)

There are a number of illustrations of this; one specific case-study is provided by Kenneth Lockridge, whose inquiry into the social context of literacy in Colonial New England leads him to conclude:

> [T]here is no evidence that literacy ever entailed new attitudes among men, even in the decades when male literacy was spreading rapidly toward universality, and there is positive evidence that the world view of literate New Englanders remained as traditional as that of their illiterate neighbors. (4)

It is even difficult to demonstrate causal links between reading and writing and changes in the economic sphere—an area that "modernization theorists" generally thought to be particularly sensitive to gains in literacy. Harvey Graff's study of social mobility in three mid-19th century towns revealed that "systematic patterns of inequality and stratification . . . were deep and pervasive and relatively unaltered by the influence of literacy." He continues:

> Class, ethnicity, and sex were the major barriers of social inequality. The majority of Irish Catholic adults, for example, were literate . . . but they

stood lowest in wealth and occupation, as did laborers and servants. Women and blacks faired little better, regardless of literacy . . . social realities contradicted the promoted promises of literacy. (*The Literacy Myth* 320–21)

Similar assertions are made closer to home by Carman St. John Hunter and David Harmon, whose overview of the research on contemporary adult illiteracy leads to this conclusion:

For most persons who lack literacy skills, illiteracy is simply one factor interacting with many others—class, race and sex discrimination, welfare dependency, unemployment, poor housing, and a general sense of power-lessness. The acquisition of reading and writing skills would eliminate conventional illiteracy among many but would have no appreciable effect on the other factors that perpetuate the poverty of their lives. (9–12. See also Ogbu.)

The oral-literate distinction can help us see differences in the communicative technologies available to the members of a society, to get a sense of formats, means, and forums through which communication occurs (Enos and Ackerman). But it appears to be historically, culturally, and economically reductive—and politically naive—to view literacy as embodying an automatic transformational power. What is called for is a contextual view of literacy: the ability to read or to write is a technology or a method or a behavior, a set of conventions that interact in complex ways with a variety of social forces to shape society and culture. It is, to use Harvey Graff's phrasing, a "myth" to assume that literacy necessarily sparks social change.

Literacy and Cognition

Let us move now from the social-cultural realm to some of the claims made about cognition. These come from two highly diverse sources: classical philological studies of epic poetry and anthropological studies of thought and language. There are problems with both.

The key work in the classicist vein is Eric Havelock's investigation of Greek culture before and after the advent of the alphabet. In books ranging from *Preface to Plato* (published in 1963) to *The Muse Learns to Write* (1986) Havelock has made the strong claim that pre-alphabetic Greeks, ingenious as they were, were barred from philosophical thought because oral discourse could not generate abstract, propositional language or self-conscious reflection on language as language. To be sure, there are times when Havelock's claims are less extreme, but even in *The Muse Learns to*

Write, a tempered book, one finds questions and statements like these: "May not all logical thinking as commonly understood be a product of Greek alphabetic literacy?" (39) and "it is only as language is written down that it becomes possible to think about it" (112). And such theorizing quickly leads to a troublesome alphabetic determinism.

Havelock's work is compelling, but we must remember that when it comes to cognition, he is operating very much in the realm of speculation. That is, he infers things about cognitive processes and the limits of reasoning ability from the study of ancient texts, some of which represent genres that one would not expect to give rise to philosophic inquiry. Furthermore, even if we accepted his method, we could find powerful counterstatements to his thesis—and some of these are contained in a festschrift issued by the Monist Press. Examining the same texts from which Havelock built his case, University of Chicago classicist Arthur W. H. Adkins provides evidence of abstraction, verbal self-consciousness, and the linguistic resources to engage in systematic thinking. He concludes that:

> Havelock has not as yet demonstrated any *necessary* link between literacy and abstract thought . . . he has not as yet demonstrated that *in fact* the stimulus to abstract thought in early Greece was the invention of writing; [and] some features denied by Havelock to be available in oral speech are found in the Homeric poems. (220. See also Margolis.)

The other line of argument about literacy and cognition comes from twentieth-century anthropological studies of the reasoning of rural farmers and primitive tribesmen. These studies tend not to be of literacy-orality per se, but are appropriated by some orality-literacy theorists. A good deal of this cross-cultural research has involved classification tasks: a set of objects (or a set of pictures of the objects) is given to a tribesman, and the investigator asks the tribesman to group the objects/pictures. The key issue is the scheme by which the tribesman completes the grouping: does he, for example, place a hoe with a potato and offer the *concrete* reason that they go together because you need one to get the other, or does he place the hoe with a knife because he reasons *abstractly* that they are both tools? The Western anthropologist considers concrete reasoning to be less advanced than abstract reasoning, and orality-literacy theorists like to pose literacy as the crucial variable fostering abstract reasoning. It is because the tribesman lacks letters that he is locked into the concrete. This is an appealing conjecture, but, as I hope the previous discussion suggests, literacy is too intertwined with schooling and urbanization, with economics, politics, and religion to be able to isolate it and make such a claim. There are other problems too, not just with the causal linking of literacy and abstraction, but with traditional comparative research itself. Cole and Means put it this way:

> [D]epartures from the typical performance patterns of American adults are not necessarily deficits, but may indeed be excellent adaptations to the life circumstances of the people involved. . . . Which type of classification is preferable will depend upon the context, that is, the number of different types of objects to be grouped and the way in which the materials are going to be used . . . preference for one type of grouping over another is really no more than that—just a matter of preference. (161–62)

In line with the above, it must be kept in mind that because "primitive" subjects tend to classify objects in ways we label concrete does not necessarily mean that they can think in no other way. Consider, as we close this section, a wonderful anecdote from anthropologist Joseph Glick, as retold by Jacqueline Goodenow:

> The investigators had gathered a set of 20 objects, 5 each from 4 categories: food, clothing, tools, and cooking utensils. . . . [W]hen asked to put together the objects that belonged together, [many of the tribesmen produced] not 4 groups of 5 but 10 groups of 2. Moreover, the type of grouping and the type of reason given were frequently of the type we regard as extremely concrete, e.g., "the knife goes with the orange because it cuts it." Glick . . . notes, however, that subjects at times volunteered "'that a wise man would do things in the way this was done.' When an exasperated experimenter asked finally, 'How would a fool do it?' he was given back groupings of the type . . . initially expected—four neat piles with foods in one, tools in another." (170–71. For fuller cross-cultural discussions of concrete vs. abstract reasoning see Ginsburg; Lave; and Tulkin and Konner.)

Literacy and Language

It is problematic, then, to claim that literacy necessarily causes a transformation of culture, society, or mind or that societies without high levels of literacy are barred from the mental activities that some theorists have come to associate with literacy: verbal self-consciousness, abstraction, etc. Perhaps, though, the orality-literacy construct does have value if one strips away the cultural-cognitive baggage; its real benefit might be its ability to help us understand the nature of the language experiences students received in their homes and communities and further help to distinguish between the oral and literate features in their writing. But even here there are problems, for the reality of speaking-writing relationships seems to be more complex than the oral-literate distinction suggests.

Certainly, there are bioanatomical and perceptual differences between speech and writing—differences in the way each is acquired, produced, and comprehended. And if you examine very different types of language (e.g., dinner-table conversation vs. academic prose), you will find significant grammatical and stylistic differences as well. (See, for example, Chafe.) But the oral-literate construct leads us to focus attention too narrowly on the channel, the mode of communication, in a way that can (a) imply a distinctive uniformity to oral modes vs. written modes and (b) downplay the complex interaction among human motive, language production, and social setting. Linguists currently working with oral narratives and written texts suggest that the notion of an oral narrative itself is problematic, for oral traditions can differ in major ways (Scollon and Scollon); that the narrative variations we see may have less to do with literateness than with cultural predispositions (Tannen, "A Comparative Analysis"); that features often defined as literate are frequently found in oral discourse and vice versa (Polanyi; Tannen, "Relative Focus"); that characteristics identified by some as a mark of preliterate discourse—e.g., formulaic expressions—are woven throughout the language of literate people (Fillmore); that while spoken sentences can be shown to differ from written sentences, they are not necessarily less complex grammatically (Halliday); and so on. Finally, it seems that many of the differences we can find between stretches of speech and writing might, as Karen Beamon suggests, depend on factors such as genre, context, register, topic, level of formality, and purpose as much as whether the passage is spoken or written.

These closer examinations of a wide variety of texts and utterances should make us wary of neat, bipolar characterizations—whether dichotomies or simple continua—of oral vs. written language. And it seems to me that this caution about the linguistic reality of the oral-literate distinction could lead to reservations about its contemporary social reality—that is, can we accurately and sensitively define, in late twentieth-century America, entire communities and subcultures as being oral and others as being literate? By what criteria, finally, will we be able to make such a distinction? In asking these questions, I am not trying to downplay the obvious: children enter school with widely different degrees of exposure to literacy activities and with significantly different experiences as to how those activities are woven into their lives. And these differences clearly have consequences for schooling.

What I do want to raise, though, is the possibility that the oral-literate continuum does not adequately characterize these differences. The continuum, because it moves primarily along the single dimension of speech-print, slights history and politics—remember, it weights literacy as *the* primary force in cognitive development and social change—and it encourages, because of its bipolarity, a dichotomizing of modes where complex interweaving seems to exist. Finally, the orality-literacy construct tends to reduce the very social-linguistic richness it is meant to describe. Here is Shirley Brice Heath on the language behaviors of two working-class communities in the Carolinas:

> The residents of each community are able to read printed and written materials in their daily lives and, on occasion, they produce written messages as part of the total pattern of communication in the community. In both communities, the residents turn from spoken to written uses of language and vice versa as the occasion demands, and the two modes of expression serve to supplement and reinforce each other. Yet, in terms of the usual distinctions made between oral and literate traditions, neither community may be simply classified as either "oral" or "literate." (*Ways with Words* 203)

Work like Heath's challenges the sociological and linguistic utility of the orality-literacy construct; in fact, elsewhere Heath directly criticizes "current tendencies to classify communities as being at one or another point along a hypothetical [oral-literate] continuum which has no societal reality" ("Protean Shapes" 116).

What is most troubling on this score is the way the orality-literacy construct is sometimes used to represent language use in the urban ghetto. What emerges is a stereotypic characterization of linguistic homogeneity— all the residents learn from the sermon but not the newspaper; they run the dozens but are ignorant of print. The literacy backgrounds of people who end up in remedial, developmental, or adult education classes are more complex than that: they represent varying degrees of distance from or involvement with printed material, various attitudes toward it and skill with it, various degrees of embracement of or complicated rejection of traditions connected with their speech. Important here is what Mina Shaughnessy and Glynda Hull so carefully demonstrate: some of the most vexing problems writing teachers face are rooted in the past attempts of educationally marginalized people *to make sense of the uses of print*. Print is splattered across the inner city, and, in effective and ineffective ways, people incorporate it into their lives.

There is a related problem. Some theorists link Piagetian notions of cognitive egocentrism with generalizations about orality and conclude that without the language of high literacy, people will be limited in their ability to "decenter," to recognize the need to "decontextualize" what they are communicating, to perceive and respond to the social and informational needs of the other. Certainly, people with poor educations will have a great deal of trouble doing such things in writing, but one must be very cautious about leaping from stunted and limited texts to inferences about deficits in social cognition or linguistic flexibility. Developmentally and sociologically oriented linguists have demonstrated for some time that human beings are not locked into one way of speaking, one register, and develop, at quite a young age, the recognition that different settings call for different kinds of speech (Hudson). Poor writers are not as a population cognitively egocentric; they are aware of the other, of "audience"—some disenfranchised people acutely so. What they lack are the opportunities to develop both oral and written communicative facility in a range of settings. Or they may resist developing that facility out of anger or fear or as an act of identity. They may prefer one way of speaking, most of us do, and thus haven't developed a fluency of voices. But rather than being cognitively locked out of other registers, other linguistic roles, other points of view, they are more likely emotionally and politically barred from them.

It is obvious that literacy enables us to do a great deal. It provides a powerful solution to what Walter Ong calls "the problem of retaining and retrieving carefully articulated thought" (34). It enables us to record discourse, scan and scrutinize it, store it—and this has an effect on the way we educate, do business, and run the courts. And as we further pursue intellectual work, reading and writing become integral parts of inquiry, enable us to push certain kinds of analysis to very sophisticated levels. In fact, as investigations of academic and research settings like Latour and Woolgar's *Laboratory Life* suggest, it becomes virtually impossible to tease writing and reading out of the conduct and progress of Western humanistic *or* scientific inquiry. One of the values of the orality-literacy construct is that it makes us aware of how central literacy is to such inquiry. But, finally, the bipolarity of the construct (as with the others we've examined) urges a way of thinking about language, social change, and cognition that easily becomes dichotomous and reductive. "The tyranny of conceptual dichotomies," Graff calls it ("Reflections" 313). If writing is thought to possess a given characteristic—say, decontextualization or abstraction—then the dichotomy requires you to place the opposite characteristic—contextualization, concreteness—in the non-writing category (cf. Elbow). We end up splitting cognition along linguistic separations that exist more in theory than in social practice.

CONCLUSION

Witkin uncovered interesting perceptual differences and led us toward a deeper consideration of the interrelations of personality, problem solving, and social cognition. Hemisphericity theorists call our attention to the neurological substrate of information processing and language production. Piaget developed an insightful, non-behaviorist method to study cognitive growth and, more comprehensively than anyone in our time, attempted to articulate the changes in reasoning we see as children develop. And the orality-literacy theorists give us compelling reflection on spoken and written language and encourage us to consider the potential relations between modes of communication and modes of thought. My intention in this essay is not to dismiss these thinkers and theories but to present the difficulties in applying to remedial writers these models of mind. For there is a tendency to accept as fact condensed deductions from them—statements stripped away from the questions, contradictions, and complexities that are central to them. Let me summarize the problems I see with the theories we've been considering.

First, the theories end up levelling rather than elaborating individual differences in cognition. At best, people are placed along slots on a single continuum; at worst they are split into mutually exclusive camps—with one camp clearly having cognitive and social privilege over the other. The complexity of cognition—its astounding glides and its blunderous missteps as well—is narrowed, and the rich variability that exists in any social setting is ignored or reduced. This reductive labelling is going on in composition studies at a time when cognitive researchers in developmental and educational psychology, artificial intelligence, and philosophy are posing more elaborate and domain-specific models of cognition.

Second, and in line with the above, the four theories encourage a drift away from careful, rigorous focus on student writing and on the cognitive processes that seem directly related to it, that reveal themselves as students compose. That is, field dependence-independence, hemisphericity, etc., lead us from a close investigation of the production of written discourse and toward general, wide-ranging processes whose link to writing has, for the most part, been *assumed rather than demonstrated*. Even orality-literacy theory, which certainly concerns language, urges an antagonism between speech and writing that carries with it sweeping judgments about cognition.

The theories also avert or narrow our gaze from the immediate social and linguistic conditions in which the student composes: the rich interplay of purpose, genre, register, textual convention, and institutional expectation (Bartholomae; Bizzell; McCormick). When this textual-institutional context is addressed, it is usually in simplified terms: the faculty—and their discourse—are literate, left-hemispheric, field-independent, etc., and underprepared students are oral, right-hemispheric, and field dependent. I hope my critical surveys have demonstrated the conceptual limits of such labelling.

Third, the theories inadvertently reflect cultural stereotypes that should, themselves, be the subject of our investigation. At least since Plato, we in the West have separated heart from head, and in one powerful manifestation of that split we contrast rational thought with emotional sensibility, intellectual acuity with social awareness—and we often link the analytical vs. holistic opposition to these polarities. (I tried to reveal the confusion inherent in such talk when discussing cognitive style and hemisphericity.) These notions are further influenced by and play into other societal notions about independence and individuality vs. communal and tribal orientations and they domino quickly toward stereotypes about race, class, and gender.

Let me say now that I am not claiming that the research in cognitive style or hemisphericity or any of the other work we surveyed is of necessity racist, sexist, or elitist. The conclusions that can be drawn from the work, however, mesh with—and could have been subtly influenced by—cultural biases that are troubling. This is an important and, I realize, sensitive point. Some assert that student writers coming from particular communities can't reason logically or analytically, that the perceptual processes of these students are more dependent on context than the processes of white, middle-class students, that particular racial or social groups are right-hemispheric, that the student writers we teach from these groups are cognitively egocentric.

A number of recent books have amply demonstrated the way 19th and early 20th century scientific, social scientific, and humanistic assessments of mental capacity and orientation were shaped by that era's racial, gender, and class biases (see, for example, Gilman; Gould; Kamin; and Valenstein). We now find these assessments repellent, but it's important to remember that while some were made by reactionary social propagandists, a number were made as well by thinkers operating with what they saw as rigorous method—and some of those thinkers espoused a liberal social philosophy. This is a powerful illustration of the hidden influences of culture on allegedly objective investigations of mind. We all try to make sense of problematic performance—that's part of a teacher's or a researcher's job—but we must ask ourselves if speculation about cognitive egocentrism and concrete thinking and holistic perception embodies unexamined cultural biases about difference—biases that would be revealed to us if we could adopt other historical and social perspectives.

These summary statements have a number of implications for research.

The leap to theory is a privileged move—it is revered in the academy and allows parsimonious interpretations of the baffling variability of behavior. But a theory, any theory, is no more than a best guess at a given time, simultaneously evocative and flawed. Especially when it comes to judging cognition, we need to be particularly aware of these flaws and limitations, for in our culture judgments about mind carry great weight. A good deal of careful, basic descriptive and definitional work must be done before we embrace a theory, regardless of how compelling it is.

A series of fundamental questions should precede the application of theory: Is the theory formulated in a way that allows application to writing; that is, can it be defined in terms of discourse? Given what we know about writing, how would the theory be expected to manifest itself—i.e., what would it mean textually and dynamically for someone to be a field-dependent writer? What will the theory allow us to explain about writing that we haven't explained before? What will it allow us to do pedagogically that we weren't able to do as well before? Will the theory strip and narrow experience and cognition, or does it promise to open up the histories of students' involvement with writing, their rules, strategies, and assumptions, the invitations and denials that characterized their encounters with print?

Beyond such general questions are more specific guidelines for those of us doing psychological research. Once we undertake an investigation of cognition we must be careful to discuss our findings in terms of the kinds of writing we investigate. Generalizing to other tasks, and particularly to broad cognitive processes, is not warranted without evidence from those other domains. If theories like the four we discussed, but others too (e.g., theories of moral development, social cognition, metacognition, etc.), are appropriated that are built on particular tests, then researchers must thoroughly familiarize themselves with the tests beneath the theories and consult with psychologists who use them. People who are going to administer such tests should take the tests themselves—see what they're like from the inside. My mentor Richard Shavelson also urges researchers to administer the tests to individual students and have them talk about what they're doing, get some sense of how students might interpret or misinterpret the instructions, the various ways they represent the task to themselves, what cognitive processes seem to come into play as the students work with the tests. Furthermore, it must be remembered that the results of testing will be influenced by the degree of familiarity the students have with the tests and by the social situation created in the administration of them. How will these conditions be adjusted for and acknowledged? Finally, the resulting data must be discussed as being specific to the students tested. Generalizing to others must be done with caution.

A special word needs to be said here about comparative studies. If we employ hi-lo designs, expert-novice studies, and the like—which can be powerfully revealing designs—we need to consider our design and our results from historical and sociopolitical perspectives as well as cognitive ones. That is, if class, gender, or race differences emerge—and they certainly could—they should not automatically be assumed to reflect "pure" cognitive differences, but rather effects that might well be conditioned by and interpreted in light of historical, socio-political realities. There is currently a lot of talk about the prospect of forging a social-cognitive orientation to composition research (see, for example, Freedman, Dyson, Flower, and Chafe; Bizzell and Herzberg). One of the exciting results of such an endeavor could be an increased sensitivity to the social forces that shape cognitive activity. I've argued elsewhere for a research framework that intersects the cognitive, affective, and situational dimensions of composing and that involves the systematic combination of multiple methods, particularly ones traditionally thought to be antagonistic. My assumption is that the careful integration of, say, cognitive process-tracing and naturalistic observation methods can both contribute to fresh and generative insight and provide a guard against reductive interpretation (Rose, "Complexity").

Much of this essay has concerned researchers and theoreticians, but at the heart of the discussion is a basic question for any of us working with poor writers: How do we go about judging the thought processes involved with reading and writing when performance is problematic, ineffective, or stunted? If I could compress this essay's investigation down to a single conceptual touchstone, it would be this: Human cognition—even at its most stymied, bungled moments—is rich and varied. It is against this assumption that we should test our theories and research methods and classroom assessments. Do our practices work against classification that encourages single, monolithic explanations of cognitive activity? Do they honor the complexity of interpretive efforts even when those efforts fall short of some desired goal? Do they foster investigation of interaction and protean manifestation rather than investigation of absence: abstraction is absent, consciousness of print is absent, logic is absent? Do they urge reflection on the cultural biases that might be shaping them? We must be vigilant that the systems of intellect we develop or adapt do not ground our students' difficulties in sweeping, essentially one-dimensional perceptual, neurophysiological, psychological, or linguistic processes, systems that drive broad cognitive wedges between those who do well in our schools and those who don't.[5]

NOTES

1. For presentation, qualification, or rebuttal of this orientation see, for example: Ann E. Berthoff, "Is Teaching Still Possible?" *College English* 46 (1984): 743–55; Thomas J. Farrell, "I.Q. and Standard English," *CCC* 34 (1983): 470–85 and the replies to Farrell by

Greenberg, Hartwell, Himley, and Stratton in *CCC* 35 (1984): 455–78; George H. Jensen, "The Reification of the Basic Writer," *Journal of Basic Writing* 5 (1986): 52–64; Andrea Lunsford, "Cognitive Development and the Basic Writer," *College English* 41 (1979): 38–46 and Lunsford, "Cognitive Studies and Teaching Writing," *Perspectives on Research and Scholarship in Composition*, Ed. Ben W. McClelland and Timothy R. Donovan, New York: MLA, (1986): 145–61; Walter J. Ong, "Literacy and Orality in Our Times," *Profession* 79, Ed. Jasper P. Neel, New York: MLA, 1979: 1–7; Lynn Quitman Troyka, "Perspectives on Legacies and Literacy in the 1980s," *CCC* 33 (1982): 252–62 and Troyka, "Defining Basic Writers in Context," *A Sourcebook for Basic Writing Teachers*, Ed. Theresa Enos, New York: Random House, 1987: 2–15; James D. Williams, "Coherence and Cognitive Style," *Written Communication* 2 (1985): 473–91. For illustration of the transfer of this issue to the broader media, see Ellen K. Coughlin, "Literacy: 'Excitement' of New Field Attracts Scholars of Literature," *The Chronicle of Higher Education* 29 (9 Jan. 1985): 1, 10.

2. For a description of the other tests—the Body Adjustment Test and the rarely used auditory and tactile embedded figures tests—see Witkin, et al.

3. Witkin later revised his theory, suggesting that the rod and frame test and the embedded figures test were tapping different dimensions of the field dependence-independence construct. This revision, however, gives rise to further problems—see Linn and Kyllonen.

4. Educators and evaluators often seem locked into a 19th century linear progress conception of the way both societies and individuals appropriate literacy. Graff presents a provocative historical challenge to such notions; here's Vygotsky on individual development: "together with processes of development, forward motion, and appearance of new forms, we can discern processes of curtailment, disappearance, and reverse development of old forms at each step . . . only a naive view of development as a purely evolutionary process. . . can conceal from us the true nature of these processes" (106).

5. Particular sections of this paper were discussed with or reviewed by specialists who provided a great deal of expert help: Susan Curtiss (neurolinguistics), Richard Leo Enos (classical studies), Sari Gilman (research psychiatry), John R. Hayes, Richard Shavelson, and Catherine Stasz (cognitive and educational psychology), Thomas Huckin (linguistics), Robert Siegler (developmental psychology). David Bartholomae, Linda Flower, Glynda Hull, David Kaufer, and Stephen Witte commented generously on the entire manuscript. The project benefited as well from rich conversation with Mariolina Salvatori and Kathryn Flannery. Versions of the paper were read at Carnegie Mellon, Pitt, Indiana University of Pennsylvania, UCLA, Berkeley, CCCC (Atlanta), Penn State, and UCSD. My thanks for all the ideas generated at those conferences and colloquia. Finally, appreciation is due to Sally Magargee for her research assistance and the Carnegie Mellon Department of English and the Spencer Foundation for their support.

WORKS CITED

Adkins, Arthur W.H. "Orality and Philosophy." Robb 207–27.

Adler, Jonathan. "Abstraction is Uncooperative." *Journal for the Theory of Social Behavior* 14 (1984): 165–81.

Arndt, Stephen, and Dale E. Berger. "Cognitive Mode and Asymmetry in Cerebral Functioning." *Cortex* 14 (1978): 78–86.

Bartholomae, David. "Inventing the University." Rose, *When a Writer Can't Write* 134–65.

Battig, William F. "Within-Individual Differences in 'Cognitive' Processes." *Information Processing and Cognition.* Ed. Robert L. Solso. Hillsdale, NJ: Erlbaum, 1975. 195–228.

Beamon, Karen. "Coordination and Subordination Revisited: Syntactic Complexity in Spoken and Written Narrative Discourse." Tannen, *Coherence in Spoken and Written Discourse* 45–80.

Beaumont, J. Graham. "Methods for Studying Cerebral Hemispheric Function." *Functions of the Right Cerebral Hemisphere.* Ed. A.W. Young. London: Academic Press, 1983. 113–46.

Beaumont, J. Graham, A.W. Young, and I.C. McManus. "Hemisphericity: A Critical Review." *Cognitive Neuropsychology* 2 (1984): 191–212.

Benson, D. Frank, and Eran Zaidel, eds. *The Dual Brain: Hemispheric Specialization in Humans.* New York: Guilford, 1985.

Berthoff, Ann E. "Is Teaching Still Possible?" *College English* 46 (1984): 743–55.

Bizzell, Patricia. "Cognition, Convention, and Certainty: What We Need to Know about Writing." *Pre/Text* 3 (1982): 213–44.

Bizzell, Patricia, and Bruce Herzberg. *The Bedford Bibliography for Teachers of Writing.* Boston: Bedford Books, 1987.

Bogen, Joseph. "The Dual Brain: Some Historical and Methodological Aspects." Benson and Zaidel 27–43.

Bogen, Joseph, et al. "The Other Side of the Brain: The A/P Ratio." *Bulletin of Los Angeles Neurological Society* 37 (1972): 49–61.

Bradshaw, J.L., and N.C. Nettleton. "The Nature of Hemispheric Specialization in Man." *Behavioral and Brain Sciences* 4 (1981): 51–91.

Brainerd, Charles J. "The Stage Question in Cognitive-Developmental Theory." *The Behavioral and Brain Sciences* 2 (1978): 173–81.

Brown, Warren S., James T. Marsh, and Ronald E. Ponsford. "Hemispheric Differences in Event-Related Brain Potentials." Benson and Zaidel 163–79.

Caplan, David. "On the Cerebral Localization of Linguistic Functions: Logical and Empirical Issues Surrounding Deficit Analysis and Functional Localization." *Brain and Language* 14 (1981): 120–37.

Carey, Susan. *Conceptual Change in Childhood.* Cambridge: MIT P, 1985.

Chafe, Wallace L. "Linguistic Differences Produced by Differences in Speaking and Writing." Olson, Torrance, and Hildyard 105–23.

Clanchy, M.T. *From Memory to Written Record: England 1066–1307.* Cambridge: Harvard UP, 1979.

Cole, Michael, and Barbara Means. *Comparative Studies of How People Think.* Cambridge: Harvard UP, 1981.

Cressy, David. "The Environment for Literacy: Accomplishment and Context in Seventeenth-Century England and New England." *Literacy in Historical Perspective.* Ed. Daniel P. Resnick. Washington: Library of Congress, 1983. 23–42.

Cronbach, Lee J. *Essentials of Psychological Testing.* New York: Harper and Row, 1960.

DeRenzi, Ennio. *Disorders of Space Exploration and Cognition.* London: Wiley, 1982.

Donaldson, Margaret. *Children's Minds.* New York: Norton, 1979.

Donchin, Emanuel, Gregory McCarthy, and Marta Kutas. "Electroencephalographic Investigations of Hemispheric Specialization." *Language and Hemispheric Specialization in Man: Cerebral Event-Related Potentials.* Ed. John E. Desmedt. Basel, NY: Karger, 1977. 212–42.

Dumas, Roland, and Arlene Morgan. "EEG Asymmetry as a Function of Occupation, Task and Task Difficulty." *Neuropsychologia* 13 (1975): 214–28.

Efron, Robert. "The Central Auditory System and Issues Related to Hemispheric Specialization." *Assessment of Central Auditory Dysfunction: Foundations and Clinical Correlates.* Ed. Marilyn L. Pinheiro and Frank E. Musiek. Baltimore: Williams and Wilkins, 1985. 143–54.

Ehrlichman, Howard, and Arthur Weinberger. "Lateral Eye Movements and Hemispheric Asymmetry: A Critical Review." *Psychological Bulletin* 85 (1978): 1080–1101.

Elbow, Peter. "The Shifting Relationships Between Speech and Writing." *CCC* 34 (1985): 283–303.

Enos, Richard Leo, and John Ackerman. "*Letteraturizzazione* and Hellenic Rhetoric: An Analysis for Research with Extensions." *Proceedings of 1984 Rhetoric Society of America Conference.* Ed. Charles Kneupper, forthcoming.

Fillmore, Charles J. "On Fluency." *Individual Differences in Language Ability and Language Behavior.* Ed. Charles J. Fillmore, Daniel Kempler, and William S.Y. Wang. New York: Academic Press, 1979. 85–101.

Flavell, John H. *Cognitive Development.* Englewood Cliffs: Prentice-Hall, 1977.

Fodor, Jerry A. *The Modularity of Mind.* Cambridge: MIT P, 1983.

Freedman, Sarah, et al. *Research in Writing: Past, Present, and Future.* Berkeley: Center for the Study of Writing, 1987.

Gardner, Howard. *Frames of Mind.* New York: Basic Books, 1983.

_____. *The Mind's New Science.* New York: Basic Books, 1985.

_____. "What We Know (and Don't Know) About the Two Halves of the Brain." *Journal of Aesthetic Education* 12 (1978): 113–19.

Gardner, Howard, and Ellen Winner. "Artistry and Aphasia." *Acquired Aphasia.* Ed. Martha Taylor Sarno. New York: Academic Press, 1981. 361–84.

Gelman, Rochelle. "Cognitive Development." *Ann. Rev. Psychol.* (1978): 297–332.

Gevins, A.S., et al. "EEG Patterns During 'Cognitive' Tasks." *Electroencephalography and Clinical Neurophysiology* 47 (1979): 704–10.

Gilman, Sander. *Difference and Pathology.* Ithaca, NY: Cornell UP, 1985.

Ginsburg, Herbert. "Poor Children, African Mathematics, and the Problem of Schooling." *Educational Research Quarterly* 2 (1978): 26–44.

Glaser, Robert. "Education and Thinking: The Role of Knowledge." *American Psychologist* 39 (1984): 93–104.

Goodenow, Jacqueline. "The Nature of Intelligent Behavior: Questions Raised by Cross-Cultural Studies." *The Nature of Intelligence.* Ed. Lauren B. Resnick. Hillsdale, NJ: Erlbaum, 1976. 168–88.

Goody, Jack. *The Domestication of the Savage Mind.* London: Cambridge UP, 1977.

Gould, Stephen Jay. *The Mismeasure of Man.* New York: Norton, 1981.

Graff, Harvey. *The Literacy Myth.* New York: Academic Press, 1979.

_____. "Reflections on the History of Literacy: Overview, Critique, and Proposals." *Humanities and Society* 4 (1981): 303–33.

Gruber, Howard E., and J. Jacques Vonèche, eds. *The Essential Piaget.* New York: Basic Books, 1977.

Halliday, M. A. K. "Differences between Spoken and Written Language." *Communication through Reading.* Vol. 2. Ed. Glenda Page, John Elkins, and Barrie O'Connor. Adelaide, SA: Australian Reading Association, 1979. 37–52.

Havelock, Eric. *The Muse Learns to Write.* Cambridge: Harvard UP, 1986.

_____. *Preface to Plato.* Cambridge: Harvard UP, 1963.

Harré, Rom, and Roger Lamb. *The Encyclopedic Dictionary of Psychology.* Cambridge: MIT P, 1983.

Heath, Shirley Brice. "Protean Shapes in Literacy Events: Ever-Shifting Oral and Literate Traditions." *Spoken and Written Language.* Ed. Deborah Tannen. Norwood, NJ: Ablex, 1982. 91–117.

_____. *Ways With Words.* London: Cambridge UP, 1983.

Hillyard, Steve A., and David L. Woods. "Electrophysiological Analysis of Human Brain Function." *Handbook of Behavioral Neurobiology.* Vol. 2. Ed. Michael S. Gazzaniga. New York: Plenum, 1979. 343–78.

Hudson, R.A. *Sociolinguistics.* Cambridge: Cambridge UP, 1986.

Hull, Glynda. "The Editing Process in Writing: A Performance Study of Experts and Novices." Diss. U of Pittsburgh, 1983.

Hunt, Earl. "On the Nature of Intelligence." *Science* 219 (1983): 141–46.

Hunter, Carman St. John, and David Harmon. *Adult Illiteracy in the United States.* New York: McGraw-Hill, 1985.

Inhelder, Barbel, and Jean Piaget. *The Growth of Logical Thinking from Childhood to Adolescence.* Trans. Anne Parsons and Stanley Milgram. New York: Basic Books, 1958.

Jensen, George H. "The Reification of the Basic Writer." *Journal of Basic Writing* 5 (1986): 52–64.

Kamin, Leon J. *The Science and Politics of I.Q.* Hillsdale, NJ: Erlbaum, 1974.

Kuhn, Deanna, Victoria Ho, and Catherine Adams. "Formal Reasoning Among Pre- and Late Adolescents." *Child Development* 50 (1979): 1128–35.

Kurtz, Richard M. "A Conceptual Investigation of Witkin's Notion of Perceptual Style." *Mind* 78 (1969): 522–33.

Latour, Bruno, and Steve Woolgar. *Laboratory Life.* Beverly Hills, CA: Sage, 1979.

Lave, Jean. "Cognitive Consequences of Traditional Apprenticeship Training in West Africa." *Anthropology and Education Quarterly* 8 (1977): 177–80.

LeDoux, Joseph E. "Cerebral Asymmetry and the Integrated Function of the Brain." *Functions of the Right Cerebral Hemisphere.* Ed. Andrew W. Young. London: Academic Press, 1983. 203–16.

Linn, Marcia C., and Patrick Kyllonen. "The Field Dependence-Independence Construct: Some, One, or None." *Journal of Educational Psychology* 73 (1981): 261–73.

Lockridge, Kenneth. *Literacy in Colonial New England.* New York: Norton, 1974.

Margolis, Joseph. "The Emergence of Philosophy." Robb 229–43.

Marrou, H.I. *A History of Education in Antiquity.* Madison, WI: U of Wisconsin P, 1982.

McCormick, Kathleen. *The Cultural Imperatives Underlying Cognitive Acts.* Berkeley: Center for The Study of Writing, 1986.

McKenna, Frank P. "Field Dependence and Personality: A Re-examination." *Social Behavior and Personality* 11 (1983): 51–55.

Messick, Samuel. "Personality Consistencies in Cognition and Creativity." *Individuality in Learning.* Ed. Samuel Messick and Associates. San Francisco: Jossey-Bass, 1976. 4–22.

Ogbu, John U. *Minority Education and Caste.* New York: Academic Press, 1978.

Olson, David R., Nancy Torrance, and Angela Hildyard, eds. *Literacy, Language, and Learning.* New York: Cambridge UP, 1981.

Ong, Walter J. *Orality and Literacy: The Technologizing of the Word.* New York: Methuen, 1982.

Ornstein, Robert E., and David Galin. "Psychological Studies of Consciousness." *Symposium on Consciousness*. Ed. Philip R. Lee et al. New York: Viking, 1976. 53–66.

Oxenham, John. *Literacy: Writing, Reading, and Social Organisation*. London: Routledge and Kegan Paul, 1980.

Perkins, D. N. "General Cognitive Skills: Why Not?" *Thinking and Learning Skills*. Ed. Susan F. Chipman, Judith W. Segal, and Robert Glaser. Hillsdale, NJ: Erlbaum, 1985. 339–63.

Piaget, Jean. "Intellectual Evolution from Adolescence to Adulthood." *Human Development* 15 (1972): 1–12.

Polanyi, Livia. *Telling the American Story: A Structural and Cultural Analysis of Conversational Storytelling*. Norwood, NJ: Ablex, 1985.

Robb, Kevin, ed. *Language and Thought in Early Greek Philosophy*. LaSalle, IL: Monist Library of Philosophy, 1983.

Rogoff, Barbara. *Everyday Cognition*. Cambridge: Harvard UP, 1984.

Rose, Mike. "Complexity, Rigor, Evolving Method, and the Puzzle of Writer's Block: Thoughts on Composing Process Research." Rose, *When a Writer Can't Write* 227–60.

———, ed. *When a Writer Can't Write: Studies in Writer's Block and Other Composing Process Problems*. New York: Guilford, 1985.

Rugg, Michael D. "Electrophysiological Studies." *Divided Visual Field Studies of Cerebral Organization*. Ed. J. Graham Beaumont. New York: Academic Press, 1982. 129–46.

Scollon, Ron, and Suzanne B. K. Scollon. "Cooking It Up and Boiling It Down: Abstracts in Athabascan Children's Story Retellings." Tannen, *Coherence in Spoken and Written Discourse* 173–97.

Shaughnessy, Mina. *Errors and Expectations*. New York: Oxford UP, 1977.

Siegler, Robert S. "Children's Thinking: The Search For Limits." *The Function of Language and Cognition*. Ed. G.J. Whitehurst and Barry J. Zimmerman. New York: Academic Press, 1979. 83–113.

Sperry, Roger W. "Consciousness, Personal Identity, and the Divided Brain." Benson and Zaidel 11–26.

Tannen, Deborah, ed. *Coherence in Spoken and Written Discourse*. Norwood, NJ: Ablex, 1984.

———. "A Comparative Analysis of Oral Narrative Strategies: Athenian Greek and American English." *The Pear Stories*. Ed. Wallace Chafe. Norwood, NJ: Ablex, 1980. 51–87.

———. "Relative Focus on Involvement in Oral and Written Discourse." Olson, Torrance, and Hildyard 124–47.

TenHouten, Warren D. "Social Dominance and Cerebral Hemisphericity: Discriminating Race, Socioeconomic Status, and Sex Groups by Performance on Two Lateralized Tests." *Intern J. Neuroscience* 10 (1980): 223–32.

Toulmin, Stephen. "Epistemology and Developmental Psychology." *Developmental Plasticity*. Ed. Eugene S. Gollin. New York: Academic Press, 1981. 253–67.

Tulkin, S. R., and M. J. Konner. "Alternative Conceptions of Intellectual Functioning." *Human Development* 16 (1973): 33–52.

Valenstein, Elliot S. *Great and Desperate Cures*. New York: Basic Books, 1986.

Vernon, Philip. "The Distinctiveness of Field Independence." *Journal of Personality* 40 (1972): 366–91.

Vygotsky, L. S. *Mind in Society*. Cambridge: Harvard UP, 1978.

Wachtel, Paul L. "Field Dependence and Psychological Differentiation: Reexamination." *Perceptual and Motor Skills* 35 (1972): 174–89.

Whitaker, Harry A., and George A. Ojemann. "Lateralization of Higher Cortical Functions: A Critique." *Evolution and Lateralization of the Brain.* Ed. Stuart Dimond and David Blizard. New York: New York Academy of Science, 1977. 459–73.

Williams, James Dale. "Coherence and Cognitive Style." Diss. U of Southern California, 1983.

Witkin, Herman A. "Psychological Differentiation and Forms of Pathology." *Journal of Abnormal Psychology* 70 (1965): 317–36.

Witkin, Herman A., et al. "Field-Dependent and Field-Independent Cognitive Styles and Their Educational Implications." *Review of Educational Research* 47 (1977): 1–64.

Wittrock, Merlin. "Education and the Cognitive Processes of the Brain." *Education and The Brain.* Ed. Jeanne S. Chall and Allen S. Mirsky. Chicago: U of Chicago P, 1978. 61–102.

Young, Andrew W. "Methodological and Theoretical Bases of Visual Hemifield Studies." *Divided Visual Field Studies of Cerebral Organisation.* Ed. J. Graham Beaumont. New York: Academic Press, 1982. 11–27.

Cognition, Convention, and Certainty

What We Need to Know about Writing

Patricia Bizzell

What do we need to know about writing? Only recently have we needed to ask this question, and the asking has created composition studies. We have needed to ask it because of changing circumstances in the classroom, and our answers will be put to the test there with a speed uncommon in other academic disciplines. The current theoretical debate over how to go about finding these answers, therefore, is not merely an empty exercise. Students' lives will be affected in profound ways.

This profound effect on students is the more to be expected because of the terms in which the "writing problem" has appeared to us—terms that suggest that students' thinking needs remediation as much as their writing. Seeing the problem this way makes it very clear that our teaching task is not only to convey information but also to transform students' whole world view. But if this indeed is our project, we must be aware that it has such scope. Otherwise, we risk burying ethical and political questions under supposedly neutral pedagogical technique. Some of our answers to the question of what we need to know about writing are riskier in this regard than others.

We now see the "writing problem" as a thinking problem primarily because we used to take our students' thinking for granted. We used to assume that students came to us with ideas and we helped them put those ideas into words. We taught style, explaining the formal properties of model essays and evaluating students' products in the light of these models. Some

Previously published in the journal *PRE/TEXT* 3.3 (1982): 213–243. Used by permission of Patricia Bizzell.

students came to us with better ideas than others, but these were simply the brighter or more mature students. All we could do for the duller, more immature students was to hope that exposure to good models might push them along the developmental path.[1]

Over the last twenty years, however, we have encountered in our classrooms more and more students whose ideas seem so ill-considered, by academic standards, that we can no longer see the problem as primarily one of expression. Rather, we feel, "Now I have to teach them to think, too!" And at the same time, students have so much trouble writing Standard English that we are driven away from stylistic considerations back to the basics of grammar and mechanics. Teaching style from model essays has not prepared us to explain or repair these students' deficiencies. The new demands on us as teachers can only be met, it seems, by a reconsideration of the relationship between thought and language. We are pretty much agreed, in other words, that what we need to know about writing has to do with the thinking processes involved in it.

Composition specialists generally agree about some fundamental elements in the development of language and thought. We agree that the normal human individual possesses innate mental capacities to learn a language and to assemble complex conceptual structures. As the individual develops, these capacities are realized in her learning a native tongue and forming thought patterns that organize and interpret experience. The mature exercise of these thought and language capacities takes place in society, in interaction with other individuals, and this interaction modifies the individual's reasoning, speaking, and writing within society. Groups of society members can become accustomed to modifying each other's reasoning and language use in certain ways. Eventually, these familiar ways achieve the status of conventions that bind the group in a discourse community, at work together on some project of interaction with the material world. An individual can belong to more than one discourse community, but her access to the various communities will be unequally conditioned by her social situation.

If composition specialists generally agree about this description, however, we disagree about what part of it is relevant to composition studies. One theoretical camp sees writing as primarily inner-directed, and so is more interested in the structure of language-learning and thinking processes in their earliest state, prior to social influence. The other main theoretical camp sees writing as primarily outer-directed, and so is more interested in the social processes whereby language-learning and thinking capacities are shaped and used in particular communities. In the current debate, each camp seeks to define what we *most* need to know about writing.

Inner-directed theorists seek to discover writing processes that are so fundamental as to be universal. Later elaborations of thinking and language-using should be understood as outgrowths of individual capacities (see Figure 1). Hence, inner-directed theorists are most interested in individual capacities and their earliest interactions with experience (locations #1 and 2, Figure 1). The inner-directed theorists tend to see the kinds of reasoning occurring at all four locations as isomorphic—all the same basic logical structures.[2] They also tend to see differences in language use at different locations as superficial matters of lexical choice; the basic structure of the language cannot change from location to location because this structure is isomorphic with the innate mental structures that enabled one to learn a language, and hence presumably universal and independent of lexical choice. Nevertheless, looking for an argument to justify teaching one form of a language, some inner-directed theorists treat one set of lexical choices as better able than others to make language embody the innate structures.

Figure 1 An inner-directed model of the development of language and thought. Arrows indicate direction of individual's development, beginning with innate capacities and issuing finally in particular instances of use.

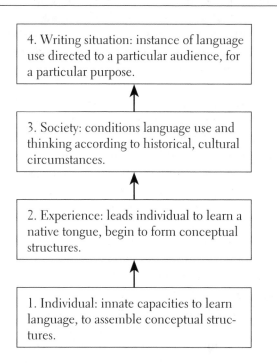

4. Writing situation: instance of language use directed to a particular audience, for a particular purpose.

3. Society: conditions language use and thinking according to historical, cultural circumstances.

2. Experience: leads individual to learn a native tongue, begin to form conceptual structures.

1. Individual: innate capacities to learn language, to assemble conceptual structures.

Insofar as these better choices fall into the patterns of, for example, a "standard" form of a native tongue, they make the standard intellectually superior to other forms.[3]

Inner-directed theorists further claim, in a similar paradox, that the universal, fundamental structures of thought and language can be taught. If our students are unable to have ideas, we should look around locations # 1 and 2 for structural models of the mental processes that are not happening in these students' minds. Once we find these models, we can guide students through the processes until the students' own thought-forming mechanisms "kick on" and they can make concepts on their own. An heuristic procedure is often presented as such a process model.[4] Similarly, if our students are unable to write English, we should look in the same locations for patterns of correct syntax, which we can then ask the students to practice until they internalize the patterns. Sentence-combining exercises offer such pattern practice.[5]

Once students are capable of cognitively sophisticated thinking and writing, they are ready to tackle the problems of a particular writing situation. These problems are usually treated by inner-directed theory as problems of audience analysis. Audience analysis seeks to identify the personal idiosyncracies of readers so that the writer can communicate her message to them in the most persuasive form. The changes made to accommodate an audience, however, are not seen as substantially altering the meaning of the piece of writing because that is based in the underlying structure of thought and language.[6]

In contrast, outer-directed theorists believe that universal, fundamental structures can't be taught; thinking and language use can never occur free of a social context that conditions them (see Figure 2). The outer-directed theorists believe that teaching style from model essays failed not because we were doing the wrong thing but because we weren't aware of what we were doing. Teaching style from model essays, in this view, is teaching the discourse conventions of a particular community—in this case, a community of intellectuals including, but not limited to, academics. But because we were unaware that we were in a discourse community, we taught the conventions as formal structures, as if they were universal patterns of thought and language. What we should do is to teach students that there are such things as discourse conventions.

The outer-directed theorists are sceptical about how we can obtain knowledge of what thinking and language-learning processes are innate. Moreover, they would argue that the individual is already inside a discourse community when she learns a native tongue, since the infant does not learn

Figure 2   An outer-directed model of the development of language and thought. Note that innate capacities have no expression outside discourse communities and that society is made up entirely of discourse communities. Individual has unequal access to different communities. Direction of development is outward from native community.

2. Society: aggregate of discourse communities that all share certain patterns of language-using, thinking conditioned by historical, cultural circumstances.

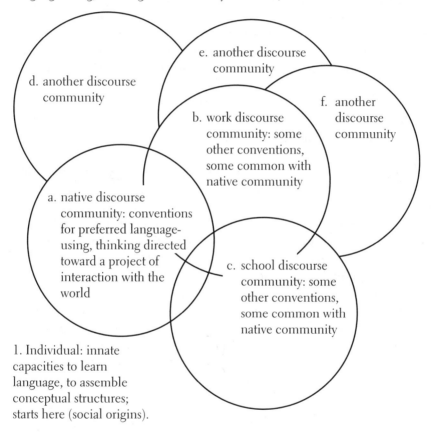

d. another discourse community

e. another discourse community

f. another discourse community

b. work discourse community: some other conventions, some common with native community

a. native discourse community: conventions for preferred language-using, thinking directed toward a project of interaction with the world

c. school discourse community: some other conventions, some common with native community

1. Individual: innate capacities to learn language, to assemble conceptual structures; starts here (social origins).

some generalized form of language but rather the habits of language use in the neighborhood, or the discourse community into which she is born.[7] Since this discourse community already possesses traditional, shared ways of understanding experience, the infant doesn't learn to conceptualize in a social vacuum, either, but is constantly being advised by more mature community members whether her inferences are correct, whether her groupings of experiential data into evidence are significant, and so on.[8] Some outer-directed theorists would go so far as to say that the lines of development of thought and language merge when the native tongue is learned, since one learns to think only by learning a language and one can't have an idea one doesn't have a word for.[9] *No A priori thought*

Outer-directed theorists would argue that we have no reason to believe, and no convincing way to determine, that our students can't think or use language in complex ways. It's just that they can't think or use language in the ways we want them to. To help them, then, we should be looking for ways to explain discourse conventions. We might find patterns of language use and reasoning that are common to all members of a society, patterns that are part of the set of conventions of every discourse community within the society. Conventions that are common in the society could be used as bridges between different discourse communities—for example, to ease the transition into the academic discourse community for students who come from discourse communities far removed from it.[10]

The staple activity of outer-directed writing instruction will be analysis of the conventions of particular discourse communities (see Figure 2). For example, a major focus of writing-across-the-curriculum programs is to demystify the conventions of the academic discourse community.[11] Discourse analysis goes beyond audience analysis because what is most significant about members of a discourse community is not their personal preferences, prejudices, and so on, but rather the expectations they share by virtue of belonging to that particular community. These expectations are embodied in the discourse conventions, which are in turn conditioned by the community's work. Audience analysis aims to persuade readers that you're right; it is to dress your argument in flattering apparel. Discourse analysis aims to enable you to make that argument, to do intellectual work of significance to the community, and hence, to persuade readers that you are a worthy co-worker.[12]

Answers to what we need to know about writing will have to come from both the inner-directed and the outer-directed theoretical schools if we wish to have a complete picture of the composing process. We need to explain the cognitive and the social factors in writing development, and even more important, the relationship between them. Therefore, we should think of the current debate between the two schools as the kind of fruitful exchange that enlarges knowledge, not as a process that will lead to its own termination, to a theory that silences debate. I would like to show here how one inner-directed theoretical model of writing can be enlarged by an outer-directed critique.

The inner-directed school has been distinguished by its fostering of research on writing that follows scientific methodology, and two of the most important researchers are Linda Flower, a professor of English at Carnegie-Mellon University, and John R. Hayes, a professor of psychology at the same school. They have been conducting research for about six years on what people do when they compose. The goal of this research is to formulate "A Cognitive Process Theory of Writing," according to the title of their recent *College Composition and Communication* essay, under review here.[13] Their work's roots in cognitive psychology can be seen in *Cognitive Processes in Writing*, also reviewed here, the proceedings of a 1978 symposium at Carnegie-Mellon.[14] Flower and Hayes see composing as a kind of problem-solving activity; what interests them are the "invariant" thought processes called into play whenever one is confronted with a writing task. In other words, they assume that although each writing task will have its own environment of purposes and constraints, the mental activity involved in juggling these constraints while moving to accomplish one's purposes does not change from task to task. This problem-solving thought process is the "cognitive process of writing."

In Figure 1, location 2 is approximately where Flower and Hayes would place what they are studying. The cognitive process is triggered by what goes on at location 4 (imposition of a particular writing task); the process may also be shaped by attitudes absorbed at location 3 and modified in the light of success or failure in problem-solving at location 4. Not everyone uses the same cognitive process in writing, some processes are more successful than others, and one's process can be consciously or unconsciously modified. Flower and Hayes seek to describe a model of the most complete and successful composing process they can find through their research.

Protocol analysis is their principle research tool. First, the researcher asks a person (the test subject) to say aloud whatever she is thinking while solving a problem posed by the researcher. For example, Flower and Hayes have asked English teachers to describe what goes through their minds while composing an article describing their jobs for the readers of *Seventeen* magazine. The transcription of what the subject says is the protocol. Next, the researcher scans the protocol looking in the subject's self-description for features predicted by the theory of cognitive activity guiding the research. Flower and Hayes have looked for descriptions of behavior common to current accounts of the writing process, such as "organizing" and "revising." In analyzing the protocol, the researcher must bridge gaps in the protocol caused by the subject's forgetting to mention some of her problem-solving steps. The theory is tested by its ability to bridge these gaps as well as by the appearance in the protocol of features it predicts (Flower and Hayes explain their procedure in "Identifying the Organization of Writing Processes," *Cognitive Processes*, pp. 3–30).

Through their research, Flower and Hayes have been gradually refining a process model of composing (see "Process Theory," p. 370). Its most current version divides the writing situation into three main parts: one, the "task environment," subdivided into "rhetorical problem" and "text produced so far"; two, the "writing process," subdivided into "reviewing" (further subdivided into "revising" and "evaluating"), "translating," and "planning" (further subdivided into "generating," "goal-setting," and "organizing"); and three, the "writer's long-term memory." The task environment is outside the writer, the writing process is inside the writer, and long-term memory can be both inside and outside—that is, in the writer's mind or in books. Task environment and memory are seen as information sources upon which the writer draws while performing the composing activities grouped under "writing process."

This model is hierarchical and recursive rather than sequential in structure; that is, Flower and Hayes do not see the writing process as an invariant order of steps. What is invariant, in their view, is the structural relation of the steps. A writer can "access" memory or task environment, and switch from one composing subprocess to another, at any time while the writing task is being completed; an entity in the model called "monitor" executes these switches. This model does not tell us how to proceed through the composing process, but only that in proceeding, there are certain subprocesses we must include if we want to compose successfully.

Flower and Hayes see this model as resolving current theoretical disagreements about what guides composing. Beginning their "Process Theory" essay with summaries of different but compatible views on composing, Flower and Hayes seem to suggest that while other theorists are like blind men describing an elephant, in the Flower-Hayes model we see the whole beast—or at least we can infer its shape when the porpoise occasionally breaks water, to switch to the animal metaphor Flower and Hayes use (*Cognitive Processes*, pp. 9–10). It is the hierarchical and recursive structure of this model, in Flower and Hayes's view, that makes it superior to other theorists' work and able to control and reconcile other theorists' work.

The Flower-Hayes model may, however, strike many readers as a surprising mix of daunting complexity and disappointing familiarity. When we finally get the new terminology straight in our minds, we find in the model's elaborate cognitive processes just the same writing activities we have been debating about. Consider, for example, the Flower-Hayes model's "monitor," the entity that executes switches between composing subprocesses. On

374

the one hand, the term, borrowed from computer programming, is rather intimidating, especially if we imagine that it names something we didn't know was there before. On the other hand, we find out eventually that "monitor" means simply "the writer's mind making decisions." Borrowing a term from programming masks the question of *why* the writer makes certain decisions. The Flower-Hayes model consistently presents a description of *how* the writing process goes on as if it were capable of answering questions about *why* the writer makes certain choices in certain situations. While it is useful for us to have an overview of the "how," such as the Flower-Hayes model offers, we should not suppose that this will enable us to advise students on difficult questions of practice. To put it another way, if we are going to see students as problem-solvers, we must also see them as problem-solvers situated in discourse communities that guide problem definition and the range of alternative solutions. Outer-directed theory can thus shore up the Flower-Hayes model in two critical areas, planning and translating.

"Translating," according to Flower and Hayes, is "the process of putting ideas into visible language" ("Process Theory," p. 373). They treat written English as a set of containers into which we pour meaning, regardless of how meaning exists before the pouring. The containers may not seem to be in convenient sizes at first—we have to struggle with their "constraints" or "special demands"—but once we internalize these, written language as a factor in the composing process essentially disappears. Writing does not so much contribute to thinking as provide an occasion for thinking—or, more precisely, a substrate upon which thinking can grow. Beyond minor matters of spelling, diction, and so on, we do not have to worry about how students are going to find out about the features of written language because these are already innate.

"Translating," then, remains the emptiest box in the Flower-Hayes model, while "planning" becomes the fullest. During planning, the writer generates and organizes ideas before struggling to put them into words. Language itself is not seen as having a generative force in the planning process, except insofar as it stands as a record of the current progress of the writer's thinking in "text produced so far." Planning processes, therefore, have to be elaborated because they are all the writer has to guide her toward a solution to the particular writing problem. What's missing here is the connection to social context afforded by recognition of the dialectical relationship between thought and language. We can have thoughts for which we have no words, I think, but learning language, though it doesn't exactly teach us to think, teaches us what thoughts matter. To put it another way, we can *know* nothing but what we have words for, if knowledge is what language makes of experience.

Vygotsky has characterized this dialectical relationship of thought and language as the development of "verbal thought." At first, language use and thinking develop separately in the child. But eventually the child comes to understand that language not only names ideas but develops and evaluates them, and then, *"the nature of the* [child's] *development itself changes,* from biological to historical."[15] The child's linguistic and cognitive development culminates in "verbal thought," which "is not a natural, innate form of behavior but is determined by a historical-cultural process and has specific properties and laws that cannot be found in the natural forms of thought and speech" (Vygotsky, p. 51). To illustrate the mature relationship between thought and language, Vygotsky uses situations that are strongly context-bound, such as conversations between lovers or among actors in a play.

Vygotsky's analysis suggests that a model that separates planning and translating will not be fruitful for describing adult language-using because these activities are never separate in adult language-using. There is, to be sure, a basis in the human organism for language-using behavior; Vygotsky calls it "biological," Flower and Hayes call it "cognitive." But while this basis is a legitimate object of study in its own right, even the most complete anatomy of it will not explain adult language-using because, as Vygotsky emphasizes, with the advent of verbal thought the very nature of language-using processes changes. The writing process can only take place after this change occurred. Vygotsky's analysis would suggest, then, not only that we should not separate planning and translating but also that we should understand them as conditioned by social context.

If we accept Vygotsky's analysis as indicating the need to fill in Flower and Hayes's empty "translating" box, then to look for knowledge to fill it, we can turn to sociolinguistics. This discipline seeks to analyze the ways thinking and language-using are conditioned by social context. In studying writing, sociolinguists look for the verbal ties with context. They argue that certain genres, implying certain relations between people, are typical of certain situations. Furthermore, readers do not perceive a text as hanging together logically unless its connections with the social context are as clear as the markers of internal coherence.[16] Therefore, for example, students who struggle to write Standard English need knowledge beyond the rules of grammar, spelling, and so on. They need to know: the habitual attitudes of Standard English users toward this preferred form; the linguistic features that most strongly mark group identity; the conventions that can sometimes be ignored; and so on. Students who do know the rules of Standard English may still seem to academics to be writing "incorrectly" if the students are insensitive to all these other features of language use in the community—then the students are using academic language in unacademic ways.[17]

Composition specialists can learn from sociolinguists to avoid what George Dillon has called the "bottom-to-top" fallacy: the notion that a writer first finds meaning, then puts it into words, then organizes the words into sentences, sentences into paragraphs, etc.[18] Dillon argues, rather, that it is the sense of her whole project that most stimulates a writer's thinking and guides her language use. The discourse gives meaning to the words and not vice versa. For example, such phrases as "it seems to me" and "these results suggest . . ." do not themselves tell us how to interpret such a pattern of qualifying statements. When we encounter these words in a student paper, we are likely to chide the writer for covering up poor research or for being unduly humble. When we encounter the very same words in a scholarly paper, we simply take them to mean that the writer is establishing a properly inquiring persona (see Dillon, p. 91).

Even something as cognitively fundamental as sentence structure takes on meaning from the discourse in which it is deployed. For this reason, for example, revising rules are notoriously unhelpful: they always require further knowledge in order to be applied. We can't "omit needless words" unless we have some additional criteria for "needlessness." We can't even "avoid passive voice" all the time. Passive voice might be preferred by a writer who wants to head her sentence with words that tie it closely to the previous sentence, especially if the kind of discourse she is producing places a high value on markers of internal coherence.[19]

"Putting meaning into words," then, cannot be seen as a mechanical process of finding the right size containers. Instead, with a form of discourse we take on a whole range of possibilities for making meaning. Language-using in social contexts is connected not only to the immediate situation but to the larger society, too, in the form of conventions for construing reality. This relationship between language and world view has prompted M.A.K. Halliday to argue that "the problem of educational failure is not a linguistic problem, if by linguistic we mean a problem of different urban dialects"; at bottom, "it is a semiotic problem, concerned with the different ways in which we have constructed our social reality, and the styles of meaning: we have learned to associate with the various aspects of it."[20] In short, educational problems associated with language use should be understood as difficulties with joining an unfamiliar discourse community.

To look at writing as situated in a discourse community is to blur over the lines between translating and planning in the Flower-Hayes model. Finding words is not a separate process from setting goals. It *is* setting goals, because finding words is always a matter of aligning oneself with a particular discourse community. The community's conventions will include instructions on a preferred form of the native tongue, a specialized vocabulary, a polite technique for establishing persona, and so on. To some extent, the community's conventions can be inferred from analyzing the community's texts. But because the conventions also shape world view, the texts can never be an adequate index of community practice.

Therefore, we should not think of what I am calling a discourse community simply as a group who have decided to abide by certain language-using rules. Rather, we should see the group as an "interpretive community," to use Stanley Fish's term, whose language-using habits are part of a larger pattern of regular interaction with the material world.[21] Because this interaction is always an historical process, changing over time, the community's conventions also change over time. This is not to say that the community's interpretive conventions are arbitrary or that they totally determine individual behavior. They are not arbitrary because they are always conditioned by the on-going work in the community and sanctioned by consensus. At any given time, community members should have no trouble specifying that some kinds of thinking and language-using are obviously appropriate to the community and some are not. Changes in conventions can only define themselves in terms of what is already acceptable (even if such definition means negation of the currently acceptable).

At the same time, some kinds of thinking and language-using are not obviously either appropriate or inappropriate; they are open to debate. An individual who abides by the community's conventions, therefore, can still find areas for initiative—adherence is slavish adherence only for the least productive community members. These "open" areas may be the unsolved problems of the community, experiences that remain anomalous in the community's interpretive scheme, or they may be areas the community has never even considered dealing with. An individual may, however, bring one of these open areas into the range of the community's discourse if her argument for an interpretation of it is sufficiently persuasive in terms the community already understands. As an example of this activity, Mina Shaughnessy has cited Freud's introductory lectures on psychoanalysis.[22]

Producing text within a discourse community, then, cannot take place unless the writer can define her goals in terms of the community's interpretive conventions. Writing is always already writing for some purpose that can only be understood in its community context. Fish has argued not only that the community of literary critics proceeds in this way but furthermore, that the main business of English studies should be to investigate the nature of discourse communities (see Fish, pp. 338–55). It is exactly this sort of analysis that the Flower-Hayes model lacks when trying to explain planning. For Flower and Hayes, "generating" (a subdivision of planning) means finding ideas by using heuristics, not by responding with individual initiative to the community's needs. "Organizing" (another subdivision) means fitting ideas into the range of logical structures available from human thought processes, not finding out what's reasonable in terms of a community's interpretive conventions. In other words, all that's needed for generating and organizing is access to the invariant, universal structures of human cognition (for a critique of this assumption, see Dillon, pp. 50–82).

The weakness of this approach is most apparent in Flower and Hayes's treatment of "goal-setting." They correctly identify goal-setting as the motor of the composing process, its most important element, but in their model they close it off in the most subordinate position (a subdivision of a subdivision of the writing process). In the "Process Theory" essay, Flower and Hayes elaborate their description into "process goals" (directions for the writing process) and "content goals" (directions for affecting the audience), and they also classify goals in terms of levels of abstraction (see "Process Theory," p. 377). Their model's structure cannot order this multifarious account.

Flower and Hayes end the "Process Theory" essay with analysis of a "good" writer's protocol, aimed to explicate the process of goal-setting. The writer is having trouble deciding how to tell *Seventeen* readers about his job as a college English teacher until he decides that many girls think of English as a "tidy" and "prim" subject and that "By God I can change that notion for them." He goes on to frame an introduction that recounts a "crazy skit" his 101 class liked on the first day of school ("Process Theory," pp. 383, 385). Of his "By God" moment of decision, Flower and Hayes say that "he has regenerated and elaborated his top-level goals," and "this consolidation leaves the writer with a new, relatively complex, rhetorically sophisticated working goal, one which encompasses plans for a topic, a persona, and an audience" (p. 383).

Notice the verbs in this explanation: "regenerating" and "elaborating" goals "leave" the writer with regenerated ("new") and elaborated ("complex") goals—which "encompass" what he needs to know to go on writing. The action described here has no force as an explanation not only because it is circular (regeneration causes regeneration), but also because we still don't know where the new goals come from. Flower and Hayes suggest that going through a process simply "leaves" one with the goals, as if the process itself brought them into being. Upon arrival, the goals are found to contain ("encompass") the necessary knowledge—but we still don't know how that knowledge got there.

The *Seventeen* article writer's process of goal-setting, I think, can be better understood if we see it in terms of writing for a discourse community. His initial problem (which seems to be typical of most subjects confronted with this writing task) is to find a way to include these readers in a discourse community for which he is comfortable writing. He places them in the academic discourse community by imagining the girls as students ("they will all have had English," p. 383). Once he has included them in a familiar discourse community, he can find a way to address them that is common in the community: he will argue with them, putting a new interpretation on information they possess in order to correct misconceptions (his "By God" decision). In arguing, he can draw on all the familiar habits of persuasion he has built up in his experience as a teacher (his "crazy skit" decision). He could not have found a way to write this article if he did not have knowledge of a discourse community to draw on.

The Flower-Hayes model does, of course, include a "long-term memory" where such knowledge could be stored, and Flower and Hayes even acknowledge its importance:

> Sometimes a single cue in an assignment, such as "write a persuasive...,"
> can let a writer tap a stored representation of a problem and bring a whole
> raft of writing plans into play. (p. 371)

A "stored representation of a problem" must be a set of directions for producing a certain kind of text—what I have been calling discourse conventions. I would argue that the writer doesn't just tap this representation sometimes but every time a writing task is successfully accomplished. Flower and Hayes give this crucial determinant of text production very off-hand treatment, however. They seem to see writing in response to discourse conventions as response to "semiautomatic plans and goals" that contrast with "goals writers create for a particular paper" (p. 381). Evidently they are seeing discourse conventions simply as rules to be internalized, similar to their treatment of the "constraints" of written English. This reduction of conventions to sets of rules is also suggested by their choice of the limerick as a good example of a "genre" (p. 379).

Hence, although Flower and Hayes acknowledge the existence of discourse conventions, they fail to see conventions' generative power, which is to say that their notion of conventions does not include the interpretive function for which I have been arguing. This neglect of the role of knowledge in composing makes the Flower-Hayes theory particularly insensitive to the problems of poor writers.

> Poor writers will frequently depend on very abstract, undeveloped top-level goals, such as "appeal to a broad range of intellect," even though such goals are much harder to work with than a more operational goal such as "give a brief history of my job." Sondra Perl has seen this phenomenon in the basic writers who kept returning to reread the assignment, searching, it would seem, for ready-made goals, instead of forming their own. Alternatively, poor writers will depend on only very low-level goals, such as finishing a sentence or correctly spelling a word. They will be, as Nancy Sommers's student revisers were, locked in by the myopia in their own goals and criteria. (p. 379)

The implication here seems to be that cognitive deficiency keeps poor writers from forming their own goals, keeps them locked in the myopia of goals appropriate to a much earlier stage of cognitive development. The physical image of poor eyesight is revealing of Flower and Hayes's assumptions about the innate sources of writing problems.

I think these students' difficulties with goal-setting are better understood in terms of their unfamiliarity with the academic discourse community, combined, perhaps, with such limited experience outside their native discourse communities that they are unaware that there is such a thing as a discourse community with conventions to be mastered. What is underdeveloped is their knowledge of the ways experience is constituted and interpreted in the academic discourse community and of the fact that all discourse communities constitute and interpret experience. Basil Bernstein has shown that British working-class students are not cognitively deficient but that, first, their native discourse community's conventions are very different from school conventions, and, second, their lack of a variety of speech partners makes it hard for them to see their problems in school as problems of learning to relate to new speech partners (or an unfamiliar discourse community).[23]

Such students may be unable to set a more operational goal because they do not know the conventions of language-using that define such goals as, for example, a "history." Without such knowledge, they may fall back on goals that worked in the past—perhaps in grammar school where close attention to spelling and grammar was rewarded. Or they may sensibly try to enlarge their knowledge by rereading the assignment, seeking clues to the conventions of this new discourse community or those "ready-made goals" without which no writing gets accomplished. Of course, their search of the assignment may be fruitless if the teacher has not been sufficiently explicit about her expectations. Academics are, perhaps, too ready to assume that such operations as "describe" or "analyze" are self-evident, when in fact they have meanings specific to the academic discourse community and specific to disciplines within that community.

To help poor writers, then, we need to explain that their writing takes place within a community, and to explain what the community's conventions are. Another way of putting this would be to borrow Thomas Kuhn's terminology and explain that "puzzle-solving" writing can go on only under the direction of an established "paradigm" for community activity.[24] As Charles Bazerman's work has shown, the writer within the academic community knows how to relate her text to "the object under study, the literature of the field, the anticipated audience, and the author's own self" via discipline-specific conventions governing "lexicon," "explicit citation and implicit knowledge," "knowledge and attitudes the text assumes that the readers will have," and the "features" of a "public face" (Bazerman, pp. 362–63).

The Flower-Hayes model of writing, then, cannot alone give us a complete picture of the process. We might say that if this model describes the *form* of the composing process, the process cannot go on without the *content* which is knowledge of the conventions of discourse communities. In practice, however, form and content cannot be separated in this way, since discourse conventions shape the goals that drive the writing process. To let the model stand alone as an account of composing is to mask the necessity for the socially situated knowledge without which no writing project gets under way. The problems of letting this model stand alone can be seen in the pedagogy emerging from Flower and Hayes's work. They are inclined to treat the model itself as an heuristic:

> Our model is a model of competent writers. Some writers, though, perhaps to their disadvantage, may fail to use some of the processes. (*Cognitive Processes*, p. 29)

Flower has recently published a textbook that aims to guide students through a complete repertoire of composing strategies.[25]

The difficulty with the textbook's view of writing as problem-solving is that it treats problem-solving as an unfiltered encounter with the underlying structure of reality—"the act of discovering key issues in a problem that often lie hidden under the noisy details of the situation" (p. 21). Having defined a problem, one should: first, "fit it into a category of similar problems"; next, decide on a possible course of action against the problem ("make the problem definition more operational"); "tree" the problem or analyze its parts into a hierarchical structure; "generate alternative solutions"; present a conclusion, which weighs alternatives and acknowledges assumptions and implications of the conclusion (see pp. 21–26). But *first,* how does one define a problem? Although Flower says that "problems are only problems for someone," she doesn't talk about this necessary link between problem definition and interpretive communities (p. 21). Rather, it seems that we will *find* (not make) the problem if we strip away the "noisy details of the situation." I would argue, in contrast, that only the noisy details of the situation can define a problem. To "define" a problem is to interact with the material world according to the conventions of a particular discourse community; these conventions are the only source for categories of similar problems, operational definitions, and alternative solutions, and a conclusion can only be evaluated as "well supported" in terms of a particular community's standards.

I certainly do not mean to suggest that students should not be encouraged to look at reality when they compose—far from it, since I have emphasized the function of writing in doing (intellectual) work in the world. But I do mean to point out that we cannot look at reality in an unfiltered way—"reality" only makes sense when organized by the interpretive conventions of a discourse community. Students often complain that they have nothing to say, whereas "real-world" writers almost never do, precisely because real-world writers are writing for discourse communities in which they know their work can matter, whereas students can see little purpose for their own attempts ("essais") other than to get a grade. For example, Erwin Steinberg has suggested that the superior organization of an electrical engineer's report, as compared to a freshman composition, stems from the engineer's superior knowledge of and experience in a field; what looks like a cognitive difference turns out to have a large social component (see "A Garden of Opportunities and a Thicket of Dangers," *Cognitive Processes,* pp. 163–165). Hence, although Steinberg is sympathetic to the project of finding writing models and heuristics, he cautions, "We must always be careful not to think in terms of a single model, because if we do we'll find one and force everyone to use it—the way English teachers used to require students to make formal outlines before they wrote" (p. 163).

The cognitive psychology approach cuts off writing-as-problem-solving from the context of a discourse community precisely because *one* model is sought (Steinberg's caveat notwithstanding). Discourse communities are tied to historical and cultural circumstances, and hence can only be seen as unenlightening instances of the general theory the cognitive approach seeks: the one model is the universal one. All of the theoretical essays in

Cognitive Processes in Writing seek to find this model. Carl Bereiter offers an account of the stages of development in children's writing processes. Like the Flower-Hayes model, his is recursive—that is, he suggests that children's development includes a certain set of stages but that the order of these stages can be changed. There is, however, a "preferred or 'natural' order of writing development," an order in which the constraints on composing imposed by the necessity of putting thoughts into words are gradually reduced by being "automatized." Bereiter suggests that this order should be adopted in the schools (see "Development in Writing," p. 89).

Collins and Gentner seek to go even further in schematizing their theory as a rule-governed model because they hope to end with a program enabling a computer to compose (see "A Framework for a Cognitive Theory of Writing," pp. 51–52). This would permit the creation of "Writing Land," where computers would guide students through the patterns of the writing process and enhance the students' cognitive activities (see "Framework," pp. 67–70). Computer-assisted composition will help students reduce the constraints imposed by the struggle to put thoughts into words by separating "idea production" and "text production" ("Framework," p. 53). Once the ideas are under control, "the next stage is to impose text structure on the ideas" ("Framework," p. 59).

During text production, Collins and Gentner confidently state, the writer can call on "structural devices, stylistic devices, and content devices"—the term "devices" suggesting rule-governed mechanisms. Yet "unfortunately for the writer, there is no one-to-one correspondence between means and end here"—in other words, no consistency in situation that would permit reliance on rule-governed mechanisms ("Framework," p. 60). Collins and Gentner's analysis frequently bumps up against language's opacity, the contribution to thinking of densely situation-bound meanings embodied in habits of language-using. Because they cannot account for this situational aspect of writing, Collins and Gentner can only define "good writing" as writing that conforms to a set of rules set by some authority (see "Framework," pp. 52–53). This approach leaves them no way to justify the authority's decisions as other than arbitrary, and hence their "rules" turn out to be situation-bound: "Delete extraneous material," "Shorten long paragraphs," and so on ("Framework," p. 65). Such advice is unhelpful to students without other knowledge that enables them to identify the extraneous and over-lengthy, as I noted earlier in my discussion of revising rules.

The fundamental problem with this approach is that it assumes that the rules we can formulate to describe behavior are the same rules that produce the behavior. As attempts to program language-using computers have shown, such structures reveal their lack of explanatory power when applied to an actual situation in which discourse conventions come into play. Programming a computer to use language comes up against a problem of infinite regress of context—or, how do we tell the computer how to tell what's important when things are important only in terms of purposive activity? How can we define, for example, what is "extraneous material," when the quality of being extraneous resides not in the material itself but in its relation to discourse? Or, to use a simpler example, how can we tell the computer when a paragraph is too long except by specifying a range of lines that constitute acceptable lengths? Is there any form of discourse in which 20-line paragraphs are acceptable and 21-line paragraphs are not? As the competence/performance debate in linguistics has suggested, it may be that we cannot have a completely descriptive theory of behavior in widely varying specific situations—that is, we cannot formulate universal rules for context-bound activities. If language-using isn't rule-governed in this sense, however, it still may be regular—that is, we may be able to group situations as likely to share a number of language-using features. But to do this is to describe the conventions of discourse communities.[26]

As I have been arguing, then, both the inner-directed and the outer-directed theoretical schools will have to contribute to a synthesis capable of providing a comprehensive new agenda for composition studies. My critique of Flower and Hayes's work is intended to contribute to such a synthesis, not to delegitimate what they are doing. I do want to raise a serious question, however, about another feature of the inner-directed school, a feature that works against fruitful discussion and synthesis: the quest for certainty. In seeking one universal model of the composing process, inner-directed theorists seek a new set of principles for our discipline that will raise their arguments, as one has put it, "above mere ideology" (Hirsch, p. 4). They seek a kind of certainty they believe is accessible only to science, and their talk of paradigm-shifting invokes Kuhn to announce that our discipline will soon have a scientific basis.[27]

This kind of certainty is presumably analogous to the commonplace elevation of fact over opinion, since it is supposed to end all debate. The inner-directed school therefore has redefined composition research to mean a search for the facts in the real world that prove a theory beyond debate. The Flower-Hayes model claims much prestige from being derived from such supposedly unimpeachable evidence. But its reliance on empirical evidence can be questioned on several grounds. For one thing, protocol analysis is a controversial method even within cognitive psychology because it tends to affect what is being observed (see Gould's remarks, *Cognitive*

Processes, p. 125). Flower and Hayes's work is particularly vulnerable because most of their adult subjects have been English teachers who are familiar with the specialized vocabulary of the theory Flower and Hayes have used to analyze the protocols. Under any circumstances, protocol analysis can lead to "self-fulfilling" prophecy because its assumption that the subject's words mirror her thinking allows the researcher to claim that certain thought processes have occurred if certain words appear in the protocol. Self-fulfilling prophecy is even more likely when test subjects share expert knowledge of these words with the researchers.

The larger point to be made here, however, is that no scientific research, no matter how rigorously it is conducted, possesses the kind of authoritative certainty inner-directed theorists are seeking.[28] It is always desirable, of course, to know more about composing, but it is also necessary to treat this knowledge as provisional, the way scientists treat their findings, if inquiry is not to end. We may wonder, then, why inner-directed theorists are so ready to invest their results with final authority and rush to pedagogical applications. I think it is that certainty appeals to composition specialists these days for various reasons. For one, until recently composition studies was a low-status enclave it was hard to escape; a powerful theory would help us retaliate against the literary critics who dominate English studies. Moreover, such a theory might help us survive what appears to be the long slide of all humanistic disciplines into a low-status enclave. A scientific-sounding theory promises an "accountability" hedge against hard times.

The strongest appeal of certainty, however, is its offer of a solution to our new students' problems that will enable us to undertake their socialization into the academic discourse community without having to consider the ethical and political dimensions of this act. We are reluctant to take up ethical and political questions about what we do because writing teachers have been under a terrific strain. Pressured with increasing asperity by our colleges to prepare students for their other courses, we have also felt anxious in the classroom both when our teaching worked—because we sensed that we were wiping out the students' own culture—and when it didn't—because we were cheating them of a chance to better their situations. Inner-directed pedagogy meets teachers' emotional needs because it can be defended on grounds that are likely to satisfy complaining faculty and administrators, and because its claim to a basis in universals assures us that when we inculcate it, we aren't touching the students' own culture but merely giving them a way around it and up the ladder of success. The corollary is that students for whom the pedagogy doesn't work need no longer be seen as victims of our incompetence but simply as innately inferior.

Invocation of certainty, then, performs the rhetorical function of invocation of the Deity. It guarantees the transcendent authority of values for which we do not need to argue but which we can now apply with the confidence of a "good cause." I would argue, however, that we must understand such a move as the assigning of superhuman authority to a human construction. All knowledge, that is, is of human origin, even scientific knowledge. Indeed, modern philosophy has centered around a critique of scientific knowledge precisely because such knowledge is most likely now to be treated as certain. As Richard Rorty has recently shown, the history of Western philosophy since the Renaissance can be seen as a series of unsuccessful attempts to fight off the admission that such claims for certainty are no longer tenable.[29] There is no way out of confrontation, except among fellow believers, with the necessity of arguing for one's ethical choices.

This confrontation is especially necessary in a pluralistic society such as the United States, in which a heterogeneous school population ensures that pedagogical choices will affect students unequally. Under such circumstances, as Rorty cautions, claims to certainty often express simply a desire for agreement which masks the question of whose interests are being served (see Rorty, p. 335). Teachers' individual ethical choices add up to political consequences, responsibility for which we cannot avoid. We are better off, then, with a disciplinary theory that encourages examination of consequences. For example, inner-directed research might come up with an heuristic that is useful in Basic Writing classes. But if we use it there, we should not imagine that the heuristic allows us to forget who the students are in Basic Writing classes, where they come from, what their prospects are — in short, why these particular students are having educational difficulties.

Ultimately, I am calling for the inspection of what some curriculum theorists have called the "hidden curriculum": the project of initiating students into a particular world view that gives rise to the daily classroom tasks without being consciously examined by teacher or students.[30] If we call what we are teaching "universal" structures or processes, we bury the hidden curriculum even deeper by claiming that our choice of material owes nothing to historical circumstances. To do this is to deny the school's function as an agent of cultural hegemony, or the selective valuation and transmission of world views. The result for students who don't share the school's preferred world views is either failure or deracination. I think we must acknowledge

387

cultural differences in the classroom, even though this means increasing our emotional strain as members of one group trying to mediate contacts among various others.

The kind of pedagogy that would foster responsible inspection of the politically loaded hidden curriculum in composition class is discourse analysis. The exercise of cultural hegemony can be seen as the treatment of one community's discourse conventions as if they simply mirrored reality. To point out that discourse conventions exist would be to politicize the classroom—or rather, to make everyone aware that it is already politicized. World views would become more clearly a matter of conscious commitment, instead of unconscious conformity, if the ways in which they are constituted in discourse communities were analyzed.

This is not to say that we can make the school an ideologically neutral place. The whole force of my argument is that there is no way to *escape* all discourse communities, stand outside them and pronounce judgment. Furthermore, I assent to most of the conventions of the academic discourse community and believe that students from other communities can benefit from learning about them, and learning them. But perhaps we can break up the failure/deracination dilemma for students from communities at a distance from academe. Through discourse analysis we might offer them an understanding of their school difficulties as the problems of a traveler to an unfamiliar country—yet a country in which it is possible to learn the language and the manners and even "go native" while still remembering the land from which one has come.

In his discussion of literary criticism and interpretive communities, Stanley Fish has offered us one set of suggestions for how such ethically and politically conscious education might proceed. Richard Rorty offers another in his vision of philosophy becoming not the arbiter of disciplines but the mediator among them. This "edifying" philosophy will have as its task making us realize that agreement that looks like certainty can occur only "because when a practice has continued long enough the conventions which make it possible—and which permit a consensus on how to divide it into parts—are relatively easy to isolate" (p. 321). Rorty's is not a positivist notion of arbitrary conventions; he sees conventions as the product of communities, situation-bound but also subject to change. Rorty generalizes Kuhn's notions of "normal" and "revolutionary" science to argue that the edifying philosopher's task is to keep reminding us that "normal" discourse is evidently clear and above debate only because we agree about its conventions. Education must begin with normal discourse but should not be limited to it, with its unhelpful distinction between facts and values (see p. 363). For the goal of discovering Truth, Rorty substitutes the goal of continuing conversation, but this will not be a dangerously relativistic goal because always conditioned by and having to answer to an historical framework. Rorty's philosophical community thus resembles Fish's interpretive community.

Finally, then, we should see our answers to the question of what we need to know about writing in the light of a new humanistic synthesis. Philosophy has moved to the position that discourse communities are all we have to rely upon in our quest for certainty. Literary criticism is analyzing how discourse communities function as historically situated interpretive communities. Composition studies should focus upon practice within interpretive communities—exactly how conventions work in the world and how they are transmitted. If the work of these disciplines continues to converge, a new synthesis will emerge that revivifies rhetoric as the central discipline of human intellectual endeavor. In view of such a synthesis, the project to make composition studies merely scientific looks obsolete.

I hope that this rhetorical synthesis, because it turns our attention to questions of value and persuasion, will also reawaken us to the collective nature of the whole educational endeavor. There should be no disgrace in discovering that one's work and the understanding that guides it cannot be achieved autonomously. Then the main casualty of our theoretical debate can be the debilitating individualism that adds so much to classroom strain. In other words, let us emphasize not only discourse but also community. I do not mean that we should seek to eliminate the conflicts that arise from our coming from different historical and cultural situations. We should recognize that being so situated is the most important thing we have in common.[31]

NOTES

1. The attitude I'm describing here has been called current-traditionalism, and it still dominates textbooks in the field; see Donald C. Stewart, "Composition Textbooks and the Assault on Tradition," *College Composition and Communication*, 29 (May 1978), pp. 171–76.

2. I am taking this sense of "isomorphic" from Frank D'Angelo, *A Conceptual Theory of Rhetoric* (Cambridge, Mass.: Winthrop, 1975), pp. 16, 26–36.

3. I have in mind here the justification for teaching Standard English advanced in E.D. Hirsch, Jr., *The Philosophy of Composition* (Chicago: Univ. of Chicago Press, 1977).

4. For example, Richard Young has recently characterized his particle-wave-field heuristic as based on "universal invariants that underlie all human experience as characteristic of rationality itself"; in "Arts, Crafts, Gifts, and Knacks: Some Disharmonies in the New Rhetoric," *Visible Language*, 14, no. 4 (1980), 347.

5. For an overview of research on sentence-combining and the arguments for teaching it, see Frank O'Hare, *Sentence Combining: Improving Student Writing without Formal Grammar Instruction* (Urbana, Illinois: NCTE, 1973).

6. A new textbook that operates from these principles of audience analysis (and other inner-directed pedagogy) is Janice M. Lauer, Gene Montague, Andrea Lunsford, and Janet Emig, *Four Worlds of Writing* (New York: Harper and Row, 1981).

7. Typically, a discourse community prefers one form of the native tongue, which may be characterized simply by level of formality and specialized vocabulary, or which may be a dialect, or a fully constituted language (in the native tongue's family) with its own grammar rules. The outer-directed theorists thus emphasize "parole" over "langue," to use de Saussure's terms, "performance" over "competence," to use Chomsky's terms. For a good account of such language differences in an American setting, see William Labov, *The Study of Nonstandard English* (1969; revised and enlarged; Urbana, Illinois: NCTE, 1975).

8. See, for example, M.A.K. Halliday, "Language as Social Semiotic," *Language as Social Semiotic* (Baltimore: University Park Press, 1978), pp. 108–26.

9. This attitude has been called the Sapir-Whorf hypothesis, because arguments are advanced for it by linguists Edward Sapir and his pupil, Benjamin Lee Whorf; for a good summary and critique of the Sapir-Whorf hypothesis, see Adam Schaff, *Language and Cognition* (1964; trans. Olgierd Wojtasiewicz, ed. Robert S. Cohen; New York: McGraw-Hill, 1973).

10. This, I think, is the gist of the analysis offered by Mina Shaughnessy, "Beyond the Sentence," *Errors and Expectations* (New York: Oxford Univ. Press, 1977), pp. 226–72.

11. A new textbook that operates from some principles of outer-directed pedagogy is Elaine Maimon, Gerald L. Belcher, Gail W. Hearn, Barbara F. Nodine, and Finbarr W. O'Connor, *Writing in the Arts and Sciences* (Cambridge, Massachusetts: Winthrop, 1981).

12. For an exemplary analysis of academic discourse conventions and how they lead to the accomplishment of the community's work, see Charles Bazerman, "What Written Knowledge Does: Three Examples of Academic Discourse," *Philosophy of the Social Sciences*, 11 (September 1981), pp. 361–87; further references in text.

13. Linda Flower and John R. Hayes, "A Cognitive Process Theory of Writing," *College Composition and Communication*, 32 (December 1981), pp. 365–87; further references in text.

14. Lee W. Gregg and Erwin R. Steinberg, editors, *Cognitive Processes in Writing* (Hillsdale, New Jersey: Lawrence Erlbaum, 1980); further references in text.

15. Lev Vygotsky, *Thought and Language* (1934; rpt. ed. & trans. Eugenia Hanfmann and Gertrude Vakar; Cambridge, Mass.: MIT Press, 1962), p. 51, author's emphasis; further references in text. Vygotsky's pupil A.R. Luria did research among Uzbek peasants which suggests that thought and language interpenetrate to such a degree that perception of optical illusions, for example, changes with cultural experience and level of education; see A.R. Luria, *Cognitive Development* (1974; rpt. trans. Martin Lopez-Morillas and Lynn Solotaroff, ed. Michael Cole; Cambridge, Mass.: Harvard Univ. Press, 1976).

16. See M.A.K. Halliday and Ruqaiya Hasan, *Cohesion in English* (London: Longman, 1976), pp. 19–26.

17. My line of argument here is based on Dell Hymes, "Bilingual Education: Linguistic vs. Sociolinguistic Bases," *Foundations in Sociolinguistics* (Philadelphia: Univ. of Pennsylvania Press, 1974), pp. 119–24; in the same volume, Hymes argues that to uncover the extralinguistic attitudes lending significance to language use, linguists need more contributions from folklorists.

18. George L. Dillon, *Constructing Texts* (Bloomington, Indiana: Indiana Univ. Press, 1981), pp. 1–20; further references in text.

19. A critique of the notion of simplicity-as-clarity has been offered by Richard Lanham, *Style: An Anti-Textbook* (New Haven, Conn.: Yale Univ. Press, 1974). Lanham's later work in composition pedagogy suggests, however, that he is cynical about the position taken in *Style* and not really ready to defend "ornate" language choices outside of special literary circumstances; see Richard Lanham, *Revising Prose* (New York: Scribner, 1979). Dillon, pp. 21–49, is more helpful on understanding the problems with revising rules.

20. Halliday, "Language in Urban Society," p. 163; Halliday suggests that our current difficulties in the composition class may be at least in part a function of the increasing number of students who come from urban areas.

21. See Stanley Fish, *Is There a Text in this Class?* (Cambridge, Mass.: Harvard Univ. Press, 1980), further references in text; the following argument is heavily indebted to Fish's work.

22. Mina Shaughnessy, "Some Needed Research on Writing," *College Composition and Communication*, 27 (December 1977), p. 319.

23. See Basil Bernstein, *Class, Codes and Control* (1971; rpt. New York: Schocken, 1975); and to correct the vulgar error that Bernstein is diagnosing a cognitive deficiency in working-class language, see "The Significance of Bernstein's Work for Sociolinguistic Theory" in Halliday, pp. 101–107. Many dangerous misinterpretations of Bernstein could perhaps have been avoided if he had not chosen to call working-class language-using habits a "restricted code" and middle-class (school-oriented) habits an "elaborated code."

24. The seminal text here is Thomas Kuhn, *The Structure of Scientific Revolutions*, 2d. edition, enlarged (Chicago: Univ. of Chicago Press, 1970). Kuhn is now going so far as to say that "proponents of different theories (or different paradigms, in the broader sense of the term) speak different languages—languages expressing different cognitive commitments, suitable for different worlds"; he announces the study of language's function in theory-making as his current project. See Thomas Kuhn, *The Essential Tension* (Chicago: Univ. of Chicago Press, 1977), pp. 22–23.

25. Linda Flower, *Problem-Solving Strategies for Writing* (New York: Harcourt Brace Jovanovich, 1981); further references in text.

26. In my discussion of Collins and Gentner, I am following the line of argument offered by Hubert L. Dreyfus, *What Computers Can't Do* (New York: Harper and Row, 1972); rpt. 2d. edition, San Francisco: Freeman, 1979). Flower and Hayes's sympathy with the Collins-Gentner approach is suggested not only by the large amount of agreement between the two accounts of composing, but also by the numerous borrowings in the Flower-Hayes model from computer terminology and by Flower and Hayes's suggestion that their model will contribute toward "building a Writer" ("Process Theory," p. 368).

27. For an example of this use of Kuhn, see Maxine Hairston, "The Winds of Change: Thomas Kuhn and the Revolution in the Teaching of Writing," *College Composition and Communication*, 33 (February 1982), pp. 76–88.

28. This argument follows the account of rhetoric's function in the scientific discourse community given by Kuhn in *Structure* and (in a more radical version) by Paul Feyerabend, *Against Method* (1975; rpt. London: Verso, 1978).

29. Richard Rorty, *Philosophy and the Mirror of Nature* (Princeton, NJ: Princeton Univ. Press, 1979); further references in text.

30. On the hidden curriculum and its reproduction of oppressive social power relations, see Michael Apple, *Ideology and Curriculum* (London: Routledge and Kegan Paul, 1979).

31. I would like to thank Bruce Herzberg for the many ideas and the editorial guidance that he has, as usual, contributed to my work.

Talking about Writing in Society

Positivism has been the dominant paradigm for Western society for nearly four centuries, its premises and assumptions rarely questioned for most of that time. It is no wonder, then, that contemporary composition studies would look to the sciences for explanations about what happens in writing. But anthropological study and various elements of critical theory, beginning in the later 1960s, put serious questions to positivism, to positivism's search for universal answers, to the very idea that we can think in terms of the universal.

Composition studies turned to three lines of inquiry in its search for alternatives to positivism. Comp turned to anthropology's social construction theory and its ethnographic research methodologies. Composition also turned to continental philosophical, psychological, and critical theories of poststructuralism. And composition turned to Stanley Fish's term *anti-foundationalism,* contained in his 1989 *Doing What Comes Naturally: Change, Rhetoric, and the Practice of Theory in Literary and Legal Studies* (Durham, NC: Duke UP). Anti-foundationalism, poststructuralism, social construction theory say in common that there can be no universal truths, no truths free from contextual particularities. Everything contains reflections, to some degree or other, of the cultural, historical, and political contexts in which inquiry takes place. And to the extent that they are political, they also include points of contact, places where cultures collide and eventually intermingle. These spaces where cultures meet (usually in unequal terms, as matters of conquest and conquered) are what linguist Mary Louise Pratt calls *contact zones,* a term which has captured the imagination of those who would turn to the social in composition studies, since it captures the cultural, the historical, the political, and the rhetorical. Scientism or positivism, on the other hand, appears inherently flawed, in its claiming to transcend the social and political, thereby failing to make explicit (or even to recognize) the effects of the social and the political in its inquiries. Pratt also introduced us to the term *autoethnography*, in which those who had been the subjects of study tell their own tales. And this tendency has extended to us all, causing us to question the nature of personal discourse. Finally, if we are to be social, we must also include social responsibility: the work of service learning.

Collaborative Learning and the "Conversation of Mankind"

KENNETH A. BRUFFEE

There are some signs these days that collaborative learning is of increasing interest to English teachers.[1] Composition teachers seem to be exploring the concept actively. Two years ago the term appeared for the first time in the list of topics suggested by the Executive Committee of the Conference on College Composition and Communication for discussion at the CCCC annual convention. It was eighth or ninth on a list of ten items. Last year it appeared again, first on the list.

Teachers of literature have also begun to talk about collaborative learning, although not always by that name. It is viewed as a way of engaging students more deeply with the text and also as an aspect of professors' engagement with the professional community. At its 1978 convention the Modern Language Association scheduled a multi-session forum entitled "Presence, Knowledge, and Authority in the Teaching of Literature." One of the associated sessions, called "Negotiations of Literary Knowledge," included a discussion of the authority and structure (including the collaborative classroom structure) of "interpretive communities." At the 1983 MLA convention collaborative practices in reestablishing authority and value in literary studies were examined under such rubrics as "Talking to the Academic Community: Conferences as Institutions" and "How Books 11 and 12 of *Paradise Lost* Got to be Valuable" (changes in interpretive attitudes in the community of Miltonists).

Reprinted from *College English* 46.7 (November 1984): 635–52. Used with permission. Readers may find more recent explorations of issues discussed in this article in Kenneth A. Bruffee, *Collaborative Learning: Higher Education, Interdependence, and the Authority of Knowledge* (Baltimore: Johns Hopkins University Press, 2nd edition, 1999).

In both these contexts collaborative learning is discussed sometimes as a process that constitutes fields or disciplines of study and sometimes as a pedagogical tool that "works" in teaching composition and literature. The former discussion, often highly theoretical, usually manages to keep at bay the more troublesome and problematic aspects of collaborative learning. The discussion of classroom practice is less fortunate. What emerges there is that many teachers are unsure about how to use collaborative learning and about when and where, appropriately, it should be used. Many are concerned also that when they try to use collaborative learning in what seem to be effective and appropriate ways, it sometimes quite simply fails.

I sympathize with these experiences. Much the same thing has happened to me. Sometimes collaborative learning works beyond my highest expectations. Sometimes it doesn't work at all. Recently, though, I think I have been more successful. The reason for that increased success seems to be that I know a little more now than I did in the past about the complex ideas that lie behind collaborative learning. This essay is frankly an attempt to encourage other teachers to try collaborative learning and to help them use collaborative learning appropriately and effectively. But it offers no recipes. It is written instead on the assumption that understanding both the history and the complex ideas that underlie collaborative learning can improve its practice and demonstrate its educational value.

The history of collaborative learning as I know it can be briefly sketched. Collaborative learning began to interest American college teachers widely only in the 1980s, but the term was coined and the basic idea first developed in the 1950s and 1960s by a group of British secondary school teachers and by a biologist studying British post-graduate education—specifically, medical education. I myself first encountered the term and some of the ideas implicit in it in Edwin Mason's still interesting but now somewhat dated polemic entitled *Collaborative Learning* (London: Ward Lock Educational Co., 1970), and in Charity James' *Young Lives at Stake: A Reappraisal of Secondary Schools* (London: Collins, 1968). Mason, James, and Leslie Smith, colleagues at Goldsmith's College, University of London, were committed during the Vietnam era to democratizing education and to eliminating from education what were perceived then as socially destructive authoritarian social forms. Collaborative learning as they thought of it emerged from this largely political, topical effort.

The collaborative forms that Mason and his colleagues proposed to establish in education had already been explored and their educational value affirmed, however, by the earlier findings of M. L. J. Abercrombie. Abercrombie's *Anatomy of Judgment* (Harmondsworth: Penguin, 1964) culminated ten years of research on the selection and training of medical students at University College, University of London. The result of her research was to suggest that diagnosis, the art of medical judgment and the key element in successful medical practice, is better learned in small groups of students arriving at diagnoses collaboratively than it is learned by students working individually. Abercrombie began her study by observing the scene that lay people think is most typical of medical education: the group of medical students with a teaching physician gathered around a ward bed to diagnose a patient. She then made a seemingly slight but in outcome enormously important change in the way that scene is usually played out. Instead of asking each individual member of the group of students to diagnose the patient on his or her own, Abercrombie asked the whole group to examine the patient together, discuss the case as a group, and arrive at a consensus, a single diagnosis that they could all agree to. What she found was that students learning diagnosis this way acquired good medical judgment faster than individuals working alone (p. 19).

For American college teachers the roots of collaborative learning lie neither in radical politics nor in research. They lie in the nearly desperate response of harried colleges during the early 1970s to a pressing educational need. A decade ago, faculty and administrators in institutions throughout the country became aware that, increasingly, students entering college had difficulty doing as well in academic studies as their native ability suggested they should be able to do. Of course, some of these students were poorly prepared academically. Many more of them, however, had on paper excellent secondary preparation. The common denominator among both the poorly prepared and the seemingly well-prepared was that, for cultural reasons we may not yet fully understand, all these students seemed to have difficulty adapting to the traditional or "normal" conventions of the college classroom.

One symptom of the difficulty these students had adapting to college life and work was that many refused help when it was offered. The help colleges offered, in the main, were tutoring and counseling programs staffed by graduate students and other professionals. These programs failed because undergraduates refused to use them. Many solutions to this problem were suggested and tried, from mandated programs that forced students to accept help they evidently did not want, to sink-or-swim programs that assumed that students who needed help but didn't seek it out didn't belong in college anyway. One idea that seemed at the time among the most exotic and unlikely (that is, in the jargon of the 60s, among the most "radical") turned out in the event to work rather well. Taking hints about the social organization of learning given by John Bremer, Michael von Moschzisker, and others writing at that time about changes in primary and secondary education, some college faculty members guessed that students were refusing help because the kind of help provided seemed merely an extension of the work, the expectations, and above all the social structure of traditional classroom learning (*The School Without Walls* [New York: Holt, 1971], p. 7). It was traditional classroom learning that seemed to have left these students unprepared in the first place. What they needed, it seemed, was help that was not an extension of but an alternative to traditional classroom teaching.

To provide that alternative some colleges turned to peer tutoring. Through peer tutoring teachers could reach students by organizing them to teach each other. And peer tutoring, it turned out, was just one way of doing that, although perhaps the most readily institutionalized way. Collectively, peer tutoring and similar modes such as peer criticism and classroom group work could be sensibly classified under the convenient term provided by our colleagues in Britain: collaborative learning. What the term meant in practice was a form of indirect teaching in which the teacher sets the problem and organizes students to work it out collaboratively. For example, in one type of collaborative learning, peer criticism (also called peer evaluation), students learn to describe the organizational structure of a peer's paper, paraphrase it, and comment both on what seems well done and what the author might do to improve the work. The teacher then evaluates both the essay and the critical response. In another type of collaborative learning, classroom group work, students in small groups work toward a consensus in response to a task set by the teacher, for example, a question about a play, a poem, or another student's paper. What distinguished collaborative learning in each of its several types from traditional classroom practice was that it did not seem to change what people learned (a supposition that now seems questionable) so much as it changed the social context in which they learned it. Students' work tended to improve when they got help from peers; peers offering help, furthermore, learned from the students they helped and from the activity of helping itself. Collaborative learning, it seemed, harnessed the powerful educative force of peer influence that had been—and largely still is—ignored and hence wasted by traditional forms of education.[2]

More recently, those of us actively interested in collaborative learning have begun to think further about this practical experience. Recent developments in philosophy seem to suggest a conceptual rationale for collaborative learning that yields some unexpected insights into pedagogical practice. A new conception of the nature of knowledge provides direction that we lacked earlier as we muddled through, trying to solve practical problems in practical ways. The better we understand this conceptional rationale, it seems, the more effective our practice of collaborative learning becomes.

In the hope that this experience will prove true for others, the following three sections outline the rationale of collaborative learning as I currently understand it and the relation of that rationale to classroom practice. The final section outlines some as yet not fully worked out implications both of collaborative learning as a practice and of some aspects of its conceptual rationale. Practice and rationale together, I will argue there, have the potential to challenge fairly deeply the theory and practice of traditional classroom teaching.

CONVERSATION AND THE NATURE OF THOUGHT AND KNOWLEDGE

In an important essay on the place of literature in education published some twenty years ago, "The Voice of Poetry in the Conversation of Mankind," Michael Oakeshott argues that what distinguishes human beings from other animals is our ability to participate in unending conversation. "As civilized human beings," Oakeshott writes,

> we are the inheritors, neither of an inquiry about ourselves and the world, nor of an accumulating body of information, but of a conversation, begun in the primeval forests and extended and made more articulate in the course of centuries. It is a conversation which goes on both in public and within each of ourselves. . . . Education, properly speaking, is an initiation into the skill and partnership of this conversation in which we learn to recognize the voices, to distinguish the proper occasions of utterance, and in which we acquire the intellectual and moral habits appropriate to conversation. And it is this conversation which, in the end, gives place and character to every human activity and utterance. (*Rationalism in Politics* [New York: Basic Books, 1962], p. 199)

Oakeshott argues that the human conversation takes place within us as well as among us, and that conversation as it takes place within us is what we call reflective thought. In making this argument he assumes that conversation and reflective thought are related in two ways: causally and functionally. That is, Oakeshott assumes what the work of Lev Vygotsky and others has shown, that reflective thought is public or social conversation internalized (see, for example, Vygotsky, *Mind and Society* [Cambridge, Mass.: Harvard University Press, 1978]). We first experience and learn "the skill and partnership of conversation" in the external arena of direct social exchange with other people. Only then do we learn to displace that "skill and partnership" by playing silently ourselves, in imagination, the parts of all the participants in the conversation. As Clifford Geertz has put it,

> thinking as an overt, public act, involving the purposeful manipulation of objective materials, is probably fundamental to human beings; and thinking as a covert, private act, and without recourse to such materials [is] a derived, though not unuseful, capability. . . . Human thought is consumately social: social in its origins, social in its functions, social in its form, social in its applications.[3]

Since what we experience as reflective thought is related causally to social conversation (we learn one from the other), the two are also related functionally. That is, because thought is internalized conversation, thought and conversation tend to work largely in the same way. Of course, in thought some of the limitations of conversation are absent. Logistics, for example, are no problem at all. I don't have to take the A train or Eastern Airlines flight #221 to get together with myself for a chat. And in thought there are no differences among the participants in preparation, interest, native ability, or spoken vernacular. Each one is just as clever as I can be, or just as dull. On the other hand, in thought some of the less fortunate limitations of conversation may persist. Limitations that may be imposed, for example, by ethnocentrism, inexperience, personal anxiety, economic interests, and paradigmatic inflexibility can constrain my thinking just as they can constrain conversation. If my talk is narrow, superficial, biased, and confined to cliches, my thinking is likely to be so too.

The relationship I have been drawing here between conversation and thought illuminates the source of the quality, depth, terms, character, and issues of thought. The assumptions underlying my argument differ considerably, however, from the assumptions we ordinarily make about the nature of thought. We ordinarily assume that thought is some sort of given, an "essential attribute" of the human mind. The view that conversation and thought are causally related assumes not that thought is an essential attribute of the human mind but that it is instead an artifact created by social interaction. We can think because we can talk, and we think in ways we have learned to talk. As Stanley Fish has put it, the thoughts we "can think and the mental

Still, it remains the case that according to this concept of mental activity many of the social forms and conventions of conversation, most of the grammatical, syntactical and rhetorical structures of conversation, and the range, flexibility, impetus, and goals of conversation are the sources of the forms and conventions, structures, impetus, range and flexibility, and the issues of reflective thought.

operations [we] can perform have their source in some or other interpretive community."[4] The range, complexity, and subtlety of our thought, its power, the practical and conceptual uses we can put it to, and the very issues we can address result in large measure directly from the degree to which we have been initiated into what Oakeshott calls the potential "skill and partnership" of human conversation in its public and social form.

To the extent that thought is internalized conversation, then, any effort to understand how we think requires us to understand the nature of conversation; and any effort to understand conversation requires us to understand the nature of community life that generates and maintains conversation. Furthermore, any effort to understand and cultivate in ourselves the kind of thought we value most requires us to understand and cultivate the kinds of community life that establish and maintain conversation that is the origin of that kind of thought. To think well as individuals we must learn to think well collectively—that is, we must learn to converse well. The first steps to learning to think better, therefore, are learning to converse better and learning to establish and maintain the sorts of social context, the sorts of community life, that foster the sorts of conversation members of the community value.

This principle has broad applicability and has implications far beyond those that may be immediately apparent. For example, Thomas Kuhn has argued in *The Structure of Scientific Revolutions*, (2nd ed.: Chicago: University of Chicago Press, 1970) that to understand scientific thought and knowledge we must understand the nature of scientific communities. Scientific knowledge changes not as our "understanding of the world" changes. It changes as scientists organize and reorganize relations among themselves (pp. 209–10). Carrying Kuhn's view and terminology further, Richard Rorty argues in *Philosophy and the Mirror of Nature* (Princeton: Princeton University Press, 1979) that to understand any kind of knowledge we must understand what he calls the social justification of belief. That is, we must understand how knowledge is established and maintained in the "normal discourse" of communities of knowledgeable peers.[5] Stanley Fish completes the argument by saying that these "interpretive communities" are the source of our thought and of the "meanings" we produce through the use and manipulation of symbolic structures, chiefly language. Fish suggests further, reflecting Erving Goffman's conclusion to *The Presentation of Self in Everyday Life* ([New York: Doubleday Anchor, 1959], pp. 252–53), that interpretative communities may also be in large measure the source of what we regard as our very selves (Fish, p. 14). Our feelings and intuitions are as much the product of social relations as our knowledge.

401

EDUCATIONAL IMPLICATIONS:
CONVERSATION, COLLABORATIVE LEARNING,
AND "NORMAL DISCOURSE"

The line of argument I have been pursuing has important implications for educators, and especially for those of us who teach English—both literature and composition. If thought is internalized public and social talk, then writing of all kinds is internalized social talk made public and social again. If thought is internalized conversation, then writing is internalized conversation re-externalized.[6]

Like thought, writing is related to conversation in both time and function. Writing is a technologically displaced form of conversation. When we write, having already internalized the "skill and partnership" of conversation, we displace it once more onto the written page. But because thought is already one step away from conversation, the position of writing relative to conversation is more complex than the position of thought relative to conversation. Writing is at once two steps away from conversation and a return to conversation. We converse; we internalize conversation as thought; and then by writing, we re-immerse conversation in its external, social medium.

My ability to write this essay, for example, depends on my ability to talk through with myself the issues I address here. And my ability to talk through an issue with myself derives largely from my ability to converse directly with other people in an immediate social situation. The point is not that the particular thing I write every time must necessarily be something I have talked over with other people first, although I may well often do just that. What I have to say can, of course, originate in thought, and it often does. But my thought itself is conversation as I have learned to internalize it. The point, therefore, is that writing always has its roots deep in the acquired ability to carry on the social symbolic exchange we call conversation.

The inference writing teachers should make from this line of reasoning is that our task must involve engaging students in conversation among themselves at as many points in both the writing and the reading process as possible, and that we should contrive to ensure that students' conversation about what they read and write is similar in as many ways as possible to the way we would like them eventually to read and write. The way they talk with each other determines the way they will think and the way they will write.

To organize students for these purposes is, in as general a way as I can put it, to organize collaborative learning. Collaborative learning provides a social context in which students can experience and practice the kinds of conversation valued by college teachers. The kind of conversation peer tutors engage in with their tutees, for example, can be emotionally involved,

402

intellectually and substantively focused, and personally disinterested. There could be no better source than this of the sort of displaced conversation—writing—valued by college teachers. Similarly, collaborative classroom group work guided by a carefully designed task makes students aware that writing is a social artifact, like the thought that produces it. Writing may seem to be displaced in time and space from the rest of a writer's community of readers and other writers, but in every instance writing is an act, however much displaced, of conversational exchange.

Besides providing a particular kind of conversation, collaborative learning also provides a particular kind of social context for conversation, a particular kind of community—a community of status equals: peers. Students learn the "skill and partnership" of re-externalized conversation, writing, not only in a community that fosters the kind of conversation college teachers value most, but also in a community that approximates the one most students must eventually write for in everyday life, in business, government, and the professions.

It is worthwhile to digress a moment here to establish this last point. In most cases people write in business, government, and the professions mainly to inform and convince other people within the writer's own community, people whose status and assumptions approximate the writer's own.[7] That is, the sort of writing most people do most in their everyday working lives is what Richard Rorty calls "normal discourse." Normal discourse (a term of Rorty's coinage based on Thomas Kuhn's term "normal science") applies to conversation within a community of knowledgeable peers. A community of knowledgeable peers is a group of people who accept, and whose work is guided by, the same paradigms and the same code of values and assumptions. In normal discourse, as Rorty puts it, everyone agrees on the "set of conventions about what counts as a relevant contribution, what counts as a question, what counts as having a good argument for that answer or a good criticism of it." The product of normal discourse is "the sort of statement that can be agreed to be true by all participants whom the other participants count as 'rational'" (p. 320).

The essay I am writing here is an example of normal discourse in this sense. I am writing to members of my own community of knowledgeable peers. My readers and I (I presume) are guided in our work by the same set of conventions about what counts as a relevant contribution, what counts as a question, what counts as having a good argument for that answer or a good criticism of it. I judge my essay finished when I think it conforms to that set of conventions and values. It is within that set of conventions and values that my readers will evaluate the essay, both in terms of its quality and in terms of whether or not it makes sense. Normal discourse is pointed;

it is explanatory and argumentative. Its purpose is to justify belief to the satisfaction of other people within the author's community of knowledgeable peers. Much of what we teach today—or should be teaching—in composition courses is the normal discourse of most academic, professional, and business communities. The rhetoric taught in our composition textbooks comprises—or should comprise—the conventions of normal discourse of those communities.[8]

Teaching normal discourse in its written form is central to a college curriculum, therefore, because the one thing college teachers in most fields commonly want students to acquire, and what teachers in most fields consistently reward students for, is the ability to carry on in speech and writing the normal discourse of the field in question. Normal discourse is what William Perry describes as discourse in the established contexts of knowledge in a field, discourse that makes effective reference to facts as defined within those contexts. In a student who can integrate fact and context together in this way, Perry says, "we recognize a colleague."[9] This is so because to be conversant with the normal discourse in a field of study or endeavor is exactly what we mean by being knowledgeable—that is, knowledge-able—in that field. Not to have mastered the normal discourse of a discipline, no matter how many "facts" or data one may know, is not to be knowledgeable in that discipline. Mastery of a knowledge community's normal discourse is the basic qualification for acceptance into that community.

The kind of writing students find most useful to learn in college, therefore, is not only the kind of writing most appropriate to work in fields of business, government, and the professions. It is also the writing most appropriate to gaining competence in most academic fields that students study in college. What these two kinds of writing have in common is that they are both written within and addressed to a community of status equals: peers. They are both normal discourse.

This point having, I hope, been established, the nature of the particular kind of community that collaborative learning forms becomes clearer. Collaborative learning provides the kind of social context, the kind of community, in which normal discourse occurs: a community of knowledgeable peers. This is one of its main goals: to provide a context in which students can practice and master the normal discourse exercised in established knowledge communities in the academic world and in business, government, and the professions.

But to say this only raises a host of questions. One question is, how can student peers, who are not members of the knowledge communities they hope to enter, who lack the knowledge that constitutes those communities, help other students enter them? The first, more concrete answer to this question is that no student is wholly ignorant and inexperienced. Every student is already a member of several knowledge communities, from canoeing to computers, baseball to ballet. Membership in any one of these communities may not be a resource that will by itself help much directly in learning to organize an essay or explicate a poem. But pooling the resources that a group of peers brings with them to the task may make accessible the normal discourse of the new community they together hope to enter. Students are especially likely to be able to master that discourse collaboratively if their conversation is structured indirectly by the task or problem that a member of that new community (the teacher) has judiciously designed.[10] To the conversation between peer tutors and their tutees in writing, for example, the tutee brings knowledge of the subject to be written about and knowledge of the assignment. The tutor brings sensitivity to the needs and feelings of peers and knowledge of the conventions of discourse and of standard written English. And the conversation is structured in part by the demands of the teacher's assignment and in part by the formal conventions of the communities the teacher represents, the conventions of academic discourse and standard English.

Such conversation among students can break down, of course, if any one of these elements is not present. It can proceed again if the person responsible for providing the missing element, usually but not always the teacher, is flexible enough to adjust his or her contribution accordingly. If, for example, tutees do not bring to the conversation knowledge of the subject and the assignment, then the teacher helps peer tutors see that their most important contribution may be to help tutees begin at the very beginning: how to go about making sufficient acquaintance with the subject matter and how to set out to clarify the assignment. If tutors lack sensitivity to language and to the feelings and needs of their peers, tutees must contribute by making those feelings and needs more clearly evident. If the task or assignment that the teacher has given is unclear or too difficult or too simpleminded to engage students effectively, then the teacher has to revise it. Throughout this process the teacher has to try to help students negotiate the rocks and shoals of social relations that may interfere with their getting on with their work together.

What students do when working collaboratively on their writing is not write or edit or, least of all, read proof. What they do is converse. They talk about the subject and about the assignment. They talk through the writer's understanding of the subject. They converse about their own relationship and, in general, about relationships in an academic or intellectual context between students and teachers. Most of all they converse about and as a part of writing. Similarly, what students do when working collaboratively in small groups in order to read a text with understanding—a poem, a story, or another student's paper—is also to converse. They converse in order to reach consensus in answer to questions the teacher has raised about the text. They converse about and as a part of understanding. In short, they learn, by practicing it in this orderly way, the normal discourse of the academic community.

COLLABORATIVE LEARNING AND THE AUTHORITY OF KNOWLEDGE

The place of conversation in learning, especially in the humanities, is the largest context in which we must see collaborative learning. To say that conversation has a place in learning should not of course seem peculiar to those of us who count ourselves humanists, a category that includes all of us who teach literature and most of us who teach writing. Furthermore, most of us believe that "class discussion" is one of the most effective ways of teaching. The truth, however, is that despite this belief the person who does most of the discussing in most of our discussion classes is the teacher.

This tends to happen because behind our enthusiasm for discussion lies a fundamental distrust of it. The graduate training most of us have enjoyed— or endured—has taught us, in fact, that collaboration and community activity is inappropriate and foreign to work in humanistic disciplines such as English. Humanistic study, we have been led to believe, is a solitary life, and the vitality of the humanities lies in the talents and endeavors of each of us as individuals. What we call discussion is more often than not an adversarial activity pitting individual against individual in an effort to assert what one literary critic has called "will to power over the text," if not over each other. If we look at what we do instead of what we say, we discover that we think of knowledge as something we acquire and wield as individuals relative to each other, not something we generate and maintain in company with and in dependency upon each other.[11]

Only recently have humanists of note, such as Stanley Fish in literary criticism and Richard Rorty in philosophy, begun to take effective steps toward exploring the force and implications of knowledge communities in the humanistic disciplines, and toward redefining the nature of our knowledge as a social artifact. Much of this recent work follows a trail blazed two decades ago by Thomas Kuhn. The historical irony of this course of events lies in the fact that Kuhn developed his notion about the nature of scientific knowledge after first examining the way knowledge is generated, established, and maintained in the humanities and social sciences. For us as humanists to discover in Kuhn and his followers the conceptual rationale of collaborative learning is to see our own chickens come home to roost.

Kuhn's position that even in the "hard" sciences knowledge is a social artifact emerged from his attempt to understand the implications of the increasing indeterminacy of knowledge of all kinds in the twentieth century.[12] To say that knowledge is indeterminate is to say that there is no fixed and certain point of reference, no Arnoldian "touchstone" against which we can measure truth. If there is no such absolute referent, then knowledge must be a thing people make and remake. Knowledge must be a social artifact. But to call knowledge a social artifact, Kuhn argues, is not to say that knowledge is merely relative, that knowledge is what any one of us says it is. Knowledge is maintained and established by communities of knowledgeable peers. It is what together we agree it is, for the time being. Rorty, following Kuhn, argues that communities of knowledgeable peers make knowledge by a process of socially justifying belief. Collaborative learning models this process.

This then is a second and more general answer to the question raised in the preceding section. How can student peers, who are not themselves members of the knowledge communities they hope to enter, help other students to enter those communities? Isn't collaborative learning the blind leading the blind?

It is of course exactly the blind leading the blind if we insist on the Cartesian model of knowledge: that to know is to "see," and that knowledge is information impressed upon the individual mind by some outside source. But if we accept the premise that knowledge is an artifact created by a community of knowledgeable peers constituted by the language of that community, and that learning is a social and not an individual process, then to learn is not to assimilate information and improve our mental eyesight. To learn is to work collaboratively to establish and maintain knowledge among a community of knowledgeable peers through the process that Richard Rorty calls "socially justifying belief." We socially justify belief when we explain to others why one way of understanding how the world hangs together seems to us preferable to other ways of understanding it. We establish knowledge or justify belief collaboratively by challenging each other's biases and presuppositions; by negotiating collectively toward new paradigms of perception, thought, feeling, and expression; and by joining larger, more experienced communities of knowledgeable peers through assenting to those communities' interests, values, language, and paradigms of perception and thought.

If we accept this concept of knowledge and learning even partially and tentatively, it is possible to see collaborative learning as a model of the way that even the most sophisticated scientific knowledge is established and maintained. Knowledge is the product of human beings in a state of continual negotiation or conversation. Education is not a process of assimilating "the truth" but, as Rorty has put it, a process of learning to "take a hand in what is going on" by joining "the conversation of mankind." Collaborative learning is an arena in which students can negotiate their way into that conversation.

COLLABORATIVE LEARNING
AND NEW KNOWLEDGE

Seen this way, collaborative learning seems unexceptionable. It is not hard to see it as comfortable, not very surprising, not even very new. In discovering and applying collaborative learning we seem to be, if not exactly reinventing the wheel, certainly rediscovering some of the more obvious implications of that familiar and useful device. Collaborative learning, it seems, is no new thing under the sun. However much we may explore its conceptual ramifications, we must acknowledge the fact that people have always learned from their peers and doggedly persist in doing so whether we professional teachers and educators take a hand in it or not. In Thomas Wolfe's *Look Homeward, Angel* Eugene Gant records how in grammar school he learned to write (in this case, form the words on a page) from his "comrade," learning from a peer what "all instruction failed" to teach him. In business and industry, furthermore, and in professions such as medicine, law, engineering, and architecture—where to work is to learn or fail—collaboration is the norm. All that is new in collaborative learning, it seems, is the systematic application of collaborative principles to that last bastion of hierarchy and individualism, the American college classroom.

This comfortable view, while appropriate, may yet be deceptive. If we follow just a bit further the implications of the rationale for collaborative learning that I have been outlining here, we catch a glimpse of a somewhat startling educational scene. Take, for example, the principle that entering an existing knowledge community involves a process of negotiation. Followed to its logical conclusion this principle implies that education is not a rite of passage in which students passively become initiated into an institution that is monolithic and unchanging. It implies that the means by which students learn to negotiate this entry, collaborative learning, is not merely a better pedagogy, a better way of initiating new members into existing knowledge communities. And it implies that collaborative learning as a classroom practice models more than how knowledge is established and maintained.

The argument pursued here implies, in short, that in the long run collaborative learning models how knowledge is generated, how it changes and grows.

This way of thinking about collaborative learning is somewhat speculative, but it is nevertheless of considerable interest and importance to teachers of English. If, as Rorty suggests, knowledge is a social artifact, if knowledge is belief justified through normal discourse, then the generation of knowledge, what we call "creativity," must also be a social process. It too must involve discourse. But the discourse involved in generating knowledge cannot be normal discourse, since normal discourse maintains knowledge. It is inadequate for generating new knowledge. Knowledge-generating discourse is discourse of quite another kind. It is, to use Rorty's phrase, abnormal discourse.

In contrast to normal discourse, abnormal discourse occurs between coherent communities or within communities when consensus no longer exists with regard to rules, assumptions, goals, values, or mores. Abnormal discourse, Rorty says, "is what happens when someone joins in the discourse who is ignorant of the conventions governing that discourse "or who sets them aside." Whereas normal discourse produces "the sort of statement which can be agreed to be true by all participants whom the other participants count as 'rational,'" "the product of abnormal discourse can be anything from nonsense to intellectual revolution." Unlike the participants in normal discourse who sound "rational" to the others in the community, a person speaking abnormal discourse sounds "either 'kooky' (if he loses his point) or 'revolutionary' (if he gains it)" (pp. 320, 339).

The importance of abnormal discourse to the discussion of collaborative learning is that abnormal discourse serves the function of helping us—immersed as we inevitably are in the everyday normal discourse of our disciplines and professions—to see the provincial nature of normal discourse and of the communities defined by normal discourse. Abnormal discourse sniffs out stale, unproductive knowledge and challenges its authority, that is, the authority of the community which that knowledge constitutes. Its purpose, Rorty says, is to undermine "our reliance upon the knowledge we have gained" through normal discourse. We must occasionally undermine this reliance because normal discourse tends to "block the flow of conversation by presenting [itself] as offering the canonical vocabulary for discussion of a given topic" (pp. 386–387).

Abnormal discourse is therefore necessary to learning. But, ironically, abnormal discourse cannot be directly taught. "There is no discipline that describes" abnormal discourse, Rorty tells us, "any more than there is a discipline devoted to the study of the unpredictable or of 'creativity'" (p. 320).

What we can teach are the tools of normal discourse, that is, both practical rhetoric and rhetorically based modes of literary criticism such as the taxonomy of figures, new-critical analysis, and deconstructive criticism.[13] To leave openings for change, however, we must not teach these tools as universals. We must teach practical rhetoric and critical analysis in such a way that, when necessary, students can turn to abnormal discourse in order to undermine their own and other people's reliance on the canonical conventions and vocabulary of normal discourse. We must teach the use of these tools in such a way that students *can* set them aside, if only momentarily, for the purpose of generating new knowledge, for the purpose, that is, of reconstituting knowledge communities in more satisfactory ways.

It is just here that, as I mentioned at the beginning of this essay, we begin to move beyond our earlier suppositions about what people learn through collaborative learning. Defining knowledge as a social artifact established and maintained through normal discourse challenges the authority of knowledge as we traditionally understand it. But by changing what we usually call the process of learning—the work, the expectations, and the social structure of the traditional classroom—collaborative learning also changes what we usually call the substance of learning. It challenges the authority of knowledge by revealing, as John Trimbur has observed, that authority itself is a social artifact. This revelation and the new awareness that results from it makes authority comprehensible both to us as teachers and to our students. It involves a process of reacculturation. Thus collaborative learning can help students join the established knowledge communities of academic studies, business, and the professions. But it should also help students learn something else. They should learn, Trimbur says, "something about how this social transition takes place, how it involves crises of identity and authority, how students can begin to generate a transitional language to bridge the gap between communities" (private correspondence).

Challenging the traditional authority of knowledge in this way, collaborative learning naturally challenges the traditional basis of the authority of those who teach. Our authority as teachers always derives directly or indirectly from the prevailing conception of the authority of knowledge. In the pre-Cartesian world people tended to believe that the authority of knowledge lodged in one place, the mind of God. In that world teachers derived their authority from their godliness, their nearness to the mind of God. In Cartesian, Mirror-of-Nature epistemology, the authority of knowledge has had three alternative lodgings, each a secular version of the mind of God. We could believe if we chose that the authority of knowledge lodged in some touchstone of value and truth above and beyond ourselves, such as mathematics, creative genius, or the universals of sound reasoning. We could believe that the authority of knowledge lodged in the mind of a person of genius: a Wordsworth, an Einstein, or a Freud. Or we could believe that the authority of knowledge lodged in the nature of the object objectively known: the universe, the human mind, the text of a poem.

Our authority as teachers, accordingly, has had its source in our nearness to one of these secular versions of the mind of God. In the first case we derive our authority from our identification with the "touchstone" of value and truth. Thus, for some of us, mathematicians and poets have, generally speaking, greater authority than, say, sociologists or literary critics. According to the second alternative we derive our authority from intimacy with the greatest minds. Many of us feel that those who have had the good fortune to study with Freud, Faraday, or Faulkner, for example, have greater authority than those who studied with their disciples; or, those who have studied the manuscripts of Joyce's fiction have greater authority than those who merely studied the edited texts. According to the third alternative, we derive our authority as teachers from being in direct touch with the objective world. Most of us feel that those whose knowledge is confirmed by hands-on laboratory experimentation have greater authority than those whose knowledge is based on a synthesis of secondary sources.

Because the concept that knowledge is socially justified belief denies that the authority of knowledge lodges in any of these places, our authority as teachers according to that concept has quite another source as well. Insofar as collaborative learning inducts students into established knowledge communities and teaches them the normal discourse of those communities, we derive our authority as teachers from being certified representatives of the communities of knowledgeable peers that students aspire to join, and that we, as members of our chosen disciplines and also members of the community of the liberally educated public at large, invite and encourage them to join. Teachers are defined in this instance as those members of a knowledge community who accept the responsibility for inducting new members into the community. Without successful teachers the community will die when its current members die, and knowledge as assented to by that community will cease to exist.

Insofar as collaborative learning helps students understand how knowledge is generated through abnormal discourse, however, our authority as teachers derives from another source. It derives from the values of a larger—indeed, the largest possible—community of knowledgeable peers, the community that encompasses all others. The interests of this largest community contradict one of the central interests of local communities such as professional disciplines and fields of study: to maintain established knowledge. The interest of the larger community is to resist this conservative tendency.

Its interest is to bridge gaps among knowledge communities and to open them to change.

The continued vitality of the knowledge communities we value—in particular the community of liberally educated people and its sub-communities, the scholarly and professional disciplines—depends on both these needs being met: to maintain established knowledge and to challenge and change it. As representatives and delegates of a local, disciplinary community, and of the larger community as well, teachers are responsible for the continued vitality of both of the knowledge communities we value. Responsible to both sets of values, therefore, we must perform as conservators *and* agents of change, as custodians of prevailing community values *and* as agents of social transition and reacculturation.

Because by giving students access to the "conversation of mankind," to return to Oakeshott's phrase, collaborative learning can serve both of these seemingly conflicting educational aims at once, it has an especially important role to play in studying and teaching English. It is one way of introducing students to the process by which communities of knowledgeable peers create referential connections between symbolic structures and "reality," that is, by which they establish knowledge and by doing so maintain community growth and coherence. To study adequately any text—student theme or play by Shakespeare—is to study an entire social symbolic process, not just part of it. To study and teach English is to study and teach the social origin, nature, reference, and function of symbolic structures.

The view that knowledge is a social artifact, furthermore, requires a reexamination of our premises as students of English and as teachers. To date, very little work of this sort has been done. One can only guess what might come of a concerted effort on the part of the profession as a whole. The effort might ultimately involve "demystifying" much that we now do as humanists and teachers of the humanities. If we bring to mind, for example, a sampling of important areas of current theoretical thought in and allied to literary criticism, we are likely to find mostly bipolar forms: text and reader, text and writer, symbol and referent, signifier and signified. On the one hand, a critique along the lines I have been following here might involve examining how these theories would differ if they included the third term missing from most of them. How would a psychoanalytically oriented study of metaphor differ, for example, if it acknowledged that psychotherapy is fundamentally a kind of social relationship based on the mutual creation or recreation of symbolic structures by therapist and patient? How would semiotics differ if it acknowledged that all "codes" are symbolic structures constituting language communities and that to understand these codes requires us to examine and understand the complex social symbolic relations among the people who make up language communities? How would practical rhetoric look if we assumed that writer and reader were not adversaries but partners in a common, community-based enterprise? How would it look if we no longer assumed that people write to persuade or to distinguish themselves and their points of view and to enhance their own individuality by gaining the acquiescence of other individuals? How would it look if we assumed instead that people write for the very opposite reason: that people write in order to be accepted, to join, to be regarded as another member of the culture or community that constitutes the writer's audience?

Once we had reexamined in this way how English is studied professionally, we could on the other hand also undertake to reexamine how English is taught as well. If we did that, we might find ourselves taking issue with Stanley Fish's conclusion that to define knowledge as a social artifact generated by interpretive communities has no effect whatsoever on the way we read and teach literature and composition. My argument in this essay suggests, on the contrary, that some changes in our pedagogical attitudes and classroom practices are almost inevitable. These changes would result from integrating our understanding of social symbolic relationships into our teaching—not just into what we teach but also into how we teach it. For example, so long as we think of knowledge as a reflection and synthesis of information about the objective world, then to teach *King Lear* seems to involve providing a "correct" text and rehearsing students in "correct" interpretations of it. "Correct" here means the text and the interpretations that, as Fish puts it, seem "obvious and inescapable" within the knowledge community, within the "institutional or conventional structure," of which we happen to be members (p. 370).

But if we think of knowledge as socially justified belief, then to teach *King Lear* seems to involve creating contexts where students undergo a sort of cultural change. This change would be one in which they loosen ties to the knowledge communities they currently belong to and join another. These two communities would be seen as having quite different sets of values, mores, and goals, and above all quite different languages. To speak in one community of a person asking another to "pray you undo this button" (V, iii) might be merely to tell a mercantile tale, or a prurient one, while in another community such a request could be both a gesture of profound human dignity and a metaphor of the dissolution of a world.

Similarly, so long as we think of learning as reflecting and synthesizing information about the objective world, to teach expository writing is to provide examples, analysis, and exercises in the traditional modes of practical rhetoric—description, narration, comparison-contrast—or examples, analysis, and exercises in the "basic skills" of writing, and to rehearse students in their proper use. But if we think of learning as a social process, the process of socially justifying belief, then to teach expository writing seems to involve something else entirely. It involves demonstrating to students that they know something only when they can explain it in writing to the satisfaction of the community of their knowledgeable peers. To teach this way, in turn, seems to require us to engage students in collaborative work that does not just reinforce the values and skills they begin with, but that promotes a sort of reacculturation.[14]

The argument I have been making here implies, in short, that students and teachers of literature and writing must begin to develop awareness and skill that may seem foreign and irrelevant to our profession at the present time. Organizing collaborative learning effectively requires doing more than throwing students together with their peers with little or no guidance or preparation. To do that is merely to perpetuate, perhaps even aggravate, the many possible negative efforts of peer group influence: conformity, anti-intellectualism, intimidation, and leveling-down of quality. To avoid these pitfalls and to marshal the powerful educational resource of peer group influence requires us to create and maintain a demanding academic environment that makes collaboration—social engagement in intellectual pursuits—a genuine part of students' educational development. And that in turn requires quite new and perhaps more thorough analyses of the elements of our field than we have yet attempted.

NOTES

1. I am indebted for conversation regarding substantive issues raised in this essay to Fellows of the Brooklyn College Institute for Training Peer Tutors and of the Asnuntuck Community College Institute in Collaborative Learning and Peer-Tutor Training, and to Peter Elbow. Both Institutes were supported by grants from the Fund for the Improvement of Postsecondary Education. I am particularly grateful to Peter Hawkes, Harvey Kail, Ronald Maxwell, and John Trimbur for reading the essay in early drafts and for offering suggestions for improvement. The essay is in many ways and at many levels a product of collaborative learning.

2. The educative value of peer group influence is discussed in Theodore M. Newcomb and Everett K. Wilson, eds., *College Peer Groups* (Chicago: Aldine, 1966).

3. *The Interpretation of Cultures* (New York: Basic Books, 1971), pp. 76–77, 360. In addition to "The Growth of Culture and the Evolution of Mind," also relevant in the same volume are "The Impact of the Concept of Man" and "Ideology as a Cultural System," parts four and five.

4. *Is There a Text in This Class?: The Authority of Interpretive Communities* (Cambridge, Mass.: Harvard University Press, 1980), p. 14. Fish develops his argument fully in part 2, pp. 303–371. On the distinction between "interiority" or "inwardness" and "internalization," see Stephen Toulmin, "The Inwardness of Mental Life," *Critical Inquiry*, 6 (1979), 1–16.

5. I have explored some of the larger educational implications of Rorty's argument in "Liberal Education and the Social Justification of Belief," *Liberal Education*, 68 (1982), 95–114.

6. I make a case for this position in "Writing and Reading as Collaborative or Social Acts," in Janice N. Hays, et al, eds., *The Writer's Mind: Writing as a Mode of Thinking* (Urbana, Ill.: National Council of Teachers of English, 1983), pp. 159–169. In the current critical climate the distinction between conversation and speech as sources of writing and thought is important to maintain. Deconstructionist critics such as Paul de Man argue (e.g., in his *Blindness and Insight* [Minneapolis: University of Minnesota Press, 1983]), following Derrida, that writing is not displaced speech but a primary act. This argument defines "writing" in a much broader sense than we are used to, to mean something like "making public" in any manner, including speech. Hence deconstructionist "writing" can be construed as a somewhat static conception of what I am here calling "conversation": a social act. So long as the conversational, hence social, nature of "writing" in the deconstructionist sense remains unrecognized, the aversion of deconstructionist criticism to the primacy of speech as embodying the phenomenological "metaphysics of presence" remains circular. The deconstructionist argument holds that privileging speech "centers" language in persons. But "persons" are fictions. The alternative proposal by deconstruction, however, that writing is "free play," invites centering once again, since the figure of play personifies language. The deconstructionist critique has thus yet to acknowledge sufficiently that language, and its products such as thought and the self, are social artifacts constituted by "interpretive communities."

7. Some writing in business, government, and the professions may of course be like the writing students do in school for teachers, that is, for the sake of practice and evaluation. Certainly some writing in everyday working life is done purely as performance to please superiors in the corporate or department hierarchy, tell them what they already know, and demonstrate to them the writer's proficiency *as* a writer. It may be true, therefore, that learning to write to a person who is not a member of one's own status and knowledge community, that is, to a teacher, has some practical everyday value. But the value of writing of this type is hardly proportionate to the amount of time students normally spend on it.

8. A textbook that acknowledges the normal discourse of academic disciplines and offers ways of learning it in a context of collaborative learning is Elaine Maimon, et al., *Writing in the Arts and Sciences* (Boston: Little Brown, 1981).

9. "Examsmanship and the Liberal Arts," in *Examining in Harvard College: A Collection of Essays by Members of the Harvard Faculty* (Cambridge, Mass.: Harvard University Press, 1963). Quoted from Kenneth A. Bruffee, *A Short Course in Writing* (Boston: Little, Brown, 1980), p. 221.

10. For examples and an explanation of this technique, see my *A Short Course in Writing*, cited above, and "CLTV: Collaborative Learning Television," *Educational Communication and Technology Journal*, 30 (1982), 26–40. Also see Clark Bouton and Russell Y. Garth, eds., *Learning in Groups* (San Francisco: Jossey-Bass, 1983).

11. I discuss the individualistic bias of our current interpretation of the humanistic tradition in "The Structure of Knowledge and the Future of Liberal Education," *Liberal Education*, 67 (1981), 181–185.

12. I trace briefly the history of the growing indeterminacy of knowledge and its relevance to the humanities in "The Structure of Knowledge," cited above.

13. Christopher Norris defines deconstruction somewhat simplistically but usefully for most purposes as "rhetorical questioning" (*Deconstruction: Theory and Practice* [London: Methuen, 1982], p. 21).

14. I suggest some possible curricular implications of the concept of knowledge as socially justified belief in "Liberal Education and the Social Justification of Belief," cited above. See also Clifford Geertz, *Local Knowledge* (New York: Basic Books, 1983), pp. 14–15, 161; Richard M. Rorty, "Hermeneutics, General Studies, and Teaching," *Synergos: Selected Papers from the Synergos Seminars*, George Mason University, 2 (Fall 1982), 1–15; and my "Learning to Live in a World out of Joint: Thomas Kuhn's Message to Humanists Revisited," *Liberal Education*, 70 (1984), 77–81.

Reality, Consensus, and Reform in the Rhetoric of Composition Teaching

GREG MYERS

I would like to raise some political questions about two methods of teaching I use in my writing classes: having small groups of students collaborate on and critique each others' writing, and having case assignments based on some actual writing situation, whether a technical proposal or an anthropology exam. My thinking about these methods is based largely on the detailed and practical suggestions of Peter Elbow and Kenneth Bruffee, and on discussion of their works with other teachers. My means of raising questions will be to compare the writings of Elbow and Bruffee to the work of an earlier writer, Sterling Andrus Leonard (1888–1931), whose Dewey-inspired English education textbook, *English Composition as a Social Problem*, suggested these two teaching methods, which I had considered new, back in 1917. I revive this now-forgotten writer and make these comparisons for two reasons: 1) the distance in time makes it easier for us to see his social context than it is to see the context of Elbow or Bruffee, and 2) the recurrence of these ideas as new ideas suggests that those of us who want to change the way writing is taught tend to overlook the efforts and the lessons of earlier reformers. As Lawrence Cremin says in his history of the progressive movement in education, of which Leonard was a part, "Reform movements are notoriously ahistorical in outlook" (8). Until recently, this ahistoricism has

Reprinted from *College English* 48.2 (February 1986): 154–71. Used with permission.

been characteristic of composition theory, with its reformist attacks on a monolithic tradition.[1]

Leonard's writings are interesting in themselves, even considered apart from their historical importance, and deserve to be rescued from the storage rooms of teachers' college libraries. Besides the comments on collaborative learning and "real" writing that I will be considering, he made a number of other criticisms and suggestions between 1914 and 1930 that could be taken from this year's issues of *College Composition and Communication* or *College English*:

> *On the composing process:* "The ideal of the finished product is absolutely vicious, except as it functions to determine the remote goal." (*English Composition* 190)
>
> *On the development of writing abilities:* "Indeed, growth in the art of writing or speaking may be defined simply as a process of becoming increasingly reader-minded." (*English Composition* 14)
>
> *On freewriting:* "Some may really do best to write first in mad and scrabble haste, for themselves only, and thus clear their thoughts before they attempt to talk or write for anyone else." (*English Composition* 111)
>
> *On the modes:* "Useful as this [classification of the forms of discourse] doubtless is for sorting completed pieces of writing, it does not view the process of writing from the side of the thoughts or ideas the writer has to express and particularly of his purpose in expressing those." ("As to the Forms of Discourse" 202)

He also makes suggestions on invention, on sentence combining, on Piaget's theories, and on the need to avoid petty criticisms of errors and unrealistic, "schoolmastering" standards of usage.[2] But what most interests me is his answer to what he calls "the central problem" of his English education work:

> How, stirred by. . . interesting problems requiring expressing, can the school class be knit into a social group organized for mutual help, and aided to move steadily forward in the arduous way of attaining effective expression? (35).

His emphases on the class as a social group, and on the real basis of writing in "interesting problems" of the students' communities inside and outside the school, anticipate the current interest in what Patricia Bizzell calls "social processes whereby language learning and thinking capacities are shaped and used in particular communities" (215). I will try to show that he also anticipates some of the political dilemmas of present-day reformers.

SOME TERMS: IDEOLOGY, CONSENSUS, AND REALITY

I will be criticizing two sorts of rhetorical appeals that Leonard, and later Elbow and Bruffee, use in arguing for the teaching of writing through groups: an appeal to the authority of consensus, and an appeal to the authority of reality. It may seem perverse to object to appeals that are so common in our field and that are apparently progressive: surely we all see the need to come to reasoned agreement within a community, and to relate our teaching to the real world. To explain why I find these appeals problematic, I need to draw on an indispensible piece of Marxist jargon, the concept of *ideology*. I am not using the word the way it is commonly used to criticize any systematic political belief, as, say, an unsympathetic reader of this article might say my views were distorted by Left wing ideology. I am using it in the sense established by Marx, and modified by twentieth-century Marxists, to describe the whole system of thought and belief that goes with a social and economic system, the thoughts that structure our thinking so deeply that we take them for granted, as the nature of the real world. The concept has been much discussed by Marxists because it helps explain the apparent stability of the capitalist system, despite all its contradictions. It helps explain why people who are oppressed seem to go along with their oppression; the ideology of the oppressive system gives them the structures through which they make sense of their world.[3]

The concept of ideology has been of particular interest to Marxist sociologists of education, who see the school as, at least in part, an institution that adapts ideology to changing economic and social conditions, and produces a new version of ideology for each generation. Schools not only teach academic knowledge; they teach work according to schedule, acceptance of authority, and competition among individuals and between groups. They also help provide a justification for the hierarchies of society, so that, for instance, people accept that manual labor should pay less than mental labor. This process of adapting and carrying on the assumptions of our society is called *reproducing ideology*, by analogy with Marx's description of the reproduction of capital. Recently, radical teachers have asked if school can also be a place where people can resist the reproduction of ideology; they have put less emphasis on the all-embracing power of ideology as a structure, and have focused on the ways students and teachers can break this unthinking acceptance of ideas that support the way things are.[4] Of course, many teachers who are not Marxists agree that the vast differences in our society between rich and poor, black and white, men and women, are bad, and many teachers agree that critical thinking is a good thing. Where Marxist teachers differ from other critics of these injustices is in arguing that the social and economic system that perpetuates the injustices builds a protective structure of ideology that prevents us from thinking critically about it. Thus, what we might think is free and progressive thought may be another way of perpetuating a system we want to change.

I will argue that ideas of *consensus* and *reality*, as they are used by Leonard, though they seem so progressive, are part of the structure of ideology. The construction of a sense of general agreement is as important to the rhetoric of composition teaching as it is to the rhetoric of national politics; look, for instance, at all the articles in this journal asserting a new paradigm in the profession. But if conflict is part of the system, and is necessary to change the system, then consensus, within the system as it is, must mean that some interests have been suppressed or excluded. Similarly, it is common in our profession to show oneself as escaping tired academic forms to enter the real world. But if what we take as reality is always a social construction, then to accept the reality we see now is to accept the structure of illusion our system gives us. Worse, it is to see reality as something natural, outside our control, rather than to see it as something we make in our actions in society.

Since many readers who see the same economic, racial, and sexist injustices I do may not share my conviction that the problems are fundamental and systematic, it may help to use a familiar example from a society all readers will believe is fundamentally and systematically unjust. Huckleberry Finn's thinking is structured by the ideology of a slave-holding society. Though Huck himself does not own any slaves or benefit from this society (recall that he has invested some capital that he found), he hates abolitionists, and he can only think about blacks and whites in the terms he has learned. (Every reader must recall the exchange he has when he tells Aunt Sally the steamboat had blown a cylinder head: "Good gracious! Anybody hurt?—No'm. Killed a nigger.—Well, it's lucky; because sometimes people do get hurt.") But for reasons Huck doesn't entirely understand, and which he would not consider as being in any way political, he is capable of some remarkable acts of resistance to this system: for instance, he makes up elaborate lies on the spur of the moment to keep slave hunters away. There is some chance for change as long as he and others are capable of such resistance. But still he consciously believes in the institution of slavery enough so that he thinks worse of Tom Sawyer, a good boy, for apparently helping free Jim. Huck himself is an agreeable sort who prefers to avoid trouble. Whenever he tries to approach the *consensus* view, to do what he believes is right, he thinks of returning his friend Jim to slavery. Towards the end of the book, he believes he is finally facing *reality* when he admits to himself that in helping Jim escape, he is guilty of stealing property from Jim's owner. Now I am not saying that the social system of present day New York or Texas or Lancashire, where I have been teaching, is like that of ante-bellum Missouri where Huck grows up; what I am saying is that our social system constructs our view of the world as slavery does Huck's, and that the appeals to consensus and to reality may support that ideological view, as they did for Huck.

STERLING LEONARD AND CONSENSUS

I have commented on how current Sterling Leonard's ideas sound today. I would argue that this is because the historical conditions of high school English education in his period, 1900–1930, have some similarities to those in college, and particularly community college, English education in our own time. The high schools then were adapting to a massive influx of immigrants, and to the enrollment of working class students who had previously left school early, if they had attended at all.[5] In a similar way, writing programs like those at the City University of New York have faced the institutional challenge of coping with a group of students who would not previously have attended a university. In both periods, the new students changed the institutions, as well as being changed by them. In both periods, the institutions were responding to the demands of business for a large workforce with a different kind of skills. And in both periods, the teachers of writing were trying to establish their own professional status. A sense of historical conditions can help us see Leonard's progressivism in a social context.

Leonard was a typical reformer of this period, and one could find ideas similar to his in the work of John Dewey, E. L. Thorndike, George Philip Krapp, Fred Newton Scott, C. C. Fries, and I. A. Richards.[6] Leonard worked with all these teachers, in his own schooling at Michigan and Columbia Teachers' College or in his later work as a professor at Wisconsin and a leader of the then new NCTE. But the most important influence on him, and an important influence still on composition theory, was the work of John Dewey. It was from Dewey that Leonard took his central theme—and the theme of most importance to us in trying to criticize his work—the idea of the school as an image of society. For instance, in *The School and Society* (1898), Dewey says, "The great thing to keep in mind, then, regarding the introduction into the school of various forms of active occupation, is that through them the entire spirit of the school is renewed. . . . It gets a chance to become a miniature community, an embryonic society" (15). This quotation refers to both the elements I want to discuss in Leonard's work, the use of the social group of the class, and the emphasis on "real projects," with their reality defined by the analogy to the world outside the school.

Leonard's emphasis on the class as a social group is not just dogmatic Deweyism; he has clearly taught and learned from classes taught this way. In *English Composition as a Social Problem*, for example, he anticipates current ideas in using group work as the basis for "prevision of ideas" (invention), for revision suggestions, and for setting standards of usage. He has practical suggestions to make on teachers' direction of class experimentation (22), on responding (or not responding) to spoken errors (42), on introducing the class to criticism of students' writing (47), on letting the class make up terminology (77), on withholding one's criticisms (97), and on restraining students' carping criticisms of each other: "We must encourage prompt condemnation of guerilla pettifogging whenever we discover signs of it" (164). These passages remind the reader today of the practical advice in Bruffee's *A Short Course in Writing* or Elbow's *Writing Without Teachers*.

But there are passages in which Leonard describes the authority of the classroom group that should make us aware of the dangers of a consensus-based method. Leonard sees his method as furthering the sort of democracy in education promised by Dewey, a democracy he does not see in the traditional classroom. "Our present classrooms are designed chiefly for securing a maximum of order and dispatch. Parliamentary practice is demanded in the custom of addressing the teacher always, and is parodied in the raising of right hands for recognition" (40). Leonard's students have much more to do with each other than this; they are "an interested group of cooperative workers" (65). The danger is that the teacher has merely embodied his or her authority in the more effective guise of class consensus. This guided consensus has a power over individual students that a teacher can not have alone. "What the class may be able, with the help and suggestion of their leader, truly to realize as quite undesirable—cheap or smart or the like—may be quietly branded by the common judgment as unacceptable, and really eliminated" (130). Any teacher who uses group discussions or projects has seen that they can, on occasion, be fierce enforcers of conformity. And Leonard welcomes this enforcement with less worry than we might have. "The erring will be helped sufficiently by a sensation of lowered class temperature, so sharp that even the least sensitive cannot escape it" (149). Leonard does not himself use, but refers to, another teacher's "device . . . of having all children look for such violations [of rules of usage] by any member of the group anywhere and report complete statements and names, and then of deputing committees to write out all such reports on the blackboard each week" (150). Such elaborate machinery might occur to a teacher only during a period of war-time red-baiting hysteria (this was written in 1917), but the tendency to unthinking conformity is always there when consensus is used to set and enforce standards.

The emphasis on the authority of the group that we see in Leonard's textbook is apparent also in his most influential research, his usage studies that attempt to show the differences between formal textbook prescriptions and the language actually used in social transactions. For him the choice is not between correct and incorrect forms, but between the real world of actual usage and the unreal world of school English: "The question appears to turn on whether we wish in these grade and high school years to cultivate excellent homely expressions to fit the daily, informal occasions that we all have to meet most often, or rather a bookish and formal type exclusively" (132). Here he attacks something like what Ken Macrorie calls "Engfish." Leonard does believe that there are some arbitrary rules that must be taught as arbitrary rules. But he believes these rules are very few; thus he is interested in the definition of what the NCTE then called "Minimum Essentials," making a short list of items to be taught by all teachers and consigning the rest of the handbook items to oblivion.

Leonard's authority for the selection of these "essential" items would be actual usage; he has nothing but scorn for the John Simons and Edwin Newmans of his day who would try to impose puristic usage by fiat. "It is easy," he wrote in an early article, "to compile and propagate handbooks of baseless prescriptions; and people will buy them, just as they will buy manuals of etiquette, simply because these announce so many things which 'aren't done' that everyone is convicted of a sin and hastens to remedy the evil. But neither language nor other phases of good manners are settled by these means" ("What About Correct English?" 255). In his Columbia dissertation, *The Doctrine of Correctness in English Usage, 1700–1800,* he traces the origins of many of the handbook rules, and shows they have no basis in the actual usage of any period. This study led to *Current English Usage,* a massive survey to show how little "cultivated usage" supports the handbooks on most disputed items.[7] His views, progressive for the time, had a strong influence on the NCTE's position on usage. But we should note that Leonard's constant appeal to consensus usage assumes the inherent superiority of certain language groups. When he compares grammar books to etiquette books, he assumes, correctly I think, that issues of grammar are debated with such heat because they conceal issues of class, and especially the uneasiness of the middle class about its status. But there is little sense in his usage studies that there might not be just one answer for each item, that different classes or regions or races might have different usages, and that conflicts between these usages reflect other social conflicts. Instead, he carefully chooses certain kinds of respondents, and carefully figures the percentages of respondents approving of each item, and takes the majority vote as the right answer. His authority, he says, is "what various judges have observed about actual use or non-use by cultivated persons" ("Current Definition of Levels in English Usage" 345). But note it is cultivated persons who are to be considered, and experts who are to be the judges. The notion of consensus in usage, while it seems democratic, ignores the conflicts that characterize language change, and leaves the authority of certain types of language unquestioned.

It may seem odd to insist that large social conflicts are behind the use of groups to critique students' papers or the decision on when to use the subjunctive. But Leonard's exercises in democracy can be seen as part of a larger effort to create consensus by eliminating or at least concealing diversity and conflict. This diversity is so well concealed that anyone reading Leonard's articles now, or reading any sampling of articles from the NCTE's *English Journal* of his period, could remain unaware that teachers in many cities would be teaching classes in which most students were foreign born.[8] The only indication of potential conflict would be the way that progressive and traditional educators alike made every class into a civics lesson. If one believes that the society of that time was basically just, and that the treatment of the immigrants and workers, and their children, was just, then the attempt to integrate these newcomers into a consensus view, into the melting pot, was a generous project. But if one reads the history of that period as a history of challenges to a system that promoted great extremes of poverty and wealth, and terrible conditions of living and work, challenges by labor unions, immigrant communities, and new black urban communities, then the attempt by educators to deny the existence of these challenges can be seen as part of a repressive response by the government and corporations. Leonard's Deweyan individualism, though it still sounds progressive to us, strips the student of any identification with class, religion, family, or origins. And these identifications, as we are now coming to see in the controversies over bi-cultural education, can be the beginnings of political action. Deweyan education reassembles these students as units in a classroom group, in which they are conscious only of the demands of a monolithic "society" as enforced by the school and by other students.

LEONARD AND REALITY

It may seem paradoxical, or even perverse, for a radical who keeps referring to the social and economic basis of education to criticize the emphasis on *reality* in the work of Leonard and other progressive educators. Aren't they trying to do, in a practical way, just what I insist on doing in theory? The difference in our views is in how we define reality. For Leonard, what is real is given; we gain knowledge of it through our senses, if we are not deceived by non-empirical assumptions, and we adapt to it as best we can. For a Marxist, reality is not a monolithic thing out there, but a process in society, an ongoing conflict between various groups, which in turn structures that society. People have no simple unmediated perception of reality; the facts we are likely to take as reality are most likely parts of another ideological structure. Think, for example, of the very limited sense "the real world" has had in recent discussion of writing courses—it becomes synonymous with the demands of employers as shown in surveys. By treating the "real world" as the bedrock of our teaching, we perpetuate the idea that reality is something outside us and beyond our efforts to change it.

We have seen that Leonard's rhetorical strategy in his attacks on what he calls "Old Purist Junk" about usage is to compare the formalism of textbooks with the way people use language in the "real world." He makes a similar appeal in replacing the teaching of the modes of discourse with a developmental classification based on the stages a child is supposed to go through in learning the presentation and interpretation of facts. In the earliest assignments a student receives, the student simply reports observations: "All these matters are to be presented as objectively as possible; they are to set forth all the writer's senses have apprehended" ("As to the Forms of Discourse" 202). The purpose of this exercise is to root out merely conventional beliefs, by making the students stick to the facts: "Nothing is of more doubtful value, as an exercise in composition or anything else, than the restatement of fact or interpretation the writer has absorbed but not lived or thought through himself" ("As to the Forms of Discourse" 204). Now I have been attacking just this handing on of uncriticized assumptions. But I disagree with Leonard's belief that the *facts* lie outside these assumptions. If what we think of as facts are determined by our ideological framework, the facts cannot themselves get us beyond that framework.[9] Leonard's textbook says, as do many textbooks today, "The whole art of helping children in writing or speaking, as this study urges it, is based on the idea of showing them how to search out and give not general but specific details" (*English Composition* 105). I too am always asking students for more details. But I am interested in what such details reveal about our assumptions, not in getting beyond assumptions to some external reality.

To take an example, Leonard asks his students to describe a place, and to cut out any statements unsupported by facts. That may lead to a more readable and more academic sounding paper, but it will not tell us what the place is really like. When, for instance, the various students in a basic writing course at Queens College write comparisons of the places they live to the places their parents lived as children, what these places are "really like" is determined by conventional frameworks of progress or nostalgia. What the place is really like might be better understood by comparing all those unsupported generalizations that various people would bring to such a description, comparing, say, the Lower East Side described as oppressive ghetto with the Lower East Side described as warm community, Forest Hills described as success and security with Forest Hills described as silent streets and alienating apartment blocks. No careful attention to the description of stoops or wide lawns will reconcile these descriptions in one objective reality. Both express deeper tensions that go beyond the rhetorical problems set by the assignment.

There is at times an alarming sound to Leonard's enthusiasm for the real world, as there is to his enthusiasm for consensus, that should make us examine our own enthusiasms today. His demand that development in school lead to the world of work and community responsibility, while it frees the school from the empty formalism of lectures, drills, and theme topics, ironically makes it more subservient to ideology. The real world is indistinguishable from the world defined by business publicists: "Meat packers, electric companies, millers, dog breeders, and others have free advertising matter and exhibits which are of the greatest value. Whatever your children want to know is likely to be covered by government or advertising material" ("Composition and Grammar in the Junior High School" 410). Despite the apparent naiveté of this view, Leonard is not by any means a promoter of a narrowly vocational education. Dewey had described the relation between business and education in broad terms.

> Though there should be an organic connection between the school and business life, it is not meant that the school is to prepare the student for any particular business, but that there should be a natural connection of the everyday life of a child with the business environment around him, and that it is the affair of the school to clarify and liberalize this connection, to bring it to consciousness, not by introducing special studies, like commercial geography and arithmetic, but by keeping alive the ordinary bonds of relation. (68)

It is not the connection of business that is in itself disturbing, but the sense of the naturalness and inevitability of this connection as the one way of reaching out to the world outside the school. For Leonard, as for Dewey, to criticize the subordination of education to the needs of business and government is to fail to face reality.

Teachers today are likely to be more skeptical about the uses of advertising. But we still assume the value of making the classroom represent "reality," and we still define this reality in very limited terms which we take uncritically from our economic system. For instance, many of the research studies that seek to define a body of good writing compare the writing of students to that of published writers. Now this makes for some valuable comparisons, but we should note how we just assume, lacking an agreed standard of writing quality, that good writing is writing that can be sold for money. Some editors of composition readers argue, using rhetoric very similar to Leonard's, that this sort of contemporary professional writing is more real than, say, readings taken from the canon of English and American literature. Or other editors of readers argue that the writing of students who have won a national essay contest is more real than the writing of professional magazine writers. All these assertions, whatever the pedagogical value of the materials they propose, beg the question of just how we come to define a real world, and accept that world as something given.

LEONARD AND REFORM

Anyone who has sat through a dull writing class (or has oneself taught a dull class with growing frustration) would recognize Leonard's descriptions of traditional methods of teaching English. He attacks these classes using a rhetoric similar to that of composition reformers today, who present themselves as fighting for more realistic views against the tradition that prevailed before the mid-1960s.[10] Much as I sympathize with the critique given by both periods of reform, I have questions about the way these reformers define themselves against the dubious practices of traditional teachers, who are often at a lower level of the hierarchy of educational prestige. The attack on tradition shifts our focus from the conflicting goals of the school in society to the simpler issue of the competence of individual teachers and the practicality of specific methods.

These questions may be raised most clearly by considering one of Leonard's articles from 1923. "How English Teachers Correct Papers" reports a study in which various groups of student-teachers and teachers were given a list of sentences from both students and famous authors and asked to mark any errors they would require a student to correct (517). Leonard's whole study is something of a trap for the unsuspecting teachers, practically all of whom "fatigued themselves to a point close to insensibility by meticulous correction of a great number of idioms in sentences by De Quincey, Lamb, Pater, Symonds, and authors of similar standing" (517), so that they were too tired to see what Leonard considered actual errors. To complete his attack, Leonard lists "constructive comments" the teachers gave on whole papers they were asked to mark, including "corrections" that made the correct incorrect, "puristic or wholly captious excisions, restatements, arrangements, and additions," and foolish or irrelevant criticisms. Leonard's suggestion that "the wisest teacher proceeds always by way of queries and suggestion, not by dogmatic rules and requirements," is a good one, and has been reiterated recently in articles in the composition journals reporting studies similar to Leonard's.[11] But Leonard's article, like some recent critiques, presents a polemic against dogmatism without either an understanding of its origins, or a model for a new method based on queries and suggestion.

The study shows how much Leonard needs bad teachers to make his argument. I would not deny that there was, and is, a plentiful supply of such teachers to provide examples of arbitrary traditionalism. But I am uneasy with the way the university expert makes them the enemy. He shows how their habits fly in the face of the "reality" revealed by current research, and he judges their judgment against an absolute level of cultivation represented by the writing of "De Quincey, Lamb, Pater, Symonds, and authors of similar standing." I would argue that this kind of top-down reform leads nowhere, because it just reinforces the hierarchy of the teaching profession, reminding teachers that the expertise is somewhere else. Thus in each generation it is the reformers who chair committees, write articles, and edit the journals; by these standards it is the reformers who are the establishment, and the opponents they label traditionalists are the outsiders. And in the 1980s we use the same sort of rhetoric, on the same sort of issues, to the same sort of teachers, to distinguish ourselves from tradition, that the members of that "tradition" used against a previous generation. What is needed to break this circle is more understanding of the conditions under which people teach, and the ideological frameworks within which they think. We should be opposing, not traditional teachers, but a system in which such repressive teaching is, in fact, perfectly appropriate.

I am annoyed with Leonard's rhetoric as a reformer because he assumes authority over other teachers and over students while denying he has it. He assumes authority as trained expert, university professor, empirical researcher, voice of the downtrodden students, bringing enlightenment to normal-school-trained teachers. But he denies his personal authority by saying the students are controlling the classroom, and his curriculum just follows the real world, and his reforms are based on the latest research. If we see that schools can be both places of liberation and places of oppression, then we have to ask how we are using what limited power over people's lives we do have.

CONSENSUS AND REALITY
IN ELBOW AND BRUFFEE

If Leonard were just a forgotten hero of composition theory, like Alexander Bain or Fred Newton Scott, to revive him and then criticize him would be unnecessary and rather unfair. But the example of Leonard can help us criticize the presentation of consensus, reality, and reform in two theorists who carry on the tradition of progressive education, Peter Elbow and Ken Bruffee.

Elbow's *Writing without Teachers* first introduced many of us to the usefulness of groups in the teaching of writing, and gave us some insights into their dynamics. But his more recent book, *Writing with Power*, shifts the emphasis away from the social context, returning to some essential internal power as a way of control of self and others. For Elbow, language may get work done in the social world, and the individual learner may use that social world as a tool to help him or her learn writing, but the system of language is produced by individuals, not by society. It is true that he seems to emphasize the social context of writing and the uses of consensus in his chapters on "Audience" and "Feedback." And he emphasizes the need to make the classroom reflect the world, using terms very much like those of Leonard: "any 'back to basics' movement in the teaching of writing needs to start by ensuring each child the most basic thing of all: a real audience for his written words—an audience that really listens and takes the interchange seriously" (184). This might seem to be a difficult need to satisfy in the composition class, but even in the artificial world of the classroom, "there is always a useful real audience available to whom writing can easily be delivered: other members of the class" (230).

For Elbow, as for Leonard, power over real audiences comes from an immediate connection with reality gained through a breaking down of stifling conventions. Writing with power requires authenticity of expression ("voice") and unmediated realism of perception in which the writer and reader must "see" the object written about (316). The problem with this call for direct experience of reality is that, as with Leonard, one must ask to which reality is one admitted. Elbow, unlike Leonard, acknowledges the existence of fundamentally different views of the world. But he still sees these views as free and individual, not acknowledging the way they are structured by ideology. So in his book, reality is divided between a cold, clear outside and a warm, messy inside. Writing consists of the negotiation between these two sides of the individual. In Elbow's model, the audience is essential to help in revision, but the best words come from deep down inside, from one's voice. Problems are solved in this model by changing the inside; change in the outside, that is, power over others, follows from this success in dealing with oneself. No wonder Elbow ends with a chapter on "Writing and Magic"; magic is the only possible source for such ineffable energies. This relentlessly internal approach to writing is both the book's strength and its weakness. *Writing with Power* consists almost entirely of vivid, often visceral, usually organic metaphors for creation.[12] These metaphors may help us see our processes of writing in new ways, but they also prevent any analysis of the social conditions of our writing. There is no real place in this model for a discourse group that gives one the structures of words one takes for granted.

Elbow has been a powerful writer for reform. Does his insistence that personal authenticity is the source of power apply to his own writing? He refers often to his own internal struggles in writing the book. I would argue, though, that its rhetorical power comes not from these struggles, but from its place in a group of texts. It gives a new metaphorical guise to familiar progressive education concepts, and makes an appeal to individualism that is a commonplace of American rhetoric. It has some affinities with a long line of straight-talking guides to self-improvement. Take, for example, the tone of hip moralism that combines with the traditional moralism of delayed reward in this passage: "If you slip into free-writing for the sake of producing good pieces of writing, then you put a kind of short-run utilitarian pressure on the process, and hinder yourself from getting all the other benefits" (*Writing with Power* 17). Now there is nothing wrong with using the jargon of self-improvement, any more than there is with using Marxist jargon as I do. My point is that both Elbow and I write within discourses developed in social processes, and that his account ignores these processes.

The work of Kenneth Bruffee can help us critique the appeal to reality that Leonard and Elbow make, especially in the recent essays in which Bruffee attempts to establish the theoretical grounds of collaborative learning. But his appeal to consensus is similar to theirs, and I think a lack of analysis of this consensus is the weak point of his theory. We might not see, at first, how different he is from Leonard and Elbow; he says in his textbook *A Short Course in Writing* that he starts with a search for a method of writing that will be *real*. "Peer criticism," he says, "is the most *real* writing students will ever do as students," because the writer has an immediate and actual audience and purpose (115). Similarly, an exercise on reminiscence tells the student, "Just begin at the beginning and tell the whole truth" (3). Where Bruffee differs from Leonard and Elbow begins to be apparent in the next exercise, when he asks the student to retell a "family story" that has become formalized with retelling over time. This exercise suggests, as the personal reminiscence assignment in most textbooks cannot, the degree to which language is given by the social group, in this case the family. The student must try to translate the private language of the family into the language of the classroom, noticing the difference.

For Bruffee, "writing is a communal activity," not just an essence of meaning given by the individual to the community. Instead of tracing language to an original voice inside, Bruffee asks questions to make the reader "see an essay as a 'thing' someone has made, like a table or a chair—something artificially designed, shaped, and put together to serve a purpose" (122). He says his system of peer criticism will enable students to "gain a stronger sense of the degree to which knowledge, like writing itself, is a social phenomenon, and the degree to which the social context in which we learn permeates what we know and how we know it" (116). In his view of knowledge, the group is there from the beginning, defining the terms of thought, and does not simply come in at the end, as an audience.

But while Bruffee shows that reality can be seen as a social construct, he does not give us any way to criticize this construct. Having discovered the role of consensus in the production of knowledge, he takes this consensus as something that just is, rather than a something that might be good or bad. For instance, in his recent essays, he argues for collaborative learning because it is the norm in business, industry, and the professions. This is true enough, but I question whether analogy to these institutions is, in itself, an argument for a teaching method. We need to look at the consensus within these institutions as the result of conflicts, not as a monolith. To decide whether the groups in our classes are introducing students to new communities of discourse, or are confining them in ideological structures, we need a clearer definition than he gives of what these interpretive communities are, and a sense of the historical processes shaping them.

Bruffee defines discourse communities in terms of certain kinds of academic or non-academic knowledge. For instance, he says, "Every student is already a member of several knowledge communities, from canoeing to computers, baseball to ballet" ("Collaborative Learning" 644). Bruffee suggests in another article that social differences are incidental to the process of education and should drop away if the students share an educational goal. "Outside the learning group . . . people may have widely different positions in the management hierarchy of a union or corporation, in the professional or student hierarchy of an educational institution, or in a system of economic or social class. But as collaborative learners all these people are peers. With regard to a course in ethnography or elementary Chinese, the vice-president of a corporation, the janitor, the English professor, the freshman, the society matron, and the shoe salesman must leave their social differences behind" ("CLTV" 38).[13]

This is an attractive and idealistic vision, but it assumes that knowledge is outside the realm of these people's social differences. Look over the list and ask who is most likely to be in a course on ethnography or elementary Chinese? Who, on the other hand, is likely to be in a course on English as a second language or on basic office skills? Who is likely to be in a basic writing course at the City University? To ask such questions is to realize that knowledge is not uniformly distributed in our society, and that it is not all of a piece. If we turn a blind eye to social factors we are likely merely to perpetuate the provision of different kinds of knowledge for the rich and the poor.

Bruffee sometimes includes non-academic knowledge in examples of discourse communities. For instance, he talks in one article about the contribution to the writing group of knowledge gained in office work, or in organizing a household. But what if one considers the knowledge of communities whose interests might be opposed, say the knowledge of social workers and the knowledge of welfare clients, or the knowledge of an accountant and the knowledge of employees in a factory to be closed? Such bodies of knowledge cannot be resolved into a consensus without one side losing something.

How are discourse communities made? Bruffee sees how society furthers thought or hinders it, but he does not see social and economic factors as providing his structures. For him, these factors are unfortunate limitations to our thought and conversation that must be eliminated as much as possible.

> Limitations that may be imposed for example, by ethnocentrism, inexperience, personal anxiety, economic interests, and paradigmatic inflexibility can constrain my thinking just as they can constrain conversation. If my talk is narrow, superficial, biased, and confined to clichés, my thinking is likely to be so too. ("Collaborative Learning" 639)

I would see such limitations as giving the structure to our thought. Ethnocentrism and economic interests are not just unfortunate habits, they are whole systems of ideas that people take for granted and use to make sense of the world. One cannot escape from one's economic interests and ethnic background, but one can try to understand how they shape one's thinking and social actions.

The model Bruffee gives for change in knowledge, adapted from Thomas Kuhn and Richard Rorty, leads us away from such analysis. It attributes the growth of knowledge and change of paradigms to factors internal to the discipline, such as the multiplication of anomalies and the shift of paradigms. The only conflict is between normal science and extraordinary science, or normal discourse and abnormal discourse. An alternative model would be in the work of historians and sociologists of science who see change in terms of social and economic factors.[14] For instance, Bruffee might call his own composition theory a new paradigm, resulting from the new models of Kuhn and Rorty. I might call it an attempt to rationalize theoretically the methods he earlier developed, and I would trace these methods to the institutional need, which he describes in his article, to deal with new kinds of university students. Similarly, I might trace my interest in these questions to my teaching of basic writing at Queens College. Ultimately, I would trace both his thinking and mine to the challenges of Open Admissions at CUNY. And Open Admissions was not the result of a paradigm shift in the philosophy of education; it emerged from the political conflicts of New York City in the 1960s.

Bruffee's recent essay points out that "The view that knowledge is a social artifact . . . requires a reexamination of our premises as students of English and as teachers" ("Collaborative Learning" 650). His suggestions for reform are excellent: he would "demystify" the humanities and the relation of teacher to student by putting them in a social context. But I think he underestimates the difficulty of the reforms he proposes, because he sees the resistance to them as a matter of habit, not of ideology. In *A Short Course*, he describes the problem he is addressing in terms of what he sees as "a conflict between two forces: the docility and dependence created in young people by American schooling and the increasing demand of modern life that human beings be autonomous, flexible, and self-possessed" (vii). But these two forces are not in conflict if we see the interests of employers, rather than "modern life" as the force that makes demands here. Students can be both docile and convinced of their autonomy, freedom of choice, and control of their lives. A school that reproduced this ideological construct would be a successful school.

In his recent article, Bruffee sees some of these dangers clearly enough. He points out the "provincial" nature of what he and Rorty call normal discourse. He also seems to recognize the kinds of possible dangers in the use of collaborative learning that I pointed out in some of Leonard's examples. He refers to the need to avoid "the many possible negative effects of peer group influence: conformity, anti-intellectualism, intimidation, and leveling-down of quality." He would do this by making "collaboration . . . a genuine part of students' educational development" (652). I would do it by emphasizing conflict as well as collaboration. I think he is referring to the same sense of a divided role I have described when he says "we must perform as conservators *and* agents of change, as custodians of prevailing community values *and* as agents of social transition and reacculturation" (650).

LESSONS FOR REFORMERS

I find I have no suggestions for assignments that are as innovative as those of the authors I am criticizing. But that is partly because what I have to suggest is not a method but a stance toward one's teaching. This stance requires a sort of doubleness: an awareness that one's course is part of an ideological structure that keeps people from thinking about their situation, but also a belief that one can resist this structure and help students to criticize it.

The sense of conflict in these three writers is clear enough when they describe their work as teachers. In each case they have a problem with existing institutions; in each case they offer an escape that I don't think works. Leonard, for instance, offers professionalism as an escape from the sense of pointlessness many teachers have: "It becomes clear how different a subject it is coming to be from the sodden, idealless drudgery of themes swoopingly red-inked and at the nearest possible moment thrown into the wastebasket" (193). Escape for him is through attention to the new research in composition in the 1920s ("Research on the Teaching of English"). But research will not change the basic antagonism of student and teacher he describes here.

Elbow, in his advice to students about writing in school, presents powerfully the role and limitations of the teacher:

> Teachers are good for giving criticism because they read papers in piles of 25 or 50. Take that criticism and use it. They are good at making you write when you don't feel like it, simply because they have authority. Instead of resenting this, try appreciating it and internalizing from it what may be the most important skill of all: the ability to write when you are in the wrong mood. They are *not* good at telling you what your writing feels like to a real human being, at taking your words seriously as messages directed to them, at praising you, or perhaps even at noticing you. Get these things elsewhere. (*Writing With Power* 234)

This is excellent advice, but Elbow's solution, that of using the tension between teacher and student, is based on his assumption that there is a world elsewhere of "real human beings." There is, of course, a world outside of school, and he is right to remind us of these other readers and writers. But the kinds of authority embodied in the school are present in the rest of the culture as well. The writer of an engineering proposal, a magazine article, or even a poem, is constrained by structures as powerful as those determining the freshman composition theme. The classroom alienation he takes for granted, in which the teacher processes batches of student raw material, is characteristic, not only of school, but of other institutions in our society. Bruffee traces his own interest in collaborative learning to a similar realization of how alienating his work had become:

> When I began teaching composition, I was still in graduate school. I had large classes, and I did not really know what I was doing. Every class hour seemed to stretch on to eternity. Grading papers took hours and was a dreadful grind. I kept hoping my classes would get smaller and the hour shorter. Instead, my classes got larger and the hour longer. I kept hoping I would learn to grade papers more easily and quickly. That did not happen either. Worst of all, I was not really sure that I was teaching anybody anything. (*Short Course* 184)

All three writers start by considering the drudgery of the work, the enormous numbers of papers, and the opposition of teachers and students. They want a change in the conditions of work, and a system that allows them to teach as well as just evaluate. They make a good case in these passages, whether they realize it or not, that our problems will not be solved just by new methods, or new theories, or new knowledge. We should begin by realizing that our interests are not the same as those of the institutions that employ us, and that the improvement of our work will involve social changes. No amount of merely educational reform will end the alienation described in these passages.

But this is not to say that all attempts at change are foiled by an all-powerful system, and that real change must wait until a revolution. Paul Willis warns other Marxist theorists against such an attitude at the end of *Learning to Labour*, his fine book on ideological reproduction in a British secondary school. He suggests the sort of double role for teachers that I have been arguing for here.

> If we have nothing to say about what to do on Monday morning then every-thing is yielded to a purist structuralist Marxist tautology: nothing can be done until the basic structures of society are changed but the structures prevent us from making any changes. There is no contradiction in asking practitioners to work on two levels simultaneously—to face immediate

problems in doing 'the best' (so far as they can see it) for their clients whilst appreciating all the time that these very actions may help to produce the structures within which the problems arise. (186)

What this approach means for, say, a basic writing teacher is that one teaches the forms of academic writing, so that students who might not finish four years of college have a better chance of finishing, without assuming that there is anything liberating about these forms or about academic discourse. One teaches job letters to the business communications students who need to get jobs downtown, without teaching that a job downtown is the answer to their problems. I have no specific new ideas for what we should do Monday morning, but I follow with interest those of other radical teachers. In this article, I am asking, not for a new kind of assignment, but for more skepticism about what assignments do to reproduce the structures of our society.

We should keep a similar skepticism about the appeals to reality and consensus in composition theory and research. There have been a number of recent articles calling for a view of writing as a social process.[15] This is a welcome corrective to the individualism of the cognitive psychology models of the 1970s. But we should not let our enthusiasm for this social view lead us to accepting social construction of knowledge as something good in itself. The kind of critique begun in *College English* by Richard Ohmann, Stanley Aronowitz, and others is even more appropriate now that we are seeing writing in a social context. I think these theories will be developed with more sophistication if we draw on critiques developed by such sociologists of education as Apple and Giroux, and on materials provided by historians of education.[16]

Leonard in the 1920s, and Elbow and Bruffee today, have made teachers aware of the need for changes in the way we teach. The work of sociologists and historians of education would help us to remain aware that the changes we propose may finally support an existing consensus and a conception of reality that supports those now in power. Our sense that something is wrong should lead us to criticize our own function in society, as well as our pedagogy. Otherwise, to use a comment of Leonard's from another, entirely different context, "It has less effect than a spoonful of water poured over a flock of ducks" ("Composition and Grammar" 448).

NOTES

1. Some recent historical studies that discuss reform in composition include those by James Berlin (whose book has an extensive bibliography), Michael Halloran, Robert Conners, Wallace Douglas, (whose article appears in a special issue of the *English Journal* devoted to the history of the profession), and Evelyn Wright.

2. See *English Composition as a Social Problem* for references to invention (81), sentence-combining (158), "schoolmastering" (183 and many other references). On Piaget, see "Relating the Teaching of English to Reality" (45).

3. For a discussion of the term, see Raymond Williams, *Keywords*. For a series of reviews of various studies of ideology, see Centre for Contemporary Cultural Studies, *On Ideology*.

4. Several detailed historical and sociological studies along these lines are collected in Michael Apple, ed., *Cultural and Economic Reproduction in Education*. Important earlier articles on ideology in education are collected in the Open University reader, Roger Dale et al., eds., *Schooling and Capitalism: A Sociological Reader*. A recent analysis of educational theories, in clear but rather abstract terms, is Henry Giroux, *Theory and Resistance in Education: A Pedagogy for the Opposition*. Current critical articles on the sociology of education often appear in the journal *Curriculum Inquiry*.

5. See Cremin; David Hogan, "Education and Class Formation: The Peculiarities of Americans," in Apple's collection; and Diane Ravitch's quite readable book on the case of New York City.

6. Biographical information on Leonard is from W. E. Leonard's *DAB* entry. Background to the period is from the books by J. N. Hook and Arthur Applebee, and from Merle Curti's contemporary study. Curti, like me, looks at these ideas from the left, but he considers Dewey's influence entirely progressive. A reviewer of my article recommended the chapter on Leonard by John Brereton in *Traditions of Inquiry* (New York: Oxford UP, 1985). The whole book should be relevant to my topic here, but it was unavailable in Britain as I revised this article.

7. Leonard's study, which he left incomplete at his death, is included in Albert Marck-wardt's *Facts About Current English Usage*.

8. On Americanization, see Cremin; Hook; Ravitch; and *English Journal in the 1920s*.

9. See Richard Ohmann, "Use Specific, Definite, Concrete Language."

10. For an example of the rhetoric of composition reform, see Donald Stewart, "Composition Textbooks and the Assault on Tradition," and some of the other articles collected in Gary Tate and Edward P. J. Corbett, eds., *The Writing Teacher's Sourcebook*.

11. Leonard's study is similar to that in Nancy Sommer's recent article, "Responding to Student Writing." Like Leonard, Sommers only gives examples of comments that are badly done. Dan Moshenberg pointed out to me the similarity of Leonard's study to the experiment in poetry criticism I. A. Richards reports in *Practical Criticism*.

12. Those who favor such visceral metaphors should see Lester Faigley's paper, "Peristalsis as Paradigm: From Process to Product."

13. See also two other essays by Bruffee, "The Structure of Knowledge and the Future of Liberal Education," and "Liberal Education and the Social Justification of Belief."

14. A good introduction to the sociology of scientific knowledge is another Open University reader, edited by Barry Barnes and David Edge.

15. See, for example, the very different approaches of Patricia Bizzell, of Bruffee ("Writing and Reading as Collaborative Social Acts"), and of Charles Bazerman ("Scientific Writing as a Social Act"). Bazerman, like Bruffee, has a textbook based on his approach (*The Informed Writer*).

16. For example, one way of seeing how deeply ingrained and uncritical are the psychological categories we use to define basic writers is to read the historical treatment of these categories in Steven Shapin and Barry Barnes, "Head and Hand: Rhetorical Resources in British Pedagogical Writing 1770–1850."

WORKS CITED

Apple, Michael, ed. *Cultural and Economic Reproduction in Education*. London: Routledge, 1982.

Applebee, Arthur. *Tradition and Reform in the Teaching of English*. Urbana: NCTE, 1974.

Aronowitz, Stanley. "Mass Culture and the Eclipse of Reason: The Pedagogical Implications." *College English* 38 (1977): 768–72.

Barnes, Barry, and David Edge, eds. *Science in Context*. Milton Keynes: Open UP, 1982.

Bazerman, Charles. *The Informed Writer*. 2nd ed. Boston: Houghton, 1985.

———. "Scientific Writing as a Social Act." *New Essays in Scientific and Technical Communication*. Ed. Carolyn Miller, et al. Farmingdale, New York: Baywood, 1983. 157–84.

Berlin, James. *Writing Instruction in Nineteenth-Century American Colleges*. Carbondale: Southern Illinois UP Press, 1984.

Bizzell, Patricia. "Cognition, Convention, and Certainty: What We Need to Know About Writing." *PrelText* 3 (1982): 213–43.

Bruffee, Kenneth. "CLTV: Collaborative Learning Television." *Educational Communication and Technology Journal* 30 (1982): 26–40.

———. "Collaborative Learning and the 'Conversation of Mankind.'" *College English* 46 (1984): 635–52.

———. "Liberal Education and the Social Justification of Belief." *Liberal Education* 68 (1982): 95–114.

———. *A Short Course in Writing*. 2nd ed. Boston: Winthrop, 1980.

———. "The Structure of Knowledge and the Future of Liberal Education." *Liberal Education* 67 (1981): 177–86.

———. "Writing and Reading as Collaborative Social Acts." *The Writer's Mind*. Ed. Janice Hays. Urbana: NCTE, 1983.

Centre for Contemporary Cultural Studies. *On Ideology*. London: Hutchinson University Library, 1978.

Connors, Robert. "The Rise and Fall of the Modes of Discourse." *College Composition and Communication* 32 (1981): 444–55.

Cremin, Lawrence. *The Transformation of the School*. New York: Vintage, 1961.

Curti, Merle. *The Social Ideas of American Educators*. New York: Scribner's, 1935.

Dale, Roger, et al., eds. *Schooling and Capitalism: A Sociological Reader*. London: Routledge, 1976.

Dewey, John. *The School and Society*. Chicago: U of Chicago P, 1898.

Douglas, Wallace. "Why Know Our History." *English Journal* 68 (1979): 16–21.

Elbow, Peter. *Writing with Power*. New York: Oxford UP, 1982.

———. *Writing without Teachers*. New York: Oxford UP, 1973.

Faigley, Lester. "Peristalsis as Paradigm: From Process to Product." Paper presented at the panel on "Nutrastylistics" at the Conference on College Composition and Communication, Minneapolis, March 1985.

Giroux, Henry. *Theory and Resistance in Education: A Pedagogy for the Opposition*. London: Heinemann Educational Books, 1983.

Halloran, Michael. "Rhetoric in the American College Curriculum: The Decline of Public Discourse." *PrelText* 3 (1982): 245–269.

Hook, J. N. *A Long Way Together*. Urbana: NCTE, 1979.

Kantor, Kevin. "Creative Expression in the English Curriculum: An Historical Perspective." *Research in the Teaching of English* 9 (1975): 5–29.

Leonard, Sterling. "As to the Forms of Discourse." *English Journal* 3 (1914): 201–211.

———. "Composition and Grammar in the Junior High School." *The Classroom Teacher* 10 (1927): 309–449.

———. "Current Definition of Levels in English Usage." *English Journal* 16 (1926): 345–59.

———. *The Doctrine of Correctness in English Usage, 1700–1800.* Madison: U of Wisconsin P, 1929.

———. *English Composition as a Social Problem.* Boston: Houghton, 1917.

———. "How English Teachers Correct Papers." *English Journal* 20 (1923): 517–31.

———. "Relating the Teaching of English to Reality." *Nation's Schools* 4 (1929): 45–48.

———. "Research on the Teaching of English." *Journal of Educational Research* 19 (1929): 317–21.

———. "What About Correct English?" *The Teachers Journal and Abstract* 6 (1931): 252–56.

Leonard, W. E. "Sterling Andrus Leonard." *Dictionary of American Biography.* 9: 168–9.

Marckwardt, Albert. *Facts About Current English Usage.* New York: Appleton-Century, 1938.

Ohmann, Richard. *English in America: A Radical View of the Profession.* New York: Oxford UP, 1976.

———. "Use Specific, Definite, Concrete Language." *College English* 41 (1979): 379–89.

Ravitch, Diane. *The Great School Wars: New York City, 1805–1973.* New York: Basic, 1974.

Richards, I. A. *Practical Criticism.* New York: Harcourt, 1929.

Shapin, Steven, and Barry Barnes. "Head and Hand: Rhetorical Resources in British Pedagogical Writing 1770–1850." *Oxford Review of Education* 2 (1976): 235–50.

Sommers, Nancy. "Responding to Student Writing." *College Composition and Communication* 32 (1982): 148–56.

Tate, Gary, and Edward P. J. Corbett, eds. *The Writing Teacher's Sourcebook.* New York: Oxford, 1981.

Williams, Raymond. *Keywords.* London: Oxford UP, 1976.

Willis, Paul. *Learning to Labour: How Working Class Kids Get Working Class Jobs.* Farnborough, England: Saxon, 1977.

Wright, Evelyn. "School English and Public Policy." *College English* 42 (1980): 327–42.

Consensus and Difference in Collaborative Learning

JOHN TRIMBUR

Kenneth A. Bruffee, Harvey S. Wiener, and others have argued that collaborative learning may be distinguished from other forms of group work on the grounds that it organizes students not just to work together on common projects but more important to engage in a process of intellectual negotiation and collective decision-making. The aim of collaborative learning, its advocates hold, is to reach consensus through an expanding conversation. This conversation takes place at a number of levels—first in small discussion groups, next among the groups in a class, then between the class and the teacher, and finally among the class, the teacher, and the wider community of knowledge. In Bruffee's social constructionist pedagogy, the language used to reach consensus acquires greater authority as it acquires greater social weight: the knowledge students put into words counts for more as they test it out, revising and relocating it by taking into account what their peers, the teacher, and voices outside the classroom have to say.

The purpose of this essay is to examine two important criticisms of the politics of collaborative learning in order to explore one of the key terms in collaborative learning, consensus. This seems worth doing because the notion of consensus is one of the most controversial and misunderstood aspects of collaborative learning.

One line of criticism argues that the use of consensus in collaborative learning is an inherently dangerous and potentially totalitarian practice that stifles individual voice and creativity, suppresses differences, and enforces conformity. Thomas S. Johnson, for example, believes that consensus is just

Reprinted from *College English* 51.6 (October 1989): 602–16. Used with permission.

another name for "group think" and conjures images of 1984. Pedro Beade worries that consensus might be used to justify the practices of "a crazy, totalitarian state" (708). These critics of collaborative learning want to rescue the sovereignty and autonomy of the individual from what Johnson calls collaborative learning's "peer indoctrination classes." Underlying these political objections is the sense, as David Foster puts it, that the human mind is "far too mysterious and fascinating" to take the social constructionist route and "ground its utterances" in a "normative social community." According to Foster, collaborative learning is based on an epistemological mistake: Bruffee's "overeager application of the social constructionist label" causes him to overvalue social practices and thus to deny the primacy of individual consciousness in creating knowledge.

A second line of criticism, on the other hand, agrees with Bruffee that things like selves, knowledge, discourse, readers, and writers are indeed socially constructed. What left-wing critics such as Greg Myers do worry about, however, is that Bruffee's social constructionist pedagogy runs the risk of limiting its focus to the internal workings of discourse communities and of overlooking the wider social forces that structure the production of knowledge. To understand the production and validation of knowledge, Myers argues, we need to know not just how knowledge communities operate consensually but how knowledge and its means of production are distributed in an unequal, exclusionary social order and embedded in hierarchical relations of power. Without a critique of the dominant power relations that organize the production of knowledge, left-wing critics hold, the social constructionist rationale for collaborative learning may, unwittingly or not, accommodate its practices to the authority of knowledge it believes it is demystifying.

In this essay I propose to extend the left critique, not to abandon the notion of consensus but to revise it, as a step toward developing a critical practice of collaborative learning. I want to concede that consensus in some of its pedagogical uses may indeed be an accommodation to the workings of normal discourse and function thereby as a component to promote conformity and improve the performance of the system. My point will be, however, that consensus need not inevitably result in accommodation. The politics of consensus depends on the teacher's practice. Consensus, I will argue, can be a powerful instrument for students to generate differences, to identify the systems of authority that organize these differences, and to transform the relations of power that determine who may speak and what counts as a meaningful statement.

Before I outline the critical and transformative projects I believe are implied in collaborative learning, I want to address the fear of conformity in the first line of criticism—the fear that collaborative learning denies differences and threatens individuality. It is important to acknowledge that this fear points to some real problems that arise when students work together in groups—problems such as parochialism, demagoguery, narrow appeals to common sense, an urge to reach noncontroversial consensus without considering alternatives. After all, we cannot realistically expect that collaborative learning will lead students spontaneously to transcend the limits of American culture, its homogenizing force, its engrained suspicion of social and cultural differences, its tendency to reify the other and blame the victim. But if the fear of conformity is a legitimate one, it is not for the reasons the first group of Bruffee's critics gives. Their effort to save the individual from the group is based on an unhelpful and unnecessary polarization of the individual and society.

The limits of these critics' fear of conformity can best be seen, I think, by emphasizing the influence of John Dewey's educational pragmatism on collaborative learning. What Bruffee takes from Dewey is a strong appreciation of the generativity of group life and its promise for classroom teaching. Consensus represents the potentiality of social agency inherent in group life—the capacity for self-organization, cooperation, shared decision-making, and common action. From a pragmatist perspective, the goal of reaching consensus gives the members of a group a stake in collective projects. It does not inhibit individuality, as it does for those who fear consensus will lead to conformity. Rather it enables individuals to participate actively and meaningfully in group life. If anything, it is through the social interaction of shared activity that individuals realize their own power to take control of their situation by collaborating with others.

For Deweyans, the effort to save the individual from the group is at best misguided and at worst reactionary. On one hand, pragmatists see no reason to rescue the individual from "normative communities" because in effect there is nowhere else the individual can be: consciousness is the extension of social experience inward. On the other hand, the desire to escape from "normative communities" and break out of the "prison house of language" by grounding utterances in the generative force of individual consciousness springs from an ideological complex of belief and practice.

Dewey's educational pragmatism recasts the fear that consensus will inevitably lead to conformity as a fear of group life itself. Pedagogies that take the individual as the irreducible, inviolate starting point of education—whether through individualized instruction, cultivation of personal voice, or an emphasis on creativity and self-actualization—inscribe a deeply contradictory ideology of individualism in classroom practice. If these pedagogies seek to liberate the individual, they also simultaneously constitute the student as a social atom, an accounting unit under the teacher's gaze, a record kept by the teacher. The fear of consensus often betrays a fear of peer group influence—a fear that students will keep their own records, work out collective norms, and take action. Rather than the liberation of the individual it claims to be, the fear of "group-think" is implicitly teacher-centered and authoritarian. It prevents a class of students from transforming themselves from an aggregate of individuals into a participatory learning community. The mode of teaching and learning remains what Bruffee calls "authoritarian-individualist": the atomization of students locks them into a one-to-one relation to the teacher, the repository of effective authority in the classroom, and cuts them off from the possibilities of jointly empowering activities carried out in the society of peers. In short, the critique of consensus in the name of individualism is baseless. Consensus does not necessarily violate the individual but instead can enable individuals to empower each other through social activity.

We may now take up the left-wing critique. Here the issue is not the status of the individual but the status of exchange among individuals. We should note, first of all, that Bruffee and his left-wing critics occupy a good deal of common ground concerning the social relationships of intellectual exchange as they are played out in the classroom. For teachers and theorists looking for a critical pedagogy, Bruffee's work has been important because it teaches us to read the classroom and the culture of teaching and learning as a social text.

How we teach, Bruffee suggests, is what we teach. For Bruffee, pedagogy is not a neutral practice of transmitting knowledge from one place to another, from the teacher's head to the students'. The pedagogical project that Bruffee initiated in the early seventies calls into question the dynamics of cultural reproduction in the classroom, a process that normally operates, as it were, behind our backs. What before had seemed commonsensical became in Bruffee's reading of the classroom as a social text a set of historically derived practices—an atomized and authoritarian culture that mystifies the production of knowledge and reproduces hierarchical relations of power and domination. Bruffee's formulation of collaborative learning in the early seventies offers an implicit critique of the culture of the classroom, the sovereignty of the teacher, the reification of knowledge, the atomized authority-dependence of students, and the competitiveness and intellectual hoarding encouraged by the traditional reward system and the wider meritocratic order in higher education.

In his early work, Bruffee sees collaborative learning as part of a wider movement for participatory democracy, shared decision-making, and nonauthoritarian styles of leadership and group life. "In the world which surrounds the classroom," Bruffee says in 1973, "people today are challenging and revising many social and political traditions which have heretofore gone unquestioned"; if education has been resistant to collaboration, "[e]lsewhere, everywhere, collaborative action increasingly pervades our society" ("Collaborative Learning" 634). In Bruffee's account, collaborative learning occurs—along with free universities, grassroots organizing, the consciousness-raising groups of women's liberation, the anti-war movement, and so on—as a moment in the cultural history of the sixties, the name we now give to signify delegitimation of power and the search for alternative forms of social and political life. I think it is not accidental that collaborative learning emerged initially within open admissions programs, as part of a wider response to political pressures from below to extend literacy and access to higher education to black, Hispanic, and working-class people who had formerly been excluded.

From the late seventies to the present, Bruffee has asked what it means to reorganize the social relations in the classroom and how the decentering of authority that takes place in collaborative learning might change the way we talk about the nature of liberal education and the authority of knowledge and its institutions. Bruffee's ongoing efforts to find a language adequate to this task—to theorize collaborative learning as a social constructionist pedagogy—have turned, in the ensuing discussion, into the source of recent left-wing challenges to his work. One of the central issues of contention concerns Bruffee's appropriation of Richard Rorty's notion of conversation.

The term conversation has become a social constructionist code word to talk about knowledge and teaching and learning as social—not cognitive—acts. Knowledge, in this account, is not the result of the confrontation of the individual mind with reality but of the conversation that organizes the available means we have at any given time to talk about reality. Learning, therefore, cannot be understood strictly on cognitive grounds; it means rather joining new communities and taking part in new conversations. Learning, as Rorty puts it, "is a shift in a person's relations with others, not a shift inside the person that now *suits* him to enter new relationships" (*Philosophy* 187). By organizing students to participate in conversation, Bruffee argues, collaborative learning forms transitional communities to help students undergo the stressful and anxiety-inducing process of moving out of their indigenous communities and acquiring fluency in the conversation of liberally educated men and women. For Bruffee, Rorty's notion of conversation provides a rationale for collaborative learning as a process of re-acculturation, of learning to participate in the ongoing discussions of new communities.

This is a powerful rationale because it translates a wider reinterpretation of knowledge taking place in contemporary critical theory to the classroom—and gives us a way to incorporate what Bruffee calls the "social turn" in twentieth-century thought into the theory and practice of teaching. Still, for left-wing teachers and theorists, there is something troubling about Rorty's notion of conversation, something in the metaphor worth unpacking.

For Rorty, the term conversation offers a useful way to talk about the production of knowledge as a social process without reference to metaphysical foundations. Rorty's notion of conversation describes a discourse that has no beginning or end, but no crisis or contradiction, either. Cut loose from metaphysical moorings and transcendental backups, the conversation keeps rolling of its own accord, reproducing itself effortlessly, responsible only to itself, sanctioned by what Rorty sees as the only sanction credible: our loyalty to the conversation and our solidarity with its practices. All we can do is to continue the conversation initiated before we appeared on the scene. "We do not know," Rorty says, "what 'success' would mean except simply 'continuance'" (*Consequences* 172).

In political terms, what Rorty calls "postmodernist bourgeois liberalism" hangs onto the "ideals of the Enlightenment" but gives up the belief in Enlightenment reason. In Rorty's hands, the metaphor of conversation invokes an eighteenth-century vision of freely constituted, discoursing subjects taking part in polite speech, in Enlightenment salons and coffee houses, in the "republic of letters" emerging in the interstices of the absolutist state. To historicize Rorty's metaphor is to disclose what Terry Eagleton calls the "bourgeoisie's dream of freedom": "a society of petty producers whose endlessly available, utterly inexhaustible commodity is discourse itself" (16–17). As Eagleton argues, the "bourgeoisie . . . discovers in discourse an idealized image of its own social relations" (16). Conversation becomes the only truly free market, an ideal discursive space where exchange without domination is possible, where social differences are converted into abstract equalities at the level of speech acts.

Only now, Rorty says, the discourse must operate without the consensus of universal reason that eighteenth-century speakers took to be the normative grounding of their utterances. Given the postmodernist's disbelief in metanarratives of reason and freedom, Rebecca Comay argues, the conversation loses its emancipatory edge and "adapts to the episodic rhythms of commercial culture" (122). If we've traded in the old metaphysical comforts for a cheerful, if ungrounded affirmation of conversation, we do so, Rorty says, so we can "read more, talk more, write more" (*Philosophy* 375). The logic of planned obsolescence drives the conversation as we look for the "new, better, more interesting, more fruitful ways of speaking" (*Philosophy* 360). In a world without foundations, "nobody is so passé as the intellectual czar of the previous generation . . . the man who redescribed all those old descriptions, which, thanks in part to his redescriptions of them, nobody now wants to know anything about" (*Consequences* xl–xli). According to the idealized exchange of a free and open market, conversation keeps circulating in a spectacle of production and consumption. The new becomes old, the fashionable out-of-date, but the conversation itself is inexhaustible. "Evanescent moments in a continuing conversation . . . we keep the conversation going" (*Philosophy* 378).

Stripped of its universalist principles, the conversation turns into an act of assimilation. Unpacked, Rorty's metaphor of conversation offers a version of nonfoundationalism without tears. The consensus that keeps things rolling is no longer based on higher purposes but instead on the recognition that if we cannot discover the truth in any final sense, what we can do is to keep on talking to each other: we can tell stories, give accounts, state reasons, negotiate differences, and so on. The conversation, that is, gives up teleological ends to reaffirm the sociability of intellectual exchange. And if, as Rorty says, the conversation is simply the way we justify our beliefs socially, then we might as well relax, get good at it, and enjoy it.

Of course there are considerable attractions to this view. But there are some problems too. Rorty acknowledges, for example, the tendency of discourse to normalize itself and to block the flow of conversation by posing as a "canonical vocabulary." The conversation, as Rorty starts to acknowledge here, is perpetually materializing itself in institutional forms, alloting the opportunity to speak and arbitrating the terms of discussion. But Rorty, finally, backs away from the full consequences of conversation's normative force. At just the point where we could name the conversation and its underlying consensus as a technology of power and ask how its practices enable and constrain the production of knowledge, privilege and exclude forms of discourse, set its agenda by ignoring or suppressing others. Rorty builds a self-correcting mechanism into the conversation, an invisible hand to keep the discourse circulating and things from going stale. This is abnormal discourse or, as Rorty says, "what happens when someone joins in the discourse who is ignorant of . . . conventions or who sets them aside" (*Philosophy* 320).

Rorty's view of abnormal discourse is, I think, a problematical one. On one hand, it identifies abnormal discourse with a romantic realm of thinking the unthinkable, of solitary voices calling out, of the imagination cutting against the grain. In keeping with this romantic figure of thought, Rorty makes abnormal discourse the activity par excellence not of the group but of the individual—the genius, the rebel, the fool, "some*one* . . . who is ignorant of . . . conventions or sets them aside." This side of abnormal discourse, moreover, resists formulation. There is, Rorty says, "no discipline which describes it, any more than there is a discipline devoted to a study of the unpredictable, or of 'creativity'" (*Philosophy* 320). It is simply "generated by free and leisured conversation . . . as the sparks fly up" (321).

At the same time, though we can't know abnormal discourse on its own terms, we can identify how it functions, but now from a pragmatist perspective, to keep the conversation going. In other words, at just the moment Rorty seems to introduce difference and destabilize the conversation, he turns crisis, conflict, and contradiction into homeostatic gestures whose very expression restabilizes the conversation. What remains, once we've removed universal reason, narratives of emancipation, or "permanent neutral frameworks" as the grounds for adjudicating knowledge claims, is civility, the agreement to keep on talking. The "power of strangeness" in abnormal discourse "to take us out of our old selves" and "to make us into new beings" (*Philosophy* 360) simply reaffirms our solidarity with the conversation.

Left-wing critics are uncomfortable with this position. They want to interrupt the conversation, to denaturalize its workings, and to talk about the way conversation legitimizes itself by its very performance. Left-wing critics worry that Rortyian conversation downplays its own social force and the conflict it generates, the discourses silenced or unheard in the conversation and its representation of itself. They suspect there are other voices to take into account—voices constituted as otherness outside the conversation. For this reason, left-wing critics want to redefine consensus by locating it in the prevailing balance of power, as a marker that sets the boundaries between discourses. As Myers suggests, we need to see consensus in terms of differences and not just of agreements, "as the result of conflicts, not as a monolith" (166). Redefining consensus as a matter of conflict suggests, moreover, that consensus does not so much reconcile differences through rational negotiation. Instead, such a redefinition represents consensus as a strategy that structures differences by organizing them in relation to each other. In this sense, consensus cannot be known without its opposite—without the other voices at the periphery of the conversation.

By looking at consensus in terms of conflict rather than agreement, we get a somewhat different picture of the relationship between normal and abnormal discourse than the one Rorty and Bruffee have offered. Redefining consensus leads us, I think, to abandon the view that abnormal discourse functions as a complement to normal discourse, something which, as Bruffee says, students can turn to from time to time to question business as usual and to keep the conversation going. Instead, abnormal discourse represents the result at any given time of the set of power relations that organizes normal discourse: the acts of permission and prohibition, of incorporation and exclusion that institute the structure and practices of discourse communities. Abnormal discourse is not so much a homeostatic mechanism that keeps the conversation and thereby the community renewed and refreshed. Instead, it refers to dissensus, to marginalized voices, the resistance and contestation both within and outside the conversation, what Roland Barthes calls acratic discourse—the discourses out of power. Abnormal discourse, that is, refers not only to surprises and accidents that emerge when normal discourse reaches a dead end, when, as Wittgenstein puts it, "language goes on holiday." In the account I'm suggesting, it also refers to the relations of power that determine what falls within the current consensus and what is assigned the status of dissent. Abnormal discourse, from this perspective, is neither as romantic nor as pragmatic as Rorty makes it out to be. Rather it offers a way to analyze the strategic moves by which discourse communities legitimize their own conversation by marginalizing others. It becomes a critical term to describe the conflict among discourses and collective wills in the heterogeneous conversation in contemporary public life.

Bruffee argues that such an emphasis on conflict has led his left-wing critics to want to "turn to 'struggle' to force change in 'people's interests'" (Response 714). I would reply that struggle is not something people, left-wing or otherwise, can "turn to" or choose to do. "Struggle," at least the way I understand it, is something we're born into: it's a standard feature of contemporary social existence. We experience "struggle" all the time in everyday life precisely because, as Bruffee points out, we "all belong to many overlapping, mutually inclusive communities." We "experience belonging to each of these communities as both limiting and liberating" (715) in part because we experience the discourses, or what Bruffee calls the "vernacular languages of the communities one belongs to," as a polyphony of voices, an internal conversation traversed by social, cultural, and linguistic differences.

Bruffee uses the term vernacular to call attention to the plurality of voices that constitute our verbal thought. The intersecting vernaculars that we experience contending for our attention and social allegiance, however, are not just plural. They are also organized in hierarchical relations of power. The term vernacular, after all, as Houston Baker reminds us, "signals" on etymological and ideological grounds "'a slave born on his master's estate'" (2). The term vernacular, that is, cannot be understood apart from the relations of domination and subordination it implies. The conversation, in Bakhtin's word, is "heteroglot," a mosaic of vernaculars, the multi-accented idiomatic expression of race, class, and gender differences. The conversation gives voice to the conflicts inherent in an unequal social order and in the asymmetrical relations of power in everyday life.

Bruffee worries that "struggle" means interrupting the conversation to "force change in people's interests." Bruffee's worries here betray what seems to me a persistent anxiety in non-foundationalist versions of social constructionist thought about its own radical disclosure: that once we give up extrahistorical and universal criteria and reduce the authority of knowledge to a self-legitimizing account of its own practices, we won't have a way to separate persuasion from force, validity claims from plays of power. As Rorty puts it, to "suggest that there is *no* . . . common ground seems to endanger rationality. . . . To question the need for commensuration seems the first step toward a return to a war of 'all against all' " (*Philosophy* 317). In the account I'm suggesting, "struggle" is not a matter of interrupting the conversation to replace consensual validation with force. It refers rather to the relations between the two terms—intellectual negotiation and power—in what we think of as rational argument and public discourse. The term "struggle" is simply a way of shifting rhetorical analysis, as Victor Vitanza has suggested, from Aristotelean persuasion or Burkean identification to an agonistic framework of conflict and difference—to a rhetoric of dissensus.

The choice, as I see it, does not consist of solidarity with a self-explaining conversation or violence. I want to preserve, along with Bruffee and Rorty, the value of civility and consensus. But to do this we will need to rehabilitate the notion of consensus by redefining it in relation to a rhetoric of dissensus. We will need, that is, to look at collaborative learning not merely as a process of consensus-making but more important as a process of identifying differences and locating these differences in relation to each other. The consensus that we ask students to reach in the collaborative classroom will be based not so much on collective agreements as on collective explanations of how people differ, where their differences come from, and whether they can live and work together with these differences.

To think of consensus in terms of dissensus is to challenge a central rationale Bruffee has offered for collaborative learning. Bruffee currently holds that one of the benefits of collaborative learning is that its consensual practices model the normal workings of discourse communities in business, government, the professions, and academia. Myers argues, correctly I think, that Bruffee's use of consensus risks accepting the current production and distribution of knowledge and discourse as unproblematical and given. The limit of Myers' critique, however, is that it concedes Bruffee's claim that consensus is in fact the norm in business, industry, and the professions. In this regard, both Bruffee and Myers seriously underestimate the extent to which the conversations of these discourse communities are regulated not so much by consensual negotiation and shared decision-making as by what

Jürgen Habermas calls a "success orientation" of instrumental control and rational efficiency.

It can be misleading, therefore, to tell students, as social constructionists do, that learning to write means learning to participate in the conversation and consensual practices of various discourse communities. Instead, we need to ask students to explore the rhetoric of dissensus that pervades writing situations. As Susan Wells argues, even such apparently prosaic and "unheroic" tasks as writing manuals for the computer-assisted redesign of an auto body section take place within a complicated network of competing and contradictory interests. In the case of the design manual that Wells cites, the technical writer faces three different audiences. Concerned with the overall operation of a computer system, the first audience of systems programmers may be just as likely to guard their professional knowledge of the system as to collaborate with others. They may, in fact, see the second audience, application programmers responsible for writing programs for specific design tasks, as "enemies" looking for ways to "tweak" or "jiggle" the system to get their work done—and who thereby threaten the overall performance of the system. The third audience of users, on the other hand, needs to know how to operate the system on narrow job-related grounds. But from both the programmers' perspective, this group is an unknown variable, men and women who may be "demonically curious" and want to play with the system, to see how it really works.

By exploring the differential access to knowledge and the relations of power and status that structure this writing situation, Wells says, students can learn not only how technical writers "write for success" by adjusting to multiple audiences. (As it turned out, the technical writer produced a separate manual containing quite different information for each of the audiences.) Students can also learn to articulate a rhetoric of dissensus that will lead them to see that the goal of discourse in this case, as Wells puts it, "is systematic misunderstanding and concealment. . . the total fragmentation and dispersal of knowledge" (256). They can learn, that is, not how consensus is achieved through collaborative negotiation but rather how differences in interest produce conflicts that may in fact block communication and prohibit the development of consensus.

Of course, it is true, as Wells notes, that not all organizations rely upon such a rigid division of labor. Collaboration and consensual decision-making, after all, have become buzz words for "new age" managers and technocrats. Part of the current conventional wisdom about the new information society is that cooperation and collaboration will replace the competitive and individualistic ethos of the entrepreneurial age of industrial capitalism. But finally what collaboration and consensus amount to are not so much new paradigms for a high-tech post-industrial order as new versions of an older industrial psychology adopted to late capitalism—human relations techniques to bolster morale, promote identification with the corporation, legitimize differential access to knowledge and status, and increase productivity. Even in the ostensibly disinterested realm of academics, the production of knowledge is motivated as much by career moves as by consensus, by the efforts of individuals to enhance their credentials and relative position in a field, to build up their fund of cultural capital.

At issue here is not whether collaborative learning reflects more accurately than traditional pedagogies the actual social relations that produce knowledge and make organizations run. Surely it does. But by modeling collaborative learning on the normal workings of discourse communities, Bruffee identifies the authority of knowledge with the prevailing productive apparatus. For social constructionists, this is an uncontroversial point. In one sense, it is the point—that the present configuration of knowledge and its institutions is a social artifact. But in another sense, this line of thought also concedes the authority of knowledge to the professional judgment of experts, to academic specialties and professional training, to the wider meritocratic order of a credentialed society.

If one of the goals of collaborative learning is to replace the traditional hierarchical relations of teaching and learning with the practices of participatory democracy, we must acknowledge that one of the functions of the professions and the modern university has been to specialize and to remove knowledge from public discourse and decision-making, to reduce it to a matter of expertise and technique. By the same token, we must acknowledge that it devalues the notion of consensus to identify it with the current professional monopolies of knowledge. If anything, the prevailing configuration of knowledge and its institutions *prevents* the formation of consensus by shrinking the public sphere and excluding the majority of the population from the conversation.

The effect of Bruffee's use of consensus is to invest a kind of "real world" authority in the discursive practices and tacit understandings that bind the discourse communities of specialists and experts together. It makes the conversation a self-explaining mechanism that legitimizes itself through its performances. "This," we tell students, "is the way we [English teachers, biologists, lawyers, chemical engineers, social workers, whatever] do things around here. There's nothing magical about it. It's just the way we talk to each other." The problem is that invoking the "real world" authority of such consensual practices neutralizes the critical and transformative project of collaborative learning, depoliticizes it, and reduces it to an acculturative technique.

To develop a critical version of collaborative learning, we will need to distinguish between consensus as an acculturative practice that reproduces business as usual and consensus as an oppositional one that challenges the prevailing conditions of production. The point of collaborative learning is not simply to demystify the authority of knowledge by revealing its social character but to transform the productive apparatus, to change the social character of production. In this regard, it will help to cast consensus not as a "real world" practice but as a utopian one.

To draw out the utopian possibilities I believe are implied in collaborative learning, we will need to distinguish between "spurious" and "genuine" consensus, as grounded and problematical as these terms may appear to be. In his theory of "communicative action," Habermas defines "genuine" consensus not as something that actually happens but instead as the counterfactual anticipation that agreement can be reached without coercion or systematic distortion. Consensus, for Habermas, is not, as it is for social constructionists like Bruffee, an empirical account of how discourse communities operate but a critical and normative representation of the conditions necessary for fully realized communication to occur. In Habermas' view, we should represent consensus not as the result at any given time of the prevailing conversation but rather as an aspiration to organize the conversation according to relations of non-domination. The anticipation of consensus, that is, projects what Habermas calls an "ideal speech situation," a utopian discursive space that distributes symmetrically the opportunity to speak, to initiate discourse, to question, to give reasons, to do all those other things necessary to justify knowledge socially. From this perspective, consensus becomes a necessary fiction of reciprocity and mutual recognition, the dream of conversation as perfect dialogue. Understood as a utopian desire, assembled from the partial and fragmentary forms of the current conversation, consensus does not appear as the end or the explanation of the conversation but instead as a means of transforming it.

To cast consensus as a utopian instead of a "real world" practice has a number of implications for the collaborative classroom. For one thing, a utopian representation of consensus offers students a powerful critical instrument to interrogate the conversation—to interrupt it in order to investigate the forces which determine who may speak and what may be said, what inhibits communication and what makes it possible. The normal workings of collaborative learning, as Bruffee describes them, ask students to generate an interpretive response to a literary work or a rhetorical analysis of a piece of writing and then to compare the results to the responses or analyses of their teacher and the community of scholars the teacher represents. The pedagogical goal is to negotiate a common language in the classroom, to draw students into a wider consensus, and to initiate them into the conversation as it is currently organized in the academy. The utopian view of consensus, on the other hand, would abandon this expert-novice model of teaching and learning. Instead consensus would provide students with a critical measure to identify the relations of power in the formation of expert judgment.

Let me give an example here. Collaborative learning in literature classes is often based on the idea that students need to avoid, on the one hand, the objectivism that assumes the meaning is in the text and, on the other, the radical pluralism that assumes we cannot distinguish the merits of one reading from another. Collaborative learning, that is, seeks to locate authority in neither the text nor the reader but in what Stanley Fish calls interpretive communities. From the perspective I am suggesting, however, the identification of collaborative learning with interpretive communities takes for granted the enterprise of interpretation as an end in itself.

In contrast, I think we need to begin collaborative classes by asking why interpretation has become the unquestioned goal of literary studies and what other kinds of readings thereby have been excluded and devalued. We would be interested in the forces which have produced dissensus about how to go about reading a literary text and about what constitutes a literary text in the first place. Students, of course, already know a good deal about all this: they are used to naming Shakespeare and Dickens and Hemingway as literature and disqualifying Stephen King, thrillers, and science fiction. What students have had less opportunity to do is to investigate collectively these implicit hierarchies in terms of the relations of power that organize them. Their literature classes have taught them to segregate kinds of reading but without asking them where these differences come from.

For this reason, we might begin the conversation in literature classes by talking not about how to read a literary text but rather about how the students in the course have been trained to read literature and how their schooled reading differs from the way they read outside of school. By examining these differences, freshmen and sophomores in introductory literature courses, I have found, can begin to examine critically the prevailing representation of literature and the institutional base on which it rests. Students rather quickly will distinguish between literature—which is assigned by teachers and is "good for you"—and the other reading they do—which is "for fun." They explain to each other and to me that literature is filled with "hidden meanings" and that the point of schooled reading is to dig them out, while the reading they do for "fun" produces strong identification with characters and teaches them about "life" or gives them the opportunity to escape from it.

The point of such discussion is not to reach agreement about what properly belongs in the realm of literature and what lies outside of it. Nor is it to abandon the usefulness of schooled reading. Rather what students begin to see is that literature exists as a social category that depends on its relation to non-literature. Students, that is, can begin to sketch the rhetoric of dissensus that structures the dominant representation of what literature is and is not and that produces marked differences in the way they read and experience texts.

Such discussions, moreover, give students permission to elaborate what they already know—namely, that schooled reading for "hidden meanings" reinforces the authority of expert readers and creates professional monopolies of knowledge. By drawing on their own experience as readers in and out of school, students regularly and spontaneously make the same telling point William E. Cain makes in *The Crisis in Criticism* that the institution of literature depends upon the "close reading" of specialist critics. In this regard, one of the most valuable things students bring to a literature class is what we as professional readers have largely forgotten—the imprecise, unanalytical act of non-close reading, the experience of ordinary readers at home, on the subway, or at the beach in the summer, the kind of reading that schooled reading marks as different.

One of the benefits of emphasizing the dissensus that surrounds the act of reading is that it poses consensus not as the goal of the conversation but rather as a critical measure to help students identify the structures of power that inhibit communication among readers (and between teachers and students) by authorizing certain styles of reading while excluding others. What students in introductory literature classes learn, I think, is to overcome the feeling that they don't get the point of literature or that they just like to read "trash." Instead, they learn why readers disagree about what counts as a reading, where the differences they experience as readers come from, and how we might usefully bring these differences into relation to each other. They learn to probe not only the ideology of the institution of literature but also the ideologies of popular reading. Just as they learn how schooled reading constitutes them as students in a complicated relationship to the authority of teachers and the institution of literature, students also learn that the reading they do outside of school is not simply a pastime but more important represents an act of self-formation that organizes their experience and desire in imaginary relations to the popular culture of late capitalism and its construction of race, class, and gender differences.

The revised notion of consensus I am proposing here depends paradoxically on its deferral, not its realization. I am less interested in students achieving consensus (although of course this happens at times) as in their using consensus as a critical instrument to open gaps in the conversation through which differences may emerge. In this regard, the Habermasian representation of consensus as a counterfactual anticipation of fully realized communication offers students a critical tool to identify the structures of power which determine who may speak and what may be said. But more important, this notion of consensus also offers students utopian aspirations to transform the conversation by freeing it from the prevailing constraints on its participants, the manipulations, deceptions, and plays of power. Through a collective investigation of differences, students can begin to imagine ways to change the relations of production and to base the conversation not on consensus but on reciprocity and the mutual recognition of the participants and their differences.

Unlike Habermas, however, I do not believe removing relations of domination and systematic distortion, whether ideological or neurotic, from the conversation is likely to establish the conditions in which consensus will express a "rational will" and "permit what *all* can want" (108). Instead, I want to displace consensus to a horizon which may never be reached. We need to see consensus, I think, not as an agreement that reconciles differences through an ideal conversation but rather as the desire of humans to live and work together with differences. The goal of consensus, it seems to me, ought to be not the unity of generalizable interests but rather what Iris Marion Young calls "an openness to unassimilated otherness" (22). Under the utopian aegis of consensus, students can learn to agree to disagree, not because "everyone has their own opinion," but because justice demands that we recognize the inexhaustibility of difference and that we organize the conditions in which we live and work accordingly.

By organizing students non-hierarchically so that all discursive roles are available to all the participants in a group, collaborative learning can do more than model or represent the normal workings of discourse communities. Students' experience of non-domination in the collaborative classroom can offer them a critical measure to understand the distortions of communication and the plays of power in normal discourse. Replacing the "real world" authority of consensus with a rhetoric of dissensus can lead students to demystify the normal workings of discourse communities. But just as important, a rhetoric of dissensus can lead them to redefine consensus as a utopian project, a dream of difference without domination. The participatory and democratic practices of collaborative learning offer an important instance of what Walter Benjamin, in "The Author as Producer," calls the "exemplary character of production"—the collective effort to "induce other producers to produce" and to "put an improved apparatus at their disposal" (233). In this regard, the exemplary character of production in collaborative learning can release collective energies to turn the means of criticism into a means of transformation, to tap fundamental impulses toward emancipation and justice in the utopian practices of Habermas' "ideal speech situation."

It would be fatuous, of course, to presume that collaborative learning can constitute more than momentarily an alternative to the present asymmetrical relations of power and distribution of knowledge and its means of production. But it can incite desire through common work to resolve, if only symbolically, the contradictions students face because of the prevailing conditions of production—the monopoly of expertise and the impulse to know, the separation of work and play, allegiance to peers and dependence on faculty esteem, the experience of cooperation and the competitiveness of a ranking reward system, the empowering sense of collectivity and the isolating personalization of an individual's fate. A rehabilitated notion of consensus in collaborative learning can provide students with exemplary motives to imagine alternative worlds and transformations of social life and labor. In its deferred and utopian form, consensus offers a way to orchestrate dissensus and to turn the conversation in the collaborative classroom into a heterotopia of voices—a heterogeneity without hierarchy.

WORKS CITED

Baker, Houston A., Jr. *Blues, Ideology, and Afro-American Literature.* Chicago: U of Chicago P, 1984.

Beade, Pedro. Comment. *College English* 49 (1987): 708.

Benjamin, Walter. "The Author as Producer." *Reflections.* Ed. Peter Demetz. New York: Schocken, 1986. 220–38.

Bruffee, Kenneth A. "Collaborative Learning: Some Practical Models." *College English* 34 (1973): 634–43.

———. Response. *College English* 49 (1987): 711–16.

Cain, William E. *The Crisis in Criticism: Theory, Literature, and Reform in English Studies.* Baltimore: John Hopkins UP, 1984.

Comay, Rebecca. "Interrupting the Conversation: Notes on Rorty." *Telos* 69 (1986): 119–30.

Eagleton, Terry. *The Function of Criticism.* London: Verso, 1984.

Foster, David. Comment. *College English* 49 (1987): 709–11.

Habermas, Jürgen. *Legitimation Crisis.* Trans. Thomas McCarthy. Boston: Beacon, 1975.

Johnson, Thomas S. Comment. *College English* 48 (1986): 76.

Myers, Greg. "Reality, Consensus, and Reform in the Rhetoric of Composition Teaching." *College English* 48 (1986): 154–74.

Rorty, Richard. *The Consequences of Pragmatism.* Minneapolis: U of Minnesota P, 1982.

_____. *Philosophy and the Mirror of Nature.* Princeton: Princeton UP, 1979.

Vitanza, Victor. "Critical Sub/Versions of the History of Philosophical Rhetoric." *Rhetoric Review* 6.1 (1987): 41–66.

Wells, Susan. "Habermas, Communicative Competence, and the Teaching of Technical Discourse." *Theory in the Classroom.* Ed. Cary Nelson. Urbana: U of Illinois P, 1986. 245–69.

Young, Iris Marion. "The Ideal of Community and the Politics of Difference." *Social Theory and Practice* 12.1 (1986): 1–26.

"Contact Zones" and English Studies

PATRICIA BIZZELL

Our Ptolemaic system of literary categories goes creaking and groaning onward, in spite of the widely acknowledged need to overhaul it in response to multiculturalism. This is not to say that there have not been attempts to revise course design in light of new materials and methods. For example, G. Douglas Atkins and Michael L. Johnson's *Writing and Reading Differently* (1985), Susan L. Gabriel and Isaiah Smithson's *Gender in the Classroom* (1990), and James A. Berlin and Michael J. Vivion's *Cultural Studies in the English Classroom* (1992) address the pedagogical consequences of deconstruction, feminist literary theory, and cultural studies, respectively, and also incorporate more diverse literatures. But these attempts to foster innovation in the individual classroom still leave the basic structure of English studies intact.

In Kristin Ross's description of the multicultural world literature and cultural studies program at the University of California at Santa Cruz, she comments indirectly on this problem when she identifies as one stumbling block to the Santa Cruz program the faculty's unwillingness "to depart from their specialized fields" (668). They fended off demands to diversify their course material with plaints like "But I don't have a PhD in South African literature" (668). Ross gives good reasons for forging ahead in spite of such protests, but she doesn't say much about the underlying structure of English studies that still makes us think our scholarship must be organized along national or chronological lines, even though these are inimical to the process of integrating new materials and methods because devised to serve and protect the old ones.

Reprinted from *College English* 56.2 (February 1994): 163–69. Used with permission.

The persistence of the old basic structure can be seen even in an impressive new collection published by the Modern Language Association with the avowed intention of fostering innovation: Stephen Greenblatt and Giles Gunn's *Redrawing the Boundaries: The Transformation of English and American Literary Studies* (1992). Even here, boundaries are not redrawn in fundamentally new ways. Rather, the old, familiar structure of English studies is visible, for instance in chapter divisions that carve literary studies into chronological periods, such as "Seventeenth-Century Studies" (British literature) and "American Literary Studies to the Civil War." Ten such chapters are followed by eleven more, most with the word "Criticism" in the title, implying that here we turn from primary to secondary texts. Yet it is here that we find the most attention to literature by women, gay people, and people of color: separate chapters are devoted, for example, to "Feminist Criticism" and "African American Criticism." Thus other traditional boundaries appear to be reasserted rather than redrawn. Moreover, the field of composition studies appears to remain behind even more impenetrable traditional boundaries. Not only is "Composition Studies" given a separate chapter (in the second set of eleven), but there must be an additional, separate chapter just to explain why composition studies is included in this book at all ("Composition and Literature").

I think we need a radically new system to organize English studies, and I propose that we develop it in response to the materials with which we are now working. Instead of finagling the new literatures and the new pedagogical and critical approaches into our old categories, we should try to find comprehensive new forms that seem to spring from and respond to the new materials. Instead of asking ourselves, for example, "How can I fit Frederick Douglass into my American Renaissance course?" we need to ask, "How should I reconceive my study of literature and composition now that I regard Douglass as an important writer?"

It could be argued that we don't need any new system of categories, that what we should do is simply to knock down the old system and then let everyone do what he or she pleases. This appears to be the approach taken by another recent attempt to chart new courses, the MLA's 1987 English Coalition Conference. Peter Elbow, in his account of this conference, *What Is English?* (1990), tells us there was a "remarkable consensus" at the conference on "the central business of English studies" (17), and it was as follows:

> *Using language* actively in a diversity of ways and settings—that is, not only in the classroom as exercises for teachers but in a range of social settings with various audiences where the language makes a difference.

Reflecting on language use. Turning back and self-consciously reflecting on how one has been using language—examining these processes of talking, listening, writing, and reading.

Trying to ensure that this using and reflecting go on in *conditions of both nourishment and challenge,* that is, conditions where teachers care about students themselves and what they actively learn—not just about skills or scores or grades. (18; emphasis in original)

The tone here, of course, is quite different from that of *Redrawing the Boundaries*—the focus is clearly on pedagogy rather than on the body of scholarly knowledge. I applaud this focus on pedagogy, and I admire the principles laid down above. But I can't help noticing that they appear to have very little to do specifically with the discipline of English studies. To me, they sound like the kind of principles I urge on faculty from all disciplines in my school's writing-across-the-curriculum program. There isn't a course at my school where these principles couldn't be put advantageously into practice. How, then, do they define "the central business of English studies"?

What these principles leave out, as Elbow himself notes, is what people read and write *about* in literary studies. He acknowledges that "you can't make meaning unless you are writing or reading about *something;* . . . practices are always practices *of* a content" (19; emphasis in original). Yet the topic of literary content appeared to be taboo at the conference. As Elbow tells it:

The question of literature was left strikingly moot. Not only was there no consensus, there was a striking avoidance of the issue. It's not that it didn't come up; the question of literature arose recurrently. . . . Yet every time we somehow slid away from the issue into something else. (96, 97)

This sounds to me like repression, not freedom, but I sympathize with the conference members. Small wonder they could not find a way to talk about literature, with the old system of organizing it discredited for lack of inclusiveness and no new system yet accepted. But I am concerned that this kind of avoidance leaves graduate and undergraduate curricula dangerously lacking in guidance—dangerously vulnerable to "cultural literacy" pundits who would shove into the breach the only system still known, namely the old, bad traditional one. Indeed, this threat appeared at the conference itself, and Elbow, although an advocate of composition pedagogies in which each writer is to do pretty much as he or she pleases, was sufficiently troubled by it that he proposes his own list of literary contents for English studies in an appendix.

But exactly how are we to develop a new system of organization from the new materials of study, supposing we agree that this is needed? To do so would seem to require that we make generalizations about the new material—about what, say, might be required to study Asian-American literature adequately—that would be extremely difficult, if not downright presumptuous, to make. I think we need an approach to the diverse world literatures written in English we are now studying that focuses not on their essential nature, whatever that may be, but rather on how they might, not "fit" together exactly, but come into productive dialogue with one another.

I suggest that we address this problem by employing Mary Louise Pratt's concept of the "contact zone":

> I use this term to refer to social spaces where cultures meet, clash, and grapple with each other, often in contexts of highly asymmetrical relations of power, such as colonialism, slavery, or their aftermaths as they are lived out in many parts of the world today. (34)

This concept can aid us both because it emphasizes the conditions of difficulty and struggle under which literatures from different cultures come together (thus forestalling the disrespectful glossing over of differences), and because it gives us a conceptual base for bringing these literatures together, namely, when they occur in or are brought to the same site of struggle or "contact zone."

A "contact zone" is defined primarily in terms of historical circumstances. It is circumscribed in time and space, but with elastic boundaries. Focusing on a contact zone as a way of organizing literary study would mean attempting to include *all* material relevant to the struggles going on there. Pratt's main example of a "contact zone" here is Peru in the late sixteenth and early seventeenth centuries, where she wants to study the interaction among texts by Native Americans (newly discovered by twentieth-century scholars) and the canonical Spanish accounts. I submit that the United States is another such contact zone, or more precisely, a congeries of overlapping contact zones, considered from the first massive immigration of Europeans in the seventeenth century up to the present day. "Multiculturalism" in English studies is a name for our recognition of this condition of living on contested cultural ground, and our desire to represent something of this complexity in our study of literature and literacy.

If we understand that we are teaching in, and about, contact zones, Pratt suggests that we must stop imagining our job to be transmitting a unitary literature and literacy. Under this old model,

The prototypical manifestation of language is generally taken to be the speech of individual adult native speakers face-to-face (as in Saussure's famous diagram) in monolingual, even monodialectal situations—in short, the most homogeneous case, linguistically and socially. The same goes for written communication. (38)

Now, Pratt suggests that we need a new model:

a theory that assumed different things—that argued, for instance, that the most revealing speech situation for understanding language was one involving a gathering of people each of whom spoke two languages and understood a third and held only one language in common with any of the others. (38)

This model treats difference as an asset, not a liability.

Given American diversity, our classrooms are getting to be more like Pratt's new model than the old one. If we respond by "teaching the contact zone," we can foster classrooms where, as in Pratt's experience,

All the students in the class . . . [heard] their culture discussed and objectified in ways that horrified them; all the students saw their roots traced back to legacies of both glory and shame; . . . [but] kinds of marginalization once taken for granted were gone. Virtually every student was having the experience of seeing the world described with him or her in it. (39)

Acknowledging its difficulties, I am suggesting that we need a new system of organization in English studies to make this kind of teaching—and scholarship—not only possible, but normative.

In short, I am suggesting that we organize English studies not in terms of literary or chronological periods, nor essentialized racial or gender categories, but rather in terms of historically defined contact zones, moments when different groups within the society contend for the power to interpret what is going on. As suggested above, the chronological, geographical, and generic parameters of any contact zone are defined on the basis of including as much material as possible that is relevant to the issue being contested. Time periods can be short or long, literatures of different groups, languages, or continents can be considered together, all genres are admitted, and so on.

For example, the New England region from about 1600 to about 1800 might be defined as a contact zone in which different groups of Europeans and Native Americans were struggling for the power to say what had happened in their relations with each other. Thus canonical Puritan histories, autobiographies, and captivity narratives would be studied in connection with historical commentaries and memoirs by non-Puritan Europeans (traditionally treated as "minor"), European transcriptions of Native American speeches (problematic but invaluable), and letters, histories, and spiritual autobiographies written by Native Americans in English (unknown in the academy until very recently). The object would not be to represent what the lives of the diverse European immigrant and Native American groups were really like. Rather, the attempt would be to show how each group represented itself imaginatively in relation to the others. We would, in effect, be reading all the texts as brought to the contact zone, for the purpose of communicating across cultural boundaries.

There are several advantages to this approach. First, it provides a rationale for integrating English studies multiculturally. No longer would we be trying to squeeze new material into inappropriate old categories, where its importance could not be adequately appreciated. We would be working with categories that treated multiculturalism as a defining feature, that assumed the richest literary treasures could be found in situations in which different histories, lifeways, and languages are trying to communicate and to deal with the unequal power distribution among them. We would no longer need to ask prejudicial questions, such as whether Frederick Douglass was as "good" on some putative absolute scale of expository value as Henry Thoreau. Rather, we would look at the rhetorical effectiveness of each writer in dealing with the matter in hand, for example, the need to promote civil disobedience in the contact zone created by white and black efforts to define and motivate action in response to slavery in the antebellum U.S.

Second, this approach fully integrates composition and rhetoric into literary studies. Studying texts as they respond to contact zone conditions is studying them rhetorically, studying them as efforts of rhetoric. The historical context provides a way to focus the rhetorical analysis. Moreover, professional and student writing can also be seen as contending in contact zones and experimenting with the textual arts of the contact zone that rhetorical analysis emphasizes. Thus boundaries between "content" (literature) and its traditional inferior, pedagogy (composition), are usefully blurred, as are the distinctions between "high" literature and other kinds of writing, including student writing. Donald McQuade makes a persuasive argument for blurring these boundaries in "Composition and Literature."

At the end of her essay, Pratt calls for the development of what she calls "the pedagogical arts of the contact zone":

> exercises in storytelling and in identifying with the ideas, interests, histories, and attitudes of others; experiments in transculturation and collaborative work and in the arts of critique, parody, and comparison (including

unseemly comparisons between elite and vernacular cultural forms); the redemption of the oral; ways for people to engage with suppressed aspects of history (including their own histories); ways to move *into and out of* rhetorics of authenticity; ground rules for communication across lines of difference and hierarchy that go beyond politeness but maintain mutual respect; a systematic approach to the all-important concept of *cultural mediation.* (40; emphasis in original)

David Bartholomae has recently suggested that we imagine these "arts" translated into exercises in an English class. Imagine, for example, a class in which literature is analyzed for the ways it moves among rhetorics of authenticity, students experiment with attending to suppressed aspects of their own history as part of establishing their writerly personae, and scholarly writing is both shared and opened for parody. Pratt calls this work "cultural mediation"; my phrase for it is "negotiating difference"—studying how various writers in various genres have grappled with the pervasive presence of difference in American life and developed virtues out of necessity. I would include analysis of student writing, for its employment of contact zone rhetorical strategies, and I would include "texts" of all kinds, as required by the contact zones under study—posters, songs, films, videos, and so forth.

Reorganizing literary studies along these lines would mean redesigning courses. For example, at Holy Cross we offer first-year students a choice of either a composition course (a course in the personal essay) or a course that introduces them to literary study by teaching the close reading of works grouped according to genre. Under the new paradigm, there would be no need for two separate courses. The abilities needed both to enter literary studies and to refine one's own writing would be the skills of analyzing and imitating rhetorical arts of the contact zone. Students would learn to critique strategies of negotiating difference in the writing of others and to practice them in their own. So we could offer just one course, writing-intensive but including some reading and analysis of literature (broadly defined).

It would also mean reorganizing graduate study and professional scholarly work in ways I hardly dare to suggest. I suppose that one would no longer become a specialist in American literature, a "Shakespeare man," or a "compositionist." Rather, people's areas of focus would be determined by the kinds of rhetorical problems in which they were interested.

My main object is to get people to work on the project. I have no coherent alternative program to present. But I believe that if we reorganize literary studies in this way, we will be giving a dynamic new direction to our profession. We will be creating disciplinary parameters within which boundaries really can be redrawn to come to terms with the demands of

465

multiculturalism. This new paradigm will stimulate scholarship and give vitally needed guidance to graduate and undergraduate curricula. It might also lead us, in the multicultural literary archives, to stories of hope that can lend us all spiritual sustenance as we renew efforts to make the United States a multicultural democracy. If we are not given to complete the task, neither are we allowed to desist from it.

WORKS CITED

Atkins, G. Douglas, and Michael L. Johnson, eds. *Writing and Reading Differently: Deconstruction and the Teaching of Composition and Literature.* Lawrence: U of Kansas P, 1985.

Bartholomae, David. "The Tidy House: Basic Writing in the American Curriculum." *Journal of Basic Writing* 12 (Spring 1993): 4–21.

Berlin, James A., and Michael J. Vivion, eds. *Cultural Studies in the English Classroom.* Portsmouth, NH: Heinemann-Boynton/Cook, 1992.

Elbow, Peter. *What is English?* New York: MLA, 1990.

Gabriel, Susan L., and Isaiah Smithson, eds. *Gender in the Classroom: Power and Pedagogy.* Urbana: U of Illinois P, 1990.

Greenblatt, Stephen, and Giles Gunn, eds. *Redrawing the Boundaries: The Transformation of English and American Literary Studies.* New York: MLA, 1992.

McQuade, Donald. "Composition and Literature." Greenblatt and Gunn 482–519.

Pratt, Mary Louise. "Arts of the Contact Zone." *Profession 91.* New York: MLA, 1991. 33–40.

Ross, Kristin. "The World Literature and Cultural Studies Program." *Critical Inquiry* 19 (Summer 1993): 666–676.

Professing Multiculturalism
The Politics of Style in the Contact Zone

MIN-ZHAN LU

In her 1991 "Arts of the Contact Zone," Mary Louise Pratt points out that while colleges and universities have increasingly deployed a rhetoric of diversity in response to the insistence of non-mainstream groups for fuller participation, the "import" of "multiculturalism" remains "up for grabs across the ideological spectrum" (39). I begin with Pratt's reminder because I want to call attention to the images of "grabbing" and "import." These depict "multiculturalism" as a construct whose "import"—meanings, implications, and consequences—is available only to those willing to expend the energy to "grab" it: to search, envision, grasp, articulate, and enact it. And these images conjure up the act of importing—of bringing in—perspectives and methods formerly excluded by dominant institutions. I want to articulate one "import" of multiculturalism here by exploring the question of how to conceive and practice teaching methods which invite a multicultural approach to style, particularly those styles of student writing which appear to be ridden with "errors." And I situate this question in the context of English Studies, a discipline which, on the one hand, has often proclaimed its concern to profess multiculturalism but, on the other hand, has done little to combat the ghettoization of two of its own cultures, namely composition teaching and student writing.

My inquiry is motivated by two concerns which I believe I share with a significant number of composition teachers. The first results from a sense of division between the ways in which many of us approach style in theory and in our teaching practices. I have in mind teachers who are aligned in theory

Reprinted from *College Composition and Communication* 45.4 (December 1994): 442–58.
Used with permission.

with a view of composition which contests the separation of form and meaning and which also argues against a conception of "academic discourse" as discrete, fixed, and unified. This alignment, while generating a critical perspective towards traditional methods of teaching style through drills in "correct usage," does not always result in any immediate revision of such methods in classroom practice. Some of us tend to resolve this gap between theory and practice in one of two ways: (1) We set aside a few weeks to teach "usage" or "copyediting" in the traditional way while spending the rest of the term helping students to revise their work on a more conceptual level; or (2) we send students who have "problems" with "usage" to the writing center. Such "resolutions" often leave the teacher frustrated. Because she recognizes the burden on those at the fringe of having to "prove" themselves to those at the center by meeting the standards set by the latter, she cannot but take seriously students' anxiety to master "correct" usage. Nevertheless, she is aware that instead of helping them to overcome such an anxiety, her teaching strategies risk increasing it, as they may reinforce students' sense of the discrepancy between their inability to produce "error-free" prose and their ability to come up with "good ideas," and they may confirm these students' impression that only those who make "errors" need to worry about issues of usage and editing. My second concern has to do with a division many of us feel between our role as composition teachers and the role we play as students, teachers, or scholars in other, supposedly more central areas of English Studies. As our interest in composition teaching, theory, and research evolves, we are increasingly interested in contesting the second-class status of work in composition. At the same time, we are often all too aware that we ourselves are guilty of perpetuating the divisions between composition and other areas of English Studies by approaching the writings of "beginners" or "outsiders" in a manner different from the approach we take to the writings of "experts."

Two stories, both of which took place around the turn of this century, illustrate part of the historical power of that kind of division. The first story comes from Gertrude Stein's *The Autobiography of Alice B. Toklas*. According to Stein, right after she had made arrangements to have her book *Three Lives* printed by Grafton Press of New York, "a very nice American young man" was sent by the press to Paris to check on her:

> You see, [the young man] said slightly hesitant, the director of the Grafton Press is under the impression that perhaps your knowledge of english. But I am an american, said Gertrude Stein indignantly. Yes yes I understand that perfectly now, he said, but perhaps you have not had much experience in writing. I suppose, said [Stein] laughing, you were under the impression

that I was imperfectly educated. He blushed, why no, he said, but you might not have had much experience in writing. Oh yes, she said, oh yes. . . . and you might as well tell [the director] . . . that everything that is written in the manuscript is written with the intention of its being so written and all he has to do is to print it and I will take the responsibility. The young man bowed himself out. (68)

This exchange between an indignant Stein and an embarrassed "young man" reveals some of the criteria used by "educated america" when dealing with an idiosyncratic style. These criteria are (a) the writer's "knowledge of english," which is seen as somehow dependent on whether she is a native speaker, and (b) the writer's "experience in writing," which is seen as related to whether she has been "[im]perfectly educated." Stein, an "American" bearing certification of a "perfect" education from Radcliffe and Johns Hopkins Medical School, knew she had the authority to maintain that everything in her manuscript was "written with the intention of its being so written." Stein's indignation and the embarrassment she elicited from the "young man" suggest that in the early 1900s, ethnic and educational backgrounds were two common denominators for determining whether style represented self-conscious and innovative experimentation or blundering "errors."

The second story took place a few years prior to the Stein event, when the style of another writer, Theodore Dreiser, was also questioned by a publisher to whom he had submitted his first novel, *Sister Carrie*. The rejection letter from Harper faults Dreiser for his "uneven" style which, according to the editors, was "disfigured by . . . colloquialisms" (*Sister Carrie* 519). Existing manuscripts of the book's revision indicate that Dreiser did not defend his style with the kind of authority Stein exhibited. Instead he sought editorial help from his wife Jug and friend Henry because he deemed both to have been better educated than himself. There is evidence in the revised manuscript that Dreiser adopted nearly all of Jug's corrections of grammar and Henry's rewording of his Germanic rhythms and cumulative sentence structures (*Sister Carrie* 580–81). Read in the context of Stein's story, Dreiser's willingness to have all aspects of his style "corrected" might be attributed in part to his acute awareness of the criteria used by "educated america" when dealing with the writing of the son of an impoverished German immigrant with extremely sporadic formal education. The early reception of *Sister Carrie* proves the validity of Dreiser's concern, as even its defenders attributed its "crude" style to his ethnic background and lack of formal education.[1]

Almost a century after these events, more and more English courses are now informed by a view of language as a site of struggle among conflicting discourses with unequal socio-political power. Students in these courses are beginning to approach the style of what they call "real" writers like Stein and Dreiser very differently. Interest in multiculturalism has also shifted the attention of some teachers to writers' success at what Bakhtin calls "dialogically coordinating" a varied and profound "heteroglossia" (295–96). Analysis of style in these classrooms often centers on the politics of the writer's stylistic decisions: (a) mapping the "heteroglossia" on the internal and external scenes of writing, (b) attending to the writer's effort to look at one discourse through the eyes of another, and (c) considering the writer's willingness to resist the centripetal forces of "official" discourses. Viewed from this multicultural perspective on style, the writings of both Dreiser and Stein could be considered in terms of the efforts of each to dialogically coordinate the profound heteroglossia within and outside official "educated" discourses. For readers adopting this perspective, neither Dreiser's ethnic background nor his "imperfect" educational background would be used to dismiss his "uneven" style solely as evidence of "error"—that is, to conclude that his style merely reflects his lack of knowledge or experience in writing. In fact, given the frequency with which writings from what Gloria Anzaldúa has called the "borderlands" are being currently assigned in some English courses and the praise this type of writing receives for its hybridization of "official" discourses, Dreiser's readiness to yield to the authority of the "better educated" now appears conservative—indicating a passive stance towards the hegemony of ethnocentrism and linguistic imperialism. In fact, the publication of the Pennsylvania edition of *Sister Carrie* in 1987 indicates that such a critical view privileging resistance was in operation when the editors decided to delete many of the changes made by the "better educated" Jug and Henry in the hope of preserving the "power and forcefulness" of Dreiser's original prose (*Sister Carrie* 581).

However, Dreiser's reaction still haunts me, especially when I move from teaching students to analyze the idiosyncratic style of "real" writers to helping them to work on their own styles. In my "literature" courses for junior- or senior-level college students or "writing" courses for first-year students, students learn to talk with considerable eloquence about the politics of stylistic decisions made by "real" writers, especially those writing from the borderlands by choice or necessity. Most of the readings I assign for these classes call attention to writers' need and right to contest the unifying force of hegemonic discourses, and thus make Dreiser's submission to the authority of the "better educated" appear dated and passive. Yet the meaning of Dreiser's submissiveness changes for me and most of my students as soon as we move to work on the style of a student writer, especially when we tinker with what we call the writer's "discursive voice"—that is, when dealing with deviations in diction, tone, voice, structure, and so on (which we loosely call the "rhetorical register"), or with punctuation, syntax, sentence structure, and so on (which we

470

refer to as the "grammatical register"). On those occasions, how to sound "right" suddenly becomes a "real" concern for my students: pervasive, immediate, and difficult for me to dismiss. My students' apparent anxiety to reproduce the conventions of "educated" English poses a challenge for my teaching and research. Why is it that in spite of our developing ability to acknowledge the political need and right of "real" writers to experiment with "style," we continue to cling to the belief that such a need and right does not belong to "student writers"? Another way of putting the question would be, why do we assume—as Dreiser did—that until one can prove one's ability to produce "error-free" prose, one has not earned the right to innovative "style"?

Again, I believe Dreiser's account of his own educational experience might shed some light on the question. In *Dawn*, Dreiser writes about his opportunity to attend the University of Indiana, Bloomington for two short terms. A former teacher made arrangements to exempt Dreiser from the preliminary examinations because, Dreiser points out, these exams would have quickly "debarred" him (342). Life as what we might today call an open admissions student at Indiana made Dreiser feel "reduced." He "grieved" at his "inability to grasp . . . such a commonplace as grammar" (378). Even though he knew he was able to apprehend many things and to demonstrate his apprehensions "quite satisfactorily" to himself, he found the curriculum "oppressive," leaving him "mute" with "a feeling of inadequacy" (425). The events surrounding the efforts of Dreiser and Stein to publish their first books indicate that the common approach of the editors, publishers, and critics to their idiosyncratic styles was not coincidental. Dreiser's experience at Indiana, his willingness to have his "uneven" style "corrected," and Stein's quick rebuttal to the "young man" all point to the institutional source of this approach. A common view of "style" as belonging only to those who are beyond "error," and a certain type of college curriculum treating matters of grammar or usage as the prerequisites to higher education, seem mutually reinforcing. It is this belief that pushes students identified as having "problems" to meet such "prerequisites" and assigns teachers trained to deal with such "problems" to the periphery or borderlands of higher education.

Dreiser's memories of Indiana seem symptomatic of the feelings of a significant number of college students I encounter. I have in mind particularly students who seem quick to admit that they are "not good" at writing because they have been identified at some point in their education as needing special—remedial, laboratory, or intensive—instruction in the "basics." Like Dreiser, they are frustrated at their inability to grasp "grammar" because they have been encouraged to view it as "such a commonplace"—something everyone who aspires to become anyone ought to be able to master. And they feel muted and reduced by the curriculum because it does not seem to recognize that they are quite able to grasp subjects other than "grammar" and demonstrate their understanding of such subjects satisfactorily to themselves, if perhaps not in writing to others. It seems to me that one way of helping students to deal with this frustration would be to connect their "difficulties" with the refusal of "real" writers to reproduce the hegemonic conventions of written English. And it seems to me that this will not take place until teachers like myself contest the distinction between "real" and "student" writers and stop treating the idiosyncratic style of the not yet "perfectly educated" solely in terms of "error." One form of contestation could be to apply to student writing the same multicultural approach we have been promoting when analyzing the work of "real" writers. Susan Miller has argued in *Textual Carnivals* that the tendency to treat student writers as "emerging, or as failed, but never as actually responsible 'authors'" has served to maintain the low status of composition studies in its relations to those "outside it, and its self-images and ways of working out its new professionalization" (195–96). An approach to student writing that treats students as real writers would undo such binaries and thus assert the right and ability of writing teachers and students to fully participate in a truly multicultural curriculum.

My aim here is to discuss a teaching method formulated out of my attempt to apply a multicultural approach to student writing: an approach which views the classroom as a potential "contact zone"—which Pratt describes as a space where various cultures "clash, and grapple with each other, often in contexts of highly asymmetrical relations of power" (34). In arguing for a multicultural approach to styles traditionally displaced to the realm of "error," I align my teaching with a tradition in "error" analysis which views even "error-ridden" student writings as texts relevant to critical approaches available to English Studies. I am particularly interested in explicitly foregrounding the category of "resistance" and "change" when helping students to conceptualize the processes of producing and interpreting an idiosyncratic style in students' own writings. In the classroom I envision, the notion of "intention" is presented as the decision of a writer who understands not only the "central role of human agency" but also that such agency is often "enacted under circumstances not of one's choosing" (West 31). I define the writer's attempt to "reproduce" the norms of academic discourses as necessarily involving the re-production—approximating, negotiating, and revising—of these norms. And I do so by asking students to explore the full range of choices and options, including those excluded by the conventions of academic discourses.

These aspects in the classroom I envision inevitably distance it from classrooms influenced by one belief prevalent in ESL courses or courses in "Basic Writing": namely, that a monolingual environment is the most conducive to the learning of "beginners" or "outsiders." This belief overlooks the dialogical nature of students' "inner voices" as well as the multicultural context of students' lives. The classroom I envision also differs from approaches to students' ambivalence towards the effects of education exemplified by Mina Shaughnessy's *Errors and Expectations.* Shaughnessy convincingly shows the relevance to error analysis of a range of feelings common to students likely to be identified as basic writers: their anxiety to "sound academic" and to self-consciously emulate the formal style (194), their low self-esteem as learners and writers, and their sense of ambivalence towards academic discourse. But as I have argued in "Conflict and Struggle," Shaughnessy's goal in acknowledging students' ambivalence is only to help them dissolve it (904–06). Because this ambivalence arises from sources well beyond the classroom—coming from the unequal power relationships pervading the history, culture, and society my students live in—not all students can or even want to get rid of all types of ambivalence. On the contrary, the experiences of writers like Gloria Anzaldúa, bell hooks, and Mike Rose suggest that, appropriately mobilized, a sense of ambivalence might be put to constructive uses in writing.

To foreground the concepts of "resistance" and "change" when analyzing the styles of a student or "real" writer, I ask students to read deviations from the official codes of academic discourses not only in relation to the writer's knowledge of these codes but also in terms of her efforts to negotiate and modify them. Aside from increasing the student's knowledge of and experience in reproducing these official forms, I am most interested in doing three things: (1) enabling students to hear discursive voices which conflict with and struggle against the voices of academic authority; (2) urging them to negotiate a position in response to these colliding voices; and (3) asking them to consider their choice of position in the context of the socio-political power relationships within and among diverse discourses and in the context of their personal life, history, culture, and society.

Because of the tendency in English Studies to ghettoize the culture of composition, I will use some student writing produced in writing courses for first-year students to illustrate how I would actually go about teaching a multicultural approach to style. And I am going to focus on features of writing styles which are commonly displaced to the realm of "error" and thus viewed as peripheral to college English teaching. In using these rather than other types of examples, I hope to illustrate as well the need to view composition as a site which might inform as well as be informed by our effort to profess multiculturalism in other, supposedly more "advanced" and "central" areas of English Studies. David Bartholomae has recently reminded us that there is no need "to import 'multiple cultures' [into the classroom, via anthologies].

They are there, in the classroom, once the institution becomes willing to pay that kind of attention to student writing" (14–15). Such attention, he explains, could produce composition courses in multiculturalism "that worked with the various cultures represented in the practice of its students" (14). My second reason for using these examples is related to the ways in which conflict and struggle have been perceived by teachers specializing in error analysis. These teachers tend to hear arguments foregrounding conflict and struggle in the classroom as sloganeering "the students' right to their own language" in order to eliminate attention to error, or as evidence of a "PC" attack on the "back to basics" movement (see, for example, Traub). The examples I use here, I hope, will demonstrate a way of teaching which neither overlooks the students' potential lack of knowledge and experience in reproducing the dominant codes of academic discourses *nor* dismisses the writer's potential social, political, and linguistic interest in modifying these codes, with emphasis on the word "potential."

When teaching first-year writing classes, I usually introduce the multicultural approach to student writing style around the mid-point of the term, when I feel that students are beginning to apply to their actual practices a view of writing as a process of re-seeing. To present the writer's experimentation with style (including what is generally called "copyediting" or the "correction of error") as an integral part of the revision process, I look for sample student writings with two characteristics. First, I am interested in writings with the kinds of "error" a majority of the class would feel they can easily "spot" and "fix." This type of writing allows me to acknowledge some potential causes of non-conventional styles and effective methods of revising them which are more widely disseminated in traditional writing classrooms and familiar to most students. Second, I look for styles which are also more conducive to my attempt to help the writer to negotiate a new position in relation to the colliding voices active in the scenes of writing.[2]

Following is a handout I have used when teaching first-year composition classes. The two segments on the handout are from the papers one student wrote in response to two assignments, one asking her to discuss an essay, "From a Native Daughter," by Haunani-Kay Trask, and another asking her to comment on the kind of "critical thinking" defined in the "Introduction" to an anthology called *Rereading America*. For the convenience of discussion in this essay, I have added emphasis to the handout:

Segment One:

As a Hawaiian native historian, Trask *can able to* argue for her people. As a Hawaiian native, she was exposed to two totally different viewpoints about her people. She was brought up in Hawaii. During this time, she heard the stories about her people from her parents. Later on she was send to America mainland to pursue higher education, in which she learnt a different stories about her people. Therefore, she understood that the interpretation of land was different between the "haole" and the native. To prove that the "haole" were wrong, she went back to Hawaii and work on the land with other native, so she *can* feel the strong bond with land her people have which the "haole" *could* not feel. The "haole" historians never bother to do so as they were more interested in looking for written evidence. That was why Trask, as a native Hawaiian historian, argued that these "haole" historians were being ignorant and ethnocentric. That is also why Trask suggested the "haole" historians learn the native tongue.

————

Segment Two:

Elements like perceiving things from different perspective, finding and validating each alternative solutions, questioning the unknown and breaking the nutshell of cultural norms are important for developing the ability of "critical thinking." . . . Most of the new universities' students are facing new challenges like staying away from family, peer pressure, culture shock, heavy college work etc. I *can* say that these are the "obstacles" to success. If a student *can able to* approach each situation with different perspectives than the one he brought from high school, I *may* conclude that this particular student has climbed his first step to become a "critical thinker." . . . However, there is one particular obstacle that is really difficult for almost everyone to overcome, that is the cultural rules. From the textbook, I found that cultural rules are deep rooted in our mind and cause us to view things from our respective cultural viewpoint. Even though cultural values lead the way of life of a particular group of people, they blind us as well. I relate to this because I truly believe that the cultural rules of my country, Malaysia, make my life here difficult. In order to achieve a "critical mind," one should try to break from his own cultural rules.

————

"can," verb:

1. to be able to; have the ability, power, or skill to. 2. to know how to. 3. to have the power or means to. 4. to have the right or qualifications to. 5. *may; have permission to. (The Random House Dictionary)*

"able," adjective:

1. having necessary power, skill, resources, or qualifications; qualified; able to lift a trunk; . . . able to vote. *(The Random House Dictionary)*

475

When using this handout, I usually begin by asking students what particularly about the two segments might be said to make the voice of the writer idiosyncratic. My students in both writing and literature classes have been fairly quick in tracing it to the "can able to" structure in the two segments. Then I ask the class to speculate on potential causes of that idiosyncrasy. Students' responses to this question usually go something like this: Here is a "foreign" speaker, a student from Malaysia, trying to use the English idiom "to be able to" and ending up with an "error." So we usually talk a little bit about the difference in grammatical function between the verb "can" and the verb "to be" in relation to the adjective "able." And I describe the writer's own initial interpretation of the cause of this "error": her native language is Chinese. With the help of a tutor, she had realized that the Chinese translation for both "can" and "be able to" is the same. When using the expression "be able to," she would be thinking in Chinese. As a result, she often ended up writing "can able to." I would refer to her own initial reading because I am interested in complicating but not denying the relationship between style and the writer's knowledge of and experience with the conventions of written English. So I try to acknowledge first that exposure to and practice in reproducing the "be able to" structure could be one of the ways to revise these segments.

I then go on to complicate this approach by also calling attention to the relationship between form and meaning. What might be the difference in meaning between "can," "be able to," and "can able to"? Most of the students I have encountered tend to see "can" as interchangeable with "be able to." To them, "can able to" appears redundant, like a double negative. To problematize this reading, I usually call attention to the two dictionary entries included in the handout, especially to definition 5 under "can." Definition 5 opens up a new reading by presenting the word "can" as having one more meaning than "to be able to." Rather than approaching the issue of ability from the perspective of what an individual possesses, definition 5 approaches it from the perspective of the external forces *permitting* something, as in the verb "may."

Most native English speakers among my students tend to argue that in actual usage, only grandmas and schoolteachers make the distinction between "can" and "may." *Everyone* uses "can" and "be able to" interchangeably nowadays. In response, I tell them the writer's position on the issue. She was aware of the distinction — she was the one who first called my attention to definition 5. At this point, a "contact zone" would begin to take shape with three conflicting positions on the meanings of "can" and "able to": the position of a speaker of idiomatic English, the position of the dictionary, and the position of a "foreign" student writer. Since the "foreign"

student writer position is here being cast as that of someone lacking knowledge and expertise in formal and idiomatic English and thus the least powerful of the three, I am most interested in furthering the students' existing
construction of that position so it is not so easily silenced.

To that end, I pose the question of whether, read in the context of the
two segments in the handout, one might argue that the "can" in the two
"can able to" structures does not take on the same meaning as the other uses
of "can" in the rest of the segments. This line of inquiry usually leads us to
compare the meaning of the "can" in the first sentence in Segment One to
the two "can's" in the seventh sentence and to the meaning of the "can" in
the "can able to" in Segment Two as well as the "can" in the previous sentence or the "may" in the second half of the same sentence. My aim here is
to get students to re-construct the voice of the writer by focusing on the various uses of the word "can" in the two segments. When exploring the question, I also try to direct attention to the passive voice (Trask was "brought up
in Hawaii" and "send to America mainland to pursue higher education") in
the sentences following the statement "Trask can able to argue for her people." I explore with the class how and why this passive voice might be read as
indicating that the student writer is approaching Trask's ability from the perspective of the external circumstances of Trask's life—using "can" in the
sense of her having the "permission to" become a native Hawaiian historian—as well as from the perspective of her having the qualifications to
argue as a historian. The two uses of "can" in sentence seven, however, present Trask's and the "haole" historians' (in)ability to "feel" the Hawaiian's
bond with the land as more related to a person's will and attitude rather than
to whether each "may"—has the permission to—learn the Hawaiian language or work with the people. ("The 'haole' historians never bother to do
so.") Similarly, in the second segment, the "can" in "a student can able to
adopt different perspectives," when read in the context of the writer's discussion of the difficulties for "everyone to overcome" the "obstacle" of cultural
rules and of her own experience of that difficulty, again foregrounds the role
of external conditions and their effect on one's ability to do something. In
that sense, this "can" is closer in meaning to the "may" in "I may conclude,"
a conclusion presented as depending more on the action of someone else
than on the ability of the "I" drawing the conclusion. At the same time, this
"can" is different from the "can" in the "I can say . . ." since the latter seems
to depend on the ability of the speaker to name the situations as "obstacles"
rather than on whether or not the speaker has permission to so name them.

In getting the class to enact a "close reading" of the two segments, I aim
to shift attention to the relationship between a discursive form, "can able to,"
and the particular meanings it might be said to create in particular contexts.

As a result, a new question often surfaces: What kind of approach to "ability" is enacted by a speaker of idiomatic English who sees "can" and "be able to" as completely interchangeable in meaning? In exploring this question, students have mentioned popular sayings such as "if there is a will, there is a way"; TV shows such as *Mr. Rogers' Neighborhood* which teach viewers to believe "everyone is special," possessing unique qualities; and various discourses promoting the power of positive thinking. Students begin to perceive the way in which a common treatment of "can" and "to be able to" as interchangeable in meaning might be seen as contributing to a popular American attitude towards the transcendental power of the individual. Once we locate these conflicting approaches to the notion of ability, it becomes clear that the revision or "correction" of the "can able to" in these two segments can no longer take place simply at the level of linguistic form. It must also involve a writer's negotiating a position in relation to value systems with unequal social power in the U.S.: one "popular" and the others "alien," "dated," or "formal" but critical. Once this structural "error" is contextualized in conflicting attitudes towards a belief in the transcendental power of the individual, the issue can no longer be merely one's knowledge of or respect for the authorities of a dictionary English versus colloquial English, or one's competency in a particular language, but also one's alignment with competing discursive positions.

At this point, we will have mapped a contact zone with a range of choices and options both among linguistic forms and among discursive alignments. As we move on to the question of how each of us might revise these two segments, I would make sure that each student further enlarges this contact zone by taking into consideration the specific conditions of her or his life. I would have already introduced my definition of the "conditions of life" in previous assignments and class discussions, a definition that includes a whole range of discursive sites, including those of race, ethnicity, gender, sex, economic class, education, religion, region, recreation, and work. I also encourage each student to think about "life" in terms of the life she has lived in the past, is living in the present, and envisions for the future. Furthermore, I stress that decisions on how to revise should also be related to each student's interpretation(s) of the two texts discussed in the segments. To summarize, the contact zone in which the revision takes place would encompass the collision of at least the following voices: the voice of a "foreign" student writer (as constructed by the class at the beginning of the discussion), the voice(s) of the writer of the two segments (as constructed by the class discussion resulting from a "close reading" of the various uses of "can"), the voice of a dictionary, the voice of a speaker of idiomatic English, the voices important to the specific conditions of each student's life, the voice of a teacher, and the voice emerging from each student's interpretation of the two texts discussed in the two segments.

Since decisions on how to revise the "can able to" structure depend on who is present, the particular ways in which the discussion unfolds, and who is doing the revision, such decisions vary from class to class and student to student. To illustrate the unpredictability of the outcome, let me use two decisions made in two different courses, one by the original writer of the two segments and one by another student whose native language is also Chinese. Like all other students in my class, during the process of a "close reading" of the uses of "can" in these two segments, the original writer encountered a construction of her "voices" which she may not have fully considered before the discussion. Therefore, when revising the two segments, she too had to negotiate with these forms of reading and constructions of voices. Upon reflecting on the conditions of her life, she reviewed the attitude towards "ability" promoted in the particular neighborhood in Malaysia where she grew up. In view of that as well as of her own experience as a daughter (especially her difficulties persuading her parents to let her rather than only their sons go abroad for college), her current difficulty in adjusting to the kind of "critical thinking" promoted in my classroom (which she felt was the direct opposite of what she was told to do in her schooling back home), and her admiration of Trask's courage to "argue for her people," the writer decided to foreground the relationship between individual ability and the conditions in which that ability "may" be realized. With the help of her classmates, she came up with several options. One was to add an "if" clause to a sentence using "be able to." Another was to change "can able to" to "may be able to." One student suggested that she use "can able to" and then tag a sentence to explain her reasoning—her view of "ability." Among the suggestions, the writer picked "may be able to" because, as she put it, it was clearly "grammatically correct" and "says what I want to say." As the term progressed, one of the students in the class used "can able to" playfully in a class discussion, and others caught on. It became a newly coined phrase we shared throughout the term.

However, a Vietnamese American student whose home language is also Chinese took a very different stance towards the hegemonic attitude toward "ability" and for a quite different reason from what led some of my American-born students to identify with the voice of an idiomatic speaker. Using examples from his immigrant community, he argued for the importance of believing in the capacity of the individual. He pointed out that the emphasis on external conditions had made some people in his community fatalistic and afraid to take up the responsibility to make changes. According to him, there is a saying in classic Chinese similar to "if there is a will, there is a way." His parents used it repeatedly when lecturing him. So he was all for using "can" and "be able to" interchangeably to foreground the power of the individual. He hoped more people in his community would adopt this outlook. Accordingly, his revision changed "can able to" to "be able to." At the same time, he also changed the passive voice in the sentences referring to Trask's childhood and education in the first segment to the active voice, arguing that there is enough basis in the essays to sustain that reading.

Given the frequency with which students opt for the voices of academic authority, I used to wonder if this kind of teaching is driven more by my view of language as a site of struggle than by the needs of students eager to internalize and reproduce the conventions of academic discourse. My conclusion is: No, this process of negotiation is particularly meaningful for students anxious to master the codes of academic discourse, especially because their discursive practices are most likely to have to take place in the kind of postmodern capitalist world critics such as Fredric Jameson have characterized. Although the product, their decision to reproduce the code, might remain the same whether it is made with or without a process of negotiation, the activities leading to that decision, and thus its significance, are completely different. Without the negotiation, their choice would be resulting from an attempt to passively absorb and automatically reproduce a predetermined form. In such cases, the student would perceive different discourses, to borrow from Bakhtin, as belonging to different, fixed, and indisputable "chambers" in her consciousness and in society. And she would evaluate her progress by the automatism with which she was able to move in and out of these "chambers." If and when this student experienced some difficulty mastering a particular code, she would view it as a sign of her failure as a learner and writer.

On the other hand, if the student's decision to reproduce a code results from a process of negotiation, then she would have examined the conflict between the codes of Standard English and other discourses. And she would have deliberated not only on the social power of these colliding discourses but also on who she was, is, and aspires to be when making this decision. If the occasion arises in the future when she experiences difficulty in reproducing a particular code, as it very likely will, her reaction may be much more positive and constructive. Learning to work on style in the contact zone is also useful for those students interested in exploring ways of resisting the unifying force of "official" discourse. First, it can help students hear a range of choices and options beyond the confines of their immediate life. Second, negotiating as a group gives them the distance they need but might not have when dealing with their own writing in isolation. Therefore, devoting a few class periods to familiarizing students with this approach to style can be fruitful, especially if students are asked to theorize their action afterwards by reflecting on its strengths and limitations.

Obviously, one of the challenges for such a teaching method is that one can only project but not predict a class discussion on the basis of the chosen sample. In fact, life in the contact zone is by definition dynamic, heterogeneous, and volatile. Bewilderment and suffering as well as revelation and exhilaration are experienced by everyone, teacher and students, at different moments. No one is excluded, no one is safe (Pratt 39). Therefore, learning to become comfortable in making blunders is central to this type of teaching. In fact, there is no better way to teach students the importance of negotiation than by allowing them the opportunity to watch a teacher work her way through a chancy and volatile dialogue. Seemingly simple markers such as skin color, native tongue, ethnic heritage or nationality can neither prescribe nor pre-script the range of voices likely to surface. How to voice and talk to rather than speaking for or about the voices of the "other" within and among cultures is thus not a question which can be resolved prior to or outside of the process of negotiation. Rather, it must remain a concern guiding our action as we take part in it.

Needless to say, this type of teaching would work better when students are also asked to try the same method when analyzing the style of "real" writers so they understand that the "problems" they have with style are shared by all writers. For example, when students in a first-year writing course were reading Trask's essay "From a Native Daughter," I asked them to discuss or write about aspects of her style which seemed to deviate from the style of other historians they had encountered. Several students observed that the paragraphs in Trask's essay are shorter, including a series of one-sentence paragraphs with parallel structures of "And when they wrote . . . they meant . . ." (123–24). Others were struck by the opening of Trask's essay, where she addresses her audience directly and asks that they "greet each other in friendship and love." She tells many more personal stories and uses fewer references for support, and she uses the imagery of a lover to depict the role of language. I urged them to examine these stylistic features in relation to the particular stance Trask seems to have taken towards the conflict between "haole" (white) culture and the native Hawaiian culture. Having approached the writing of a "real" writer from the perspective of the relationship between meaning, form, and social identifications, students are likely to be more motivated in applying this perspective to their own style and its revision.

At the same time, using a student paper to enact a negotiation in the contact zone can create a sense of immediacy and a new level of meaningfulness about abstract concepts discussed or enacted in the assigned readings for students in "literature" and "critical theory" classes. For example, I have used the handout with the "can able to" construction in senior-level critical theory courses when discussing Bakhtin's notion of "internal dialogism," Raymond Williams's concept of "structures of feeling," Cornel West's "prophetic critics and artists of color," and "dense" critiques of colonial discourse by such writers as Edward Said or Homi K. Bhabha. In the process of revising the "can able to" structure in the handout, in actively negotiating conflict in a contact zone, students in literature and cultural critical theory courses can gain a concrete opportunity to test the theories of various critics against their own practice. This type of activity reduces the "alienation" students often experience when asked to "do" theory. Testing theories against their own writing practices can also enable students to become more aware of the specific challenges such theories pose as well as the possibilities they open up for the individual writers committed to practicing these viewpoints. And I have used this method in upper-level literature courses when teaching such "borderland" literature as Sandra Cisneros's short story "Little Miracle, Kept Promises" or *Breaking Bread* by Cornel West and bell hooks. Reading and revising a student text, students can become more sensitive to the ways in which a "real" writer negotiates her way through contending discourses. At the same time, such reading and revision of their own writing allows students to enter into dialogue with "real" writers as "fellow travelers," active learners eager to compare and contrast one another's trials and triumphs.

One reaction to teaching style in the contact zone is fear that it will keep students from wanting to learn the conventions of academic discourse. My experience so far suggests that the unequal sociopolitical power of diverse discourses exerts real pressures on students' stylistic choices. After all, students choose to come to college, the choice of which speaks volumes on that power. The need to write for professors who grade with red pens circling all "errors" is also real for a majority of our students in most classrooms outside English departments. Therefore, although the process of negotiation encourages students to struggle with such unifying forces, it does not and cannot lead them to ignore and forget them. It acknowledges the writer's right and ability to experiment with innovative ways of deploying the codes taught in the classroom. It broadens students' sense of the range of options and choices facing a writer. But it does not choose for the students. Rather, it leaves them to choose in the context of the history, culture, and society in which they live.

NOTES

1. See Anderson, "An Apology for Crudity"; Kazin, *On Native Grounds*; and Mencken, "The Dreiser Bugaboo."

2. For an extended discussion of teaching editing that informs my own, see Horner, "Rethinking," especially pages 188–96.

WORKS CITED

Anderson, Sherwood. "An Apology for Crudity." *The Stature of Theodore Dreiser: A Critical Survey of the Man and His Work.* Ed. Alfred Kazin and Charles Shapiro. Bloomington: Indiana UP, 1965. 81–84.

Anzaldúa, Gloria. *Borderlands/La Frontera: The New Mestiza.* San Francisco: aunt lute, 1987.

Bakhtin, Mikhail. *The Dialogic Imagination.* Ed. Michael Holquist. Trans. Caryl Emerson and Michael Holquist. Austin: U of Texas P, 1981.

Bartholomae, David. "The Tidy House: Basic Writing in the American Curriculum." *Journal of Basic Writing* 12 (1993): 4–21.

Dreiser, Theodore. *Dawn.* New York: Fawcett, 1931.

———. *Sister Carrie: The Pennsylvania Edition.* Philadelphia: U of Pennsylvania P. 1981.

Horner, Bruce. "Mapping Errors and Expectations for Basic Writing: From the 'Frontier Field' to 'Border Country.'" *English Education* 26 (1994): 29–51.

———. "Rethinking the 'Sociality' of Error: Teaching Editing as Negotiation." *Rhetoric Review* 11 (1992): 172–99.

Kazin, Alfred. *On Native Grounds: An Interpretation of Modern American Prose Literature.* New York: Harcourt, 1942.

Lu, Min-Zhan. "Conflict and Struggle: The Enemies or Preconditions of Basic Writing?" *College English* 54 (1992): 887–913.

Mencken, H. L. "The Dreiser Bugaboo." *Seven Arts* 2 (1917): 507–17.

Miller, Susan. *Textual Carnivals: The Politics of Composition.* Carbondale: Southern Illinois UP, 1991.

Pratt, Mary Louise. "Arts of the Contact Zone." *Profession* 91 (1991): 33–40.

Shaughnessy, Mina. *Errors and Expectations: A Guide for the Teacher of Basic Writing.* New York: Oxford UP, 1977.

Stein, Gertrude. *The Autobiography of Alice B. Toklas.* New York: Vintage, 1933.

Trask, Haunani-Kay. "From a Native Daughter." *Rereading America: Cultural Contexts for Critical Thinking and Writing.* 2nd ed. Ed. Gary Colombo, Robert Cullen, and Bonnie Lisle. Boston: Bedford, 1989. 118–27.

Traub, James. "P.C. vs. English: Back to Basic." *The New Republic* 8 Feb. 1993: 18–19.

West, Cornel. "The New Cultural Politics of Difference." *Out There: Marginalization and Contemporary Cultures.* Ed. Russel Ferguson, Martha Gever, Trinh T. Minh-Ha, and Cornel West. Cambridge, MA: MIT P, 1990. 19–36.

Acknowledgments: Earlier versions of this paper were delivered at the 1993 CCCC and at the University of Washington. My thanks go to the respondents in the audiences at both occasions. I am also grateful for comments on drafts of this piece from Elizabeth Robertson, Ira Shor, Anne Herrington, and James Seitz. Work on this essay was supported by a grant from the Drake University Center for the Humanities. And I offer special thanks to Bruce Horner for his contributions to the conception and revisions of this essay.

Beyond the Personal

Theorizing a Politics of Location in Composition Research

GESA E. KIRSCH AND JOY S. RITCHIE

In recent years, feminist scholarship has begun to inform much research in composition studies. One particular emphasis has been on admitting the "personal" into our public discourse, on locating ourselves and research participants in our research studies. In what Adrienne Rich calls "a politics of location," theorizing begins with the material, not transcending the personal, but claiming it. The goal is, Rich says in an echo of Hélène Cixous, "to reconnect our thinking and speaking with the body of this particular living human individual, a woman" (213).[1] This new emphasis on the personal, on validating experience as a source of knowledge, raises a number of recurring questions: How does a politics of location inform—and change—research practices? How do we both affirm the importance of "location," and yet understand the limitations of our ability to locate ourselves and others? How do issues of power, gender, race, and class shape a politics of location? What ethical principles are consistent with feminist scholarship and can guide researchers? Although these questions are clearly important in feminist scholarship, they are not merely feminist issues. They mark an important point where feminist theories can inform composition studies. And although we believe women's experiences are an important starting point for research because they have been ignored and omitted in studies of many kinds, we also believe that what can be learned from women's experiences and from

Reprinted from *College Composition and Communication* 46.1 (February 1995): 7–29. Used with permission.

feminist theory has wider implications for composition research; it can become a location for reconsidering what counts as knowledge and for revitalizing research in composition.

In this article, we begin by examining what it means to bring a politics of location to composition research and by foregrounding some of the difficulties of assuming that perspective. We argue that it is not enough to claim the personal and locate ourselves in our scholarship and research. In doing so, we risk creating another set of "master narratives," risk speaking for and essentializing others, and risk being blinded by our own culturally determined world views. Instead, we propose that composition researchers theorize their locations by examining their experiences as reflections of ideology and culture, by reinterpreting their own experiences through the eyes of others, and by recognizing their own split selves, their multiple and often unknowable identities. Further, we propose changes in research practices, such as collaborating with participants in the development of research questions, the interpretation of data at both the descriptive and interpretive levels, and the writing of research reports. Finally, we raise ethical questions that arise from these new research practices. We illustrate our argument with examples drawn from composition, including our own research, but also from scholarship in anthropology, oral history, and sociology. Scholars in those fields have a long history of using ethnomethodological research, have reflected on the role of the personal in research, and have encountered a range of ethical dilemmas.

A POLITICS OF LOCATION
IN FEMINIST RESEARCH

We begin this essay by locating ourselves in this writing, although we recognize that any location is fluid, multiple, and illusive. The impulse to write this article came from a day-long conversation among several women during a workshop on feminism and composition at the 1992 CCCC.[2] These women, though mostly tenured and tenure-tracked and with successful teaching and publication records, were nevertheless frustrated because of the conflicts they experience as feminists in composition living in English departments. The issues we talked about that day suggested that we have been taught to devalue our own experiences as researchers and writers, our relationships with students and other teachers, and our own histories as sources for research and scholarship. As a result, we have often stripped the personal from our writing and research.

As we continued to think about the conflicts women expressed in that group, we began to realize that in part, these conflicts arise from our varied and shifting locations in our discipline, particularly from attempts to hold feminist values and to focus on issues of gender in research, while we still accept the existing epistemologies and methodologies in the field—methodologies that often presuppose objectivity and gender-neutrality. We recognize this tension in our own research. Instead of working to question, resist, and transform traditional research practices, we often find ourselves attempting to live within the contradictions between our feminist beliefs and those traditionally valued in our discipline, even as we write this essay. As we explored these contradictions, we found that many feminists in other disciplines have already begun this work.

We believe researchers in composition must engage in the same kinds of discussions that feminist researchers are having in other disciplines concerning the "politics of location" in research. We hope to advance that discussion by presenting some of the feminist critiques of philosophical, methodological, and ethical assumptions underlying traditional research. In doing so we assert the importance of interrogating the motives for our research and the unspoken power relationships with the "subjects" of our research, considerations we hope will assist us in developing a more ethical approach to research.[3]

If we are to move beyond what Sandra Harding calls an "add women and stir" approach to research (*Feminism* 3), we need to examine just what a politics of location means for research, what are its implications and its limitations. How might we achieve a more problematized politics of location? Rich says that we can no longer utter phrases like "women always. . . ." Instead, she argues: "If we have learned anything in these years of late twentieth-century feminism, it's that that 'always' blots out what we really need to know: When, where, and under what conditions has the statement been true" (214)? But Rich does not suggest that research simply needs to provide the ethnographer's "thick descriptions" of context or to engage in superficial reflexivity. It is not enough to make the facile statements that often occur at the beginning of research articles, to say, "I am a white, middle-class woman from a Midwestern university doing research." She urges women to investigate what has shaped their own perspectives and acknowledge what is contradictory, and perhaps unknowable, in that experience.

In addition to acknowledging our multiple positions, a politics of location must engage us in a rigorous ongoing exploration of *how* we do our research: What assumptions underlie our approaches to research and methodologies? And a politics of location must challenge our conception of *who* we are in our work: How are our conflicting positions, histories, and desires for power implicated in our research questions, methodologies, and conclusions? A politics of location allows us to claim the legitimacy of our experience, but it must be accompanied by a rigorously reflexive examination of ourselves as researchers that is as careful as our observation of the object of our inquiry (Harding, *Whose Science?* 149–50, 161–63). Thus, for example, researchers need to acknowledge the way race (and for most composition scholars this means examining their whiteness), social class, and other circumstances have structured their own thinking and how that, in turn, has shaped their own questions and interpretations. Rich observes: "Marginalized though we have been as women, as white and Western makers of theory, we also marginalize others because our lived experience is thoughtlessly white, because even our 'women's cultures' are rooted in some Western tradition" (219).

Finally, a postmodern feminist perspective leads us to continually question our ability to locate ourselves as researchers and to locate the participants in our research. We need to take into account what psychoanalytic, hermeneutic, and postmodern critics have already shown us about the limitations of our ability to fully understand our own motivations and perspectives. These scholars remind us that we can never fully step outside our culture in order to examine our assumptions, values, and goals. Pretending to do so amounts to what Stanley Fish calls the "theory hope of antifoundationalism" (qtd. in Bizzell 40), the belief that although we reject foundational truth as the basis of knowledge, we can nevertheless use critical analysis to interrogate the historical, political, and social contexts of our knowledge. But, as Fish reminds us, no attempt at analyzing our assumptions is neutral or value-free; it is always a culturally and politically charged activity.

This problematized "politics of location" may seem to make our task impossible; it may make us wonder if we can claim anything for our research. But instead of falling into inaction and despair, we move forward with the awareness that we can only approximate an understanding, noticing the multiple and contradictory positions researchers and participants occupy, complicating and politicizing our investigation, valuing the individual and the local, although we can never hope to understand them fully. We move forward with a willingness to pursue the difficulties inherent in a politics of location accompanied by an equal willingness to be unrelentingly self-reflective.

THE RISK OF ESSENTIALISM

While locating research questions in ourselves and our own experience is vital, it also creates unsettling problems and possibilities for the way we think about knowledge, authority, and power. Feminists have rightly challenged the claims to objectivity in traditional research, arguing that inattention to the researcher's location and subjectivity has led to what Donna Haraway calls the "god trick," researchers' false claims to an ahistorical and universal perspective that has caused gross omissions and erasures in claims of knowledge (qtd. in Harding, *Whose Science?* 153). But feminist theorists have also argued against the uncritical celebration of female experience situated in a fixed or "natural" female identity (Ritchie 255). In fact, it would be dangerous for women, as Teresa Ebert argues, to invest so much in the "local," the individual, the unique, that we forget the global power structures that oppress women (902).

It is not enough, then, to begin locating ourselves and our experiences. In doing so naively, we risk ignoring hierarchies and creating the same unifying and totalizing master narratives that feminist scholars have sought to revise and oppose. More specifically, we risk defining gender biologically rather than recognizing it as a varied set of social relationships. We risk limiting our definitions to a binary of male and female as opposite, inherently different human beings, without seeing the multiple permutations of gendered experience. Jane Flax argues that this will prevent us from adequately asking and answering the questions we need to articulate in order to understand how both men and women are affected by cultural contexts (*Thinking Fragments* 182).

In composition studies we risk making essentializing distinctions about writers: If they are male they must write or think *this* way; if they are female, they must write or think another. New research on gender and writing has made important contributions to composition studies and moved the field from being "gender-blind to [being] gender-sensitive" (Peaden 260), but there remains the tendency to polarize—to essentialize—accounts of gender differences.[4] Don Kraemer suggests that in considering gender and language we look at the "range of social relations they imply" rather than read gender as "one monolithic language" (328). We argue that composition researchers need to resist the drive to generalize about men and women, that we can learn much from studying the multiple ways in which both men and women can express themselves, and that composition teachers need to develop pedagogical practices that encourage students to write in a wide variety of discourse forms, a task that Lillian Bridwell-Bowles has begun to map out successfully in "Discourse and Diversity."

Claiming our experience, then, may be as inadequate for making claims to knowledge as traditional claims from objectivity are. Harding points out that "our experience may lie to us" just as it has lied to male researchers who believed their positions were value-free or universal (*Whose Science?* 286). A number of African American, lesbian, and third world feminists, including bell hooks, have argued that simply privileging our experience may lead us to posit rigid and exclusionary definitions of experience that erase the interlocking structures of race, social class, and heterosexist oppression for men and women ("Feminist Politicization" 107–08). The result is that we create definitions of experience that produce dominant group "common-sense" norms so exclusive that the experience of nonwhite, nondominant people is eliminated, while dominant gender, class, race, and sexuality produce more airtight, fastened down, comprehensive theories. Sidonie Smith observes that feminist researchers "from the dominant culture" can easily appropriate the experiences of others if they are "unselfconscious about the possibility of such cultural appropriation" (401). Consider, for example, the experience that taught one of us (Ritchie) about the problems of cultural appropriation and representation.

Joy Ritchie: As I observed the writing of two women students in an advanced composition class—Manjit Kaur, a Punjabi from Malaysia and BeeTin Choo, a Chinese woman from Singapore—I was struck by the rich and contradictory construction of selfhood in their writing. When I decided to report on their writing, I quickly recognized the political and ethical problems involved in writing *about* them, speaking *for* them, or attempting to represent their experiences. Instead, I invited them to co-author an article, thinking that allowing them to speak for themselves would help me avoid appropriating their writing for my purposes. But I discovered that we still faced many difficult decisions because of the complexity and multiplicity of each of our identities and motivations, most obviously because of our cultural differences, because of the complex power relations between students and professor, and because of the constraints of academic writing. For example, during the time we were writing our essay, after our proposal had been accepted by the editors, BeeTin became increasingly committed to a Christian perspective and was, therefore, uncomfortable with the feminist theoretical framework the other two of us favored. Both women were concerned particularly that their representations of their cultures, written in the relative safety of a classroom, would be misinterpreted by readers and used to solidify existing negative stereotypes of their culture. Whose theory, whose language, whose interpretation, and whose narrative voice would prevail? We had to negotiate these and other questions. I drafted the introduction and conclusion for the essay because I felt some responsibility for ensuring coherence among our three distinct voices, but I struggled, without complete success, to minimize the dominance of my narrative voice.

In a continuing dialogue as we wrote together, I learned more about the way my own cultural context constrained my perspective and often caused me to objectify "others." First, I had to recognize that my assumptions about international students and "Asian women students" led to limited and essentialized understanding of their lives as students, as women, and as writers. BeeTin's silence was not Asian acquiescence to authority; it was a form of resistance. Manjit's exploration of the roles of women in Malaysia and in the United States did not necessarily fit within my western feminist assumptions about women's oppression. I realized that I set apart Manjit and BeeTin as essentialized "others" as I sought to define their voices and to analyze the style, form, and rhetorical features of their writing according to my own training in rhetoric. Although we finished the article, we considered abandoning it at several points because each of us felt at least slightly compromised in the essay that resulted (Ritchie, Kaur, Choo Meyer).

If researchers are to preserve the value of experience as a source of knowledge, they need to locate the experience of others, especially those previously excluded or devalued. But they also need to recognize the impossibility of ever fully understanding another's experiences and to question their motives in gathering, selecting, and presenting those stories. It is important to step back from our own experience, to understand it as a reflection of ideology and culture. But this may not be enough. As Ritchie's work with her students suggests, the tendency to essentialize is only one symptom of what Michelle Fine calls the "knotty entanglement" of self and other (72). As researchers examine more carefully the relationship between themselves and participants, they will need to consider the provocative advice of Trinh Minh-ha: "In writing close to the other of the other, I can only choose to maintain a self-reflexively critical relationship toward the material, a relationship that defines both the subject written and the writing subject undoing the I while asking 'what do I want, wanting to *know* you—or me?'" (76).

Since researchers cannot assume that they understand what is relevant in the lives of others or even what are the important questions to ask, research participants must be invited to articulate research questions, to speak for themselves, to choose the occasions for and forms of representing their experiences. Inevitably, as in Ritchie's work with her students, participants' perspectives will reshape the assumptions and methodologies on which research is based, leading to more collaborative, complex, and "knottily entangled" research practices.

RELATIONSHIP OF THE KNOWER TO THE KNOWN

We have been focusing on the "knower" and her perspective on research. But feminist researchers have another significant and related concern—the "known" and its relationship to the "knower." One of the methodological changes proposed by feminist scholars is to establish more interactive, collaborative, and reciprocal relations between researchers and participants. These changes have come to us from pioneering work of scientists like Barbara McClintock and Evelyn Fox Keller, whose ideas about "objectivity" and the relationship between subject and object of study have complicated feminist research. McClintock's discoveries (documented by Keller) about genetic transposition in maize arose from her unconventional view of the role of the scientist and the relationship of observer and the observed. She no longer thought of the scientist as combative, manipulative, or dominant but rather in a relationship of intimacy and empathy with nature (Keller 117).

As scholars in composition we are uniquely positioned to interact closely with participants since much of our work involves us directly in the lives of students, teachers, and writers as we study their written and oral language. Our research strategies often bring us into lived daily relationships with research participants in ways not possible for biologists or even sociologists. Shirley Brice Heath's *Ways with Words* provides examples of daily lived interactions among research participants and researcher, although she mentions them only occasionally in her narrative: Heath's children played with the children in her study; she transported them in her car; she socialized with them in homes and churches. In the context of her work, Heath's participants became partners in research. Black and white teachers, mill workers, businessmen, and parents whose communities Heath was studying, began themselves to observe and analyze the patterns of language use around them and could therefore begin to formulate questions and initiate change.

One of the assumptions underlying collaboration between researchers and participants is that it will benefit all parties involved in the interaction: Researchers can gather additional insights by getting to know participants in the context of their daily lives, and participants can gain new knowledge about themselves and their lives through the research project. Collaborative research practices often bring about methodological changes as well. One frequently quoted example of methodological innovation resulting from collaborative research is Ann Oakley's interview study of working-class pregnant women. When Oakley encountered women who asked her about prenatal care or other medical information, for example, she found that she could not follow traditional interview procedures: to deflect questions, withhold information, and maintain the role of distanced interviewer. Instead, Oakley decided that she had a moral obligation to assist these women in their quest for information. Consequently, she changed her research methodology in response to research participants: she engaged in dialogue with the women, provided them with information available to her, and helped them get access to prenatal care. Thus, she launched one of the early feminist critiques of social science research methodology. In composition studies, we need to be similarly sensitive to research procedures. Whether we study basic or professional writers, we need to ask participants to collaborate with us, to help us design our research questions, to ask for their feedback, to answer their questions, and to share our knowledge with them.

This formulation of collaborative research still does not go far enough. A feminist politics of location would require the learning about self to be as *reciprocal* as possible—with the researcher also gaining knowledge about her own life or at least reexamining her cultural and gender biases. Sherry Gorelick suggests that "the researcher is transformed in the process of research—influenced and taught by her respondent-participants as she influences them. Theory and practice emerge from their interaction" (469). In composition there are few published accounts in which researchers reflect on the knowledge they gained about themselves and their relations with others due to the research they conducted, and in the few places where such accounts appear, they are often relegated to a preface or epilogue. We suspect this has to do with the format of traditional research reports which do not invite researchers' self-reflections and introspections. But we have anecdotal evidence from colleagues and friends who have discovered that interactive, collaborative research leaves them with a changed understanding of themselves. We have already mentioned one such example: the collaborative writing project Ritchie undertook with two students and the profound questions it raised for her and her position as a white female university professor. Another example emerged in an interview study Kirsch conducted with academic women (*Women Writing the Academy*).

Gesa Kirsch: In my effort to learn more about the concerns of academic women in different disciplines and at different stages of their careers, I invited participants to collaborate with me during various stages of the research: I developed interview questions with the help of women who participated in the study, adding and revising questions in response to initial conversations. I also collaborated with women in the interpretation of interviews. As I began to record and transcribe interviews, I consulted with women about the themes I identified as important in their lives. Thus, I entered into a cycle of conversation whereby both researcher and participants shaped, to some extent, the interpretation of interviews. In many cases, the collaboration between myself and participants was mutually beneficial: the stories women told me transformed my sense of self as writer, as scholar, and as participant in the academic community; women themselves also reported gaining insights into their writing and research processes through the interviews. In some cases, the interviews led to friendships that extended well beyond the duration of my research.

But the cycle of collaboration also had limitations. For example, it was cut short by time constraints I faced as researcher and by participants' interest, availability, and willingness to collaborate with me. I also have to assume that some participants may have felt disappointed, misunderstood, or even manipulated. Although no woman directly expressed this sentiment to me, lack of interest in follow-up conversations and resistance to collaboration suggest that possibility.

Relations between researcher and participants will always retain the potential for misunderstandings, even exploitation—much like other human relationships do. This potential risk, however, should not lead to inaction; rather, researchers can learn to explore sites of conflict for the shifting, multiple, and contradictory positions researchers and participants inevitably occupy and for the ethical questions raised by collaborative research.

ETHICAL QUESTIONS: ISSUES OF POWER AND COLONIZATION

So far we have argued that a politics of location must begin with researchers who recognize their own subjectivity, who draw on their experiences to formulate research questions even as they recognize the limitations of their perspective, experiences, and understanding. Researchers' reflective and critical stance, however, is only the beginning. They must also investigate the relation between the knower and the known and explore the possibilities of collaboration with participants as they develop research questions, collect data, interpret findings, and write research reports. Finally, they must be open to change themselves, reexamining their own perspective continually as they collaborate with participants and come to recognize how their cultural, ethnic, gendered, and personal histories influence the shape of their research. Ideally, a politics of location enables reciprocal, dialogic, collaborative, and mutually beneficial relations between researchers and participants. However, this "ideal" research scenario often remains just that—an ideal. More often, researchers encounter epistemological, methodological, and—perhaps most troubling—ethical dilemmas. We now turn to ethical issues, such as questions of power and colonization, that scholars are likely to face in the research process.

The work of Michel Foucault and others has allowed us to see how observation, classification, and codification in the discourse of the academy are always exercises of power, sometimes more coercive than others. Issues of power and colonization can become particularly prominent in studies of oppressed or disenfranchised groups, as the example of Daphne Patai's work illustrates. She reflects on her experience of interviewing working-class women in Brazil, many of whom lived in poverty and lacked access to adequate health care and education.

> The dilemma of feminist researchers working on groups less privileged than themselves can be succinctly stated as follows: is it possible—not in theory, but in the actual conditions of the real world today—to write about the oppressed without becoming one of the oppressors? (139)

Patai ultimately answers this question in the negative, arguing that the material, economic, and political conditions that separate privileged feminist researchers from disenfranchised or oppressed women cannot easily be overcome, no matter how emancipatory the research methods are or how much good will the researcher brings to the project. She does not, however, suggest that scholars abandon all research that involves oppressed or disenfranchised people; instead, she suggests that scholars abandon their naiveté and learn to make professional judgments about the context, consequences, and potential benefits and drawbacks of their work.

Other ethical dilemmas can emerge when researchers solicit highly personal information from participants. Judith Stacey, a sociologist, faced an ethical dilemma when she interviewed a fundamentalist Christian woman. This woman revealed that she had been involved in a lesbian relationship before her marriage, but asked Stacey not to disclose that information. Thus, the researcher faced a dilemma:

> What feminist ethical principles could I invoke to guide me here? Principles of respect for research subjects and for a collaborative, egalitarian research relationship demand compliance, but this forced me to collude with the homophobic silencing of lesbian experience, as well as consciously to distort what I considered to be a crucial component of the ethnographic "truth" in my study. Whatever we [the interviewer and interviewee] decided, my ethnography was forced to betray a feminist principle. (114)

At times researchers will find that feminist principles are at odds with ethnographic ones. Feminist principles urge researchers to listen to women's voices, to cooperate with women in the telling of their stories, and to honor their trust. Ethnographic principles, on the other hand, urge researchers to be as accurate, exhaustive, and frank as possible in the process of gathering and presenting information about other people and cultures.

The kinds of ethical dilemmas Patai and Stacey describe also concern composition researchers. While composition research does not necessarily involve "disenfranchised groups," it often concerns groups who have less power and fewer resources than the researchers, such as students, basic writers, K–12 teachers, minorities, and women. Furthermore, composition scholars frequently solicit highly personal information from research participants, much in the same way that writing teachers who assign autobiographical essays can find themselves confronted with details about their students' lives that they never anticipated.[5] Researchers need to consider, for example, the dynamics of the interview situation. Although it may be dishonest to assume the stance of objective, detached interviewer, Sheila Riddell points out that it is equally problematic to position oneself as "just another woman" whose concerns in life are similar to those of the research participant (83–84). Because it creates a false atmosphere of equality and mutuality in which women are often eager to talk, this stance may seem to break down barriers between the researcher and participants, but it may also be manipulative or even coercive, while giving participants a false sense of control. Riddell's interviews with teenaged girls led her to speculate that women may talk more openly in some situations because of their social powerlessness and are thus easily exploited. In a long-term study of English teachers Ritchie faced similar issues.

Joy Ritchie: As my colleague David Wilson and I conducted a study of teachers' developing knowledge of their discipline and its pedagogy, I interviewed Carol Gulyas, one of our participants, several times over a period of four years while she completed her course work and began teaching. Because of the many hours I spent in interviews with her and because of her position as a student in some of our classes and as a research and teaching assistant in our project, we developed a closer relationship with Carol than with other participants, a relationship she described as one of "love and caring." My position of authority, but also our frequent and extended contacts, as well as my position as a woman with similar concerns about children and parents, for example, no doubt caused Carol to be less reserved in revealing connections between her personal life and the development of her voice as a writer, as a teacher, and as a woman. According to Carol, our frequent prompts to reflect on and articulate her learning over several semesters encouraged and deepened her learning. Because Carol was so articulate, self-reflective, and astute in her analyses of herself and her peers, the data she provided, and especially the connection between her personal history and her theoretical learning, were crucial in shaping our conclusions. David and I recognized that our representation of her personal experience in our writing might be a distortion or an appropriation. But because we had been so intrusive in Carol's life, we could not withdraw—nor would we have wanted to—from Carol after the study was over.

We felt more than the usual obligation to become an advocate for Carol in her emerging career, to encourage her to write her own account of her learning, even in counterpoint to our representation of it, and to continue to learn from her as a colleague (Gulyas; Wilson and Ritchie).

A final ethical dilemma we want to discuss concerns anthropologists, oral historians, and composition scholars alike: How can or should researchers respond to participants who do not share the researcher's values, who oppose feminist research goals, or who do not identify with feminist causes? We draw on another example from oral history to illustrate this ethical issue. Sondra Hale, an anthropologist who studies African and Middle Eastern women, reports on the dissonance she experienced in interviews with women who either did not identify themselves as feminists or did not share the researcher's notion of what it means to be a feminist. Hale describes her disappointment with an interview of a Sudanese women's movement leader who ignored Hale's invitation to reflect on her role and position in the movement. Instead, the woman chose to use the interview as an occasion to promote the "party line," to enhance the image of the Sudanese women's movement, even when it meant providing inaccurate information or exaggerating accomplishments. In composition studies, we can face similar dissonances in our interactions with research participants. In the interview study of academic women mentioned above, Kirsch also faced questions of how to interpret women's lives.

Gesa Kirsch: I interviewed a history professor who chose to distance herself from the feminist movement and repeatedly disavowed any interest in, sympathy with, or connections to feminist ideas. Yet she had been a "pioneer" in a field dominated by men and made many comments that were feminist in nature, such as pointing to the discrepancy between her values and those of her male colleagues, describing herself as a woman living in a "foreign" male culture, and expressing an interest in experimenting with forms of writing that went "against the academic grain." How was I to represent her views and comments? Should I use her comments that emphasized dissonance from feminist ideas, or should I offer my feminist reading of her interview? Taking my cues from feminist scholars, I addressed these questions by doing both; I juxtaposed her comments (in extended interview quotes) with my analysis and commentary, thereby giving readers evidence that allowed both perspectives to emerge. Of course, as the writer of the research report, I still retain authority by selecting interview quotes, arranging the text, and drawing on supporting theories.

To some degree, researchers cannot escape a position of power and the potential for appropriating or manipulating information. The point here, however, is not to suggest that scholars ignore or omit data that seem to contradict their views. Rather, the point is to encourage researchers to view dissonances as opportunities to examine deeply held assumptions and to allow multiple voices to emerge in their research studies, an act that will require innovation in writing research reports. (We discuss possibilities for new forms of writing below.) Only in that manner will researchers be able to allow readers to see the conflicting pieces of information they often gather in their work and the potential contradictions inherent in their interpretations.

We are not advocating a relativist approach to research here, however. Instead, we argue that feminist research goals should guide researchers' decisions. Feminist research can be distinguished from other research traditions by its emancipatory goals.[6] Feminist researchers not only set out to study and describe women's lives and experiences, but actively seek to understand and change the conditions of women's social and political realities. Thus, feminist researchers advocate using guiding questions like these for responding to ethical dilemmas: Who benefits from the research/theories? What are the possible outcomes of the research and the possible consequences for research participants? Whose interests are at stake? How and to what extent will the research change social realities for research participants? There are no easy solutions to the range of ethical dilemmas researchers can face. Like Patai, we do not think

> that generic solutions can be found to the dilemmas feminists [and other researchers] face in conducting research, nor do [we] for an instant hold out the hope of devising exact "rules" that will resolve these issues for us. In [our] view, this is impossible because ethical problems do not arise as absolutes requiring "blind justice." (145)

Researchers will face difficult decisions in the research process, but a politics of location requires that researchers interrogate their relations with the people they study and the power they hold over them. Linda Alcoff suggests that "in order to evaluate attempts to speak for others in particular instances, we need to analyze the probable or actual effects of the words on the discursive and material context" (26). At times, researchers will have to refocus their research questions, find additional or different participants, assume roles other than that of participant-observer, leave some data unpublished, or even abandon a research project.

TOWARDS AN ETHICS OF RESEARCH

In the previous section we have raised some of the ethical questions inherent in a feminist politics of location. Although we do not claim to have all the answers, we want to suggest how composition researchers can begin to address these questions. As we have shown, these questions are intertwined with—and highlight the necessity for articulating—ethical concerns. However, as we have attempted earlier in this essay to problematize our understanding of a politics of location, we also need to problematize ethics, informing our view with the vigorous discussion of ethics in which feminists from various disciplines have recently engaged.[7] First we will consider how we might revise our definition of ethics based on caring, collaborative relationships with participants. Next, we suggest changes in research methods and forms of writing to meet these ethical demands, changes that allow multi-vocal, dialogic representations in our research narratives. Finally, we propose a reexamination of the goals and implications of research in a further attempt to examine an ethical stance in our work.

Feminist discussions of ethics call for a fundamental change in the way ethics is conceived. Traditional ethics are based on a fixed set of principles determined through rational means to guide one's approach to all problems. That approach assumes a universal applicability and fails to question beliefs in objectivity and neutrality. It also homogenizes differences in contexts and perspectives and fails to take into account the connection between political and moral questions. In general, feminist philosophers disavow traditional rule-governed ethics based on "universal" principles and on unbending rules, because acting from principle entails acting without experience and context, without a politics of location (e.g., Noddings; Schweickart; Young). An ethic of care often comes to different conclusions than an ethic of principle. Ethical behavior must be guided by natural sentiment or what Noddings calls "caring" within the context of human relationships. Unlike rule-bound ethics, "caring" requires one to place herself in an empathetic relationship in order to understand the other's point of view. For this reason an ethic of care is dependent on the engagement of "the personal"—a particular person of ethical character engaged in the examination of context, motivations, relationships, and responsibility (Tronto, "Beyond Gender" 657–58).

But empathy is not an unproblematic concept. Gregory Clark, paraphrasing Wyschogrod, notes that "an act of empathy is inherently an interpretation that eclipses, at least partially, the full reality of another's difference: it directs me to 'understand' another in my own terms" (66). Feminist critics, while acknowledging the importance of an ethic of care, point out the inherent hierarchies, paternalism, and inequalities even in this "caring" ethical model. Patrocinio Schweickart observes that "an ethic of care is no guarantee against self-deception—a discourse of care can be used to mask exploitative and uncaring conditions" (187). Further, Sarah

Hoagland suggests that Noddings's ethic still posits a one-way relationship rather than a truly reciprocal relationship between the caring and cared-for. Such unidirectional relationships of care, she argues, reinforce oppressive institutions (250–53).

Hoagland's concern seems especially relevant for composition researchers because of the problems inherent in seemingly benevolent but unequal relationships. It suggests that researchers continually interrogate their relations with participants, working toward dialogic, mutually educative, caring relations while at the same time recognizing that the complex power dynamics between researcher and participants can undermine, threaten, or manipulate those relations. Engaging in more collaborative approaches to research can help reduce the distance between researchers and participants. Participants can be brought in as co-researchers; those who have been marginalized can be encouraged to join in posing research questions that matter to them. Not only should participants co-author the questions, they can also work with researchers to negotiate the interpretations of data at both the descriptive and interpretive level. bell hooks is most insistent that white, privileged researchers and writers stop asking disempowered women to tell their stories so that these women can rewrite them in their own language, making their stories their own ("Choosing the Margin" 152). Madeleine Grumet provides further suggestions for reciprocal relationships between researchers and participants.

> So if telling a story requires giving oneself away, then we are obligated to devise a method of receiving stories that mediates the space between the self that tells, the self that told, and the self that listens: a method that returns a story to the teller that is both hers and not hers, that contains her self in good company. (70)

Inevitably caring, reciprocal, collaborative research will lead to complications, but it may also lead to richer, more rigorously examined results. Despite the potential problems of an ethic of care, we prefer, along with Tronto, "a moral theory that can recognize and identify these issues [problems of otherness, privilege, and paternalism] . . . to a moral theory that, because it presumes that all people are equal, is unable even to recognize them" (*Moral Boundaries* 147).

Reciprocal relations also imply that researchers attempt to open themselves to change and learning, to reinterpreting their own lives, and to reinventing their own "otherness" (Harding, *Whose Science?* 217). This means doing more than listening to and becoming more sensitive to the experiences of those who are disenfranchised. It requires researchers to attempt to identify what may be repressed and unconscious in their own experiences, and to claim their own contradictory social and gendered identities. Women can explore their marginality, for example, by considering that a woman scholar is at some level a contradiction in terms, that women in the academy still continue to occupy marginal positions because of their gender (Harding, "Who Knows?" 103). Marginality is not merely determined by sex or skin color; we sometimes make choices that place us in such positions. Men in composition studies, for example, can explore how their work as teachers and scholars often positions them as "other" in English departments that tend to privilege the study of literature and critical theory.[8] African American scholars have theorized the importance of using this perspective to generate new understandings of our discipline (Collins 40–41; hooks, "Choosing the Margin" 149). Collins argues that our own devalued identities can be powerful resources for knowing because the tension that arises from assuming the perspective of "outsiders within" allows us to see what privileged insiders cannot (59). Patricia J. Williams in *The Alchemy of Race and Rights* combines her privileged perspective as a legal scholar and her marginalized personal history as an African American woman to analyze the social and political contexts of such seemingly arcane matters as contract law.[9]

Working from a marginal position also offers the potential for research that moves beyond analyzing gender or race as though they are someone else's problem—not ours. It can lead the more privileged to consider themselves as potential "subjects" of study, and, therefore, reveal more clearly their privileged positions as well as their unacknowledged marginality. In her analysis of self-other relations, Michelle Fine describes the study of one of her students, Nancy Porter. Porter interviewed white "Main Line" women in Philadelphia and revealed how white people's lives are protected from surveillance and how scholars have "sanitized" evidence of the dysfunctional in such privileged lives (73).[10] Historian Minnie Bruce Pratt provides another example of this process. She uses her identity as a white Southerner at the center, but also her identity as a lesbian on the margin, to analyze her understanding of Southern history, to see how her white perspective is challenged by the perspective of African American lives, and by her own "outsider" position as a lesbian. We are not suggesting that scholars engage in self-indulgent privileging of their own stories or that they superimpose their stories on those of others; instead, we suggest that they can place their stories and those of their research participants in dialogue with each other to gain new insights into their own and others' lives. As the women in our discussion group at CCCC acknowledged, because our gender and our position in composition still locates us in a marginal position in many English departments, it gives us one important site from which to see with the perspective of outsiders.

We have already asserted the importance of rigorous self-reflection on the part of the researcher in order to avoid essentializing others and to clarify her own motives, desires, and interests. We also understand that to some extent these will always remain unconscious and unknowable. However, neutrality and objectivity are also myths that mask the power-relations always present in research endeavors. That does not mean that relativism is the only alternative, however. Harding's notion of "strong objectivity" may help us understand how to negotiate this apparent dichotomy between a humanist belief in our ability to represent experience and a paralyzed postmodernist stance that denies the possibility of making any claims or taking action. "Strong objectivity" recognizes the historical, social, culturally situated nature of our motives and values, continually theorizes the impact of those values on our work, and searches for what is being eliminated, distorted, or masked in the process (*Whose Science?* 145–47).[11] As part of this activity we can look at the relationship between our theories and our conclusions. The questions that guide our data collection, the stories we decide to tell or eliminate from our research narratives, the range of conclusions we suppress or include—all are guided by our own positionality and must be acknowledged. This process is difficult because "working from a perspective in which we are trained to want to give a reasoned and connected account, we face live material [such as interviews and ethnographic observations] that is constantly in the process of transformation, that is not organized in the way of academic theories" (Acker, Barry, and Esseveld 149).

In addition to acting from an ethic of care and from the perspective offered by rigorous ongoing scrutiny of our motivations and methods, an ethical stance also suggests that we encode in our research narratives the provisional nature of knowledge that our work generates and the moral dilemmas inherent in research. We need to reconsider our privileging of certain, coherent, and univocal writing and include multiple voices and diverse interpretations in our research narratives, highlighting the ideologies that govern our thinking as well as those that may contradict our own. These "rupturing narratives," as Michelle Fine describes them, "allow us to hear the uppity voices of informants and researchers" (78). Finally, of course, we must be prepared to make the case for new forms of research and writing in our discipline as McCarthy and Fishman and others have begun to do. Traditional research reports, for example, urge writers to come to conclusions and announce their findings. That process demands that researchers make coherent what might be fragmented, and thus that they might sometimes reduce complex phenomena or erase differences for the sake of developing coherent theories.[12]

To avoid such erasing of differences, we need to continue experimenting with new ways of reporting research. In composition, a number of scholars have begun to invent writing that highlights multiple narratives and diverse perspectives. Several examples come to mind: Beverly Clark and Sonja Wiedenhaupt published an article on writers' block that took the form of a dialogue between the researcher and the writer, thereby allowing two distinct voices to tell the story from two different vantage points; Jill Eichhorn, Sara Farris, Karen Hayes, Adriana Hernandez, Susan Jarratt, Karen Powers-Stubbs, and Marian Sciachitano used a symposium to reflect on and theorize their experiences as feminist teachers, writing "both as a collective and in [their] seven different voices" (297); and Susan Miller collaborated and co-authored a study of "academic underlife" with several of her undergraduate students, Worth Anderson, Cynthia Best, Alycia Black, John Hurst, and Brandt Miller.[13] Such innovative writing challenges scholars to find new ways of presenting research, challenges journal editors to develop a greater tolerance for ambiguity and unconventional forms of discourse, and challenges readers to learn new ways of reading and interpreting texts. Fine observes, "When we construct texts collaboratively, self-consciously examining our relations with/for/despite those who have been contained as Others, we move against, we enable resistance to, "Othering" (74). Multivocal reports also disrupt the smooth research narratives we have come to know and expect, highlight rather than suppress the problems of representation in our writing, and expose the multiple, shifting, and contradictory subject positions of researchers and participants.[14]

Finally, a problematized politics of location leads us to research centered in the local and the individual while at the same time acknowledging that research has social consequences in the world. If we work from an ethic of care, we cannot ignore the political and cultural conditions that place us in unequal power relationships with the participants of our research (Hoagland 260). We have seen in the studies of Patai and Oakley and in our own research how deeply implicated issues of power are, in our work. Patti Lather is one of many feminist thinkers who argues strongly that we cannot be satisfied with more research and better data concerning women (or other groups we choose to study). If our research is centered on a politics of location it demands an extra measure of responsibility and accountability on our part. It requires using research as "praxis" to help those who participate with us in research to understand and change their situation, to help those who have been marginalized to speak for themselves. Under these circumstances, it will not be possible to walk away from the research site or those who live in it. Our research instead will need to extend to theory-generating in a self-reflexive and mutually dialogic context to help researchers and participants challenge and change the conditions that keep oppressive structures in place. Only in this extra measure of "care" can our research truly be ethical.

Pursuing the difficulties inherent in a politics of location may lead us beyond some of the frustrations we experience in our work in English departments, because these discussions will inevitably lead us to question our accommodation with the status quo in our discipline, to more seriously question the discipline's traditional ways of asking and answering research questions, to examine the internalized structures, the standard conventions for generating and communicating knowledge in the discipline, and to reshape our agendas for research and action in the field. It will engage us in a rigorous process of analyzing the meaning of the "personal" in our work.

NOTES

1. We frame our article with Adrienne Rich's words realizing that she has been criticized for some of her earlier writing in which she seems to advocate an essentialist position that reinscribes bourgeois individualism and an unproblematic universal feminism. We think her position is an important starting point for discussions of a politics of location, however, because Rich was one of the early theorists attempting to reintroduce the personal in order to challenge the impersonal authority and false universality of interpretive practices that exclude women's writing and women's lives altogether from the academy and other public sites. In the essay we quote, she does acknowledge the social and psychological construction of women's lives and defines "location" as a space in which we move, not as a fixed site. She also foregrounds the tension we want to explore between the degendered, depoliticized subject of post-modernist aesthetics and the universalizing, unified, humanist subject—both positions which can erase the specificity and lived experience of particular women.

2. We realize that our attempt to locate the origins of this article in a single event misrepresents the many origins our work inevitably has. In the first place we had to be motivated to attend the workshop, a motivation we could trace to our reading of feminist literature, to conversations with colleagues and friends, and to our lived everyday experiences as women in the academy and in the culture at large. If we continue this search for origins, we quickly come to realize that questions of location are complex and call for an analysis of the many conflicting layers of reality we experience in our multiple and shifting subject positions.

3. People participating in research studies are traditionally called "subjects." This term, however, is problematic, implying a division if not hierarchy between researchers and subjects, thereby positioning participants as objects of study, not as the complex and contradictory human beings they are. Since we are questioning precisely this division between researchers and subjects, we have chosen to use the terms "research participants" or simply "participants" throughout this article when we are referring to human beings involved in research studies.

4. Heather Brodie Graves, for example, argues that traditional "feminine" and "masculine" traits can be found in writers of both genders; she analyzes the writing of Kenneth Burke for "feminine" traits and that of Julia Kristeva for "masculine" traits to illustrate her point.

5. For discussions of writing teachers faced with highly personal and at times disturbing information in their students' writing, see Carole Deletiner; Cheryl Johnson; Richard E. Miller.

6. For discussions of feminist research goals and methods, see *Beyond Methodology* (Fonow and Cook), *Feminism and Methodology* (Harding), *Feminist Research Methods* (Nielsen), *Feminist Methods in Social Research* (Reinharz).

7. Space does not permit a full discussion of feminist approaches to ethics, particularly an ethic of care. We refer interested readers to discussions in political science (Tronto; Young), in feminist theory and philosophy (Card; Friedman; Hoagland; Houston; Lather; Schweickart), in education and psychology (Fine; Gilligan; Grumet; Noddings; Punch), and in composition studies (Clark; Mortensen and Kirsch).

8. We do not mean to suggest that only scholars who are marginalized can engage in feminist or care-based approaches to research. Rather, we argue for a sense of location that one can actively learn to choose. But we believe that attending to the experiences of marginalized people as well as examining aspects of one's identity that are suppressed are important points of departure for a critical perspective on research.

9. We do not wish to minimize differences among women of different backgrounds, generations, race, class, ethnicity, or other identity-shaping factors. In fact, the position of African American women in the academy is distinctly different from those of white, middle class women and has caused much debate and tension among feminist theorists. We use this example only to suggest that a marginal position can be a source of strength and insight, allowing researchers to formulate new research questions and gain knowledge not readily available to those who occupy more privileged positions.

10. For another revealing study of "whiteness," see *White Women, Race Matters: The Social Construction of Whiteness* by Ruth Frankenberg.

11. Harding's concept of "strong objectivity" is not unproblematic. Flax, for example, argues that it is still based on a notion of "transcendental truth" because it suggests that once we eliminate or reduce gender biases we will have come closer to 'the truth' (Disputed Subjects 141–47). We concur with Flax's critique but find Harding's notion useful as a working concept for researchers trying to assess the ethical dimensions of their work.

12. We recognize the irony of the text we have produced: a relatively univocal, coherent text that argues for experimental, multivocal writing. We have attempted to present multivocality by writing in our individual voices when describing our own research projects and in our collective voice in other sections of this text, but we can imagine more experimental and innovative ways of writing.

13. We list names of all collaborators/authors here to give full credit to the nature of collaborative work; all too often multiple authors disappear in the "et al." convention, a practice that reinforces the dominant single-author model of scholarship.

14. The multivocal texts we advocate are not without risk; besides making new demands on readers, writers, and editors, these texts pose special risks for untenured faculty and graduate students who still have to "prove"—or feel that they still have to prove—their disciplinary membership by using conventional research methods and forms.

WORKS CITED

Acker, Joan, Kate Barry, and Johanna Esseveld. "Objectivity and Truth: Problems in Doing Feminist Research." *Beyond Methodology: Feminist Scholarship as Lived Research.* Ed. Mary Fonow and Judith Cook. Bloomington: Indiana UP, 1991. 133–53.

Alcoff, Linda. "The Problem of Speaking for Others." *Cultural Critique* 20 (1991–92): 5–32.

Anderson, Worth, Cynthia Best, Alycia Black, John Hurst, Brandt Miller, and Susan Miller. "Cross-Curricular Ablex: A Collaborative Report on Ways with Academic Words." *College Composition and Communication* 41 (1990): 11–36.

Bizzell, Patricia. "Foundationalism and Anti-Foundationalism in Composition Studies." *Pre/Text* 7 (1986): 37–56.

Bridwell-Bowles, Lillian. "Discourse and Diversity: Experimental Writing within the Academy." *College Composition and Communication* 43 (1992): 349–68.

Card, Claudia, ed. *Feminist Ethics*. Lawrence: UP of Kansas. 1991.

Clark, Beverly Lyon, and Sonja Wiedenhaupt. "On Blocking and Unblocking Sonja: A Case Study in Two Voices." *College Composition and Communication* 43 (1992): 55–74.

Clark, Gregory. "Rescuing the Discourse of Community." *College Composition and Communication* 45 (1994): 61–74.

Collins, Patricia Hill. "Learning from the Outsider Within: The Sociological Significance of Black Feminist Thought." *(En)Gendering Knowledge: Feminists in Academe*. Ed. Joan Hartman and Ellen Messer-Davidow. Knoxville: U of Tennessee P, 1991. 40–65.

Deletiner, Carole. "Crossing Lines." *College English* 54 (1992): 809–17.

Ebert, Teresa. "The 'Difference' of Postmodern Feminism." *College English* 53 (1991): 886–904.

Eichhorn, Jill, Sara Farris, Karen Hayes, Adriana Hernandez, Susan Jarratt, Karen Powers-Stubbs, and Marian Sciachitano. "A Symposium on Feminist Experiences in the Composition Classroom." *College Composition and Communication* 43 (1992): 297–322.

Fine, Michelle. "Working the Hyphens: Reinventing Self and Other in Qualitative Research." *Handbook of Qualitative Research*. Ed. Norman Denzin and Yvonna Lincoln. Thousand Oaks, CA: Sage, 1994. 70–82.

Flax, Jane. *Thinking Fragments: Psychoanalysis, Feminism, and Postmodernism in the Contemporary West*. Berkeley: U of California P, 1990.

——. *Disputed Subjects: Essays on Psychoanalysis, Politics, and Philosophy*. New York: Routledge, 1993.

Fonow, Mary Margaret, and Judith A. Cook, eds. *Beyond Methodology: Feminist Scholarship as Lived Research*. Bloomington: Indiana UP, 1991.

Frankenberg, Ruth. *White Women, Race Matters: The Social Construction of Whiteness*. Minneapolis: U of Minnesota P, 1993.

Friedman, Marilyn. "Beyond Caring: The De-Moralization of Gender." *Science, Morality, and Feminist Theory*. Ed. Marsha Hanen and Kai Nielsen. Calgary: U of Calgary P, 1987. 87–110.

Gilligan, Carol. *In a Different Voice: Psychological Theory and Women's Development*. Cambridge, MA: Harvard UP, 1982.

Gorelick, Sherry. "Contradictions of Feminist Methodology." *Gender and Society* 4 (1991):459–77.

Graves, Heather Brodie. "Regrinding the Lens of Gender: Problematizing 'Writing as a Woman.'" *Written Communication* 10 (1993):139–63.

Grumet, Madeleine R. "The Politics of Personal Knowledge." *Stories Lives Tell: Narrative and Dialogue in Education*. Ed. Carol Witherell and Nel Noddings. New York: Teachers College P, 1991. 67–77.

Gulyas, Carol. "Reflections on Telling Stories." *English Education* 18 (1994): 189–94.

Hale, Sondra. "Feminist Methods, Process, and Self-Criticism: Interviewing Sudanese Women." *Women's Words: The Feminist Practice of Oral History*. Ed. Sherna Gluck and Daphne Patai. New York: Routledge, 1991. 121–36.

Haraway, Donna. "Situated Knowledges: The Science Question in Feminism and the Privilege of Partial Perspective. *Feminist Studies* 14 (1988): 575–99.

Harding, Sandra, ed. *Feminism and Methodology: Social Science Issues.* Bloomington: Indiana UP, 1987.

———. "Who Knows? Identities and Feminist Epistemology." *(En)Gendering Knowledge: Feminists in Academe.* Ed. Joan Hartman and Ellen Messer-Davidow. Knoxville, TN: U of Tennessee P, 1991. 100–15.

———. *Whose Science? Whose Knowledge? Thinking from Women's Lives.* Ithaca: Cornell UP, 1991.

Heath, Shirley Brice. *Ways with Words: Language, Life, and Work in Communities and Classrooms.* New York: Cambridge UP, 1983.

Hoagland, Sarah Lucia. "Some Thoughts about 'Caring'." *Feminist Ethics.* Ed. Claudia Card. Lawrence: UP of Kansas, 1991. 246–63.

hooks, bell. "Feminist Politicization: A Comment." *Talking Back: Thinking Feminist, Thinking Black.* Boston: South End P, 1985. 105–11.

———. "Choosing the Margin as a Space of Radical Openness." *Yearning: Race, Gender, and Cultural Politics.* Boston: South End P, 1990. 145–54.

Houston, Barbara. "Rescuing Womanly Virtues: Some Dangers of Moral Reclamation." *Science, Morality, and Feminist Theory.* Ed. Marsha Hanen and Kai Nielsen. Calgary: U of Calgary P, 1987. 237–62.

Johnson, Cheryl L. "Participatory Rhetoric and the Teacher as Racial/Gendered Subject." *College English* 56 (1994): 409–19.

Keller, Evelyn Fox. "Dynamic Objectivity: Love, Power, and Knowledge." *Reflections on Gender and Science.* New Haven: Yale UP, 1985. 115–26.

Kirsch, Gesa, E. *Women Writing the Academy: Audience, Authority, and Transformation.* Carbondale: Southern Illinois UP, 1993.

Kraemer, Don J. "Gender and the Autobiographical Essay: A Critical Extension of the Research." *College Composition and Communication* 43 (1992): 323–39.

Lather, Patti. *Getting Smart: Feminist Research and Pedagogy With/In the Postmodern.* New York: Routledge, 1991.

McCarthy, Lucille Parkinson, and Stephen M. Fishman. "A Text for Many Voices: Representing Diversity in Reports of Naturalistic Research." *Ethics and Representation in Qualitative Studies of Literacy.* Ed. Peter Mortensen and Gesa E. Kirsch. Urbana, IL: National Council of Teachers of English, 1996. 155–76.

Miller, Richard E. "Fault Lines in the Contact Zone." *College English* 56 (1994): 389–408.

Minh-ha, Trinh T. *Women, Native, Other: Writing Postcoloniality and Feminism.* Bloomington: Indiana UP, 1989.

Mortensen, Peter, and Gesa Kirsch. "On Authority in the Study of Writing." *College Composition and Communication* 44 (1993): 556–72.

Nielsen, Joyce McCarl, ed. *Feminist Research Methods: Exemplary Readings in the Social Sciences.* San Francisco: Westview, 1990.

Noddings, Nel. *Caring: A Feminine Approach to Ethics and Moral Education.* Berkeley: U of California P, 1984.

Oakley, Ann. "Interviewing Women: A Contradiction in Terms?" *Doing Feminist Research.* Ed. Helen Roberts. New York: Routledge, 1981. 30–61.

Patai, Daphne. "U.S. Academics and Third World Women: Is Ethical Research Possible?" *Women's Words: The Feminist Practice of Oral History.* Ed. Sherna Gluck and Daphne Patai. New York: Routledge, 1991. 137–53.

Peaden, Catherine Hobbs. Rev. of *Gender Issues in the Teaching of English*. Ed. Nancy McCracken and Bruce Appleby. *Journal of Advanced Composition* 13 (1993): 260–63.

Pratt, Minnie Bruce. "Identity: Skin Blood Heart." *Yours in Struggle: Three Feminist Perspectives on Anti-Semitism and Racism*. Ed. Elly Bulkin, Minnie Bruce Pratt, and Barbara Smith. Ithaca, NY: Long Haul P, 1984. 11–63.

Punch, Maurice. "Politics and Ethics in Qualitative Research." *Handbook of Qualitative Research*. Ed. Norman Denzin and Yvonna Lincoln. Thousand Oaks, CA: Sage, 1994. 83–97.

Reinharz, Shulamit. *Feminist Methods in Social Research*. New York: Oxford UP, 1992.

Rich, Adrienne. "Notes on a Politics of Location." *Blood, Bread, and Poetry*. New York: Norton, 1989. 210–31.

Riddell, Sheila. "Exploiting the Exploited? The Ethics of Feminist Educational Research." *The Ethics of Educational Research*. Ed. Robert Burgess. New York: Falmer, 1989. 77–99.

Ritchie, Joy S. "Confronting the Essential Problem: Reconnecting Feminist Theory and Pedagogy." *Journal of Advanced Composition* 10 (1990): 249–71.

Ritchie, Joy S., Manjit Kaur, and Bee Tin Choo Meyer. "Women Students' Autobiographical Writing: The Rhetoric of Discovery and Defiance." *Situated Stories: Valuing Diversity in Composition Research*. Ed. Emily Decker and Kathleen Mary Geissler. Portsmouth, NH: Boynton/Cook Heinemann, 1998. 173–89.

Schweickart, Patrocinio. "In Defense of Femininity: Commentary on Sandra Bartky's Femininity and Domination." *Hypatia* 8 (1993): 178–91.

Smith, Sidonie. "Who's Talking/Who's Talking Back? The Subject of Personal Narrative." *Signs: Journal of Women in Culture and Society* 18 (1993): 392–407.

Stacey, Judith. "Can There Be a Feminist Ethnography?" *Women's Words: The Feminist Practice of Oral History*. Ed. Sherna Gluck and Daphne Patai. New York: Routledge, 1991. 111–19.

Tronto, Joan. "Beyond Gender Difference to a Theory of Care." *Signs: Journal of Women in Culture and Society* 12 (1987): 644–63.

————. *Moral Boundaries: A Political Argument for an Ethic of Care*. New York: Routledge, 1993.

Williams, Patricia J. *The Alchemy of Race and Rights*. Boston: Harvard UP, 1991.

Wilson, David E., and Joy S. Ritchie. "Resistance, Revision, and Representation: Narrative in Teacher Education." *English Education* 18 (1994): 177–88.

Young, Iris Marion. *Justice and the Politics of Difference*. Princeton: Princeton UP, 1990.

———————

Acknowledgments: We wish to thank colleagues, friends, and CCC reviewers for their comments and encouragement as we developed this essay: Lil Brannon, Robert Brooke, Gregory Clark, Lisa Ede, Elizabeth Flynn, Min-Zhan Lu, and Kate Ronald.

The Public Intellectual, Service Learning, and Activist Research

ELLEN CUSHMAN

While I support the good intentions of those who have recently proposed definitions of the public intellectual, I find these definitions problematic in their narrow delineation of the word "public"—they focus on a "public" consisting of middle and upper class policy makers, administrators, and professionals, and, in doing so, omit an important site for uniting knowledge-making and political action: the local community. Canvassing the letters submitted to the October 1997 *PMLA* forum on intellectual work in the twenty-first century, one notices numerous tensions regarding the larger public role of the intellectual:

> New and old intellectuals in the twenty-first century need to try to answer such questions as: "What do people(s) want?" and "What is the meaning of the political?" (Alina Clej; Forum 1123)

> In the next century, the intellectual must be willing to take more risks by choosing exile from confining institutional, theoretical, and discursive formations. (Lawrence Kritzman 1124)

> American intellectuals appear to have entered a period of non-engagement, cherishing their autonomy over engagement and retreating into the ivory tower. (Patrick Saveau 1127)

> If there is a task ahead for the kind of intellectual I have in mind, it lies in the attempt to forge a more secure link between the love of art and human decency. (Steven Greenblatt 1131)

Reprinted from *College English* 61.3 (January 1999): 328–36. Used with permission.

[The modern intellectual's] goal would be to enact in one's research an informed concern with specific questions of public value and policy. (Dominick Lacapra 1134)

A postoccidental intellectual [is] able to think at the intersection of the colonial languages of scholarship and the myriad languages subalternized and banned from cultures of scholarship through five hundred years of colonialism. (Walter Mignolo 1140)

Taken together, these statements indicate a growing pressure for intellectuals to make knowledge that speaks directly to political issues outside of academe's safety zones. This urgency comes in part from administrators and legislators who demand accountability, but it also comes from academics who have grown weary of isolation and specialization and who hope their work might have import for audiences beyond the initiated few. They wonder if knowledge-making can take risks while both cultivating aesthetics and leading to political action. Above all, these quotations reveal the nagging suspicion that academics have yet to realize their full potential in contributing to a more just social order. I believe public intellectuals can indeed contribute to a more just social order, but to do so they have to understand "public" in the broadest sense of the word.

The kind of public intellectuals I have in mind combine their research, teaching, and service efforts in order to address social issues important to community members in under-served neighborhoods. You know these neighborhoods: they're the ones often located close by universities, just beyond the walls and gates, or down the hill, or over the bridge, or past the tracks. The public in these communities isn't usually the one scholars have in mind when they try to define the roles of "public" intellectuals. For example, Pierre Bourdieu recognizes that the intellectual has dual and dueling agendas: "on the one hand, he [*sic*] must belong to an autonomous intellectual world; . . . on the other hand, he must invest the competence and authority he has acquired in the intellectual field in a political action" ("Fourth Lecture" 656). Yet Bourdieu advocates only one kind of political action: "the first objective of intellectuals should be to work collectively in defense of their specific interests and of the means necessary for protecting their own autonomy" (660). Granted, academics must have the secure position that autonomy (typically gained through tenure) provides if the knowledge they make is to be protected from censorship. Yes, academics need to defend their positions, particularly in this socio-economic climate where big business ethics of accountability, total quality management, downsizing, and overuse of part-time labor conspire to erode academics' security within the university. However, the fight for our own autonomy is a limited and self-serving form of political action addressed only to an elite "public" of decision-makers.

Another type of public intellectual, in the limited sense of the word *public*, believes in protecting scholarly autonomy through popularizing intellectual work. Here's Michael Bérubé on this kind of public intellectual: "the future of our ability to produce new knowledges for and about ordinary people—and the availability of education *to* ordinary people—may well depend on how effectively we can . . . make our work intelligible to nonacademics—who then, we hope, will be able to recognize far-right rant about academe for what it is" (176). Going public, turning to mass media, dressing our work in plain garb may help preserve autonomy, may even get intellectuals a moment or two in the media spotlight, but how will this help individuals who have no home, not enough food, or no access to good education? Popularizing scholarship may help solve problems on academe's front lines, but such action does not seem to do democracy any great favors. Popularizing suggests that public intellectuals simply translate their thinking into less specialized terms, then publish in the *New Yorker* or *Academe*. Yet publishing to a greater number of elite audiences works more to bolster our own positions in academe than it does to widen the scope of our civic duties as intellectuals.

Bourdieu and Bérubé belong to the modern ranks of public intellectuals, among whom I might include such currently prominent figures as Henry Louis Gates, Jr., and Stanley Fish. They all share an implied goal of affecting policy and decision-making, and they reach this goal by using their positions of prestige as well as multiple forms of media (newspapers, radio, and television) in order to influence a public beyond the academy, though this public will usually be limited to the educated upper echelons of society. In their dealings with this public, moreover, they typically remain scholars and teachers, offering their superior knowledge to the unenlightened.

When public intellectuals not only reach outside the university, but actually *interact* with the public beyond its walls, they overcome the ivory tower isolation that marks so much current intellectual work. They create knowledge with those whom the knowledge serves. Dovetailing the traditionally separate duties of research, teaching, and service, public intellectuals can use the privilege of their positions to forward the goals of both students and local community members. In doing so, they extend access to the university to a wider community. Academics can reach these goals in two ways: service learning and activist research.

SERVICE LEARNING

To enact citizenship in the larger sense, and to unify the locations of research, teaching, and service, the public intellectual can begin by developing service learning or outreach courses. Service learning asks students (both graduate and undergraduate) to test the merit of what they learn in the university classroom against their experiences as volunteers at local sites such as philanthropic agencies, primary and secondary schools, churches, old-age homes, half-way houses, and shelters. When students enter communities as participant observers, they "begin not as teachers, but as learners in a community setting where the goals and purposes of a 'service' effort are not established beforehand" (Schutz and Gere 145). Students enter the community in a sincere effort to both engage in and observe language use that helps address the topics that are important to community members. When activist fieldwork is a cornerstone of the course, students and community residents can develop reciprocal and dialogic relations with each other; their relationship is a mutually beneficial give-and-take one.

As participant observers, students take fieldnotes that reflect on their experiences with community members and how these experiences relate to the set of readings chosen by the professor. These fieldnotes serve a twofold purpose. First, they offer students a ready supply of examples to analyze in their essays, and second, they become potential source material for the professor. The professors' own notes, video and audio tape recordings, evaluations from the public service organization or area residents, and other literacy artifacts constitute a rich set of materials for knowledge-making. Since the professors also volunteer, teach, and administer the service learning course, they have first-hand familiarity with the important social issues and programmatic needs at the local level, and they tailor the curriculum to fit these. Thus, when activist methods are employed, knowledge-making in outreach courses happens *with* the individuals served. The course must respond to the immediate concerns and longstanding problems of the area in order to remain viable.

In their most limited sense, service learning courses unite in a single mission the traditionally separate duties of research, teaching, and service.

The research contributes

- ♦ to teaching by informing a curriculum that responds to both students' and community members' needs, and
- ♦ to service by indicating emerging problems in the community which the students and curriculum address.

The teaching contributes

- ♦ to research by generating fieldnotes, papers, taped interactions and other materials, and
- ♦ to service by facilitating the community organization's programmatic goals with the volunteer work.

The service contributes

- ♦ to research by addressing political and social issues salient in every-day lived struggles, and
- ♦ to teaching by offering students and professors avenues for testing the utility of previous scholarship in light of community members' daily lives and cultural values.

Because service learning includes an outreach component, the knowledge generated together by the area residents, students, and the professor is exoteric (as opposed to esoteric) and is made in interaction (as opposed to isolation).

Among composition and rhetoric scholars, Bruce Herzberg, Linda Flower, and Aaron Schutz and Anne Ruggles Gere, to name a few, have created community literacy projects which include service learning. Joan Schine has recently discussed elementary and secondary programs in service learning, and Barbara Jacoby addresses the practical and political aspects of developing outreach courses at the university level. Although scholars have begun to develop these outreach initiatives, few have offered a methodology that integrates the civic-minded mission of service learning with the politics of research in local settings.

ACTIVIST RESEARCH

One limitation of service learning courses can be students' perception of themselves as imparting to the poor and undereducated their greater knowledge and skills. Instructors in the service learning course that Anne Ruggles Gere and her colleagues developed noted that "their students often entered seeing themselves as 'liberal saviors,' and that the structure of tutoring had the potential to enhance the students' vision of this 'savior' role" (Schutz and Gere 133). Indeed, if the university representatives understand themselves as coming to the rescue of community residents, students will enact this missionary ideology in their tutoring. Service learning courses can avoid this liberal do-gooder stance when they employ activist research methodologies.

Activist research combines postmodern ethnographic techniques with notions of reciprocity and dialogue to insure reciprocal and mutually beneficial relations among scholars and those with whom knowledge is made. Since a central goal of outreach courses is to make knowledge *with* individuals, scholars need a methodology that avoids the traditional top-down approaches to ethnographic research: "The Bororos of Brazil sink slowly into their collective death, and Lévi-Strauss takes his seat in the French Academy. Even if this injustice disturbs him, the facts remain unchanged. This story is ours as much as his. In this one respect, . . . the intellectuals are still borne on the backs of the common people" (de Certeau 25). Traditional forms of ethnographic fieldwork yield more gains for the intellectual than the community residents. On the other hand, activist ethnographic research insures that, at every level of the ethnographic enterprise—from data collection through interpretation to write-up—the researcher and participants engage in openly negotiated, reciprocal, mutually beneficial relations.

Theories of praxis can be united with notions of emancipatory pedagogy in an effort to create a theoretical framework for activist methodology. Scholars who advocate praxis research find the traditional anthropological method of participant observation unsatisfactory because it has the potential to reproduce an oppressive relationship between the researcher and those studied (Oakley; Lather; Bleich; Porter and Sullivan). Instead of emphasizing observation, research as praxis demands that we actively participate in the community under study (Johannsen; for a thoughtful exploration of the connections between critical ethnography and critical pedagogy, see Lu and Horner). Applied anthropology provides theoretical models for how praxis—loosely definable as ethical action to facilitate social change—enters into the research paradigm, but many scholars still need to do the work of intervention, particularly at the community level.

Praxis research can take emancipatory pedagogy as its model for methods of intervention, since notions of emancipatory pedagogy work with the same types of theoretical underpinnings. Paulo Freire's *Pedagogy of the Oppressed* exemplifies the pragmatic concerns of politically involved teaching aimed at emancipating students. His work teaching illiterate peasants in Latin America has been adapted to American educational needs in schooling institutions (Apple and Weis; Giroux; Luke and Gore; Lankshear and McLaren). Emancipatory teaching can only go so far in instantiating activist research, though, because teachers often apply liberating teaching only in the classroom, and they are hard pressed to create solidarity and dialogue within the institutionalized social structure of American schools. In order to adapt Freire's pedagogy to the United States, we must also practice it outside the academy, where we can often more easily create solidarity. In a conversation with Donaldo Macedo, Freire says: "it is impossible to export pedagogical practices without re-inventing them. Please, tell your fellow American educators not to import me. Ask them to recreate and rewrite my ideas" (Macedo xiv). Our revisions of his pedagogy can be more fully expanded if we move out of the institutionalized setting of classrooms and into our communities. In this way, liberatory teaching can be brought together with praxis research to create the activist research useful to service learning.

Although I have conducted a three-and-a-half year long ethnography of literacy in an inner city (Cushman), Spring 1998 offered me the first opportunity to bridge activist research and service learning through a course called "Social Issues of Literacy." The course links Berkeley undergraduates with the Coronado YMCA in Richmond, a place residents of the East Bay call "the forgotten inner city." Undergraduates read scholarship on literacy, volunteer at the YMCA, write fieldnotes, and then integrate theory and data in case studies. The course has met with initial success in three ways.

First, students immediately saw the tight integration of literacy theory and practice. Their essays revealed careful attention to the scholarship and some rigor in challenging the limitations of these readings against their own observations. One student's paper noted that Scribner and Cole's famous work on Vai literacy showed their limited access to Vai females' literacy practices. Her paper then illustrated two interactions where she noticed how girls were excluded by the boys during storytelling, playing, and writing. She considered methods of participant observation that might invite more of the girls to engage in these activities. At the same time, she conducted informal interviews with the YMCA members in order to understand better how their values for oral and literate language shifted along gender lines. She did this with an eye toward filling gaps in knowledge that she saw in the scholarship on literacy that we read in class.

Second, the outreach course has filled a very real need for the YMCA staff. While this particular YMCA had numerous programs, including African dance, sports, teen pregnancy prevention, and scouting, they needed adults to engage youths in language use that would promote their reading and writing—without reproducing a school atmosphere. As one supervisor told me, "if the undergraduates come in here with too much school-like structure, they could turn the kids off to the reading and writing that they'll need to get ahead in school. So let's create a flexible structure for activities." Her point was subtle; area children hold schoolwork in low esteem, but the adults value the reading and writing needed to succeed in education.

With the supervisor's goals in mind, the undergraduates and I ask the YMCA members what kinds of activities they would like to do and offer a broad range of reading, writing, and artistic events in which they can engage. One ongoing literacy event centers around the creation of personal journals. Shawn, a nine-year-old, told me he wanted his "own journal here [at the YMCA] where I can keep all my stories and things." Together with the undergraduates, the children have produced journals with decorated covers bound with staples or yarn. Inside the journals, they keep their stories, math homework, spelling words, drawings, and letters to the undergraduates and myself. Leafing through a set of completed journals, the YMCA supervisor noted that the children "don't even realize that all the art, math, and writing they're doing in these journals will help them with their schoolwork." At the intersection where university representatives and community members meet, these journals offer a brief illustration of the way in which public intellectuals and community members can work together to identify and ameliorate local-level social issues. In this case, we together found ways to engage in reading and writing that would bridge a problematic split in generational values attached to literacy.

Finally, "Social Issues of Literacy" has met with some success in terms of research: the course has generated numerous literacy artifacts and events which could potentially serve as data for an extended study of community literacy. In exchange for the hours I have invested in curriculum development, site coordination, grant writing, and local research, I have the immediate reward of writing this paper. Thus, at least the initial results indicate that everyone seems to benefit from the service learning and activist research in this project.

However, even with examples of outreach and activist research like this, literary scholars may be hard pressed to see their intellectual work as amenable to service learning courses. To put a finer point on it, can outreach courses help forge a more secure link "between the love of art and human decency" (as Greenblatt put it in the *PMLA* forum), between intellectual work which cultivates aesthetics and work which speaks to common, lived conditions of struggle in the face of vast and deepening social inequalities? If public intellectuals hope to find and generate overlaps between aesthetics and politics, they need to first understand that what they count as art or political choices does not necessarily match what community members count as art or political choices. Because university representatives tend to esteem their own brand of knowledge more than popular forms of knowledge, they deepen the schism between universities and communities. Bourdieu described well the production of legitimate (read specialized, publishable, esoteric, academic) language, which gains material, cultural and symbolic capital by implicitly devaluing nonstandard (read colloquial, vernacular, common, vulgar) language. The educational system, particularly higher education, "contributes significantly to constituting the dominated uses of language as such by consecrating the dominant use as the only legitimate one" through "the devaluation of the common language which results from the very existence of a literary language" (*Language* 60–61). How can public intellectuals link the love of art and human decency if we continue to value university-based knowledge and language more than community-based knowledge and language? Unless the love of art and human decency, as they manifest themselves in university culture, justify themselves against local cultural value systems, academic knowledge-making will remain esoteric, seemingly inapplicable, remote, and elitist.

Public intellectuals challenge the value system of academe by starting with the assumption that all language use and ways of knowing are valuable and worthy of respect. To enact this principle, service learning offers meeting places for community and university values, language, and knowledge to become mutually informative and sustaining, places where greater numbers of people have a say in how knowledge is made, places where area residents, students, and faculty explore works of art, literature, and film to find ways in which these works still resonate with meaning and inform everyday lived struggles. Service learning "mak[es] rhetoric into a social praxis . . . assigning students to effective agency in the ongoing struggle of history" (France 608). Public intellectuals can use service learning as a means to collapse harmful dichotomies that traditional university knowledge espouses: literary/vernacular; high culture/low culture; literature/literacy; objective/subjective; expert/novice. Because these dualities place faculty members in a presumably higher social position, they distance academics from those they hope their knowledge serves—from those their knowledge must serve.

Public intellectuals can use their service, teaching, and research for the benefit of those inside and outside the university. Their knowledge, created with students and community members, can have political implications in contexts beyond the university. Their positions as faculty members can have readily apparent accountability, and their intellectual work can have highly visible impact. In the end, public intellectuals can enact the kind of civic-minded knowledge-making that engages broad audiences in pressing social issues.

WORKS CITED

Apple, Michael, and Lois Weis, eds. *Ideology and Practice in Schooling.* Philadelphia: Temple UP, 1983.

Bérubé, Michael. *Public Access: Literary Theory and American Cultural Politics.* London: Verso, 1994.

Bleich, David. "Ethnography and the Study of Literacy: Prospects for Socially Generous Research." *Into the Field: Sites of Composition Studies*. Ed. Anne Ruggles Gere. New York: MLA, 1993. 176–92.

Bourdieu, Pierre. "Fourth Lecture. Universal Corporatism: The Role of Intellectuals in the Modern World." *Poetics Today* 12.4 (1991): 655–69.

———. *Language and Symbolic Power*. Cambridge: Harvard UP, 1991.

Cushman, Ellen. *The Struggle and the Tools: Oral and Literate Strategies in an Inner City Community*. Albany: SUNY P, 1998.

de Certeau, Michel. *The Practice of Everyday Life*. Berkeley: U of California P, 1984.

Flower, Linda. *The Construction of Negotiated Meaning*. Carbondale: Southern Illinois UP, 1994.

Forum. *PMLA* 112.5 (October 1997): 1121–41.

France, Alan. "Assigning Places: The Function of Introductory Composition as a Cultural Discourse." *College English* 55.6 (1993): 593–609.

Giroux, Henry. *Ideology, Culture, and the Process of Schooling*. Philadelphia: Temple UP, 1981.

Herzberg, Bruce. "Community Service and Critical Teaching." *College Composition and Communication* 45.3 (Oct. 1994): 307–19.

Jacoby, Barbara. *Service-Learning in Higher Education*. San Francisco: Jossey-Bass, 1996.

Johannsen, Agneta. "Applied Anthropology and Post Modernist Ethnography." *Human Organization*. 50.1 (1992): 71–81.

Lankshear, Colin, and Peter McLaren, eds. *Critical Literacy: Politics, Praxis, and the Postmodern*. Albany: SUNY P, 1993.

Lather, Patti. "Research as Praxis." *Harvard Education Review* 56 (1992): 257–77.

Lu, Min-Zhan, and Bruce Horner. "The Problematic of Experience: Redefining Critical Work in Ethnography and Pedagogy." *College English* 60.3 (March 1998): 257–77.

Luke, Carmen, and Jennifer Gore. *Feminism and Critical Pedagogy*. New York: Routledge, 1992.

Macedo, Donaldo. *Literacies of Power: What Americans Are Not Allowed to Know*. Boulder: Westview P, 1994.

Oakley, Anne. "Interviewing Women: A Contradiction in Terms." *Doing Feminist Research*. London: Routledge, 1981. 30–62.

Schine, Joan. *Service Learning*. Chicago: NSSE/U of Chicago P, 1997.

Schutz, Aaron, and Anne Ruggles Gere. "Service Learning and English Studies: Rethinking 'Public' Service." *College English* 60.2 (1998): 129–49.

Sullivan, Pat, and James Porter. *Opening Spaces: Writing Technologies and Critical Research Practices*. Greenwich, CT: Ablex, 1997.

Talking about Selves and Schools
On Voice, Voices, and Other Voices

Once we claim that all knowledge is socially constructed, imbricated in times and places and cultures, we are compelled to articulate those times and places and cultures. What is the academic discourse community? Is it as homogeneous as it appears? And if it is, what does that suggest—that there are cultures (which includes the cultures as defined by gender and sexual preferences) which are not part of, or at least not recognized by, the academic community? Who comprises the academic community? Who are its students? Each question generates another.

The first answer says, "Let's hear from the members of the community, its teachers and its students." The essay form returns to a central place in the curriculum, narrative discourse, the autobiographical. There was precedent. In the 1930s Fred Newton Scott of the University of Michigan advocated a writing instruction consisting of the relation between personal experience and the external world, an individual within society, a matter of civic responsibility. Scott's theory would regain popularity in the 1980s, though the curriculum would be associated with the Brazilian pedagogical theorist Paulo Freire rather than Scott, insofar as Freire adds an overtly political impetus to literacy and to writing from what one knows experientially.

When in the early 1970s the City University of New York opens its doors to any high school graduate wanting admission, the social and the political join the discussion on the value of narrative and the value of more conventional forms of academic discourse. With open admissions the colleges of the CUNY system were besieged by scores of students who would not have been able to attend college under older admissions policies. These were students—mainly from among the poor and mainly people of color—who believed themselves college material. And their college teachers agreed that these students were otherwise bright—except that the students' reading and

519

writing abilities were so significantly lower than what would be necessary for success in college that, as we have seen, many came to believe that the students were victims of some sort of cognitive shortcoming.

The colleges were baffled. A new range of research was developed to confront and assist these "new" students, nontraditional students, remedial, developmental students. Finally, Mina Shaughnessy coins the term *basic writers,* and in the first truly empathetic research work on basic writers, she looks to patterns of error in these students' writing, not cognitive dysfunction. This takes shape as *Errors and Expectations* (New York: Oxford UP, 1977).

But for all its sympathy, there are those who would go a step further, would try to understand the social processes that could relegate such a large number to the trouble-heap, a large number with two essential qualities in common—being poor and not being from the racial or ethnic majority. And in trying to understand, this newer line of scholarship tries to circumvent the reproduction of a school system that has traditionally failed to educate the woman, the poor, or the person of color at the same grade of efficiency as others. This gets complicated as rhetorical theory looks to how language is not just the conveyor of knowledge; language is the way knowledge becomes known.

Women show a way. They assert their role within the society at large and within the academy. The central role of women in composition studies makes feminist issues unignorable, with women making up the greater portion of the teaching force, with women playing key roles in developing contemporary composition, figures like Janet Emig, Mina Shaughnessy, Andrea Lunsford, to name too few. And given American feminism's turn to the autobiographical in its popular and its academic writing, composition's turn to narrative receives further reinforcement.

Others follow suit. In some sense, Richard Rodriguez's *Hunger of Memory* (New York: Bantam, 1983) opens the door, as he writes of his experiences in acquiring abilities in English literacy, the child of Mexican immigrants who becomes a doctoral candidate in British literature. Gloria Anzaldúa publishes *Borderlands/La Frontera* in 1987 (San Francisco: Aunt Lute), crossing ancient native languages, Spanish, English, and exploring matters of sexuality. Mike Rose, already a known figure in composition studies, writes in *Lives on the Boundary* (New York: Penguin, 1990) of his experiences as a working-class remedial student who eventually succeeds, thanks to some wonderful teachers. A year after Mike Rose's book, Keith Gilyard's *Voices of the Self* (Detroit: Wayne State UP, 1991) is released, the story of an African American growing up in New York. His is a story in multiple genres—autobiography and linguistic analysis of code switching in alternating chapters. Two years later, Victor Villanueva publishes *Boot-straps* (Urbana: NCTE, 1993), a mix of several genres including autobiography, now firmly located within rhetoric and composition studies. In 1994 bell hooks comes out with *Teaching to Transgress* (New York: Routledge). The concerns with "voice" that had arisen in the 1960s and 1970s thanks to pioneers like Ken Macrorie, Walker Gibson, Donald Murray, and especially Peter Elbow emerge in the writings of women and people of color. But what James Berlin had seen as a too-strong concern with individualism in these "expressionists" is responded to by the women and people of color writing critical autobiographies. The turn to autobiography becomes auto-biography *as* social and political, with some asking if the political has any place in the composition classroom.

Inventing the University

David Bartholomae

Education may well be, as of right, the instrument whereby every individual, in a society like our own, can gain access to any kind of discourse. But we well know that in its distribution, in what it permits and in what it prevents, it follows the well-trodden battle-lines of social conflict. Every educational system is a political means of maintaining or of modifying the appropriation of discourse, with the knowledge and the powers it carries with it.
— *Michel Foucault*, The Discourse on Language

. . . the text is the form of the social relationships made visible, palpable, material.
— *Basil B. Bernstein*, Codes, Modalities and the Process of Cultural Reproduction: A Model

I

Every time a student sits down to write for us, he has to invent the university for the occasion—invent the university, that is, or a branch of it, like history or anthropology or economics or English. The student has to learn to speak our language, to speak as we do, to try on the peculiar ways of knowing, selecting, evaluating, reporting, concluding, and arguing that define the discourse of our community. Or perhaps I should say the *various* discourses of our community, since it is in the nature of a liberal arts education that a

Reprinted from *When a Writer Can't Write: Studies in Writer's Block and Other Composing-Process Problems.* Ed. Mike Rose. New York: Guilford, 1985. 134–65. Copyright © 1985 by the Guilford Publications.

student, after the first year or two, must learn to try on a variety of voices and interpretive schemes—to write, for example, as a literary critic one day and as an experimental psychologist the next; to work within fields where the rules governing the presentation of examples or the development of an argument are both distinct and, even to a professional, mysterious.

The student has to appropriate (or be appropriated by) a specialized discourse, and he has to do this as though he were easily and comfortably one with his audience, as though he were a member of the academy or an historian or an anthropologist or an economist; he has to invent the university by assembling and mimicking its language while finding some compromise between idiosyncrasy, a personal history, on the one hand, and the requirements of convention, the history of a discipline, on the other hand. He must learn to speak our language. Or he must dare to speak it or to carry off the bluff, since speaking and writing will most certainly be required long before the skill is "learned." And this, understandably, causes problems.

Let me look quickly at an example. Here is an essay written by a college freshman.

> In the past time I thought that an incident was creative was when I had to make a clay model of the earth, but not of the classical or your everyday model of the earth which consists of the two cores, the mantle and the crust. I thought of these things in a dimension of which it would be unique, but easy to comprehend. Of course, your materials to work with were basic and limited at the same time, but thought help to put this limit into a right attitude or frame of mind to work with the clay.
>
> In the beginning of the clay model, I had to research and learn the different dimensions of the earth (in magnitude, quantity, state of matter, etc.) After this, I learned how to put this into the clay and come up with something different than any other person in my class at the time. In my opinion, color coordination and shape was the key to my creativity of the clay model of the earth.
>
> Creativity is the venture of the mind at work with the mechanics relay to the limbs from the cranium, which stores and triggers this action. It can be a burst of energy released at a precise time a thought is being transmitted. This can cause a frenzy of the human body, but it depends on the characteristics of the individual and how they can relay the message clearly enough through mechanics of the body to us as an observer. Then we must determine if it is creative or a learned process varied by the individuals thought process. Creativity is indeed a tool which has to exist, or our world will not succeed into the future and progress like it should.

I am continually impressed by the patience and goodwill of our students. This student was writing a placement essay during freshman orientation. (The problem set to him was: "Describe a time when you did something you felt to be creative. Then, on the basis of the incident you have described, go on to draw some general conclusions about 'creativity.'") He knew that university faculty would be reading and evaluating his essay, and so he wrote for them.

In some ways it is a remarkable performance. He is trying on the discourse even though he doesn't have the knowledge that would make the discourse more than a routine, a set of conventional rituals and gestures. And he is doing this, I think, even though he *knows* he doesn't have the knowledge that would make the discourse more than a routine. He defines himself as a researcher working systematically, and not as a kid in a high school class: "I thought of these things in a dimension of . . ."; "I had to research and learn the different dimensions of the earth (in magnitude, quantity, state of matter, etc.)." He moves quickly into a specialized language (his approximation of our jargon) and draws both a general, textbook-like conclusion — "Creativity is the venture of the mind at work . . ." — and a resounding peroration — "Creativity is indeed a tool which has to exist, or our world will not succeed into the future and progress like it should." The writer has even picked up the rhythm of our prose with that last "indeed" and with the qualifications and the parenthetical expressions of the opening paragraphs. And through it all he speaks with an impressive air of authority.

There is an elaborate but, I will argue, a necessary and enabling fiction at work here as the student dramatizes his experience in a "setting" — the setting required by the discourse — where he can speak to us as a companion, a fellow researcher. As I read the essay, there is only one moment when the fiction is broken, when we are addressed differently. The student says, "Of course, your materials to work with were basic and limited at the same time, but thought help to put this limit into a right attitude or frame of mind to work with the clay." At this point, I think, we become students and he the teacher giving us a lesson (as in, "You take your pencil in your right hand and put your paper in front of you"). This is however, one of the most characteristic slips of basic writers. (I use the term "basic writers" to refer to university students traditionally placed in remedial composition courses.) It is very hard for them to take on the role — the voice, the persona — of an authority whose authority is rooted in scholarship, analysis, or research. They slip, then, into a more immediately available and realizable voice of authority, the voice of a teacher giving a lesson or the voice of a parent lecturing at the dinner table. They offer advice or homilies rather than "academic" conclusions. There is a similar break in the final paragraph, where the conclusion that pushes for a definition ("Creativity is the venture of the mind at work with the mechanics relay to the limbs from the cranium") is replaced by a conclusion that speaks in the voice of an elder ("Creativity is indeed a tool which has to exist, or our world will not succeed into the future and progress like it should").

It is not uncommon, then, to find such breaks in the concluding sections of essays written by basic writers. Here is the concluding section of an essay written by a student about his work as a mechanic. He had been asked to generalize about work after reviewing an on-the-job experience or incident that "stuck in his mind" as somehow significant.

> How could two repairmen miss a leak? Lack of pride? No incentive? Lazy?
> I don't know.

At this point the writer is in a perfect position to speculate, to move from the problem to an analysis of the problem. Here is how the paragraph continues, however (and notice the change in pronoun reference).

> From this point on, I take *my* time, do it right, and don't let customers get under *your* skin. If they have a complaint, tell them to call your boss and he'll be more than glad to handle it. Most important, worry about yourself, and keep a clear eye on everyone, for there's always someone trying to take advantage of you, anytime and anyplace. (Emphasis added)

We get neither a technical discussion nor an "academic" discussion but a Lesson on Life.[1] This is the language he uses to address the general question, "How could two repairmen miss a leak?" The other brand of conclusion, the more academic one, would have required him to speak of his experience in our terms; it would, that is, have required a special vocabulary, a special system of presentation, and an interpretive scheme (or a set of commonplaces) he could have used to identify and talk about the mystery of human error. The writer certainly had access to the range of acceptable commonplaces for such an explanation: "lack of pride," "no incentive," "lazy." Each commonplace would dictate its own set of phrases, examples, and conclusions; and we, his teachers, would know how to write out each argument, just as we know how to write out more specialized arguments of our own. A "commonplace," then, is a culturally or institutionally authorized concept or statement that carries with it its own necessary elaboration. We all use commonplaces to orient ourselves in the world; they provide points of reference and a set of "prearticulated" explanations that are readily available to organize and interpret experience. The phrase, "lack of pride" carries with it its own account of the repairman's error, just as at another point in time a reference to "original sin" would have provided an explanation, or just as in certain university classrooms a reference to "alienation" would enable writers to continue and complete the discussion. While there is a way in which these terms are interchangeable, they are not all permissible: A student in a composition class would most likely be turned away from a discussion of original sin. Commonplaces are the "controlling ideas" of our composition textbooks, textbooks that not only insist on a set form for expository writing but a set view of public life.[2]

When the writer says, "I don't know," then, he is not saying that he has nothing to say. He is saying that he is not in a position to carry on this discussion. And so we are addressed as apprentices rather than as teachers or scholars. In order to speak as a person of status or privilege, the writer can either speak to us in our terms—in the privileged language of university discourse—or, in default (or in defiance) of that, he can speak to us as though we were children, offering us the wisdom of experience.

I think it is possible to say that the language of the "Clay Model" paper has come *through* the writer and not from the writer. The writer has located himself (more precisely, he has located the self that is represented by the "I" on the page) in a context that is finally beyond him, not his own and not available to his immediate procedures for inventing and arranging text. I would not, that is, call this essay an example of "writer-based" prose. I would not say that it is egocentric or that it represents the "interior monologue or a writer thinking and talking to himself" (Flower, 1981, p. 63). It is, rather, the record of a writer who has lost himself in the discourse of his readers. There is a context beyond the intended reader that is not the world but a way of talking about the world, a way of talking that determines the use of examples, the possible conclusions, acceptable commonplaces, and key words for an essay on the construction of a clay model of the earth. This writer has entered the discourse without successfully approximating it.

Linda Flower (1981) has argued that the difficulty inexperienced writers have with writing can be understood as a difficulty in negotiating the transition between "writer-based" and "reader-based" prose. Expert writers, in other words, can better imagine how a reader will respond to a text and can transform or restructure what they have to say around a goal shared with a reader. Teaching students to revise for readers, then, will better prepare them to write initially with a reader in mind. The success of this pedagogy depends on the degree to which a writer can imagine and conform to a reader's goals. The difficulty of this act of imagination and the burden of such conformity are so much at the heart of the problem that a teacher must pause and take stock before offering revision as a solution. A student like the one who wrote the "Clay Model" paper is not so much trapped in a private

527

language as he is shut out from one of the privileged languages of public life, a language he is aware of but cannot control.

II

Our students, I've said, have to appropriate (or be appropriated by) a specialized discourse, and they have to do this as though they were easily or comfortably one with their audience. If you look at the situation this way, suddenly the problem of audience awareness becomes enormously complicated. One of the common assumptions of both composition research and composition teaching is that at some "stage" in the process of composing an essay a writer's ideas or his motives must be tailored to the needs and expectations of his audience. Writers have to "build bridges" between their point of view and the reader's. They have to anticipate and acknowledge the reader's assumptions and biases. They must begin with "common points of departure" before introducing new or controversial arguments. Here is what one of the most popular college textbooks says to students.

> Once you have your purpose clearly in mind, your next task is to define and analyze your audience. A sure sense of your audience—knowing who it is and what assumptions you can reasonably make about it—is crucial to the success of your rhetoric. (Hairston, 1978, p. 107)

It is difficult to imagine, however, how writers can have a purpose before they are located in a discourse, since it is the discourse with its projects and agendas that determines what writers can and will do. The writer who can successfully manipulate an audience (or, to use a less pointed language, the writer who can accommodate her motives to her reader's expectations) is a writer who can both imagine and write from a position of privilege. She must, that is, see herself within a privileged discourse, one that already includes and excludes groups of readers. She must be either equal to or more powerful than those she would address. The writing, then, must somehow transform the political and social relationships between students and teachers.

If my students are going to write for me by knowing who I am—and if this means more than knowing my prejudices, psyching me out—it means knowing what I know; it means having the knowledge of a professor of English. They have, then, to know what I know and how I know what I know (the interpretive schemes that define the way I would work out the problems I set for them); they have to learn to write what I would write or to offer up some approximation of that discourse. The problem of audience awareness, then, is a problem of power and finesse. It cannot be addressed, as it is in most classroom exercises, by giving students privilege and denying the situation of the classroom—usually, that is, by having students write to an outsider, someone excluded from their privileged circle: "Write about 'To His Coy Mistress,' not for your teacher but for the students in your class"; "Describe Pittsburgh to someone who has never been there"; "Explain to a high school senior how best to prepare for college"; "Describe baseball to an Eskimo." Exercises such as these allow students to imagine the needs and goals of a reader, and they bring those needs and goals forward as a dominant constraint in the construction of an essay. And they argue, implicitly, what is generally true about writing—that it is an act of aggression disguised as an act of charity. What these assignments fail to address is the central problem of academic writing, where a student must assume the right of speaking to someone who knows more about baseball or "To His Coy Mistress" than the student does, a reader for whom the general commonplaces and the readily available utterances about a subject are inadequate.

Linda Flower and John Hayes, in an often quoted article (1981), reported on a study of a protocol of an expert writer (an English teacher) writing about his job for readers of *Seventeen* magazine. The key moment for this writer, who seems to have been having trouble getting started, came when he decided that teenage girls read *Seventeen*; that some teenage girls like English because it is tidy ("some of them will have wrong reasons in that English is good because it's tidy—can be a neat tidy little girl"); that some don't like it because it is "prim" and that, "By God, I can change that notion for them." Flower and Hayes's conclusion is that this effort of "exploration and consolidation" gave the writer "a new, relatively complex, rhetorically sophisticated working goal, one which encompasses plans for topic, a persona, and the audience" (p. 383).[3]

Flower and Hayes give us a picture of a writer solving a problem, and the problem as they present it is a cognitive one. It is rooted in the way the writer's knowledge is represented in the writer's mind. The problem resides there, not in the nature of knowledge or in the nature of discourse but in a mental state prior to writing. It is possible, however, to see the problem as (perhaps simultaneously) a problem in the way subjects are located in a field of discourse.

Flower and Hayes divide up the composing process into three distinct activities: "planning or goal-setting," "translating," and "reviewing." The last of these, reviewing (which is further divided into two subprocesses, "evaluating" and "revising"), is particularly powerful, for as a writer continually generates new goals, plans, and text, he is engaging in a process of learning and discovery. Let me quote Flower and Hayes's conclusion at length.

> If one studies the process by which a writer uses a goal to generate ideas, then consolidates those ideas and uses them to revise or regenerate new, more complex goals, one can see this learning process in action. Furthermore, one sees why the process of revising and clarifying goals has such a broad effect, since it is through setting these new goals that the fruits of discovery come back to inform the continuing process of writing. In this instance, some of our most complex and imaginative acts can depend on the elegant simplicity of a few powerful thinking processes. We feel that a cognitive process explanation of discovery, toward which this theory is only a start, will have another special strength. By placing emphasis on the inventive power of the writer, who is able to explore ideas, to develop, act on, test, and regenerate his or her own goals, we are putting an important part of creativity where it belongs—in the hands of the working, thinking writer. (1981, p. 386)

While this conclusion is inspiring, the references to invention and creativity seem to refer to something other than an act of writing—if writing is, finally, words on a page. Flower and Hayes locate the act of writing solely within the mind of the writer. The act of writing, here, has a personal, cognitive history but not a history as a text, as a text that is made possible by prior texts. When located in the perspective afforded by prior texts, writing is seen to exist separate from the writer and his intentions; it is seen in the context of other articles in *Seventeen*, of all articles written for or about women, of all articles written about English teaching, and so on. Reading research has made it possible to say that these prior texts, or a reader's experience with these prior texts, have bearing on how the text is read. Intentions, then, are part of the history of the language itself. I am arguing that these prior texts determine not only how a text like the *Seventeen* article will be read but also how it will be written. Flower and Hayes show us what happens in the writer's mind but not what happens to the writer as his motives are located within our language, a language with its own requirements and agendas, a language that limits what we might say and that makes us write and sound, finally, also like someone else. If you think of other accounts of the composing process—and I'm thinking of accounts as diverse as Richard Rodriguez's *Hunger of Memory* (1983) and Edward Said's *Beginnings* (1975)—you get a very different account of what happens when private motive enters into public discourse, when a personal history becomes a public account. These accounts place the writer in a history that is not of the writer's own invention; and they are chronicles of loss, violence, and compromise.

It is one thing to see the *Seventeen* writer making and revising his plans for a topic, a persona, and an audience; it is another thing to talk about discovery, invention, and creativity. Whatever plans the writer had must finally have been located in language and, it is possible to argue, in a language that is persistently conventional and formulaic. We do not, after all, get to see the *Seventeen* article. We see only the elaborate mental procedures that accompanied the writing of the essay. We see a writer's plans for a persona; we don't see that persona in action. If writing is a process, it is also a product; and it is the product, and not the plan for writing, that locates a writer on the page, that locates him in a text and a style and the codes or conventions that make both of them readable.

Contemporary rhetorical theory has been concerned with the "codes" that constitute discourse (or specialized forms of discourse). These codes determine not only what might be said but also who might be speaking or reading. Barthes (1974), for example, has argued that the moment of writing, where private goals and plans become subject to a public language, is the moment when the writer becomes subject to a language he can neither command nor control. A text, he says, in being written passes through the codes that govern writing and becomes "de-originated," becomes a fragment of something that has always been *already* read, seen, done, experienced" (p. 21). Alongside a text we have always the presence of "off-stage voices," the oversound of all that has been said (e.g., about girls, about English). These voices, the presence of the "already written," stand in defiance of a writer's desire for originality and determine what might be said. A writer does not write (and this is Barthes's famous paradox) but is, himself, written by the languages available to him.

It is possible to see the writer of the *Seventeen* article solving his problem of where to begin by appropriating an available discourse. Perhaps what enabled that writer to write was the moment he located himself as a writer in a familiar field of stereotypes: Readers of *Seventeen* are teenage girls; teenage girls think of English (and English teachers) as "tidy" and "prim," and, "By God, I can change that notion for them." The moment of eureka was not simply a moment of breaking through a cognitive jumble in that individual writer's mind but a moment of breaking into a familiar and established territory—one with insiders and outsiders; one with set phrases, examples, and conclusions.

I'm not offering a criticism of the morals or manners of the teacher who wrote the *Seventeen* article. I think that all writers, in order to write, must imagine for themselves the privilege of being "insiders"—that is, the privilege both of being inside an established and powerful discourse and of being granted a special right to speak. But I think that right to speak is seldom conferred on us—on any of us, teachers or students—by virtue of the fact that we have invented or discovered an original idea. Leading students to believe that they are responsible for something new or original, unless they understand what those words mean with regard to writing, is a dangerous and counterproductive practice. We do have the right to expect students to be active and engaged, but that is a matter of continually and stylistically working against the inevitable presence of conventional language; it is not a matter of inventing a language that is new.

When a student is writing for a teacher, writing becomes more problematic than it was for the *Seventeen* writer (who was writing a version of the "Describe baseball to an Eskimo" exercise). The student, in effect, has to assume privilege without having any. And since students assume privilege by locating themselves within the discourse of a particular community— within a set of specifically acceptable gestures and commonplaces—learning, at least as it is defined in the liberal arts curriculum, becomes more a matter of imitation or parody than a matter of invention and discovery.

To argue that writing problems are also social and political problems is not to break faith with the enterprise of cognitive science. In a recent paper reviewing the tremendous range of research directed at identifying general cognitive skills, David Perkins (in press) has argued that "the higher the level of competence concerned," as in the case of adult learning, "the fewer *general* cognitive control strategies there are." There comes a point, that is, where "field-specific" or "domain-specific" schemata (what I have called "interpretive strategies") become more important than general problem-solving processes. Thinking, learning, writing—all these become bound to the context of a particular discourse. And Perkins concludes:

> Instruction in cognitive control strategies tends to be organized around problem-solving tasks. However, the isolated problem is a creature largely of the classroom. The nonstudent, whether operating in scholarly or more everyday contexts, is likely to find himself or herself involved in what might be called "projects"—which might be anything from writing a novel to designing a shoe to starting a business.

It is interesting to note that Perkins defines the classroom as the place of artificial tasks and, as a consequence, has to place scholarly projects outside the classroom, where they are carried out by the "nonstudent." It is true, I think, that education has failed to involve students in scholarly projects, projects that allow students to act as though they were colleagues in an academic enterprise. Much of the written work that students do is test-taking, report or summary—work that places them outside the official discourse of the academic community, where they are expected to admire and report on what we do, rather than inside that discourse, where they can do its work and participate in a common enterprise.[4] This, however, is a failure of teachers and curriculum designers, who speak of writing as a mode of learning but all too often represent writing as a "tool" to be used by an (hopefully) educated mind.

It could be said, then, that there is a bastard discourse peculiar to the writing most often required of students. Carl Bereiter and Marlene Scardamalia (in press) have written about this discourse (they call it "knowledge-telling"; students who are good at it have learned to cope with academic tasks by developing a "knowledge-telling strategy"), and they have argued that insistence on knowledge-telling discourse undermines educational efforts to extend the variety of discourse schemata available to students.[5] What they actually say is this:

> When we think of knowledge stored in memory we tend these days to think of it as situated in three-dimensional space, with vertical and horizontal connections between sites. Learning is thought to add not only new elements to memory but also new connections, and it is the richness and structure of these connections that would seem . . . to spell the difference between inert and usable knowledge. On this account, the knowledge-telling strategy is educationally faulty because it specifically avoids the forming of connections between previously separated knowledge sites.

It should be clear by now that when I think of "knowledge" I think of it as situated in the discourse that constitutes "knowledge" in a particular discourse community, rather than as situated in mental "knowledge sites." One can remember a discourse, just as one can remember an essay or the movement of a professor's lecture; but this discourse, in effect, also has a memory of its own, its own rich network of structures and connections beyond the deliberate control of any individual imagination.

There is, to be sure, an important distinction to be made between learning history, say, and learning to write as an historian. A student can learn to command and reproduce a set of names, dates, places, and canonical interpretations (to "tell" somebody else's knowledge); but this is not the same thing as learning to "think" (by learning to write) as an historian. The former requires efforts of memory; the latter requires a student to compose a text out of the texts that represent the primary materials of history and in accordance with the texts that define history as an act of report and interpretation.

Let me draw on an example from my own teaching. I don't expect my students to *be* literary critics when they write about *Bleak House*. If a literary critic is a person who wins publication in a professional journal (or if he or she is one who could), the students aren't critics. I do, however, expect my students to be, themselves, invented as literary critics by approximating the language of a literary critic writing about *Bleak House*. My students, then, don't invent the language of literary criticism (they don't, that is, act on their own) but they are, themselves, invented by it. Their papers don't begin with a moment of insight, a "by God" moment that is outside of language. They begin with a moment of appropriation, a moment when they can offer up a sentence that is not theirs as though it were their own. (I can remember when, as a graduate student, I would begin papers by sitting down to write literally in the voice—with the syntax and the key words—of the strongest teacher I had met.)

What I am saying about my students' essays is that they are approximate, not that they are wrong or invalid. They are evidence of a discourse that lies between what I might call the students' primary discourse (what the students might write about *Bleak House* were they not in my class or in any class, and were they not imagining that they were in my class or in any class—if you can imagine any student doing any such thing) and standard, official literary criticism (which is imaginable but impossible to find). The students' essays are evidence of a discourse that lies between these two hypothetical poles. The writing is limited as much by a student's ability to imagine "what might be said" as it is by cognitive control strategies.[6] The act of writing takes the student away from where he is and what he knows and allows him to imagine something else. The approximate discourse, therefore, is evidence of a change, a change that, because we are teachers, we call "development." What our beginning students need to learn is to extend themselves, by successive approximations, into the commonplaces, set phrases, rituals and gestures, habits of mind, tricks of persuasion, obligatory conclusions and necessary connections that determine the "what might be said" and constitute knowledge within the various branches of our academic community.[7]

Pat Bizzell is, I think, one of the most important scholars writing now on "basic writers" (and this is the common name we use for students who are refused unrestrained access to the academic community) and on the special characteristics of academic discourse. In a recent essay, "Cognition, Convention, and Certainty: What We Need to Know about Writing" (1982a), she looks at two schools of composition research and the way they represent the problems that writing poses for writers.[8] For one group, the "inner-directed theorists," the problems are internal, cognitive, rooted in the way the mind represents knowledge to itself. These researchers are concerned with discovering the "universal, fundamental structures of thought and language" and with developing pedagogies to teach or facilitate both basic, general cognitive skills and specific cognitive strategies, or heuristics, directed to serve more specialized needs. Of the second group, the "outer-directed theorists," she says that they are "more interested in the social processes whereby language-learning and thinking capacities are shaped and used in particular communities."

> The staple activity of outer-directed writing instruction will be analysis of the conventions of particular discourse communities. For example, a main focus of writing-across-the-curriculum programs is to demystify the conventions of the academic discourse community. (1982a, p. 218)

The essay offers a detailed analysis of the way the two theoretical camps can best serve the general enterprise of composition research and composition teaching. Its agenda, however, seems to be to counter the influence of the cognitivists and to provide bibliography and encouragement to those interested in the social dimension of language learning.

As far as basic writers are concerned, Bizzell argues that the cognitivists' failure to acknowledge the primary, shaping role of convention in the act of composing makes them "particularly insensitive to the problems of poor writers." She argues that some of those problems, like the problem of establishing and monitoring overall goals for a piece of writing, can be

> better understood in terms of the unfamiliarity with the academic discourse community, combined, perhaps, with such limited experience outside their native discourse communities that they are unaware that there is such a thing as a discourse community with conventions to be mastered. What is underdeveloped is their knowledge both of the ways experience is constituted and interpreted in the academic discourse community and of the fact that all discourse communities constitute and interpret experience. (1982a, p. 230)

One response to the problems of basic writers, then, would be to determine just what the community's conventions are, so that those conventions could be written out, "demystified" and taught in our classrooms. Teachers, as a result, could be more precise and helpful when they ask students to "think," "argue," "describe," or "define." Another response would be to examine the essays written by basic writers—their approximations of academic discourse—to determine more clearly where the problems lie. If we look at their writing, and if we look at it in the context of other student writing, we can better see the points of discord that arise when students try to write their way into the university.

The purpose of the remainder of this chapter will be to examine some of the most striking and characteristic of these problems as they are presented in the expository essays of first-year college students. I will be concerned, then, with university discourse in its most generalized form—as it is represented by introductory courses—and not with the special conventions required by advanced work in the various disciplines. And I will be concerned with the difficult, and often violent accommodations that occur when students locate themselves in a discourse that is not "naturally" or immediately theirs.

III

I have reviewed 500 essays written, as the "Clay Model" essay was, in response to a question used during one of our placement exams at the University of Pittsburgh: "Describe a time when you did something you felt to be creative. Then, on the basis of the incident you have described, go on to draw some general conclusions about "creativity." Some of the essays were written by basic writers (or, more properly, those essays led readers to identify the writers as basic writers); some were written by students who "passed" (who were granted immediate access to the community of writers at the university). As I read these essays, I was looking to determine the stylistic resources that enabled writers to locate themselves within an "academic" discourse. My bias as a reader should be clear by now. I was not looking to see how a writer might represent the skills demanded by a neutral language (a language whose key features were paragraphs, topic sentences, transitions, and the like—features of a clear and orderly mind). I was looking to see what happened when a writer entered into a language to locate himself (a textual self) and his subject; and I was looking to see how, once entered, that language made or unmade the writer.

Here is one essay. Its writer was classified as a basic writer and, since the essay is relatively free of sentence level errors, that decision must have been rooted in some perceived failure of the discourse itself.

> I am very interested in music, and I try to be creative in my interpretation of music. While in highschool, I was a member of a jazz ensemble. The members of the ensemble were given chances to improvise and be creative in various songs. I feel that this was a great experience for me, as well as the other members. I was proud to know that I could use my imagination and feelings to create music other than what was written.
>
> Creativity to me, means being free to express yourself in a way that is unique to you, not having to conform to certain rules and guidelines.

Music is only one of the many areas in which people are given opportunities to show their creativity. Sculpting, carving, building, art, and acting are just a few more areas where people can show their creativity.

Through my music I conveyed feelings and thoughts which were important to me. Music was my means of showing creativity. In whatever form creativity takes, whether it be music, art, or science, it is an important aspect of our lives because it enables us to be individuals.

Notice the key gesture in this essay, one that appears in all but a few of the essays I read. The student defines as his own that which is a commonplace. "Creativity, *to me,* means being free to express yourself in a way that is unique to you, not having to conform to certain rules and guidelines." This act of appropriation constitutes his authority; it constitutes his authority as a writer and not just as a musician (that is, as someone with a story to tell). There were many essays in the set that told only a story—where the writer established his presence as a musician or a skier or someone who painted designs on a van, but not as a person at a remove from that experience interpreting it, treating it as a metaphor for something else (creativity). Unless those stories were long, detailed, and very well told—unless the writer was doing more than saying, "I am a skier" or a musician or a van-painter—those writers were all given low ratings.

Notice also that the writer of the "Jazz" paper locates himself and his experience in relation to the commonplace (creativity is unique expression; it is not having to conform to rules or guidelines) regardless of whether the commonplace is true or not. Anyone who improvises "knows" that improvisation follows rules and guidelines. It is the power of the commonplace—its truth as a recognizable and, the writer believes, as a final statement—that justifies the example and completes the essay. The example, in other words, has value because it stands within the field of the commonplace.[9] It is not the occasion for what one might call an "objective" analysis or a "close" reading. It could also be said that the essay stops with the articulation of the commonplace. The following sections speak only to the power of that statement. The reference to "sculpting, carving, building, art, and acting" attest to the universality of the commonplace (and it attests the writer's nervousness with the status he has appropriated for himself—he is saying, "Now, I'm not the only one here who has done something unique"). The commonplace stands by itself. For this writer, it does not need to be elaborated. By virtue of having written it, he has completed the essay and established the contract by which we may be spoken to as equals: "In whatever form creativity takes, whether it be music, art, or science, it is an important aspect of *our* lives because it enables *us* to be individuals." (For me to break that contract, to argue that *my* life is not represented in that essay, is one way for me to begin as a teacher with that student in that essay.)

All of the papers I read were built around one of three commonplaces: (1) creativity is self-expression, (2) creativity is doing something new or unique, and (3) creativity is using old things in new ways. These are clearly, then, key phrases from the storehouse of things to say about creativity. I've listed them in the order of the students' ratings: A student with the highest rating was more likely to use number three than number one, although each commonplace ran across the range of possible ratings. One could argue that some standard assertions are more powerful than others, but I think the ranking simply represents the power of assertions within our community of readers. Every student was able to offer up an experience that was meant as an example of "creativity"; the lowest range of writers, then, was not represented by students who could not imagine themselves as creative people.[10]

I said that the writer of the "Jazz" paper offered up a commonplace regardless of whether it was true or not; and this, I said, was an instance of the power of a commonplace to determine the meaning of an example. A commonplace determines a system of interpretation that can be used to "place" an example within a standard system of belief. You can see a similar process at work in this essay.

> During the football season, the team was supposed to wear the same type of cleats and the same type socks, I figured that I would change this a little by wearing my white shoes instead of black and to cover up the team socks with a pair of my own white ones. I thought that this looked better than what we were wearing, and I told a few of the other people on the team to change too. They agreed that it did look better and they changed there combination to go along with mine. After the game people came up to us and said that it looked very good the way we wore our socks, and they wanted to know why we changed from the rest of the team.
>
> I feel that creativity comes from when a person lets his imagination come up with ideas and he is not afraid to express them. Once you create something to do it will be original and unique because it came about from your own imagination and if any one else tries to copy it, it won't be the same because you thought of it first from your own ideas.

This is not an elegant paper, but it seems seamless, tidy. If the paper on the clay model of the earth showed an ill fit between the writer and his project, here the discourse seems natural, smooth. You could reproduce this paper and hand it out to a class, and it would take a lot of prompting before the students sensed something fishy and one of the more aggressive ones said something like, "Sure he came up with the idea of wearing white shoes and white socks. Him and Billy 'White-Shoes' Johnson. Come on. He copied the very thing he said was his own idea, 'original and unique.' "

The "I" of this text—the "I" who "figured," "thought," and "felt"—is located in a conventional rhetoric of the self that turns imagination into origination (I made it), that argues an ethic of production (I made it and it is mine), and that argues a tight scheme of intention (I made it because I decided to make it). The rhetoric seems invisible because it is so common. This "I" (the maker) is also located in a version of history that dominates classrooms, the "great man" theory: History is rolling along (the English novel is dominated by a central, intrusive narrative presence; America is in the throes of a Great Depression; during football season the team was supposed to wear the same kind of cleats and socks) until a figure appears, one who can shape history (Henry James, FDR, the writer of the "White Shoes" paper), and everything is changed. In the argument of the "White Shoes" paper, the history goes "I figured . . . I thought . . . I told . . . They agreed . . ." and, as a consequence, "I feel that creativity *comes from when* a person lets his imagination come up with ideas and he is not afraid to express them." The act of appropriation becomes a narrative of courage and conquest. The writer was able to write that story when he was able to imagine himself in that discourse. Getting him out of it will be a difficult matter indeed.

There are ways, I think, that a writer can shape history in the very act of writing it. Some students are able to enter into a discourse but, by stylistic maneuvers, to take possession of it at the same time. They don't originate a discourse, but they locate themselves within it aggressively, self-consciously. Here is another essay on jazz, which for sake of convenience I've shortened. It received a higher rating than the first essay on jazz.

> Jazz has always been thought of as a very original creative field in music. Improvisation, the spontaneous creation of original melodies in a piece of music, makes up a large part of jazz as a musical style. I had the opportunity to be a member of my high school's jazz ensemble for three years, and became an improvisation soloist this year. Throughout the years, I have seen and heard many jazz players, both professional and amateur. The solos performed by these artists were each flavored with that particular individual's style and ideas, along with some of the conventional premises behind improvisation. This particular type of solo work is creative because it is, done on the spur of the moment and blends the performer's ideas with basic guidelines.
>
> I realized my own creative potential when I began soloing. . . .
>
> My solos, just as all the solos generated by others, were original because I combined and shaped other's ideas with mine to create something completely new. Creativity is combining the practical knowledge

and guidelines of a discipline with one's original ideas to bring about a new, original end result, one that is different from everyone else's. Creativity is based on the individual. Two artists can interpret the same scene differently. Each person who creates something does so by bringing out something individual in himself.

The essay is different in some important ways from the first essay on jazz. The writer of the second is more easily able to place himself in the context of an "academic" discussion. The second essay contains an "I" who realized his "creative potential" by soloing; the first contained an "I" who had "a great experience." In the second essay, before the phrase, "I had the opportunity to be a member of my high school's jazz ensemble," there is an introduction that offers a general definition of improvisation and an acknowledgment that other people have thought about jazz and creativity. In fact, throughout the essay the writer offers definitions and counterdefinitions. He is placing himself in the context of what has been said and what might be said. In the first paper, before a similar statement about being a member of a jazz ensemble, there was an introduction that locates jazz solely in the context of this individual's experience: "I am very interested in music." The writer of this first paper was authorized by who he is, a musician, rather than by what he can say about music in the context of what is generally said. The writer of the second essay uses a more specialized vocabulary; he talks about "conventional premises," "creative potential," "musical style," and "practical knowledge." And this is not just a matter of using bigger words, since these terms locate the experience in the context of a recognizable interpretive scheme — on the one hand there is tradition and, on the other, individual talent.

It could be said, then, that this essay is also framed and completed by a commonplace: "Creativity is combining the practical knowledge and guidelines of a discipline with one's original ideas to bring about a new, original end result, one that is different from everyone else's." Here, however, the argument is a more powerful one; and I mean "powerful" in the political sense, since it is an argument that complicates a "naive" assumption (it makes scholarly work possible, in other words), and it does so in terms that come close to those used in current academic debates (over the relation between convention and idiosyncrasy or between rules and creativity). The assertion is almost consumed by the pleas for originality at the end of the sentence; but the point remains that the terms "original" and "different," as they are used at the end of the essay, are problematic, since they must be thought of in the context of "practical knowledge and guidelines of a discipline."

The key distinguishing gesture of this essay, that which makes it "better" than the other, is the way the writer works against a conventional point of view, one that is represented within the essay by conventional phrases that the writer must then work against. In his practice he demonstrates that a writer, and not just a musician, works within "conventional premises." The "I" who comments in this paper (not the "I" of the narrative about a time when he soloed) places himself self-consciously within the context of a conventional discourse about the subject, even as he struggles against the language of that conventional discourse. The opening definition of improvisation, where improvisation is defined as spontaneous creation, is rejected when the writer begins talking about "the conventional premises behind improvisation." The earlier definition is part of the conventional language of those who "have always thought" of jazz as a "very original creative field in music." The paper begins with what "has been said" and then works itself out against the force and logic of what has been said, of what is not only an argument but also a collection of phrases, examples, and definitions.

I had a teacher who once told us that whenever we were stuck for something to say, we should use the following as a "machine" for producing a paper: "While most readers of _____ have said _____, a close and careful reading shows that _____." The writer of the second paper on jazz is using a standard opening gambit, even if it is not announced with flourish. The essay becomes possible when he sets himself against what must become a "naive" assumption—what "most people think." He has defined a closed circle for himself. In fact, you could say that he has laid the ground work for a discipline with its own key terms ("practical knowledge," "disciplinary guidelines," and "original ideas"), with its own agenda and with its own investigative procedures (looking for common features in the work of individual soloists).

The history represented by this student's essay, then, is not the history of a musician and it is not the history of a thought being worked out within an individual mind; it is the history of work being done within and against conventional systems.

In general, as I reviewed essays for this study, I found that the more successful writers set themselves in their essays against what they defined as some more naive way of talking about their subject—against "those who think that . . ."—or against earlier, more naive versions of themselves—"once I thought that. . . ." By trading in one set of commonplaces at the expense of another, they could win themselves status as members of what is taken to be some more privileged group. The ability to imagine privilege enabled writing. Here is one particularly successful essay. Notice the specialized vocabulary, but notice also the way in which the text continually refers to its own language and to the language of others.

> Throughout my life, I have been interested and intrigued by music. My mother has often told me of the times, before I went to school, when I would "conduct" the orchestra on her records. I continued to listen to music and eventually started to play the guitar and the clarinet. Finally, at about the age of twelve, I started to sit down and to try to write songs. Even though my instrumental skills were far from my own high standards, I would spend much of my spare time during the day with a guitar around my neck, trying to produce a piece of music.
>
> Each of these sessions, as I remember them, had a rather set format. I would sit in my bedroom, strumming different combinations of the five or six chords I could play, until I heard a series of which sounded particularly good to me. After this, I set the music to a suitable rhythm, (usually dependent on my mood at the time), and ran through the tune until I could play it fairly easily. Only after this section was complete did I go on to writing lyrics, which generally followed along the lines of the current popular songs on the radio.
>
> At the time of the writing, I felt that my songs were, in themselves, an original creation of my own; that is, I, alone, made them. However, I now see that, in this sense of the word, I was not creative. The songs themselves seem to be an oversimplified form of the music I listened to at the time.
>
> In a more fitting sense, however, I *was* being creative. Since I did not purposely copy my favorite songs, I was, effectively, originating my songs from my own "process of creativity." To achieve my goal, I needed what a composer would call "inspiration" for my piece. In this case the inspiration was the current hit on the radio. Perhaps, with my present point of view, I feel that I used too much "inspiration" in my songs, but, at that time, I did not.
>
> Creativity, therefore, is a process which, in my case, involved a certain series of "small creations" if you like. As well, it is something, the appreciation of which varies with one's point of view, that point of view being set by the person's experience, tastes, and his own personal view of creativity. The less experienced tend to allow for less originality, while the more experienced demand real originality to classify something a "creation." Either way, a term as abstract as this is perfectly correct, and open to interpretation.

This writer is consistently and dramatically conscious of herself forming something to say out of what has been said *and* out of what she has been saying in the act of writing this paper. "Creativity" begins in this paper as "original creation." What she thought was "creativity," however, she now says was imitation; and, as she says, "in a sense of the word" she was not "creative." In another sense, however, she says that she *was* creative, since she didn't purposefully copy the songs but used them as "inspiration."

While the elaborate stylistic display—the pauses, qualifications, and the use of quotation marks—is in part a performance for our benefit, at a more obvious level we as readers are directly addressed in the first sentence of the last paragraph: "Creativity, therefore, is a process which, in my case, involved a certain series of 'small creations' if you like." We are addressed here as adults who can share her perspective on what she has said and who can be expected to understand her terms. If she gets into trouble after this sentence, and I think she does, it is because she doesn't have the courage to generalize from her assertion. Since she has rhetorically separated herself from her younger "self," and since she argues that she has gotten smarter, she assumes that there is some developmental sequence at work here and that, in the world of adults (which must be more complete than the world of children) there must be something like "real creativity." If her world is imperfect (if she can only talk about creation by putting the word in quotation marks), it must be because she is young. When she looks beyond herself to us, she cannot see our work as an extension of her project. She cannot assume that we too will be concerned with the problem of creativity and originality. At least she is not willing to challenge us on those grounds, to generalize her argument, and to argue that even for adults creations are really only "small creations." The sense of privilege that has allowed her to expose her own language cannot be extended to expose ours.

The writing in this piece—that is, the work of the writer within the essay—goes on in spite of, or against, the language that keeps pressing to give another name to her experience as a songwriter and to bring the discussion to closure. (In comparison, think of the quick closure of the "White Shoes" paper.) Its style is difficult, highly qualified. It relies on quotation marks and parody to set off the language and attitudes that belong to the discourse (or the discourses) that it would reject, that it would not take as its own proper location.

David Olson (1981) has argued that the key difference between oral language and written language is that written language separates both the producer and the receiver from the text. For my student writers, this means that they had to learn that what they said (the code) was more important than what they meant (the intention). A writer, in other words, loses his primacy at the moment of writing and must begin to attend to his and his words' conventional, even physical presence on the page. And, Olson says, the writer must learn that his authority is not established through his presence but through his absence—through his ability, that is, to speak as a god-like source beyond the limitations of any particular social or historical moment;

to speak by means of the wisdom of convention, through the oversounds of official or authoritative utterance, as the voice of logic or the voice of the community. He concludes:

> The child's growing competence with this distinctive register of language in which both the meaning and the authority are displaced from the intentions of the speaker and lodged "in the text" may contribute to the similarly specialized and distinctive mode of thought we have come to associate with literacy and formal education. (1918, p. 110)

Olson is writing about children. His generalizations, I think I've shown, can be extended to students writing their way into the academic community. These are educated and literate individuals, to be sure, but they are individuals still outside the peculiar boundaries of the academic community. In the papers I've examined in this chapter, the writers have shown an increasing awareness of the codes (or the competing codes) that operate within a discourse. To speak with authority they have to speak not only in another's voice but through another's code; and they not only have to do this, they have to speak in the voice and through the codes of those of us with power and wisdom; and they not only have to do this, they have to do it before they know what they are doing, before they have a project to participate in, and before, at least in terms of our disciplines, they have anything to say. Our students may be able to enter into a conventional discourse and speak, not as themselves, but through the voice of the community; the university, however, is the place where "common" wisdom is only of negative values—it is something to work against. The movement toward a more specialized discourse begins (or, perhaps, best begins) both when a student can define a position of privilege, a position that sets him against a "common" discourse, and when he or she can work self-consciously, critically, against not only the "common" code but his or her own.

IV

Pat Bizzell, you will recall, argues that the problems of poor writers can be attributed both to their unfamiliarity with the conventions of academic discourse and to their ignorance that there are such things as discourse communities with conventions to be mastered. If the latter is true, I think it is true only in rare cases. All the student writers I've discussed (and, in fact, most of the student writers whose work I've seen) have shown an awareness that something special or something different is required when one writes for an academic classroom. The essays that I have presented in this chapter all, I think, give evidence of writers trying to write their way into a new community. To some degree, however, all of them can be said to be unfamiliar with the conventions of academic discourse.

Problems of convention are both problems of finish and problems of substance. The most substantial academic tasks for students, learning history or sociology or literary criticism, are matters of many courses, much reading and writing, and several years of education. Our students, however, must have a place to begin. They cannot sit through lectures and read textbooks and, as a consequence, write as sociologists or write literary criticism. There must be steps along the way. Some of these steps will be marked by drafts and revisions. Some will be marked by courses, and in an ideal curriculum the preliminary courses would be writing courses, whether housed in an English department or not. For some students, students we call "basic writers," these courses will be in a sense the most basic introduction to the language and methods of academic writing.

Our students, as I've said, must have a place to begin. If the problem of a beginning is the problem of establishing authority, of defining rhetorically or stylistically a position from which one may speak, then the papers I have examined show characteristic student responses to that problem and show levels of approximation or stages in the development of writers who are writing their way into a position of privilege.

As I look over the papers I've discussed, I would arrange them in the following order: the "White Shoes" paper; the first "Jazz" essay; the "Clay Model" paper; the second "Jazz" essay; and, as the most successful paper, the essay on "Composing Songs." The more advanced essays for me, then, are those that are set against the "naive" codes of "everyday" life. (I put the terms "naive" and "everyday" in quotation marks because they are, of course, arbitrary terms.) In the advanced essays one can see a writer claiming an "inside" position of privilege by rejecting the language and commonplaces of a "naive" discourse, the language of "outsiders." The "I" of those essays locates itself against the specialized language of what is presumed to be a more powerful and more privileged community. There are two gestures present then—one imitative and one critical. The writer continually audits and pushes against a language that would render him "like everyone else" and mimics the language and interpretive systems of the privileged community.

At a first level, then, a student might establish his authority by simply stating his own presence within the field of a subject. A student, for example, writes about creativity by telling a story about a time he went skiing. Nothing more. The "I" on the page is a skier, and skiing stands as a representation of a creative act. Neither the skier nor skiing are available for interpretation; they cannot be located in an essay that is not a narrative essay (where skiing might serve metaphorically as an example of, say, a sport where set movements also allow for a personal style). Or a student, as did the one who wrote the "White Shoes" paper, locates a narrative in an unconnected rehearsal of commonplaces about creativity. In both cases, the writers have finessed the requirement to set themselves against the available utterances of the world outside the closed world of the academy. And, again, in the first "Jazz" paper, we have the example of a writer who locates himself within an available commonplace and carries out only rudimentary procedures for elaboration, procedures driven by the commonplace itself and not set against it. Elaboration, in this latter case, is not the opening up of a system but a justification of it.

At a next level I would place student writers who establish their authority by mimicking the rhythm and texture, the "sound," of academic prose, without there being any recognizable interpretive or academic project under way. I'm thinking, here, of the "Clay Model" essay. At an advanced stage, I would place students who establish their authority as *writers*; they claim their authority, not by simply claiming that they are skiers or that they have done something creative, but by placing themselves both within and against a discourse, or within and against competing discourses, and working self-consciously to claim an interpretive project of their own, one that grants them their privilege to speak. This is true, I think, in the case of the second "Jazz" paper and, to a greater degree, in the case of the "Composing Songs" paper.

The levels of development that I've suggested are not marked by corresponding levels in the type or frequency of error, at least not by the type or frequency of sentence-level error. I am arguing, then, that a basic writer is not necessarily a writer who makes a lot of mistakes. In fact, one of the problems with curricula designed to aid basic writers is that they too often begin with the assumption that the key distinguishing feature of a basic writer is the presence of sentence-level error. Students are placed in courses because their placement essays show a high frequency of such errors, and those courses are designed with the goal of making those errors go away. This approach to the problems of the basic writer ignores the degree to which error is less often a constant feature than a marker in the development of a writer. A student who can write a reasonably correct narrative may fall to pieces when faced with a more unfamiliar assignment. More important, however, such courses fail to serve the rest of the curriculum. On every campus there is a significant number of college freshmen who require a course to introduce them to the kinds of writing that are required for a university education. Some of these students can write correct sentences and some cannot; but, as a group, they lack the facility other freshmen possess when they are faced with an academic writing task.

The "White Shoes" essay, for example, shows fewer sentence-level errors than the "Clay Model" paper. This may well be due to the fact that the writer of the "White Shoes" paper stayed well within safe, familiar territory. He kept himself out of trouble by doing what he could easily do. The tortuous syntax of the more advanced papers on my list is a syntax that represents a writer's struggle with a difficult and unfamiliar language, and it is a syntax that can quickly lead an inexperienced writer into trouble. The syntax and punctuation of the "Composing Songs" essay, for example, shows the effort that is required when a writer works against the pressure of conventional discourse. If the prose is inelegant (although I confess I admire those dense sentences) it is still correct. This writer has a command of the linguistic and stylistic resources—the highly embedded sentences, the use of parentheses and quotation marks—required to complete the act of writing. It is easy to imagine the possible pitfalls for a writer working without this facility.

There was no camera trained on the "Clay Model" writer while he was writing, and I have no protocol of what was going through his mind, but it is possible to speculate on the syntactic difficulties of sentences like these: "In the past time I thought that an incident was creative was when I had to make a clay model of the earth, but not of the classical or your everyday model of the earth which consists of the two cores, the mantle and the crust. I thought of these things in a dimension of which it would be unique, but easy to comprehend." The syntactic difficulties appear to be the result of the writer's attempt to use an unusual vocabulary and to extend his sentences beyond the boundaries of what would have been "normal" in his speech or writing. There is reason to believe, that is, that the problem was with *this* kind of sentence, in this context. If the problem of the last sentence is that of holding together the units "I thought," "dimension," "unique" and "easy to comprehend," then the linguistic problem was not a simple matter of sentence construction. I am arguing, then, that such sentences fall apart not because the writer lacked the necessary syntax to glue the pieces together but because he lacked the full statement within which these key words were already operating. While writing, and in the thrust of his need to complete the sentence, he had the key words but not the utterance. (And to recover the utterance, I suspect, he would need to do more than revise the sentence.) The invisible conventions, the prepared phrases remained too distant for the statement to be completed. The writer would have needed to get inside of a discourse that he could in fact only partially imagine. The act of constructing a sentence, then, became something like an act of transcription in which the voice on the tape unexpectedly faded away and became inaudible.

Shaughnessy (1977) speaks of the advanced writer as one who often has a more facile but still incomplete possession of this prior discourse. In the case of the advanced writer, the evidence of a problem is the presence of dissonant, redundant, or imprecise language, as in a sentence such as this: "No education can be *total*, it must be *continuous*."

Such a student, Shaughnessy says, could be said to hear the "melody of formal English" while still unable to make precise or exact distinctions. And, she says,

> the pre-packaging feature of language, the possibility of taking over phrases and whole sentences without much thought about them, threatens the writer now as before. The writer, as we have said, inherits the language out of which he must fabricate his own messages. He is therefore in a constant tangle with the language, obliged to recognize its public, communal nature and yet driven to invent out of this language his own statements. (1977, pp. 207–208)

For the unskilled writer, the problem is different in degree and not in kind. The inexperienced writer is left with a more fragmentary record of the comings and goings of academic discourse. Or, as I said above, he or she often has the key words without the complete statements within which they are already operating.

Let me provide one final example of this kind of syntactic difficulty in another piece of student writing. The writer of this paper seems to be able to sustain a discussion only by continually repeating his first step, producing a litany of strong, general, authoritative assertions that trail quickly into confusion. Notice how the writer seems to stabilize his movement through the paper by returning again and again to recognizable and available commonplace utterances. When he has to move away from them, however, away from the familiar to statements that would extend those utterances, where he, too, must speak, the writing—that is, both the syntax and the structure of the discourse—falls to pieces.

> Many times the times drives a person's life depends on how he uses it. I would like to think about if time is twenty-five hours a day rather than twenty-four hours. Some people think it's the boaring or some people might say it's the pleasure to take one more hour for their life. But I think the time is passing and coming, still we are standing on same position. We should use time as best as we can use about the good way in our life. Everything we do, such as sleep, eat, study, play and doing something for

ourselves. These take the time to do and we could find the individual ability and may process own. It is the important for us and our society. As time going on the world changes therefor we are changing, too. When these situation changes we should follow the suitable case of own. But many times we should decide what's the better way to do so by using time. Sometimes like this kind of situation can cause the success of our lives or ruin. I think every individual of his own thought drive how to use time. These affect are done from environmental causes. So we should work on the better way of our life recognizing the importance of time.

There is a general pattern of disintegration when the writer moves off from standard phrases. This sentence, for example, starts out coherently and then falls apart: "*We should use time as best as we can* use about the good way in our life." The difficulty seems to be one of extending those standard phrases or of connecting them to the main subject reference, "time" (or "the time," a construction that causes many of the problems in the paper). Here is an example of a sentence that shows, in miniature, this problem of connection: "*I think every individual* of his own thought drive how to use *time.*

One of the remarkable things about this paper is that, in spite of all the syntactic confusion, there is the hint of an academic project here. The writer sets out to discuss how to creatively use one's time. The text seems to allude to examples and to stages in an argument, even if in the end it is all pretty incoherent. The gestures of academic authority, however, are clearly present, and present in a form that echoes the procedures in other, more successful papers. The writer sets himself against what "some people think"; he speaks with the air of authority: "But I think. . . . Everything we do. . . . When these situation changes. . . ." And he speaks as though there were a project underway, one where he proposes what he thinks, turns to evidence, and offers a conclusion: "These affect are done from environmental causes. So we should work. . . ." This is the case of a student with the ability to imagine the general outline and rhythm of academic prose but without the ability to carry it out, to complete the sentences. And when he gets lost in the new, in the unknown, in the responsibility of his own commitment to speak, he returns again to the familiar ground of the commonplace.

The challenge to researchers, it seems to me, is to turn their attention again to products, to student writing, since the drama in a student's essay, as he or she struggles with and against the languages of our contemporary life, is as intense and telling as the drama of an essay's mental preparation or physical production. A written text, too, can be a compelling model of the "composing process" once we conceive of a writer as at work within a text and simultaneously, then, within a society, a history, and a culture.

It may very well be that some students will need to learn to crudely mimic the "distinctive register" of academic discourse before they are prepared to actually and legitimately do the work of the discourse, and before they are sophisticated enough with the refinements of tone and gesture to do it with grace or elegance. To say this, however, is to say that our students must be our students. Their initial progress will be marked by their abilities to take on the role of privilege, by their abilities to establish authority. From this point of view, the student who wrote about constructing the clay model of the earth is better prepared for his education than the student who wrote about playing football in white shoes, even though the "White Shoes" paper is relatively error-free and the "Clay Model" paper is not. It will be hard to pry loose the writer of the "White Shoes" paper from the tidy, pat discourse that allows him to dispose of the question of creativity in such a quick and efficient manner. He will have to be convinced that it is better to write sentences he might not so easily control, and he will have to be convinced that it is better to write muddier and more confusing prose (in order that it may sound like ours), and this will be harder than convincing the "Clay Model" writer to continue what he has already begun.

ACKNOWLEDGMENTS

Preparation of this chapter was supported by the Learning Research and Development Center of the University of Pittsburgh, which is supported in part by the National Institute of Education.

NOTES

1. David Olson (1981) has made a similar observation about school-related problems of language learning in younger children. Here is his conclusion: "Hence, depending upon whether children assumed language was primarily suitable for making assertions and conjectures or primarily for making direct or indirect commands, they will either find school texts easy or difficult" (p. 107).

2. For Aristotle, there were both general and specific commonplaces. A speaker, says Aristotle, has a "stock of arguments to which he may turn for a particular need."

> If he knows the *topoi* (regions, places, lines of argument)—and a skilled speaker will know them—he will know where to find what he wants for a special case. The general topics, or *common*places, are regions containing arguments that are common to all branches of knowledge. . . . But there are also special topics (regions, places, *loci*) in which one looks for arguments appertaining to particular branches of knowledge, special sciences, such as ethics or politics. (1932, pp. 154–155)

And, he says, "the topics or places, then, may be indifferently thought of as in the science that is concerned, or in the mind of the speaker." But the question of location is "indifferent" *only* if the mind of the speaker is in line with set opinion, general assumption. For the speaker (or writer) who is not situated so comfortably in the privileged public realm, this is indeed not an indifferent matter at all. If he does not have the commonplace at hand, he will not, in Aristotle's terms, know where to go at all.

3. Pat Bizzell has argued that the *Seventeen* writer's process of goal-setting

> can be better understood if we see it in terms of writing for a discourse community. His initial problem . . . is to find a way to include these readers in a discourse community for which he is comfortable writing. He places them in the academic discourse community by imagining the girls as students. . . . Once he has included them in a familiar discourse community, he can find a way to address them that is common in the community: he will argue with them, putting a new interpretation on information they possess in order to correct misconceptions. (1982a, p. 228)

4. See Bartholomae (1979, 1983) and Rose (1983) for articles on curricula designed to move students into university discourse. The movement to extend writing "across the curriculum" is evidence of a general concern for locating students within the work of the university; see Bizzell (1982a) and Maimon *et al.* (1981). For longer works directed specifically at basic writing, see Ponsot and Deen (1982) and Shaughnessy (1977). For a book describing a course for more advanced students, see Coles (1978).

5. In spite of my misgivings about Bereiter and Scardamalia's interpretation of the cognitive nature of the problem of "inert knowledge," this is an essay I regularly recommend to teachers. It has much to say about the dangers of what seem to be "neutral" forms of classroom discourse and provides, in its final section, a set of recommendations on how a teacher might undo discourse conventions that have become part of the institution of teaching.

6. Stanley Fish (1980) argues that the basis for distinguishing novice from expert readings is the persuasiveness of the discourse used to present and defend a given reading. In particular, see the chapter, "Demonstration vs. Persuasion: Two Models of Critical Activity" (pp. 356–373).

7. Some students, when they come to the university, can do this better than others. When Jonathan Culler says, "the possibility of bringing someone to see that a particular interpretation is a good one assumes shared points of departure and common notions of how to read," he is acknowledging that teaching, at least in English classes, has had to assume that students, to be students, were already to some degree participating in the structures of reading and writing that constitute English studies (quoted in Fish, 1980, p. 366).

Stanley Fish tells us "not to worry" that students will violate our enterprise by offering idiosyncratic readings of standard texts:

> The fear of solipsism, of the imposition by the unconstrained self of its own prejudices, is unfounded because the self does not exist apart from the communal or conventional categories of thought that enable its operations (of thinking, seeing, reading). Once we realize that the conceptions that fill consciousness, including any conception of its own status, are culturally derived, the very notion of an unconstrained self, of a consciousness wholly and dangerously free, becomes incomprehensible. (1980, p. 335)

He, too, is assuming that students, to be students (and not "dangerously free"), must be members in good standing of the community whose immediate head is the English teacher. It is interesting that his parenthetical catalogue of the "operations" of thought, "thinking, seeing, reading," excludes writing, since it is only through written records that we have any real indication of how a student thinks, sees, and reads. (Perhaps "real" is an inappropriate word to use here, since there is certainly a "real" intellectual life that goes on, independent of writing. Let me say that thinking, seeing, and reading are valued in the academic community *only* as they are represented by extended, elaborated written records.) Writing, I presume, is a given for Fish. It is the card of entry into this closed community that constrains and excludes dangerous characters. Students who are excluded from this community are students who do poorly on written placement exams or in freshman composition. They do not, that is, move easily into the privileged discourse of the community, represented by the English literature class.

8. My debt to Bizzell's work should be evident everywhere in this essay. See also Bizzell (1978, 1982b) and Bizzell and Herzberg (1980).

9. Fish says the following about the relationship between student and an object under study:

> we are not to imagine a moment when my students "simply see" a physical con-figuration of atoms and *then* assign that configuration a significance, according to the situation they happen to be in. To be in the situation (this or any other) is to "see" with the eyes of its interests, its goals, its understood practices, values, and norms, and so to be conferring significance *by* seeing, not after it. The categories of my students' vision are the categories by which they understand themselves to be functioning as students . . . and objects will appear to them in forms related to that way of functioning rather than in some objective or preinterpretive form. (1980, p. 334)

10. I am aware that the papers given the highest rankings offer arguments about creativity and originality similar to my own. If there is a conspiracy here, that is one of the points of my chapter. I should add that my reading of the "content" of basic writers' essays is quite different from Lunsford's (1980).

REFERENCES

Aristotle. (1932). *The rhetoric of Aristotle* (L. Cooper, Trans.) Englewood Cliffs, NJ: Prentice-Hall.

Barthes, R. (1974). *S/Z* (R. Howard, Trans.). New York: Hill & Wang.

Bartholomae, D. (1979). Teaching basic writing: An alternative to basic skills. *Journal of Basic Writing, 2*, 85–109.

Bartholomae, D. (1983). Writing assignments: Where writing begins. In P. Stock (Ed.), *Forum* (pp. 300–312). Montclair, NJ: Boynton/Cook.

Bereiter, C., & Scardamalia, M. (in press). Cognitive coping strategies and the problem of "inert knowledge." In S. S. Chipman, J. W. Segal, & R. Glaser (Eds.), *Thinking and learning skills: Research and open questions* (Vol. 2). Hillsdale, NJ: Erlbaum.

Bizzell, P. (1978). The ethos of academic discourse. *College Composition and Communication, 29*, 351–355.

Bizzell, P. (1982a). Cognition, convention, and certainty: What we need to know about writing. *Pre/text, 3*, 213–244.

Bizzell, P. (1982b). College composition: Initiation into the academic discourse community. *Curriculum Inquiry, 12*, 191–207.

Bizzell, P., & Herzberg, B. (1980). "Inherent" ideology, "universal" history, "empirical" evidence, and "context-free" writing: Some problems with E. D. Hirsch's *The Philosophy of Composition*. *Modern Language Notes, 95,* 1181–1202.

Coles, W. E., Jr. (1978). *The plural I.* New York: Holt, Rinehart & Winston.

Fish, S. (1980). *Is there a text in this class? The authority of interpretive communities.* Cambridge, MA: Harvard University Press.

Flower, L. S. (1981). Revising writer-based prose. *Journal of Basic Writing, 3,* 62–74.

Flower, L., & Hayes, J. (1981). A cognitive process theory of writing. *College Composition and Communication, 32,* 365–387.

Hairston, M. (1978). *A contemporary rhetoric.* Boston: Houghton Mifflin.

Lunsford, A. A. (1980). The content of basic writers' essays. *College Composition and Communication, 31,* 278–290.

Maimon, E. P., Belcher, G. L., Hearn, G. W., Nodine, B. F., & O'Conner, F. X. (1981). *Writing in the arts and sciences.* Cambridge, MA: Winthrop.

Olson, D. R. (1981). Writing: The divorce of the author from the text. In B. M. Kroll & R. J. Vann (Eds.), *Exploring speaking–writing relationships: Connections and contrasts.* Urbana, IL: National Council of Teachers of English.

Perkins, D. N. (in press). General cognitive skills: Why not? In S. S. Chipman, J. W. Segal, & R. Glaser (Eds.), *Thinking and learning skills: Research and open questions* (Vol. 2). Hillsdale, NJ: Erlbaum.

Ponsot, M., & Deen, R. (1982). *Beat not the poor desk.* Montclair, NJ: Boynton/Cook.

Rodriguez, R. (1983). *Hunger of memory.* New York: Bantam.

Rose, M. (1983). Remedial writing courses: A critique and a proposal. *College English, 45,* 109–128.

Said, E. W. (1975). *Beginnings: Intention and method.* Baltimore: The Johns Hopkins University Press.

Shaughnessy, M. (1977). *Errors and expectations.* New York: Oxford University Press.

When the First Voice You Hear
Is Not Your Own

Jacqueline Jones Royster

This essay emerged from my desire to examine closely moments of personal challenge that seem to have import for cross-boundary discourse. These types of moments have constituted an ongoing source of curiosity for me in terms of my own need to understand human difference as a complex reality, a reality that I have found most intriguing within the context of the academic world. From a collectivity of such moments over the years, I have concluded that the most salient point to acknowledge is that "subject" position really is everything.

Using subject position as a terministic screen in cross-boundary discourse permits analysis to operate kaleidoscopically, thereby permitting interpretation to be richly informed by the converging of dialectical perspectives. Subjectivity as a defining value pays attention dynamically to context, ways of knowing, language abilities, and experience, and by doing so it has a consequent potential to deepen, broaden, and enrich our interpretive views in dynamic ways as well. Analytical lenses include the process, results, and impact of negotiating identity, establishing authority, developing strategies for action, carrying forth intent with a particular type of agency, and being compelled by external factors and internal sensibilities to adjust belief and action (or not). In a fundamental way, this enterprise supports the sense of rhetoric, composition, and literacy studies as a field of study that embraces the imperative to understand truths and consequences of language use more fully. This enterprise supports also the imperative to reconsider the beliefs and values which inevitably permit our attitudes and actions in discourse

Reprinted from *College Composition and Communication* 47.1 (February 1996): 29–40. Used with permission.

communities (including colleges, universities, and classrooms) to be systematic, even systemic.

Adopting subjectivity as a defining value, therefore, is instructive. However, the multidimensionality of the instruction also reveals the need for a shift in paradigms, a need that I find especially evident with regard to the notion of "voice," as a central manifestation of subjectivity. My task in this essay, therefore, is threefold. First, I present three scenes which serve as my personal testimony as "subject." These scenes are singular in terms of their being my own stories, but I believe that they are also plural, constituting experiential data that I share with many. My sense of things is that individual stories placed one against another build credibility and offer, as in this case, a litany of evidence from which a call for transformation in theory and practice might rightfully begin. My intent is to suggest that my stories in the company of others demand thoughtful response.

Second, I draw from these scenes a specific direction for transformation, suggesting dimensions of the nature of voicing that remain problematic. My intent is to demonstrate that our critical approaches to voice, again as a central manifestation of subjectivity, are currently skewed toward voice as a spoken or written phenomenon. This intent merges the second task with the third in that I proceed to suggest that theories and practices should be transformed. The call for action in cross-boundary exchange is to refine theory and practice so that they include voicing as a phenomenon that is constructed and expressed visually and orally, *and* as a phenomenon that has import also in being a *thing* heard, perceived, and reconstructed.

SCENE ONE

I have been compelled on too many occasions to count to sit as a well-mannered Other, silently, in a state of tolerance that requires me to be as expressionless as I can manage, while colleagues who occupy a place of entitlement different from my own talk about the history and achievements of people from my ethnic group, or even about their perceptions of our struggles. I have been compelled to listen as they have comfortably claimed the authority to engage in the construction of knowledge and meaning about me and mine, without paying even a passing nod to the fact that sometimes a substantive version of that knowledge might already exist, or to how it might have already been constructed, or to the meanings that might have already been assigned that might make me quite impatient with gaps in their understanding of my community, or to the fact that I, or somebody within my ethnic group, might have an opinion about what they are doing. I have been compelled to listen to speakers, well-meaning though they may think they are, who signal to me rather clearly that subject position is everything. I have come to recognize, however, that when the subject matter is me and the voice is not mine, my sense of order and rightness is disrupted. In metaphoric fashion, these "authorities" let me know, once again, that Columbus has discovered America and claims it now, claims it still for a European crown.

Such scenes bring me to the very edge of a principle that I value deeply as a teacher and a scholar, the principle of the right to inquiry and discovery. When the discovering hits so close to home, however, my response is visceral, not just intellectual, and I am made to look over a precipice. I have found it extremely difficult to allow the voices and experiences of people that I care about deeply to be taken and handled so carelessly and without accountability by strangers.

At the extreme, the African American community, as my personal example, has seen and continues to see its contributions and achievements called into question in grossly negative ways, as in the case of *The Bell Curve*. Such interpretations of who we are as a people open to general interrogation, once again, the innate capacities of "the race" as a whole. As has been the case throughout our history in this country, we are put in jeopardy and on trial in a way that should not exist but does. We are compelled to respond to a rendering of our potential that demands, not that we account for attitudes, actions, and conditions, but that we defend ourselves as human beings. Such interpretations of human potential create a type of discourse that serves as a distraction, as noise that drains off energy and sabotages the work of identifying substantive problems within and across cultural boundaries and the work also of finding solutions that have import, not simply for "a race," but for human beings whose living conditions, values, and preferences vary.

All such close encounters, the extraordinarily insidious ones and the ordinary ones, are definable through the lens of subjectivity, particularly in terms of the power and authority to speak and to make meaning. An analysis of subject position reveals that these interpretations by those outside of the community are not random acts of unkindness. Instead, they embody ways of seeing, knowing, being, and acting that probably suggest as much about the speaker and the context as they do about the targeted subject matter. The advantage with this type of analysis, of course, is that we see the obvious need to contextualize the stranger's perspective among other interpretations and to recognize that an interpretive view is just that—interpretive. A second advantage is that we also see that in our nation's practices these types of interpretations, regardless of how superficial or libelous they may actually be within the context of a more comprehensive view, tend to have considerable consequence in the lives of the targeted group, people in this case whose own voices and perspectives remain still largely under considered and uncredited.

Essentially, though, having a mechanism to see the under considered helps us see the extent to which we add continually to the pile of evidence in this country of cross-cultural misconduct. These types of close encounters that disregard dialectical views are a type of free touching of the powerless by the power-full. This analytical perspective encourages us to acknowledge that marginalized communities are not in a good position to ward off the intrusion of those authorized in mainstream communities to engage in willful action. Historically, such actions have included everything from the displacement of native people from their homelands, to the use of unknowing human subjects in dangerous experiments, to the appropriation and misappropriation of cultural artifacts—art, literature, music, and so on. An insight using the lens of subjectivity, however, is a recognition of the ways in which these moments are indeed moments of violation, perhaps even ultimate violation.

This record of misconduct means that for people like me, on an instinctive level, all outsiders are rightly perceived as suspect. I suspect the genuineness of their interest, the altruism of their actions, and the probability that whatever is being said or done is not to the ultimate benefit and understanding of the people who are subject matter but not subjects. People in the neighborhood where I grew up would say, "Where is their home training?" Imbedded in the question is the idea that when you visit other people's "home places," especially when you have not been invited, you simply can not go tramping around the house like you own the place, no matter how smart you are, or how much imagination you can muster, or how much authority and entitlement outside that home you may be privileged to hold. And you certainly can not go around name calling, saying things like, "You people are intellectually inferior and have a limited capacity to achieve," without taking into account who the family is, what its living has been like, and what its history and achievement have been about.

The concept of "home training" underscores the reality that point of view matters and that we must be trained to respect points of view other than our own. It acknowledges that when we are away from home, we need to know that what we think we see in places that we do not really know very well may not actually be what is there at all. So often, it really is a matter of time, place, resources, and our ability to perceive. Coming to judgment too quickly, drawing on information too narrowly, and saying hurtful, discrediting, dehumanizing things without undisputed proof are not appropriate. Such behavior is not good manners. What comes to mind for me is another saying that I heard constantly when I was growing up, "Do unto others as you would have them do unto you." In this case, we would be implored to draw conclusions about others with care and, when we do draw conclusions, to use the same type of sense and sensibility that we would ideally like for others to use in drawing conclusions about us.

This scene convinces me that what we need in a pressing way in this country and in our very own field is to articulate codes of behavior that can sustain more concretely notions of honor, respect, and good manners across boundaries, with cultural boundaries embodying the need most vividly. Turning the light back onto myself, though, at the same time that my sense of violation may indeed be real, there is the compelling reality that many communities in our nation need to be taken seriously. We all deserve to be taken seriously, which means that critical inquiry and discovery are absolutely necessary. Those of us who love our own communities, we think, most deeply, most uncompromisingly, without reservation for what they are and also are not, must set aside our misgivings about strangers in the interest of the possibility of deeper understanding (and for the more idealistic among us, the possibility of global peace). Those of us who hold these communities close to our hearts, protect them, and embrace them; those who want to preserve the goodness of the minds and souls in them; those who want to preserve consciously, critically, and also lovingly the record of good work within them must take high risk and give over the exclusivity of our rights to know.

It seems to me that the agreement for inquiry and discovery needs to be deliberately reciprocal. All of us, strangers and community members, need to find ways to sustain productivity in what Pratt calls contact zones (199), areas of engagement that in all likelihood will remain contentious. We need to get over our tendencies to be too possessive and to resist locking ourselves into the tunnels of our own visions and direct experience. As community members, we must learn to have new faith in the advantage of sharing. As strangers, we must learn to treat the loved people and places of Others with care and to understand that, when we do not act respectfully and responsibly, we leave ourselves rightly open to wrath. The challenge is not to work with a fear of abuse or a fear of retaliation, however. The challenge is to teach, to engage in research, to write, and to speak with Others with the determination to operate not only with professional and personal integrity, but also with the specific knowledge that communities and their ancestors are watching. If we can set aside our rights to exclusivity in our own home cultures, if we can set aside the tendencies that we all have to think too narrowly, we actually leave open an important possibility. In our nation, we have little idea of the potential that a variety of subjectivities—operating with honor, respect, and reasonable codes of conduct—can bring to critical inquiry or critical problems. What might happen if we treated differences in subject position as critical pieces of the whole, vital to thorough understanding, and central to both problem-finding and problem-solving? This society has not, as yet, really allowed that privilege in a substantial way.

SCENE TWO

As indicated in Scene One, I tend to be enraged at what Tillie Olsen has called the "trespass vision," a vision that comes from intellect and imagination (62), but typically not from lived experience, and sometimes not from the serious study of the subject matter. However, like W. E. B. Du Bois, I've chosen not to be distracted or consumed by my rage at voyeurs, tourists, and trespassers, but to look at what I can do. I see the critical importance of the role of negotiator, someone who can cross boundaries and serve as guide and translator for Others.

In 1903, Du Bois demonstrated this role in *The Souls of Black Folk*. In the "Forethought" of that book, he says: "Leaving, then, the world of the white man, I have stepped within the Veil, raising it that you may view faintly its deeper recesses—the meaning of its religion, the passion of its human sorrow, and the struggle of its greater souls" (1). He sets his rhetorical purpose to be to cross, or at least to straddle, boundaries with the intent of shedding light, a light that has the potential of being useful to people on both sides of the veil. Like Du Bois, I've accepted the idea that what I call my "home place" is a cultural community that exists still quite significantly beyond the confines of a well-insulated community that we call the "mainstream," and that between this world and the one that I call home, systems of insulation impede the vision and narrow the ability to recognize human potential and to understand human history both microscopically and telescopically.

Like Du Bois, I've dedicated myself to raising this veil, to overriding these systems of insulation by raising another voice, my voice in the interest of clarity and accuracy. What I have found too often, however, is that, unlike those who have been entitled to talk about me and mine, when I talk about my own, I face what I call the power and function of deep disbelief, and what Du Bois described as "the sense of always looking at one's self through the eyes of others, of measuring one's soul by the tape of a world that looks on in amused contempt and pity" (5).

An example comes to mind. When I talk about African American women, especially those who were writing non-fiction prose in the nineteenth century, I can expect, even today after so much contemporary scholarship on such writers, to see people who are quite flabbergasted by anything that I share. Reflected on their faces and in their questions and comments, if anyone can manage to speak back to me, is a depth of surprise that is always discomforting. I sense that the surprise, or the silence, if there is little response, does not come from the simple ignorance of unfortunate souls who just happen not to know what I have spent years coming to know. What I suspect is that this type of surprise rather "naturally" emerges in a society that so obviously has the habit of expecting nothing of value, nothing of consequence, nothing of importance, nothing at all positive from its others, so that anything is a surprise; everything is an exception; and nothing of substance can really be claimed as a result.

In identifying this phenomenon, Chandra Talpade Mohanty speaks powerfully about the ways in which this culture co-opts, dissipates, and displaces voices. As demonstrated by my example, one method of absorption that has worked quite well has been essentially rhetorical. In discussing nineteenth century African American women's work, I bring tales of difference and adventure. I bring cultural proofs and instructive examples, all of which invariably must serve as rites of passage to credibility. I also bring the power of storytelling. These tales of adventure in odd places are the transitions by which to historicize and theorize anew with these writers re-inscribed in a rightful place. Such a process respects long-standing practices in African-based cultures of theorizing in narrative form. As Barbara Christian says, we theorize "in the stories we create, in riddles and proverbs, in the play with language, since dynamic rather than fixed ideas seem more to our liking" (336).

The problem is that in order to construct new histories and theories such stories must be perceived not just as "simple stories" to delight and entertain, but as vital layers of a transformative process. A reference point is Langston Hughes and his Simple stories, stories that are a model example of how apparent simplicity has the capacity to unmask truths in ways that are remarkably accessible—through metaphor, analogy, parable, and symbol. However, the problem of articulating new paradigms through stories becomes intractable, if those who are empowered to define impact and consequence decide that the stories are simply stories and if the record of achievement is perceived, as Audre Lorde has said, as "the random droppings of birds" (Foreword xi).

If I take my cue from the life of Ida Wells, and I am bold enough and defiant enough to go beyond the presentation of my stories as juicy tidbits for the delectation of audiences, to actually shift or even subvert a paradigm, I'm much more likely to receive a wide-eyed stare and to have the value and validity of my conceptual position held at a distance, in doubt, and wonderfully absorbed in the silence of appreciation. Through the systems of deep disbelief I become a storyteller, a performer. With such absorptive ability in the systems of interpretation, I have greater difficulty being perceived as a person who theorizes without the mediating voices of those from the inner sanctum, or as a person who might name myself a philosopher, a theorist, a historian who creates paradigms that allow the experiences and the insights of people like me to belong.

What I am compelled to ask when veils seem more like walls is who has the privilege of speaking first? How do we negotiate the privilege of interpretation? When I have tried to fulfill my role as negotiator, I have often walked away knowing that I have spoken, but also knowing, as Anna Julia Cooper knew in 1892, that my voice, like her voice, is still a muted one. I speak, but I can not be heard. Worse, I am heard but I am not believed. Worse yet, I speak but I am not deemed believable. These moments of deep disbelief have helped me to understand much more clearly the wisdom of Audre Lorde when she said: "I have come to believe over and over again that what is most important to me must be spoken, made verbal and shared, even at the risk of having it bruised or misunderstood" (*Sister* 40). Lorde teaches me that, despite whatever frustration and vulnerability I might feel, despite my fear that no one is listening to me or is curious enough to try to understand my voice, it is still better to speak (*Black* 31). I set aside the distractions and permeating noise outside of myself, and I listen, as Howard Thurman recommended, to the sound of the genuine within. I go to a place inside myself and, as Opal Palmer Adisa explains, I listen and learn to "speak without clenching my teeth" (56).

SCENE THREE

There have been occasions when I have indeed been heard and positively received. Even at these times, however, I sometimes can not escape responses that make me most weary. One case in point occurred after a presentation in which I had glossed a scene in a novel that required cultural understanding. When the characters spoke in the scene, I rendered their voices, speaking and explaining, speaking and explaining, trying to translate the experience, to share the sounds of my historical place and to connect those sounds with systems of belief so that deeper understanding of the scene might emerge, and so that those outside of the immediacy of my home culture, the one represented in the novel, might see and understand more and be able to make more useful connections to their own worlds and experiences.

One very well-intentioned response to what I did that day was, "How wonderful it was that you were willing to share with us your 'authentic' voice!" I said, "My 'authentic' voice?" She said, "Oh yes! I've never heard you talk like that, you know, so relaxed. I mean, you're usually great, but, this was really great! You weren't so formal. You didn't have to speak in appropriated academic language. You sounded 'natural.' It was nice to hear you be yourself." I said, "Oh, I see. Yes, I do have a range of voices, and I take quite a bit of pleasure actually in being able to use any of them at will." Not understanding the point that I was trying to make gently, she said, "But this time, it was really you. Thank you."

The conversation continued, but I stopped paying attention. What I didn't feel like saying in a more direct way, a response that my friend surely would have perceived as angry, was that all my voices are authentic, and like bell hooks, I find it "a necessary aspect of self-affirmation not to feel compelled to choose one voice over another, not to claim one as more authentic, but rather to construct social realities that celebrate, acknowledge, and affirm differences, variety" (12). Like hooks, I claim all my voices as my own very much authentic voices, even when it's difficult for others to imagine a person like me having the capacity to do that.

From moments of challenge like this one, I realize that we do not have a paradigm that really allows for what scholars in cultural and postcolonial studies (Anzaldúa, Spivak, Mohanty, Bhabha) have called hybrid people—people who either have the capacity by right of history and development, or who might have created the capacity by right of history and development, to move with dexterity across cultural boundaries, to make themselves comfortable, and to make sense amid the chaos of difference.

As Cornel West points out, most African Americans, for example, dream in English, not in Yoruba, or Hausa, or Wolof. Hybrid people, as demonstrated by the history of Africans in the Western hemisphere, manage a fusion process that allows for survival, certainly. However, it also allows for the development of a peculiar expertise that extends one's range of abilities well beyond ordinary limits, and it supports the opportunity for the development of new and remarkable creative expression, like spirituals, jazz, blues, and what I suspect is happening also with the essay as genre in the hands of African American women. West notes that somebody gave Charlie Parker a saxophone, Miles Davis a trumpet, Hubert Laws a flute, and Les McCann a piano. I suggest that somebody also gave Maria Stewart, Gertrude Mossell, Frances Harper, Alice Walker, Audre Lorde, Toni Morrison, Patricia Williams, June Jordan, bell hooks, Angela Davis and a cadre of other African American women a pencil, a pen, a computer keyboard. In both instances, genius emerges from hybridity, from Africans who, over the course of time and circumstance, have come to dream in English, and I venture to say that all of their voices are authentic.

In sharing these three scenes, I emphasize that there is a pressing need to construct paradigms that permit us to engage in better practices in cross-boundary discourse, whether we are teaching, researching, writing, or talking with Others, whoever those Others happen to be. I would like to emphasize, again, that we look again at "voice" and situate it within a world of symbols, sound, and sense, recognizing that this world operates symphonically. Although the systems of voice production are indeed highly integrated and appear to have singularity in the ways that we come to sound, voicing actually sets in motion multiple systems; prominent among them are systems for speaking but present also are the systems for hearing. We speak within systems that we know significantly through our abilities to negotiate noise and to construct within that noise sense and sensibility.

Several questions come to mind. How can we teach, engage in research, write about, and talk across boundaries *with* others, instead of for, about, and around them? My experiences tell me that we need to do more than just talk and talk back. I believe that in this model we miss a critical moment. We need to talk, yes, and to talk back, yes, but when do we listen? How do we listen? How do we demonstrate that we honor and respect the person talking and what that person is saying, or what the person might say if we valued someone other than ourselves having a turn to speak? How do we translate listening into language and action, into the creation of an appropriate response? How do we really "talk back" rather than talk also? The goal is not, "You talk, I talk." The goal is better practices so that we can exchange perspectives, negotiate meaning, and create understanding with the intent of being in a good position to cooperate, when, like now, cooperation is absolutely necessary.

When I think about this goal, what stands out most is that these questions apply in so much of academic life right now. They certainly apply as we go into classrooms and insist that our students trust us and what we contend is in their best interest. In light of a record in classrooms that seriously questions the range of our abilities to recognize potential, or to appreciate students as non-generic human beings, or to appreciate that they bring with them, always, knowledge, we ask a lot when we ask them to trust. Too often, still, institutionalized equations for placement, positive matriculation, progress, and achievement name, categorize, rank, and file, while our true-to-life students fall between the cracks. I look again to Opal Palmer Adisa for an instructive example. She says:

> Presently, many academics advocate theories which, rather than illuminating the works under scrutiny, obfuscate and problematize these works so that students are rendered speechless. Consequently, the students constantly question what they know, and often, unfortunately, they conclude that they know nothing. (54)

Students may find what we do to be alienating and disheartening. Even when our intentions are quite honorable, silence can descend. Their experiences are not seen, and their voices are not heard. We can find ourselves participating, sometimes consciously, sometimes not, in what Patricia Williams calls "spirit murder" (55). I am reminded in a disconcerting way of a troubling scene from Alex Haley's *Roots*. We engage in practices that say quite insistently to a variety of students in a variety of ways, "Your name is Toby." Why wouldn't students wonder: Who can I trust here? Under what kinds of conditions? When? Why?

In addition to better practices in our classrooms, however, we can also question our ability to talk convincingly with deans, presidents, legislators, and the general public about what we do, how we do it, and why. We have not been conscientious about keeping lines of communication open, and we are now experiencing the consequences of talking primarily to ourselves as we watch funds being cut, programs being eliminated, and national agencies that are vital to our interests being bandied about as if they are post-it notes, randomly stuck on by some ill-informed spendthrift. We must learn to raise a politically active voice with a socially responsible mandate to make a rightful place for education in a country that seems always ready to place the needs of quality education on a sideboard instead of on the table. Seemingly, we have been forever content to let voices other than our own speak authoritatively about our areas of expertise and about us. It is time to speak for ourselves, in our own interests, in the interest of our work, and in the interest of our students.

Better practices are not limited, though, even to these concerns. Of more immediate concern to me this year, given my role as Chair of CCCC, is how to talk across boundaries within our own organization as teachers of English among other teachers of English and language arts from kindergarten through university with interests as varied as those implied by the sections, conferences, and committees of our parent organization, the National Council of Teachers of English (NCTE). Each of the groups within NCTE has its own set of needs, expectations, and concerns, multiplied across the amazing variety of institutional sites across which we work. In times of limited resources and a full slate of critical problems, we must find reasonable ways to negotiate so that we can all thrive reasonably well in the same place.

In our own case, for years now, CCCC has recognized changes in our relationships with NCTE. Since the mid-1980s we have grown exponentially. The field of rhetoric and composition has blossomed and diversified. The climate for higher education has increasingly degenerated, and we have struggled in the midst of change to forge a more satisfying identity and a more positive and productive working relationship with others in NCTE who are facing crises of their own. After 50 years in NCTE, we have grown up, and we have to figure out a new way of being and doing in making sure that we can face our challenges well. We are now in the second year of a concerted effort to engage in a multi-leveled conversation that we hope will leave CCCC well-positioned to face a new century and ongoing challenges. Much, however, depends on the ways in which we talk and listen and talk again in crossing boundaries and creating, or not, the common ground of engagement.

As I look at the lay of this land, I endorse Henry David Thoreau's statement when he said, "Only that day dawns to which we are awake" (267). So my appeal is to urge us all to be awake, awake and listening, awake and operating deliberately on codes of better conduct in the interest of keeping our boundaries fluid, our discourse invigorated with multiple perspectives, and our policies and practices well-tuned toward a clearer respect for human potential and achievement from whatever their source and a clearer understanding that voicing at its best is not just well-spoken but also well-heard.

WORKS CITED

Adisa, Opal Palmer. "I Must Write What I Know So I'll Know That I've Known It All Along." *Sage: A Scholarly Journal on Black Women* 9.2 (1995): 54–57.

Anzaldúa, Gloria. *Borderlands/La Frontera*. San Francisco: Aunt Lute, 1987.

Bhabha, Homi K. *The Location of Culture*. London: Routledge, 1994.

Christian, Barbara. "The Race for Theory." *Cultural Critique* 6 (1987): 335–45.

Cooper, Anna Julia. *A Voice from the South*. New York: Oxford UP, 1988.

Du Bois, W. E. B. *The Souls of Black Folk*. New York: Grammercy, 1994.

Haley, Alex. *Roots*. Garden City: Doubleday, 1976.

Hernstein, Richard J., and Charles Murray. *The Bell Curve: Intelligence and Class Structure in American Life*. New York: Free, 1994.

hooks, bell. *Talking Back: Thinking Feminist, Thinking Black*. Boston: South End, 1989.

Lorde, Audre. *The Black Unicorn*. New York: Norton, 1978.

_____. Foreword. *Wild Women in the Whirlwind*. Ed. Joanne M. Braxton and Andree Nicola McLaughlin. New Brunswick: Rutgers UP, 1990. xi–xiii.

_____. *Sister Outsider*. Freedom: The Crossing Press, 1984.

Mohanty, Chandra Talpade. "On Race and Voice: Challenges for Liberal Education in the 1990s." *Cultural Critique* 14 (Winter 1989–90): 179–208.

_____. "Decolonizing Education: Feminisms and the Politics of Multiculturalism in the 'New' World Order." Ohio State University, Columbus, April 1994.

Olsen, Tillie. *Silences*. New York: Delta, 1978.

Pratt, Mary Louise. "Arts of the Contact Zone." *Profession* 91 (1991): 33–40.

Spivak, Gayatri Chakravorty. *In Other Worlds: Essays in Cultural Politics*. New York: Routledge, 1988.

Thoreau, Henry David. *Walden*. New York: Vintage, 1991.

Thurman, Howard. "The Sound of the Genuine." Spelman College, Atlanta, April 1981.

West, Cornel. "Race Matters." Ohio State U, Columbus, OH, February 1995.

Williams, Patricia. *The Alchemy of Race and Rights*. Cambridge: Harvard UP, 1991.

Memoria Is a Friend of Ours

On the Discourse of Color

VICTOR VILLANUEVA

A memory. Seattle, 1979.

She is a contradiction in stereotypes, not to be pegged. He likes her right off. She wants to go to Belltown, the Denny Regrade, to take photos. He wants to go along. He does, feeling insecure and full of bravado, slipping into the walk of bravado he had perfected as a child in Brooklyn. Stops into a small café at the outskirts of downtown, at the entry to the Regrade. It's a French-style café, the Boulangerie, or some such. To impress her, he speaks French.

"Une tasse de café, s'il vous plaît. Et croissants pour les deux." Don't laugh. It's how he said it.

He's an English major, a senior, quite proud of having gotten this far in college. But he's insecure about what this will lead to (since he had only gotten as far as deciding to stay in college till he's finally in over his head). He tells her of a novel he will write someday. His description goes something like this:

> *I've been thinking about a novel about a white Puerto Rican kid who buys into the assimilation myth, hook, line, and sinker. He does all the right things — learns the language, learns how to pronounce "r's" in words like "motherrr" and "waterrr" and how not to trill the "r" when he says "three," and he does well in school. He's even a war hero. Does it all, only to realize that assimilation just can't happen. Yet he can't really be Puerto Rican. So maybe he goes to Puerto Rico to find out who he might have been and what he is tied to. I don't have it all worked out.*

Reprinted from *College English* 67.1 (2004): 9–19. [First published in *Personal Effects: The Social Character of Scholarly Writing*. Ed. Deborah H. Holdstein and David Bleich, Logan: Utah State UP, 2001.] Copyright 2001 by Utah State University Press. Reprinted with permission.

The plot line might not have been worked out, but this was the impulse nevertheless—to keep alive the memory of assimilation denied, a truism turned to myth, to try to hold on to, maybe even to regain, that which had been lost on the road to assimilation.

A reminiscence:

> *That morning I had spoken with Ceci, my friend the Cuban English profes-sor. Her husband had said something to me over the phone that I had to unravel quickly, immediate translation from my first language to my only language, slipping the Spanish into English to understand. Their baby, I'm told, used to translate into Spanish for her mother when someone spoke in English at home, translated the English into Spanish so that the English professor would understand. Cute.*
>
> *During that phone conversation, I tried to come up with a familiar Spanish saying about how Cubans and Puerto Ricans are two wings of the same bird. It was there: at the tip of the mind. But I could never. I said it in English. Ceci said it for me in Spanish. Quickly. Then again more slowly. I heard it. I understood it. I recognized it. I still feel unsure that I could pro-duce it. My Spanish is limited to single sentences, never extended stretches of discourse. I can't. At least I don't believe I can. And I listen to salsa and mambo and bomba and plena—the music of my childhood. But I can't dance to it in front of anyone. And phrases from the CDs slip by me, untrans-lated. I am assimilated. I am not.*
>
> *So I was driving home from some chore or other on the afternoon of the morning I had spoken to Ceci. And in the midst of a left turn I thought: "I'm fifty now, maybe a third of my life left. I wonder if I'll die without ever being fluent in the language that first met my ears." English is the only language I know, really. Yet Spanish is the language of my ear, of my soul. And I try to pass it on to my children. But I'm inadequate.*

In some sense, the impulse of the book I had described twenty-one years ago gets worked out in *Bootstraps*, the assimilation myth explicit in the title; the story told then elaborated upon with research and with theory. It's an attempt to play out a kind of Freirean pedagogy: the political explored through the experiential. And it does more. It's

> an autobiography with political, theoretical, pedagogical considerations. The story includes ethnographic research. The story includes things tried in classrooms. The story includes speculations on the differences between immigrants and minorities, the class system and language, orality and liter-acy, cultural and critical literacy, Freire, ideology, hegemony, how racism continues and the ways in which racism is allowed to continue despite the profession's best efforts. And in [so doing] the story suggests how we

are—all of us—subject to the systemic. This is the personal made public and the public personalized, not for self-glory nor to point fingers, but to suggest how, maybe, to make the exception the rule. (xviii)

I wrote that in 1992. Now some part of that first impulse reasserts itself, fictionalizing, telling the story, reaching back to the heritage that is at risk of passing away quickly. To the kids before my father died last spring:

> *Remember to call your grandpa abuelo. He'll like the sound of that, since none of my sister's kids have called him that. If you let him, he'll just watch baseball day and night and not say much. Push him for the stories of Puerto Rico during his childhood. Ask him about catching shrimp with his hands, and the stories of how the neighborhood boys got a Model A Ford, about the revolutionary who hid out in El Yunque, about his time in the Army. Ask about my grandfather, Basilio, and gardening, and working as a groundskeeper and gardener for the university. And ask about Tío Benito, the tall farmer, inland, on the coffee hills. "Inland" is important about knowing about being Puerto Rican, about Puerto Rico. I remember when I met him. A tall PR. Man, that was very cool. And he gave me sugar cane from his farm, and a coffee bean, and a lemon that he had cut a hole on the top of. And he told me to chew on the bean, squeeze lemon juice on the tongue, and chew on the cane. I wish I could give you that memory, mi'jitas.*
>
> *Now, Mom is easier. She loves to talk. But she'd rather forget the past. And I don't want the past forgotten, so press her too.*

A poem: Victor Villanueva y Hernándes

Triste lucha la del árbol con espinas	Sad struggle of the tree of thorns
Fuerte ardor que solo a su alma	Fierce feeling covered solely by
se cobija.	your soul
Vano empeño para el ser que vive,	Vain striving for he who lives,
En tratar de comprender su propia vida.	In trying to understand his own life.
Muy dulce es percivir de la noche	So sweet to see your caresses in
sus caricios;	the night
Pero es terrible saber	But so terrible to know
Que más tarde en la madrugada	That later in the light of day
Agonizando todos ellos quedan. . . .	All the agonies remain. . . .
Triste lucha del árbol con espinas	Sad struggle of the tree of thorns
triste lucha la del que ya un	sad struggle of that which is
poquito tarde,	already a little late,
Ni siquiera el más leve	Without even the lightest
suspiro	sigh
su alma alienta.	your soul's breath

Triste e interminable lucha	Sad and interminable struggle
esta que jamás se aleja	that which will never leave
¡Oh, que triste lucha ésta	Oh, how sad this struggle
que a mi pecho	Weighing so on my chest!
Tanto apena!	
¡Triste lucha . . . triste lucha!	Sad struggle . . . sad struggle!
—"En el pasado versa tu presente"	—"In the past turns the present"
19 de enero 1951	19 January 1951

The fiction, the *Bootstraps* retold and fictionalized, would have to begin back then, not quite a generation after the change of hands, when the Spanish colony was handed over to the United States, the changes seen by three generations—*Boricua* to Nuyorican to the middle class of color far removed from the cultural soil of either of the generations, maybe even a wheat field in Eastern Washington. It's important. The memory.

So many have said this so well, that it's hard for me to reiterate without breaking into the academic discourse of cite-and-quote—Adell, JanMohamed and Lloyd, Omi and Winant, Saldívar, San Juan, Singh, Skerrett, and Hogan, Smorkaloff, and the "standards" like Anzaldúa or hooks—all have written about the connections between narratives by people of color and the need to reclaim a memory, memory of an identity in formation and constant reformation, the need to reclaim a memory of an identity as formed through the generations. And I'd say the need to reclaim and retain the memory of the imperial lords, those who have forcibly changed the identities of people of color through colonization.

Nelly, the department's graduate secretary, hands me a flyer for a meeting of the Pacific Islanders' group, inviting me to join the students, staff, and faculty (which includes two department chairs I work with often). We smile at each other. Her cultural ways—Filipina—and mine are so different really— except that we have two out of three imperial lords in common: Spain and the United States. It binds us. Our first imperial lord was there before the world got large, more local: the Japanese and the Caribes. We laugh, while others look and listen on with looks of wondering. It's not their memory.

Memory simply cannot be adequately portrayed in the conventional discourse of the academy.

I am grateful for the acknowledgment of perceptions that academic discourse provides, for the resources the conventions of citation make available, for the ideocentric discourse that displays inductive or deductive lines of reasoning, a way to trace a writer's logical connections.

Academic discourse is cognitively powerful!

But the cognitive alone is insufficient. It can be strong for *logos*. It can be strong for *ethos*. But it is very weak in *pathos*. Academic discourse tries, after all, to reach the Aristotelian ideal of being completely logocentric, though it cannot be freed of the ethical appeal to authority. A demonstration: Agustín Lao, in "Islands at the Crossroads: Puerto Ricanness Traveling between the Translocal Nation and the Global City," writes that

> Puerto Ricans (like other racialized diasporas) function within multiple and ambiguous registers of race and racism. As colonized subjects, all Puerto Ricans are "colored" by colonial discourses. On the other hand, differential processes of racialization can either nominalize Puerto Ricans as "ethnic" and/or allow some light-skinned Puerto Ricans to "pass" as "white." [. . .] A single Puerto Rican "transmigrant" can be classified as *trigueña* on the island, black in Ohio, and Latina in New York. (178–79)

Now consider the rhetorical effect of Professor Lao's assertion (though with qualification) and a couple of stories from this light-skinned Puerto Rican. Both take place during the Summer of 2000:

> *He was picked up at the registration desk of the hotel in Iowa City. The limousine (really a van) driver walks up, a man in his late fifties or early sixties, buzz cut, thick build, surely one more accustomed to hard physical labor, a farmer, one would imagine, given the locale. Says at least the guest is on time, kind of to the person behind the registration desk, kind of to himself, maybe even to the guest. He goes on to say that the last guest he'd picked up had been fifteen minutes late, then didn't pay the fare.*
>
> *Once in the van, the story of the deadbeat develops. It was a family of four, including an infant. No car seat.*
>
> *"I could've had my license pulled, with no car seat for the baby. Then he tries to pay me with a $100 travelers' check, like I carry that kind of money at five in the morning."*
>
> *"Were they foreigners?" assuming the passengers would have overestimated the fluidity of travelers' checks.*
>
> *"Who can know these days. The guy wore a turban. What are you?"*
>
> *Internal soliloquy: He didn't say "rag head," so maybe this is more the condition of the international seaports flowing into the middle of America, the in-migration of the newest immigrants and those new immigrants from the 1930s, a land no longer completely owned by those of Scandinavian and German ancestry. But 1898 and 1917 really should mean something in a situation like this.* [NB: 1898: the U.S. acquisition of Puerto Rico; 1917: US citizenship conferred on all Puerto Ricans]

"Me? I'm American."
"Coulda fooled me!"
"Yeah, well. I'm from New York."
The conversation ends. The next passenger turns out to be a black man with a crutch coming out of an upper-middle-class home in the suburbs of Iowa City. Kind of felt sorry for the driver and his comfortable assumptions.

Second story:

It was another one of those receptions produced by the dean of the graduate school. This one was to welcome doctoral fellows in residence. Most were persons of color. I was there as a department chair and as one of the mentors to a couple of the fellows.

The scene: Back porch of the house, clusters of folks with drinks in hand or paper plates with guacamole and chips, talking, smiling, overlooking cows grazing in the valley below and green soft rolling hills nearby, maybe three hundred yards away, where there will soon be wheat blowing beautifully in the wind.

A conversation ensues with one of the fellows, a woman who grew up in the black area of Boston, Roxbury. Listening in is an associate dean, originally from Central Asia, overtly happy to be away from Russian bureaucracy. The conversation turns to race in the wheatland.

VV: "Around here folks don't know if I'm Spanish, Jewish, Italian, from the Middle East, or from South Asia."

Associate Dean: "I would have thought you were Italian."

Roxbury: "I don' know. He looks pretty Portorican to me."

Sure, she knows the hue, she sees the "niggerlips," one of those names I endured as a child, just like Martín.

Martín Espada:

Niggerlips was the high school name
for me.
So called by Douglas
the car mechanic, with green tattoos
on each forearm,
and the choir of round pink faces
that grinned deliciously
from the back row of classrooms,
droned over by teachers
checking attendance too slowly.

Douglas would brag
about cruising his car

572

near sidewalks of black children
to point an unloaded gun,
to scare niggers
like crows off a tree,
he'd say.

My great-grandfather Luis
was un negrito too,
a shoemaker in the coffee hills
of Puerto Rico, 1900.
The family called him a secret
and kept no photograph.
My father remembers
the childhood white powder
that failed to bleach
his stubborn copper skin,
and the family says
he is still a fly in milk.

So Niggerlips has the mouth
of his great-grandfather,
the song he must have sung
as he pounded the leather and nails,
the heat that courses through copper,
the stubbornness of a fly in milk,
and all you have, Douglas,
is that unloaded gun.

Professor Lao, I would contend, is not quite right. Those of us who are light-skinned don't pass for white; we're just not automatically sorted into the appropriate slot. But more to the point is that Lao's academic discourse (complete with scare quotes and nominalizations) is insufficient, lacks emotional appeal. And though Aristotle thought it not right to sway with emotional appeals, he knew that the greatest impact on listeners is in fact the emotional. The personal here does not negate the need for the academic; it complements, provides an essential element in the rhetorical triangle, an essential element in the intellect—cognition *and* affect. The personal done well is sensorial and intellectual, complete, knowledge known throughout mind and body, even if vicariously.

And for the person of color, it does more. The narrative of the person of color validates. It resonates. It awakens, particularly for those of us who are in institutions where our numbers are few. We know that though we really are Gramsci's exceptions—those who "through 'chance' [. . . have] had opportunities that the thousand others in reality could not or did not have"—our experiences are in no sense unique but are always analogous to other experiences from among those exceptions. So more than narrating the life of one of color so that "one creates this possibility, suggests the process, indicates the opening," in Gramsci's terms (*Selections from Cultural Writings* 132), we remember the results of our having realized the possibility, discovered the process, found the opening, while finding that there is in some sense very little change on the other side. This is what Ellis Cose describes as *The Rage of a Privileged Class*. This is Luis Rodriguez's call, that we'll read below.

Ellis Cose, I've written before ("On Colonies"), explains, mainly by way of anecdote, the reasons African Americans in particular continue to be angry even after having crossed over to the other side. He explains the ways in which little slights continue to display the racism inherent in our society. Those "Dozen Demons" are

1. Inability to fit in.
2. Exclusion from the club.
3. Low expectations.
4. Shattered hopes.
5. Faint praise.
6. Presumption of failure.
7. Coping fatigue.
8. Pigeonholing.
9. Identity troubles.
10. Self-censorship and silence.
11. Mendacity.
12. Guilt by association. (57–68)

I haven't been called a "spic" in many years (except by others of color, perhaps, in fun, I hope). Yet little things happen that betray the underlying racism that affects us all, no matter how appalled by racism we might be. I read Anzaldúa or hooks or the poetry of Espada or Cruz or Esteves or any other writing of color, and I know I haven't become clinically paranoid. I know that I've been poked by one of the demons. Some of the slights signified by Cose are self-imposed, instances of Frantz Fanon's internal colonialism. Some are externally imposed. All can be laid bare through the personal made public.

There's the story of the academics of color who wrote about the subtle ways in which they find themselves victims of some of Cose's demons—exclusion, expecting less, presuming failure, pigeonholing as "brown-on-brown" research rather than disinterested research (read: white and classical-empirical). Someone far away reads the essay once published and files suit for slander. The authors had never heard of the person. This is a very funny story to people of color who have heard it — the laughter of verification and white guilt gone awry.

The converse:
"Man, I loved your book [or article or essay]. I could relate. The same things have happened to me," something I've heard time and again wherever I travel. Identity minus troubles among Cose's demons, association guiltless, a new club formed.

Somehow, the spic does remain, despite all the good fortune and accolades, not only from within but from without. While a good academic piece would help me to remember, rich narrative does more for the memory.

And the precedent is old. *Memoria* was the mother of the muses, the most important of the rhetorical offices. Now rhetorics of writing seem to go no further than invention, arrangement, and style; when delivery is still there, it's the matter of "voice." But memory is tied in as well, surely for people of color. It's as if we have accepted Plato's prophecy that literacy would be the downfall of memory, leading only to remembrance. We have to remember Plato, because his writing is significant by virtue of its genre, an attempt at representation of dialogue, of storytelling, of the play. Plato's literacy took shape not as logocentric discourse but as a representation of discourse in action. Though folks like Volosinov have shown that all discourse, written as well as spoken, is dialogic, Plato is maybe the coolest of the philosophers because of the resonance of the dialogue, the possibility for humor, the clear presence of all three points in the rhetorical triangle and the often unspecified dimension which is context. I don't mean to be waxing Platonic, really, only to suggest that there's something to Plato's notion of memory as more than recollection and to his leaning on a written discourse that approximates orality as a means toward arriving at Memory. The narratives of people of color jog our memories as a collective in a scattered world and within an ideology that praises individualism. And this is all the more apparent for the Latino and Latina, whose language contains the assertion of the interconnectedness among identity, memory, and the personal. There is a common saying among Puerto Ricans and Cubans: *Te doy un cuento de mi historia*, literally rendered as "I'll give you a story about my history": me, history and memory, and a story.

A thousand years before the first Europeans arrived on Puerto Rico, the native peoples of the mainland and the lesser Antilles migrated to Puerto

Rico, where they could live in relative peace, able to fish and live off the fresh vegetation—pineapple and varieties of tuber that have no name in English. We don't know the names of the first inhabitants of Puerto Rico. Our history is the history told by the Europeans, who, conferring their values on the land, took the language of the local imperial lords. We only know the names given the first Puerto Ricans by their first colonizers, the first to raid them, the first to enslave them, the ones the Europeans honored by naming the region after them. These first colonizers were the peoples of Carib. And they named the people of that island Arawak *and the culture of the Arawak was called* Taino. *And their island was named Boriquén.*

Then came Columbus (or Columbo or Colón. I'm glad we've stopped translating people's names, or I'd have to walk around with the name Conqueror Newton). And then Ponce de León. Then the priests.

And when the slaves of Puerto Rico rebelled, slaves from Africa were brought in, and the Boricuas ran inland, away from the fortressed walls of El Morro, *acquiescing to the Spanish yet surreptitiously trading with Dutch and English, French and Italian pirates who would find other ways to enter the island. This subversion became* jaibería. *So I understand Angel Rama, when he says that it is in the Caribbean that "the plural manifestations of the entire universe insert themselves" (qtd. in Smorkaloff vii). My mother's name is Italian (the line is never lost in the Spanish tradition: my father's mother—Hernándes and my mother becoming María Socorro Cotto de Villanueva, my father was thus Victor Villanueva y Hernándes and me Victor Villanueva y Cotto until we both were Americanized and I became "Jr."). My mother's name: Italian. The memory of that first Italian, whether family or slavemaster (which is how so many of the Tainos got their names, just like the African Americans of the mainland)—lost.*

Centuries after the first Europeans later, I am Puerto Rican—a product of the first migrations of Puerto Ricans to New York in the late 1940s, though my mother arrived through what was euphemistically called "indentured servitude," what others called "white slavery," as if somehow more barbaric than the slavery of Africans. And I assimilate. And I don't. But I know how to seem to be—jaibería—and I have the memory—the memory provided by stories told. Memory does hunger. And it's fed through the stories told.

I'm trying to figure this out, somehow: who I am, from where, playing out the mixes within. It isn't a question for me, whether public or private discourses. I am contradictory consciousness. The discourse should reflect that. I am these uneasy mixes of races that make for no race at all yet find themselves victim to racism. The discourse should reflect that. I am an American (in every sense—a boy from Brooklyn, jazz and rock 'n' roll, and from the Americas, with an ancestry dating back before the Europeans), an academic, a person of color—an organically grown traditional intellectual, containing both of Gramsci's intellectual formations, yet not quite his new intellectual. The discourse should reflect that as well. And I am in a wheatfield, attempting to pass on a memory as I attempt to gather one. Personal discourse, the narrative, the auto/biography, helps in that effort, is a necessary adjunct to the academic.

Looking back, we look ahead, and giving ourselves up to the looking back and the looking ahead, knowing the self, and, critically, knowing the self in relation to others, maybe we can be an instrument whereby students can hear the call.

A poem by Luis J. Rodriguez:

The calling came to me
while I languished
in my room, while I
whittled away my youth
in jail cells
and damp *barrio* fields.

It brought me to life,
out of captivity,
in a street-scarred
and tattooed place
I called body.

Until then I waited silently,
a deafening clamor in my head,
but voiceless to all around;
hidden from America's eyes,
a brown boy without a name.

I would sing into a solitary
        tape recorder,
music never to be heard.
I would write my thoughts
in scrambled English;
I would take photos in my mind
        plan out new parks,
        bushy green, concrete free,
        new places to play
        and think.

Waiting.
Then it came.
The calling.
It brought me out of my room.

It forced me to escape
night captors
in street prisons.

It called me to war,
to be writer,
to be scientist
and march with the soldiers
    of change.

It called me from the shadows,
out of the wreckage
of my *barrio*—from among those
who did not exist.

I waited all of 16 years
for this time.

Somehow, unexpected,
I was called.

Memoria calls and pushes us forward. *Memoria* is a friend of ours. We must invite her into our classrooms and into our scholarship.

WORKS CITED

Adell, Sandra. *Double Consciousness/Double Bind: Theoretical Issues in Twentieth-Century Black Literature.* Urbana: U of Illinois P, 1994.

Cose, Ellis. *The Rage of a Privileged Class.* New York: Harper, 1993.

Espada, Martín. "Niggerlips." *Cool Salsa: Bilingual Poems on Growing Up Latino in the United States.* Ed. Lori M. Carlson. New York: Fawcett, 1994. 73–74.

Fanon, Frantz. *Black Skin, White Masks.* Trans. Charles Lam Markmann. New York: Grove, 1967.

Gramsci, Antonio. *Selections from Cultural Writings.* Ed. David Forgacs and Geoffrey Nowell-Smith. Trans. William Boelhower. Cambridge: Harvard UP, 1985.

——. *Selections from the Prison Notebooks.* Ed. and trans. Quintin Hoare and Geoffrey Nowell-Smith. New York: International, 1971.

Grosfoguel, Ramón, Frances Negrón-Muntaner, and Chloé S. Georas. "Beyond Nationalist and Colonialist Discourses: The *Jaiba* Politics of the Puerto-Rican Ethno-Nation," *Puerto Rican Jam: Rethinking Colonialism and Nationalism.* Ed. Frances Negrón-Muntaner and Ramón Grosfoguel. Minneapolis: U of Minnesota P, 1997. 1–36.

JanMohamed, Abdul R., and David Lloyd, eds. *The Nature and Context of Minority Discourse.* New York: Oxford UP, 1990.

Lao, Agustín, "Islands at the Crossroads: Puerto Ricanness Traveling between the Translocal Nation and the Global City." *Puerto Rican Jam: Rethinking Colonialism and Nationalism.* Ed. Frances Negrón-Muntaner and Ramón Grosfoguel. Minneapolis: U of Minnesota P, 1997. 169–88.

Omi, Michael, and Howard Winant. *Racial Formation in the United States: From the 1960s to the 1990s.* New York: Routledge, 1994.

Rodriguez, Luis J. "The Calling." *Cool Salsa: Bilingual Poems on Growing Up Latino in the United States.* Ed. Lori M. Carlson. New York: Fawcett, 1994. 123–24.

Saldívar, Ramón. *Chicano Narrative: The Dialectics of Difference.* Madison: U of Wisconsin P, 1990.

San Juan, E. *Racial Formations/Critical Transformations: Articulations of Power in Ethnic and Racial Studies in the United States.* Atlantic Highlands, NJ: Humanities, 1992.

Singh, Amritjit, Joseph Skerrett, Robert E. Hogan, eds. *Memory, Narrative, and Identity: New Essays in Ethnic American Literature.* Boston: Northeastern UP, 1994.

Smorkaloff, Pamela Maria. *Cuban Writers on and off the Island: Contemporary Narrative Fiction.* New York: Twayne, 1999.

Villanueva, Victor. *Bootstraps: From an American Academic of Color.* Urbana, IL: NCTE, 1993.

——. "On Colonies, Canons, and Ellis Cose's Rage of a Privileged Class." *JAC* 16 (1996): 159–69.

Composing as a Woman

Elizabeth A. Flynn

*It is not easy to think like a woman in a man's world, in the world of the pro-
fessions; yet the capacity to do that is a strength which we can try to help our
students develop. To think like a woman in a man's world means thinking
critically, refusing to accept the givens, making connections between facts
and ideas which men have left unconnected. It means remembering that every
mind resides in a body; remaining accountable to the female bodies in which
we live; constantly retesting given hypotheses against lived experience. It
means a constant critique of language, for as Wittgenstein (no feminist) observed, "The limits of my language are the limits of my world." And it means
that most difficult thing of all: listening and watching in art and literature, in
the social sciences, in all the descriptions we are given of the world, for silences, the absences, the nameless, the unspoken, the encoded—for there we
will find the true knowledge of women. And in breaking those silences, naming ourselves, uncovering the hidden, making ourselves present, we begin to
define a reality which resonates to us, which affirms our being, which allows
the woman teacher and the woman student alike to take ourselves, and each
other, seriously: meaning, to begin taking charge of our lives.*

—Adrienne Rich, "Taking Women Students Seriously"

The emerging field of composition studies could be described as a feminization of our previous conceptions of how writers write and how writing should
be taught.[1] In exploring the nature of the writing process, composition specialists expose the limitations of previous product-oriented approaches by

Reprinted from *College Composition and Communication* 39.4 (December 1988): 423–35.
Used with permission.

demystifying the product and in so doing empowering developing writers and readers. Rather than enshrining the text in its final form, they demonstrate that the works produced by established authors are often the result of an extended, frequently enormously frustrating process and that creativity is an activity that results from experience and hard work rather than a mysterious gift reserved for a select few. In a sense, composition specialists replace the figure of the authoritative father with an image of a nurturing mother. Powerfully present in the work of composition researchers and theorists is the ideal of a committed teacher concerned about the growth and maturity of her students who provides feedback on ungraded drafts, reads journals, and attempts to tease out meaning from the seeming incoherence of student language. The field's foremothers come to mind—Janet Emig, Mina Shaughnessy, Ann Berthoff, Win Horner, Maxine Hairston, Shirley Heath, Nancy Martin, Linda Flower, Andrea Lunsford, Sondra Perl, Nancy Sommers, Marion Crowhurst, Lisa Ede. I'll admit the term foremother seems inappropriate as some of these women are still in their thirties and forties—we are speaking here of a very young field. Still, invoking their names suggests that we are also dealing with a field that, from the beginning, has welcomed contributions from women—indeed, has been shaped by women.

The work of male composition researchers and theorists has also contributed significantly to the process of feminization described above. James Britton, for instance, reverses traditional hierarchies by privileging private expression over public transaction, process over product. In arguing that writing for the self is the matrix out of which all forms of writing develop, he valorizes an activity and a mode of expression that have previously been undervalued or invisible, much as feminist literary critics have argued that women's letters and diaries are legitimate literary forms and should be studied and taught alongside more traditional genres. His work has had an enormous impact on the way writing is taught on the elementary and high school levels and in the university, not only in English courses but throughout the curriculum. Writing-Across-the-Curriculum Programs aim to transform pedagogical practices in all disciplines, even those where patriarchal attitudes toward authority are most deeply rooted.

FEMINIST STUDIES
AND COMPOSITION STUDIES

Feminist inquiry and composition studies have much in common. After all, feminist researchers and scholars and composition specialists are usually in the same department and sometimes teach the same courses. Not surprisingly, there have been wonderful moments when feminists have expressed their commitment to the teaching of writing. Florence Howe's essay, "Identity and Expression: A Writing Course for Women," for example, published in *College English* in 1971, describes her use of journals in a writing course designed to empower women. Adrienne Rich's essay, "'When We Dead Awaken': Writing as Re-Vision," politicizes and expands our conception of revision, emphasizing that taking another look at the texts we have generated necessitates revising our cultural assumptions as well.

There have also been wonderful moments when composition specialists have recognized that the marginality of the field of composition studies is linked in important ways to the political marginality of its constituents, many of whom are women who teach part-time. Maxine Hairston, in "Breaking Our Bonds and Reaffirming Our Connections," a slightly revised version of her Chair's address at the 1985 convention of the Conference on College Composition and Communication, draws an analogy between the plight of composition specialists and the plight of many women. For both, their worst problems begin at home and hence are immediate and daily. Both, too, often have complex psychological bonds to the people who frequently are their adversaries (273).

For the most part, though, the fields of feminist studies and composition studies have not engaged each other in a serious or systematic way. The major journals in the field of composition studies do not often include articles addressing feminist issues, and panels on feminism are infrequent at the Conference on College Composition and Communication.[2] As a result, the parallels between feminist studies and composition studies have not been delineated, and the feminist critique that has enriched such diverse fields as linguistics, reading, literary criticism, psychology, sociology, anthropology, religion, and science has had little impact on our models of the composing process or on our understanding of how written language abilities are acquired. We have not examined our research methods or research samples to see if they are androcentric. Nor have we attempted to determine just what it means to compose as a woman.

Feminist research and theory emphasize that males and females differ in their developmental processes and in their interactions with others. They emphasize, as well, that these differences are a result of an imbalance in the social order, of the dominance of men over women. They argue that men have chronicled our historical narratives and defined our fields of inquiry. Women's perspectives have been suppressed, silenced, marginalized, written out of what counts as authoritative knowledge. Difference is erased in a desire to universalize. Men become the standard against which women are judged.

A feminist approach to composition studies would focus on questions of difference and dominance in written language. Do males and females compose differently? Do they acquire language in different ways? Do research methods and research samples in composition studies reflect a male bias? I do not intend to tackle all of these issues. My approach here is a relatively modest one. I will survey recent feminist research on gender differences in social and psychological development, and I will show how this research and theory may be used in examining student writing, thus suggesting directions that a feminist investigation of composition might take.

GENDER DIFFERENCES IN SOCIAL AND PSYCHOLOGICAL DEVELOPMENT

Especially relevant to a feminist consideration of student writing are Nancy Chodorow's *The Reproduction of Mothering*, Carol Gilligan's *In a Different Voice*, and Mary Belenky, Blythe Clinchy, Nancy Goldberger, and Jill Tarule's *Women's Ways of Knowing*. All three books suggest that women and men have different conceptions of self and different modes of interaction with others as a result of their different experiences, especially their early relationship with their primary parent, their mother.

Chodorow's book, published in 1978, is an important examination of what she calls the "psychoanalysis and the sociology of gender," which in turn influenced Gilligan's *In a Different Voice* and Belenky et al.'s *Women's Ways of Knowing*. Chodorow tells us in her preface that her book originated when a feminist group she was affiliated with "wondered what it meant that women parented women." She argues that girls and boys develop different relational capacities and senses of self as a result of growing up in a family in which women mother. Because all children identify first with their mother, a girl's gender and gender role identification processes are continuous with her earliest identifications whereas a boy's are not. The boy gives up, in addition to his oedipal and preoedipal attachment to his mother, his primary identification with her. The more general identification processes for both males and females also follow this pattern. Chodorow says,

> Girls' identification processes, then, are more continuously embedded in and mediated by their ongoing relationship with their mother. They develop through and stress particularistic and affective relationships to others. A boy's identification processes are not likely to be so embedded in or mediated by a real affective relation to his father. At the same time, he tends to deny identification with and relationship to his mother and reject

what he takes to be the feminine world; masculinity is defined as much negatively as positively. Masculine identification processes stress differentiation from others, the denial of affective relation, and categorical universalistic components of the masculine role. Feminine identification processes are relational, whereas masculine identification processes tend to deny relationship. (176)

Carol Gilligan's *In a Different Voice,* published in 1982, builds on Chodorow's findings, focusing especially, though, on differences in the ways in which males and females speak about moral problems. According to Gilligan, women tend to define morality in terms of conflicting responsibilities rather than competing rights, requiring for their resolution a mode of thinking that is contextual and narrative rather than formal and abstract (19). Men, in contrast, equate morality and fairness and tie moral development to the understanding of rights and rules (19). Gilligan uses the metaphors of the web and the ladder to illustrate these distinctions. The web suggests interconnectedness as well as entrapment; the ladder suggests an achievement-orientation as well as individualistic and hierarchical thinking. Gilligan's study aims to correct the inadequacies of Lawrence Kohlberg's delineation of the stages of moral development. Kohlberg's study included only male subjects, and his categories reflect his decidedly male orientation. For him, the highest stages of moral development derive from a reflective understanding of human rights (19).

Belenky, Clinchy, Goldberger, and Tarule, in *Women's Ways of Knowing,* acknowledge their debt to Gilligan, though their main concern is intellectual rather than moral development. Like Gilligan, they recognize that male experience has served as the model in defining processes of intellectual maturation. The mental processes that are involved in considering the abstract and the impersonal have been labeled "thinking" and are attributed primarily to men, while those that deal with the personal and interpersonal fall under the rubric of "emotions" and are largely relegated to women. The particular study they chose to examine and revise is William Perry's *Forms of Intellectual and Ethical Development in the College Years* (1970). While Perry did include some women subjects in his study, only the interviews with men were used in illustrating and validating his scheme of intellectual and ethical development. When Perry assessed women's development on the basis of the categories he developed, the women were found to conform to the patterns he had observed in the male data. Thus, his work reveals what women have in common with men but was poorly designed to uncover those themes that might be more prominent among women. *Women's Ways of Knowing* focuses on "what else women might have to say about the development of their minds and on alternative routes that are sketchy or missing in Perry's version" (9).

Belenky et al. examined the transcripts of interviews with 135 women from a variety of backgrounds and of different ages and generated categories that are suited for describing the stages of women's intellectual development. They found that the quest for self and voice plays a central role in transformations of women's ways of knowing. Silent women have little awareness of their intellectual capacities. They live—selfless and voiceless—at the behest of those around them. External authorities know the truth and are all-powerful. At the positions of received knowledge and procedural knowledge, other voices and external truths prevail. Sense of self is embedded either in external definitions and roles or in identifications with institutions, disciplines, and methods. A sense of authority arises primarily through identification with the power of a group and its agreed-upon ways for knowing. Women at this stage of development have no sense of an authentic or unique voice, little awareness of a centered self. At the position of subjective knowledge, women turn away from others and any external authority. They have not yet acquired a public voice or public authority, though. Finally, women at the phase of constructed knowledge begin an effort to reclaim the self by attempting to integrate knowledge they feel intuitively with knowledge they have learned from others.

STUDENT WRITING

If women and men differ in their relational capacities and in their moral and intellectual development, we would expect to find manifestations of these differences in the student papers we encounter in our first-year composition courses. The student essays I will describe here are narrative descriptions of learning experiences produced in the first of a two-course sequence required of first-year students at Michigan Tech. I've selected the four because they invite commentary from the perspective of the material discussed above. The narratives of the female students are stories of interaction, of connection, or of frustrated connection. The narratives of the male students are stories of achievement, of separation, or of frustrated achievement.

Kim's essay describes a dreamlike experience in which she and her high school girlfriends connected with each other and with nature as a result of a balloon ride they decided to take one summer Sunday afternoon as a way of relieving boredom. From the start, Kim emphasizes communion and tranquility: "It was one of those Sunday afternoons when the sun shines brightly and a soft warm breeze blows gently. A perfect day for a long drive on a country road with my favorite friends." This mood is intensified as they ascend in the balloon: "Higher and higher we went, until the view was overpowering. What once was a warm breeze turned quickly into a cool crisp wind. A feeling of freedom and serenity overtook us as we drifted along slowly." The group felt as if they were "just suspended there on a string, with time non-existent." The experience made them contemplative, and as they drove quietly home, "each one of us collected our thoughts, and to this day we still reminisce about that Sunday afternoon." The experience solidified relationships and led to the formation of a close bond that was renewed every time the day was recollected.

The essay suggests what Chodorow calls relational identification processes. The members of the group are described as being in harmony with themselves and with the environment. There is no reference to competition or discord. The narrative also suggests a variation on what Belenky et al. call "connected knowing," a form of procedural knowledge that makes possible the most desirable form of knowing, constructed knowledge. Connected knowing is rooted in empathy for others and is intensely personal. Women who are connected knowers are able to detach themselves from the relationships and institutions to which they have been subordinated and begin to trust their own intuitions. The women in the narrative were connected doers rather than connected knowers. They went off on their own, left their families and teachers behind (it was summer vacation, after all), and gave themselves over to a powerful shared experience. The adventure was, for the most part, a silent one but did lead to satisfying talk.

Kathy also describes an adventure away from home, but hers was far less satisfying, no doubt because it involved considerably more risk. In her narrative she makes the point that "foreign countries can be frightening" by focusing on a situation in which she and three classmates, two females and a male, found themselves at a train station in Germany separated from the others because they had gotten off to get some refreshments and the train had left without them. She says,

> This left the four of us stranded in an unfamiliar station. Ed was the only person in our group that could speak German fluently, but he still didn't know what to do. Sue got hysterical and Laura tried to calm her down. I stood there stunned. We didn't know what to do.

What they did was turn to Ed, whom Kathy describes as "the smartest one in our group." He told them to get on a train that was on the same track as the original. Kathy realized, though, after talking to some passengers, that they were on the wrong train and urged her classmates to get off. She says,

> I almost panicked. When I convinced the other three we were on the wrong train we opened the doors. As we were getting off, one of the conductors started yelling at us in German. It didn't bother me too much because I couldn't understand what he was saying. One thing about trains in Europe is that they are always on schedule. I think we delayed that train about a minute or two.

In deciding which train to board after getting off the wrong one, they deferred to Ed's judgment once again, but this time they got on the right train. Kathy concludes, "When we got off the train everyone was waiting. It turned out we arrived thirty minutes later than our original train. I was very relieved to see everyone. It was a very frightening experience and I will never forget it."

In focusing on her fears of separation, Kathy reveals her strong need for connection, for affiliation. Her story, like Kim's, emphasizes the importance of relationships, though in a different way. She reveals that she had a strong need to feel part of a group and no desire to rebel, to prove her independence, to differentiate herself from others. This conception of self was a liability as well as a strength in the sense that she became overly dependent on the male authority figure in the group, whom she saw as smarter and more competent than herself. In Belenky et al.'s terms, Kathy acted as if other voices and external truths were more powerful than her own. She did finally speak and act, though, taking it on herself to find out if they were on the right train and ushering the others off when she discovered they were not. She was clearly moving toward the development of an authentic voice and a way of knowing that integrates intuition with authoritative knowledge. After all, she was the real hero of the incident.

The men's narratives stress individuation rather than connection. They are stories of individual achievement or frustrated achievement and conclude by emphasizing separation rather than integration or reintegration into a community. Jim wrote about his "Final Flight," the last cross-country flight required for his pilot's license. That day, everything seemed to go wrong. First, his flight plan had a mistake in it that took $1\frac{1}{2}$ hours to correct. As a result, he left his hometown 2 hours behind schedule. Then the weather deteriorated, forcing him to fly as low as a person can safely fly, with the result that visibility was very poor. He landed safely at his first destination but flew past the second because he was enjoying the view too much. He says,

Then I was off again south bound for Benton Harbor. On the way south along the coast of Lake Michigan the scenery was a beautiful sight. This relieved some of the pressures and made me look forward to the rest of the flight. It was really nice to see the ice flows break away from the shore. While enjoying the view of a power plant on the shore of Lake Michigan I discovered I had flown past the airport.

He finally landed and took off again, but shortly thereafter had to confront darkness, a result of his being behind schedule. He says,

The sky turned totally black by the time I was half-way home. This meant flying in the dark which I had only done once before. Flying in the dark was also illegal for me to do at this time. One thing that made flying at night nice was that you could see lights that were over ninety miles away.

Jim does not emphasize his fear, despite the fact that his situation was more threatening than the one Kathy described, and his reference to his enjoyment of the scenery suggests that his anxiety was not paralyzing or debilitating. At times, his solitary flight was clearly as satisfying as Kim's communal one. When he focuses on the difficulties he encountered, he speaks only of his "problems" and "worries" and concludes that the day turned out to be "long and trying." He sums up his experience as follows: "That day I will long remember for both its significance in my goal in getting my pilot's license and all the problems or worries that it caused me during the long and problem-ridden flight." He emerges the somewhat shaken hero of his adventure; he has achieved his goal in the face of adversity. Significantly, he celebrates his return home by having a bite to eat at McDonald's by himself. His adventure does not end with a union or reunion with others.

Jim's story invites interpretation in the context of Chodorow's claims about male interactional patterns. Chodorow says that the male, in order to feel himself adequately masculine, must distinguish and differentiate himself from others. Jim's adventure was an entirely solitary one. It was also goal-directed—he wanted to obtain his pilot's license and, presumably, prove his competence to himself and others. His narrative calls into question, though, easy equations of abstract reasoning and impersonality with male modes of learning since Jim was clearly as capable as Kim of experiencing moments of exultation, of communion with nature.

Joe's narrative of achievement is actually a story of frustrated achievement, of conflicting attitudes toward an ethic of hard work and sacrifice to achieve a goal. When he was in high school, his father drove him twenty miles to swim practice and twenty miles home every Tuesday through

Friday night between October and March so he could practice for the swim team. He hated this routine and hated the Saturday morning swim meets even more but continued because he thought his parents, especially his father, wanted him to. He says, "I guess it was all for them, the cold workouts, the evening practices, the weekend meets. I had to keep going for them even though I hated it." Once he realized he was going through his agony for his parents rather than for himself, though, he decided to quit and was surprised to find that his parents supported him. Ultimately, though, he regretted his decision. He says,

> As it turns out now, I wish I had stuck with it. I really had a chance to go somewhere with my talent. I see kids my age who stuck with something for a long time and I envy them for their determination. I wish I had met up to the challenge of sticking with my swimming, because I could have been very good if I would have had their determination.

Joe is motivated to pursue swimming because he thinks his father will be disappointed if he gives it up. His father's presumed hold on him is clearly tenuous, however, because once Joe realizes that he is doing it for him rather than for himself, he quits. Finally, though, it is his gender role identification, his socialization into a male role and a male value system, that allows him to look back on his decision with regret. In college, he has become a competitor, an achiever. He now sees value in the long and painful practices, in a single-minded determination to succeed. The narrative reminds us of Chodorow's point that masculine identification is predominantly a gender role identification rather than identification with a particular parent.

I am hardly claiming that the four narratives are neat illustrations of the feminist positions discussed above. For one thing, those positions are rich in contradiction and complexity and defy easy illustration. For another, the narratives themselves are as often characterized by inconsistency and contradiction as by a univocality of theme and tone. Kathy is at once dependent and assertive; Joe can't quite decide if he should have been rebellious or disciplined. Nor am I claiming that what I have found here are characteristic patterns of male and female student writing. I would need a considerably larger and more representative sample to make such a claim hold. I might note, though, that I had little difficulty identifying essays that revealed patterns of difference among the twenty-four papers I had to choose from, and I could easily have selected others. Sharon, for instance, described her class trip to Chicago, focusing especially on the relationship she and her classmates were able to establish with her advisor. Diane described "An Unwanted Job" that she seemed unable to quit despite unpleasant working conditions. Mike, like Diane, was dissatisfied with his job, but he expressed his dissatisfaction and was fired. The frightening experience Russ described resulted from his failed attempt to give his car a tune-up; the radiator hose burst, and he found himself in the hospital recovering from third-degree burns. These are stories of relatedness or entanglement; of separation or frustrated achievement.

The description of the student essays is not meant to demonstrate the validity of feminist scholarship but to suggest, instead, that questions raised by feminist researchers and theorists do have a bearing on composition studies and should be pursued. We ought not assume that males and females use language in identical ways or represent the world in a similar fashion. And if their writing strategies and patterns of representation do differ, then ignoring those differences almost certainly means a suppression of women's separate ways of thinking and writing. Our models of the composing process are quite possibly better suited to describing men's ways of composing than to describing women's.[3]

PEDAGOGICAL STRATEGIES

The classroom provides an opportunity for exploring questions about gender differences in language use. Students, I have found, are avid inquirers into their own language processes. An approach I have had success with is to make the question of gender difference in behavior and language use the subject to be investigated in class. In one honors section of first-year English, for instance, course reading included selections from Mary Anne Ferguson's *Images of Women in Literature*, Gilligan's *In a Different Voice*, Alice Walker's *Meridian*, and James Joyce's *A Portrait of the Artist as a Young Man*. Students were also required to keep a reading journal and to submit two formal papers. The first was a description of people they know in order to arrive at generalizations about gender differences in behavior, the second a comparison of some aspect of the Walker and Joyce novels in the light of our class discussions.

During class meetings we shared journal entries, discussed the assigned literature, and self-consciously explored our own reading, writing, and speaking behaviors. In one session, for instance, we shared retellings of Irwin Shaw's "The Girls in Their Summer Dresses," an especially appropriate story since it describes the interaction of a husband and wife as they attempt to deal with the husband's apparently chronic habit of girl-watching. Most of the women were sympathetic to the female protagonist, and several males clearly identified strongly with the male protagonist.

The students reacted favorably to the course. They found Gilligan's book to be challenging, and they enjoyed the heated class discussions. The final journal entry of one of the strongest students in the class, Dorothy, suggests the nature of her development over the ten-week period:

> As this is sort of the wrap-up of what I've learned or how I feel about the class, I'll try to relate this entry to my first one on gender differences.
>
> I'm not so sure that men and women are so similar anymore, as I said in the first entry. The reactions in class especially make me think this. The men were so hostile toward Gilligan's book! I took no offense at it, but then again I'm not a man. I must've even overlooked the parts where she offended the men!
>
> Another thing really bothered me. One day after class, I heard two of the men talking in the hall about how you just have to be really careful about what you say in HU 101H about women, etc. *Why* do they have to be careful?! What did these two *really* want to say? That was pretty disturbing.
>
> However, I do still believe that MTU (or most any college actually) does bring out more similarities than differences. But the differences are still there—I know that.

Dorothy has begun to suspect that males and females read differently, and she has begun to suspect that they talk among themselves differently than they do in mixed company. The reading, writing, and discussing in the course have clearly alerted her to the possibility that gender affects the way in which readers, writers, and speakers use language.

This approach works especially well with honors students. I use somewhat different reading and writing assignments with non-honors students. In one class, for instance, I replaced the Gilligan book with an essay by Dale Spender on conversational patterns in high school classrooms. Students wrote a paper defending or refuting the Spender piece on the basis of their experiences in their own high schools. I have also devised ways of addressing feminist issues in composition courses in which the focus is not explicitly on gender differences. In a course designed to introduce students to fundamentals of research, for instance, students read Marge Piercy's *Woman on the Edge of Time* and did research on questions stimulated by it. They then shared their findings with the entire class in oral presentations. The approach led to wonderful papers on and discussions of the treatment of women in mental institutions, discrimination against minority women, and the ways in which technology can liberate women from oppressive roles.

592

I return now to my title and to the epigraph that introduces my essay. First, what does it mean to "compose as a woman"? Although the title invokes Jonathan Culler's "Reading as a Woman," a chapter in *On Deconstruction*, I do not mean to suggest by it that I am committed fully to Culler's deconstructive position. Culler maintains that "to read as a woman is to avoid reading as a man, to identify the specific defenses and distortions of male readings and provide correctives" (54). He concludes,

> For a woman to read as a woman is not to repeat an identity or an experience that is given but to play a role she constructs with reference to her identity as a woman, which is also a construct, so that the series can continue: a woman reading as a woman reading as a woman. The noncoincidence reveals an interval, a division within woman or within any reading subject and the "experience" of that subject. (64)

Culler is certainly correct that women often read as men and that they have to be encouraged to defend against this form of alienation. The strategy he suggests is almost entirely reactive, though. To read as a woman is to avoid reading as a man, to be alerted to the pitfalls of men's ways of reading.[4] Rich, too, warns of the dangers of immasculation, of identifying against oneself and learning to think like a man, and she, too, emphasizes the importance of critical activity on the part of the woman student—refusing to accept the givens of our culture, making connections between facts and ideas which men have left unconnected. She is well aware that thinking as a woman involves active construction, the recreation of one's identity. But she also sees value in recovering women's lived experience. In fact, she suggests that women maintain a critical posture in order to get in touch with that experience—to name it, to uncover that which is hidden, to make present that which has been absent. Her approach is active rather than reactive. Women's experience is not entirely a distorted version of male reality, it is not entirely elusive, and it is worthy of recuperation. We must alert our women students to the dangers of immasculation and provide them with a critical perspective. But we must also encourage them to become self-consciously aware of what their experience in the world has been and how this experience is related to the politics of gender. Then we must encourage our women students to write from the power of that experience.

NOTES

1. I received invaluable feedback on drafts of this essay from Carol Berkenkotter, Art Young, Marilyn Cooper, John Willinsky, Diane Shoos, John Flynn, Richard Gebhardt, and three anonymous *CCC* reviewers.

2. The 1988 Conference on College Composition and Communication was a notable exception. It had a record number of panels on feminist or gender-related issues and a number of sessions devoted to political concerns. I should add, too, that an exception to the generalization that feminist studies and composition studies have not confronted each other is Cynthia Caywood and Gillian Overing's very useful anthology, *Teaching Writing: Pedagogy, Gender, and Equity*. In their introduction to the book, Caywood and Overing note the striking parallels between writing theory and feminist theory. They conclude, "[T]he process model, insofar as it facilitates and legitimizes the fullest expression of the individual voice, is compatible with the feminist re-visioning of hierarchy, if not essential to it" (xiv). Pamela Annas, in her essay, "Silences: Feminist Language Research and the Teaching of Writing," describes a course she teaches at the University of Massachusetts at Boston, entitled "Writing as Women." In the course, she focuses on the question of silence—"what kinds of silence there are; the voices inside you that tell you to be quiet, the voices outside you that drown you out or politely dismiss what you say or do not understand you, the silence inside you that avoids saying anything important even to yourself, internal and external forms of censorship, and the stress that it produces" (3–4). Carol A. Stanger in "The Sexual Politics of the One-to-One Tutorial Approach and Collaborative Learning" argues that the one-to-one tutorial is essentially hierarchical and hence a male mode of teaching whereas collaborative learning is female and relational rather than hierarchical. She uses Gilligan's images of the ladder and the web to illustrate her point. Elisabeth Daeumer and Sandra Runzo suggest that the teaching of writing is comparable to the activity of mothering in that it is a form of "women's work." Mothers socialize young children to insure that they become acceptable citizens, and teachers' work, like the work of mothers, is usually devalued (45–46).

3. It should be clear by now that my optimistic claim at the outset of the essay that the field of composition studies has feminized our conception of written communication needs qualification. I have already mentioned that the field has developed, for the most part, independent of feminist studies and as a result has not explored written communication in the context of women's special needs and problems. Also, feminist inquiry is beginning to reveal that work in cognate fields that have influenced the development of composition studies is androcentric. For an exploration of the androcentrism of theories of the reading process see Patrocinio P. Schweickart, "Reading Ourselves: Toward a Feminist Theory of Reading."

4. Elaine Showalter, in "Reading as a Woman: Jonathan Culler and the Deconstruction of Feminist Criticism," argues that "Culler's deconstructionist priorities lead him to overstate the essentialist dilemma of defining the *woman* reader, when in most cases what is intended and implied is a *feminist* reader" (126).

WORKS CITED

Annas, Pamela J. "Silences: Feminist Language Research and the Teaching of Writing." *Teaching Writing: Pedagogy, Gender, and Equity*. Ed. Cynthia L. Caywood and Gillian R. Overing. Albany: State U of New York P, 1987. 3–17.

Belenky, Mary Field, et al. *Women's Ways of Knowing: The Development of Self, Voice, and Mind*. New York: Basic Books, 1986.

Britton, James, et al. *The Development of Writing Abilities (11–18)*. London: Macmillan Education, 1975.

Caywood, Cynthia L., and Gillian R. Overing. Introduction. *Teaching Writing: Pedagogy, Gender, and Equity*. Ed. Cynthia L. Caywood and Gillian R. Overing. Albany: State U of New York P, 1987. xi–xvi.

Chodorow, Nancy. *The Reproduction of Mothering: Psychoanalysis and the Sociology of Gender.* Berkeley: U of California P, 1978.

Culler, Jonathan. *On Deconstruction: Theory and Criticism after Structuralism.* Ithaca: Cornell UP, 1982.

Daeumer, Elisabeth, and Sandra Runzo. "Transforming the Composition Classroom." *Teaching Writing: Pedagogy, Gender, and Equity.* Ed. Cynthia L. Caywood and Gillian R. Overing. Albany: State U of New York P, 1987. 45–62.

Gilligan, Carol. *In a Different Voice: Psychological Theory and Women's Development.* Cambridge: Harvard UP, 1982.

Hairston, Maxine. "Breaking Our Bonds and Reaffirming Our Connections." *College Composition and Communication* 36 (October 1985): 272–82.

Howe, Florence. "Identity and Expression: A Writing Course for Women." *College English* 32 (May 1971): 863–71. Rpt. in Howe, *Myths of Coeducation: Selected Essays, 1964–1983.* Bloomington: Indiana UP, 1984. 28–37.

Kohlberg, Lawrence. "Moral Stages and Moralization: The Cognitive-Development Approach." *Moral Development and Behavior.* Ed. T. Lickona. New York: Holt, 1976. 31–53.

Perry, William G. *Forms of Intellectual and Ethical Development in the College Years.* New York: Holt, Rinehart & Winston, 1970.

Rich, Adrienne. "Taking Women Students Seriously." *On Lies, Secrets, and Silence: Selected Prose, 1966–1978.* New York: W.W. Norton, 1979. 237–45.

———. "'When We Dead Awaken': Writing as Re-Vision." *On Lies, Secrets, and Silence: Selected Prose, 1966–1978.* New York: W.W. Norton, 1979. 33–49.

Schweickart, Patrocinio P. "Reading Ourselves: Toward a Feminist Theory of Reading." *Gender and Reading: Essays on Readers, Texts and Contexts.* Ed. Elizabeth A. Flynn and Patrocinio P. Schweickart. Baltimore: Johns Hopkins UP, 1986. 31–62.

Showalter, Elaine. "Reading as a Woman: Jonathan Culler and the Deconstruction of Feminist Criticism." *Men and Feminism.* Ed. Alice Jardine and Paul Smith. New York: Methuen, 1987. 123–27.

Stanger, Carol A. "The Sexual Politics of the One-to-One Tutorial Approach and Collaborative Learning." *Teaching Writing: Pedagogy, Gender, and Equity.* Ed. Cynthia L. Caywood and Gillian R. Overing. Albany: State U of New York P, 1987. 31–44.

Feminism in Composition
Inclusion, Metonymy, and Disruption

Joy Ritchie and Kathleen Boardman

At a time when composition is engaged in clarifying its theoretical, political, and pedagogical histories, it is appropriate to construct a story of feminism's involvement in the disciplinary conversations. Despite the recent burgeoning of feminist perspectives in our discipline, it is not easy to delineate how feminism has functioned over the past three decades to shape and critique our understandings of the gendered nature of writing, teaching, and institutions. Although some accounts suggest that feminism, until recently, has been absent or at least late-blooming in the field, we find a more complex relationship in our rereading of essays and books in composition written from a feminist perspective—in particular, the many accounts of personal experience in the field written by feminists and by women since the 1970s. In this essay we look, and look again, at the few articles and notes that appeared in *CCC*, *College English*, and *English Journal* in the early 1970s. We also focus on feminist retrospective accounts—re-visions of composition written since the mid-1980s.

In writing this brief critical historical survey, we have found ourselves working from various impulses. First, we want to document and celebrate the vitality of feminism in composition, from its early manifestations in the small scattering of essays published in the 1970s (some of them frequently cited, others forgotten) to the explosion of feminist theory and well-documented feminist practice of the last decade. We wish to point out that much early feminist work in composition is not documented in our official publications,

Reprinted from *College Composition and Communication* 50.4 (June 1999): 585–606. Used with permission.

having occurred in informal conversations, in classrooms, and in committee meetings. At the same time, we want to suggest ways to examine and theorize experiential accounts—both published and unpublished—of feminism in composition. We must also consider seriously the causes and consequences of the delay in feminism's emergence in the published forums of our discipline and the extent to which feminism, despite its recent vitality, has remained contained or marginalized in composition. Finally, we hope to speculate on the positive and negative potential of inclusive, metonymic, and disruptive strategies for feminism's contribution to composition's narratives.

In the past decade, feminists have been visibly active in our discipline. They have examined the subjectivity of the gendered student and the position of women writers in the profession. Questioning assumptions about genre, form, and style, they have provided an impetus to seek alternative writing practices. Feminist perspectives have produced analyses of the gendered nature of the classroom, the feminization of English teaching, the working conditions for female teachers, and the implications of feminist theory for scholarship. Feminist scholars like Andrea Lunsford and Cheryl Glenn have begun rewriting the rhetorical tradition by reclaiming, refiguring, and regendering "Rhetorica." They are also critiquing earlier constructions of history and scholarship in composition. And from a different direction, scholars are drawing upon feminist, African American, lesbian, Native American, and class-based examinations of difference in order to complicate definitions of diversity within composition. Two recent essay collections, Susan Jarratt and Lynn Worsham's *Feminism and Composition Studies: In Other Words*, and Louise Phelps and Janet Emig's *Feminine Principles and Women's Experience in American Composition and Rhetoric*, especially highlight the strength of feminism(s) in composition and show how important feminism has been in shaping women's definitions of themselves, their work, and their commitment to pursuing questions of equity in the field.

Yet in the 1970s, while the work of composition as an emerging discipline was occurring right next door to, down the hall from, or in the basement under the work of feminist linguists and literary scholars, composition's official published discussions were largely silent on issues of gender. There is little explicit evidence of systematic theorizing about gender from the 1950s to the late 1980s. As late as 1988, Elizabeth Flynn could write, "For the most part . . . the fields of feminist studies and composition studies have not engaged each other in a serious or systematic way" (425). Indeed, when we began this study, we framed it as a paradox: prior to the mid-1980s, feminism seemed absent from composition but present among compositionists. From those early investigations we pulled one useful reminder: that the connections of composition and feminism have not been an inevitable result of the presence of so many women in the field. But subsequent conversations with a number of longtime teachers and scholars, who spoke to us about their own feminist beliefs and activities in composition dating back to the 1960s, reminded us that the near-absence of feminism from our publications does not constitute absence from the field.

The absence-presence binary also did not help us explain our own history as feminists in composition. As secondary English teachers, teaching women's literature and applying our feminist perspectives to high school courses in the 1970s, we moved into graduate courses and tenure track jobs in composition in the late 1980s and 1990s. Reflecting on our own experience, we recognized that much of the creative feminist energy in composition's history is not visible in the publications we searched: it appeared in informal conversations, in basement classrooms, and in committees on which women served. This energy might be viewed as ephemeral, yet we can testify, along with others, that it created solidarity among women, influenced students and colleagues, and helped form an epistemology on which later feminist work could grow. Sharon Crowley reminds us further that composition allowed and acknowledged women's participation in teaching and scholarship before many other disciplines began to do so—as we see from the important work of Josephine Miles, Winifred Horner, Ann Berthoff, Janet Emig and others. Still, Theresa Enos' collection of anecdotes from women in the field over the last several decades cautions us that the job conditions and security for many of these practitioners were terrible.

Crowley's and Enos' different perspectives point again to a history of women and feminism in composition that cannot be constructed in a tidy narrative. In the documents and accounts we have read and heard, we find three overlapping tropes that shed light on the roles feminism has played in composition and in the strategies women have used to gain a place in its conversations: (1) Following the pattern of developing feminist thought in the 1970s and 1980s, many early feminist accounts in composition sought *inclusion* and equality for women. (2) More recent accounts like those of Louise Phelps and Janet Emig posit feminism as a "subterranean" unspoken presence (xv), and Susan Jarratt and Laura Brady suggest the *metonymy* or contiguity of feminism and composition. (3) Also developing during this time has been what feminist postmodernists define as *disruption* and critique of hegemonic narratives—resistance, interruption, and finally redirection of composition's business as usual.

While it's tempting to posit this as a linear, evolutionary set of tropes— that women have grown out of and into as we've matured theoretically—we find it too restrictive to do so. These narratives coexist and have multiple functions, often depending on the historical or theoretical context in which they are read. For example, some early attempts at inclusion, based on experiential accounts, function also as disruptive narratives, and a number of very recent accounts might be characterized as primarily metonymic narratives. Furthermore, each of these tropes has both advantages and disadvantages for feminism in composition: for example, a narrative aimed at *including* women may also function to *contain* feminism within narrow boundaries. We also emphasize that we are not interested in categorizing narratives (and narrators) as "inclusionist," "disruptionist," and so on. Rather we hope to tease out the tropes, show how these narratives can be reread in multiple ways, and suggest how each one enacts one or more epistemological positions with respect to women's experience, identity, and difference.

As we reread for these rhetorical strategies, we find that the conceptions of experience in each of these sets of narratives also require examination. Most of the feminist writing in composition is grounded in accounts of personal experience. For example, many women have told powerful stories of their first recognition of their marginality in a field they had previously thought of as theirs. We must beware of reading these moving accounts too transparently and untheoretically. In her essay "Experience," Joan W. Scott offers a useful caution:

> When experience is taken as the origin of knowledge, the vision of the individual subject (the person who had the experience or the historian who recounts it) becomes the bedrock of evidence upon which explanation is built. Questions about the constructed nature of experience, about how subjects are constituted as different in the first place, about how one's vision is structured—about language (or discourse) and history—are left aside. (25)

Scott reminds us that narratives of experience should be encountered not as uncontested truth but as catalysts for further analysis of the conditions that shape experience.

We want to be clear about our view of experience: we are not dismissing such accounts but only suggesting ways to read and listen to them. The problem is not that these narratives are personal or that they are experiential, but that they are often untheorized. In understanding both the value and the limitations of feminist uses of experience in our field, we have found the work of Scott and of Rosemary Hennessy particularly useful. Both address "experience" as a construct and show ways to continue to value women's experiences as sources of knowledge; but they also suggest ways to theorize experience to make it a more critical rhetorical tool. Scott advises us to keep in mind that "experience is at once always already an interpretation and is in need of interpretation. What counts as experience is neither self-evident nor straightforward; it is always contested, always therefore political" (37). Hennessy views experience as a critical tool for examining the values and ideologies used to construct women's experiences, but she adds an important qualification for ensuring that women's experience is not narrowly read. Any critical theorizing of women's experience must be undertaken in the context of a continual "re-contextualization of the relationship between personal and group history and political priorities" (Minnie Bruce Pratt, qtd. in Hennessy 99) and in relation to the "counterhegemonic discourses" of others (99). We have found that by attending to certain feminist tropes in our discipline, we can not only begin to tease out the relationships between composition and feminism, but also gain a better sense of the important dialectical relationships between experience and theory.

ADDING WOMEN: NARRATIVES AIMED AT INCLUSION

Correcting the long absence of women from intellectual and political landscapes, inserting women's perspectives into contexts dominated by patriarchy, and giving women equal status with men have constituted one of the central feminist projects—that of *inclusion*. This effort to add women has been criticized retrospectively as ineffective because it arises from Enlightenment conceptions of individual autonomy and the unquestioned "truth" of individual experience. Discussions of inclusion of women *as* women may reinforce essentialist or biological definitions of gender, and they often neglect to theorize the discourses that keep women and minorities marginalized. Most critically, many attempts to include women in the conversations of the field have in fact added only white, middle-class, heterosexual women. Despite these criticisms, we need to reread these attempts from their cultural context and for their first steps toward gender awareness. As Suzanne Clark reminds us, "feminists challenging a certain kind of feminism in composition represent a luxury: women now have a sufficient number to play out [their] anxieties of influence" (94). Our analyses need to take into account cultural and historical contexts out of which women were working that made these assumptions viable at the time.

Some of the first published evidence of the initiative to add women to the conversation came in NCTE publications aimed primarily at secondary teachers. The March 1972 *English Journal* printed "The Undiscovered," Robert A. Bennett's NCTE presidential address of the previous November.

In highlighting "the undiscovered human resources of our professional organization" (352), Bennett includes girls and women among "those peoples of American society who have not yet been allowed to make their fullest contribution":

> The talents of the great number of women teachers who are today still non-members of the Council or who are inactive in Council affairs, provide another undiscovered resource. As a professional organization, we must reach out to these women and encourage them . . . to become full partners in our common effort. (353)

After urging the organization to examine wage and promotion policies, document discriminatory practices, and work for recognition of women in curriculum and pedagogy, Bennett declares, "NCTE must take a stand for recognition of the contribution of women to society and to our profession. We have not done it. Let's get at it" (353).

Two months later, *English Journal* carried a short "Open Letter from Janet Emig, Chairwoman, NCTE Committee on the Role and Image of Women," asking the membership to nominate committee members and to send information about any "instances of discrimination against women in the profession, either in the form of a brief narrative or, if you are the woman involved, as a signed or as an anonymous case history" (710). A direct result of NCTE's new commitment to include women, Emig's committee was soliciting stories that would potentially disrupt business-as-usual in the profession, (a practice that Theresa Enos repeated more than 20 years later for *Gender Roles and Faculty Lives in Rhetoric and Composition*). The CCCC Committee on the Status of Women also continues to solicit narratives, in various forums, in order to ascertain more clearly the status of women in the field.

While a review of *CCC* from the late 1960s through the late 1980s uncovers few essays or other documents that would indicate a gendered feminist consciousness in composition, two landmark special issues of *College English*, in 1971 and 1972, report on the newly formed MLA Commission on the Status of Women in the Profession and document courses designed by feminists in English to reshape the curriculum from the standpoint of women students. The narratives in these special issues set the pattern for the impulse a decade or more later in composition to add women to its perspectives. Arising from the writers' own consciousness-raising experiences, the narratives articulate the potential for student and teacher subjectivities that are not neutral or universal but uniquely influenced by the textual, social, and political context of gender. Florence Howe's impassioned 1971 essay, in which she inserts her own personal account of discrimination, reports the inequities in women's status she uncovered as chair of the MLA commission. In addition to these first attempts to address women's low status in the profession, Howe and Elaine Showalter both illustrate their efforts to rectify the lack of women's texts and perspectives in English courses. Showalter describes her newly organized course, "The Educated Woman in Literature," in practical terms, and Howe presents a writing course she designed to help women alter their self-image "from centuries of *belief* in their inferiority, as well as from male-dominated and controlled institutions" (863). A second special issue of *College English* (October 1972) contains important essays concerning women's inclusion in the discipline of English, among them Tillie Olsen's "Women Who Are Writers in Our Century: One Out of Twelve" and Adrienne Rich's "When We Dead Awaken: Writing as Re-vision." Each of these essays seeks to insert women—their perspectives, their writing, their lived experiences—into a discipline from which they had been excluded.

In "Taking Women Students Seriously," her important 1978 essay emphasizing the necessity of including women's perspectives in education, Adrienne Rich described how the experience of changing from one teaching context to another allowed her to translate the critical questions she asked as a writing instructor of minority students into parallel questions she needed to ask about women students:

> How does a woman gain a sense of her *self* in a system . . . which devalues work done by women, denies the importance of female experience, and is physically violent toward women? . . . How do we, as women, teach women students a canon of literature which has consistently excluded or depreciated female experience? (239)

These early essays set a pattern for subsequent inclusive questions that women in composition began asking. Beginning by describing their own consciousness-raising experiences in their essays, the writers moved on to document the concrete changes in teaching and critical perspectives they advocated. What are women's experiences in classrooms, in institutions? How do women use language? How are women writers different from male writers? Questions like these included women in ways that had not been possible in a "gender-blind" field of composition; they set the stage for writers in the 1980s like Pamela Annas and Elizabeth Flynn to engage them further in work that again sought women's inclusion in the field and sparked feminist discussions for a newer generation of women.[1]

In the late 70s, the trope of inclusion appeared in essays applying feminist language research to composition by investigating claims made by

Robin Lakoff in her 1975 *Language and Woman's Place*—that women, by using a ladylike middle-class language, contributed to their own oppression. Lakoff's argument reflected the "dominance" approach to women's language use that was prominent among feminists of the 70s: attributing gender differences in language mainly to social oppression of women. Joan Bolker's 1979 *College English* article, "Teaching Griselda to Write," is a practitioner's account of her experience struggling with the absence of voice and authority in the work of "good-girl" student writers. The many citations of this short article in the past 19 years suggest that it has resonated with feminists in composition. In 1978, two articles examining women's "different" style appeared in CCC. In "The Feminine Style: Theory and Fact," Mary P. Hiatt discusses her study of the stylistic features of women's and men's writing. She reports "clear evidence of a feminine style . . . [that] is in fact rather different from the common assumptions about it" (226). Contrary to Lakoff's generalizations about women's oral language, women's written style, according to Hiatt, has "no excesses of length or complexity or emotion" (226). In "Women in a Double-Bind: Hazards of the Argumentative Edge," Sheila Ortiz Taylor draws composition instructors' attention to the "invisible, though real, disadvantage" that women students face in writing courses because "both the methods and the goals of such classes are alien to them" (385). She argues that the competitive, impersonal style of traditional argument alienates women; she urges instructors to validate "conversational tone, dramatic technique, and intimate reader involvement" (389).

Among the first composition articles to train the spotlight on women's language experiences, these essays highlight deficiency. (Ironically, as in Lakoff's book, an essentialized "woman" is both *included* and *found lacking*.) Bolker, Taylor, and Hiatt respond differently to the idea that women students must have special problems because a feminine style represents deficiency. Taylor uses the language of victimization to describe the woman student: "She must feel that something is wrong with her, a self-destructive disapproval common enough in women. . . . of course, much of the damage has been done by the time our students reach us. They have been taught a special language" (385). But Taylor adds that a feminine style of argument is only "deficient" because society has refused to validate it. Bolker believes that with more self-esteem and voice, the good girl can be a contender in the arena of the dominant discourse. Hiatt implies that readers need to be more discerning about the gender differences they *think* they see. None of these articles is heavily theorized; with the possible exception of Hiatt's, they arise from and return directly to classroom experience. Because they do not attend closely to larger systemic issues of power and discourse, these studies also make it possible for feminist concerns to be contained, encapsulated, or dismissed as "women's issues." Yet essays like these deserve credit for challenging the field's gender-blindness by insisting that women be included in narratives of classroom writing practices. They have contributed to a sense of intuitive connection between composition and those who ask, at least implicitly, "What difference might it make if the student (or teacher) is female?"

MAKING INTUITIVE CONNECTIONS: NARRATIVES OF METONYMIC RELATIONSHIP

In their introduction to *Teaching Writing: Pedagogy, Gender, and Equity*, one of the first books to connect writing and feminism in composition, Cynthia Caywood and Gillian Overing say that despite the absence of explicit discussion, they had experienced as practitioners an "intuitive understanding" of a "fundamental connection" between feminism and revisionist writing theory. While highlighting an absence of attention to gender, they also posit a more complicated reading of this absence by pointing to the nearly parallel lives of composition and feminist theory. According to this story, the two have run for years in the same direction, along close trajectories; to bring the fields together it is necessary only to notice the shared goals and common directions, and to make connections more visible and explicit. Caywood and Overing ask, "At what point did our parallel interests in feminism and revisionist writing theory converge?" (xi). More recently Susan Jarratt, Laura Brady, Janet Emig, and Louise Phelps have suggested that the boundaries have been permeable between feminist work in literary studies, the social sciences, and composition. This resonates with our own sense, as practitioners in the 70s, that boundaries between feminism and composition were often marked by unarticulated overlaps and crossovers. This permeability may have been partly the result of the interdisciplinary nature of composition, which drew for its theoretical substance from linguistics, cognitive and developmental psychology, and literary criticism. But while this intuitive connection may have created alliances among women in composition and feminists in other fields, it may also have delayed the emergence of feminist theory and continued its marginalization in the field.

Various factors account for the intuitive sense of connection that many of us have experienced and narrated. First, emerging pedagogical theories spoke a language that resonated with feminism's concerns of the time: coming to voice and consciousness, illuminating experience and its relationship to individual identity, playing the believing game rather than the doubting game, collaborating rather than competing, subverting hierarchy in the classroom. These watchwords characterized composition's link to liberal political and social agendas shared by feminist scholars in other disciplines and aimed at challenging established traditions, epistemologies, and practices of the academy.[2] Sharon Crowley explicitly connects Dewey's progressivism with Janet Emig's development of "process pedagogies," arguing that this link between progressivism and process pedagogies was vitally important in reconceptualizing composition "as an art rather than a course," and "because its theorists discovered a way to talk about student writing that authorized teachers to think of themselves as researchers" (17). This reconceptualization resonated for feminists theoretically and politically.

Secondly, at that time many women in the profession were doing double-duty as composition and literature teachers. Among the *College English* authors represented in the special issues we have pointed out, Florence Howe taught composition and wrote about how her course focused on women, and Adrienne Rich taught writing with Mina Shaughnessy in the SEEK program at CCNY. Many feminist composition instructors, coming from literary critical backgrounds, continued reading in their fields and appropriating whatever feminist approaches seemed useful—much as compositionists of the 80s and 90s have appropriated the work of Belenky, Clinchy, Goldberger, and Tarule and poststructuralist feminists.

The material conditions surrounding women in composition have also contributed to a felt sense of the feminist connections to our work. Composition was and still is constructed as women's work, and the majority of workers were women; many of us teaching writing or working on composition degrees during the 70s and 80s were newly arrived from secondary teaching. Surrounded by colleagues with similar career patterns, we entered conversations that enacted an interplay between our lives and our professional work. The drawbacks of the "feminization" of the field were not theorized until several years later.

Finally, as the field developed in the 1970s, although journal editors and the professional hierarchy were primarily male, the names of women were also moving into prominent places: Mina Shaughnessy, Janet Emig, Ann Berthoff, Sondra Perl, Anne Gere, Lillian Bridwell-Bowles, and others were writing many of the important articles and books we studied. Many feminists refer with appreciation to the "foremothers," first for their presence as models, and secondly for their ideas which, though not articulated in terms of gender, are often read, in retrospect, as consistent with feminist practice. In many cases, these ideas have to do with nurturing, collaboration, revisioning, and decentering.

Some retrospective accounts use theory to make the composition-feminism connections less intuitive, more explicit. Turning from foremothers

606

to "midwives," Carolyn Ericksen Hill uses feminist theory to read composition history through the gendering of practices, of theories, and of the field itself.[3] She reads the label "midwives" back onto male composition theorists active in the 60s and early 70s: Peter Elbow, Ken Macrorie, John Schultz, and William Coles, Jr. Without necessarily claiming them as feminists, she can, with the aid of postmodern theory, gender their approach as feminine and place their work in a certain feminist context: they helped "birth" the experiential self. The expressivist/nurturing feminist connection has often been made in passing, but Hill's label "midwives" claims these key composition figures for feminist theorizing—and also marginalizes them. In the 1990s, Hill argues, these four "expressivist" figures have been pushed to the edge of a newly theorized and professionalized field; their gender-blindness and humanistic model of the autonomous self have had to make way for gender difference and shifting subject positions, powerful constructs for feminist analysis. Hill sees in the compartmentalization—rather than dynamic rereading—of the four men's so-called expressivism a parallel with the "othering" of "woman," and of feminism, that continues to occur.

The rereading of "foremothers"—or even "midwives"—as feminist precursors may also be problematic if it ignores context and complexity, as we see from a few examples of foremothers who resist labeling. In the late 1970s, Ann Berthoff roundly rejected the gendering of logic and the either/ or-ism of all discussions of women's ways of knowing; she reaffirmed this rejection at the 1998 CCCC convention. Still, the foremother figures can both exemplify and disrupt the notion of the feminization of the field. As fore*mothers* they are both marginalized and typically characterized as nurturers. But insofar as they are envisioned as *fore*mothers, as founders, they are not feminized but rather constructed in a traditionally masculine position.

Evidence that stories of connection continue to resonate with us may be found in Jan Zlotnik Schmidt's introduction to *Women/Writing/Teaching*, a 1998 collection of essays by women writers and teachers. Schmidt emphasizes the importance of women's experience in making writing-teaching connections and expresses her hope that readers will also "explore their own life stories, their development of selfhood, their multiple identities as writers, teachers, and writing teachers" (xii). Retrospective narratives that create foremothers, midwives, connections, and nurturing community in composition's history foreground the double potential of the metonymic relationship between feminism and composition. This intuitive connection helps to create a sense of solidarity and vitality. But it may also reinforce the very structures that keep feminist perspectives contained in a separate, benign category rather than giving feminist analysis a central place, or at least keeping it insistently, vocally disruptive of the discipline's metanarratives. For example, some feminist practitioners have told powerful stories about replacing hierarchical, agonistic classroom environments with decentered, nurturing classrooms based on an ethic of care. But, as Eileen Schell argues, "femin*i*nist pedagogy, although compelling, may reinforce rather than critique or transform patriarchal structures by reinscribing what Magda Lewis calls the 'woman as caretaker ideology'" ("The Cost" 74, our italics).

Granting feminism's intuitive connections with a discipline that challenged current-traditional conceptions of language and introduced new decentered writing pedagogies, it is also important to recognize that some feminist agendas were more likely to disrupt than to aid composition's early progress toward full disciplinary status. Composition needed to build institutional legitimacy in the traditional academy; a fundamental feminist goal was to disrupt rather than extend patriarchal discourses and their assumptions about knowledge. Composition sought a single theory of the writing process and the writing subject; feminist theorists challenged notions of a singular universal concept of truth. The trope of metonymy may have difficulty expanding to cover some of these adversarial relationships.

FEMINIST DISRUPTIONS

Composition has many narratives of feminist disruption which emphasize neither inclusion nor intuitive connection but rather represent some form of feminism (newly experienced or theorized) reaching back to reread and even reconfigure past experience and practice. We see increasing numbers of current feminists drawing on postmodern theories to analyze and critique the basic "process" narratives of composition's first 20 years, to raise questions about difference(s), and to critique disciplinary practices and structures that have shaped composition. Disruption is often linked to postmodern theories of power, discourse, and ideology rather than to consciousness-raising sessions, discussions of pedagogy, or attempts to create equitable and inclusive conditions for women. In order to intervene significantly in power structures that keep women subordinate, feminists investigate and uncover the contradictions in those dominant structures. The feminist narratives we have reread remind us, however, that efforts at inclusion, connection, and disruption often work synthetically rather than as adversaries or as unequal partners. As Theresa Enos says, her book's "most powerful use of 'data' is the narrative, in the stories that help us define our places in academia so that we can better trace our future" (1).

The explicit recognition of composition's lack of attention to women's material lives has led women in anger, frustration, and recognition to tell the stories of their coming to awareness. A classic feminist narrative of the early 70s is the story of a "good girl," silenced by her compulsion to please, whose recognition of her oppression releases an anger strong enough to overcome politeness and fear; thus she finds both her voice and an agenda for change. The consciousness-raising sessions of the late 60s and early 70s provided a model for this narrative, as did the two special women's issues of *College English*, 1971–72, that we have mentioned. In "When We Dead Awaken," Rich told her own story of frustration at the demands that she be good at all the roles women were supposed to play, while Howe, after narrating how she had acquiesced in years of inequitable treatment, wrote, "Eighteen months as commission Chairwoman [of the MLA Commission on the Status of Women] has eroded that wry smile. I feel now a growing anger as I come to realize that . . . I am not alone in my state" (849).

Many of today's feminist accounts of the 60s and 70s follow a similar pattern. Lynn Z. Bloom's essay, "Teaching College English as a Woman" (1992), is a scathing look at the bad old days in college English, when a woman in the field—whether student or teacher—would be exploited if she did not get angry and speak up. Bloom recalls a conversion experience when, as a part-time composition instructor, she finally was able to obtain office space: in a basement room full of desks, on the floor under the stairs, next to the kitty litter. Surveying these wretched conditions, she told herself, "If I ever agree to do this again, I deserve what I get" (821). Separated by more than 20 years, Bloom's and Howe's angry accounts illustrate what we might call individual, liberal disruption: the idea that once a woman sees clearly, her life is changed, and she is thus empowered to become effectively active for change and reform. These accounts show the "revisioning" that feminist thinking has enabled individual women to do. We read these accounts as disruptive because in addition to realizing that the liberal Enlightenment agenda hasn't included *her*, each of these women also recognizes that she must take action to disrupt and change the structures that have kept her subordinate.

Other women who are currently doing feminist work in composition studies have provided similar testimonies of naive compliance, oppressed silence, eventual recognition, and new outspokenness.[4] That we now have so many such narratives may mean that women in composition today are finally in a position to claim the authority of the autobiographical; it may also mean that, largely due to feminist efforts, the conventions of scholarly discourse have expanded to include the personal narrative as a way of situating oneself in one's scholarship. But perhaps the personal testimony remains an effective—and still necessary—tool of disruption. Many of these stories are disruptive because they expose "the pattern of well-rewarded, male supervision of under-rewarded, female workers" that has existed in composition and "is entrenched in our whole culture" (Enos vii). The disruption that is so central to the consciousness-raising narrative itself also highlights gaps in our reading of our past and of business as usual. Rereading the consciousness-raising essays that have recurred in composition over the past 25 years can show us more sites where women have been silent but where feminists want to rupture that silence.

Many narratives deal with experiences in teaching and department politics, but a 1993 retrospective account by Nancy McCracken, Lois Green, and Claudia Greenwood tells how they acquiesced as researchers to a field characterized by "a persistent silence on the subject of gender" in its "landmark research studies on writing development and writing processes" (352). Now writing collaboratively, they return to studies of teacher responses to student writing that they had published earlier (and separately), reinterpreting those studies in terms of gender differences. These authors emphasize that until the late 80s the climate in composition studies had made it difficult to notice or report gender differences in empirical studies: "None of us went looking for gender differences. When the data began to speak of gender, we dared not listen" (356). They recount their worries about being accused of biological determinism, about seeming to exclude men, about appearing unprofessional, and about calling attention to themselves as women. Now, they say, they feel empowered not only to note gender difference but to insist on it. Theirs is not a story of breaking silence by themselves. Instead, the current "research environment in which it is both important and safe to study the interplay between students' gender and their development as writers" (354) has made it possible to revise their findings. Their story is not about singular heroism but about collaboration, in a network of mutual support, in a research/scholarly environment that has made discursive structures more visible. Their story is not about going solo against a hostile discipline but about rereading the field and their own complicity. Their reading disrupts, among other things, their *own* research, by requiring that they return to it and revise it.

Some of the early disruptive narratives we have mentioned are reformist, and they may even be read as attempts at inclusion as well as disruption. Another form of disruptive narrative is less grounded in the impulse for individual disruption and change, but seeks wider consideration of difference. Such critiques often create conflict and may evoke more resistance because they demand changes in institutional and epistemological structures that conflict with composition's continuing need to establish legitimacy. They support the emergence of different perspectives rather than suppressing them. In these accounts difference is expanded from the single male/female binary to differences, taking into account multiple inflections of social class, sexual orientation, and race. For example, Harriet Malinowitz's study of lesbian and gay students in writing classes and Shirley Wilson Logan's writing on the confluence of race and gender in composition both attempt to expand our understanding of what differences can mean in composition classrooms. They articulate the connections among differences as well as show the privileging or erasure of some categories by others. Writing out of her own experience as a Chinese student speaking several languages, Min-Zhan Lu has drawn upon third-world and minority feminisms as well as other cultural theorists to disrupt composition teachers' view of the conflicts students face in negotiating the political, linguistic, and rhetorical "borderlands" between home and school. She reopens a debate about the processes of acculturation and accommodation at work in writing classrooms, particularly those that serve minority and immigrant students. In doing so, she rereads the work of Mina Shaughnessy, Thomas Farrell, Kenneth Bruffee, and others in light of current contexts in order to critique the wider public debates about literacy and to highlight the cultural conflicts and necessary resistances of today's students on the margins.

At times these disruptions can create tension and anger even among feminists, highlighting the way feminism itself is shaped by and embedded in existing hierarchical discourses. This conflict may seem to undermine any sense of solidarity that existed when feminism appeared in a more intuitive rather than carefully articulated and scrutinized form. But in fact, such conflict may produce one of feminism's most important benefits—the proliferation of differences. Nedra Reynolds argues: "Feminists daring to criticize other feminists have opened up spaces for analyzing difference; they interrupted the discourses of feminism in the singular to make possible feminism in the plural" (66). Other disruptive narratives of difference are only now emerging and await further exploration. Constructs like Gloria Anzaldúa's *mestiza*, Trinh T. Minh-ha's subject-in-the-making, Donna Haraway's cyborg, and Judith Butler's performer of gender extend postmodern notions of difference in disruptive directions with their advocacy of multiplicity, fluidity, hybridity, and indeterminacy.

Feminists in composition in the past decade have used postmodern theories to reread the feminization and the femin*in*ization of composition as problematic and to seek to revise institutional frameworks. The preponderance of women in composition has not led inevitably to the triumph of feminist interests and values in the field. For example, Susan Miller tells the story of the "sad women in the basement" and describes feminization as the "female coding" of the "ideologically constructed identity for the teacher of composition" (123); it involves constructing composition as "women's work." Feminization refers to the gendering of the entire field of composition and of various activities that have taken place within it (nonhierarchical pedagogy, the writing process movement, "romantic" philosophies, nurturing of writers). For Miller, feminization points to the devaluation of the composition instructor, and the subordination of composition to literature, throughout the history of the field. For Rhonda Grego and Nancy Thompson, compositionists "still reside within our gendered roles," but we are not limited to a traditional "wifely" role because the field has lately been "developing terms and methods through which to name our work at least to ourselves, if not yet fully to the ruling apparatus of the academic system" (68). In *Gypsy Academics and Mother Teachers*, Eileen Schell combines materialist feminist and postmodern perspectives, labor and institutional history, and the personal narratives of women nontenure-track teachers to analyze the gendered division of labor in composition and to critique femin*in*ization—the coopting of the "ethic of care." She also provides strategies for coalition-building and tangible plans of action for reconceptualizing women's positions and reshaping institutional structures. Feminization narratives like these work disruptively in two directions: their analysis foregrounds the political position of composition within institutional structures, but it also highlights tensions within women's roles and interests in composition.

Finally, disruptive narratives in composition have begun to analyze the established narratives of the discipline and the agency of students and teachers constructed by those narratives. They explore the ideologies underlying the discourses where composition has been situated, including those espoused by feminists, to underscore the contradictions and dangers that those create for women as well as for the field in general. An early example is Susan Jarratt's rereading of Peter Elbow's work and of the tendency in feminism and expressivism to suppress conflict and promote consensus.[5] She argues that such a stance fails to arm women students and teachers with the tools to confront the power relations inherent in their positions. An important recent example of disruption is Nedra Reynolds' rereading of several major narratives in the field. Reynolds emphasizes that interruption—talking back, forcibly breaking into the prevailing discourse of a field—is a way to create agency: "Agency is not simply about finding one's own voice but also about intervening in discourses of the everyday [this would include personal experience narratives] and cultivating rhetorical tactics that make interruption and resistance an important part of any conversation" (59). She points out the tendency of "some of the most important voices in composition today . . . to ignore work in feminism that might complement or complicate their ideas" (66). She not only "interrupts" some of the major cultural studies theorists but also analyzes the conceptions of subjectivity and agency in the work of James Berlin, John Trimbur, and Lester Faigley. She criticizes the dominant narrative's tendency to compartmentalize inter-rupters and disrupters as "rude women," thereby denying them agency. As part of the evidence for her argument, she tells stories about a cultural stud-ies conference where bell hooks and other women participants analyzed the "terror" of the typical "white supremacist hierarchy" (65). Reynolds urges women to develop strategies for interrupting dominant discourses in compo-sition and challenges them to offer their students the means to resist rigid forms of discourse.

CONCLUSION: IN EXCESS

These three different but also converging narratives of feminism suggest a rich tradition of feminist thought and activity in composition: pushing for admission, working intuitively alongside, and interrupting the conversation. We believe these three tropes may help us read and revise feminism's evolv-ing place in the narratives of composition; they provide useful insight for feminists about existing tensions in the relationship of theory to experience and practice; and they point to strategies feminists may seek to promote or avoid in the future.

In composition's last three decades, the impulse has been toward legiti-mation, theory-building, and consolidation. The disruption and the asser-tion of difference that feminists and others represent have come slowly and with struggle; they have been delayed and even suppressed by the need to build a more unified disciplinary discourse. In several recent metanarratives that assess where composition has come from and where it is going, we find traces of these three lines of feminist thought that may help us see where feminism might most usefully lead composition and where they might go together. These recent commentaries demonstrate that tropes of inclusion and metonymic connection still define feminism's relationship to the field.

In *Fragments of Rationality*, Lester Faigley practices inclusion as he cred-its feminism for its efforts to theorize a postmodern subject with agency; he also cites the contributions of feminists in foregrounding important pedagogi-cal and political questions. James Berlin's *Rhetorics, Poetics, Cultures* does not mention feminism, but this book, like Faigley's, does cite several post-modern feminists' efforts to theorize subjectivity and difference. In Joseph Harris' A *Teaching Subject: Composition Since 1966*, the connections

between women practitioners, feminism, and "the teaching subject" are neither articulated nor connected; they remain an unspoken presence. Like Berlin, Sharon Crowley argues in *Composition in the University* that despite its
progress over the past 30 years, composition has remained a conservative discipline, still trapped in current-traditionalism, still shackled to the service
role of Freshman English, and still bound to the limitations of humanism in
English departments. Unlike Berlin, she looks to feminist thought for its disruptive power, as one of several theoretical perspectives that might help dis-
lodge composition from narrow disciplinary confines.

The representation of feminist perspectives in these recent commentaries suggests that in the future these relationships will persist—with unspoken alliances between feminist thought and composition, and inclusive
reliance on postmodern feminism(s) where they advance the general argument. But it is to the disruptive strategy, framed in dialogue with inclusivity
and metonymy, that we return. It is tempting to see disruption as the newest
and best hope for feminism and to privilege theorizing as the most worthwhile activity for feminism and composition. But it's also clear that different
emphases may be more effective as rhetorical contexts shift and historical
moments change. While efforts at inclusion suffer from the limitations
we've outlined, and untheorized or unarticulated practices also create risks
of marginalization and erasure, disruptive strategies, by themselves, also
have limitations. The history of feminism suggests that it is necessary to do
more than interrupt a disciplinary conversation. Disruption may be only
temporary, and as Reynolds and others point out, it's easy to push disrupters
to the sidelines, to stop listening to them and to marginalize them once
again. In addition, the task of disruption requires rhetorical skill. Those who
interrupt may gain momentary attention, but those who can't sustain the
conversation, hold up the argument, or tell an absorbing story will soon
drop—or be dropped—from the discussion.

Certainly feminists in composition have provided the field with models
for persuasive and beautiful writing that tells and disrupts stories of experience. (Lynn Worsham's "After Words: A Choice of Words Remains" is a
recent example.) If theorizing and disruption are detached from lived experience and material history, they may remain irrelevant. And if disruption only
fractures and doesn't again create connection, a sense of an even tentatively
inclusive agenda, it will lack the vital energy and supportive alliances to sustain its own taxing work. Over the last 30 years, feminists have demonstrated
that critique and disruption are never finished and that coalition-building
and collaboration are vital for change.

Our rereading of 30 years of feminist writing suggests that in both early
and more recent work, feminism has been most challenging and disruptive

and also provided a sense of alliance and inclusion when it has maintained a dialogical relationship between theory and experience. Despite its short history, feminist work in composition can certainly provide many revitalizing demonstrations of this dialogical relationship as one of its contributions to academic feminism. Virtually all the feminist work we've reviewed and see emerging has, at least in part, claimed, interpreted, and revised accounts of experience and history: the personal history of one's life as a woman, the practice of the teacher, or the experience of the scholar. As Suzanne Clark points out, narratives of experience theorized become possible sites of agency: "At the same time that stories of personal experience invoke and re-cite determinant categories of identity . . . such stories also produce an excess not easily retrofitted as the norm" (98). Rather than dismissing stories of experience, Clark suggests that we look at them for what is "excessive," that is, for parts of the narrative that do not fit our current explanations: "What refuses, despite the sometimes daunting applications of straitjacket pseudo-sciences, to be contained?" (98). One of feminism's most potentially powerful tools is the deployment of what is excessive, what is other. Difference, "otherness," disrupts, as Rosemary Hennessy argues, because the "gaps, contradictions, *aporias*" that otherness creates force dominant perspectives into crisis management to "seal over or manage the contradictions. . . . But they also serve as the inaugural space for critique" (92).

Many gaps remain for feminists to explore in composition and in its relationship to English and the broader culture. Although researchers have now examined from a feminist perspective the status of women in composition and the feminized status of composition within English studies, many women still teach composition in the "basement," and the wider institutional, economic, and cultural conditions continue to create barriers against improving their status. Although women and men in our field have considered how class, gender, and race may shape their pedagogy, we have not thoroughly come to terms with students' or teachers' gendered, classed, or raced position in the academy—or the continuing failure to provide a viable education for many minority students or encouragement for minority colleagues in our field. Although various critics have highlighted the gender blindness of liberatory and critical pedagogies, we have not thoroughly considered how such theories and pedagogies stop short of realizing their goals where women students, minorities, and gay and lesbian students are concerned. Although we have a body of metacommentary on research methodologies and ethical representation of research subjects, we have only begun to explore effective ways to connect our research to wider public concerns and debates about literacy.

Our own interest in diversity and multiplicity makes us curious about the possible uses of "excess" as a trope for feminists in composition of the present and future. Already we are exploring feminist or "diverse discourses," which are in excess of what a singular linear argument requires. We are pushing for notions and accounts of agency that exceed limited ideas of the determined subject. Might the re-visionary stories of the next generation refer to greedy visions of *more* as well as angry recognitions of *lack*? Can we envision narratives of a disruptive practice that overflows as well as challenges? Excess might be proposed as inclusion with a difference: uncontained and without limits.

At this time when composition is reviewing its past and seeking to chart new directions, a glance beyond the academy suggests that political and economic conditions will create continuing intellectual and practical "straitjackets" in composition's next 50 years. The energy of feminists will be vital to the disruption of restrictive theory and practice. This energy will be important for sustaining coalitions for change; it is our best hope for inclusion and proliferation of difference, multiplicity, and uncontainable excess.

NOTES

1. In two recent collections of essays on composition, Villanueva's *Cross-Talk in Comp Theory*, and Bloom, Daiker, and White's *Composition in the Twenty-First Century*, the only essay specifically from a feminist perspective is Flynn's 1988 "Composing as a Woman." The frequent inclusion of this essay suggests the impact it has had; the fact that it is the only one included suggests that, in some venues at least, it has been used to contain feminism at the same time.

2. For example, the February 1970 issue of CCC contains articles by Donald Murray and by William Coles articulating many of the crucial progressive assumptions emerging in composition: the value of individual students' writing as an articulation of agency and self-hood rather than merely as an object of diagnosis and correction. The CCC journals of that year also contain several proposals for alternative freshman English courses for minority students, and the October 1972 issue contains the CCCC Executive Committee's Resolution, "The Student's Right to His Own Language." Although they remain steadfastly gender-blind, essays like these attest to the profession's increasing attempts in the late 60s and 70s to redefine writing and writing instruction. These disciplinary calls for cultural diversity in the curriculum and for the students' rights to their own language caused a great deal of ferment in the profession and foregrounded issues of difference, yet they still did not open a discursive space for women to speak as women writers and teachers or to consider the gendered implications of Coles' goal for writing: "to allow the student to put himself together" (28).

3. Belenky, Clinchy, Goldberger, and Tarule are noted for their use of "midwife" in their discussion of educators who promote constructed knowledge. But the term was applied to writing instructors much earlier. In 1970, Stephen Judy wrote in *English Journal* (which he was later to edit): "We need to discard the structure of the composition teacher as one who passes on knowledge about writing, makes assignments, and corrects errors on themes. A more appropriate role can be described as that of coach or catalyst, or one that I prefer, that of midwife: one who assists in the process of bringing something forth but does not participate in the process himself" (217). This passage suggests possibilities for metonymy; the

masculine pronoun may simply illustrate composition's gender-blindness, but it may also be a trace of the gender-shifting that Hill does twenty years later. Judy adds, "It would be difficult for a midwife to do *her* job adequately if the expectant mother knew she were going to be graded on the results" (217, italics ours).

4. Wendy Bishop, Lillian Bridwell-Bowles, Louise Phelps, and Nancy Sommers are just a few of the women who have written personal narratives that practice and reflect on disruption of a status quo. Jacqueline Jones Royster writes, "I have been compelled on too many occasions to count to sit as a well-mannered Other" (30). Theresa Enos' *Gender Roles and Faculty Lives in Rhetoric and Composition* contains a number of anonymous stories from women in composition, along with her narrative of her own experience as an "academically battered woman" (ix). Gesa Kirsch's interviews with women in various academic disciplines explore their interpretations of their experiences as writers and raise "questions of gender and language, women's participation in public discourse, and women's 'ways of writing'" (xvii). A new collection, *Women/Writing/Teaching*, edited by Jan Zlotnik Schmidt presents ten previously published and ten new essays by women that examine their personal experiences as writers and teachers.

5. We could cite numerous other examples: Patricia Sullivan's rereading of Stephen North's *The Making of Knowledge in Composition*; Nancy Welch's use of feminist theory and her own experience to reread Lacan and other theorists and to disrupt composition's conceptualization of revision; and the important work of increasing numbers of feminists rereading and regendering the rhetorical tradition from Aspasia to Ida B. Wells, from Gertrude Buck to Toni Morrison.

WORKS CITED

Annas, Pamela J. "Style as Politics: A Feminist Approach to the Teaching of Writing." *College English* 47 (1985): 360–71.

Belenky, Mary Field, Blythe McVicker Clinchy, Nancy Rule Goldberger, and Jill Mattuck Tarule. *Women's Ways of Knowing: The Development of Self, Voice, and Mind.* New York: Basic, 1986.

Bennett, Robert A. "NCTE Presidential Address: The Undiscovered." *English Journal* 61 (1972): 351–57.

Berlin, James. *Rhetorics, Poetics, and Cultures: Refiguring College English Studies.* Urbana: NCTE, 1996.

Berthoff, Ann E. "Rhetoric as Hermeneutic." *CCC* 42 (1991): 279–87.

Bishop, Wendy. "Learning Our Own Ways to Situate Composition and Feminist Studies in the English Department." *Journal of Advanced Composition* 10 (1990): 339–55.

Bloom, Lynn Z. "Teaching College English as a Woman." *College English* 54 (1992): 818–25.

Bloom, Lynn Z., Donald A. Daiker, and Edward M. White, eds. *Composition in the Twenty-First Century: Crisis and Change.* Carbondale: Southern Illinois UP, 1996.

Bolker, Joan. "Teaching Griselda to Write." *College English* 40 (1979): 906–08.

Brady, Laura. "The Reproduction of Othering." Jarratt and Worsham 21–44.

Bridwell-Bowles, Lillian. "Freedom, Form, Function: Varieties of Academic Discourse." *CCC* 46 (1995): 46–61.

Caywood, Cynthia, and Gillian Overing, eds. *Teaching Writing: Pedagogy, Gender, and Equity.* Albany: State U of New York P, 1987.

Clark, Suzanne. "Argument and Composition." Jarratt and Worsham 94–99.

Coles, William, Jr. "The Sense of Nonsense as a Design for Sequential Writing Assignments." *CCC* 21 (1970): 27–34.

Crowley, Sharon. *Composition in the University: Historical and Polemical Essays.* Pittsburgh Series in Composition, Literacy, and Culture. Pittsburgh: U of Pittsburgh P, 1998.

Enos, Theresa. *Gender Roles and Faculty Lives in Rhetoric and Composition.* Carbondale: Southern Illinois UP, 1996.

Faigley, Lester. *Fragments of Rationality: Postmodernity and the Subject of Composition.* Pittsburgh Series in Composition, Literacy, and Culture. Pittsburgh, U of Pittsburgh P, 1992.

Flynn, Elizabeth A. "Composing as a Woman." *CCC* 39 (1988) : 423–35.

Fontaine, Sheryl I., and Susan Hunter, eds. *Writing Ourselves into the Story: Unheard Voices from Composition Studies.* Carbondale: Southern Illinois UP, 1993. 1–17.

Grego, Rhonda, and Nancy Thompson. "Repositioning Remediation: Renegotiating Composition's Work in the Academy." *CCC* 47 (1996): 62–84.

Harris, Joseph. *A Teaching Subject: Composition Since 1966.* Upper Saddle River: Prentice, 1997.

Hennessy, Rosemary. *Materialist Feminism and the Politics of Discourse.* Thinking Gender Series. New York: Routledge, 1992.

Hiatt, Mary P. "The Feminine Style: Theory and Fact." *CCC* 29 (1978): 222–26.

Hill, Carolyn Ericksen. *Writing from the Margins: Power and Pedagogy for Teachers of Composition.* New York: Oxford UP, 1990.

Howe, Florence. "A Report on Women and the Profession." *College English* 32 (1971): 847–54.

——. "Identity and Expression: A Writing Course for Women." *College English* 32 (1971): 863–71.

Jarratt, Susan C. "Feminism and Composition: The Case for Conflict." *Contending with Words: Composition and Rhetoric in a Postmodern Age.* Ed. Patricia Harkin and John Schilb. New York: MLA, 1991. 105–23.

Jarratt, Susan C.,and Lynn Worsham, eds. *Feminism and Composition Studies: In Other Words.* New York: MLA, 1998.

Judy, Stephen. "The Search for Structures in the Teaching of Composition." *English Journal* 59 (1970): 213–18.

Kirsch, Gesa E. *Women Writing the Academy: Audience, Authority, and Transformation.* Studies in Writing and Rhetoric. Carbondale: Southern Illinois UP, 1992.

Kirsch, Gesa E., and Patricia A. Sullivan, eds. *Methods and Methodology in Composition Research.* Carbondale: Southern Illinois UP, 1992.

Lakoff, Robin. *Language and Woman's Place.* New York: Harper, 1975.

Logan, Shirley W., ed. *With Pen and Voice: The Rhetoric of Nineteenth Century African-American Women.* Carbondale: Southern Illinois UP, 1995.

Lu, Min-Zhan. "Conflict and Struggle: The Enemies or Preconditions of Basic Writing?" *College English* 54 (1992): 887–913.

——. "From Silence to Words: Writing as Struggle." Perl 165–76.

Malinowitz, Harriet. *Textual Orientations: Lesbian and Gay Students and the Making of Discourse Communities.* Portsmouth: Boynton, Heinemann, 1995.

McCracken, Nancy, Lois Green, and Claudia Greenwood. "Gender in Composition Research: A Strange Silence." Fontaine and Hunter 352–73.

Miller, Susan. *Textual Carnivals: The Politics of Composition.* Carbondale: Southern Illinois UP, 1991.

Murray, Donald M. "The Interior View: One Writer's Philosophy of Composition." *CCC* 21 (1970): 21–26.

Olsen, Tillie. "Women Who Are Writers in Our Century: One Out of Twelve." *College English* 34 (1972): 6–17.

"Open Letter from Janet Emig, Chairwoman, NCTE Committee on the Role and Image of Women." *English Journal* 61 (1972): 710.

Perl, Sondra, ed. *Landmark Essays on Writing Process.* Landmark Essays Series 7. Davis: Hermagoras, 1994.

Phelps, Louise W. "Becoming a Warrior: Lessons of the Feminist Workplace." Phelps and Emig 289–339.

Phelps, Louise W., and Janet Emig, eds. *Feminine Principles and Women's Experience in American Composition and Rhetoric.* Pittsburgh Series in Composition, Literacy, and Culture. Pittsburgh: U of Pittsburgh P, 1995.

Reynolds, Nedra. "Interrupting Our Way to Agency: Feminist Cultural Studies and Composition." Jarratt and Worsham 58–73.

Rich, Adrienne. "When We Dead Awaken: Writing as Re-vision." *College English* 34 (1972): 18–25.

_____. "Taking Women Students Seriously." *On Lies, Secrets, and Silence: Selected Prose 1966–1978.* New York: Norton, 1979. 237–45.

Royster, Jacqueline Jones. "When the First Voice You Hear Is Not Your Own." *CCC* 47 (1996): 29–40.

Schell, Eileen. *Gypsy Academics and Mother-Teachers: Gender, Contingent Labor, and Writing Instruction.* Portsmouth: Boynton, 1998.

_____. "The Costs of Caring: 'Feminism' and Contingent Women Workers in Composition Studies." Jarratt and Worsham 74–93.

Schmidt, Jan Zlotnik, ed. *Women/Writing/Teaching.* Albany: State U of New York P, 1998.

Scott, Joan. "Experience." *Feminists Theorize the Political.* Ed. Judith Butler and Joan W. Scott. New York: Routledge, 1992. 22–40.

Showalter, Elaine. "Women and the Literary Curriculum." *College English* 32 (1971): 855–62.

Sommers, Nancy. "Between the Drafts." Perl 217–24.

Sullivan, Patricia A. "Feminism and Methodology." Kirsch and Sullivan 37–61.

Taylor, Sheila Ortiz. "Women in a Double-Bind: Hazards of the Argumentative Edge." *CCC* 29 (1978): 385–89.

"The Students' Right to Their Own Language." *CCC* 25 Special Issue (1974): 1–32.

The Secretary's Report of Executive Committee. "The Student's Right to His Own Language." *CCC* 21 (1970): 319–28.

Villanueva Jr., Victor, ed. *Cross-Talk in Comp Theory.* Urbana: NCTE, 1997.

Welch, Nancy. *Getting Restless: Rethinking Revision in Writing Instruction.* Portsmouth: Boynton, 1997.

Worsham, Lynn. "After Words: A Choice of Words Remains." Jarratt and Worsham 329–56.

On the Subjects of
Class and Gender in
"The Literacy Letters"

LINDA BRODKEY

In "The Discourse on Language," Michel Foucault dramatizes the desire to be "on the other side of discourse, without having to stand outside it, pondering its particular, fearsome, and even devilish features" (215) in this whimsical colloquy between the individual and the institution.

> Inclination speaks out: "I don't want to have to enter this risky world of discourse; I want nothing to do with it insofar as it is decisive and final; I would like to feel it all around me, calm and transparent, profound, infinitely open, with others responding to my expectations, and truth emerging, one by one. All I want is to allow myself to be borne along, within it, and by it, a happy wreck." Institutions reply: "But you have nothing to fear from launching out; we're here to show you discourse is within the established order of things, that we've waited a long time for its arrival, that a place has been set aside for it—a place that both honours and disarms it; and if it should have a certain power, then it is we, and we alone, who give it that power." (215–16)

What Foucault and other poststructuralists have been arguing the last fifteen or twenty years is considerably easier to state than act on: we are at once constituted and unified as subjects in language and discourse. The discursive subject is of particular interest to those of us who teach writing because language and discourse are understood to be complicit in the representation of

Reprinted from *College English* 51.2 (February 1989): 125–41. Used with permission.

self and others, rather than the neutral or arbitrary tools of thought and expression that they are in other modern theories, not to mention handbooks and rhetorics. Among other things, this means that since writers cannot avoid constructing a social and political reality in their texts, as teachers we need to learn how to "read" the various relationships between writer, reader, and reality that language and discourse supposedly produce.

New theories of textuality are inevitably new theories of reading. And in the field of writing, those who teach basic writers and welcome new ways to read their texts are perhaps the most likely to recognize the possibilities of discursive subjectivity. The poststructural David Bartholomae of "Inventing the University," for example, writes less confidently but more astutely of what student errors may signify than the Bartholomae of "The Study of Error," published some years earlier at the height of the field's enthusiasm for empirical research and error analysis. For the startling power of a discourse to confer authority, name errors, and rank order student texts speaks more readily to the experience of reading basic writing than promises of improved reliability or validity in the empirical study of errors. While empiricality is far from moot, it makes little difference if one is right if one is not talking about that which most concerns writing and the teaching of writing. Or, as Sharon Crowley has put it, "the quality of the power that is associated with writing varies with the degree of authority granted by a culture to its texts" (96). In this society the authority that teachers are empowered to grant to or withhold from student texts derives from the theory of textuality governing their reading.

The question then is how to read what students write. And at issue is the unquestioned power of a pedagogical authority that insists that teachers concentrate on form at the expense of content.

> I'm siting at home now when I have more time to write to you I enjoyed rending your letters. I under stand reading them one word I had a little trouble with the word virginia but know about me well that is hard but I will try.

The errors in spelling and punctuation in this passage are serious, but not nearly as egregious, I suspect, as the tradition that warrants reducing a text to its errors. Remember the anger you feel when someone corrects your pronunciation or grammar while you are in the throes of an argument, and you can recover the traces of the betrayal students must experience when a writing assignment promises them seemingly unlimited possibilities for expression, and the response or evaluation notes only their limitations. The errors are there, and the passage is hard to read. Yet to see only the errors strikes me as an unwarranted refusal to cede even the possibility of discursive subjectivity and authority to the woman who wrote this passage, barring of course that of basic writer which an error analysis would without question grant her.

CHANGING THE SUBJECT

This is an essay about the ways discourses construct our teaching. In postmodern theories of subjectivity:

1. all subjects are the joint creations of language and discourse;
2. all subjects produced are ideological;
3. all subject positions are vulnerable to the extent that individuals do not or will not identify themselves as the subjects (i.e., the effects) of a discourse.

Those who occupy the best subject positions a discourse has to offer would have a vested interest in maintaining the illusion of speaking rather than being spoken by discourse. Postmodern rhetoric would begin by assuming that all discourses warrant variable subject positions ranging from mostly satisfying to mostly unsatisfying for those individuals named by them. Each institutionalized discourse privileges some people and not others by generating uneven and unequal subject positions as various as stereotypes and agents. Hence, it is at least plausible to expect most, though not all, of those individuals whose subjectivity is the most positively produced by a discourse to defend its discursive practices against change. And it is equally plausible to expect some, though again not all, of those individuals whose subjectivity is the most negatively produced to resist its discursive practices. Feminists, for example, regularly resist discursive practices that represent female subjectivity solely in terms of reproductive biology. Of course, neither verbal resistance nor other material forms of protest to such reduced subject positions are universal among women.

Discursive resistance requires opportunities for resistance. Altering an institutionalized discourse probably requires an unremitting negative critique of its ideology, a critique that is most often carried out in the academy by attempting to replace a particular theory (e.g., of science or art or education or law) with another. Recently, theoretical battles have proliferated to such an extent that a cover term, *critical theory,* has come to refer to a variety of ideological critiques of theory, research, and practice across the academy: critical legal studies, critical practice, critical anthropology, critical pedagogy, and so on.

Discursive resistance, however, need not be conducted in such abstract terms as we have recently witnessed in the academy. The more usual practice would be for those individuals who are ambivalent or threatened by their subject positions in a given discourse to interrupt the very notion of the unified self—the traditional Cartesian notion that the self is a transcendent and absolute entity rather than a creation of language and ideology—in their spoken and written texts. Such interruptions are likely to take one of two forms: reversing the negative and positive subject positions in a given discourse—as Carol Gilligan does in her feminist revision of the research on the development of moral reasoning among adolescent girls; or re-presenting a stereotype as an agent in a discourse the least committed to the preservation of the stereotype—as Toni Morrison does when representing Afro-American women and men as the agents rather than the victims of events in her novels.

Studies of these and other interruptive practices, rhetorics of resistance in which individuals shift subject positions from one discourse to another or within a discourse in their speaking and writing, would constitute empirical inquiry into the postmodern speculation that language and discourse are material to the construction of reality, not simply by-products reflecting or reproducing a set of non-discursive, material social structures and political formations. Knowledge of multiple subject positions makes possible both the practical and the theoretical critiques that interrupt the assumption of unchanging, irreversible, and asymmetrical social and political relations between the privileged and unprivileged subjects represented in a particular discourse (see Williams, esp. 75–141).

What is needed is research that addresses what Stuart Hall has recently called "a theory of articulation," which he describes as "a way of understanding how ideological elements come, under certain conditions, to cohere together within a discourse, and a way of asking how they do or do not become articulated, at specific junctures, to certain political subjects" (53). Since articulation separates intentions from effects, or production from reception, Hall has reinserted the possibility of human agency into post-structural theory. More specifically, articulation distinguishes between the desire to be unified in a discourse and what happens in practice, namely, what individuals do in and with the unified subject positions offered them by such recognizable institutional discourses as, say, science, art, education, law, and religion or ethics.

624

"THE LITERACY LETTERS"

What I mean by research on the rhetorics of discursive practice and attendant practices of resistance is amply illustrated in a curriculum project I have referred to elsewhere as "the Literacy Letters" (see Brodkey). The letters were generated in the discourse of education, since they were initiated by six white middle-class teachers (four women and two men) taking my graduate course on teaching basic writing and sustained by six white working-class women enrolled in an Adult Basic Education (ABE) class. The woman who was teaching the ABE class and taking my course hoped that corresponding would provide the students in her class with what she called an authentic reason to write—on the order of a pen-pal experience for adults. The experienced English teachers from my class, most of whom had not taught basic writing, set out to learn more about the reading and writing concerns of their adult correspondents. As for me, I welcomed the chance to study correspondence itself, which seemed to me a remarkable opportunity to examine both the production and reception of self and other in the writing and reading of personal letters.

Permission to photocopy the letters as data for research was granted by all correspondents before the first exchange. For the two months that they wrote, the correspondents agreed not to meet or talk on the phone. The data, then, are the letters written by the six pairs who wrote regularly: one pair exchanged letters eight times; one pair seven times; two pairs six times; and two pairs five times.

When the teachers first reported that they found writing the letters stressful, I attributed their anxiety to the fact that I would be reading and evaluating their letters as well as those written by the students in the ABE class. But their uneasiness persisted despite repeated assurances that I couldn't look at or read the letters until the semester's end, a standard procedure meant to protect the educational rights of those who agree to participate in classroom research. After reading and thinking about the letters, however, I am no longer so inclined to assume that my presence as such was as threatening or intrusive as I first thought, though doubtless it contributed some to their anxiety.

Learning to Read "The Literacy Letters"

Research on basic writers as well as my own experience teaching amply prepared me for the ungainly prose produced by the women in the ABE class (e.g., Bartholomae, Perl, Shaughnessy). But nothing I had read or remembered from my own teaching prepared me for occasional moments of linguistic as well as discursive awkwardness from the teachers. I am not referring to the necessary clumsiness with which the teachers sought their footing before they knew anything about their correspondents, but to intermittent improprieties that occurred once several letters had been exchanged. In fact, I found these occasional lapses so perplexing that it's fair to say that the teachers' unexpected errors, rather than the students' expected ones, led me to think about the literacy letters in terms of the poststructural discursive practices of reproduction and resistance. Only discourse, more specifically the power of a discourse over even its fluent writers, I decided, could begin to explain the errors of these otherwise literate individuals.

That educational discourse grants teachers authority over the organization of language in the classroom, which includes such commonplace privileges as allocating turns, setting topics, and asking questions, is clear from sociolinguistic studies of classroom language interaction (e.g., Stubbs). Many teachers, including those in this study, attempt to relinquish their control by staging opportunities for students to take the privileged subject position of teacher in, say, group discussions or collaborative assignments that grant them, at least temporarily, a measure of control over educational discursive practice. Attempts to transform classroom discussions into conversations between peers are thwarted to the extent that teachers fail to realize that their interpersonal relationships with students, as well as their institutional ones, are constituted by educational discourse. While the power of a discourse is not absolute, neither is it vulnerable to change by individuals who ignore its power, only by those who interrupt or resist or challenge the seemingly immutable reality of unified subjectivity. In much the same way that you don't resist racism by denying that racism exists, but by confronting it in yourself and others, teachers cannot divest themselves of those vestiges of authority that strike them as unproductive by ignoring the institutional arrangements that unequally empower teachers and students.

At the outset, the teachers in this study attempted to mitigate the power of educational discourse over themselves and their correspondents by "playing" student. Their letters are replete with the desire to represent themselves as students of writing pedagogy and their correspondents as their teachers. The longest running correspondence, for instance, was initiated by a teacher who wrote: "I think that some of the things you could tell me might help me to understand what I can do better when I try to help my students learn to improve thier (sic) writing." Since none of the students made suggestions about either curriculum or instruction, roles were not reversed. But making the requests seems to have mooted the possibility of the teachers practicing the most authoritarian "dialect" of educational discourse in their correspondence. To wit, no teacher reduced personal correspondence to spelling or grammar lessons; nor, for that matter, did any of the students from the ABE class ask to be taught or corrected.

Bear in mind that the writers of the literacy letters are not held by the usual arrangements between teachers and students. To be sure, the teachers are teachers and the students are students. But theirs is what might be called an extracurricular relationship, arranged by the authorized teacher. While the teachers assiduously avoided lessons and hence avoided even the possibility of displacing the classroom teacher's authority, there are nevertheless times in the letters when it certainly looks as if by ignoring rather than contesting the authority of educational discourse, they retained control over such discursive privileges as determining what is and what is not an appropriate topic. The teachers exercise their authority infrequently, but decisively, whenever one of their correspondents interrupts, however incidentally, the educational discursive practice that treats class as irrelevant to the subjectivity of teachers and students. Telegraphed by linguistic and/or discursive lapses, the refusal that signals the teachers' unspoken commitment to a classless discourse provokes additional and more pronounced discursive resistance from the ABE writers.

Personal Narratives in "The Literacy Letters"

Discursive hegemony on the part of the teachers is most obvious and discursive resistance on the part of the students is most dramatic during storytelling episodes. Personal correspondence evokes personal narratives. The teachers tell a variety of stories in which they represent themselves as busy professionals trying to resolve conflicts among work, family, and school. Social research on storytelling suggests that in exchange for being granted the time it takes to tell a story, the teller is expected to make it worth the listener's while by raising for evaluation or contemplation that which is problematic or unusual about the narrative conflict and its resolution (see Labov, Pratt). That the teachers tell stories representing themselves as guilty about their inability to find enough time is not surprising, since their busy lives have been made all the more complicated by recently adding course work to schedules already overburdened by responsibilities at work and home. Nor are the responses to their stress stories unexpected, for the women from the Adult Basic Education class console and commiserate with the teachers in much the way that research suggests interlocutors ordinarily do. The teachers, however, occasionally respond in extraordinary ways when their correspondents reciprocate with stories about their lives.

The ABE students do not tell narratives about not having the time to fulfill their obligations to the three spheres of work, school, and family. Nor are their stories about internal conflicts like guilt. Instead, they write most frequently about external threats to the well-being of themselves and their families or their neighbors. While work and education often figure in their stories, they are important only insofar as they materially affect their lives: a family is besieged by the threat of layoffs; lack of educational credentials means the low paychecks and the moonlighting that robs families of time with the overworked wage earner.

Clearly teachers and students alike told class-based narratives. Yet the teachers' markedly inept responses to their correspondents' narratives suggest that the hegemony of educational discourse warrants teachers not only to represent themselves as subjects unified by the internal conflicts like guilt that preoccupy professionals, but to disclaim narratives that represent a subject alternatively unified in its conflicts with an external material reality. This refusal to acknowledge the content of their correspondents' narratives, most explicable as a professional class narcissism that sees itself everywhere it looks, alienates the ABE writers from educational discourse and, more importantly, from the teachers it ostensibly authorizes.

Don and Dora

The seven-letter exchange between the teacher and student I'll call Don and Dora is disarming. Frequency alone suggests that both teacher and student found corresponding satisfying. For some weeks they wrote about movies, food, and their families, all topics introduced by Don who represented himself in his initial letter as a complex subject, specifically, as a young man beset by personal failings his correspondent would find amusing:

> I won't tell you how long I like to stay in bed in the morning—though I do stay up very late at night (watching old movies)—but let's just say that it's past 11 AM. Oh well, we all have to have at least one vice. Unfortunately, I have more than one. One of my others is Chinese food. There's a Chinese food cart parked right outside the window of the library where I work, so every afternoon I dash out when the line slacks off . . . I usually try to get some vegetable dishes, even though I most always end up getting the most highly caloric item on the menu.

His comedic self-presentation is amplified by this final request: "Please let me know what you're doing: do you like Chinese food (and if so, what kind?), do you like old movies (and if so, which ones?), do you think I'm too weird to write back to? I'll look forward to your responses, comments, complaints, etc." In her response letter, Dora picks up the topics of movies and food. "I to enjoy the old movies and (love Chinese food)," she writes, but then goes on to conclude about them both, "so [I] guess that make two of us that are (weird)." Notice that while she responds to his question, "do you think I'm too weird to write back to?", writing back is itself material evidence that Dora doesn't find Don's tastes *too* weird. Dora is, as she puts it, "looking forward to writing back this is my first letter I ever wrote."

Over the next few weeks, their letters follow this pattern. Don writes extended and humorous anecdotes that portray him as a man at odds with himself at work, school, and home, and Dora offers consolation by letting him know how amusing she and the other women in her class find his stories: "Rachel [her teacher] ask me to read your letter to the class we all though that your grandmother and father was funning about the candy." After dutifully playing audience for some weeks, however, Dora dramatically reverses the pattern when she not only asserts herself as a narrator, but as the narrator of tragic rather than comedic events, in this letter which in its entirety reads as follows:

> I don't have must to siad this week a good frineds husband was kill satday at 3:15 the man who kill him is a good man he would give you the shirt off of his back it is really self-defense but anyway I see police academy three it was funny but not is good as the first two

Dora's narrative limns as stark a reality as any represented in the literacy letters. However, the abrupt shift from herself as a narrator who reflects on the aftermath of violence to herself as the student who answers a teacher's questions—"but anyway I see police academy three it was funny but not is good as the first two"—is, for me, one of those moments when the power of discourse seems the most absolute.

It's not implausible to imagine that in telling a narrative Dora is trying out the more positive subject position afforded narrators by the discourse of art, and that Don has held throughout their correspondence. But art is only a respite, it seems, for Dora shifts quickly from narrator back to student. Yet in that brief moment when she inserts herself as the narrator, Dora takes on the more complex subjectivity afforded by the discourse of art to narrators. Though short, the story she tells is one in which the narrator's sympathies are clearly divided between the survivors—the friend and the murderer—a narrative position that Dora grounds in the extenuating circumstances of moral character (a good man "would give you the shirt off of his back") and law ("it is really self-defense"). Her narrative point of view considers not the grisly fact of murder and not even what motivated the murder, but the notion that murder is a consequence of circumstances rather than character.

Narrative strikes me as a potentially effective mode of resistance, for the rules governing storytelling more or less require Don to respond to the content of Dora's narrative. Since Dora attentuated the full interruptive force of the discourse of art on educational discourse, however, by interjecting the comment about the movie, she effectively lost her hold on the rhetorical practice in which the narrative critiques a teacher's exclusive right to initiate topics. The abrupt shift from narrator back to audience returns, or offers to return, teacher and student alike to the already established subject positions of teacher/narrator and student/audience.

Even if Dora's interjection is understood as hesitation, Don might have assisted her by simply responding to the content of her story. He might have asked about motive or even asked why she says nothing about the victim. But Don's response suggests only that he is nonplussed:

> I'm sorry to hear about the problem that you wrote about last week. It's always hard to know what to say when the situation is as unusual as that one. I hope that everything is getting a little better, at least for you trying to know what to say and do in that situation.

Several issues about the fragility of the unity that even the most privileged subjects are able to achieve in language and discourse come immediately to mind. Most obvious, perhaps, is the syntactic lapse in the final sentence ("I hope that everything is getting a little better, at least for *you* trying to know what to say and do in that situation"). Less obvious, though equally to the point, is the way that Don's linguistic facility, under the circumstances, only amplifies the discursive inadequacy of this passage as a response to the content of her narrative.

Bearing in mind that she has just told a story in which the "problem" is the aftermath of murder—her friend's husband is dead and the good man who killed him presumably faces prison—the assertion that this is a matter of manners—"It's always hard to know what to say when the situation is as unusual as that one"—is not simply inappropriate. It constitutes a discursive retreat that threatens to reconstitute Don and Dora in the most profoundly alienated subject relationship of all—self and other—and to give over their more or less satisfying discursive relationship as narrator and audience. Even the demonstrative adjective, *that*, underscores the distance Don places between himself and the world in which he resides and the other and the world in which she resides. The contrast between this awkward first paragraph and the plans to visit his grandmother on Mother's Day that complete his letter effectively reiterates the terms of their continued correspondence.

In her next letter, Dora again responds to the content of Don's letter, "I am glad to hear that you are going to see your grandmother." And though she makes no further mention in this or any letter of the murder, she writes "I hope you get more energy about work," which remark is followed by:

> I wouldn't want to see you living in Kensington with the rest of us bums, ha ha

It certainly looks as if she has acknowledged the threat of othering by noting that his self-proclaimed and amply documented laziness throughout their correspondence would, in the eyes of many, make him one of the others—"the rest of us bums"—whose subjectivity he's denying. That her class antagonism increases after the next letter, in which he narrates in the usual humorous detail his visit with his grandmother, is evident in the fact that for the first time she makes no reference to his anecdote and ends a brief account of her own Mother's Day with, "I got call back to work today. I am very nervous about it. it like started a new job." In his next letter, in which he makes no mention of her job, Don follows yet another extended narrative about a day at the beach with "Keep cool and write soon!" But this time Dora ignores both the narrative and the imperatives and does not write again.

Don's response is characteristic of the kind of discursive uneasiness that arises whenever one of the students interrupts the educational practice that deems such working-class concerns as neighborhood violence irrelevant. And while this is admittedly one of the more dramatic examples, it suggests the extent to which unacknowledged tension over the control of subject positions contributes to rather than alleviates class antagonism, for we see that the teacher's desire to be preserved as the unified subject of an educational discursive practice that transcends class overrides the student's desire to narrate herself as a subject unified in relation to the violence that visited her working-class neighborhood.

Rita and Esther

The second example comes from the six-letter exchange between an experienced secondary English teacher I'll call Rita and the most fluent and prolific writer from the ABE class, a student I'll call Esther. The set itself is unusual, since these are the only correspondents whose letters are often of similar length. From the outset, it's easy to see that Esther is not only actively resisting playing "student" but sometimes even tries to play "teacher." In response to Rita's initial letter, for instance, Esther first compliments her—"My classmates and I read your wonderful letter"—but then faults her for what she neglected to mention: "you never stated your age or your country in the letter. And also where your Grandmother's home was." And unlike the other ABE writers, in her first and subsequent letters, Esther asks for information that Rita has neither offered nor alluded to:

> What is it like where you live and what are the shopping areas like. How is the transportation and the Climate there. What kind of food do you like to eat. You didn't say if you were married, or if you have children. Please write back and let me know.

Though this is admittedly an insight considerably improved by hindsight, the class antagonism that erupts later can probably be traced to Rita's ambivalance about their relationship, for she seems unable either to accept Esther's assumption that they are peers or to assert herself as a teacher. Rita's reluctance to declare herself as either a teacher or a peer may explain her refusal to do more than name the suburb she lives in or the nearby mall in answer to questions like "What is it like where you live and what are the shopping areas like." In short, Rita replies but does not answer Esther's questions.

In a letter near the end of their correspondence, following yet one more futile effort to establish what Rita's life is like—"Do you live near a beach or the shore? Are you going anywhere special this Summer?"—Esther writes this explanation in response to Rita's comment that she sounded "a little discouraged" in her last letter:

> I'm going to have to look for another house because, the Restate is Selling the house unless somebody invests in it and wants me to stay his or her tennant. That is why I was a little discourage because I didn't have a chance to save any money. I'll still answer your letters. Thank you for writing back.

This is a remarkable passage if only because it is one of the few times in the literacy letters when anyone mentions money by name. There are plenty of coded references to money: vacations taken or not taken, the buying of gifts, the cost of public transportation and food. But this particular statement is about money, about the simple economic fact that changing housing requires capital. And given what Esther has written, Rita's response strikes me as a perverse misreading:

> It is difficult to save money. Do you have any idea where you will move? What kind of home are you planning to buy? Interest rates are low now.

The peculiarity arises in the increasing unconnectedness of Rita's sentences to Esther's assertions. The first sentence is a response to Esther's assertion that she hasn't "had a chance to save any money." And the second sentence relates to Esther's claim that she will probably have to move. But in light of what Esther wrote, the assumption that Esther is planning to buy a house or that interest rates are of any consequence to her is, to say the least, surprising. That the question confounds Esther is evident in her next letter, which begins with a passing reference to Rita's sister, whose illness Rita mentioned in her last letter, followed by a brief but pointed attempt to correct the misunderstanding:

> I'm very sorry to hear about your sister. I hope she gets better. About the house. The only way I could buy a house is by hitting a number in the Lotto.

As lessons in elementary economics go this is about as clear as any I know. Yet Rita's response to this assertion is, on the face of it, even more bizarre than her statement that "Interest rates are low now." To wit, she ignores Esther's topic, which is housing, and reintroduces gambling, Lotto, as a topic they might discuss:

> Do you play Lotto frequently? I never think that I can ever win one of those lotteries. Did you ever know anyone who won? Some people play faithfully.

This is a near perfect example of cross-talk, for two conversations are now in play—one about housing and another about gambling. And were this a conversation between peers, Rita would be charged with illicitly changing the topic, since it is she who played the conversational gambit in which Esther's instructive hyperbole—"the only way I could buy a house is if I win the Lotto"—is taken at its face value, and Lotto, which is not the topic but the comment, is transformed into the topic, now in the form of questions about gambling. It's a familiar teacher's gambit for controlling what does and does not count as knowledge, a remnant, perhaps, of the institutionalized silencing that Michelle Fine suggests "more intimately informs low-income, public schooling than relatively privileged situations" (158).

The salient fact here is that educational discourse empowers teachers to determine what is worthwhile in a student's contributions, presumably even if that judgment has little or no linguistic basis and even if a teacher-student relationship is not entirely warranted. Remember that Esther has been representing herself as an adult whose financial status is precarious and that she has gone to some pains not to occupy the student position that Rita has finally assigned her. It is in Esther's final letter, in which she makes one last attempt to establish subjective parity between herself and Rita, that we see the devastating pedagogical consequences of preserving this particular privilege of educational discursive practice.

> I don't play the Lotto everyday except on my birthday when it July 11 (7/11). I'm really messing up this letter. I'm going to an award dinner on May 30th at 7 p.m. And when I get a lucky number. I don't know anyone that ever won. Thank you for your nice letter. Bye for now.

Esther wrote better letters at the beginning than at the end of the semester. The disintegration of syntax in this her last letter ("when it" for "which is") augurs the disappearance of the working-class adult subject she has been representing and the articulation of the Adult Basic Writer, a subject unified by its errors, its sentence fragments ("And when I get a lucky number") and its rhetorical disjunctures (the sentences and phrases whose meanings are recoverable only by association). That Esther sees the failure as her own, "I'm really messing up this letter," echoes Foucault's assertion that it is the power of discourse to create the illusion that "it is we, and we alone, who give it that power." Finally overwhelmed by educational discourse, the adult subject retreats into silence.

Ellen and Pat

The eight-letter exchange between the student and teacher I'll call Pat and Ellen is by many standards, including my own, the most successful not simply because they wrote the most often, but because Pat's letters grew longer and her errors fewer over the two months she corresponded with Ellen. While she shares the other teachers' aversion to class, Ellen differs considerably from them in her initial and repeated representation of herself as unified in relation to family: "I have been married for 21 years," "[I am] the mother of two teenagers," "I'm a very family-centered person." Ellen's representation of her familial self is often completed or articulated by Pat, when, for example, she writes "I'm all so marry for $22^1/_2$ year. I have 4 kids." The self unified in relation to family is reminiscent of that represented in many of the working-class narratives, except that the self articulated in their letters is decidedly female.

That gender is a crucial dimension of their subjectivity first becomes apparent when Ellen responds to Pat's physical description of herself with this measured assertion of identification: "It sounds as though you and I look somewhat alike." In this instance, it is Ellen who articulates or completes a representation of self initiated by Pat and hence Ellen who identifies herself as the embodied female subject represented in Pat's physical description. This particular articulation stands out because it is the only corporeal representation of self in the letters and because it is also the only self-representation offered by one of the students with which a teacher identifies or articulates. To be sure, Ellen's articulation is tenuous, qualified immediately by "somewhat," and later by assertions such as "I'm trying to lose some weight before the summer season comes so I won't be so embarrassed in my bathing suit" that suggest the middle-class woman's all too familiar and uneasy relationship to her body.

In the course of their reciprocal articulation, and the co-construction of themselves as gendered subjects, Pat and Ellen tell and respond to stories that narrate their shared concerns as mothers. And it is as mother-women that they ignore the class differences that overwhelm the correspondents in the other two examples. Their mutual concern for their children's education, for instance, overrides material differences between their children's actual access to education. Ellen writes that she and her husband will be traveling to Williamsburg to bring their daughter home from college for the summer: "So far, each year that we've gone we've had to move her in the rain. It would be nice to be able to keep dry for once during all of the trips back and forth to the car." Pat advises Ellen to "think positive," attending not to the fact that Ellen's daughter attends a private college while her son goes to a local community college, but to the prediction that it will probably rain. In what appears to be yet another attempt to lift Ellen's spirits, Pat then recalls that she, her husband, and three children took a trip to Williamsburg eight years earlier, about which she has only this to say: "Williamsburg is a beautiful place."

Toward the end of their correspondence, Ellen and Pat recount their Mother's Days. Ellen's story is short:

> I hope you had an enjoyable Mother's Day. Did your family treat you to dinner? B [Ellen's daughter] cooked the meal and we had a combination Mother's Day and birthday celebration. My husband was one of those Mother's Day presents when he was born so every eighth year his birthday and Mother's Day fall on the same weekend so it was quite a festive time with lots going on.

Pat responds with an elaborate narrative, at least four times longer than any letter she has written, in the course of which she introduces class concerns that unify her identity as the mother and hence differentiate her experience as a mother from Ellen's. In other words, Pat's narrative interrupts their mutually constructed gender identity with a representation of herself as a subject unified in relation to Mother's Day that differs considerably from the self represented in Ellen's narrative.

In the first of five episodes, Pat establishes mood, explaining that on the Thursday evening before Mother's Day, after finally succeeding in bathing and putting the younger children to bed, she found herself "down hartit" and worrying about how hard her husband works at his two jobs and how his not being at home much means that she feels "like a mom and a dad." She follows this orientation to her state of mind with a second episode in which her two older children ask what she wants for Mother's Day. She reports telling her son that "a card will do" but confiding to her daughter that "what I want you can't affordit." Pressed by the daughter to tell, she admits to wanting "a ciling fane for my dinning room." Pat indicates that a ceiling fan is out of the question by writing "she laugh and so did I laugh." The third episode, which opens with an account of the complicated childcare arrangements made in order for her son to take her window shopping for ceiling fans that Friday evening, includes: a brief description of the shopping spree ("there are lots of fanes to look at but I like this one fane a lots"); a scene in which the son surprises her by giving her the money to buy the fan; and an account of what happens when they return home where the children are waiting ("They all where happy for mom but not as thrill as I was inside of me"). On Saturday, the fourth episode begins with a gift of flowers from her son and his "girl friend" and concludes with dinner with the younger children at McDonald's, where a young woman at the counter tells Pat that her son "is an inspiration to the young people here" who "miss he but there is hope for the future." (In a previous letter Pat has explained that her son worked at McDonald's for a year and a half while attending a local community college, but had since taken a job at a hospital where, after three promotions, he was making 10% more than he had as manager of the night shift at McDonald's.) She concludes the fourth episode with "I was so proud of him. Went I was told this." The fifth and final episode begins on Mother's Day morning with her husband making breakfast, after which she receives a box of candy from the smaller children, a card containing ten dollars from all the children, two "short sets" from her grandson, and yet another box of candy from the son's "girl friend." Reflecting on events in the conclusion of her letter, Pat writes: "I was surprize it was a beautiful motherday weekend. I feel like I writing a book so I am lifeing now."

The demonstrations of familial affection in Pat's narrative apparently resolve her internal conflict (discouragement). In a family where money is scarce—the husband works two jobs, the son holds a full-time job while attending community college, and the daughter is employed—the members shower the mother with cash and commodities. Rather than confine their celebration of the mother to service—cooking for her or dining out—the family extends it to include both the material tokens—the flowers, the fan, the clothes, and the candy—and the thrill of consumption—the material event of shopping and paying for the fan. The ritual acts of consumption and service that dramatize the mother's value in this working-class family temporarily align all its members with the economy. In other words, the economic realities that are continually threatening its unity are replaced by a four-day fantasy in which the family compensates the mother for her emotional and physical labor.

Middle-class families do not ordinarily celebrate motherhood with consumption rituals. What Ellen has described is the familiar middle-class service ritual in which the mother is released from the specific task of cooking, a symbol of the domestic responsibilities that threaten to alienate those mothers who also work outside the home from their families. In response to Pat's narrative, Ellen writes, "I enjoyed hearing about all your very nice Mother's Day surprises. It sounds as though you have a very loving and considerate family. They must really appreciate how hard you work and all of the many things you do for them." Ellen's is a gracious comment that fully acknowledges their shared understanding of mothers' work and once again articulates their mutual identity as gendered subjects. But Ellen's response fails to articulate Pat's representation of her own and, by extension, Ellen's subjectivity as contingent on class. It's not just that their families understand the mother differently. I suspect that the working-class celebration of the mother would strike Ellen as too much and that the middle-class celebration would strike Pat as too little. Differences in their material circumstances separate them as mothers (neither Ellen nor her middle-class family need ritual relief from economic hardships), and Ellen's comment fails to acknowledge that Pat's class-based narrative places them in distinct rather than the same subject positions as women.

Ellen concludes her letter with a suggestion that draws Pat's attention to what is not said. "Since this is the last week of your classes you can wrtie (sic) me at my home address if you think that you will have the time and would like to continue writing. I know that I would enjoy hearing from you." Pat understands the absence of any expressed desire to write as well as read her letters to mean that Ellen has lost the enthusiasm for writing she expressed in earlier correspondence: "At first I was nervous about writing to someone I didn't know, but now I enjoy writing them and look forward to your letter each week." By invoking the institutional auspices under which they have been corresponding—"this is the last week of your classes"—Ellen effectively shifts from the discourse of art in which they have both been representing and articulating their subjectivity as mothers in personal narratives to the educational discourse in which Pat would presumably be a student writing for a teacher.

Pat interrupts the shift in discourse and subject positions that Ellen has suggested when she writes: "I would like to know, if you would still writing me, or not if not it has been nice writing to you. I don't know if it help you are not, I know it has help me a lot. Thank you very must." Pat offers yet another version of their educational relationship in which she and Ellen would continue to learn from one another by corresponding, but she makes it clear, I think, that the decision to write as well as read is Ellen's. And Ellen chooses not to write back.

CONCLUSION

Since the late 1970s, that is, since the publication of Pierre Bourdieu and Jean-Claude Passeron's *Reproduction in Education, Society and Culture*, many teachers and parents, and some administrators and social theorists and social scientists, have been concerned about the extent to which schools not only tolerate but legitimate the very forms of classism, racism, and sexism that American education is publicly charged with eliminating. I mention this by way of pointing out that law provides educational opportunity for those it designates as the subjects of social and economic discrimination. Indeed, it is the state that provides a good deal of the funding for the Adult Basic Education program that the working-class students in the study were attending. Yet the data remind us that law does not protect these students from the dialect of educational discourse in which a teacher's control over discursive practice is contingent on the ideology that classroom language transcends class, race, and gender.

The teachers in this study are not ogres—far from it. They are energetic and inventive practitioners committed to universal education. In their writing, however, that commitment manifests itself in an approach to teaching and learning that many educators share in this country, a view that insists that the classroom is a separate world of its own, in which teachers and students relate to one another undistracted by the classism, racism, and sexism that rage outside the classroom. Discursive hegemony of teachers over students is usually posed and justified in developmental terms—as cognitive deficits, emotional or intellectual immaturity, ignorance, and most recently, cultural literacy—any one of which would legitimate asymmetrical relationships between its knowing subjects, teachers, and its unknowing subjects, students. To the credit of the teachers who participated in this study, none took the usual recourse of justifying their discursive control by focusing on errors in spelling, grammar, and mechanics that are indubitably there and that make reading the literacy letters as difficult as reading Lacan, Derrida, Foucault, or Althusser. Yet the teachers frenetically protected educational discourse from class, and in their respective refusals to admit class concerns into the letters, they first distanced and then alienated themselves from their correspondents.

While educational discourse defends its privileged subjects against resistance, against the violence that Dora narrates, against Esther's lesson in economics, and even against Pat's much celebrated mother, the linguistic and rhetorical uneasiness with which these attempts to articulate working-class subjectivity were met suggests that the class-free discourse that seems immutable in theory is, in practice, a source of some ambivalence for the teachers in this study. What is immediately challenged by the narratives is the rhetorical practice in which the privileges of one subject—to tell stories or decide what the topic is—materially diminish the rights of other subjects. What is ultimately challenged is the ideology that class, and by extension race and gender differences, are present in American society but absent from American classrooms. If that's true, it is only true because the representation by students of those concerns inside educational discourse goes unarticulated by teachers.

To teach is to authorize the subjects of educational discourse. We have all been faced with the choice that Pat gave Ellen. To say no to writing is to say no to differences that matter to those students who live on the margins of an educational discourse that insists that they articulate themselves as the subjects teachers represent, or not at all. To say yes to writing is to say yes to those alternative subjectivities that Dora, Esther, and Pat represent in their writing and that are left unchallenged when unarticulated by Don, Rita, and Ellen. In this instance, teachers and students alike lose the opportunity to question the extent to which class figures in any individual's rendering of a unified self. Resistance inside educational discourse is then a practice in cooperative articulation on the part of students and teachers who actively seek to construct and understand the differences as well as similarities between their respective subject positions.

WORKS CITED

Bartholomae, David. "Inventing the University." *When a Writer Can't Write.* Ed. Mike Rose. New York: Guilford P, 1985. 134–65.

———. "The Study of Error." *College Composition and Communication* 31 (1980): 253–69.

Bourdieu, Pierre, and Jean-Claude Passeron. *Reproduction in Education, Society and Culture.* Beverly Hills: Sage, 1977.

Brodkey, Linda. "Topics of Literacy." *Journal of Education* 168 (1986): 47–54.

Crowley, Sharon. "writing and Writing." *Writing and Reading Differently: Deconstruction and the Teaching of Composition and Literature.* Ed. Douglas Atkins and Michael L. Johnson. Lawrence: UP of Kansas, 1985. 93–100.

Fine, Michelle. "Silencing in the Public Schools." *Language Arts* 64 (1987): 157–74.

Foucault, Michel. "The Discourse on Language." *The Archeology of Knowledge.* New York: Harper & Row, 1976. 215–37.

Hall, Stuart. "On Postmodernism and Articulation: An Interview with Stuart Hall." Ed. Larry Grossberg. *Journal of Communication Inquiry* 10 (1986): 45–60.

Labov, William. *Language in the Inner City: Studies in the Black English Vernacular.* Philadelphia: U of Pennsylvania P, 1972.

Perl, Sandra. "The Composing Processes of Unskilled College Writers." *Research in the Teaching of English* 13 (1979): 317–36.

Pratt, Mary Louise. *Toward a Speech Act Theory of Literary Discourse.* Bloomington: Indiana UP, 1977.

Shaughnessy, Mina. *Errors and Expectations: A Guide for the Teacher of Basic Writing.* New York: Oxford UP, 1977.

Stubbs, Michael. *Language, Schools and Classrooms.* London: Methuen, 1976.

Williams, Raymond. *Marxism and Literature.* New York: Oxford UP, 1977.

Inviting the Mother Tongue

Beyond "Mistakes," "Bad English," and "Wrong Language"

PETER ELBOW

Every time I say something the way I say it, she correct me until I say it some other way. Pretty soon it feel like I can't think. My mind run up on a thought, git confuse, run back and sort of lay down. . . . Look like to me only a fool would want you to talk in a way that feel peculiar to your mind. (Alice Walker 183–84)

. . . Alice Walker's . . . subject . . . writes herself to a personal freedom and to a remarkable level of articulation in the dialect voice in which Hurston's protagonist speaks. (Henry Louis Gates, Jr. 169, emphasis in the original)

[T]he eradication of one tongue is not prerequisite to the learning of a second. (Keith Gilyard 160)

This essay grows out of feeling torn between conflicting goals or obligations. I think most teachers of first year college writing courses also feel this conflict, and I experience it acutely as director of a university writing program. On the one hand, I feel an obligation not to force all my students to conform to the language and culture of mainstream English. (See "The Students' Right to Their Own Language" [Committee].) On the other hand, I feel an obligation to give all my students access to the written language of power and prestige.

The written language of power and prestige. This is not a very precise formulation, and I will use an equally imprecise but common label for it:

First published in JAC 19.3 (1999): 359–88. Reprinted with permission.

Standard Written English (SWE). Precision is not possible here. The conventions of SWE, or what is called correct by prestige readers, can vary from one setting to another—from business to journalism to the academy and even within disciplines. (For example, some will say that SWE forbids all run-ons, fragments, split infinitives, or any use of a capital after a colon; others will say such usages are correct if used well.) But for the purposes of this paper I can side-step such ambiguities and use a highly pragmatic definition of SWE. I say here what I say to my students: "Standard Written English is the usage, grammar, syntax, punctuation, and spelling that will pass muster with most university faculty around here as correct or at least acceptable. Faculty members will differ from each other a bit, but on *most* of these language matters, they will agree."

The most common attitude toward "wrong" language is to want to get rid of it. Citizens of all sorts—whether they are teachers in the schools, college faculty, members of the mainstream general public, spokespersons for culture, or legislators—are likely to agree that a teacher's job is to *"improve"* students' language. And students often feel the same goal for themselves—as we ourselves are likely to feel in relation to our own speaking and writing: if the words that come naturally to our mouth or pen are labeled wrong, we feel ourselves to have a problem.

Historical conditions can intensify these impulses to improve language. There has been a series of influxes into higher education of diverse populations whose native dialect was not the correct or accepted one:

> [T]he push for "proper" grammar and word usage has been shown to coincide with a dramatic change in the demographics of the college population brought on by relatively more open admission policies in the years after the Civil War (Ohmann 234). No longer could the homogeneous student population of the pre-War years be assumed, as more and more young people from non-elite backgrounds came to fill the universities in search of access to the privileges of high socio-economic rank (Berlin 73; Rudolph 151). [from Boyd 57–58]

During this period, as Robert Connors tells us, textbooks emphasized grammar to an unprecedented degree:

> Between 1865 and 1895, such elements of mechanical correctness as grammar, punctuation, spelling, and capitalization, which would never have been found in textbooks before 1850, came to usurp much of the time devoted in class to rhetorical instruction and most of the marking of student writing (Connors 65). [from Boyd 57]

After World War II, returning GIs created another wave of "new students" into higher education. Then came open admissions in the 1960s. And now we live in yet another time of extensive immigration into the country and into higher education. In our college and university classrooms, we find an unprecedented number of speakers of nonmainstream dialects and students for whom English is a second language. In addition, it seems to many college faculty and outside commentators that even the monolingual natives—students who grew up with the mainstream dialect—arrive in college with "bad English." Historical situations like these, then, can fuel desires to preserve the standard or accepted or prestige language intact—to keep it from being misused, debased, corrupted. No wonder we hear strong calls for "English Only."

But I am *not* trying to get rid of what people call wrong language, errors, carelessness, or nonmainstream language. On the contrary, I'm trying to make a safer place for all of it. I may sound perverse to some readers, but my main goal in this essay is to show how the *writing classroom* can be a safer place for such language than most sites of language use—a place where, for a good deal of the time, students can put out of mind any worries about whether anyone might consider their language wrong or incorrect.

The problem is that students cannot have that crucial experience of safety for writing *inside* our classrooms unless we can also show them how to be safe *outside*—that is, unless we can also help them produce final drafts that conform to Standard Written English. It is because I care so much about making room for the mother tongue and making the classroom safe for what people call wrong that I want to insist that my students learn to produce SWE too. (By "mother tongue" I mean dialects of English, not languages other than English.)

How can we possibly pull this off—especially in a one-semester course for first year students? Especially if it's their only writing course, or their only course except for some "writing intensive" courses or a junior year writing course—a common situation in colleges and universities. Before I offer some concrete proposals, I need to explore the two goals themselves: safety inside our classrooms for the mother tongue and language people call wrong, and also the ability to produce correct SWE.

Because the second goal is so clear and simple, let me start with it: correct Standard Written English. Teachers of other subjects sometimes penalize students more for what they call wrong language and surface mistakes than for other weaknesses in their writing. Issues of correctness become even more weighty from the perspective of race. Lisa Delpit is surely right when she criticizes white "liberal" teachers for handicapping students of color by ignoring their need to master the dialects of power:

To imply to children or adults . . . that it doesn't matter how you talk or how you write is to ensure their ultimate failure. . . . [T]here is a political power game that is also being played, and if they want to be in on that game there are certain games they too must play. ("Silenced Dialogue" 292)

But what about my first goal of safety? It's not that I love language that people call wrong *because* they call it wrong (though my wife thinks I do). What I love is the mother tongue. Most people cannot really feel comfortable or at home writing, and cannot use writing as naturally as speaking, unless they are taught to write in their home voice—that is, in whatever language comes naturally to hand and mouth. People can't learn to write well unless they write a great deal and with some pleasure, and they can't do that unless they feel writing to be as comfortable as an old shoe—something they can slip into naturally and without pinching.

After all, we experience our language or dialect not just as something we use but as a deep part of *us*. Our home language is not just inside us; we are also inside it (see Pierce, Norton, and many of the essays in the volume by Severino, Guerra, and Butler). The metaphor of "mother tongue" is no joke. How do you think I'll feel if you shout at me, "Aaahhh, your mother tongue wears combat boots," or "Your mother tongue spends her life on her back"?

I grew up in the comfortable white middle class. Both my parents went to college and they respected teachers—professors more so. They admired most things intellectual, and along with that, "good" language. Indeed, my mother was a bit disappointed when I came home from two years' study at Oxford with no English accent, thus revealing a not so uncommon feeling that American English is inferior to British English (meaning "good" British English). I also grew up, I should add, with another mother who spoke Black English.

Despite my linguistic blessings, I have come to notice something interesting when I am trying to copy-edit away my mistakes for a final draft: not just that copy-editing is a bother because it takes so much time and trouble. What strikes me more, now that I've come to notice and acknowledge it to myself, is a feeling of resentment against the *actual acquiescence* to correctness. I feel a little sheepish about admitting what seems to be such a childish feeling, but I have a hunch I'm not the only one: "I want you to take me as I *am*."

There is a crucial larger point here: *Standard Written English is no one's mother tongue.* People like me have a mother tongue much closer to SWE than many others do, but there is still a distance. The words and constructions that come naturally to my tongue are often inappropriate for writing.

Speech and writing are different dialects. For writing, there is still a need to acquiesce—to "give in."[1]

If *I* feel I have to give in when I write, then what must many of our students be feeling? When students turn in final drafts full of mistakes, we often say, "How careless!" or "How lazy!" But now I'm suspecting that plenty of them may be saying—consciously or unconsciously: "If you won't take me the way I am, then screw you."

What if I'd been raised poor or working class and speaking a nonmainstream dialect? Furthermore, what if it weren't just nonmainstream but *bad*? That is, certain dialects are widely seen as inferior, defective, or broken (e.g., African-American English, Latino or Hispanic English, Puerto Rican English, Mexican-American English, or Hawai'ian Creole English). If I spoke a stigmatized dialect, my speech would be widely experienced as stupid—and I along with it. And I might get this message not only from speakers of mainstream English. Even my mother—whose tongue it is—might call our shared natural speech "bad English" or "trash" talk. Jesse Jackson publicly characterized Ebonics or black English in just such terms. Yes, his response was blurted, and he later qualified it, but his blurt said a lot. ("[S]ome of the most scornful and negative criticism of AAVE [African American Vernacular English] speakers comes from African Americans" [Lippi-Green 200]. Note that my real mother also harbored the hope that I'd abandon her perfectly respectable dialect for a "superior" one.)

Of course, middle class white speakers may also be told that their mistakes are "bad English" that imply ignorance. But such mistakes are seldom experienced as implying stupidity. Spanish speakers from Spain who are struggling with English will not feel that their dialect is inherently stupid or trash. The mistakes of ESL speakers from an Asian background are often experienced by teachers as poetic and insightful.

I try to imagine what it would be like if I had grown up with a stigmatized dialect. If I found myself a student in your class and you asked me to write in mainstream English (and I wasn't comfortably bi-dialectal), your request would be problematic. If I went along with you, I would know, consciously or not, that I would have to give in to a culture that thinks my language is defective or bad—or even that a core part of my very self is stupid or bad. Not only that: I would also have to give in to a culture that has been trying to wipe out my culture and what I experience as part of my core self. Besides, some of my best buddies or family members might make fun of me or even disown me if I were to give in and start using your English. ("Over at my school, if they—first time they catch you talkin' white, they'll never let it go. Even if you just quit talking like that, they'll never let it go!" [Lippi-Green 191]. "In the group I most loved, to be fully hip meant to repudiate a school system in which African-American consciousness was undervalued or ignored" [Gilyard 160]. See also Fordham and Ogbu.)

It wouldn't matter how understanding and supportive you were: I'd still be liable *not* to want to give in to mainstream or prestige English—or at least not till I've done some hard chewing and unpleasant swallowing. Yet if you don't find some way around this problem, you will have no success as my writing teacher. For even if you somehow do get me to write correctly—by carrot or stick—I'll be building anger and resentment into the very activity of writing.

If I were a student in that situation, how might you get me to write without resentment—and write more than the minimal required amount? You would have to try to set up the following conditions:

- ♦ You would have to show me that you respect my dialect and accept it as a full, complete, sophisticated language—in no way inferior or defective compared to Standard Written English. Fortunately for you, this is something that most linguists agree on.

- ♦ You would have to show me that you see me as smart. And not just smart but linguistically sophisticated. Fortunately for you, there is a simple obvious fact here—though I and others in the class will constantly need to be reminded of it: even though I am less skilled in SWE than most speakers of prestige English, I possess a linguistic sophistication that most of them lack. I have had lots of practice in hearing and understanding *multiple* dialects. In fact, I have probably learned to switch codes quickly and easily. My mainstream classmate speakers are usually less linguistically sophisticated and more blind to some of the social realities of linguistic variation.

- ♦ You would have to make your class a place where I can *use* my mother tongue as much as I want. *Or* as little as I want. That is, you have to offer me a real invitation to use my mother dialect, yet you can't come across like bell hooks' teacher and fellow students who told her that her voice was only "true" and "authentic" when she used a Southern black dialect (hooks 11).

- ♦ Ideally you would have to set things up so that *other students* see me and my language as fully sophisticated and rich. But let's hope that I would understand that chauvinist, classist, and racist attitudes of some of my fellow students cannot be changed by a teacher in a single course.

I don't mean to imply that all speakers of stigmatized dialects are resistant or angry. Some have internalized the feeling that their mother dialect is indeed inferior or wrong. Such a feeling is understandable for many reasons. Lippi-Green points out that any black student who feels her language to be as good as mainstream English will have to live with "an unresolvable conflict": "*'I acknowledge that my home language is viable and adequate'* and *'I acknowledge that my home language will never be accepted'*" (186, emphasis in the original). Students who have internalized a sense of inferiority about their mother tongue may be compliant and docile, but that very outlook is likely to undermine them as strong users of language.

Yet how can I reconcile this goal of a completely safe place in our classrooms for the mother tongue and language that people call wrong with my other goal of producing essays that conform to Standard Written English? I'll give my argument in a minute, but first one more delay — one more reason why I want so much for the writing classroom to be a safe haven for the mother tongue.

Walter Ong repeatedly points to the obvious fact that the mother tongue is more deeply connected to the unconscious than any dialect or language we learn later. When language is in touch with the unconscious and draws on it, that language usually has more force and resonance. Writing gains energy, life, and voice when it is fed by the various linguistic elements that permeate the unconscious, but many of these elements are wrong or incorrect in writing: slang, colloquialisms, childishness, idiosyncratic voice, so-called deviant or nonmainstream dialects — and all the kinds of instinctive and bodily-linked utterances and partial utterances that Julia Kristeva calls "semiotic" rather than "symbolic" discourse.

I'm not arguing that the mother tongue and these elements from the unconscious are the only sources of power and vitality in writing. But they are strong sources, and more to the point, *they are the sources most readily accessible to unskilled writers* — especially writers who grew up using nonprestige dialects of English. It is for all these reasons, then, that I take it as my goal to make the first year writing course (indeed, every writing course) a place where our students' own comfortable and natural language can flourish — the language that comes instinctively to mind, ear, and tongue. (Unfortunately I cannot take this goal for speakers of languages other than English.)

I've been talking so much about dialects the mainstream culture seems bent on wiping out that perhaps you'll think I have no interest in apple pie mistakes that mainstream speakers produce through carelessness or ignorance of the conventions. Not so. Even if mainstream students don't have the handicap of a nonprestige dialect, they still have a serious disadvantage in writing that needs just as much safety. That is, very few of them have ever had the experience of writing for a teacher while their minds were *focused wholeheartedly on their meaning, topic, or thinking.* Even mainstream English speakers tend to devote a large amount of their attention to questions of correctness in grammar, spelling, and so forth.

How must our writing suffer if some of our attention is always leaking away from our meaning, our reasoning, and our organizing to matters of correct language—wondering what a reader with authority over us will call wrong? Full attention to thinking and rhetoric is not possible unless we can make the classroom a place that is safe for *all* forms of language considered wrong.

HOW CAN I ACHIEVE BOTH GOALS?

So where am I? I'm seeking safety for all language that comes naturally to the tongue, and yet I know that such language *cannot* be safe, and that the mother tongue cannot flourish, unless we also help our students produce final drafts that conform to the conventions of SWE. In the face of this dilemma, I could simply repeat what people might expect from my past writing: "Just relax about propriety or correctness on early and middle drafts, but then be vigilant about copy-editing at the end. Learn to alternate between opposite mentalities."

This answer is all very well in general, but it's too general to help us in a one semester writing course that is the only one students are likely to get. Too many students are simply incapable of getting their final drafts to conform to what we call SWE—no matter how vigilantly they copy-edit. We could try to *teach* them everything they need for successful copy-editing, but some students don't need this teaching at all while others need more than we can provide even if we did nothing else. (If I were an English teacher in elementary or high school, I would make the teaching of grammar a substantial part of my curriculum, but I would be with my students more hours per week and more weeks per year than I now get in my college course, and I'd also know that they take English in every grade.)

We could also restrict our *regular* one semester first year writing class to those students who don't need instruction in conventions of usage or copy-editing, and put the others in remedial or basic classes devoted to those matters. But if we take that path, we tend to focus the basic course on "error" and send just the wrong message to students who are least skilled at SWE: "If you want to learn to write, you must first concentrate most of your attention on grammar and correctness. Only after you master surface features do you get to concentrate your attention wholeheartedly on the substance of your thinking." Also, segregation on the basis of surface features of language can result in segregation on the basis of race and class. I am not arguing against all basic writing courses, but I am troubled by how they often function. (See Royer and Gilles for a promising approach to placement into basic writing.)

So I'm stuck with the same conflict of goals or obligations I started with, and yet I've dug myself deeper into a hole. By becoming even more committed to safety for the mother tongue, I've made it harder to achieve my goal of giving students power and control over the kind of language that most teachers and most employers will insist on as correct. It seems as though I'll have to give in a bit on correctness. This is, of course, a well trodden path: simply to become a bit more tolerant of final drafts with grammar, syntax, and spelling that deviates from SWE. But Delpit's indictment continues to ring in my ears: that white "liberal, middle class" teachers ensure "that power . . . remains in the hands of those who already have it" ("Silenced Dialogue" 285). I want *all* students to produce the language they need in order to avoid stigmatization by other teachers and readers.

Therefore, in this essay I will suggest another path—one that I have begun to follow in my teaching. Instead of relaxing the "tough" goal of successful copy-editing, I can *reframe* it or rethink it. That is, I can demand and try to teach a slightly different writerly ability—one that is both more important yet in fact more teachable than the ability singlehandedly to get all grammar, syntax, and spelling to conform to SWE. I'm talking about the practical ability to take whatever steps are necessary to get the desired grammar, syntax, punctuation, and spelling—*even if that means getting help.*

"Whatever steps are necessary." It's surprising how many students can copy-edit successfully if they just focus their wholehearted attention and commitment to the job. They can access knowledge of conventions that they sometimes trick us into thinking they lack. But of course many students cannot get rid of all deviations from SWE no matter how much they care or how hard they try. They will have to call on help. I urge these students to seek help from various sources: spell checkers, grammar programs (admittedly problematic), writing centers, learning labs, roommates, friends, loved ones, and even paid typists or editors. I offer *help* during my office hours too, though like the writing center, I won't copy-edit for them. We have no qualms about requiring *typed* papers from students, even if that means some of them pay for the job. We don't object when professional writers are given free copy-editing by publishers. Why should we object if students also get help? As teachers of writing, we need to recognize that taking whatever steps are needed for successful copy-editing is an important and inherent part of what it means to be a writer. (Of course, speakers of a nonmainstream dialect may need more than just copy-editing. More about this later.)

The central thing here is a shift in what we require: not the impossible demand that all our students know enough about English grammar and conventions of usage to do it all without help, but rather the pragmatic and feasible demand that they know how to take charge of their writing process and do what is needed. I now simply make this a required part of my course—like attendance—for the four or five most important essays of the semester.

In one sense, this policy is a move toward *softness*—letting students off the hook and condoning "cheating." But help in copy-editing is not plagiarizing—unless you want to say that all published authors are guilty of plagiarism. It makes me happy when students figure out how to get the help they need. This is feasible knowledge, and it is crucial for success in future courses and jobs. If I say they have to copy-edit successfully without help, I am setting them up for inevitable failure, no matter how hard I try to teach grammar and spelling.

And as for real or substantive plagiarism, this approach is actually a big help. It is much easier to know if students are really writing their own papers when I see early and middle and even late drafts that are very much in their own tongue—for it is inherent in this approach to use at least three drafts on major essays as we move toward an additional copy-edited, "publication draft." I also have them do plenty of informal writing in class and I see a certain amount of that.

But in another sense, this policy is a move toward *toughness*: students who need the most help will often have the fewest friends and loved ones who can copy-edit well—and the least money to buy help. This could be called unfair, but I've reconciled myself to it because I find the alternatives unacceptable: making the class less safe for the mother tongue or letting these students turn in final drafts that will undermine their chances of success with other teachers and employers. And as I've begun to use this policy, I've discovered that students who speak a nonmainstream dialect (and also second-language students) are usually more understanding of the need for these copy-editing steps. They can usually manage my requirement with the help of writing centers and friends; a few pay. It's the complacent mainstream speakers who resent the requirement or can't comprehend that they need help. Mainstream speakers also need to know the pragmatic truth about the power and politics of language. You have to turn in correct final drafts if you want to avoid stigma; but you don't have do all the correcting yourself.

Admittedly, a *few* stickler teachers mark down students on matters of surface mechanics on in-class essay exams where there is no chance for help in copy-editing. But my nonmainstream dialect students will be worse off in such situations if they can't even put their best thinking into comfortable and clear language. There are also a few jobs that demand the ability to copy-edit memos on the spot with no chance for help. But these jobs are pretty rare, and I don't think it makes sense to design a first year, one-semester writing course as preparation for them.

PUTTING THIS POLICY INTO PRACTICE

This policy can seem contradictory and confusing to students. Some of them think I don't really care about good copy-editing since I invite the mother tongue and carelessness about surface language on early and mid-process drafts. Others think I am "hung up about correctness" with my blanket demand for conformity to SWE on final drafts. And some students are confused when I push them for good thinking, organization, and clarity on *midprocess* drafts while nevertheless not pushing them on correctness. (If a student really wants feedback on surface features on early drafts, I'll give it, but only if this doesn't deflect attention from thinking, organization, and clarity of meaning.) But few students have trouble understanding the policy when I relate it to the political realities of language use. I make it clear that I'm not calling SWE inherently better than other dialects. I'm emphasizing that they can't have success in most college courses and most job situations without writing that conforms to the conventions of SWE.

More to the point, I engage in some concrete practices that I think are worth spelling out briefly:

- ◆ I make this copy-editing demand on only four or five major essays. I assign lots of quickwrites, exercises, and informal assignments that needn't be well copy-edited.

- ◆ On major essays, I find it crucial to specify copy-editing as a separate assignment with a separate due date. On my course calendar I have one due date for the "third and almost final draft" (which does not have to be well copy-edited), and then a due date one or two classes later for the fourth or "publication draft," and this must be successfully copy-edited. When I used to stop with a third draft, I finally realized that I was asking students to do two conflicting cognitive tasks at once: revise for content, organization, and style, *and* copy-edit for surface features. It doesn't bother me that some students will find the copy-editing assignment quite easy. In the second half of the semester, I sometimes ask for a bit of other homework for the same class.

651

♦ I find it helpful to define copy-editing as a blunt yes/no requirement rather than something I grade along a continuum. I compare it to the requirement that they come to class, or that they turn in all previous drafts with later drafts, or do process writing. If I "grade" copy-editing, I am treating it as a matter of talent. Yes, good copy-editing *is* a talent, but I'm purposely taking it out of that realm and putting it into the realm of responsibility, diligence, and self-management — something done or not done. That's the message I'm trying to send: "If you want to pass this course you simply have to manage yourself and do the things that writers do — one way or another."

♦ I try to exploit what seems to me the biggest help in copy-editing: the human voice. Many students have never *heard* what they have written. When they read out loud with any degree of presence and they actually *hear* their words, they make many improvements in the surface features of their words. No, the ear won't help with spelling mistakes or even usually with forms like "would of," but the improvements from reading out loud are extensive — *as long as* I train students to be braver and speak with full intonation and to listen with care (see Chafe). Therefore, I get students to do lots of reading out loud: in pairs, in small groups, sometimes to the whole class — and often to me in frequent conferences. I use many short conferences for hearing them read their papers out loud and then responding on the spot (instead of taking the papers home to respond in writing). Of course, speakers of nonmainstream dialects don't by any means notice all deviations from SWE by ear, but they do in fact notice and correct a remarkably large number of them, especially problems in punctuation. Much of their knowledge of the mainstream dialect is in their ears.

♦ In our program we have always used lots of publication. Four or five times a semester every teacher publishes every student's essay in a class magazine. Students have an easier time taking copy-editing seriously when they see their "publication drafts" in a magazine in their classmates' hands. We use a lab fee to pay for photocopying class magazines.

♦ And of course I try to soften my "hard" requirement with concrete help:

  • I teach some mini-lessons in usage, grammar, punctuation, occasionally a point of spelling, and we do a few exercises in copy-editing a sample paper.

- I take some class time for discussing ways to get help in copy-editing—just like getting help having papers typed. I talk about what the Writing Center can and cannot do. I try to help them make better use of spell checkers. (I want to learn how to help them make better use of grammar/style checkers.) We talk about trying to find friends or loved ones who can do a good job, and ways of bartering for help.

- On their first major essay, when I get their third drafts, I write in copy-editing suggestions for the first page or two, and suggest copy-editing strategies they might need to use for the rest of the paper. I may call in a few students who face a big copy-editing job and give them some help in conference—but I concentrate on getting them to talk about the steps *they* need to take to get more help.

- On the days when I return third drafts, I often set up peer copy-editing teams in class. I wander around a bit and try to have some whole-class discussion of specific questions that come up.[2]

AN OBJECTION TO THIS APPROACH FOR SPEAKERS OF NONMAINSTREAM DIALECTS

Your approach may be fine for mainstream students, but you can't invite speakers of other dialects of English to do most of their writing in the mother tongue and then at the end say, "Now just copy-edit out the surface features of the dialect." Dialects consist of more than just different third-person verb endings. A dialect carries deeper habits of rhetoric and organization. Speakers of nonmainstream dialects who write early drafts in their mother tongue will have to rewrite much of the substance and even thinking of their essays at the end in order to have a college essay in Standard Written English. Where does one find a partner or hire an editor for that job? Thought and language are deeply linked, but your proposal implies that they can be handily separated.

This objection connects with the scholarship in contrastive rhetoric that shows how culture is linked with language, rhetoric, thinking, and even modes of identity. There is extensive research about how people in different cultures argue and persuade and present ideas differently. For one example, Arnetha Ball, one of the prime researchers of African American English (AAE), researched the modes of organizing and presenting ideas that were used and preferred by a group of African American students and compared them to results for a group of mainstream students. She found that AAE students had a greater tendency to use and to prefer narrative and circumlocutionary modes for presenting their thinking or experience. (For interesting contributions to contrastive rhetoric, see Coleman, De and Gregory, Fox, and Shen. For an ambitious overview of studies in contrastive rhetoric, see Connor.)

This objection also connects with the almost universally accepted advice about learning a new language: "don't formulate your thoughts in your home language and then *translate* them into the new language; it's far better to operate *in* the new language so you can learn to get comfortable in it." In short, if culture, language, thinking, and perhaps even identity are deeply linked, it would seem to follow that we shouldn't ask students to write in their home dialect when it carries a different culture of thinking and rhetoric from what they are supposed to end up with.

In response to this strong objection, I want to propose three arguments.

1. **I am not writing about ESL.** Most of the research in contrastive rhetoric about the links between culture and rhetoric, and about the difficulties of students who were raised in one culture trying to write in a new one, involves *different languages*. (Arnetha Ball's research on dialects, just mentioned, is an exception; I'll take up her findings below. Helen Fox emphasizes the difficulty and anxiety for students moving across entire languages.) In this essay I am not suggesting that students move from one language to an entirely different one, but rather that they move a much shorter distance from one dialect of English to another.

   Yet even "translating" may not be so bad. For even though I'm not suggesting that we should invite speakers of Japanese or Turkish to write early drafts in their home language, perhaps it's not such a wild idea. Some startling research on total translation from one language to another provides interesting support for my suggestion that students engage in a much milder form of "translation" between dialects of the same language. In a careful research study of forty-eight Japanese university students writing in English, Kobayashi and Rinnert compared the quality of their compositions using two composing processes: writing directly in English, and writing in Japanese and then translating into English. They found that all students produced higher quality compositions through translation—though high English-proficiency students benefited much less:

   > In the translation versions, these students developed more ideas with explanations and specifics, which captured the readers' attention, and they also used more sophisticated vocabulary and a

greater variety of form. These results suggest that composing initially in the first language allows students, especially those of lower language proficiency, easier and freer discovery of meaning (e.g., as discussed by Zamel, 1982 and Spack, 1984) and support Lay's (1982) and Cumming's (1989) observations about the benefits of first-language use in second-language writing. (201)

2. **The hardest journey may be from oral to literate.** Most nonmainstream or stigmatized dialects of English are oral and not written. Therefore, the journey for speakers of these dialects in writing college essays may not be so much a journey from one language to another, *per se*, nor from one ethnic culture to another, *per se*, as it is a journey from oral modes of thinking and rhetoric to written modes of thinking and rhetoric. Ball writes: "[S]peakers of AAE . . . because of their cultural and linguistic experiences, rely on oral discourse features" and have "vernacular-based preferences in expository patterns" ("Cultural Preference" 520). That is, the changes in rhetoric and thinking needed for writing college essays are difficult not because the home dialect is a *different dialect* but rather because the home dialect is an *oral dialect*.

    Therefore, the strategy of asking these students to write out their oral thinking and rhetoric as it comes to the tongue will serve as a helpful midway stage in their journey from oral to written modes of thinking and rhetoric. If we want our students to take on the power of full mainstream literacy, we can never remove the difficulty or even identity anxiety that some of them may experience in having to move past an oral culture (not necessarily to leave it) and take on a culture of literacy. But we can substantially mitigate their anxiety by inviting them to take on *full literacy* in their oral dialect. And let's not forget that *lots* of mainstream students in our first year writing classes have not read or written very much; therefore, they too cannot really be considered to have entered the culture of literacy. Many of them also show the same tendencies toward an oral-based rhetoric of narrative, circumlocution, and indirectness.

3. **Links are not chains.** There may indeed be deep links between language, thinking, culture, and identity, but links are not chains. Even a knowledgeable authority about contrastive rhetoric like Ilona Leki insists that a culture does not consist of just one way of thinking:

> Despite a possible resurrection of the Sapir-Whorf hypothesis (see Connor's essay in this volume), contrastive rhetoric cannot show us the thought patterns of another culture. Rhetorical choices are not

directly linked to thought patterns; they are made in response to social, political, and rhetorical contexts and histories. . . . [And] yet the findings of contrastive-rhetoric research on a single text type (or a small number of text types) have sometimes been promulgated as discoveries about an entire cultural group's general rhetorical preferences. . . . How many writing teachers of native English-speaking (NES) students would be willing to accept descriptions of English rhetorical patterns based on essays by a randomly selected group of NES freshmen writing in a language other than English, even one as close to English as French, let alone Chinese? (236. Leki is writing in a rich and impressive collection of essays that will probably interest readers of this essay: *Writing in Multicultural Settings*. Severino, Guerra, and Butler, editors.)

The mere *use* of a dialect or language does not lock someone into one way of thinking or prevent other ways of thinking. Shall we say, for example, that people cannot analyze or think abstractly if they are using AAE? Smitherman is at pains to show otherwise in her *Talkin and Testifyin* and in some remarkable research findings noted below. (See Thomas Farrell for a striking contrary assertion that such links are indeed chains. He argues that Black children get lower IQ scores because their dialect is oral and lacks "the full standard deployment of the verb 'to be' and depends too much on additive and appositional constructions rather than embedded modification and subordination" [481].)

Does mainstream English or SWE "own" certain discourses? Do people have to give up their cultural identity to take on certain rhetorical or intellectual or cognitive tasks? Surely not. I believe we can validly invite speakers of AAE or other dialects and cultures to take on academic tasks and write an academic essay *in* their home dialects—*as* Latinos, African Americans, or Caribbeans. (Note a related case. The discourses of abstraction, analysis, and logic are genuinely and deeply *linked* with white, male, Western culture, yet plenty of women have insisted that they don't have to give up their identity as women to use these discourses. See Nussbaum for a vigorous statement of this position.)

TWO STRATEGIES FOR CHANGING THINKING

So where are we? I've been trying to address this objection: *"We shouldn't ask speakers of nonmainstream dialects to compose in their mother tongue and*

656

copy-edit later, because they will have to make substantive changes in their rhetoric and thinking at the end—instead of just copy-editing." I hope I've given convincing answers to the first part of the objection. That is, I've given reasons why it *is* valid to invite these students to compose in their mother tongue (though not to force them to do so). But I have *not* answered the second part of the objection. That is, I fully agree that many of these students will indeed have to make substantive changes in their rhetoric and thinking if they want to end up with strong college essays that conform to the conventions of SWE. Language and thinking *are* deeply linked or intertwined, and therefore my teaching approach makes special difficulties for students who have strong roots in a nonmainstream culture. Let me describe two teaching strategies that I use to deal with these difficulties. I choose one or the other, depending on the assignment, the student, or the point in the semester.

First strategy. I use this strategy when I am pushing for an essay of fairly standard or orthodox structure—that is, an essay that makes a single main point that is well supported with reasons and evidence. I start by inviting students to write about something they care about and to produce exploratory writing or a draft that follows whatever path comes most naturally or comfortably. From a male African American student I get an initial piece of writing that shows various features, some of which are the ones that Ball talks about: it is short; it is narrative based; it treats a personal situation in a personal, conversational way with lots of first person; it has an angry tone and sometimes drifts into hostile second-person address; and it is indirect in that it implies or suggests an overall point but doesn't really make it. In addition, it uses many surface dialect features of AAE.

As a first step, I get the writer to make it longer by explaining more and by giving more details and examples. But I don't ask for any changes in the surface dialect. Next, on the basis of feedback from me and/or classmates, I ask the student to settle on a main point and give more reasons and argument for it. In addition, I get him to think more about purpose and audience and lead him not to direct his anger *at his reader*, but rather to explain in a less angry fashion to *other* readers why his anger at certain people makes sense. (In doing this I am also teaching him about the genre of academic discourse—where you are supposed to speak in the third person to a group of "general readers" rather than speaking directly in the second person to the people you are actually annoyed at.) Only at the end do I get him to make the changes in surface dialect that are needed to get his final draft to conform to the conventions of correct SWE—giving him *some* help but still leaving a lot of responsibility on his shoulders.

This process raises an intriguing question as to the nature of dialect: as he gradually transforms his essay—first in thinking, rhetoric, and organization and finally in grammar, syntax, and spelling—at what point has he abandoned AAE? I think the answer will be a matter of fruitful debate, but however it is settled, it is clear that I am asking him to make substantive changes in his thinking as he moves his drafts to mainstream or academic or "white" modes of thinking and presentation. And thus I have to acknowledge to him that he might experience some of the difficulty or even anxiety that students sometimes experience as they try to adopt rhetorical modes of a different culture from the one they grew up in.

Nevertheless, I would still be able to emphasize to him that he need not, throughout this difficult work, worry at all about his surface language. As he struggles to change his pattern of thinking and organizing, he is still free simply to put down whatever words, syntax, grammar, and spellings that come to mouth and hand, without having to notice, question, or doubt them. So even though I don't want to *minimize* the task this student faces as he tries to change his larger rhetoric, I would argue that this approach considerably reduces the size of his struggle by postponing one very large battle. For the allegedly "minor" or surface features of our dialect are often the peskiest or even the most disturbing elements to try to change.

Of course, some students will not *want* to start off writing in their home dialect. They've always tried to write in mainstream English and it feels too odd to do otherwise. Some even feel it would "pollute" their home dialect: "If I have to end up with a white essay, I want to start off writing white." Fair enough; I make it clear that this is fine with me. This is the bi-dialectal path that most speakers of nonmainstream dialects have traditionally chosen: one dialect for speech, another for writing. But I want to show such students that they have a *choice*: they don't *have* to start out with mainstream English if they want to end up with mainstream English. And I suggest to these students that they *try* drafting in AAE on some other occasions—perhaps in low-stakes freewrites or quickwrites. The whole point here is to give students more choice about language and dialect. Till now, most students were obliged always to try to write in the mainstream dialect of English—and made to feel that they had a big problem if they had trouble doing so.

Second strategy. I use this strategy when the final essay doesn't have to follow a strictly conventional academic organization. And this time let me picture a female student, since some argue (Fox in particular) that women in some nonmainstream cultures have special difficulty moving from a rhetoric of indirectness to the full, blunt, hierarchical explicitness that most teachers want in school essays. This could be someone of Latino or Hawai'ian background (or in fact many seemingly mainstream U.S. backgrounds, as De and Gregory point out [122]). In this strategy I encourage her and help her along in writing it "her way"—perhaps beginning with a story or digression, and only gradually circling around to her main point—a point that she finally makes somewhat indirectly and without any oppositional confrontation with contrary views. I try to help her make her essay as good as she can in "her rhetoric." I give her feedback on early drafts to help her make it better, but without trying to get her to change her rhetorical approach.

But then for her final stages of revision, I suggest a way she can try to *fit* this draft to mainstream readers—even academic readers. I show her how she can add a tiny introductory section to this effect:

> In my essay I am making the following point: [and here she needs to state her point directly and briefly]. But I think I can develop and transmit my point most effectively if I work up to it slowly and state it subtly, weaving it together with various suggestive narratives and scenes.

And if the ending seems abrupt or inconclusive to me—that is, if it doesn't do what we think of as "concluding" in an academic culture—I might suggest adding a comparable blunt note at the end. Of course, she might find these opening or closing sentences offensive, clunky, rude, or even difficult to write. But I would suggest to her that this approach is easier than trying to transform the rhetoric of her whole essay. Thus, where the first strategy involves moving step by step away from one's home rhetoric and dialect— first in matters of rhetoric and organization and finally in surface details— the second strategy invites the student to hang on to home thinking and rhetoric till the end.

This second strategy calls attention to a powerful rhetorical principle: the opening of any discourse has a disproportionate effect on responses by the audience. The opening usually determines whether readers are cooperative or resistant as they read the rest of the text. Cooperative readers often appreciate and even praise the very things they would criticize if they were reading in a resistant frame of mind. An explanatory opening like the one I've just described tends to give readers that crucial feeling: "Yes, I'm in safe hands. This writer seems to know what she is doing." When readers have a sense of where the essay is trying to end up, they are less likely to feel lost if the path wanders. (This holds even for surface features: readers are usually much less upset over spelling and grammar problems if they don't see any in the first page or two.) Similarly, the closing of a text often determines how a reader decides on a final evaluation of a text.

In describing this second strategy I also need to insist on an important cultural observation. Not all successful academic or published writing uses the slam bam thank you ma'am style: first tell 'em what you're going to say, then tell 'em what you are saying, and finally tell 'em what you told 'em. (The five paragraph essay is the paradigm of slam bam.) Many teachers are grateful for subtlety, finesse, movement, and even indirection, *as long as* they can see the writer's skill and control, and as long as they get the help necessary for not feeling lost or bewildered. In the last few decades, academic readers have become accustomed to an astounding range of rhetorical strategies that are anything but four-square. And our journals are rife with first year writing faculty and writing-across-the-curriculum faculty describing adventuresome forms for academic writing (see Bridwell-Bowles for a classic statement).

In fact, I look forward to pushing the second strategy even further. That is, I could invite this student to forget about providing any introductory or concluding assistance to mainstream readers and instead go straight to the final copy-editing. Consider the result. She might well end up with an essay that starts with an anecdote or story and circles around digressively to a main point that is only brushed in. This could be viewed as a very nonmainstream or even "non-Western" essay, but in fact it wouldn't be very different from much writing published in any number of magazines and literary journals. Remember, this essay will not be "carelessly" nonacademic and nonmainstream. The writer will have worked hard—with the teacher's help—to make it as good as it can be in "her rhetoric." And it will be in impeccably correct SWE. Indirection and subtlety are much valued and published—as long as they are handled well. Students from stigmatized dialects need to know this. We need to ponder the point that Victor Villanueva makes in looking back at his writing as an undergraduate college student. He points out that his essays were grounded in what he calls a "Sophist" rhetoric—a "Latino sophistic" that neglected logic—yet these essays were highly successful with his teachers because he made his grammar and spelling flawless (87). Citing and analyzing Villanueva, Pat Bizzell argues for opening the door in our college writing classes to "Rhetorics of 'Color'" (her title).

MAYBE SPEAKERS OF STIGMATIZED DIALECTS DON'T HAVE TO CHANGE THEIR RHETORIC

I've been at pains to acknowledge that speakers of nonmainstream dialects will have to change their rhetoric and thinking, not just tweak their grammar and syntax. I like to acknowledge this because it suggests a larger truth about our job as teachers of writing: whether our students are from the mainstream or not, we usually spend most of our energy trying to affect students' thinking and rhetoric—not just their grammar and syntax. But the examples of Villanueva, Bizzell, and Bridwell-Bowles suggest that perhaps there is a bit more room for variation than is sometimes assumed.

For further and more substantive evidence, we can look at research conducted by Geneva Smitherman and a team of readers who analyzed student exams written for the National Assessment of English Proficiency (NAEP). Their main finding was this:

> For 1984 imaginative and 1984 and 1988 persuasive NAEP essays, a team of experienced writing instructors was able to identify a discernible black discourse style [involving rhetorical and structural features—which they distinguished from black grammar and syntax] and establish criteria for rating the "blackness" of student essays. The team achieved a 90 percent agreement for 867 essays. Results indicated that students who employed a black expressive discourse style received higher NAEP scores than those who did not. In the case of primary trait scores, this finding held regardless of the frequency of BEV [Black English Vernacular] syntax. . . . ("The Blacker the Berry" 94)

Smitherman argues that language and rhetorical norms have changed over time. Her team looked at essays from two earlier tests (1969 and 1979), and found that black discourse style did *not* correlate with higher scores then. She concludes:

> As cultural norms shift focus from "book" English to "human" English, the narrativizing, dynamic quality of the African American Verbal Tradition will help students produce lively, image-filled, concrete, readable essays, regardless of rhetorical modality—persuasive, informative, comparison-contrast, and so forth (95).

One of the important correlative findings by the Smitherman team was that black language and black discourse were *not* necessarily linked. "No correlation was found between a discernibly African American discourse style and the production of BEV syntax" (94).

Of course, Smitherman's is only one study (actually she calls on another one too), and her team did not look at college level writing. Still, her results suggest that we shouldn't be too quick to assume speakers of stigmatized dialects must abandon *all* the rhetorical and linguistic habits of their culture. When people like De and Gregory point to rhetorical losses for students from other cultures writing for mainstream teachers, they usually base their findings on texts produced when students were trying to start off writing in "proper English." Indeed, many of their examples are taken from timed exams—surely a poor window into students' language and thinking. Students may well pay a smaller rhetorical price when they actually get a chance to compose in their home dialect.

There is another price that students pay when they start off trying to write in "proper English": what ESL teachers have called "production errors." That is, students create *additional* deviations from SWE because they are stretching for correctness in an unfamiliar dialect—errors that wouldn't show up if they wrote in their home dialect. Of course, the home dialect produces its own deviations from SWE, but the important point here is this: the grammar and syntax of a nonmainstream dialect of English in the United States is usually *less* alien from SWE than many students think. Every teacher is familiar with the destructive effects of students stretching for an unnecessary "propriety" in writing.

A LONG-TERM GOAL

My short term goal is crudely pragmatic: to help speakers of nonmainstream dialects come up with good essays in *correct* SWE as quickly and easily as possible. But my long term goal is probably no secret: to honor and help pre-serve multiple dialects of English and to legitimize their use *in writing*. Do we really want a world with fewer and fewer dialects? Listen to Toni Morrison:

> The worst of all possible things that could happen would be to lose that language. There are certain things I cannot say without recourse to my language. It's terrible to think that a child with five different present tenses comes to school to be faced with those books that are less than his own language. And then to be told things about his language, which is him, that are sometimes permanently damaging. . . . This is a really cruel fallout of racism. I know the Standard English. I want to use it to help restore the other language, the lingua franca. (quoted in Lippi-Green 185–86)

Linguists tell us that dialects tend to drift toward the dominant language and to die out. I don't think minority dialects can survive and flourish unless they come to be legitimate for writing. Given the growing recognition of English as a *world* language rather than merely the language of the United Kingdom and the United States, however, it's not unrealistic to imagine a future where multiple and very distinct dialects of English *are* legitimate and widely used for writing.

So even in a one semester writing course, while we try to make sure that all students get the final drafts of their major essays to conform to the conventions of SWE, I think we can also honor writing in nonmainstream dialects.

We can invite students to leave their exercises and low stakes writing in the home dialect—helping send the message that nonmainstream dialects don't need to be "corrected" into SWE to be legitimate. And even on major essays, we can invite copy-editing into *two* final drafts: one into correct SWE and one into the best form of the student's home dialect.

Speakers of stigmatized dialects need to know how much good writing is currently being published in these dialects. They need to know about the works of writers like Gloria Anzaldúa, Zora Neale Hurston, Darrell Lum, Sapphire, "Sistren," Alice Walker, and Lois-Ann Yamanaka. As Gates and others have noted, nonprestige dialect tends to appear first as reported speech in poetry and fiction. Gradually it spreads to narrators and to nonfiction. Geneva Smitherman uses African American English even for scholarly and academic writing.

Knowing this, students will be more adventuresome in finding audiences for their writing in nonprestige dialects—audiences that do exist. They will have friends and peers who will appreciate such pieces, and this kind of work is already starting to be published in some campus literary magazines and even at times in the student newspaper. As teachers we may find, as I have, that *we* enjoy it—particularly because writing in nonmainstream dialects tends to have a stronger and livelier voice. Given how much is now being published in nonprestige dialects, I see a day when many more mainstream readers will also appreciate it.

Some people say nonmainstream dialects are not meant to be written; orality is their essence. I have heard this even from native speakers of these dialects. But Middle English literature and a good deal of Renaissance literature in English is nothing *but* writing in local, oral dialects that varied widely according to region. And much of this literature was widely published—some of it by means of copying and circulating, some of it actually printed. Only later did *one* of these dialects become "standard" because it happened to be the dialect of the region that became economically and politically dominant. This tradition of publication in the vernacular continued past the Renaissance with writers like Robert Burns and, more recently, James Kelman. I suspect that the same thing happened in other countries. Dante wrote in a vernacular of the people that was looked down on by many academics for that reason. All our modern European languages started out as nonmainstream oral vernaculars.

So the truth about writing in oral dialects is more curved and interesting than we might have thought: it *used* to be common and it is getting common again; but we have been living through a long period—in England and the United States anyway—when writing in nonprestige oral dialects seems to have been relatively rare. Our present situation highlights a question that is coming more and more to the fore—a dominant question that was the focus of the Spring 1997 special issue of *TESOL Quarterly*: "Who owns English?" In the introductory essay, Bonny Norton asks "whether English belongs to native speakers of English, to speakers of mainstream English, to White people, or to all of those who speak it, irrespective of their linguistic and sociocultural histories" (422).

BRIEF RESPONSES TO TWO OTHER OBJECTIONS

1. I imagine an objection from even a *champion* of nonprestige dialects. I'm thinking of people like De and Gregory who worry about minority dialects being "colonized," engulfed, or tamed when they interact with English and "Western epistemic practices" (120) and with the "rigors of academic thinking and writing" (123). I can imagine them saying that this colonization process will accelerate if we invite students to compose in their home dialect and then revise into SWE. Perhaps nonmainstream dialects can only be preserved intact by *heightening* their separation—and keeping them oral.

I suspect that the strategy I am describing might lead to more mixing and hybridity; and I admire the pedagogical suggestions De and Gregory offer in their efforts to help students keep the logics of two cultures distinct (they focus more on logic than rhetoric). Still, I suspect that dialects can only survive and prosper if they are widely used—in writing and for various purposes. This will probably result in some change, but I'm worried about the survival of dialects if people try too hard to preserve them in their "pure" or unmixed form. Change is the rule when it comes to language and especially dialect. Standard English itself has changed substantially because of contact with nonmainstream dialects. English, perhaps more than most languages, is itself a hybrid. Pratt argues as a linguist that interaction among languages and dialects is the norm and that linguistic homogeneity is the exception, the "utopia." William Labov (see Fasold, Stevens), studying Black English, and Charlene Sato, studying Hawai'ian Creole English, both observe an interesting phenomenon: even though creoles *tend* to drift toward the dominant language (in this case mainstream English), Black English and Hawai'ian Creole English are halting in this drift and resisting being swallowed by the mainstream dialect. When students can write early drafts in home dialect and home rhetoric, I think that both their language and their thinking will be stronger and be more their own—even if not remaining pure.

2. Am I just a "well intentioned white liberal" with a sentimental attachment to other dialects because I already have access to the dialect of power? A friend has called my proposal "lily white." Lisa Delpit criticizes teachers

who introduce "dialect readers" into the early grades and who also, in their liberal looseness, veil their authority and offer students too much choice and therefore too little access to the language of power. Such teachers may be well intentioned, she says, but their behavior serves "to prevent the schools from teaching the linguistic aspects of the culture of power, thus dooming Black children to a permanent outsider caste" ("Silenced Dialogue" 285).

The substantive question is not about my color, I hope, but about whether my proposal sufficiently achieves Delpit's goal of offering access to the language of power for students of stigmatized dialects. This is probably the most important question raised by this essay, and I acknowledge that the answer is debatable. For my approach here might seem to involve mixed messages about teacher authority, student choice, and the demand for competence in the language of power. On the one hand, I am offering students a new choice of writing early drafts in their home dialect. And I am also inviting them to get help in copy-editing into SWE rather than trying to insist that they be able to do it on their own. Yet on the other hand, I'm insisting that students learn to turn in final drafts in the language of power. In doing so I'm not using what Delpit calls "veiled commands" (289); I make it a blunt requirement. I'm not sure what Delpit would say about this mixed approach, especially since her criticisms seem to be addressed more to teachers in the schools than to teachers in colleges. (It's important to remember that I'm talking about a one-semester first year college course, not English courses in the schools.) But she recently made a suggestion about the teaching of writing that is not so different from what I am suggesting here:

> Unlike unplanned oral language or public reading, writing lends itself to editing. While conversational talk is spontaneous and must be responsive to an immediate context, writing is a mediated process which may be written and rewritten any number of times before being introduced to public scrutiny. Consequently, writing is more amenable to rule application— one may first write freely to get one's thoughts down, and then edit to hone the message and apply specific spelling, syntactical, or punctuation rules. ("Ebonics and Culturally Responsive Instruction" 7)

Geneva Smitherman makes a similar recommendation:

> I am often asked "how far" does the teacher go with this kind of writing pedagogy. My answer: as far as you can. Once you have pushed your students to rewrite, revise; rewrite, revise; rewrite, revise; and once they have produced the most powerful essay possible, then and only then should you have them turn their attention to BEV grammar and matters of punctuation, spelling, and mechanics. ("The Blacker the Berry" 95)

Arnetha Ball writes that

> students can continue to use their informal language patterns while acquiring competence in new academic registers. These kinds of curricula mandate further research on creating bridges between patterns used in students' home discourse communities and those required for school success. ("Cultural Preferences" 525)

Patricia Bizzell has well earned her stripes as not-a-white-liberal, and so it is interesting to hear her thinking in this area. In a short paper for a recent conference, she wrote, "It may no longer be necessary, or even accurate, to say that all students must write only in traditional academic discourse and Standard English to satisfy academic expectations" ("The Need for a Common Language: A Constraint on Civic Literacy?"). In a recent full essay she seems to restrict her focus to "Rhetorics of 'Color'" rather than grammar and syntax of color. In her first paragraph, she acknowledges that "we have a responsibility to teach the standard forms" (1), but in the second paragraph, she turns and devotes the rest of the essay to arguing that nevertheless,

> the academy should allow culturally diverse students to retain their home habits of language use and adapt these to academic writing. This means that the academy would have to accept alternative forms of academic discourse, forms that reflect the students' own cultural diversity. (2)

I look forward to more research and conversation as to whether the approach I suggest in this essay provides students of stigmatized dialects enough access to the language of power.

TO CONCLUDE

After these excursions into complex and often theoretical matters of dialect and culture, I want to move back to the concrete realm of the classroom. Consider the criteria that most teachers use in judging most essays: sticking to the topic or question or assignment; getting the information or concepts right; having good ideas of one's own; reasoning carefully; giving enough arguments, evidence, and examples; organizing effectively; and making meaning clear at the sentence level. *It is possible to meet every one of those criteria and still use lots of language people call wrong.* Thus it is possible to meet all those criteria before worrying about grammar, syntax, and spelling. (A few matters of punctuation will come up in trying to achieve clear meaning at the sentence level.) And thus it is possible to give students feedback on *all* these criteria and help them satisfy every one—and never once talk about surface features of language.

Once a draft has become strong and clear on *all* these substantive criteria, it's usually not so hard to make the changes needed in grammar, syntax, and spelling for conformity to SWE. Students can get better at this job relatively quickly, and get help with it—*after* they've worked on all the other criteria without worrying about surface features (as Smitherman emphasizes). It may be difficult for speakers of nonmainstream dialects to copy-edit final drafts, but not as difficult as trying to write *all* their drafts in SWE. The same goes for "giving in": it may be galling to give in on final drafts to a culture that seems bent on destroying your culture—but not as galling as giving in on all drafts, all writing.

But this approach can put a strain on teachers. It's not uncommon to hear teachers say they can't pay attention to substance if there are too many mistakes; they need to "clean up the language" enough to see the thinking and structure. Here's a comment I recently overheard on a list serve discussion among writing teachers: "Only now can I really address the underlying thinking and understanding problems because previously the writing was so atrocious that I couldn't see them." This is a common reaction—I occasionally feel it myself. But it's a reaction we need to get over. Premature attention to surface correction has created a serious handicap for many students—plenty of them speakers of the mainstream dialect. Over the years, the writing of these students has not improved enough because they have not been pushed hard enough or held accountable enough on the *substance* of their thinking. Their thinking and rhetoric have been too much ignored because their teachers have too often addressed only problems in grammar, syntax, and spelling. Think about the effects of never being pushed about weakness in thinking, organization, or even clarity of explanation and only being pushed about your language.

In short, providing safety about language does not mean discarding standards and evaluation. Carelessness about surface language is not the same as carelessness about meaning, thinking, organization, and clarity. We can make it clear to students that our invitation not to worry about grammar, syntax, and spelling on early drafts is our method of asking them to give *more* attention to meaning, thinking, organization, and clarity. We can give them more feedback and hold them more responsible on these matters of substance if we are not trying to correct grammar and syntax on early and mid drafts.

Since I've been trying to cover such a lot of territory in this essay, let me conclude by summarizing my main hypotheses and suggestions:

♦ It is possible and often beneficial to do most of our writing using all sorts of language that people call wrong and only at the end make changes to get the text to conform to the conventions of Standard Written English.

♦ Plenty of students will need help in making those final changes, but it is reasonable to invite them to get that help if we are teaching the only writing course they have in college or in their first two years. In teaching such a course, we do not need to take it as our goal that all students know how to make their final drafts conform to correct SWE without help. But we can and should insist that they know how to manage themselves as writers so as to do what is necessary to get their final drafts into SWE — the language of prestige and power.

♦ Students *can* use nonprestige dialects for whatever cognitive and rhetorical tasks face them. In doing so, they will usually find writing more comfortable and inviting and will usually be able to find more words and ideas and get more force, power, energy, and voice into their writing. This approach might help stigmatized dialects and their cultures to persist and flourish.

♦ We can make the writing classroom one of the most *hopeful of all sites of language use*: a place where students can learn to put their entire attention on their meaning and not on surface propriety — and where students can use their mother tongue as much as they want (or as little as they want). We can communicate respect for all dialects and help all students realize that speakers of nonmainstream dialects are usually more linguistically sophisticated than speakers of mainstream English.

Perhaps this is the most important benefit for speakers of stigmatized dialects. We can show them that *writing* provides a safer site for language use than speaking — easier access to linguistic power. That is, when they *speak* to mainstream listeners they must use correct mainstream English — even down to intonation — or risk stigmatization; but when they write to mainstream readers, they can do most of their work in their mother tongue and still end up with a text in SWE.

Finally, I want to call attention to an underlying principle of great generality. Everything in this essay reflects a recent discovery that will stand as one of the most important and enduring principles of literacy: *Anyone at any time can write anything he or she can say; writing is easier than reading and hence serves as a much more empowering doorway to literacy*. It was only a few years ago that Donald Graves (with the powerful help of people like

Nancie Atwell) learned that tiny children could be taught how to write before they could read—if only they were shown how to make use of squiggles and invented spelling. Now, kindergarteners and first graders all over the country are learning that they can put their words on paper as naturally and easily as they speak. Children in these elementary classrooms become literate much more quickly and comfortably when they start by writing in their idiosyncratic dialect. Even their relationship to reading improves. Since virtually everyone is far more linguistically sophisticated in speaking than in writing, we do well to call on speech in order to import that sophistication into writing. Putting it another way, more and more teachers are learning to build more bridges to literacy by blurring the boundaries between speech and writing.[3]

NOTES

1. An adult graduate student, teacher of writing, and serious writer (also white and middle class) responded to an earlier draft of this paper with an example that is telling because it is something so trivial that nevertheless still sticks in her craw.

> In an essay, I wrote that my parents were going "down to the store." The teacher lived in our town, our geography, but he corrected the English: "to the store." I was baffled at the time (I can remember this, even though it was 5th grade) because that is exactly the prepositional phrasing my family used and the phrasing matched our physical reality (the store was down hill). But it was also my mother tongue, in a way. Though only a phrase, I felt a bit taken back. I can't even begin to fathom what African American students, say, feel in a composition class. (Alex Peary, written response, 12/3/97)

2. Long ago in the Bard Writing and Thinking Program I experimented timidly with shared responsibility for copy-editing. Small groups were officially responsible, as groups, for the copy-editing of all their members. If any single member's paper was not well copy-edited, none of their papers were acceptable. See Johnson and Johnson, Sharan, and Slavin for more about this dimension of cooperative learning in various school subjects and levels. I would like to explore this kind of thing again (and would love to hear about successful uses of it for copy-editing).

3. I have shared various versions of these thoughts on various occasions and I am indebted to helpful feedback I have gotten from far too many people to name here. But I would especially thank Marcia Curtis, Diana Eades, and Suzie Jacobs.

WORKS CITED

Anzaldúa, Gloria. *Borderlands / La Frontera: The New Mestiza.* San Francisco: Spinters-Aunt Lute, 1987.

Atwell, Nancie. *In the Middle: Writing, Reading, and Learning with Adolescents.* Portsmouth NH: Boynton/Cook Heinemann, 1987.

Ball, Arnetha F. "Cultural Preference and the Expository Writing of African-American Adolescents." *Written Communication* 9.4 (1992): 501–32.

———. "Expository Writing Patterns of African American Students." *English Journal* 85 (January 1996): 27–36.

Ball, Arnetha and Ted Lardner. "Dispositions toward Language: Teacher Constructs of Knowledge and the Ann Arbor Black English Case." *College Composition and Communication* 48 (1997): 469–85.

Berlin, James. *Writing Instruction in Nineteenth-Century American Colleges.* Carbondale: Southern Illinois UP, 1984.

Bizzell, Patricia. "The Need for a Common Language: A Constraint on Civic Literacy?" Position paper for "New Directions for Programs in Writing, Rhetoric and Composition Studies: Visual and Civic Literacy." Conference at the University of Rhode Island, May 28, 1998.

———. "Rhetorics of 'Color': The Example of *Bootstraps.*" *Race, Rhetoric, and Composition.* Ed. Keith Gilyard. Portsmouth, NH: Heinemann Boynton/Cook. In press.

Boyd, Richard. "'Grammatical Monstrosities' and 'Contemptible Miscreants': Sacrificial Violence in the Late Nineteenth-Century Usage Handbook." *The Place of Grammar in Writing Instruction.* Eds. Susan Hunter and Ray Wallace. 1995. Portsmouth, NH: Heinemann/Boynton Cook. 54–70.

Bridwell-Bowles, Lillian. "Discourse and Diversity: Experimental Writing within the Academy." *College Composition and Communication* 43 (October 1992): 349–68.

Chafe, Wallace. "Punctuation and the Prosody of Written Language." Technical Report No. 11, Center for the Study of Writing, Berkeley, CA and PA, 1987.

Coleman, Charles F. "Our Students Write with Accents." *College Composition and Communication* 48 (1997): 486–500.

Committee of the Conference on College Composition and Communication. "Students' Right to Their Own Language." *College Composition and Communication* 25 (1974): 1–18.

Connor, Ulla. "Contrastive Rhetoric: Implications for Teachers of Writing in Multicultural Classrooms." In Severino, Guerra, Butler. 198–208.

Connors, Robert J. "Mechanical Correctness as a Focus in Composition Instruction." *College Composition and Communication* 36 (1985): 61–72.

Cook, William. "Writing in the Spaces Left." *College Composition and Communication* 44 (1993): 9–25.

De, Esha Niyogi and Donna Uthus Gregory. "Decolonizing the Classroom: Freshman Composition in a Multicultural Setting." In Severino, Guerra, Butler. 118–32.

Delpit, Lisa. "Ebonics and Culturally Responsive Instruction." *Rethinking Schools* 12.1 (Fall 1997): 6–7.

———. "The Silenced Dialogue: Power and Pedagogy in Educating Other People's Children." *Harvard Educational Review* 58.3 (1988): 280–98.

Elbow, Peter. "The War between Reading and Writing—and How to End It." *Rhetoric Review* 12.1 (Fall 1993): 5–24.

Farr, Marcia and Harvey Daniels. *Language Diversity and Writing Instruction.* New York: ERIC, 1986.

Farrell, Thomas. "IQ and Standard English." *College Composition and Communication* 34.4 (December 1983): 470–84.

Fasold, Ralph W. (introd.). Labov, William. "Are Black and White Vernacular Diverging?" *Papers from the NWAVE XIV Panel Discussion. American Speech* 62.1 (Spring 1987).

Fordham, Signithia and John Ogbu. "Black Students' School Success: Coping with the 'Burden of "Acting White.""" *Urban Review* 18 (1986): 176–206.

Fox, Helen. *Listening to the World*. Urbana IL: NCTE, 1994.

Gates, Henry Louis Jr. *The Signifying Monkey: A Theory of African-American Literary Criticism*. New York: Oxford UP, 1988.

Gilyard, Keith. *Voices of the Self: A Study of Language Competence*. Detroit: Wayne State UP, 1991.

Graves, Donald. *Writing: Teachers and Children at Work*. Portsmouth, NH: Heinemann, 1983.

hooks, bell. "'When I Was a Young Soldier for the Revolution': Coming to Voice." In *Talking Back: thinking feminist, thinking black*. Boston: South End Press, 1988. 10–18.

Hurston, Zora Neale. *Their Eyes Were Watching God; A Novel*. NY: J. B. Lippincott Co, 1937.

Johnson, David W. and Johnson, Frank P. *Joining Together: Group Theory and Group Skills*. 2nd ed. Englewood Cliffs: Prentice Hall, 1982.

Jordan, June. "Nobody Mean More to Me Than You: And the Future Life of Willie Jordan." *On Call: Political Essays* (Boston: South End, 1985). 123–39.

Kobayashi, Hiroe and Carol Rinnert. "Effects of First Language on Second Language Writing: Translation versus Direct Composition." *Language Learning* 42:2 (June 1992): 183–215.

Kristeva, Julia. *Revolution in Poetic Language*. Trans. Margaret Waller. New York: Columbia UP, 1984.

———. "The System and the Speaking Subject." *Times Literary Supplement*, 12 Oct. 1973: 1249–52.

Leki, Ilona. "Cross-Talk: ESL Issues and Contrastive Rhetoric." In Severino, Guerra, Butler. 234–44.

Lippi-Green, Rosina. "The Real Trouble with Black English." In *English With an Accent: Language, Ideology and Discrimination in the United States*. London: Routledge, 1997. 176–201.

Lisle, Bonnie and Sandra Mano. "Embracing a Multicultural Rhetoric." In Severino, Guerra, Butler. 12–26.

Lum, Darrell H. Y. *Pass On, No Pass Back*. Honolulu: Bamboo Ridge P, 1990.

Norton, Bonny. "Language, Identity, and the Ownership of English." *TESOL Quarterly* 31.3 (1997): 409–29.

Nussbaum, Martha. "Feminists and Philosophy." Rev. of *A Mind of One's Own: Feminist Essays on Reason and Objectivity*, ed. Louise M. Antony and Charlotte Witt. *New York Review of Books*, 20 Oct. 1994: 59–63.

Ohmann, Richard. *Politics of Letters*. Middletown, CT: Wesleyan UP, 1987.

Ong, Walter. *Orality and Literacy: The Technologizing of the Word*. New York: Methuen, 1982.

Pierce, Bonny Norton. "Social Identity, Investment, and Language Learning." *TESOL Quarterly* 29.1 (1995): 9–31.

Pratt, Mary Louise. "Linguistic Utopias." *The Linguistics of Writing*. Ed. Nigel Fabb et al. Machester: Manchester UP, 1987. 48–66.

Royer, Dan and Roger Gilles. "Putting Assessment in Its Place with Directed Self-Placement." *College Composition and Communication* 50.1 (September 1998): 54–70.

Rudolph, Frederick. *Curriculum: A History of the American Undergraduate Course of Study Since 1636*. San Francisco: Jossey-Bass, 1981.

Sapphire. *Push: A Novel.* New York: Knopf, 1996.

Sato, Charlene J. "Language Change in a Creole Continuum: Decreolization?" *Progression and Regression in Language: Sociocultural, Neuropsychological, and Linguistic Perspecitves.* Ed. Kenneth Hyltenstam and Ake Viberg. Cambridge: Cambridge UP, 1993.

Severino, Carol, Juan C. Guerra, and Johnnella E. Butler, eds. *Writing in Multicultural Settings.* New York: MLA, 1997.

Sharan, Shlomo, ed. *Handbook of Cooperative Learning Methods.* Westport, CT: Greenwood P, 1994.

Shen, Fan. "The Classroom and the Wider Culture: Identity as a Key to Learning English Composition." *College Composition and Communication* 40 (1989): 459–66.

Sistren, with Honor Ford Smith, editor. *Lionheart Gal: Life Stories of Jamaican Women.* London: The Women's Press, 1986.

Slavin, Robert E. *Cooperative Learning: Theory, Research, and Practice.* Boston: Allyn and Bacon, 1995.

Smitherman, Geneva. "'The Blacker the Berry, the Sweeter the Juice.' African American Student Writers." *The Need for Story: Cultural Diversity in the Classroom and Community.* Urbana, IL: NCTE, 1994. 80–101.

——. *Talkin and Testifyin: The Language of Black America.* Detroit: Wayne State UP, 1986.

Stevens, W. K. "Study Finds Blacks' English Increasingly Different." *New York Times,* March 15, 1985, A14.

Troutman, Denise. "Whose Voice Is It Anyway? Marked Features in the Writing of Black English Speakers." In Severino, Guerra, Butler. 27–39.

Villanueva, Victor, Jr. *Bootstraps: From an American Academic of Color.* Urbana, IL: NCTE, 1993.

Walker, Alice. *The Color Purple.* New York: Harcourt Brace, 1982.

Yamanaka, Lois-Ann. *Blue's Hanging.* New York: Farrar, Straus and Giroux, 1997.

——. *Saturday Night at the Pahala Theater.* Honolulu: Bamboo Ridge P, 1993.

Composition Studies
and ESL Writing
A Disciplinary Division of Labor

PAUL KEI MATSUDA

Specialization leads to its own problems. The discipline or department can become an end in itself.

> —Joel Colton, "The Role of the Department in the Groves of Academe," 317

Although the number of nonnative speakers of English in U.S. institutions of higher education has been increasing continuously during the last four decades, the development of composition studies does not seem to reflect this trend.[1] Until fairly recently, discussions of English as a Second Language (ESL) issues in composition studies have been few and far between. Few composition theorists include second-language perspectives in their discussions, and only a handful of empirical studies written and read by composition specialists consider second-language writers in their research design, interpretation of data, and discussion of implications. It almost seems as though the presence of over 457,000 international students in colleges and universities across the nation (Davis 2) does not concern writing teachers and scholars.[2]

The presence of ESL students should be an important consideration for all teachers and scholars of writing because ESL students can be found in many writing courses across the United States. As Jessica Williams' survey of ESL writing program administration suggests, the vast majority of institutions

Reprinted from *College Composition and Communication* 50.4 (June 1999): 699–721. Used with permission.

continue to require undergraduate ESL students to enroll in first-year composition courses, often in addition to special ESL writing courses. In many cases, they are also required by their departments to take professional writing courses. Thus, it is becoming increasingly likely that writing teachers at one point or another will encounter ESL writers in their classrooms. Although working with these students is "not radically different from teaching writing to native English speakers" (Leki xi), some of the linguistic and cultural differences they bring to the classroom pose a unique set of challenges to writing teachers. In a review of empirical research comparing ESL writers and native speakers of English, Tony Silva states that the former not only produced texts that were characterized by native-English-speaking readers as "distinct from and often simpler and less effective" but also "planned and reread their writing less, wrote with more difficulty because of a lack of lexical resources, and exhibited less ability to revise intuitively by ear" ("Differences" 215).[3] In *Teaching ESL Writing*, Joy Reid also writes that "the needs, backgrounds, learning styles, and writing strategies of most ESL students differ dramatically" (vii) from those of native English speakers. Furthermore, she points out that there is considerable diversity even among ESL students "in terms of language and cultural backgrounds, prior education, gender, age, and ESL language proficiency" (vii), which may make working with ESL students challenging for some writing instructors. While there also are many similarities, these and many other differences continue to "cause anxiety and misunderstandings" (Leki xi), suggesting the need for writing instructors to become more sensitive to the unique needs of ESL writers.

This absence of second-language writing discussions reflects and is reflected in the way composition studies has been constructed in its historical context. The second-language component does not appear in the work of influential historians of composition studies—such as James Berlin, Robert Connors, Susan Miller, and David Russell—because ESL writing has not been considered as part of composition studies since it began to move toward the status of a profession during the 1960s. This omission poses a serious problem for the status of second-language issues in composition studies because historical studies provide narratives that shape the practice within the profession. That is, the lack of second-language elements in the history of composition studies, and therefore in our sense of professional identity, continues to reinscribe the view that the sole responsibility of teaching writing to ESL students falls upon professionals in another intellectual formation: second-language studies, or more specifically, Teaching English as a Second Language (TESL).[4] This view of the interdisciplinary relationship, or what I call the "disciplinary division of labor," seems to reflect the values of the two intellectual formations that sought, especially during their formative years, to establish their own unique identities as respectable professions or academic "disciplines." As I will argue, this desire to claim their own areas of expertise led to the division of writing scholarship into first- and second-language components. This division of labor, however, is inadequate as a metaphor for the relationship between composition studies and TESL because ESL students, just like their native-speaker counterparts, continue to be affected by the institutional practices within composition studies because of their continued presence in composition classes. Yet, this metaphor not only keeps writing teachers from applying the insights from the growing body of second-language writing scholarship in working with ESL writers in their classrooms but also creates a tension that further divides teachers and researchers in the two fields.[5]

To construct an interdisciplinary relationship that is more responsive to the needs of ESL students in composition programs, it is necessary to understand the historical context in which the disciplinary division of labor is situated. In this essay, I examine how this division emerged between composition studies and TESL. Specifically, I will show how the professionalization of TESL over the period of 1941 to 1966—just when composition studies was also undergoing a revision of its own disciplinary identity—inadvertently contributed to the creation of the disciplinary division of labor that continues to influence the institutional practices in composition programs across the nation.

THE BIRTH OF A PROFESSION

It is not enough for the foreign language teacher to be able to speak English; to be most effective he should know English—its sound system, its structural system, and its vocabulary—from the point of view of a descriptive analysis in accord with modern linguistic science.

—*Charles C. Fries*, Teaching (13)

Prior to the 1940s, the teaching of ESL was not regarded as a profession in the United States, although this is not to say that the teaching of English to nonnative speakers had not taken place. By the 19th century, the teaching of English to Native American children was well under way (Spack, *Americas*), and Americanization programs provided some formal English language instruction to immigrants in urban areas during the late 19th century and the early 20th century.[6] At the college level, ESL instruction began to take place during the early 20th century. Harold B. Allen notes that the first English class for international students was taught in 1911 by J. Raleigh Nelson at the

University of Michigan. Harvard University offered a similar course in 1927, followed by George Washington University in 1931 ("English" 307).[7] Other institutions, however, failed to recognize the special needs of international ESL students, although by 1930 there were already almost 10,000 international students, mostly from Asia and Europe (Institute of International Education 232–35). Consequently, many ESL students were forced into the sink-or-swim approach to language learning. The teaching of ESL generally did not receive serious attention in the United States, and there seemed to be little respect for ESL teachers (Allen, "English" 307; "Freshman" 156).

A significant change was brought to the status of the ESL teaching profession with the development of U.S. foreign policy. Following President Franklin D. Roosevelt's announcement of the Good Neighbor policy at the Pan-American Conference in 1933, the teaching of English to nonnative speakers—especially in Latin American countries—became a serious concern of the federal government. The subsequent development prompted the U.S. Department of State to promote the teaching of the English language to nonnative speakers as well as the preparation of English language teachers. In the fall of 1939, the State Department funded, in cooperation with the Rockefeller Foundation, a conference at the University of Michigan to decide on a theoretical basis for the teaching of ESL (Allen, "English" 299; Alatis 382). Two of the most promising proposals were presented, according to Allen, by I. A. Richards and by Charles C. Fries:

> Richards, who had just come to Harvard University from England and his association there with C. K. Ogden in developing Basic English, offered a plan to teach English as a foreign language through a combination of lessons involving word and picture correspondence and vocabulary acquisition through the use of Basic English. In sharp contrast, Fries's proposal not only relied heavily upon the principles of Henry Sweet but also added a significant dimension taken from current linguistic theory. This dimension provided for controlled drills, structural study of English and the native language of the learner. ("English" 299)

Fries's proposal convinced the Rockefeller Foundation to provide him with a grant in 1940 to develop teaching materials for Latin American students. In 1941, with additional grants from the Department of State and the Rockefeller Foundation, the English Language Institute (ELI) at the University of Michigan came into being with Fries as its first director.

The opening of the ELI at Michigan was one of the most significant events in the history of TESL in the United States. At the 1956 meeting of the Conference on College Composition and Communication, Paul R. Sullivan of the University of Minnesota referred to the Institute as the starting point of modern English language teaching methods ("Studies" 163–64). Allen later characterized the ELI as "the nation's most dynamic single force in the teaching of English as a second or foreign language" ("English" 298). Indeed, the creation of the ELI at Michigan had a significant influence on the development of TESL as a profession. One of the primary missions of the ELI was to provide specialized intensive language instruction to ESL students. Influenced by the U.S. foreign policy, the ELI initially provided courses designed primarily for Spanish speaking students from Latin American countries, but later it opened itself up to ESL students from other countries who were brought by the conclusion of the World War II. During its first ten years of operation, 2,100 international ESL students at the University of Michigan were enrolled in the intensive language courses offered by the ELI. The Institute also provided a professional preparation program for ESL teachers, thus promoting a sense of professionalism among ESL teachers. In fact, one of the most important consequences of the creation of the Michigan ELI was the rise of what may be called "Michigan professionalism," the principle on which the Institute was founded.

Before the Michigan ELI was established in 1941, it was commonly believed that anyone whose native language was English was qualified to teach English to nonnative speakers—much as some thought any literate person could teach writing. In fact, one of the most significant contributions that Fries's ELI made to the profession was to dispel this myth. As Fries later wrote:

> The native speaker himself however, unless he has been specially trained to observe and analyze his own language processes, finds great difficulty in describing the special characteristics either of the sounds he makes or of the structural devices he uses. His comments about his own language more often mislead than help a foreigner. ("As We See It" 13)

With the creation of the professional preparation program at the University of Michigan, however, the teaching of ESL began to move toward the status of a respectable profession.

The meaning of "professionalism" that emerged among applied linguists at Michigan during the 1940s was quite different from the sense of professionalism embraced by practitioners of TESL during the 1960s. Allen's characterization of the language teaching profession in the inaugural issue of the *TESOL Quarterly* in 1966, for instance, focused on the sense of belonging to a group of teachers who shared common concerns and problems:

> Nor without an organization can a large number of people with common interests effectively further those interests. Without an organization, teachers having a common discipline and a common subject matter will not

easily come to consider themselves a professional group. ("TESOL and the Journal" 3)

In contrast, professionalism, as defined by Fries and his colleagues at Michigan, privileged the knowledge of structural linguistics. What professionalism in language teaching meant to them was the application of the principles of linguistics, hence the use of the term "applied linguistics" in describing the profession of language teaching. The term, in the words of Robert B. Kaplan, was "initially nearly inextricably tied to language teaching," although it has, at least in the United States, acquired a broader meaning (374).[8] In A *History of English Language Teaching*, A. P. R. Howatt points out that Fries' view of applied linguistics was "a hierarchical one" with the linguist "at the 'top'" producing the "basic, scientific descriptions of the source and target languages" to be applied by language teachers (267). That Fries decried the lack of knowledge about linguistic principles among language teachers was apparent in the preface to his *Teaching and Learning English as a Foreign Language* (1945), a textbook for second-language teachers that continued to be influential until the 1970s. He wrote:

> In spite of the fact that there has been more than a hundred years of vigorous linguistic investigation in accord with sound scientific methods, very little of the results of this investigation has actually got into the schools to affect the materials and methods of teaching language and the actual conditions under which language teaching is attempted. (i)

He went on to quote structural linguist Leonard Bloomfield, who complained in 1925 that teachers at all levels "do not know what language is, and yet must teach it, and in consequence waste years of every child's life and reach a poor result" (Bloomfield 5, qtd. in Fries, *Teaching* i). Influenced by a Bloomfieldian view of linguistics as a body of knowledge with practical applications, Fries saw the development of teaching materials at the Michigan ELI as "an attempt to interpret, in a practical way for teaching, the principles of modern linguistic science and to use the results of scientific linguistic research" (*Teaching* i).

Fries's view of professionalism was not always welcomed by language teachers, however, because his hierarchical notion of applied linguistics struck them as condescending. As William G. Moulton notes, Fries's idea of "instruction being based on 'sound linguistic principles' and being supervised by a 'trained linguist' struck them [language teachers] as professional exaggeration, not to say arrogance, on the part of the linguists" (97). Yet, Michigan professionalism became increasingly pervasive both nationally and internationally due to the enormous success in reproducing the values of Fries's ELI through the graduates of its teacher preparation program. Although the number of programs that offered graduate courses and certificate programs in TESL had increased to 22 by the end of the 1950s (Institute of International Education 123), the creation of many teacher preparation programs at various institutions across the nation did not so much diversify the view of the profession as it perpetuated the already influential Michigan professionalism because many of those programs were developed or staffed by people who were associated with the Michigan ELI in one way or another.[9] As Allen wrote:

> Even in many of these newer programs is felt the pervasive influence of Charles C. Fries, for dominant in the list of those who founded or now direct or teach in principal other programs are the names of persons who were either trained in the English Language Institute or, now a second generation, were trained by former graduates or staff members. ("English" 302)

Another significant event that contributed to the perpetuation of Michigan professionalism was the creation of a journal. Graduate students at the Michigan ELI had established the Research Club in Language Learning and, in 1948, began the publication of *Language Learning: A Quarterly Journal of Applied Linguistics*, the first journal of its kind in the United States.[10] It was also "the first journal in the world to carry the term 'applied linguistics' in its title," although L. W. Lockhart had already used the term in the subtitle of his book in 1931 (Editorial 1). The goal of the journal, according to Howatt, was "to bring the ideas developed at Fries's English Language Institute at the University of Michigan to the attention of a wider public" as well as to promote the understanding of linguistics and applied linguistics in general (265). As Robert Lado also noted in his 1960 editorial for the journal, the stated goal of the Research Club in publishing the journal was clearly in line with Fries's view of the profession: "to publish articles exploring the application and implications of linguistics in foreign language teaching" (v). Lado further wrote:

> *Language Learning* steadily continued to fill the need for the publication and distribution of those articles that more or less deliberately applied linguistics to language teaching. . . . *Language Learning* has dared to publish articles which would be rejected as too linguistic for the non-linguist and not linguistic enough for the pure linguist. (v)

The initial goal of the Research Club was met successfully; the journal became widely accepted—in the first ten years of the publication, the circulation rose from 200 U.S. subscribers to 1,200 subscribers in 76 countries (Lado v).

The journal continued to adhere to Fries's view of the language teaching profession until the late 1960s. As a 1967 editorial stated, the journal had been publishing articles that "dealt with applications of linguistic theory in the teaching and learning of languages." However, it was no longer possible to ignore the broadening definition of applied linguistics, which came to include "studies in first language acquisition, in bilingualism, translation (human and machine), in linguistic statistics, in sociolinguistics, in psycholinguistics, in the development of writing systems for unwritten languages, in the development of 'new' national languages, and so on." For this reason the editor announced that the journal would also consider articles "in these and other branches of applied linguistics" but only "to the extent that they are at least of marginal interest to those applied linguists whose primary concern is with language learning and teaching" (1).

The growth of Michigan professionalism and its view of second-language teaching as the application of linguistic principles had a profound impact on the way ESL writing was positioned in the emerging field of composition. Before discussing how the rise of professionalism in TESL contributed to the division of labor, however, it is necessary to understand the place of ESL issues in composition studies during that time. I now turn to a discussion of how ESL issues became a concern among teachers of composition and how they were handled in composition programs.

ESL CONCERNS AT CCCC

Many colleges and universities in the United States, especially large institutions with a reputation abroad, are constantly faced with the problem of what to do with foreign students who do not have a knowledge of English adequate for keeping up, on an even basis, with native students.

—*George Gibian, (157)*

Despite the development of the Michigan ELI and other innovative local ESL programs, such as the program developed at Queens College (Schueler), the number of institutions that developed specialized ESL programs for international students during the early 1940s was rather small. As Allen reported, "there was no noticeable increase in the numbers of foreign students" and "no one saw any major problem." As a consequence, few institutions were prepared for the large numbers of international ESL students who came to the United States at the conclusion of the Second World War ("English" 307). The development of the Conference on College Composition and Communication during the first decade after the war reflected

680

rising concerns about ESL students. When CCCC was first established in 1947, ESL was not a major component of the organization. Yet, as the number of ESL students continued to increase during the 1950s, institutions were no longer able to ignore the presence of this population, and ESL became an important issue at the annual meetings of the Conference.

In the late 1950s, the problems associated with international ESL students often became a topic of discussion at the annual spring meetings of CCCC. A number of panels and a series of workshops on issues surrounding international students were presented between 1955 and 1966, and were included in the workshop reports printed annually in *CCC*, a practice that continued until the 1970s. The names of prominent ESL specialists—including Kenneth Croft of Georgetown University, Robert B. Kaplan of the University of Southern California, Robert Lado of the University of Michigan, and Paul R. Sullivan of Georgetown University—appeared regularly in those workshop reports.

Among the scholars and teachers who were active in both TESL and composition studies was linguist Harold B. Allen, who later presided over NCTE in 1961 and became the first president of Teachers of English to Speakers of Other Languages (TESOL) in 1966.[11] Allen was a key player during the formative years of CCCC. In a historical review of *CCC*, Phillips, Greenberg, and Gibson count Allen among the most frequently published authors of major articles as well as the most frequently cited authors between 1950 and 1964. Characterizing him as one of the "early shapers of the discipline," they also note that Allen "was active in the national organization" and that "his reprinted speeches about the future of the profession were often referred to in *CCC* articles" (452). Allen was a member of the general committee for the first CCCC meeting in 1949, and he chaired a workshop the following year. At the business meeting on November 24, 1950, he was elected associate chair of the committee. He then chaired the Conference in 1952.

Although the lack of English language proficiency was one of the most important concerns among English teachers, it was obvious to many that the difficulties that ESL students faced were not only linguistic. For this reason, discussions at CCCC meetings included a wide variety of topics. The participants in the workshop called "The Foreign Student in the Freshman Course" at the 1955 meeting "quickly agreed that satisfactory handling of the foreign student's problems with English involved more than materials and methods of classroom instruction" ("Foreign Student" 1955, 138). Indeed, topics of discussion in this and subsequent workshops often included a wide range of issues: the need for and the availability of English language proficiency tests, models of special ESL curriculum, the issue of granting college credits for ESL courses, evaluation standards in English classes, admission criteria for international students, the need for orientation programs, and the role of English teachers in the students' cultural adjustment process.

The presence of a large number of ESL students in the English classroom was a serious concern not only among ESL specialists but among teachers whose professional interest or preparation did not include the teaching of ESL. The issue of increasing linguistic diversity in English classrooms was highlighted in a 1956 panel entitled "Studies in English as a Second Language." The panel chair, Paul R. Sullivan, began the session by noting that "all teachers of English frequently teach English as a second language" in effect because of the presence of students who spoke a differing variety of English, if not another language, outside of school. He also pointed out the need to provide specialized instruction for the increasing number of international ESL students ("Studies" 163–64). In the following year, Sullivan chaired another panel on the application of TESL principles to the regular English classes. In this panel, he once again pointed out that it had become "increasingly evident that many teachers are finding themselves faced with the problem of teaching English as a second language" ("English" 10). For this reason ESL workshops attracted many non-ESL specialists; in 1956, faculty from institutions without ESL programs constituted the majority of the participants in the CCCC workshop. One of the central topics of discussion at this workshop was the question of how to deal with international ESL students in the regular composition course at institutions where neither ESL specialists nor separate ESL courses were available—a question that continues to be relevant today. The report also indicated that participants in this workshop "represented an immense range in the kinds of programs (or lack of them) now existing" ("Foreign Student" 1956, 122).

Despite the increasing recognition throughout the 1950s of the presence of ESL students in English classrooms and the unique problems they brought with them, the vast majority of institutions continued to place ESL students into sections of English courses designed only for native speakers of English without making any adjustments or providing sufficient linguistic support. Others placed international ESL students into basic writing courses, or "remedial subfreshman courses" as they were then called, although the needs of international ESL students tended to be quite different from those of basic writers and immigrant ESL students.[12] These courses were often taught by teachers whose interest and preparation were limited to literary studies. Some institutions even sent ESL students to "speech clinics where speech therapists treated them as suffering from speech defects" (Allen, "English" 307).

At other institutions, where a large number of ESL students were enrolled, the problem of writing instruction for ESL students became "too conspicuous to be brushed under the freshman English rug" (307). One type of solution, deemed most desirable by applied linguists at the time, was the creation of intensive English language programs modeled after the ELI at Michigan. Many of those programs, often located outside the traditional institutional structure of the English department, were staffed by specially trained ESL instructors. However, the "special training" for the teachers meant at the time coursework in structural linguistics. The intensive programs were able to meet the needs of beginning or intermediate ESL students who had limited or no background in the English language, but they did not address the needs of ESL students in composition courses. Fries's approach to language teaching, which he termed the "oral approach," focused on the "mastery" of the sound system of the English language and was not intended for the teaching of writing to ESL students at the college level. In Fries's words,

> The practice which the student contributes must be *oral practice*. No mat-
> ter if the final result desired is only to *read* the foreign language[,] the mas-
> tery of the fundamentals of the language—the structure and the sound
> system with a limited vocabulary—must be through speech. The speech *is*
> the language. The written record is but a secondary representation of the
> language. To "master" a language it is not necessary to read it, but it is
> extremely doubtful whether one can really *read* the language without first
> mastering it orally. (*Teaching* 6)

To Fries, a language was nothing more than "a set of habits for oral production and reception," and writing, or "written symbols," was used only to the
extent that it assisted in the mastery of the spoken language (6). Partly due to
the dominance of Fries's view of applied linguistics, the study of written language or the teaching of writing to ESL students did not attract serious attention from applied linguists until the 1960s, and intensive English programs
did not pay much attention to the teaching of writing beyond grammar drills
at the sentence level.

At many institutions where ESL enrollment was relatively low, creating
a separate program staffed by ESL specialists was not a feasible option.
Instead, special remedial writing courses were created for ESL students and
were often taught by instructors from foreign language departments or English departments. In "College English for Foreign Students" (1951), George
Gibian wrote that a special section of remedial English was developed at
Harvard in 1949 to meet the "peculiar needs" of "a small group of European
students, all of whom seemed to need extra aid" (157). The goal of this
course was to teach students communication skills—including writing and
reading as well as oral communication—that were necessary to succeed in
college courses. Sumner Ives of Tulane University also reported in 1953 the

creation of a special ESL writing course offered only in the fall. Although this course was offered on a non-credit basis by default, it sometimes became credit bearing when a significant number of students demonstrated the ability to succeed in the second-semester writing course. While this course was primarily concerned with writing, the curriculum and materials from Michigan's ELI were adopted to help students who needed extra linguistic support. Similarly, William F. Marquardt of the University of Washington created a three-credit ESL course in which writing was the focus of instruction.

Those who were committed to the teaching of ESL argued for the division of labor on the basis of the need for a specially trained ESL instructor. As Ives wrote: "This course should . . . be taught by someone on the permanent staff, for an essential feature is the continuity of judgment which is involved. Moreover, it should be taught by someone with linguistic training" (143). Although these courses were intended to provide the needed linguistic support for ESL students, they were also motivated by the need to release composition specialists from the extra "burden" of teaching ESL students in their classes. Gibian argued, for instance, that "distributing the burden of extra aid and consideration among all instructors of courses which the foreign student takes, without helping by providing a special course, is an inefficient process, wasteful and lacking in organization" (157). The creation of these programs was one of the factors that contributed to the division between first- and second-language specialists. However, it was the combination of this and other factors, such as the rise of applied linguistics and the professionalization of both TESL and composition studies, that ultimately led to the institutionalization of the disciplinary division of labor.

INSTITUTIONALIZATION OF
THE DIVISION OF LABOR

If we are to be a profession, we must have standards that the professional worker meets. If we are to be a profession, some agency must establish those standards. If we are to be a profession, some agency must recognize appropriately those institutions that acceptably prepare teachers to meet those standards.

—*Harold B. Allen, "The Pros Have It" (117)*

As the number of ESL programs and teacher preparation programs increased, more teachers began to receive specialized training in TESL, and the need for professionalization of TESL was increasingly felt. Yet, many institutions continued to staff their ESL programs with junior faculty and graduate students from English and foreign language departments whose primary interest and training were in literary studies and not in the teaching of ESL. This tendency was deemed unacceptable both by applied linguists, who were increasingly committed to promoting the application of linguistic principles, and by TESL specialists who sought to increase the professional status of ESL teachers. As William Slager wrote:

> For linguistic science has made it clear that to teach English (effectiveness, organization and usage) to native-born Americans, and to teach English as a foreign language (mastery of the sound and structure system), are as widely different as two tasks can be. The first in many ways deals with language as an art. The other deals with language as a science: its subject matter and its classroom techniques require special background and training. That both courses are often taught in the same department is coincidental. (24)

To Slager and others, the teaching of ESL required "enough linguistic training to make phonemic and structural comparisons" across languages ("Foreign Student" 1955, 139), and the division of labor between composition teachers and ESL teachers was often suggested as a desirable, if not the only acceptable, solution to the problem of teaching ESL students. In the report from the 1961 CCCC panel, "The Freshman Whose Native Language is Not English," chair Ernest A. Boulay argued for the creation of special programs as a solution to the increasing concerns about ESL students. Implicit in this argument was the division of labor between writing teachers and ESL teachers. He argued for a "separate preparatory course" taught by "a linguistic expert, or experts, so that the student may be prepared for and oriented to some of the vagaries of the English language before the Freshman English teacher meets him" (156). At the same session, other panelists also addressed the issue of teacher qualification and argued for the division of labor. Clara M. Siggins of Boston College argued that the course for ESL students "should not be given by the beginning English teacher in order to 'pick up' experience, nor should it be given as extracurricular activity" and that "a program such as this calls for careful course organization and a special faculty." Clifford H. Prator of the University of California, Los Angeles was of the same opinion. He argued that ESL teaching "can be well done only by a specialist with an analytical knowledge of English and with deep insights into the way the student's native tongue interferes with his learning of the new language. The usual freshman composition instructor is not equipped to do the work, to say nothing of the person whose only qualification is that he speaks English as his mother tongue" (156). Prator's argument was motivated by the need for professionalization:

> The teaching of English as a second language is a perfectly respectable academic field which offers immense opportunities for serious research. This discipline needs more practitioners who will devote their entire career to it and not regard it as a temporary way of winning one's bread while preparing to teach courses in linguistic[s] or literature. It is definitely not a job which some university departments of English can continue with impunity to wish off on the newest member of the faculty and on its most defenseless member. (156)

The arguments for the division of labor were also motivated by Michigan professionalism, which sought to establish, in the language teaching arena, the place of the structural linguists who had "become increasingly interested in applying the results of linguistic methods of analysis to the solution of language problems" (156). In 1965, members of the CCCC workshop, chaired by Robert B. Kaplan, formalized the attitude of ESL specialists at the Conference by putting forth a recommendation that "[w]here it is feasible, speakers of English as a second language should be taught *in special classes* by teachers who have had training in teaching English as a second language" ("ESL Programs" 203).

Some ESL specialists were wary of the possible implications of the division of labor. When professionalization was realized by the creation of TESOL, Allen cautioned TESL specialists that the argument for professionalization should not become an argument for "the *reductio ad absurdum* that no one should legally be entitled to teach a single English word to non-English speaking persons without having obtained a license to practice" ("Pros" 114). Although the argument for professionalization did not lead to a ban on the teaching of ESL by non-TESL specialists, it did lead to a decline of interest in ESL issues among composition specialists. In effect, composition teachers were being told by applied linguists and TESL specialists that they lacked the needed expertise to teach ESL students. At the same time, however, composition teachers might have welcomed the same argument because it would release them from the "burden" of acquiring new knowledge and skills to teach ESL students and from the extra time that they had to spend in working with the unique problems that ESL students brought to the classroom.

The decline of interest in ESL issues among composition teachers was evident as the number of participants at CCCC workshops on ESL issues decreased; in fact, nobody attended the 1965 workshop. Discouraged by the lack of interest in ESL issues among CCCC members, the ESL workshop in 1966, chaired again by Kaplan, made a decision that would, in effect, remove ESL elements from composition studies almost entirely. The "small but loquacious group" of ESL specialists at the workshop resolved "somewhat sadly . . . that, given the small attendance at this workshop for several years under the aegis of CCCC, the group should meet hereafter only at NCTE meetings" ("Teaching" 198). In the same year, TESOL was started as a professional organization to serve the needs of a growing number of ESL specialists (Alatis 386–87; Allen, "English" 315–16; Hook 218). The creation of a professional organization that devoted itself entirely to ESL issues and the decline of interest in those issues among composition specialists led to the separation of writing issues into first-language and second-language components. The disciplinary division of labor was thus institutionalized.

The immediate effect of the institutionalization of the division of labor can best be illustrated by considering the exchange that took place between Joseph H. Friend of Southern Illinois University and Gordon Wilson of Miami University, Ohio. At the CCCC executive committee meeting on April 1967, Friend asked "whether problems of teaching composition to non-English speakers should not be included in the program." Wilson, who was the executive committee chair at the time, responded to Friend's inquiry by pointing out that the "competition of TESOL might prevent a sufficient number of people from attending a workshop." Although Wilson suggested that "a panel [on ESL issues] might be advisable" (Burke 1967, 205), sessions concerning nonnative speakers of English—either in the form of panels or workshops—remained absent from CCCC conventions at least for the next ten years.

Richard Braddock of the University of Iowa, who was the convention chair in 1967, was more sympathetic to Friend's cause. During the same meeting, he appointed Friend to act as a liaison between CCCC and TESOL (Burke 1967, 206–7). When Braddock chaired the executive committee meeting in November 1967, he responded to Friend's brief report by asking him to "continue submitting such reports to CCCC" and by saying that "CCCC is always willing to cooperate with TESL" (Hettich 262). However, the TESOL reports continued only during Braddock's tenure in the executive committee. Friend made another report in April 1968 (Burke 1968), but his name disappeared from these meetings after the November 1968 meeting, when Friend "had no report on TESOL" (Burke 1969, 267). ESL concerns had perhaps vanished even earlier, since the content of neither of Friend's reports were recorded in the secretary's reports on executive committee meetings.

BEYOND THE DIVISION OF LABOR

That there is, and will be, a clash of cultures between the two disciplines is . . . beyond doubt, and as long as it remains, the immediate needs of the students will not be met as constructively as they might be if L1 [composition] and ESL specialists worked jointly and cooperatively.

— *Terry Santos (89)*

As I have argued, the division of labor between composition specialists and ESL specialists was inadvertently created between the 1940s and the 1960s as a byproduct of the professionalization of TESL as well as of composition studies. The division of labor has had a lasting impact on the relationship between the two professions. Guadalupe Valdés observes, for instance, that "individuals who focus on the teaching of English to native speakers generally belong to organizations such as NCTE . . . and CCCC" while "individuals . . . who focus on the teaching of English to nonnative speakers of English are generally members of TESOL . . . or NABE (National Association of Bilingual Education)." She continues:

> Even though there are segments within CCCC and NCTE that specialize in the writing of nonmainstream students, these two organizations are not generally known for their expertise on matters related to the teaching of English to students from non-English-speaking backgrounds. (88)

Indeed, one of the consequences of the disciplinary division of labor is the lack of concern about the needs of ESL writers among composition specialists that continues even today. As Alice Roy suggests, there is a "tendency among administrators and English Department faculties to look for linguists and ESL specialists to 'deal with' second language writers" (20; see also Ransdell). Ann Johns also points out that, while some ESL specialists have been trying to suggest ways to increase the understanding of ESL issues among composition specialists, ESL panels at CCCC "seem to attract only the ESL people who attend this conference" ("Too Much" 86). Composition specialists, Johns further writes, "have shown little interest, so far, in who we are, who our students are, and what we do" (86). Although ESL issues have become somewhat visible at CCCC meetings—thanks to the work of people such as Carolyn Chitereer Gilboa, Barbara Kroll, Nancy Duke S. Lay, Ann Raimes, Alice Roy, Tony Silva, and Lynn Quitman Troyka—most CCCC members seem to remain oblivious to the needs and characteristics of ESL writers.

As a view of the interdisciplinary relationship between composition studies and second-language studies, the division of labor is far from adequate because it is based on the "myth of transience" (Rose; Russell; Zamel, "Strangers")—the assumption that ESL writing can be broken down neatly into a linguistic component and a writing component and that the linguistic problems will disappear after some additional instruction in remedial language courses. Yet, this is often not the case. Even when ESL students are enrolled in special ESL courses before taking required writing courses, the unique difficulties that ESL writers encounter in English composition are not likely to disappear completely after a semester —or even a few years—of additional language instruction, as Ruth Spack demonstrated in her longitudinal study of a Japanese international student ("Acquisition"). Leki also points out that, "after ten years of studying English in classrooms abroad, ESL students still may have trouble writing effectively in English . . . and students who can recite grammar rules . . . are not always able to use those rules in producing language" (23). Similarly, Williams argues that it is unrealistic to expect that ESL writers "should have put their second language problems behind them and be ready to take on the challenges of the composition classroom without further support" (175). Furthermore, ESL students may not be familiar with the culturally constructed values and expectations that are tacitly understood and shared by the majority of teachers and students in the composition program, as a number of studies have suggested (Atkinson; Atkinson and Ramanathan; Fox; Li; Ramanathan and Kaplan). Since ESL students in most cases are required to enroll in composition courses, and since many ESL writers also take professional writing courses, ESL writing issues should be as much a concern for composition specialists as they are for second-language specialists.

I am not arguing, however, that composition studies and second-language studies should be merged. Although the disciplinary division of labor has created a number of serious and unresolved problems for the two intellectual formations, the solution to these problems does not lie in eliminating the division entirely. Since both composition studies and second-language studies have established their institutional identities and practices over the last three decades, attempting to consolidate the diverse practices in the two distinct professions would be unrealistic and even counterproductive. Rather, second-language writing should be seen as an integral part of both composition studies and second-language studies, and specialists in both professions should try to transform their institutional practices in ways that reflect the needs and characteristics of second-language writers in their own institutional contexts.

How, then, can composition studies integrate second-language elements into its institutional practices? One logical place to start is for composition specialists to begin learning about ESL writing and writers by reading relevant literature and by attending presentations, workshops, and special interest group meetings on ESL-related topics at professional conferences. Research on second-language writing also appears regularly in second-language journals—such as *College ESL, English for Specific Purposes, Journal of Second Language Writing, Language Learning,* and *TESOL Quarterly.* In addition, a few journals in composition studies—most notably the *Journal of Basic Writing, Teaching English in the Two-Year College,* and *Written Communication*—have come to include an increasing number of articles concerning second-language writing issues. A number of bibliographic sources on ESL writing are also available. Dan Tannacito's *A Guide to Writing in English as a Second or Foreign Language: An Annotated Bibliography* provides a fairly comprehensive bibliography through the end of 1993, and the *Journal of Second Language Writing* also has been publishing annotated bibliographies of recent scholarship on the subject since 1993.

Composition scholars, regardless of their areas of interest or modes of inquiry, should also try to consider second-language perspectives in their work because theories of composition that exclude second-language writers and writing "can at best be extremely tentative and at worst totally invalid" (Silva et al. 402). In conducting empirical studies, composition researchers should acknowledge the presence of ESL writers in writing classrooms and try to include second-language writers in their research design, analysis, and discussion of implications—rather than excluding them as "outliers" or "exceptions," as many researchers have done. As Paul Prior points out:

> Although nonnative speakers (NNS) of English, whether resident or international students, are now found in many university classes, only one study of writing in the disciplines (Sternglass, 1988) has even mentioned such students, and that mention was brief. The different language, cultural, and educational backgrounds that NNS bring to their courses raise both theoretical and practical questions that deserve careful attention. (271)

Valdés also writes, "research on bilingual minority writers must be carried out by mainstream researchers as well as minority researchers and viewed as a legitimate focus of activity" (128).

Graduate programs in composition studies should also try to incorporate second-language writing into their curricula because graduate school is where institutional values are instilled in new members of the profession. At some institutions, graduate students in composition studies can take a second-language writing course offered through a graduate program in TESL, although the number of TESL programs offering a course in second-language writing is still small, and various institutional practices may discourage them from taking the course. An alternative is to create second-language writing courses or components within graduate programs in composition studies. A second-language component can easily be added to courses in composition theory and history as publications concerning second-language writing are becoming more readily available (Kroll, *Second Language*; Severino et al.). In empirical research courses, students can discuss how the consideration of second-language writers may complicate research designs and analyses. Readings from second-language writing research can also be included in courses dealing with almost any topic in composition studies, including writing in the disciplines (Belcher and Braine; Johns, *Text*; Zamel and Spack), literacy (McKay; Rodby), assessment (Hamp-Lyons), reading and writing (Carson and Leki), writing program administration (Braine, "ESL"; Kroll, "Rhetoric/Syntax"; Roy; Silva, "Examination"; Williams), and written discourse analysis (Connor; Connor and Johns; Connor and Kaplan; Purves).

Another important site of institutional practice is writing program administration. Since ESL students continue to enroll in writing courses, writing program administrators should make every effort to provide an ESL-friendly learning environment. This can be accomplished in a number of ways. One approach is to place ESL writers into basic writing or "mainstream" sections of composition that are taught by writing teachers prepared to work with ESL writers. Creating an ESL section of required composition courses is also a common response to the presence of ESL writers. Another approach is to create a special section of composition where native and non-native English speakers are systematically integrated and taught by a teacher who has preparation and experience in working with both types of students (Reichelt and Silva). As Silva suggests, what is important is "to offer ESL students as many of these options (and more) as resources permit" ("Examination" 41). Some institutions, however, may not be able to hire enough writing teachers with ESL preparation because of the lack of financial resources or the shortage of such teachers (Kroll, "Teaching"). In those situations, administrators may need to provide opportunities for writing teachers to learn how to work with ESL writers. This can be accomplished, for example, by offering pre-service and inservice workshops on teaching ESL writing, such as the one described by Braine ("Starting"), or by creating a local e-mail list for the discussion of ESL writing concerns. A number of introductory textbooks are available to facilitate the development of new ESL writing teachers (Campbell; Ferris and Hedgcock; Leki; Reid).

The needs of ESL students differ from individual to individual and from institution to institution, and it is not possible to create one solution that fits all situations. Yet, the solution cannot be found in total isolation from other disciplinary perspectives, either. For more than 30 years, ESL specialists have been working to improve the institutional practices for ESL writers in second-language classrooms by incorporating insights from composition studies; it is time for composition specialists to learn from them in developing institutional practices that can meet the needs of an increasing number of ESL students in writing classrooms—and beyond.

NOTES

1. The primary focus of this essay, which covers the period between 1941 and 1966, is on international ESL students at the undergraduate level rather than immigrant ESL students because, whereas the former began to increase in the 1940s, the latter did not reach a critical mass until the late 1960s. The distinction between international, or "foreign," students and immigrant students, who are permanent residents or citizens (as opposed to "non-immigrant aliens") of the United States, was a salient one during the formative years of composition studies and TESL. (See Slager, for example.) Although this dichotomy tends to oversimplify differences within the two groups of students, it continues to be a significant distinction because immigrant ESL students have needs and advantages that are different than those of international students (Leki 42–43). The presence of immigrant ESL students warrants another historical study, which is beyond my scope here.

2. According to the Institute of International Education, the total number of international students in the 1996–1997 academic year was 457,984, including 227,305 undergraduate students (Davis 130). Although not all international students are ESL students, most of them come from countries where English is not the dominant language.

3. It is important to remember that not all ESL texts are "simple" or "ineffective"— overgeneralization of research findings should be avoided at all cost—and that these are relative characterizations based on the expectations of native-English-speaking readers. Texts written by ESL students are often complex in ways that are different than those written by native speakers of English, and the effectiveness of the text is also context dependent. However, my experience as a second-language writer as well as my interaction with ESL students also suggest that ESL writers, especially in the early stages of language learning, often feel frustrated because they are not able to write with the kind of complexity and effectiveness that they can achieve more easily when writing in their native languages.

4. My use of the term "intellectual formation" is inspired by Michel Foucault, whose notion of formation implies dynamic and complex discursive relations rather than a static and coherent body of knowledge. I thank Patricia Harkin for her insightful comment on this point.

5. I do not mean to imply that there has not been any interaction between the two intellectual formations. Second-language writing researchers have been borrowing theoretical and methodological frameworks from composition studies since the 1960s. (See, for example, Kaplan, "Cultural"; Raimes; Zamel, "Teaching," "Recent"). During the 1970s and the 1980s, Mina Shaughnessy, Alice Horning and others also made efforts to incorporate insights from second-language studies in general, although their goal was to help basic writers rather than ESL writers.

6. Spack, "America's"; Allen, "English" 295; see Brown and Singh for accounts of English language instruction to immigrants before 1920.

7. See Rogers for an account of the program at George Washington University.

8. Kaplan claims to be the first in the United States to bear the title of Professor of Applied Linguistics (Kaplan, "TESOL" 374).

9. There were, of course, some exceptions, including programs created at Georgetown University, American University, and the University of Texas, Austin (Moulton 105).

10. The term "Quarterly" was later dropped from the title because of the initial difficulty in maintaining its regular production schedule.

11. Allen contributed significantly to the creation of TESOL and its journal by conducting a status study of the ESL teaching profession (i.e., Allen, *Survey*) and by organizing conferences on ESL teaching between 1964 and 1966 (Hook 218).

12. Slager was among the first to discuss the differing needs of international ESL students and immigrant ESL students, and the placement issue of ESL students continues to be an important topic of discussion among ESL specialists. See Leki for a succinct review of differences between ESL writers and basic writers (27–38), and Silva ("Examination") for a comprehensive review of available placement options.

WORKS CITED

Alatis, James E., with Carol LeClair. "Building an Association: TESOL's First Quarter Century." *State of the Art TESOL Essays: Celebrating 25 Years of the Discipline.* Ed. Sandra Silberstein. Alexandria: TESOL, 1993. 382–413.

Allen, Harold B. "English as a Second Language." *Current Trends in Linguistics: Linguistics in North America.* Vol. 10. Ed. Thomas A. Sebeok. The Hague: Mouton, 1973. 295–320.

———. "The Pros Have It." *TESOL Quarterly* 2 (1968): 113–20.

———. *A Survey of the Teaching of English to Non-English Speakers in the United States.* Champaign: NCTE, 1966.

———. "TESOL and the Journal." *TESOL Quarterly* 1 (1967): 3–6.

Atkinson, Dwight. "A Critical Approach to Critical Thinking in TESOL." *TESOL Quarterly* 31 (1997): 71–94.

Atkinson, Dwight, and Vai Ramanathan. "Cultures of Writing: An Ethnographic Comparison of L1 and L2 University Writing/Language Programs." *TESOL Quarterly* 29 (1995): 539–68.

Belcher, Diane, and George Braine, eds. *Academic Writing in a Second Language: Essays on Research and Pedagogy.* Norwood: Ablex, 1995.

Bloomfield, Leonard. "Why a Linguistic Society?" *Language* 1 (1925): 1–5.

Braine, George. "ESL Students in First-Year Writing Courses: ESL Versus Mainstream Classes." *Journal of Second Language Writing* 5 (1996): 91–107.

———. "Starting ESL Classes in Freshman Writing Programs." *TESOL Journal* 3.4 (1994): 22–25.

Brown, Steven. "ESL Textbooks and Teaching in the Progressive Era." *The Mid-Atlantic Almanac* 6 (1997): 81–94.

Burke, Virginia M. "Secretary's Report No. 56." *CCC* 18 (1967): 204–7.

———. "Secretary's Report No. 58." *CCC* 19 (1968): 263–65.

———. "Secretary's Report No. 59." *CCC* 20 (1969): 266–68.

Campbell, Cherry. *Teaching Second-Language Writing: Interacting with Text.* Boston: Heinle, 1998.

Carson, Joan G., and Ilona Leki, eds. *Reading in the Composition Classroom: Second Language Perspectives*. Boston: Heinle 1992.

Colton, Joel. "The Role of the Department in the Groves of Academe." *The Academic's Handbook*. 2nd ed. Ed. A. Leigh DeNeef and Craufurd D. Goodwin. Durham: Duke UP, 1995. 315–33.

Connor, Ulla. *Contrastive Rhetoric: Cross-Cultural Aspects of Second Language Writing*. New York: Cambridge UP, 1996.

Connor, Ulla, and Ann M. Johns, eds. *Coherence in Writing: Research and Pedagogical Perspectives*. Alexandria: TESOL, 1990.

Connor, Ulla, and Robert B. Kaplan, eds. *Writing Across Languages: Analysis of L2 Text*. Reading: Addison, 1987.

Davis, Todd M., ed. *Open Doors 1996–97: Report on International Educational Exchange*. New York: Institute of International Education, 1997.

Editorial. *Language Learning* 17.1/2 (1967): 1–2.

"ESL Programs: Composition and Literature." CCC 16 (1965): 203.

Ferris, Dana, and John Hedgcock. *Teaching ESL Composition: Purpose, Process, and Practice*. Mahwah: Erlbaum, 1998.

"The Foreign Student in the Freshman Course." CCC 6 (1955): 138–40.

"The Foreign Student in the Freshman Course." CCC 7 (1956): 122–24.

Fox, Helen. *Listening to the World: Cultural Issues in Academic Writing*. Urbana: NCTE, 1994.

"The Freshman Whose Native Language Is Not English." CCC 12 (1961): 155–57.

Fries, Charles C. "As We See It." *Language Learning* 1.1 (1948): 12–16.

_____. *Teaching and Learning English as a Foreign Language*. Ann Arbor: U of Michigan P, 1945.

Gibian, George. "College English for Foreign Students." *College English* 13 (1951): 157–60.

Hamp-Lyons, Liz, ed. *Assessing Second Language Writing in Academic Contexts*. Norwood: Ablex, 1991.

Hettich, David W. "Secretary's Report No. 57." CCC 19 (1968): 261–63.

Hook, J. N. *A Long Way Together: A Personal View of NCTE's First Sixty-Seven Years*. Urbana: NCTE, 1979.

Horning, Alice S. *Teaching Writing as a Second Language*. Carbondale: Southern Illinois UP, 1987.

Howatt, A. P. R. *A History of English Language Teaching*. New York: Oxford UP, 1984.

Institute of International Education. *Handbook on International Study: For Foreign Nationals*. New York: Institute of International Education, 1961.

Ives, Sumner. "Help for the Foreign Student." CCC 4 (1953): 141–44.

Johns, Ann M. *Text, Role, and Context: Developing Academic Literacies*. New York: Cambridge UP, 1997.

_____. "Too Much on Our Plates: A Response to Terry Santos' 'Ideology in Composition: L1 and ESL.'" *Journal of Second Language Writing* 2 (1993): 83–88.

Kaplan, Robert B. "Cultural Thought Patterns in Inter-cultural Education." *Language Learning* 16 (1966): 1–20.

_____. "TESOL and Applied Linguistics in North America." *State of the Art TESOL Essays: Celebrating 25 Years of the Discipline*. Ed. Sandra Silberstein. Alexandria: TESOL, 1993. 373–81.

Kroll, Barbara. "The Rhetoric/Syntax Split: Designing a Curriculum for ESL Students." *Journal of Basic Writing* 9.1 (1990): 40–55.

_____. ed. *Second Language Writing: Research Insights for the Classroom.* New York: Cambridge UP, 1990.

_____. "Teaching Writing IS Teaching Reading: Training the New Teachers of ESL Composition." *Reading in the Composition Classroom: Second Language Perspectives.* Ed. Joan G. Carson and Ilona Leki. Boston: Heinle, 1992. 61–81.

Lado, Robert. "New Perspectives in Language Learning." Editorial. *Language Learning* 10.1/2 (1960): v–viii.

Leki, Ilona. *Understanding ESL Writers: A Guide for Teachers.* Portsmouth: Boynton/ Cook, 1992.

Li, Xiao-Ming. *"Good Writing" in Cross-Cultural Context.* Albany: State U of New York P, 1996.

Marquardt, William F. "Composition and the Course in English for Foreign Students." *CCC* 7 (1956): 29–33.

McKay, Sandra Lee. *Agendas for Second Language Literacy.* New York: Cambridge UP, 1993.

Moulton, William G. "Linguistics and Language Teaching in the United States 1940–1960." *Trends in European and American Linguistics 1930–1960.* Ed. Christine Mohrmann, Alf Sommerfelt, and Joshua Whatmough. Utrecht: Spectrum, 1961. 82–109.

Phillips, Donna Burns, Ruth Greenberg, and Sharon Gibson. "*College Composition and Communication:* Chronicling a Discipline's Genesis." *CCC* 44 (1993): 443–65.

Prior, Paul. "Contextualizing Writing and Response in a Graduate Seminar." *Written Communication* 8 (1991): 267–310.

Purves, Alan C., ed. *Writing Across Languages and Cultures: Issues in Contrastive Rhetoric.* Thousand Oaks: Sage, 1988.

Raimes, Ann. "What Unskilled ESL Students Do As They Write: A Classroom Study of Composing." *TESOL Quarterly* 19 (1985): 229–58.

Ramanathan, Vai and Robert B. Kaplan. "Some Problematic 'Channels' in the Teaching of Critical Thinking in Current L1 Composition Textbooks: Implications for L2 Student-Writers." *Issues in Applied Linguistics* 7.2 (1996): 225–49.

Ransdell, D. R. "Important Events: Second Language Students in the Composition Classroom." *Teaching English in the Two-Year College* 21 (1994): 217–22.

Reichelt, Melinda, and Tony Silva. "Cross-Cultural Composition." *TESOL Journal* 5.2 (1995–1996): 16–19.

Reid, Joy M. *Teaching ESL Writing.* Englewood Cliffs: Prentice, 1993.

Rodby, Judith. *Appropriating Literacy: Writing and Reading in English as a Second Language.* Portsmouth: Boynton, 1992.

Rogers, Gretchen L. "Freshman English for Foreigners." *School and Society* 61 (1945): 394–96.

Rose, Mike. "The Language of Exclusion: Writing Instruction at the University." *College English* 47 (1985): 341–59.

Roy, Alice M. "ESL Concerns for Writing Program Administrators: Problems and Policies." *Writing Program Administration* 11.3 (1988): 17–28.

Russell, David R. *Writing in the Academic Disciplines, 1870–1990: A Curricular History.* Carbondale: Southern Illinois UP, 1991.

Santos, Terry. "Response to Ann Johns." *Journal of Second Language Writing* 2 (1993): 89–90.

Severino, Carol, Juan C. Guerra, and Johnnella E. Butler, eds. *Writing in Multicultural Settings.* New York: MLA, 1997.

Schueler, Herbert. "English for Foreign Students." *Journal of Higher Education* 20.6 (1949): 309–16.

Shaughnessy, Mina P. *Errors and Expectations: A Guide for the Teacher of Basic Writing.* New York: Oxford UP, 1977.

Silva, Tony. "An Examination of Writing Program Administrator's Options for the Placement of ESL Students in First Year Writing Classes." *Writing Program Administration* 18.1/2 (1994): 37–43.

———. "Differences in ESL and Native-English-Speaker Writing: The Research and Its Implications." *Writing in Multicultural Settings.* Ed. Carol Severino, Juan C. Guerra, and Johnnella E. Butler. New York: MLA, 1997. 209–19.

Silva, Tony, Ilona Leki, and Joan Carson. "Broadening the Perspective of Mainstream Composition Studies: Some Thoughts from the Disciplinary Margins." *Written Communication* 14 (1997): 398–428.

Singh, Frances. "Teaching English to Adult Speakers of Other Languages: 1910– 1920." *College ESL* 2.1 (1992): 44–53.

Slager, William. "The Foreign Student and the Immigrant: Their Different Problems as Students of English." *Language Learning* 6.3/4 (1956): 24–29.

Spack, Ruth. "The Acquisition of Academic Literacy in a Second Language: A Longitudinal Case Study." *Written Communication* 14 (1997): 3–62.

———. *America's "Second Tongue": The Ownership of English and American Indian Education, 1860s-1900.* Diss. Lesley College, 1998.

Sternglass, Marilyn S. *The Presences of Thought: Introspective Accounts of Reading and Writing.* Norwood: Ablex, 1988.

"Studies in English as a Second Language." *CCC* 7 (1956): 163–65.

Sullivan, Paul R. "English as a Second Language: Potential Applications to Teaching the Freshman Course." *CCC* 8 (1957): 10–12.

Tannacito, Dan J. *A Guide to Writing in English as a Second or Foreign Language: An Annotated Bibliography of Research and Pedagogy.* Alexandria: TESOL, 1995.

"Teaching English as a Second Language." *CCC* 17 (1966): 198–99.

Valdés, Guadalupe. "Bilingual Minorities and Language Issues in Writing: Toward Professionwide Response to a New Challenge." *Written Communication* 9 (1992): 85–136.

Williams, Jessica. "ESL Composition Program Administration in the United States. *Journal of Second Language Writing* 4 (1995): 157–79.

Zamel, Vivian. "Strangers in Academia: The Experiences of Faculty and ESL Students Across the Curriculum." *CCC* 46 (1995): 506–21.

———. "Teaching Composition in the ESL Classroom: What We Can Learn from Research in the Teaching of English." *TESOL Quarterly* 10 (1976): 67–76.

———. "Recent Research on Writing Pedagogy." *TESOL Quarterly* 21 (1987): 697–715.

Zamel, Vivian, and Ruth Spack, eds. *Negotiating Academic Literacies: Readings on Teaching and Learning Across Cultures.* Mahwah: Erlbaum, 1998.

Acknowledgments: I am grateful to Tony Silva and Irwin Weiser, whose comments and encouragement helped me in developing this essay. I also thank Robert B. Kaplan for his valuable insights, Ruth Spack for discussing many important points with me, and Dwight Atkinson, Margie Berns, Laurie Cubbison, Ted Gallagher, Vai Ramanathan, Carlos Salinas, Michele Simmons, and John Swales for their thoughtful comments and suggestions.

SECTION SIX

Virtual Talk
Composing Beyond the Word

In 1985 a new journal came into the profession, the former newsletter *Computers and Composition*. It marked the beginning of discussions about what would first be termed *computer-assisted writing* and what would eventually become an integral part of all that we do. The journal is the hallmark of a turn in composition studies, but the conversations were cropping up in all of our work in the 1980s. Though some were cautious about this new paradigm, the trend seemed to support the sense that everything about reading and writing was changing, at least online. In 1993, Richard Lanham, in *The Electronic Word: Democracy, Technology, and the Arts* (Chicago: U of Chicago P, 1993), fleshed out previous arguments about the ways in which new electronic media redefine the word, now comprising text, sight, and sound, no longer even necessarily linear. This new mode of discourse, hypertext, became the topic of discussion about new methods of reading, writing, and knowing.

Composition turned to hypertextual software (such as Storyspace) and the classroom use of MUDs and MOOs (digital spaces in which users can interact through textual communication and the building of various worlds); some began using listservs and message boards to hold classroom discussions. All this gave rise to discussions on synchronous and asynchronous practices, culminating in the popularity of Lester Faigley's *Fragments of Rationality: Postmodernity and the Subject of Composition* (U of Pittsburgh P, 1992). In examining what happens in disrupted written discourse, the stuff of MUDs and MOOs and message boards and listservs, Faigley speculated about the creation of a new epistemology, considering whether "it [would] be more difficult to preserve the rational, autonomous subject" in this new online environment (165), arguing as well that the new paradigm had the potential to dismantle teacher authority and grant greater authority to those who would otherwise be silenced, though he acknowledged that that potential is not always realized. The ways in which computer-mediated communication is, or is not, empowering became a common topic of discussion.

One of the earliest "proceed with caution" arguments within English studies came from Richard Ohmann in the article included in this section. Gail Hawisher and Cynthia Selfe offered *Critical Perspectives on Computers and Composition Instruction* as early as 1989 (New York: Teachers College P), providing balanced accounts of the virtues and pitfalls of the digital paradigm from that time to the present day. Within literary studies, Katherine Hayles, in *How We Became Posthuman: Virtual Bodies in Cybernetics, Literature, and Informatics* (Chicago: U of Chicago P, 1999), asked how technology shifts the ways in which we define ourselves. Folks like Kristine Blair and Pamela Takayoshi examined how online spaces affect, and are affected by, women, and Beth Kolko, Lisa Nakamura, and Gilbert Rodman looked at *Race in Cyberspace* (New York: Routledge, 2000). Such discussions and reminders to pay attention to the material reality of lived bodies continue.

While the enthusiasm for hypertextual theory in the 1980s and early 1990s may have called for radical departures from past media, Jay David Bolter and Richard Grusin's *Remediation: Understanding New Media* (Cambridge, MA: MIT P, 2000) argued that digital technologies are not divorced from previous technologies, that we shouldn't think of them in this way. Instead, new media work because they refashion the old—that is, they re-mediate. To think of any technology as separate and isolated from previous technologies may prove a disservice to our theories and practices. If our literacies have changed to include the multimodal and the digital more than ever before, then perhaps it is more effective to think of those literacies as Lawrence Lessig or Henry Jenkins ask—as a Remix or a Convergence.

Literacy, Technology, and Monopoly Capital

RICHARD OHMANN

My late, lamented colleague Vernon Dibble once told me this rule of thumb: if a title comprises three words or phrases in a series, and their order makes no difference, then the lecture or article will be nonsense. (Vernon used a stronger word than "nonsense," actually.) I hope to make some sense in this essay, although the three terms of my title could as well come in any sequence.[1] In fact, the five sections of the essay might themselves be rearranged. They represent five pieces of what I take to be a Big Picture, so big that to fill it all in would require a fat volume which I do not plan to write. So I ask the courteous reader to bear with my somewhat fragmentary method, here, and with an argument that cannot be decisive, only suggestive.

It may help if I indicate where I am heading. I claim that exhortations about the need for "computer literacy" have much in common with longer-standing debates about literacy itself; that both kinds of discussion usually rest on a serious misconception of technology and its roles in history; and that we can best understand the issues that trouble us by situating them within the evolution of our present economic and social system—a very recent historical process, going back little more than a hundred years. The whole discussion presumes that questions of literacy and technology are inextricable from political questions of domination and equality.

Reprinted from *Politics of Letters* by Richard Ohmann (Wesleyan University Press, 1987); originally published in *College English* 47.7 (1985): 675–89.

1. HISTORY

The earliest citations for the word "literacy" in the OED come from the 1880s. The word "illiteracy," in the common modern sense, appears only a bit earlier. (Before that, it referred to lack of cultivation, or to ignorance.) The adjectives "literate" and "illiterate" have a much longer history; but again, before the late nineteenth century they had a global, qualitative meaning—well-read and civilized, or the reverse—rather than indicating a line that divided those who could read and write from those who could not.

If this were 1850, we could not talk about literacy in the language we use now, nor with the same concepts. Of course people had been discussing for centuries the ability to read and write, and who should have it. But they did so without a mass noun that isolated that ability from other human practices and that referred to it as a measurable attribute of individuals, groups, or whole societies. That seems odd to me. Why did the concept and the term "literacy" come into play just when they did, toward the end of the last century?

We can get a hint by looking at the discourse within which writers (and doubtless speakers) began to use the words "literacy" and "illiteracy." One of the OED's earliest citations for "literacy" points us to *The New Princeton Review*, Nov., 1888.[2] The word turns up in an article by George R. Stetson, called "The Renaissance of Barbarism," which laments and analyzes the rise in crime—statistically documented—since mid-century. He sees this quite specifically as a class phenomenon. There has been a widening "separation of those who have, from those who have not, a complete control of their appetites and passions"; the latter, he calls "the brutalized class," and to them he attributes almost all "the outrageous, inhuman, and barbarous crimes." That is why, although "Education is more general, our literacy greatly increased," moral degeneracy is also on the rise—with immigrants and Negroes contributing far more than their share (336–7).

A companion article in the same issue, by James P. Munroe, ponders "The Education of the Masses." Munroe, like Stetson, worries about moral degeneration, idleness, and crime; like Stetson, he writes of these dangers in terms of class. There is a "dangerous class," composed mainly of immigrants, which may easily contaminate the class next to it, "the so-called working class." (His theory of class interaction: "Below a certain stratum of the social structure, all populations have a tendency toward degeneration,—a tendency enormously increased by contact with classes upon a still lower plane.") Munroe's concern is to provide the right education for these "slowly-plodding millions, without fame, almost without identity. . . ."

In this context he, too, uses one of the new words. He does *not* advocate repeal of compulsory education laws: "Not for one moment would

I advocate illiteracy," he writes, even though at the moment, "the evils of mal-education" are "perhaps greater . . . than those of illiteracy. . . . " His solution: take the children of the masses—who are "unfitted or indisposed" to educate their children—from the parents at age two or three, put them in "kindergartens," and train them "to habits of cleanliness, order, neatness, and punctuality." To offset the cost of such education, Munroe advocates the abolition of free high schools, whose "higher education" is wasted upon most of the lower classes (348–52 *passim*). I would note that Stetson also fixes upon education as a cause, and possible cure, for crime: a purely "intellectual" schooling has pushed out "religious and manual training," expanding literacy but not moral character (342–3).

I don't want to make these two articles bear too much weight, but I suggest that we think about the soil in which our main concept took root. The argument over education for poor people had been joined long before the 1880s, of course. What catches my attention is how easily the new idea slid into that discourse. For it was a top-down discourse from the start, and its participants almost invariably took the underlying question to be: how can we keep the lower orders docile? Thus, for instance, Bernard de Mandeville: "Going to School . . . is Idleness, and the longer Boys continue in this easy sort of Life, the more unfit they'll be when grown up for downright Labour. . . ." (180). And, on the other side, Adam Smith: "An instructed and intelligent people . . . are always more decent and orderly than an ignorant and stupid one" (269; see Altick for a useful treatment of this debate). Once the lower orders came to be seen as masses and classes, the term "literacy" offered a handy way to conceptualize an attribute of theirs, which might be manipulated in one direction or the other for the stability of the social order and the prosperity and security of the people who counted.

From these origins, the concept evolved naturally to serve purposes of social diagnosis and reform. One could *measure* literacy scientifically. The first study of illiteracy in the United States was published in 1870 (Leigh),[3] but it was not until World War I, when thirty percent of recruits were unable to take the written intelligence test, that a movement toward systematic literacy testing got underway (Resnick and Resnick 381–82). Literacy *tests* and census questions become evidence to fix the literacy *rate* of a society. After that, of course, we may thrill to periodic literacy *crises*, followed by back-to-basics movements. And international agencies may attack low literacy rates in third world countries with literacy *campaigns* designed to hasten modernization. (Modernization theory held that a literacy rate of forty percent was necessary for "take-off" to occur.)

All of this—the analytic division of people into measurable quantities, the attempt to modify these quantities, the debate among professionals and political leaders over what's good for the poor—all this legacy still inheres in the discourse of literacy, even now, when almost everyone takes it for granted that literacy is a Good Thing, and when it would be hard to find a Mandeville to argue that the poor should be kept illiterate in order to keep them content.

2. MONOPOLY CAPITAL

By coincidence—or maybe not—the term "literacy" came into use roughly at the beginning of the epoch of monopoly capital.[4] A word about the transformation I have in mind: in the mid- and late-nineteenth century, *competitive* capitalism ran its energetic course, building a huge industrial system with unparalleled speed. The familiar movement from farm and shop to factory, from country to city, can be expressed in any number of statistics. For instance, the value of manufactured goods increased seven-fold in the last four decades of the century, far outdistancing the value of farm products. The number of factories quadrupled, and the number of people working in them tripled. Profits were large, and most of them went into the building of more industrial capacity: industrial capital quadrupled just in the last three decades of the century, and the *rate* of capital formation reached the highest point before or since, in the 1890s. Production changed utterly, and businessmen were in command of the nation's future

But as they raced ahead, making fortunes and transforming the society, they were experiencing painfully the contradictions of the system they had built. Every decade between 1870 and 1900 brought a major depression; crises of overproduction were apparently untamable. Within this volatile *system*, individual businesses led precarious existences; competition was fierce, and none of the legal or illegal attempts to restrain it worked. The rate of profit began to decline. And attempts on the part of businessmen to counter these dangers by reducing wages led to all but open class warfare in 1877, 1885, and the early 1890s. (These conflicts sponsored the discourse of dangerous classes, and what to do about them, to which I referred earlier; just as in England the Hyde Park riots provided an impetus for Arnold's *Culture and Anarchy*.) By concentrating their energies on production and on price competition, businessmen had built an empire, but one they could not govern, either as a class or individually—one whose anarchy led to great instability, killing risk, falling profits, and social rebellion.[5]

What emerged from this extended crisis—and partially resolved it—was the system I am calling monopoly capitalism. This is no time to characterize it in detail; it is, in any case, the ocean in which we now swim, as familiar to all of us as our bodies. I will mention only a few of its main features, as they bear on the themes of this essay. Please keep in mind that every aspect of monopoly capitalism was a response to the crisis of which I have spoken, and an effort to control and rationalize processes that felt—to businessmen as well as to most other people—chaotic and threatening. In fact, one might characterize monopoly capitalism by its powerful drive toward *planning*— its attempt to replace Adam Smith's invisible hand with the visible hand of management.

I take that phrase from Alfred D. Chandler's *The Visible Hand: The Managerial Revolution in American Business*, a classic study of monopoly capitalism's main institutional form, the giant corporation, which emerged in the last two decades of the nineteenth century. Where before, entrepreneurs had built factories and concentrated on getting out the goods, from the 1880s on, the impersonal corporation became dominant. Characteristically, it brought the entire economic process within its compass, from extraction of raw materials through manufacturing through distribution. Far too complex for the supervision of a single businessman (and his family), it brought into existence the modern table of organization, with divisions and subdivisions and layers of hired management. It attempted to coordinate every stage of making and selling, so as to eliminate uncertainty from the process. That project never succeeded entirely, of course, but it did establish an economic order that has proved supple enough through our century.

Before redirecting these large, pear-shaped thoughts toward technology and literacy, I want to mention two ways in which the new corporations carried out this design. First, monopoly capital took control of the labor process, far more precisely and intrusively than had been done before. It developed the approach that came to be known as scientific management, following that magical moment when Frederick Winslow Taylor, overseeing the work of a "Dutchman" named Schmidt, got him to move far more pigs of iron in a day than had previously been thought possible. Taylor analyzed labor into its minutest components, divided the process among various workers, and created the techniques which culminated in Ford's assembly line. He built on three principles: (1) dissociate the labor process from the vested skills and knowledge of workers; (2) separate conception from execution; and (3) reserve understanding for management, and use it to control each step of production. (As Studs Terkel's workers put it, one way and another, "a robot could do my job.") Harry Braverman, from whom I draw this understanding, sums up the role of management thus:

> to render conscious and systematic, the formerly unconscious tendency of capitalist production. It was to ensure that as craft declined, the worker

would sink to the level of general and undifferentiated labor power, adaptable to a large range of simple tasks, while as science grew, it would be concentrated in the hands of management. (120–21)

The second main movement of monopoly capital was to add control of *sales* to control of production. This was a change of great complexity and unevenness, working through the evolution of department stores, chain stores, mail order houses, the railroads, the telegraph, and the postal system, as well as the new corporate structure and its sales division. The outcome was a universal, national market, increasingly managed by the same corporations that produced the goods. To enter national markets successfully, they quickly developed a number of new practices: uniform packaging (as opposed to the barrel of anonymous pickles or crackers); brand names to help form habits of loyalty among buyers; trademarks to link a *second* sign to the product and enhance its aura; slogans, jingles, and cartoon characters to penetrate every buyer's mind. In short, they came to depend on advertising as a direct channel of instruction from manufacturer to customer. And piggy-back on the new advertising industry, there arose for the first time a national mass culture, whose main product was not the magazine, the newspaper, the radio or TV broadcast, but the *attention of the audience*, sold in blocks to advertisers. I assert that this characteristic feature of modern society and contemporary humanity—mass culture—derives from exactly the same forces that transformed labor. In fact, the two are obverse and reverse, in a social mode that had polarized work and leisure, production and consumption, worker and consumer.

3. TECHNOLOGY

Against this background, I will now marshal some reflections on technology—unsystematic, but I hope suggestive. First, as a kind of loosening-up exercise, I ask you to imagine some instances of the almost unimaginable.

a. Suppose that writing (a technology, as Walter Ong rightly insists) had been invented by slaves—say, in the Roman Empire—and for purposes of survival, resistance, and rebellion. How might they have devised a writing system to advance those purposes? Might it have been a shifting code, to preserve its secrets from masters? Might there have been a common form that could encode the different languages spoken by slaves? I don't know, but my guess is that writing would not have evolved as it did, had its inventors wanted it as an aid to solidarity and revolt.

b. What about printing? You may recall that when Raphael Hythloday, Thomas More's traveler, showed European books to the Utopians, they quickly re-invented printing and papermaking: their sole purpose was to make available thousands of copies of the Greek classics, so that all who wished might pursue wisdom and the study of nature. Shortly after More wrote, the English adapted printing to a different use, in the *Great Boke of Statutes:* organizing the laws for their more rational administration and enforcement.[6] Would the Utopians, with their purely humanistic and relatively egalitarian aims, have developed the technology of printing in ways different from those that served state power? Certainly the printing technology that served English radicals of the 1790s, with their plethora of small presses, pamphlets, and journals was sharply different from the technology developed for mass circulation magazines, with gigantic rotary presses and photoengraving, to address people as a mass audience rather than as participants in a common discourse. (The 1790s term, "corresponding societies," suggests a very different setting for technology than does our term, "mass communications.")

c. Suppose that wireless communication had evolved, not under the guidance and for the needs of the British Navy, the United Fruit Company, and commercial advertisers, but among women tinkering in their homes, sharing knowledge about domestic production, establishing networks of childcare and concern. Every receiver is in principle a transmitter as well. Might we have had electronic systems that actually merited the name "communication," rather than or in addition to *broadcasting?*

d. And what if the computer . . . ? I don't even know the right bizarre question to ask, but I do know that computers are an evolving technology like any other, shaped within particular social relations, and responsive to the needs of those with the power to direct that evolution. I will return to this subject shortly, for a mixture of anxiety and excitement about computers inevitably surrounds any discussion of literacy and technology today.

First, though, let me state the point of the in-some-ways absurd thought experiments I just asked you to conduct. Following Raymond Williams's helpful clarifications (10–14), I have meant to call into question technological determinism (the idea that, e.g., TV somehow got invented, and from that accident many consequences have inexorably followed), and also what Williams calls "symptomatic technology" (the idea that TV was invented on the margins of the social process, and was simply deployed by other forces that dictate the direction of society—so that it is a *symptom* of consumerism, mass culture, passivity, or whatever). This second view is close to what I might call "neutral technology"—the idea that every invention, still thought of as appearing independently, can be put to an infinite number of uses—humane and inhumane, tyrannical and democratic.

I agree with Williams that these views err in abstracting technology from society, sometimes in a way that makes it seem like a miraculous intervention in history. The history of radio and television, as told by Williams, or by Eric Barnouw in *Tube of Plenty*, reveals quite a different process. The technology developed over a century and more, in ways far from accidental. Those with the vision, the needs, the money, and the power gradually made it what they wanted—a mass medium. (I exaggerate only a bit.) Technology, one might say, is itself a social process, saturated with the power relations around it, continually reshaped according to some people's *intentions*. The point is borne out with respect to electric lighting, the telephone, the chemical industry, etc., in David Noble's fine study, *America by Design*. As a recent TV commercial aptly put it: "The future is being driven by technology, and Martin Marietta is masterminding it."

Perhaps I can make the point another way by entering a friendly objection to some characteristic formulations of Walter Ong, one of our most stimulating and learned writers on these matters. In *Interfaces of the Word*, for instance, he writes of "technological devices . . . which enable men to . . . shape, store, retrieve, and communicate knowledge in new ways" (44). Again, "writing and print and the computer enable the mind to constitute within itself . . . new ways of thinking. . . ." (46). And, "the alphabet or print or the computer enters the mind, producing new states of awareness there. . . . the computer actually releases more energy for new kinds of exploratory operations by the human mind itself . . ." (47). My objections are, first, to phrases like "*the* computer," as if it were one, stable device; second, to these phrases used as grammatical agents ("the computer enables the mind . . ."), implying that the technology somehow came before *someone's* intention to enable *some* minds to do *some* things; and third, to phrases like "man," "the mind," and "the human mind," in these contexts, suggesting that technologies interact with people or with "culture" in global, undifferentiated ways, rather than serving as an arena of interaction among classes, races, and other groups of unequal power. Certainly Fr. Ong is no stranger to such ideas, and he may well agree with most of what I am saying. My point is just that technological determinism is a powerful ideology which tends to infiltrate our minds when we look the other way. I think we need to be on guard against it, when thinking about literacy or any other technology, including:

4. COMPUTERS

About which I know remarkably little—so that I may now air my prejudices with only slight interference from the facts.

We are told (in the language of technological determinism) that computers will transform the workplace and the home, not to mention the school, and that in anticipation of this change, we need to provide "computer literacy" for everyone, or at least for the young. Paul A. Strassmann, vice president for "strategic planning" at Xerox's Information Products Group, holds that we are now at the end of the Gutenberg era and "the beginning of the 'electronic display' era." Adults ignorant of computers will soon be as restricted as those who today are unable to read. Software will become the language of the future, and "the dominant intellectual asset" of the human race, so that an "understanding of software . . . will be a primary component of literacy in the electronic age" (116, 119). Many of those who worry about education see things the same way. The National Council of Teachers of Mathematics committed itself a few years ago to the proposition that "an essential outcome of contemporary education is computer literacy." The National Science Foundation then funded a study to define computer literacy; its findings appeared in *Mathematics Teacher* (Johnson, et al.).[7] The article lists sixty-four objectives for computer education (including forty "core" objectives), ranging from a grasp of how computers work to familiarity with computer crime. The authors acknowledge that achievement of these objectives would require more than a single course. There is already a lot of pressure on schools to provide such education.

Behind such pressure, of course, is the fear of parents and students that computer literacy will be required for many or most good jobs in the future. People like Strassmann encourage that view. He predicts that almost 30 million people—roughly one-quarter of the workforce—will have "electronic workstations" by 1990, and use this means of communication about one-half the time they are at work (117). I don't know just what Strassmann has in mind, but one may perhaps allay one's anxiety *or* euphoria, in anticipating this revolution, by looking around oneself right now.

For example: in my own department of 23 full-time workers, only one has an electronic workstation, and is required to possess a small degree of computer literacy. She is the junior secretary, and, at $10,000 a year, the worst paid of the 23. (I don't believe that the computer has improved her life or her temperament.) All the workers at my travel agency have electronic workstations, which have considerably routinized (and dehumanized) their work. So does the baggage agent at the airline. So does the teller at my bank. And I wonder if Strassmann's count included the check-out clerks at my supermarket, with their recently installed, computerized scanners, which have reduced the skill required to an almost entirely manual one of the most repetitive kind. Or how about the young people behind the fast-food counter, whose computer keyboards no longer carry numbers and letters, but pictures of food items, so that the work could be done by someone who is both computer-illiterate and just plain illiterate? Predictions that 50 to 75 percent of jobs will be "computer-related" by 1990 sound intimidating, but how many of those jobs will call for even the slightest understanding of computers ?[8]

I am suggesting that, seen from the side of production and work, the computer and its software are an intended and developing technology, carrying forward the deskilling and control of labor that goes back to F. W. Taylor and beyond, and that has been a main project of monopoly capital. As Taylor consciously sought to transfer all understanding of production to management and reduce the worker's role to that of a conduit for the transfer of commands into physical energy, engineers are shaping computers now so that those who work at them will be only keyboard operators. As Phil Kraft puts it, "all the skill is embodied in the machines" — in fact, that could be a definition of the term "user-friendly." ("Designing for idiots is the highest expression of the engineering art," in David Noble's words.)[9] In a special irony, engineers are programming some of their *own* skill into obsolescence, along with that of technicians, in the booming field of Computer-Assisted Design/ Computer-Assisted Manufacture — "CAD/CAM." And predictably, there begin to be programs for *programming*, aimed at reducing the need for intelligent programmers even as schools and colleges scramble to train them.

Of course there will be more jobs in the computer field itself. But that doesn't amount to much, as against the deskilling that is underway (or indeed, against the number of jobs *eliminated* through computerization). It seems that a decade from now there will be only half a million or so additional jobs in this field, compared to 800,000 new jobs for janitors (Pincus 7). Furthermore, the field is layered into specialties, which will be dead ends for most people in them. Operators seldom become programmers; programmers seldom become systems analysts; analysts seldom become designers or computer scientists (Corson 35). Graduates of MIT will get the challenging jobs; community college grads will be technicians; those who do no more than acquire basic skills and computer literacy in high school will probably find their way to electronic workstations at McDonald's. I see every reason to expect that the computer revolution, like other revolutions from the top down, will indeed expand the minds and the freedom of an elite, meanwhile facilitating the degradation of labor and the stratification of the workforce that have been hallmarks of monopoly capitalism from its onset.[10]

After this brief look at production, an even briefer glance now at consumption, before I skip back to literacy. Microcomputers *will* be in the homes of most people, without question (some forecasts see them penetrating the home market almost as universally as television has done). And to judge from some of my friends who are buffs, hobbyists, and addicts, some people *will* have their horizons widened and their minds challenged. (Though I also forecast even more broken marriages from this cause than have resulted from TV football coverage.) But I remain skeptical about the import of the change. Apparently, eighty percent of home computers are used *exclusively* for games (Douglas Noble 42, another helpfully critical source). I bet many of them will fall into disuse, like other new toys. Yet the manufacturers are selling them hot and heavy, often appealing to the hopes and anxieties of parents in quite unscrupulous ways. Thus, a radio commercial that I often heard last year featured a dad saying to a mom that if they bought a personal computer it could change their daughter's whole life. To Mom's incredulity, Dad explained that their daughter would get an edge on other kids at school that could get her into a prestigious college, and *that* could even affect whom she might *marry!* Mom was convinced. This appeal to hope and anxiety calls to mind strongly the pitch of door-to-door encyclopedia salespeople, thirty years ago.

Seen from *this* side of the market, computers are a commodity, for which a mass market is being created in quite conventional ways. And their other main use in the home, besides recreation, most likely will be to facilitate the marketing of still *more* commodities, as computerized shopping becomes a reality. Thus our "age of technology" looks to me very much like the age of monopoly capital, with new channels of power through which the few try to control both the labor and the leisure of the many.

And the education? That is not my subject here; but a brief aside may be in order, to connect the instructional use of computers to my argument. Only two years ago, Stanley Pogrow lamented that schools were not responding well to the new "information economy." There were only 96,000 microcomputers in the schools, and they were not being used to improve learning for most students. He saw a high likelihood that in this decade, the dissatisfaction of parents and employers will go beyond "political activism" to *abandonment* of public schools, and to "environmental collapse" of a school system unable to adapt, with industry taking over this side of education (92–94). Two other specialists in this area—Tim O'Shea and John Self—are confident that computers will become standard furniture in classrooms, but pose the danger and the choices in this way:

> Computers will cause great changes in education. Already there are examination halls in American universities where rows of nervous students type

answers to multiple-choice questions at computer consoles and anxiously await their grade. There are also experimental classrooms where young children happily and confidently command a computer to draw pictures or play music, and articulately explain their latest computer program. Motivated by cost-effectiveness and efficiency, educators may try to use computers to turn classrooms into human battery farms. But there is a possibility that computers will be used to enhance the educational process and equip each learner with an exciting medium for problem-solving and individual tuition. (1)

Most people I've asked agree that O'Shea and Self's first alternative is ascendant at the moment, with computers being used as little more than electronic workbooks and data banks. That the liberatory possibilities explored by O'Shea and Self lag behind may have something to do with the way that Pogrow's forecast is already proving to be wrong. There are now about 500,000 computers in American schools, many of them gifts or nearly so from the manufacturers and from other companies. The motives for such generosity are not hard to imagine. Apparently, business will take care that its needs are met without the "enviromental collapse" of public schools, and one cannot expect those needs to include many of the liberatory classrooms mentioned by O'Shea and Self. This is the first area of public education to be so stimulated and directed by business. Most likely, the technology of classroom computers—especially software—will serve purposes I have already described.

Now, none of these developments is foreordained. The technology is malleable; it does have liberatory potential. Especially in education, we have something to say about whether that potential is realized. But its fate is not a technological question: it is a political one.

5. LITERACY

I have stated my outlook on these themes in enough ways, now, that you will know whether you find it congenial or not. I will not develop it in detail, with respect to the prospects for literacy in the United States today, but will just reflect on some of its implications.

Plainly, from this perspective it is not helpful to think of literacy as an invariant, individual skill, or as a skill whose numerically measurable distribution across a society (as in "literacy rate") will tell us much of scholarly interest or human relevance. Literacy is an activity of social groups, and a necessary feature of some kinds of social organization. Like every other human activity or product, it embeds social relations within it. And these relations always include *conflict* as well as cooperation. Like language itself, literacy is an exchange between classes, races, the sexes, and so on. Simply recall the struggle over black English, or think on the continuing conflict over the CCCC statement, "Students' Right to Their Own Language," or the battle over generic male pronouns, for times when the political issues have spilled out into the open. But explicit or not, they are always there, in every classroom and in every conversation—just as broadcasting technology is an exchange which has up to now been resolved through control by the dominant classes, and participation by the subordinate classes in the form of Neilson ratings and call-in shows.

That means that we can usefully distinguish between literacy-from-above and literacy-from-below.[11] From the 1790s to roughly the 1830s, popular literacy in England was broad and vigorous (among men, at least), as artisans and the new industrial working class taught one another to read, formed corresponding societies, drafted petitions, put out pamphlets and books, held meetings. *The Rights of Man* sold 1.5 million copies by the time of Paine's death—equivalent to sales of 25 million in the United States today. This happened in a context where, as Donald puts it,

> what we now specify as politics, education, literacy, journalism and recreation were still bound inextricably together. Their division into separate institutions was one effect of the ruling bloc's new techniques of power. (56)

Those techniques won out, both in England and in the United States, as literacy was subsumed within state-run school systems. As we well know, the results here have been such as to provoke both patriotic self-congratulation and repeated literacy "crises" over the last 75 years—the latter meaning a periodic rediscovery by those at the top and their allies that after ten or twelve years of instruction in "English," very many citizens read and write badly.

But why should it be otherwise? Isn't the functional literacy rate just about what you'd expect, given how schooling relates to the needs and life chances of the working class? (Shouldn't we expect similar results in computer literacy, once people understand the false promises behind that movement?) Likewise, top-down literacy campaigns in "developing" countries have been almost universally failures. In Cuba, on the other hand, during the single year of 1961, 750,000 illiterate adults learned to read and write, leaving only 250,000 illiterates there, or about four percent of the population. I've suggested that a literacy *rate* is in itself mystifying; but you can sense the *kind* of literacy and the context that supported it by reading some of the letters that "students" wrote to Castro, as their final "exam."

Dr. Fidel Castro Ruz
Dear Comrade:
I write this to let you know that now I know how to read and write thanks to
our Socialist and democratic Revolution. That's why I'm writing to you, so
that you can see with your own eyes. I take leave with a firm Revolutionary
and democratic salute.
I used to be illiterate
Patria o Muerte
Teaching, we shall triumph.

Comrade Fidel Castro:
I am very thankful because I know how to write and read. I would like you
to send me the Follow-Up books to improve my knowledge more in the
reading and in the writing. To be an educated people is to be free. (Kozol,
"A New Look at the Literacy Campaign in Cuba" 358–59)

These peasants had learned to read and write in the context of a revolution, and with the aim of becoming full participants in it, not of passing from
third grade into fourth or of meeting a college requirement. Their learning
was saturated with politics, an activity of conscious liberation. Of course it
did not happen spontaneously, and it *began* at the top in that Castro initiated the campaign. But he spoke for nearly all the people of Cuba when he
articulated the goal of full literacy, and those people responded with energy
because they saw the revolution as theirs, and literacy as contributing to it.

Cuba at that time had only 35,000 teachers, and they stayed in their
classrooms teaching kids. The *brigadistas* who went out into the hills to live
and work with peasant families were students, ninety percent of them
between ten and nineteen years old, mainly from the cities. Over 100,000
volunteered after Castro's call, in spite of the distances they would travel
from home, the crude shacks they would live in, and the strangeness of their
task (after just ten days of training). "I knew nothing about reading" (said a
woman who was 16 in 1961). My first motive . . . was not to teach. It was to
be part of a great struggle. It was my first chance to take a stand" (Kozol,
Children of the Revolution 31). They learned to use a primer and a book of
readings, which began, not with "See Jane run," but with key political terms:
"OEA," Spanish acronym for the Organization of American States; "INRA,"
the National Institute of Agrarian Reform. From the first day, the project of
literacy was for these *campesinos* connected to their needs and their situation in the world. As David Harman (an adult literacy worker in Israel) said
to Kozol, the pedagogical theories and classroom techniques don't matter a
lot: "None of it works . . . unless it is allied with something else. That 'something else' is what they did in Cuba. It is the promise of a better life for every

man and woman in the land" (*Children of the Revolution* 77). The more recent literacy campaign in Nicaragua, which also offered "something else," used similar methods with similar results (Arnove).

Technique is less important than context and purpose in the teaching of literacy; and the *effects* of literacy cannot be isolated from the social relations and processes within which people become literate.

Enough. The age of computer technology will bring us some new tools and methods for teaching literacy. I hope we (or rather, those of us teachers who are on my side!) will manage to shape that technology to democratic forms.

But this age of technology, this age of computers, will change very little in the social relations—the *class* relations—of which literacy is an inextricable part. Monopoly capital will continue to saturate most classrooms, textbooks, student essays, and texts of all sorts. It will continue to require a high degree of literacy among elites, especially the professional-managerial class. It will continue to require a meager literacy or none from subordinate classes. And yet its spokesmen—the Simons and Newmans and Safires and blue ribbon commissions on education—will continue to kvetch at teachers and students, and to demand that all kids act out the morality play of literacy instruction, from which the moral drawn by most will be that in this meritocracy they do not merit much.

But then monopoly capital will *also* continue to generate resistance and rebellion, more at some times than at others. I hope many of us will find ways to take part in that resistance, even in our daily work. Apparently we must learn to fight mindless computer literacy programs, as we have sometimes fought mindless drills in grammar and usage. We should remember that most programmed instruction, in addition to being mindless, builds in imperatives other than ours and other than those of our students. Computerized testing is likely to be undemocratic, not because the computer is, but because it will help realize the impulse toward inequality that is implicit in all standardized testing. We should be critically analyzing the politics of all these tendencies, trying to comprehend them historically, and engaging our students in a discussion of literacy and technology that is both historical and political. It's worth trying to reconstitute literacy as a process of liberation— but also to remember that work for literacy is not in itself intrinsically liberating. The only way to have a democracy is to make one.

NOTES

1. This essay is a revised talk, given at the Wyoming Conference on Freshman and Sophomore English, June, 1984. The theme of the conference was "Literacy in an Age of

Technology," and my original title, implying a critique of that conceptualization, was "Literacy in an Age of Monopoly Capital."

2. Actually, the OED says *December*. It had never occurred to me that the OED could be wrong about something.

3. Thanks to my colleague, Gerald Burns, for this reference. Burns also tells me that Horace Mann referred to the "stigma of illiteracy" as early as 1838, in his *Second Annual Report*, but I think this was the older usage of the term.

4. I follow Baran and Sweezy and many other Marxists in the use of this term and in my characterization of our economic system. Other terms—"advanced capitalism," "late capitalism," etc.—imply different theories of history, but point to the same social formation. Terminology aside, almost everyone agrees that a new stage of capitalism emerged around the turn of the century.

5. Here and at the end of this section, I adapt the argument and some phrasing from Ohmann, 1981.

6. See Eisenstein (58–59) for some of the social consequences of this printing innovation. I'm suggesting that social purposes like this had an impact on the technology as well.

7. Thanks to Marilyn Frankenstein and Bob Rosen for pointing me to this and other articles on computers, and to Rosen for helpfully reading a draft of this article.

8. Corson (35) reports these predictions (by the U.S. Labor and Commerce Departments and by corporations like IBM) and discusses this question.

9. Corson (35) is my source for both of these quotations.

10. Pincus (7) reports Bureau of Labor statistics suggesting that however much high tech *gear* may be around, high tech *employment* may be no more important in 1995 than it is today.

11. As does James Donald, whose discussion I found particularly helpful, both for its historical account and for its theoretical position, and I have drawn upon it here. Myron Tuman also offers a good discussion of literacy as cause and effect.

WORKS CITED

Altick, Richard D. *The English Common Reader: A Social History of the Mass Reading Public 1800–1900.* Chicago: U of Chicago P, 1957.

Arnove, Robert F. "The Nicaraguan National Literacy Crusade of 1980." *Comparative Education Review* 25 (1981): 244–60.

Baran, Paul A., and Paul M. Sweezy. *Monopoly Capital: An Essay on the American Economic and Social Order.* New York: Modern Reader Paperbacks, 1966.

Barnouw, Eric. *Tube of Plenty: The Evolution of American Television.* New York: Oxford UP, 1982.

Braverman, Harry. *Labor and Monopoly Capital: The Degradation of Work in the Twentieth Century.* New York: Monthly Review, 1974.

Chandler, Alfred D. *The Visible Hand: The Managerial Revolution in American Business.* Cambridge, MA: Harvard UP, 1977.

Corson, Ross. "Computer Revolution." *The Progressive* Sept. 1982: 32, 34–36.

Donald, James. "Language, Literacy and Schooling." *The State and Popular Culture 1*, a unit in the Open University course on popular culture. Milton Keynes: The Open University, 1982.

Eisenstein, Elizabeth L. "Some Conjectures about the Impact of Printing on Western Society and Thought: A Preliminary Report." *Literacy and Social Development in the West: A Reader.* Ed. Harvey J. Graff. Cambridge, Eng.: Cambridge UP, 1981. 53–68.

Johnson, David C., Ronald E. Anderson, Thomas P. Hansen, and Daniel L. Klassen. "Computer Literacy—What Is It?" *Mathematics Teacher* 73 (1980): 91–96.

Kozol, Jonathan. *Children of the Revolution: A Yankee Teacher in the Cuban Schools.* New York: Delacorte, 1978.

———. "A New Look at the Literacy Campaign in Cuba." *Harvard Educational Review* 48 (1978): 341–77.

Leigh, Edwin. "Illiteracy in the United States." *Annual Report of the Commissioner of Education,* 1870: 467–502.

Mandeville, Bernard de. "Essay on Charity and Charity Schools." *The Fable of the Bees.* 1723. London, 1795.

Munroe, James P. "The Education of the Masses." *The New Princeton Review.* Nov. 1888: 346–54.

Noble, David. *America by Design: Science, Technology, and the Rise of Corporate Capitalism.* New York: Knopf, 1977.

Noble, Douglas. "The Underside of Computer Literacy." *Raritan* 3 (1984): 37–64.

Ohmann, Richard. "Where Did Mass Culture Come From? The Case of Magazines." *Berkshire Review* 16 (1981): 85–101.

Ong, Walter J. *Interfaces of the Word: Studies in the Evolution of Consciousness and Culture.* Ithaca: Cornell UP, 1977.

O'Shea, Tim, and John Self. *Learning and Teaching with Computers.* Englewood Cliffs, NJ: Prentice, 1984.

Pincus, Fred. "Students Being Groomed for Jobs That Won't Exist." *The Guardian* 9 May 1984: 7.

Pogrow, Stanley. *Education in the Computer Age: Issues of Policy, Practice, and Reform.* Beverly Hills: Sage, 1983.

Resnick, Daniel P., and Lauren B. Resnick. "The Nature of Literacy: An Historical Exploration." *Harvard Educational Review* 47 (1977): 370–85.

Smith, Adam. *The Wealth of Nations,* 2 vols. London: J. M. Dent and Sons, 1910. Vol. 2.

Stetson, George R. "The Renaissance of Barbarism." *The New Princeton Review.* Nov. 1888: 336–45.

Strassmann, Paul A. "Information Systems and Literacy." *Literacy for Life: The Demand for Reading and Writing.* Ed. Richard W. Bailey and Robin Melanie Fosheim. New York: Modern Language Association, 1983. 115–21.

Tuman, Myron. "Words, Tools, and Technology." *College English* 45 (1983): 769–79.

Williams, Raymond. *Television: Technology and Cultural Form.* New York: Schocken, 1975.

Blinded by the Letter

Why Are We Using Literacy as a
Metaphor for Everything Else?

ANNE FRANCES WYSOCKI AND
JOHNDAN JOHNSON-EILOLA

Too easily does "literacy" slip off our tongues, we think, and get put next to other terms: visual literacy, computer literacy, video literacy, media literacy, multimedia literacy, television literacy, technological literacy. Too much is hidden by "literacy," we think, too much packed into those letters—too much that we are wrong to bring with us, implicitly or no.

So:

Our first question in this essay: *what are we likely to carry with us when we ask that our relationship with all technologies should be like that we have with the technology of printed words?*

Our second question: *what other possibilities might we use for expressing our relationships with and within technologies?*

> "Examining titles in the ERIC database for 1980–94, inclusive, indicates that educators felt moved to discuss almost two hundred different kinds of literacy during those fifteen years; that is, two hundred different kinds of modified literacy as opposed to plain, unmodified literacy." This is from Dianne G. Kanawati's article, "How Can I Be Literate: Counting the Ways," where the author found, among the 197 total references in the ERIC database, Cash-culture Literacy, Christian Literacy, Discipline Literacy, Risk Literacy, Somatic Literacy, Water Literacy, Competitive Literacy, and Post-Literacy.

Reprinted from *Passions, Pedagogies, and 21st Century Technologies.* Ed. Gail E. Hawisher and Cynthia L. Selfe. Logan: Utah State UP and Urbana, IL: NCTE, 1999. 349–368. Copyright 1999 by Utah State University Press. Reprinted with permission.

FIRST

There are two bundles we carry with us when we ask that our relationship with all technologies should be like that we have with printed words. There is, first, a bundle of stories we have accumulated about what literacy is and does; second, there is our regard for the object to which we relate within literacy.

1

THE BUNDLE OF STORIES

a

"Of course you can learn how to read. Do you want to try?"

—Ransom Stoddard (James Stewart) to Hallie (Vera Miles),
his future wife, in *The Man Who Shot Liberty Valance*

At almost the ending of *The Man Who Shot Liberty Valance*, Ransom Stoddard and his wife Hallie are returning by train to Washington D.C. for what he says will be his last term as senator. He has recently finished recounting how he, a lawyer opposed to guns, helped bring law—and order—and statehood—and "book learning"—to the open territory around Shinbone (an unidentified territory in the U.S. West).

Hallie looks out the train window and says to Ransom, "It was once a wilderness. Now it's a garden."

In an earlier scene in a makeshift schoolroom (with "Education is the basis of law and order" written on the blackboard at the front), Ransom asks Pompey, a man of middle years and a student in the class, to talk about "the basic law of the land." Pompey, who works for Tom Donovan (John Wayne), starts to talk, with hesitant pauses in his sentences but with pride, about the Constitution; Jimmy Stewart corrects him: Pompey means the Declaration of Independence. Pompey starts again: "We hold these truths to be, uh, self-evident, that . . ."

He stops. Ransom finishes for him, ". . . all men are created equal." "I knew that, Mr. Ranse," says Pompey, "but I just plumb forgot it."

The room is disrupted by Tom entering to tell of how the cattlemen—who are fighting statehood because it will close off the free range—will bring violence down upon the townspeople and farmers who want a state. But, of course, eventually, Jimmy Stewart's gentle and learned ways help tame the area into statehood.

b

February 13, 1996

President Clinton announced today his intent to nominate Mary D. Green to the National Institute for Literacy Board...

The National Institute for Literacy was created to assist in upgrading the workforce, reducing welfare dependency, raising the standard of literacy and creating safer communities.

(http://www.ed.gov./PressRelease/02-1996/whpr24.html)

c

People who read, according to our reading of McLuhan, do nothing; they are helpless as the words they read pass through their eyes to shape them:

. . . print causes nationalism and not tribalism; and print causes price systems and markets such as cannot exist without print. (50)

. . . the assumption of homogeneous repeatability derived from the printed page, when extended to all the other concerns of life, led gradually to all those forms of production and social organization from which the Western world derives many satisfactions and nearly all of its characteristic traits. (144)

. . . the mere accustomation to repetitive, lineal patterns of the printed page strongly disposed people to transfer such approaches to all kinds of problems. (151)

And quantification means the translation of non-visual relations and realities into visual terms, a procedure inherent in the phonetic alphabet. (161)

Or, as Walter J. Ong puts it in *Orality and Literacy*, literacy fulfils our destiny:

> ... without writing, human consciousness cannot achieve its fuller potentials, cannot produce other beautiful and powerful creations. . . . Literacy . . . is absolutely necessary for the development not only of science but also of history, philosophy, explicative understanding of literature and of any art, and indeed for the explanation of language (including oral speech) itself. (15)

X X X

It is thus a large but not unruly bundle that comes with "literacy": John Wayne, Jimmy Stewart, the taming of the U.S. west, democracy, an upgraded workforce, less welfare dependency, our forms of production and social organization, science, and philosophy. The various descriptions and quotations above (a small selection from many possible) argue that if we acquire the basic skills of reading and writing—if we are literate—we have, or will have, all the goods the stories bundle together, no matter who or where or when we are.

"We think," writes Glynda Hull, "of reading and writing as generic, the intellectual equivalent of all-purpose flour, and we assume that, once mastered, these skills can and will be used in any context for any purpose, and that they are ideologically neutral and value-free" (34).

When we speak of "technological literacy," then, or of "computer literacy" or of "[fill-in-the-blank] literacy," we probably mean that we wish to give others some basic, neutral, context-less set of skills whose acquisition will bring the bearer economic and social goods and privileges. Aimée Dore says as much in an article titled "What Constitutes Literacy in a Culture with Diverse and Changing Means of Communication?":

> ... most people in education and communication are comfortable using the term "literacy" for [describing a relation to print, visual objects, television, and computer] because the various literacies have in common the image of people able to use symbol systems and the media or technologies in which they are instantiated in order to express themselves and to communicate with others, to do so effectively, and to do so in socially desirable ways. (145)

The same belief in a discrete set of basic skills shows itself in a recent White House document:

AMERICA'S TECHNOLOGY LITERACY CHALLENGE

February 15, 1996

"In our schools, every classroom in America must be connected to the information superhighway with computers and good software and well-trained teachers. . . . I ask Congress to support this education technology initiative so that we can make sure this national partnership succeeds."
President Clinton, State of the Union, January 23, 1996

NATIONAL MISSION TO MAKE EVERY YOUNG PERSON TECH-NOLOGICALLY LITERATE: The President has launched a national mission to make all children technologically literate by the dawn of the 21st century, equipped with communication, math, science, and critical thinking skills essential to prepare them for the Information Age. He challenges the private sector, schools, teachers, parents, students, community groups, state and local governments, and the federal government, to meet this goal by building four pillars that will:

1. Provide all teachers the training and support they need to help students learn through computers and the information superhighway;

2. Develop effective and engaging software and on-line learning resources as an integral part of the school curriculum;

3. Provide access to modern computers for all teachers and students;

4. Connect every school and classroom in America to the information superhighway.

But—and (unfortunately) of course—this notion of discrete skills is only a partial view of "literacy." The bundle of meanings and implications that comes with this word is, we argue alongside many other writers, much denser and messier.

In "Arts of the Contact Zone," Mary Louise Pratt describes a 1200 page manuscript, dated 1613, discovered in Copenhagen in 1908:

Written in a mixture of Quechua and ungrammatical, expressive Spanish, the manuscript was a letter addressed by an unknown but apparently literate Andean to King Phillip III of Spain. . . .

The second half of the epistle . . . combines a description of colonial society in the Andean region with a passionate denunciation of Spanish exploitation and abuse. (34–35)

But:

No one, it appeared, had ever bothered to read it or figured out how. (34)

In *The Man Who Shot Liberty Valance*, reading and writing don't get Pompey (an African-American man) or Hallie (the white wife) or the Mexican children in Ransom's classroom or their parents the right to vote in the move towards statehood; that privilege is reserved for the white men in the movie—some of whom cannot read and write. In the non-film reality of our present time, becoming literate in English does not help a young Navajo woman feel that she has a real place in Anglo culture, as Anne DiPardo describes, nor does it help the Native Alaskans or African-Americans about whom Lisa Delpit writes feel that they really belong as students in graduate programs or as teachers in U.S. schools. Hull provides a catalogue of writers who warn that U.S. supremacy in business will be eroded by illiteracy in the workforce, but then Hull describes the experiences of two African-American women whose "failure" at a job (processing checks for a bank) was due not to their lack of literacy skills but to day care and transportation and economic problems unacknowledged by their employers.

In spite of the stories we quoted above, literacy alone—some set of basic skills—is not what improves people's lives.

Both Harvey J. Graff, in the early 1980s, and Ruth Finnegan, in the early 1990s, use "literacy myth" to name the belief that literacy will bring us everything the stories above promise; according to Finnegan,

> This story has been around for a long time. It reflects popular and still widely held assumptions: that literacy is a good thing, both the sign and the cause of progress, and that without it we and others would still be in the dark ages. Although it is under attack from a number of directions, this view is still in many circles the conventional wisdom and has played a large part in the rhetoric—and to some extent, therefore—in the practice of educationalists and "development" experts. (32)

Brian Street argues that the idea of such an autonomous literacy, whose acquisition necessarily causes progress, has played a part in the practice of

national and international literacy programs; using programs in Iran, Great Britain, and Mozambique as examples, he argues that such programs—which claim to bring economic growth by giving people a simple neutral skill—ignore and override and irrevocably change the lives and culture of those who are made literate: "[T]hese grandiose claims for 'academic' literacy," he writes, "are merely those of a small elite attempting to maintain positions of power and influence by attributing universality and neutrality to their own cultural conventions" (224).

In *The Violence of Literacy*, Elspeth Stuckey's words are equally strong for those who believe that literacy is or can be neutral:

> In the United States we live the mythology of a classless society. . . . In a society bound by such a mythology, our views about literacy are our views about political economy and social opportunity. . . . Far from engineering freedom, our current approaches to literacy corroborate other social practices that prevent freedom and limit opportunity. (vii)

And:

> We must take responsibility for the racism throughout schooling, the racism leveled most brutally and effectively in children's earliest years of schooling by literacy whose achievements can be seen in the loss of a third or more poor students by schooling's end. (122)

Or, as Finnegan puts it:

> The myth can be seen as playing an essential ideological function for the governing social, political, or educational order, whether manifested by earlier imperial expansion or by current national or international inequalities. So, when people might want, for example, houses or jobs or economic reform, they are instead given literacy programs. (41)

When we speak then of "literacy" as though it were a basic, neutral, contextless set of skills, the word keeps us hoping—in the face of lives and arguments to the contrary—that there could be an easy cure for economic and social and political pain, that only a lack of literacy keeps people poor or oppressed.

And when we believe this—that poverty and oppression result from a lack of a simple, neutral set of skills—we have trouble understanding why everyone and anyone can't acquire the skills: there must be something wrong with someone who can't correctly learn what most of us acquired easily, in our early years in home or school. Delpit describes classrooms where students and teachers have cultural and grammatical differences, with the teachers then judging their students' "actions, words, intellects, families, and communities as inadequate at best, as collections of pathologies at worst" (xiv). According to Stanley Aronowitz, Walter Lippman and John Dewey argued for the importance of education and literacy because they thought that "lacking education the 'people' are inherently incapable of governing themselves" (298). When people aren't literate—when under this conception of literacy they are not economically secure or part of the culture of the rest of us—it is because of some (inherent?) failure of theirs. We ask them, by using a conception of literacy that allows us to ask them, to blame themselves. We overlook, if not forget, the economic and social and political structures that work to keep people in their places.

> If "literacy" is a deceptive promise of basic skills that on their own will fix someone's life, why do we wish to use this term when we speak of the relationship we desire for our students and others to have with newer technologies?

2

THE SECOND BUNDLE: THE OBJECTS WE ADDRESS THROUGH THE RELATION OF LITERACY

a

> The paged book became the physical embodiment, the incarnation, of the text it contained. (Bolter 86)

b

> . . . if, in an era of uncertain values, we want to keep alive respect for ideas and knowledge, it is important to give books a form that encourages respect. (Levarie 306)

c

d

Prepare a narrative of all which has held it.

Prepare a narrative of all which has held it.

Prepare a narrative of prepare a narrative of all which has held it.

Out of the whole.

Out of the whole wide world I chose it.

Out of the whole wide world I chose it. (Stein 253)

X X X X

The other day, in *Dear Abby*, this was part of the opening letter:

> An ongoing cycle of illiteracy haunts children on the edges of poverty.
> When teachers ask their students to bring a favorite book to class to share,
> these children show up with an advertisement or a coupon book because
> they have no books at home.
>   Abby, please help these children learn to love books and reading.
> (*Daily Mining Gazette*, Houghton, MI, 11/19/96)

As we have argued above, we believe that "literacy" is presented as a necessary and sufficient set of skills for entree to the good life when it is really a
diversion from social and political situations. We do not, however, deny that
reading and writing can be a useful set of skills amongst all the skills and
practices and behaviors and attributes we all need in order to flourish in our
present culture . . .
    . . . but why should anyone love books — the objects — in and of themselves?

In "Literacy and the Colonization of Memory," Walter D. Mignolo
argues that when the Spaniards colonized the area we now call Mexico, they
were so steeped in book culture that they believed the Mexica had no sense
of history — because the Mexica recorded their pasts in paintings rather than
in words in books — and hence that the Mexica "lacked intelligence and
humanity" (96).

> (For a more detailed description of this meeting between the Inca and the
> Spanish — and more about how this incident hinging on a [the?] book can
> be tied to other consequences of literacy, see Diamond 68–81.)

Constance Classen, in *Worlds of Sense: Exploring the Senses in History
and Across Cultures*, describes an incident in the Spanish colonization of
the Inca, whose cosmology relied on hearing:

. . . the Spanish priest accompanying the expedition gave a brief summary of Christian doctrine, denounced Inca religion as invented by the Devil, and demanded that Atahualpa become the vassal of the Holy Roman Emperor. While giving his address the priest held a book, either the Bible or a breviary, in one hand. Atahualpa, deeply offended by this speech, . . . demanded of the priest by what authority he made these claims. The friar held up the book to him. Atahualpa examined it, but as it said nothing to him he dropped it to the ground. This rejection of the essence of European civilization was the excuse the Spanish needed to begin their massacre. (110)

This attachment to books as essence hasn't changed in the hundreds of years following that massacre; witness Sven Birkerts' words from *The Gutenberg Elegies: The Fate of Reading in an Electronic Age*:

I stare at the textual field on my friend's [computer] screen and I am unpersuaded. Indeed, this glimpse of the future—if it is the future—has me clinging all the more tightly to my books, the very idea of them. If I ever took them for granted, I do no longer. I now see each one as a portable enclosure, a place I can repair to release the private, unsocialized, dreaming self. A book is a solitude, privacy; it is a way of holding the self apart from the crush of the outer world. Hypertext—at least the spirit of hypertext, which I see as the spirit of the times—promises to deliver me from the "liberating domination" of the author. It promises to spring me from the univocal linearity which is precisely the constraint that fills me with a sense of possibility as I read my way across fixed acres of print. (164)

Birkerts' attachment to books is more self-conscious than the Spanish friar's, perhaps, but it is nonetheless just as closed off to other forms of expression that might offer other senses of possibility. For both men, dream and value and self and culture and world seem to be fully enclosed within literacy, objectified in—and not separable from—the book.

Birkerts' words call to our minds Habermas, who wrote that a necessary (but not sufficient) step in the development of a critical public in the 18th century was that men read to themselves: in the privacy of their reading they developed a sense of individuated self, a self that could hold a position in the public sphere (45–56). Robert Romanyshyn puts an earlier date to the book's relation to this individuation:

Linear perspective vision was a fifteenth-century artistic invention for representing three-dimensional depth on the two-dimensional canvas. It was a geometrization of vision which began as an invention and became a convention, a cultural habit of mind. . . . At approximately the same time that Alberti's procedures [for perspective] are mapping the world as a geometric grid, laying it out in linear fashion, the book will be introduced and mass-produced. The linearity of the geometric world will find its counterpart in the linear literacy of the book, where line by line, sentence by sentence, the chronological structures of the book will mirror the sequential, ordered, linear structure of time in the sciences. In addition, the interiorization of individual subjectivity within the room of consciousness will find apt expression in the private act of reading and in silence, unlike the manuscript consciousness of the Middle Ages, where reading was done aloud. (349–351)

The exact date of this interiorization of a self is not important to our words here; rather, what we wish to call attention to is how writers like McLuhan and Ong, and Birkerts accept that books—once they have somehow acquired the form we now take for granted, small enough for us to hold and carry about, and containing texts that encourage us to see continuity stretching like words linearly over the time of many pages—ask us to think of ourselves as selves. These writers' words are like commands—or interpellations—hailing us to see our selves and the possibilities of our world delimited between the covers of the book; Ivan Illich and Barry Sanders put it the following way in *ABC: The Alphabetization of the Popular Mind:*

> The idea of a self that continues to glimmer in thought or memory, occasionally retrieved and examined in the light of day, cannot exist without the text. Where there is no alphabet, there can be neither memory conceived as a storehouse nor the "I" as its appointed watchman. With the alphabet both text and self became possible, but only slowly, and they became the social construct on which we found all our perceptions as literate people. (72)

Here are other descriptions (several possibilities from among many) of our relationship with books, and of how that relationship is to shape us:

> Ramus was entirely right in his insistence on the supremacy of the new printed book in the classroom. For only there could the homogenizing effects of the new medium be given heavy stress in young lives. Students processed by print technology in this way would be able to translate every kind of problem and experience into the new visual kind of lineal order. (McLuhan 146)

> What is written has a disembodied existence; knowledge is no longer contained within human bodies but exists separately from them. In a literate society, therefore, knowledge—and by extension, the cosmos—is devitalized,

de-personalized, and reified. The literate world is a silent, still world, one in which the primary means of gaining knowledge is by looking and reflecting. . . . (Classen 110)

. . . print is a singularly impersonal medium. Lay preachers and teachers who addressed congregations from afar [through texts] often seemed to speak with a more authoritative voice than those who could be heard and seen within a given community. (Eisenstein 148)

To the book, then, the writers we have quoted attribute our sense of self, our memories, our possibilities, the specific linear forms of analysis we use, our attitude towards knowledge, our belief in the authority of certain kinds of knowledge, our sense of the world.

What has been encompassed by the book, then, is the second (but still not unruly) bundle we promised in our beginning. If the first bundle that comes with "literacy" is the promise of social, political, and economic improvement, it is because the second bundle is the book, which covers

who we are and what we might be and the institutions in which we act. If the Spanish friar had not thought this, if he had not acted out of a notion of "literacy" so tied to the singular object of the book, there would have been no massacre.

What else might we be—or be open to—if we did not see ourselves and our world so defined in books?

Y

When we discuss "technological literacy" or "computer literacy" or "[fill in the blank] literacy," we cannot pull "literacy" away from the two bundles of meanings and implications we have described. We may argue that we want to use "literacy" because it is a handy shortcut for covering a wide range of skills and procedures and practices; we may argue, "That's not what we meant at all; we really meant something broader, more open." But we are still using "literacy," which, unless we deny our histories, comes to us in the bundles we have just begun to unpack.

And our unpacking allows us now to offer up a response to the question that titles our work here: why are we using literacy as a metaphor for everything else? If we have unpacked "literacy" at all adequately, we hope we can now argue that "literacy" gets put behind "technological" or "computer" because "literacy" is already used to encompass everything we think worthy of our consideration: the term automatically upgrades its prefix. If "literacy" is already closely tied to our sense of how the world was colonized and settled and tamed, if "literacy" is already (deceptively) tied to political and social and economic improvement, if "literacy" already is the boundary of our sense of who we are, then why not apply the notion to newer technologies?

But. When we speak of the relationship we hope to establish—for ourselves and for our students—with newer technologies, do we want to carry forward all these particular attachments and meanings and possibilities?

Do we want to speak in the context of a set of practices and beliefs those with decision-making powers use to cultivate, to settle, to tame those without—so that those without remain without and blame themselves? When we say or write "technological literacy" how can we not expect others to hear, even if only partially, that we believe there is some minimum set of technological skills everyone should have—and that it is their own fault if they do not have them? And that it is therefore their own fault if they are not successful and mainstream? How can we not expect others to hear that this literacy constitutes not only a necessary but a sufficient condition for attaining The Good Life?

Do we want to use a word that contains within it a relation to a singular object that we use to narrow our sense of who we are and what we are capable of? Do we want to continue a relationship that is externalized, linear, private, visual, static, and authoritative? When we say, "computer literacy," for example, what part of this relationship to the book are we asking ourselves or our students to establish with, within, and through computers?

Why aren't we instead working to come up with other terms and understandings—other more complex expressions—of our relationship with and within technologies?

SECOND

SO: WHAT OTHER POSSIBILITIES MIGHT WE USE FOR EXPRESSING OUR RELATIONSHIPS WITH TECHNOLOGIES?

In what follows (in only visually linear form) we analyze and reconstruct new approaches to communication that prioritize ways of knowing other than those dependent on "literacy."

There are two bundles in our writing here as well, but they are far from neat and tidy bundles, and we must pull them together rather than unpack them. These bundles unravel even as we write and revise and as you (and you and you) read: first we will offer an interpretation of what it might mean to think of literacy under postmodernism; second, we will begin to shift terms, suggesting other ways to think of literacy that begin moving away from the baggage outlined in the bundles above. And rather than simplifying any of the issues we have unbundled in the first section of our writing, the sorts of "literacy" we are about to discuss (we will abandon the term eventually) complicate, question, challenge, and make contingent.

1

LITERACY IN SPACE

a

Chia suspected that her mother's perception of time differed from her own in radical and mysterious ways. Not just in the way that a month, to Chia's mother, was not a very long time, but in the way that her mother's "now" was such a narrow and literal thing. News-governed, Chia believed. Cable-fed. A present honed to whatever very instant of a helicopter traffic report.

Chia's "now" was digital, effortlessly elastic, instant recall supported by global systems she'd never have to bother comprehending.

(The requisite William Gibson quotation, 13–14)

b

Having everything on-line is fantastic. Now as soon as a transfer is completed, it's there! You can really look up what you need. If someone calls, you know exactly what's going on. Sometimes you are looking for a part of a case that someone else has. You used to have to go looking for it, and maybe you wouldn't find it. Now you can see where it is without getting up from your seat. It's all right there at my fingertips. (Clerk in Stock and Bond Transfer Department in a recently computerized insurance under-writer, quoted in Zuboff 157–158).

c

The great obsession of the nineteenth century was, as we know, history: with its themes of development and of suspension, of crisis and cycle, themes of the ever-accumulating past, with its great preponderance of dead men and the menacing glaciation of the world. The nineteenth century found its essential mythological resources in the second principle of thermodynamics. The present epoch will perhaps be above all the epoch of space. We are in the epoch of simultaneity: we are in the epoch of juxtaposition, the epoch of the near and far, of the side-by-side, of the dispersed. We are at a moment, I believe, when our experience of the world is less that of a long life developing through time than that of a network that connects points and intersects with its own skein. One could perhaps say that certain ideological conflicts animating present-day polemics oppose the pious descendents of time and the determined inhabitants of space. (Foucault 22)

@

Begin here, in a linear flow of text that suggests a flow of time, by imagining what literacy might be if we conceived it primarily as a spatial relation to information.

Although literacy has long been bound up with spaces (consider the geopolitical stories in the bundles we discussed above/earlier, for example), literacy changes profoundly if we choose to prioritize space over time. This shift has been frequently described by others with the term "postmodernism," although that term has become so complex and contradictory—so rich—that we use it to gesture generally rather than to point accurately: we are not here to argue whether the "postmodern condition" is indeed the one in which we find ourselves, but rather to use the thinking of different writers identified with postmodernism to lay out some possible relations with and within communication technologies.

> I believe the most striking emblem of this new mode of thinking relationships can be found in the work of Nam June Paik, whose stacked or scattered television screens, positioned at intervals within lush vegetation, or winking down at us from a ceiling of strange new video stars, recapitulate over and over again prearranged sequences or loops of images which return at dyssynchronous moments on various screens. The older aesthetic is then practiced by viewers, who, bewildered by this discontinuous variety, decided to concentrate on a single screen, as though the relatively worthless image sequence to be followed there had some organic value in its own right. The postmodernist viewer, however, is called upon to do the impossible, namely, to see all the screens at once, in their radical and random difference. . . . (Jameson 31).

How is it that we are able to see all the screens at once? Prioritizing space over time—and so looking away from time and also then from history—removes origins, futures, and progress: we see "all the screens"—all the information—all at once. In a spatially organized understanding of communication and knowledge, past and future can only merely be other locations in space. We are left with a sort of spread-out and flat simultaneity through which we travel.

> On a flat world, it is difficult to build an argument or to move directly from one point to the next because surfaces can be very slippery. Glissage or sliding is the preferred mode of transport. (Hebdige 170)

This "simultaneity" could be a way of thinking about how we have wired our communications and our "working knowledge" to new technologies. The speed with which we can move amongst screens of information—their visual, near instantaneous presence to us all at once—suggests that it is possible to describe information not as something we send from place to place, in books or on paper, over time, but as something we move (and hence think) within. Where "intertextuality" has long been understood at a conceptual level—text citing text citing text in an unseen network of reference—we now have conditions that allow it the possibility of it being material, visible and navigable, writable and readable, on our computer screens. "Literacy"—if we describe it as some set of skills that allows us to work with the information structures of our time—then becomes the ability to move in the new-technology spaces of information, the ability to make the instantaneous connections between informational objects that allow us to see them all at once.

> As long as the game is not a game of perfect information, the advantage will be with the player who has knowledge and can obtain information. By definition, this is the case with the student in a learning situation. But in games of perfect information, the best performativity cannot consist in obtaining additional information in this way. It comes rather from arranging the data in a new way, which is what constitutes a "move" properly speaking. This new arrangement is usually achieved by connecting together series of data that were previously held to be independent. This capacity to articulate what used to be separate can be called imagination. Speed is one of its properties. (Lyotard 52)

But seeing information (and hence "literacy") in that way plays itself back on how we conceive of the space we are creating by and within new communication technologies. The speed of our imaginations—our ability to make instantaneous connections—relies on the construction of information spaces that can be navigated so quickly that space seems compressed for us. With new communication technologies, we want to be able to—we feel we can—move from one end of space to another nearly instantaneously; we can bring any set of places—any set of things—together into one.

In one way of looking, then, this is not just about privileging space over time, but about time and space collapsing into each other . . . and if we can work as though time does not ration out what we can do, then we can work as though space doesn't either: with new communication technologies, space, like information, can become less something we experience and more something we simply work with/in, making creative connections and reconnections.

> For flatness is corrosive and infectious. Who, after all, is Paul Virilio anyway? The name sounds as if it belongs to a B movie actor, a member of *Frankie Goes to Hollywood*, a contestant in a body-building competition. I know that "he" writes books but does such a person actually exist? In the land of the gentrified cut-up, as in the place of dreams, anything imaginable can happen, anything at all. The permutations are unlimited: high / low / folk culture; pop music / opera; street fashion / haute couture; journalism / science fiction / critical theory; advertising / critical theory / haute couture. . . . With the sudden loss of gravity, the lines that hold the terms apart waver and collapse. (Hebdige 161)

In this way of looking, the collapse of our experience of "technological" space can also correspond to a collapse of "real" space. Two steps are at work here: first, physically distant locations are wired up, so that it seems the one with whom I am communicating is just on the other side of the screen; second, the possibility that virtual spaces are collapsible leads to the idea that real spaces are likewise. This may sound like faulty logic, but, instead, the shift is straightforward: if communication is real, then the spaces in which it occurs are also real.

But what are we, then, in this space of all spaces all at once and no temporal flow? Under the sense of literacy we unpacked in the earlier/previous part of this writing, we rely on our ability to construct ourselves at some nexus between past and future, to have faith in the present as the point where past and future meet like (exactly like) a reader progressing through a linear text, uniting what has gone before with what is now and with what will come.

[P]ersonal identity is itself the effect of a certain temporal unification of past and future with one's present. . . . If we are unable to unify the past, present, and future of the sentence, we are similarly unable to unify the past, present, and future of our own biographical experience or psychic life. (Jameson 27)

When everything is all at once, what do we do?

Long ago, there must have been a golden age of harmony between heaven and earth. High was high; low was low; inside was in; and outside was out. But now we have money. Now, everything is out of balance. They say, "Time is money." But they got it all wrong: Time is the absence of money. (Wenders.)

The shift towards privileging space over time — what so many say is a hall-mark of now — can have a frightening and dangerous result: the shift towards postmodernism acts in a radical unbinding of history from subjec-tivity. The unbinding can become so overpowering that it colonizes sub-jectivities and tears them apart; with no guarantees of either a stable past or a connected future, it is impossible to believe in the unity of a single, stable subject — the subject of our previous discussions of literacy.

But the unbinding can also be under-stood as opening up room for another view of ourselves: in understanding the implications of a postmodern worldview, we open ourselves to the possibility of remaking cultural meanings and identi-ties. The connotations of literacy, as we discussed it in the first sections of our writing, suggest a process of mechanical and passive individual reception: the book gives us who we are, the book sets the limits for who we allow into the realms of privilege. If we under-stand communication not as discrete bundles of stuff that are held together in some unified space, that exist linearly through time, and that we pass along, but as instead different possible constructed relations between infor-mation that is spread out all before us, then . . . living becomes movement among (and within) sign systems.

Data Warehouse. *noun* 1: a process that collects data from various applications in an organization's operational systems, integrates the information into a logical model of business subject areas, stores it in a manner accessible to decision makers and delivers it to them through report-writing and query tools. The goal is to put standardized and comparable corporate information into employees' hands, enabling an enterprisewide view of the business. (McWilliams DW/ 2)

Symbolic analysts solve, identify, and broker problems by manipulating symbols. They simplify reality into abstract images that can be rearranged, juggled, experimented with, communicated to other specialists, and then, eventually, transformed back into reality. The manipulations are done with analytic tools, sharpened by experience. (Reich 178)

Here is the possibility of understanding our relation to our communication technologies as not being one through which we are passively, mechanically shaped. There is the possibility of seeing ourselves as not just moving through information, but of us moving through it and making and changing conscious constructions of it as we go. This is not about handing books to children or high-school dropouts or the underdeveloped, and hoping that they will pick up enough skills to be able to lose themselves in reading (and so to come back with different selves that better fit a dominant culture); it is instead about how we all might understand ourselves as active participants in how information gets "rearranged, juggled, experimented with" to make the reality of different cultures. This involves, of course, understanding our selves within the making and changing.

And this involves, then, not just thinking that we should pass along discrete sets of skills to others—or pretending that those discrete sets of skills are all that it takes to have a different life. There are certainly skills needed for connecting and reconnecting information—but the relationships to communication technologies we are describing now and here ask, in necessary addition, for a shared and discussed, ongoing, reconception of the space and time we use together and in which we find (and can construct) information and ourselves.

This reconception is thus not about handing down skills to others who are not where we are, but about figuring out how we all are where we are, and about how we all participate in making these spaces and the various selves we find here.

2

ARTICULATING LITERACY

So what else? We hope to have made it clear by now that our questions never have simple, bounded answers. No single term—such as "literacy"—can support the weight of the shifting, contingent activities we have been describing.

There are many possibilities—other than literacy, other than postmodernism—for how we might conceive our relationships with communication technologies (and no single correct answer). We can work from Stuart Hall's term "articulation" to suggest something else yet again.

> In England, the term [articulation] has a nice double meaning because "articulate" means to utter, to speak forth, to be articulate. It carries that sense of language-ing, of expressing, etc. But we also speak of an "articulated" lorry (truck): a lorry where the front (cab) and the back (trailer) can, but need not necessarily, be connected to one another. The two parts are connected to each other, but through a specific linkage, that can be broken. An articulation is thus the form of the connection that can make a unity of two different elements, under certain conditions. It is a linkage which is not necessary, determined, absolute and essential for all time. You have to ask, under what circumstances can a connection be forged or made? (Hall 53)

Under this understanding of relationships, then, we could describe literacy not as a monolithic term but as a cloud of sometimes contradictory nexus points among different positions. Literacy can be seen as not a skill but a process of situating and resituating representations in social spaces.

> So the so-called "unity" of a discourse is really an articulation of different, distinct elements which can be re-articulated in different ways because they have no necessary "belongingness." The "unity" which matters is a linkage between that articulated discourse and the social forces with which it can, under certain historical conditions, but need not necessarily, be connected. Thus, a theory of articulation is both a way of understanding how ideological elements come, under certain conditions, to cohere together within a discourse, and a way of asking how they do or do not become articulated, at specific conjunctures, to certain political subjects. Let me put that the other way: a theory of articulation asks how an ideology discovers its subject rather than how the subject thinks the necessary and inevitable thoughts which belong to it; it enables us to think how an ideology empowers people, enabling them to begin to make some sense or intelligibility of their historical situation, without reducing those forms of intelligibility to their socioeconomic or class location or social position. (Hall 53)

With the notion of connection, in articulation, comes the notion of potential disconnection. Literacy here shifts away from receiving a self to the necessary act of continual remaking, of understanding the "unity" of an object (social, political, intellectual) and simultaneously seeing that that unity is contingent, supported by the efforts of the writer/reader and the cultures in which they live.

> With and through articulation, we engage the concrete in order to change it, that is, to rearticulate it. To understand theory and method in this way shifts perspective from the acquisition or application of an epistemology to the creative process of articulating, of thinking of relations and connections as how we come to know and as creating what we know. Articulation is, then, not just a thing (not just connections) but a process of creating connections, much in the same way that hegemony is not domination but the process of creating and maintaining consensus or of co-ordinating interests. (Slack 114)

Articulation is only one among many ways of re-presenting literacy. Jim Collins, paralleling Jameson's discussions, offers an "architectural" model as one possibility:

> Appropriation is not simply an anti-Romantic stance opposed to the mythology of pure genius; this shift also involves profound changes in regard to the mutability of both information and the forms of cultural authority which govern (or used to govern) its circulation. To appropriate is to take control over that which originated elsewhere for semiotic/ideological purposes. . . .

> The determination to take possession . . . does not signify the denial of cultural authority but, rather, the refusal to grant cultural *sovereignity* to any institution, as it counters one sort of authority with another. (Collins 92–93)

Still other possible terms abound: Deleuze and Guattari describe the rhizomic nature of the nomad; Pratt offers linguistic contact zones; Giroux constructs border spaces; Anzaldua occupies borderlands. With such new bundles, we suggest new ways of relating to technologies (including texts) and to each other: both a process and a structure bound up (literally and figuratively) with social change.

BUT . . .

None of these terms exhausts new possibilities for "literacy," but only suggests productive ways of questioning our current positions, of unpacking old bundles and remaking new ones. Unpack ours and make your own.

A NOTE ON THE ILLUSTRATIONS

The drawings of people with books (and the one illustration of a woman with a television) come from a collection of clip art produced by the Volk Corporation and the Harry Volk Jr. Art Studio, both in Pleasantville, NJ, from 1959 through 1968. In the various small books of clip art from which these illustrations come, all the people are white and clearly middle class; there are many illustrations of women and children holding books; if men have printed matter in their hands, it is account books or newspapers—unless they are shown reading to their families (as one illustration here shows).

REFERENCES

Birkerts, Sven. 1994. *The Gutenberg Elegies.* New York: Ballantine.

Bolter, Jay David. 1991. *Writing Space: The Computer, Hypertext, and the History of Writing.* Hillsdale, NJ: Erlbaum.

Clinton, William J. 1998. Remarks at Technology '98 Conference. *Federal Document Clearing House Political Transcripts.* 26 Feb.

Eisenstein, Elizabeth L. 1979. *The Printing Press as an Agent of Change.* Cambridge: Cambridge UP.

Habermas, Jürgen. 1990. *Moral Consciousness and Communicative Action,* trans. Christian Lenhardt and Shierry Weber Nicholsen. Cambridge, MA: The MIT P.

Jameson, Fredric. 1991. *Postmodernism, Or, the Cultural Logic of Late Capitalism.* Durham, NC: Duke UP.

Lyotard, Jean-François. 1988. *The Differend: Phrases in Dispute,* trans. Georges Van Den Abbeele. Minneapolis: U of Minnesota P.

Ong, Walter J. 1982. *Orality and Literacy.* New York: Methuen.

Street, Brian V. 1984. *Literacy in Theory and Practice.* Cambridge: Cambridge UP.

Stuckey, J. Elspeth. 1991. *The Violence of Literacy.* Portsmouth, NH: Boynton/Cook.

Zuboff, Shoshana. 1988. *In the Age of the New Machine: The Future of Work and Power.* New York: Basic Books.

The Politics of the Interface

Power and Its Exercise in Electronic Contact Zones

CYNTHIA L. SELFE AND RICHARD J. SELFE, JR.

Over a casual lunch at a recent professional conference, Trent Batson, a professor at Gallaudet University, told us a story that made us think about borders and their effects. He had been visiting Mexico on a short day trip in the company of an academic colleague who taught at Mt. Holyoke but had been born in India. On the way back into the United States, these colleagues entered two separate lines at the stations marking the official re-entry point to this country. Border guards, observing the darker skin of the one colleague stopped him—as they did all people who, in Batson's words, "looked vaguely Mexican." The Indian colleague, having lived and worked in this country for a number of years, had made the mistake of thinking that this border, this country, was an open one. He carried only a photocopy of the green card that identified him as a "resident alien," rather than the card itself, as required by United States law.

Given these relatively unexceptional circumstances, what followed seemed significant to us—the Indian-born colleague was detained by officials and eventually fined—even though he carried additional materials identifying him as a professor at Holyoke. Batson was not stopped or questioned. He was also not allowed to accompany his friend, who was taken to an office by the border guards where he was detained for half an hour. Batson was allowed to watch the proceedings through a window, to gaze on the administration and application of American law.

On the surface of the story, no real harm was done: the detainment was short term, the fine minimal, the laws for resident aliens clear. But for us, as

Reprinted from *College Composition and Communication* 45.4 (December 1994): 480–504. Used with permission.

citizens of the United States, the telling of this story had a chilling effect. We were ashamed not only about the assumptions that the border guards seem to have made but also of the cultural values that the story revealed. As Midwesterners who live relatively far from the border in question, we were taken aback by the story—by the guards' reactions, by the feelings these reactions suggest about Mexican nationals, and by the treatment that people of color receive every day in our own country. We should not, of course, have been surprised at all. It is at the geopolitical borders of countries that the formations of social power, normally hidden, are laid embarrassingly bare—where power in its rawest form is exercised.

If at the time of this story's original telling we didn't like what it made us think about our country, it was not until we had reflected more closely on the incident that we began to unpack the various ways in which it seemed meaningful and bothersome to us—in general, for our own professional lives as teachers and, in specific, for the more specialized instructional work that we do in computer-supported writing and learning environments. The longer we thought about it, the more we realized that the borders represented in this story, the values built into them and constituted continually by them, were—and are—present in our own classrooms as well. These borders are represented and reproduced in so many commonplace ways, at so many levels, that they frequently remain invisible to us. One place in which such borders remain quite visible, we realized, is in the computers that we, and many other teachers of English, use within classrooms. When re-considering this story in light of our own experiences, we began to see how teachers of English who use computers are often involved in establishing and maintaining borders themselves—whether or not they acknowledge or support such a project—and, thus, in contributing to a larger cultural system of differential power that has resulted in the systematic domination and marginalization of certain groups of students, including among them: women, non-whites, and individuals who speak languages other than English.

This article represents our further thinking about these realizations. In it, we begin the task of describing some of the political and ideological boundary lands associated with computer interfaces that we—and many other teachers of composition—now use in our classrooms. We also talk about the ways in which these borders are at least partly constructed along ideological axes that represent dominant tendencies in our culture, about the ways in which the borders evident in computer interfaces can be mapped as complex political landscapes, about the ways in which the borders can serve to prevent the circulation of individuals for political purposes, and about the ways in which teachers and students can learn to see and alter such borders in productive ways. At the end of the paper, we talk about tactics that teachers can use to enact a radical pedagogy of electronic borders and borderlands.

As a way into this examination, we look at computer interfaces as linguistic contact zones, in Mary Louise Pratt's words, "social spaces where cultures meet, clash, and grapple with each other, often in contexts of highly asymmetrical relations of power, such as colonialism, slavery, or their aftermaths as they are lived out in many parts of the world today" (34). Within this context, we talk about computer interfaces as maps that enact—among other things—the gestures and deeds of colonialism, continuously and with a great deal of success. This is not to claim, of course, that the *only* educational effects computers have is one of re-producing oppression or colonial mentalities. Indeed, from the work of computers and composition specialists, it is clear that computers, like other complex technologies, are articulated in many ways with a range of existing cultural forces and with a variety of projects in our educational system, projects that run the gamut from liberatory to oppressive. However, because recent scholarship on computers has tended to focus in overoptimistic ways on the positive contributions that technology can make to English composition classrooms, our goal in this piece is to sketch the outlines of an alternative vision for teachers, one that might encourage them to adopt a more critical and reflective approach to their use of computers.[1] Such a picture provides a necessary balance, we believe. An overly optimistic vision of technology is not only reductive, and, thus, inaccurate, it is also dangerous in that it renders less visible the negative contributions of technology that may work potently and effectively against critically reflective habits and efforts of good teachers and students. Our goal is to help teachers identify some of the effects of domination and colonialism associated with computer use so that they can establish a new discursive territory within which to understand the relationships between technology and education.

COMPUTERS AS LEARNING ENVIRONMENTS: HISTORY AND MOTIVATION

For the last decade, English composition teachers have been using computers in classrooms to create electronic forums—on local-area networks (LANs) and wide-area networks (WANs)—within which writers and readers can create, exchange, and comment on texts. These spaces, it has been noted, have the potential for supporting student-centered learning and discursive practices that can be different from, and—some claim—more engaging and democratic than those occurring within traditional classroom settings.[2] Such a vision is all the more tantalizing given our recognition that the education taking place in traditional classrooms—despite our best intentions—contributes, in part, to a continuing cultural tendency to marginalize and oppress groups of people due to their race, gender, or ethnic background. Gomez, for example, citing Wheelock and Dorman, compares the 12% dropout rate for white students to the 17% rate for African American students, 18% for Hispanic students, and 29.2% for Native American students (319–20). Giroux notes that "in many urban cities the dropout rate for nonwhite children exceeds 60% (with New York City at 70%)" (111). As teachers of English, we recognize, in other words, that we work in an educational system that instructs students about oppression and inequity, by example, even as we strive to erase such lessons from the official curriculum. This situation and these figures, as June Jordan notes, are all the more dramatic in light of the fact that only 15% of the entrants into the American workforce will be white males by the year 2000 and that some states like California will have 61% non-white students in their populations by the year 2010 (22). And as Mary Louise Gomez further reminds us, most schools can expect 30–40% of their student population to come from a non-English language background by the end of this decade (319).

This continuing pattern has encouraged many teachers of English to turn to—among other things—computer-supported writing environments as places within which they and students can try to enact educational practices that are more democratic and less systematically oppressive: for example, student-centered, on-line discussion groups in which individuals discover their own motivations for using language; on-line conferences in which students' race, gender, age, and sexual preference may not figure in the same ways that they do in more conventional face-to-face settings; collaborative groups in which students learn to negotiate discursive power. To create and maintain these communities—to defend their use and value—we have often used what Hawisher and Selfe have identified as an overly positive "rhetoric of technology" (55) that portrays computer-supported forums—among ourselves, to administrators, to students—as democratic spaces, what Mary Louise Pratt might call "linguistic utopias"(48) within which cues of gender, race, and socioeconomic status are minimized; students speak without interruption; and marginalized individuals can acquire more central voices. And if this rhetoric is helpful in that it describes what we *want* to happen—and sometimes, to some extent, *does* happen—in our classrooms, it is also dangerous. Through its use, we legitimate the status quo of computer use and, as Hawisher and Selfe note, "de-legitimate critique"(53)—thus allowing ourselves to think erroneously that the use of computers and networks provides discursive landscapes that are, in Mary Louise Pratt's words, "the same for all players" (38).

The rhetoric of technology obscures the fact that, within our current educational system—even though computers are associated with the potential for great reform—they are not necessarily serving democratic ends. Computer interfaces, for example, are *also* sites within which the ideological and material legacies of racism, sexism, and colonialism are continuously written and re-written along with more positive cultural legacies.[3] Perhaps the most salient evidence for this claim lies in the different uses to which computers are put in minority classrooms and majority classrooms. Sheingold, Martin, and Endreweit, for example, note that in schools with large minority enrollments computers are used primarily to provide basic skills instruction delivered by drill-and-practice software. . . . In contrast, computer use in majority schools is characterized by its emphasis on the use of computers as tools to develop higher order literary and cognitive skills as objects of study (e.g., instruction focused on computer literacy and programming" (89). Charles Piller, in a recent article in *MacWorld*, notes that minority populations and lower socioeconomic populations are America's growing "technological underclass" (218) and, thus, that these students are the least likely to gain skills during their public schooling experience that will serve them well in a world increasingly dependent on technology.

The recognition of this situation, for many computer-using teachers of English, is not possible without a great deal of pain. It demands our realization that—while we, as individual English teachers, may very strongly support democratic reform, broad involvement, or egalitarian education, and while our teaching and computer use may be aimed toward these ends—we are also simultaneously participating in a cultural project that, at some level and to some degree, seems to support racist, sexist, and colonial attitudes. This is true even as our profession broadly supports more productive and progressive forms of educational action. If we hope to get English composition teachers to recognize how our use of computers achieves both great good and great evil—often at the same time, as Joseph Weizenbaum points out—we have to educate them to be technology *critics* as well as technology users. This recognition requires that composition teachers acquire the intellectual habits of reflecting on and discussing the cultural and ideological characteristics of technology—and the implications of these characteristics—in educational contexts. With such a realization, we maintain, English composition teachers can begin to exert an increasingly active influence on the cultural project of technology design.

MAPPING THE INTERFACE OF COMPUTERS AS EDUCATIONAL SPACE

The project that we have described is not a simple one, nor is it one that we can describe fully here. We can, however, provide an extended example of the agenda we want to pursue by focusing in particular ways on computer *interfaces*, those primary representations of computer systems or programs that show up on screens used by both teachers and students. Within the virtual space represented by these interfaces, and elsewhere within computer systems, the values of our culture—ideological, political, economic, educational—are mapped both implicitly and explicitly, constituting a complex set of material relations among culture, technology, and technology users. In effect, interfaces are cultural maps of computer systems, and as Denis Wood points out, such maps are never ideologically innocent or inert. Like other maps that Wood mentions—the medieval *mappaemundi* that offer a Christian-centered vision of the 13th century world or the Mercater projection that provides a Euro-centric view of the Earth's geography in the 20th century—the maps of computer interfaces order the virtual world according to a certain set of historical and social values that make up our culture. The users of maps, as a result, read cultural information just as surely as they read geographical information—through a coherent set of stereotyped images that the creators of maps offer as "direct testimony" (Berger 69) of the world, of social formations and socially organized tendencies, of a culture's historical development (Wood 145). The enhanced power of maps, growing out of their long association with the projects of science and geography, resides in the fact that they purport to represent fact—the world, a particular space—as it is in reality, while they naturalize the political and ideological interests of their authors (Wood 2).

Given this background, we can better understand why it is important to identify the cultural information passed along in the maps of computer interfaces—especially because this information can serve to reproduce, on numerous discursive levels and through a complex set of conservative forces, the asymmetrical power relations that, in part, have shaped the educational system we labor within and that students are exposed to. What is mapped in computer interfaces—just as what is mapped in other social and cultural artifacts such as our educational system—is both "ownership" and opportunity (Wood 21). In this sense, we maintain, the "ferocious" (Wood 25) effectiveness of computer interfaces as maps is established as much by what they do *not* show about American culture as by what they *do*. Primary computer interfaces do not, for example, provide direct evidence of different cultures and races that make up the American social complex, nor do they show much evidence of different linguistic groups or groups of differing economic status. It is only when we recognize these gestures of omission for what they are, as interested versions of reality, that we can begin to examine the naturalizing functions of computer interfaces and, as educators, break the frame to extend the discursive horizon (Laclau and Mouffe 19) of the landscape we have created and that, in turn, creates us and the students in our classes.

Once we recognize these functions, we also begin to understand the ideological gesture of the interface's map as a "flawed, partial, incomplete" (Wood 26) and interested vision of reality, at least partly constructed from the perspective of, and for the benefit of, dominant forces in our culture. In particular—given that these technologies have grown out of the predominately male, white, middle-class, professional cultures associated with the military-industrial complex—the virtual reality of computer interfaces represents, in part and to a visible degree, a tendency to value monoculturalism, capitalism, and phallologic thinking, and does so, more importantly, to the exclusion of other perspectives. Grounded in these values, computer interfaces, we maintain, enact small but continuous gestures of domination and colonialism. To examine these claims, we have to turn directly to examples that illustrate the ways in which such maps "name, marginalize, and define difference as the devalued Other" (Giroux 33)—not in a totalizing fashion but through many subtly potent gestures enacted continuously and naturalized as parts of technological systems. Such examples are not difficult to come by if we examine the borderland of the interface from the perspective of non-dominant groups in our culture.

Interfaces as Maps of Capitalism and Class Privilege

In general, computer interfaces present reality as framed in the perspective of modern capitalism, thus, orienting technology along an existing axis of class privilege. The graphically intuitive Macintosh interface provides a good example of this orientation. That interface, and the software applications commonly represented within it, map the virtual world as a *desktop*—constructing virtual reality, by association, in terms of corporate culture and the values of professionalism. This reality is constituted by and for white middle- and upper-class users to replicate a world that they know and feel comfortable within. The objects represented within this world are those familiar primarily to the white-collar inhabitants of that corporate culture: manila folders, files, documents, telephones, fax machines, clocks and watches, and desk calendars. We can grasp the power of this ideological orientation—and thus sense its implications—by shifting our perspective to what it does *not* include, what it leaves unstated. The interface does not, for example, represent the world in terms of a kitchen counter top, a mechanic's workbench, or a fast-food restaurant—each of which would constitute the virtual world in different terms according to the values and orientations of, respectively, women in the home, skilled laborers, or the rapidly increasing numbers of employees in the fast-food industry.

Built into computer interfaces are also a series of semiotic messages that support this alignment along the axes of class, race, and gender. The white pointer hand, for example, ubiquitous in the Macintosh primary interface, is one such gesture, as are the menu items of the Appleshare server tray and hand, calculator, the moving van (for the font DA mover), the suitcase, and the desk calendar. Others images—those included in the HyperCard interface commercial clip art collections, and in the Apple systems documentation—include a preponderance of white people and icons of middle- and upper-class white culture and professional, office-oriented computer use. These images signal—to users of color, to users who come from a non-English language background, to users from low socio-economic backgrounds—that entering the virtual worlds of interfaces also means, at least in part and at some level, entering a world constituted around the lives and values of white, male, middle- and upper-class professionals. Users of color, users from non-English language background, users from a low socio-economic class who view this map of reality, submit—if only partially and momentarily—to an interested version of reality represented in terms of both language and image.

When users recognize the corporate orientation of the interface, they also begin to understand more about how computers as a technology are ideologically associated with capitalism. Computer interfaces, for example, can serve to reproduce a value on the commodification of information. On the Macintosh desktop, for instance, the raw material of information is gathered in databases and files, stored in folders and on hard drives, accumulated within artificially expanded memory spaces, and finally manipulated and written in the form of documents that acquire their own authority and value within a capitalist economy.

All of these information products—following the prevailing model of text-as-commodity established in what Jay D. Bolter calls the "late age of print" (1)—are "owned" by an author who can protect work with a "password" and accord "privileges" to readers according to the relationship and involvement she would like them to have with a text. This commodification of information is also played out at additional levels within computer interfaces. Through interfaces, for example, students now learn to access and depend on sources like BITNET or Internet, library systems in other states, and information bases around the world for the information they need.

These electronic spaces—which are subject to increasing legislation and control—are at the same time becoming more expensive and more rigidly aligned along the related axes of class privilege and capitalism. The refinement and use of packet charging technologies, for example, and the increasing exploitation of large-scale commercial networks that appeal to the public will continue to support such an alignment. Recent figures published in a recent *New York Times* article indicate that commercial public networks such as Prodigy and Compuserve charge approximately $50 for starter kits on their systems, between $8 and $15 for basic use each month, and some additional per-message or per-minute charges as well. The capital stake that commercial groups have in promoting these electronic systems to citizens is not a small one: Information-as-commodity is big business—approximately 3.4 million people subscribe to commercial networks at the rates we have mentioned (Grimes 13–15).

Interfaces as Maps of Discursive Privilege

The orientation of the interface along the axis of class privilege is made increasingly systematic by the application of related discursive constraints. Primary interfaces, for example, also generally serve to reproduce the privileged position of Standard English as the language of choice or default, and, in this way, contribute to the tendency to ignore, or even erase, the cultures of non-English language background speakers in this country. Although the global expansion of technology is exerting an increasingly strong influence on the computer industry—and thus interfaces in other languages are becoming more common—these influences are resisted at many levels and in many ways, and this resistance is represented vividly in the maps of computer interfaces. A more particular example of this orientation exists in most word-processing programs—those tools we present students with so that they can "express" themselves in the language of our choosing. Many such programs commercially distributed in this country present their menued items only in English, despite the fact that, as Mary Louise Gomez reminds us, most schools can expect 30–40% of their student population to come from a non-English language background by the end of the decade (319). Those word-processing programs that *do* present an alternative-language interface market their non-English language background products separately, adding additional cost; or market them only in other countries, making them difficult to obtain especially with education discounts; or retain the privileged position of English simply by default. WordPerfect 5.1 for the IBM, for instance, which presents English menus as the default interface, does allow users to operate in other languages—among them three versions of English

(Australian, Great Britain, and United States) and only one of Spanish, in addition to Catalan (*WordPerfect for DOS* 325). To write or edit in another language, users must go to a "Layout" pull-down menu and then select — with some irony, we hope — the item labeled "Other" (324). As the manual for WordPerfect notes, moreover, the thesaurus and spell checkers accompanying the regular WordPerfect package come only in English. One can order versions of this thesaurus and spell checker in other languages, but they come at an additional cost. The telephone number which one uses to place such an order, the *Reference* manual notes, further, is "not toll-free" (326).

This decision to use English as a default language — articulated, as we have pointed out, with the custom of identifying non-English language background speakers as a marginalized "Other" and the socio-economic forces that limit access to software in other languages — clearly has important implications for our educational system, for teachers and for students. In schools, this default position means that students from other races and cultures who hope to use the computer as a tool for empowerment must — at some level — submit to the colonial power of language and adopt English as their primary means of communication, even if this submission is only partial or momentary. Few schools and few teachers can find a realistic perspective from which to resist the tendential forces associated with this default to English as a standard. Certainly, those schools that may most need fully functional bi- and tri-lingual interfaces are the *least* likely to have the monies available to purchase additional packages. This characteristic focus of interfaces on Standard English is further supported and exacerbated by the fact that style and grammar packages are generally based on an overly narrow — and erroneous — vision of "correct" language use and spelling checkers that exert a continuously normative influence (LeBlanc) within the setting of colonial discourse. Both kinds of software can serve to de-value linguistic diversity and inscribe nonstandard language users as Other within the interface, the classroom, the educational system, and the culture.

We got an idea of just how powerful and evenly dispersed this cultural inscription is — how systematically it operates — when we attended the 1992 convention of the National Council of Teachers of English. At that gathering, a software company demonstrated a word-processing package designed to present a bilingual (Spanish/English) interface. The package was available in a low-cost, school-edition package for approximately $300 and in a site-license, networkable version for approximately $1500. As the package's literature pointed out, users could employ a pull-down menu system to select the Spanish mode — where all menus, dialog boxes, help, and messages appear in Spanish. When we tested the software in the Spanish mode, however, we found the keystroke options did not change correspondingly to the same language. In fact those options, which depend, for the most part on mnemonic aids—apple-D for "delete"—remain keyed to the English words even when the corresponding Spanish menu items—"eliminar," for example—start with different letters. A student using this program, then, should she want to use the keystroke options, might be able to write in Spanish, but would have to think at some level in English.

This value on English as the privileged language of computer interfaces—and the effects of the design decisions that support this system—are certainly not limited to the United States. For example, a recent international gathering on computer-based instruction (Teleteaching '93) sponsored by the International Federation for Information Processing and focused on the use of computers for global distance education projects, required all sessions and discussions to be conducted in English—even though the conference was held in Norway and many representatives from non-English speaking countries were in attendance. This decision, presented to participants as a necessary convenience, recognized the extent to which Americans have influenced computer design, computer use, and computer applications over the past decade, and the fact that English has been, during this same period, the world language of science and technology. The language of computers has thus become English by default: The majority of standard interfaces are English, much of the documentation for these interfaces and the machines they operate on is in English, and the systems that currently support global computing networks rely on English as a standard exchange language. At the conference in question, several presenters from non-English speaking countries, for instance, noted that the educational conversations and projects they set up for French, German, Russian, or Slovakian students were conducted in English because these exchanges relied on the ability to link computers and systems through a common exchange standard called American Standard Code for Information Interchange (ASCII) that does not adequately support languages other than English. ASCII—because it was originally based on a 7-bit code—can handle, as Charles Petzold points out, only "26 lowercase letters, 26 uppercase letters, 10 numbers, and 33 symbols and punctuation marks" unless it is extended by 8-bit byte computer systems that allow it to handle 128 additional characters. Even with these additional characters, ASCII's alphabetic limitations preclude the full and adequate representation of Greek, Hebrew, Cyrillic, and Han characters (374–75).

In a recent article about Unicode—a proposed international replacement for ASCII—Petzold explores some of the implications of relying solely on ASCII:

There's a big problem with ASCII and that problem is indicated by the first word of the acronym. ASCII is truly an *American* standard, but there's a whole wide world outside our borders where ASCII is simply inadequate. It isn't even good enough for countries that share our language, for where is the British pound sign in ASCII? . . . ASCII . . . is not only inadequate for the written languages of much of the world, but also for many people who live right in my own neighborhood. . . . We simply can't be so parochial as to foster a system as exclusive and limiting as ASCII. The personal computing revolution is quickly encompassing much of the world, and it's totally absurd that the dominant standard is based solely on English as it is spoken in the U.S. (375)

Although this limitation may not represent a large problem to academic professionals, such a limited system makes global computer communications unnecessarily difficult for student learners who speak languages other than English. What remains most interesting about this situation—especially given that teachers, scholars, and computer designers generally acknowledge the limitations of ASCII—is that the change to a more broadly accommodating system has been so slow, even though the technological means for representing other alphabetic systems (e.g., the memory, the programming mechanics, the computer hardware) have been available for some time now. To change ASCII, however, is to work against a complex set of tendential forces encouraging inertia—because changing ASCII means changing existing software, hardware, documentation, and programming approaches. It also requires that individuals and groups in the computer industry abandon English as the *natural* language of, the natural standard for, computer technology. Such changes do not happen easily or quickly.

Interfaces as Maps of Rationalism and Logocentric Privilege

If the map of the interface is oriented simultaneously along the axes of class, race, and cultural privilege, it is also aligned with the values of rationality, hierarchy, and logocentrism characteristic of Western patriarchal cultures. IBM's DOS environment, for example, is fundamentally dependent on an hierarchical representation of knowledge, a perspective characteristically—while not exclusively—associated with patriarchal cultures and rationalistic traditions of making meaning. This way of representing knowledge within computer environments, although not essentially limiting or exclusive by itself, becomes so when linked to a positivist value on rationality and logic as *foundational* ways of knowing that function to exclude other ways of knowing, such as association, intuition, or bricolage. This validation of positivism, rationality, hierarchy, and logic as the only authorized contexts for "knowing" and representing knowledge continues to inform—and limit—many formal aspects of computer programming and technology design. As Winograd and Flores note, the current rationalistic framework that informs the design of computers and their interfaces is "based on a misinterpretation of the nature of human cognition and language," one that provides "only impoverished possibilities for modeling and enlarging the scope of human understanding" (78). As a result, these authors continue, "We are now witnessing a major breakdown in the design of computer technology—a breakdown that reveals the rationalistically oriented background of discourse within which our current understanding [of technology] is embedded" (78–79). A similar case has been made by Ted Nelson, a pioneer in the design of hypertext interfaces, who has referred to the conceptual structure of hierarchical file systems as an "enormous barrier" to creative thinking. Nelson has characterized the effects of such systems as both "oppressive and devastating." The "tyranny" of hierarchical systems, Nelson contends, "imposes intricate, fixed pathways that we must commit to memory" and "forbid acting on inspiration." He adds, further, that such systems cause programmers to "oversimplify" their representation of data and the uses of such data within computer interfaces (83–84).

As Sherry Turkle and Seymour Papert point out, this conventional validation of—and dependence on—hierarchy, rationality, and logic is all the more potent because it is operative at all levels of computer interface design and programming. Computer programmers are educated to solve problems using hierarchical approaches to problem solving and to represent relationships in programs abstractly, within a strict syntactical system of linear propositional logic. This "formal, propositional" way of constructing knowledge (129) has come to constitute a "canonical style" (133) for programmers who are solving problems and representing information, a privileged way of relating ideas one to the other that has become "literally synonymous with knowledge" (129) in computer science. So synonymous has this way of thinking become with knowledge, in fact, that computer scientists have come to see propositional thinking not as *one* way of knowing, but as the *only* way of knowing. It has become equated with "formal" and "logical" thinking, and given "a privileged status" (133) within computer science.

Recently, however, increasing numbers of computer specialists have begun to identify the limitations inherent in relying on hierarchical approaches and data representations—in dealing with learners who have varying levels and kinds of visualization skills, in training programmers to apply epistemologically diverse approaches to programming problems, and in representing non-hierarchically organized information structures like *wicked* or *fuzzy* problems (complex problems with no definitive formulations or solutions), and in coping with natural language input.[4]

Several programming paradigms have been suggested as alternatives and supplements to hierarchical representations of knowledge, such as object-oriented programming systems (OOPS) and iconic interfaces that represent knowledge, concepts, or programs through small pictures, called *objects* or *icons*. Such methods of programming and designing computer interfaces, some computer designers contend, can support alternative approaches to constructing meaning—though "bricolage," for example, a term that Turkle and Papert (135) use in reference to the work of Claude Levi-Strauss. Bricolage, as Turkle and Papert employ the term, refers to the construction of meaning through the arrangement and rearrangement of concrete, well-known materials, often in an intuitive rather than logical manner. Bricoleurs get to know a subject by interacting with it physically, by manipulating materials, or symbols, or icons in rich associative patterns, by arranging and re-arranging them constantly until they fit together in a satisfying or meaningful way. Bricoleurs reason "from within" (144) to come to an understanding of a problem through a direct "physical path of access" (145) rather than reasoning with the help of a traditionally validated pattern of logical representation that depends on objective distancing.

Turkle and Papert contend that allowing for bricolage as a way of representing knowledge will encourage an "epistemological pluralism" within the "computer culture" (153) that might especially benefit individuals who feel "more comfortable with a relational, interactive, active, and connected approach to objects" (150). In particular, Turkle and Papert link bricolage with approaches to problem solving that are culturally determined and articulated with gender. Drawing on the work of Carol Gilligan, Evelyn Fox Keller, and Sandra Harding and Merrill Hintikka, these authors suggest that women, in particular, might benefit from conceptual frameworks that would support bricolage, but not exclude rationalistically determined approaches such as hierarchical representations. It could be a mistake, however, as Judith Butler points out, to see gender itself in such fixed terms or to consider the continual construction and re-constructions of gender identities as other than complex, momentary, and contradictory "intersections" (3) of cultural and political forces. As played out realistically within the maps of computer interfaces, Turkle and Papert's suggestions prove more problematic. The Macintosh interface, for instance, allows for both bricolage and rationalistically determined representations of hierarchy—that is, documents, folders, and text nodes can be arranged and re-arranged according to alternative relations of space, time, association, and intuition *or* according to more traditional logical relations of hierarchy and classification. As we have tried to indicate, however, the alignment of these cultural maps along the articulated axes of capitalism, class, gender, and race creates a set of tendential forces that continues to value approaches associated primarily with dominant ideological positions.

Given the characteristics of the interface as a linguistic contact zone, our uses of computers in English classrooms certainly seem capable of supporting what Henry Giroux calls "imperialist master narratives" (57) of colonial dominance, even as they make the promise of technological liberation and progress. Students who want to use computers are continually confronted with these grand narratives which foreground a value on middle-class, corporate culture; capitalism and the commodification of information; Standard English; and rationalistic ways of representing knowledge. These values simultaneously do violence to and encourage the rejection of the languages of different races and the values of non-dominant cultural and gender groups. When students from these groups enter the linguistic borderlands of the interface, in other words, they often learn that they must abandon their own culture or gender and acknowledge the dominance of other groups. As Pratt and Said, among others, note, such individuals are forced, at some level, into "simultaneously identifying with dominant groups" and disassociating themselves from the colonial values of these groups (Pratt 59, citing Moreau).

This is, as we see it, one of the ways in which educators use computers—albeit unconsciously—to enact what Elspeth Stuckey calls "the violence of literacy." Each time we ask students from a marginalized cultural group to use computers, we ask them—require them—to learn a system of literacy that "distance[s] them from the ways of equality" (94). When we connect the regularly dispersed violence of literacy education to the use of computers, as technology critics like C. Paul Olson and Andrew Feenberg point out, we get more than the sum of the parts. We get, indeed, a master narrative that resonates all too successfully with modernist myths of technological progress: Civilization and reason, as manifested in an increasingly literate people, are supported in their historical evolution by continual improvements of industry and science. If teachers hear this resonance, we think they understand the need to identify and correct the tone.

WHAT TO DO?

Scholars who use technology and educators who teach with technology will, no doubt, find it difficult to study the maps of computer interfaces in a critical light to identify the many layers of culture and ideology they represent. As Denis Wood suggests, the greatest difficulty of all comes when we understand that we must locate ourselves in relation to the map. At this point, we end up asking ourselves where we stand in this colonial landscape, how we have cast our own multiple subjective positions within the territory that we have created and examined. Are we the cartographers who compose the map in our own cultural image—as white-collar professionals, many of us white or privileged? Are we members of a dominant group that profits from the map's reproductive function—as official representatives of an educational system and, in the case of many institutions of higher learning, the State? In part, of course, we do (already and always, as they say) stand in these places, but we can also—by revealing the partial and flawed nature of the map, by acknowledging our own role in composing the map—claim other vantage places as well. In particular, we can take with increasing seriousness the role of serving as technology critics when we use computers in the classroom and when we work with other teachers to integrate technology within these learning spaces. As Elspeth Stuckey, in *The Violence of Literacy,* says of literacy education in general—when we finally get around to "seeing" how a system supports repression, we can also find ways to alter the nature of our involvement in it:

> A system takes a lot of trouble. A system must be devised and implemented. To be sure, much of its design is tacit, its implementation an extension of usual modes of comfortable life. That is why uncomfortable people can often change a system. They can see it. (126)

So what do we do as educators and as the teachers of teachers? In our own classrooms, the continuing process has to be centered on a continuing foregrounding of the problems we have sketched out here, which leads us to suggest some related strategies for re-drawing the territory of the interface with students. To begin, however, we have to learn to recognize—and teach students to recognize—the interface as an interested and partial map of our culture and as a linguistic contact zone that reveals power differentials. We need to teach students and ourselves to recognize computer interfaces as non-innocent physical borders (between the regular world and the virtual world), cultural borders (between the haves and the have-nots), and linguistic borders. These borders we need to recognize as cultural formations "historically constructed and socially organized within rules and regulations that limit and enable particular identities, individual capacities, and social forms" (Giroux 30). We also need to teach students and ourselves useful strategies of crossing—and demystifying—these borders. It is important to understand that we continually re-map and renegotiate borders in our lives.

One of the ways to come to this understanding is through working with students and computer specialists to re-design/re-imagine/re-create interfaces that attempt to avoid disabling and devaluing non-white, non-English language background students, and women. Our goal in creating these new interfaces should be to help rewrite the relationships between the center and the margins of our culture and, in Henry Giroux's words, "extend rather than erase the possibility for enabling human agency" (27) among currently marginalized and oppressed groups represented within the culture and the educational system. Although it is important to recognize—given the strong tendential forces of our cultural and the regularly dispersed nature of ideological systems—that any progress we make toward these goals will be partial, temporary, and contradictory, there are a few practices (what de Certeau might call *tactics*) that could help us enact a border pedagogy in computer-supported writing environments. We would like to spend the last part of this article identifying a few of these practical approaches that might be of use in composition programs at the college and university level.

Becoming Technology Critics as Well as Technology Users

One tactic for responding to the interested nature of computer interfaces has to do with encouraging a general level of critical awareness about technology issues on the part of both pre-service and in-service teachers. Currently, most teachers of composition studies at the collegiate level are educated to deal with technology not as critics but as users—if, indeed, they are educated to deal with it at all. Few programs that educate college-level teachers of composition, for example, require students to take coursework in technology studies. If they are lucky, new faculty or graduate teaching assistants at an institution may be introduced—during an orientation for instructors or during a graduate course in teaching composition—to a computer facility that they can use for their teaching. Often, these introductions accomplish nothing more than exposing teachers to one or more software programs available for use in the classroom, and allowing time for some minimal hands-on practice with the software. Few composition programs or English departments, however, make a systematic effort to provide parallel instruction on technology issues as they touch on educational projects—stressing readings and discussions on technology criticism, or on the growing body of scholarship and research associated with computers and composition studies.[5] As a result, teachers of composition—and prospective teachers of composition—may learn to use technology, but not to think carefully about the implications of its use within their own classrooms.

Influencing this situation is an additional set of forces that encourage relatively conservative teaching strategies in connection with technology and relatively little room for reflection on these strategies. Given the costs involved in computing, most composition programs and English departments must depend on access to generic *computing* environments rather than facilities designed specifically to provide computer-supported *writers'* environments. Such generic facilities, because they are administered and maintained by computer specialists rather than teachers of English, foreground an emphasis on the machine and its use rather than on a critical approach to teaching composition with computer support. Characteristic of these facilities, often located in interior rooms or basements, are rows of numbered machines arranged to look very much like traditional classrooms and often networked so that they can be controlled from a single teacher's workstation at the front of the room. In such settings, and often armed with very little preparation or training, teachers of composition also have little encouragement to make changes in conventionally influenced teaching approaches they observe in regular classrooms, as Klem and Moran note (5–22). In such an environment, for example, it may become difficult to have students working in flexible groupings, to avoid a teacher-centered classroom, or to provide students room to take some charge of their own learning.

Operating within these parameters, it is recognizably difficult to educate teachers of composition as technology critics and to inculcate the intellectual habit of reflecting critically on the effects that technology might have within composition classrooms. Writing program administrators and individual teachers can, however, take some steps toward this goal by making sure that their programs—whether pre-service or in-service—are spending at least as much time educating teachers about important technology issues (access to technology, design of technology, ideologies associated with technology) as they are on training them to use technology. Among the efforts that might be undertaken by teachers and program administrators in support of this goal are collecting and circulating articles and books that provide critical as well as optimistic visions of technology, setting up research groups and teaching observations to encourage reflective teaching habits in computer-supported writing facilities, encouraging faculty to participate in e-mail lists that discuss technology issues as they are manifested in English composition classrooms, and sponsoring talks by informed scholars who examine technology issues from critical perspectives.[6]

Contributing to Technology Design

A second tactic for addressing the interested nature of computer interfaces is more narrowly and specifically focused on the efforts of those faculty who are computers and composition specialists. Given the embryonic state of this field and the traditional educational reward structures within which computers and composition specialists must function to earn tenure, promotion, and professional recognition, these colleagues have focused most of their efforts during the past fifteen years on identifying, exploring, and testing pedagogical uses of available computer technologies—suggesting, for example, effective ways to integrate the use of word-processing packages, on-line conferences, or idea generation packages into the teaching of English composition classes.[7] Less effort, therefore, has been available to invest in software design efforts—which can be costly in terms of resources and professional advancement, as LeBlanc points out—and almost no involvement has been encouraged in the design of primary interfaces. Without such an involvement by humanist scholars and teachers—especially those individuals who are familiar with language and learning theory, who understand issues raised by technology studies and cultural studies—interface design will continue to be dominated primarily by computer scientists and will lack perspectives that could be contributed by humanist scholars.

Fortunately, avenues for involvement in software design efforts are becoming more accessible. Computers and composition specialists who find the penalties associated with the effort to design specific software packages to be overly costly in terms of tenure, promotion, and advancement, can also influence software design through collective professional action aimed at general technology design efforts. Professional organizations such as the Alliance for Computers in Writing,[8] International Federation of Information Processing, and even the National Council of Teachers of English (through committees like the Instruction Technology Committee, and the CCCC Committee on Computers) currently influence the design of software through various formal and informal strategies of collective action: by identifying groups of teachers and professional educators who can engage directly in conversations with software manufacturers and vendors, by charging committees to take on the task of making systematic suggestions to these manufacturers after consulting with reflective computer-using teachers, by identifying outstanding efforts in software design, by publishing papers and reviews that include critical examinations of design implications in the classroom, and by identifying the kinds of products that are limited in their classroom usefulness. Many of these committees and organizations also hold ongoing discussions of computer issues of interest to teachers of composition on the Internet. Within these forums—which often are global in their participation and include a mix of computer scientists, educators, software designers, and content specialists—computers and composition specialists can encourage discussions that focus on interfaces, language issues, cultural reproduction, learning theories, and critical theories of language use. Through these conversations, computers and composition specialists can contribute to an increasingly critical awareness of technology issues on the part of individuals involved directly in the design of technology. Such conversations—if they can serve to extend and transform the existing intellectual and political terrain for various groups of people—could have, in Laclau and Mouffe's words, a "profound subversive power" (155).

Re-Conceiving the Map of the Interface

A third suggestion for addressing the interested map of reality offered by computer interfaces is to involve composition teachers and students in composition classes in an ongoing project to revise interfaces as *texts*. The purpose of these map-making sessions would be to come up with ideas for changing the interface to reflect a range of cultural, linguistic, and ideological perspectives. Faculty who specialize in computers and composition studies can serve as key resource people in this effort, although the goal is to involve *all* computer-using teachers and students in conceptualizing alternative maps of computer interfaces. The outcome of such sessions should not be to redesign interfaces in a technical sense, but rather to reconceive of them according to the experiences of a broad range of writers and teachers of writing: identifying desirable features generally unavailable in primary interfaces (a light pen for writing in the margins of documents, or a highlighter for color coding related documents), suggesting ways of customizing interfaces for the needs of various writers and readers (adding a read-aloud option for writers who want to hear how their texts sound), or imagining productive metaphors around which interfaces can be built (mechanics' workbenches, kitchen countertops, garages). In these sessions—to further reduce the focus on technical expertise—teachers and students can represent their interface re-revision ideas either through prose descriptions or pencil-and-pen drawings.

For those faculty and teachers who are more adventurous in terms of technology, some relatively simple computer-based tools already exist that could support these projects at a level accessible to non-specialists. Teachers and students can use the computer-based drawing and illustration packages they are already familiar with, for example, to create representations of re-designed interface screens to which they add new features. In addition, software designers for the Macintosh have already published scores of alternative icons and images that can be used by English composition teachers, and students, to customize primary computer interfaces. Matrix Communication Associates of Pittsburgh, for instance, is now marketing a package of African American computer graphics and has plans to market graphics packages that more adequately represent other ethnic groups as well (Creedy). With such packages, faculty and graduate students who have very little familiarity with computers can illustrate how they would like to incorporate various features into primary interfaces—creating icons for bulletin boards, on-line conferences, multiple user dimensions, or other student-centered learning spaces that they would like to include in an interface. It is possible that the representations identified by writing teachers and students can later be used by software and hardware design specialists as the basis for more technical projects that might actually produce working versions of alternative interfaces.

To support these conceptual redesign efforts, computers and composition specialists can also work with both teachers and students to assemble expanded libraries of images that appeal to writers of different ages, races, sexual preferences, classes, and lifestyles. These icons should be chosen to resonate with a range of different cultural and ideological positions—delicatessens and 7-Elevens, babies and rocking chairs, rosetta stones and piñatas, apartment buildings and subway maps, powwow dances and storytellers—which can be used to customize systems for different groups of writers. The goal in identifying these images and icons, in Henry Giroux's words, would be to help students and teachers focus on the act of crossing borders "moving in and out of borders constructed around coordinates of difference and power," learning and negotiating "the shifting parameters of place, identity, history, and power" (136). This project may help us and students to see that the interests represented within maps are "neither singular nor simple" (Wood 94) and that interests concealed in one map, one representation of a culture, can be revealed and foregrounded in another.

TOWARD A CRITICAL READING OF INTERFACES

For both teachers and students, Giroux notes, the project of eliminating oppression based on class, race, and gender involves "an ongoing contest within every aspect of daily life," a continual project of mapping and re-mapping the educational, political, and ideological spaces we want to occupy." He continues, "no tradition should ever be seen as received in this project" (155–56). In this sense, English teachers cannot be content to understand the maps of computer interfaces as simple, uncomplicated spaces. Rather, we need to prepare ourselves and the students with whom we work to map these virtual spaces as sites of "multiple and heterogeneous borders where different histories, languages, experiences, and voices intermingle amidst diverse relations of power and privilege" (Giroux 169). At the same time, it is prudent to acknowledge the complications and contradictions inherent in such work. As Winograd and Flores point out, our continuing efforts toward revealing the interested nature of computer interfaces will, in part, contribute to concealment because "as carriers of a tradition, we cannot be objective observers of it." This realization, however, cannot provide an excuse for inaction. We must also, as these authors note, take on the responsibility of continuing to "work towards unconcealment . . . and let our awareness guide our actions in creating and applying technology" (179).

ACKNOWLEDGMENTS

We owe a great deal of gratitude to colleagues who helped us work through the ideas in this article. The generosity and intellectual contributions of Marilyn Cooper, Jim Sosnoski, and Joe Janangelo are evident in the best aspects of this paper.

NOTES

1. For more critical discussions of the overly optimistic rhetoric associated with computer use in composition classrooms, see Faigley's description of a synchronous network conversation (*Fragments* 163–99), Barton's discussion of the dominant discourses associated with technology ("Interpreting the Discourses of Technology"), Hawisher and Selfe's exploration of teachers' claims about computer use ("The Rhetoric of Technology"), and Romano's discussion of bias in on-line conversations ("The Egalitarianism Narrative").

2. Readers who want to explore the potential of electronic forums on WANs or LANs may want to consult: Barker and Kemp's "Network Theory"; Bruce, Peyton, and Batson's *Networked Classrooms*; Cooper and Selfe's "Computer Conferences"; Eldred's "Computers, Composition and the Social View"; Faigley's "Subverting the Electronic Notebook"; Handa's *Computers and Community*; Kiesler, Siegel, and McGuire's "Social Psychological Aspects"; and Spitzer's "Computer Conferencing."

3. Discussions of the ways in which racism, sexism, and power relationships related to colonialism are enacted in connection with technology use can be found in Gomez's "The Equitable Teaching of Composition," Hawisher and Selfe's "Rhetoric of Technology," Jessup's "Feminism and Computers," and LeBlanc's "Competing Ideologies."

4. For descriptions of the challenges associated with wicked problems and fuzzy logic, readers may want to refer to: Ambler, Burnett, and Zimmerman; Kurzweil; Seagull and Walker; Turkle and Papert; and Winograd and Flores.

5. For criticism related to technology, we recommend the works of Feenberg, Kramare, Olson, Ohmann.

6. Several such lists exist for teachers of composition. Megabyte University (MBU), for instance, focuses on issues surrounding the use of computers in writing-intensive classrooms and BreadNet serves to connect English teachers who have attended Breadloaf seminars. To obtain information on Megabyte University, contact Fred Kemp, the founder of MBU, at Texas Tech University (YKFOK@TTACS1.TTU.EDU). To obtain additional information about BreadNet, contact Bill Wright (BWRIGHT@TMN.COM). The National Council of Teachers of English is currently engaged in designing a computer network that will connect teachers of English across the country. For additional information on NCTENet, contact

Tharon Howard, Chair of the NCTE Instructional Technology Committee, at Clemson University (THARON@HUBCAP.CLEMSON.EDU).

7. The advent of computers and composition studies is typically dated from 1975, when Ellen Nold's *CCC* article, "Fear and Trembling," gave voice to the concerns English composition teachers had about technology (and thus gave impetus to focused work in this area), or from 1979, when Hugh Burns published the first dissertation that systematically examined the effects of computer-assisted instruction on student writers' invention efforts. The first fully assembled microcomputer, the Apple II, marketed in 1976, provided the actual technological means of introducing computers into composition classrooms in a meaningful way. These machines provided composition teachers with word-processing systems that were far easier to teach and far less difficult to use than the clumsy line-editors offered on mainframe computers in the seventies.

8. The Alliance for Computers in Writing is a national coalition of teachers, publishers, professional organizations, and educational institutions interested in promoting the effective use of computers in English composition classrooms. For more information on the Alliance for Computers and Writing, contact Trent Batson, Gallaudet University (TWBATSON@GALLUA.BITNET).

WORKS CITED

Ambler, Allen L., Margaret M. Burnett, and Betsy A. Zimmerman. "Operational versus Definitional: A Perspective on Programming Paradigms." *Computer* (September 1992): 28–43.

Barker, Thomas T., and Fred O. Kemp. "Network Theory: A Postmodern Pedagogy for the Writing Classroom." *Computers and Community: Teaching Composition in the Twenty-First Century.* Ed. Carolyn Handa. Portsmouth, NH: Boynton 1–27.

Barton, Ellen. "Interpreting the Discourses of Technology." *Literacy and Computers: The Complications of Teaching and Learning on Technology.* Ed. Cynthia L. Selfe and Susan Hilligoss. New York: MLA, 1994. 56–75.

Batson, Trent. "The ENFI Project: A Networked Classroom Approach to Writing Instruction." *Academic Computing* (February/March 1988): 32–33, 55–56.

Berger, John. *Ways of Seeing.* New York: Penguin Books, 1972.

Bolter, Jay D. *Writing Space: The Computer, Hypertext, and the History of Writing.* Hillsdale, NJ: Erlbaum, 1991.

Bruce, Bertram, Joy Freeft Peyton, and Trent Batson. *Network-Based Classrooms: Promises and Realities.* New York: Cambridge UP, 1993.

Burns, Hugh. "Stimulating Rhetorical Invention through Computer-Assisted Instruction." Diss. U of Texas at Austin, 1979.

Butler, Judith. *Gender Trouble: Feminism and the Subversion of Identity.* New York: Routledge, 1990.

Cooper, Marilyn M., and Cynthia L. Selfe. "Computer Conferences and Learning: Authority, Resistance, and Internally Persuasive Discourse." *College English* 52 (1990): 847–69.

Creedy, Steve. "Local Firm's African-American Computer Graphics Fill Void." *Pittsburgh Post Gazette* 23 August 1993: B8.

de Certeau, Michel. *The Practice of Everyday Life.* Trans. Steven Randall. Berkeley: U of California P, 1984.

Deleuze, Gilles, and Félix Guattari. *A Thousand Plateaus: Capitalism and Schizophrenia.* Trans. Brian Massumi. Minneapolis, MN: U of Minnesota P, 1987.

Eldred, Janet C. "Computers, Composition, and the Social View." *Critical Perspectives on Computers and Composition Studies.* Ed. Gail E. Hawisher and Cynthia L. Selfe. New York: Teachers College P, 1989. 201–18.

Faigley, Lester. "Subverting the Electronic Notebook: Teaching Writing Using Networked Computers." *The Writing Teacher as Researcher: Essays in the Theory and Practice of Class-Based Research.* Ed. Donald A. Daiker and Max Morenberg. Portsmouth, NH: Boynton, 1990. 290–311.

Faigley, Lester. *Fragments of Rationality: Postmodernity and the Subject of Composition.* Pittsburgh: U of Pittsburgh P, 1992.

Feenberg, Andrew. *Critical Theory of Technology.* New York: Oxford UP, 1991.

Flores, Mary J. "Computer Conferencing: Composing a Feminist Community of Writers." *Computers and Community: Teaching Composition in the Twenty-First Century.* Ed. Carolyn Handa. Portsmouth, NH: Boynton, 1990. 106–17.

Foucault, Michel. "Space, Knowledge, and Power." *The Foucault Reader.* Ed. Paul Rabinow. New York: Pantheon, 1984. 239–56.

Gilligan, Carol. *In a Different Voice: Psychological Theory and Women's Development.* Cambridge, MA: Harvard UP, 1982.

Giroux, Henry A. *Border Crossings: Cultural Workers and the Politics of Education.* New York: Routledge, 1992.

Gomez, Mary L. "The Equitable Teaching of Composition." *Evolving Perspectives on Computers and Composition Studies.* Ed. Gail E. Hawisher and Cynthia L. Selfe. Urbana, IL: NCTE, 1991. 318–35.

Grimes, William. "Computer as a Cultural Tool." *New York Times* 1 December 1992: C 13–15.

Handa, Carolyn, ed. *Computers and Community: Teaching Composition in the Twenty-First Century.* Portsmouth, NH: Boynton, 1990.

Harding, Sandra, and Merrill B. Hintikka, eds. *Discovering Reality: Feminist Perspectives on Epistemology, Metaphysics, Methodology, and Philosophy of Science.* London: Reidel, 1983.

Hawisher, Gail E., and Cynthia L. Selfe. "Voices in College Classrooms: The Dynamics of Electronic Discussion." *The Quarterly* 14 (Summer 1992): 24–28, 32.

——. "The Rhetoric of Technology and the Electronic Writing Class." CCC 42 (1991): 55–65.

——. "Tradition and Change in Computer-Supported Writing Environments." *Theoretical and Critical Perspectives on Teacher Change.* Ed. P. Kahaney, J. Janangelo, and L. A. M. Perry. Norwood, NJ: Ablex, 1993. 155–86.

Janangelo, Joseph. "Technopower and Technoppression: Some Abuses of Power and Control in Computer-Assisted Writing Environments." *Computers and Composition* 9 (November 1991): 47–64.

Jessup, Emily. "Feminism and Computers in Composition Instruction." *Evolving Perspectives on Computers and Composition Studies: Questions for the 1990s.* Ed. Gail E. Hawisher and Cynthia L. Selfe. Urbana, IL: 1991. 336–55.

Jordan, June. *ON CALL: Political Essays.* Boston, MA: South End 1985.

——. "Toward a Manifest New Destiny." *The Progressive* (February 1992): 18–23.

Keller, Evelyn F. *Reflections on Gender and Science.* New Haven: Yale UP, 1985.

Kiesler, Sara, Jane Siegel, and Timothy W. McGuire. "Social Psychological Aspects of Computer-Mediated Communication." *American Psychologist* 39 (1984): 1123–34.

Klem, Elizabeth, and Charles Moran. "Teachers in a Strange LANd: Learning to Teach in a Networked Writing Classroom." *Computers and Composition* 9 (August 1992): 5–22.

Kramare, Cheris, ed. *Technology and Women's Voices: Keeping in Touch.* New York: Routledge, 1988.

Kremers, Marshall. "Adams Sherman Hill Meets ENFI: An Inquiry and a Retrospective." *Computers and Composition* 5 (August 1988): 69–77.

Kurzweil, Raymond. *The Age of Intelligent Machines.* Cambridge, MA: MIT P, 1990.

Laclau, Ernesto, and Chantel Mouffe. *Hegemony and Socialist Strategy: Towards a Radical Democratic Politics.* London: Verso, 1985.

LeBlanc, Paul. "Competing Ideologies in Software Design for Computer-Aided Composition." *Computers and Composition* 7 (April 1990): 8–19.

Moreau, N. B. "Education, Ideology, and Class/Sex Identity." *Language and Power.* Ed. Cheris Kramarae. Beverly Hills, CA: Sage, 1984. 43–61.

Nelson, Theodor H. "The Tyranny of the File." *Datamation* 15 December 1986: 83–86.

Nold, Ellen. "Fear and Trembling: A Humanist Approaches the Computer." *CCC* 26 (1975): 269–273.

Ohmann, Richard. "Literacy, Technology, and Monopoly Capitalism." *College English* 47 (1985): 675–689.

Olson, C. Paul. "Who Computes?" *Critical Pedagogy and Cultural Power.* Ed. David Livingstone. South Hadley, MA: Bergin, 1987. 179–204.

Petzold, Charles. "Move Over, ASCII! Unicode Is Here." *PC Magazine* 12 (26 October 1993): 374–376.

Piller, Charles. "Separate Realities: The Creation of the Technological Underclass in America's Public Schools." *MacWorld* (September 1992): 218–30.

Pratt, Mary Louise. "Linguistic Utopias." *The Linguistics of Writing.* Ed. Nigel Fabb et al. Manchester: Manchester UP, 1987. 48–66.

———. "Arts of the Contact Zone." *Profession* 91(1991): 33–40.

Romano Susan. "The Egalitarianism Narrative: Whose Story? Which Yardstick?" *Computers and Composition* 10 (August 1993): 5–28.

Said, Edward. "Reflections on Exile." *Out There: Marginalization and Contemporary Cultures.* Ed. Russell Fergeson, Martha Gever, Trinh T. Minh-ha, and Cornell West. Cambridge, MA: MIT P, 1990. 357–68.

Seagull, J. F., and N. Walker. "The Effects of Hierarchical Structure and Visualization on Computerized Information Retrieval." *International Journal of Human-Computer Interaction* 4 (1992): 369–485.

Selfe, Cynthia L. "English Teachers and the Humanization of Computers: Networking Communities of Readers and Writers." *On Literacy and Its Teaching: Issues in English Education.* Ed. Gail E. Hawisher and Anna O. Soter. Albany, NY: State U of New York P, 1990. 190–205.

———. "Technology in the English Classroom: Computers through the Lens of Feminist Theory." *Computers and Community: Teaching Composition in the Twenty-First Century.* Ed. Carolyn Handa. Portsmouth, NH: Boynton, 1990. 118–39.

Selfe, Cynthia L., and Paul R. Meyer. "Testing Claims for On-Line Conferences." *Written Communication* 8 (1991): 163–92.

Sheingold, Karen, L. M. Martin, and M. W. Endreweit. "Preparing Urban Teachers for the Technological Future." *Mirrors of Minds: Patterns of Experience in Educational Computing.* Ed. Roy D. Pea and Karen Sheingold. Norwood, NJ: Ablex, 1987. 67–85.

Spitzer, Michael. "Computer Conferencing: An Emerging Technology." *Critical Perspectives in Computers and Composition Instruction.* Ed. Gail E. Hawisher and Cynthia L. Selfe. New York: Teachers College P, 1989. 187–200.

Springer, Claudia. "The Pleasure of the Interface." *Screen* 32 (1991): 303–23.

Stuckey, Elspeth. *The Violence of Literacy.* Portsmouth, NH: Boynton, 1991.

Turkle, Sherry, and Seymour Papert. "Epistomological Pluralism: Styles and Voices within the Computer Culture." *Signs* 16 (1990): 128–57.

Virilio, Paul. *Speed and Politics: An Essay on Dromology.* Trans. Mark Polizzotti. New York: Semiotext(e), 1987.

Weizenbaum, Joseph. "Not without Us: A Challenge to Computer Professionals to Use Their Power to Bring the Present Insanity to a Halt." *Fellowship* (October/ November 1986): 8–10.

Wheelock, Ann, and Gail Dorman. *Before It's Too Late.* Boston, MA: Massachusetts Advocacy Commission, 1989.

Winograd, Terry, and Fernando Flores. *Understanding Computers and Cognition: A New Foundation for Design.* Reading, MA: Addison, 1986.

Wood, Denis. *The Power of Maps.* New York: Guilford, 1992.

WordPerfect for DOS: Reference for IBM Personal Computers and PC Networks, 1989.

From Analysis to Design

Visual Communication in the Teaching of Writing

DIANA GEORGE

In some respects . . . words cannot compare in effectiveness with pictures. The mere outlines in a Greek vase painting will give you a more immediate appreciation of the grace and beauty of the human form than pages of descriptive writing. A silhouette in black paper will enable you to recognize a stranger more quickly than the most elaborate description in words. (166)

—*John Hays Gardiner, George Lyman Kittredge, and Sarah Louise Arnold, 1902*

How's this for a visual argument: In response to reading Adam Hochschild's *King Leopold's Ghost*,[1] Boikhutso Jibula, a first-year student from Botswana, reproduces three maps of Africa, each on a transparency. In the first, the continent is empty except for what look like random circles primarily in the sub-Saharan region. The circles outline areas traditionally occupied or claimed by various tribes or communities before colonization. Boikhutso then superimposes a second map—this one of colonized Africa. He points out the English, French, and German names of places that now have well-defined borders, most of which cut through the original circles, splitting

Reprinted from *College Composition and Communication* 54.1 (September 2002): 11–39. Used with permission.

traditional regions into new nations, neither named for nor controlled by the people whose places he had identified in the original map. Over that second map, Boikhutso superimposes a third—this one is postcolonial Africa. The names, he points out, are changed. German East Africa is now mainly Tanzania. The Congo Free State is, on this map at any rate, Zaire. Colonization has ended, he tells us, but the boundaries are much the same, the people dispersed or gone, the languages and kingdoms and villages still split or destroyed. It takes very few words for Boikhutso to tell the class what these maps show them: Precolonial Africa cannot be recovered. There is no possibility of going back to what was there before the colonizer. African people must work as nations within the nations now outlined on this third map.

Or picture this: In the same course, Grace VanCamp from lower Michigan creates a dinner place setting, Judy Chicago style. On a place mat, she arranges a plastic plate, knife, fork, spoon, and Coca-Cola© glass. On the face of the plate, Grace has glued a map of the African continent. The place card reads, "King Leopold."

And finally: Deirdre Johns shows the class a remaking of Leopold of Belgium's Congo Free State flag. Like the original, her redesign features a bold

Original design by Deirdre Johns.

yellow star in the center of a deep blue field. She tells the class that in her research she learned of the reasoning for the design: the star was to signify the light of Europe being brought in to the Dark Continent. In Deirdre's flag, the blue field is now covered with images of precolonial African art. The gold star is covered in images of slavery, faces of explorers, photos from the rubber and ivory trade. "This is what Europe really brought to Congo," she tells the class.

There are others I could describe—graphs and oil paintings and Web pages and digital designs and book covers and more—but they would tell much the same story. The work of these students and others like them has convinced me that current discussions of visual communication and writing instruction have only tapped the surface of possibilities for the role of visual communication in the composition class.[2] Or, even more to the point—our students have a much richer imagination for what we might accomplish with the visual than our journals have yet to address.

From W. J. T. Mitchell's claim that the second half of the twentieth century was marked by "the pictorial turn" (11–34) to the New London Group's call for a pedagogy of "multiliteracies," we are experiencing yet another push to incorporate visual language into the composition course.[3] It is, of course, true that an insistence on the importance of visual literacy is an old and perennial one. In fact, it has become common today to talk of multiple literacies, to encourage the uses of visual communication in the teaching of writing, and to argue that writing is itself a form of visual communication.

Even so, there remains much confusion over what is meant by *visual communication, visual rhetoric,* or, more simply, *the visual* and where or whether it belongs in a composition course. What's more, to the extent that this confusion remains unaddressed, visual and written communication continue to be held in a kind of tension—the visual figuring into the teaching of writing as a problematic, something added, an anomaly, a "new" way of composing, or, somewhat cynically, as a strategy for adding relevance or interest to a required course. Only rarely does that call address students as producers as well as consumers or critics of the visual. More rarely does the call acknowledge the visual as much more than attendant to the verbal.

My aim in what follows is not to define visual communication or visual rhetoric in a way that would eliminate that tension. I actually believe that some tug of war between words and images or between writing and design can be productive as it brings into relief the multiple dimensions of all forms of communication. For my purposes here, at any rate, there is little reason to argue that the visual and the verbal are the same, are read or composed in the same way, or have the same status in the tradition of communication instruction.

In place of a resolution, then, I am after a clearer understanding of what can happen when the visual is very consciously brought into the composition classroom as a form of communication worth both examining *and* producing. What, for example, might it mean to ask, as I did of the students whose work opens this paper, for a visual argument? Are we posing a new relationship between composition and communication or resurrecting an older one? How does the visual both promise and threaten to change the composition course?

At this point, I should make an important distinction. I will be examining primarily the places of visual literacy in the *composition* classroom. It is quite true that a concern for visual

> "*Remember that graph-and-chart reading is not one of the three R's*" (180).
>
> —*Rudolph Flesch, 1949*

literacy/visual communication has been an ongoing one in the teaching of scientific, technical, and professional communication. In fact, for a number of compositionists over the years, the technical writing course was exactly where the visual belonged. (Witness, for example, Rudolph Flesch's rather Gradgrindian declaration that one mainstay of technical writing instruction, understanding the uses of graphs and charts, "is not one of the three R's.") My focus is on arguments that have been made for including the visual in composition courses because these arguments are linked closely to discussions of basic literacy and even to English departments' investments in literary studies rather than to professional communication's emphasis on the functions or uses of visual information. That is not at all to dismiss the extensive work that characterizes professional communication's engagement with the visual. Instead, it is my attempt to bring composition studies into a more thoroughgoing discussion of the place of visual literacy in the writing classroom.

In the end, I argue that the terms of debate typical in our discussions of visual literacy and the teaching of writing have limited the kinds of assignments we might imagine for composition. I do not make a claim that our students have a special talent for the visual or that their knowledge of the visual is necessarily more sophisticated than their teachers'. Instead, I would argue that if we are ever to move beyond a basic and somewhat vague call for attention to "visual literacy" in the writing class, it is crucial to understand how very complicated and sophisticated is visual communication to students who have grown up in what by all accounts is an aggressively visual culture. Such a move must first address how relationships between visual communication and writing instruction have been typically configured.

In order to get to that argument, however, I find it necessary first to set what I'd call one curricular context through which visual literacy has entered the teaching of writing, at least as it emerges in scholarly journals and text-book assignments for more than fifty years. The history of how visual literacy has entered the teaching of writing, at least as it emerges in scholarly journals and textbook assignments for more than fifty years, is not a smooth or consistent one in which writing instruction and visual literacy move seamlessly from image analysis to design. Instead, it is one that can best be related through major themes that have dominated the English classroom since at least the 1940s. I begin, in fact, at what might seem a far remove from the college writing classroom: examining arguments in elementary and secondary education for including visual instruction alongside lessons more familiar to English language arts. It is here that we see most clearly how visual studies has been perceived as a threat to language and literature instruction.

VISUAL LITERACY IN THE ENGLISH CLASSROOM

In 1946, the instructor's edition of the popular Dick and Jane elementary reader series alerted teachers to the reality that teaching reading demanded attention to more than print literacy. It meant teaching students to read pictures as well as words:

> Skill in interpreting pictures is becoming increasingly important as a means of securing pleasure and information. Adults today are exposed to "picture" magazines, cartoons, advertisements, movies, and many types of diagrammatic schemes for the presentation of facts. Children are surrounded with picture books and "read" the funnies long before they enter school. Regardless of age or situation, the individual who can "read" pictorial material effectively has access to a vast world of new ideas. (Kismaric and Heiferman 88)

Fifty years later, the New London Group issued their report through which they identified the ability both to read and use visual information/visual signs as primary among multiliteracies:

> [W]e argue that literacy pedagogy now must account for the burgeoning variety of text forms associated with information and multimedia technologies. *This includes understanding and competent control of representational forms* that are becoming increasingly significant in the overall communications environment, such as visual images and their relationship to the written word—for instance, visual design in desktop publishing or the interface of visual and linguistic meaning in multimedia. (61, emphasis added)

The two reports sound a common theme about visual communication that might be summed up in this way: Literacy means more than words, and visual literacy means more than play.

Coming as it did at the beginning of a media revolution of sorts, the Dick and Jane statement was repeated in a number of ways for the next thirty years or so. During much of the second half of the twentieth century, mass media became a focus for study or a problem to confront in literacy instruction, and so I turn briefly to school talk about television, the visual medium that, throughout the 1950s and 1960s, threatened (or promised) to change the English classroom permanently.

In 1961, NCTE issued its report from the Commission on the Study of Television, *Television and the Teaching of English*. Neil Postman, who twenty-five years later would publish his own critique of the culture of television (*Amusing Ourselves to Death*), was its primary author. For Postman

> "Whatever the future may hold, teachers of English can face it with equanimity if they avoid the temptation to pit television or any other medium against print." (13)
>
> —Neil Postman, 1961

and the members of his commission, the job at hand was to convince English teachers that television was not only a proper subject for the English classroom but a necessary one, even though "We do not mean to suggest by its use that television is the equivalent of *belles lettres* but rather that certain kinds of television programs employ language and action in ways that duplicate the functions of traditional literary forms" (39–40). The commission's incentive for bringing the study of television into the English class will likely sound somewhat dated but still very familiar: "To the extent that their responses to television are *informed, discriminating,* and *creative,* we may be assured that our language and literature, as well as the lives of our students, will be enriched by contact with television. *But taste and critical judgment are learned habits of mind*" (1, emphasis added). Here, the points of concern are explicit: Television is what our children are watching. It surrounds them daily. It is their "primary source of literary experience" (1). The English teacher's job, then, is to foster "taste and critical judgment," two qualities that lift the schooled above the unschooled. This judgment was deemed important because, according to the commission's figures, already in 1961 (only thirteen years after the 1948 postwar boom in television production) 88 percent of American households in the U.S. owned at least one television (30). It was a "literary experience" that threatened to replace those forms more common (and more comfortable) to the English class. "Teachers of English," the report states, "must help the children qualify their enthusiasm with thoughtful criticism" (73).

Though not quite the call for relevance that became common in the 1960s, this report, like the Dick and Jane instructors' manual fifteen years earlier and the New London Group's manifesto thirty-five years later, does acknowledge a changing world in which "a redefinition of 'literacy' is required, one that would extend beyond the printed page" (12). In the end, although the Commission on the Study of Television was not persuaded of the need for a new literacy, its members did accept the challenge to extend the content of the English classroom to include a new literature—television as literary text.

It is here, then, in these early lessons on the uses of visual texts in the reading and writing classroom that literacy instruction and literary studies meet. Visuals (be they paintings, films, comic books, or television narratives) were to be studied in the same way as literary texts, as subjects of close analysis—a use of the visual that continues throughout the history of writing instruction.

In 1962, only one year after the publication of the Postman report, NCTE published William Boutwell's *Using Mass Media in the Schools*, a report from The Committee on the Use of Mass Media. In it, Boutwell writes, "No rain forest in darkest Africa ever confronted men with more unknowns or a stranger mixture of enthusiasm, excitement, fears, and hopes than the tangled strands of communication we call 'mass media'" (v). As Boutwell tells us in his preface to the report, mass media (everything from newspapers and magazines to radio, television, motion pictures, and comic books) "often seems to be a force beyond human control" (vi).

An air of resignation over the influence of mass media permeates this collection, even in such writing assignments as Nina T. Fleir's proposal that teachers use students' favorite television shows rather than poetry, drama, or fiction as prompts for writing (150–52).

> "Every teacher must, sooner or later, face the fact that television is here to stay." (254)
>
> —Anita J. Willens, *in* Using Mass Media in the Schools, 1962

Only rarely do we encounter a suggestion that students might become producers as well as receivers or victims of mass media, especially visual media. As a tool for literacy instruction, then, this collection uses visual media as little more than a prompt for student essays and stories, a substitute for more traditional literary forms, or a subject of scrutiny.

By contrast, the 1996 New London Group report would also direct students' attention toward mass media but not as a subject of scrutiny or an invention prompt alone. Instead, the New London Group adds to the older model of media study the notion of *design* as a way of understanding literacy acquisition. What the New London Group urges, then, is not a closer relationship to media but the use of media to encourage the development of "multi-modal designs" that relate

> . . . all the other modes in quite remarkably dynamic relationships. For instance, mass media images relate the linguistic to the visual and to the gestural in intricately designed ways. Reading the mass media for its linguistic meanings alone is not enough. Magazines employ vastly different visual grammars according to their social and cultural content. A script of a sitcom such as *Roseanne* would have none of the qualities of the program if you didn't have a "feel" for its unique gestural, audio, and visual meanings. A script without this knowledge would only allow a very limited reading. Similarly, a visit to a shopping mall involves a lot of written text. However, either a pleasurable or a critical engagement with the mall will involve a multimodal reading that not only includes the design of language, but a spatial reading of the architecture of the mall and the placement and meaning of the written signs, logos, and lighting. (80–81)

What these scholars urge, then, is not simply the inclusion of mass media as objects of study but the use of media to encourage the development of multimodal designs.

I will return to this issue of design, but for the moment it is important to point out that thinking of composition as *design* shifts attention, if only momentarily, from the product to the act of production. We might say that despite their concern for the influence of television on students' writing and reading abilities, even the 1962 Boutwell collection in some ways prefigured the work of the New London Group. Yet, without a concept like the notion of design, these older media assignments seem to be stuck in a kind of literacy civil war—one that pits poetics against the popular and words against pictures.

VISUAL LITERACY IN THE WRITING CLASS: THE CASE OF *WRITING WITH A PURPOSE*

The treatment of the visual in postsecondary writing instruction has been a tentative one in many of the same ways as those early attempts to bring mass media into English classrooms. As a case in point, the story of how visual elements were incorporated into successive editions of a single and very popular twentieth-century college writing text (James McCrimmon's *Writing with a Purpose*) can serve to mirror the history of the visual in writing classes, especially as it indicates a clear impulse to include the visual but not always a consistent or stable way of doing that.[4]

Although some visual elements (primarily charts, graphs, and diagrams) were present even in 1950 in the first edition,[5] it wasn't until 1972 when *Writing with a Purpose* introduced a visual assignment, organized around eighteenth-century British artist William Hogarth's prints *Beer Street* and *Gin Lane*, that the textbook used visuals as an integral part of any writing assignment. According to Dean Johnson of Houghton Mifflin,

> The Hogarth pictures were introduced in the fifth edition (cy 1972) and used through the eighth edition (cy 1984). Originally they were the stuff of an exercise to support observation as a means of gathering material. In each edition, however, they were treated differently. In the seventh edition, for example, they were used to illustrate a so-called "three step method of interpretation" (e.g., observe, interpret, infer).[6]

By the eighth edition, the Hogarth prints were linked to lessons in the chapter on planning strategies.

In his discussion of how the 1970s editions of *Writing with a Purpose* reflected the changes in the student population, Robert Connors points to the visual design of the fifth edition as indicating a "lowered evaluation of its audience's abilities" signaled by "wide margins and a two-color format to open up the text's appearance" (107). Later editions, Connors writes, are even more prone to a visual appearance that suggests a dumbing down. The 1976 edition, for example, "goes in deeply for the 'visual observation' invention methods . . . It is filled with photos, cartoons, illustrations, all meant to add spice to the text" (108). And, while I would argue that the visual is not at all a simpler form of communication than the verbal, it seems clear that Connors is very likely correct in his assessment of the editorial motives for changing the visual format of *Writing with a Purpose* and, in particular, for adding visuals like the Hogarth prints.

At the outset, the *Beer Street* and *Gin Lane* prints were meant to teach students the art of observation and develop the skill of creating vivid word images—much in the tradition of *ut pictora poesis*, popularized in literary criticism in the late 1950s and early 1960s, especially by Jean Hagstrum's *The Sister Arts*.[7] According to Johnson, the Hogarth prints remained in McCrimmon's text primarily because teachers liked them. Thus, the prints stayed on for several editions because they were popular with faculty who, no doubt, recognized them as not mere popular culture but popular culture in the literary tradition. Assignments linked to the prints changed with changing composition pedagogy.

This last bit of information is useful to keep in mind in the context of a discussion on the place of visuals in the writing classroom. In many respects, the Hogarth prints were absolutely peripheral to whatever writing assignment might be attached to them. Nearly any pair of images might have been used as prompts for the same writing assignments. Within the tradition of verbal/visual communication I am outlining here, only certain kinds of "visual" assignments seem possible for a writing course. Primarily, these would be assignments that use visual images as prompts for essay writing.

Such a tactic was not new with McCrimmon, of course. Lucille Schultz found similar uses of the visual to be common in writing textbooks as far back as the nineteenth century:

> [These texts] rely heavily on illustrations as a teaching tool . . . fairly detailed and complex illustrations were used abundantly in many of the lesser known mid-19th century first books of composition; in addition to common objects, they depicted scenes of home life, school life, and work life, and the illustrations served as writing prompts for young writers who were asked to describe what they saw in the picture. In these books, the illustrations were not simply embellishment or ornament, they were an integral part of the book's instructional practice. (12)

Though these early texts commonly used pictures (often reproductions of paintings) as prompts for student compositions, the aim of each exercise was to bring students to a more vivid or accurate use of written language.[8] Often, the authors made an elaborate case for the advantage or superiority of words over pictures. The Gardiner, Kittredge, and Arnold comment that opens this paper, for example, appears at first to be an argument for the primacy of the visual over the verbal, but the authors go on to say, "what can a picture tell you about wind or heat, about sound or smell, about motion, about the feeling of roughness or moisture? Nothing *directly*; it can only *suggest*" (166, emphasis in original).

"*Drawings are generally more accessible than essays to those college students who are inadequately prepared in reading.*" (vii)

—Lewis Meyers, 1980

Of course, other kinds of assignments involving visuals do occur in college writing pedagogies. Visual analysis (especially advertising analysis) has been commonplace in postsecondary writing instruction for at least fifty years as a part of the post-World War II emphasis on propaganda and semantics characteristic of many composition and communication courses beginning in the 1940s,[9] but that practice did not always or consistently include careful consideration of how images, layout, or graphics actually communicated meaning. Instead, advertising was treated as a subject for critique rather than itself a form of communication that employed both word and image. A 1975 CCC article by D. G. Kehl describes an advertising analysis assignment typical for composition in the seventies. Though Kehl does make a brief reference to the images (the pictures) in particular ads, he does so only to suggest that the ad image functions to replicate the "controlling idea" or "central thesis" of a traditional argument essay of the sort students might be assigned to write. Like the McCrimmon assignments, Kehl used advertising as a sort of shadow essay, a form once removed from the actual written essay students would produce. Kehl's stated motive for using advertising at all is one repeated by many of his colleagues throughout this period: He argues that this is a good assignment, especially "For students who are visually but not necessarily verbally sensitive" (135). Running through much of the composition literature of the period, assignments linked to images carried with them a call for relevance, the need to make this dull, required class more interesting, and the suggestion that less verbal students would perhaps succeed with pictures where they could not with words. These were sometimes arguments for using popular culture in the writing class but not always.[10]

For many instructors during this same period, the use of visuals went hand in hand with expressivist pedagogies. In 1972, for example, Harcourt Brace Jovanovich published Joseph Frank's *You*, a trendy writing text loaded with photos, paintings, ads, drawings, and graphic designs. The basic assumption of this text was that each student was an individual who had something to say and could find a voice with which to say it. The focus is clearly on the self as Frank tells students, "*You* is also concerned with perception, for how and what you perceive determines who you are" (iii). Thus, assignments tied to visuals asked students how a particular image made them feel or of what an image reminded them. One assignment even juxtaposes a Rorschach-like inkblot with an abstract painting to get at how an image can be created "deliberately trying to expand both [the painter's] and the viewer's consciousness" (100). And, of course, Walker Gibson's *Seeing and Writing*, written around this same time, makes much the same argument for using visual media in the writing classroom.

Throughout much of the work mentioned so far, there runs an ongoing suspicion that the visual must somehow be important to writing. It just isn't entirely clear how.

> "*Learning to see well helps students write well.*"
>
> —*Donald and Christine McQuade, 1999*

Are images strategies for getting students to pay attention to detail? Do they mimic the rhetoric of verbal argument? Are they a dumbing down of writing instruction making visible to nonverbal students what the verbally gifted can conceptualize? Certainly, there is the message in much of this work that images may be useful, even proper stimuli for writing, but they are no substitute for the complexity of language.

THE TURN TO CULTURAL THEORY

When David Bartholomae and Anthony Petrosky reprinted a portion of John Berger's *Ways of Seeing* in their 1987 composition reader (and named their text *Ways of Reading* in a nod to Berger's work), they connected the visual arts very directly with the world of language. Berger's *Ways of Seeing* initially shook the world of art history with its insistence upon the social production of art. As a text about meaning and culture, *Ways of Seeing* has been even more important to a broader audience.[11] Berger begins his argument simply:

> Seeing comes before words. The child looks and recognizes before it can speak. But there is also another sense in which seeing comes before words. It is seeing which establishes our place in the surrounding world; we explain that world with words, but words can never undo the fact that we are surrounded by it. The relation between what we see and what we know is never settled. . . . The way we see things is affected by what we know or what we believe. In the Middle Ages when men believed in the physical existence of Hell the sight of fire must have meant something different from what it means today. (7–8)

That idea, that images are not a reflection of a fixed reality, that, instead, our ways of understanding the world around us are somehow commingled with how we represent the world visually was a notion that appealed to teachers of writing like Bartholomae and Petrosky who were searching for ways of incorporating cultural theory into the composition classroom.

What was radical about Berger's work was his insistence on breaking down the barriers that separated high culture (in this case art history) from low (advertising). Bartholomae and Petrosky's *Ways of Reading* made that message available to the writing class. In this textbook, not only was meaning no longer restricted to the verbal, the visual was also not used as a gentle step into the "more serious" world of the verbal. As an extract published in a composition reader, *Ways of Seeing* certainly did lead writing teachers to ask students to examine images as culturally informed texts. Yet, the complete written text of Berger's argument was *visually* much farther reaching than any discussion of image analysis might suggest or, at least, than the design of composition readers at the time would allow for.[12]

In a "Note to the Reader" that opens *Ways of Seeing*, Berger writes, "The form of the book is as much to do with our purpose as the arguments contained within it" (5). Berger points particularly to "essays" that consist only of images that "are intended to raise as many questions as the verbal essays" (5). And, yet, he could just as well have been talking about the text's heavy font, the cover design that reproduces the opening remarks of the first essay, or the ragged-right margins that call attention to page design. It would be many years before this very conscious attention to design and its relation to meaning would have much impact at all on college composition courses.

Instead, the push in the eighties was to continue to explore what visuals could teach students about their written compositions. In 1986, for example, William Costanzo, then chair of the NCTE Committee on Film Study, reported in *CCC* on a 1979 NEH project to teach film *as* composition. He lists four arguments for the use of film in teaching writing:

(1) The basic steps of filmmaking can serve as a working model of the composing process . . . (2) . . . An understanding of the visual code which enables us to "read" a movie can help to clarify the conventions of English diction, syntax, punctuation, and usage. (3) Many of the rhetorical principles of film composition (for organizing inchoate experience into meaningful sequence, for achieving a suitable style, for selling a product or an idea) can be applied directly to specific writing tasks. (4) When students' notions of composition are widened to include these more familiar, visual forms, the writing class seems less remote. (79–80)

This urge to tie the use of images in any way possible to "the composing process" was a common one throughout this period.

Costanzo's report would seem rather ordinary, certainly right in line with attitudes we have already witnessed, if it weren't for an afterword he included as the article was being readied for press. In it, Costanzo acknowledges that his report was written five years earlier and that his understanding of the role of film in writing classes has changed considerably since that time. By 1986, Costanzo is no longer making a simple link between the study of film and the teaching of composing strategies. Instead, he writes: "If I once regarded film study as a path to better writing, I now see film and writing as equal partners traveling along the same road" (86). His concluding remarks signal a significant shift in the way he, at least, had begun to think of the role of visual media in the writing class:

> Much of what once seemed revelatory about the role of visual media in our students' lives is now widely accepted, even taken for granted. Film and television continue to dominate a major portion of their formative years, creating expectations, shaping attitudes, influencing language patterns, and providing a common frame of reference. . . . At the same time, ground-breaking work in semiotics, neurophysiology, and cognitive psychology has made strong connections between visual forms of thought and written language. It now appears that the act of writing involves more visual thinking than we recognized in traditional composition classes. (86)

Here, Costanzo was no longer talking about the visual as a convenient heuristic but, instead, asking that compositionists pay attention to "visual thinking" as one way of understanding the written word. Significantly, Costanzo's report appears in the same issue of *CCC* as Stephen Bernhardt's "Seeing the Text," an article arguing for the importance of teaching not images in the writing classroom but writing-as-image or, at least, of noting that the design of a text as well as the words used in the text conveyed meaning. Bernhardt's work indicated a change in the ways many compositionists began to think of "the visual" as it relates to the teaching of writing. For many, that change was most evident in attention to design.

THE INFLUENCE OF DESIGN

Throughout the history of writing instruction in this country, there has been some attention to the visual nature of written compositions, if only, in the earliest textbooks, to emphasize the importance of handwriting or penmanship as a visual representation of the writer's character.[13] And, of course, even today, the one visual reproduction we can count on in even the most contemporary texts is that snapshot of the research paper, complete with title page and works cited. In these lessons on producing the research paper, such visual marks as margins, page layout, and font size take on the utmost importance, again, in visually representing the seriousness and thoroughness with which the student has approached the assignment. In effect, they become a sign of academic decorum.

For many years, in fact, the research paper section was literally the only place in a composition textbook where we might encounter any reference to page design, layout, or font choices; primarily, we found a reminder to double space, choose a readable font appropriate for serious work (12-point Times, perhaps), and use "normal" margins. That has begun to change, especially since the first edition of John Trimbur's *Call to Write*, which includes a brief chapter on document design as well as attention to visual communication throughout in genres as various as flyers, posters, Web pages, and public service ads.[14]

In his most recent scholarship, Trimbur examines the "materiality of literacy from the perspective that writing is a visible language produced and circulated in material forms" ("Delivering" 188). This attention to the production of text as visible language, emphasizing "the composer's work . . . to make the special signs we call writing" (189) is one that links literacy practice with production and distribution of text and to the history and theory of graphic design (see also Trimbur, "Composition"). Perhaps even more useful for the future of visual communication and writing studies is Trimbur's use of the work of Walter Benjamin who "offers a way to think about how the study and teaching of writing might take up the visual . . . as more than just new texts and topics . . . to write about" ("Delivering" 199–200). As this work suggests, recent emphasis on design history, research, and theory marks a turn in the way scholars and teachers might begin thinking of composition and its relation to graphic design.

Such a turn is, however, very recent. Even as late as 1987, discussion of page design was minimal and often tied to word processing technology or desktop publishing. In March 1987, for example, *College English* ran a Macintosh™ ad entitled "A lesson in English Composition." The ad copy suggests that a Mac can make proofreading, copyediting, and formatting easier. The sample page offered in the ad—"created on a Macintosh"—tells a very different story. This very professional looking page clearly argues that it is the visual dimension of this composition that is most intriguing—layout, graphics, fonts, pull-out quotes. "With a Macintosh your students can prepare compositions that look like classics," the ad reads. "The rest is for posterity to judge."

Perhaps more than any other technology, desktop publishing has moved writing instruction into the world of design, despite, I suspect, our best efforts to contain composition in the essay of the sort familiar in *Harper's* or *Esquire* or *The Atlantic*.[15] To talk of literacy instruction in terms of *design* means to ask writers to draw on available knowledge and, at the same time, transform that knowledge/those forms as we redesign. Design, the New London Group writes, "will never simply reproduce Available Designs. Designing transforms knowledge in producing new constructions and representations of reality" (76; see also Buchanan on the rhetoric of design).[16]

> *"What are we likely to carry with us when we ask that our relationship with all technologies should be like that we have with the technology of printed words?" (349)*
>
> —Anne Wysocki and Johndan
> Johnson-Eilola, 1999

If I have given the impression that the media revolution of the fifties and sixties was a tough one for composition teachers, then I must say here that the world of graphic design, electronic text, and Web technologies certainly will prove even more difficult, though ultimately perhaps more useful for future understandings of composition as design. As with written compositions, Web pages must have an internal coherence; they must, in other words, be navigable. Unlike written compositions, the internal logic of a Web piece is likely to appear first in the visual construction of the page—not only in the images chosen but the colors, the placement of text or links, the font, the use of white space, and other elements linked more closely to the world of graphic design than to composition pedagogy. The work of Anne Wysocki is useful here as she challenges writing teachers to rethink their notions of what composition means—beyond the word and inclusive of the visual. Wysocki writes, "When we ask people in our classes to write for the Web we enlarge what we mean by composition. None of us are unaware of the visuality of the Web, of how that initial default, neutral grey has a different blankness than typing-paper" ("Monitoring Order"). And whether it is true or not that their teachers are aware of the difference between the blank screen and the blank page, our students are certainly aware of this difference. Many already compose for the Web. Many have worked in the realm of the visual (or the *virtual*) as constitutive of composing texts of all sorts years before they get to their first-year college courses.

THE PLACE OF THE VISUAL IN COMPOSITION TODAY

At this point (feeling just a bit like Tristram Shandy telling the story of his life), I must back up once more before I go forward, this time to emphasize how much has changed in the ways we have thought about our students' work in composition over the past twenty-five years or more. In 1975, Harris K. Leonard, writing about his use of *Superman* comics to teach concepts from the classics, expresses concern over his students' request to make their own comics. This is how he describes the situation:

> Once the students realized how influential comic books were, some of them began to inquire why they could not write their own comics, reflecting their own heritage and their own reality. This was a difficult question,

but as a teacher of the classics I had only one way to answer it. When they finished the course they would be able to write their own comics. However, the reason they were in college was not to learn comic book writing, but to counter the comic book mentality of our age with a more educated vision. The classics provide that vision. The classics are classics because they represent the finest and most humane statement on the universal human condition. . . . (406)

Nearly twenty-five years later, Lester Faigley in "Material Literacy and Visual Design," describes several Web sites he has encountered that are composed by teens as young as fifteen. "I find these sites remarkable for a number of reasons," Faigley writes, "not the least of which is the considerable design talent of these adolescents" (173). He goes on to compare these teens' thought-provoking and creative uses of image, text, and technology to the dull sameness of official sites created for mainstream companies. At no point in this article does Faigley seem remotely worried that these students are not learning what they should be learning in school. He seems to be asking, instead, why it is that we (their teachers) don't seem to understand how sophisticated these literacy practices actually are.

I don't mean to target Leonard here. His response is one that had a certain currency at the time and is right in line with what I've been describing throughout this discussion. Comics might have seemed like a useful way to get students into the "real" work of the course, but the notion that students should want to create their own comics "reflecting their own heritage and their own reality" would have seemed silly to many good teachers even in the fourth quarter of the last century.

I began by claiming that our students have a much richer imagination for how the visual might enter composition than our journals have yet to address, and so I return here to those students whose work opens this paper. In my assignment (see Appendix), I simply asked for a *visual argument*. The form, medium, and aim of the argument was up to the students. The course was a first-year seminar meant to introduce students to university-level work and to make a passing nod, at any rate, in the direction of oral, written, and visual communication practices. For many faculty across campus, I suspect such a course might represent precisely what Leonard was after in 1975, an introduction to the "great works of western culture."

The visual argument is an assignment I have given for at least five years now, but, like Faigley in his encounter with student work, I was struck in the fall of 2000 by how many more students seemed comfortable in the realm of visual design than had in years before and by how very few of them asked what I meant by visual argument. Moreover, these students turned to all sorts of visual design, as the assignment sheet suggested they might, for their projects. Those less comfortable with "art work" chose to create charts, diagrams, or maps. Those like Jake Betzold or Andy Waisanen, more comfortable with digital design and Web technologies, worked with PhotoShop® to make digital "paintings" or set up Web sites devoted to the course. Deirdre's flag was created by using colored construction paper, scissors, glue, and a photocopier. Not one of these students seemed to think that their visual argument was any less complicated or took less research or thought than the typical argument essay that they were also assigned in the course.

When I told other faculty teaching sections of the same course that I would be asking my students to construct a visual argument, many were more than skeptical. They wanted to know if such a genre exists and, if it does, how can it be taught, and for what reason might I use it—except, perhaps, to keep students doing "interesting projects." Primarily, faculty asked how I could evaluate visual arguments since some students, according to these faculty, are just more visual/more visually talented than others. Perhaps the most important of these questions is the first: What is a visual argument?

In 1996, analytic philosopher J. Anthony Blair, writing on "The Possibility and Actuality of Visual Arguments," just barely manages to agree that a visual argument, possessing all of the "salient properties of arguments," could actually be said to exist, and if it could be said to exist, it would have to be quite strictly "non-verbal visual communication" (26). To summarize Blair briefly, an argument must make a claim (an assertion), motivated by reasons for the claim, communicated to an audience in an attempt to convince that audience (the recipient) to accept the claim on the basis of the reasons offered (24). In this definition, drawn from the work of D. J. O'Keefe, claims must be "linguistically explicable" though not necessarily expressed linguistically. In other words, there is room here for the possibility of a non-verbal assertion.

To be faithful to Blair's position, I would have to say that, though he does acknowledge that visual argument is possible and even that visual arguments have been made, he does not hold out much hope for making one that is either propositionally complex or at all unique. Of course, in order to make his own argument, Blair must assert that the visual is open to interpretation in a way that words are not.[17] Such an assertion can only be made if one believes that the verbal and visual both involve communication of meaning. Certainly, parallels between verbal and visual communication do exist, which is why Blair finds himself agreeing, if grudgingly, that visual argument is *possible*.

My own requirements for visual argument are less rigid than Blair's, though I certainly accept his primary description of argument and ask that visual arguments make a claim or assertion and attempt to sway an audience by offering reasons to accept that claim. The simplest way for me to explain visual argument (and one I use with my own students) is to begin with visual parody, especially of the sort familiar to readers of *Adbusters* or the Guerilla Girls. Visual parody, like verbal parody, does make an overt claim, assertion, or proposition that draws particularly on comparison, juxtaposition, and intertextuality to offer the assertion to an audience for acceptance.[18] But visual arguments do not need to be parodic. All sorts of visuals make assertions and develop those assertions with visual information.

Though I would reject Blair's notion that a visual argument must be entirely nonverbal, I would say that a visual argument must make its case primarily through the visual. Deirdre's argument, for example, makes use of the flag as a visual expression of nationhood. Through research, she learned what the original Congo Free State flag was supposed to be saying about that nation. Her assertion, that what Europeans really brought to Africa was not enlightenment but slavery is carried through visually. To make an argument that would convince her audience, she used visuals familiar to that audience, in this case, a class of first-year students in a seminar called Africa in the Popular Imagination. She drew from books the class had read and images the class had seen. In other words, her argument was visually powerful and easily read by her target audience. Though some readers might consider her assertion somewhat sentimental or oversimplified, I do not read it that way at all. The students in this course, including students from Rwanda, Botswana, and Ghana had not heard the history of Leopold's Congo before the course—in particular, the international human rights movement generated by events of the time. The American students began the course recalling stories they had heard or read of African exploration, and most assumed that explorers had opened the Congo, as well as other areas of the continent, up to development of the best sort. Deirdre's decision to turn Leopold's flag back on him, to show it for what it was, represents an attempt on her part to ask her audience to reread the history of Congo exploration and to rethink the state of civilization and art that thrived there before Leopold's Congo Free State.

The same could be said of Boikhutso's map and Grace's place setting. Grace took from the course Leopold's statement that he meant to get for himself "a piece of this magnificent African cake" and extended that to the ludicrous: the king who sees an entire continent as his to feast upon. This, in contrast to the propaganda at the time in which Leopold represented himself as a great philanthropist taking the Congo region under his protection in order to end slavery and ensure international free trade. Her audience knew the background for her argument, and so her piece was shaped for that audience.

Boikhutso's map series aims for a much more difficult position statement. Though his argument might be read as obvious (it is obvious that we can never return to a precolonial Africa), that is not necessarily a position available to everyone involved. Boikhutso began the course by wanting to explain current Zimbabwe land disputes: why some Africans might feel that white settlers should be run off the land no matter the cost. These land disputes, which have become quite bloody, are for some involved an attempt to return Africans to land that was once theirs. As Boikhutso illustrates, theirs is a fruitless attempt if they believe that they can return to precolonial Africa. As he said in his presentation, "African people must learn to deal with what is here; not to try to recover what cannot be recovered." And, though some might see that argument as self-evident or one only useful for a first-year seminar in a small town, it is an argument Boikhutso felt needed to be made to the people involved today in actual violent and ongoing land battles.

The students in these classes were clearly very serious about the arguments they were making. They were also quite serious about how a visual argument should be evaluated. Given an opportunity to design evaluation criteria, students turned to the same criteria we would find common for written arguments: Does the visual make an argument? How well does the visual communicate that argument? Is the argument relevant to the course and to the assignment? Is it interesting? Is it clear or focused?

In other words, these students and others like them took the visual in its broadest sense as a form of communication through which they could make a sophisticated and relevant argument. And, though their evaluation criteria could certainly come under scrutiny within the context of schooling and how schooling elevates certain values/certain ways of thinking over others, I choose to offer them as one way of illustrating how the students saw these assignments fitting into their course work as it is typically evaluated.

COMPOSITION IN A VISUAL AGE

The history I have outlined clearly links words to high culture and the visual to low, words to production and images to consumption. And yet, as Cynthia Selfe has suggested, teachers of English composition have not, until very recently, had the means to produce communication that went very far beyond the word.[19] Many of us still remember producing dittos and stencils. We worked long and tedious hours armed with razor blades, correcting fluid, and as much patience as we could muster given the state of our fingers and hands covered with ink and cracking from printing chemicals. The idea of *producing* anything that went beyond that often blotched or botched handout would have been unthinkable. As well, most English teachers have not been trained in visual thinking beyond the level of *ut pictora poesis* or of media criticism. My own abilities in graphic design are very clearly limited by my willingness to learn software, to the clipart and borders available in that software, and to my barely tutored eye for design and page layout.[20]

Teachers who have been interested in using the visual in writing classes have generally limited their discussions to analysis because there were few ways of doing otherwise. Certainly, more recent access to the Internet and to desktop publishing has given teachers ways of incorporating visual thinking into the writing class, but even that will take time and money and equipment and training. And, again, while some teachers have access to state-of-the-art technology, many others have trouble finding an overhead projector that works or arrives in the classroom on time. My guess is that many of these difficulties will not ease up in yet another age of back-to-basics talk and threats of outcomes-based funding. Yet, our students will continue to work with whatever technology—much of it primarily visual—they can get their hands on.

For those scholars and teachers like Wysocki, Faigley, Trimbur, Johnson-Eilola, and others who are raising new questions about verbal and visual communication, the issue seems to be less one of resources than of emphasis or, rather, relationship. The question for me is not whether, "Learning to see well helps students write well," as Donald and Christine McQuade claim in their 1999 textbook *Seeing and Writing* (vii). Instead, the question is much closer to one Anne Wysocki and Johndan Johnson-Eilola ask: "What are we likely to carry with us when we ask that our relationship with all technologies should be like that we have with the technology of printed words?" (349).

Whether that question will lead us, as the New London Group and others suggest, toward multiliteracies or toward composition as design or simply toward a more complete way of understanding verbal and visual communication practices is not resolved. What such a question, and others like it, does lead to, however, is a new configuration of verbal/visual relationships, one that does allow for more than image analysis, image-as-prompt, or image as dumbed-down language. For students who have grown up in a technology-saturated and an image-rich culture, questions of communication and composition absolutely will include the visual, not as attendant to the verbal but as complex communication intricately related to the world around them.

ACKNOWLEDGMENTS

In my world, all scholarship is collaborative, and so I would like to thank the many friends and colleagues who took time to read and advise me on this article as it went through several incarnations. Among them, I particularly thank John Trimbur, Jeanette Harris, Diane Shoos,

Cindy Selfe, Anne Wysocki, Julia Jasken, and Robert Johnson. Marilyn Cooper, Jack Selzer, and Joseph Harris provided careful and invaluable commentary in the final shaping of the article. I am especially grateful to MTU students Boikhutso Jibula, Deirdre Johns, Grace VanCamp, Derrick Siebert, Jake Betzold, and Andy Waisanen for permission to use or refer to their compositions in this article.

APPENDIX

Africa in the Popular Imagination
Making a Visual Argument

So far this term, we have talked about how popular ideas and ideals are conveyed in film and in explorers' journals and reports. As well, we have talked about how these ideas can be changed, corrected, enriched by such investigations as Hochschild's *King Leopold's Ghost* or E. D. Morel's reports on the conditions in the Congo at the turn of the century. You have also looked at maps to note how a map can convey a particular argument or idea.

For this next assignment, I want you to make a **visual argument** about Africa and its people. We have been focusing on events in the Congo and on early explorations and reports, so it will be easiest if you focus your work on the issues, people, or ideas you have found in your reading and in the films you have watched.

You'll notice, for example, that even the cover of Hochschild's history makes a visual argument by layering a photo of mutilated African villagers on top of the portrait of Leopold to suggest the two are intricately connected.

A visual argument can take any form you wish. Here are a few suggestions:

1. Make a new cover for one of the books you have read—*Tarzan* or *King Leopold's Ghost* or *Through the Dark Continent* or *Heart of Darkness* or *Travels in West Africa*.

2. Draw a map that conveys an idea of the changing nature of Africa after Leopold— changing populations, exports of raw materials vs. imports, changing political boundaries, changing transportation systems, etc.

3. Design a chart or visually powerful table to convey one or more of these changes.

4. Create a Web page (just the opening page for now) that introduces readers to the issues you think are important.

5. Make a flyer.

6. Create a collage of photos and maps you find that help you convey an argument.

7. Make a painting.

8. Draw a diagram.

You will present your argument to the class. Be sure to tell the class what decisions you made to create your argument and how well you think you got your position across.

The visual can cover any of the material from the beginning of the course through our discussions of *Heart of Darkness*.

NOTES

1. *King Leopold's Ghost* is a history of Leopold of Belgium's colonization of the Congo.

2. I first began assigning visual arguments several years ago at a suggestion from John Trimbur whose work very much informs my own here.

3. The New London Group formed in September 1994 at a meeting in New London, New Hampshire. The ten women and men who make up the group are Courtney B. Cazden, Bill Cope, Norman Fairclough, James Paul Gee, Mary Kalantzis, Gunther Kress, Carmen Luke, Sarah Michaels, Martin Nakata, and Joseph Lo Bianco. Their original manifesto appeared in the *Harvard Educational Review* in 1996 and is cited here under "New London Group." A version of that original piece also appears as the first chapter of the book-length collection *Multiliteracies: Literacy Learning and the Design of Social Futures* cited here under Cope and Kalantzis. For more information on the group, see Trimbur, "Review of *Multiliteracies.*"

4. I choose *Writing with a Purpose* here partially because of its popularity and long life but also because Robert Connors (*Composition-Rhetoric*) chose it as a text illustrative of composition pedagogy from the 1950s into the 1970s. Moreover, this was in no way a media-based composition book, and so an examination of McCrimmon's inclusion of the visual for this text can serve to suggest how the visual entered many non-media-based composition classrooms for many years.

5. In Robert Connors's discussion of this text he notes that there were "no illustrations at all in the first three editions, but by the mid-1970s *Writing with a Purpose* contained over thirty pictures and photographs" (106). Actually, there were illustrations in that first edition though no photographs. The illustrations occur in the research paper assignment where McCrimmon has reproduced several graphs and charts.

6. Personal e-mail correspondence with author, April 7, 1996.

7. Jean Hagstrum argues that, though the typical rendering of the phrase came to be "Let a poem be like a painting," there is little warrant for that particular interpretation (9–10).

8. See Lucille Schultz's discussion (18–19) of John Frost's 1839 text, *Easy Exercises in Composition* and A. R. Phippen's 1854 *The Illustrated Composition Book*.

9. See Diana George and John Trimbur ("Communication Battle") for a further discussion of this period in writing instruction.

10. In fact, a brief survey of *CCC* during this period reveals a growing desire to explain how and why we might bring images into the writing class though the assignments are all slightly different, each with different aims. For example, a 1974 "Staffroom Interchange" piece reports on the benefits of assigning a cassette-slide show in required composition as a way to reach what the authors called "non-verbal/right-hemisphere-dominated" students who "find it up-to-date and relevant to their world of movies and TV" (Burnett and Thomason 430). In 1977, Jack Kligerman argued for the use of photography in the composition class to teach students to see objectively, to learn to detail what they see in an image before they try to interpret that image. Here, photography is used as a kind of heuristic aiding the art of selection, planning, arranging, and observing because, Kligerman says of students, "as writers, one of their main problems is to learn to 'capture' a scene in language, to make or re-make part of the world" (174). In his article, Kligerman expressed special concern that students simply weren't ready to interpret what they saw until they could objectively list the details of the world surrounding them: "For unless we can get our students to record what they see in the most unmetaphorical, uninterpretive way," Kligerman writes, "then as teachers we are merely helping them confirm what they already believe. Moreover, we could be reinforcing habits and making it impossible

for them to discover a world 'out there' and, perhaps, a basis for inductive reasoning" (176). The picture as evidence of a fixed and knowable outside reality is the lesson here.

11. *Ways of Seeing* was a BBC television series before it came out in book form.

12. Publishers have, off and on, attempted to play with the more traditional design of writing texts. Joseph Frank's *You*, mentioned above, is one example of that. However, it has not been until very recently, perhaps with the publication of Donald McQuade and Christine McQuade's *Seeing and Writing*, that design allowed the visual to take much more than an illustrative role as a supplement to the written text or as a way of making the written text more appealing to the eye.

13. See, for example, Brainard Kellogg's 1891 discussion of letter writing with its emphasis on penmanship in A *Text-Book on Rhetoric Supplementing the Development of the Science with Exhaustive Practice in Composition.*

14. The shift toward normalizing the visual in writing instruction is also one impulse behind many of the assignments in Diana George and John Trimbur's *Reading Culture*, particularly in Visual Culture, Mining the Archive, and Fieldwork sections.

15. In "Delivering the Message," John Trimbur provides a brief bibliographic sketch indicating how design studies is beginning to make itself felt in writing studies.

16. For a further discussion of design and multiliteracies, see Gunther Kress, "Design and Transformation"; Bill Cope and Mary Kalantzis, "Designs for Social Futures"; and Kress, "Multimodality."

17. See, for example, J. Anthony Blair's assertion that "the conditions of visual expression are indeterminate to a much greater degree than is the case with verbal expression" (27).

18. See Diana George and Diane Shoos for a more thorough discussion of intertextuality and George and Trimbur (*Reading Culture*, 211–15) for assignments based on visual parody.

19. As Cynthia Selfe points out, "I don't think people remain unconvinced that the visual is important, but I don't think they know how to make that turn" from words to the visual. These comments were made during a telephone conversation with the author, December 4, 2000.

20. Add to that the fact that (as we often tell each other about computers in the classroom) technology is unevenly distributed. Ten years ago, it would have been a luxury for many faculty to have consistent access to a video player and inexpensive videos not to mention the capacity for making videotapes of their own. Copyright laws have made some copying, even some video rental for classroom, difficult. Both videotapes and DVDs are now produced without any permission rights for public showing. In the end, just showing an ad or a clip of a film or television program for class discussion can be considered off-limits if some of the most conservative interpretations of copyright laws are observed.

If a classroom is not wired for Internet use, the expense of visuals can be far beyond the reach of most English teachers. Some of the most useful tapes for teaching media analysis, for example, are extremely expensive if individual teachers must purchase them, running from as low as $19.95 to as high as $295 for tapes from such sources as Media Education Foundation. Even cheap rentals are not a wholly satisfying solution to the problem I outline here.

WORKS CITED

Bartholomae, David, and Anthony Petrosky. *Ways of Reading*. Boston: St. Martin's, 1987.
Berger, John. *Ways of Seeing*. London: BBC and Penguin, 1977.
Bernhardt, Stephen. "Seeing the Text." *College Composition and Communication* 37 (1986): 66–78.

Blair, J. Anthony. "The Possibility and Actuality of Visual Arguments." *Argumentation and Advocacy* 33 (1996): 23–39.

Boutwell, William D., ed. *Using Mass Media in the Schools.* New York: Appleton-Century-Crofts, 1962.

Buchanan, Richard. "Declaration by Design: Rhetoric, Argument, and Demonstration in Design Practice." *Design Discourse: History, Theory, Criticism.* Ed. Victor Margolin. Chicago: Chicago UP, 1989. 91–109.

Burnett, Esther, and Sandra Thomason. "The Cassette-Slide Show in Required Composition." *College Composition and Communication* 25 (1974): 426–30.

Connors, Robert J. *Composition-Rhetoric: Backgrounds, Theory, and Pedagogy.* Pittsburgh: Pittsburgh UP, 1997.

Cope, Bill, and Mary Kalantzis. *Multiliteracies: Literacy Learning and the Design of Social Futures.* London: Routledge, 2000.

———. "Designs for Social Futures." Cope and Kalantzis 203–34.

Costanzo, William. "Film As Composition." *College Composition and Communication* 37 (1986): 79–86.

Faigley, Lester. "Material Literacy and Visual Design." *Rhetorical Bodies: Toward a Material Rhetoric.* Ed. Jack Selzer and Sharon Crowley. Madison: U of Wisconsin P, 1999. 171–201.

Flesch, Rudolf. *The Art of Readable Writing.* New York: Harper, 1949.

Frank, Joseph. *You.* New York: Harcourt Brace Jovanovich. 1972.

Gardiner, John Hays, George Lyman Kittredge, and Sarah Louise Arnold. *The Mother Tongue: Elements of English Composition, Book III.* Boston: Ginn & Company, 1902.

George, Diana, and Diane Shoos. "Dropping Breadcrumbs in the Intertextual Forest: or, We Should Have Brought a Compass." Ed. Gail Hawisher and Cynthia Selfe, *Passions, Pedagogies, and Twentieth-First Century Technologies.* Logan: Utah State UP, 1999. 115–26.

George, Diana, and John Trimbur. "The Communication Battle, or, Whatever Happened to the Fourth C?" *College Composition and Communication* 50 (1999): 682–98.

———. *Reading Culture: Contexts for Critical Reading and Writing,* 4th ed. New York: Longman, 2001.

Gibson, Walker. *Seeing and Writing.* 2nd ed. New York: D. McKay Co., 1974.

Hagstrum, Jean H. *The Sister Arts: The Tradition of Literary Pictorialism and English Poetry from Dryden to Gray.* Chicago: Chicago UP, 1958.

Hochschild, Adam. *King Leopold's Ghost.* Boston: Houghton Mifflin, 1998.

Kehl, D. G. "The Electric Carrot: The Rhetoric of Advertisement." *College Composition and Communication* 26 (1975): 134–40.

Kellogg, Brainerd. *A Text-Book on Rhetoric Supplementing the Development of the Science with Exhaustive Practice in Composition.* New York: Effingham Maynard, 1891.

Kismaric, Carole, and Marvin Heiferman. *Growing Up with Dick and Jane.* San Francisco: Collins, 1996.

Kligerman, Jack. "Photography, Perception, and Composition," *College Composition and Communication* 28 (1977): 174–78.

Kress, Gunther. "Design and Transformation: New Theories of Meaning." Cope and Kalantzis 153–61.

———. "Multimodality." Cope and Kalantzis 182–202.

Leonard, Harris K. "The Classics—Alive and Well with Superman," *College English* 37 (1975): 405–07.

McCrimmon, James. *Writing with a Purpose*. Boston: Houghton Mifflin, 1950.

McCrimmon, James, Joseph F. Trimmer, and Nancy Sommers. *Writing with a Purpose*. 8th ed. Boston: Houghton Mifflin, 1984.

McQuade, Donald, and Christine McQuade. *Seeing and Writing*. Boston: Bedford/St. Martin's, 2000.

Meyers, Lewis. *Seeing Writing*. New York: Harcourt Brace Jovanovich, 1980.

Mitchell, W. J. T. *Picture Theory*. Chicago: U of Chicago P, 1994.

New London Group. "A Pedagogy of Multiliteracies: Designing Social Futures." *Harvard Educational Review* 66 (1996): 60–92.

Postman, Neil. *Amusing Ourselves to Death*. New York: Penguin, 1985.

——. *Television and the Teaching of English*. New York: Appleton-Century-Crofts, Inc., 1961.

Schultz, Lucille M. "Elaborating Our History: A Look at Mid-19th Century First Books of Composition." *College Composition and Communication* 45 (1994): 10–30.

Trimbur, John. *The Call to Write*. New York: Longman, 1999.

——. "Composition and the Circulation of Writing." *College Composition and Communication* 52 (2000): 188–219.

——. "Delivering the Message: Typography and the Materiality of Writing." *Composition As Intellectual Work*. Ed. Gary Olson. Carbondale: Southern Illinois UP, 2002. 188–202.

——. "Review of *Multiliteracies: Literacy Learning and the Design of Social Futures*." *College Composition and Communication* 52 (2001): 659–62.

Willens, Anita. "TV—Lick It or Join It?" Boutwell, 254-56.

Wysocki, Anne Frances. "Monitoring Order: Visual Desire, the Organization of Web Pages, and Teaching the Rules of Design." *Kairos* 3.2 (Fall 1998). 12 Jun. 2002 <http://www.hu.mtu.edu/~awysocki>.

Wysocki, Anne Frances, and Johndan Johnson-Eilola. "Blinded by the Letter: Why Are We Using Literacy As a Metaphor for Everything Else?" *Passions, Pedagogies, and Twenty-First Century Technologies*. Ed. Gail Hawisher and Cynthia Selfe. Utah State UP, 1999. 349–68.

Made Not Only in Words

Composition in a New Key

KATHLEEN BLAKE YANCEY

Words strain,

Crack and sometimes break, under the burden,

Under the tension, slip, slide, perish,

Decay with imprecision, will not stay in place,

Will not stay still.

Sometimes, you know, you have a moment.

For us, this is one such moment. In coming together at CCCC, we leave our institutional sites of work; we gather together—we quite literally convene—at a not-quite-ephemeral site of disciplinary and professional work.

At this opening session in particular, inhabited with the echoes of those who came before and anticipating the voices of those who will follow—we pause and we commence.

We have a moment.

I come to this podium this morning fully conscious of the rather daunting responsibility attached to this occasion—a responsibility heightened by what my distinguished predecessors have said in their Chair's Addresses.

—Anne Ruggles Gere 1994

Reprinted from *College Composition and Communication* 56.2 (December 2004): 297–328. Used with permission. Due to space constraints, material originally set as sidebars is now set as centered, italic text within two lines.

These moments: they aren't all alike, nor are they equal. And how we value them is in part a function of how we understand them, how we connect them to other moments, how we anticipate the moments to come. For compositionists, of this time and of this place, this moment—this moment *right* now—is like none other.

Never before has the proliferation of writings outside the academy so counterpointed the compositions inside. Never before have the technologies of writing contributed so quickly to the creation of new genres. The consequence of these two factors is the creation of a writing public that, in development and in linkage to technology, parallels the development of a reading public in the 19th century. And these parallels, they raise good questions, suggest ways that literacy is created across spaces, across time.

On March 22, 2004, I delivered the "Chair's Address." This talk was twenty-six pages, more or less, double-spaced, and composed in Garamond 12. While I talked, two synchronized PowerPoint slide shows ran independently, one to my right, another to my left. Together, the two slide shows included eighty-four slides.[1] There was one spotlight on me; otherwise, the theatre was dark, lit only by that spot and the slide shows. Oddly, I found myself "delivering" the Chair's Address to an audience I could not see. As Chris Farris pointed out to me later, given this setting, the talk was more dramatic performance than address.

Or: what genre was I invoking?

Literacy today is in the midst of a tectonic change. Even inside of school, never before have writing and composing generated such diversity in definition. What do our references to writing mean? Do they mean print only? That's definitely what writing is if we look at national assessments, assuming that the assessment includes writing at all and is not strictly a test of grammar and usage. According to these assessments—an alphabet soup of assessments, the SAT, the NEAP, the ACT—writing IS "words on paper," composed on the page with a pen or pencil by students who write words on paper, yes—*but* who *also* compose words and images and create audio files on Web logs (blogs), in word processors, with video editors and Web editors and in e-mail and on presentation software and in instant messaging and on listservs and on bulletin boards—and no doubt in whatever genre will emerge in the next ten minutes.[2]

Note that no one is *making* anyone *do* any of this writing. Don't you wish that the energy and motivation that students bring to some of these other genres they would bring to our assignments? How is it that what we teach and what we test can be so different from what our students know as

> *But the main insight I have about my own literacy history is that none of the important or meaningful writing I have ever produced happened as a result of a writing assignment given in a classroom.*
>
> —*Lillian Bridwell Bowles 1995*

writing? What *is* writing, really? It includes print: that seems obvious. But: Does it include writing for the screen? How visual is it? Is it the ability to move textual resources among spaces, as suggested by Johndan Johnson-Eilola? Is composing, as James Porter suggests, not only about medium but also specifically about technology? Suppose I said that basically writing is interfacing? What does that add to our definition of writing? What about the circulation of writing, and the relationship of writing to the various modes of delivery?

In planning this address—what some called a script, others a transcript—I designed a multi-genred and mediated text that would embody and illustrate the claims of the talk. To accomplish this aim, I developed "stock" of two kinds. I collected verbal material, based on readings, some of my own writings, and some of my students' work. Concurrently, I collected images, again from my own work, photographs from places I knew, and images from the public domain. Collecting these different materials and putting them in dialogue with each other was a key part of this composing process.

And what do these questions mean with respect to another kind of delivery, the curricular and pedagogical delivery of college composition, in classroom to seminar room to online chat room to studio?

Collectively, these questions sound a moment for composition in a new key.

To explain what I mean by this more fully, I'll detail what this moment is, and why and how it matters for us, and what it is that we might want to do about it in a talk I have subtitled Composition in Four Quartets.

QUARTET ONE

In my beginning is my end.

We have a moment.

In some ways our moment is like that in 19th-century Britain when a new reading public composed of middle- and working-class peoples came into being. Technology played a major role in this creation: with a new steam printing press and cheaper paper, reading material became more accessible. There were political and economic reasons as well. Economic changes of the 19th century came in the context of a globalization connected to travel, adventure, colonialism, and a massive demographic shift from farm to city changing the

material conditions of work and life.[3] Economically, what has been called the Industrial Age promoted a "rising" middle class, indeed a bourgeoisie, that had the funds to buy print reading material and the leisure in which to read it and that began to have some political rights—and to press for more. From the perspective of literature, the genre receiving the most attention was the novel, which is said to have encouraged readers and in some ways to have created them. As important for our purposes, these novels were often *published in another form first*, typically in serial installments that the public read monthly. In other words, the emergence of this reading public co-occurred with the emergence of a multiply genred and distributed novel. All of Dickens's novels, for instance, were so published, "generally in monthly parts." And the readers were more than consumers; they helped shape the development of the text-in-process. Put differently, the "fluctuations of public demand" influenced the ways that Dickens and other novelists developed future episodes. The British novels of the 19th century were from the very beginning developed and distributed in multiple genres made possible by a new technology, the novelist writing in the context of and for very specific readers who, in turn, provided responses influencing the development of the text in question.

The images, in other words, did not simply punctuate a written text; together words and images were (and are) the materials of composition.[4]

The Chair's Address is, of course, one genre, what Mike Palmquist has called a "call to action" genre. In medium, this address was plural— delivered simultaneously through the human voice and through the PowerPoint slides, both in relation to and also mediated by the twenty-six pages of written text.[5] In response to some requests for the script, I created a version of it in the spirit of an executive summary. *Another version is being developed for* CCC *Online; its logic is different still. And then there is the text you are reading now, which includes a limited number of slides (reproduced) that are arranged anew. This "Chair's Address" also includes new images and new verbal text—like the meta-text you are reading now.*

All of which leads me to ask: how many compositions are in this text?

People read together, sometimes in "reading circles," sites of domestic engagement, but also in public places. Technological constraints—bad lighting, eyesight overstrained by working conditions[6] —encouraged such communal readings, since in this setting no single pair of eyes was overly strained. People also gathered frequently to hear authors read their own works in staged readings. For these 19th-century novels, the patterns of circulation thus included both oral and written forums. Or: new forms of writing—the serials, the newspapers, the triple-decker Victorian novel— encouraged new reading publics who read for new purposes.

And all of this happened outside of school.

Today, we are witnessing a parallel creation, that of a *writing* public made plural, and as in the case of the development of a reading public, it's taking place largely outside of school—and this in an age of universal education. Moreover, unlike what

> *Modern physics long since made us learn that the world out there has more space than stuff anyway, and it is in the spaces that we find relationships.*
>
> *—Richard Lloyd Jones 1978*

happens in our classes, *no one is forcing this public to write.* There are no As here, no Dean's lists, no writing teacher to keep tabs on you. Whatever the exchange value may be for these writers—and there are millions of them, here and around the world—it's certainly not grades. Rather, the writing seems to operate in an economy driven by use value. The context for this writing public, expanded anew, is cause for concern and optimism. On the one hand, a loss in jobs in this country caused (it is said) by globalization is connected to a rise in corporate profits detailed in one accounting report after another, and we are assured by those in Washington that such job loss is actually *good* for us. As one commentator on NPR put it in early March, we've moved from just-in-time jobs to just-in-time people. Such an approach to labor is not news to those of us in composition: we apparently got there first. On the other hand, those committed to another vision of globalization see in it the chance for a (newfound) cooperation and communication among peoples, one with potential to transform the world and its peoples positively. At best, it could help foster a world peace never known before. At least, as we have seen over the course of the last year, it is (finally) more difficult to conduct any war in secret.

It's worth asking what the principles of all these compositions are. Pages have interfaces, although like much that is ubiquitous, we don't attend to such interfaces as we might. The fact that you have one interface governing the entire text, however, does provide a frame. What is the frame for (and thus the theory governing) a composition in multiple parts? For that matter, how does this text—with call outs, palimpsest notes, and images—cohere?

And:
How do we create such a text?
How do we read it?
How do we value it?

Not least, how will we teach it?

Like 19th-century readers creating their own social contexts for reading in reading circles, writers in the 21st century self-organize into what seem to be overlapping technologically driven writing circles, what we might call a series of newly imagined communities, communities that cross borders of all kinds—nation state, class, gender, ethnicity. Composers gather in Internet chat rooms; they participate in listservs dedicated to both the ridiculous and the sublime; they mobilize for health concerns, for political causes, for research, and for travel advice. Indeed, for Howard Dean's candidacy we saw the first blog for a presidential candidate. Many of the Internet texts are multiply genred and purposed: MoveOn.com sends e-mails, collects money, and hosts a Web site simultaneously. Flash mobs gather for minutes-long social outings; political flash mobs gather for purposes of political reform. And I repeat: like the members of the newly developed reading public, the members of the writing public have learned—in this case, to write, to think together, to organize, and to act within these forums—largely without instruction and, more

Because we are essentially in partnership with the wider community attempting to share meaningfully in the working out of a community responsibility, we must be in communication with the other parts of the community.

—Vivian Davis 1979

to the point here, largely without *our* instruction. They need neither self-assessment nor our assessment: they have a rhetorical situation, a purpose, a potentially worldwide audience, a choice of technology and medium—and they write.

The literacies that composers engage in today are multiple. They include print literacy practices (like spelling) that URL's require; they include visual literacy; they include network literacy. As important, these literacies are textured and in relationship to each other. Perhaps most important, these literacies are social in a way that school literacy all too often only pretends to be.

Some of these new Internet genres—e-mail, instant messaging, and so on—divide along lines based in age and in formal schooling. Faculty—the school insiders—use e-mail daily, considering it essential to academic and personal life. In contrast, students use instant messaging at least as often, and unlike most of us, they *like* it. Faculty see blogs—if they see them at all—as (yet) another site for learning, typically in school; students see blogs as a means of organizing social action, a place for geographically far-flung friends to gather, a site for poets and musicians to plan a jam. But our experiences are the same in one key way: most faculty and students alike *all have learned these genres on our own, outside of school.* Given *this* extracurricular writing curriculum and its success, I have to wonder out loud if in some pretty important ways and within the relatively short space of not quite ten years, we may already have become anachronistic.

Of course, as Anne Gere demonstrated in her own Chair's Address, writing has always been embedded in an extra-curriculum. Public institutions now design for such a curriculum, bringing together what computer game designer Frank Lantz calls a convergence of digital and physical space. Examples include new public libraries, especially those in Salt Lake City and in Seattle. In their designs, both architectural and curricular, these institutions overlap and interplay "domestic spaces" (like Seattle's "living room" inside the library), "conventional" library spaces, and electronic spaces.[7]

Kandinsky, Composition VII

Some disturbing data suggests that traditional English departments already are. According to the list of departmental administrators published in the PMLA, over the last twenty years, we have seen a decline in the number of departments called English of about 30%. Let me state this more dramatically: of the number of English departments whose administrators were included on the list in 1985, about one in three has disappeared. Why? They may have simply stopped being represented for any number of reasons: a shortage of funds, a transfer of the listing elsewhere. Naturally, this statistic doesn't mean that English is disappearing as an institutional unit. Most obviously, it means that fewer units calling themselves English are listed in the PMLA. And when plotted against another trend line—the *increase* of units called something other than English, like departments of communication and divisions of humanities—it seems more plausible that *something* reductionist in nature is happening to English departments generally. They are being consolidated into other units or disappearing.[8] Another data point tells the same story: according to the Association of Departments of English (ADE), if English departments were graduating English majors at the same rate graduated in 1966, we would congratulate 100,000 students this year. Instead, we will offer English degrees to half that number—50,000.[9] And these data points may well explain why the number of tenure-line jobs in English continues its now altogether-too-familiar decline (which makes the continuing increase in tenure-line jobs in rhetoric and composition all the more remarkable). Of course, for many of us, this may be a moot point. We may not be housed in English departments ourselves, and most of us don't teach courses in the major because the major continues to be defined as *territorias literati*, a point to which I will return. Still, enough of us do reside in English to understand that as English goes, so may we.

Although interpretations of data around the status of English departments vary, here something in English studies is clearly underway. The data points I report plot one trend line, a line that in its downward direction contrasts with the upward swing of the plot line for rhetoric and composition. In the midst of this moment, a new discourse that repositions English and humanities is emerging. The latest evidence: As I write this, literary scholar Helen Vendler, in her NEH Jefferson Address, has attempted an English-centric redefinition of the humanities that excludes both history and philosophy.

These shifts: are they minor tremors signifying routine academic seismic activity that makes the world more stable? Alternatively, are they tremors occurring along the fault lines of tectonic plates that will in the not-too-distant future change the very topography of higher education?

These questions assume greater significance as evidence of other tremors within higher education make themselves felt. In the last two decades, we've seen a shift in the way the country views higher education. According to a 2004 edition of *U.S. News & World Report* (Shea), beginning in the Reagan era, the U.S.

> *Composition is a part of a higher education and the persistent problems in composition are tied to larger issues in the world, in our country, in higher education generally and in each academic institution specifically.*
>
> —Miriam Chaplin 1988

began moving away from the view that college is good for the *country*, a view that enfranchises all of us, and began shifting toward the view that higher education is good for the *individual*. Given this shift, perhaps it makes a perverse kind of sense that even though more than half of college students work, they still graduate with debt exceeding $15,000. During this same period, public institutions became state-supported institutions, then state-assisted schools, then state-affiliated schools, and now state-located schools. States haven't abandoned support of education: rather, they have redirected the revenue streams away from the institutions and toward the consumers, the students. In other words, historically, public funds went to public institutions; today, in many states, including mine, they go directly to the students—chiefly through scholarships titled Hope or Freedom, which one economist has likened to vouchers for K–12. And the worst-case scenario has already been proposed in Colorado: take all funding for public institutions and distribute it not to them but directly to students.[10] Educationally, in the words of Robert Putnam, we are increasingly bowling alone, and apart from the damage it will do to the individual schools, I worry about the damage it will do to the country as a commons.

Additional evidence of our unwillingness, as members of a commons, to support higher education is abundant. Again, as I write this, President Bush's plan to maintain the level of funding for Pell Grants goes almost unchallenged. Given that tuition costs have risen and the number of eligible students has likewise risen, what this means is less support for students.

Relevant to literacy specifically, we can record other tremors, specifically those associated with the screen, and in that focus, they return us to questions around what it means to write. Further, I'd suggest that they constitute a serious challenge to us. As articulated by Elizabeth Daley, dean of the University of Southern California School of Television & Cinema, this view of literacy makes a clear distinction—both in practice and in institutional home—between print literacy and screen literacy. Linking what happens outside of school to what we might do inside, Daley observes that both in metaphorical analogy and in use, the screen has become ubiquitous. "Metaphors from the screen have become common in our daily conversation," she says ("Expanding" 34). Think about these everyday terms: close up, flash back, frame, cut to the chase, segue. Our daily communicative, social, and intellectual practices are screen-permeated. Further, her argument is that *the screen is the language of the vernacular*, that if we do not include it in the school curriculum, we will become as irrelevant as faculty professing in Latin. "No longer," she declares, "can students be considered truly educated by mastering reading and writing alone. The ability to negotiate through life by combining words with pictures with audio and video to express thoughts will be the mark of the educated student" ("Speaking"). Specifically, she proposes that the literacy of the screen, which she says *parallels* oral literacy and print literacy, become a *third* literacy required of all undergraduates. Not surprisingly, she believes such literacy should be taught not in composition classrooms but in media studies programs. Not least, Daley argues that education needs to get in step with life practices and should endeavor to assist students to negotiate through life.

Part of what's at issue with screen literacy is how it too enables the making of stories, a common question we ask of literary texts, a common question we ask of students and of ourselves. As Daley suggests, the screen is very much part of the thinking around narrative. In reviewing 21 Grams, *for instance, film critic Roger Ebert brings the issue into relief (perhaps ironically?) when he says: "Imagining how heartbreaking the conclusion would have been if we had arrived at it in the ordinary way by starting at the beginning, I felt as if an unnecessary screen of technique had been placed between the story and the audience."*

What do these conceptions of reading and writing publics, these tremors in the world and in higher education and in English have to do with composition?

QUARTET TWO

A people without history
Is not redeemed from time, for history is a pattern
Of timeless moments.

We have a moment.

What we make of this moment is contextualized by our own history as a discipline. Many have noted the role that first-year composition played in the formation of CCCC: it was our raison d'etre—and a worthy cause. We focused then on the gatekeeping

Someone has estimated that there are at least nine thousand of us teaching in college courses in composition and communication.

—John Gerber 1950

moment, the moment when students enter college and in particular on that transition moment between high school and college. It's worth considering, however, how this gatekeeping situation has changed in the last fifty-five years.

Early in the decade when CCCC was formed, in 1949, only 30% of students graduated from high school; only 20% of high school graduates even began college, typically at four-year liberal arts institutions; and fewer than 6% graduated. Today, depending on your source, about 89% of students graduate from high school, and some 65% begin college ("America's"). In other words, at various times—in high school in AP classes and dual-enrollment classes, just after high school, years after completing high school—many students—indeed most students—do begin college.[11]

It's almost impossible to know how many students finish high school. Some finish after four years; some finish after another year or two in an alternative setting; some finish through the GED program. And it is so that some don't finish at all. Where they don't finish, typically in urban settings and in impoverished states, life is harder all the way around. Still, if we in college could graduate the same percentage of students as our colleagues in high school do, we'd nearly triple our graduation rate.

But what happens? They don't finish: only 28% of Americans complete four years of college. It looks bleaker as you go to certain categories: 17% of African Americans have college degrees, 10.6% of Latinos, even fewer Native Americans (Wright). Still, too often we define ourselves as that first-year course. Suppose that if instead of focusing on the gatekeeping year, we saw composition education as a *gateway*? Suppose that we enlarged our focus to include *both* moments, gatekeeping and gateway? And further suppose, to paraphrase Elizabeth Daley, that we designed a curriculum in composition that prepared students to become members of the writing public and to nego-

tiate life. How might that alter what we think and what we do?

Such an agenda is consistent with data that account for successful college experiences. Richard Light, for instance, demonstrates that one of the key factors students and alumni cite in studies of how college can work well is writing. The National Survey of Student Engagement—in both two- and four-year school versions—sounds the same note. We know that writing makes a difference—both at the gatekeeping moment and as students progress through the gateway.

Of course, in this moment in composition's history, I'm making certain assumptions about writing that as a disciplinary community, we are still ambivalent about. What should be the future shape of composition? Questioning the role of technology in composition programs—shall we teach print, digital, composition, communication, or all of the above?—continues to confound us. Do we want to confine our efforts to print literacy only—or, alternatively, to print literacy predominately? Given a dearth of

resources—from hardware to professional development, from student access to what Gail Hawisher calls the bandwidth digital divide—many of us continue to focus on print. Given a concern that postmodernism and infobits could undermine a sustained rational discourse that is fundamental to democracy, many of us vote for the known that is, not, coincidentally, what our colleagues expect us to deliver in the composition classroom: the print of CCCC—coherence, clarity, consistency, and (not least) correctness.

In the Portraits of Composition Research Study, respondents spoke in chorus about the move to digital texts. Nearly all respondents expect students to submit texts composed in a word processor; nearly half of the respondents respond to student texts via e-mail. But very few—less than 30%—use a course management system. [12]

At the same time, when reviewed, our own practices suggest that we have already committed to a theory of communication that is both/and: print and digital. Given the way we *produce* print—sooner or later inside a word processor—we are digital already, at least in process. Given the course management systems like Blackboard and WebCT, we have committed to the screen for administrative purposes at least. Given the oral communication context of peer review, our teaching requires that students participate in mixed communicative modes. Given the digital portfolios coming into their own, even the move by CCCC to provide LCD's and Internet connects to panelists upon request and for free, we teachers and students seem to have moved already—to communication modes assuming digital literacy. And thinking about our own presentations here: when we consider how these presentations will morph into other talks, into articles for print and online journals,[13] into books, indeed into our classrooms, it becomes pretty clear that we *already* inhabit a model of communication practices incorporating multiple genres related to each other, those multiple genres remediated across contexts of time and space, linked one to the next, circulating across and around rhetorical situations both inside and outside school.

This is composition—*and* this is the *content* of composition.

That composition has a content at all—other than process—is a radical claim. The CCCCs was founded with a concern about what the content of first-year composition should be, and it is a concern that continues to energize us even today.

If we cannot go home again to the days when print was the sole medium, what will the new curricular home for composition look like?

QUARTET THREE

Words, after speech, reach
Into the silence. Only by the form, the pattern,
Can words or music reach
The stillness, as a Chinese jar still
Moves perpetually in its stillness.

We have a moment.

At this moment, we need to focus on three changes: Develop a new curriculum; revisit and revise our writing-across-the-curriculum efforts; and develop a major in composition and rhetoric.[13]

Since the limits of time and space preclude my detailing all three, I will focus on the first, developing *a new curriculum for the 21st century*, a curriculum that carries forward the best of what we have created to date, that brings together the writing outside of school and that inside. This composition is located in a new vocabulary, a new set of practices, and a new set of outcomes; it will focus our research in new and provocative ways; it has as its goal the creation of

> *To accept rhetoric and composition . . .*
> *as legitimate parts of the graduate*
> *curriculum is not a sign of dissolution,*
> *dispersion, and decomposition. It is,*
> *rather a sign that we are regaining our*
> *composure, taking composure to mean*
> *composition in all of its senses.*
>
> —*Frank D'Angelo 1980*

thoughtful, informed, technologically adept writing publics. This goal entails the other two: extending this new composition curriculum horizontally throughout the academy and extending it vertically through our own major. In other words, it is past time that we fill the glaringly empty spot between first-year composition and graduate education with a composition major.

And in the time and space that's left, I want to sketch briefly what this new curriculum might look like.

To begin thinking about a revised curriculum for composition, we might note the most significant change that has occurred in composition over the last thirty years: the process movement. Although not everyone agrees that the process movement radically altered the teaching of composition (see Crowley; Matsuda), most do think that process—as we defined it in the research of scholars like Janet Emig and Linda Flower and as brought into the classroom by teachers like us—did revolutionize the teaching of writing. We had a new vocabulary, some of it—like invention—ancient, some of it—writing process and rewriting and freewriting—new. We developed pedagogy anew: peer review, redrafting, portfolio assessment. But nothing stays still, and process approaches have given way to other emphases. Recently, we have seen several approaches seeking to update that work, some on the left in the form of cultural studies and post-process; some more interested in psychological approaches like those located in felt sense; others more interested in the connections composition can forge with like-minded educational initiatives such as service learning and first-year experience programs.

Erika Lindemann's work on the bibliographic categories that organize and construct composition reveals the role that process both has and has not played in the discipline. Lindemann notes that while in the 1986 CCCC Bibliography process was included in three of twelve categories (or 25%), it is completely absent in the 2001 MLA successor to the Cs bibliography.

What no one, including writing teachers, foresaw twenty years ago was the extent to which the creation of wealth would be divorced from labor and redistributed, leaving the United States the most economically polarized among industrialized nations, with the divide between rich and poor continuing to widen.

—*Lester Faigley 1997*

What's interesting is that regardless of the changes that are advocated as we attempt to create a post-process compositional curriculum, most (not all but most) attempt this without questioning or altering the late-20th-century basis of composition. To put the point directly, composition in this school context, and in direct contrast to the *world* context, remains chiefly focused on the writer qua writer, sequestered from the means of production. Our model of teaching composing, as generous, varied, and flexible as it is in terms of aims and as innovative as it is in terms of pedagogy—and it is all of these—(still) embodies the narrow and the singular in its emphasis on a primary and single human relationship: the writer in relation to the teacher. In contrast to the reading public nearly two centuries ago, the "real" reading public of school is solitary, the teacher whose reading consists of print text delivered on the teacher's desk. In contrast to the development of a writing public, the classroom writer is not a member of a collaborative group with a common project linked to the world at large and delivered in multiple genres and media, but a singular person writing over and over again—to the teacher.

John Trimbur calls our school model of writing the in loco parentis model: we are the parents who in our practices continue to infantilize our students as we focus their gaze and their energy and their reflection on the moments of creation, on process. I tend to think of it in another, complementary way, as a remediated tutorial model of writing. In other words, it seems to me that in all our efforts to improve the teaching of composition—to reduce class size, for instance, to conference with students, to respond vociferously to each student paper, and to understand that in our students' eyes we are the respondent who matters—we seek to approximate the one-to-one tutorial model. Quite apart from the fact that such an effort is doomed—about a hundred years ago, Edwin Hopkins asked if we could teach composition under the current conditions,[14] which conditions then are the same conditions we work in today, and immediately answered, "NO"—I have to wonder why we want to work this way, wonder why *this* is the neo-Platonic mode to which we continuously aspire. Not that the process model is bad, I hasten to add: students do engage with each other, often do write to the world, and frequently do develop elaborated processes—all to the good. But if we believe that writing is social, shouldn't the system of circulation—the paths that the writing takes—extend beyond and around the single path from student to teacher?

I am interested in the terms we use to constitute our subject, the terms we take for granted and the degree to which we take them for granted. Today I'll stick to the three terms of our name, composition, communication, conference. These terms are our legacy; we must not betray those who have given them to us. They are also our problem, our burden, since they resist reflection and change.

—*David Bartholomae 1989*

More to the point, the list of what students aren't asked to do in the current model—and what they might—is long:

- consider the issue of intertextual circulation: how what they are composing relates or compares to "real world" genres;

- consider what the best medium and the best delivery for such a communication might be and then create and share those different communication pieces in those different media, to different audiences;

- think explicitly about what they might "transfer" from one medium to the next: what moves forward, what gets left out, what gets added—and what they have learned about composing in this transfer process;

- consider how to transfer what they have learned in one site and how that could or could not transfer to another, be that site on campus or off;[15]

- think about how these practices help prepare them to become members of a writing public.

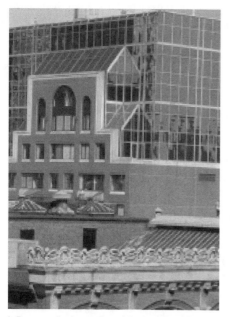

A Boston skyline, the old juxtaposed with the new, old and new interfaced. An architectural intertextuality.

What I'm proposing is that we move to a new model of composing where students are explicitly asked to engage in these considerations, to engage in these activities, to develop as members of a writing public. Such a model of composition is located in three key expressions:

Circulation of composition

Canons of rhetoric

Deicity of technology

Let me begin with circulation: although they are related, I will here outline and exemplify two kinds: (1) the circulation of texts generally, and (2) the circulation of a student's own work within an educational culture. Texts circulate: they move across contexts, between media, across time. Writers compose in the context of other writers and thinkers and speakers. They imitate them directly and indirectly; they quote them, write in direct reference to them, paraphrase them, and frame their own work in these contexts. This circulation is the one, perhaps, with which we are most familiar: we often talk about it as intertextuality, as a conversation that we invite students to join. The conversation, of course, occurs through genres and is really many conversations, with texts circulating in multiple, interrelated ways.

Conceptually, composition itself is in circulation. From music and art, it carries an aesthetic dimension. From chemistry and architecture, it carries an interest in materials. Pedagogically, borrowing from Joe Janangelo and Pablo Picasso, I have talked elsewhere about students as "ongoing compositions." We see such humans-as-compositions in any collected work, summarized minimally in a resume or vita; developed and illustrated more fully and reflectively in a portfolio. Regardless of whether we see such composing or not, it is always in play. In the context of compositionists as professionals, we compose ourselves, both individually, in the words of Elizabeth Flynn, and as participants of a community, in the words of Andrea Lunsford's Chair's Address.

What I am calling circulation can go by other names: Charles Bazerman and David Russell, for instance, call it activity theory, but basically it's the same point: As they explain,

> Writing is alive when it is being written, read, remembered, contemplated, followed—when it is part of human activity. . . . The signs on the page serve to mediate between people, activate their thoughts, direct their attention, coordinate their actions, provide the means of relationship. It is in the context of their activities that people consider texts and give meaning to texts. And it is in the organization of activities that people find the needs, stances, interactions, tasks that orient their attention toward texts they write and read. So to study text production, text reception, text meaning, text value apart from their animating activities is to miss the core of text's being.

So: circulation.

With the help of David Russell and Arturo Yañez, let me put a classroom face on what this might look like in terms of curriculum. They tell the story of a student caught in an all-too-familiar dilemma. Beth, the student, is an aspiring journalist convinced of the integrity and objectivity of reportorial accounting; moreover, she believes that good writing is good writing is good writing, regardless of the discipline. Which means, of course, that good writing is the writing she understands and practices. The problem: she's enrolled in an Irish literature class that she needs for graduation, a class where good writing—located in interpretation and exercise of judgment—looks very different. To her, this historical writing feels inexact and duplicitous; and it makes history, which she has understood as an exercise in "Just the facts, ma'am"—as completely alien. What activity theory adds to this mix is a means of making sense of these seemingly disparate texts and ways of knowing.

> Professional historians . . . critically examine and interpret (and reinterpret) primary documents according to the methods (rules, norms) of history. They argue and debate to persuade other experts. And when enough experts (or the enough powerful experts) arrive at consensus, that consensus is put into textbooks for high school students and generally perceived as "fact." And, perhaps, that consensus is eventually put into popular history books, of the kind that journalists review and the rest of us Big Picture People sometimes read—to find the "facts" of history. (Russell and Yañez)

> *Who writes the "first draft" of history can change, of course, as can patterns of circulation. Concerns around such issues are not merely academic, as is clear in the following* New York Times *commentary on the relationship between genres and the roles they are currently playing in* this *historical moment: "The sudden outpouring of inside details in books about the Bush administration is all the more remarkable because of the administration's previous success at controlling the flow of information to the press about its workings. It is a phenomenon that is creating an unusual reversal in which books—the musty vessels traditionally used to convey patient reflection into the archives—are superceding newspapers as the first draft of history, leaving the press corps to cover the books themselves as news."*

Thinking in terms of circulation, in other words, enables students to understand the epistemology, the conventions, and the integrity of different fields and their genres. Using that as a point of departure allows students to complete the task *and* move closer to the big picture of writing. Trimbur makes an analogous point in outlining a curricular approach where students in health sciences understand how different genres even within the same field function epistemologically: research genres to make scientific knowledge; public health articles deriving from the research genres both diluting and distributing it, each according to its own logic and conventions. His purpose?

> I want students to see that the shift in register and genre between a journal article and a news report amounts to a shift in modality—the relative credibility and authoritativeness invested in written statements—that marks

journal articles as 'original' contributions and news reports as secondary and derivative. (213)

Media themselves provide another example of circulation. As Jay Bolter and Richard Grusin explain in *Remediation,* and as McLuhan suggested before that, nearly every medium is re/mediated on another

> *We look at the present through a rear-view mirror. We march backwards into the future.*
>
> — *Marshall McLuhan 1964*

medium. In other words, consciously or otherwise, we create the new in the context of the old and based on the model of the old. Television is commonly understood to be remediated on film, for example, and the Web is commonly understood to be remediated on print. Remediation can be back-ended as well, as we see in the most recent CNN interface on TV, which is quite explicitly remediated on the Web. The new, then, repeats what came

before, while at the same time remaking that which it models. This isn't a new phenomenon, however, as we remember from the development of that 19th-century novel, which appeared in multiple genres and media: serials, triple-deckers, performances. Fast forward to the 21st century: imagine that in composition classes students, like Victorian novelists before them,

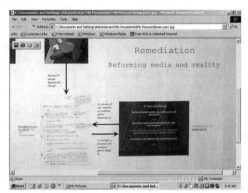

focus on remediating their own texts. Beginning with a handout or one pager, they define a key term of the course and revise that on the basis of class response; in addition, they move the material of that handout to a five-slide Power-Point show presented to the class and itself revised. Suppose that they move this material to a poster, then to a presentation, then to a conventional written text. For the conventional written text, they brainstorm in class and on a blog, thinking individually and communally about which of these tasks "counts" as writing—and why. As they move from medium to medium, they consider what they move forward, what they leave out, what they add, and for each of these write a reflection in which they consider how the medium itself shapes what they create. The class culminates with text in which they write a reflective theory about what writing is and how it is influenced or shaped or determined by media and technology. Located in the rhetoric of purpose, audience, genre, this model of circulation is particularly oriented to medium and technology; it permits a student, as Brian Morrison does here, to define composition as "the thoughtful gathering, construction, or reconstruction of a literate act in any given media."

Speaking of Remediation . . .

Have you heard Sheryl Crow's version of Rod Stewart's "The First Cut Is the Deepest"?

Or how about Moulin Rouge?

These three related approaches: all oriented to the circulation of texts, to genre, to media, and to ways that writing gets made, both individually and culturally. As important, all three of these approaches, in their analysis of textual relationships and contexts, in their theories and examples of how writing works, and in their situating the student as a maker of knowledge, map the content for new composition. And if you are saying, but I can't do all this in first-year composition, I'm going to reply, "Exactly." First-year composition is a place to begin; carrying this forward is the work of the major in composition and rhetoric.

What is the relationship between and among remediating texts, carrying forward materials, finding new sources, and representing and inventing a self?

One thing that is clear to me as I compose this text for the page is that this remediation feels less like a small morphing of a text from one medium to another than it does like creating a new text. And it's not mere perception: this composition is longer by over 2,000 words, most of which comment on, extend, and complicate the earlier voiced text.

A second kind of circulation, occurring within the bounds of school and often within the classroom, has to do with the variety of academic texts that students create, with the places in which those texts are created and distributed, and with how *this circulation* contributes to student development in writing. We have some fine research in this sense of circulation that accounts for students moving forward in their writing: research conducted by Lee Ann Carroll, Nancy Sommers and Laura Saltz, Marilyn Sternglass, Richard Haswell, and Elizabeth Chiseri-Strater. Typically, such studies focus on how and what students "transfer" from one site to another; Anne Beaufort's study asks the same question but applied to the site of work. And often we ask students to engage in this activity themselves: in their reflections, students account for the progress (or not) of their texts; of what they have learned in the construction of such texts; in their portfolios—be they digital or print—students comment and demonstrate the circulation of the course.

A vignette composed by Paul Prior and Jody Shipka shows us another way to think about circulation that focused exclusively on a single text.

> A psychology professor reports to us that when she is revising an article for publication she works at home and does the family laundry. She sets the buzzer on the dryer so that approximately every 45 minutes to an hour she is pulled away from the text to tend the laundry downstairs. As she empties the dryer, sorts and folds, reloads, her mind wanders a bit and she begins to recall things she wanted to do with the text, begins to think of new questions or ideas, things that she had not been recalling or thinking of as she focused on the text when she was upstairs minutes before. She perceives this break from the text, this opportunity to reflect, as a very productive part of the process.

What Prior and Shipka point out, of course, is that this text is produced through two activity systems: the domestic and the disciplinary.[16] They raise provocative questions about the role the buzzer plays in the drafting process, about the spaces created here for reflection, about the role reflection plays in composing.

This too is circulation; this too is composition.

A map of his writing process by first-year writer Josh Reynolds.

Bill Watterson, the creator of Calvin and Hobbes, *talks about how circulation of another kind can influence the development of a creator, in this case of a cartoonist. He notes, "The challenge of any cartoonist is not just to duplicate the achievements of the past, but to build on them as well" (9–10).*

He argues it is thus necessary for the cartoonist to have access to earlier cartoons, through their collection and republication—in book form.[17]

As I move into the second expression, the canons of rhetoric—invention, arrangement, style, memory, and delivery—I'm aware that these are hardly new. I wonder about how we understand them, however. Like others before me, I would note that we have separated delivery and memory from invention, arrangement, and style in ways that are counterproductive. Let me further say that too often we treat them as discrete entities when in fact they are interrelated. Let me share with you an image. Don't ask me why, but I have always understood each canon as sitting on a rhetorical shelf, as though a freshly laundered cotton blanket in a laundry closet. I take one canon down—my favorite, if truth be told, is invention—use it, then put it neatly back on the shelf. But as my options for delivering texts have widened—from the page to the screen to the networked screen and then back to the page anew—I've begun to see the canons not as discrete entities like those blankets on shelves but, rather, as related to each other in much the same way as the elements of Burke's pentad are related: the canons interact, and through that interaction they contribute to new exigencies for invention, arrangement, representation, and identity. Or: they change what is possible.

It's instructive to attempt to map the relationship between and among the canons. As I continue to explore delivery—of text, of instruction, of public extracurricula—delivery seems at the heart of the relationship, but I can see how at other times, other canons take that place.

The revolution, if there is one, is the social one of interconnectivity.

—James Porter 2003

Richard Lanham, of course, has argued that with the addition of the digital to the set of media in which we compose, delivery takes on a critical role, and I think that's so. But much more specifically, what a shift in the means of delivery does is bring invention and arrangement into a new relationship with each other. The writer of the page has fundamentally different opportunities than the creator of a hypertext. Anne Wysocki is right about the interface of the page—that is, it has one, and it's worth paying attention to—but even so, as we read the pages of an article, we typically do so line by line, left to right, as you do now: page one before page two. This is the fixed default arrangement. The writer *invented* through such a text is a function of that arrangement. In other words, you can only invent inside what an arrangement permits—and different media permit different arrangements. By contrast, the creator of a hypertext can create a text that, like the page, moves forward. In addition, however, hypertext composers can create other arrangements, almost as in three rather than two dimensions. You can move horizontally, right branching; you can then left branch. The writer invented in a medium permitting these arrangements is quite different—a difference of kind, not degree.

We used to have a stable definition of composing and of the author. These have changed. The freedom to invent, to arrange multiply, can be a wonderful thing. It can also evoke anxiety, somewhat akin to discovering that the tectonic plates underlying the continents are not stable but, in fact, are shifting constantly.

The tectonic plate theory of continental drift was "discovered" in 1965. Rohman and Wlecke's stage-model of writing was "discovered" a year earlier; Rohman's CCC article detailing prewriting was published the year following, in 1965.

Given my own teaching and research interests, I see such differences, particularly in portfolios. In a print portfolio, remediated on a book, the arrangement is singular. In a digital portfolio, remediated on a gallery, the arrangements are plural. And the students invented in each are quite different. In a print portfolio, the tendency is to tell a single story, one with a single claim and an accumulating body of evidence. In arrangement, a digital portfolio—again, by contrast—is multiple, is defined by links. Because you can link externally as well as internally and because those links are material, you have more contexts you can link to, more strata you can layer, more

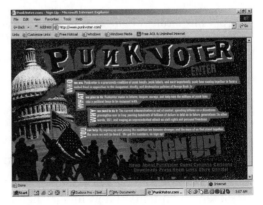

"you" to invent, more invention to represent. In sum, the potential of arrangement is a function of delivery, and *what and how you arrange*—which becomes a function of the medium you choose—*is who you invent.*[18] Moreover, I suspect that as multiple means of delivery become more routinized, we will understand *each* of the canons differently, and we will understand and be able to map their interrelationships.

My third and final expression is the deicity of technology. *Deixis*, linguistically, refers to words like *now* and *then*, words whose "meanings change quickly depending on the time or space in which they are uttered" (Leu et al.) or read. The word *Now* when I wrote this text is one time; as I read the word *Now* in San Antonio was a second time; and now, when this talk is published in *CCC* and who knows how many people do (or do not!) read *this* Chair's Address, it will be many, many other times. Literacy is deictic. The speed of technological change has affected literacy, as we know. The particular claim that D. J. Leu, C. K. Kinzer, J. Coiro, and D. Cammack (among others) have made is this: "technological change happens so rapidly that the changes to literacy are limited not by technology but rather by our ability to adapt and acquire the new literacies that emerge." Deixis, they say, "is a defining quality of the new literacies of the Internet" and other information communication technologies.

Leu and his colleagues note how our working in a context of deixis changes the way we teach. No longer, they say, can we speak from the podium with the expertise of old. Instead, faculty and students will consider questions and use various technologies to help address them, with the faculty member guiding the work, and in some cases learning along with the students. In composition, we need to learn how to read and write e-texts—synthesizing, questioning, evaluating, and importing from them—databases and catalogues, hyper-texts and archives, Web essays and portfolios.

And this means we all need to learn more about how to use images and sources, how to document them appropriately, how to create our own.

According to Leu and his coauthors, there are three sources for this deictic nature of literacy:

1. transformations of literacy because of technological change,

2. the use of increasingly efficient technologies of communication that rapidly spread new literacies, and

3. envisionments of new literacy potentials within new technologies.

Although deixis might be a new term to many of us, the first two claims are familiar. As we saw in the case of the 19th-century reader, technology changes literacy: that's the kind of trans-

By paying critical attention to lessons about technology, we can re-learn important lessons about literacy.

—Cindy Selfe 1999

formation we are seeing now with regard to writers. Technology, of course, has always been ubiquitous: as Dennis Baron points out, a pencil is a technology. At the same time, however, *this* digital, networked technology continuously promotes itself and new literacies—through the marketing efforts of the corporations that develop these technologies; through open source and shareware and freeware; through our ability to download new programs and formats that are essentially new engines for a literacy no one can quite predict. The dissemination of this potential capacity is built into this model of technology. Given its worldwide distribution and its democratization of authorship, that's new.

The third source—what Leu calls "envisionments of new literacy potentials within new technologies"—is provocative. Here is what he is referring to: the ability of someone to take a given technology and find a use for it that may be at odds with its design. The example he provides is this. Suppose that you are writing an e-mail but decide to compose the e-mail inside a word processor, which is a different (if related) technology. In this scenario,

> a word processor can be transformed into a tool for composing e-mail messages, a purpose for which it was not designed, but a function it fills admirably. This potential only comes to life when a person envisions a new function for a technology and *enacts this envisionment*. In essence, we can say that she envisioned how to repurpose a technology for a new and different function. Envisionments such as this happen regularly as individuals encounter new problems and seek solutions in new and creative uses of existing technologies. (Leu et al.)

Envisionment is a practice most of us engage in, typically without thinking about it as such. Teachers use a spreadsheet for grading purposes. A colleague uses a spreadsheet for a digital portfolio template for her class of 120 students. Elementary teachers use PowerPoint for reluctant writers. High school teachers use textboxes for peer review and links for research hypercards. College teachers invite blocked writers to draft in an e-mail program.

A modest proposal: one outcome for all writers is the ability to use many kinds of technologies for their intended purposes and for other purposes, as needed and as imagined.

Or: writers use technology rhetorically.

Writing, by its very nature, encourages abstraction, and in the shuttling process from the past to the present, from the particular to the general, from the concrete to the abstract, we seek relationships and find meaning.

—*William Irmscher 1979*

And let me provide another example. For the last several years, I have worked with graduate students in architecture, and one of their practices is meeting monthly to talk about how their projects and theses are developing. Now, given that it's architecture, they do more than talk: they *show*—in pinups on the walls, in a one-page handout, and in a set of PowerPoint slides. Something that grabbed my attention almost immediately was how those slides were being used: not for *presentation* of a finished idea, as the design of them would have it—and as the name, presentation software, suggests—but, rather, for a different purpose: for exploration, in fact as a new space for drafting ideas. Since then, in several different classes, I've used PowerPoint in just this way, as a site for a rough draft, shared with a real audience. Or: envisionment. What other technologies might be re-envisioned and to what effects? What envisionments have students already created that we don't know about? And how do we build this ability—envisioning—into our curriculum?

This new composition includes rhetoric and is about literacy. New composition includes the literacy of print: it adds on to it and brings the notions of practice and activity and circulation and media and screen and networking to our conceptions of process. It will require a new expertise of us as it does of our students. And ultimately, new composition may require a new site for learning for all of us.

QUARTET FOUR

Time present and time past
Are both perhaps present in time future,
And time future contained in time past.

We have a moment.

In her study *Institutionalizing Literacy,* Mary Trachsel makes the argument that when we separate an activity related to curriculum from it, faculty lose control over curriculum to the detriment of students and faculty alike. Trachsel, of course, is speaking of assessment, and how historically it has been cleaved from curriculum, particularly at the gatekeeping moment when students enter college— and she cites the SAT as evidence of the claim. I would make the same observation about technology. If we continue to partition it off as just something technical, or outside the parameters governing composing, or limit it to the screen of the course management system, or think of it in terms of the bells and whistles and templates of the Power-Point screen, students in our classes learn only to *fill up* those templates and *fill in* those electric boxes—which, in their ability to invite intellectual work, are the moral equivalent of the dots on a multiple choice test. Students will not compose and create, making use of all the means of persuasion and all the possible resources thereto; rather, they will complete someone else's software package; they will be the invention of that package.

These spaces—the intertextual, overlapping curricular spaces—between school and the public, including print and screen, are still ours to study, to examine, to work in, and to claim. They are the province of first-year composition but are not limited to it. This curricular change includes renewed attention to WAC. It includes a new major in whatever site: English department, writing studies depart-

> *It is time to speak for ourselves, in our own interests, in the interest of our own work, and in the interest of our students.*
>
> — *Jacqueline Jones Royster 1996*

ment, rhetorical studies program. The institutional site is less important than the major itself, which can begin to secure our position in the academy while it makes space for the writing that students do on their own, now, without us.

The metaphors we use to describe also construct. The metaphor of tectonic change, particularly when used in the context of the changes of the 19th century, can help us understand how pervasive our current challenges are, how necessary our efforts to adapt.

So this talk: yes, it's about change. Change, as we saw in the 19th century, and as we see now, can be very difficult, can be unnerving. I used the metaphor of tremors intentionally. A little more than twenty years ago we talked about "winds of change" (Hairston); today the changes are those of tremors. These are *structural* changes—global, educational, technological. Like seismic tremors, these signal a re-formation in process, and because we exist on the borders of our own tectonic plates—rhetoric, composition and communication, process, activity, service and social justice—we are at the very center of those tremors.

Perhaps the most important of the plates on which we stand is advocacy, especially at this moment. As the Dixie Chicks point out, voting is an excellent means of self-expression. In helping create writing publics, we also foster the development of citizens who vote, of citizens whose civic literacy is global in its sensibility and its communicative potential, and whose commitment to humanity is characterized by consistency and generosity as well as the ability to write for purposes that are unconstrained and audiences that are nearly unlimited.

It's an ambitious agenda I laid before you in San Antonio and that I lay before you in these pages today, but yes, this is made not only in words: composition in a new key.

ACKNOWLEDGMENTS

Gracious thanks to the CCCC audience in San Antonio and to those who helped me before I arrived there: Kristi and Shawn Apostel, Michael Crawford, Will Dickert, Teddi Fishman, Morgan Gresham, Doug Hesse, Martin Jacobi, Brian Morrison, Michael Neal, Josh Reynolds, Summer Smith Taylor, and Irwin Weiser. For special help in the selection and placement of images and in the overall design of this text, many thanks to Marilyn Cooper.

Thanks also to the following for permission to reprint. Lines from "Burnt Norton" on pages 297, 308 and 320 from *Four Quartets* by T.S. Eliot, copyright 1936 by Harcourt, Inc., and renewed 1964 by T.S. Eliot, reprinted by permission of the publisher. A line from "East Coker" on page 299 from *Four Quartets* by T.S. Eliot, copyright 1940 by T.S. Eliot and renewed 1968 by Esmc Valerie Eliot, reprinted by permission of Harcourt, Inc. Lines from "Little Gidding" on page 305 from *Four Quartets* by T.S. Eliot 1942 and renewed 1970 by Esmc Valerie Eliot, reprinted by permission of Harcourt, Inc. *Composition VII* by Wassily Kandinsky on page 303, copyright 2004 Artists Rights Society (ARS), New York/ADAGP, Paris, reprinted by permission.

NOTES

1. The slides were arranged so that duplicates showed up simultaneously at various points in the presentation: two screens showed the same slide. Also, as the performance progressed, some slides were repeated, in part to provide some contour to the performance, in part to provide some coherence. I attempt to explain the logic of this composition in *Composition in a New Key*, forthcoming.

2. In the 1980's, compositionists were excited about the role that process was playing—in our teaching, in the assessment of student work, in our own research. Given the disparity between the out-of-school, often digitally composed genres that students currently work in and the form that current assessments are taking—even the much ballyhooed new SAT "writing test" includes a component on grammar and usage that is allowed *more* time than the pencil-and-paper draft portion—Marshall McLuhan's point about marching backwards into the future sounds all too true. For a compelling analysis of the disjunction between what we teach and what is being assessed, see Miles McCrimmon, "High School Writing Practices in the Age of Standards: Implications for College Composition."

3. The relationship between and among technology, literacy practices, nation states, and centralized control is considerably more complicated than I can pursue here. For an analysis that focuses on the materiality of literacy practices and technology, see Lester Faigley's *Material Literacy and Visual Design*; for a discussion that emphasizes the centralization of the nation state as related to literacy and technology, see Ronald Deibert's *Parchment, Printing, and Hypermedia: Communication in World Order Transformation* and Deborah Brandt's *Literacy in American Lives*.

4. Digital compositions include other materials as well: audio files, for instance. For a discussion of such materials in the context of remediation and composition, see Scott Halbritter.

5. The talk I delivered was not precisely the same as the written text. For historical purposes, CCCC videotapes the talk, and what seemed obvious to me at the time is so in retrospect: the two "talks" differ.

6. How various technologies—from technology producing light to that associated with various printing presses—interact to influence the development of literacy (and whose needs this literacy serves) is a (another) question worth pursuing.

7. You don't have to be present to see them: online, you can see the home pages for the Seattle Public Library and the Salt Lake City Library. For a fuller discussion of the lessons regarding these spaces that libraries have to teach us, see Yancey, "Episodes in the Spaces of the Plural Commons."

8. The idea that English departments are being consolidated into other units was first drawn to my attention by Tina Good, at Suffolk County Community College, who has conducted a study of the SUNY system, verifying the claim in that context.

9. As David Lawrence, the executive director of the Association of Departments of English (ADE), has pointed out to me, there's no reason to regard the number of majors from 1966 as the ideal or the norm, and it is the case that English majors still rank in the top ten of all majors (calculated based on a U.S. government database). Point taken. Still, this seems small comfort to me (as a member of an English department) when I remember that more students go to college and graduate today, in 2004, than did in 1966, so the numbers for the English major, it seems to me, ought to grow, not hold steady. In a population that is increasing, maintaining constitutes a decline, as the numbers attest. One reply to such a view, as explained in the *ADE* report "The Undergraduate English Major," is to put the numbers in

larger historical perspective. In this case, that entails the observation that the "semicaptive" audience of majors that English used to have—that is, women—are now choosing to major in other fields, especially biology, psychology, and business, which given our interest in gender equity is a good thing. *Of course.* Still, the trend lines—number of majors, number of tenure-line hires, number of English departments—plot a narrative that those of us who are aligned with English should not ignore.

10. On May 10, 2004, the Colorado legislature passed this bill, which provides funding vouchers to all college students in the state to be applied to all kinds of postsecondary institutions, including private schools. The implications of this bill are widespread: for an early analysis, see Chris Kampfe and Kyle Endres.

11. As this list indicates, a number of so-called college classes are actually *delivered* in high school: what does this say about college composition? With several others, I attempt to answer this question: see Yancey, *Delivering College Composition: The Fifth Canon,* Heinemann 2004.

12. The respondents included more than 1,800 faculty members from forty-eight states, split about 40/60 between two-year and four-year faculty. In terms of faculty status, 17% identified as graduate students and 23% as adjunct faculty. For a fuller description and analysis of the results, see Yancey et al., "Portraits of Composition: How Writing Gets Taught in the Early Twenty-First Century."

13. The idea for a major in rhetoric and composition is not new. Keith Miller was kind enough to point me toward the George Tade, Gary Tate, and Jim Corder article in *CCC,* "For Sale, Lease, or Rent: A Curriculum for an Undergraduate Program in Rhetoric." And some 25 years later, Robert Connors makes the philosophical argument in his Afterword to *Coming of Age.*

14. For a full account of the influence of Edwin Hopkins, see the article by John Heyda and Randall Popken.

15. As I look over the list of items here, the key word seems to be transfer: from composing site to composing site, from classroom to classroom, from one experience to the next. As I have suggested elsewhere, Donald Schon's notion of "reflective transfer" is crucial to this development. See Yancey, *Reflection in the Writing Classroom.*

16. The activity systems mapped by Paul Prior and Jody Shipka parallel the spaces architects are designing into various kinds of buildings: both conceive of human activity organized into multiple overlapping spaces. Another way to theorize composition of the 21st century is through the overlapping curricular, activity, and physical spaces where it occurs now and where it might occur. In this construct, the circulation of composition takes yet another definition.

17. Bill Watterson has several books that in their commentary on processes, media, and transfer are models for the observation, analysis, and insight we often find in portfolio reflections.

18. For a fuller account of both kinds of portfolios, see Yancey, "Postmodernism, Palimpsest, and Portfolios: Theoretical Issues in the Representation of Student Work" and *Teaching Literature as Reflective Practice,* especially chapter five.

WORKS CITED

ADE. "Report of the Undergraduate English Major." Report of the 2001–2002 ADE Ad Hoc Committee on the English Major. *ADE* (Fall/Winter 2003): 68–91.

"America's Fortunes." Atlantic Online (January/February 2004) 21 Mar 04 <http:www. theatlantic.com/cgi-bin/send.cgi?pae=http%3A//www.the atlantic.com/issues>.

Baron, Dennis. "From Pencils to Pixels." *Passions, Pedagogies, and 21st Century Technologies*. Ed. Gail Hawisher and Cynthia Selfe. Logan: Utah State UP, 1999. 15–34.

Bartholomae, David. "Freshman English, Composition, and CCCC." *College Communication and Composition* 40.1 (1989): 38–50.

Bazerman, Charles, and David Russell, eds. *Writing Selves, Writing Societies: Research from Activity Perspectives*. Fort Collins, CO: The WAC Clearinghouse and Mind, Culture, and Activity. 1 June 2004 <http://wac.colostate.edu/books/selves_societies/intro.cfm>.

Beaufort, Anne. *Writing in the Real World: Making the Transition from School to Work*. New York: Teachers College P, 1999.

Bolter, Jay David, and Richard Grusin. *Remediation: Understanding New Media*. Cambridge: MIT P, 2000.

Brandt, Deborah. *Literacy in American Lives*. New York: Cambridge UP, 2001.

Bridwell-Bowles, Lillian. "Freedom, Form, Function: Varieties of Academic Discourse." *College Communication and Composition* 46.1 (1995): 46–61.

Carroll, Lee Ann. *Rehearsing New Roles: How College Students Develop as Writers*. Carbondale: Southern Illinois UP, 2002.

Chaplin, Miriam T. "Issues, Perspectives, and Possibilities." *College Composition and Communication* 39.1 (1988): 52–62.

Chiseri-Strater, Elizabeth. *Academic Literacies: The Public and Private Discourse of University Students*. Portsmouth, NH: Boynton/Cook, 1991.

Connors, Robert. Afterword. *Coming of Age: The Advanced Writing Curriculum*. Ed. Linda K. Shamoon, Rebecca Moore Howard, Sandra Jamieson, and Robert A. Schwegler. Portsmouth, NH: Boynton/Cook, 2000. 143–49.

Crowley, Sharon. *Composition in the University: Historical and Polemical Essays*. Pittsburgh: U of Pittsburgh, 1998.

D'Angelo, Frank. "Regaining Our Composure." *College Composition and Communication* 31.4 (1980): 420–26.

Daley, Elizabeth. "Expanding the Concept of Literacy." *Educause Review* 38.2 (2003): 33–40.

———. "Speaking the Languages of Literacy." Speech, University of Michigan, April 2003. 9 Aug. 04 <http://web.si. umich.edu/news/news-detail.cfm? NewsItemID=350>.

Davis, Vivian I. "Our Excellence: Where Do We Grow from Here?" *College Composition and Communication* 30.1 (1979): 26–31.

Deibert, Ronald. *Parchment, Printing, and Hypermedia: Communication in World Order Transformation*. New York: Columbia UP, 1997.

Ebert, Roger. Review of *21 Grams*. *Chicago Sun Times* (2003) 1 June 2004 <http://www. suntimes.com/ebert/ebert_reviews/2003/11/112606.html>.

Emig, Janet. *The Composing Processes of Twelfth Graders*. Urbana, IL: NCTE, 1971.

Faigley, Lester. "Literacy after the Revolution." *College Composition and Communication* 48.1 (1997): 30–43.

———. "Material Literacy and Visual Design." In *Rhetorical Bodies: Toward a Material Rhetoric*. Ed. Jack Selzer and Sharon Crowley. Madison: U of Wisconsin P, 1999. 171–201.

Flower, Linda, and John Hayes. "A Cognitive Process Theory of Writing." *College Composition and Communication* 32.4 (1981): 365–87.

Flynn, Elizabeth. "Composing as a Woman." *College Composition and Communication* 39.4 (1988): 423–35.

Gerber, John C. "The Conference on College Composition and Communication." *College Composition and Communication* 1.1 (1950): 12.

Gere, Anne Ruggles. "Kitchen Tables and Rented Rooms: The Extracurriculum of Composition." *College Composition and Communication* 45.1 (1994): 75–92.

Good, Tina. Personal discussion, 25 April 2003.

Hairston, Maxine. "The Winds of Change: Thomas Kuhn and the Revolution in the Teaching of Writing." *College Composition and Communication* 33.1: 76–88.

Halbritter, Scott. "Sound Arguments: Aural Rhetoric in Multimedia Composition." PhD diss. University of North Carolina, 2004.

Haswell, Richard. *Gaining Ground in College: Tales of Development and Interpretation.* Dallas, TX: Southern Methodist UP, 1991.

Hawisher, Gail. Personal discussion. Feb 2004.

Heyda, John. "Industrial-Strength Composition and the Impact of Load on Teaching." *More Than 100 Years of Solitude: WPA Work before 1976.* Ed. Barbara L'Eppateur and Lisa Mastrangelo. Forthcoming.

Hopkins, Edwin. "Can Good English Composition Be Done under the Current Conditions?" *English Journal* 1 (1912): 1–8.

Irmscher, William F. "Writing as a Way of Learning and Developing." *College Composition and Communication* 30.3 (1979): 240–44.

Johnson-Eilola, Johndan. "Writing about Writing." Speech, Computers and Writing Town Hall Meeting, 2002, Illinois State University.

Jones, Richard Lloyd. "A View from the Center." *College Composition and Communication* 29.1 (1978): 24–29.

Kampfe, Chris, and Kyle Endres. "Vouchers to Change the Way Higher Ed is Funded." *The Rocky Mountain Collegian.* 10 May 2004. <http://www.collegian.com/vnews/display.v/ART/2004/05/07/409b21d2bfdee?in_archive=1>.

Lanham, Richard. *The Electronic Word: Democracy, Technology, and the Arts.* Chicago: U of Chicago P, 1993.

Lawrence, David. E-mail to author. April 2004.

Leu, D. J., C. K. Kinzer, J. Coiro, and D. Cammack. "Toward a Theory of New Literacies Emerging from the Internet and Other ICT." *Theoretical Models and Processes of Reading.* 5th ed. Ed. R. Ruddel and Norman Unrau. D. E. International Reading Association, 2004. 4 Aug. 2004 (Preprint version) <http://www.readingonline.org/newliteracies/leu>.

Light, Richard J. *Making the Most of College: Students Speak Their Minds.* Cambridge: Harvard UP, 2001.

Lindemann, Erika. "Early Bibliographic Work in Composition Studies." *Profession* (2002): 151–58.

Lunsford, Andrea. "Composing Ourselves: Politics, Commitment, and the Teaching of Writing." *College Composition and Communication* 41.1 (1990): 71–82.

McCrimmon, Miles. "High School Writing Practices in the Age of Standards: Implications for College Composition." Forthcoming.

McLuhan, Marshall. *Understanding Media: The Extensions of Man.* 1964. Cambridge: MIT P, 1994.

Matsuda, Paul. "Process and Post Process: A Discursive History." *Journal of Second Language Writing* 12 (2003): 65–83.

Palmquist, Michael. "Review: Made Not Only in Words: Composition in a New Key." 15 April 2004. *Across the Disciplines* at the WAC Clearinghouse. 1 June 2004 <http://wac. colostate.edu/atd/reviews/cccc2004/viewmessage.cfm?messageid =61>.

Popken, Randall. "Edwin Hopkins and the Costly Labor of Composition Teaching." *College Composition and Communication* 55.4 (2004): 618–42.

Porter, James. "Why Technology Matters to Writing: A Cyberwriter's Tale." *Computers and Composition* 20.3 (2003): 375–94.

Prior, Paul, and Jody Shipka. "Chronotopic Laminations: Tracing the Contours of Literate Activity." *Writing Selves, Writing Societies: Research from Activity Perspectives.* Ed. Charles Bazerman and David Russell. Fort Collins, CO: The WAC Clearinghouse, and Mind, Culture, and Activity, 180–238. 1 June 2004 <http://wac.colostate.edu/books/ selves_ societies/prior>.

Putnam, Robert. *Bowling Alone.* New York: Simon and Schuster, 2000.

Reynolds, Josh. "Writing Process Map." *My English Portfolio.* 1 June 2004 <http://people. clemson.edu/~jsreyno/Process. htm>.

Rohman, D. Gordon. "Prewriting: The Stage of Discovery in the Writing Process." *College Composition and Communication* 16.2 (1965): 106–12.

Rohman, D. Gordon, and Albert O. Wlecke. "Pre-Writing: The Construction and Applications of Models for Concept Formation in Writing." Cooperative Research Project No. 2174. USOE: Washington, DC.

Royster, Jacqueline Jones. "When the First Voice You Hear Is Not Your Own." *College Composition and Communication* 47.1 (1996): 29–40.

Russell, David, and Arturo Yañez. "Big Picture People Rarely Become Historians: Genre Systems and the Contradictions of General Education." *Writing Selves, Writing Societies: Research from Activity Perspectives.* Ed. Charles Bazerman and David Russell. Fort Collins, CO: The WAC Clearinghouse, and Mind, Culture, and Activity. 1 June 2004 <http://wac.colostate.edu/books/selves_societies/russell>.

Selfe, Cynthia L. "Technology and Literacy: A Story about the Perils of Not Paying Attention." *College Composition and Communication* 50.3 (1999): 411–36.

Shea, Rachel Hartigan. "How We Got Here." *U.S. News and World Report*, 9 Aug 2004: 70–73.

Sommers, Nancy, and Laura Saltz. "The Novice as Expert: Writing the Freshman Year." *College Composition and Communication* 56.1 (2004): 124–49.

Sternglass, Marilyn. *Time to Know Them: A Longitudinal Study of Writing and Learning at the College Level.* Mahwah, NJ: Lawrence Erlbaum Associates, 1997.

Tade, George, Gary Tate, and Jim Corder. "For Sale, Lease, or Rent: A Curriculum for an Undergraduate Program in Rhetoric." *College Composition and Communication* 26.1 (1975): 20–24.

Trachsel, Mary. *Institutionalizing Literacy: The Historical Role of College Entrance Examinations in English.* Carbondale: Southern Illinois UP, 1992.

Trimbur, John. "Composition and the Circulation of Writing." *College Composition and Communication* 52.2 (2000): 188–219.

Vendler, Helen. "The Ocean, the Bird, and the Scholar." NEH Jefferson Address, 6 May 2004. 9 Aug. 04 <http://www.neh. gov/whoweare/vendler/lecture.html>.

Watterson, Bill. *Sunday Pages 1985–1995: An Exhibition Catalogue.* Kansas City, MO: Andrews McMeel Publishing, 2000.

Wright, John ed. *New York Times 2004 Almanac*. New York: Penguin, 2003.

Wysocki, Anne, and Julia Jasken. "What Should Be an Unforgettable Face." *Computers and Composition* 21.1 (2004): 29–49.

Yancey, Kathleen Blake. "Episodes in the Spaces of the Plural Commons: Curriculum, Administration, and Design of Composition in the 21st Century." Speech, Writing Program Administration, Delaware, 14 July 2004.

———. "Postmodernism, Palimpsest, and Portfolios: Theoretical Issues in the Representation of Student Work." *College Composition and Communication* 55.4 (2004): 738–61.

———. *Reflection in the Writing Classroom*. Logan: Utah State UP, 1998.

———. *Teaching Literature as Reflective Practice*. Urbana, IL: NCTE, 2004.

Yancey, Kathleen Blake, Teddi Fishman, Morgan Gresham, Michael Neal, and Summer Smith Taylor. "Portraits of Composition: How Postsecondary Writing Gets Taught in the Early Twenty-First Century." Forthcoming.

Oakland, the Word, and the Divide

How We All Missed the Moment

ADAM J. BANKS

I once thought I could never imagine what it would have been like to be among the newly freed slaves after the shock of it all when the word finally came down, after the Juneteenth celebrations, after the pained attempts to locate lost family and loved ones, when the difficult work of reconstruction sat there waiting to be done. Same thing with those who helped to build Black lives and opportunities anew after the decades long struggle of African American leftists, moderates, liberals, and conservatives resulted in the temporary victories of the Civil Rights and Voting Rights Acts. It all seemed so basic when I learned bits of the histories of those moments: how could we not have gotten further? How could the rare coalescence of a national political will to change and legislation attempting to make that will some kind of reality not result in more tangible progress? How could Washington and DuBois still be debating what should have been obvious more than 30 years after emancipation? How could activists be left with such shambles of an education system 50 years after *Brown v. Board* when Blackfolk were infected with a euphoria that had them chanting "free by 63!"?

Why is it that we end up in this endless cycle when we learn about Black freedom struggle? Over and over and over again, victory, then inertia, then contentiousness then the sickening feeling that such history making

Reprinted from *Race, Rhetoric, and Technology: Searching for Higher Ground* by Adam J. Banks (Mahwah, NJ: Lawrence Erlbaum and Urbana, IL: NCTE, 2006). Used by permission.

victories made little difference in the long run? As an undergraduate with all of the idealism of 18- and 20-year-olds everywhere and all of the certitude that things were so clear and so easy, none of this made sense. The crack epidemic making shambles of my family and neighborhood at the exact same time Dr. King's birthday was being recognized as a national holiday? Surely the Negroes in whatever parallel universe might be watching us were shaking their heads as I was. Then I saw, on a much smaller scale, admittedly, how these travesties take place: the Digital Divide and Oakland. What happened (and didn't happen) with the alignment of these two national discussions in rhetoric and composition's theorizing and teaching, showed me what happens when Black warriors get caught on the wrong end of time warps being forced yet again to defend Black humanity, and when both well meaning and reactionary elements of the mainstream refuse to change. This is partially out of their insistence on subjecting that very humanity to debate and partially out of a blindness to the grounds on which we're all forced to live out our collective humanity, shifting rapidly while forcing that very, very old debate, in a nation where seemingly promising legislation or policy turned out to be nearly bankrupt.

This is exactly what happened in the late 1990s—the Department of Commerce introduced the Digital Divide as a concept to acknowledge the systematic differences in technology access that African Americans, other racial minorities and those in rural areas experienced and attempted policy initiatives that members of the Clinton administration thought would help to erase those gaps. Although what seemed to be a promising bit of political will emerged for educators to address problems of technology access in their schools, colleges, and universities, this issue failed to even make it onto academics' collective radar, with few exceptions. And a major part of why educators all over the country, at all levels, missed it, is because of their inability to avoid, yet again, the debate over Black humanity—in this case, educability in standardized English, because of the Oakland controversy.

Rhetoric and composition, as well as the technology sector in American society, have functioned very much in the same way as the legal system (that I examine in chapter four), in that each rests on a history that has branded African Americans as utter outsiders, unworthy of full, equitable, and just access because they are non-technological, unable to learn Standard English, in essence, non-citizens. Because of the persistence of these constructions, access to technologies and the discursive practices that determine power relations in our society, the Digital Divide, and the larger history of African Americans, is essentially a rhetorical problem. And because African American exclusions from the educational system that determines access to employment (and therefore the technologies that undergird the American economy) are so rooted in the specter of the Ebonics speaker and writer, the rhetorical problems that dominate understandings of race in our discipline are technological problems.

The history of these constructions extends back into Enlightenment notions of race and forward into the present. Neither rhetoric and composition nor the technology sector have found ways to discuss their continued exclusions of Black people, both continuing to define the rhetor and the technology user as White by default. This longstanding theoretical blind spot is especially pronounced in a field like English Studies, where race, technology, and questions of access are all addressed, sometimes even energetically, but where the connections between them are almost never explored. This chapter is an exploration of that odd silence as it has been carried out in the major journals and some other writings in composition and technical communication over the last 10 years, as well as in the development of African American rhetoric since it entered the university as an area of study. I examine this problem of representation by looking at the flashpoint where the Digital Divide and the Oakland controversy collided, and I argue that while there are staggering silences on the connections between these issues, silences that were made even more profound by the missed opportunities that national conversations about the Digital Divide provided, the twin sites of composition and technical communication are especially productive sites from which to address problems of technological access. African American rhetorical study can help bridge those sites, end those silences, and bring new theoretical tools to bear on the conversations about the relationships between technologies, literacies, and discourses that English Studies more broadly has plunged itself into.

RACE AND TECHNOLOGY ACCESS DURING THE GREAT EBONICS DEBATE

It might seem entirely irrelevant to some, but I'm fascinated with the fact that during the period of what is often called the greatest advance in technology in the last 100 years—and what many still like to suggest is the most important communication technology to emerge since the printing press—the nation and English departments throughout were mired helplessly in yet another Ebonics debate we'd already been through decades ago.

I'm still fascinated with the simultaneity of these events, nearly 10 years later, for many reasons: I wonder why the Oakland School Board's claim on federal resources for educating Black children caused such a furor two decades after the Ann Arbor trial, 30 years after the CCCC "Students'

Right" document, and almost 50 years after the Brown decision; why, almost to a person, Black "leaders" and advocates sounded just like White conservatives (and still do, given the despair and rage in Bill Cosby's recent rants about Black children not wanting to learn Standard English and their parents not caring enough to ensure that they do); and why assumptions about the supposed inferiority of African American varieties of English that have been dismantled consistently by Black and White linguists alike over the last several decades still hold such force, especially with language teachers and professionals. The most important reason I'm still fascinated with the connection between these events is because of what wasn't happening during that debate: serious, thoughtful discussion about race and the problem of access to computers, the Internet, and information technologies.

Although African American engineers and science professionals, and even some mainstream policymakers, have long understood the importance of equal access to these technologies, writing and communication teachers of all races have been mostly silent on the subject. If, however, the most important characteristic of computers and the Internet is their role as communication technologies—if, as Jay David Bolter and many others have argued, these tools have begun a revolution in communication more significant than any other in the 500 years since Gutenberg's printing press—the results for African Americans, who have consistently and often systematically been denied access to these technologies, will be catastrophic.

This said, English departments (specifically rhetoric and composition and technical communication programs) have been staggeringly silent about the problematic relationship between race and technology access that became crystallized in the term "Digital Divide." This silence is a peculiar one, given the facts that composition as a field owes its existence in many ways to the project of making equal access to higher education real, and has worked diligently, if not always effectively, at important points in its history to address the role of race in those struggles, especially as that struggle has been made manifest in scholars' and practitioners' longstanding debates about Ebonics. The silence is even more stark if one really considers technology access to be a rhetorical problem, because if it is, technical communication and rhetoric and composition more broadly are the intellectual spaces within English Studies, and maybe even the university as a whole, that have the potential to do the most to address it. I use the rest of this chapter to examine that silence over the last decade as it echoes throughout journals and books published in composition and technical communication, as well as in African American rhetoric, to show just how little has been said, offer an assessment of those attempts scholars have made, and identify places where we can speak across the divides inside our own discipline that maintain the severity of the Digital Divide that remains so pervasive. The point of this rehearsal of the work that has been done is not to castigate individual scholars or the allegiances that exist within our discipline. Rather, it is to show the opportunity we all missed but can still grasp, in adding depth to the shallow treatment technology access received when it finally did attract the attention of policymakers in the Clinton and Bush administrations; to show just how promising extended dialogue across our own disciplinary lines could be in making real progress in improving technology access for African Americans and all Americans, in making inquiry into technological issues a real part of the intellectual work of rhetoric and composition; and possibly—if genuine dialogue across those disciplinary silences ever begins—reshape the futures of rhetoric/composition, technical communication, and African American rhetorics.

During the last ten years since the Digital Divide and broader technology access issues emerged in the national conversation, not a single article in the three major technical communication journals, *Technical Communication, Technical Communication Quarterly*, and the *Journal of Technical Writing and Communication*, addresses the Divide or any technology access issue, although all of these journals frequently take up questions of the promises and perils of computers and the Internet. No article in *Technical Communication* addresses any issue related to race and technology—in fact, no article in the journal takes up the question of race at all—in spite of a significant presence of African-American and Latino/a engineers (because engineering and science students are the major audience for many technical communication programs and courses) in the workplace. When "cultural" issues are raised, the subject is broached in the service of global capitalism, focused on international students, employees, or clients. International in these cases often means those from Arab, Asian, or European countries. *Technical Communication Quarterly* manages a grudging nod in the direction of Black people with Heather Brodie Graves and Robert Graves' contribution on the need for cultural sensitivity in technical editing, "Masters, Slaves, and Infant Mortality." The *Journal of Technical Writing and Communication* continues the silence on access, but includes two articles on African Americans and communication: a study of Ebonics that purports to examine student attitudes toward the language variety by "translating" a Jesse Jackson speech into Ebonics. This article says nothing about the specific features of African American varieties of English their translation used, however, or why their version focused on the features it did. The authors of the second article present it as "a descriptive study of the Black communication style by African Americans within an organization." This 1997 article, "A Descriptive Study of the Use of the Black Communication

Style by African Americans within an Organization," by Vonnie Corsini and Christine Fagliasso, ends with the familiar call for an awareness of cultural differences.

Composition hasn't done much better. The discipline's major journal, *College Composition and Communication,* has published very few articles on technology access and writing instruction: Cynthia Selfe's 1997 chair's address to the annual conference, "Technology and Literacy: A Story about the Perils of Not Paying Attention," and "The Politics of the Interface: Power and Its Exercise in Electronic Contact Zones," a 1994 article by Cindy and Richard Selfe demonstrating that computer and other technology interfaces can uphold the very exclusions many thought they would eradicate. The good news is that their work has helped to push composition in a more progressive direction than technical communication, one that acknowledges the political and social forces at work in the development and use of any technology—and acknowledges racism as one of those forces. Unfortunately, that's about it.

How is it that the convergence of race and technology in the problem of differentiated access is ignored, evaded, or elided in a discipline that has long struggled with issues of race and access, and one that sees its work as teaching students and professionals to become critical users of technologies? How is it that the ways African Americans and other people of color use digital technologies are entirely neglected even in the few conversations that do take place? This discursive divide occurs in part because both areas have simply been slow to make the connection. Charles Moran calls scholars to this theoretical nexus in his essay "Access: The 'A' Word in Technology Studies," arguing that composition has to carefully, thoughtfully engage problems of race, gender, and wealth differences and what their resulting problems of access portend for teaching, research, and writing. This article appears in 1999, almost 2 decades after the emergence of the journal, *Computers and Composition,* and almost 5 years since the Department of Commerce's landmark Digital Divide reports, with Moran acknowledging that his work represents first steps for this kind of inquiry: "most of us simply do not deal with the relationship between wealth and access. I think of some of the major texts in our field . . . none of which raises the question of access in a substantial way" (p. 210). Moran continues, with a reflection on the institutional side of this neglect, "I would add to this list too, university alumni magazines and public relations documents that boast of their institution's technology without mentioning the fact that it is available only to a privileged few" (p. 210), and adds that scholarly anthologies in composition are complicit as well. Moran's critique of university public relations organs might seem trivial compared with the curricular and infrastructure work that does not happen, or universities' policy failures and their inability to reach out to communities and school districts that are desperate for their leadership and support, but his point is that institutional chest thumping to reach out to those who have been privileged while those failures remain is hypocritical, especially when many such guides and newsletters and magazines often find women and people of color to pose for token pictures to tout their commitments to "diversity."

James Porter does important work to clear out space for issues of access in the discipline in his book *Rhetorical Ethics and Internetworked Writing* that starts to take into account social and pedagogical issues, even if the book seems, at first glance, not to directly address how race and ethnicity might affect the definition of access he offers. Porter notes that access "may well be the number one ethical issue for internetworked writing" (p. 102), citing a need for scholars to move beyond the focus of most conversations about technology and access on the "haves" and find ways to genuinely include the "have nots." Cynthia Selfe also calls attention to the importance of access, and explores the importance of race in that conversation in her book-length treatment, *Technology and Literacy in the Twenty-First Century: The Importance of Paying Attention:*

> But if the project to expand technological literacy has been justified as a means of achieving positive social change and new opportunity, to date it has failed to yield the significant positive social progress or productive changes that many people have come to hope for. Indeed, the American school system as a whole, and in the culture that this system reflects, computers continue to be distributed differentially along the related axes of race and socioeconomic status, and this distribution contributes to ongoing patterns of racism and to the continuation of poverty. It is a fact, for instance, that schools primarily serving students of color and poor students continue to have access to fewer computers than do schools primarily serving affluent students or White students. And it is a fact that schools primarily serving students of color and poor students continue to have less access to the Internet, to multimedia equipment, to CD ROM equipment, to local-area networks, and to videodisk technology than do schools primarily serving more affluent and White students. (p. 6)

Selfe tells a truth we're loath to admit when we have to think about systemic exclusions: they *still* exist, and they're *still* tied to race. Selfe's project as she outlines it in this part of her book is significant not just because it begins to explore race and technology access. She also uses the book to examine the social and political implications that are involved in, but often hidden in, conversations about technologies by looking at the Clinton administration's

"Technology Literacy Challenge." What appeared to be a positive agenda by President Clinton, with its stated goals of "wiring every school in America," posed the danger, according to Selfe, of merely providing technology producers with the perfect market for their products: passive consumers dependent on those technologies, but unable to effect any meaningful change in the lives of those who have been marginalized.

Meaningful access to any technology involves political power and literacies: "in a formulation that literacy educators will feel most keenly, the project to expand technological literacy implicates literacy and illiteracy—in their officially defined forms—in the continued reproduction of poverty and racism. And it implicates teachers as well" (p. 7). That implication has become much more explicit in the years since Clinton's departure from office, because even those policies, with all their attendant dangers that Selfe points out, have been completely reversed. So not only did the Department of Commerce remove all of the "Falling through the Net" reports from its Web sites immediately upon the arrival of the new administration and reduce the Divide to a case of class envy (as I'll detail later), but the Department of Education stole and cruelly used the Children Defense Fund's "No Child Left Behind" slogan to sell policies that cut funding for schools that needed it most and identified thousands of schools serving poorer students and students of color as irrevocably "failing." But the subtitle of Selfe's book shows us just how much work remains for all of us in composition, computers and writing, and technical communication: "The Importance of Paying Attention." Both Selfe and Moran note that the field has not paid attention as of the turn of the century, imploring the field to finally catch up and take things digital and access to them seriously.

While race, and especially the connections between race and technology access, serve as what Catherine Prendergrast would call the "absent presence in composition," conveniently contained within easy labels that prevent action on an anti-racist agenda (like tolerance, multiculturalism, and diversity, to take those in common parlance these days) (p. 36), the silence is not all-engulfing, as small numbers have begun to pay attention. There is important work being done with, and in response to, Selfe and Porter, even if that work still amounts to rumors and rumblings where strength and passion are needed.

Moran and Selfe, in an article published in *English Journal*, geared primarily to K–12 English and Language Arts teachers, "Teaching English Across the Technology/Wealth Gap," continue their call for teachers to place the Digital Divide at the center of research, teaching, and activism for writing specialists, and acknowledge the critical role race places in access to digital technologies. They also press on to identify important problems for those who take up the challenge. Selfe and Moran argue in the article that embracing technology uncritically can not only contribute to worsening the wealth gap and power differences between people of color and Whites, but also make teachers the best allies a global capitalist society could hope for:

> Advocates for technology often have an agenda that has nothing to do with our students' learning. If one is a politician or academic administrator in this decade, it is almost mandatory to call for technology in our schools, not because of any proven link between technology and learning—there really is no consistent evidence of such a link, especially in language arts and literacy studies—but because technology is seen as a quick and cheap fix for the perceived problems in our educational system. Anything associated with technology has a special glow these days. We note this in regard to the extraordinary bubble in technology stocks that is helping to drive the stock market. . . . In language arts and English classrooms, we need to recognize that we can no longer simply educate students to become technology users—and consumers on autopilot—without helping them learn how to understand technology issues from socially and politically informed perspectives . . . [otherwise] we may, without realizing it, be contributing to the education of citizens who are habituated to technology but who have little critical awareness about, or understanding of, the complex relationships among humans and machines and the cultural contexts within which the two interact. (pp. 48, 52)

An investigation into the conditions of technology access and its relationship to education by the *Baltimore Sun* shows just how serious the problem is. Even when there is decent material access to computers, software, and internet connections, educators, students, and parents are still often hoodwinked, bamboozled, run amok, led astray, as Malcolm would put it. The fact that the grounds of officially sanctioned literacies are always changing, while students and schools in Black, Brown, and poor school districts are continually labeled as needing remediation as they navigate the seismic shifts in those grounds, in the high-stakes version of my electronic games parable in the prologue, leads to a collective desperation by parents, educators, and students themselves. Caught between the rock of political invective labeling them as failures and the hard place of magic pill solutions sold to them by technology companies, families and schools often make huge investments in technologies and still never escape the cycle.

The *Baltimore Sun* series "Poor Schools, Rich Targets" shows the devastation the convergence of forces Selfe calls us to attend: the Prince George's County, Maryland, school district, in response to the pressure of being designated a school in need of improvement under reporting standards included in the No Child Left Behind Act, held trials for an Algebra software package it might purchase. According to the article, this package, named "Plato," costs on average about $60,000 per school. Huge investments like these are not abnormal. Camden, New Jersey's school district, with 19,000 students, paid almost $11 million in site licenses to Compass Learning and a suite of educational video games from Lightspan. These programs are typically of the skill/drill/kill variety, and often only offer remediation. Compositionists can only wonder what happened to all of the intellectual struggle they waged over the last fifty years to move writing instruction beyond such a narrow focus, especially in schools and districts that have habitually reserved such instruction for poor students and students of color while children in Camden are stuck in labs working on grammar baseball games:

> One girl who was working on a punctuation drill was told to insert a comma in the appropriate place in the following sentence: "Robots will teach science in high school trade schools and kindergarten." The girl stared at the screen, which was illustrated with a picture of a robot, and then moved the mouse to place the comma between "school" and "trade." The screen lit up: She was right! Then it gave her another sentence to test the same skill: "The robots of 2019 will be able to see feel and have a better understanding of the world." Staring at the screen, the girl moved to add the comma to the correct spot again. (MacGillis, *Baltimore Sun*, 2004)

This is what Camden paid $11 million for, and the site licenses are only good for 3 years, after which time, of course, new versions will have been released costing even more. Administrators often feel that the expense is the only choice they have—a more justifiable use of funds than spending it on recruiting and paying signing bonuses to stronger teachers they often feel will not remain with the districts for any significant length of time.

Given these problems, Selfe and Moran articulate an agenda based on activism for equitable access across racial and economic lines, but for an access that is critically informed. This is the most important point for me, when we consider the ways Black students are continually dumbed down by skills-only curricula, whether in the name of "raising standards" which usually results in remediation and those same exclusions based on Black students not being prepared enough for whatever the new dominant understanding of literacy is in place at a given time. Technology issues must be as much the work of writing and communication teachers and scholars as writing and communication are, and we must find ways to build students' and teachers' digital literacies in the current environment of poorly funded schools and racialized education politics.

Toward the end of making the Digital Divide a central issue in curricula and pushing professional organizations to take public stands on technology policy issues, Selfe and Moran call on teachers to find ways to use any and all tools available in the project to expand access now. They suggest that given the expense of cutting-edge technologies and the fact that there is always some new cutting-edge software package or hardware tool being sold as the next great answer, the job of promoting digital literacies and writing abilities might often be best accomplished with lower-end tools (p. 52). Regardless of whether one pursues this strategy or not, the most important change in perspective for writing teachers is that they must make sure clearly articulated pedagogical goals drive all technology decisions so that purchases, training, and planning related to technology implementation remains relevant to the learning, social, political, and economic needs of those we hope to serve.

So a theoretical framework for initial action is in place in the field, if the voices offering it remain isolated ones. Jeffrey Grabill makes gestures toward filling an important void in computers and writing scholarship with his 1998 *Computers and Composition* article, "Utopic Visions, the Technopoor, and Public Access: Writing Technologies in a Community Literacy Program." This void is the need to engage some of the nascent policy/political/theoretical commitments in studies of how issues of access are played out in specific learning and teaching sites. Grabill's work is significant not only because it is concerned with access, but also because he argues that it is time for computers and writing specialists to take their work outside the composition classroom, to consider how "our understanding of how people write with computers will change because work in nonschool settings will alter inquiries and the knowledge produced" (p. 311). Grabill's understanding of access is built on Porter's definition (infrastructure, literacies, acceptance) and Porter's argument that access—who gets the resources, where they get access, what the environments will look like, and who will make decisions on all of these questions—is the key ethical issue that must drive all of our conversations about technologies and their relationship to written communication (p. 301). The Adult Basic Education program that Grabill studies serves primarily White women, but it clears valuable theoretical ground for composition and computers and writing faculty interested in community technology issues, and could link up in important ways with work on African American literacies outside the classroom as Elaine Richardson (2003) and Beverly Moss (2003) take it up in their respective books, *African American Literacies* and *A Community Text Arises*.

A few other pieces, mainly Susan Romano's (1993) "The Egalitarianism Narrative: Whose Story? Whose Yardstick?" and Kristine Blair's "Literacy, Dialogue, and Difference," advocate the use of computer-mediated communication technologies in the writing classroom, and attempt to disrupt simplistic assumptions that computers will magically create equal, democratic environments—moves that speak back in important ways to technology theorists like William Mitchell, whose *City of Bits* offers an architecture and urban planning model for the development of cyberspace with no consideration of the relationship between the racist histories of those professions and those who employ them and live and flee from the spaces they have designed and planned. Romano's and Blair's studies foreground valuable questions of Hispanic identity online, but are not overtly concerned with access.

One piece that does directly examine the connections between race and technology access as they affect African Americans is Elaine Richardson's "African American Women Instructors: In a Net." In her case study of three Black female writing instructors, Richardson works to show the political forces involved in their decisions to become more technologically literate, and to employ digital tools in their teaching. Richardson acknowledges the importance of technology access from the outset, but notes that women of color, because of the positions they often occupy as untenured or contingent faculty, do not have the luxury of adopting critical positions on technological issues or "opting out" based on their critiques that other members of the academy, and particularly English departments, tend to have. This constraint, when combined with obstacles that hinder these three instructors from gaining meaningful access (increased teaching loads, graduate study, publishing requirements, family and other responsibilities), can make access, even when it is achieved, highly problematic. Richardson's study helps shed light on the complexities of access, showing that it certainly includes all of the elements of Porter's initial definition, but also extends beyond materials, skills, and community acceptance. The burden of access is not only the responsibility of those seeking it, but is a systemic burden as well.

Although many African American scholars and teachers are concerned about how new technologies might open up possibilities for resistance to racism and participation in American society on their own terms, the pressing need for these writers has often been to address the perception that African Americans just don't "do" science and technology. In "Computers on Campus: The Black-White Technology Gap," a *Journal of Blacks in Higher Education* article published in 1993, Terese Kreuzer quotes Richard Goldsby, an African American teaching Biology at Amherst College at the time: "They aren't likely to be hackers or computer nerds. Computers are not part of Black culture" (p. 93). A jarring comment, even if made 12 years ago, but one repeated many times in different ways in the scholarship on African Americans and science and technology. In another *JBHE* article, "Will Blacks in Higher Education Be Detoured off the Information

Superhighway," Raymond Slater recognizes the difficult selling job in store for those who care about access:

> Black kids are not going to have the access to computers or online informa-
> tion services. We need to turn educators on to this problem. We are not
> sure how it's going to be done, but if it doesn't happen the technology gap
> between the races is going to widen. It's already wide, but it's going to get
> worse. (1999, p. 98)

Lois Powell (1990) begins an article in the *Journal of Negro Education* with the heading "The Black Scientist, a Rare Species." Some claim that there is no real problem with access to science and technology fields, but as recently as 2000, the National Action Council for Minorities in Engineering (NACME), a consortium of fellowship programs, faculty, foundation members, and National Science Foundation representatives working to solve this problem, published *Access Denied: Race, Ethnicity, and the Scientific Enterprise*, examining the systemic factors limiting the participation of people of color in the sciences, engineering, and mathematics.

Knowledge of the systemic barriers that Black people have faced in the sciences and technology doesn't help much here. Goldsby's comment still echoes: "computers are not part of Black culture." However laced with the same kinds of self-defeating stereotypes about Black people that undergirded the Ebonics debate, Goldsby's concern points to the perception that the sciences and technology have never been central to African American struggles against racism and for equal participation in American society. Almost 25 years ago, Herman and Barbara Young (1977), in "Science and Black Studies," urged Black Studies programs to make study of the sciences a more central part of their curricula: "most Black studies programs have been concentrated in the fields of humanities, history, and the social sciences. They have neglected one area of special significance in achieving their objectives, which is the contributions of Black men to the fields of science" (p. 381). They argue that African Americans have a long history of achievement in the sciences, and that more focus on those achievements would help meet all of Black Studies' major disciplinary goals, including "provid[ing] alternative ideologies for social change" (p. 380).

A quarter of a century later, few African American Studies programs have answered the call. Abdul Alkalimat, African American Studies director at the University of Toledo, is one of those who has, however, by explicitly linking technology to inquiry in African American Studies. In addition to creating eBlack, the online presence of Toledo's Africana Studies program, and in Alkalimat's words, the "virtualization of the Black experience," he

uses the current moment's conversations about technology to keep reflections about what African Americans can and should do with technolog(ies)
grounded in past struggle.

As he argues in an article published on cy.Rev (www.cyRev.com),
"Technological Revolution and Prospects for African American Liberation
in the 21st Century" (2001a), the relationship between technological
change and the economic, social, cultural, and political struggle of African
American people is the missing link in the "history of African American history." Technological advances that improved the mechanization of the cotton and auto industries bring this relationship into relief for Alkalimat:
"[c]otton and auto, as the leading sectors of the US economy—19th century
agricultural and 20th century industrial production—helped to structure
more than 150 years of African American labor. It has been this economic
structure of how agriculture and industry have utilized African American
labor that has set the stage for all of African American history." The perfection of the cotton gin provides the quintessential example of this relationship between technology innovation and African American struggle in
Alkalimat's analysis, as it is the creation of the cotton gin that made cotton
King and slavery even more profitable than it had been by the 1800s.

What makes this relationship important for the study of African American rhetoric is the fact that not only did these technological changes structure the conditions in which African American people lived, but they
influenced the environments in which they organized to resist those conditions. Just as the cotton gin mechanized the cleaning of cotton and created
incredible demands for slave labor, Alkalimat notes, the mechanical cotton
picker made sharecroppers obsolete, and was thus another important factor
in what is commonly known as the "second great migration" of African
Americans to the North (those migrating from the South after 1940) and led
to conditions becoming favorable for the Civil Rights movement to emerge.
He shows a similar pattern of high demand for African American labor being
created, and then obliterated by technological change in the automobile
industry, and points to the staggering unemployment statistics for African
American men in the 1980s and 1990s in northern cities as evidence.

One need not agree with the breadth of Alkalimat's claim that "the most
profound historical changes are linked to changes in technology" to take
from his analysis an understanding that there are important connections
between technological history in the United States and African American
struggle. An important part of this connection is the relationship between
communication technologies and rhetorical production. It is this relationship that I want to point to, as a way of extending Alkalimat's argument and
making it relevant for African American rhetorical study.

Advances in communication technologies do not simply amount to minor changes in the medium. All technologies come packaged with a set of politics: if those technologies are not inherently political, the conditions in which they are created and in which they circulate into a society are political and influence their uses in that society (Winner, 1986), and those politics can profoundly change the spaces in which messages are created, received, and used. The potential of the changes in these spaces can be staggering when considered in light of the communicative possibilities they can either open up or shut down. One's ability to understand and operate within those changed spaces determines whether her or his linguistic dexterity is even relevant—as any faculty member who has been flamed (translation: dissed) on an e-mail listserv will be happy to explain.

Radio provides a better example: what it represents as a communication space and its potential as a medium for both entertainment and activism are not only dependent on the transmission of sound through amplified or frequency modulations or the broadcasting power that determines a radio station's reach. The politics of the Federal Communications Commission's decision to expand the numbers of stations individual companies can own in a particular market has turned a local medium into a national one and had effects ranging as wide a spectrum as wholesale changes in programming formats and the near elimination of the Disc Jockey as a relevant figure in the life of a community, beyond making paid advertising appearances for those businesses who can afford them. These effects produce both rhetorical problems and opportunities, as the Tom Joyner Morning Show demonstrates. Sophisticated rhetors and technology users must be aware not only of the politics that come packaged with technologies, but also of the responses they both enable and limit.

African Americans' ability to make the move from "ideology to information," and to take African American experience into new technological spaces, to digitize African American history, struggle, and celebration, is important not only to survival for Alkalimat. It is also a move that offers possibilities that did not exist before: "[w]hile ideological struggle has persisted the information revolution has undercut the material conditions for ideological ignorance. The information revolution has increased our capacity to produce, store, distribute, and consume all texts—written, oral, and visual" (Alkalimat, 2001b). eBlack, as a model of what is possible when African American Studies, traditions, and struggle are digitized, is currently comprised of 5 programs or parts:

- ◆ Professional connection and discourse: eBlack edits and manages H Afro-Am, a listserv designed to connect faculty and graduate students in professional conversations in and about African American Studies. In the 3 years of its existence, it has attracted 1,000 members, and allows conversations that might never happen between scholars and students across wide geographic distances.

- Curriculum development through distance education: eBlack is developing a Pan-African studies program via the Internet, using distance education.

- Community Service: eBlack works to create websites for local churches in the Toledo area, and teach church members to create and maintain websites.

- Continuing Struggle, the African American Radical Congress: eBlack used the web to convene African American activists to "reinvigorate African American radicalism." Alkalimat notes that although many of the activists involved were skeptical about whether cyberspace could be an important site of struggle, organizing in this way not only allowed participants to document their work in spaces they could control, but that also prevented "factionalism and a hardening of ideological lines."

- Research Web site on Malcolm X: Alkalimat sees the web as an opportunity to combat the exclusions that are inherent in those institutions that have developed major archives of the papers of African Americans, like the Schomburg Center and many university libraries. The potential cyberspace provides for digitizing African American history can not only open up access to important figures like Malcolm X, but help to recover lost voices as well, including African American women, who Alkalimat notes, have been all but ignored by major archives.

What is important about Alkalimat's work with eBlack is not just that the histories and work of African American leaders, activists, and organization can be put online, but that cyberspace can transform that work because it is a space that, for all of the barriers to access that exist now, can allow more direct control of one's message than other media. As the Internet is currently constructed, a person who has a connection can view any site she wishes (that is not password protected, of course). Those with messages to share can target them directly to people they want to reach, unhindered by a television network's assumptions about African American people, or the limited range of AM radio or Cable television public access channels, for example. And it is far easier to own the means of production than it is a television station, radio station, newspaper, or magazine. So the possibilities for individual activists and rhetors are impressive, but they are just as bright for students and scholars of African American rhetoric.

Imagine, for example, if as a result of eBlack's work with churches in the Toledo area, or of any effort in any town, that twenty years from now, 2 or 5 or 10 churches in that area have Web sites that have archived all of their pastors' sermons (either in print, audio, video, or some combination of forms) over that 20 year period, with examples of church bulletins, directories, activities, and newsletters as well. One of the most studied forms in African American rhetoric, the sermon becomes much easier to study thoroughly, because many of the five challenges to offering rhetorical criticism of sermons that Lyndrey Niles identifies can be greatly minimized:

♦ Most African American sermons were not and are not prepared in manuscript form.

♦ Most African American sermons through the centuries were not and are not tape-recorded during delivery.

♦ Some preachers are reluctant to release copies for criticism.

♦ Because most African American sermons are in dialogue form, manuscripts may not satisfactorily represent what actually took place in the church.

♦ Sermons in the African American tradition were not written to be read. Much of the real impact, therefore, is lost unless the critic knows how the words would have sounded, and can picture the delivery in his or her mind as he or she reads the manuscript.

As I noted earlier and Niles' problems show, African American rhetoric has always been multimedia, has always been about body and voice and image, even when they only set the stage for language. Even within a definition of African American rhetoric as being about the word, careful considerations of how current technologies can extend its study will provide a much richer body of work for rhetorical criticism and analysis.

This connection is not just about the politics of a particular writing, speaking, or designing space, nor is it just about the benefits that can exist for students and scholars of rhetoric. Technologies shape all five of the classical canons of Rhetoric, and greatly affect the rhetorical situation, however one might define the concept. Whether the technology involved is a soapbox, a megaphone, printing press, typewriter, telegraph, microphone, television, radio, or Web site, the tools available affect the means available because of how they configure relationships between rhetors and their potential audiences.

Black intellectuals have always been concerned with improving African American participation in the sciences and technology, and to the degree that the humanities and social sciences are privileged, that emerges from the specific nature of the intellectual underpinnings of Western racism. Henry Louis Gates, Jr. and Nellie McKay (1997) look directly at this privileging of the humanities, offering some understanding of why literary production has had such a central role in African American struggle against racism for more than 200 years: "African American slaves, remarkably, sought to write themselves out of slavery by mastering the Anglo-American belletristic tradition" in ways "that both talked `Black' and, through its unrelenting indictment of the institution of slavery, talked back" (pp. xxvii, xxviii). Literature—and literacies—hold this important place for several reasons, Gates and McKay contend. Black inferiority was a dominant theme in Enlightenment philosophy and science, as they show through extensive quotations from Immanuel Kant, David Hume, and Thomas Jefferson. Many people already know the story of Enlightenment justifications of racism, but the assumptions that Black people had "no ingenious manufacturers amongst them, no arts, no sciences" (p. xxx) was accompanied by a draconian body of public laws, making two forms of literacy punishable by law: the mastery of letters and the mastery of the drum" (p. xxix). Gates' introduction to *Race, Writing, and Difference* quotes a passage from Hume that makes these assumptions explicit:

> I am apt to suspect the negroes, and in general all the other species of men (for there are four or five different kinds) to be naturally inferior to the Whites. There never was a civilized nation of any other complexion than White, nor even any individual eminent either in action or speculation. No ingenious manufacturers amongst them, no arts, no sciences . . . . Such a uniform and constant difference could not happen, in so many countries and ages, if nature had not made an original distinction betwixt these breeds of men. Not to mention our colonies, there are negroe slaves dispersed all over Europe, of which none ever discovered any symptoms of ingenuity . . . . In Jamaica indeed they talk of one negroe as a man of parts and learning [Francis Williams, the Cambridge-educated poet who wrote verse in Latin]; but 'tis likely he is admired for very slender accomplishments, like a parrot, who speaks a few words plainly. (1986, p. 10)

Given this legal and intellectual history, it becomes easy to read African Americans' commitment to literacy as a technological commitment and all of the means they have employed toward achieving literacy as technological mastery.

This connection between Black language and literary traditions and political struggle becomes even more explicit in Larry Neal's manifesto defining the Black Arts Movement. It is the Black Arts Movement that "is the aesthetic and spiritual sister of the Black Power concept" (p. 122). While the Black Arts Movement articulated goals for literary production that were very different from those of Phillis Wheatley or writers in the Harlem Renaissance, the larger purpose remained the same—to undermine Western racism based in pseudo science by using literature to talk back by talking Black, as

> writing, many philosophers argued in the Enlightenment, stood alone among the fine arts as the most salient repository of "genius," the visible sign of reason itself. In this subordinate role, however, writing, although secondary to reason, was nevertheless the medium of reason's expression. We know reason by its representations (Gates and McKay, 1997, p. xxx).

The fact that this literacy and literary activity was always engaged in a relationship with scientific and technological discourse cannot be overstated. V. P. Franklin and Bettye Collier-Thomas show this relationship in their reflection on Carter G. Woodson's (1969) work in founding the *Journal of Negro History*. They note that Woodson made it clear that this was to be "a quarterly scientific magazine" committed to publishing scholarly research and documents on the history and cultures of Africa and the peoples of African descent around the world. Woodson understood that publishing these articles and collecting these materials was the only way "that the Negro could escape the awful fate of becoming a negligible factor in the thought of the world." The activities pursued by the members of the Association for the Study of Negro Life and History (ASNLH) would "enable scientifically trained men and women to produce treatises based on the whole truth." V. P. Franklin used the life writings of African American literary artists and political leaders to demonstrate that "race vindication" was a major activity for Black intellectuals from the 19th century. African American preachers, professors, publishers, and other highly educated professionals put their intellect and training in service to the race to deconstruct the discursive structures erected in science, medicine, the law, and historical discourse to uphold the mental and cultural inferiority of African peoples (p. 1).

In other words, the chasm between literary and cultural production on one hand and scientific and technological pursuits on the other is not a part of the Black intellectual tradition, at least for one of the greatest intellectuals of that tradition, Dr. Carter G. Woodson. But just as dangerous as assumptions that Black people are not technologically inclined, is the assumption that race is, and should be, irrelevant online.

The case I make throughout this book for an African American digital rhetoric probably seems contrary to some. It might even seem odd to attempt to argue that the entire African American rhetorical tradition can and should be read with a focus on the importance of technologies and African Americans' access to them. After all, the story of African American rhetoric to this point has been primarily understood as being about mastery of "the word," written and especially oral, throughout our history. Examples of this focus on speeches and essays abound, from foundational texts defining the scope of Black rhetorical study to articles analyzing specific rhetorical performances, regardless of the disciplinary homes (English Studies or Speech and Communication) of their authors. The titles of some of the major works in the field demonstrate this focus: Alice Moore Dunbar Nelson's (2000) *Masterpieces of Negro Eloquence*, Arthur Smith's (now Molefi Asante) *Voice of Black Revolution*, Philip Foner's (1975) anthology *Voice of Black America*, Foner and Branham's (1998) follow-up edition *Lift Every Voice*, Geneva Smitherman's (1986) trailblazing theoretical work *Talkin and Testifyin: The Language of Black America* and Gerald Early's (1992) collection on the African American essay *Speech and Power: The Afro American Essays and Its Cultural Contents from Polemics to Pulpit* are but a few examples. This is not to say that individual scholars in African American rhetoric have not discussed technology issues, but rather that traditions of Black mastery of spoken and written language and their use of it in collective struggle remains the frame that organizes the field.

Using such a frame works, obviously, for many reasons—not only because of its congruence with the events of that history from Frederick Douglass' ability to trick White playmates into teaching him to read when it was illegal for him to learn, to Ida B. Wells' crusading uses of argument in "A Red Record" to condemn state-supported terror and lynchings of Black people, to Barack Obama's celebrated 2004 speech at the Democratic National Convention (a speech far more worthy of note for its poetic delivery than for any new Black progressive agenda, as it offered none)—but because it allows a relatively coherent view of that history. Because African American history has been so much about anti-racist struggle, because that struggle has been so consistently about making the argument for equal and meaningful participation in the nation, and because our greatest victories often emerge from the linguistic and argumentative brilliance of activists, poets, teachers, grassroots organizers, preachers, politicians, essayists, and musicians, it makes sense to organize that study around the spoken and written word.

It also allows for a somewhat stable narrative. One can link the power and commitment of Stevie Wonder's music to the development of Malcolm X's political voice and his ability to simultaneously take the best elements of the African American homiletic tradition and turn that tradition on its head. Carol Mosely Braun's fly signifyin on Jesse Helms in formal legislative debate (Crenshaw, 1997) can be connected to innumerable unnamed people across historical eras and social, political, and economic circumstances based on their use of argument to pursue a collective agenda on behalf of African American people, whether that agenda be one of resistance and revolution (Smith) or access to some notion of "the good life" (Golden & Rieke). Just as important, the word as the organizing trope of African American rhetorical study provides scholars and students with a ground on which to offer that narrative unshaken by the rapid changes that occur in communication media. It doesn't matter whether we talk about poetry that had to be authenticated by 18 of Boston's "most prominent citizens" because it could not be conceived that it was written by an African American person, as in the case of Phillis Wheatley, or the multimedia connectivity of Tom Joyner's attempts to get African American folks to "party with a purpose," the same analytical tools allow for conversations about all African American rhetorical production.

This promise of analytical stability across rhetorical situations and across communication media is a tempting one. So tempting, in fact, that to claim that technologies can be just as important a concept as the word is to take on a challenge, and might even seem to border on the heretical. Technology issues seem to be entirely unconnected to the making of arguments, and everyone knows how troubling African American relationships with technologies have been. But that's just the argument I want to make. Alongside our understanding of the centrality of language to African American rhetorical production, a parallel examination of how African American rhetors have used and manipulated communication technologies can foster both access and transformation.

As strenuously as I follow Abdul Alkalimat's lead, arguing that African American rhetoric has always been about technology issues, and that study in African American rhetoric should be opened up to examine more carefully those writing, designing, and performative acts that are acknowledged (but not appreciated as rhetorical in nature), I also argue that these other acts and texts need to be included *with*, not instead of, oratory. I believe, with Philip Foner and Branham, editors of *Lift Every Voice*, that even now, with all of our technologies, oratory is still the genre of public engagement—the genre where the work any group of people commit to begins. As important as the Internet, books, magazines, journals, songs, dances, nightclubs, church services, and many other spaces are, it's still the sermon, the conference, the convention, the political speech, where the people make their commitments known. This is even more the case in African American communities, where Black people place an even greater emphasis on one's speaking ability, as those who are seen as African American public intellectuals themselves would have to attest. Had Cornel West never written any of the 20 books he has written, or written 20 more, his influence in African American communities would still depend to a large extent on his ability to "make it plain, reb," and make whatever knowledge he has translate at the podium. That said, work in African American rhetoric has to involve examining the technology issues involved in oratory at least as much as opening up Black rhetorical traditions to visual, electronic, and design issues.

Beth Kolko shows what is possible when scholars across this discursive divide do pay attention to each other, however. She argues that the history of racialized exclusions and their attendant assumptions of utter Black difference and irrelevance are programmed right into the interface of online environments like MOOs and MUDs—writing spaces similar to chats that accounted for much of the initial popularity of "cyberspace." Her essay, "Erasing @race: Going White in the (Inter)face," questions how race as a category has been elided in such media through various design choices, and it further investigates how the construction of "raceless" interfaces affects the communicative possibilities of virtual worlds (p. 214). This elision is a hallmark not only of the MOO and MUD environments with which Kolko is concerned—"the history of online communities demonstrates a dropping-out of marked race within cyberspace" (p. 214).

Kolko builds on the work of Richard and Cynthia Selfe (1994) with her examination of the interface as a raced yet e-raced space. This problem is important, in her words, because

> what this line of inquiry seems to represent is a growing awareness that technology interfaces carry the power to prescribe representative norms and patterns, constructing a self-replicating and exclusionary category of "ideal" user, one that, in some very particular instances of cyberspace, is a definitively White user. (p. 218)

This is a very different conclusion about racelessness in online spaces than that reached by many theorists caught up in the initial technological rapture, who frequently assumed that cyberspace as raceless space would mean that race, gender, and economic class would no longer matter and would usher in new, equal, and thoroughly democratic worlds—both online and off.

Elaine Richardson and Samantha Blackmon are among very few African Americans in Rhetoric and Composition who address these issues. Their work, along with that of individuals like Kolko, Richard and Cynthia Selfe, James Porter, Jeff Grabill, and Johndan Johnson-Eilola, is important for several reasons. It takes technology access seriously as an intellectual and activist project for Rhetoric and Composition and Technical Communication instruction; it acknowledges directly the connections that exist between gender, class, and racism rather than attempting to reduce the Digital Divide to an outbreak of class envy, as has current FCC Chair (and son of U.S. Secretary of State, Colin Powell) Michael Powell; and it offers glimpses into an agenda for addressing the Digital Divide that goes beyond the mere existence of hardware and software to the quality of that hardware and software and Internet connections, technological literacies, and critical understandings of technology that are needed to gain meaningful access to any technology. Unfortunately, the fact that I can name the individuals who have attended to these concerns and review the work done to address them in the space of a decade has kept the Digital Divide firmly in place for Blackfolk and in the academy. In fact, we are guilty of exacerbating its persistence when, for a brief moment from 1995 to 2001, there existed some amount of political will to do something about it, even if the Clinton administration's efforts to address the Digital Divide seemed based on a definition that amounts to the same access African American children have to public education or Black Floridians to the franchise: a vaguely articulated right to be in the same space *if* one navigates all the other barriers that prevent that presence. An examination of Clinton's policy initiatives on technology access and some of the shortsighted (sometimes well-intentioned, sometimes not) debates about whether a Divide even exists and how important it might be will begin to show one of the many ways technology access is a rhetorical problem and the need for our critical focus on it.

While one reason for the persistence of the Digital Divide is the reduction of African Americans to the level of people who have neither language, rhetoric, nor technology, another reason is the level of contest that exists around the term, especially when it is connected to race. Thus, the Digital Divide involves both contest and silence: debate over whether there is a Divide at all, waged by politicians, foundations, and business interests now; debate over whether race is a factor in whatever problems in technology access might exist; and concern that the use of a term like *Digital Divide* represents African Americans unfairly and does more to further the erasure of Black people by continuing to cast them as the utter outsider. These debates all carry assumptions about what constitutes access to computers, the Internet, or any digital technology that, even when guided by the best of intentions, threaten disaster if not addressed. This danger exists because those assumptions will guide legal, corporate, and educational policies that can trap Black people into roles as passive consumers of technologies rather than producers and partners, and worse, lead to continued electronic invisibility and economic, educational, and political injustice.

While African Americans have often at least implicitly understood technological issues as central to Black advancement, public recognition of race as a factor affecting access to digital technologies is a recent phenomenon, and largely due to the work of Larry Irving and many others on "Falling through the Net," the series of U.S. Department of Commerce reports that introduced the term *Digital Divide* to the lexicon in 1995. "Falling through the Net," in all four of its versions, acknowledged race as a factor just as important as education, income level, and geography in determining who is and is not able to obtain technology access. The first of the four reports, subtitled "A Survey of the Haves and Have Nots in Rural and Urban America," published in July 1995, examined access to the NII or National Information Infrastructure, by measuring the rates of telephone, computer, and modem "penetration" (i.e., the numbers of people who had telephones, computers, and computer modems in their homes). The major findings of the report were that education, age, and residence either in rural areas or central cities were important factors determining access to the Internet, but that race was just as crucial. Rural and city African Americans had the lowest rates of computer ownership, but the few who were online were significant in how they used the tools. Those African Americans were more likely than many other groups to use the Net to look for jobs, to take classes online, and access government reports. The policy recommendations of "Falling through the Net" focused on connectivity: to develop more specific profiles of those who had telephones, computers and modems, and to provide assistance, primarily through an interim tactic of supporting community access providers like libraries and public schools. The fundamental assumption of the first report was the concept of universal access—that every household that wanted to connect to the National Information Infrastructure should, and ultimately, would be able to do so.

Three years later, the Department of Commerce and NTIA released a revision of the report, "Falling through the Net II: New Data on the Digital Divide." The focus of this revision was primarily in providing a clearer look at the patterns that emerged from the first study, using 48,000 door-to-door surveys completed by the Census Bureau in 1997. In other words, the goals were to be able to better aggregate and disaggregate the data about who was connected and who was not, and to gauge the degree to which the patterns presented in the first report held or changed. The NTIA found that even with significant growth in computer ownership and Internet connectivity, the gap between numbers of African Americans who had access and the broader population *increased* between 1994 and 1997 (a difference of 21.2%

in computer ownership rates in 1997 as opposed to a 16.4% difference in 1994). Further, as ubiquitous as telephone usage seemed to be for many during the 1980s and 1990s, there were still large gaps in telephone penetration across racial lines. Data collected for this report revealed that Whites were more than twice as likely to own a computer as Black people (40% vs. 19%) and almost three times more likely to be connected to the Net from home (21.2% vs. 7.7%). The policy recommendations in the second report remained the same; namely that more needed to be done to get people connected to the Internet, and that public access points would be an important means for providing that access. Again, the focus was on computer, telephone, and modem ownership as constituting access, and the report failed to engage the implications of Black, Latino/a and Native American people being disproportionately forced to share access in cramped public spaces while others worked in the comfort of home, with the leisure of learning skills and nuances of how the technologies worked. This assumption that mere physical proximity to a technology or ownership of the products is all there is to access is a troubling one that still dominates many studies on technology access.

The next of the reports, released in 1999 and subtitled "Defining the Digital Divide," concludes by acknowledging the likely persistence of the Divide, and begins to offer data on computer and Internet usage in schools and libraries. The connections that some of us now take for granted between technologies, literacies, and education thanks to Cindy Selfe's book emerge here, as this version of the report warns the nation that it will be impossible to eliminate race as a problem in American society without addressing technology and information access. The report noted that economic survival would soon be tied to information access, and recommended policies and strategies aimed at filling the gaps that still existed in computer ownership and Internet connectivity, including lower prices, lease arrangements, and free computers, but took what amounts to a laissez-faire, free-markets-solve-most-problems pass given to those in the technology sector, arguing that increasing price competition between companies trying to gain market share would do much to minimize many of these gaps. This version of the report made references to issues of the relevance of technologies in peoples' lives and content (such as software and documentation), but these references were brief and did more to skip over these problems than address them. The report called for outreach that would "let them know why they should care—how new technologies can open new opportunities for them and their children." To use an old missionary metaphor, salvation was only possible if the heathen saw the error in their ways and converted while government and business could continue to operate as usual.

The final version of the report, published in October 2000, sounds like a reelection campaign speech, proclaiming mission accomplished. It reported major progress among all groups, based on the same notion of connectivity (computer, telephone, and modem ownership) as the only important elements determining one's overall access, although it also considered computer use in public places as the third version did. The final report accounted more fully for how those with access used the Net, with information broken down into categories recognizing work, research, shopping, personal, and entertainment uses. Again, access is still defined as mere connectivity: not as literacies and community acceptance, as Porter argued for; not as critical awareness or change in the lives of individuals or communities, as African American rhetors have always argued for.

Other studies were undertaken to pursue some of the questions sparked by the "Falling through the Net" series. Two of the more widely cited of these reports were Donna Hoffman and Thomas Novak's "Bridging the Digital Divide: The Impact of Race on Computer Access and Internet Use" and the Pew Internet and American Life Project's "African Americans and the Internet," both also released in 2000. While the Hoffman and Novak report acknowledges significant differences in access to the Internet by race, that access is also still defined by the access = connectivity model: questions focused on whether and how one used the Internet (in the last week, in the last 6 months),and whether that use took place at home or work, or at other locations. What is important about the Hoffman and Novak study is that, as the later NTIA reports do, it controls for education and income and shows that the Digital Divide is significantly connected to race. The conclusions from their work were that more African Americans were online than previously thought, and that African Americans need multiple points of access because home computer ownership rates are so different across racial lines.

The Pew report looked more at how African Americans used the Net than on questions of connectivity. Tracking a sample of 12,571 adults—2,087 of them African American—for 6 months, the study concluded that African Americans are more likely to have looked for job information, religious information, music, video, and audio clips, and more likely to have looked for places to live online than the general population. The Pew study, however, interpreted all of its results solely by comparison with the uses to which White Americans put computers and the Internet, repeating the erasure Beth Kolko argued is a fundamental characteristic of technology decision makers, making Whites' uses of these tools a technological default, rather than viewing the results through a lens focused on African Americans' needs, experiences, and histories with the technologies. The major result of the Pew study was that the Divide, in their view, was narrowing, and this conclusion has generated much conversation about whether or not people need to continue to view the Digital Divide as an "African American" problem.

Regardless of the problems in definition of access operative in the initial "Falling through the Net" studies, however, Larry Irving, its principal author, was very clear about trying to call the nation's attention to it as a problem of the legacy of racial exclusions in this country (no matter how muted the language might seem), calling it not only a major economic issue for Black people, but a Civil Rights issue as well. The reports on the Divide were used to support policies throughout President Clinton's administration that had universal access for all Americans as their stated goal. The potential these policies offered educators, even with all of their flaws in defining access as mere connectivity, was short-lived, however, because the concept of a Digital Divide that was deeply rooted in the stubbornness of racial exclusions came under attack from several quarters. Some politicians and public figures attacked the notion that such a phenomenon as a systematic Divide in technology access even existed, while others argued that its determining factor was class, and therefore, irrelevant, since, after all, class differences will always exist. Finally, even some Blackfolk committed to digital progress for African Americans grew weary of what seemed to be the same old, same old: more definitions of Black people as behind, and intentional silence about the technological innovation that has always been there, obscured by the story of a Divide.

In widely reported comments from his first press conference as the new chair of the Federal Communications Commission, Michael Powell maliciously reduced the Digital Divide to a toy fetish, announcing for all, from the beginning, that the Bush administration wasn't havin it, saying, "I think there's a Mercedes Divide. I'd like to have one, but I can't afford one." He continued, "I don't mean to be completely flip about this . . . but it shouldn't be used to justify the notion of essentially the socialization of the deployment of the infrastructure," a contention completely contradicting the "Falling through the Net" reports' tepid strategies of wiring schools and libraries and its mild, responsibility-evading conclusions that the marketplace would eliminate any problems in access that remained. Of course, under Powell's leadership, the FCC would later mandate that televisions makers equip sets with high-definition technology rather than allowing free market forces that Republicans and Democrats alike often tout to allow consumers to decide whether they wanted such changes, a kind of "socialism" for Sony and Magnavox and other television makers, but such ironies did not matter when the FCC made the later decision. Intervention on behalf of technology producers to force innovation, force the obsolescence of millions of perfectly good television sets in the next decade was more important than intervention to help African Americans, American Indians, Latino/Hispanic peoples, and poor Whites in urban and rural areas achieve anything resembling "basic" access to the National Information Infrastructure. After referring to the "so-called Digital Divide," Powell added in the same press conference, "I think the term sometimes is dangerous in that it suggests that the minute there's a new and innovative technology in the market, there's a divide unless it is equitably distributed among every part of the society." And in what became the ultimate sign of disrespect, given the FCC's later policy decisions, he added, "You know what? It's going to be the wealthier people who have the largess to go out and buy $4,000 high-definition TVs first. Does that mean there's an HDTV divide? No." Now, of course, no political leader, corporate executive, researcher, or teacher has ever argued that Mercedes Benz cars or HDTVs will be necessary for people to gain employment or participate in democracy, as politicians and legions of academics, community leaders and others have about computer-related communication technologies. However, this point was clearly irrelevant to Powell, who was content to dismiss all of these concerns and the nation's racist past and present as just the latest case of economic playa-hatin.

Not everyone challenging the concept of the Digital Divide or the racial element of the Divide are as polemical, political, or maliciously short-sighted as Chairman Powell was in his attempt to deflate the entire concept of the Information Superhighway (as the NII was called) to a high-end import car and a form of television the public still hasn't decided it wants to adopt yet, despite the FCC's activism on its behalf. Some African Americans in the technology industry have made moves to re-center conversations about the Divide away from race and toward class as the major factor. Barry Cooper and David Ellington are among those technology professionals. A Salon.com (Rawlinson, 1999) article quotes Cooper, the CEO of BlackVoices.com, as saying that "people have legitimate concerns, but if [there] is a divide, it is economic." Ellington, founder and CEO of NetNoir.com, concurs: "I don't feel there is much of a divide anymore. The Internet is becoming relevant in our lives as a result of e-mail and chat sites, and African Americans are going online in droves." In these cases, the same understanding of access as mere connectivity and usage, the same assumptions that drove the major early studies of the Divide, were being used to dismantle the concept.

A collection of Black academics known as AfroGeeks also have serious problems with the persistence of the Divide as a trope, calling attention to the serious gaps in access that Black people continue to face. The group presents its motto as "from technophobia to technophilia" and is far more concerned with the ways discussions about the Digital Divide have "erased" the contributions of technology innovators. The group's home on the web, http://www.afrogeeks.com, hosted on the University of California at Santa Barbara server, announces boldly:

> In recent years, African Americans, especially, have been portrayed as poster children for the digital divide discourse. Though rarely represented as full participants in the information technology revolution, Black people are among the earliest adopters and comprise some of the most ardent and innovative users of IT. It is too often widespread ignorance of African Diasporic people's long history of technology adoption that limits fair and fiscally sound IT investments, policies and opportunities for Black communities locally and globally. Such racially aligned politics of investment create a self-fulfilling prophesy or circular logic wherein the lack of equitable access to technology in Black communities produces a corresponding lack of technology literacy and competencies.
>
> Thus, necessary high-tech investments are not made in such under-served communities because many consider it fiscally irresponsible, which, in turn, perpetuates this vicious cycle. Despite such formidable odds, Black people continue to break out of this cycle of socially constructed technological determinism. It is this way that African Disaporic people's many successes within new media and information technologies are too often overshadowed by the significant inequalities in technology access.

In other words, "you ignorant niggas is keeping me from getting mine, with all that noise about the access you ain't got." This seems like a harsh assessment of an argument that clearly speaks some truth, but the assessment is just for several reasons. The Digital Divide is not the equivalent of national "why Johnny can't read" campaigns that brand Black people illiterate in the service of continued American racism, but rather, was deployed by Black technology innovators in the Clinton administration (namely Irving and William Kennard, the FCC chair who preceded Michael Powell), community organizations, academics like Abdul Alkalimat, and activists in order to call attention to systemic inequalities—the same inequalities that the Afro-Geeks acknowledge in their rant. Moreover, their embrace of technologies is unequivocal, lumping those with any critical consciousness about the ills they could cause or exacerbate as Luddites and technophobes who are part of the problem by announcing that the transition must be from phobia to philia. More worrisome than either of these issues, however, is the fact that they see their erasure as the *result of* the struggle for equitable access rather than part of the larger problem of the Divide, reflecting the same crabs-in-the-barrel mentality, the same scorn for Black people who have been systematically denied the educations and digital literacies they enjoy that were the worst excesses of turn of the 20th-century uplift ideology.

Although there are no absolute unities and many middle and upper-middle class Blackfolk will not have the same commitments as those who still struggle against systematic exclusion, middle class invisibility and the utter exclusion of working and poor Black people from the technologies, politics, and economies of mainstream American life still emerge from the same history of racism rather than problems we might have with each other. Rhetors like Marcus Garvey preached this incessantly, appealing for unity as we fight the issues that affect us rather than attacking each other over superficial differences. Unfortunately, these appeals for unity came out as bitter attacks on those Garvey saw as Black liberals imitating Whites, but the spirit of his argument beyond the rancor in his need to write himself into the discourse remain. In "An Exposé of the Caste System Among Negroes," Garvey (1923) writes, "unfortunately, there is a disposition on the part of a certain element of our people in America, the West Indies, and Africa, to hold themselves up as the 'better class' or 'privileged' group" (p. 268). Garvey saw this developing caste as rooted in class, which at that point in time often meant skin complexion. Rather than skin politics, the issue here is digital politics, where the AfroGeeks charge that it is Black technology activists and their allies, rather than larger systems of racism, that have denied them due recognition for their achievements.

I want to temper the charge just a bit at this point, because I do not believe the group intends to target Black activists as they do. It seems they misread the Digital Divide and the work toward equitable access it sparked as yet another in the long line of efforts I detailed earlier in the chapter, identifying Black students as Ebonics students needing remediation, and Black technology users and potential users as digital illiterates needing remediation. But to confuse Larry Irving and William Kennard for Rod Paige and Michael Powell is every bit as disingenuous—especially because the AfroGeeks are academics—as some of Garvey's well-known charges that W. E. B. DuBois worked against Black interests. By identifying "Digital Divide discourse" as the problem denying them their respect, the AfroGeeks risk the problem of seeming to try to write themselves into the larger digital discourse at the expense of young people and adults who can't eat or get decent jobs in an education system that has never yet answered the essential challenge of the *Brown vs. Board* case and verdict from 50 years ago.

DEFINING ACCESS—AND A NEW VISION FOR AFRICAN AMERICAN RHETORIC

Fortunately, not all African American technology professionals view the Divide as Powell, Ellington, and Cooper do, nor do they all argue that we must stop talking about the Divide. And, in spite of the numerous debates that mark this territory, there is hope that those concerned with equal technology access for Black people can make that argument and demand that long traditions of Black technology innovation can be recognized. More sophisticated approaches to these debates can point us to higher ground, to more nuanced understandings of exactly what constitutes access, and a vision of what African American rhetoric might look like in this digital age. Let me begin this section with another version of the call I've issued:

> What is usually missing in our celebrations of African American history is a focus on how technological change contributes to the structural basis of African American history. . . . The entire sweep of African American history needs to be examined on the basis that technological change creates the main structural context for the grand historical narrative of enslavement and the subsequent freedom struggle. (Alkalimat, 2001a)

And one possible response, given the context of the Digital Divide we find ourselves in:

> The folks promoting this nonsense—I call them "tricknologists"—are the high tech equivalent of the three card monty dealers you see on street corners. You know the game: they get you to follow one card, and all the while the real action is somewhere else. Well, that's exactly what the New Age tricknologists are doing with the Digital Divide debate. The trick is simple: the first step is to narrow the definition of the Divide, by saying that computer ownership and Internet usage are how we measure minority participation in the new, high-tech economy. In fact, all these statistics prove is that minorities are closing the gap in becoming consumers of technology, not in being producers or equal partners. . . . Saying that the Digital Divide is closing because minorities have greater access to computers is like saying minorities have a stake in the automobile industry because they drive cars, or that they are Bill Gates because they own Microsoft Office 2000. (Taborn, 2001, p. 8)

You won't find too many engineers in African American rhetoric anthologies, but Tyrone Taborn, as publisher of *U.S. Black Engineer: Information Technology*, is obviously grounded in the tradition. His magazine is billed as "the African American community's technology magazine," continuing in the history of periodicals committed to advocacy for African American people. As is clear in the previous quote, taken from the February 2001 "Community Awareness" issue, Taborn understands technology as one of the major battlegrounds for African American struggle in this era of post–Civil Rights retrenchment. More than just an intriguing rhetorical performance in its own right, with its comparison of technology decision makers with everyday slicksters, Taborn's article shines a spotlight on the connections that have always existed between communication technologies, questions of access, and the African American rhetorical tradition. These connections can allow a new look at that tradition and how scholars might engage it in a new century, toward the combined ends of full participation in American society and the preservation and celebration of African American identity.

The history of African American rhetoric is, in many ways, one of individuals and collectives of writers, speakers, visual artists, and designers mastering, manipulating, and working around available technologies, even when access to them had been denied the masses of Black people. Through concentrating on this connection between communication technologies and rhetorical production, by looking forward to African American futures to look back through traditions of struggle, African American rhetorical scholars can not only offer far richer analyses of those speeches and writings considered to be within the tradition, but can also open those traditions up beyond just the word and show it has always been multimedia, using *all* the available means in resisting racism and pursuing justice and equal access on behalf of African American people.

Taborn helps us to understand that the AfroGeeks are partially right, but that Larry Irving and William Kennard are as well, as is Abdul Alkalimat in his work over the last decade. We must complicate access, and use our understanding of it to look forward, imagining Black futures, then back through African American rhetorical traditions and legacies of struggle, understanding histories to be created in the service of the futures we want.

What exactly, then, constitutes technology access, and how can it, whatever it is, sustain new visions of African American rhetoric, and rhetoric and composition, more broadly? Before moving to that central point, I want to reiterate that this current context of technology access—of the Digital Divide and its connection to America's larger racial ravine—is an especially productive one in which to offer a new look forward to a new conception of African American rhetoric. This is because the Divide itself is a rhetorical problem at least as much as it is a technical or material one, and because technology issues have always functioned as a metaphor for imagining collective Black futures. As a field that has always had to address issues of access either directly or indirectly, African American rhetoric becomes central to both broader rhetorical and digital theory. And study at this important intersection of issues can continue the work of transforming the nation by eliminating that Divide, by addressing the real effects of technological exclusions, just as those rhetors we study always have. There are: the continual removal of Black labor from the workforce, inadequate health care, a legal system that operates on the presumption of Black guilt, a continual White flight into and out of urban centers, voting systems that conveniently do not work in major elections, and computer and information industries that operate comfortably under the assumption that Black people are non-technological while they spend billions of dollars to recruit, train, and develop temporary talent from overseas—when companies don't just send the jobs themselves overseas. All of this is at least possible—if technological issues make it onto our maps of the field, and if we end the silences that have prevented composition, computers and writing, and other elements of English Studies from taking Black intellectual traditions seriously.

A technological reading of African American rhetorical history offers at least three benefits beyond the obvious one of a more thorough appreciation of Black contributions to, challenges to, and even transformations of, the nation:

♦ A richer set of tools for analyzing those speeches and texts that have always been considered part of the tradition;

♦ A wider set of texts, images, sounds, and issues to address, and

♦ A chance to develop the arguments and policies that will end the Digital Divide and challenge the nation to accept responsibility for the exclusions programmed into its technologies rather than continue to assume that technologies are neutral and that there is nothing systematic about the differences in American life that remain tied significantly to race.

Attempting a useful definition of meaningful access is a difficult task, but all of the partial answers that have emerged throughout this chapter show that it is possible: Porter's call for literacies and community acceptance in addition to the black boxes that dominate the Digital Divide reports; equal distribution of the black boxes themselves; the Selfes' and Charles Moran's call for critical awareness of the roles technologies play so that we avoid becoming passive consumers; even the AfroGeeks' insistence that we eliminate the centuries-old constructions of Black people as utterly illiterate and therefore unworthy of participation in the society and the technologies that govern it. All of these can contribute to an understanding of access that goes beyond the material and move us closer to the transformative ideals that unify Black rhetorical traditions.

One of the difficulties in defining access lies in the stubbornness of common understandings of technologies as merely the instruments people use to extend their power and comfort. Technologies also include the systems of knowledge we must acquire to use any particular tool and the networks of information, economic, and power relations that enable that tool's use. An example might help clarify this point. Law enforcement is a technological system for protecting the persons and property in a society, as well as the desired patterns of relations between them. Regardless of the availability of individual tools to police in their work (guns, nightsticks, pepper spray, hands, feet, squad car computers, dashboard video cameras) and the wide range of force those tools represent, young Black and Latino men (and increasingly, women) are killed, injured, arrested, charged, and convicted at higher rates than other groups of people in this country.

Observers from different academic disciplines would offer very different explanations for why these patterns endure, why as a nation we were not horrified enough by the cases of Amadou Diallo and Abner Louima to demand fundamental change in policing, although we were (I use *we* sarcastically here) angry enough to press for changes to the judicial system in the aftermath of the Simpson verdict. I have no desire to take up those disagreements here. My point is simply this: any decision about how police use the tools and force they have is largely a result of what they have been taught about when and how to use them and the mandates police forces are given that construct crime and criminals in particular ways. Because of these literacies and processes and encoded forms of knowledge, one will almost always hear a defense of officers being within the law or policy of using the "maximum allowable force" in answering a brutality complaint rather than being expected to use the minimum force necessary to subdue a suspect.

The Clinton administration efforts I've cited throughout this chapter to "wire every school in America" in the mid to late 1990s offer another example. Many technologists and educators argued passionately that computers and the Internet connections in schools would be the great equalizer in American education. Ensuring that all students had networked computers in their schools would not only avail them of information that had never been distributed equally in their land-based schools, but would make their teachers better and motivate students to learn. For all of the passion that went into creating programs and writing grants to install hardware, software, and connections in schools, no mechanisms were in place to ask how the new computers would be used. Few resources existed for school systems to teach either students or faculty how to even use these tools, much less integrate them into anti-racist democratic teaching agendas. Few considered the difference that anywhere from a 5 to a 25 year head start would make for teachers, students, and parents who had already been indoctrinated into digital culture, and more importantly, had been made comfortable enough with computers and the Net to take advantage and ownership of the technologies. And when people did begin to consider these issues in the last few years, almost no African Americans were present where the decisions were being made, either in technology companies, policy think tanks, university faculties, consulting companies, vendors, IST or technical writing faculties, or the policies, documentation, content, interfaces and environments, or training efforts any of them created.

The problem with the Digital Divide as a concept for addressing systematic differences in access to digital technologies is that it came to signify mere material access to computers and the Internet, and failed to hold anyone responsible for creating even the narrow material conditions it prescribed. Beyond the tools themselves, meaningful access requires users, individually and collectively, to be able to use, critique, resist, design, and change technologies in ways that are relevant to their lives and needs, rather than those of the corporations that hope to sell them. Let me sketch what I believe is a more effective matrix for understanding technology access and then conclude with some reflections on what this changed understanding might mean for writing instruction—the work of composition, computers and writing, technical communication, and African American rhetoric.

Of course, one has to own or be near places that will allow him or her to use computers, software, Internet connections, and other communication technologies when needed. The "Falling through the Net" reports, along with many other studies, brought this need to our attention. I call this *material access*, and meaningful access begins with equality in the material conditions that drive technology use or nonuse. To really play out the implications of this statement would mean that there can be no real digital equality without fundamental transformations of the economic relations in our nation. But even that "revolution" alone would not be enough.

For material access to have any effect on people's lives or on their participation in the society, they must also have the knowledge and skills necessary to use those tools effectively, or what I'll label as *functional access*. I use this term because, just like functional literacy, it is insufficient for economic or political power or for many kinds of participation in the nation's social or cultural structures. Porter's call for us to understand access as involving the skills and knowledge necessary to benefit from technologies is partially a call for this kind of access.

Porter also notes that people must actually embrace the technologies involved, that there must be a level of community awareness and acceptance in order for those technologies to mean anything. Beyond the tools themselves and the knowledge and skills necessary for their effective use, people must actually use them; they must have *experiential access*, or an access that makes the tools a relevant part of their lives. In addition to discerning relevance in the technologies, people must have some involvement in the spaces where technologies are created, designed, and planned and where policies and regulations are written. They must be present in the processes by which technologies come to mean what they mean for us. This notion of experiential access is a kind of fusion of Porter's understanding of access and Taborn's insistence that access also includes power in the creation and shaping of our technologies.

Richard and Cynthia Selfe's work, along with that of Charles Moran, show us that not even these layers of access, alone, are enough. Members of a particular community must also develop understandings of the benefits and problems of any technology well enough to be able to critique, resist, and avoid them when necessary as well as using them when necessary. School districts must know when the wonderful sales pitches of computer companies—and maybe even their donations—won't work for their budgets, curricula, and strategic plans. I term this ability *critical access*. Let me offer what might seem to be a simplistic non-technological example here. Just as we make decisions about what foods are healthy for us or not healthy for us, or which ones fit our bodies' needs at a particular time when at a supermarket or restaurant, any group of people must know how to be intelligent users and producers of technology if access is to mean more than mere ownership of or proximity to random bits of plastic and metal.

Supermarket savings cards provide a more relevant—and seemingly ubiquitous—technological example. These cards, offered by large supermarket chains, are used to track consumer purchases. These chains then use, sell, and trade this information with many other corporations in order to create demographic profiles of communities and make decisions on whether to expand or withhold products and services to them, just as credit card companies and other corporations do. Oscar Gandy describes the potential for racism in the ways corporations gather and use this information in his article "It's Discrimination, Stupid!" Given the obvious value and use of this information and the way supermarkets virtually force consumers to sign up for these cards with pricing strategies that make any product savings dependent on one's ownership of a savings card, and given the pricing disparities that often exist in grocery stores that major chains operate in inner cities, African Americans and many other groups of people face important decisions about whether or not they should own or use these cards, and if they do, under what terms. Just as Operation Breadbasket organized consumer education and boycotts in the 1970s to encourage Black consumers to withhold their business from companies that did not hire Black people, it is past time for African Americans to engage in targeted and mass protests and boycotts of supermarkets, science and technology departments in universities, and corporations in the technology sector that fail to recruit, hire, or promote African Americans and members of other underrepresented groups while they spend billions of dollars on myriad programs (including the H1B visa program) to recruit technical talent from overseas.

The understanding of access I take here echoes the language of literacies that has become common even in non-academic circles, and is informed by Stuart Selber and Johndan Johnson-Eilola's (2001) framework of "thinking, doing, and teaching" that they argue can provide the multidimensional basis that instruction in technical communication needs to better prepare its students for the complexities involved in the technologies with which they will live and work (p. 4). It is also one that locates technology as a site and means for African Americans' continued efforts to "carve out free spaces in oppressive locations such as the classroom, the streets, the airwaves" (p. 16), as Elaine Richardson documents as the purpose of other Black literate practices. In other words, technology is both one of those sites of struggle and a possible means of liberation, something we can not only survive but transform in our own interests.

This taxonomy of access that I have begun to piece together—to quilt—from the patches of others' definitions and debates is best thought of rhetorically as taking place along the related axes of critique, use, and design. The larger project of making access meaningful for African Americans and other marginalized groups must combine participation, resistance, and the re-creation, the reimagining of technological systems, artifacts, processes, and the economic, power, and social relations that are embedded within them. Table 1 begins to establish the relations between the items on my list and the traditions of critique, use, and design that often govern explorations at the intersection of rhetoric and technology. The questions I include within it represent only the merest of beginnings, but include issues I address later in the book as well as concerns taken up by others like Tyrone Taborn, Cynthia Selfe, James Porter, and others.

It bears repeating at this point that computers, the Internet, and other technologies included in the Digital Divide are only a part of the larger racial ravine—the complex of technological divides that have always operated in American history, and have always been used to maintain exclusions connected to race. The ways racial exclusions are built into our technologies and into our society operate to continue and even ensure those exclusions while allowing individual members of that society to avoid responsibility for that exclusion. This helps to explain why the computer industry—the only major American industry to truly emerge in the aftermath of the Civil Rights and Black Power movements—remains the most segregated in the American workforce. At the same time individual companies continue to congratulate themselves for having inclusive advertising

Table 1

Critique	Use	Design
What are the patterns of computer and technology ownership by race? How are those patterns overdetermined by present patterns of racial exclusion?	How does the distribution of a technology affect how people use it (material access)?	How can the aesthetics and functions of technological artifacts and interfaces be made more culturally relevant?
Where do African Americans use computers, and how do the policies and assumptions about education at work in those spaces affect the uses that are available to them (material access, critical access, functional access, experiential access)?	What cultural retentions do African Americans and other people of color bring to the technologies they use? What relationships exist between these retentions and the acquisition of digital literacies (functional access)?	How can the cultural relevance of design questions like this affect the degree to which users embrace technologies and take ownership of them (experiential access)?
What economic and policy factors influence those patterns (material access)?	How can technical communication address race and culture more effectively in areas like the writing and design of documentation and policy (functional access, experiential access)?	What specific visual and design traditions can African Americans bring to technology design?
What tools do activists, scholars, teachers, users have available to interrupt and intervene in closed technological systems (critical access)?	How can educators avoid being swindled by technology companies eager to manipulate their desperation? How can they make better spending decisions with the limited resources they have? What pedagogical aims direct technology spending choices (functional access, critical access)?	How can African Americans counter the design processes and practices of technology firms that have rigorously excluded them (critical access)?
	How does one decide when to promote low-tech solutions to specific users' and learners' needs (critical access, material access)?	

campaigns or for funding individual "minority" science and engineering programs or offering occasional grants and "legacy" (translation, 2nd, 3rd generation or older) machines and stripped down education versions of software programs in order to foster brand loyalty.

Ownership of computers and other digital technologies, knowledge of their uses, participation in their processes, and even critique of their failings are not enough either, however. The way of looking at race and technologies, and of a meaningful technology access, goes further: to transformation. This kind of look at race and technology posits that our nation is a construct, or system, maybe even a technological system, and the Constitution, federal, state, and local laws, are part of the code that runs it. Social spaces like schools, cities, the workplace, and the court system are all interfaces where people use that system. African American struggle as reflected in its rhetorical traditions was always an attempt to both change the interfaces of that system and fundamentally change the codes that determine how the system works. My exploration of technology issues in African American rhetoric, then, is intended to document the ways Black people have hacked or jacked access to *and* transformed the technologies of American life to serve the needs of Black people and all its citizens. My goal here is not merely to encourage long-denied appreciation of these traditions of struggle, but to enable new (as well as ever present but unrecognized) strategies and tactics for pursuing African American freedom in this recalcitrant racial moment.

African American rhetoric has been about all of this and more; Black people have continually worked for a *transformative access* to all of the technologies that make up American life. By transformative access, I mean that African Americans have always argued for a genuine inclusion in technologies and the networks of power that help determine what they become, but never merely for the sake of inclusion. African American rhetorical practices call attention to the ways that the interfaces of American life, be they public facilities, education, employment, transportation, the legal system, or computer technologies, have always been bound up in contests over language, and have always been rhetorical—about the use of persuasion, in these cases, toward demonstrably tangible ends.

One might argue, that at best, the United States has adopted what we can call a "user-friendly" racism in the aftermath of Black freedom struggles of the middle and late 20th century: a language of tolerance and facile efforts to make individual interfaces more accessible (such as public facilities and education) in a system that remains fundamentally unchanged, and in constant contest over even those minimal efforts. Just as Civil Rights struggle was about far more than the right to sit next to White people at lunch counters or in schools, technological struggle in this century must be about much more than merely owning or being near computers or any other technological tool. The question is not about how many of our schools are wired, but rather, as Martin King put it in one of his final speeches, "Remaining Awake through a Great Revolution," the problem of how "through our technological and scientific genius, we have made of this world a neighborhood and yet, we have not had the ethical commitment to make of it a brotherhood . . . [we live with the] unhappy truth that racism is a way of life . . . spoken and unspoken, acknowledged and denied, subtle and not so subtle" (1991, p. 270). King's point in this speech, which I take up in more detail in the next chapter, is that the racism in our society infects our technologies just as it infects our media, our schools, our politics, our economy, and that the technologies themselves must be transformed. What does this transformative ideal look like? What set of attitudes, commitments, and goals might enable one to pursue this kind of transformation?

REFERENCES

AfroGeeks. Retrieved from http://research.ucsb.edu/cbs/projects/afrogeeks.html. Accessed October 15, 2004.

Alkalimat, A. (2001a). Technological revolution and prospects for Black liberation in the 21st century. *cy.rev.* World Wide Web. Accessed June 13, 2001 from http://www.cyrev.net.

Alkalimat, A. (2001b). eBlack: A 21st century challenge. *eBlackStudies.* World Wide Web. Accessed June 13, 2001 from http://eblackstudies.net/eblack.html.

Asante, M. K. (1969). *Rhetoric of Black revolution.* Boston: Allyn & Bacon.

Blair, K. (1998). Literacy, dialogue, and difference in the "electronic contact zone." *Computers and Composition, 15,* 317–329.

Bolter, J. D. (1991). *Writing space: The computer, hypertext, and the history of writing.* Hillsdale, NJ: Lawrence Erlbaum Associates.

Corsini, V., & Fogliasso, C. (1997). A descriptive study of the use of the Black communication style by African-Americans within an organization. *Journal of Technical Writing and Communication, 27*(1), 33–47.

Crenshaw, C. (1997). Resisting Whiteness' rhetorical silence. *Western Journal of Communication, 61*(3), 253–278.

Dunbar-Nelson, A. M. (2000). *Masterpieces of Negro eloquence.* Mineola, NY: Dover Publications.

Early, G. (Ed.). (1992). *Speech and power: The African-American essay and its cultural contents from polemics to pulpit: Vol. 1.* Hopewell, NJ: The Ecco Press.

Falling through the Net: A survey of the "have nots" in rural and urban America. NTIA July 1995 http://www.ntia.doc.gov/ntiahome/fallingthru.html.

Falling through the Net II: New data on the Digital Divide. NTIA July 1998 http://www.ntia.doc.gov/ntiahome/net2/.

Falling through the Net III: Defining the Digital Divide. NTIA July 1999 http://www.ntia.doc.gov/ntiahome/fttn99/contents.html.

Falling through the Net IV: Toward digital inclusion. NTIA July 2000 http://www.ntia.doc.gov/ntiahome.fttn00/contents00.html.

Foner, P. S. (1975). *Voice of Black America*. New York: Capricorn Books.

Foner, P. S., & Branham, R. J. (Eds.). (1998). *Lift every voice*. Tuscaloosa: University of Alabama Press.

Franklin, V. P., & Collier-Thomas, B. (1990). Biography, race vindication, and African American intellectuals: Introductory essay. *Journal of Negro History, 81*(1), 1–16.

Gandy, O. (1995). It's discrimination, stupid! In J. Brook & I. Boal (Eds.), *Resisting the virtual life: The culture and politics of information* (pp. 35–47). San Francisco: City Lights.

Garvey, M. (1923). An exposé of the caste system among Negroes. In M. Marable & L. Mullings (Eds.), *Let nobody turn us around: Voices of reform, resistance, and renewal*. Lanham, MD: Rowan and Littlefield.

Gates, H. L. (1986). *Race, writing, and difference*. Chicago: University of Chicago.

Gates, H., & McKay, N. (1997). *The Norton anthology of African American literature* (pp. xxxvii–xli). New York: W. W. Norton & Company.

Grabill, J. T. (1998). Utopic visions, the technopoor, and public access: Writing technologies in a community literacy program. *Computers and Composition, 15*, 297–315.

Hoffman, D., & Novak, T. (1998). *Bridging the Digital Divide: The impact of race on computer access and computer use*. Accessed December 5, 2001 from wwww2000.ogsm.vanderbilt.edu/papers/race/science.html.

King, M. L. (1991). Remaining awake through a great revolution. In M. Washington (Ed.), *Testament of hope: The essential writings and speeches of Martin Luther King, Jr.* (pp. 197–201). San Francisco: Harper.

Kolko, B. E. (2000). Erasing @race: Going White in the (inter)face. In B. E. Kolko, L. Makamura, & G. B. Rodman (Eds.), *Race in cyberspace* (pp. 213–232). New York: Routledge.

Kreuzer, T. (1993). Computers on campus: The Black-White technology gap. *Journal of Blacks in Higher Education, 12*(4), 88–95.

MacGillis, A. (2004, September 19–25). Poor schools, rich targets. Retrieved October 15, 2004 from the *Baltimore Sun* http://www.baltimoresun.com/nationworld/balte.software21sep21,1,1793980.story?ctrack=1&cstet=true.

Mitchell, W. J. (1995). *City of bits: Space, place, and the infobahn*. Cambridge, MA: Massachusetts Institute of Technology Press.

Moran, C. (1999). Access: The a-word in technology studies. In G. E. Hawisher & C. L. Selfe (Eds.), *Passions, pedagogies, and 21st century technologies* (pp. 205–220). Logan, UT: Utah State University Press and Urbana, IL: National Council of Teachers of English.

Moran, C., & Selfe, C. L. (1999). Teaching English across the technology/wealth gap. *English Journal, 88*(6), 48–55.

Moss, B. (2003). *A community text arises: A literate text and a literacy tradition in African American churches*. Creskill, NJ: Hampton Press.

Neal, L. (1999). The Black aesthetic. In H. A. Ervin (Ed.), *African American literary criticism* (pp. 122–128). New York: Twayne.

Porter, J. E. (1998). *Rhetorical ethics and internetworked writing*. Greenwich, CT: Albex.

Powell, L. (1990). Factors associated with the underrepresentation of African Americans in mathematics and science. *Journal of Negro Education, 59*(3), 292–298.

Prendergrast, C. (1998). Race: The present absence in composition studies. *College Composition and Communication, 50*(1), 36–53.

Rawlinson, R. (1999). Can Robert Johnson bring more Blacks online? Accessed December 1, 2001 from http://archive.salon.com/tech/feature/1999/10/06/bet_johnson/print.html.

Richardson, E. (1997). African American women instructors: In a net. *Computers and Composition, 14*(2), 279–287.

Richardson, E. (2003). *African American literacies.* London: Routledge.

Romano, S. (1993). The egalitarianism narrative: Whose story? Whose yardstick? *Computers and Composition, 10*(3), 7–28.

Selber, S., & Johnson-Eilola, J. (2001). Sketching a framework for graduate education in technical communication. *Technical Communication Quarterly, 10,* 403–437.

Selfe, C. L. (1999). *Technology and literacy in the twenty-first century: The importance of paying attention.* Carbondale, IL: Southern Illinois University Press.

Slater, R. (1994). Will Blacks in higher education be detoured off the information superhighway? *Journal of Blacks in Higher Education, 3,* 96–99.

Smitherman, G. (1986). *Talkin and testifyin: The language of Black America.* Detroit, MI: Wayne State University Press.

Taborn, T. (2001). The art of Tricknology. *U.S. Black engineer: Information technology.* Baltimore, MD: Career Communication Group.

Winner, L. (1986). *The whale and the reactor: A search for limits in an age of high technology.* Chicago: University of Chicago.

Woodson, C. G. (1969). *Negro orators and their orations.* New York: Russell & Russell.

Young, H. A., & Young, B. H. (1977). Science and Black studies. *Journal of Negro Education, 46*(4), 380–387.

A List of Resources

Anzaldúa, Gloria. *Borderlands/La Frontera*. San Francisco: Aunt Lute Books, 1999.

Applebee, Arthur N. *Tradition and Reform in the Teaching of English: A History*. Urbana, IL: NCTE, 1974.

Aristotle. *The Rhetoric and the Poetics of Aristotle*. Trans. W. Rhys Roberts and Ingram Bywater. Ed. Edward P. J. Corbett. New York: Random House, 1984.

Bain, Alexander. *English Composition and Rhetoric: A Manual*. London: Longman, 1866.

Ball, Arnetha F., and Ted Lardner. *African American Literacies Unleashed: Vernacular English and the Composition Classroom*. Carbondale: Southern Illinois UP, 2005.

Banks, Adam J. *Race, Rhetoric, and Technology: Searching for Higher Ground*. Mahwah, NJ: Erlbaum and Urbana, IL: NCTE, 2006.

Bartholomae, David, and Anthony Petrosky, eds. *Facts, Artifacts, and Counterfacts: Theory and Method for a Reading and Writing Course*. Upper Montclair, NJ: Boynton/Cook, 1986.

_____, eds. *Ways of Reading: An Anthology for Writers*. 4th ed. Boston: St. Martin's, 1996.

Belanoff, Pat, and Marcia Dickson, eds. *Portfolios: Process and Product*. Portsmouth, NH: Boynton/Cook, 1991.

Benson, Thomas W., and Michael H. Prosser, eds. *Readings in Classical Rhetoric*. Boston: Allyn and Bacon, 1969.

Berlin, James A. *Rhetoric and Reality: Writing Instruction in American Colleges, 1900–1985*. Carbondale: Southern Illinois UP, 1987.

_____. *Rhetorics, Poetics, and Cultures: Refiguring College English Studies*. Urbana: NCTE, 1996.

_____. *Writing Instruction in Nineteenth-Century American Colleges*. Carbondale: Southern Illinois UP, 1984.

Bizzell, Patricia. *Academic Discourse and Critical Consciousness*. Pittsburgh: U Pittsburgh P, 1992.

Blair, Kristine, and Pamela Takayoshi, eds. *Feminist Cyberscapes: Mapping Gendered Academic Spaces*. Stamford, CT: Ablex, 1999.

Britton, James, et al. *The Development of Writing Abilities, 11–18*. Schools Council Research Studies series. London: Macmillan, 1975.

Brody, Miriam. *Manly Writing: Gender, Rhetoric, and the Rise of Composition*. Carbondale: Southern Illinois UP, 1993.

Cooper, Charles R., and Lee Odell, eds. *Evaluating Writing: Describing, Measuring, Judging*. Urbana, IL: NCTE, 1977.

Corbett, Edward P. J. *Classical Rhetoric for the Modern Student*. 3rd ed. New York: Oxford UP, 1990.

Crowley, Sharon. *The Methodical Memory: Invention in Current-Traditional Rhetoric*. Carbondale: Southern Illinois UP, 1990.

———. *Ancient Rhetorics for Contemporary Students*. New York: Macmillan, 1994.

Daiker, Donald A., Andrew Kerek, and Max Morenberg. *The Writer's Options: College Sentence Combining*. New York: Harper and Row, 1979.

Elbow, Peter. *What Is English?* New York: Modern Language Association; and Urbana, IL: National Council of Teachers of English, 1990.

———. *Writing without Teachers*. New York: Oxford UP, 1973.

———. *Writing with Power: Techniques for Mastering the Writing Process*. New York: Oxford UP, 1981.

Emig, Janet. *The Composing Processes of Twelfth Graders*. NCTE Research Report No. 13. Urbana, IL: NCTE, 1971.

Flower, Linda. *The Construction of Negotiated Meaning: A Social Cognitive Theory of Writing*. Carbondale: Southern Illinois UP, 1994.

Fowler, Shelli B., and Victor Villanueva, eds. *Included in English Studies: Learning Climates That Cultivate Racial and Ethnic Diversity*. Washington, DC: American Association for Higher Education, 2002.

Enos, Theresa, ed. *A Sourcebook for Basic Writing Teachers*. New York: Random House, 1987.

Faigley, Lester. *Fragments of Rationality: Postmodernity and the Subject of Composition*. Pittsburgh: U of Pittsburgh P, 1992.

Freire, Paulo. *Cultural Action for Freedom*. Cambridge, MA: Harvard Educational Review, 1970.

———. *Pedagogy of the Oppressed.* Trans. Myra Bergman Ramos. New York: Herder and Herder, 1970.

Freire, Paulo, and Donaldo Macedo. *Literacy: Reading the Word and the World.* South Hadley, MA: Bergin & Garvey, 1987.

Gere, Anne Ruggles. *Writing Groups: History, Theory, and Implications.* Carbondale: Southern Illinois UP, 1987.

Gibson, W. Walker. *Tough, Sweet & Stuffy: An Essay on Modern American Prose Styles.* Bloomington, IN: Indiana UP, 1966.

Gilyard, Keith, ed. *Race, Rhetoric, and Composition.* Portsmouth, NH: Boynton/Cook, 1999.

———. *Voices of the Self : A Study of Language Competence.* Detroit: Wayne State UP, 1991.

Golden, James L., and Edward P. J. Corbett. *The Rhetoric of Blair, Campbell, and Whately.* New York: Holt, Rinehart and Winston, 1968.

Gramsci, Antonio. *Selections from the Prison Notebooks of Antonio Gramsci.* Ed. and Trans. Quintin Hoare and Geoffrey Nowell Smith. New York: International, 1971.

———. *Selections from Cultural Writings.* Ed. David Forgacs and Geoffrey Nowell-Smith. Trans. William Boelhower. Cambridge: Harvard UP, 1985.

Graves, Richard L., ed. *Rhetoric and Composition: A Sourcebook for Teachers and Writers.* 2nd ed. Upper Montclair, NJ: Boynton/Cook, 1984.

Havelock, Eric A. *Preface to Plato.* Cambridge, MA: Harvard UP, 1963.

Hawisher, Gail E., and Cynthia L. Selfe, eds. *Global Literacies and the World-Wide Web.* New York: Routledge, 2000.

Heath, Shirley Brice. *Ways with Words: Language, Life, and Work in Communities and Classrooms.* New York: Cambridge UP, 1983.

hooks, bell. *Teaching to Transgress: Education as the Practice of Freedom.* New York: Routledge, 1994.

Horner, Bruce, and Min-Zhan Lu. *Representing the "Other": Basic Writers and the Teaching of Basic Writing.* Urbana, IL: NCTE, 1999.

Irmscher, William. *Teaching Expository Writing.* New York: Holt, Rinehart and Winston, 1979.

Jarratt, Susan C. *Rereading the Sophists: Classical Rhetoric Refigured.* Carbondale: Southern Illinois UP, 1991.

Kells, Michelle Hall, and Valerie Balester, eds. *Attending to the Margins: Writing, Researching, and Teaching on the Front Lines.* Portsmouth, NH: Boynton/Cook, 1999.

Kennedy, George. *Classical Rhetoric and Its Christian and Secular Tradition from Ancient to Modern Times.* 2nd ed. Chapel Hill: U of North Carolina P, 1999.

Kent, Thomas, ed. *Post-Process Theory: Beyond the Writing-Process Paradigm.* Carbondale: Southern Illinois UP, 1999.

Kolko, Beth E., Lisa Nakamura, and Gilbert B, Rodman, eds. *Race in Cyberspace.* New York: Routledge, 2000.

Lessig, Lawrence. *Remix: Making Art and Commerce Thrive in the Hybrid Economy.* New York: Penguin, 2008.

Lindemann, Erika. *A Rhetoric for Writing Teachers.* 4th ed. New York: Oxford UP, 2001.

Locke, John. *An Essay Concerning Human Understanding.* Ed. Peter H. Nidditch. Oxford: Clarendon, 1975.

Macrorie, Ken. *The I-Search Paper.* Portsmouth, NH: Boynton/Cook, 1988.

———. *Uptaught.* New York, Hayden, 1970.

Marrou, H. I. *A History of Education in Antiquity.* New York: Sheed and Ward, 1956.

Mathieu, Paula. *Tactics of Hope: The Public Turn in English Composition.* Portsmouth, NH: Boynton/Cook, 2005.

Matsen, Patricia P., Philip Rollinson, and Marion Sousa. *Readings from Classical Rhetoric.* Carbondale: Southern Illinois UP, 1990.

Mellon, John C. *Transformational Sentence-Combining: A Method for Enhancing the Development of Syntactic Fluency in English Composition.* NCTE Research Report No. 10. Urbana, IL: NCTE, 1969.

Miller, Susan, ed. *The Norton Book of Composition Studies.* New York: Norton, 2009.

Moffett, James. *Teaching the Universe of Discourse.* Boston: Houghton Mifflin, 1983.

Murphy, James J., ed. *A Short History of Writing Instruction: From Ancient Greece to Twentieth-Century America.* Davis, CA: Hermagoras, 1990.

———. *Rhetoric in the Middle Ages: A History of Rhetorical Theory from St. Augustine to the Renaissance.* Berkeley: U of California P, 1974.

———, ed. *The Rhetorical Tradition and Modern Writing.* New York: MLA, 1982.

Murray, Donald. *A Writer Teaches Writing.* Boston: Houghton Mifflin, 1968.

Nelson, Cary, and Lawrence Grossberg, eds. *Marxism and the Interpretation of Culture.* Urbana: U of Illinois P, 1988.

Ohmann, Richard M. *English in America: A Radical View of the Profession.* New York: Oxford UP, 1976.

Ong, Walter J. *Orality and Literacy: The Technologizing of the Word.* London: Methuen, 1982.

Piaget, Jean. *The Language and Thought of the Child.* Trans. Marjorie Gabain. New York: World, 1973.

Plato. *Phaedrus.* Trans. R. Hackforth. Cambridge: Cambridge UP, 1952.

Quintilian. *On the Teaching of Speaking and Writing.* Ed. James J. Murphy. Carbondale: Southern Illinois UP, 1987.

Reynolds, Nedra. *Geographies of Writing: Inhabiting Places and Encountering Difference.* Carbondale: Southern Illinois UP, 2004

Rose, Mike. *Lives on the Boundary: A Moving Account of the Struggles and Achievements of America's Educational Underclass.* New York: Penguin, 1989.

Schroeder, Christopher, Helen Fox, and Patricia Bizzell, eds. *ALT DIS: Alternative Discourses and the Academy.* Portsmouth, NH: Boynton/Cook, 2002.

Scott, Tony. *Dangerous Writing: Understanding the Political Economy of Composition.* Logan: Utah State UP, 2009.

Scribner, Silvia, and Michael Cole. *The Psychology of Literacy.* Cambridge, MA: Harvard UP. 1981.

Shaughnessy, Mina. *Errors and Expectations: A Guide for the Teacher of Basic Writing.* New York: Oxford UP, 1977.

Shor, Ira, and Paulo Freire. *A Pedagogy for Liberation: Dialogues on Transforming Education.* South Hadley, MA: Bergin & Harvey, 1987.

Swearingen, C. Jan. *Rhetoric and Irony: Western Literacy and Western Lies.* New York: Oxford UP, 1991.

Tate, Gary, ed. *Teaching Composition: Twelve Bibliographical Essays.* Rev. ed. Ft. Worth: Texas Christian UP, 1987.

Tate, Gary, and Edward P. J. Corbett, eds. *The Writing Teacher's Sourcebook.* 2nd ed. New York: Oxford UP, 1988.

Villanueva, Victor, Jr. *Bootstraps: From an American Academic of Color.* Urbana, IL: NCTE, 1993.

Vygotsky, Lev. *Thought and Language.* Cambridge, MA: MIT P, 1962.

Yagelski, Robert P. *Literacy Matters: Writing and Reading the Social Self.* New York: Teachers College P, 2000.

Young, Richard E., Alton L. Becker, and Kenneth L. Pike. *Rhetoric: Discovery and Change.* New York: Harcourt, Brace and World, 1970.

Index

Mexico, colonization and literacy of, 725–726
Michigan professionalism, 677–680, 686
"Midwives," 607, 616n3
Mignolo, Walter, 725
Miller, George, 132, 133, 134, 151–152
Miller, James, 242, 243
Miller, Susan, 472, 611–612
Miller, Thomas, 116
Mills, John, 214
Minot, Walter, 85–86
Miscue analysis
  in composition process studies, 24–25, 29–30, 31
  and errors in writing, 36–37
Mitchell, Ruth, 77, 79–82, 80
Mitchell, William, 838
MLA Commission on the Status of Women in the Profession, 602–603
Modeling processes, 256–257
Modern Dogma and the Rhetoric of Assent (Booth), 82
Moffett, James, 8, 87–88, 251, 253
Monitor, in cognitive process model, 257, 263, 374–375
Monopoly capital, 702–704, 708, 713
Morais, José, 214
Moral development, stages of, 585
Moran, Charles, 832–833, 834–837, 859, 862
Morgan, Arlene, 338–339
Morgan, M. J., 336
Morris, C. W., 132, 133
Morrison, Toni, 662
Moscowitz, Irene, 214
Mother tongues. *See* Dialects, nonprestige English
Motives, location in language, 530
Moulton, William, 678
Mullin, Joan, 121
Multiculturalism. *See* Contact zones; Cross-boundary discourse
Multiliteracies, pedagogy of, 766, 769
Multivocal research reports, 503
Munroe, James, 700–701
Murphy, Christina, 121
Murray, Donald, 92–93
Muse Learns to Write, The (Havelock), 350–351
"My Pedagogic Creed" (Dewey), 118–119
Myers, Greg, 442, 448, 450, 452
Mythological function of language, 131, 132

Narrative discourse
  audience fictionalization in, 61–69, 74
  of feminist disruptions, 599–600, 608–613, 614
  of metonymic relationship, 605–608, 613
  and narrative theorizing, 561
  by people of color, 573–578
  in "The Literacy Letters," 627–638
  trends in, 520–521
  and women's inclusion in composition, 600, 601–605, 613

Narrative theorizing, 561
Nashe, Thomas, 67–68
National Council of Teachers of English (NCTE), 565–566, 601–602, 757
National Council of Teachers of Mathematics, 707
National Institute for Literacy, 719
National Science Foundation, 707
Nature of Narrative, The (Scholes), 56–57, 69
NCTE (National Council of Teachers of English), 565–566, 601–602, 757
Negotiating difference, 465, 480–482
Nelson, Ted, 751
Neo-Aristotelian (Classicist) pedagogy and rhetoric, 237–239, 245, 246, 247, 248
Neo-Platonic (Expressionist) pedagogy and rhetoric, 241–243, 245, 246, 247, 248, 807
Neuleib, Janice, 205–206, 207, 208–209
Neumann, Erich, 144–146
Neutral technology, 706
New London Group, 769, 771–772, 779, 787n3
New Rhetoric, 244–245, 247, 248
"Nice Derangement of Epitaphs, A" (Davidson), 111
Nicomachean Ethics (Aristotle), 71
Niles, Lyndrey, 843
Nold, Ellen, 262
Normal discourse
  among community of peers, 403–404
  in conflict-based view of consensus, 448–449
  within knowledge communities, 404–405, 411, 412
  Rorty's philosophical view of, 388
  teachable tools of, 410
  vs. abnormal discourse, 409, 448–449
Novak, Thomas, 852

Oakeshott, Michael, 399
Oakley, Ann, 492–493
Odell, Lee, 17–18, 253, 281
Odyssey (Homer), 61
Olsen, Leslie, 216–217
Olson, David, 543–544, 550n1
Olson, Gary, 97, 108
One-to-one tutorial model of composition, 806–807
Ong, Walter
  audience-invoked perspective, 82–88, 90
  literacy, 355, 720
  mother tongue-unconscious connection, 647
  technology and ways of thinking, 706
Open admissions programs, 519, 642
Opinion, as function of language, 132, 133
Oppenheimer, Robert, 314
Oral verbalization. *See* Oral vs. written verbalization; Speech
Oral vs. written discourse
  in African American communities, 847–848
  basic writers' understanding of, 296

Editors

Victor Villanueva is currently Regents Professor at Washington State University but will join the English faculty at Auburn University in June 2011. He is a former chair of the Conference on College Composition and Communication and was honored with the organization's 2009 Exemplar Award. All of his efforts have centered on the connections between language and racism.

Kristin L. Arola is assistant professor and Buchanan Scholar at Washington State University, where she directs the Digital Technology and Culture program. She is interested in the ways that the design and functionality of online spaces encourage particular uses for particular groups of people (particularly American Indians), and works on ways of teaching students to be more critical of the online spaces within which they work and live. To these ends, she writes about design, identity, and agency, and how best to incorporate multimodal practices into the composition classroom. She resides in Pullman, Washington, with her amazing husband and charming dog.

This book was typeset in 11/13 Electra by Precision Graphics.
Typefaces used on the cover and spine were Electra and Gill Sans.
The book was printed on 50-lb. Opaque Offset by Versa Press, Inc.